5th edition

Child and Adolescent Development

Kelvin L. Seifert
The University of Manitoba

Robert J. Hoffnung
University of New Haven

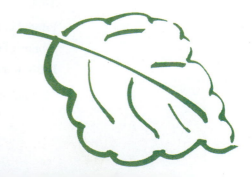

Houghton Mifflin Company   Boston   New York

To my students, whether currently children or formerly children.
K.L.S.

For my sister Michele and my brother Dan.
R.J.H.

Senior sponsoring editor   Kerry T. Baruth
Basic book editor   Karla Paschkis
Senior project editor   Rosemary Winfield
Senior production/design coordinator   Jill Haber
Senior cover design coordinator   Deborah Azerrad Savona
Senior manufacturing coordinator   Marie Barnes
Senior marketing manager   Pamela Laskey

Cover design: Rebecca Fagan; *cover image:* "Higher Education" by Kevin Ghiglione

Anatomical and biological illustrations by Nancy Kaplan: Figures 4.3, 5.2, 12.1
Illustrations by Patrice Rossi: Figure 2.1
Illustrations by Elizabeth Seifert: Figure 8.4
All other credits appear on page A-1, which constitutes an extension of the copyright page.

Printed in the U.S.A.

Library of Congress Catalog Card Number: 99-71931

ISBN: 0-395-96426-1

23456789-VH-03 02 01 00

Brief Contents

Contents

Special Features

Preface

We are delighted that again we have had an opportunity to refine, enhance, and update *Child and Adolescent Development*. The fifth edition remains a comprehensive introduction to the field, of course, but it is more than that: it is a tool for kindling students' enthusiasm about children and youth, for helping them to become more thoughtful about developmental processes, and for assisting them in thinking about the relevance of developmental psychology to current careers and social issues. We hope, as you get to know this new edition of the book, that you will see these values in it as well.

As a text, *Child and Adolescent Development* is appropriate for all undergraduates taking a first course in development, regardless of the department in which the course is taught. To accommodate the range of interests among students and instructors, the fifth edition incorporates important changes in emphasis, while at the same time retains the strengths that have accounted for its success in the past. As in earlier editions, we seek the following:

- To communicate to students the freshness and vitality of real, fully dimensional children and the idea that development, above all, is a human process. In the fifth edition, however, we seek to convey this sense of "real children and youth" even more strongly, since readers have found it helpful in understanding developmental psychology.

- To convey that the developmental psychologist's understanding of children and youth is based on scientifically derived information and, further, that good science involves a synthesis of classic and recent findings. In keeping with this goal, we have added new and updated research throughout the book while keeping important studies from the past that have served as benchmarks for later thinking and studies.

- To keep our writing clear, low-key, and nontechnical and to weave abundant concrete details about children and youth into our discussions.

- To explore the influence of cultural and social factors on development, such as the impact of ethnicity, of language background, of gender, and of socioeconomic status. The multicultural emphasis has long been a hallmark of this book. Because of our own beliefs in its importance, we have continued to strengthen and elaborate on multicultural information and research in the fifth edition.

- To help students appreciate the connections among the key developmental domains: physical, cognitive, and psychosocial. In Chapter 15, for example, we have added and revised a discussion of school influences on youth, framing these as both cognitive and social.

- To explore, for both scientific and practical reasons, the roles of the adults who nurture, care for, and educate children. Throughout the book, for example, are found interviews with adults who work with children; some of these are new to this edition.

Continued Emphasis on Applications

As in previous editions, we have included material related to occupations and vocations that use knowledge from developmental psychology. In every chapter of the fifth edition, there is no missing the relevance and importance of developmental processes in daily life! Students who read this book—and especially those who also discuss its ideas with interested instructors and classmates—will find their practical interests respected, encouraged, and stimulated. These benefits will happen, of course, in the context of learning sound information from developmental research.

Here is a sampling of some of the applied, research-based information that is new to the fifth edition. In addition to these topics, there are numerous others that we have retained from earlier editions and updated appropriately with newer research:

- Behavioral theories as they apply to behavior modification and the treatment of ADHD (Chapter 2)

- Childbearing with a disability (Chapter 3)

- Categorical and anticipatory thought in infancy (Chapter 6)

- Consequences of child care arrangements on children's attachment (Chapter 7)

- Significance of individual differences in motor skill development in early childhood (Chapter 8)

- Long-term impact of early friendships (Chapter 10)

- Impact of schooling on the social participation of children (Chapter 12)

- Relationships between custodial and noncustodial parents following divorce (Chapter 13)

- Relationships of athletics and eating disorders (Chapter 14)

- Longitudinal studies of delinquency and antisocial behavior (Chapter 16)

In addition to this new and updated coverage, each chapter contains an interview (called "*Working With*") with a professional who works with children or youth and whose work depends on applying knowledge of developmental psychology. This feature is described in greater detail below.

Strong Multicultural Coverage

In the fifth edition, we have continued to strengthen the multicultural coverage in the book beyond what it contained in previous editions. This trend reflects our commitment to inclusivity, both in the field of developmental psychology and in society itself. We are convinced that all children are worthy of study, throughout both society and the world, and that knowledge of a respect for human diversity is indeed a fundamental purpose of developmental psychology as a field. To this end we have retained a specially designated multicultural topic in each chapter, presented in a box called *A Multicultural View,* which is described more fully below. More important, but less immediately visible, multicultural findings such as those listed here have been added generously throughout the text:

- Chapter 1 includes a new discussion of street children in cross-cultural context.

- In Chapter 4, our coverage of modern midwives and doulas emphasizes the social context of the birth process.

- In Chapter 5, we place our discussion of infant nutrition in its international context.

- In Chapter 7, we include an expanded discussion of sleeping arrangements on the kibbutzim of Israel.

- In Chapter 9, we revised the coverage of language development to emphasize more strongly the cultural differences in language acquisition and language styles.

- In Chapter 12, our discussion of school influences considers social biases that affect school learning.

- In Chapter 13, we discuss children's play for its relevance to the two peer "cultures" of boys and girls.

- In Chapter 16, we relate research on parenting styles specifically to styles of control used in African American families.

Enhanced Illustration Program

Because we are aware that a picture is worth a thousand words, we have enhanced the illustration program in the fifth edition. We have added numerous new graphs, figures, and tables to make key explanations, ideas, and concepts more clear. All students, and especially those who prefer or need to learn in visual, as well as verbal ways, will find these additions helpful.

Responses to the photo programs in earlier editions were so positive that we have retained the same approach to illustrating key ideas by choosing photographs that emphasize the multicultural, contemporary, and human aspects of child and adolescent development.

Special Features

The fifth edition of *Child and Adolescent Development* includes a number of unique features designed to enhance students' understanding of developmental psychology. Some of these have been mentioned already but deserve fuller explanation:

A Multicultural View   A series of boxed inserts called *A Multicultural View* focus on important multicultural topics related to child and adolescent development. Appearing in each chapter, they cover such topics as breast-feeding practices in contrasting societies, cultural variations in parent-child language interactions, beliefs about the nature of "intelligence" in diverse societies, social stereotypes about physical attractiveness in different cultures, and cross-cultural differences in attachment. The most successful, relevant, and current multicultural boxes have been retained from the previous edition, and two new *Multicultural View* boxes have been added: one about street children in cross-cultural perspective (Chapter 1) and one about differing cultural views of juvenile delinquency (Chapter 16). We hope that these boxes will increase readers' awareness of the importance of cultural context in the development of children and youth and of the importance of an inclusive perspective about human problems. A complete list of topics appears on page xi.

Working With   Each chapter includes an interview with an experienced professional who works with children or adolescents in some way and whose work depends on knowledge of developmental psychology. In conducting the *Working With* interviews, we talked with people in careers that students of developmental psychology are likely to consider, and so the interviews offer glimpses of where students might eventually go with their working lives and why developmental psychology might help them once they get there. Each individual has been selected because his or her work relates to a theme or domain of the chapter. Because Chapter 5 is about physical development in infancy, for example, we interview a pediatric nurse about her experiences on a maternity ward. Among the occupations represented are a genetic counselor, an infant day care coordinator, and a nutritionist. Three new interviews have been added to the fifth edition: one with a psychiatric social worker (Chapter 2), one with a private family day care provider (Chapter 8), and one with a high school mathematics teacher (Chapter 15). For a complete list of careers and topics featured, see page xi.

A Talk With   Interviews with children and adolescents reinforce and bring to life the text's coverage of concepts and theories. *A Talk With* interviews convey some of the experience of childhood and adolescence (and the delight that is possible from close observation of young people!). They are based on an extensive collection of tape-recorded interviews conducted especially for this text by one of the authors (Robert Hoffnung). A full list appears on pages xi–xii.

Perspectives   We extend the text discussions in *Perspectives* boxed inserts, which highlight significant research on human development or identify issues of social policy related to the welfare of children. The *Perspectives* boxes emphasize the connectedness of developmental psychology with all aspects of the human condition, both intellectual and practical. In Chapter 3, for example, the race and intelligence controversy and its social policy implications are explored, while the *Perspectives* box in Chapter 8 documents the close relationship between SES and children's health and suggests ways of making health care more equitable for children and youth. The fifth edition includes new boxes about eating disorders and athletics (Chapter 14) and about managing conflicts between parents about child-rearing goals (Chapter 13). Also, every *Perspectives* box now includes follow-up questions. See page xi for a complete list of *Perspectives* topics.

What Do You Think?   We recognize the importance of dialogue in constructing knowledge about children and youth and invite students to enter that dialogue via *What Do You Think?* questions, which stimulate reflection on issues and concepts of developmental psychology. *What Do You Think?* sections are located periodically throughout every chapter and can be used as a basis for classroom discussions and activities. Many of the questions are intended to encourage collaboration among classmates. Because of their success in previous editions, we have expanded the *What Do You Think?* questions in the fifth edition to appear in the *Working With* and *Perspectives* boxes as well.

Special Learning Aids   Other pedagogical features include opening chapter outlines and initial focusing questions, in-chapter margin definitions of all key terms, and end-of-chapter summaries of key points, lists of key terms. By organizing important information from the text, these features help students significantly to understand important themes, ideas, and concepts. Indirectly, by assisting in the mastery of content, they free students to develop their personal perspectives about the field of developmental psychology and about its practical uses.

Ancillaries

Many useful materials designed to augment the teaching and learning experience accompany the fifth edition of *Child and Adolescent Development*. The study guide, test bank, and instructor's resource manual share learning objectives and are well integrated with the text. New to this edition is a comprehensive CD-ROM for instructors.

Study Guide   The student Study Guide contains learning objectives, a chapter overview and outline, a fill-in review of key terms and concepts, and an expanded and updated list of suggested further readings. Each chapter also includes two sets of multiple-choice practice questions—one tests the student's factual knowledge and the other tests applied knowledge. The multiple-choice answer key explains why each option is correct or incorrect, a feature particularly appreciated by students.

Test Bank   The Test Bank includes 100 multiple-choice and three essay questions per chapter. Each multiple-choice question is keyed to a learning objective and a text page number, and identified as requiring factual, applied, or conceptual knowledge. Emphasis is on providing a wealth of applied and conceptual questions. The essay questions include sample response guides.

Computerized Test Bank   The test items on disk give instructors the flexibility to generate tests electronically, edit test items, or add their own.

Instructor's CD-ROM   The Transparencies and Instructor's Resource Manual are available on CD-ROM. The Instructor's Resource Manual offers a number of methods to facilitate course preparation and student assessment. Chapters begin with a map that keys activities or questions to particular points in the text chapters. Additional resources include chapter overviews, outlines, learning objectives, examples and strategies for helping students, lecture topics, relevant news stories, journal writing topics, in-class activities, out-of-class projects, and recommended Internet links, videos, transparencies, and readings. The CD-ROM also includes a full set of overhead transparencies containing images from within and outside the text.

Videos   Videos covering a wide range of topics relevant to child development are available to qualified adopters. See your Houghton Mifflin representatives for details.

Video Rental Policy   Qualified adopters can also borrow films or videos free of charge through a consortium of university film libraries.

Acknowledgments

A number of reviewers made constructive suggestions and provided thoughtful reactions at various stages in the development of the fifth edition, and we are very appreciative of the help we received from them. In particular, we wish to thank:

Marlene Adelman, Norwalk Community College
Sheridan DeWolf, Grossmont College
Teresa Elliott, American University
Catherine Gillespie, Drake University
John R. Hranitz, Bloomsburg University of Pennsylvania
Herbert Merrill II, Erie Community College
Mary Kay Reed, York College of Pennsylvania
Daniel J. Robin, Indiana University
Holly Scrivner, Shasta College

We would like to thank the many people who have made this book possible; there are so many, after five editions, that it is now difficult to list them all! For the fifth edition, special thanks go to Karla Paschkis and Sheralee Connors for their insightful comments in developing the manuscript, as well as commendably dogged awareness of deadlines and their implications. As always, families and close personal relationships have made room for us to work on this project; those people, along with our students, are in some indirect sense the creators of the book.

Kelvin L. Seifert   Robert J. Hoffnung

PART 1

Studying Development

As infants grow into children and children grow into adolescents, a great many changes occur. Some of these changes are small and fleeting, and many are relatively profound and long-lasting. These developmental changes are the subject of this book and of the field of study known as *developmental psychology*.

The study of development offers much insight into human nature: why we are what we are and how we became that way. Because describing development is a complex task, this book begins with two chapters that orient you to what lies ahead. They explain just what development is and describe some of the most important tools of developmental psychology, namely the theories and methods that guide understanding of child and adolescent development. As you read the chapters, though, keep in mind one of the most important sources of the theories: the children themselves.

Introduction: Studying Human Development

Focusing Questions

- What in general is human development?
- Why is it important to know about development?
- What general themes or issues are important in developmental psychology?
- How do developmental psychologists go about studying children and adolescents?
- What ethical considerations should guide the study of children?

D o you remember your past? When thinking back, each of us remembers different details, of course, but all personal memories share a paradoxical quality: when comparing the past and the present, we all feel as though we have changed, yet also stayed the same. As a preschooler, for example, one of the authors (Seifert) had trouble tying a shoelace. As a child and a teenager, he could tie laces easily, but he admits he never enjoyed or excelled at tasks calling for delicate or precise physical skills. In this small way, Seifert both changed and stayed the same. You yourself may remember experiences with this same dual quality. As a schoolchild—and in contrast to many classmates—perhaps you loved spelling "bees" or contests. Later, as a high school and then a college student, you no longer participated in spelling contests, and lost some of your earlier ability to figure out and remember truly unusual spellings. But you could still spell better than many adults of your age, and you still have a general knack for handling verbal information of other kinds—like computer languages—without getting mixed up. Or imagine another example. As a teenager, you may have constantly wondered whether you would ever overcome shyness and be truly liked and respected by peers. As an adult, in contrast, you finally feel that you have good, special friends; but you have to admit that it took effort to become sociable enough to acquire them.

Continuity in the midst of change marks every human life. Sometimes change seems more obvious than continuity, such as when a speechless infant becomes a talkative preschooler. Other times continuity seems more obvious than change, such as when a sixteen-year-old still feels like a six-year-old whenever he talks with his parents. But close scrutiny of examples like these suggests that both factors may be operating, even when one of them is partially hidden. The talkative four-year-old still has much the same temperament, or personality, that she had as a "speechless" infant. The sixteen-year-old may still feel like a young child, but at the same time feel different. It takes both continuity and change to be fully human: I must be connected to my past somehow, but also not locked into it or fully determined by it.

The Nature of Human Development

This book is about continuity and change throughout childhood and adolescence. Sometimes these processes are called "human development," although this term is sometimes used to emphasize changes rather than constancies in physical growth, feelings, and ways of thinking. As we will see in later chapters, a focus on change may indeed be appropriate at certain points in a person's life. A girl experiencing her first menstrual period, for example, may undergo a number of important changes at the same time, and rather suddenly: her body begins looking different, she begins thinking of herself differently, and other people begin treating her differently. But at other periods, continuity dominates over change. Observing an

Sometimes human behavior can be pretty puzzling! The field of human development can help in understanding apparent contradictions and inconsistencies—as when this child first does not, and then does, want to take a bath.

eight-year-old settled into school and living in a stable family, for example, we might conclude that life is rather stable from day to day or month to month. Since this book surveys a wide span of life (from birth to adolescence), it will make the most sense to keep both factors in mind—continuity *and* change—without privileging one over the other in advance. When we speak of **human development** in this book, therefore, we will mean the mix of continuities and changes that occur throughout a person's life, but especially from birth through the end of adolescence.

Note that both continuity and change can take many forms. Changes can be relatively specific, such as when an infant takes his first unassisted step. But it can also be rather general and unfold over a long time, such as when a teenager becomes aware of the qualities she prefers in "best" friends. The same can be said of continuity. Sometimes *continuity* seems to refer only to short periods of time: an eight-year-old who enjoys athletics, for example, is likely to become a nine-year-old who enjoys athletics. Other examples seemingly last a lifetime: an extroverted child—one who seeks and enjoys social companionship—is likely to still seek and enjoy companionship as an eighteen-year-old.

These examples may make the notion of *human development* seem very broad, but note that not every change or continuity is truly "developmental," and some human developments are easily overlooked or discounted. Consider the impact of the weather. A sudden cold snap makes us behave differently: we put on warmer clothing and select indoor activities more often. A continuous spell of cold weather, on the other hand, creates constancy in behavior: we wear the same type of clothing for a period of time and engage in the same (indoor) set of activities repeatedly. In both cases, our behavior does not quality as "development" because it is triggered by relatively simple external events and has no lasting impact on other behaviors, feelings, or ways of thinking.

And true human developments also sometimes occur, but are overlooked or dismissed as something other than development. Personal identity or sense of "self" is an example. A concept of who "I" am always seems to be with me, and often it seems so constant that I ignore it, making it "part of the woodwork" of my mind. Kelvin Seifert (or the other author, Robert Hoffnung) always seems to be Kelvin Seifert (or Robert). This fact is so much a part of our lives that it is easy to overlook its importance, or to fail to notice changes in self-concepts when they occur. Yet sense of identity does evolve and change as we grow older, and the changes make us act in new ways and make new choices.

Three Domains of Development

As these examples suggest, human development can take many forms. For convenience in discussing it, this book distinguishes among three major types, or **domains,** of development: physical, cognitive, and psychosocial. The division is reflected in the organization of the book, which alternates chapters about physical, cognitive, and psychosocial changes. The domain of **physical development,** or bi-

• • •

human development Long-term continuities and changes in growth, thinking, and social relationships.

domain A realm of psychological functioning.

physical development Long-term continuities and changes related to growth, motor skills, and sensory perception.

cognitive development Long-term continuities and changes related to thinking and learning.

psychosocial development Long-term continuities and changes related to personality, social knowledge, and emotions.

ological change, includes changes in the body itself and how a person uses the body. Some of these changes may be noticeable to a casual observer, such as the difference in how a person walks when he is two years old compared to twenty years old. Others may be essentially invisible without systematic observation, such as the difference in ability to hear between a one-year-old infant and her seven-year-old sister. Like other forms of development, physical changes often span very long periods—literally years or even decades—though not always. Changes in height and weight occur rather rapidly during the early teenage years, for example, but only slowly during middle age.

Cognitive development involves change in styles of thinking, language ability and use, and memory. We tend to think of these abilities as located "inside" individuals. A person is said to "have" a good memory, for example, as if he or she carries that skill around all the time and can display it anywhere with equal ease no matter what the situation. As later chapters will point out, however, viewing cognitive development in this way may be more convenient than accurate: memory, language, and thinking are all heavily dependent on supports (and impediments) both from other people and from circumstances. In this sense, cognitive changes "belong" to more than the individual who displays them, and cognitive development is best understood in conjunction with physical and social changes rather than separately from them.

Psychosocial development is about change in feelings or emotions as well as in relations with other people. It includes interactions with family, peers, classmates, and coworkers, but it also includes a person's personal identity, or sense of self. Because identity and social relationships evolve together, we often discuss them together in this book. And as already pointed out, they also evolve in combination with physical and cognitive changes. Children with satisfying family relationships are apt to feel—and to be— more competent than children who have difficult family relationships. And they are even likely to stay physically healthier as well. Each domain—physical, cognitive, and psychosocial—influences each of the others.

Figure 1.1 shows some of the major landmarks of development in each of the three domains. It also hints at some of the connections among specific developments, both between domains and within each single domain. For example, gender-role awareness is noted as emerging in early childhood; it sets the stage for gender segregation in middle childhood. But gender-role learning also influences the physical and cognitive skills. Young boys tend to engage in rougher games and activities, for example, and young girls tend to acquire skills involving fine or delicate motor coordination. To the extent that the two sexes do so, a gender-role difference gradually contributes to physical sex differences in strength and coordination. But numerous other relationships exist between and within domains of development. In later chapters we will try to point these out explicitly wherever appropriate. Meanwhile, to get a better sense of what development means, consider a more extended, complete example.

Changes happen in all domains at once— physical, cognitive, and psychosocial. As this toddler learns the physical skills of walking, she deepens her attachment to her caregiver. As the young boy develops his athletic skills, he also develops new self-respect and new knowledge of his overall competence.

One Individual's Development: Jodi

So far, though we have talked about the importance of relationships among various forms of development, our examples have been a bit diverse and fragmented. How would developments tie together in the life of a real person? What relationships among them could we see then? These are not simple questions to answer fully, but you can begin to get partial answers by considering a child whom one of the authors knew personally: Jodi.

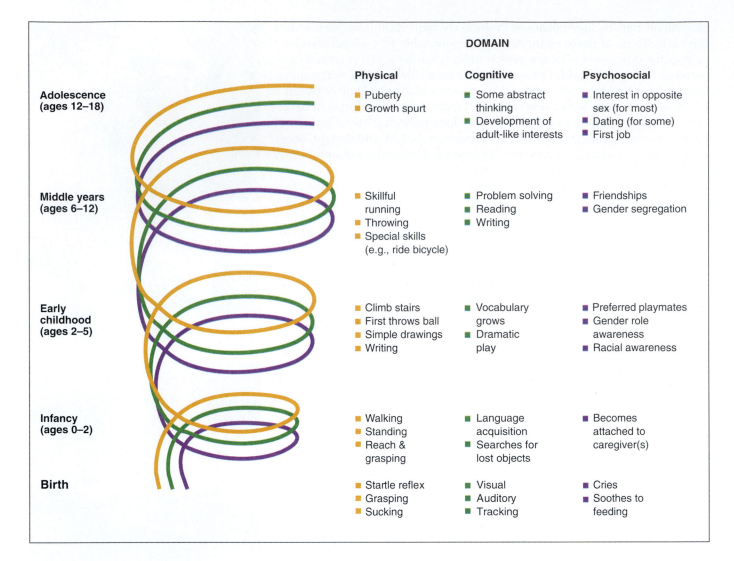

FIGURE 1.1

Selected Landmarks of Development

Development is a continual unfolding and integration of changes in all domains, beginning at birth. Changes in one domain often affect those in another domain.

When Jodi was four, one of her brothers died. Roger had been 2½ years older, a friendly kid and a decent sibling. Jodi played with him more than with her sister and other brother, who were both older than Roger. He died suddenly one winter from complications of chicken pox. The doctors said he may have reacted to the aspirin he had taken for his fever. They said you weren't supposed to give aspirin to children, but Jodi didn't know that, and apparently her parents didn't know it either.

For a few years after that, they were a three-child family "with a hole in the middle," said Jodi to her best friend, where Roger was supposed to be. It was not ideal for Jodi, but it was tolerable: she didn't have the playmate she used to have, but she did have her family ("What's left of it!") and her friends from school. Life got back to normal—sort of.

When Jodi was nine, her parents adopted another child, a boy of twelve, about the same age Roger would have been had he lived. Frank had lived in numerous foster care homes, some of which had not been happy experiences for him. In two homes the discipline had been extremely strict, but it was hard for Jodi to know this, because Frank did not tell her as much as he told the social workers or his new adopted parents, and her parents did not say much about Frank's past. In fact, Frank said little to Jodi about anything; he seemed distinctly cool toward all three of his new siblings.

Except for his periodic visits to Jodi's room at night. The first time it happened, Jodi was startled out of her sleep: Frank was standing by her bed and demanded that she take off her nightgown. That was all for that time. But he came back every few weeks, each time asking for more than the time before and threatening to hurt her badly if she revealed "our secret."

So Jodi learned not to sleep deeply. She also learned to avoid being alone in the house with Frank. In school she learned to avoid talking to boys very much, except in a joking way and in the presence of lots of other kids. In class she learned to look interested in what the teacher said even on the morning after a visit from Frank. And she learned to keep awake during the day, even when, as she later put it, "I was sleeping inside." Jodi learned a lot from Frank, though not things she wanted to learn and not things most of her classmates were learning.

Jodi's story shows several things about human development. It shows, for example, that the domains of development all unfold together. Jodi's thoughts and feelings about Frank occurred in the context of physical changes happening to herself. Being physically older or younger may not have protected her from abuse, but it probably would have altered the experience, both in impact and in quality.

Jodi's story also suggests the importance of unique, personal experiences when exploring human development in general. Some things about Jodi may always be unique because of her encounters with Frank; she may always be a bit mistrustful of boys and men, for example. But other things about Jodi can be understood as examples of human changes that are universal or nearly universal. In experiencing abuse, for example, Jodi responds to gender-role differences that pervade nearly all societies; in most societies, women experience less power than men.

To help organize thinking about developmental psychology, the developmental psychologist Urie Bronfenbrenner has originated a widely used framework for thinking about the multiple influences on children like Jodi (Bronfenbrenner, 1989; Garbarino, 1992a). He describes the contexts of development as *ecological systems*, which are sets of people, settings, and recurring events that are related to one another, have stability, and influence the child over time. (See Figure 1.2 and Table 1.1.)

1. The *microsystem* refers to situations in which the child has face-to-face contact with influential others. For Jodi, the microsystem consists of her immediate family (though note that the membership of this family changed over time) as well as her teachers and peers at school.

2. The *mesosystem* refers to the connections and relationships that exist between two or more microsystems and influence the child because of their relationships. An example would be the contacts between Jodi's parents and the social workers responsible for Frank's adoption: their contacts led them (perhaps wrongly) to withhold information about Frank from Jodi.

3. The *exosystem* consists of settings in which the child does not participate but still experiences decisions and events that affect him or her indirectly. An example in Jodi's case might be the medical system, which either lacked the knowledge needed to save Roger at the time of his death or had been organized in a way that interfered with communicating needed medical knowledge to Jodi's parents.

4. The *macrosystem* is the overarching institutions, practices, and patterns of belief that characterize society as a whole and take the smaller micro-, meso-, and exosystems into account. An example that affected Jodi was gender role: a widespread belief that men should dominate women may have contributed to Frank's coercive actions against Jodi, though of course it probably was not the only reason for them.

In the pages ahead we will try to keep in mind these multiple systems, such as those implied by Jodi's story, as well as the importance both of long-term continuity and of change in the lives of children and youth. Only in this way will we be able to convince you that developmental psychology has something to say about particular human lives: about how you, I, or a friend of yours changes and grows and what the changes and growth signify for our lives as a whole. In taking this perspective, we want to emphasize that developmental changes often have consequences that are multiple, complex, and interrelated. Jodi's response to abuse one month or one year after the experience may—or may not—be the same as her response many years later. At both times her responses are likely to influence not only her social relationships but also her learning. By being cautious with her teachers and with certain classmates, for example, Jodi may limit what she can learn from them academically and socially. We encourage you to think of her story as a reminder of developmental complexities like these, which pervade every human life.

Why Study Development?

Knowing about human development can help you in five major ways. First, it can give you realistic expectations for children and adolescents. Developmental psychology tells you, for example, when infants usually begin talking, and it suggests when schoolchildren tend to begin reasoning abstractly. Admittedly, it generally tells you only averages for children: when a "typical" child acquires a particular skill, behavior, or emotion. Nonetheless, knowledge of these averages can help you know what to expect from specific, individual children.

Second, knowledge of development can help you respond appropriately to children's actual behavior. If a preschool boy tells his mother that he wants to marry her, should she ignore his remark or make a point of correcting his misconception? If a third-grade child seems more interested in friends than in schoolwork, should her teacher discourage contact with friends or try to figure out ways to use the friends

TABLE 1.1   Ecological System Levels

Ecological Level	Definition	Examples	Issues Affecting Children
Microsystem	Situations in which the child has face-to-face contact with influential others	Family, school, peer group, church	Is the child regarded positively? Is the child accepted? Is the child reinforced for competent behavior? Is the child exposed to enough diversity in roles and relationships? Is the child given an active role in reciprocal relationships?
Mesosystem	Relationships between micro-systems; the connections between situations	Home–school, home–church, school–neighborhood	Do settings respect each other? Do settings present basic consistency in values?
Exosystem	Settings in which the child does not participate but in which significant decisions are made affecting the child or adults who do interact directly with the child	Parents' place of employment, school board, local government, parents' peer group	Are decisions made with the interests of parents and children in mind? How well do supports for families balance stresses for parents?
Macrosystem	"Blueprints" for defining and organizing the institutional life of the society	Ideology, social policy, shared assumptions about human nature, the "social contract"	Are some groups valued at the expense of others (e.g., sexism, racism)? Is there an individualistic or a collectivistic orientation? Is violence a norm?

Source: Garbarino (1982).

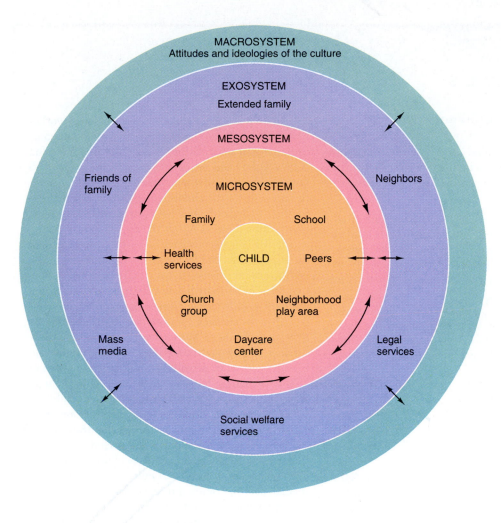

MACROSYSTEM
Attitudes and ideologies of the culture

EXOSYSTEM
Extended family

MESOSYSTEM

Friends of family

MICROSYSTEM

Neighbors

Family   School

Health services   CHILD   Peers

Church group   Neighborhood play area

Mass media   Daycare center   Legal services

Social welfare services

● ● ● ● ● ● ● ● ● ● ● ● ●

FIGURE 1.2

Bronfenbrenner's Four Ecological Settings for Developmental Change

Bronfenbrenner describes human development as a set of overlapping ecological systems, as shown. All of them operate together to influence what a child becomes as he or she grows into an adult. In this sense development is not exclusively "in" the person, but is also "in" the person's environment.
Source: Garbarino (1982).

to support the child's school studies? Developmental psychology can help answer such questions by indicating the sources and significance of many of the thoughts, feelings, and behaviors of children.

Third, knowledge of development can help you recognize when departures from the typical or average are truly significant. If a child talks very little by age two, should her parents and doctors be concerned? What if she still does not talk much by age three or four? If a teenager admits to having had sexual intercourse "once or twice" by age fifteen, should his parents worry that he is becoming promiscuous? How about if he is only thirteen or even eleven? We can answer these questions more easily if we know what usually happens to children and adolescents. And knowing what *usually* happens—being aware of the universal trends—makes up a great deal of the content of developmental psychology.

Fourth, studying development can help you understand yourself. Developmental psychology makes explicit the processes of psychological growth, processes that each of us may overlook in our personal, everyday lives. Even more important, it can help you make sense out of your own experiences, such as whether it really mattered that you reached puberty earlier (or later) than your friends did.

Finally, studying development can make you a better advocate for the needs and rights of children. By knowing in detail the capacities and potential of youngsters, you will be in a good position to persuade others of the importance and value of children. The "others" are diverse: they include parents, professionals who work with children, and political and business leaders. These groups, which include most

PERSPECTIVES

Wanted: A Child and Family Policy

• • • • •   Parents generally do value their children, want the best for them, and make sacrifices on their behalf. In spite of this support, though, the lives of children are often difficult:

- In the early 1990s, more than 20 percent of all children in the United States under age six lived in families that were officially poor (Huston, 1994). This is more than twice the rate of poverty in Canada and about ten times the rate of poverty in Sweden.

- A similar proportion of children have failed to receive routine immunizations against polio, measles, and other childhood diseases. Here too the United States ranks much lower than many other developed countries.

- About a third of all children living today will eventually experience the divorce of their parents, with all of the stress it brings (Hetherington, 1995). One of the stresses will be poverty, because the parent who usually has major custody, the mother, tends to earn much less than the father.

- In the United States, on average, an infant is born into poverty every thirty-five seconds, a child is physically punished in school every four seconds, and a preschooler is murdered every fourteen hours (Children's Defense Fund, 1995).

A major reason these problems exist is that the United States lacks a comprehensive, integrated set of policies for caring for its children. Programs to remedy social problems have tended to focus on problems selectively rather than recognizing the impact of one problem on another. School programs to assist with learning difficulties, for example, tend to work with children individually, even though health, nutrition, illness, and family disruptions contribute to learning difficulties in major ways. A more effective approach is to provide a set of related and coordinated services to support families: pediatric care, combined with

special help at school and a supportive social worker or nurse to visit parents at home to provide encouragement and information. When Victoria Seitz and Nancy Apfel tried this approach with some low-SES families, they found improvements in cognitive abilities not only for the children originally at risk but also for their siblings who had not even been a focus of the intervention (Seitz & Apfel, 1994)!

Similar conclusions have followed from studies of the supports needed by low-SES single mothers who wish to attend college (Kates, 1995). The most effective form of support has not been restricted to the mothers as individuals. Career counseling and campus advocacy services, for example, are useful for low-SES single mothers. More useful is to combine these services with supports for the mother's family and friends, such as by providing child care as needed or help with finding housing. Best of all is to include, along with these services, programs to actively develop awareness of these students' needs among university faculty and administrators so that they in turn can help the students find what they need.

Such combined approaches to children's welfare may look expensive and difficult when organized as special demonstration projects, but experience in other developed countries suggests that costs decrease markedly when implemented universally and that organizational problems can in fact be solved (Chafel, 1993; U.S. General Accounting Office, 1993). The real challenge, it seems, may be political: enlisting the support of leaders in government and business to develop comprehensive policies for children, and thereby ensuring the future of society.

What Do You Think?

If coordination of services is a good idea, why do you think it has not been done more often? Assuming the providers of services all intend to improve the lives of the people they serve, what barriers stand in the way of coordinating their activities?

readers of this book, have a common interest in the future of society and therefore in the future of children. Yet, as the accompanying Perspectives box indicates, we as a society can do a better job of supporting child development than we in fact have done.

WHAT DO YOU THINK ?   What do *you* hope to gain by studying developmental psychology (besides a college credit, of course!)? Take a minute to think about this question—maybe even jot down some notes about it. Then share your ideas with two or three classmates. How do they differ?

Past Understandings of Human Development

Until just a few hundred years ago, children in Western society were not perceived as full-fledged members of society or even as genuine human beings (Ariès, 1962). During medieval times, infants tended to be regarded rather like talented pets: at best interesting and even able to talk, but not creatures worth caring about deeply. Children graduated to adult status early in life, around age seven or eight, by taking on major, adultlike tasks for the community. At that time, children who today would be attending second or third grade might have been caring for younger siblings, working in the fields, or apprenticed to a family to learn a trade.

Because children took on adult responsibilities so soon, the period we call *adolescence* was also unknown. Teenagers assumed adult roles. Although these roles often included marriage and childrearing, most people in their teens lived with their original families, helping with household work and with caring for others' children until well into their twenties.

Although this may all seem harsh by modern, middle-class standards, it was not necessarily bad in the context in which it occurred. Historians and sociologists have pointed out that children and youth did have to work, but they tended to do only tasks for which they were capable, and they earned modest respect (if not wealth) from the community because they made true economic contributions to it (Haraven, 1986; Somerville, 1990)—an advantage that modern children experience much less often. Adults at that time also showed more awareness than now of the profound differences among children's formative, childhood experiences. The modern tendency to view all children as innocent and needing protection has also led, ironically, to much more uniform views about the nature of childhood and insensitivity to the impact of culture and economic class (Hendrick, 1997; Seifert, in press).

Early Precursors to Developmental Study

Why did awareness of childhood as a special time of life eventually emerge? Society was becoming less rural and more industrialized. During the eighteenth century, factory towns began attracting large numbers of workers, who often brought their children with them. "Atrocity stories" became increasingly common: reports of young children in England becoming caught and disabled in factory machinery and of children being abandoned to the streets. Partly because of these changes, many people became more conscious of childhood and adolescence as unique periods of life, periods that influence later development. At the same time, they became concerned with arranging appropriate, helpful experiences for children.

Without a doubt, the change in attitudes eventually led to many social practices that we today consider beneficial to children and youth. But there were losses at the same time. One positive gain was compulsory education, instituted because children needed to be prepared for the adult world rather than be simply immersed in it. Another was the passage of laws against child labor to protect children from physical hardships of factory life and make it less tempting for them to go to work instead of to school. But these gains also had a dark side. Viewing children as innocent also contributed to increasing beliefs that children are incompetent, their activities are unimportant, and the people who care for children deserve less respect than other people. That is why, it was argued, children cannot do "real" work and why they need education (Cannella, 1997). This view also contributed to the idea that children are essentially passive and lacking in opinions and goals worth respecting; that is why, it was thought, adults have to supervise them in school and pass laws on their behalf (Glauser, 1997; Kitzinger, 1997). These were early signs of what later came to be

The concept of childhood as a distinct period in a person's life is a relatively new invention, at least as judged by how children have been portrayed in paintings over the centuries. Until the nineteenth century, painters generally depicted children as miniature adults, with adultlike clothing, facial expressions, and bodily proportions. By the nineteenth century, though, childhood had come to be seen—and valued—as a unique time, one quite different from adulthood. Children were expected to wear special types of clothing and hairstyles and engage in their own kind of activities and pastimes.

called **ageism,** a prejudice against individuals based on their age, which eventually also affected social attitudes about adults as well, especially the elderly.

The Emergence of Modern Developmental Study

During the nineteenth and twentieth centuries, the growing recognition of childhood led to new ways of studying children's behavior. One of these was the **baby biography,** a detailed diary of a particular child, usually the author's own. One of the most famous English biographies was written and published by Charles Darwin (1877) and contained lengthy accounts of his son Doddy's activities and accomplishments. The tradition of rich description continued in the twentieth century with Arnold Gesell, who observed children at precise ages doing specific things, such as building with blocks, jumping, and hopping (Gesell, 1926). After studying more than five hundred children, Gesell generalized standards of normal development, or **norms**—behaviors typical of children at certain ages. Although the norms applied primarily to white, middle-class children and to specific situations and abilities, they gave a wider-ranging picture of child development than was possible from baby biographies alone.

The method of descriptive observation in child development research has persisted into the present. An influential observer in this century has been Jean Piaget, who described many details of his own three children's behavior as infants (Piaget, 1963). He did not observe all of the children's possible behaviors but focused on those that illustrated their cognitive skills, or ability to think. Piaget has influenced modern developmental psychology to such an extent that we discuss his work at length later in this book.

• • •

ageism Prejudice or bias against an individual on account of the individual's age.

baby biography A detailed narrative or history of an infant's development.

norms Behaviors typical at certain ages and of certain groups; standards of normal development.

WHAT DO YOU THINK ? What are the merits and problems of descriptive study of children? One way to find out is for you and two or three classmates to make separate written observations of the "same" events. Visit a place with people in it (even your developmental psychology classroom), and separately write about what you see one particular person doing. Afterward, compare notes. How well do they agree, and when and how do they differ?

Pamela Mitchell, **Primary School Teacher**

The Many Purposes of Play

Pamela Mitchell taught kindergarten for many years. Most recently she has been responsible for an innovative program that deliberately integrates first-, second-, and third-grade children into one class. She spoke eloquently about her students and the changes she sees in them as a result of activities that engage them in class. As she talked, it became clear that Pamela deeply cares about giving children *choices*, so I asked her to talk more about that.

Kelvin: *How do you provide for choice in the classroom?*

Pamela: One thing I do is put aside an hour every morning for "Choice Time." I set up materials around the room that relate to the current theme—things like cooking, science experiments, new activities on the computer, building blocks, games, or new art activities. If the kids don't want to choose one of them, that's OK too. There are so many possibilities!

Kelvin: *Isn't Choice Time what most of us would call "play"? Why not just call it that?*

Pamela: You're right, it really is play. If you walked into my room, you would see kids "playing" every morning for an hour. I always call it Choice Time, though, because I think *choice* highlights what play accomplishes, both for me and for the kids.

Kelvin: *Which is . . . ?*

Pamela: [*smiling broadly*]: You know what? Choice Time is probably the most valuable time of the day. It gives me a chance to see each child holistically—to see how each one sets priorities, combines what they're learning and seeing. Choice Time lets the kids "put it all together"; it's when they organize their knowledge.

Kelvin: *It sounds pretty "cognitive" in its benefits.*

Pamela: Yes, Choice Time—play—definitely has cognitive benefits, but it has social and emotional benefits too. It also helps with motor skills!

In the cognitive area, play helps children with their language. They have to listen and talk with others. Of course, talking is also a social activity—the kids have to negotiate how to share or how to work their way into an activity. They're figuring out *what* to say and *when* to talk and when to keep silent.

Playing with others can be pretty emotional, too! I've had children shed tears when someone else was using a book or an activity they wanted. Children learn to deal with those things through play.

Kelvin: *What about motor skills? Your classroom seems pretty small, which might limit your options.*

Pamela: You'd be surprised. Building with blocks takes motor skills; so does drawing. When the kids go out in the hallway to measure just how long a twenty-six-foot dinosaur would be, it takes motor skills to lay out the tape measure, along with cooperation and strategizing about how to measure such a big distance. But you're right—we don't do running-around, gym-type games in here.

Kelvin: *I should think that some people might consider Choice Time a poor use of class time. Some parents or even some other teachers might say, "it's just play," belittling its value.*

Pamela: But it isn't just play—it's the element of *choice* that makes it so valuable. The kids choose an activity that interests them, and that makes them feel empowered to learn. If a parent seems unsure about Choice Time, I might say, "Think about how you learn something new. Say you recently learned to use a computer. You didn't just read a book about using it; you *played* with it!" That's how we all learn.

Kelvin: *For all the good things about Choice Time, do you see any pitfalls?*

Pamela: You have to be really involved during Choice Time; it's probably the busiest time of my day. I'm talking to individual kids, following up on their initiatives and maybe suggesting other materials or activities to support them further. I try to check in with as many of the children as possible during that time. It's critical to connect what the kids choose to do, what I've done with them earlier, and what I'll be doing later.

Kelvin: *So involvement is a key to success with children's play?*

Pamela: You could say that. The key is to believe in your heart that children learn by choosing and by constructing knowledge on their own initiative. When you do, it changes your whole attitude about teaching and learning.

What Do You Think?

1. Do you agree with Pamela's ideas about play? If you were teaching a primary-grade class, would you feel comfortable organizing it the way she has?

2. Think back to an activity or a skill that you do well, and ponder *how* you learned it. Did your mastery involve periods of play and/or free exploration? Compare your experience with those of two or three classmates. Does everyone seem to have needed playful exploration, or only some people?

3. If play is so closely intertwined with cognitive learning, social development, and motor development, why is it not more common in school programs? What factors do you think might limit its use? After you formulate your own answer, you might find it helpful to get the opinion of an experienced teacher about this question.

Basic Issues in Developmental Study

As child development has evolved as a discipline, four basic issues about the nature of human development have emerged: continuity and discontinuity, nature and nurture, context and universality, and deficit and difference in development. These issues influence how developmental psychology is organized, and therefore also influence what you can expect when you study it. They are summarized in Table 1.2.

Continuity and Discontinuity

Continuity and **discontinuity** are the issues to which we called attention at the beginning of the chapter. Developmental psychologists have noted what we pointed out earlier: that some long-term changes seem like obvious continuations of earlier qualities and skills, whereas others seem new and unprecedented. Take memory: older children usually can recall and define more words than younger children, as if this developmental change were simply a matter of accumulating more numerous verbal memories. But is that all there is to it? In recalling and using terms, is an older child really just doing "more" of what a younger child does or doing something altogether different? Michelene Chi wondered about this question and, through some ingenious memory tests (Chi, 1985), concluded that later memory is not necessarily more of earlier memory but the same memory organized differently. She asked a first-grade girl to recall the names of as many of her classmates as possible. The girl performed this task quite well, but by using a strategy different than that used by most older children and adults: instead of recalling classmates' names alphabetically, as older children and adults probably would have done, the girl recalled them according to the children's seating arrangement in the classroom. When asked to recall a list of unfamiliar names in alphabetical order, on the other hand, she performed poorly compared to adults. The child's memory was discontinuous with the adult's, at least on this task, in that child and adult followed different rules for organizing information. But the adult's memory was also continuous with the child's in two important ways. One continuity was that both individuals used *some* sort of rules of organization. The second continuity was that in certain situations, the adult probably also used the *same* rules of organization (remembering by social grouping) that the child did.

continuity Long-term stability in a human quality, behavior, or ability.

discontinuity Long-term gaps or changes in a human quality, behavior, or ability.

nature In the study of human development, the essential and/or inborn qualities of a person.

nurture In the study of human development, the environmental influences and experiences that affect a person's development.

Nature and Nurture

How much are you the result of genetic, inborn qualities, and how much the result of learning and experience? The first alternative (genetics and inborn qualities) is your **nature,** and the second (learning and experience) is your **nurture.** It seems sensible to expect that each of us combines nature and nurture in a lot of ways. Your height depends on how tall your parents are (nature), but it also depends on the nutrition and exercise you get as you grow up (nurture).

Developmental psychologists have many questions about exactly how nature and nurture interact and whether one is sometimes more important than the other. Robert Plomin and his associates, for example, studied the temperaments (or emotional styles) of two groups of infants: one a group of identical twins, and therefore completely the same genetically, and the other fraternal twins, and therefore only as similar genetically as ordinary siblings (Plomin et al., 1993). The identical twins were somewhat more simi-

TABLE 1.2	Basic Issues In Developmental Psychology	
Issue	**Crucial Question**
Continuity and discontinuity	How much does development simply continue earlier acquisitions, and how much does it lead to qualitatively new behaviors and skills?
Nature and nurture	How much are qualities, behaviors, and skills inborn, and how much are they acquired through experience?
Universal and context-specific development	How much can developmental psychology identify developmental changes that happen to everyone throughout the world, and how much should it take specific human and cultural contexts into account?
Deficit and difference	Are certain developmental changes and milestones inherently more desirable than others?

An important issue in developmental psychology has to do with accounting for diversity among individuals, families, and communities. Are there principles that hold true for all people—including this Amish family and this African American family—regardless of circumstances?

lar to each other in their emotional reactions than were the fraternal twins—they responded to strangers with similar degrees of shyness, for example—suggesting that genetics influenced their reactions and styles. But the tendency to be more similar was only modest, suggesting that experiences since birth also affected the babies' emotional temperaments.

Universal and Context-Specific Development

As a practical matter, most of us (including developmental psychologists) recognize that who we are and become depends in various ways on the settings and situations in which we grow up—that is, it is context-specific. If I grow up among English-speaking adults, I will learn to speak English, not some other language. If I grow up on the streets of Paraguay, as described in the accompanying Multicultural View box, my entire personality will develop differently than if I grow up in a small-town family in the midwestern United States. What makes developmental psychologists curious is the extent and importance of such influences: when are they superficial and limited (such as wearing one color of clothing instead of another), and when are they profound, far-reaching, and part of our human essence? When is development **universal,** and when **context-specific**?

Patricia Greenfield studied routine parent-teacher conferences between Anglo teachers and Hispanic mothers in terms of differences in personal and family values between the two groups (Greenfield, 1995). During the conferences, the Anglo

● ● ●
universal development Changes or continuities that occur to all, or at least most, human beings.

context-specific development Continuities or changes that happen only to certain individuals because of unique circumstances that they experience.

A Multicultural View ....

Street Children: Comparing Paraguay and North America

Like all countries of Latin America, Paraguay contains children and youths who are popularly call "street children." They are a serious concern for the authorities in this country, as indeed they are everywhere, including in North America. Who are the street children, and what do they need? The sociologist and social worker Benno Glauser investigated these questions in Paraguayan society, using interviews and case studies of street children and their families. He was surprised to find it was not at all clear what street children have in common with one another or what they therefore needed (Glauser, 1997). The ambiguities he encountered have implications for how we should think about and deal with street children in more developed societies such as the United States or Canada.

In Paraguay, political leaders, social workers, and other makers of public opinion used the term "street children" to refer to youngsters in cities who lacked a home or family, spent nights on the street, and either begged or worked at various semilegal or illegal activities to get money for food. Yet Glauser found that real street children were much more diverse than this definition implies. Some still slept with their families, for example, and usually spent days on the street only to attend to a job (e.g., selling flowers). Some deliberately slept out, but only occasionally or for selected periods because of their employment (e.g., giving street directions to tourists for money could be done only in the tourist season). Some never saw their parents, but slept in the home of another relative or some other responsible adult. And some (a minority) fit the definition of the authorities: they never saw

family or relatives, banded together with other homeless children for mutual protection, and always slept on the street. This last group was much more vulnerable to physical abuse, more likely to become sick, and more likely to become involved in criminal and other illicit activities (e.g., drugs or child prostitution). This finding has been confirmed by other research on street children (Campos et al., 1994).

Unfortunately, as Glauser discovered, the authorities tended to treat all street children as if they belonged to this last group and therefore were all in need of rather heavy-handed protection from abuse, disease, and poverty. Policies and actions favored (1) interrupting children's economic activities (e.g., washing car windshields at street corners), (2) moving children out of sight by having police pick them up and take them to more remote areas of the city, and (3) encouraging children to attend school and their caregivers to support children's attendance. Most of these actions proved either inappropriate or ineffective. Usually, for example, a child's job was not a "hobby" in spite of its informal status. Poor families often needed the child's income, or at least needed the child not to be an economic burden on the family. So parents and other relatives did not regret a child working. In fact, they often believed that a job developed character and a sense of responsibility. School, on the other hand, was widely regarded as a bad investment among poor families, since it led to few jobs and cost money for tuition once a child moved beyond the earliest grades (schoolchildren, in fact, often felt *more* rather than less pressure to work simply to pay the costs of education). And removing children from sight, as the police frequently did, accomplished little in the long term. Children simply walked back to their workplaces or living places and began again—though often after experiencing humiliation at the hands of

teachers uniformly sought to highlight the individual achievements of the child ("Carmen is doing well with her spelling"). But many of the Hispanic mothers preferred to direct the conversation toward how the child fit into the family and into the classroom group ("Carmen is such a help to me, and so friendly"). The parents' remarks reflected differences in general cultural values—the Anglo parents valuing independence somewhat more, but the Hispanic parents (sometimes) valuing *inter*dependence more. The result was frustration with the conference on the part of both teachers and parents and less effective support for the children in their efforts to succeed socially and academically. Note, though, that even among these parents and teachers, there were differences: some parents and teachers did adjust to each other's conversational priorities, regardless of ethnic background.

Deficit and Difference

When children develop in different ways, are some children deficient or lacking in some way, or are they merely different from others? Are certain developmental mile-

Research about street children in Latin America has found diversity, not uniformity, in the motives and circumstances of the children. Some are relatively content with their situation, as this boy may be, and well protected by a network of relatives or trustworthy friends. Others are not.

the police. For two reasons, in fact, Glauser suspected that Paraguayan policies and practices regarding street children were serving the interests not of the children but of well-off adults. The first was the emphasis by the police (and other leaders of society) on simply getting street children out of sight, a strategy all too common in some American communities as well (Vissing, 1996). The second was the neglect of children who might need protection and help but are "hidden" from public view, such as unpaid child servants, child prostitutes, or child soldiers in the Paraguayan army. These groups were at least as common as street children, but were ignored in all public discourse.

The Paraguayan experience has two important implications about street children in more economically developed countries such as the United States. One implication is about diversity: it is likely here, as in Paraguay, that "street children" come in different types, from those who merely work the street during the day, to those who sleep there intermittently, to those who live there essentially full time. All may need protection, though not necessarily to the same extent or in the same way. As in Paraguay, street children do not necessarily lose touch totally with parents, other relatives, or other responsible adults. Alternative living arrangements (e.g., a foster home) may—or may not—be better for a child in any particular case, especially for children who already receive significant, though partial, care from their biological parents or other close relatives.

A second point is that in a developed country such as the United States, we understandably hope that school is a more productive investment than may be the case in Paraguay. Here, therefore, police and social workers may be more justified in encouraging street children to attend school than they are in less developed countries. But such reasoning may be more hope than reality even in the United States, where living conditions for poor families sometimes approach Third World conditions in spite of proximity to wealth, and where schools face tremendous educational challenges as a result (Dalglish, 1998; Kozol, 1991, 1995). Children of the First World, or at least some of them, may not be so very different from children of the Third World.

stones inherently more desirable than others? To the extent that developmental psychologists (as well as the rest of the world) can agree on which changes are truly desirable, they (and other professionals) can actively work to encourage them and to discourage unwanted or undesirable directions of growth and change in children.

At some general level, some changes surely must be more desirable than others. Nearly everyone would agree, for example, that acquiring some sort of language is better than acquiring no language at all, because language gives a child a way to communicate with others. But as often as not, one developmental change is not clearly "better" than another. Although acquiring language in general may be good for a child, it may not matter *which* particular language is acquired: Spanish, Chinese, American Sign Language, and all dialects (or "accents") of English are equally capable of expressing the full range of human thoughts and feelings. Speaking (or signing) these various languages makes children different, but does not make some children deficient compared to others.

The effort to identify general developmental trends sometimes makes developmental psychologists prone to equate **differences** in children with **deficits.** Recently a number of psychologists have explored an example of this tendency in

difference In human development, a continuity or change regarded as making an individual distinctive but not better or worse than other individuals.

deficit In human development, a continuity or change regarded as limiting the competence and potential of an individual.

studying how children and adults develop morality—a sense of ethics, or of right and wrong. Until the early 1980s, the psychological study of moral development focused on children's general sense of justice or fairness (Colby et al., 1983). Is it always right, for example, to pay a person in proportion to his or her productivity? Is it always wrong to steal? More mature (and therefore "better") development seemed to be associated with the ability to reason abstractly about principles of fairness. An implication was that people who cannot or do not reason as abstractly as others are not just different but deficient in their moral reasoning.

More recent research has suggested that this view of moral development is unfair to many people's ethical ideas. Carol Gilligan interviewed adolescent girls and young women who were considering having abortions and found that their sense of right and wrong focused much less on general principles of fairness ("Is abortion always/sometimes/never right?") and more on the welfare of the particular people affected (the baby, the father, the woman herself, her family). This approach, an "ethic of care" rather than of justice, becomes well developed in many women (and some men) and is used by them to resolve a variety of ethical dilemmas (Brown & Gilligan, 1992; Colby & Damon, 1992). Its existence suggests a new way of thinking about moral reasoning: perhaps children develop not toward a common endpoint but toward multiple possible endpoints. Some may develop moral reasoning oriented toward general principles of justice, whereas others develop an ethic of care. One orientation would be different from the other, but not necessarily deficient.

Perspective of This Book on Issues of Development

As developmental psychologists, our thinking about children has been affected importantly by the four issues described in the previous section—by the problems of continuity and change, of nature and nurture, of universality and context, and of deficit and difference. But as human beings, we bring our own perspective to these issues, a perspective that at times may be as noticeable as the issues themselves. In particular, we bring a strong commitment to supporting the welfare of children in all its forms, to understanding children's lives and minds in their naturally occurring contexts, and to acquainting ourselves with real, live children as a way to test and challenge our ideas about them. These goals are interrelated and influence how we understand each of the basic issues about developmental psychology.

Supporting the Welfare of Children   For us, developmental psychology is full of implications for benefiting the lives of children and youth, through making recommendations to parents, teachers, nurses, and other adults responsible for the young. This belief makes us especially interested in the "nurture" side of the nature/nurture issue: we are concerned with how experiences can make children's lives better or (unfortunately) sometimes worse. The Working With and Perspectives boxes in each chapter reflect our interest in how adults in all walks of life can have a positive impact on children. But the same interest is woven into the text itself, which offers numerous references to how the adults in children's lives can (and should) assist children's development.

Understanding Children's Lives in Context   An outcome of our concern for the welfare of children is our interest in the diverse circumstances and conditions of children's lives. This attitude has made us especially interested in context-specific development and inclined to see variation among children as developmental differences rather than as developmental deficits. We are fascinated with the diversity among children, families, and communities. An obvious expression of our interest is the Multicultural View boxes in each chapter, which describe some aspect of development as it occurs outside of middle-class North American society. A subtler expression of our commitment to context lies in the evidence we present about concepts and theories of developmental psychology: while we see merit in highly general explanations about children, we are interested at the same time in factors that qualify or limit the generalities in the lives of particular children. Why does a theory seem to work for one child or youngster and not for another? What additional information must be taken into account to make a developmental concept or theory "work" in particular circumstances?

Real Lives, Real Children   Seeking to understand development in context leads naturally to an interest in real, live children: in specific children and youth the authors have known. A few of their voices appear in boxes called "A Talk with . . .", where these individuals comment on particular topics relevant to developmental psychology. Experiences with other children we have known also turn up at key places in the text, such as at the beginnings of chapters (they have been somewhat fictionalized, though, to protect the children's privacy). And we invite you frequently to think about children whom you know or to think about your own childhood. The most obvious invitations are the What Do You Think? questions embedded periodically throughout every chapter. Many of these questions draw out the relationships between continuity and change that exist in the lives of particular children, as well as in your own lives.

WHAT DO YOU THINK ?   A psychologist once said that "every parent believes in nurture until they have their *second* child." What do you think she was getting at with this comment? If you happen to be a parent of at least two children, share your opinion of the comment with a classmate who is not a parent or with one who is a first-time parent. And vice versa: if you've raised no children, or only one, compare your opinions to those of a second- or third-time parent.

Methods of Studying Children and Adolescents

As a field of study, developmental psychology bases its knowledge on systematic research, the study or investigation of continuity and change in human beings. The methods used are quite diverse, but all bear some relationship to the **scientific method,** procedures to ensure objective observations and interpretations of observations. As noted below, the scientific method allows for considerable variety in how research studies might be conducted. In fact, it is more accurate to speak of *many* scientific methods rather than just one.

Scientific Methods

All scientific research studies have a number of qualities in common, whatever their specific topic. For various practical reasons, the qualities cannot always be realized perfectly, but they form ideals to which to aspire (Cherry, 1995; Levine & Parkinson, 1994).

1. *Formulating research questions* Research begins with questions. Sometimes these questions refer to previous studies, such as when a developmental psychologist asks, "Are Professor Deepthought's studies of thinking consistent with studies of thinking from less developed countries?" Other times they refer to issues important to society, such as "Does preschool education make children more socially skilled later in childhood?"

2. *Stating questions as hypotheses* A **hypothesis** is a statement that expresses a research question precisely. In making a hypothesis out of the preschool education question above, a psychologist needs to be more specific about the terms *preschool education* and *socially skilled*. Does *preschool education* mean a

scientific methods Systematic procedures for ensuring objective observations and meaningful interpretations of observations.

hypothesis A statement that expresses a research question precisely and is capable of being tested scientifically.

part-time nursery or a full-time child care center? Does *socially skilled* refer to a child who initiates activities or only to a child who smiles frequently and co-operates? By custom, however, a hypothesis usually is phrased as an assertion that can be tested (Hypothesis: "Preschool education makes children more so-cially skilled later in childhood") rather than as a question ("Does preschool ed-ucation make children more socially skilled later in childhood?").

3. *Testing the hypothesis* Having phrased a research question as a hypothesis, re-searchers can conduct an actual study about it. As the next section describes further, they can do this in a number of ways. The choice of method usually de-pends on convenience, ethics, and scientific appropriateness. No method of in-vestigation is perfect, although some are more suited than others for particular research questions.

4. *Interpreting and publicizing the results* After conducting the study itself, psy-chologists have a responsibility to report its outcomes to others by presenting them at conferences and publishing them in journal articles. Their reports should include reasonable interpretations or conclusions based on the results and enough details to allow other psychologists to replicate (or repeat) a study themselves to test the conclusions. In practice, the limits of time (at a confer-ence presentation) or space (in a journal) sometimes compromise this ideal.

There is a wide range of ways to carry out these steps, each with its own strengths and limitations. Viewed broadly, studies can vary in time frame, the extent of intervention and control, and the sampling strategies used. These dimensions of-ten get combined in various ways, depending on the questions the studies are in-vestigating. Table 1.3 summarizes the various possible methods, and the following sections explain them more fully.

Variations in Time Frame

In general, developmental psychologists can either compare people of different ages at one point in time (called a **cross-sectional study**) or compare the same people at different times as they get older (called a **longitudinal study**). Each method has its advantages and problems.

Cross-sectional Study   A cross-sectional study compares children of different ages at a single point in time. One such study compared preschool children (age

• • •

cross-sectional study A develop-mental study that compares individu-als of different ages at the same point in time.

longitudinal study A developmen-tal study that compares the same in-dividual(s) with themselves at earlier or later ages.

TABLE 1.3	Methods of Studying Children and Adolescents
Method	**Purpose**
Cross-sectional study	Observes children of different ages at one point in time
Longitudinal study	Observes same group(s) of children at different points in time
Sequential study	Combines features of cross-sectional and longitudinal studies
Naturalistic study	Observes children in naturally occurring situations or circumstances
Experimental study	Observes children where circumstances are carefully controlled
Correlational study	Observes tendency of two behaviors or qualities of a child to occur or vary together; measures this tendency statistically
Survey	Brief, structured interview or questionnaire about specific beliefs or behaviors of large numbers of persons or children
Interview	Face-to-face conversation used to gather complex information from children or adults
Case study	Investigation of just one individual or a small number of individuals using a variety of sources of information

four) and early-school-age children (age six) on their ability to distinguish between real and apparent emotions (Joshi & MacLean, 1994). Half of the children lived in India, and the other half lived in Great Britain. All of the children listened to stories in which a character sometimes had to conceal his or her true feelings (such as when an uncle gives a child a toy that the child did not really want) and described both how the character really felt as well as how the character seemed to feel. The results shed light on how children distinguish sincerity from tactfulness. The older children were more sensitive to this distinction than the younger ones, but the Indian children (especially girls) also were more sensitive to it than the British children.

Longitudinal Study   A longitudinal study observes the same individuals periodically over a relatively long period, often years. A recent example is the twenty-three-year follow-up of the effects of a demonstration preschool program for low-income children that originally took place in 1967. The four-year-old "graduates" of the program were assessed (and continue to be) every few years following the program; at the latest report, they were all twenty-seven years old (Schweinhart et al., 1993). Researchers gathered interviews, school achievement test results, and reports from teachers and (later) employers and compared them to results from an equivalent group of four-year-olds who had been identified at the time of the program but did not participate in it. The results are gratifying: the graduates have succeeded in school and employment better than the nongraduates and cost taxpayers less by needing less public aid and fewer medical and police services.

Longitudinal studies are especially well suited to studying long-term constancy and change in particular individuals or groups. This brother and sister keep much of the same look across the years—though perhaps they have "exchanged" their styles of smiling.

Cross-sectional and longitudinal studies both have their advantages and limitations. Cross-sectional studies can be completed more quickly, but they do not guarantee to show actual change *within* individuals. In the study of children's knowledge of emotions, for example, the fact that older children were more knowledgeable does not ensure that each *individual* child becomes more knowledgeable. It shows only an average trend for the group; in certain individuals knowledge of emotions may improve little as they get older, or even decrease, whereas other individuals may experience a huge leap in knowledge! Why these differences in individual change occur remains a question—and an urgent one if you work with children as a teacher, a nurse, or a counselor.

Longitudinal studies therefore may be more truly "developmental" because they show the steps by which individuals actually change. But they too pose a practical problem: by definition, they take months or even years to complete. Over this much time, some of the original children may move away; investigators may become hopelessly bogged down with other work and fail to complete the original study; or government funding to support the work may disappear prematurely. Given these problems, psychologists have organized cross-sectional studies much more often than longitudinal studies, despite the latter's special value.

Sequential Study   Sometimes the dilemmas of the time frame are solved by combining elements of cross-sectional and longitudinal studies. In the case of the ability to distinguish real from apparent emotions, children of different ages can be compared at one point in time (cross-sectional) and then followed for a few years before being tested again (longitudinal). Six-year-olds and nine-year-olds can be compared

In much naturalistic research, psychologists observe children's behavior as it normally occurs in everyday settings. These children standing in line for a drink, for example, suggest ideas about how relationships form among peers and about the nature of friendship in childhood.

initially and observed again three years later. Like a cross-sectional study, a *sequential study* produces relatively immediate results; like a longitudinal study, it traces individuals' actual development. As a compromise, therefore, sequential studies have much to recommend them.

Variations in Control: Naturalistic and Experimental Studies

Developmental studies also vary in how much they attempt to control the circumstances in which children are observed. When children are observed in naturally occurring settings, the studies are naturalistic; when circumstances are controlled tightly, the studies are experimental.

Naturalistic Studies   At one extreme, **naturalistic studies** purposely observe behavior as it normally occurs in natural settings, such as at home, on a playground, or in a classroom. Reed Larson and Maryse Richards (1994) used this strategy to explore the daily emotional lives of parents and their adolescent children. For several weeks, each member of the family carried an electronic pager that beeped at random intervals to remind the person to report on his or her current moods and activities by telephoning a prearranged number. In every other respect, however, the family members engaged in their normal daily activities—school, job, homemaking, or whatever. The researchers discovered many interesting facts about individuals' responses to family life. Being at home *relieved* stress for fathers ("Then I can relax"), for example, but often *created* it for mothers ("Home is my 'second job'"). Figure 1.3 illustrates this trend. Teenage children felt far more hassled by small daily chores than their parents realized ("They don't notice it when they overdo the reminders about chores").

Experimental Studies   In contrast to naturalistic studies, **experimental studies** arrange circumstances so that just one or two factors or influences vary at a time. For example, Henry Wellman and Anne Hickling (1994) investigated how children understand the human mind: do they think of "the mind" as the center of a person, as adults do, or more as an impersonal switchboard, perhaps like a computer or the motor of a car? To study this question, the investigators designed an experiment in which children had to explain the meanings of metaphorical statements about the mind ("My mind wandered" or "His mind played tricks on him"). Many conditions of the experiment were held constant: all children were interviewed in the same room, by the same person, and asked exactly the same questions. Children were selected from specific ages between 2½ and 10 to allow investigators to infer when the

• • •

naturalistic study A research study in which behavior is observed in normal or natural circumstances and without significant intervention by the researcher.

experimental study A research study in which circumstances are arranged so that only one or two known factors influence the participants at a time.

children began believing in a personified view of the mind. (The result? At 2½ children had only hazy notions of the mind as human or personified, but by age 8 most children did. Figure 1.4 depicts part of this trend.)

Because this study was an experiment, Wellman and Hickling held constant all the factors that might influence children's responses to metaphorical notions *except* age, the one they were studying. This deliberately varied factor is often called the **independent variable**. The factor that varied as a result of the independent variable—in this case, the children's success at interpreting metaphorical statements about the mind—is often called the **dependent variable**.

The experimental method also requires making decisions about the population, or group, to which the study refers. When every member of the population has an equal chance of being chosen for the study, the people selected comprise a **random sample**. If not everyone in a population has an equal chance of being chosen, the sample is said to be *biased*. Investigators can never be completely sure that they have avoided systematic bias in selecting children to study, but they can improve their chances by defining the population they are studying as carefully as possible and then selecting participants (in this case, children) only from that population. When Wellman and Hickling studied children's beliefs about the human mind, for example, the population to which they limited their observations consisted only of children of a certain age range—2½ to 10 years—and they sampled children within this range at random. Interpretations of their results therefore apply only to this population of children. In later studies, they (or other investigators) could sample other populations, such as children of other ages or specific ethnic backgrounds.

Experimental studies incorporate a number of precautions to ensure that their findings have **validity**, meaning they measure or observe what they intend to measure. One way to improve validity is to observe not one but two sample groups, one an experimental, or treatment, group and the other a control group. The **experimental group** receives the treatment or intervention related to the purposes of the experiment. The **control group** experiences conditions that are as similar as possible to the conditions of the experimental group, but without experiencing the crucial experimental treatment. Comparing the results for the two groups helps to

independent variable A factor in an experimental study that a researcher manipulates (or varies) to determine its influence on the participants.

dependent variable A factor measured in an experimental study that depends on or is controlled by one or more independent variables.

random sample In a research study, a group of participants chosen from a larger population such that each has an equal chance of being chosen.

validity The extent to which research findings measure or observe what is intended.

experimental group In an experimental study, the participants who experience an experimental treatment while in other ways experiencing conditions similar or identical to those of the control group.

control group In an experimental study, the participants who experience conditions similar or identical to the experimental group, but without experiencing the experimental treatment.

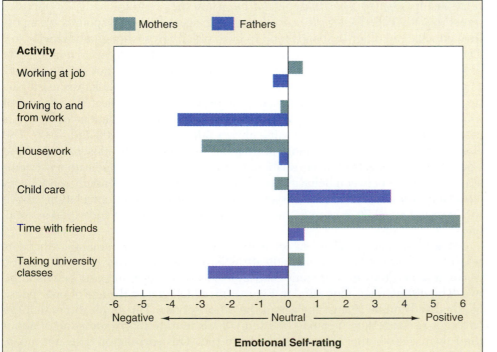

FIGURE 1.3

Mothers' and Fathers' Self-Rated Emotions During Various Activities

The idea of "his" marriage and "her" job contains some truth. In this naturalistic study, in which family members reported their emotions at random intervals, mothers and fathers rated a number of activities differently.
Source: Larson & Richards (1994).

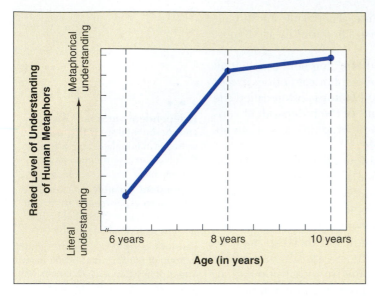

Rated Level of Understanding of Human Metaphors

Metaphorical understanding

Literal understanding

6 years   8 years   10 years

Age (in years)

●●●●●●●●●●●●●●●●●●●

FIGURE 1.4

Children's Understanding of Human Metaphors of Mind

In this experimental study, children were asked to explain statements that contained metaphorical expressions for the human mind (e.g., "my mind fell asleep"). Results suggested that children begin understanding these expressions as metaphors sometime after their sixth birthday, but do not achieve full understanding until age ten. *Source: Adapted from Wellman & Hickling (1994).*

● ● ●

correlation An association between two variables in which changes in one tend to accompany changes in the other without implying that one variable causes changes in the other.

explicitly establish the effects of the experimental treatment.

Comparisons of experimental and control groups are widespread in developmental research, but especially for problems involving interventions to improve the welfare of infants or children. One team of investigators used the strategy to study the impact of a program to develop literacy skills in low-income preschoolers (Whitehurst et al., 1994). The investigators used classrooms from Head Start, a nationwide early intervention program. They randomly assigned certain classrooms to an experimental group, which received the special literacy program. Other classrooms were randomly assigned to the control group, which received the usual Head Start program.

At the end of one year, they tested all classrooms in both groups for improvements in literacy skills. As you might expect, the experimental group improved more than the control group; children in the literacy program could identify more letters and their own names, for example. What is especially important is that the control group *also* improved somewhat, just by growing older; so the investigators were able to make allowances for this fact in evaluating the impact of the literacy program.

Because of its logical organization, the experimental method often gives clearer results than naturalistic studies do. But because people sometimes do not behave naturally in experimental situations, one criticism of the experimental method is that its results can be artificial. Naturalistic research does not face this particular problem, but it does run a greater risk of ambiguity in its results.

Correlations   Whether naturalistic or experimental, most research studies look for correlations among variables. A **correlation** is a systematic relationship, or association, between two behaviors, responses, or human characteristics. When the behaviors, responses, or characteristics tend to change in the same direction, the relationship is called a *positive correlation*; when they tend to change in opposite directions, it is called a *negative correlation*. The ages of married spouses are a positive correlation: older husbands tend to have older wives (though not strictly so). The age of a child and the frequency of bed wetting is a negative correlation: the older the child, the less frequent the bed wetting (though again, not strictly so).

When correlated factors can be expressed numerically, psychologists use a particular statistic, the *correlation coefficient* (abbreviated r), to indicate the degree of relationship between two behaviors or characteristics. The correlation coefficient is calculated in such a way that its value always falls between +1.00 and −1.00. The closer to +1.00 the value, the more positive the correlation; the closer to −1.00 the value, the more negative the correlation. Correlations near 0.00 indicate no systematic relationship between behaviors or characteristics, or an essentially random relationship. For various reasons, psychologists tend to consider correlations above +0.70 or below −0.70 as strong ones and those between +0.20 and −0.20 as weak ones.

When you read or talk about correlations, it is important to remember that correlations by themselves do not indicate whether one behavior or characteristic *causes* another; they indicate only that some sort of association exists between the two. The distinction is illustrated in Figure 1.5, which graphs the age of one spouse in a married couple against the age of the other spouse. The graph shows that the two ages rise together, meaning that individuals tend to marry someone of about their own age, whether that age is young or old. This correlation does not mean, however, that one spouse *causes* the other to be similar in age. More likely, the correlation reflects the influence of society's beliefs about appropriate ages for spouses or the way modern schooling is age-segregated and therefore facilitates meeting people of roughly your own age. A correlation only challenges us to consider these possible explanations; further research would be needed to determine their truth or importance.

Variations in Sample Size

In addition to all the variations described so far, developmental studies vary in how many people they observe or collect information about.

Surveys   At one extreme are large-scale **surveys**, specific, focused interviews of large numbers of people. Grace Kao (1995) used this method to examine patterns of school achievement among Asian American youth. She was particularly interested in a common stereotype of Asian youth as "model students": the belief that they always excel academically. Using interviews with about fifteen hundred Asian American students, parents, and teachers, as well as with about twenty-five thousand Anglo American counterparts, Kao compared family incomes, educational levels, and ethnic backgrounds with academic achievement. She found that the stereotype of the "model student" is rather misleading. Academic success varies substantially among particular Asian ethnic groups. It also depends more heavily on how much time and money particular parents invest in education for their particular children than on the educational, financial, or ethnic backgrounds of the family as such. In these ways, the Asian American youth were no different from their Anglo American counterparts.

These conclusions seem especially persuasive because of the rather large sample of families on which they are based—an advantage of the survey method. But the method also has limitations. Survey questions tend to be "cut and dried" to ensure that responses can be compared among large numbers of respondents. They tend not to explore subtleties of thinking or the reasons people have for taking certain actions or holding certain beliefs. Did some of Kao's Asian American families invest more in education because their culture encourages them to do so or because they correctly sensed the danger of discrimination due to their ethnic background and regarded education as insurance against such discrimination? To answer questions such as these, researchers need methods that invite respondents to comment more fully, such as interviews and case studies.

Interviews   A research study that seeks complex or in-depth information may use **interviews**, or face-to-face directed conversations. Because they take time, interview studies usually focus on a smaller number of individuals than surveys do, perhaps several dozen or so. Carol Gilligan and her colleagues (Brown & Gilligan, 1992; Taylor et al., 1995) used interviews to learn more about how teenage girls coped with the stresses caused by gender-role expectations as they grew up under different conditions. Some interviews involved girls who were attending a private girls' boarding school and were from economically well-off families; others included girls who were attending a public high school in a racially mixed, lower-income community. The interview format allowed Gilligan to explore the girls' perspectives in depth and to find out when and how differences in their circumstances influenced their development as young women. As it turned out, economic and family supports did matter, but not always as Gilligan expected. A constant challenge for all girls was to find and remain true to their own perspective (or *voice*, as Gilligan

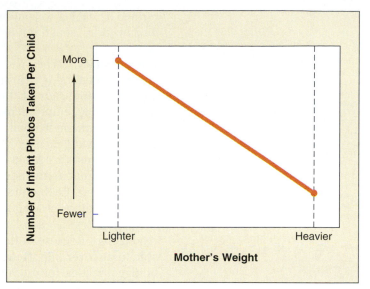

● ● ● ● ● ● ● ● ● ● ● ● ●
FIGURE 1.5

Correlation Is Not Causation

The number of baby pictures taken of an infant correlates (or varies) with the weight of the child's mother, with heavier mothers taking fewer pictures. But this does not mean that gaining weight *causes* mothers to stop taking pictures or that taking pictures causes mothers to gain weight. More likely a third factor, such as number of previous children to which the mother has given birth, causes both factors separately. Mothers tend to gain weight after each birth, but they also have less time for picture taking as a result of additional children in the house.

● ● ●

survey A research study that samples specific knowledge or opinions from a large number of individuals.

interview A face-to-face, directed conversation used in a research study to gather in-depth information.

termed it). Doing so could sometimes prove harder for well-off girls than for lower-income girls, though not necessarily.

Case Studies   When a study uses just one or a few individuals, it is called a **case study**. In general, a case study tries to pull together a wide variety of information and observations about the individual case and then present the information as a unified whole, emphasizing relationships among specific behaviors, thoughts, and attitudes in the individual. An example is a study by Robert Jimenez, Georgia Garcia, and David Pearson (1995) comparing the language skills and knowledge about reading of just three school-age children: one proficiently bilingual Hispanic student, one proficiently monolingual Anglo student, and one modestly bilingual Hispanic student. Each child was interviewed at length about her perceptions of her own skills with each language. Each was also invited to "think aloud" while reading samples of text in each language (that is, the child told about her thoughts as she read along). Because of the time taken with each individual, the investigators were able to discover important subtleties about how each student read. The proficient bilingual reader, for example, thought of *each* language as an aid to understanding the other language, whereas the less fluent bilingual reader believed simply that her Spanish assisted her English.

By its nature a case study can explore an aspect of child development, looking for new or unexpected connections among the child's behaviors, needs, or social relationships. This is the most common use of case studies. Second, it can confirm whether connections previously found in experimental studies actually occur in everyday, nonexperimental situations, even when conditions are not carefully controlled. The second use resembles the naturalistic studies described earlier in this section.

WHAT DO YOU THINK ?   Are some methods of child study inherently more effective than others? Try answering this question by organizing a multisided debate. Pick a successful developmental study (you can use any of the ones described in this chapter, for example), and assign each of three or four debating teams to design and argue the merits of some *alternative* method of studying the same question. In a second round of the debate, each team can try to refute the arguments of any of the other teams. Remember: there will be more than two sides to this discussion!

Ethical Constraints on Studying Development

Sometimes ethical concerns influence the methods that can be used to study a particular question about development. Take the question of punishment: what kinds of punishment work best with children, and for what reasons? For ethical reasons, we may be unable to study certain aspects of this problem directly. Observing parents actually scolding and reprimanding their children would require delicacy at best. At worst, if the punishment became severe or physical, ethics might require our active intervention simply to protect the child from abuse.

For ethically sensitive questions, we may instead have to satisfy ourselves with less direct but more acceptable methods of study. We can interview a variety of parents about the methods of punishment they use, or we can ask experts who work directly with families what methods they think parents typically use. A few courageous families might allow us to observe their daily activities, with the understanding that we are interested in observing how they punish their children. But by being volunteers, these few families may not represent other families very well.

Generally, research about human beings faces at least three ethical issues: confidentiality, full disclosure of purposes, and respect for the individual's freedom to participate (American Psychological Association, 1992). In developmental psychol-

case study A research study of a single individual or small group of individuals considered as a unit.

ogy, all of these issues are complicated by the youthfulness of the participants and by their parents' responsibilities for them.

1. *Confidentiality* If researchers collect information that might damage individuals' reputations or self-esteem, they should take care to protect the identities of the participants. Observing parents' methods of punishment might require this sort of confidentiality. Parents may not want just anyone knowing how much and how often they experience conflicts with their children. Chances are that the children would not want this information made public either. In such cases, investigators should not divulge the identities of participating families without their consent, either during the conduct of the study or afterward when the results are published.

2. *Full disclosure of purposes* Parents (and their children) are entitled to know the true purposes of any research study in which they participate. Most of the time, investigators understand and follow this principle carefully. But at times it can be tempting to mislead participants. In studying parents' punishment techniques, researchers might suspect that stating this purpose honestly will cause certain families to avoid participation, especially those with the most discipline problems. Or investigators might suspect that telling families the truth about the study will make them distort their behavior, perhaps making them self-consciously hide their worst conflicts. According to this argument, therefore, intentional misleading of parents would produce more complete observations of conflicts and parental punishment techniques. In this sense, dishonesty might make the research more "scientific." But investigators would purchase this benefit at the cost of their long-run reputations with the participants. Purposeful deception may sometimes be permissible, but only when no other method is possible and when participants are fully informed after the study of the deception and its reasons.

3. *Respect for individual's freedom to participate* As much as possible, researchers should avoid pressuring parents or children to participate in research studies. This may not be as simple as it first appears. Because psychologists have a relatively high status in society, some parents may be reluctant to decline an invitation from them to participate in "scientific research." Investigators therefore may have to bend over backward to assure parents that participation is indeed voluntary. They cannot simply assume parents or children will automatically feel free to decline if approached. After all, what parent wants to interfere with the progress of science?

When all three principles are closely followed, they allow for what psychologists call **informed consent:** the people or groups being studied understand the nature of the research, believe their rights are being protected, and feel free to either volunteer or refuse to participate. Informed consent therefore forms a standard, or ideal, for research to aim for and one that most studies do in fact approximate.

As the preceding discussion indicates, however, a completely informed consent may prove difficult to achieve in some cases. This is especially so for research about children, who tend to be dependent on the goodwill and wisdom of parents and other adults, including researchers. In studying children, investigators may sometimes wonder whether their participants can fully understand the purposes of a study, even when those purposes are explained. How well can children really understand why investigators want to observe conflicts between them and their parents? Even if such a goal makes sense to children, can they really feel free to participate or to decline? Or will children usually think they must cooperate with whatever adult investigators request? If the children are very young, perhaps parents can decide on their behalf, but when do children become mature enough to be consulted directly?

• • •

informed consent An agreement to participate in a research study based on understanding the nature of the research, protection of privacy, and the right to withdraw from the study at any time.

As these questions imply, the developmental level of the child should influence the way investigators resolve ethical issues in studying children (Thompson, 1990b). As a rule, younger children understand the purposes of a research project less well than do older children, making it less crucial that the younger ones themselves be thoroughly informed but more important that the parents be informed. Younger children also are more vulnerable to stressful research procedures, such as experimentation with the effects of personal criticism on the child. Older children, on the other hand, are more prone to self-consciousness and are more likely to detect—and survive—implied personal criticisms. Thus, investigators need to be more careful in studying problems that might shame a child publicly (such as by asking, "How often do you cry?" or "What problems have you had because your parents are divorced?").

Wherever possible, the right to decide about whether to participate in a research study rests with the child, provided the child understands the nature of the study and feels truly free to decline participation. When these conditions hold only partially, such as with young children, parents share the ultimate right to decide with the child. When the conditions do not hold at all, such as with infants, parents essentially take over the right to decide about participation.

However, these guidelines do not relieve research investigators of responsibility for the child's decision to participate, particularly when the child is young. Investigators must still follow a principle called **in loco parentis,** a Latin phrase meaning "in place of parents." The principle of in loco parentis requires investigators to act at all times in the best interests of the children being studied, much as the children's parents do in everyday affairs (Steininger et al., 1984). This means not only respecting parents' and children's decisions about participating but also looking after the children's welfare once a study is under way. If a study of children's games led (accidentally) to aggression or hurt feelings, in loco parentis would require the investigator to do whatever the parents might do to remedy the problem, including stopping the games.

WHAT DO YOU THINK ? Are there some research questions that are *never* ethical to study with children? What would they be, and why would they not be acceptable for study? What would be the consequences for society of permanently ignoring careful study of those topics?

Strengths and Limitations of Developmental Knowledge

As this chapter has demonstrated, human development has to be studied in particular ways and with certain limitations in mind. Because time is a major dimension of development, its impact must be approached thoughtfully. Yet the very nature of time poses real problems for studying at least some major questions. Sometimes people "take too long" to develop within the time frame available to study them. Also, because developmental psychologists deal with people, they must treat participants with respect and abide by the usual standards of decency and consideration for human needs. Finally, because they deal with especially young people, developmental psychologists sometimes must take extra care to determine the true best interests of participants, even when the participants do not know what they are being asked to do or do not feel free to refuse even when they do know.

Lest these limitations sound overly discouraging, be assured that in spite of them, developmental psychologists have accumulated considerable knowledge of children and adolescents in recent decades, and continue to do so. The remaining chapters of this book should make that point amply clear. Developmental psychology may not have definitive answers for all important questions about human nature, but it *does* have the answers for a good many.

• • •
in loco parentis In developmental research, the principle that investigators should act in the best interests of the child at all times.

Summary of Major Ideas

The Nature of Human Development

1. Developmental psychology concerns how thoughts, feelings, personality, social relationships, and motor skills evolve as individuals get older.

2. Development occurs in three major domains: physical, cognitive, and psychosocial.

3. The domains of development interact in many ways, and individuals always develop as whole persons rather than in separate parts.

Why Study Development?

4. Studying development can help give you appropriate expectations about the behavior of children and adolescents.

5. A knowledge of development can help you respond appropriately to children's actual behavior.

6. A knowledge of development can help you recognize when unusual behaviors are cause for concern.

7. Studying development can give you self-knowledge and understanding of your past.

8. Studying development can make you a better advocate for the needs and rights of children.

Past Understandings of Human Development

9. Until just a few hundred years ago, childhood and adolescence were not regarded as distinct periods of life.

10. Societal changes in the eighteenth century led to awareness of children's unique needs.

11. In the nineteenth and twentieth centuries, the first research studies of children consisted of baby biographies and structured observations of children at specific ages.

Basic Issues in Developmental Study

12. In general, developmental psychology focuses on four major issues: the extent of continuity and discontinuity in development, the impact of nature and nurture, the universality of development, and the problem of deficit and difference in development.

13. The authors of this book hold a perspective that emphasizes the importance of adults in children's lives, of the circumstances or context of children's lives, and of the value of knowing particular real-life children.

Methods of Studying Children and Adolescents

14. Research about developmental psychology tries to follow the scientific method: formulating research questions, stating them as hypotheses, testing the hypotheses, and interpreting and publicizing the results.

15. Studies vary in the time frame (cross-sectional or longitudinal), in control of the context (naturalistic or experimental), and in sampling strategies used (surveys, interviews, or case studies).

16. Cross-sectional studies compare individuals of different ages at one point in time.

17. Longitudinal studies observe human change directly by following the same children over relatively long periods of time.

18. Naturalistic methods observe children in natural contexts as much as possible.

19. Experimental methods try to control or hold constant extraneous conditions while varying only one or two specified variables.

20. Surveys, interviews, and case studies each sample different numbers of people, and each has unique advantages and problems.

Ethical Constraints on Studying Development

21. Ethical considerations guide how development can be studied and sometimes rule out certain studies altogether.

22. Generally, developmental studies should be guided by the principles of confidentiality, full disclosure of purposes, and respect for the individual's freedom to participate.

23. Research about children should strive for informed consent from children and their parents.

24. The specific ethical concerns in studying development depend on the age or developmental level of the children being studied as well as on the content of the study itself.

25. Even after a study has begun, researchers should follow the principle of in loco parentis, acting according to the best interests of the child.

Key Terms

ageism (12)	hypothesis (19)
baby biography (12)	in loco parentis (28)
case study (26)	independent variable (23)
cognitive development (4)	informed consent (27)
context-specific development (15)	interview (25)
continuity (14)	longitudinal study (20)
control group (23)	naturalistic study (22)
correlation (24)	nature (14)
cross-sectional study (20)	norms (12)
deficit (17)	nurture (14)
dependent variable (23)	physical development (4)
difference (17)	psychosocial development (4)
discontinuity (14)	random sample (23)
domain (4)	scientific methods (19)
experimental group (23)	survey (25)
experimental study (22)	universal development (15)
human development (4)	validity (23)

Theories of Development

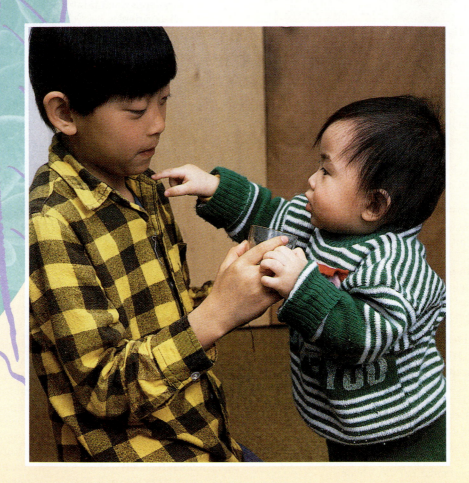

Focusing Questions

- What are developmental theories and how are they useful?

- How have psychodynamic theories influenced thinking about development?

- How have developmental theories based on learning principles contributed to our understanding of developmental change?

- How do cognitive developmental theories help us understand changes in thinking and problem solving from birth through adolescence?

- How have contextual approaches to development broadened our view of developmental change?

- Given the variety of developmental theories, how do you decide which theory or combination of theories is best for you?

W hen Elizabeth, age three, began nursery school, she cried and screamed every day when her mother left her. "Home!" and "Mama!" were the only words she seemed able to produce between sobs, which continued for much of each morning. Her concerned teachers met to discuss what to do about Elizabeth.

"It's best to ignore the crying," said one teacher. "If you give her lots of special attention because of it, you will reinforce the crying, and she'll just keep going longer."

"But we can't just ignore a crying child," said another. "This is a new and strange situation, and her crying shows that she's feeling insecure and abandoned. Look at her! She needs comfort and emotional support so that she can feel safer and more secure. At least give her a hug!"

"I think she's unsure whether her mother really will come back for her," said a third teacher. "Maybe we can find ways to help her understand and remember our daily routine here."

The teachers decided to follow all of this advice. They agreed not to fuss too much over Elizabeth's tears and to give her lots of comfort and support when she was not crying. They also helped Elizabeth draw a picture chart of the daily schedule and tape it to her cubbyhole. Finally, they talked with her mother about what they had observed and the solutions they were trying.

How well did it work? Elizabeth stopped crying—more quickly, in fact, than any of the teachers had expected. Although all three teachers agreed that Elizabeth clearly was happier and more at ease, no one was sure exactly how or why the change had come about.

Another question we might ask is: How might the theories we will encounter in this chapter and throughout this text help us to understand the physical, cognitive, and psychosocial developmental changes that we will see in Elizabeth as she moves through early childhood, the school years, and adolescence? How will developmental theories help Elizabeth, her family, and her teachers to better anticipate and respond to these changes in ways that are most helpful to her? In what ways will Elizabeth's development be similar to that of Jodi (discussed in Chapter 1), in what ways will it differ, and why? In this chapter, we will explore the nature of developmental theories and how they help us to understand the important developmental changes that take place from birth through adolescence.

The Nature of Developmental Theories

Each of Elizabeth's teachers' approaches reflects a different set of ideas and beliefs about children and their development. Whether they know it or not, most people—teachers, parents, students, and even children themselves—are guided by "informal theories" of human development.

What Is a Developmental Theory?

As we point out in Chapter 1, *human development* refers to long-term changes that occur during a person's lifetime and the patterns of those changes. Theories are useful because they help us to organize and make sense of large amounts of sometimes conflicting information about children's development, a task that at times can be complicated and confusing. For example, how do we decide whether day care is good for children and, if so, what type of day care is developmentally best? For that matter, how do we make developmental sense of different approaches to parenting and family life or education? In contrast to informal theories, the more formal developmental theories we are about to discuss attempt to provide clear, logical, and systematic frameworks for describing and understanding the events and experiences that make up developmental change and discovering the principles and mechanisms that underlie the process of change.

What qualities should a good theory ideally have? First, a theory should be *internally consistent,* meaning its different parts fit together in a logical way. Second, a theory should *provide meaningful explanations* of the actual developmental changes we are interested in, be they changes in children's thinking with age or the long-range effects of divorce on their social adjustment. Third, a theory should be *open to scientific evaluation* so that it can be revised or discarded if new or conflicting evidence appears or if a better theory is proposed. Fourth, a theory should *stimulate new thinking and research.* Finally, a theory should *provide guidance* to parents and professionals in their day-to-day work with children and adolescents.

How Developmental Theories Differ on Four Developmental Issues

While all developmental theories explore human experiences at various points from childhood through adolescence, they also differ in some important ways. In this chapter, we look at how each theory addresses basic questions about human development: To what degree is a given developmental change due to maturation (nature) and to what degree is it due to experience (nurture)? Is development a continuous process or a series of discontinuous stages? Does the individual take an active or a passive role in his or her own development? And broadly or narrowly, does the theory itself define the aspects of developmental change it seeks to explain?

Maturation or Experience?   Theories differ in the importance they assign to maturation and experience as causes of developmental change. *Maturation* refers to developmental changes that seem to be biologically determined because they occur in all infants and children relatively independently of their particular experiences. Examples of changes due to maturation include growth in height and weight and increases in the muscle coordination involved in sitting up, walking, and running. Examples of changes due to experience include increasing skill in playing baseball, basketball, or tennis, which clearly seems to be due mostly to formal and informal learning. But for many developmental changes, the relative contributions of maturation and experience are less clear. Talking is a good example. To what degree do all children learn to talk regardless of their particular learning experiences? How much does their talking depend on their particular experiences in the family, community, and culture in which they grow up?

Process or Stages?   Developmental theories also differ in whether they propose that development is made up of a series of small, continuous changes or whether it consists of distinct, stagelike steps. Theorists such as Erik Erikson and Jean Piaget assume that developmental change occurs in distinct stages. All individuals follow the same sequence, or order. Each successive stage is qualitatively unique from all other stages, is increasingly complex, and integrates the developmental changes and accomplishments of earlier stages.

Erikson's theory, for example, assumes that an infant must first master the crisis of *trust versus mistrust;* that is, she must come to trust her caregiver's ability to meet her needs. Only then can she move on to tackle the crisis that defines the next stage: *autonomy versus shame and doubt. Autonomy* refers to a child's capacity to be independent and self-directed in her activities. These and other stages of development proposed by Erikson are discussed later in the chapter.

Many motor skills, such as jumping rope or riding a bike, develop in predictable sequences or stages.

Learning theories on the other hand, see development as a relatively smooth and continuous process. The development of trust and autonomy, or of more sophisticated thinking and problem-solving skills, is thought to occur through the many, many small changes that unfold as a child interacts with his environment.

Still other theories see developmental change as a sequence of more rounded, overlapping slopes rather than as one continuous incline or a series of sharply defined stages.

Active or Passive Role of the Child?   Developmental theories also differ in their view of how actively children contribute to their own development. For instance, behavioral learning theorists believe developmental change is caused by events in the environment that stimulate individuals to respond, resulting in the learned changes in behavior that make up development. Theorists who are interested in how thinking and problem-solving abilities develop, such as Jean Piaget, propose that such changes depend on the child's active efforts to master new intellectual problems of increasing difficulty. Likewise, Erik Erikson's theory of identity development proposes that a child's personality and sense of identity are strongly influenced by his or her active efforts to master the psychological and social conflicts of everyday life (Hall & Lindzey, 1978; Miller, 1993).

Broad or Narrow Focus?   Finally, developmental theories differ in how broadly (or narrowly) they define the range of factors and circumstances that may influence development, in how many areas of developmental change they seek to explain, and in the number of specific developmental processes and mechanisms they propose. For example, Uri Bronfenbrenner's *ecological systems theory* emphasizes the broad range of situations and contexts in which development occurs. These include the child's direct and indirect experiences with family, school, work, and culture, all of which act together to create developmental change. However, these theories say little about the specific processes or mechanisms involved. On the other hand, *social learning theories* explain just a few specific issues, such as the development of gender roles and aggression, but describe several mechanisms—in this case, types of learning—that are involved.

WHAT DO YOU THINK ?   Does developmental change occur in stages, or is it a continuous process? How might different answers to this question affect how parents raise their children? How might they affect how teachers educate their students?

Psychodynamic Developmental Theories

Psychodynamic theorists believe development is an active, dynamic process that is influenced by both a person's inborn, biological drives and his or her conscious and unconscious social and emotional experiences. According to Sigmund Freud, a child's development is thought to occur in a series of stages. At each stage, the child experiences unconscious conflicts that he must resolve to some degree before going on to the next stage. Other influential psychodynamic approaches, such as those of Erik Erikson and object relations theorists, place less emphasis on biological drives and unconscious conflict. These theorists focus more on the development of a sense of identity as a result of important social, emotional, and cultural experiences.

Freudian Theory

Sigmund Freud (1856–1939) was the creator of *psychoanalysis,* the approach to understanding and treating psychological problems on which psychodynamic theory is based. Much of Freud's formal theory is outdated. However, his ideas continue to influence our understanding of personality development, including such areas as early infant-caregiver attachment, diagnosis and treatment of childhood emotional disorders, adolescent identity formation, and the long-range consequences of divorce.

The Three-Part Structure of Personality   Freud described each individual's personality as consisting of three hypothetical, or imaginary, mental structures: the id, the ego, and the superego.

The **id,** which is present at birth, is unconscious. It impulsively tries to satisfy a person's inborn biological needs and desires by motivating behaviors that maximize pleasure and avoid discomfort with no regard for the realities involved. In this view, the newborn infant is all id, crying for food and comfort but having no idea of how to get them because he cannot distinguish between wishful fantasy and reality.

The **ego** is the largely rational, conscious, problem-solving part of the personality. It is closely related to a person's sense of self. The ego functions according to the *reality principle,* a process by which the infant learns to delay her desire for instant satisfaction and redirect it into more realistic and appropriate ways of meeting her needs. This involves a shift of psychological energy from fantasy to the real parents and other caregivers who can in fact meet the infant's needs. Thus, a hungry infant shifts from imagining that the wish for food will satisfy her hunger to a more realistic focus on anticipating the appearance of her parent or other caregiver, who will feed her. An infant's developing ego, or sense of self, is based on her internalized mental images of her relationships with these caregivers.

The **superego** is the moral and ethical component of the personality. It develops at the end of early childhood. The superego includes the child's emerging sense of *conscience,* or right and wrong, as well as the *ego-ideal,* an idealized sense of how he should behave. The superego acts as an internalized, all-knowing parent. It punishes the child for unacceptable sexual or aggressive thoughts, feelings, and actions with guilt and rewards him for fulfillment of parental standards with heightened self-esteem. The superego sometimes can be overly moralistic and unreasonable, but it provides the child with standards by which to regulate his moral conduct and take pride in his accomplishments.

Stages of Psychosexual Development   Freud believed development occurs through a series of *psychosexual* stages. Each stage focuses on a

id In Freud's theory, the part of an individual's personality that is present at birth, unconscious, impulsive, and unrealistic, and that attempts to satisfy a person's biological and emotional needs and desires by maximizing pleasure and avoiding pain.

ego According to Freud, the rational, realistic part of the personality; coordinates impulses from the id with demands imposed by the superego and by society.

superego In Freud's theory, the part of personality that acts as an all-knowing, internalized parent. It has two parts: the conscience, which enforces moral and social conventions by punishing violations with guilt, and the ego-ideal, which provides an idealized, internal set of standards for regulating and evaluating one's thoughts, feelings, and actions.

Sigmund Freud and his daughter Anna, who became a psychoanalyst herself and whose work with young children has been influential.

different area of the body that is a source of excitation and pleasure. At each stage, developmental changes result from conflicts among the id, ego, and superego. These conflicts can threaten the child's ego, or sense of self. Pressures from the id push the child to act impulsively to achieve immediate pleasure; pressures from the ego encourage her to act more realistically by delaying satisfaction until it can be attained, and pressures from the superego push her to meet standards of moral behavior and achievement that may be overly strict or unrealistically high. Table 2.1 summarizes Freud's psychosexual stages and the developmental processes that occur in each stage.

The ego uses defense mechanisms to protect itself from such conflicts. *Defense mechanisms* are unconscious distortions of reality that keep conflicts from the ego's (self's) conscious awareness. One such defense mechanism is *repression,* in which unacceptable feelings and impulses are forced from memory and forgotten. Another is *projection,* in which a person's conflict-producing feelings, such as feelings of aggression, are mistakenly attributed to another person.

Even young infants, such as the one pictured here with her father, have an inner emotional life, feel connected with their caregivers, and participate actively in their own development.

According to Freud, unresolved id-ego and superego-ego conflicts can lead to a *fixation,* or a blockage in development. Fixation can also result from parenting that is not appropriately responsive to a child's needs. For example, overindulgence during the oral stage (see Table 2.1) may result in excessive dependence on others later in life. On the other hand, infants who experience severe deprivation and frustration of their needs may later feel they have to exploit or manipulate others to meet their needs. In this view, an individual's personality traits reflect the patterns typical of the stage at which a fixation occurred.

Erikson's Psychosocial Theory

Erik Erikson (1902–1994) grew up in Europe. He studied psychoanalysis with Freud's daughter, Anna, who strongly influenced his ideas about personality development. The accompanying Perspectives box describes the relationship between Erikson's life and his theory.

TABLE 2.1   Freud's Psychosexual Stages and Developmental Processes

Psychosexual Stage	Approximate Age	Description
Oral	Birth–1 year	The mouth is the focus of stimulation and interaction; feeding and weaning are central.
Anal	1–3 years	The anus is the focus of stimulation and interaction; elimination and toilet training are central.
Phallic	3–6 years	The genitals (penis, clitoris, and vagina) are the focus of stimulation; gender role and moral development are central.
Latency	6–12 years	A period of suspended sexual activity; energies shift to physical and intellectual activities.
Genital	12–adulthood	The genitals are the focus of stimulation with the onset of puberty; mature sexual relationships develop.

Developmental Processes

Development occurs through a series of psychosexual stages. In each stage the child focuses on a different area of her body, and how she invests her libido (sexual energy) in relationships with people and things reflects the concerns of the stage she is in. New areas of unconscious conflict among the id, ego, and superego, the three structures of personality, also occur. Conflicting pressures from the id to impulsively achieve pleasure, from the ego to act realistically by delaying gratification, and from the superego to fulfill moralistic obligations and to achieve idealistic standards all threaten the ego. The ego protects itself by means of unconscious defense mechanisms, which keep these conflicts from awareness by distorting reality.

In Erikson's view, personality development is a *psychosocial* process, meaning internal psychological factors and external social factors are both very important. Developmental changes occur throughout a person's lifetime and are influenced by three interrelated forces: (1) the individual's biological and physical strengths and limitations; (2) the person's unique life circumstances and developmental history, including early family experiences and degree of success in resolving earlier developmental crises; and (3) the particular social, cultural, and historical forces at work during the individual's lifetime (for example, racial prejudice, poverty, rapid technological change, or war).

Psychosocial Stages of Development   Erikson proposed that development occurs in a series of eight stages, beginning with infancy and ending with old age. Each stage is named for the particular *psychosocial crisis,* or challenge, that every child must resolve to be able to move on to the next. Successful mastery of the psychosocial crisis at a particular stage results in a personality strength, or *virtue,* that will help the individual meet future developmental challenges (Miller, 1993). Table 2.2 summarizes Erikson's stages and developmental processes.

Stage 1: trust versus mistrust.   The earliest basic trust is indicated by the infant's capacity to sleep, eat, and excrete in a comfortable and relaxed way. Parents who reliably ensure daily routines and are responsive to their infant's needs provide the basis for a trusting view of the world. The proper ratio, or balance, between trust and mistrust leads to the development of hope. *Hope* is the enduring belief that one's wishes are attainable. Failure to develop such trust may seriously interfere with a child's sense of security and compromise her ability to successfully master the challenges of the stages that follow.

Stage 2: autonomy versus shame and doubt.   As mentioned earlier, *autonomy* refers to a child's capacity to be independent and self-directed in his activities. It also reflects his ability to balance his own demands for self-control with demands for control from his parents and others. *Shame* involves a loss of self-respect due to a failure to meet one's own standards (Lewis, 1992). During toilet training, for example, a child will sometimes have accidents. A child who is treated with firmness,

• • •

trust versus mistrust In Erikson's theory, the psychosocial crisis of children from birth to one year involving whether they can rely on their parents to reliably meet their physical and emotional needs.

autonomy versus shame and doubt According to Erikson, the psychosocial crisis of children ages one to three involving the struggle to control their own thoughts, feelings, and actions; the second of Erikson's developmental stages.

TABLE 2.2   Erikson's Psychosocial Stages and Developmental Processes

Psychosocial Stage	Approximate Age	Description
Trust versus mistrust	Birth–1 year	Focus on oral-sensory activity; development of trusting relationships with caregivers and of self-trust (hope)
Autonomy versus shame and doubt	1–3 years	Focus on muscular-anal activity; development of control over bodily functions and activities (will)
Initiative versus guilt	3–6 years	Focus on locomotor-genital activity; testing limits of self-assertion and purposefulness (purpose)
Industry versus inferiority	6–12 years (latency period)	Focus on mastery, competence, and productivity (competence)
Identity versus role confusion	12–19 years (adolescence)	Focus on formation of identity and coherent self-concept (fidelity)
Intimacy versus isolation	19–25 years (early adulthood)	Focus on achievement of an intimate relationship and career direction (love)
Generativity versus stagnation	25–50 years (adulthood)	Focus on fulfillment through creative, productive activity that contributes to future generations (care)
Ego integrity versus despair	50 and older	Focus on belief in integrity of life, including successes and failures (wisdom)

Developmental Processes

Development of the ego, or sense of identity, occurs through a series of stages, each building on the preceding stages and focused on successfully resolving a new psychosocial crisis between two opposing ego qualities. No stage is fully resolved, and more favorable resolution at an earlier stage facilitates achievement of later stages.

PERSPECTIVES

Erik Erikson's Identity Crisis: An Autobiographical Perspective

• • • • •   *How do theorists' own life experiences influence their theories of development? Here is what Erik Erikson has written about his own identity crises and how they influenced his developmental theory.*

Erik Erikson was born in 1902 and died in 1994. He grew up in southern Germany with his mother, who was Danish, and her husband, a German pediatrician. Erikson recalls that "all through my earlier childhood, they kept secret from me the fact that my mother had been married previously; and that I was the son of a Dane who had abandoned her before my birth" (E. Erikson, 1975, p. 27).

As Erikson entered puberty and adolescence, identity conflicts intensified. "My stepfather was the only professional man in an intensely Jewish small bourgeois family, while I . . . was blond and blue-eyed, and grew flagrantly tall. Before long, then, I was referred to as a 'goy' [outsider] in my stepfather's temple, while to my schoolmates I was a 'Jew.' . . . Although during World War I, I tried desperately to be a good German chauvinist, [I] soon became a 'Dane' when Denmark remained neutral" (pp. 27, 28).

During this period, Erikson decided he would be an artist and a writer, rejecting his family's more middle-class values and expectations. He spent most of his time traveling, painting, writing, occasionally taking art classes, and teaching art. In looking back at these years, Erikson said that he now considered them to be an important part of his training (pp. 25, 26).

Using Freud's theory as a starting point, Erik Erikson expanded it to cover the life-span and modified the stages to place more emphasis on social encounters.

In fact, it was not until Erikson was almost thirty and moved to Austria that his career as a psychoanalyst and developmental theorist really began. His training in psychoanalysis was conducted by Anna Freud, who accepted him as a student after observing his work with children as a teacher in a small private school. After studying and practicing psychoanalysis in Vienna, Erikson was forced to leave Austria by the rise of Hitler. He emigrated to the United States, where he lived and worked the rest of his life.

Erikson achieved his outstanding accomplishments as a teacher, scholar, and therapist without the benefit of even a college degree, much less any other professional credentials. In the 1930s, Erikson worked as a psychoanalyst with children and debated whether to return to school for a professional degree. Instead, he accepted a research appointment at Yale Medical School and the Yale Institute of Human Relations, where he worked with an interdisciplinary team of psychologists, psychiatrists, and anthropologists and conducted field studies of the Sioux Indians in South Dakota.

In the 1940s, Erikson moved to California to study the life histories of children living in Berkeley and then the lives of the Yurok Indians. He joined the faculty of the University of California at Berkeley in the early 1950s, but was soon fired because of his opposition to the Korean War and refusal to sign a "loyalty oath," part of the fanatical anticommunist crusade of Senator Joe McCarthy. Erikson was reinstated as politically dependable, but resigned in support of others who were not rehired. Erikson says of this experience, "As I think back on that controversy now, it was a test of our American identity; for when the papers told us foreign-born among the nonsigners to 'go back where we came from,' we suddenly felt quite certain that our apparent disloyalty to the soldiers in Korea was, in fact, quite in line with what they were said to be fighting for. The United States Supreme Court has since confirmed our point of view" (pp. 42–43).

Erikson wrote this about that period: "It would seem almost self-evident now how the concepts of 'identity' and 'identity crisis' emerged from my personal, clinical, and anthropological observations in the thirties and forties. I do not remember when I started to use these terms; they seemed naturally grounded in the experience of emigration, immigration, and Americanization. . . . I will not describe the pathological side of my identity confusion, which included disturbances for which psychoanalysis seemed, indeed, the treatment of choice. . . . No doubt, my best friends will insist that I needed to name this crisis and to see it in everybody else in order to really come to terms with it in myself" (pp. 26, 43).

What Do You Think?

How did Erikson's own life experiences influence his developmental theory? What aspects of your own experiences have influenced your ideas about development?

According to Erikson, during the school years youngsters devote a great deal of time and energy to achieving new physical and social skills and to mastering the developmental crisis of industry versus inferiority.

initiative versus guilt Erikson's third crisis, during which a child's increasing ability to initiate verbal and physical activity and expanding imaginative powers lead to fantasies of large and sometimes frightening proportions.

industry versus inferiority Erikson's fourth crisis, during which children concern themselves with their capacity to do good work and thereby develop confident, positive self-concepts or else face feelings of inferiority.

identity versus role confusion The fifth of Erikson's psychosocial crises, in which one must integrate one's many childhood skills and beliefs and gain recognition for them from society.

reassurance, and respect for her failures as well as for her successes eventually will achieve autonomy (independence and self-direction) in this area. A child who is consistently shamed may have difficulty developing confidence in his ability to express himself freely and to self-regulate his thoughts, feelings, and behaviors. A successful outcome for this stage is the virtue of will. *Will* is the capacity to freely make choices based on realistic knowledge of what is expected and what is possible.

Stage 3: initiative versus guilt. During this stage, the child focuses on her genitals as a source of pleasure and on achieving greater mastery and responsibility. *Initiative* combines autonomy with the ability to explore new activities and ideas and to purposefully pursue and achieve tasks and goals. *Guilt* involves self-criticism due to failure to fulfill parental expectations. This crisis often involves situations in which the child takes on more than he can physically or emotionally handle, including the powerful sexual and aggressive feelings children often act out in their play. If a child's conflicting feelings of love and hate and conflicting impulses to be independent and dependent are ignored, belittled, or ridiculed, destructive feelings of guilt can result. If a child is treated respectfully and helped to formulate and pursue her goals without feeling guilty, she will develop the virtue of *purpose* in her life.

Stage 4: industry versus inferiority. This stage runs roughly from ages six to twelve. As a child leaves the protection of his family and enters the world of school, he must come to believe in his ability to learn the basic intellectual and social skills required to be a full and productive member of society and to start and complete tasks successfully. The virtue of *competence* is the result. A failure to feel competent can lead to a sense of inferiority. The child who consistently fails in school is in danger of feeling alienated from society or of thoughtlessly conforming to gain acceptance from others.

Stage 5: identity versus role confusion. This stage coincides with the physical changes of *puberty* and the psychosocial changes of adolescence. A successful resolution of this crisis is the development of the virtue of *fidelity,* the ability to sustain loyalties to certain values despite inevitable conflicts and inconsistencies. *Identity* involves a reliable, integrated sense of who one is based on the many different roles one plays. *Role confusion* refers to a failure to achieve this integration of roles. During this stage, teenagers undergo reevaluation of who they are in many areas of identity development, including the physical, sexual, intellectual, religious, and career areas. Frequently conflicts from earlier stages resurface. A successful resolution of this crisis is the development of the virtue of *fidelity,* the ability to sustain loyalties to certain values despite inevitable conflicts and inconsistencies. Failure to resolve this crisis may lead to a premature choice of identity, a prolonged identity and role confusion, or choosing a permanently "negative" identity that may be associated with antisocial and delinquent behavior. We take a closer look at identity development during adolescence in Chapter 16.

Erikson's final three stages occur after adolescence.

Stage 6: intimacy versus isolation. Successful resolution of this stage results in the virtue of being able to experience *love.* The young adult must develop the ability to establish close, committed relationships with others and cope with the fear of losing her own identity and separate sense of self that such intense intimacy raises.

Stage 7: generativity versus stagnation. This stage occurs during adulthood and midlife. Successful resolution brings the virtue of *care,* or concern for others. *Generativity* is the feeling that one's work, family life, and other activities are both personally satisfying and socially meaningful in ways that contribute to future generations. *Stagnation* results when life no longer seems purposeful.

Stage 8: ego integrity versus despair. This stage occurs during later adulthood and old age. Successful resolution brings the virtue of *wisdom. Ego integrity* refers to the ability to look back on the strengths and weaknesses of one's life with a sense of dignity, optimism, and wisdom. It is in conflict with the despair resulting from health problems, economic difficulties, social isolation, and lack of meaningful work experienced by many elderly persons in our society.

According to Erikson, psychosocial conflicts are never fully resolved. Depending on his or her life experiences, each individual achieves a more or less favorable ratio of trust to mistrust, industry to inferiority, ego integrity to despair, and so on. Therefore, conflicts from earlier stages may continue to affect later development.

Other Psychodynamic Approaches

A number of psychodynamic theorists have sought to extend Freud's basic insights about the importance of a child's object relations. **Object relations** refer to the child's relationships with the important people (called *objects*) in his environment and the process by which their qualities become part of his personality and mental life. Object relations theorists such as Margaret Mahler, Daniel Stern, and Heinz Kohut study how children internalize the images, memories, and values of people who are important to them and with whom they have strong emotional attachments (Barlow & Durand, 1995).

Object relations theorists have largely rejected Freud's idea that all developmental change is based on the satisfaction of primary inborn, biological drives such as hunger and sex. Instead, they cite research evidence with humans and other animals supporting the view that human infants possess an inborn tendency to develop close physical and emotional attachments with their caregivers that are *independent* of the basic drives of hunger, sex, and aggression (Eagle, 1984; Hamilton, 1989). (See Chapter 7 for a discussion of attachment.)

Margaret Mahler, for example, proposes that during the first three years of life, children go through four phases in developing a psychological sense of self. A newborn infant begins life in an *autistic phase,* meaning she is self-absorbed and has little psychological awareness of the world around her. Next, during the *symbiotic phase,* the infant experiences herself as being completely connected with and dependent on her primary caregiver rather than as a psychologically separate person. During the *separation-individuation phase,* she begins to develop a separate sense of self. Finally, during the *object constancy phase,* the infant achieves a more stable sense of self based on her increasing ability to form reliable mental representations of her primary caregivers (called *objects*) and their responses to her (Mahler et al., 1975). (See Table 2.3.)

An alternative description of the development of the psychological self is offered by Daniel Stern, who studied infant-parent interactions both in the laboratory and in naturalistic settings. According to Stern, an integrated *core self* based on the infant's mental *representations of past interactions that have been generalized,* or *RIGs,* emerges between two and six months. RIGs can be thought of as flexible mental structures that incorporate several actual experiences or interactions and form a model to represent them all. For example, after the first game of peek-a-boo, the infant lays down a memory of that specific episode. After the second, third, or twelfth experience of slightly different peek-a-boo episodes, the infant will have

intimacy versus isolation The sixth of Erikson's psychosocial crises, in which young adults must be able to develop intimate relationships with others while dealing with the fear of loss of identity that such intimacy entails.

generativity versus stagnation The seventh of Erikson's psychosocial crises, reached in middle adulthood, in which one must balance the feeling that one's life is personally satisfying and socially meaningful with feelings of purposelessness.

ego integrity versus despair According to Erikson, the final psychosocial crisis, reached during late adulthood and old age, in which one looks back on one's life with dignity, optimism, and wisdom while facing the despair resulting from the negative aspects of old age.

object relations The child's relationships with the important people (called *objects*) in his or her environment and the process by which their qualities become part of the child's personality and mental life.

TABLE 2.3	Mahler's Phases of Development	

Phase	Approximate Age	Description
Autistic phase	0–2 months	Safe, sleeplike transition into the world
Symbiotic phase	2–6 months	Development of an emotionally charged mental image of the primary caregiver
Separation-individuation phase	6–24 months	Functions as a separate individual
Hatching subphase	6–10 months	Responds differently to primary caregivers versus others
Practicing subphase	10–16 months	Safe separation and disengagement
Rapprochement subphase	16–24 months	Experiments more fully with leaving and returning to the safe home base of the caregiver
Object Constancy Phase	24–36 + Months	Maintains stable and reliable mental images of the primary caregivers

formed a RIG of peek-a-boo, that is, a memory or mental representation of peek-a-boo that is based on all of his previous peek-a-boo experiences. Next, a *subjective self,* based on an organized mental representation of relationships with others, appears between six and twelve months. Finally, a *verbal self* emerges between twelve and eighteen months with the development of language and symbolic thought.

According to Stern, these language and symbolic thinking skills continue to emerge throughout childhood and adolescence, and form the basis of internal working models. *Internal working models* describe how infants (as well as older children, adolescents, and adults) organize thoughts, feelings, experiences, and expectations about their relationships with the significant individuals in their lives and guide their understandings and expectations of themselves and others throughout their lives. Internal working models are broader than RIGs, which provide the basic building blocks from which they are constructed and may change as new RIGs are added or deleted. For example, an infant and her caregiver will each form an internal working model of their attachment relationship based on past and current patterns of RIGs, which in turn are based on their interactions with each other. (Stern, 1985a, 1995; Cushman, 1991). (See Table 2.4.)

A third theorist, Heinz Kohut, suggests that a newborn infant's sense of self is at first fragmented and incomplete. Through a process called *empathic mirroring,* a caregiver responds to the infant in ways that accurately and sensitively reflect, or *mirror,* her awareness and appreciation of the baby's feelings, needs, and experiences. This empathic mirroring allows the infant to form a progressively more complete and well-organized set of mental representations of himself and his caregivers. From these mental portraits, the infant eventually constructs a reliable and independent sense of self (Eagle, 1984).

Evaluation of Developmental Issues in Psychodynamic Approaches

This section evaluates psychodynamic approaches with regard to the four developmental themes discussed at the beginning of the chapter.

Maturation or Experience?   Freud and, to a lesser extent, Erikson believed biologically determined maturational processes play a significant role in developmental change, but they also emphasized the importance of experience. For example, in Freud's theory inadequate parenting at any stage can contribute to weak or overly rigid defenses and to later personality problems in the child. Erikson emphasized not only the child's unique life circumstances and experiences but also the broader social, cultural, and historical forces that influence development and shape the identity crises each individual confronts. Object relations theorists generally place even less emphasis on maturation and propose that a child's social and emotional experiences with caregivers play a very central role in development.

Process or Stages?   Both Freud's and Erikson's theories strongly support a stage view of developmental change. Mahler, Stern, and Kohut view stages as a way to organize observations of children rather than as a central mechanism of change.

Active or Passive Role of the Child?   All of the psychodynamic theories discussed view the child as a participant in his or her own development. However, Freud puts the least emphasis on the child's active role, whereas Erikson and object relations theorists emphasize it more.

Broad or Narrow Focus?   Freud's theory is broad in that it attempts to explain the development of adult personality through childhood experiences. It is also narrow in its focus on the psychosexual domain of experience to the exclusion of physical, cognitive, and broader social, cultural, and historical factors. While Erikson covers the entire lifespan, including social, cultural, and historical forces, in his theory, he too says little about physical or cognitive development. Mahler, Stern, and Kohut emphasize important social, emotional, and, to some extent, cognitive aspects of development, but limit their explanations to infancy and early childhood.

Applications of Psychodynamic Developmental Theories to Everyday Life

Psychodynamic theories help us to understand the formation of **attachment,** the strong and enduring emotional bond that develops between infant and caregivers during the infant's first year of life (Chapter 7); the development of autonomy and self-control during infancy and toddlerhood (Chapter 7); and the development of intimate relationships during adolescence and adulthood (Chapter 16). These theories also alert us to the social and emotional importance of early childhood play (Chapter 10), and help us to deal with death, loss, and grieving during middle childhood (Chapter 13) and with eating disorders, depression, and delinquency during adolescence (Chapters 14 and 16).

Erikson's psychosocial theory will help us see that resolving the crisis of *identity versus role confusion,* a major task of adolescence, has its origins in earlier stages of identity development. Object relations theories, such as Mahler's, help us to better understand the process of separation-individuation during the first three years, and Ruthellen Josselson uses similar ideas to help teenagers and their parents deal with the sometimes difficult task of separating from each other during the adolescent years (Chapter 16). Finally, Stern's concept of *internal working models* furthers our understanding of how a parent's distorted mental portrait of his or her child can

• • •

attachment The strong and enduring emotional bond that develops between an infant and his or her caregivers during the infant's first year of life.

TABLE 2.4	**Stern's Stages of Development**	
Stage	**Approximate Age**	**Description**
Emergent self	0–2 months	Active seeking of stimulation; more mature regulation of sleeping, eating, responsiveness, and emotional state
Core self	2–6 months	Development of sense of integrated self based on mental Representations of past Interactions that have been Generalized (RIGs)
Subjective self	6–12 months	Organized perspective about relationships with others
Sense of verbal self	12 Months +	Development of language and symbolic thinking skills

WORKING WITH
Jeffrey Friedman, **Clinical Social Worker**

The Value of Development Theory for Helping Children and Families

Jeffrey Friedman, a clinical social worker, specializes in child development. He was interviewed in his office at a community mental health center where he helps children, adolescents, and families with their developmental problems and consults with pediatricians about the developmental problems they encounter in their practices.

Robert: *Do you find developmental theories useful in your work?*

Jeffrey: They help a lot if you use them in a practical way and don't treat them like cookbook recipes to follow in every case. Theories also help me to avoid mistakes. They correct myths about people that most of us are taught to believe. Sometimes they remind me to keep the whole person in mind when I am focused on a single pressing problem, and sometimes they help me to divide a big, vague problem into small, discrete parts that are easier to work with. They add things that I couldn't figure out from my own experience and common sense.

Robert: *Such as?*

Jeffrey: Before I studied development, when I spent time with children I assumed that they thought the same way adults do, because I couldn't remember how I thought when I was their age. Reading the work of theorists who studied children closely and working under the guidance of teachers who applied these theories has helped me to understand better the peculiar ways in which children think about and experience the world.

Robert: *Could you give an example?*

Jeffrey: Think of the way a child conceptualizes death. When a child talks about her uncle dying and being buried, you might assume that she kind of knows what death is. If you haven't read about how children understand death, it probably wouldn't occur to you to ask the child what she means so that you could help her feel better about it. Because if you *did* ask her, she might tell you that they're going to plant her uncle in the ground, and next spring he's going to grow up like a flower and she'll have him back again.

Robert: *Or she might think that her uncle went to sleep, but since she doesn't understand the difference between death and sleep, could be terrified that if she goes to sleep, she might also die.*

Jeffrey: Exactly.

Robert: *How do you apply theories when you work with children and families?*

Jeffrey: You find people in family relationships all tied up in knots, doing things they don't expect or even want to do, feeling things they don't want to feel. For children, the feelings and experiences of their primary caregivers turn out to have an enormous impact on development.

Robert: *As I recall, you once worked with a group of children whose problems in their relationships with their parents were so severe that they actually stopped growing. What was this problem called?*

Jeffrey: It's called psychosocial dwarfism. I'm glad that you remembered that, because it's a very dramatic instance of how psychological theory helped to explain a very perplexing disorder!

Robert: *Can you give me some details?*

Jeffrey: They were young kids, mostly 6, 7, 8 years old and some as old as 10 or 11. They all were extremely small, and most were two or three years below the normal height and weight for children their age. They were also intensely angry and unhappy and were doing poorly both at home and in school. People thought they were so small for their age because of malnutrition.

Robert: *Was that the problem?*

contribute to abuse, and how changes in these internal working models can help to prevent abuse (Chapter 10).

WHAT DO YOU THINK? Erikson proposed that cultural and social forces play a major role in developmental change. With this in mind, how might growing up as a member of an ethnic minority, growing up in poverty, or growing up female influence how an adolescent deals with the crisis of identity versus role confusion?

Behavioral Learning and Social Cognitive Learning Developmental Theories

Learning is generally defined as relatively permanent changes in observable behavior that result from experience. According to the learning theories, the learning ex-

Jeffrey: Well, no. Their metabolism and growth hormones were highly abnormal, although the glands that produced the growth hormones were fine—and when the children were given growth hormones, they didn't grow. But when these children were put in the hospital away from their families, a surprising thing happened: their mental and physical conditions improved dramatically. They started to grow, gaining on average almost a centimeter a month. When the children returned home to their families, we were in for another surprise. Their mental states again deteriorated and the growth stopped completely.

Robert: *What were their parents like?*

Jeffrey: They weren't physically abusive, neglectful, or anything like that. In fact, they loved their children very much. Most were middle class people who lived in nice houses and had good jobs. Often they had other children who were doing just fine. As we got to know the parents better, though, we discovered that in every case at least one parent had very disturbed ways of thinking about their child, though they weren't aware of them.

Robert: *Do you mean their "internal working models"?*

Jeffrey: Yes, the working models or mental portraits that these parents held about their dwarfed children were severely defective. Developmental theory helped me to appreciate how, in the context of intense love relationships, patterns of thoughts and feelings that parents are barely aware of can profoundly affect the psychosocial, physical, and cognitive well being and development of their own children. Over time, I came to recognize the disturbed and irrational feelings that the parents were expressing indirectly to their children. Once the theory helped me find what was hidden, I could then help the parent and the child understand what was going on, so they could start to improve the situation. Although it took many months, once the quality of these parent-child relationships improved, the psychological adjustment of the children also improved. They all grew up to be of normal height and weight.

Robert: *Are similar problems in parent-child relationships found in other instances?*

Jeffrey: Yes, they are. Frequently, physical and sexual abuse of children by parents and others who are very close to them arises from problems in the working models they hold about their children. To understand those disturbed relationships and their impact on children's minds and bodies—and to know how best to improve things—you need developmental theories to help you understand the people involved, the factors in the situation, and the way they interact to affect a particular child and his or her family.

What Do You Think?

1. Why does Jeffrey Friedman believe that developmental theory is essential to understanding and helping individuals and their families?

2. What are your views of the differences between children's ways of thinking and those of adults? How has developmental theory influences those views?

3. What are your thoughts about the discussion of psychosocial dwarfism? In what way were you surprised about the power of mental life to influence development? In what were you not surprised?

periences that occur over a person's lifetime are the source of developmental change. Thus, changes in existing learning opportunities or the creation of new ones can modify the course of an individual's development.

We first discuss the work of two founders of the behavioral learning approach, Ivan Pavlov and B. F. Skinner. Next, we briefly review the social cognitive learning approach of Albert Bandura. Although few developmental theorists today are strict behaviorists, the ideas of Pavlov and Skinner continue to play an influential role.

Behavioral Learning Theories

The behavioral learning theories of Pavlov and Skinner provide key concepts for understanding how learning experiences influence development and for helping individuals to acquire new, desirable behaviors and alter or eliminate problematic behaviors.

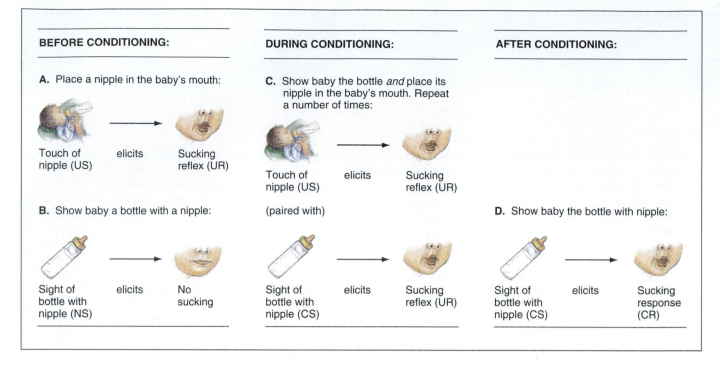

BEFORE CONDITIONING:

A. Place a nipple in the baby's mouth:

Touch of nipple (US)   elicits   Sucking reflex (UR)

B. Show baby a bottle with a nipple:

Sight of bottle with nipple (NS)   elicits   No sucking

DURING CONDITIONING:

C. Show baby the bottle *and* place its nipple in the baby's mouth. Repeat a number of times:

Touch of nipple (US)   elicits   Sucking reflex (UR)

(paired with)

Sight of bottle with nipple (CS)   elicits   Sucking reflex (UR)

AFTER CONDITIONING:

D. Show baby the bottle with nipple:

Sight of bottle with nipple (CS)   elicits   Sucking response (CR)

FIGURE 2.1

Illustration of Classical Conditioning

In this example, the nipple in the baby's mouth is an unconditioned stimulus (US), which with no prior conditioning brings about, or elicits, the sucking reflex, an unconditioned response (UR). (A) the nipple in the mouth elicits a sucking reflex; (B) the sight of a bottle is a neutral stimulus (NS) and has no effect; (C) once the sight of the bottle (neutral stimulus) is repeatedly paired with the nipple in the mouth (UCS), the sight of the bottle becomes a conditioned (learned) stimulus (CS), which now elicits sucking, the conditioned response (CR).

classical conditioning According to Pavlov, learning in which a neutral stimulus gains the power to bring about a certain response by repeated association with another stimulus that already elicits the same response.

operant conditioning According to Skinner, a process of learning in which a person or an animal increases the frequency of a behavior in response to repeated reinforcement of that behavior.

Pavlov: Classical Conditioning   Ivan Pavlov (1849–1936), a Russian scientist, first developed his behavioral theory while studying digestion in dogs. In his well-known experiments, Pavlov rang a bell just before feeding a dog. Eventually the dog salivated whenever it heard the bell, even if it received no food. Pavlov called this process **classical conditioning.** He named the salivation itself the *conditioned response,* the food stimulus the *unconditioned stimulus,* and the dog's salivatory response the *unconditioned response.* The last was so named because the connection between the food stimulus and the dog's response was an inborn, *unconditioned reflex,* that is, an involuntary reaction similar to the eyeblink and knee-jerk reflexes.

Through the processes involved in classical conditioning, reflexes that are present at birth may help infants to learn about and participate in the world around them. For example, conditioning of the sucking reflex, which allows newborn infants to suck reflexively in response to a touch on the lips, has been reported using a tone as the conditioned stimulus (Lipsitt & Kaye, 1964). Other stimuli, such as the sight of the bottle and the mother's face, smile, and voice, may also become conditioned stimuli for sucking and may elicit sucking responses even before the bottle touches the baby's lips. Although even newborns' behavior may be classically conditioned, it cannot be reliably observed over a wide range of reflexes until about six months of age (Lipsitt, 1990). Figure 2.1 illustrates the process of classical conditioning.

Skinner: Operant Conditioning   B. F. Skinner (1904–1991) is best known for his learning theory, also known as **operant conditioning.** This theory is based on the idea that the future likelihood of any behavior is influenced by the consequences that follow that behavior. Two types of consequences, positive and negative reinforcement, increase the future likelihood of the behaviors they follow. *Positive reinforcement* refers to situations in which the future likelihood of a particular behavior (a baby saying "da-da") is increased by adding something pleasant to the environment (a father saying "good boy") following the occurrence of that behavior. *Negative reinforcement* refers to situations in which the future likelihood of a behavior is increased by removing something unpleasant from the environment following the occurrence of that behavior. Despite many past requests, Jason, age twelve, was unwilling to pick up his books, CDs, and various "projects" that had been cluttering up the living room for some time. His mom decided to play music that Jason hates on the living room stereo and turn off the music, as a negative reinforcer, whenever Jason made progress in cleaning up his clutter.

Two types of consequences decrease the future likelihood of a behavior that they follow. *Punishment* following a child's undesirable behavior decreases the future likelihood of that behavior by adding something unpleasant to the environment when the behavior occurs. When Alice, Jason's younger sister, refused to do her weekend chores, her mom punished her by adding an extra chore for every week the chores remained undone. *Response cost* decreases the future likelihood of an unwanted behavior by removing something pleasant from the environment following that behavior. When Billy, Jason's nine-year-old brother, persisted in misbehaving at the dinner table, his parents suspended his television viewing privileges for five days, to be reinstated only if no additional occurrences of dinnertime disruption had occurred.

Extinction refers to the disappearance of a response when the consequences that reinforced or maintained it are removed. Frequently the best way to extinguish an undesirable behavior is to ignore it and reinforce a more desirable alternative. *Shaping* occurs when a child learns to perform new responses not already in her repertoire, or "collection." This is achieved by starting with an existing response and then modifying, or shaping, it by reinforcing small changes that bring it closer and closer to the desired behavior. Consider a dad who wishes to teach his seven-year-old daughter to hit a ball with a bat. Since she already can swing a bat, careful encouragement (a good reinforcer) for better and better swings and eventually for actually making contact with the ball (which is itself a good reinforcer) will transform, or shape, his daughter's bat-swinging behavior into ball-hitting behavior, a far more enjoyable and useful one.

B.F. Skinner developed one of the best-known forms of behaviorism—operant conditioning. Its success may stem from its many practical applications to child and adolescent development.

Social Cognitive Learning Theory

Albert Bandura believes that developmental change occurs largely through **observational learning,** or learning by observing others. Learning is *reciprocally determined,* meaning it results from interactions between the child (including his behaviors, cognitive processes, and physical capacities) and his physical and social environment.

Observational learning takes two forms: imitation and modeling. In *imitation,* a child is directly reinforced for repeating or copying the actions of others. In *modeling,* the child learns the behaviors and personality traits of a parent or other model through vicarious (indirect) reinforcement. A child learns to behave in ways similar to those of a parent or other model by merely observing the model receiving reinforcement for his or her actions. How influential the model will be depends on a variety of factors, including the model's relationship to the child, his or her personal characteristics, and how the child perceives them (Bandura, 1989; Miller, 1993). Children's levels of cognitive development strongly influence their ability to observe, remember, and later perform in ways similar to the models they have watched.

The social cognitive learning approach has been useful in explaining gender development, the development of aggression, and the developmental impact of television and other media. It has also been useful to counselors and therapists who work with problems in the parent-child relationship and with children with a variety of

● ● ●

observational learning The tendency of a child to imitate or model behavior and attitudes of parents and other nurturant individuals.

It is likely that observational learning plays an important role as these girls learn to prepare bread dough.

behavioral and adjustment difficulties in both outpatient and residential treatment settings. Now let's look at how these theories view the four developmental themes.

Evaluation of Developmental Issues in Behavioral and Social Cognitive Learning Approaches

Maturation or Experience?   The learning theories of Pavlov and Skinner are striking in their exclusive emphasis on experience as the sole source of developmental change. Although Bandura's social cognitive approach notes that cognitive maturation plays a developmental role, it too focuses mainly on learning as the source of developmental change.

Process or Stages?   Pavlov, Skinner, and learning theorists in general view development as continuous rather than stagelike. While Bandura's most recent revision of his theory makes some mention of stages, stages play a relatively minor role in his view.

Active or Passive Role of the Child?   Both Pavlov and Skinner assume the child is a passive reactor rather than an active participant in the learning process and exclude the cognitive processes required for a more active role. Bandura views the child as a highly active participant in the social and cognitive learning interactions responsible for developmental change.

Broad or Narrow Focus?   Although learning approaches have proposed to explain all of developmental change using relatively few principles and processes focused on how learning occurs, until fairly recently they have maintained a relatively narrow focus on observable social behavior. More current cognitive learning approaches have expanded their views to include cognitive development and certain emotional processes. Nevertheless, they are still limited in these areas.

Applications of Behavioral Learning and Social Cognitive Learning Developmental Theories to Everyday Life

Pavlov's and Skinner's behavioral learning theories have proven particularly useful in helping us to understand development from infancy through adolescence. For example, classical conditioning has been used to teach infants to respond to different stimuli by sucking on a pacifier in order to study the development of objective perception in young infants. Operant conditioning and observational learning have guided the study of cognitive development during the first two years (Chapter 6) and helped to explain the development of autonomy in infancy and toddlerhood (Chapter 7). **Behavior modification,** a specific set of techniques based on operant conditioning and social cognitive learning, has been essential in helping school-age children and their families deal with **attention deficit hyperactivity disorder (ADHD)** (Chapter 13) and in helping adolescents with eating disorders and delinquent behavior (Chapters 14 and 16). Both behavioral and social cognitive learning theories help to explain how language is acquired during early childhood (Chapter 9). Social cognitive learning theories help us to understand the role of vicarious (indirect) reinforcement and self-reinforcement in early childhood play.

WHAT DO YOU THINK ?   Think of some examples of developmental changes in a young child's behavior that might be accurately explained using behavioral learning theories. Then think of an example of a developmental change that doesn't seem to fit the behavioral model.

Cognitive Developmental Theories

In this section, we discuss three theoretical approaches to cognitive development: Piaget's cognitive theory, neo-Piagetian theories, and information-processing theory. All of these theories share a strong focus on how children's thinking and problem solving develop and how such cognitive activities contribute to the overall process of child and adolescent development.

Piaget's Cognitive Theory

Jean Piaget (1896–1980) was one of the most influential figures in developmental psychology. Just as Freud's ideas radically changed thinking about human emotional development, Piaget's ideas have changed our understanding of the development of human thinking and problem solving, or *cognition.*

Key Principles of Piaget's Theory   Piaget believed that children's thinking develops in a series of increasingly complex stages, or periods, each of which incorporates and revises those that precede it. Piaget's cognitive stages and developmental processes are summarized in Table 2.5. His theory is discussed in greater detail in the chapters on cognitive development.

What exactly makes a child develop from one stage of thinking and problem solving to the next? Piaget believed that three processes are involved: (1) direct learning, (2) social transmission, and (3) maturation.

Direct learning results when a child actively responds to and interprets new problems and experiences based on patterns of thought and action he already knows. Piaget called these existing patterns of thought and actions *schemes.* A **scheme** is a systematic pattern of thoughts, actions, and problem-solving strategies that helps the child to deal with a particular intellectual challenge or situation.

• • •

behavior modification Techniques based on the principles of learning theory that can be used by parents, teachers, therapists, and other professionals to help children, adolescents, and adults to reduce or eliminate undesirable behaviors and learn desirable ones.

attention deficit hyperactivity disorder (ADHD) A disorder of childhood characterized by impulsivity, excessive motor activity, and an inability to focus attention for appropriate amounts of time.

scheme According to Piaget, a behavior or thought that represents a group of ideas and events in a child's experience.

According to Piaget, an infant's first understanding of the world is based on a limited number of *innate schemes* made up of simple patterns of unlearned reflexes that are inherited at birth, such as sucking, grasping, and looking. These schemes rapidly change as the infant encounters new experiences through the complementary processes of *assimilation* and *accommodation*.

Assimilation is the process by which an infant interprets and responds to a new experience or situation in terms of an existing scheme. For example, a two-month-old baby who is presented with a bottle for the first time understands what is needed to suck from the bottle based on her existing sucking scheme for her mother's breast. The infant has assimilated a new situation, sucking from a bottle, into her existing scheme for sucking.

As children grow older, schemes involve increasingly complex mental processes. For example, a preschooler sees a truck but calls it a "car" because the concept of *car* is already well established in his thinking. But this same child correctly uses the concept of *bird* to refer to several very different winged creatures—say, a chicken, a pigeon, and a parakeet.

In **accommodation,** a child changes existing schemes, or ways of thinking, when faced with new ideas or situations in which the old schemes no longer work. Instead of calling a truck by the wrong name, the preschooler searches for a new name and begins to realize that some four-wheeled objects are not cars. According to Piaget, development results from the interplay of assimilation and accommodation, a process called *adaptation*. **Adaptation** results when schemes are deepened or broadened by assimilation and stretched or modified by accommodation.

Social transmission, Piaget's second explanation for development, is the process through which one's thinking is influenced by learning from social contact with and observation of others rather than through direct experience. *Physical maturation,* Piaget's third explanation for developmental change, refers to the biologically determined changes in physical and neurological development that occur relatively independently of specific experiences. For example, a child must reach a certain minimal level of biological development to be able to name an object.

According to Piaget, a central goal of intellectual activity is to establish *equilibrium*, a stable and harmonious balance between one's thought processes and one's experiences with the environment. If an earlier way of thinking or acting does not work in a new situation, cognitive change is stimulated. Such changes increase the sophistication and maturity of a child's thinking and allow the child to move into a new phase of development—a new cognitive stage.

While research at least partially supports many of Piaget's ideas, it has found a number of shortcomings. One problem is how to explain why, in many instances,

assimilation According to Piaget, a method by which a child responds to new experiences by using existing concepts to interpret new ideas and experiences.

accommodation According to Piaget, the process of modifying existing ideas or action-skills to fit new experiences.

adaptation Piaget's term for the process by which development occurs; concepts are deepened or broadened by assimilation and stretched or modified by accommodation.

TABLE 2.5	Piaget's Cognitive Stages and Developmental Processes	
Cognitive Stage	**Approximate Age**	**Description**
Sensorimotor	Birth–2 years	Coordination of sensory and motor activity; achievement of object permanence
Preoperational	2–7 years	Use of language and symbolic representation; egocentric view of the world
Concrete operational	7–11 years	Solution of concrete problems through logical operations
Formal operational	11–adulthood	Systematic solution of actual and hypothetical problems using abstract symbols

Developmental Processes

The earliest and most primitive patterns, or schemes, of thinking, problem solving, and constructing reality are inborn. As a result of both maturation and experience, thinking develops through a series of increasingly sophisticated stages, each incorporating the achievements in preceding stages. These changes occur through the processes of assimilation, in which new problems are solved using existing schemes, and accommodation, in which existing schemes are altered or adapted to meet new challenges. Together, these processes create a state of cognitive balance or *equilibrium*, in which the child's thinking becomes increasingly stable, general, and harmoniously adjusted to the environment.

According to Piaget, children think in qualitatively different ways as they develop. Very young children usually think about objects and experiences by looking and touching. Many adolescents, on the other hand, can plan and reason abstractly.

tasks that are logically equivalent are mastered at very different points in children's development. It is also hard to explain why a child's cognitive performance on two logically similar tasks is often very different. Finally, Piaget's exclusive emphasis on the predetermined "logical" aspects of children's functioning often does not match the actual thought processes children appear to use and largely ignores the social, emotional, and cultural factors that influence children's thinking (Case, 1992; Rogoff & Chavajay, 1995). Some of these issues are discussed in the Multicultural View box that appears later in this chapter.

Neo-Piagetian Approaches

Neo-Piagetian theories are new or revised models of Piaget's basic approach that attempt to go beyond Piaget's thinking. While these theories generally agree with Piaget's basic ideas about overall stages of cognitive development, they disagree about some of the details of how these broad changes work.

Robbie Case, for example, proposes that cognitive development results from increases in the child's mental space. *Mental space* refers to the maximum number of schemes the child can apply simultaneously at any given time (Case, 1991b, 1991c, 1991d). During early childhood, most cognitive structures are rather specific and concrete, such as drawing with a pencil, throwing a ball, or counting a set of objects. As the structures guiding these actions become coordinated with one another, they form new, more efficient, higher-level cognitive structures, which in turn begin to be coordinated with other, similar structures. Thus, a child's ability to use increasingly general cognitive structures enables him to think more abstractly. Different forms of the same logical problem may require different processing skills and capacities. As a result, a child's performance on two logically similar tasks may differ significantly, and mastery of each task may occur at very different points in her development.

Kurt Fischer, another neo-Piagetian theorist, also accepts Piaget's basic idea of stages. However, Fischer uses specific *skills* instead of *schemes* to describe the cognitive structures children use in particular problem-solving tasks or sets of tasks. The breadth of a skill is determined by both the level of maturation a child's central nervous system has reached and the range of specific learning environments to which the child has been exposed (Fischer, 1980; Fischer & Pipp, 1984). Thus, support from parents, teachers, and others in the environment is important for skill acquisition. Also, at any given point in each child's development, there is an optimal level of skill performance that cannot be exceeded without further central nervous

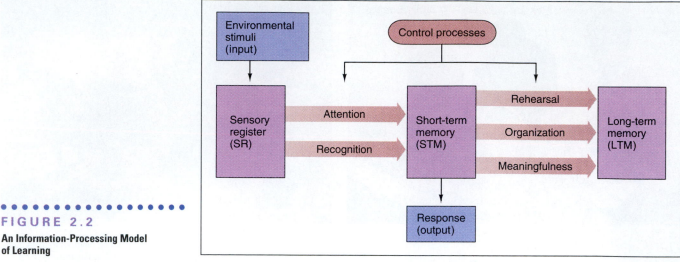

FIGURE 2.2
An Information-Processing Model
of Learning

system development. Fischer's "breadth of skill" idea has much in common with Lev Vygotsky's *zone of proximal development,* which you will read about later in this chapter.

Information-Processing Theories

Another alternative to Piaget's cognitive theory is **information-processing theories,** which focus on the precise, detailed features or steps involved in mental activities (Klahr, 1992; Seifert, 1993). Like a computer, the mind is viewed as having distinct parts that make unique contributions to thinking and problem solving in a specific order.

Key Principles of Information-Processing Theories   *Information-processing theories* concern how information gets into memory and how it is stored, retrieved, organized, and manipulated during thinking and problem solving. Figure 2.2 shows one information-processing model of human thinking. According to this model, when a person tries to solve a problem, she first takes in information from her environment through her senses. The information gained in this way is held briefly in the *sensory register,* the first memory store. The sensory register records information exactly as it originally receives it, but the information fades or disappears within a fraction of a second unless the person processes it further.

Information to which a person pays special attention is transferred to *short-term memory (STM),* the second memory store. The short-term memory corresponds roughly to "momentary awareness," or whatever the person is thinking about at a particular instant. The short-term memory can hold only limited amounts of information—in fact, only about seven pieces of it at any one time. After about twenty seconds, information in short-term memory is either forgotten or processed further. At this point, it moves into *long-term memory (LTM),* the third memory store.

Information can be saved permanently in long-term memory. But doing so requires various cognitive strategies, such as rehearsing information repeatedly or organizing it into familiar categories. Unlike short-term memory, long-term memory probably has unlimited capacity for storage of new information. The problem comes in retrieving information. As odd as it sounds, a person cannot always remember how to recall something. Most of us experience this problem when an old acquaintance's name is on the tip of our tongue or when we remember only that the person's name "begins with the letter *w,* I think." But most of us can remember certain events that occurred long ago better than many more recent events.

information-processing theory
Explanations of cognition that focus on the precise, detailed features or steps of mental activities. These theories often use computers as a model for human thinking.

Developmental Changes in Information Processing   As children grow older, they experience several cognitive changes that allow them to process information more efficiently and comprehensively. Changes occur in cognitive control processes, in metacognition (knowledge about knowledge), and in the amount of knowledge itself.

Control Processes   The most important developmental change in information processing is the acquisition of control processes. *Control processes* direct an individual's attention toward particular input from the sensory register and guide the response to new information once it enters short-term memory. Usually control processes organize information in short-term memory, such as when a student reads an arithmetic problem, ponders it in his head, and immediately announces the answer. Sometimes control processes also relate information in STM to previously learned knowledge from LTM, such as when a youth hears a song on the radio and notes its similarity to another song heard previously. And sometimes control processes consist of strategies for learning information effectively, such as strategies for remembering a person's telephone number.

Metacognition   As children grow older, they develop metacognition. **Metacognition** is an awareness and understanding of how thinking and learning work, and it assists learning in a number of ways. It allows a person to assess how difficult a problem or learning task will be and therefore to plan appropriate ways to approach it. More specifically, metacognition involves knowledge of self, knowledge of task variables, and knowledge of which information-processing strategies are effective in which situations (Forrest-Pressley et al., 1985).

Knowledge Base   In addition to metacognition, children acquire many other kinds of knowledge. Some children gradually become comparative experts in particular areas, such as math, sports, or getting along with peers. *Knowledge base* refers to children's current fund of knowledge and skills in various areas. A child's knowledge base in one area makes acquiring further knowledge and skills in the same area easier because the child can relate new information to prior information more meaningfully.

According to many information-processing theorists, changes in the knowledge base are not general, stagelike transformations such as those proposed by Piaget (Chi et al., 1989). Instead, they are specialized developments of expertise based on the gradual accumulation of specific information and skills about a field, including

● ● ●

metacognition Knowledge and thinking about cognition, how learning and memory operate in everyday situations, and how one can improve cognitive performance.

The chess-playing abilities of both this young girl and her father are closely tied to the knowledge of chess and awareness and understanding of their own thought processes and problem-solving strategies that each has achieved.

information and skills about *how* knowledge in the field is organized and learned efficiently. A very good chess player is an expert in chess but is not necessarily advanced in other activities or areas of knowledge. Her skill probably reflects long hours spent in one major activity: playing chess games. Each hour of play enables her to build a larger knowledge base about chess: memories of board patterns, moves, and game strategies that worked in the past.

Now let's see how the cognitive developmental theories stand in regard to the four major developmental themes.

Evaluation of Developmental Issues in Cognitive Approaches

Maturation or Experience?   Piaget's theory assigns important roles to both maturation and experience. While maturational factors are necessary to the unique structural qualities of the stages and to the progression from lower to higher stages, without experience cognitive development would not occur. Neo-Piagetian theories also accept the importance of maturation, but emphasize the child's specific experiences in interacting with the environment as the source of cognitive development. The information-processing approach assumes the processes and structures involved in cognitive development are primarily a product of the child's experiences.

Process or Stages?   Piaget's theory places major emphasis on developmental stages that are closely tied to maturation of the capacity to perform certain predetermined logical operations. The stages that neo-Piagetian theorists propose are similar to Piaget's, but are more closely tied to the increases in processing efficiency and skill level that result from specific experiences than to predetermined operations. Information-processing theories view developmental change as a continuous rather than stagelike process.

Active or Passive Role of the Child?   Piaget believes children play a relatively active role in their own development. Neo-Piagetian theorists and information-processing approaches stress the child's active participation even more strongly.

Broad or Narrow Focus?   Both Piaget's theory and the neo-Piagetian revisions limit their focus to the domain of cognitive change. They say little about the role of social, emotional, and physical factors in cognitive development or the ways cognitive development may influence these domains. The information-processing approach limits its focus to developing and testing models to explain the role of memory and information processing in cognitive change.

Applications of Cognitive Developmental Theories to Everyday Life

Piaget's cognitive theory and the more recent neo-Piagetian approaches have provided the central conceptual framework for understanding the development of thinking and problem solving throughout childhood and adolescence. In Chapter 6, for example, Piaget's theory helps to explain sensorimotor development during the first two years, and the Working With interview with Gillian Luppiwiski, an infant care provider, will discuss how cognitive theory can be used to foster thinking and intellectual development in infants. Cognitive theory also helps to explain the development of symbolic thought and language in preschoolers (Chapter 9) and how growth in thinking and problem-solving abilities affects relationships with friends and peers in middle childhood (Chapter 12). In Chapter 15, we will see how cognitive theory is used to design programs to foster critical thinking in adolescents; to better understand *adolescent egocentrism, imaginary audience,* and *personal fable;* and to understand moral development and the ethics of care during adolescence.

WHAT DO YOU THINK ? How might the cognitive approach be useful to an elementary school math teacher who is preparing lesson plans? Would this theoretical approach be of any use in a health education class?

Contextual Developmental Theories

Contextual approaches view development as a process of reciprocal, patterned interactions between the developing child and his physical and social environment. A leading example of this approach is the ecological systems theory of Urie Bronfenbrenner. As we saw in Chapter 1, *ecological systems theory* proposes that a child's development is influenced by four interactive and overlapping contextual levels: (1) the *microsystem*—the face-to-face physical and social situations that directly affect the child (family, peer group, classroom); (2) the *mesosystem*—connections and relationships among the child's microsystems; (3) the *exosystem*—the settings or situations that indirectly influence the child (parent's place of employment, the school board, the local government); and (4) the *macrosystem*—the values, beliefs, and policies of society and culture that provide frameworks, or "blueprints," for organizing our lives and indirectly influence the child through their effects on the exosystem, mesosystem, and microsystem.

Another interesting example of contextual theory was developed by the Russian psychologist Lev Vygotsky (1896–1934). Vygotsky was interested in how changing historical and cultural contexts within which children's activities occur influence their cognitive development. According to Vygotsky, higher mental functions grow out of the social interactions and dialogues that take place between a child and parents, teachers, and other representatives of the culture. Through these interactions, children internalize increasingly mature and effective ways of thinking and problem solving. Some of these changes occur through discoveries that the child initiates on her own.

Many developmental tasks, however, occur in what Vygotsky called the *zone of proximal development.* The **zone of proximal development** refers to the range of tasks that a child cannot yet accomplish without active assistance from parents and others with greater knowledge (Blanck, 1990; Rogoff, 1990; Wertsch, 1989). Vygotsky's ideas are useful in helping teachers and parents to provide children with the right amounts of structure and guidance and in understanding how children's private speech (talking to themselves) may help them to regulate their own behavior when adult guidance is not available (Berk, 1994; Karpov & Haywood, 1998). (See the accompanying Multicultural View box for a discussion of culture and cognitive development.)

Richard Lerner's contextual approach emphasizes the dynamic, interactive relationships between the individual's development and the changing contexts in which his or her development occurs (Lerner, 1996; Fischer & Lerner, 1994). Developmental changes during adolescence are a good example. Adolescents, their families, and the communities and societies in which they live all experience systematic and successive developmental changes over time. Changes within one level of organization, such as cognitive or psychosocial changes within the individual, influence and are influenced by developmental changes within other levels, such as changes in caregiving patterns or relationships between husband and wife within the familial level of organization. According to Lerner, these reciprocal changes among levels of

• • •

zone of proximal development (ZPD) According to Vygotsky, the level of difficulty at which problems are too hard for children to solve alone but not too hard when given support from adults or more competent peers.

A Multicultural View ....

Cultural Context and Cognitive Development

According to Lev Vygotsky's theory, cognitive development is largely "context specific," meaning it must be understood in terms of the particular social, cultural, and historical processes of people's everyday experiences (Vygotsky, 1978; Wertsch, 1985). Individuals growing up in different societies, cultures, and historical periods are likely to display differences in how they think and solve problems and in how cognitive development occurs. This view is very different from that of Jean Piaget, who believed cognitive development is largely "universal," meaning all individuals progress through the same developmental stages at approximately the same ages relatively independently of their particular situations and experiences.

Research based primarily on observations of children from Western industrialized societies, where formal schooling is heavily stressed, has generally supported Piaget's ideas. Studies of children growing up in other societies and cultures, however, have been more consistent with Vygotsky's views.

Children growing up in cultures with little formal schooling have been found to take much longer to achieve the *concrete operational stage* of thinking and appear unable to achieve the *formal operational stage* of thinking, Piaget's final stage (Rogoff & Chavajay, 1995). Michael Cole, a pioneer in studying culture and cognitive development, concluded that the superior performance of children who had formal schooling was due to the common structure and activities of schooling and tests of cognitive development rather than to the effects of schooling on children's thinking (Cole, 1990).

Performance on tasks that require participants to classify test items into categories is one good example. Whereas individuals from Western countries typically classify test items based on their type (for example, putting animals in one group, food items in another, and tools in a third), individuals in many other nations sort the same items based on their function (for example, putting a hoe with a potato because a hoe is used to dig up a potato) (Rogoff & Chavajay, 1995).

Logical tasks that require a person to draw conclusions based on abstract, hypothetical reasoning rather than on direct personal experience are another example. Nonliterate

---

organization are both the cause and the product of changes within levels. For example, parents' "styles" of childrearing influence children's personality and cognitive development; the child's unique personality, cognitive style, and the choices he or she makes, in turn, affect parental behaviors and styles and the quality of family life.

Glen Elder (1998) suggests that education, work, and family create the **social trajectories,** or pathways, that guide individual development. Important life transitions, such as birth of a sibling, school entry, and graduation, give these social trajectories distinctive shape and meaning for each individual. Historical changes such as wars, economic depressions, and technological innovations shape the social trajectories of family, education, and work, which in turn influence individual development. While individuals are able to select the paths they follow by asserting their *human agency,* or free will, those choices are not made in a social vacuum; they depend on the opportunities and constraints of social structure and culture, which themselves change over time (Elder, 1998; Hernandez, 1997).

The future developmental changes that Elizabeth, the preschooler discussed at the beginning of this chapter, is likely to experience illustrate Elder's ideas. For example, entry into first grade, transitions to middle school, high school, and college, entering the world of work, getting married, and having a child are all likely to be important parts of the pathway that will give her long-term development distinctive meaning and form. At the same time, political, economic, and technological changes in society will influence Elizabeth's family, education, and work, which in turn will influence her behaviors and the particular directions her developmental choices take. Although Elizabeth will have considerable potential to assert her agency and freely choose the paths she will follow, such life choices will also depend on the opportunities and constraints that she encounters.

• • •

social trajectory The pathway, or direction, that development takes over an individual's life course, which is influenced by the school, work, family, and other important social settings in which he or she participates.

individuals who are able to make excellent logical judgments when dealing with the immediate, practical problems of their everyday life experiences may, for cultural reasons, be unwilling to demonstrate similar reasoning abilities in situations that are not culturally familiar. The following example, taken from an interview with a nonliterate Central Asian peasant, illustrates this point:

Interviewer: In the Far North, where there is snow, all bears are white. Novaya Zemlya is in the Far North and there is always snow there. What color are the bears there?

Peasant: . . . We always speak of only what we see; we don't talk about what we haven't seen.

Interviewer: But what do my words imply?

Peasant: Well, it's like this: our tsar isn't like yours, and yours isn't like ours. Your words can be answered only by someone who was there, and if a person wasn't there he can't say anything on the basis of your words.

Interviewer: But on the basis of my words—in the North, where there is always snow, the bears are white—can you gather what kind of bears there are in Novaya Zemlya?

Peasant: If a man was sixty or eighty and had seen a white bear and had told me about it, he could be believed, but I've never seen one and hence I can't say. (Luria, 1976, pp. 108–109, quoted in Rogoff & Chavajay, 1995, p. 861)

Differences in performance of common cognitive tasks may also reflect cultural differences in how a problem is defined and how it should be solved (Goodnow, 1976). European Americans, for example, believe intelligence involves technical rather than social skills. Kipsigis (Kenyan) parents include responsible participation in family and social life in their definition. For the Ifaluk of the western Pacific, intelligence means not only having knowledge of good social behavior but also performing it. Ugandan villagers associate intelligence with being slow, careful, and active, whereas westernized groups associate it with speed (Rogoff & Chavajay, 1995).

Future research will provide additional evidence regarding the social and cultural contexts of cognitive development.

Ethological Theory

The ethological approach attempts to apply the principles of evolutionary biology and ethology to behavioral and psychological characteristics (Bowlby, 1988; Hinde, 1989; Miller, 1989). This approach has its roots in *ethology,* the study of various animal species in their natural environments. Ethology emphasizes the ways widely shared species behaviors evolved through the process of natural selection to ensure species survival. Developmental ethologists are interested in how certain behavioral and psychological traits or predispositions that appear to be widely shared among human beings may have developed to help ensure the evolutionary survival of the human species.

An underlying assumption is that just as human evolution has imposed certain constraints on our physical development, it may have influenced the range and nature of our behavioral development. Developmental ethologists also attempt to understand how individual differences in traits such as aggressiveness, shyness, competitiveness, and altruism reciprocally interact with the social environment to mutually influence development.

One area of ethological interest has been the study of infant emotions and *temperament*—relatively enduring individual differences in infant responsiveness and self-regulation that appear to be present at birth (see Chapter 7). A second important application of the ethological approach is the study of infant-caregiver *attachment*—the mutually reinforcing system of physical, social, and emotional stimulation and support between infant and caregiver. This pattern of attachment behaviors has been observed in other species, and ethologists presume it has survival value for humans as well (see Chapter 7).

The particular cultural context in which the celebration of Passover and other important events occur can significantly influence a child's development.

Evaluation of Developmental Issues in Contextual Approaches

Maturation or Experience?   With the exception of ethological theory, contextual approaches focus almost exclusively on the child's experiences in multiple contexts as the moving force in developmental change. Bronfenbrenner and Vygotsky propose that developmental change occurs primarily through patterns of reciprocal interaction rather than through maturational influences. Ethological theorists, on the other hand, strongly believe that certain inborn physical and behavioral tendencies and characteristics predispose children to develop in certain ways. However, ethological theory also emphasizes that developmental change reflects how behavioral tendencies interact with the environmental and cultural contexts in which the child lives.

Process or Stages?   Stages are not a feature of contextual theories. Development is seen as a continuous process.

Active or Passive Role of the Child?   All of the contextual theories view the child as a highly active participant in his own development and see development as the product of highly reciprocal, mutually determined interactions between the child and the multiple contexts in which he exists.

Broad or Narrow Focus?   Contextual approaches include a broad range of social, cultural, and historical developmental influences. On the other hand, they tend to focus on social development and less on emotional, cognitive, and physical development. Similarly, they tend to emphasize a limited range of developmental issues rather than a comprehensive and balanced view of developmental change.

Applications of Contextual Developmental Theories to Everyday Life

Contextual theories have become increasingly useful in explaining how individual development is influenced by and interacts with the changing life contexts in which development occurs. The discussion of Jodi and her multiple contexts of development in Chapter 1 is an excellent illustration of how Urie Bronfenbrenner's ecological systems theory helps us to understand individual development. Ecological systems theory has been especially useful for understanding the multiple factors and contexts involved in divorce, teen parenthood, and juvenile delinquency and for designing programs to assist troubled adolescents and to prevent those problems from occurring (Chapter 16).

Vygotsky's sociocultural approach and his concept of *zone of proximal development* can help us to understand the development of problem-solving skills and intelligence during middle childhood (Chapter 13). Finally, ethological theory has helped to explain the contribution of differences in *temperament* that are observable at birth to development through childhood and adolescence. It has also helped us to understand the importance of *attachment* in the development of relationships from early infancy onward, a topic that we noted in our earlier discussion of applications of psychodynamic theory.

WHAT DO YOU THINK ?   To what degree does your informal theory of development include the different developmental contexts these theorists propose? Are there any you would add? Any you would delete?

Developmental Theories Compared and Their Implications for the Student

We have reached the end of our review of several of the most important theories in developmental psychology. What conclusions might we draw? In what ways are these theories useful as we investigate children's development in the remainder of this book? As we suggested at the beginning of this chapter, theories are useful because they help us to systematically organize and make sense of large amounts of sometimes inconsistent information about children's development. Theories also stimulate new thinking and research and guide parents and professionals in their day-to-day work with children.

Although each theory we explored in this chapter has significantly expanded knowledge in its particular area of focus, none should be thought to provide a complete explanation of development. Taken together, the theories are complementary and can be used in conjunction with one another to provide a fairly comprehensive view of child and adolescent development. Table 2.6 summarizes the main features and key concepts for each theoretical approach discussed.

Theories help us to understand and actively participate in our own development. Theories can also broaden and deepen our understanding of ourselves, the factors influencing our development, and the choices we have. They can help us to better understand how our family dynamics and relationships may have influenced our current personalities and our struggles with issues such as identity, intimacy, gender role, and sexuality.

However, uncritical reliance on theories has several pitfalls. Because theories guide and direct our perceptions of and thinking about children, reliance on a given theory may lead us to focus on certain aspects of development, make certain assumptions, and draw conclusions about development that are consistent with the theory but not necessarily accurate. For example, overreliance on Piaget's cognitive approach may lead a teacher to underestimate the contributions of social and emotional factors to a child's academic difficulties. Similarly, parents who tend to interpret their child's irresponsible behavior in terms of psychological conflict may overlook the fact that the same behavior is frequently modeled and reinforced by the child's older sibling.

TABLE 2.6   Developmental Theories Compared

Theoretical Approach	Main Focus	Key Concepts	Basic Assumptions
Psychodynamic			
Freud	Personality (social, emotional)	Id, ego, superego; psychosexual conflict; defense mechanisms	This broadly focused stage theory assumes a moderate role for maturation, a strong role for experience, and a moderately active developmental role for the individual.
Erikson	Personality (social, emotional, identity)	Lifespan development; psychosocial crises	This broadly focused stage theory assumes a weak to moderate role for maturation, a strong role for experience, and a highly active role for the individual.
Mahler	Personality (social, emotional self)	Birth of psychological self; separation-individuation	This narrowly focused stage theory assumes a strong role for maturation, a moderate role for experience, and a moderately active role for the developing individual.
Stern	Personality (interpersonal, cognitive, emotional, self)	Interpersonal sense of self; RIGs (representation of past interactions that have been generalized)	This moderately focused stage theory assumes a moderate role for maturation, a strong role for experience, and a highly active role for the developing individual.
Behavioral Learning			
Pavlov; Skinner	Learning specific, observable responses	Classical and operant conditioning; extinction; reinforcement; punishment	These narrowly focused, process-oriented theories assume a weak role for maturation, a strong role for experience, and a highly active role for the developing individual.
Social-Cognitive Learning			
Bandura	Learning behavior, cognitive response patterns, social roles	Imitation, social learning, modeling, cognitive learning, reciprocal determinism, skills capabilities	This moderately focused, process-oriented theory assumes a weak role for maturation, a strong role for experience, and a highly active role for the developing individual.
Cognitive			
Piaget	Cognitive (thinking, problem solving)	Schemes, assimilation, accommodation, equilibrium, mental space, routinization of schemes	This moderately focused stage theory assumes a strong role for maturation, a moderate role for experience, and a moderately active role for the developing individual.
Case; Fischer	Cognitive; problem-solving skills and capabilities	Skill acquisition; optimal level of performance, higher-level skills	These moderately focused, process-oriented theories assume a moderate role for both maturation and experience and a highly active role for the developing individual.
Information Processing	Cognitive; steps and processes involved in problem solving and other mental abilities	Sensory register, short-term memory (STM), long-term memory (LTM), metacognition, knowledge base, control processes	This narrowly focused, process-oriented theory assumes a strong role for maturation, a moderate role for experience, and a highly active role for the developing individual.
Contextual Approaches			
Bronfenbrenner	Contextual; interactive contextual influences	Ecological contexts; microsystem, ecosystem, mesosystem, macrosystem	This broadly focused, process-oriented theory assumes a strong role for maturation, a moderate role for experience, and a highly active role for the developing individual.
Vygotsky	Contextual; cultural/historical influences	Dialogues; zone of proximal development	This moderately focused, process-oriented theory assumes a weak role for maturation, a strong role for experience, and a highly active role for the developing individual.
Ethological	Adaptation to biological and ethological contexts	Behavioral dispositions; evolutionary adaptations	These moderately focused, process-oriented theories assume a moderate role for maturation, a weak to moderate role for experience, and a moderately active role for the developing individual.
Lerner; Elder	Individual change within changing social and historical contexts	Multiple organizational levels of reciprocal, dynamic change; social trajectories (pathways)	These broadly focused, process-oriented theories assume a weak role for maturation, a strong role for experience, and a highly active role for the developing individual.

As you read the chapters that follow, notice that the theories are applied selectively based on the ages and developmental issues being discussed. We encourage you to refer back to this chapter whenever you have questions about the material and to make your own judgments about which theory (or theories) fits best. Finally, keep an eye on how your own theories of development change as you read the book and talk with your instructor and classmates. By the end of the course, if not sooner, you are likely to have a much clearer idea of your preferred theoretical orientation(s), as well as a much clearer perspective of what development is all about.

WHAT DO YOU THINK ? Remember three-year-old Elizabeth at the beginning of this chapter? Now that you have learned more about theories of development, which theory (or theories) do you think is most useful in understanding her situation and helping her adjust to her first days of nursery school? Why?

Summary of Major Ideas

The Nature of Developmental Theories

1. Theories are useful in organizing and explaining the process of development and in stimulating and guiding developmental research, theory, and practice.
2. Developmental theories differ in the degree to which they emphasize maturation versus experience, continuous versus stagelike development, active versus passive participation, and breadth of theoretical focus.

Psychodynamic Developmental Theories

3. The theories of Freud and Erikson view development as a dynamic process that occurs in a series of stages, each involving psychological conflicts that the developing person must resolve.
4. According to Freud, personality development is energized by three conflicting functions: the unconscious, irrational, pleasure-seeking id; the largely conscious, rational, realistic ego; and the superego, which is the voice of conscience and morality.
5. The Freudian approach describes five stages of psychosexual development: oral, anal, phallic, latency, and genital.
6. Erikson's psychosocial theory outlines eight developmental stages encompassing the lifespan, each defined by a unique psychological crisis that is never completely resolved.
7. During infancy, a basic sense of trust (versus mistrust) results in *hope.* During toddlerhood and the preschool years, a child achieves a sense of autonomy (versus shame and doubt) and initiative (versus guilt), resulting in *will* and *purpose.*
8. During the school years a child must resolve the crisis of industry (versus inferiority), and during adolescence the crisis of identity (versus role confusion), resulting in *competence* and *fidelity.*
9. Erikson's final three stages occur after adolescence. They include young adulthood and the crisis of intimacy (versus isolation), adulthood and the crisis of generativity (versus stagnation), and old age and the crisis of ego integrity (versus despair). Successful resolution brings *love, care,* and *wisdom.*
10. Object relations approaches emphasize development as resulting from a child's internalized mental representations of early social and emotional relationships with parents and important others.
11. According to Mahler, the infant goes through autistic, symbiotic, separation-individuation, and object constancy phases in developing a psychological sense of self. For

Stern, the process involves a core self, a subjective self, and a verbal self. For Kohut, empathic mirroring by caregivers helps the infant to develop a cohesive and reliable set of mental representations out of which a sense of self emerges.

Behavioral Learning and Social Cognitive Learning Developmental Theories

12. Pavlov's theory emphasizes learning through classical conditioning as the main process by which developmental changes occur.
13. Skinner's operant conditioning theory emphasizes the influence of reinforcement, punishment, and extinction on developmental change.
14. Bandura's social cognitive theory emphasizes reciprocal and interactional processes involving both direct observational learning and vicarious reinforcement.

Cognitive Developmental Theories

15. Piaget's theory explains the underlying structures and processes involved in the development of children's thinking and problem solving.
16. According to Piaget, thinking develops in a series of increasingly complex and sophisticated stages, or periods, each of which incorporates the achievements of those preceding it.
17. New ways of thinking and problem solving are achieved through the joint processes of assimilation (fitting a new scheme of thinking or action into an existing one) and accommodation (changing an existing scheme to meet the challenges of a new situation).
18. The neo-Piagetian theories emphasize the roles of mental space, skill acquisition, and information-processing capacity in cognitive development.
19. Information-processing theories focus on the steps involved in thought processes. Information is first stored in the sensory register, then in short-term memory, and finally in long-term memory. As children grow older, they experience cognitive changes in control processes, metacognition, and their knowledge bases.

Contextual Developmental Theories

20. Bronfenbrenner's ecological systems theory proposes that the microsystem, mesosystem, exosystem, and macrosystem form interactive and overlapping contexts for development. Vygotsky emphasizes the contributions of history and culture to development that take place within a child's zone of proximal development. Lerner and Elder

emphasize individual change within changing social and historical contexts.

21. Ethological theory focuses on the developmental roles of behavioral dispositions and traits, such as temperament and attachment, that are thought to have evolutionary survival value for the human species.

Developmental Theories Compared and Their Implications for the Student

22. Although developmental theories differ in both focus and explanatory concepts, together they provide a fairly comprehensive view of the process of developmental change.

23. By systematically organizing what we already know about development and proposing explanations that can be tested through formal and informal observations, developmental theories are so useful for experts and nonexperts alike that they are well worth the effort required to understand them.

Key Terms

accommodation (48)
adaptation (48)
assimilation (48)
attachment (41)
attention deficit/hyperactivity disorder (ADHD) (47)
autonomy versus shame and doubt (36)
behavior modification (47)
classical conditioning (44)
ego (34)
ego integrity versus despair (39)
generativity versus stagnation (39)
id (34)
identity versus role confusion (38)

industry versus inferiority (38)
information-processing theory (50)
initiative versus guilt (38)
intimacy versus isolation (39)
metacognition (51)
object relations (39)
observational learning (45)
operant conditioning (44)
scheme (47)
social trajectory (54)
superego (34)
trust versus mistrust (36)
zone of proximal development (53)

PART 2

Beginnings

Although you may think human development starts in infancy, it actually begins at the moment of conception. We become individuals partly because of our genetic endowments, which are determined the moment sperm meets egg; partly because of events we experience while still in our mothers' wombs; and partly because of events that occur in the wider environment.

The next two chapters look at these influences. They show some of the ways heredity and environment affect who a child becomes, not only physically but cognitively and socially. They describe what actually happens during the thirty-eight weeks or so before birth, as well as the events surrounding birth itself. By childbirth—a time of wonder, anxiety, and joy—the baby already has undergone many changes. But there is plenty of room to learn from experience, and the child will undergo many more changes throughout his or her life.

Genetics

Focusing Questions

- How does inheritance work?
- How are genetic differences usually transmitted from one generation to the next?
- How do heredity and environment jointly influence developmental change?
- What is known about common genetic abnormalities and their causes?
- How can experts help parents discover and respond to potential genetic problems?
- How do we sort out the unique contributions heredity and environment make to the development of individual children?

I nheritance affects a vast number of human qualities, from the color of our eyes and how tall we are to more complex characteristics such as athletic ability, intelligence, and temperament. What makes these things "run in families"? How is genetic information passed on from one generation to the next?

In this chapter, we explore answers to these questions. First, we describe the basic biological processes involved in human reproduction. Then we explain how genetic information from two individuals is combined and conveyed from parents to children. Genetic abnormalities receive special attention, not because they outnumber normal genetic processes but because they shed considerable light on those processes. Then we address an issue that psychologists have found especially important: the relationship between heredity and environment and how both contribute to individual development. Finally, we describe ways to use knowledge of these relationships to benefit parents and their children.

Mechanisms of Genetic Transmission

The process by which genetic information is combined and transmitted begins with **gametes,** the reproductive cells of a child's parents. In the father the gametes are produced in the testicles, and each is called a **sperm** cell. In the mother they develop in the ovaries, and each is called an **ovum,** or *egg cell.* The sperm and egg cells contain genetic information in molecular structures called **genes,** which form threads called **chromosomes.** Thus, chromosomes contain the genetic material that the child will inherit from the parent. Each human sperm or egg cell contains twenty-three chromosomes. All other cells of the body contain forty-six chromosomes and approximately one hundred thousand genes. A single chromosome may contain as many as twenty thousand genes. Figure 3.1 shows a picture, or *karyotype,* of the chromosomes for a normal human male.

The Role of DNA

The genes themselves are made up of **DNA (deoxyribonucleic acid).** All DNA molecules have a particular chemical structure—a double helix, or spiral—that allows them to divide easily and create new, duplicate DNA molecules reliably. DNA contains the complex protein code of genetic information that directs the form and function of each body cell as it develops (see Figure 3.2).

gamete A reproductive cell (sperm or ovum).

sperm Male gametes, or reproductive cells; produced in the testicles.

ovum The reproductive cell, or gamete, of the female; the egg cell.

gene A molecular structure, carried on chromosomes, containing genetic information; the basic unit of heredity.

chromosome A threadlike, rod-shaped structure containing genetic information that is transmitted from parents to children; each human sperm or egg cell contains twenty-three chromosomes, and these determine a person's inherited characteristics.

deoxyribonucleic acid (DNA) A molecule containing hereditary information; has a chemical structure of two chains of polynucleotides arranged in a double helix or spiral.

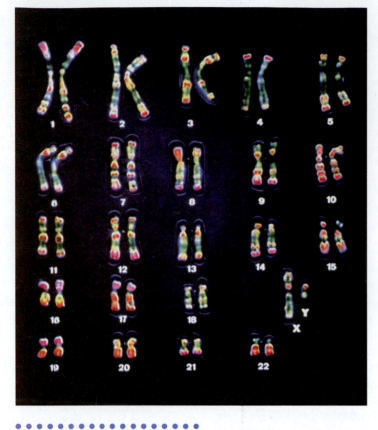

● ● ● ● ● ● ● ● ● ● ● ● ● ● ● ● ● ● ●

FIGURE 3.1

Chromosomes for the Normal Human Male
This karyotype depicts the twenty-two pairs of chromosomes and the two sex chromosomes for the normal human male. In females, the twenty-third pair of chromosomes consists of an XX instead of an XY pair.

● ● ● ● ● ● ● ● ● ● ● ● ● ● ● ● ● ● ●

FIGURE 3.2

Genetic Structures

DNA shares this information at conception, when a sperm from the father penetrates an egg from the mother. Within a few hours, the walls of the sperm cell and the *nucleus*, or center, of the egg cell both begin to disintegrate, allowing each one to release its chromosomes, which join to form a new cell. The new cell formed by the egg and sperm is called a **zygote** (see Figure 3.3). At this point, the zygote is still so small that hundreds of them could fit on the head of a pin. Yet it contains all of the necessary genetic information in its DNA molecules to develop into a unique human being. A fuller discussion of the process of conception appears at the beginning of Chapter 4.

Meiosis and Mitosis

All of the cells that make up a human being develop from this original zygote through a process of cell division. As mentioned earlier, the sperm and ova contain only twenty-three chromosomes, making them unique from other body cells. This ensures that when an egg and sperm cell join to form a new zygote during conception, the zygote will contain the complete set of forty-six chromosomes (twenty-three pairs). This is important, because the zygote contains the genetic material from which all of an individual's cells are formed.

To accomplish this, reproductive cells, or *gametes*, divide by a process called *meiosis* and recombine into a zygote at conception. All of the other cells that make up a unique human being will develop from this original zygote through a simple division of their genes, chromosomes, and other cellular parts by means of a process called *mitosis*.

Meiosis involves the following steps. First, the twenty-three chromosomes of the egg (or sperm) cell duplicate themselves. Then they break up into smaller pieces and randomly exchange segments of genetic material with each other. Next, the new chromosome pairs divide to form two different cells. Finally, the two new cells divide again. Each new cell now ends up with only *one-half* the usual number of chromosomes carried by all other cells—just twenty-three chromosomes instead

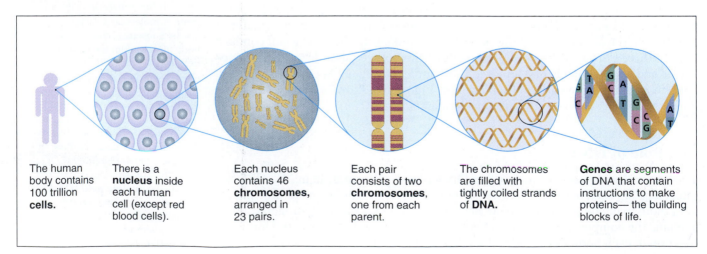

The human body contains 100 trillion **cells.**

There is a **nucleus** inside each human cell (except red blood cells).

Each nucleus contains 46 **chromosomes,** arranged in 23 pairs.

Each pair consists of two **chromosomes,** one from each parent.

The chromosomes are filled with tightly coiled strands of **DNA.**

Genes are segments of DNA that contain instructions to make proteins— the building blocks of life.

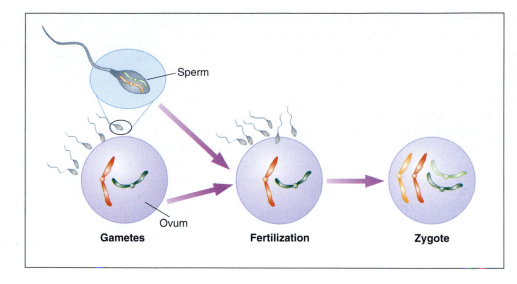

● ● ● ● ● ● ● ● ● ● ● ● ● ● ● ● ●
FIGURE 3.3
Gametes and Zygote
Each gamete, whether sperm or ovum, contains twenty-three single chromosomes. (Two chromosomes are shown in each gamete here.) At fertilization, sperm and ovum combine to form a zygote with forty-six chromosomes in twenty-three pairs. (Two pairs are shown here.) In each pair, one chromosome is from the mother and one is from the father.

of forty-six. This ensures that the single-cell zygote formed during conception will contain the normal forty-six chromosomes: twenty-three chromosomes from the egg and twenty-three from the sperm. Figure 3.4 illustrates the process of meiosis for sperm cells. The process for egg cells is the same.

Once the zygote forms, it and all of its descendants divide through the process called *mitosis*. **Mitosis** involves the following steps. First, the twenty-three pairs of chromosomes of a cell duplicate themselves and divide into two identical sets. Next, the two sets of chromosomes move to opposite sides of the cell. Finally, a new wall forms between them, resulting in two new, identical cells containing the same unique set of chromosomes, genes, and DNA-based genetic

● ● ● ● ● ● ● ● ● ● ● ● ● ● ● ●
FIGURE 3.4
The Process of Meiosis for Sperm Cells
As meiosis begins, (a) DNA replicates as in mitosis. However, before the replicated arms split apart, one member of each pair of chromosomes moves to become part of each first-generation daughter cell (b). Once the first generation of daughter cells is established, DNA copies then split as part of the second meiotic division (c). Thus, one copy of one member of the pair of chromosomes is contributed to each second-generation daughter cell (d). These two successive divisions produce four cells, each with twenty-three chromosomes.

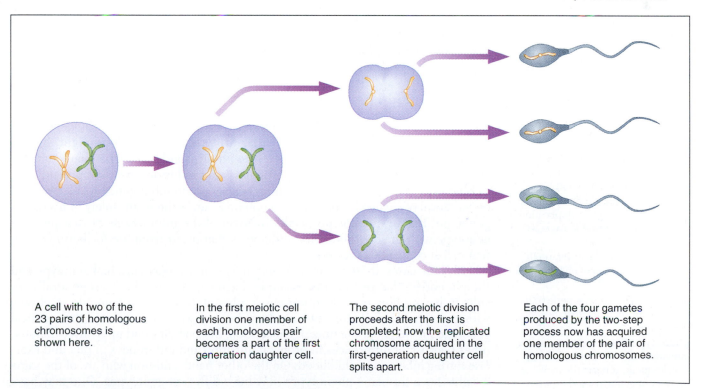

A cell with two of the 23 pairs of homologous chromosomes is shown here.

In the first meiotic cell division one member of each homologous pair becomes a part of the first generation daughter cell.

The second meiotic division proceeds after the first is completed; now the replicated chromosome acquired in the first-generation daughter cell splits apart.

Each of the four gametes produced by the two-step process now has acquired one member of the pair of homologous chromosomes.

• • • • • • • • • • • • • • • • • •

FIGURE 3.5

The Process of Mitosis

Mitotic cell division produces all the cells of the body except the gametes. During mitosis, each chromosome replicates to form two chromosomes with identical genetic blueprints. As the cell divides, one member of each identical pair becomes a member of each daughter cell. In this manner, complete genetic endowment is replicated in nearly every cell of the body.

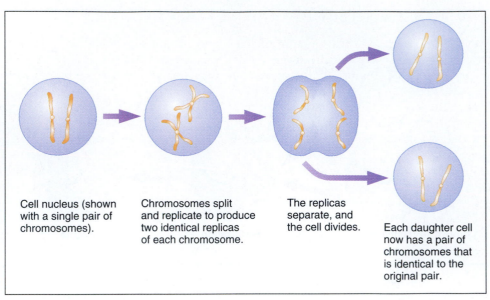

Cell nucleus (shown with a single pair of chromosomes).

Chromosomes split and replicate to produce two identical replicas of each chromosome.

The replicas separate, and the cell divides.

Each daughter cell now has a pair of chromosomes that is identical to the original pair.

This micrograph of cell division shortly after human conception shows the two-cell stage of human embryonic development.

codes that will help guide the new organism's development. Figure 3.5 depicts the process of mitosis.

WHAT DO YOU THINK? Sometimes a good way to check your understanding of rather complex material is to explain it to another person. Team up with a classmate and explain the roles of meiosis and mitosis to him or her in your own words. Then ask your classmate to explain it back to you. What unanswered questions do you still have?

Individual Genetic Expression

How does the genetic information contained in our cells influence the development of our unique physical, intellectual, social, and emotional characteristics? In the following section, we explore this question.

Genotype and Phenotype

Genotype refers to the genes a person inherits, that is, to the specific genetic information that may influence a particular trait such as eye color, height, intelligence, or shyness. **Phenotype** refers to the physical and behavioral characteristics an individual actually exhibits at a particular point in his or her development, such as blue eyes; a height of five feet ten inches; a certain intelligence test score; or a certain level of shyness. A person's phenotype is never the result solely of his or her genotype. Rather, phenotype results from all of the interactions of that person's genotype with the environmental influences that occur from the formation of the first cell at conception onward.

In some cases, there is a close match between a person's original genotype and the phenotype that results. For example, having genes for blue eyes generally results in having blue eyes. In other cases, phenotype does not coincide so closely with genotype. For example, two newborn infants may have inherited the identical genotype for weight at the time of conception, but one may end up heavier than the other because of differences in prenatal nutrition and differences in diet and exercise during infancy and childhood. On the other hand, children who are of the same weight (have the same phenotype) may have different genotypes. One may have reached that weight by dieting and the other simply by eating whatever she wanted.

zygote The single new cell formed when a sperm cell attaches itself to the surface of an ovum (egg).

meiosis A complex process by which gametes form; involves duplication and division of reproductive cells and their chromosomes.

mitosis The creation of new cells through duplication of chromosomes and division of cells.

genotype The set of genetic traits inherited by an individual. See also *phenotype*.

phenotype The set of traits an individual actually displays during development; reflects the evolving product of genotype and experience. See also *genotype*.

Dominant and Recessive Genes

Genes are inherited in pairs, one from each parent. Some genes are dominant and others are recessive. A **dominant gene** will influence a child's phenotype even if it is paired with a recessive gene. A **recessive gene,** however, must be paired with another recessive gene to be able to influence the phenotype. If it is paired with a dominant gene, its influence will be controlled or blocked. More than one thousand human characteristics appear to follow the dominant-recessive pattern of inheritance (McKussick, 1988, 1995). Table 3.1 lists a number of common dominant and recessive traits.

Eye color is a good example. Suppose human eyes came in only two colors, blue and brown. Most Caucasian children are born with blue eyes, but from about six months of age, a child's eyes remain blue only under certain conditions. Because blue eyes are a recessive trait and brown eyes are a dominant trait, a child's eyes will remain blue only if he has received the appropriate blue-producing gene from both parents. If he has received it from only one parent or from neither, he will end up with brown eyes.

Even for simple traits such as eye color, however, the dominant-recessive distinction does not explain phenotype fully. Very few physical traits have a completely either-or quality—even eye color, for that matter. If you look carefully at all of your friends, you will probably see that a few have hazel or greenish eyes and some have darker-brown eyes than others. How can we account for variations such as these?

Transmission of Multiple Variations

The genes responsible for eye color—and, in fact, for any other trait—often take on two or more alternative forms called **alleles.** Earlier we assumed that the gene responsible for eye color can take only two allele forms, blue and brown. In reality, the gene for eye color occasionally takes on a third allele, which often leads to hazel or green eyes. A person who inherits two identical alleles for a particular trait is **homozygous** for that trait. A person who inherits two different alleles for the trait is **heterozygous** for that trait. In the case of eye color, a heterozygous person (one brown and one blue/hazel/green allele) therefore will show the phenotype of the

• • •

dominant gene In any paired set of genes, the gene with greater influence in determining physical characteristics that are physically visible or manifest.

recessive gene In any paired set of genes, the gene that influences or determines physical characteristics only when no dominant gene is present.

allele One of several alternative forms of a gene.

homozygous A genetic condition in which an individual inherits two identical genes at a particular location on a particular chromosome.

heterozygous Describes a genotype consisting of distinct forms of chromosomes for the same gene.

TABLE 3.1   Some Common Dominant and Recessive Traits

Dominant Trait	Recessive Trait	Dominant Trait	Recessive Trait
Brown eyes	Gray, green, hazel, or blue eyes	Short fingers	Fingers of normal length
Hazel or green eyes	Blue eyes	Double-fingers	Normally jointed fingers
Normal vision	Nearsightedness	Double-jointedness	Normal joints
Farsightedness	Normal vision	Type A blood	Type O blood
Normal color vision	Red-green color blindness	Type B blood	Type O blood
Brown or black hair	Blond hair	Rh positive blood	Rh negative blood
Nonred hair	Red hair	Normal blood clotting	Hemophilia
Curly or wavy hair	Straight hair	Normal red blood cells	Sickle-cell disease
Full head of hair	Baldheadedness	Normal protein metabolism	Phenylketonuria (PKU)
Normal hearing	Some forms of congenital deafness	Normal physiology	Tay-Sachs disease
Normally pigmented skin	Albino (completely white) skin	Huntington disease	Normal central nervous system functioning in adulthood
Facial dimples	No dimples	Immunity to poison ivy	Susceptibility to poison ivy
Thick lips	Thin lips		

Note: Many common traits show dominant or recessive patterns. Sometimes too, a pattern may be dominant with respect to one trait but recessive with respect to another

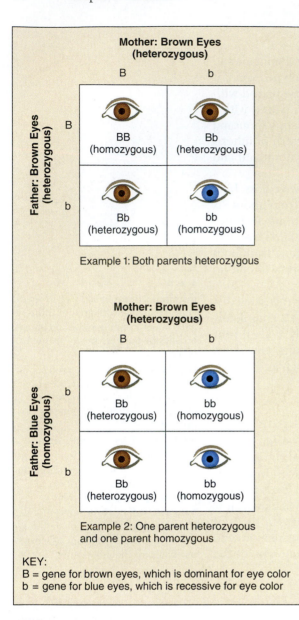

KEY:
B = gene for brown eyes, which is dominant for eye color
b = gene for blue eyes, which is recessive for eye color

● ● ● ● ● ● ● ● ● ● ● ● ● ● ● ● ● ●

FIGURE 3.6

Genetic Transmission of Eye Color

Example 1: Three out of four offspring will have brown eyes, and one out of four will have blue eyes. Example 2: Two out of four offspring will have brown eyes, and two out of four will have blue eyes.

dominant allele and thus have brown eyes. Only a person who is homozygous will display the phenotype of one of the recessive alleles and have blue or hazel eyes. From a genetic standpoint, there are three times as many ways to have brown eyes as there are to have blue or green ones. Figure 3.6 illustrates this example.

Keep in mind, however, that although all of the patterns of inheritance for dominant and recessive traits are possible, each genotype will not necessarily occur in each family, since genes are inherited randomly. In Figure 3.6 (example 1), for instance, although it is possible that two parents will have children with the eye color genotypes of BB, Bb, or bb, all of their children may in reality be BB or bb. Thus, the increased probability of a particular genotype (e.g., Bb) does not mean that genotype will definitely occur. In the genetic transmission of a sex-linked trait such as hemophilia (discussed later) (see Figure 3.8), it is possible that no offspring will receive the genotype for the disorder. There is, however, a 25 percent chance that any daughter will be a carrier of the genotype but no chance that she will develop the disorder, and a 25 percent chance that any son will inherit the genotype, with 100 percent chance that he will then develop the phenotype for hemophilia.

Many genes have more than two alleles. As a result, the traits they govern can vary in more complex ways. The four major human blood types, for example, are based on three alleles of the same gene. Two of these alleles, type A and type B, are dominant forms, and the O allele is recessive. Figure 3.7 illustrates how these three alleles for blood type can combine in six possible ways but produce only four blood types, A, B, O, and AB. The AB blood type is an example of *codominance,* a situation in which the characteristics of both alleles are independently expressed in a new phenotype rather than one or the other being dominant, or as a mixture of the two. Because each blood type has a unique chemistry that allows it to mix only with certain other blood types, determining the compatible blood genotype is very important for people who receive blood transfusions.

Not all alleles occur with equal frequency. One of the three alleles of blood type does not occur nearly as often as the other two do, and different parts of the world's population inherit the blood-typing alleles with different frequencies. In fact, population geneticists have used blood samples from two thousand communities and tribes to map the worldwide geographic distribution of allele frequencies for such traits as blood type, eye and skin color, and body shape. Perhaps their most important finding is that although some group differences in alleles for such surface traits exist, there is little genetic evidence to support the idea of different "races." In fact, groups previously thought to be racially different are remarkably alike in their genetic makeup, whereas genetic diversity among individuals within these groups is enormous (Subramanian, 1995).

Polygenic Transmission

Unlike with eye color and blood type, which can vary only in a limited number of qualitatively distinct ways, the inheritance of most physical traits—including height, weight, hair and skin color, and complex personality and behavioral traits such as intelligence, extroversion, introversion, emotionality, shyness, alcoholism, depression, and schizophrenia—does not fit the simple single-gene model just described. These traits are called *polygenic,* meaning they involve *many* genes, each with small effects, as well as environmental influences. In all these cases, children show a marked tendency to have a phenotype that is intermediate between those of their parents, and for the most part, the exact mechanisms of inheritance for such traits are still unknown (Plomin et al., 1994; Plomin, 1989, 1990).

Because polygenic phenotypes vary by small degrees, environment can influence them in relatively important ways. An overweight person can become more slender through a change in diet, for example, and a shy person can learn to be more outgoing. Such experiences matter less for traits that are simply transmitted by a single gene; there is no way to change eye color, even though you can cover your irises with tinted contact lenses.

The Determination of Sex

One pair of chromosomes among the usual twenty-three pairs is largely responsible for determining whether a child develops as a male or a female. In women, this pair looks pretty much like any other pair of matched chromosomes. In men, one member of the pair is noticeably shorter than the other. The longer reproductive or sex chromosome in either gender is called *X*, and the shorter one in men is called *Y*. Genetically normal men therefore always have a mixed combination, XY, whereas normal women always have an XX combination.

Whether a child becomes male or female depends on events at conception. All ova, or egg cells, contain a single X chromosome, whereas a sperm cell may contain either an X or a Y. If a Y-bearing sperm happens to fertilize the egg, a male (XY) zygote develops; if the sperm is X-bearing, a female (XX) zygote develops.

How does this work? During the first several weeks following conception, the developing male or female embryos possess a set of bisexual gonadal, or sex, tissues, meaning they can develop into either male or female sex structures. Between the fourth and eighth weeks of the embryo's development, the gonadal tissue develops into testes or ovaries depending on the presence or absence of a small section of the Y chromosome, referred to as *TDF*, or *testis-determining factor*. Fertilized ova that lack the Y chromosome (and TDF) develop into embryos that are female. For ova

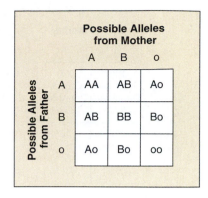

		Possible Alleles from Mother		
		A	B	o
Possible Alleles from Father	A	AA	AB	Ao
	B	AB	BB	Bo
	o	Ao	Bo	oo

● ● ● ● ● ● ● ● ● ● ● ● ● ● ● ● ●
FIGURE 3.7

Inheritance of Blood Type

In blood type inheritance, both A and B alleles are dominant and the 0 allele is recessive. Therefore, the following proportions of blood types are likely to occur in the general population:
Type A (AA or AO): 3/9
Type B (BB or BO): 3/9
Type AB: 2/9
Type O (OO): 1/9

Most physical traits result from the combined influences of gene pairs inherited from both parents. The degree of resemblance between a child and a given parent depends on the particular pattern of gene variations involved.

Carrier Mother

	X	X
Normal Father X	XX Normal Daughter (25%)	XX Carrier Daughter (25%)
Y	XY Normal Son (25%)	XY Hemophilic Son (25%)

● ● ● ● ● ● ● ● ● ● ● ● ● ● ● ●

FIGURE 3.8

Inheritance of Hemophilia, a Sex-Linked Disorder

In this example of the inheritance of hemophilia, the mother is a carrier of the disease. Each daughter has a 50 percent chance of inheriting a pair of normal chromosomes (XX) and a 50 percent chance of being a carrier (XX) like her mother. However, she herself will not be affected by the disorder because her second X chromosome protects her. Each son has a 50 percent chance of being normal (XY) and a 50 percent chance of inheriting the abnormal chromosome and being hemophilic. This is because as a male, his second chromosome is a Y, which does not protect him from the disorder.

● ● ●

sex-linked recessive traits Recessive traits resulting from genes on the X chromosome.

hemophilia A disease in which the blood fails to clot properly and therefore is characterized by excessive bleeding; example of a sex-linked recessive trait.

genetic imprinting A method of genetic transmission in which genes are chemically marked to result in a different phenotype if inherited from the mother than if inherited from the father.

fertilized by a Y-bearing sperm, TDF is present, and male embryos result (Page et al., 1987).

More Y sperm than X sperm succeed in fertilizing the ovum, resulting in about 30 percent more male than female zygotes. By birth, however, baby boys outnumber baby girls by about 6 percent, on average, and by age thirty-five, women begin to outnumber men, suggesting that males may be more vulnerable than females. Much of this vulnerability is related to *sex-linked transmission*. Recall that unlike females, who carry XX chromosomes, males carry XY chromosome pairs. Because the Y chromosome carried by all males is much shorter than its matching X chromosome and therefore may lack many of the gene locations of its matching X chromosome, many genes from the mother may not be matched or counteracted with equivalent genetic material from the father. As a result, genetic abnormalities on the single complete X chromosome are more likely to result in phenotypic abnormalities in males than in females. Table 3.2 lists a number of **sex-linked recessive traits,** abnormalities that are transmitted on the single complete X chromosome.

One such trait is **hemophilia,** an inability of the blood to clot and therefore to stop itself from flowing. Since clotting is so slow, internal bleeding can at times be life threatening, as can the risk of contracting AIDS from transfusions with blood that hasn't been carefully screened (American College of Obstetricians and Gynecologists [ACOG], 1990; McKussick, 1995). Because the gene for hemophilia is located on the X chromosome, a female carrier is protected by having a normal gene on her second X chromosome. Daughters who get the gene will be carriers, like their mothers, while sons will develop hemophilia because they lack a second X chromosome to counteract the gene's effects. (See Figure 3.8.)

Most human characteristics that have been studied follow the pattern of dominant-recessive and codominant inherence, and in most instances, a gene that has been inherited influences development in the same manner whether it was contributed by the biological mother or the father. However, geneticists have discovered a new mode of inheritance called **genetic imprinting,** in which genes are chemically marked, or *imprinted,* such that identical sections of the same chromosome will result in different phenotypic outcomes, depending on whether the chromosome was inherited from the mother or the father. This imprint is most often temporary and may disappear in the next generation (Cassidy, 1995).

An example of genetic imprinting is Prader-Willi syndrome, which leads to shortness of stature, mental retardation, and insatiable appetite. This syndrome is

TABLE 3.2   Sex-Linked Recessive Traits

Condition	Description
Colorblindness	Inability to distinguish certain colors, usually reds and greens
Hemophilia	Deficiency in substances that allow the blood to clot; also known as *bleeder's disease*
Muscular dystrophy (Duchenne's form)	Weakening and wasting away of muscles, beginning in childhood
Diabetes (two forms)	Inability to metabolize sugars properly because the body does not produce enough insulin
Anhidrotic ectodermal dysplasia	Lack of sweat glands and teeth
Night blindness (certain forms)	Inability to see in dark or very dim conditions
Deafness (certain forms)	Impaired hearing or total hearing loss
Atrophy of optic nerve	Gradual deterioration of vision and eventual blindness

Note: All of the above traits are carried by the X chromosome, and all are recessive. As a result, they occur less often in females than in males.

caused by the absence of a portion of chromosome 15. If an offspring inherits a defective chromosome 15 from the father, Prader-Willi results. However, if the same defective chromosome 15 is inherited from the mother, the result is a very different disorder called Angelman's syndrome, which causes constant, uncontrollable outbursts of laughter and jerky motions. It is likely that modifier genes that are different in the mother and the father cause different chemical alterations in the affected areas of chromosome 15 so that different disorders result.

WHAT DO YOU THINK ?   Now that you know how eye color and blood type are inherited, see if you can figure out how you inherited *your* eye color. How about your blood type?

Genetic Abnormalities

Once in awhile, genetic reproduction goes wrong. Sometimes too many or too few chromosomes transfer to a newly forming zygote. Sometimes the chromosomes transfer properly but carry particular defective genes that affect a child physically, mentally, or both. The changes almost always create significant disabilities for the child, if they do not prove fatal.

A large-scale international research effort called the *human genome project* is currently under way. Its goal is to map the locations and describe the biochemical composition of all of the approximately one hundred thousand genes that comprise the twenty-three pairs of human chromosomes. Approximately 40 percent of the human X chromosomes have been mapped so far. Genes associated with twenty-six inherited diseases have been reproduced and genes associated with fifty others identified. Most of these abnormalities are either fatal to a fetus or put it at serious medical risk (Cooperative Human Linkage Center, 1996; Garver & Garver, 1994).

Disorders Due to Abnormal Chromosomes

Most of the time, inheriting one too many or one too few chromosomes proves fatal. After all, one extra chromosome forces several thousand "wrong" genes on the

Children with Down syndrome, like this girl, learn academic material very slowly. But with special educational help and proper social support, they can lead satisfying lives.

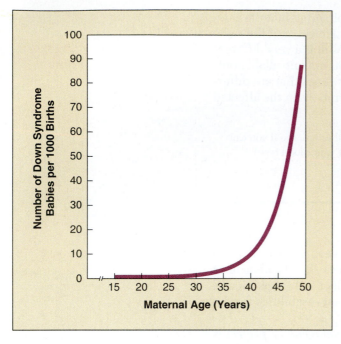

FIGURE 3.9

Relationship Between Maternal Age and the Incidence of Down Syndrome

As women get older, their chances of giving birth to a baby with Down syndrome increase. At age twenty-one, 1 in every 1,500 babies is born with Down syndrome. At age thirty-nine, 1 in 150 babies is born with the disorder. At age forty-nine, 1 in 10 babies is born with Down.

developing fetus, and it certainly cannot cope easily with so much genetic misinformation. In a few cases, however, children with an extra or a missing chromosome survive past birth and even live fairly normal lives. Three such cases are mentioned here; each is named after the doctor who first published a description of it.

Down Syndrome   *Down syndrome* is also called *trisomy 21* because it is generally caused by an extra twenty-first chromosome or the translocation, or transfer, of part of the twenty-first chromosome onto another chromosome. People with this disorder have almond-shaped eyes, round heads, and stubby hands and feet. Many also have abnormalities of the heart and intestinal tract, and facial deformities. They also show greater than usual vulnerability to a number of serious diseases, such as leukemia. Most children with Down syndrome live until middle adulthood, but about 14 percent die by age one and 21 percent die by age ten.

Although children with Down syndrome achieve many of the same developmental milestones that normal children do, as they get older they fall farther and farther behind developmentally and never "catch up" with their peers. By adulthood, most individuals with Down syndrome plateau at a moderately retarded level of cognitive functioning. They are able to learn and follow simple routines and hold routine jobs, but because they are easily confused by change and have difficulty making important decisions, they usually cannot live independently and require extensive, ongoing support from their families and community service programs (Sloper et al., 1990; Stratford, 1994).

Down syndrome is much more frequent in babies of mothers over age thirty-five and among older fathers. This is because as men and women grow older, they experience longer exposure to environmental hazards, such as chemicals and radiation, that may affect their ovaries and sperm. In addition, since a woman's ova are formed before she is born, they are likely to undergo progressive deterioration with age (Halliday et al., 1995). Figure 3.9 summarizes the risk of having a Down syndrome baby for women of different ages.

Klinefelter Syndrome   *Klinefelter syndrome* (XXY) results from inheriting at least one extra chromosome, usually an extra X chromosome, creating an XXY pattern. A person with this syndrome is phenotypically male but tends to have small testes even after puberty and to remain sterile throughout his lifetime. However, hormonal supplements allow individuals with this disorder to achieve normal sexual functioning. Note that individuals with Klinefelter syndrome have normal intelligence. Klinefelter affects about one in eight hundred newborn males (ACOG, 1990).

Turner Syndrome   *Turner syndrome* (XO) results from having only one sex chromosome; thus, affected individuals are, by default, female. The presence of a single X chromosome provides genetic information to form a viable infant, although she will develop specific learning disabilities and will not be fully sexually differentiated. (Note that if only a single Y chromosome were present, a viable embryo would not be possible.) Individuals with Turner syndrome grow up to be very short as adults (between four and five feet) and have short, "webbed" necks and ears that are set lower than usual. During puberty, they generally fail to develop secondary sexual characteristics such as breasts and pubic hair. These women are not mentally retarded, but do develop specific learning problems involving memory and judgment.

Disorders Due to Abnormal Genes

Even when a zygote has the proper number of chromosomes, it may inherit specific genes that can create serious medical problems for the child after birth. In many cases, these problems prove lethal. In others, genetic diseases are at least manageable, if not fully curable.

There are three main types of genetic disorders: *dominant gene disorders, recessive gene disorders,* and *multifactorial gene disorders.* Table 3.3 lists some common examples of each and the risk of their presence at birth.

Dominant Gene Disorders   Dominant gene disorders require only one abnormal gene from either parent to affect a child. Figure 3.10 illustrates the inheritance of a dominant gene disorder.

Huntington Disease   *Huntington disease* is a dominant gene disorder that results in a gradual deterioration of the central nervous system, causing uncontrollable movements and mental deterioration. Typically it does not appear until affected people are in their thirties or forties, and it always proves fatal. Before that age, people usually have no way of knowing whether they will get the disease (ACOG, 1990).

Researchers have recently identified specific sections, or markers, of human genome that are exclusively linked to Huntington disease. The gene for the disorder appears to be located somewhere on chromosome 4. Although it may now be possible to develop a genetic blood test for Huntington, an understanding of how the gene actually causes the disease and treatments are likely to be many years away (Cooperative Human Linkage Center, 1996; Horgan, 1993).

Recessive Gene Disorders   Recessive gene disorders (see Table 3.3) can occur when the fetus inherits a pair of recessive genes, one from each parent. Figure 3.11 illustrates the inheritance of a recessive gene disorder.

Cystic Fibrosis   *Cystic fibrosis* is the most common genetic disease among people of northern European descent. This disability involves the production of abnormally thick mucus, clogging the lungs and causing serious difficulties in breathing and digestion, delayed growth and sexual maturation, high vulnerability to infections, and shortened life expectancy (ACOG, 1990).

Sickle-Cell Disease   In **sickle-cell disease,** the oxygen-carrying protein of the red blood cells takes on a rigid *sickle* shape inside the cells rather than the normal round, *doughnut* shape. These abnormal red blood cells get caught in the blood vessels, cutting off circulation, reducing the oxygen supply, and causing pain. Other symptoms include increased bacterial infections and degeneration of organs that need a great deal of oxygen, including the brain, kidneys, liver, heart, spleen, and muscles. Infants with this illness must be given daily doses of oral penicillin beginning at two months of age to reduce the chance of infection. Even with careful care, however, the majority of victims die before age twenty and few live past age forty (Diamond, 1989; Selekman, 1993).

By now you may be wondering why so many harmful genetic abnormalities evolved or why they do not disappear as the generations pass, given the serious health problems they cause. Sickle-cell disease suggests one possible answer to this question. Sometimes a genetic condition may benefit people in general even though it hurts individuals in particular. About 1 in 635 African Americans are affected with sickle-cell disease, and about 1 in 10 are carriers of it. Sickle-cell disease is especially common in tropical climates such as Africa, the Mediterranean, India, and the Middle East.

Individuals who are heterozygous (having both one abnormal and one normal allele) show a few signs of sickle-cell disease but also a strong immunity to malaria, which is common in the tropics. There is some physical cost, however. Most live

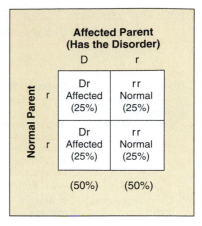

● ● ● ● ● ● ● ● ● ● ● ● ● ● ● ● ● ●

FIGURE 3.10

Inheritance of a Dominant Gene Disorder

When one parent has a dominant gene disorder, each child has a 50 percent chance of inheriting the dominant abnormal gene for the disorder (D) and a 50 percent chance of inheriting a pair of recessive genes (rr) and being unaffected.

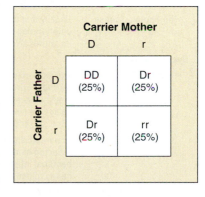

● ● ● ● ● ● ● ● ● ● ● ● ● ● ● ● ● ●

FIGURE 3.11

Inheritance of a Recessive Gene Disorder

When both parents are carriers of a recessive gene disorder, each child faces the following possibilities: (1) a 25 percent chance of inheriting the pair of recessive genes (rr) required to inherit the disorder; (2) a 25 percent chance of inheriting a pair of dominant genes (DD) and being unaffected; or (3) a 50 percent chance of inheriting one dominant and one recessive gene (Dr) and being a carrier like both parents.

● ● ●

sickle-cell disease A genetically transmitted condition in which a person's red blood cells intermittently acquire a curved, sickle shape. The condition sometimes can clog circulation in the small blood vessels.

TABLE 3.3   Risk of Selected Genetic Disorders

Disorder	Description	Risk of Having a Fetus with the Disorder	
		Overall	**With One Affected Child**
Chromosomal			
Down syndrome	Extra or translocated twenty-first chromosome. Symptoms include almond-shaped eyes, round head, stubby hands and feet, abnormalities of the heart and intestinal tract, facial deformities, and vulnerability to disease. Most children with Down syndrome live until middle adulthood, but about 14 percent die by age one and 21 percent die by age ten.	1/800	1–2%
Klinefelter syndrome (XXY)	At least one extra chromosome, usually an X. Affected individual is phenotypically male, but has small testes and is sterile.	1/800 men	N/S[1]
Fragile X syndrome	The most common inherited form of mental retardation. Caused by an abnormal gene on the bottom end of the X chromosome. Causes spectrum of learning difficulties ranging from mild problems to severe mental retardation.	1/1,200 male births 1/2,000 female births	N/S[1]
Turner syndrome (XO)	Affects only females born with a single X in the sex chromosome. Grow to be very short as adults, "webbed" necks and ears set lower than usual; fail to develop secondary sexual characteristics; problems with spacial judgment, memory, and reasoning.	1/3,000 women	N/S[1]
Dominant Gene			
Polydactyly	Extra fingers or toes. Fairly common. Correctable by surgery.	1/300–1/100	50%
Achondroplasia	Rare disorder of the skeleton; afflicted person has shorter than normal arms and legs.	1/2,300	50%
Huntington disease	Usually first affects people in their 30s and 40s; gradual deterioration of the central nervous system, causing uncontrollable movements, mental deterioration, and death.	1/15,000–1/5,000	50%
Recessive Gene			
Cystic fibrosis	The most common genetic disease among white persons of Northern European descent. Abnormally thick mucus clogs the lungs, causing serious difficulties in breathing and digestion, delayed growth and sexual maturation, high vulnerability to infection, and shortened life expectancy.	1/2,500 white persons (risk of being a carrier is 1/25)	25%
Sickle-cell disease	Abnormal, sickle-shaped red blood cells clog blood vessels, reducing blood supply and causing pain. May cause increased bacterial infections and degeneration of brain, kidneys, liver, heart, spleen, and muscles. Shortened lifespan.	1/625 African Americans (risk of being a carrier is 1/10)	25%
Tay-Sachs disease	Found mostly in persons of Eastern European Jewish descent. Chemical imbalance of central nervous system. Symptoms first occur at six months of age, progressively causing severe mental retardation, blindness, seizures, and death by third year due to lowered resistance to disease.	1/3,600 Eastern European Jews (risk of being a carrier is 1/30–1/300)	25%
X Linked			
Hemophilia	Lack of substance needed for blood clotting. Risk of life-threatening internal bleeding; risk of AIDS from transfusions.	1/2,500 male babies	50% for boy, 0% for girl
Multifactorial			
Congenital heart disease	Structural and/or electrical abnormalities of the heart. May respond to medication or corrective surgery performed after birth.	1/125	2–4%
Neural tube defect	Tube enclosing the spine fails to close completely or normally. Brain may be absent or underdeveloped (anencephaly) or spinal cord and nerve bundles may be exposed. Death or severe retardation or other long-term problems for children who survive.	1–2/1,000	2–5%
Cleft lip/cleft palate	Gap or space in lip or hole in roof of mouth. May cause difficulties in breathing, speech, hearing, and eating. Corrective surgery at birth can repair most clefts.	1/1,000–1/5,000	2–4%

[1]No significant increase.

Sources: ACOG (1990); Blatt (1988); Diamond (1989); Hagerman (1996); Selekman (1993); Stratford (1994).

normal lives, but when deprived of sufficient oxygen, such as during intense physical exercise or at high altitudes, the *sickling* of their red blood cells can be triggered, causing pain. Individuals who are homozygous (having two dominant or two recessive genes) either avoid sickle-cell disease completely by having two dominant genes or suffer badly from it because they have two recessive genes. Either way, they contract malaria at very high rates. As it turns out, very large percentages of individuals in tropical areas are heterozygous. The troublesome allele seems to have evolved for their benefit and at the expense of people who contract sickle-cell disease.

Although no cure exists yet for this disease, a new drug called *hydroxyurea* appears to reduce the production of sickle cells by switching on a gene that triggers the production of fetal hemoglobin, a type produced by babies before and shortly after birth that does not sickle (Leary, 1995).

Tay-Sachs Disease   *Tay-Sachs disease* is a disorder of the nervous system that occurs most frequently among people of German or Eastern European Jewish origin (ACOG, 1990; Muir, 1983). Tay-Sachs disease disturbs the chemical balance in an infant's nerve cells. At birth the baby may seem fairly normal, but by about six months of age she or he may show poor tolerance for sudden loud noises and seem weak and slow to develop. Motor skills initially acquired may later be "forgotten" or lost, and the baby becomes progressively apathetic and irritable. Eventually, deterioration of the nervous system may cause convulsive seizures and lead to deafness and blindness. Most Tay-Sachs babies die by their third birthday, most frequently from a common illness such as pneumonia, because of their reduced resistance to disease.

Phenylketonuria   *Phenylketonuria (PKU)*, which occurs in five to ten out of every one hundred thousand births, is a disorder that severely diminishes a child's ability to utilize an amino acid called *phenylalanine*, which is found in protein-based foods, such as milk and meat, that are essential to normal nutrition and growth. The disorder is caused by a single recessive allele carried by a relatively small percentage of people. But because PKU is recessive, many people are carriers without realizing it. Left untreated, PKU causes phenylalanine to build up to dangerous levels in the child's blood and spinal fluid. This appears to damage the *prefrontal cortex* of the brain, causing deterioration in cognitive functioning and mental retardation. Because very small increases in phenylalanine can affect the brain, prenatal detection, early diagnosis, and a carefully planned diet from birth onward may be required to prevent the symptoms.

Long-term continuation of an extremely restrictive diet is very difficult for children and their families. In addition, pregnant women must maintain a restrictive diet to avoid passing on high levels of phenylalanine to their fetuses. These strategies help individual children and their families, but do not remove the gene that causes the problem in the first place (Diamond, 1993; Mazzocco et al., 1994).

PKU illustrates clearly the difference between genotype and phenotype. Depending on the nutrition their environment provides, infants with one particular genotype, the PKU deficiency, can either grow into a healthy phenotype or get sick enough to die. Infants with two different genotypes, one normal and one abnormally sensitive to PKU, can end up with similar, healthy phenotypes when conditions are right.

Multifactorial Disorders   **Multifactorial disorders,** which result from a combination of genetic and environmental factors, are an excellent illustration of the theme of developmental context discussed in Chapter 1. The incidence of these disorders varies widely in different parts of the world, largely because of the great differences in existing environmental contexts. (See Table 3.3.)

Neural tube defects result when the tube enclosing the spinal cord fails to close completely or normally. In some instances, the upper part of the brain is absent or

• • •
multifactorial disorders that result from a combination of genetic and environmental factors.

underdeveloped; in others, the lower part of the neural tube fails to close properly, leaving the spinal cord and nerve bundles exposed. Both conditions are generally fatal or result in severe retardation or other serious long-term problems for children who do survive (ACOG, 1990). Neural tube defects are believed to have multiple causes, including hereditary tendencies (whether a family is genetically predisposed to these defects), environmental insults (such as pollutants; poor nutrition, including a diet deficient in ascorbic acid, folate, and zinc), and certain medications (prescribed, over-the-counter, or street drugs), and diseases (including diabetes mellitus). The frequency of neural tube defects is affected by geographical location and racial/ethnic background. The British Isles have the highest overall incidence (four to five per one thousand births); other high-frequency areas include Egypt, Pakistan, India, and some Arab countries. The frequency in the United States is one to two per one thousand births, with the highest incidence occurring in the Appalachian region. Countries with the lowest incidence (fewer than 0.5 per one thousand births) include Finland, China, Japan, and Israel. African Americans, Asians, and Ashkenazi Jews have the lowest occurrence, while the Irish and Sikhs have the highest (Barnes, 1993).

Cleft palate/lip is a condition in which the upper lip and/or roof of the mouth (palate) fail to grow together, resulting in a "cleft," or split. The two conditions may occur separately or together. Depending on severity, they may lead to difficulties in breathing, speech, hearing, and eating. Corrective surgery at birth can repair most clefts (Blatt, 1988).

Congenital heart disease refers to structural and/or electrical abnormalities in the formation of the heart. Depending on the type of defect, medication may be prescribed or corrective surgery performed after birth (Blatt, 1988).

WHAT DO YOU THINK?   Woody Guthrie, the famous folk singer and father of Arlo Guthrie (also a famous folk singer), died of Huntington disease. Based on your new knowledge about this disorder, what questions might you ask Arlo about how his genetic inheritance has affected his life decisions, such as whether or not to have children?

Genetic Counseling and Prenatal Diagnosis

Some genetic problems can be reduced or avoided by sensitive counseling for couples who may carry genetic disorders. Couples in need of such counseling may know of relatives who have suffered from genetic diseases. Or they may belong to an ethnic group at risk for a particular disorder, such as African Americans, who are at risk for sickle-cell disease. More immediate signs of genetic risk include the birth of an infant with some genetic disorder or the spontaneous abortion of earlier pregnancies. Table 3.4 presents guidelines for determining who should seek prenatal genetic counseling.

Genetic counselors use potential parents' medical and genetic histories and tests to help couples estimate their chances of having a healthy baby and discuss alternatives from which a couple can choose. Once the actual genetic risk is clarified, counselors can discuss alternatives from which a couple can choose. One obvious alternative is to avoid conception completely and, perhaps, to adopt a baby. A second is to take the risk in the hope of conceiving a healthy baby. Modern methods of prenatal diagnosis (discussed shortly) can now be used to detect genetic disorders after conception but before birth, allowing the parents the choice of terminating the pregnancy during the first trimester if a serious problem is detected. In addition, medical intervention early in infancy may help repair damage caused by a genetic disorder, depending on its severity. Finally, *preimplantation diagnosis,* which refers to a variety of methods to screen ova (eggs) and early embryos *before* they are implanted into the uterus, is being developed as an alternative to prenatal screening, which can be used only after a pregnancy has been established (see the Working With interview on page 81).

Most methods of preimplantation diagnosis use *in vitro* or "test tube" fertilization to identify the presence of recessive genes for hereditary and genetic conditions by selecting for fertilization only those eggs that appear to be free of abnormalities. Proponents of this method believe it is a more suitable option for couples who are opposed to abortion or may have difficulty deciding to terminate a pregnancy in which the fetus may be at risk. Some critics have questioned the accuracy of the method. Others are concerned that techniques designed solely to screen embryos based on carefully considered and ethically acceptable medical reasons will be used as a new form of *eugenics* to engineer "better babies" based on beliefs or prejudices about which human qualities are currently desirable and which are not, thus limiting the gene pool on which human diversity depends (Hubbard, 1993; Pappert, 1993).

Genetic Screening   The rapid advances made in new technologies to screen for genetic disorders raise important ethical and social policy concerns about who should control these technologies and how they should be used. One danger is that people who are carriers of genetic disorders will be denied health care coverage on the basis that they have a *pre-existing condition.* In one recent survey of the country's main types of health care insurers, approximately 75 percent of health maintenance organizations (HMOs), 40 percent of commercial insurers, and 35 percent of Blue Cross/Blue Shield plans agreed that the carrier of a genetic disease trait has a pre-existing condition. In an increasing number of cases, employers, HMOs, and adoption agencies have used genetic information to discriminate against individuals with genetic abnormalities, even when they were carriers who were healthy or had extremely mild symptoms (Rennie, 1994).

Privacy is another important issue. If someone is a carrier of a defective gene or has a genetic disease, does someone else have the right to know? When asked this question in a recent survey, 57 percent of the respondents answered yes, 41 percent said no, and 2 percent were uncertain. Furthermore, if someone else deserves to know, who should it be? When those who believe someone else does deserve to know were asked this question, 100 percent said that a spouse or fiancé should know, 70 percent said family members, approximately 59 percent said the insurer, and about 32 percent said the employer (Rennie, 1994).

A third issue concerns how such tests should be regulated or controlled. Should private companies whose goal of maximizing investor profits may conflict with insuring high-quality and affordable health care for all be allowed to control the

TABLE 3.4   **Who Should Seek Prenatal Counseling?**
1. Couples who already have a child with some serious defect such as Down syndrome, spina bifida, congenital heart disease, limb malformation, or mental retardation
2. Couples with a family history of a genetic disease or mental retardation
3. Couples who are blood relatives (first or second cousins)
4. African Americans, Ashkenazi Jews, Italians, Greeks, and other high-risk ethnic groups
5. Women who have had a serious infection early in pregnancy (rubella or toxoplasmosis) or who have been infected with HIV
6. Women who have taken potentially harmful medications early in pregnancy or habitually use drugs or alcohol
7. Women who have had X rays taken early in pregnancy
8. Women who have experienced two or more of the following: stillbirth, death of a newborn baby, miscarriage
9. Any woman thirty-five years or older

Source: Adapted from Feinbloom & Forman (1987) p. 129.

A Multicultural View

Cultural Difference and Genetic Counseling

The growing Asian American population in the United States tends to use genetic counseling infrequently. Reasons for this include lack of information and misperceptions about such services and cultural attitudes that strongly discourage seeking outside help for family problems.

In traditional Asian cultures, the family is the most important social unit. It is a source of material, social, and emotional support for its members and is responsible for maintaining the cultural and religious traditions that connect the present generation with past and future ones. The personal decisions and actions of an individual regarding pregnancy and genetic counseling reflect not only on herself but on her *nuclear family* (spouse and children), her *extended family* (parents, siblings, and other relatives), and *past and future generations* of her family (Chan, 1991; Wang & Marsh, 1992). John Roland, a psychologist who has studied personality development in India and Japan, believes that in addition to an *individual* and a *spiritual* sense of self, individuals growing up in such traditional societies develop a powerful *familial* self. Within this sense of self, a person experiences himself as an inseparable part of the family unit and one whose actions will be largely determined by family needs and expectations (Roland, 1988; Segall et al., 1998).

Three other areas of cultural difference are important for genetic counselors to understand: (1) *collective versus personal autonomy,* (2) *shame and stigma,* and (3) *directive versus nondirective authority* (Wang & Marsh, 1992).

Collective Versus Personal Autonomy

A belief in *personal autonomy* is a cornerstone of Western genetic counseling, which views the patient as a self-determining individual who is largely free from the external control of family and other outside influences. The counselor's goal is to help the patient make an informed, autonomous decision about what is best by providing information in a nondirective and value-free way. This approach, however, frequently conflicts with cultural expectations of Asian patients, who hold a *collective* view of autonomy.

Collective autonomy presumes that a patient is an inseparable part of the traditional family unit and one whose actions will be largely determined by family interests. Family roles and responsibilities are rigidly and hierarchically defined based on generation, age, and gender, with the father occupying a position of unquestioned leadership and authority. This pattern serves to minimize family conflict by allowing little room for individuality and independence on the part of its members and to maintain family harmony and further the family's welfare and reputation (Wang & Marsh, 1992).

---

development, costs, and use of such tests? Or should technology that is so central to people's well-being be regulated by our democratically elected government representatives?

Differences in cultural beliefs and expectations can affect who receives genetic counseling and the forms it takes. The accompanying Multicultural View box discusses this issue.

Prenatal Diagnostic Techniques

Sometimes genetic disorders can be detected after conception but before birth using various diagnostic techniques. This section discusses current diagnostic techniques to screen for genetic disorders. (See Table 3.5.)

Ultrasound   With **ultrasound,** high-frequency sound waves are projected through the mother's womb. When they bounce off the fetus, they create a television image of the size, shape, and position of the fetus. Ultrasound can be used throughout a pregnancy to assess the age of the fetus, multiple pregnancies, and gross physical defects in external and internal organs. It now can also be used to detect Down syndrome, which is identified by a characteristic extra skin fold on the back of the neck. Ultrasound is also used to guide instruments during prenatal procedures such as amniocentesis, chorionic villus sampling, fetoscopy, and PUBS (discussed shortly). So far, any potential negative effects of ultrasound have not been discovered (Blatt, 1988; D'Alton & DeCherney, 1993).

● ● ●
ultrasound A prenatal diagnostic method that allows medical personnel and others to view the fetus by projecting high-frequency sound waves through the mother's womb.

Shame and Stigma

In traditional Asian culture, which places tremendous importance on successfully marrying off a daughter, infertility is viewed as a handicapping stigma that will make a young woman unmarriageable and bring shame to herself and her family. Such problems are therefore managed within the family. To seek outside help from a genetic counselor would be a public admission of failure (Sue & Zane, 1987; Wang & Marsh, 1992).

Directive Versus Nondirective Authority

A *nondirective approach to authority* is a second cornerstone of genetic counseling that directly conflicts with the cultural expectations of Asian patients. This approach assumes the patient is responsible for making her own decisions and should not be influenced by the counselor's own views and values. In contrast, the *directive approach* assumes that as an expert authority, the counselor should provide the patient with clear and highly structured guidance about what he should do.

The directive approach is much more consistent with the authority relations and role expectations in Asian families. It therefore is more likely to relieve high levels of anxiety, shame, and doubt by providing practical and immediate solutions to problems (Wang & Marsh, 1992). Stanley Sue, who has written extensively about these issues, suggests that families from Asian and other traditional cultures will seek help from professionals who earn credibility and trust by responding to their need for directive, immediate assistance while also working with them to achieve more self-directed, long-term solutions (Sue, 1998; Sue et al., 1994).

As in the case of this multigenerational Asian American family, effective genetic counseling must be responsive to cultural differences.

Amniocentesis   **Amniocentesis** is performed at weeks fourteen through eighteen of pregnancy. With the aid of ultrasound, a slender needle is carefully inserted through the mother's abdomen into the uterus and the amniotic sac, and a tiny sample of the amniotic fluid is withdrawn. This fluid contains cells that have the fetus's genetic makeup rather than the mother's, so it can be used to determine whether the fetus has abnormal chromosomes. It can also be tested for alpha-fetoprotein, a protein produced by the fetus that is present in the amniotic fluid and in the mother's blood. Fetal cells are then cultured in the laboratory over a two-to-four-week period and prepared so that their chromosomes can be studied under a microscope. The test reveals the presence of chromosomal disorders such as Down syndrome (an extra chromosome), and neural tube defects, as well as the gender of the baby.

Minor complications, such as uterine cramping, vaginal bleeding from the uterus, and leaking of amniotic fluid through the vagina, occur in about one out of one hundred procedures. A small increase in the rates of miscarriage (approximately 0.5 percent), maternal bleeding at birth, or injury to the fetus is associated with this procedure (ACOG, 1990; Feinbloom & Forman, 1987).

Chorionic Villus Sampling   **Chorionic villus sampling (CVS)** tests for most of the same genetic disorders that amniocentesis does. Because it can be performed between the eighth and tenth weeks of pregnancy and results obtained within about ten days, it allows for earlier detection than does amniocentesis. CVS involves collecting and analyzing tissue by inserting a thin, hollow tube (catheter) through the

• • •

amniocentesis A prenatal diagnostic method in which a sample of amniotic fluid is withdrawn and tested to detect chromosomal abnormalities.

chorionic villus sampling (CVS) A medical procedure for detecting genetic abnormalities before birth in which a small bit of tissue surrounding the embryo is removed and examined microscopically.

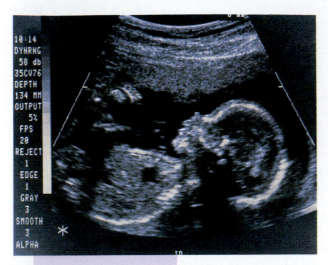

Ultrasound images such as the one of a healthy baby in this photo help parents and their professional caregivers monitor fetal development.

vagina into the uterus between the uterine lining and the chorion. The *chorion* is a tissue layer that surrounds the embryo for the first two months of its development and later develops into the placenta. A syringe attached to the tube sucks up several of the *chorionic villi,* projections of tissue that transfer oxygen, food, and waste between the mother's and embryo's circulatory systems and are genetically identical with the embryo.

This technique allows parents to know in the very early weeks of pregnancy whether the fetus has inherited a serious defect and gives them time to decide whether to have a therapeutic abortion. However, CVS cannot detect more subtle chromosomal abnormalities; therefore, amniocentesis sometimes is also required. A second limitation is that CVS currently is available only in a small number of major teaching hospitals. The primary risk of CVS is miscarriage, which at present occurs in about 0.2 percent of the cases studied (ACOG, 1990; D'Alton & DeCherney, 1993).

Fetoscopy   *Fetoscopy* involves inserting a fetoscope—a thin, telescopelike instrument with a fiber-optic lens—through the mother's abdomen into the uterus to observe the amniotic fluid, placenta, and fetus. Usually performed fifteen to eighteen weeks after conception, fetoscopy is used to confirm results from a prior prenatal test or to assess the severity of a disability already identified, such as a cleft lip or a missing limb seen on ultrasound. It can also help determine the prospects for performing fetal surgery in utero (Blatt, 1988).

Maternal Serum Alpha-fetoprotein   *Maternal serum alpha-fetoprotein (MSAFP)* is a test that measures the amount of alpha-fetoprotein (AFP) in the mother's blood and is performed between weeks fifteen and eighteen of pregnancy. Alpha-fetoprotein is produced by the fetus and passes from the amniotic fluid through the placenta into the mother's bloodstream. Abnormally high levels of AFP are associated with various problems. The test will identify 90 percent of fetuses with anencephaly (lacking a brain), 75 percent of fetuses with spina bifida (having an opening in the back that exposes the spinal cord), and about 25 percent of fetuses with

TABLE 3.5	Conditions That Prenatal Diagnosis Can Detect	
Procedure	**Timing**	**Conditions Detected**
Ultrasound	Throughout pregnancy	Pregnancy; multiple pregnancies; fetal growth and abnormalities such as limb defects; tubal (ectopic) pregnancy; multiple pregnancies; atypical fetal position
Amniocentesis	14–18 weeks	Chromosomal disorders such as Down syndrome; neurological disorders; gender of the baby
Chorionic villus sampling (CVS)	9–13 weeks	Tests for most of the same genetic disorders as amniocentesis, but is less sensitive to more subtle abnormalities
Fetoscopy	15–18 weeks	Used to confirm results from a prior prenatal test or to assess the severity of a disability already identified
Maternal serum alpha-fetoprotein (MSAFP)	15–18 weeks	Various problems, including neural tube defects and Down syndrome; positive first test is followed by additional testing, such as ultrasound and amniocentesis
Percutaneous umbilical blood sampling (PUBS)	18–36 weeks	Down syndrome, neural tube defects, Tay-Sachs disease, cystic fibrosis, sickle-cell disease; gender of the fetus; fetal infections such as rubella, toxoplasmosis, or AIDS

Sources: ACOG (1990); Blatt (1988); D'Alton & DeCherney (1993); Feinbloom & Forman (1987).

WORKING WITH

Gail Gardner, Genetic Counselor

Advising Parents about Potential Problems

Gail Gardner has worked as a genetic counselor at a university medical center for the last three years. Gail developed an interest in genetics as an undergraduate biology major and went on for a master's degree in the field. The interview took place in her office next to the genetics laboratories.

Rob: *What does a genetic counselor do?*

Gail: My basic work involves meeting families and helping them understand what their risks are, or might be in the future, for having children with genetic problems. Some families don't yet have children and aren't expecting a child, but want to know from their family medical history, and maybe occupational exposure history, what risks they face if they have children. I also see couples who are currently expecting and want to know their risk for having a child with a genetic problem. Then there are families with either a child or an adult member with a known genetic condition. I also counsel individuals about chances for developing problems themselves in the future.

Rob: *What do you do when you meet with a family?*

Gail: Based on their family medical history and life circumstances, I help them to assess their risks of having children with genetically related problems. I explain the condition and recommend tests where appropriate. I try to help the family or individual reach the best decision for them given their particular religious, cultural, and emo-tional situation. I also try to help them cope with the decision they do make, and remain available to help them live with those decisions.

Rob: *This sounds like a potentially sensitive discussion.*

Gail: Oh, it is. I don't just deal with gathering information and passing it along; the issues are very personal and have a lot of psychological implications for each parent and for their relationship with each other. For example, if one parent is found to be a carrier, meaning the parent passes a condition to a child but doesn't actually cause it, there may be a lot of guilt. A lot of blaming could occur.

Rob: *Do you ever need to refer families to a psychologist or psychiatrist for additional professional help?*

Gail: Sometimes I do. And if it looks as if there's a really difficult moral dilemma, I might refer to clergy, if that's appropriate.

Rob: *Can you give an example of how you work with a particular genetic disorder?*

Gail: Tay-Sachs disease is a good example. Jewish people of Ashkenazi or Western European background have a one in thirty chance of carrying a gene for Tay-Sachs disease compared to only one in three hundred in the general population. It's inherited in a recessive fashion—both parents must carry the gene for their children to get it. A simple blood test will identify whether parents are carriers or not.

Rob: *What can a couple do if both carry the Tay-Sachs gene?*

Gail: Well, one option is to go ahead and take their chances and have their own children. They have a 25 percent, or one in four, chance of having a child who inherits double recessive genes for the disease. Two out of four times a child will inherit only one recessive gene and become a carrier, and one out of four times no Tay-Sachs gene will be inherited.

Rob: *What are the other options?*

Gail: Other options include artificial insemination, in vitro fertilization, and, of course, adoption. Preimplantation genetic testing is also a possibility now, but is very expensive. This involves taking ova and sperm selected from the mother and father and fertilizing and growing them in the laboratory. We then analyze the DNA of the pre-embryos, and if successful, we select those that don't have the Tay-Sachs trait and implant them in the mother, where one of them will hopefully survive to term.

What Do You Think?

1. What are the most challenging aspects of the job for a genetic counselor? Why?

2. Given what you've learned about dominant/recessive traits in the chapter, what kinds of questions about family history do you think a genetic counselor would ask?

3. What other questions might you ask Gail about her work?

Down syndrome in women under age thirty-five. Because only a small percentage of women who test positive actually have problems, a positive first test is followed by additional testing that may include ultrasound and amniocentesis (ACOG, 1990).

Percutaneous Umbilical Blood Sampling *Percutaneous umbilical blood sampling (PUBS)* is an experimental method of sampling fetal blood by guiding a needle through the mother's abdomen and uterus into the umbilical vein. PUBS can be performed between weeks eighteen and thirty-six of pregnancy. It is used to help identify a number of conditions associated with genetic abnormalities that were discussed earlier in this chapter. These include Down syndrome, neural tube defects, Tay-Sachs disease, cystic fibrosis, and sickle-cell disease. PUBS is also used to determine the gender of the fetus and to test for the presence of certain antibodies to fetal infections such as rubella, toxoplasmosis, and HIV. This method provides a direct connection to the fetus, so it can also be used for intrauterine blood transfusions, to administer medications, and, perhaps in the future, to replace missing enzymes or proteins (Blatt, 1988; D'Alton & DeCherney, 1993).

Implications of Genetic and Prenatal Testing

Fortunately, approximately 95 percent of fetuses examined through prenatal diagnosis are normal. If a problem is detected and a couple decides to continue an abnormal pregnancy to term, medical treatments sometimes can alleviate or even eliminate certain genetic disorders. As we already discussed, the effects of PKU can be avoided by careful planning of an infant's diet to avoid the particular amino acids that PKU babies cannot utilize. Rh disease, which produces an incompatibility between the baby's and mother's blood, can be treated even after it affects a pregnancy through blood transfusions to the fetus or newborn infant.

More often than not, however, genetic disorders cannot be cured or controlled effectively. Couples at genetic risk need to face this fact and decide what they want to do about it. Genetic counselors cannot make these choices for couples. They can only lay out the facts and alternatives and offer support for whatever choices couples make in the end.

As we have seen, genetic inheritance has a profound impact on an individual's development. The environmental context in which a person grows up also plays an important role. In the next section, we examine how genetics and environment interact to influence the course of developmental change.

WHAT DO YOU THINK?   Do modern medical techniques unwittingly maintain several hereditary disorders by keeping alive many abnormal children who in the past might have died? If so, does this pose an ethical problem?

Relative Influence of Heredity and Environment

The importance of hereditary (genetic) influences on individual differences in development has gained wide acceptance. Interestingly, the very same data from behavior-genetic research that support the significance of heredity also provide the best available evidence for the importance of environmental influence. This is because most complex behaviors of interest to psychologists and society, such as temperament, intelligence, and personality, are influenced at least as heavily by environmental factors as by genetic ones (Plomin, 1989).

Key Concepts of Behavior Genetics

Untangling the effects of heredity, or nature, from those of environment, or nurture, has become the special focus of behavior genetics. **Behavior genetics** is the scientific study of how genetic inheritance (*genotype*) and environmental experience *jointly* influence physical and behavioral development (*phenotype*). In fact, every characteristic of an organism is the result of the unique interaction between the organism's genetic inheritance and the sequence of environments through which it has passed during its development. For some traits, the variations in envi-

• • •

behavior genetics The scientific study of the relationship between genotype and phenotype, especially with regard to intelligence, personality, and mental health.

How much of the physical resemblance between this family and the interests that they share are due to heredity and how much due to environment?

ronment have minimal effect. Thus, once the genotype is known, the eventual form or phenotype of the organism is pretty much specified. For other traits, knowing the genetic makeup may be a poor predictor of the eventual phenotype. Only by specifying both the genotype and the environmental sequence can the character, or phenotype, of the organism be predicted. In the section that follows, we first discuss four key concepts of behavioral genetics: range of reaction, canalization, the gene-environment relationship, and measures of hereditary influence.

Range of Reaction   **Range of reaction** refers to the range of possible phenotypes that an individual with a particular genotype might exhibit in response to the specific sequence of environmental influences he or she experiences (Turkheimer & Gottsman, 1991). For example, if three infants start life with different genetic inheritances (genotypes) for intelligence—one low, one middle, and one high—the different levels of intelligence they actually develop (phenotypes), as measured by IQ tests, will depend on how well each child's intellectual development is nurtured and supported by his or her experiences from conception onward, including the conditions created by the child's family, school, and community. Thus, in an enriched environment, the child with low genetic endowment may achieve an IQ that is actually equal to (or even higher than) that of the child with a middle-range endowment who grows up in a restricted or below-average environment. Nevertheless, the first child cannot be expected to achieve an IQ score equal to that of children with high genetic endowment, because this is beyond the upper limit of that child's range of reaction: the highest level of intellectual functioning possible for that child. Figure 3.12 illustrates range of reaction for intelligence. Theorists such as Robert Sternberg (1988) and Howard Gardner (1993a) believe that intelligence is best understood as consisting of several different factors or dimensions, and thus range of reaction may differ according to which aspect of intelligence is being measured. We look more closely at these theories when we examine cognitive development in middle childhood in Chapter 12.

Canalization   **Canalization** refers to the tendency of genes to narrowly direct or restrict the development of certain phenotypic characteristics to a single or relatively limited number of outcomes in spite of environmental pressures toward other

• • •

range of reaction The range of possible phenotypes that an individual with a particular genotype might exhibit in response to the particular sequence of environmental influences he or she experiences.

canalization The tendency of many developmental processes to unfold in highly predictable ways under a wide range of conditions.

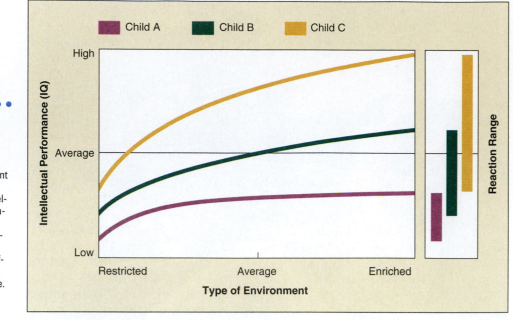

● ● ● ● ● ● ● ● ● ● ● ● ● ● ● ● ●

FIGURE 3.12

The Concept of Range of Reaction for Intellectual Performance

Range of reaction refers to the range of possible phenotypes as a result of different environments interacting with a specific genotype. As this figure shows, while intellectual performance will be retarded or facilitated for all children depending on whether the environment is restricted, average, or enriched, the range of potential intellectual performance in reaction to different environments will be limited by the child's genetic inheritance for intelligence. *Source: Gottesman (1963); Turkheimer & Gottesman (1991).*

● ● ●

gene-environment relationship
May be passive, active, or evocative, depending on whether an infant or a child passively accepts, stimulates (evokes), or actively seeks and creates situations and experiences that support or increase genetically influenced behavioral traits such as shyness or intelligence.

outcomes. The more deeply canalized a genetic predisposition is, the more resistant it will be to environmental influence (Waddington, 1966). For example, the stages of a normal infant's perceptual-motor development (sucking, turning over, sitting up, crawling, and walking) are strongly canalized and will predictably occur for all infants within a wide range of family and cultural childrearing environments. Social and cognitive development are also canalized, though perhaps to a lesser extent. For example, Jerome Kagan (1984) studied Guatemalan children who had experienced extreme malnutrition as infants, and found that they showed normal social and cognitive development during childhood.

More recently, however, Esther Thelan (1995) has challenged this view. She has suggested that even the stepping reflex performed by newborns, which has always been presumed to be genetically preprogrammed (highly canalized), may in fact be the product of a mutual and active process of gene-environment interaction. The *stepping reflex* consists of a well-coordinated, alternating-step-like pattern of movements when the infant is held upright with her feet resting on a supporting surface. However, it mysteriously disappears within a few months, reappearing later when the child begins to stand and walk. Thelan suggests that the disappearance is due not to some canalized genetic program but to the rapid gain in body fat (but not muscle or strength) that babies of this age experience. Although the stepping reflex is still there, this weight gain temporarily makes the infant's chubby legs too heavy to lift from an upright, stepping position. Infants are able to perform the stepping reflex when submerged in waist-deep warm water (which makes their legs lighter). They can also lift their chubby legs when lying down, a movement that involves exactly the same actions the stepping reflex does but is made easier by gravity as the leg is raised from this position. Clearly, sorting out the sources of developmental change is not a simple task!

Many other important developmental characteristics, such as personality, temperament, and intellectual functioning, appear to be minimally canalized and are strongly influenced by environmental factors that include family, school, and culture.

The Gene-Environment Relationship   The **gene-environment relationship** refers to the patterns of interaction between a newborn infant and his caregiving environment and the extent to which that pattern supports the expression and development of the child's inborn traits. Parents directly influence their children's traits, such as athletic ability or shyness, through the genes their children inherit. They may also exert this influence indirectly by displaying their own genetically influenced behavioral traits (athletic ability or shyness) that support the development of similar traits in their children.

A *passive gene-environment relationship* exists if support for the development of certain traits comes mainly from others (parents and other family members), with the infant or child having little or no influence over this development. For example, parents who are themselves genotypically inclined to be good athletes or to be shy will probably expose their children to environments that support athletic activities or shy behavior in addition to having already given them a similar genetic endowment for these traits at birth.

An *evocative gene-environment relationship* exists when a child's early expression of her genetic endowment (such as a display of athletic ability or shyness) evokes support for these behaviors from others.

Finally, as children grow older and broaden their experiences to include environments outside the family, a third relationship often occurs. An *active gene-environment relationship* exists when a child with a particular genetic endowment actively seeks out and creates environmental situations, or *niches,* that support and increase his tendencies. A child who is athletic may sign up for Little League and choose friends who like sports, whereas a child who is shy may join the computer club and choose friends who are also shy. This tendency for children to choose environments that support their traits has been humorously referred to as *niche picking* (Scarr & McCartney, 1983).

Measures of Hereditary Influence   Two statistical measures are used to describe the influence of heredity on various complex human characteristics or traits. **Heritability estimates** measure the *degree* of genetic influence for traits that vary in degree rather than in an all-or-none way. Examples of such traits include height, athletic ability, intelligence, and shyness. To calculate the heritability of a particular trait, such as intelligence, the average correlation between the IQ scores for pairs of *fraternal twins* (50 percent shared genes) is subtracted from the average correlation for IQ scores for *identical twins* (100 percent shared genes) and then doubled.

Heritability scores range from 0.00 (no genetic influence) to 1.00 (complete genetic determination). For example, the heritability estimate for height is .90, meaning 90 percent of the variation in height is accounted for by genetic variation, while .10, or 10 percent, is due to diet and other environmental factors. Heritability estimates of intelligence are around .50, meaning about half of the variation we observe in children's intelligence appears to be due to differences in their genes (Horgan, 1993; Plomin, 1989).

Concordance rates are used to quantify the influence of heredity on traits that are thought to occur in an all-or-none way. These include certain physical disorders, such as cystic fibrosis, and mental disorders, such as schizophrenia and major depressive disorders. The concordance rate is stated as the percentage of instances in which both members of a pair of genetically similar individuals (such as identical twins) display a given trait, such as cystic fibrosis or schizophrenia.

Adoption and Twin Studies

Adoption Studies   **Adoption studies** compare the degree of physical or behavioral similarity between adoptive children and members of their adoptive families (with whom they have little in common genetically) with the degree of physical or behavioral similarity between these same children and members of their biological families (with whom they share half of their genes). If adoptive children share similar environments but not genes with their adoptive family members, differences in trait similarity with their adoptive versus biological relatives should tell something

• • •

heritability estimate The degree to which variation among an individual's phenotypic behaviors can be attributed to genetic influences.

concordance rate The percentage of instances in which both members of a genetically similar pair of individuals (e.g., identical twins) display a particular all-or-none trait such as cystic fibrosis, Huntington's disease, or schizophrenia.

adoption study A research method for studying the relative contributions of heredity and environment in which genetically related children reared apart are compared with genetically unrelated children reared together.

about the influence of their genetic differences. For example, if the IQ scores of adopted children correlated more highly with the IQ scores of their biological families versus their adoptive families, we might conclude that heredity made a strong contribution to intelligence. However, if the IQ scores of these adoptive children were significantly higher (or lower) than those of their biological parents, this might also indicate the influence of family circumstances and other environmental factors.

One major limitation of family comparisons is that because many different *mini* environments exist within the same family, two children raised in the same family may have very different developmental experiences based on the unique set of expectations and interactions that develop.

Twins and Twin Studies   When the uterus contains more than one fetus, a *multiple pregnancy* exists, and if all goes well, a *multiple birth* results. The most common type of multiple birth is *fraternal* or *dizygotic twins*, which result when two ova (eggs) are simultaneously released from the mother's ovaries and each is fertilized by a different sperm cell to form two separate zygotes. With fraternal twins, each embryo usually has its own placenta and amniotic sac. Because each develops from a zygote formed by a different egg and sperm, the twins are no more genetically alike than any brother or sister.

Identical or *monozygotic twins* are formed when a single zygote divides and develops into two separate embryos, each with the identical set of genetic characteristics. They share a placenta, but each usually has its own amniotic sac. Twins occur naturally about once in every ninety births and triplets once in every nine thousand births. Fraternal twins occur in approximately eight out of every one thousand white births, twelve to sixteen out of one thousand African American births, and four out of every one thousand Asian births. The likelihood of fraternal twins increases with the use of fertility drugs, with additional births, with increasing maternal age until thirty-five, and in women who are normal to large in physical size. The likelihood of fraternal twins decreases with poor maternal nutrition and for women who are physically small. The frequency of identical twins is approximately four out of every one thousand births and appears to be unaffected by such factors (ACOG, 1990; Little & Thompson, 1988).

Twin studies compare pairs of *identical twins* raised in the same family with pairs of *fraternal twins* (50 percent shared genes) raised in the same family. Since identical twins have the exact same genetic makeup, greater similarity between identical twins than between fraternal twins on a trait such as intelligence or shyness probably would reflect the influence of heredity.

Twin Adoption Studies   Studies of identical twins reared apart since birth provide the most reliable method for understanding the gene-environment relationship in humans. Identical twins inherit exactly the same genes. Therefore, if we could compare pairs of identical twins raised in truly different family environments, we would be able to separate out the relative contributions of heredity and environment. The catch is to find twins who are growing up in adoptive families. An additional problem is that adoptive families are most frequently chosen with the goal of offering twins similar socioeconomic, cultural, and religious conditions and experiences, raising the question of how different their adoptive family environments really are. Despite these limitations, studies of twins reared apart and of adopted children have shed a great deal of light on the relative contributions of heredity and environment to human development (Horgan, 1993).

Linkage and Association Studies   Linkage and association studies allow researchers to identify *polymorphisms*—certain segments of human DNA that are inherited together in a predictable pat-

twin study A research method for studying the relative contributions of heredity and environment in which the degree of similarity between genetically identical twins (developed from a single egg) is compared with the similarity between fraternal twins (developed from two eggs).

The shared inheritance of genetically identical twins such as these provides researchers with an opportunity to study the relative contributions of heredity and environment to human development.

tern—as genetic markers for the genes near which they are located. *Linkage studies* seek to discover polymorphisms that are coinherited, or "linked," with a particular trait in families unusually prone to that trait. This was the case in the discovery of genetic markers for Huntington disease and fragile X syndrome, which were described earlier in this chapter. *Association studies* compare the relative frequency of polymorphisms in two populations, one with the trait and one without it (Horgan, 1993).

Intelligence   General intelligence—as measured by standardized IQ tests, for example—shows both hereditary and environmental components. While considerable controversy revolves around how much genetic inheritance contributes to intelligence, most researchers agree that genotype makes some contribution. Close relatives tend to have more similar IQ scores than distant relatives do, and relatives in general have more similar scores if they live together than if they live apart. Studies generally have found that about 50 percent of the difference among individuals *within* a given group is genetic. Longitudinal studies have found that genetic influence on IQ increases substantially during childhood and that these differences continue into adulthood (Plomin et al., 1988).

Separated at birth, the Mallifert twins meet accidentally.

Shared genes or shared experiences? Studies of genetically identical twins who are reared in different environments from birth attempt to evaluate the degree to which shared behavioral characteristics are determined by shared genes versus shared experiences.

There is also some evidence based on twin and adoption studies that genetic inheritance may substantially influence verbal and spatial abilities and specific areas of academic achievement such as English usage, mathematics, social studies, and natural sciences. The Colorado Adoption Study longitudinally studied the cognitive development of more than two hundred adopted children and their birth and adoptive parents and that of a control group of children raised by their biological parents from early childhood through adolescence. The verbal and spatial abilities of the adopted children in the Colorado study came to resemble those of their birth parents as much as the abilities of children who were raised by their birth parents. In contrast, adopted children's skills were not similar to those of their adoptive parents, suggesting that most of the family resemblance in these cognitive skills was caused by genetic rather than environmental factors (Plomin & DeFries, 1998).

Critics of twin studies caution that in some studies, identical twins supposedly raised apart were sometimes in fact raised by members of their families or by unrelated families in the same neighborhood and that some have had extensive contact with each other while growing up. The media coverage and publicity associated with such studies motivate participants to downplay previous contacts and exaggerate their similarities (Hagerman, 1996; Horgan, 1993).

Our understanding of how genes and environment influence intelligence has major social policy implications as well. The accompanying Perspectives box discusses this issue.

Animal Studies

Animal studies use selective breeding for certain traits, such as endurance, speed, intelligence, and aggressiveness, *and* control of environmental conditions to better understand the relative contributions of heredity and environment. Because genetic partners can be selected based on their observable traits and environmental influences can be carefully controlled, the effects of genes can be systematically studied. The breeding of racehorses is a very successful example of this approach.

PERSPECTIVES

The Race and Intelligence Controversy: Social Policy Implications

The practical importance of understanding how genes and environment influence development is vividly demonstrated by recent claims that group differences between blacks and whites in average IQ test scores are due to genetic rather than environmental differences (Hernstein & Murray, 1994; Jensen, 1969a, 1969b). Most twin adoption studies report average heritability scores of about .50 for *within-group differences* in IQ among pairs of individuals who have a *known degree* of genetic similarity but have been raised in unequal environments. This, however, tells us nothing about average IQ differences *between groups*. This is because even though a trait such as IQ may be equally heritable for pairs of individuals *within* two different groups (say, blacks and whites), the two groups are very likely to differ in their average IQ scores if, on the average, their members grow up in environments that provide unequal support and opportunities.

Unfortunately, this appears to be the case for whites and blacks in our society. Large differences in pre- and postnatal health care, income, education, and general living conditions continue to exist despite a variety of efforts to reduce them (Holmes, 1995). Until we have convincing evidence that these between-group differences in environment have been eliminated, such environmental inequalities will remain the most likely explanation for differences in average group IQ scores. Additional support for this explanation comes from studies showing that when black and white children are raised in environments that are equally supportive of their intellectual development, average between-group differences disappear (Gordon, 1995; Lane, 1994).

On what basis, then, do people such as Hernstein and Murray conclude that group differences in intelligence are genetically based? Part of the answer appears to lie in confusion about race. While a great deal of evidence exists that race serves as a *social and cultural* category that influences attitudes, perceptions, and behaviors, existing scientific evidence lends little support for a *genetics*-based concept of race. Population geneticists working with the Human Genome Diversity Project, for example, recently completed a worldwide mapping of human genetic characteristics. They found that with very minor variations, all humans share a single genetic makeup and therefore belong to a single genetic or racial group.

What appear to be racial differences based on readily observable physical differences are mainly allelic adaptations to climate that evolved as people migrated from their common African origin to their current locations around the world. For example, although Australian aborigines and Africans share such superficial traits as skin color and body shape, Australians are in fact genetically most different from Africans and genetically most similar to Southeast Asians, their geographic neighbors (Garver & Garver, 1994; Montagu, 1975).

Another reason group genetic differences are unlikely to underlie group differences in IQ has to do with the concept of intelligence itself. Ideas of what intelligence is and how it is demonstrated vary so widely across different cultures and have changed so much over time that it is highly unlikely that the genes that have evolved for "intelligence" are related to any culturally specific definition of that trait, such as IQ. Since the very trait we are predicting is influenced by differing and changing cultural assumptions and behaviors, it is likely that the genetic contribution to intelligence will turn out to be quite general and flexible rather than specific to a particular cultural or ethnic group. In fact, human evolution has been *biosocial* rather than strictly biogenetic. This means our social and cultural evolution, including language, problem solving, and sophisticated use of tools, occurred simultaneously with our genetic evolution, raising the question of whether genetic and cultural contributions to intelligence can ever be separated (Kamin, 1995; Montagu, 1975).

Some critics have suggested that supporters of a racial-genetic view of group differences in IQ may be politically motivated. They point out that the conclusion that racial differences in intelligence are genetic is based on insufficient evidence and misleading applications of the principles of behavior genetics. They assert that proponents of this view use it to attack social programs designed to reduce economic and social inequality, claiming that group differences in IQ are inherited and therefore unchangeable (Gordon, 1995; Kamin, 1995; Lane, 1994; Lerner, 1992).

What Do You Think?

While little evidence currently exists to support the idea of a genetic basis for a racial-genetic view of group difference in IQ, what should be done if such differences were actually found? What values regarding human diversity might guide your recommendations?

Newly developed *targeted gene replacement* techniques have been used to study the genome, or genetic makeup, of mice. In this method, a healthy gene on a chromosome of a mouse embryo is replaced with a gene that has been mutated with a DNA-damaging chemical that is chemically marked so that its effects on the embryo's development can be studied. Next, mice that now carry the targeted mutation are bred with normal mice, producing offspring that are heterozygous, meaning they have one mutated copy and one normal copy of the gene. Finally, when heterozygous mice are mated, 25 percent of the offspring will display abnormalities that will reveal the normal functions of the target gene in all of their tissues (Cepecchi, 1994).

If you are wondering what mice and people have in common, you may be surprised to learn that an estimated 99 percent or more of the genes in mice and humans are the same and serve similar purposes. As a result, behavioral genetic studies of mice may eventually help us to better understand the more than five thousand human genetic defects. However, a note of caution is in order. Although this approach has already helped us to better understand the inheritance of the gene for cystic fibrosis, most genetic disorders are not tied to a single gene. Rather, they are the result of the complex series of interactions of many genes and many environmental factors that emerge from conception onward (Cepecchi, 1994).

Since neither selective breeding, environmental manipulation, nor target gene replacement are likely to be ethically acceptable choices for research with human beings, methods based on "naturally occurring" opportunities, such as those described above, must be relied on to sort out the relative contributions of heredity and environment to human development.

Cautions and Conclusions About the Influence of Heredity and Environment

Though substantial evidence exists that genetic inheritance plays at least a moderate role in differences in physical, intellectual, and personality traits, it is likely that such differences are influenced by *both* heredity and environmental experience. Our understanding of the mechanisms of behavioral genetics has increased substantially, but the degree and manner in which genes and environment influence development still remain unclear.

Even for children who grow up in the same family, environmental influences tend to operate on an individual-by-individual rather than a family-by-family basis. Thus, they tend to make children in the same family different from one another rather than making the same family different from other families. Siblings in the same family appear to experience considerably different environments in terms of parental treatment and their interactions with one another and their peers (Plomin, 1989). The pattern by which genes and environment interact to influence the long-term development of any individual can be understood only on a case-by-case basis that reflects that person's particular developmental contexts and experiences. The contribution of heredity tends to remain most stable where there is a passive relationship between heredity and environment and most subject to change when an active relationship between heredity and environment exists. Thus, an infant who is irritable at birth will be more likely to continue to exhibit that trait if her family and other experiences support it and less likely to do so if they do not. Even with our greatly increased knowledge of the biochemistry of genetics, successful prediction of long-term intellectual and personality characteristics may never be possible given that we can neither predict nor control the continuing changes they will undergo over the individual's course of development.

Currently, however, there is a growing trend toward minimizing environmental contributions in favor of a *genetic determinism:* a belief that most, if not all, human characteristics, from intellectual functioning to gender roles and career choice, are determined primarily by genes. This tendency may in part be a reaction to *environmental determinism,* an equally simplistic view that sees environmental experience as the central or sole cause of developmental change and dismisses the possibility that genes may also make a significant contribution. It may also reflect the explosive growth in biotechnology and the overly optimistic view it appears to have generated.

Neither biogenetic nor environmental determinism can ever provide an adequate understanding of human development. Rather, human development is always the product of multiple levels of biogenetic and environmental influences and human agency—the self-determining choices that each individual makes.

WHAT DO YOU THINK ?   Based on what you have just read, how do you view the relationship between genes and environment? To what degree do you believe that most or all of human development will someday be explainable in terms of genetics? Where, in your judgment, does human agency or free will fit in?

Genetics and Developmental Psychology

Despite its limitations, knowledge of human genetics contributes to human welfare in two ways. First, it clarifies the origins of many behaviors. According to conventional wisdom, behaviors are either "learned" or "inborn"; human genetics suggests instead that many behaviors are actually both. Second, knowledge of genetics can suggest realistic limits as to how much to expect from many ordinary life experiences. How much can education really make people "more intelligent?" How much can parents expect a child with an active temperament to learn to be quieter? After learning the complex answers genetics usually gives to questions such as these, professionals can—and should—shift attention to individuals: How can we know whether *this* child will develop normally or whether *that* child will experience a chronic disorder? For these more personal questions, we need more knowledge of individual development, such as that genetic counseling offers. Such an orientation is also provided by other branches of developmental psychology, which we describe in the following chapters.

Summary of Major Ideas

Mechanisms of Genetic Transmission

1. Genetic information is contained in a complex molecule called *deoxyribonucleic acid (DNA).*

2. Most body cells produce tissue by simple division of their genes, chromosomes, and other cellular parts by means of a process called *mitosis.*

3. Reproductive cells, or gametes, divide by a process called *meiosis* and recombine into a zygote at conception.

4. The process of meiosis gives each gamete one-half of its normal number of chromosomes; conception brings the number of chromosomes up to normal again and gives the new zygote equal numbers of chromosomes from each parent.

Individual Genetic Expression

5. A person's phenotype is the pattern of traits the person actually shows during his or her life.

6. A person's genotype is the set of inherited genetic traits; it depends on the pattern of chromosomes and genes inherited at conception.

7. Although most genes exist in duplicate, some—called *dominant genes*—may actually influence the phenotype if only one member of the pair occurs.

8. Recessive genes do not influence the phenotype unless both members of the pair occur.

9. Many genetic traits are transmitted by the combined actions of several genes.

10. Gender is determined by one particular pair of chromosomes, called the *X* and *Y* chromosomes, and a testis-determining factor (TDF) located on a small section of the Y chromosome. In genetic imprinting, identical sections of the same chromosome yield different phenotypic outcomes depending on whether the chromosome came from the father or the mother.

Genetic Abnormalities

11. Some genetic abnormalities occur when an individual inherits too many or too few chromosomes.

12. The most common abnormalities of this type are Down syndrome, Klinefelter syndrome, and Turner syndrome.

13. Other genetic abnormalities occur because particular genes are defective or abnormal even though their chromosomes are normal. Examples are Huntington disease, cystic fibrosis, sickle-cell disease, Tay-Sachs disease, and phenylketonuria (PKU).

Genetic Counseling and Prenatal Diagnosis

14. Experts on genetics can provide parents with information about how genetics influences the development of children and about the risks of transmitting genetic abnormalities from one generation to the next.

15. Several methods now exist for diagnosing genetic problems before a baby is born, including amniocentesis, CVS, ultrasound, and various blood tests.

16. Given the permanence and importance of genetic problems when they occur, genetic counselors should help couples reach informed decisions about pregnancy that take personal circumstances as well as scientific information into account.

17. Cultural differences in beliefs and expectations significantly affect the counseling situation.

Relative Influence of Heredity and Environment

18. According to behavioral geneticists, every characteristic of an organism is the result of the unique interaction between the genetic inheritance of that organism and the sequence of environments through which it has passed during its development.

19. Behavioral geneticists use the concepts of range of reaction, canalization, heritability, and concordance to describe the strength and directness of genetic predisposition.

20. The gene-environment relationship can be passive, active, or evocative.

21. Studies of identical twins and of adopted children suggest that heredity and environment operate jointly to influence developmental change.

22. Linkage and association studies use repeated DNA segments called *polymorphisms* as genetic markers to locate abnormal genes.

23. Certain personality traits, such as shyness, may be inherited to a certain extent, but they are also substantially influenced by environmental experiences.

24. When environmental factors are significant, they operate on an individual rather than a family basis.

25. The controversy over the reasons for between-group differences in IQ demonstrates the practical social policy implications of the concepts of behavioral genetics.

Key Terms

adoption study (85)
allele (67)
amniocentesis (79)
behavior genetics (82)
canalization (83)
chorionic villus sampling (CVS) (79)
chromosome (63)
concordance rate (85)
DNA (deoxyribonucleic acid) (63)
dominant gene (67)
gamete (63)
gene (63)
gene-environment relationship (84)
genetic imprinting (70)
genotype (66)

hemophilia (70)
heritability estimate (85)
heterozygous (67)
homozygous (67)
meiosis (66)
mitosis (66)
multifactorial disorder (75)
ovum (63)
phenotype (66)
range of reaction (83)
recessive gene (67)
sex-linked recessive traits (70)
sickle-cell disease (73)
sperm (63)
twin study (86)
ultrasound (78)
zygote (66)

Prenatal Development and Birth

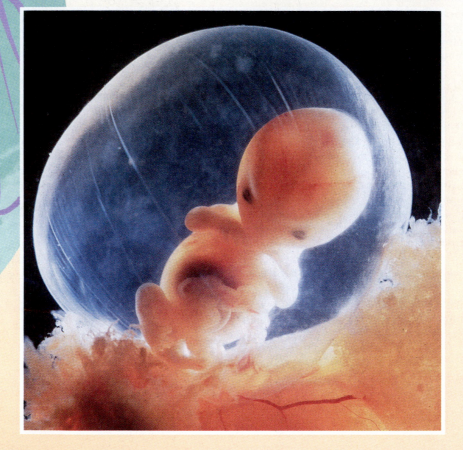

Focusing Questions

- What must happen for normal conception to occur? What alternatives are currently available for couples who have problems conceiving a child?

- What happens to the developing embryo during the three stages of prenatal development that occur between conception and birth?

- What risks do a mother and baby normally face during pregnancy, and how can they best be minimized?

- What methods are currently available to help parents prepare for the birth process?

- What happens during the three stages of the birth process? What are the possible difficulties, and how are they handled?

From the moment of conception, a child becomes a biological entity. Early during its nine months inside the womb, a fetus acquires all the essential human physical features and some rudimentary human behaviors. It is influenced by changes in its environment, by its own rapid physical growth, and by the well-being of its mother and the stresses and supports that affect her. Together these internal and external influences create a truly unique person.

How do microscopic cells become people? In this chapter, we describe the events and processes that occur from conception through birth and how they may affect later development. We also look at certain risks and problems of prenatal development and of birth and their long-term impact on the child.

Stages of Prenatal Development

Prenatal development begins with conception and continues through discrete periods, or stages. The first is the **germinal stage,** or *period of the ovum,* which occurs during the first two weeks of pregnancy; the **embryonic stage** lasts from the third week to the eighth week; and the **fetal stage** lasts from the eighth week until birth.

Conception

Let us look first at the microscopic actors of prenatal development, the gametes we described in Chapter 3. One gamete is the *ovum,* or *egg cell.* The egg cells develop in two small, almond-shaped organs, the ovaries, which normally release one egg cell during each menstrual cycle. The egg travels down one of the fallopian tubes toward the uterus, where the baby will develop. The opening of the uterus, the cervix, connects to the woman's vagina, which receives the male's penis during intercourse and, upon ejaculation, the male's reproductive cells.

Egg cells start to develop well before a girl begins having menstrual cycles or is otherwise ready for intercourse. In fact, at birth a girl's ovaries contain several hundred thousand ova, which are already partially developed. Many of these ova degenerate or die during the dozen or so years before the girl begins menstruating, and many more fail to mature fully after that. Thus, a woman ends up with approximately four hundred ova, a fixed supply that must last her entire reproductive life (Silber, 1991). In this respect, she differs markedly from a man.

Male reproductive cells are called *spermatozoa,* or *sperm cells.* They develop in the testes, which are located in the bag of skin called the *scrotum* that is underneath and behind the penis. The sperm get a late start compared to ova; the testes do not begin producing sperm in quantity until puberty, or about age twelve to fourteen

germinal stage The stage in prenatal development that occurs during the first two weeks of pregnancy; characterized by rapid cell division. Also called the *period of the ovum.*

embryonic stage Stage in prenatal development that lasts from week 2 through week 8.

fetal stage The stage in prenatal development that lasts from the eighth week of pregnancy until birth.

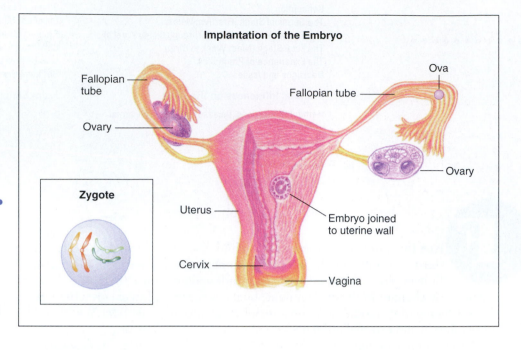

Implantation of the Embryo

Fallopian tube

Ova

Fallopian tube

Ovary

Ovary

Zygote

Uterus

Embryo joined to uterine wall

Cervix

Vagina

● ● ● ● ● ● ● ● ● ● ● ● ● ● ● ●

FIGURE 4.1

The Germinal Stage of Prenatal Development

The sperm and ovum join to form a single-celled *zygote,* which then divides and redivides and becomes a multicelled *blastocyst.* The blastocyst buries, or *implants,* itself in the uterine wall. The fully implanted blastocyst is now called an *embryo.*

years. They soon make up for lost time, however, by producing millions of sperm, and production continues relatively undiminished well into a man's old age. Each sperm cell has a head and a long tail, rather like a tadpole, that helps it to swim through the female reproductive organ.

Conception normally occurs when one of the approximately 360 million sperm contained in the *semen,* which the man has ejaculated into the woman's vagina during intercourse, swims through the *cervix* (opening of the uterus) into the fallopian tube and successfully attaches itself to the surface of an ovum, or egg, released from one of the woman's ovaries (Wilcox et al., 1995). (See Figure 4.1.) As noted in the Perspectives box on page 103, some couples have difficulty conceiving through intercourse. In some cases, various technological alternatives exist to join sperm and egg. For a couple to conceive successfully, each of the following conditions must be met:

1. The ovaries must release one healthy egg cell.

2. The egg cell must migrate most of the way down the fallopian tube.

3. Millions of sperm cells must be deposited as far as possible up the vagina, preferably at or near the cervix.

4. At least some of the sperm must swim in the right direction: up through the uterus to the fallopian tubes.

5. At least some of these sperm must survive the journey; the woman's uterus is slightly acidic and therefore toxic to sperm.

6. A few sperm must reach the ovum.

7. One sperm must penetrate the ovum to form a zygote.

Timing is crucial in this process. The ovum normally lives only about twenty-four hours after it is released and the sperm only about forty-eight hours (Silber, 1991). These limits give a couple about three days, or seventy-two hours, each month when intercourse is likely to result in conception and pregnancy. The period lasts from about two days before the egg is released (the sperm can survive that long) until about one day afterward (when the egg dies). This fertile period usually occurs about halfway through a woman's menstrual cycle, but it may occur at some other time.

● ● ●

conception The moment at which the male's sperm cell penetrates the female's egg cell (ovum), forming a zygote.

Other, less direct factors also affect whether conception occurs. For example, some men produce much denser concentrations of sperm than others do, although even a relatively low concentration usually contains more than enough gametes to ensure conception if the sperm can reach the ovum. Also, the number of sperm is reduced considerably if intercourse already occurred recently—say, within the previous twenty-four hours. And conception becomes less likely if either partner is more than forty years old (Silber, 1991). Apparently age diminishes the man's concentration of sperm somewhat; more important, it may lead to an increased number of defective gametes in either the man or the woman. Stress also can reduce the chances of conception. Stress can interfere directly by discouraging lovemaking or indirectly by somehow preventing ovulation or implantation of the zygote.

Of course, all of these influences can amount to either obstacles or preventatives, depending on whether a woman wants to become pregnant. Either way, they can be frustrating because of the indirectness with which they operate. And either way, getting pregnant can prove as difficult for some couples as it is easy for others. A significant number of individuals have difficulty conceiving normally.

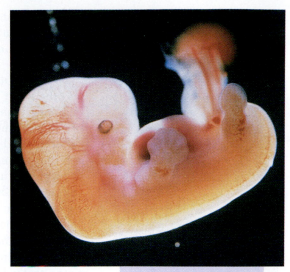

The environment and anatomy of an embryo change dramatically during the first two months of pregnancy. By the end of the third week, the embryo is surrounded by a thin sac of fluid, which cushions it from bumps and provides a more uniform temperature. The embryo shown here is at the end of the fifth week after conception. Note its leg buds and eyes.

The Germinal Stage (First Two Weeks)

Once a sperm and an ovum join successfully, the resulting zygote begins to divide and redivide. The original cells form a tiny sphere called a *blastocyst*, which looks something like a miniature mulberry. After about three days, the blastocyst contains about sixty cells, but these become smaller as the cells increase in number, so the blastocyst is still scarcely larger than the original zygote. While these divisions occur, the blastocyst floats down the remainder of the fallopian tube, helped in part by gentle squeezing motions similar to the digestive motions of the intestines.

The blastocyst, which is filled with fluid, rapidly undergoes a number of important changes. The cells along one of its sides thicken to form the embryonic disk, out of which the baby will eventually develop. The blastocyst also differentiates into three layers. The *ectoderm,* or upper layer, later develops into the epidermis, or outer layer of skin, nails, teeth, and hair, as well as the sensory organs and nervous system. The *endoderm* (lower layer) becomes the digestive system, liver, pancreas, salivary glands, and respiratory system. The *mesoderm,* or middle layer, develops somewhat later and becomes the dermis (inner layer of skin), muscles, skeleton, and circulatory and excretory systems. In a short time the *placenta, umbilical cord,* and *amniotic sac* (to be discussed shortly) also will form from blastocyst cells.

After a few more days—about one week after conception—*implantation* occurs. During **implantation,** the blastocyst buries itself like a seed in the wall of the uterus. The fully implanted blastocyst is now referred to as the **embryo.** Implantation takes about another week to complete, so it ends about the time the woman might expect another menstrual period. It also signifies the end of the germinal stage and the beginning of the next phase of prenatal growth, during which the developing child begins to grow differentiated cells. Figure 4.1 illustrates the changes that occur during the germinal stage of prenatal development.

The Embryonic Stage (Third Through Eighth Weeks)

Growth during the embryonic stage (and the fetal stage that follows) occurs in two patterns: a *cephalocaudal* (head-to-tail) pattern and a *proximodistal* (near-to-far,

• • •

implantation The attachment of the blastocyst to the wall of the uterus.

embryo The fully implanted blastocyst; refers specifically to the developing human from the second to eighth week after conception.

from the center of the body outward) pattern. Thus, the head, blood vessels, and heart—the most vital body parts and organs—begin to develop earlier than the arms, legs, hands, and feet. Figure 4.3 (upper portion) on page 106 illustrates these changes.

At *three weeks,* the head, tail, brain, and circulatory system begin to develop, and the heart has begun beating. At *four weeks,* the embryo is little more than an inch long. The beginnings of a spinal cord, arms, and legs are evident, a small digestive system and a nervous system have developed, and the brain has become more differentiated. The embryo's parts do not have the fully adult shapes, but nonetheless they are unmistakable (Harris, 1983). During *week five,* hands and lungs begin to form. During *week six,* the head grows larger, the brain becomes more fully developed, and hands, legs, and feet become more fully formed. During *weeks seven and eight,* muscles form and the cerebral cortex begins to develop.

While these developments are taking place, a placenta forms between the mother and the embryo. The **placenta** is an area on the uterine wall through which the mother supplies oxygen and nutrients to the embryo and the embryo returns waste products from her bloodstream. In the placenta, thousands of tiny blood vessels from the two circulatory systems intermingle. Although only minute quantities of blood can cross the separating membranes, nutrients pass easily from one bloodstream to the other. Some of them are pushed actively from one to the other as though by a pump, and others float freely through the vessel walls by a process called *osmosis.* Although many toxic chemicals and drugs in the mother's system do not spread easily by osmosis, others do. As we discuss later, seemingly harmless chemicals sometimes prove devastating to the child.

The **umbilical cord** connects the embryo to the placenta. It consists of three large blood vessels, one to provide nutrients and two to carry waste products into the mother's body. The cord enters the embryo at a place that becomes the baby's belly button, or navel, after the cord is cut following birth. The cord contains no nerves, so cutting it hurts neither the mother nor the child. For the same reason, mother and child can exchange no neural signals or messages through the cord before birth, even though they certainly communicate in other ways.

By the end of the eighth week, an amniotic sac has developed. The **amniotic sac** is a tough, spongy bag filled with salty fluid that completely surrounds the embryo and serves to protect it from sudden jolts and maintain a fairly stable temperature. The baby floats gently in this environment until birth, protected even if its mother goes jogging, sits down suddenly, or shovels heavy snow.

The Fetal Stage (Ninth Week to Birth)

At about *eight weeks* of gestation, the embryo develops its first bone cells, which marks the end of differentiation into the major structures. At this point the embryo acquires a new name, the **fetus,** and begins the long process of developing relatively small features, such as fingers and fingernails and eyelids and eyebrows. Their smallness belies their importance, however. For example, the eyes undergo their greatest growth during this stage of development. The fetus's newly developing eyelids fuse shut at about ten weeks and do not reopen until the eyes themselves are essentially complete, at sixteen to twenty weeks.

Not only the eyes but most other physical features become more adult looking during this period and more truly human in proportion (Harris, 1983). The head becomes smaller relative to the rest of the body (even though it remains large by adult standards), partly because the fetus's long bones, the ones supporting its limbs, begin growing significantly. Thus, its arms and legs look increasingly substantial.

By *twelve weeks,* the fetus is about three inches long and able to respond reflexively to touch. By *sixteen weeks,* it has grown to about 4½ inches in length. If its palm is touched, it exhibits a grasp reflex by closing its fist; if the sole of its foot is

---

• • •

placenta An organ that delivers oxygen and nutrients from the mother to the fetus and carries away the fetus's waste products, which the mother will excrete.

umbilical cord Three large blood vessels that connect the embryo to the placenta, one to provide nutrients and two to remove waste products.

amniotic sac A tough, spongy bag filled with salty fluid that surrounds the embryo, protects it from sudden jolts, and helps to maintain a fairly stable temperature.

fetus An embryo that has developed its first bone cells, after about eight weeks of gestation.

touched, its toes spread (Babinski reflex); and if its lips are touched, it will respond with a sucking reflex. In addition, the fetal heartbeat can now be heard through the wall of the uterus.

Between the *fourth* and *fifth months* (sixteen to twenty weeks), hands and feet become fully developed, eyes can open and close, hearing is present, lungs become capable of breathing in and out, and nails, hair, and sweat glands develop. Around the sixteenth week, most pregnant women feel *quickening*, the movement of the fetus inside the womb. Actually these movements have been going on for many weeks by the time most mothers notice them, but as the womb becomes more crowded, the fetus inevitably hits its walls more often. In fact, studies of fetal movement cycles observe "jerky," or "sporadic," head and neck movements as early as the seventh gestational week and fetal respiratory movement at ten weeks. Fetal movements appear to grow progressively stronger and more frequent from eighteen weeks on, reaching a maximum between twenty-eight and twenty-nine weeks, after which they diminish somewhat until delivery. Fetal movements are an indicator of central nervous system integrity and function, and can be studied through maternal perceptions as well as with ultrasound, fetal heart rate monitors, and other electromechanical devices (Primeau, 1993).

Although the fetus's weight increases throughout pregnancy, large gains do not occur until near the end of pregnancy. By twenty weeks, or about halfway to birth, the fetus typically measures about 50 percent of its final prenatal length but only about 10 percent of its final weight (Hamilton, 1984). That makes the fetus about twelve inches long and only about ten ounces in weight; it is still a very tiny baby. But this weight gain seems slow only relative to the development lying ahead; compared with what has already happened, the fetus has made impressive gains.

By the beginning of the *seventh month*, the fetus is about sixteen inches long and weighs approximately three to five pounds. It is able to cry, breathe, swallow, digest, excrete, move about, and suck its thumb. The reflexes mentioned earlier are fully developed. Because of these capacities, the fetus is said to have attained *age of viability*, meaning it could survive if born at this point.

By the *eighth month*, the fetus weighs between five and seven pounds and has begun to develop a layer of body fat that will help it to regulate its body temperature after birth, and by *nine months* it has achieved its full birth weight. Toward the end of nine months, the average baby is about 7.5 pounds and almost 20 inches long. Growth in size stops, although fat continues to be stored, heart rate increases, and internal organ systems become more efficient in preparation for birth and independent life outside the womb.

The developing fetus is also responsive to stimuli in the external environment. One study recorded changes in fetal heart rate in response to sound and vibration (Kisilevsky et al., 1992). This raises the question of the effects of prenatal stimulation on behavior after birth. In an intriguing study designed to help answer this question, pregnant mothers were asked to read a children's story, Dr. Seuss's *The Cat in the Hat,* out loud to their unborn babies twice a day for the final six weeks of pregnancy. A few days after birth, the infants were exposed to the same story or to one they had not heard before. To test which story they preferred, the infants were given a special pacifier that allowed them to turn each recording on and off by

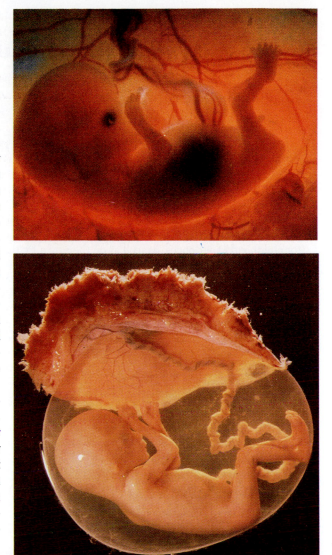

By the twelfth week, arms, hands, fingers, toes, and feet are clearly visible. The fetus begins exercising its limbs almost as soon as they develop, but it is not until sometime around the fourth or fifth month that the mother begins feeling these movements. The umbilical cord connecting the fetus to the placenta remains taut—and therefore untangled—because it is constantly filled with blood. Vessels and arteries proliferate throughout the fetus's body and are easily visible because the skin is still rather transparent.

During the middle trimester of pregnancy, the fetus grows rapidly, as you can see by comparing this sixteen-week-old fetus with the eleven-week-old fetus in the previous photograph. By sixteen weeks, the fetus looks quite human, but it still cannot survive outside the womb.

A Multicultural View

Reasons for Having a Child in the United States and Eight Other Countries

Attitudes of Parents in the United States

Pregnancy is a beginning, and expectant parents prepare for the birth of their baby and parenthood by creating, often unconsciously, a set of images of what being parents will be like (Galinsky, 1987). These images of parenthood are based partly on memories of the couple's own actual and wished-for childhood experiences, as well as on their own firsthand (or secondhand) experiences with parenthood and wishes for the future. Images are also influenced by life circumstances, one of the most important being the reasons for wanting (or not wanting) the child.

When researchers asked prospective parents, "Why do you want to have a child?", the following reasons were most frequently given:

1. Validation of adult status and social identity

2. Expansion of self, including ties to the future and a sense of immortality

3. Achievement of moral values in the sense that one is doing something "good" by having and raising a child

4. The need to obtain primary-group ties and affection by creating a family larger than just husband and wife

5. Stimulation, novelty, and fun

6. Achievement, competence, and creativity (people take pride in producing a baby)

7. Power and influence through directing and controlling the baby's life

8. Economic utility, based on the expectation that when grown, the baby will help provide economic and emotional support for the family (Hoffman, 1988; Hoffman & Hoffman, 1973).

For parents who already have a child, the desire to provide a sibling for the first child is a major reason for having a second one. Another common reason for wanting a child, particularly for teenagers, is to have someone to love and be loved by. A person's reasons for wanting a child and whether a pregnancy is planned or unplanned also can influence feelings about pregnancy. For example, women who planned their pregnancies and who wanted children for self-growth reasons have been found to be more positive about having children than women who did not. These women see parenthood as an opportunity to expand their sense of self and to intensify and enrich their marriages. Women who are more negative about becoming a parent either have unplanned pregnancies, see having a child as a way to escape current life circumstances, or consider a child to be a source of status or security (Leifer, 1977).

A Cross-Cultural Comparison

Do reasons for having children differ across cultures? A cross-cultural study of the advantages of having children as reported by mothers in the United States and eight other countries suggests that they do (Hoffman, 1988). As the accompanying table shows, the three most common needs

---

increasing or decreasing the interval of time between sucks. The infants increased their rate of sucking each time they heard *The Cat in the Hat,* but did not do so with the new story. They showed an obvious preference based on their prenatal experience with the Dr. Seuss story. A more recent study using a short children's rhyme found similar results (DeCasper et al., 1994).

The Experience of Pregnancy

Pregnancy involves many physical changes for the expectant mother. In this section, we discuss these changes and how they are experienced.

Sudah is nearing the end of her pregnancy—just eight weeks to go! She has been careful to eat a good, balanced diet and has gained about twenty-four pounds, which her doctor says is fine for her size and weight. Lately her belly feels like a basketball, and she sometimes worries whether Dan, her husband, still finds her attractive and whether she will ever get her prepregnancy figure back. During the first two months of pregnancy, Sudah felt nauseous a lot of the time and found it hard to keep food down. She found that eating small amounts of food (especially plain crackers) throughout the day helped, as did resting more frequently—which was hard to do, since she was still working full time.

Reasons for Having Children, as Reported by Mothers, by Country (Percentage)

	United States	Turkey	Indonesia (Japanese)	Indonesia (Sudanese)	Philippines	Thailand	Korea	Taiwan	Singapore
Economic-utility	6.0	54.0	94.1	79.6	71.3	74.6	35.7	44.4	46.8
Primary ties and affection	66.1	34.3	14.0	34.7	46.1	12.9	36.8	44.8	58.6
Stimulation and fun	60.0	21.7	12.8	38.2	58.2	9.2	46.8	68.6	70.9
Expansion of self	35.3	10.4	28.6	41.5	8.9	4.7	23.7	38.1	21.2
Adult status and social identity	21.9	13.8	2.1	4.7	5.9	2.0	5.8	8.3	9.1
Achievement	11.1	4.6	7.8	7.7	3.4	1.8	30.1	2.8	3.0
Morality	6.8	6.7	0.5	0.4	1.9	1.9	2.3	0.4	0.2
Power	2.2	1.8	0.1	0.2	2.0	0.1	1.2	0.1	0.2
n	1,259	1,539	984	965	1,567	2,288	1,433	2,103	904

children satisfy are economic utility; the need for primary-group (family) ties, love, and affection; and the need for fun and stimulation.

Considerable variation exists, however. In Turkey, Indonesia, the Philippines, and Thailand, the most common value of children mentioned is economic utility. Primary ties and affection are the most common reason in the United States, whereas stimulation and fun are the reason most frequently given in Korea, Taiwan, and Singapore. Because the number of responses given and coded differed somewhat from country to country, it is more meaningful to compare the relative importance of the reasons for having a child in each country than the actual percentages of any particular response.

These cross-cultural differences likely reflect societal differences in how intensely each need is felt, the extent to which children are seen as a way to satisfy the need, and what sources other than children exist for satisfying the particular need.

Until recently, aside from getting tired more easily, Sudah has felt pretty good. During the last few weeks, however, she has had some swelling in her legs and some back pain, and has had to go to the bathroom much more frequently because of the pressure of the baby on her bladder. Although she and Dan both can't wait for the baby to arrive, they are somewhat apprehensive about whether they are grown up enough to be parents and take on the responsibilities of parenthood.

Sudah's complaints are fairly typical of those associated with the hormonal and physiological changes of pregnancy. More than 50 percent of pregnant women experience some degree of nausea during the first trimester, but this usually disappears by the twelfth week. Strategies for relieving nausea include eating small amounts of food frequently, increasing protein intake, eating dry crackers or plain yogurt, and resting more often during the day. Frequent urination is another symptom of early pregnancy and is due to hormonally induced softening of the pelvic muscles, which allows the enlarged uterus to press on the bladder. Other symptoms include fatigue, headaches, dizziness and fainting, constipation, leg cramps, heartburn, shortness of breath, swelling of legs, hands, or face, varicose veins, and backache (Davis, 1993). Pregnant women with premature contractions or other problems (discussed later in the chapter) are often confined to complete bedrest for several weeks, which can be tedious.

For the family pictured here, pregnancy is an event that affects all of its members.

In addition to the influence of hormonal changes, some of these symptoms are due to weight gain during pregnancy. Both a woman's weight before pregnancy and her weight gain during pregnancy influence the baby's birth weight. Current recommendations are that women of normal weight before pregnancy gain about thirty pounds, women who are overweight about twenty pounds, and women who are underweight about thirty-four pounds, with the exact amount reflecting the woman's height and prepregnancy weight.

Where does the weight gain go? The increased size of the uterus, breast tissue, blood volume, body fluid, and extra fat to prepare the woman to produce milk for breast feeding all contribute to the additional pounds (ACOG, 1990). Table 4.1 summarizes how the average weight gain during pregnancy is distributed.

The physical changes of pregnancy, of course, make a woman's body dramatically different than the one she started out with, and most women have mixed feelings about their changed appearance. A big concern is whether their bodies will ever return to their normal size and shape. The answer is generally yes, although typically it takes some time and a reasonable approach to eating and exercise for this

TABLE 4.1 Average Weight Gain During Pregnancy	
Maternal stores (fat, protein, and other nutrients)	7.0 pounds
Increased fluid volume	4.0 pounds
Increased blood volume	4.0 pounds
Breast enlargement	2.0 pounds
Uterus	2.0 pounds
Baby	7.5 pounds
Amniotic fluid	2.0 pounds
Placenta	1.5 pounds
Total weight gain	30.0 pounds

Source: ACOG (1990).

to occur. Women who are conscious of diet and exercise before and during pregnancy are likely to have an easier time returning to their prepregnancy appearance than women who are not.

Pregnancy is a powerful experience that can significantly affect how both the mother and the father feel about themselves and each other. For most prospective parents, it raises the question "Am I ready to be emotionally and economically responsible for this baby?" Couples who are experiencing pregnancy together may wonder, "How will having a baby affect our relationship with each other?" The feelings and expectations associated with pregnancy are related to reasons for having a baby, which are discussed in the accompanying Multicultural View box.

Decisions and Issues

Prenatal development tends to follow a predictable path after conception. However, the road to conception itself can take some unexpected turns. People who want to conceive may find it difficult to do so. Others may want to carefully time conception or to avoid conception altogether. Still others may seek to end a pregnancy.

Infertility

Letisha and Alvin had always wanted children, but put off conceiving until both were in their early thirties and had established successful careers. After almost two frustrating years of unsuccessful attempts at conception, they finally decided to go to a fertility clinic to get help in finding out what might be causing the problem and what could be done about it.

Alvin and Letisha's situation is not uncommon. Approximately 15 percent of American couples experience *infertility*, meaning they are unable to conceive or carry a pregnancy to term after one year of unprotected intercourse. In about 80 to 90 percent of couples receiving medical treatment, it is possible to discover a clear medical reason for the infertility (American College of Obstetricians and Gynecologists [ACOG], 1990; Greil, 1993a). The social and emotional consequences of infertility can be considerable. In America, parenthood remains an important part of the transition, or "rite of passage," to adulthood. Although the number of couples choosing not to have children has risen, studies still find that 90 to 95 percent of American women view childlessness as an undesirable state for themselves and for others. Given the continuing importance attached to childbearing and parenting, infertility can become a symbol of significant role failure and a cause of personal and marital conflict and unhappiness (Greil, 1993b).

A problem during any part of the complex process of conception can make a couple infertile. If the problem is in the male's reproductive system, it usually is related to the quantity or strength of the sperm produced. If the problem is due to the female's reproductive system, it is likely the result of structural abnormalities in the fallopian tubes or uterus or of failure to ovulate and release mature eggs from the ovaries. An estimated 1 million American women a year develop *pelvic inflammatory disease* when sexually transmitted infections such as *chlamydia* spread into the uterus and fallopian tubes, and one in four women with the disease lose their ability to conceive. Indeed, sexually transmitted diseases account for one-fifth of infertility cases. Other causes include genetic or chromosomal abnormalities; exposure to harmful chemicals or radiation; excessive exercise, weight loss or gain, or drug or alcohol use; and infections other than sexually transmitted diseases (Liebmann-Smith, 1993; McTigue, 1993).

If infertility has been diagnosed and structural problems ruled out, the first course of treatment is fertility drugs that increase ovulation and chances of pregnancy, even in cases where a woman's ovulation is normal but sperm quality or production is a problem. A growing number of new reproductive technologies are now available as alternatives to normal conception for couples who are infertile. These alternatives are discussed in the accompanying Perspectives box.

Contraception   *Family planning* is regarded as the best way to reduce unwanted or unplanned pregnancies and improve maternal and child health. Family planning programs provide information and contraceptives to enable people to voluntarily regulate both the number and spacing of their children. *Contraception* refers to voluntary methods of preventing unintended pregnancy. Reversible methods of contraception include hormonal methods (oral contraceptives, injection, implant, or vaginal ring), intrauterine devices (diaphragm, condom, spermicide, foam, sponge, or cervical cap), periodic abstinence (natural family planning, or rhythm method), and withdrawal (coitus interruptus, the removal of the penis from the vagina before ejaculation). More permanent and largely irreversible methods of contraception, which are also known as *sterilization,* are tubal ligation for women and vasectomy for men (Waldman, 1993).

Abortion   Social attitudes about abortion, the termination of pregnancy before the embryo or fetus is capable of independent life, have varied significantly over time and from place to place. Ideas about the appropriateness of intervention by government, religious, or medical authorities change. Fertility rates change too, along with attitudes toward women, fetuses, and motherhood (Simonds, 1993). Historically, abortion has been a universally relied-on method to terminate pregnancy. Today an estimated 90 percent of the approximately 45 million abortions that take place worldwide each year occur in poorer, developing countries. Approximately 45 percent of these abortions are performed under unsafe and often illegal conditions. Every year some eighty thousand deaths result, 95 percent of them among women living in less developed nations. Many more women die of miscarriages due to health problems or poor prenatal care. Only 5 members of the United Nations currently prohibit abortion to save the life of the mother, and the remaining 184 member countries permit abortion under certain conditions (Crosette, 1998). (See Figure 4.2 and Table 4.2.)

In the United States, it was not until the middle 1800s that laws restricting abortion were enacted. In 1973, in *Roe v. Wade,* the Supreme Court ruled that a

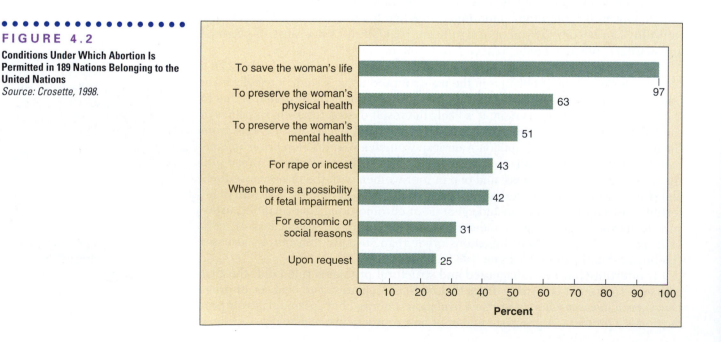

FIGURE 4.2

Conditions Under Which Abortion Is Permitted in 189 Nations Belonging to the United Nations
Source: Crosette, 1998.

PERSPECTIVES

Technological Alternatives to Normal Conception

Earlier in this century, the only alternative for couples who were infertile was to adopt a child or to remain childless. But today's medical techniques offer a growing number of alternative options. These alternatives vary in practicality and popularity, but from a strictly medical standpoint they all work fairly reliably.

Artificial (donor) insemination (DI) is used in cases where infertility is caused by problems in sperm quality or production. In this procedure, fresh or previously frozen sperm from a donor are inserted into the woman's vagina and held in place for a few hours. While in most cases the donor is anonymous, he can also be a friend or a relative. Artificial insemination is safe and easy to carry out and induces pregnancy as effectively as does normal intercourse between fertile partners—a 20 percent success rate in any one month (Liebmann-Smith, 1993; Silber, 1991). A controversial application of artificial insemination is *surrogate mothering,* in which sperm from the future father are inserted into the womb of a woman who agrees (usually for a fee) to give up the baby once it is born.

In vitro fertilization (IVF) is used if both eggs and sperm are normal and infertility is caused by blocked fallopian tubes that cannot be surgically repaired. With IVF, ovulation is induced with medications that cause multiple eggs to be produced. With the aid of a laparoscope and ultrasound, one or more eggs are then removed through the woman's vagina under local anesthesia. They are mixed in a laboratory dish with sperm from the male and allowed to fertilize in an incubator. Two days later, the fertilized egg or zygote is transferred back into the woman's uterus through her vagina. Additional embryos can be frozen (cryopreserved) for future use. Although fertilization rates are high, getting the embryos to implant is much harder to achieve. Pregnancy rates with IVF are about 15 percent (Liebmann-Smith, 1993; Silber, 1991).

Gamete intrafallopian tube transfer (GIFT), a variation of IVF, solves the implantation problem and can be used by women with healthy fallopian tubes. The GIFT procedure is exactly the same as IVF, except that the sperm and eggs are both surgically placed directly into the woman's fallopian tube, where they are naturally fertilized, and then moved to the uterus at the appropriate time. Pregnancy rates with GIFT are approximately three times higher than with IVF. With GIFT,

it is also possible to use donor eggs when a woman no longer ovulates or has a genetic condition she wants to avoid passing on to her offspring (Silber, 1991).

Zygote intrafallopian transfer (ZIFT) is a modification of GIFT and IVF. After the egg and sperm are fertilized in the laboratory, the resulting embryo, or zygote, is placed in the fallopian tube rather than the uterus (with IVF, the "test-tube" embryo is placed in the uterus; with GIFT, the unfertilized sperm and eggs are placed in the fallopian tube). ZIFT is used when the sperm's ability to fertilize the woman's eggs is questionable. It also allows the surgeon to select and transfer only eggs that have been fertilized, thus increasing the chances of a pregnancy (Silber, 1991). GIFT and ZIFT produce identical pregnancy rates. However, whereas GIFT requires only a short (forty-five-minute) operation, ZIFT involves egg retrieval (aspiration) and in vitro fertilization, followed two days later by a procedure to transfer the embryo into the fallopian tube.

Finally, *micromanipulation (microfertilization)* is an experimental procedure in which a few sperm are microsurgically placed directly into the outside layer (zona) of the egg, making it possible for a man with very few viable sperm to fertilize his partner's egg.

What are the experiences of families with children conceived by the new reproductive technologies? In a recent British study that compared families with a child conceived by in vitro fertilization or donor insemination with families whose children were conceived naturally or adopted, Susan Golombok and her associates found no group differences in the quality of children's emotions, behavior, or overall relationships with their parents (Golombok et al., 1995). Mothers of IVF and DI children, in fact, showed greater warmth toward and deeper emotional involvement with their children, and both mother- and father-child interactions were more positive. At least for the families studied, genetic ties appeared to be less important for family functioning than a strong desire to become a parent.

What Do You Think?

If now (or in the future) you and your partner wished to have a child but were unable to do so through normal conception, what reservations might you have about using the new technological alternatives? How have the results of Susan Golombok's study influenced your thinking?

woman's right to privacy and self-determination regarding pregnancy is constitutionally protected. Since then, organizations opposing abortion (which have labeled themselves "pro-life") and organizations supporting access to abortion (which have labeled themselves "pro-choice") have battled to prevent or protect women's access to abortion, respectively. In 1992, the Supreme Court upheld the right of individual states (in that case, Pennsylvania) to restrict access to abortion by, for example, requiring parental notification or waiting periods. The abortion debate appears to involve competing moral frameworks: those opposed to abortion focus on the fetus as an innocent life that must be protected, whereas those who support access to abortion emphasize women's right to control pregnancy on the grounds that it takes place within or is part of their bodies (Simonds, 1993).

Over the past two decades, general support for the continued availability of abortion has remained at around 70 percent, but also varies with the circumstances. People tend to see abortion as appropriate when the pregnancy endangers the woman's life, when the pregnancy resulted from rape or incest, and when the fetus is seriously impaired. Support declines when the decision is based on more individual considerations, such as the woman's financial inability to afford any more children, unwillingness to marry the father, and conflicting work and educational plans. Support for abortion is correlated with more years of education; with a more liberal or moderate, versus conservative, political orientation; with knowing someone who has had an abortion or having had an abortion oneself; with being younger; and with being unmarried. Opposition is strongly tied to religious beliefs (Simonds, 1993).

Most clinics and medical offices that perform abortions provide education for their clients in small groups and offer individual counseling when requested or when clinic staff identify a problem. Support in the procedure room may be provided by a counselor, a specially trained aide, or a nurse. The pregnant woman and her partner, a supportive family member, or a friend are encouraged to make decisions jointly when possible, although the final decision is hers. The goals of pre-abortion counseling are to (1) ensure that the woman has considered her alternatives and made an uncoerced choice; (2) obtain informed consent by fully explaining the procedure and its potential risks and complications; (3) assess the suitability of an outpatient procedure for the particular individual and refer her to an inpatient procedure, if appropriate; (4) assist the woman in reviewing her decision, her feelings, and her ability to handle the mixed emotions associated with the pregnancy, her circumstances, and the choice of abortion; (5) help the woman prepare for the procedure and deal with anxiety by providing relaxation and pain management techniques; and (6) discuss

TABLE 4.2   Death Rates from Safe and Unsafe* Abortions in Rich and Poor Nations

	Rich (Developed) Nations		Poor (Developing) Nations	
	Number of Abortions	Number of Deaths	Number of Abortions	Number of Deaths
Legal and Safe Abortions	11 million (84.6%)	500 (.045/1,000)	14 million (44.0%)	500 (.036/1,000)
Unsafe Abortions	2 million (15.4%)	700 (.035/1,000)	18 million (56.0%)	69,300 (3.85/1,000)
Totals	13 million	1,200	32 million	69,800

*An abortion is unsafe if performed by persons lacking the necessary skills or in an environment lacking the minimal medical standards. In poor, developing nations, 56 percent of abortions are unsafe compared to 15.4 percent in rich, developed nations, resulting in 3.85 deaths per thousand versus .035 deaths per thousand in richer nations.
Source: Crosette (1998).

with the woman her contraceptive history and assist her in making appropriate contraceptive choices to use after the abortion (Beresford, 1993).

WHAT DO YOU THINK ? For those of you who have already experienced pregnancy, what was it like? For those of you who haven't, what do you imagine the experience might be like for you? How has what you have read so far in this chapter influenced your views about pregnancy?

Prenatal Influences on the Child

As we have noted, physical structures develop in a particular sequence and at fairly precise times. Psychologists and biologists sometimes call such regularity *canalization*. **Canalization** refers to the tendency of genes to narrowly direct or restrict growth and development of particular physical and behavioral characteristics to a single (or very few) phenotypic outcomes and to resist environmental factors that push development in other directions (McCall, 1981).

Typically prenatal development is a highly reliable process, so prospective parents generally worry much more than they need to about whether their baby will be "all right." In fact, 97.5 percent of human infants are perfect at birth, and of the 2.5 percent who are not, half have only minor defects such as hammertoes, extra fingers or toes, or birthmarks (Guttmacher & Kaiser, 1984).

But certain conditions can interfere with even the highly canalized processes of fetal development. These conditions are sometimes called *risk factors* because they increase the chance that the future baby will have medical problems but do not guarantee that these problems will actually appear. One set of risk factors are the mother's biological characteristics, including age and physical condition, as well as biological factors that are influenced by psychological and social stresses. Other risks include exposure to diseases, drugs, chemicals, and other environmental hazards during pregnancy.

Harmful Substances, Diseases, and Environmental Hazards

As the complex sequence of prenatal growth proceeds, the timing of the development of each new organ or body part is particularly important. **Critical period** refers to a time-limited period during which certain developmental changes are particularly sensitive to disruption. This "window of opportunity" is dictated by complex genetic codes in each cell *and* by the particular set of prenatal conditions that must be in place for each change to occur. If development is disturbed or blocked during a critical period, the changes that were scheduled to occur may be disrupted or prevented from occurring at all. Figure 4.3 shows the critical periods in human development.

Especially during the early weeks of its life, development of the embryo is particularly vulnerable to disruption if the embryo is exposed (through the mother) to certain harmful substances called *teratogens*. A **teratogen** is any substance or other environmental influence that can interfere with or permanently damage an embryo's growth. Named after an ancient Greek word meaning "monster-creating," teratogens can result in serious physical malformations and even the death of the embryo. Teratogens are most harmful if exposure occurs during the critical period for the particular physical change to occur (see Figure 4.3). Teratogens include many *medicinal and nonmedicinal drugs; other chemicals; diseases* (viruses and bacteria); and certain *other harmful environmental influences*, such as radiation. A substance is classified

• • •

canalization The tendency of many developmental processes to unfold in highly predictable ways under a wide range of conditions.

critical period Any period during which development is particularly susceptible to an event or influence, either negative or positive.

teratogen Any substance a pregnant woman is exposed to that can harm the developing embryo or fetus.

as a teratogen based on its ability to disrupt prenatal development. Teratogens can be contracted from a variety of sources, including from other individuals who have communicable diseases; from drugs; from ingesting foods that have been contaminated; and from exposure to chemicals, X-rays, and radioactivity in the workplace and in nonwork environments.

Several factors influence a teratogen's effects. The first is the *timing of exposure*. The nine months of pregnancy generally are divided into three *trimesters*, each lasting three months. Disruptions during the first trimester, when the critical periods for embryonic and fetal development occur, are most likely to result in spontaneous abortion or serious birth defects. During the third week, for example, teratogens can harm the basic structures of the heart and central nervous system, which are just beginning to form. The effects of exposure in the second and third trimesters generally are less severe.

The impact of a teratogen is also influenced by the *intensity and duration of exposure*. For example, the higher the dose (intensity) and the longer the exposure to a harmful drug such as alcohol or cocaine, the greater the chances that the baby will be harmed and that the harm will be more severe than if dose and duration are less. The *number of other harmful influences* that are present also makes a difference; the greater the number, the greater the risk. Finally, the *biogenetic vulnerability of mother and infant* will influence a teratogen's effects. Mothers and their infants will differ in the degree to which they will be affected by exposure to a particular type and level of teratogen. For example, whereas heavy and prolonged drinking is likely to affect almost all babies, very moderate drinking may cause considerable harm for one infant but no measurable harm for another.

● ● ● ● ● ● ● ● ● ● ● ● ●

FIGURE 4.3

Timing and Effects of Teratogens During Sensitive or Critical Periods

This figure illustrates the sensitive or critical periods in human development. The dark band indicates highly sensitive or critical periods; the light band indicates stages that are less sensitive to disruption caused by teratogens. Note that each structure has a critical period during which its development may be disrupted. Note also that development proceeds from head to tail (cephalocaudal) and from the center of the body outward (proximodistal).
Source: Reprinted from Before We Are Born: Basic Embryology and Birth Defects, *2nd ed., by K. L. Moore, p. 111, with permission of W. B. Saunders Company, ©1983.*

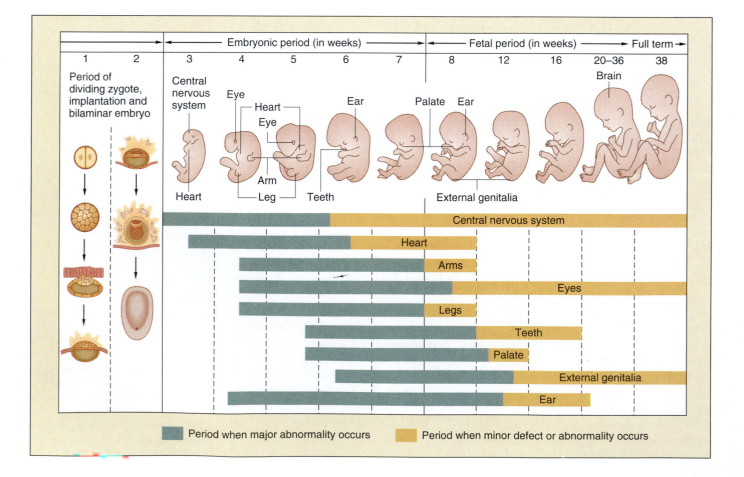

Medicinal Drugs Medical science has developed countless drugs with highly beneficial effects, from curing illness to relieving pain. Yet a medication with positive effects overall may negatively affect a child's development if taken during pregnancy. A drug called *thalidomide* illustrates dramatically how such damage can occur. It also illustrates the political, economic, and social policy implications of new medical and scientific discoveries that affect human growth and development.

Thalidomide is a seemingly harmless sedative that during the late 1950s and early 1960s was widely prescribed for calming the nerves, promoting sleep, and reducing morning sickness and other forms of nausea during the early weeks of pregnancy. Although it was advertised as being completely safe, between 1958 and 1962 thousands of babies were born with birth defects that included missing, shortened, or misshapen arms and legs, deafness, severe facial deformities, seizure disorders, dwarfism, and brain damage. It took until 1961 for the drug to be banned in the United States, in part because the effects of teratogens were less understood then and because the federal Food and Drug Administration (FDA) was under political pressure from the drug industry to keep thalidomide on the market (Stout, 1993).

It is estimated that there are currently about eight thousand thalidomide-affected adults and that twice that many babies were stillborn (dead at birth) or died shortly afterward because of defects caused by thalidomide (Stout, 1993). Teratogenic drugs pose an even greater developmental risk in developing countries in South America, Africa, and Asia, where drugs are less strictly regulated than in the United States. In Brazil, one of the world's largest producers of thalidomide, the drug is used to help treat the symptoms of leprosy, which afflicts almost 300,000 people in that country. This has led to a growing number of birth defects in babies born to mothers with leprosy who have taken the drug because they are not aware of its effects (Gorman, 1993).

Unfortunately, the damage done by toxic drugs or chemicals does not always show itself as obviously or as soon as in the case of thalidomide. For about twenty-five years following World War II, another drug, *diethylstilbestrol (DES)*, was taken by 3 million to 6 million pregnant women with histories of spontaneous abortions to prevent miscarriages. The drug was especially useful during the early months, when miscarriages occur most often. At birth the babies of women who took DES seemed perfectly normal, and they remained so throughout childhood. As they became young adults, however, abnormal development of vaginal cells and structural abnormalities of the uterus were found in all female babies who had been exposed, and about one in one thousand eventually developed cancer of the vagina or of the cervix. The sons of DES mothers developed abnormalities in the structure of their reproductive organs and have a higher rate of testicular cancer. Even the daughters who did not get cancer had significantly more problems than usual with their own pregnancies, including higher rates of spontaneous abortion and stillbirth, as well as more minor problems, and they had them whether or not their families had histories of difficult births. More recently, as most of the people exposed to DES before birth are now reaching midlife, there is growing evidence of increased risk for autoimmune disorders such as pernicious anemia, myasthenia gravis (a nerve-muscle disorder), serious intestinal disorders, and multiple sclerosis as a result of DES damage to the immune system (Brody, 1993). DES support networks and social action groups for affected individuals and families have been formed in both Canada and the United States (Linn et al., 1988; Sato, 1993).

Other medications that can harm the fetus include *isotreitinoin (accutane)*, a treatment for acne; *streptomycin*, an antibiotic used to treat tuberculosis; and *tetracycline*, an antibiotic used to treat a wide variety of infections.

Nonmedicinal Drugs   Not surprisingly, drugs such as *heroin, cocaine*, and *alcohol* also affect the fetus.

Heroin   At birth, the child of a woman who uses heroin immediately begins to have withdrawal symptoms, including vomiting, trembling, irritability, fever, disturbed sleep, and an abnormally high-pitched cry. Unfortunately, the symptoms may not become noticeably serious until several days after birth, when the baby has left the hospital. Even when the infant has recovered from withdrawal, she or he often develops slowly during the first year, exhibiting less attentiveness to the environment and poor motor skill performance. Some infants display longer-term attention deficits in their childhood years, but others do not (de Cubas & Field, 1995; East & Steele, 1987; Vorhees & Mollnow, 1987).

Cocaine   Mothers who use cocaine and cocaine derivatives such as *crack* generally have a greater than normal risk of miscarriage or premature delivery. Their babies are more likely to have lower than normal birth weight, be more irritable, and be more susceptible to serious respiratory problems. There is growing evidence that cocaine is also associated with genital and urinary tract deformities, heart defects, and central nervous system problems (Bartol, 1986; Chasnoff et al., 1989; MacGregor et al., 1987).

Alcohol   Even in biblical times, people suspected that alcohol harms an unborn child: "Behold, thou shalt conceive and bear a son; and now drink no wine nor strong drink, neither eat any unclean thing" (*Judges 13:7*). Both then and now, many babies born to mothers who consume alcohol during pregnancy display fetal alcohol effects (FAEs), and the most severely affected babies exhibit a cluster of defects known as *fetal alcohol syndrome (FAS). Fetal alcohol effects* refer to a set of symptoms that include lower birth weight, lack of responsiveness and arousability, and increased occurrences of heart rate and respiratory abnormalities in infants. These infants achieve lower mental development scores at eight months and at four years and have higher rates of learning disabilities (Barr et al., 1990; Streissguth et al., 1989).

Symptoms of **fetal alcohol syndrome (FAS)** include central nervous system damage and physical abnormalities such as heart defects, small head, distortion of joints, and abnormal facial features, including a flattened mid-face region and a thin upper lip; mental retardation and/or behavioral disorders such as hyperactivity and poor impulse control; and impaired growth and/or failure to thrive (discussed in Chapter 5). Babies of heavy drinkers, particularly in the last three months of pregnancy, are at much greater risk for these problems. It is estimated that 50 to 75 percent of infants born to chronically alcoholic women may be affected. Longitudinal studies show that problems with vigilance, attention and short-term memory may occur in adolescents who experienced exposure to alcohol prenatally (Streissguth et al., 1995).

You may be wondering what level of alcohol consumption is safe for a pregnant woman. At present, the only completely safe answer is *none*. Even moderate daily drinking during pregnancy (two ounces of hard liquor, nine ounces of wine, or two beers) is associated with an increase in these disorders. The chance of fetal alcohol effects in the infant of a mother who consumes more than four drinks daily is estimated to be about 33 percent and about 10 percent for a woman who consumes between two and four drinks per day. However, no completely proven safe dosage of alcohol for a pregnant woman has yet been determined (Feinbloom & Forman, 1987).

Despite our knowledge of the risks of drinking, the national Centers for Disease Control (CDC) report that the rate of FAS increased almost sevenfold over a fifteen-year period from 1 per 10,000 births in 1979 to 6.7 per 10,000 births in 1993 (*New York Times*, 1995a). FAS could be prevented if alcohol were not consumed during pregnancy, but this goal has not been easy to achieve. As with a number of other problem drugs, alcohol use is deeply embedded in many aspects of people's lives, including their individual histories; family, neighborhood, and work situations; social and economic conditions; and ethnicity and culture. Drug use can be seen as an attempt to self-medicate to relieve the pain and unhappiness of a difficult life, a pattern that is difficult to break without significant societal changes. In the case of

• • •

fetal alcohol syndrome (FAS) A congenital condition exhibited by babies born to mothers who consumed too much alcohol during pregnancy. They do not arouse easily and tend to behave sluggishly in general; they also have distinctive facial characteristics.

The development of each of these girls has been affected by fetal alcohol syndrome (FAS).

alcohol (and tobacco, which is discussed shortly), widespread use has been strongly encouraged and financed by powerful economic interests. Sales of alcohol play a major role in our economy in terms of jobs, profits, and tax revenues, and for many people alcohol use is supported by long-standing cultural practice.

Programs to help pregnant mothers curb their drinking have had best results for the children when they emphasize the importance of not drinking at all, even if only for the last few months of pregnancy. Mothers who cut back throughout pregnancy give birth to healthy, alert babies more often than do mothers who only cut back early and resume drinking later in their pregnancies (Rosett et al., 1980).

Tobacco   Cigarette smoking also can harm the fetus, but the effects are more general than those for alcohol. Two key elements of cigarette smoke, nicotine and carbon monoxide, appear to interfere with the supply of oxygen to the fetus and to contribute to increased fetal heart rate. Smoking during pregnancy has been associated with reduced birth weight, increased risk of spontaneous abortion, prematurity, higher infant mortality during the birth process, and poorer postnatal adjustment. Even exposure to smoke from others (passive smoke) can adversely affect pregnant women and their fetuses (Armstrong, 1992; McDonald et al., 1992a, 1992b). It is estimated that smoking during pregnancy causes the deaths of about 5,600 babies and 115,000 miscarriages every year, contributes to 53,000 low-birth-weight babies and 22,000 babies who require intensive care at birth, and is implicated in 1,900 annual cases of sudden infant death syndrome (discussed in Chapter 5) (*New York Times,* 1995b).

Women who stop smoking before becoming pregnant or during the first trimester are likely to have infants of normal birth weight. Women who stop smoking before their thirtieth week will, on average, have higher-birth-weight infants than women who continue to smoke throughout pregnancy. Despite growing awareness of the dangers of smoking, however, between 24 and 30 percent of pregnant smokers continue to smoke during pregnancy (U.S. Department of Health and Human Services, 1990).

It is estimated that elimination of smoking during pregnancy could prevent 5 percent of fetal/infant deaths, 20 percent of low-birth-weight deliveries, and 8 percent of premature deliveries each year in the United States. For young, unmarried, and/or uneducated mothers—groups with a high prevalence of smoking (and other pregnancy risk factors)—elimination of smoking could prevent 10 percent of fetal/infant deaths, 35 percent of low-birth-weight deliveries, and 15 percent of premature births (M. Miller, 1993). As in the case of other teratogens, reducing the incidence of smoking during pregnancy is not easy. Smoking is difficult to give up because of its addictive and habit-forming qualities, particularly for women whose lives are high in stress and low in social support. While better education and cessation programs that offer adequate social support for women who smoke can help, reducing the promotion and sale of cigarettes may prove to be more effective. Heavy tobacco industry advertising in popular magazines and at sporting events that targets teenagers and young adults is a big part of the problem. Among people age twenty-four or younger, the percentage of female smokers is now higher than that for male smokers. Furthermore, it is expected that female smokers of all ages will soon outnumber male smokers because more girls than boys start smoking and women quit less often than men do (M. Miller, 1993).

TABLE 4.3   Teratogens and Their Effects

Teratogen	Effects
Drugs	
Medicinal Drugs	
Thalidomide	Birth defects such as missing, shortened, or misshapen arms and legs, deafness; severe facial deformities; seizure disorders; dwarfism; brain damage; fetal/infant death
Diethylstilbestrol (DES)	*Grown daughters:* vaginal and cervical cancer; spontaneous abortions and stillbirth; autoimmune disorders such as pernicious anemia, myasthenia gravis (a nerve-muscle disorder), intestinal disorder, multiple sclerosis; *grown sons:* abnormalities in reproductive organs, testicular cancer
Nonmedicinal Drugs	
Heroin	Withdrawal symptoms, including vomiting, trembling, irritability, fever, disturbed sleep, an abnormally high-pitched cry; delayed social and motor development
Cocaine	Miscarriage or premature delivery, low birth weight, irritability, respiratory problems, genital and urinary tract deformities, heart defects, central nervous system problems
Alcohol	*Fetal alcohol effects (FAEs):* lower birth weight, lack of responsiveness and arousability, heart rate and respiratory abnormalities; delayed cognitive development; learning disabilities; *fetal alcohol syndrome (FAS):* central nervous system damage, heart defects, small head, distortions of joints, abnormal facial features; mental retardation; behavioral disorders such as hyperactivity and poor impulse control; impaired growth and/or failure to thrive
Tobacco	Spontaneous abortion, prematurity, fetal/infant death, reduced birth weight, poorer postnatal adjustment
Maternal Diseases	
Rubella	*First trimester:* blindness, deafness, heart defects, damage to central nervous system, mental retardation; *second trimester:* problems with hearing, vision, and language
Syphilis and gonorrhea	Fetal death, jaundice, anemia, pneumonia, skin rash, bone inflammation, dental deformities, hearing difficulties, blindness
Genital herpes	Disease of skin and mucous membranes, blindness, brain damage, seizures, and developmental delay
Cytomegalovirus	Jaundice, microcephaly (very small head), deafness, eye problems, increased risk for severe illness and infant death
AIDS	Abnormally small skull; facial deformities; immune system damage; enlarged lymph glands, liver, spleen; recurrent infections; poor growth; fever; brain disease; developmental delay; deteriorated motor skills
Toxoplasmosis	Spontaneous abortion, prematurity, low birth weight, enlarged liver and spleen, jaundice, anemia, congenital defects, mental retardation, seizures, cerebral palsy, retinal disease, blindness

Maternal Diseases   Exposure of a pregnant woman to certain viral, bacteriological, and parasitic diseases can adversely affect her baby's development. Table 4.3 summarizes the teratogenic effects of exposure to selected diseases and drugs during pregnancy. In addition, some diseases can be directly transmitted from mother to fetus, often with devastating consequences; these include syphilis and gonorrhea.

Rubella   Also called *German measles*, the rubella virus apparently can infect the embryo or fetus by passing through the placenta into the fetal bloodstream. During the first two months of pregnancy, it is likely to cause blindness, deafness, heart defects, damage to the central nervous system, and mental retardation. During the second trimester, after the fetus is fully formed, rubella's effects are less severe but may include hearing, vision, and language problems. Because of the successful public health efforts to inoculate schoolchildren and women at risk, on the average only twenty new cases of rubella are reported per year in the United States (Blackman, 1990).

Syphilis and Gonorrhea   A pregnant woman with untreated syphilis can transmit the disease to her fetus. In 25 percent of cases, death of the fetus results, usually during the second trimester. An additional 25 percent of infected fetuses die soon after birth. Of those who survive, about 25 percent show symptoms such as jaundice, anemia, pneumonia, skin rash, and bone inflammation (Blackman, 1990).

Fetuses that contract gonorrhea in the birth canal may later develop eye infections or become blind. It is now standard practice to put drops of silver nitrate or penicillin in newborns' eyes to protect them against these conditions, because gonorrhea may be present in the mother without obvious symptoms.

Genital Herpes   Genital herpes causes blisters on the genitalia of both men and women. It is most frequently transmitted to the baby at birth as the newborn comes through the birth canal and in contact with herpes sores on the mother's genitals (Feinbloom & Forman, 1987; Hanshaw et al., 1985). The incidence of neonatal herpes infection ranges from 0.03 to 0.3 per 1,000 live births.

There are two types of neonatal herpes infection. In the first type, the infant develops a mild disease of the skin and mucous membranes of the mouth and eyes. In the second, more severe type, about 33 percent of infected newborns die and another 25 to 35 percent suffer disabilities such as blindness, permanent brain damage, seizures, and developmental delay. Transmission of herpes by mothers with active herpes infections can be prevented by caesarean delivery, a procedure in which the baby is surgically delivered through the mother's abdomen. Herpes infection in newborns is now treated with antiviral drugs (Blackman, 1990).

Cytomegalovirus   Cytomegalovirus (CMV) is a viral infection that is difficult to detect because people who have it rarely show symptoms. When symptoms occur, they are similar to those of mononucleosis and include fever, fatigue, swollen lymph glands, and sore throat. CMV can be passed to the baby through the placenta, the vagina, or breast milk. Although the risk of a primary infection in a woman is only 2 percent, about 50 percent of fetuses are infected, with 10 percent developing symptoms at birth. Infants who have symptoms are at higher risk for severe illness, death, or disabilities, and are more likely to have problems such as jaundice, microcephaly (a very small head and mental retardation), deafness, and eye problems (ACOG, 1990). Infected newborns can harbor and excrete CMV for months, so pregnant women and child care workers should practice careful handwashing techniques after handling the babies or their diapers (Feinbloom & Forman, 1987). HIV, which leads to pediatric AIDS, can also be directly transmitted from mother to fetus through the placenta, although as we will see shortly, children are most often infected during the delivery.

Toxoplasmosis   At some point in their lives, about 25 percent of the U.S. population contracts and develops antibodies to *toxoplasmosis*, a disease caused by a parasite present in uncooked meat and in the feces of infected cats. The approximate incidence of toxoplasmosis is about one or two per one thousand live births.

Toxoplasmosis may result in spontaneous abortion or premature delivery. Affected infants are characterized by low birth weight, an enlarged liver and spleen, jaundice, and anemia. Congenital defects include hydrocephalus, microcephaly, and calcifications in the brain. Later problems include mental retardation, seizures, cerebral palsy, and diseases of the retina that result in blindness. It is strongly recommended that women avoid all contact with cat litter boxes during pregnancy (Blackman, 1990).

Pediatric AIDS   Pediatric AIDS is a huge problem worldwide. Each year 2 million HIV-infected women worldwide become pregnant; an estimated 680,000 babies were born with AIDS in 1997. In the same year, nearly 6 million people (close to 16,000 a day) acquired HIV and nearly 2.3 million died from it, including 460,000 children. Approximately 1.6 million children worldwide lost their mothers to AIDS. The United Nations recently began a new pilot program to slow the transmission of AIDS by providing AZT treatment to about 30,000 HIV-infected pregnant women. Critics have objected to the small scale of the project and to the fact that no treatment will be provided for these mothers following delivery (Mann & Tarantola, 1998; Wilfert & McKinney, 1998).

Seventy-eight percent of AIDS cases in children involve perinatal (at the time of birth) transmission from an infected mother to her child, either through the placenta or through contact with HIV-contaminated blood at the time of delivery (American Academy of Pediatrics, 1991; Wilfert & McKinney, 1998). In the majority of these cases, the mother's infection can be linked to her own intravenous (IV) drug use or that of her sexual partner. African American and Hispanic children make up three-quarters of all pediatric AIDS cases in the United States, although they account for only one-fourth of all American children. Because AIDS has an incubation period of up to five years in adults, pregnant women may be unaware that they have the virus or that it can be transmitted to their offspring.

Although most children infected *perinatally* show symptoms before age one, some may live for years without symptoms. Because newborns retain the protective antibodies they receive from their mothers for several months after birth, testing a newborn for HIV antibodies can give accurate information only about the mother (Lee, 1995; Richter, 1993).

AIDS may also cause serious malformations in the developing embryo and fetus. Prenatal AIDS infection can lead to an abnormally small skull and facial deformities that include a prominent, boxlike forehead, eyes that are widely spaced and off center, and thickened lips. These abnormalities are more severe and appear in the first year of life when the virus was transferred to the fetus early in the fetus's development. Other symptoms of AIDS relate to a damaged immune system and include enlargement of lymph glands, liver, and spleen, recurrent infections, poor growth, and fever. There may also be disease of the brain resulting in developmental delay, deterioration of motor skills and intellectual abilities, and behavioral abnormalities. Seventy-five percent of babies born with AIDS die before their second year (American Academy of Pediatrics, 1991; Wilfert & McKinney, 1998).

Treatment of HIV-infected mothers and their children with antiviral drugs is still in its early stages. Recent studies suggest that women who take the drug AZT during pregnancy and labor can reduce the risk of having an HIV-infected baby from 15 to 30 percent to about 8 percent. Treatment of the secondary infections that result from the immunodeficiency has improved, but it is unlikely that a cure for this terminal illness will be found in the near future. Although children with AIDS appear to survive longer than AIDS-afflicted adults, the typical life expectancy of a child born with AIDS is not yet known (Lee, 1995; Wilfert & McKinney, 1998).

Therapies for children with HIV present special problems. Most drugs are designed for adults, and because many children cannot swallow pills, they may need liquids and syrups, but certain anti-HIV compounds are insoluble in water or have a terrible taste. In addition, since drug companies typically test new medications on adults first, knowledge of the effects of these drugs on children of different ages is still limited. Finally, the treatment regime for HIV is extraordinary even for adults. Three or more drugs must be given two or three times a day, every day, 365 days a year. If doses are missed, HIV can become resistant to the medications. Even for a family that is not under stress, it is easy to forget to give a child medicine for a simple ear infection. The majority of families of HIV-positive children are low income, under a great deal of life stress, and often poorly equipped to deal with the very stringent demands of intensive anti-HIV therapy. Many families are also reluctant to tell others about their child's HIV status, and as a result may allow their child to skip medicine doses at day care or school (Wilfert & McKinney, 1998).

The psychological as well as the medical consequences of AIDS/HIV are devastating. A multidisciplinary team approach that works with the medical, psychological, social, and economic problems and stresses caused by AIDS has been found to be most effective in caring for afflicted infants and children (Task Force on Pediatric AIDS, 1989).

Environmental Hazards A broad range of environmental hazards can be destructive to prenatal development. These include exposure to radiation from nuclear explosions, nuclear plant accidents, industrial materials, and medical X-rays; to industrial chemical pollutants such as carbon monoxide, "passive" cigarette smoke, lead, mercury, and PCBs in the air or water; to fertilizers, herbicides, and pesticides in the food supply; to food additives; and even to excessive heat and humidity. Although the careful parent may take steps to avoid some of these hazards, many are beyond individual control and require efforts on a national or even international scale.

Currently the majority of women are employed outside the home, and most women who are employed when they become pregnant continue working throughout their pregnancies. Many of the environmental hazards to pregnant women and their babies are encountered in the workplace. These include (1) physical hazards such as noise, radiation, vibration, stressful physical activity, and materials handling; (2) biological hazards such as viruses, fungi, spores, and bacteria; and (3) chemical hazards such as anesthetic gases, pesticides, lead, mercury, and organic solvents. As yet, there is no consistent overall finding regarding the effects of such workplace hazards on prenatal development (Bernhardt, 1990). A mother's age and physical characteristics may also cause complications during pregnancy, as we will see in the next section.

Several other physical characteristics of the mother during pregnancy can increase the chance of spontaneous abortion or miscarriage (McKenzie, 1983):

1. Having had several previous pregnancies (at least four or five), especially if some of them involved medical problems

2. Being very overweight or underweight, that is, more than about 25 percent over or under the average weight for the mother's height and frame (being only a little overweight or underweight does not create risk)

3. Being very short (under five feet tall, to be specific) and small in size of frame

But many women who live with risks such as these have no problems at all with their pregnancies. This is especially true of women who have only one risk factor, but it is even true of women with more than one. Being "at risk" means only that there is a higher than usual chance of having problems; it does *not* mean a certainty. The distinction is important for all risks to pregnancy, including those we discuss in the following sections.

Maternal Age and Teenage Pregnancy

Healthy women over age thirty-five are not at significantly greater risk for complications during pregnancy than younger women, although they are at greater risk for Down syndrome and infertility (ACOG, 1990). Very young mothers, especially those in their early teens, however, are at significantly greater risk of having low-birth-weight infants, stillbirths, or problems during delivery. They also have higher rates of neurological defects and are more likely to die during their first year. They are also more likely to encounter developmental problems during their preschool and school years. This is partly because teenage mothers have not completed their own growth, so their bodies are unable to meet the extra nutritional demands of a developing fetus. Teenage mothers are more likely to be poor and less likely to get adequate prenatal care and to have the maturity of judgment to adapt their lifestyles to the demands of pregnancy (Coley & Chase-Lansdale, 1998; Fraser et al., 1995; Furstenberg et al., 1989).

The United States has the highest rate of teenage pregnancy of all industrialized countries. The direct cause of teenage pregnancy is the failure to use effective and consistent methods of birth control. For many teens who become pregnant, the prospect of having a baby of their own represents one of the few routes available to feel needed and loved and to achieve adult status. In contrast, their families, schools, and neighborhoods may provide little opportunity to achieve these things. Teenage pregnancy and its prevention are discussed more fully in Chapter 16.

Domestic Violence

Domestic violence poses another serious hazard for pregnant women and their babies. Studies of prenatal clinic patients report that between 7 and 8 percent of pregnant women are beaten by their partners, and that women who are battered have twice as many miscarriages as women who are not. While 87.5 percent of pregnant women who are battered had been abused before, it is estimated that 1 percent of all pregnant women with no history of being battered will be abused during pregnancy (Helton et al., 1987). These rates probably are actually higher, since poor and teenage mothers, who are at greatest risk for abuse, are less likely to receive prenatal care or to be included in such studies. Abuse during pregnancy is correlated with unemployment, substance abuse, poverty, and family dysfunction, making it difficult to determine the relative contribution of each of these risks (Herzberger, 1996).

Four factors appear to play a particularly strong role in the battering of pregnant women. First, in high-risk families, the stresses associated with pregnancy and the transition to parenthood may combine with already high levels of stress and family dysfunction to precipitate violence. Second, violence toward a pregnant woman may be intended to hurt the baby or terminate an unwanted pregnancy. Adults who themselves were abused as children may see violence as a normal part of family life, another factor that may contribute to the battering of pregnant women, especially in households that view abortion as unacceptable. Finally, the physical condition of pregnancy makes pregnant women less able to protect themselves, and concern for their babies' safety may place them at risk because of the anger it may stimulate in a jealous partner. Strategies to prevent violence against pregnant women include programs to reduce the stresses of an unwanted pregnancy, planned parenthood programs, dissemination of birth control, and the availability of safe, legal abortions. In addition, prenatal education that prepares men and women for the changes and challenges associated with pregnancy, childbirth, and parenthood can help. Finally, informal and formal support and intervention programs for at-risk families or families already experiencing battering can reduce or prevent this problem (Beveridge, 1993; Herzberger, 1996).

Prenatal Health Care

Adequate early prenatal care is critical to infant and maternal health, and mothers who begin prenatal care early in pregnancy have improved pregnancy and newborn outcomes, including decreased risk of low birth weight and preterm delivery. The quality of prenatal care is strongly influenced by the woman's life circumstances, with race and economics playing a major role.

How can the prenatal care of high-risk mothers be improved? The *Prenatal/ Early Infancy Project* conducted by David Olds and his colleagues is one promising answer to this question (Olds, 1997). The program was designed to improve low-income women's prenatal health habits, infant caregiving skills, use of informal social support and community services, and educational and occupational achievement. Beginning in the second trimester of pregnancy, nurses established helping relationships with the women through regular home visits. They provided education about diet and weight gain; the effects of cigarettes, alcohol, and drugs; signs of pregnancy complication; the importance of regular rest, exercise, and personal hygiene; preparation for labor and delivery and early care of the newborn; effective use of the health care system; planning for subsequent pregnancies; returning to school; and finding employment. Nurses also educated mothers about early infant temperament and how to promote infants' social, emotional, and cognitive development. Finally, nurses helped mothers to expand their informal support network to include husbands, boyfriends, and other family and friends and to develop reliable, ongoing relationships with their pediatricians and other health and human service providers. Participation in the program lasted for two years, and a follow-up study was conducted when the children were four years old.

Pregnant women who participated in the program made more use of formal services, experienced greater informal social support, improved their diets more, and reduced the number of cigarettes smoked compared to similar women not in the program. Very young teenagers in the program showed a significant improvement in their babies' birth weights, and smokers showed a 75 percent reduction in preterm deliveries. After delivery, these women displayed higher levels of infant and child care and made better use of health and social services. There was also a 75 percent reduction in verified cases of child abuse and neglect and a 42 percent decrease in subsequent pregnancies among poor, unmarried women in the program (Olds, 1997).

Diet and Nutrition   For mothers with poor diets, rates of prematurity and infant mortality are higher, birth weights are lower, and the risk of congenital malformations increases. Nutritionally deprived infants are less responsive to environmental stimulation and are irritable when aroused. Malnourished infants are found to have a significantly reduced number of brain cells, especially when the malnutrition occurred during the last trimester or during the first three months following birth (Lozoff, 1989). Each year in the United States, between 80,000 and 120,000 infants are born with serious malnutrition. The federally sponsored *Special Supplemental Food Program for Women, Infants, and Children (WIC)* provides foods such as milk and cheese to about 60 percent of poor and low-income women; however, due to inadequate funding, only 60 percent of those eligible receive this help (ACOG, 1990; Children's Defense Fund, 1995).

Recent research conducted by Larry Brown and Ernesto Pollitt (1996) in Guatemala found that when poor mothers and their infants regularly received a nutritious food supplement called *Atole* (a hot soup made from maize, a local grain), the rate of infant mortality decreased by 69 percent compared to a similar group of mothers and infants receiving a less nutritious supplement called *Fresco*. The children who received Atole displayed significantly greater gains in motor skills, physical growth, and social and emotional development than the children who received

WORKING WITH

Katie Glover, OB-GYN Nurse Practitioner

Preparing for Childbirth

Katie Glover was interviewed in her office at the primary health care clinic where she works. Despite her hectic schedule, Katie has a relaxed and unhurried manner. She has a three-year-old son and is currently seven months pregnant. Our interview focused on preparation for childbirth.

Rob: *What advice do you give pregnant women about their nutrition?*

Katie: Pregnant women need three to four glasses of milk a day and should increase consumption of fruits and vegetables, which many people don't eat regularly. As a bottom line, we recommend a balanced diet plus a few extra calories and vitamin supplements. We also recommend a twenty-five-to-thirty-pound weight gain over the course of a pregnancy, depending on the woman's size, build, and weight.

Rob: *Why do you recommend weight gain?*

Katie: If you figure the average baby weighs roughly 6½ to 7½ pounds and the average placenta weighs maybe 3 to 5 pounds, and add the extra fluid a woman retains and extra subcutaneous fat her body stores as added protection, that's about twenty to twenty-five pounds right there.

Rob: *How do weight gain and other changes of pregnancy affect women?*

Katie: They certainly change their body image. How a woman feels about that directly relates to how she feels about being pregnant. Someone who's thrilled about pregnancy will be happy to see her belly getting bigger. Someone who resents the pregnancy is likely to have a harder time with her body's changes. It's not just that her breasts are getting larger or her stomach is getting bigger. She can't run up and

down the stairs as easily, and she can't find a comfortable position to sleep in. Pregnancy gets in the way of your life. You have to alter how you move and how you eat and how often you go to the bathroom—day and night. When all you really want is a good eight hours of sleep, you may start wondering if it's all worth it!

Rob: *Pregnancy can be stressful, then.*

Katie: Yes. In a way, pregnancy is a crisis. How a person copes with that crisis has a lot to do with her feelings about being pregnant as well as what her social and emotional support system is like. If her partner, parents, or friends provide good, solid support and appreciation for what she's experiencing, pregnancy is likely to be a more positive experience than if she doesn't have such support.

Rob: *What preparation for childbirth do you offer your patients?*

Katie: Most medical practices encourage some kind of childbirth classes. Classes typically cover the various stages of pregnancy, physiological and psychological changes a woman might experience, changes in the couple's relationship. We talk about labor and what the hospital will be like. We talk about the different kinds of pain medications that might be offered, their effects, and the risks and benefits. Most classes also teach basic relaxation and breathing techniques, which are very important. Knowing what to expect and how to deal with the anxiety and pain can really help make labor a more positive experience.

Rob: *How do you feel about birth clinics and home deliveries?*

Katie: For many people who don't want to give birth in a hospital, a birth cen-

ter is ideal, whether it's freestanding or directly attached to a hospital. It offers a little more freedom of movement, a little more comfort, a different atmosphere, and reassurance that medical backup is available if needed, including quick transfer to a fully equipped hospital. Of course, parents who come to a birth center should be carefully screened beforehand for any potential medical complications.

Rob: *What about home birth?*

Katie: I think it's a good option for the very small percentage of people who are truly suited for it.

Rob: *Why is that?*

Katie: It takes a very high level of commitment to arrange a home birth. Real problems can arise if it's not something both partners agree on and believe in deeply. If both partners are always there for each other, if the home situation is a nice, clean, supportive place, and if a pediatrician and a well-trained, experienced obstetrician or midwife and good emergency medical backup are available, then go for it!

What Do You Think?

1. Katie suggests that pregnancy is a type of crisis and that how a woman copes with it will depend on her attitudes toward pregnancy and the social support she receives. How might this knowledge be used to design programs to help pregnant teenagers cope better with the "crisis" of pregnancy?

2. How might a woman's pregnancy affect the father and other family members?

3. Katie discusses alternatives to hospital birth. What additional information might you need to consider these alternatives for yourself?

Fresco. A long-term study of adolescents and adults who had been exposed to Atole or Fresco, both prenatally and for at least two years after birth, found that those who had received Atole early in life performed significantly better on academic achievement and general intelligence tests.

Although the effects of moderate undernutrition are likely to be less severe than those of malnutrition, it is still very important that a pregnant woman maintain a diet that provides adequate nutrition for both her baby and herself. Every diet should include proteins, carbohydrates (sugars and starches), fats, vitamins, and minerals selected from the four major food groups: (1) fruits and vegetables; (2) whole-grain or enriched breads and cereals; (3) milk and milk products; and (4) meat, poultry, fish, eggs, nuts, and beans (ACOG, 1990).

What constitutes a nutritious diet during pregnancy? As Katie Glover mentions in the Working With interview on p. 116, pregnant women should increase consumption of fruits, vegetables, and calcium-rich foods and strive to eat a balanced overall diet. Nutritionists also agree that a pregnant woman should eat between two hundred and one thousand calories more per day than she ate before pregnancy, as long as the extra calories consist mainly of carbohydrates and protein. As noted earlier in this chapter, experts now recommend that women of normal weight before pregnancy gain about thirty pounds, women who are obese around twenty pounds, and women who are underweight about thirty-four pounds, with the exact amount reflecting their height and prepregnancy weight.

Pregnant women are also advised to get extra calcium (usually by drinking milk) to provide for the growing bones of the fetus and sometimes for breast feeding, and also to use multiple vitamin and mineral supplements. Currently folic acid is commercially added to foods such as flours to reduce birth defects such as *spina bifida,* which may result from a dietary shortage of that nutrient. It is especially important that low-income women who have had a poor prepregnancy diet obtain at least adequate amounts of nutrients during prenatal development. Vitamin balance is also important. Too much of vitamins, such as A, can also cause problems. That's why it's usually better to stick with prescribed multivitamin supplements rather than to self-medicate.

Stress and Health   *Stress* refers to chronic feelings of worry and anxiety. Most mothers (and fathers) feel significant stress simply about having a baby, which is something of a crisis even in the most well-adjusted families. Parents often feel surprised or even shocked at the news of pregnancy, even if they have planned to have a child. Later they may worry about whether the baby will be normal, whether they really can afford to have it, and whether they are psychologically ready to be parents. These feelings are all stressful, but when kept within reasonable bounds, they are quite normal and cause no long-run damage to the baby.

Women who experience severe and prolonged anxiety just before or during pregnancy, however, are more likely to have medical complications and to give birth to infants with abnormalities than women who do not. Emotional stress has been associated with greater incidence of spontaneous abortion, difficult labor, premature birth and low birth weight, newborn respiratory difficulties, and physical deformities. Maternal stress and anxiety during late pregnancy have been associated with newborns who are hyperactive, irritable, and irregular in their feeding, sleeping, and elimination, but this is probably due to the mothers' continuing anxiety after childbirth (Glover, 1997; Lou et al., 1994). Although these findings suggest that maternal stress is associated with certain difficulties, no causal relationship between maternal stress and infant problems has yet been established.

WHAT DO YOU THINK?   If good prenatal diet and health care are so closely related to healthy prenatal and postnatal development, why don't all expectant mothers follow nutritious diets and receive good health care? How can adequate health care be made available to all pregnant women?

Birth

After thirty-eight weeks in the womb, the fetus is considered to be "full term," or ready for birth. At this point it will weigh around 7½ pounds, but it can weigh as little as 5 or as much as 10 pounds and still be physically normal. The fetus measures about twenty inches or so at this stage, almost one-third of its final height as an adult.

During the last weeks, the womb becomes so crowded that the fetus assumes one position more or less permanently. This orientation is sometimes called *fetal presentation*. **Fetal presentation** (or *orientation*) refers to the body part of the fetus that is closest to the mother's cervix. The most common fetal presentation, and the most desirable one medically, is head pointing downward (called a *cephalic presentation*). Two other presentations also occur: feet and rump first (*breech presentation*) or shoulders first (*transverse presentation*). These two orientations used to jeopardize an infant's survival, but modern obstetric techniques have greatly reduced their risk.

• • •

fetal presentation Refers to the body part of the fetus that is closest to the mother's cervix; may be head first (cephalic), feet and rump first (breech), or shoulders first (transverse).

• • • • • • • • • • • • • • • • • •

FIGURE 4.4

The Process of Delivery

(a) Before labor begins; (b) during the first stage of labor; (c) crowning, during the second stage of labor; (d) emergence of the head, near the end of the second stage of labor; (e) expulsion of the afterbirth.

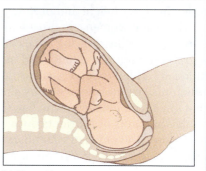

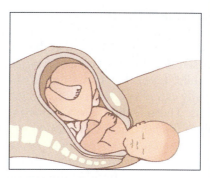
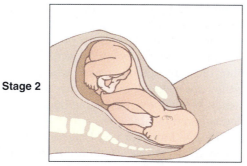

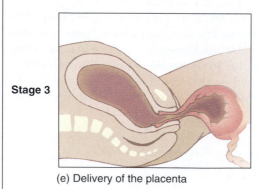

Stage 1

(a) Dilation and effacement of the cervix   (b) Transition

Stage 2

(c) Pushing   (d) Birth of the baby

Stage 3

(e) Delivery of the placenta

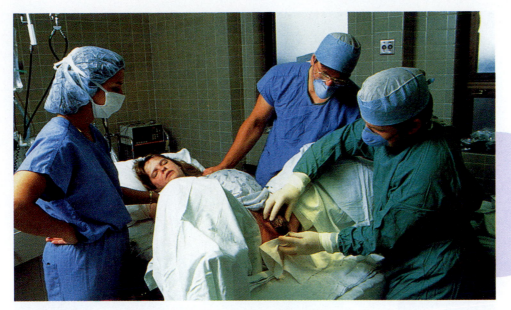

Crowning—when the baby's head can first be seen at the opening of the vagina—marks the beginning of the second stage of labor.

Although parents and doctors often dearly wish they could predict the exact moment of the onset of labor, so far no one has been able to do so. However, several theories have been suggested to explain why labor begins when it does. It may be that the uterus becomes stretched beyond some natural limit and as a result evacuates itself, rather as an overly full intestine does. Or perhaps certain hormones in the fetus combine with hormones in the mother (in particular, *oxytocin*) to initiate the process; the combination may reach some crucial concentration or balance. If so, then to some extent the fetus tells the mother when it is ready.

Most fetuses develop normally for the usual thirty-eight to forty weeks and face their birth relatively well prepared. When the labor process begins, it too usually proceeds normally. The uterus contracts rhythmically and automatically to force the baby downward through the vaginal canal (see Figure 4.4). The contractions occur in a relatively predictable sequence of stages, and as long as the baby and mother are healthy and the mother's pelvis is large enough, the baby usually is out within a matter of hours.

Stages of Labor

It is common for the mother to experience "false labor," or *Braxton-Hicks contractions*, in the last weeks of pregnancy as the uterus "practices" contracting and relaxing in preparation for actual labor. These contractions do not open the cervix as real labor contractions do.

Labor consists of three stages. The **first stage of labor** is the longest; it lasts from the first true contraction until the cervix (the opening of the uterus) is completely open, or *dilated* to 10 centimeters (4.5 inches), which is the usual U.S. standard for full dilation. It usually begins with relatively mild and irregular contractions of the uterus. As contractions become stronger, more regular, and more frequent, *dilation*, or widening, of the cervix increases until there is enough room for the baby's head to fit through. As it stretches and dilates, the cervix also becomes thinner, a process referred to as *effacement*.

Toward the end of this first stage of labor, which may take from eight to twenty-four hours for a first-time mother, a **period of transition** begins. The cervix approaches full dilation, contractions become more rapid, and the baby's head begins to move into the birth canal. Although this period generally lasts for only a few minutes, it can be the most intense and challenging one because contractions become

* * *

first stage of labor In childbirth, the stage that begins with relatively mild and irregular contractions of the uterus. As contractions grow stronger, the cervix dilates enough for the baby's head to begin fitting through. May take from eight to twenty-four hours for a first-time mother.

period of transition A very brief period between the first and second stages of labor during which the cervix approaches full dilation, contractions become more rapid and intense, and the baby's head moves into the birth canal.

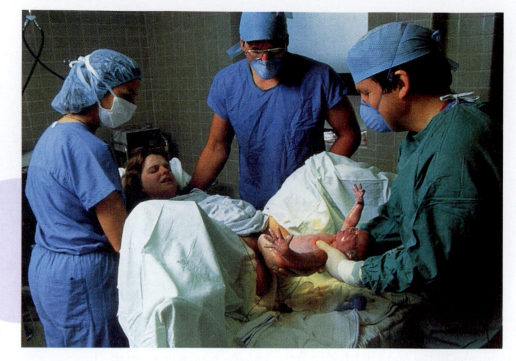

After a few additional pushes by the mother, the head emerges, followed shortly thereafter by the newborn's shoulders, chest, legs, and feet.

stronger and more deeply felt, lasting from forty-five to ninety seconds each. Managing each contraction involves a great deal of concentration and energy; women typically use the period between contractions to catch their breath and prepare for the next contraction. During transition, a woman often experiences a variety of physical changes, including trembling, shaking, leg cramps, nausea, back and hip pain, burping, and perspiring, and tends to be preoccupied with feelings of pain, pressure, and hoped-for relief (McKay, 1993).

The **second stage of labor** ranges from complete dilation of the cervix to birth. Contractions continue, but may be somewhat shorter, lasting forty-five to sixty seconds. Although the baby now has only a few more inches to move down the vagina to be born, the process can be slow, usually lasting between one and two hours for a first baby and less than a half-hour for women who have previously given birth. Although dilation is complete, for most women the reflexive urge to push the baby out by bearing down full strength usually develops toward the end of this stage, and often becomes irresistible. When a woman first begins to push, she may be uncoordinated and need to learn to push "with" the contraction and rest in between. How hard she pushes will depend on the strength of the contractions, which varies throughout labor. If a woman doesn't feel the urge to push, guidance from a partner can help, particularly if she had an epidural block or other local anesthetic that interferes with her bearing-down reflex.

During the **third stage of labor,** which lasts between five and twenty minutes, the afterbirth, which consists of placenta and umbilical cord, is expelled. Contractions still occur but are much weaker, and the woman may have to push several times to deliver the placenta. The medication oxytocin is frequently given to help the placenta to detach from the side of the uterus. Putting the baby to the mother's breast also can help, because stimulation of the nipple naturally releases oxytocin (McKay, 1993).

Childbirth Settings and Methods

Until the 1800s, births in the United States generally took place in the woman's home. Usually it was attended by midwives, friends, neighbors, and family mem-

• • •

second stage of labor The period of labor that starts with "crowning," the first moment the baby's head can be seen, and ends with the baby's birth; usually lasts between sixty and ninety minutes.

third stage of labor The final stage of labor, in which the afterbirth (placenta and umbilical cord) is expelled; normally lasts only a few minutes.

bers, and was viewed as a natural process rather than as a medical procedure. The **midwife** was a woman experienced in pregnancy and childbirth who traditionally served as the primary caregiver during pregnancy, childbirth, and the month or so following birth. During the 1800s, political and social factors and the emergence of medicine as a scientifically based and politically powerful profession led to the replacement of midwives by physicians as the chief birth attendants. In the 1900s, delivery was moved to the hospital, where it was increasingly treated as a medical rather than a naturally occurring community event (Bogdon, 1993; Steiger, 1993).

These changes brought the benefits of modern medical technology to the birth process and resulted in decreased mortality rates for mothers and their babies, particularly in the case of high-risk pregnancies. However, they also shifted the birth process from being a natural event controlled by the pregnant woman, her family, her friends, and the community to a medical event controlled by physicians. As a result, all babies and their mothers were exposed to the risks associated with hospital-based medical procedures, including overreliance on medication and on procedures such as episiotomies and caesarian sections (discussed a bit later).

Hospital Births   Currently more than 90 percent of all births in the United States occur in hospitals under the supervision of a physician. Until recently, a typical hospital birth called for a sterilized, clinical delivery room full of bright lights and imposing equipment and attended mostly by comparative strangers, the doctors and nurses. In recent years, the maternity wards of many hospitals have modified their environments to be more comfortable and supportive of pregnant women and their families. A growing number of hospitals now have *birthing rooms* with more comfortable furniture, muted colors and lighting, and soft music, and facilities for *rooming in* that allow mother and baby to stay together until both are ready to leave the hospital. Most hospitals now allow a partner to be present during the delivery, a practice that was rarely allowed just two decades ago. Nurse-midwives currently assist in only 5 percent of all births. This is due primarily to political and legal obstacles to practicing, which include issues of licensing, third-party reimbursement, malpractice insurance, and resistance from obstetrician-gynecologists who currently control access to medically supervised births, rather than to lack of adequate training (Steiger, 1993).

Nonhospital Settings   **Freestanding birth centers (FBCs)** are nonhospital facilities organized to provide family-centered maternity care for women who are

• • •

midwife A woman experienced in pregnancy and childbirth who traditionally served as the primary caregiver during pregnancy, childbirth, and the month or two following delivery.

freestanding birth center (FBC) Nonhospital facilities organized to provide family-centered maternity care for women who are at low risk for obstetrical complications.

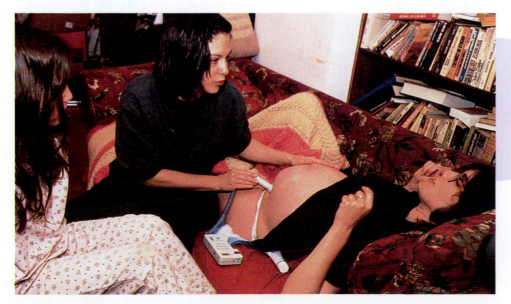

A nurse/midwife is assisting this mother with a home birth.

judged to be at low risk for obstetrical complications. Approximately 240 centers currently operate in both urban and rural areas as for-profit and nonprofit medical centers and office practices run by nurse-midwives, physicians, investors, and other individuals. Equipped and staffed to handle all but the most serious medical emergencies and designed like simple but comfortable hotels, birth centers encourage the active involvement of the mother, her family, and her friends in a birth process that minimizes technical intervention deemed to be medically unnecessary and physiologically and psychologically stressful in low-risk deliveries (Eakins, 1993).

Recent large-scale studies concluded that low-risk women delivering at freestanding birth centers are no more likely to have poor birth outcomes than are low-risk women delivering in hospitals. Birth centers were much less likely to employ *caesarean section* (surgical delivery) than were hospitals with patients of similar risk, and had very low neonatal and maternal mortality rates. Almost all major health insurance companies now cover birth center delivery, which is about one-third the cost of a normal hospital birth due to the type of facility used, the use of nurse-midwives rather than obstetrician-gynecologists, and the reduced need for certain costly medical equipment (Eakins, 1989, 1993; Rooks et al., 1989).

Home birth is another alternative to hospital birth available for low-risk pregnancies. In a typical home birth, normal daily activities continue through the first stage of labor. When contractions increase, the nurse-midwife or physician is called to monitor the labor. Backup arrangements with a doctor or hospital generally are in place should they be needed, and women planning on home birth are carefully screened to minimize last-minute complications requiring hospital equipment or procedures. In addition to the widely held view that hospitals are the place of choice for birth, difficulty in obtaining malpractice insurance and resistance by the medical profession are major barriers to widespread acceptance of home birth.

Prepared Childbirth   In the past two decades or so, the majority of hospitals and nonhospital birth settings have offered programs to help women and their partners prepare for the physical and psychological experience of birth. These include preparatory visits to the hospital or birth facility, where pregnant women and their partners can become familiar with the physical setting and procedures. Various methods of **prepared childbirth** have been devised to help parents rehearse, or simulate, the actual sensations of labor well before the projected delivery date. Although these methods differ from one another in certain details, all generally emphasize educational, physical, and emotional preparation for the birth process and active involvement of the mother and father (or other partner). Typically they encourage the mother to find a coach (often her spouse or a relative) to give her personal support during labor (Lamaze, 1970; Livingston, 1993a, 1993b, 1993c).

The earliest proponent of prepared or "natural" childbirth was Grantly Dick-Read, an English physician who believed that the pain women experience during childbirth is not natural but due to a combination of fear and tension caused by cultural ignorance of the birth process and by the isolation and lack of emotional and social support women receive during labor and in hospital delivery rooms (Livingston, 1993a). The Read method consisted of educating women about the anatomy and physiology of labor and training them in progressive relaxation techniques to reduce tension, fatigue, and pain. Read also encouraged obstetricians and nurses to be more patient and to rely less heavily on medication in the birth process.

Currently the most widely used approach to prepared childbirth in the United States is the Lamaze method, which was originated in the Soviet Union; brought to France in the 1950s by Fernand Lamaze, the head of a maternity hospital; and then popularized in the United States by Marjorie Karmel, an American who had given birth to her first child at Lamaze's hospital in France and wanted to use the method for the birth of her second child in the United States. The Lamaze method differs from the Read approach in that it strongly encourages the active participation of *both* mother and father (or labor partner) during the weeks preceding delivery it-

• • •
prepared childbirth A method of childbirth in which parents have rehearsed or simulated the actual sensations of labor and delivery well before the actual delivery date.

Pregnant women and their "birth coaches" attend a Lamaze birth class to help them prepare for the experience of childbirth.

self (Livingston, 1993b). The Lamaze method encourages labor either without drugs or with minimal drugs, and stresses the importance of birth as a shared emotional experience.

Another widely used method of natural childbirth was introduced by Robert Bradley, an American obstetrician who modified Read's technique. Bradley's husband-coached childbirth method stresses the importance of the father as comforter, supporter, and caregiver before and during the delivery. Bradley also emphasizes relaxation and controlled breathing in a calm, quiet, physically comfortable environment (Livingston, 1993c).

Women who have participated in prepared childbirth also report more favorable attitudes toward labor and delivery, decreased stress during the birth process, and more sensitive interaction with the newborn baby (Lindell, 1988). Not only the mother benefits from the Lamaze or similar methods. A father's involvement in preparing for delivery and in the delivery process itself has been found to positively influence his experience of birth, his behavior toward mother and baby during delivery, and his relationship to his new infant (M. Hoffnung, 1992; Markman & Kadushin, 1986).

Modern Midwives and Doulas   Throughout human history and around the world, midwives have helped other women to give birth. Today midwives in the United States are trained and licensed to give care and advice to women during pregnancy, labor, and the postpartum period, to conduct deliveries, and to care for newborn infants. Midwives also provide counseling and education not only to women giving birth but to the families and communities as well, providing prenatal education and preparation for parenthood, family planning, and child care (Davis, 1987; Steiger, 1993).

Two kinds of midwives practice in the United States. *Direct-entry midwives (DEMs)* are self-trained or have learned midwifery skills through apprenticeship to individual practicing midwives. *Certified nurse-midwives (CNMs)* are registered nurses (RNs) with additional hospital and academic training in obstetrics. Direct-entry midwives practice mainly at home births and at privately run, freestanding birth centers, but generally are not licensed to assist in hospital deliveries. Certified nurse-midwives are licensed to practice in a wide variety of settings, including hospitals, freestanding birth centers, and home births, and generally work under the supervision of a physician. Midwives historically have played an important role in poor, rural areas, particularly in the South, where a long-standing tradition of midwife-assisted births exists among African American women who were denied access to medical care through segregation and economic discrimination. In 1990, midwives assisted about 5 percent of all births in the United States (Holmes, 1993; Steiger, 1993).

The term *doula* applies to an individual who cares for the new mother, especially when breast feeding begins. Like midwives, doulas have helped with the birth process around the world since the beginning of human history. Doulas do not deliver babies, but they may assist a mother and midwife in the process. Depending on the culture, the role of doula may be filled by one or more relatives or friends or, at times, by a midwife. The use of doulas has increased in the United States over the last decade. Research suggests that women who receive social and emotional support from doulas have shorter labors, have fewer labor and delivery complications and fewer caesareans, and appear better able to cope with the demands of motherhood (Gilbert, 1998; Raphael, 1993).

Medicinal Methods During Delivery   Despite adequate psychological preparation, most mothers feel some pain during labor contractions. Under good conditions, many mothers can endure this pain until the baby is delivered. But conditions are not always good: sometimes labor takes an unusually long time, and sometimes a mother finds herself less prepared than she thought. In such cases, pain-reducing drugs such as narcotics or other sedatives can make the experience bearable. But such medications must be used cautiously. Most pain relievers cross the placenta and therefore can seriously depress the fetus if given at the wrong time or in improper amounts.

During the final stages of delivery, two other forms of pain relief are available. Doctors may inject a sedative into the base of the woman's spine. The two most

---

TABLE 4.4   Major Medications During Childbirth and Their Effects on the Baby

Type	Administration	Positive Effects for Mother	Negative Effects for Baby
Analgesics	By injection (in controlled doses) during the first stage of labor to reduce pain	Reduces pain, causes some drowsiness and euphoria (sense of well-being and tranquility); women participate in labor and delivery	May cause drowsiness and decreased responsiveness for first few hours after birth or longer; naloxone hydrochloride (Narcon) can be used to reverse these effects
Local anesthesia			
Spinal	By injection into spinal canal in controlled doses when cervix is fully dilated (beginning of second stage of labor); numbs sensory and motor nerves so that mother's pelvic area and legs cannot move voluntarily	Mother can remain awake and aware during labor and delivery; can be used for either vaginal or caesarean birth; is highly effective in eliminating pain	No negative effects reported
Epidural	By injection during active phase of first stage of labor to numb sensory nerves after their exit from spinal canal	Pain and sensations are generally eliminated; mother is awake; some voluntary movement is preserved, although it is less effective because a woman's sense of position and tension are blocked by the medication	No negative effects reported
General anesthesia	A mixture of nitrous oxide and oxygen is inhaled; is less commonly used than blocking agents	Easily administered, rapid onset of effect; anesthetic of choice in emergencies in which time is critical and baby must be delivered quickly	Decreased alertness and responsiveness following birth

Source: Feinbloom & Forman (1987).

common of these procedures are an *epidural* and a *spinal.* They allow the mother to remain awake and alert during the final stages of labor, but unfortunately they also prevent her from controlling her contractions, a capability that normally is quite helpful when the baby is finally expelled. Nitrous oxide, which dentists commonly use, also has been used to take the edge off the pain of the peak contractions while allowing the mother to remain conscious.

Giving a mother either a general or a local anesthetic before delivery removes all pain, of course, but both mother and child may take a long time to recover from it. Mothers who receive general anesthetics for delivery stay in the hospital for more days after delivery, on the average, than do mothers who receive other kinds of medication. This is partly because it takes several days for them to recover from the medication (Hamilton, 1984). In addition, the bonding between mother and child is delayed while both are recovering from the effect of anesthesia. Table 4.4 lists the major types of medications used during labor and delivery, their administration, and their effects (Feinbloom & Forman, 1987).

Perceptions of Pain During Childbirth   An important issue in modern childbirth involves decisions about whether and when medication should be used to manage the discomfort and pain often associated with the birth process. Professionals who assist women in deliveries find it difficult to determine how much discomfort or distress a laboring woman is in and how to respond appropriately. Cultural differences in how pain or discomfort is experienced and expressed also complicate such assessments.

To better understand cultural differences in perceptions of pain related to childbirth, Janice Morse and Caroline Park studied expectant parents from four cultural groups living in western Canada: English-speaking Canadians, Ukrainians, Hutterites, and East Indians (Morse & Park, 1988). These parents, who were about to have hospital deliveries, were asked to compare the pain of childbirth with eight other painful events: heart attack, kidney stone, severe burn, toothache, gallstones, eye injury, broken bone, and migraine. Figure 4.5 shows the mean pain ratings of women and men from each cultural group.

The Canadian parents expected the most pain. Like most middle-class Americans, they planned to use a variety of nonmedicinal methods to prepare for it. However, they also knew that if labor became too uncomfortable, they would be offered medications to relieve the pain. The East Indian parents were next highest in expected pain. The emphasis on purity and innocence in East Indian culture means females are not taught directly about the process of birth. During labor, East Indian women frequently expressed their discomfort by vocalizing (crying, yelling, or complaining) continually.

The Hutterite parents anticipated considerably less pain. Hutterites live in a collection of religious and agricultural communities that reject technology and maintain strict traditional and patriarchal customs and values that rigidly restrict women to the maternal role. Contraception is not allowed unless maternal health is threatened, and family size averages 10.4 children. During pregnancy there is no change in a woman's work role or diet, and the discomfort of childbirth is viewed as God's will. The Ukrainian parents reported the lowest overall ratings of discomfort during childbirth. Ukrainians are also an agricultural community with strong religious values, but are more flexible regarding the use of contraception and the roles of women. Deliveries for both the Hutterite and Ukrainian parents were relatively calm and unemotional, with the women dealing with their discomfort in a quiet and uncomplaining manner.

Morse and Park note that the two cultures that rate childbirth discomfort the highest (Canadians and East Indians) do not consider childbirth to be a natural event, as reflected in the medicalization of childbirth in Canadian culture and the withholding of information about birth in East Indian culture. On the other hand, the Hutterite and Ukrainian cultures consider childbirth to be a natural event that

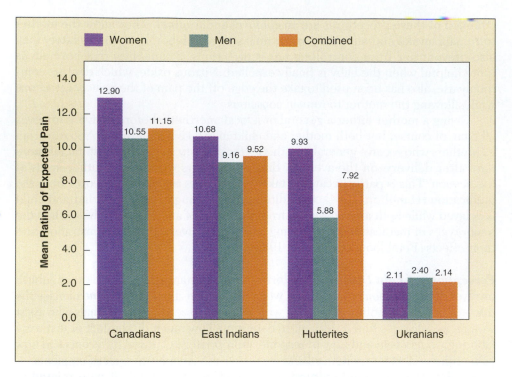

FIGURE 4.5

Differences in Mean Ratings of Expected Pain During Childbirth among Four Cultural Groups

As the bar graphs show, Canadian parents expected the most pain, followed by East Indian parents and Hutterite parents. Ukrainian parents anticipated the least pain, with ratings much lower than those for the three other groups.
Source: Morse & Park (1988).

need not be extensively managed or purposefully ignored. Whatever their causes, such differences in cultural expectations may affect the amount of distress actually experienced during labor and delivery. It is important that they be considered by professionals and others involved in the labor and delivery processes.

Problems During Labor and Delivery

Interference with labor and delivery can occur in three ways: through *faulty power* in the uterus, a *faulty passageway* (the birth canal), or a *faulty passenger* (the baby itself). These problems actually interconnect in various ways, but it is convenient to distinguish among them (Buckley & Kulb, 1983).

Faulty Power   Sometimes the uterus does not contract strongly enough to make labor progress to a delivery. The problem can occur at the beginning of labor or develop midway through a labor that began quite normally, especially if the mother tires after hours of powerful contractions. In many cases, the doctor can strengthen the contractions by giving the mother an injection of the hormone oxytocin. Such *induced labor* must be monitored carefully, so that the artificial contractions it stimulates do not harm both baby and mother by forcing the baby through the canal before the canal is ready.

In about one in two thousand deliveries, the uterus ruptures because of the power of its contractions (Hamilton, 1984). This condition is quite serious; the mother may bleed to death in just a few moments if she is unattended, and in the process the baby almost always dies. Because uterine rupture occurs somewhat more often among mothers who have previously delivered babies surgically, hospitals used to require such mothers to plan on delivering all future babies by caesarean section (discussed shortly). Recent improvements in surgical techniques, however, have left these mothers with stronger uterine walls. As a result, many doctors now permit mothers to attempt natural labor as long as the hospital staff watches carefully for any signs of rupture. If problems develop, a caesarean section can still be arranged and performed quickly and safely.

Faulty Passageway   Sometimes the placenta partially or completely blocks the cervix and prevents the baby from moving down the birth canal during labor. This condition, called *placenta previa,* occurs late in pregnancy and causes bleeding when the cervix starts to open. Because this bleeding is painless, mothers (and doctors) tend to underestimate its significance. If left untreated, it may leave the fetus somewhat undernourished, because it prevents sufficient blood from reaching it. Sometimes it blocks a normal delivery entirely so that the baby must be delivered by caesarean section.

Even if the placenta implants far enough away from the cervix, it occasionally partly separates from its base against the wall of the womb, a condition called *placenta abruptio.* This condition also causes vaginal bleeding and can be quite painful. As a result, doctors are more likely to detect the problem relatively soon after it occurs. No sure remedy exists, although doctors sometimes advise complete bed rest if they believe substantial portions of the placenta have separated (Hamilton, 1984).

Faulty Passenger   Usually a baby enters the birth canal head first, but occasionally one turns in the wrong direction during contractions. A *breech presentation*—with the bottom leading—is risky for the baby, for its spine can be broken if a contraction presses it too hard against the mother's pelvis. Or the baby may not get enough oxygen because it cannot begin breathing on its own until after its nose comes out. In some cases a skilled midwife or doctor can deliver a breech baby with no problem, but if the baby gets stuck partway out of the vagina, medical staff may use *forceps* to pull it the rest of the way out. In most cases, breech babies are either turned to the right position during delivery or delivered surgically by caesarean section.

A small but significant proportion of babies are simply too big to pass through the mother's pelvis and vaginal canal, a problem sometimes called *cephalopelvic disproportion (CPD)*—literally, a disproportion of the head and pelvis. Extra hours of labor do not help to push such babies through; their heads are too big to fit, although often by only a fraction of an inch. Such a mismatch of size can result from genetic influence, but ironically it also results from an especially healthy, well-nourished pregnancy, which creates an exceptionally large baby. If the mismatch is too severe and threatens the life of mother or child, the doctor may interrupt the labor and deliver the baby surgically.

Caesarean Section   **Caesarean section,** or *C-section,* is a procedure used in cases where the baby cannot be safely delivered through the vagina and therefore has to be removed surgically. Techniques for this surgery have improved substantially over the past decades. The operation now takes only about half an hour, most of which is devoted to sewing the mother up after getting the baby out. Also, the incision is smaller than it used to be (just a few inches), generally oriented horizontally, and located rather low on the mother's abdomen.

Partly because of these improvements, the number of C-sections for live births almost quadrupled between 1970 and 1988. Much of this increase was due to a sharp rise in C-section rates for teenagers and women in their twenties. By the early 1990s the C-section rate leveled off at about one in four births, but many experts and parent advocates are concerned that the rates are still too high and reflect medical practices that are not in the best interests of mothers and their babies (Taffel, 1989, 1993). Recent efforts by commercial managed care and insurance corporations to cut costs by drastically reducing hospital stays (resulting in so-called "drive-by" deliveries) may also be increasing reliance on C-sections, which can be prescheduled for hospital efficiency and are reimbursable as a medical procedure.

Both supporters and critics of caesarean birth agree there are a number of good reasons to select a C-section as the safest way to deliver a baby. These include some of the problems of placenta previa, abruptio placenta, and cephalopelvic disproportion already noted, as well as prolapsed cord, where the umbilical cord cuts off the

* * *

caesarean section A childbirth procedure in which the baby is removed surgically from the mother's abdomen.

baby's oxygen; unusual positions of the baby that make vaginal delivery impossible; severe fetal distress that cannot be corrected; and active herpes, which the baby may contract through vaginal birth.

Selection of a caesarean delivery purely for the convenience of the managed care company or the physician, a previous caesarean delivery (currently the most common reason for doing the procedure), inactive herpes, and suspected cephalo-pelvic disproportion not confirmed by a period of strong, frequent contractions are all no longer accepted as valid reasons for a caesarean delivery. Reasons for considering a vaginal birth after a previous C-section include less risk of surgical complications, shorter recovery time, and the opportunity for greater involvement of the mother in the delivery process (ACOG, 1990).

Fetal Monitoring   Most hospitals use *electronic fetal monitoring* to record uterine contractions and the fetal heart rate. Uterine contractions are externally measured by a pressure gauge strapped to the mother's abdomen that electronically represents changes in the shape of the uterus on graph paper. Fetal heart rate can be picked up by an *external* ultrasound monitor placed on the abdomen over the uterus or *internally* by a wire, leading through the vagina and screwed into the fetus's scalp, that records more subtle electrical changes in the fetus's heart.

Although internal fetal monitoring is extremely helpful in high-risk and emergency situations, experts have questioned its routine use for low-risk deliveries. Because the amniotic membranes must be ruptured to permit attachment of the electrode to the baby's scalp, the very procedure designed to identify the fetus at risk of distress may itself contribute to fetal distress. In addition, the mother must lie in bed for as long as the wires are attached (Feinbloom & Forman, 1987). Experts have also noted that "high-tech" birth imposes psychological burdens as well by shifting the center of focus from the experience of mother and baby to readouts from the equipment. This makes birth a less "human" experience (Davis-Floyd, 1986).

Childbearing with a Disability

Having a baby poses challenges for all parents, but the challenges for men and women who have a disability or chronic illness are even greater. Laura has suffered from multiple sclerosis since she was a teenager. Her wheelchair is her main mode of getting around, although she can walk for short distances with the aid of crutches.

TABLE 4.5   How Professional Caregivers Can Assist Prospective Parents with Disabilities
• Provide accurate and appropriate family planning advice
• Present a realistic picture of risks to prospective parents and their baby prior to conception and refer to genetic counselors or other specialists as needed
• Provide appropriate prenatal care and realistic advice about potential effects of pregnancy on the disability, and vice versa (including the effects of medication on the fetus or on the infant via breast feeding)
• Provide information about appropriate prenatal exercise, options for labor positions, pain relief, and sources of nonmedical support
• Help ensure accessibility of needed equipment and space in labor and postnatal wards
• Discuss child care methods and adaptation of baby equipment as necessary
• Provide appropriate medical care as well as support and encouragement both in labor and postnatally
• Provide information about local and national self-help organizations for expectant parents with disabilities

Source: Adapted from Campion (1993).

When Laura and her husband, Peter, who is not disabled, decided to have a baby, they encountered many of these challenges. For one thing, they faced the widespread misconception that people with disabilities cannot be adequate parents. Paradoxically, they also found that many people expected them to be "superparents," an ideal that few others are expected to meet. They discovered a strong tendency to stereotype all people with disabilities as either heroes or victims. Many people seemed to focus on Laura's disability and thus denied her normalcy. Laura and Peter also found that the prenatal classes, clinics, hospital labor wards, and postnatal wards they visited often were poorly equipped to accommodate individuals with disabilities. Laura would have to negotiate narrow doorways, staircases, high-sided baths that were not wheelchair accessible, beds that couldn't be lowered, and baby cribs and changing tables that couldn't be reached from her wheelchair. Expectant parents with disabilities may also experience anxiety due to lack of information and support and to doubts about the long-term effects of their disabilities on their capacity to meet the new challenges of being parents. Individuals who are deaf or blind may face additional barriers to getting the information they need (Campion, 1993; Shapiro, 1993). Table 4.5 lists ways professional caregivers can help parents with disabilities to cope with the challenges of having a baby.

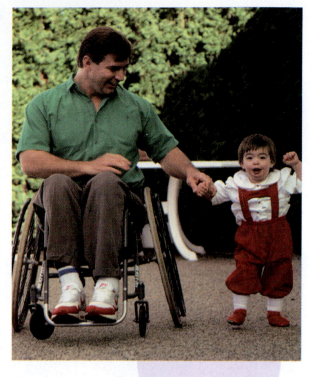

The challenges of parenting with a physical disability clearly have not prevented the father and daughter in this picture from taking delight in her newly developing ability to walk.

Low-Birth-Weight Infants

The average weight of a full-term newborn infant is about 7.5 pounds (3,400 grams). **Low-birth-weight** infants, in contrast, weigh 5.5 pounds or less at birth. These babies account for between 6 and 7 percent of all births in the United States. The incidence of low birth weight varies widely among developed and underdeveloped countries, due largely to differences in rates of poverty, famine, and malnutrition. Percentages of low-birth-weight infants range from 50 percent in Bangladesh; 20 percent in the Philippines; less than 5 percent in France, Japan, New Zealand, and Australia; and less than 4 percent in Sweden, Finland, Netherlands, and Norway (Grant, 1986; Sen, 1993).

The majority of low-birth-weight infants are also preterm. *Preterm* (commonly called *premature*) refers to babies who are born three or more weeks early and therefore are immature in their prenatal development compared to babies who have the full thirty-nine weeks to prepare for birth. Preterm babies account for approximately 10 percent of live births in the United States. Some low-birth-weight infants are *small for date*, which refers to infants who are born on time (close to their due dates) but weigh less than the average for babies of the same gestational age.

Low-birth-weight infants generally are at risk for a wide range of developmental, neurological, and health problems, with the risks increasing as birth weight and maturity decrease. If they are *preterm*, they are likely to suffer from *respiratory distress syndrome (RDS)*, a leading cause of death in newborns, and to have more abnormalities in physical growth, motor behavior, neurological functioning, and intellectual development than full-term babies. Small-for-date infants are at somewhat greater risk than other low-birth-weight infants, having higher rates of death, susceptibility to illness, and neurological problems during their first year and greater developmental difficulties than preterm infants as they get older (Teberg et al., 1988). One promising program to prevent low-birth-weight pregnancies was discussed earlier in the chapter, and additional coverage of this topic appears in Chapter 5.

• • •

low birth weight A birth weight of less than 2,500 grams (about 5½ pounds).

Birth is a family event. Involving children in the preparation for birth can play a very important role in helping them adjust to the changes.

Birth and the Family

The arrival of a new baby can be particularly difficult for parents who lack the economic resources and social and emotional support that are so important in adjusting to the complicated demands of caring for a new baby. Having a baby that is low birth weight can be particularly traumatic. Though it is unwise to generalize too broadly, adolescent parents, single parents, and parents who are educationally and economically disadvantaged are more likely to find parenthood difficult.

Nevertheless, the great majority of births in this country occur without significant problems and to families whose economic, social, and psychological resources enable them to become effective parents. For women (and their partners) who receive good preparation and training for the birth process and obtain adequate social and emotional support from family, friends, and culture, birth is likely to be a very positive and welcome event. For most families, the arrival of a new baby brings many changes that take some time to adjust to. For first-time parents, learning to care for a new baby and rearranging family schedules to be able to provide the almost constant attention a newborn requires are very big challenges, to say the least.

For parents who already have children, a newcomer to the family also creates stresses. Children naturally worry they will lose their special place in the family and the exclusive attention they enjoy once the newcomer arrives. Involving the child in the preparation for birth, for the period when the mother is in the hospital, and for the changes that will occur with the new arrival are all important ways to help a child adjust to the changes. Talking to the child about these things and listening carefully to his questions and concerns are particularly important. Especially with preschoolers, providing concrete information about birth, newborn babies and what they are like, and the specific changes that will occur in the family before and after the baby's birth can help to allay their fears.

After the new baby arrives home, parents can do a number of things to assist the adjustment process. Giving the older child lots of verbal reassurance helps, but concrete actions speak louder than words. One strategy is to give the child an important role in the event by providing special activities, asking friends and family members to bring a gift for the child as well as for the new baby, and including the child in daily activities with the new infant. High priority should also be placed on continuing routine activities with the older child and ensuring that each parent spends lots of special time just with her.

WHAT DO YOU THINK? How might the process of birth vary depending on a family's circumstances such as age, marital status, income, race, and culture? To explore this question, have yourself and several classmates play the roles of expectant parents from different life circumstances. What did you discover?

From Biological to Psychological Development

The process of prenatal development presents a contradictory picture. On the one hand, it seems highly predictable and insensitive to the influences that might change its course. Starting from a single cell, the process rapidly unfolds and develops in an increasingly complex sequence of interrelated patterns of change, all of which have become highly canalized over the thousands of years of human evolution. It is as though from the moment of conception, the emergence of the newborn baby nine months later were never in doubt. Although deviations from these normal developmental pathways occur, they are not genuine departures from normal prenatal development; rather, they seem to further emphasize the predictability of most embryos and fetuses.

On the other hand, although birth marks the end of prenatal development, it is only the beginning of the incredible range of developmental changes that follow—changes that are much less canalized or predictable. The fact that biology seems to lose its hold on the child once she or he emerges from the womb and the environment and experience take over may be overwhelming to a new parent. Nevertheless, as we discover in the chapters that follow, biology and experience remain too closely intertwined to be sharply distinguishable from each other. The path a child's development takes will be only partly determined by the child's experiences, including the efforts of the parents.

Summary of Major Ideas

Stages of Prenatal Development

1. Prenatal development begins with conception, in which a zygote is created by the union of a sperm cell from the father and an egg cell, or ovum, from the mother.

2. Prenatal development consists of discrete periods, or stages.

3. The germinal stage occurs during the first two weeks following conception; the zygote forms a blastocyst, which differentiates into three distinct cell layers and then implants itself in the uterine wall to form the embryo.

4. During the embryonic stage, which lasts from the third through eighth weeks of pregnancy, the placenta and umbilical cord form and the basic organs and biological systems begin to develop.

5. During the fetal stage, which lasts from the ninth week until the end of pregnancy, all physical features complete their development.

6. The experience of pregnancy includes dramatic changes in a woman's physical functioning and appearance, as well as significant psychological changes, as prospective mothers and fathers anticipate the birth of a baby.

7. Infertility is the inability to conceive or carry a pregnancy to term after one year of unprotected intercourse. Family planning allows people to decide on the number and spacing of their children. Methods of contraception allow families to voluntarily prevent unintended pregnancy. Abortion is used to terminate pregnancy.

Prenatal Influences on the Child

8. Although prenatal development is highly canalized, or directed, there are critical periods (particularly during the first trimester) when embryonic development is highly vulnerable or at risk to disruption from teratogens.

9. Teratogens are substances or other environmental influences that can permanently disrupt and damage an embryo's growth. Their effects depend on the timing, intensity, and duration of exposure, the presence of other risks, and the biological vulnerability of baby and mother.

10. Risk factors for prenatal development include medicinal drugs such as thalidomide and DES and nonmedicinal drugs such as heroin, cocaine, alcohol, and tobacco. These also can have teratogenic effects on prenatal development.

11. Diseases such as rubella, syphilis, genital herpes, and AIDS are also teratogens that can irreversibly harm the embryo or fetus, particularly during critical periods of development.

12. Environmental hazards such as radiation or industrial pollution can harm the developing embryo or fetus.

13. The risk of domestic violence increases during pregnancy and is highest for women who are teenagers and living in impoverished and dysfunctional families and communities.

14. Risk factors for prenatal development are associated with the physical and biological characteristics of the mother, including her age, physical size, and state of health.

15. Teenage pregnancy increases risks to healthy prenatal and postnatal development, as well as developmental risks to the mother.

16. Adequate prenatal nutrition and health care for the mother and her developing baby is associated with a successful pregnancy, a normal birth, and healthy neonatal development.

Birth

17. Labor occurs in three distinct overlapping stages. During the first stage of labor, the uterine contractions increase in strength and regularity, and the cervix dilates sufficiently to accommodate the baby's head. The second stage of labor lasts from the complete dilation of the cervix until birth and takes from sixty to ninety minutes. During the third stage of labor, which lasts only a few minutes, the afterbirth is expelled.

18. Nonhospital birth centers and home birth are two alternatives to hospital-based birth.

19. Prepared childbirth is now widely used in both hospital and nonhospital birth settings to help women actively and comfortably meet the challenge of giving birth.

20. Many babies are now delivered by midwives who provide caregiving during pregnancy, childbirth, and the weeks following delivery. Doulas do not deliver babies, but help the mother during birth and with her newborn.

21. Pain-reducing medications can make the experience of childbirth more comfortable, but in recent years they have been used more cautiously because of their potentially adverse effects on the recovery of both infant and mother.

22. One problem that may arise during labor and delivery is insufficient uterine contractions, or faulty power. A faulty passageway caused by blockage of the birth canal by the placenta (placenta previa) is another potential problem. A faulty passenger may occur if the baby's physical position or large head size prevents completion of the journey through the birth canal.

23. Childbearing and delivery for parents with a disability pose specific challenges that can be overcome by clarifying misconceptions and providing appropriate information, equipment, and social and emotional support.

24. Most hospitals use electronic fetal monitors to keep track of fetal heart rate and uterine contractions.

25. Low-birth-weight babies may experience significant complications after birth; however, the bigger and more mature they are at birth, the greater are their chances for survival and healthy development.

26. While learning to care for a new baby is a welcome challenge for most new parents, it may be especially difficult for adolescent parents, single parents, and parents who are educationally and economically disadvantaged.

Key Terms

amniotic sac (96)	germinal stage (93)
caesarean section (127)	implantation (95)
canalization (105)	low birth weight (129)
conception (94)	midwife (121)
critical period (105)	period of transition (119)
embryo (95)	placenta (96)
embryonic stage (93)	prepared childbirth (122)
fetal alcohol syndrome (FAS) (108)	second stage of labor (120)
	teratogen (105)
fetal stage (93)	third stage of labor (120)
fetal presentation (118)	umbilical cord (96)
fetus (96)	
first stage of labor (119)	
freestanding birth center (FBC) (121)	

PART 3

The First Two Years

As parents and other proud relatives continually discover, infants grow and change more rapidly than the rest of us. Parents who take snapshots of their children find they must do so every few months, or even weeks, to keep up with all these changes. In a matter of months, infants are able to smile, sit, and babble. In just a few more months, they acquire language and the earliest symbolic skills and take their first tentative steps. And during their first year of life, they also acquire close attachments to particular caregivers.

These changes are crucial in many ways. They make infants seem much more "human" than they appeared as newborns. They also lay important foundations for all future development. The next three chapters describe these critical changes.

Physical Development in the First Two Years

Focusing Questions

- What do newborn infants look like, and how do they act during the first two years of life?

- How do infants' sleep and wakefulness patterns change as they get older? Can parents influence these patterns?

- How do infants' senses operate at birth?

- What are some motor skills that evolve during infancy?

- What do infants need nutritionally?

- What are the relative advantages of breast milk and formula?

- What nutritional deficiencies are common in North America and around the world?

- What are the risks of low birth weight on infant development?

Anne was looking at the journal she had kept about her daughter since Michelle was seven months old.

- February 7: This week Michelle began pushing herself backward on her stomach to get around—not very efficient, but it works!

- April 9: For two weeks she has been *creeping,* not crawling. She raises up her tummy, pushes her body forward (like a seal!), and plops down. Jim and I can't help laughing—she looks so ridiculous.

- June 10: Crawling all over the place—mostly after the dog. Gets mad when King walks away; then she cries and "forgets" how to locomote.

- August 10: Michelle's really working at walking. Three to five steps at a time, mostly when one of us is encouraging her. She really looks different, especially now that she's vertical.

As Anne can attest, during the first months of life a baby's behaviors evolve rapidly. In this chapter, we trace some of these physical developments through the first two years of life. We begin by discussing what young infants look like. Then we investigate babies' nervous systems, including the growth of their brains and how they are affected by sleep patterns. We go on to discuss the development of the senses. Then we turn to how infants develop motor skills, sampling both early, inborn reflexes and major early voluntary skills, such as walking. Next, we discuss infants' nutritional needs: what food they need immediately at birth, how their nutritional needs change as they get older, and how diet can affect their physical development or even their very survival.

As we will see, when compared to other periods of life, physical development during infancy proceeds more quickly and predictably. Growth occurs now like at no other time of life! Babies change daily, putting on pounds and inches; "You can almost *see* them grow," said one mother. Each week and month brings improvements in sensory abilities: they see and hear, and become able to organize sights and sounds. Basic motor skills develop out of the earliest, most primitive reflexes. Instead of sucking and grasping at objects automatically, a baby becomes able to search for an object and to examine it deliberately. Proud parents, of course, notice these changes, and often love to talk about them.

Appearance of the Young Infant

As we saw in the last chapter, birth continues rather than initiates physical development. Most organs have already been working for several weeks, or even months, prior to this event. The baby's heart has been beating regularly, his muscles have been contracting sporadically, and his liver has been making its major product, bile, which is necessary for normal digestion after birth. Even some behaviors, such as sucking and arm stretching, have already developed. Two physical functions, however, do begin at birth: breathing and ingestion (the taking in of foods).

The First Few Hours

When it first emerges from the birth canal, a newborn infant (also called a **neonate**) definitely does not resemble most people's stereotypes of a beautiful baby. No matter what its race, its skin often looks rather red—redder than parents usually expect, especially if they have never paid close attention to young babies before. The infant may be covered with various substances, such as fluid from the amniotic sac, blood from the placenta, and bits of brownish fluid from its own bowels. If born a bit early, it may also have a white, waxy substance called *vernix* on its skin, and its body may be covered with fine, downy hair called *lanugo*. If the baby was born vaginally rather then delivered surgically, its head may be somewhat elongated or have a noticeable point on it; the shape comes from the pressure of the birth canal, which squeezes the baby's skull for several hours during labor. Within a few days or weeks, the head fills out again to a more rounded shape, leaving gaps in the bones. The gaps are sometimes called *fontanelles*, or "soft spots," although they are actually covered by a tough membrane that can withstand normal contact and pressure. The gaps eventually grow over, but not until the infant is about eighteen months old.

Healthy newborns react vigorously to their surroundings during the first fifteen or thirty minutes of life. They may cry, look around, or suck, using the inborn reflexes described later in this chapter. Before long, though, they fall asleep (labor can wear them out, too!) and do not wake for a few hours.

Is the Baby All Right? The Apgar Scale

Because hospitals cannot always afford to have a pediatrician (a doctor with special expertise in children and infants) attend every birth, doctors and nurses need a way

neonate A newborn infant.

TABLE 5.1	The Apgar Scale		
		Score	
Characteristic	**0**	**1**	**2**
Heart rate	Absent	Less than 100 beats per minute	More than 100 beats per minute
Efforts to breathe	Absent	Slow, irregular	Good; baby is crying
Muscle tone	Flaccid, limp	Weak, inactive	Strong, active motion
Skin color	Body pale or blue	Body pink, extremities blue	Body and extremities pink
Reflex irritability	No response	Frown, grimace	Vigorous crying, coughing, sneezing

Source: Apgar (1953).

to decide quickly which newborns need immediate medical attention and which are healthy enough to wait a bit longer. The **Apgar scale** (named after its originator, Dr. Virginia Apgar) helps to meet this need (Apgar, 1953). The scale consists of ratings that are simple enough for nonspecialists to make, even amid the distractions surrounding the moment of delivery. To use it, someone present at the delivery calculates the baby's heart rate, breathing effort, muscle tone, skin color, and reflex irritability and assigns a score of 0 to 2 to each of these five characteristics. Babies are rated one minute after they emerge from the womb and again at five minutes. For each rating they can earn a maximum score of 10, as shown in Table 5.1. Most babies earn nine or ten points, at least by five minutes after delivery. A baby who scores between four and seven points at one minute is given immediate special medical attention, which usually includes examination by a pediatrician, and is then carefully observed during the next few hours and days for any problems that may develop (Brazelton & Nugent, 1997; Wyly, 1997).

Newborns who score less than 4 on the Apgar Scale face serious medical risk. Their heart rates are slow, their breathing is irregular and labored, and their muscle tone is weak. Instead of having the healthy reddish-pink color that results from an ample supply of oxygen in their blood, babies with low Apgar ratings may look blue in their extremities or even all over their bodies. Also, they do not respond strongly when stimulated; a sudden noise, for example, produces no startle reaction. Such babies need intensive care immediately if they are to survive. Their most immediate problem usually concerns breathing: often they need extra oxygen and special apparatus to facilitate breathing. If intensive care is available, however, most low-Apgar babies do survive.

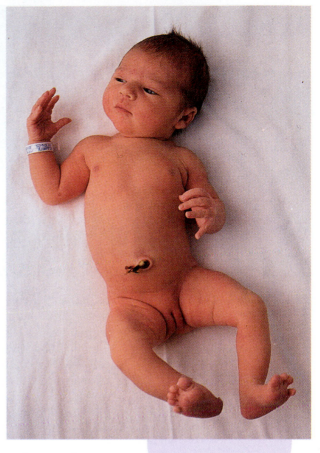

In the first few minutes after birth, healthy newborn babies are quite alert and responsive to sights and sounds. Soon, however, they begin spending most of their time asleep—perhaps just as well for mothers who are tired after labor.

Newborn Weight

At birth a typical baby weighs about 7½ pounds, or 3,400 grams, about as much as an average cat or a small dog. Because they are small, neonates have a rather large surface area relative to their weight. As a result, they lose heat more rapidly than adults do, and they have to consume more calories just to keep warm. But neonates also need to gain weight during the earliest months; by four or five months of age, they typically have doubled their birth weight. (See Figure 5.1.) How, then, can they keep themselves warm and gain quite a lot of weight at the same time?

The answer is: they eat. Because they still have no teeth, they have to drink all their calories. A newborn usually consumes about one quart of breast milk or infant formula in twenty-four hours. As a proportion of body weight, this is the same as an adult drinking ten to twenty quarts per day. And, of course, the baby must excrete after capturing the valuable nutrients from these huge amounts. No wonder, then, that diapers and feedings form the center of a newborn's life.

Size and Bodily Proportions

Lying down, a newborn baby measures about twenty inches, or fifty centimeters. Her length matches her adult size more closely than her weight does: her twenty inches represent more than one-quarter of her final height, whereas her 7½ pounds represent only a small percentage of her adult weight.

• • •

Apgar scale A system of rating newborns' health immediately following birth based on heart rate, strength of breathing, muscle tone, color, and reflex irritability.

The normal facial features of infants—large forehead and eyes, high cheekbones, small mouth—may help to stimulate attachment in adults. Similar facial proportions exist in the young of many other animals; puppies, for example, have larger eyes and cheekbones than adult dogs.

This fact suggests that newborns should look skinny, but actually they usually look chubby or even overweight. Babies' heads take up almost one-quarter of their length, and their limbs are disproportionately short. (See Figure 5.2.) Their chests seem small compared to their stomachs, which often stick out like a middle-aged person's pot belly. Bones contribute much less to overall weight than they do for adults; they are small and thin in proportion to the baby's size. For all these reasons, babies tend to look rather fat and cute.

Babies' proportions and general physical appearance may have psychological consequences by fostering **attachments,** or bonds, between infants and the people who care for them. Such bonds promote feelings of security. The cuteness of infants' faces in particular seems to help. No matter what their racial or ethnic background, most babies have unusually large foreheads, features that are concentrated in the lower part of the face, eyes that are large and round, and cheeks that are high and prominent. Dolls and cartoon characters have these facial features too, although often in exaggerated form, and so do a variety of animal species. The pattern of babyish features occurs so widely among animals, in fact, that biologists who study animal behavior suspect it has a universal and genetically based power to elicit parental or nurturing responses among adult animals (Archer, 1992; Lorenz, 1970). Mothers in some species of ducks, for example, take care of baby ducks even when the babies are not their own.

Cuteness apparently affects humans in comparable ways, although not as automatically as among other animals. The mere sight of a babyish face creates interest in most people and in a wide variety of situations. This interest is both conscious and unconscious. Not only do people say they find babies attractive; their bodies respond to babies with enlarged pupils and a faster heartbeat. Unlike many other ani-

---

● ● ● ● ● ● ● ● ● ● ● ● ●

FIGURE 5.1

Height and Weight Growth During the First Two Years

Girls and boys gain rapidly in height and weight during infancy. The colored bands show the range of sizes possible for all but the tallest and shortest 5 percent of children and for all but the most and least heavy 5 percent. The line in the middle of each band indicates average height and weight for each age. Note that although girls are slightly shorter and lighter than boys, the genders overlap more than they differ.

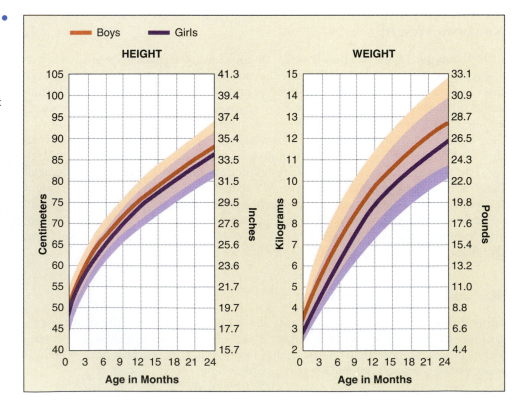

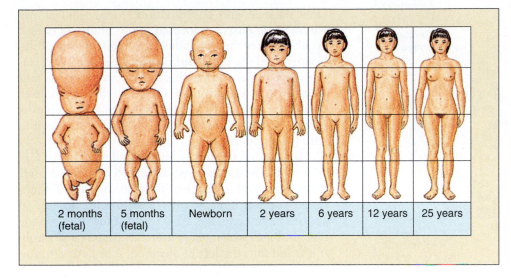

| 2 months (fetal) | 5 months (fetal) | Newborn | 2 years | 6 years | 12 years | 25 years |

● ● ● ● ● ● ● ● ● ● ● ● ● ● ● ● ●
FIGURE 5.2
Body Proportions, Fetal Period Through Adulthood

In addition to increases in size, growth involves major changes in the proportions of various body parts. From conception to adulthood, the head steadily becomes proportionately smaller than the body and the limbs become proportionately larger. The chest and abdomen remain in relatively constant proportion.

mal species, humans are interested in infants even if they are not parents or other adults; babies, for example, seem very interested in other babies and even in their own images in a mirror (Priel & Zeidman, 1990).

WHAT DO YOU THINK ?   What do you think attracts parents to their newborn children? Explore this question with the parents of a physically handicapped infant. How did they feel about their child (and about themselves) when the child was first born?

Development of the Nervous System

The **central nervous system** consists of the brain and nerve cells of the spinal cord, which together coordinate and control the perception of stimuli as well as motor responses of all kinds. The more complex aspects of this work are accomplished by the brain, which develops rapidly from just before birth until well beyond a child's second birthday. At seven months past conception, the baby's brain weighs about 10 percent of its final adult weight, but by birth it has more than doubled to about 25 percent of final adult weight. By the child's second birthday, it has tripled to about 75 percent of its final adult weight (Freund et al., 1997).

Most of this increase results not from increasing numbers of nerve cells, or **neurons,** but from the development of a denser, or more fully packed, brain. This happens in two ways. First, the neurons put out many new fibers that connect them with one another. Second, certain brain cells called *glia* put out fatty sheathing, or *myelin,* that gradually encases the neurons and their fibers. Because impulses can travel relatively easily through myelin sheaths, myelin allows nerve fibers to transmit impulses much more quickly (more than ten times!) as well as more reliably. The myelin acts like the insulation on an electric cord: it keeps impulses from short-circuiting on other fibers and ensures that they discharge only at designated places along the nerve fibers.

Growth of the Brain

At birth and for about the first six months thereafter, neural activity is dominated by the relatively primitive, or "lower," areas of the brain called the **brainstem** and the **midbrain,** which regulate relatively automatic functions such as breathing, digestion, and general alertness or consciousness. Another part, the **cerebellum,** regu-

● ● ●

attachment The strong and enduring emotional bond that develops between an infant and his or her caregivers during the infant's first year of life.

central nervous system The brain and nerve cells of the spinal cord.

neurons Nerve cell bodies and their extensions or fibers.

brainstem A relatively primitive, or "lower," area of the brain; along with the midbrain, this area regulates relatively automatic functions such as breathing, digestion, and consciousness.

midbrain The area of the brain that, together with the brainstem, regulates relatively automatic functions such as breathing, digestion, and consciousness.

cerebellum The part of the brain that coordinates muscles and maintains physical balance.

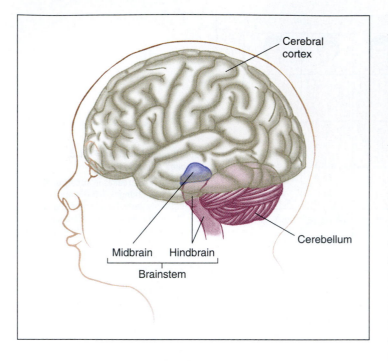

Cerebral
cortex

Midbrain   Hindbrain

Brainstem

Cerebellum

• • • • • • • • • • • • • • • • • •

FIGURE 5.3

The Brain

Different parts of the brain regulate different human functions. The midbrain regulates automatic activities such as breathing and digestion; the cerebellum regulates physical coordination; and the cerebral cortex regulates "higher" functions such as thinking and speaking.

lates balance and coordination. Figure 5.3 shows where these parts are located in the brain. As babies approach their first birthday, the "higher" part of the brain, called the **cerebral cortex,** becomes more active. Although even newborns respond to sights and sounds, it is not until age one that their responses seem conscious and they can perform at will coordinated motor actions such as reaching and grasping with their fingers.

By the end of infancy, the overall anatomical features of the brain are reasonably well established, but its various parts continue to develop specialized functions. The left hemisphere, for example, appears to specialize in language. As a result, most three-year-olds understand language more accurately and easily if it is fed into the left hemisphere (compared to the right) of their brains with special earphones (Hellige, 1993). Despite such specialization, however, other facts suggest that children's brains retain flexibility for many years. Children whose normal brain language centers are damaged, for example, usually recover most of their language ability as long as the damage occurred before adolescence. Apparently they recover because their brains find new areas of the brain to devote to language processing.

States of Sleep and Arousal

One important function of the brain is to control infants' states of sleep and wakefulness. Thus, the brain regulates the amount of stimulation infants experience, both externally and internally. Periodic sleep helps infants to shut out external stimulation and thereby allows them to obtain general physical rest.

Sleep   Very young infants move from deep sleep to wakefulness, with much more of the former than the latter. In the days immediately after birth, newborns sleep an average of sixteen hours per day, although some sleep as little as eleven hours a

Infants spend more time sleeping than doing anything else. Even by age two, most babies still need to sleep twelve hours a day. But like adults, they vary in how deeply they sleep and in how long they sleep at one time.

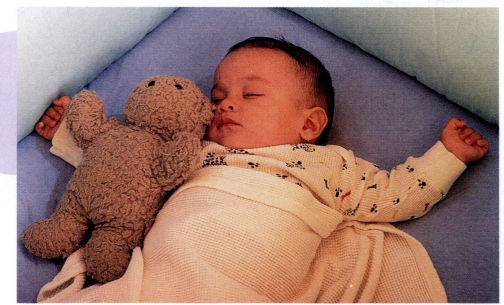

day and others as much as twenty-one (Michelsson et al., 1990). For most infants, the amount of sleep decreases steadily with each passing month. By age six months babies average just thirteen or fourteen hours of sleep per day, and by twenty-four months only eleven or twelve. But these hours still represent considerably more sleeping time than is typical for adults.

Newborns divide their sleeping time about equally between relatively active and quiet periods of sleep (see Figure 5.4). The more active kind is named **REM sleep,** after the "*rapid eye movements,*" or twitchings, that usually accompany it. REM sleep generally seems restless: sometimes infants' limbs or facial muscles twitch, and their breathing seems faster and more irregular. In the quieter kind of sleep, **non-REM sleep,** infants breathe regularly and more slowly, and their muscles become much limper. During the night, infants experience cycles of REM and non-REM sleep. For young infants, the night begins with REM sleep, and each cycle lasts about one hour.

Unfortunately for parents, a baby's extra sleep time does not usually include long, uninterrupted rest periods, even at night. In the first few months, it is more common for the baby to waken frequently—often every two or three hours—but somewhat unpredictably. Studies of brain development suggest that much of the unpredictability may result from the physical immaturity of the baby's nervous system: his brain may have frequent, accidental "storms" of impulses because it is not yet fully formed (Sheldon et al., 1992). In most cases the irregularities pose no problem for an infant, but in a very small percentage, irregularities may be related to "crib death," or sudden infant death syndrome (see the accompanying Perspectives box).

• • • • • • • • • • • • • • • • • •
FIGURE 5.4
Developmental Changes in Sleep Requirements

Sleep changes in nature as children grow from infancy to adulthood. Overall they sleep less (shown by the top line decreasing to the right), and the proportion of REM (rapid-eye-movement) sleep decreases sharply during infancy and childhood (shown by the space decreasing between the two lines).

Source: Reprinted with permission from Roffwary, Muzio & Dement, 1966 (revised 1969).

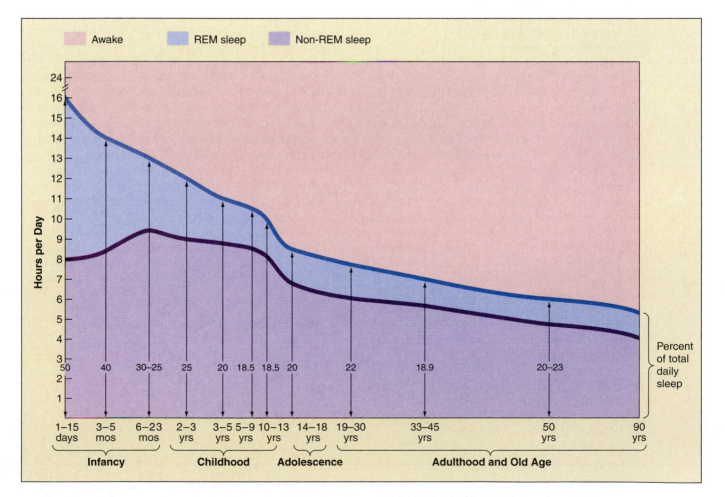

PERSPECTIVES

Sudden Infant Death Syndrome

• • • • • Each year about one out of every one thousand young infants die in their sleep for no apparent reason. Doctors call this phenomenon **sudden infant death syndrome (SIDS),** or "crib death." The problem is most frequent among infants between ages two months and four months, although SIDS can affect babies as young as one month and as old as one year. It is the leading cause of death among infants who survive the first few weeks after delivery.

SIDS is disturbing because it is so mysterious. Typically parents put a seemingly healthy baby down to sleep as usual, but when they come in to get her up again, they discover she is dead. Sadly, because the baby had exhibited no health problems, the parents often blame themselves for the death, suspecting that somehow they neglected their child or hurt him in some way (Kaplan, 1995). Even more unfortunately, friends and relatives often concur in blaming the parents, simply because they can think of no other way to explain SIDS. Other obvious causes simply do not happen. The baby does not choke, vomit, or suffocate; she just stops breathing.

What causes SIDS? One theory is that SIDS is an exaggerated form of normal *sleep apnea,* temporary cessations of breathing during sleep (Hunt, 1992). Another theory suggests that SIDS occurs primarily at a special transition in development, just when inborn reflexive control of breathing begins to fade in importance but before infants have firmly established voluntary control of breathing. For most infants, this transition occurs at about two to four months of age, just when SIDS strikes most often. A third theory suggests that SIDS infants suffer from heart problems: their nervous systems may fail to prompt regular, strong heartbeats and in essence cause them to suffer a heart attack (Gunther et al., 1995). Unfortunately, no clear evidence points to any of these alternative explanations.

If medical researchers could identify a basic cause, they would help future infants at risk for SIDS. Those babies could wear monitors that would indicate interruptions in breathing (if lungs are the problem) or heart rate (if that is it) and prompt parents or medical personnel to give the baby immediate, appropriate help. But so far the use of monitors has not been practical on a widespread scale because they can be cumbersome, cause a lot of unnecessary alarm, and occasionally fail to function properly.

Medical research has identified several factors that make a particular family or infant more likely to experience SIDS (Byard & Cohle, 1994). Very young mothers and fathers (less than twenty years) stand a greater chance of having a SIDS infant; so do mothers who smoke cigarettes or have serious illnesses during pregnancy. Mothers who are poorly nourished during pregnancy also carry more risk than mothers who keep reasonably well nourished. But certain babies also are at greater risk for SIDS independently of their parents' qualities or behaviors. Boys die of SIDS more often than girls, for example, and infants born small (less than seven pounds) die more often than bigger infants. These relationships do not mean, however, that being a boy or being small actually *causes* SIDS; they imply only that for reasons still not understood, SIDS seems to strike boys and small infants more frequently.

Even taken together, these factors do not predict SIDS very accurately. The vast majority of high-risk infants never die, whereas some infants with few risk factors die of SIDS anyway. This circumstance creates problems in translating the studies of risk factors into concrete recommendations for medical personnel and parents, because taking the risk indications too literally can arouse fears in parents unnecessarily. The most useful recommendations tend to be valid for all families, whether or not they are at risk for SIDS (Carroll & Siska, 1998). For example, it is a good idea to recommend that parents not smoke and that an infant's room be humidified, if possible, whenever the baby catches a cold. Recent research also has found that SIDS is less likely to occur if infants sleep on their backs rather than on their stomachs. These are good pieces of advice for everyone, but unfortunately they do not guarantee complete protection from SIDS. For parents whose babies do die, many hospitals and communities have created support groups in which couples can share their grief and come to terms with it.

What Do You Think?

If you were counseling a parent who lost a baby to SIDS, what would be your most important concern? What might you say to the parent? What might you also say to a relative of the parent who suspects neglect may have caused the death?

The unpredictability of infants' sleep can create chronic sleep deprivation in some parents; obviously somebody has to wake up during the night to calm or feed a crying baby! Some of the cure for fussiness depends on physical maturation, but parents can also influence their infant's sleep patterns by developing regular (though not rigid) times for and methods of waking, feeding, and sleeping that involve the infant. One study found that infants change toward more adultlike levels of wakefulness and sleep within six weeks after arriving home, provided routines are (relatively) regular (Bamford et al., 1990). Another study (described further in the Multicultural View box on p. 238 of Chapter 8) found that regularity offers dividends later in childhood: comparisons of Dutch and American families found fewer sleep problems among the young children of Dutch families, whose culture encourages regularity of daily routines more strongly than North American society does (Harkness & Keefer, 1995).

The advice to strive for (relatively) regular routines is widely supported among parent advice experts, but it makes crucial assumptions that not all families can meet. In some families, routines cannot be made regular because of competing pressures from other children, because of exhaustion from work or from earlier ill-timed wakings or feedings, or because the family has only one parent to begin with. Under these conditions, parents need additional support from friends, extended family, or social service workers. They cannot do it all themselves.

States of Arousal   Although infants show various states of arousal from the day they are born, as they get older their patterns of arousal begin to resemble those of older children (Ferber & Kryger, 1995). Table 5.2 summarizes the various states. The largest share of time, even among older infants, goes to the most completely relaxed and deepest form of sleep.

Variations in arousal make a practical difference to parents, other caregivers, and babies themselves. During the alert times, the baby is most likely to look at her surroundings and begin forming initial impressions of them. She begins noticing human faces almost immediately after birth, but increasingly so throughout the first year. Sometime before her six-month birthday, she begins to show a special preference for the faces of the people who care for her the most. She also begins to notice that various sounds and sights usually occur together—that a mouth opening and shutting, for example, usually occurs when a human voice comes her way. These experiences may stimulate perceptual abilities and early attachments, provided the child is awake to have them!

TABLE 5.2	States of Arousal in Infants
State	**Behavior of Infants**
Non-REM sleep	Complete rest; muscles relaxed; eyes closed and still; breathing regular and relatively slow
REM sleep	Occasional twitches, jerks, facial grimaces; irregular and intermittent eye movements; breathing irregular and relatively rapid
Drowsiness	Occasional movements, but fewer than in REM sleep; eyes open and close; glazed look; breathing regular, but faster than in non-REM sleep
Alert inactivity	Eyes open and scanning; body relatively still; rate of breathing similar to drowsiness, but more irregular
Alert activity	Eyes open, but not attending or scanning; frequent, diffuse bodily movements; vocalizations; irregular breathing; skin flushed
Distress	Whimpering or crying; vigorous or agitated movements; facial grimaces pronounced; skin very flushed

Source: Ferber and Kryger (1995).

cerebral cortex The "higher" part of the brain; along with the cerebrum, it controls vision, hearing, and touch, as well as motor actions such as lifting an arm.

REM sleep A relatively active period of sleep, named after the rapid eye movements that usually accompany it. See also *non-REM sleep.*

non-REM sleep A relatively quiet, deep period of sleep. See also *REM sleep.*

sudden infant death syndrome (SIDS) "Crib death" syndrome in which apparently healthy infants stop breathing unaccountably and die in their sleep; most frequently strikes infants between ages two and four months.

A fully alert state may not be the only condition under which young babies learn. Infants fail to *habituate,* or get used to, sounds and other stimuli that occur during more active REM sleep. Heart rates speed up in reaction to such stimulation, suggesting that infants may do some sort of mental processing of the stimulation even while asleep. On the other hand, it may also show neural *dis*organization. Babies who are born prematurely or who are extremely small for their age show more variability in heart rate when they hear sounds in their sleep (Spassov et al., 1994).

WHAT DO YOU THINK ?   How do parents deal with differences in children's sleep patterns? Ask a classmate or friend who is a parent of more than one child, or ask your own parent(s), how he or she responded to sleep differences in the children as infants. Combine your information with several other classmates'. Do you see any trends?

Sensory Development

All of the human senses operate at birth. This conclusion is supported by a variety of observations and experiments with neonates. For example, newborn infants sometimes prefer slight changes in brightness, as shown by their staring longer at a light that changes slightly in intensity than at one that does not. Behaviors and responses such as these show that newborns have the use of their senses. But observations also reveal that they have certain sensory limitations as well.

Visual Acuity

Infants can see at birth, but without the clarity of focus, or *acuity* (keenness), characteristic of adults with good vision. They can track a bright light even before they leave the hospital delivery room, as long as the light lies near their line of vision and moves fairly slowly. For a newborn to see a single line, the line must be about ten times as wide as necessary for adults, and if the line lies off to one side of the infant's line of vision, it must be even wider (Aslin, 1987). When looking at stationary contours and objects, newborns see more clearly at short distances, especially at about eight to ten inches—about the distance, incidentally, between a mother's breast and her face. Their vision is better when tracking moving objects, but even so their overall vision is rather poor until about one month of age (Seidel et al., 1997).

Visual acuity improves a lot during infancy, but it does not reach adult levels until the end of the preschool years. An older infant (ages one to two) often has 20/30 or 20/40 vision, meaning he can see fine details at twenty feet that adults can see at thirty or forty feet. This quality of vision is quite satisfactory for everyday, familiar activities; in fact, many adults can see no better than this, without even realizing it. But this level of visual acuity does interfere with seeing distant objects.

The sensory acuity of infants means that parents may be partly right when they claim their newborn child recognizes them even from birth. What parents may be noticing is their newborn's immediate responsiveness to sights and sounds. They are right to exclaim over it: by taking an interest in the environment, the child creates conditions where she can begin organizing (or *perceiving*) sights and sounds, and attaching meanings to them. As we will see in the next chapter, certain kinds of lines, shapes, and contours are especially interesting to a young infant. So are certain kinds of sounds. Fortunately for the development of family ties, parents are able to provide many of the most interesting sights and sounds with their own faces and voices; and partly in this way, attachments between parents and children are born.

Auditory Acuity

Auditory acuity refers to sensitivity to sounds. Infants can hear at birth, but not as well as adults. Any sudden loud noise, such as that caused by dropping a large book on the floor, demonstrates they can hear. The sound produces a dramatic startle reaction, called a *Moro reflex:* the neonate withdraws her limbs suddenly, sometimes shakes all over, and may also cry (see also the discussion later in this chapter). Not all noises produce this reaction; pure tones, such as the sound of a flute, cause relatively little response. Complex noises containing many different sounds usually produce a stronger reaction; a bag of nails spilling on the floor, for example, tends to startle infants reliably.

Even when they do not startle overtly, however, newborn infants respond internally to sounds. Electrodes attached to their heads register minor electrical responses to most ordinary noises that are moderately loud, suggesting that newborns can even discriminate between certain common consonant sounds, such as *b* and *p*. Quiet sounds or noises do not evoke electrical responses, even when they are loud enough to do so in adults. Judged in this way, infants seem a bit hard of hearing compared to adults, although of course they are far from deaf. These differences persist through much of the second year of life (Northern, 1996).

Children begin to sense very soft sounds sometime toward the end of infancy, judging both by the electrical brain waves just described and by their increasingly overt responses to sounds, language, and music as observed by parents. Frequency (or pitch) discrimination shows comparable improvements. By about five months, infants respond to small differences in high pitches—those at the upper third of a piano keyboard—as well as adults do, although it takes them longer than this to learn to discriminate among low pitches.

Taste, Smell, and Touch

Even at birth, infants clearly prefer sweet tastes; they suck faster when an artificial nipple delivers sugar water than when it delivers plain water. When assessed by their sucking, however, other taste preferences seem much less clear-cut than they are among children and adults. Newborn infants will suck *less* for saltwater, for example, but only if the saltwater is delivered automatically between bursts of sucking. If saltwater comes as a result of each suck, they show no significant decrease from their normal rates of sucking. Other tastes (bitterness and sourness) have even less effect on sucking behavior and take time to develop to adult levels (Beauchamp & Bartoshuk, 1997).

Newborns also react to a variety of smells, both good and bad. A faint odor of ammonia or vinegar, for example, makes one-week-old infants grimace and avert their heads. On the other hand, they can also recognize the odor of their mothers' breasts (Cernoch & Porter, 1985). If two breast pads, only one of which has previously been worn by a nursing mother, are hung in front of one-month-old infants, the babies spend more time facing or looking at the pad that has come from the nursing mother, presumably because of its aroma. Even non-breast-fed infants, who have not had the opportunity to learn the smell of mother's milk, show this preference. Infants also prefer the odor of mother's milk even if it did not originate with their own mothers, though they do show a preference for their own mothers' aroma when given a choice (Makin & Porter, 1989).

What about touch? Newborns exhibit many reflexes that imply sensitivity to touch. A light stroke on the cheek, for example, normally causes a baby to turn his head in the direction of the stroke, and placing a finger on the baby's lips typically causes him to make sucking motions. Parents in many cultures have discovered that wrapping newborn infants in a cloth or blanket, or even just holding them firmly,

WORKING WITH

Helen Turman, **Pediatric Nurse**

Continuity and Change in Infants' Behavior

Helen Turman has been a public health nurse for nearly twenty years. She has worked with infants and their mothers and other relatives in the postpartum nursery of a hospital, looking after newborns and helping mothers and babies get used to each other; as a public health nurse, visiting mothers and babies recently discharged from the hospital; and at "well baby" clinics run by public health nurses. Helen talked about her experiences in the postpartum nursery.

Kelvin: *What are some of the differences that you see among babies? Surely they differ among themselves . . .*

Helen: Well, they do and they don't; it depends on how you look at it. It seems to me that *all* babies need certain things: cuddling, the warmth of a human body, feeding at the right times. And bundling—wrapping them up snugly—usually quiets them right down. All babies respond to these things from day one, but they keep needing them for quite awhile too.

Kelvin: *What about the differences?*

Helen: One of the earliest differences is in feeding patterns. Some babies nurse often but take in smaller amounts; others eat less frequently but stay on the breast longer and take more. You see variety in sucking patterns. Some babies seem businesslike: they lock on to the mother's breast and won't let go for anything until they're done! The mother can talk, eat her dinner with one hand, even walk around, and the baby will keep nursing.

Other babies get distracted. They won't start feeding right away, even when the mother offers the breast and even if the baby has been fussing like she's hungry. Then they get distracted at the least thing, like if someone is talking across the room. Feeding takes forever.

Kelvin: *Do these differences in "style" seem to last beyond infancy?*

Helen: Oh, for sure. Some babies don't seem very hungry when they're first born; maybe mucus is filling their stomachs or something. That can be disturbing. Mothers worry when their baby won't eat! And their breasts become engorged—it's uncomfortable.

Kelvin: *Can you see the differences while you work in the postpartum nursery? It seems like your time with individual babies would be pretty short.*

Helen: Yes, it is indeed short. These days, if a birth is uncomplicated and mother and child are both healthy, the two of them might go home twenty-four hours after delivery! But you actually see them longer than that because of our hospital's new system of "family-oriented care." That's where labor, delivery, and recovery all happen in the same room, even if the mother needs a surgical delivery! In that case, though, mother and child would stay longer.

Kelvin: *What kinds of differences do you see among the mothers?*

Helen: Well, pretty quickly you sense which mothers are apprehensive, which have a lot of questions, and which seem receptive to "teaching" from me or the other nurses.

Kelvin: *"Teaching" about what?*

Helen: About getting started with breast feeding, and nutrition for themselves, and help with diaper changes. Mothers vary dramatically in how much they involve us, the nurses, during the time after delivery and in how much they care for their own infants. Some act like they already know how much work the baby is going to be, so they want *me*, the nurse, to do as much as possible now so they can get some rest. Others want to do it all themselves;

then I don't get to know the mother or the baby as well.

Kelvin: *Does age make a difference? Are older mothers different with their babies than younger mothers?*

Helen: Yes, but not always the way you might expect. Some teenage mothers I've seen actually don't worry as much as the older mothers, the thirty-five-year-olds. A teenager can be very giving and nurturant with her baby. Maybe she just doesn't know yet what there is to worry about, so she relaxes and enjoys the baby. Trouble might come later, when she has to juggle the responsibilities of school, child care, maintaining relationships with the baby's father or with her own parents, and so on.

What Do You Think?

1. Given differences such as those Helen points out, how helpful is it to speak of "typical" infant development? Take another look at the chapter's discussion of breast feeding and sleep patterns, for example, and think about how you might rewrite the material to better account for individual differences.

2. What factors do you think might influence a mother's level of involvement with her newborn infant in the postpartum nursery? Previous childrearing experience? Extent and nature of family relationships at home? Amount of career and work involvement? Compare your opinions about these possibilities with those of a classmate.

3. Ask a classmate about his or her own preferred times and ways of eating. Are they more or less regular than yours? Speculate about how eating patterns get established and whether they are connected to an individual's personality.

tends to reduce crying and fussing. In part such quieting implies sensitivity to touch, although it may also result from the interesting sights and sounds that accompany being swaddled or held.

In newborns, in fact, touch may assist development in many ways. Much of the benefit occurs by way of the central nervous system. The closeness brought on by touching, holding, and carrying relaxes both the baby and the caregiver (Hover-Kramer, 1996). Thus, tactual behaviors seem to encourage healthy physical development in the baby on the one hand and stimulate the caregiver to be more alert and attentive to the baby on the other.

At birth, one particular tactile sensation, pain, seems less developed than among slightly older infants or children (Spanshott, 1997). It is possible to evoke a response of pain or other negative reaction to a pinprick, such as that a baby might receive for a blood test, in one-day-old infants. But most infants this young seem somewhat less sensitive to painful stimuli than they do even a few days later. The insensitivity may help newborn infants to endure the highly stressful experience of birth itself; or, alternatively, the stress of birth itself may release hormones that reduce the baby's sensitivity to pain for a short time after birth.

WHAT DO YOU THINK?   Do parenting books agree with our comments that young infants have the use of their senses? Check the comments made in two or three books about the capabilities of newborn babies. Do they seem consistent, or at least not *inconsistent*?

Motor Development

The infant's very first movements appear to be inborn and automatic, and are called **reflexes.** During the first months of life, most reflexes disappear or become incorporated into relatively purposeful or voluntary movements. When they have these qualities, they are called **skills.** Both reflexes and skills are also called **motor abilities** (the term *motor* refers to movement or motion).

Early Reflexes

Pediatricians have identified more than two dozen inborn reflexes. A few of these reflexes, such as sucking, clearly help the baby to adapt to the new life outside the womb. Others look more like evolutionary vestiges of behaviors that may have helped earlier versions of *Homo sapiens* to cope, for example, by clinging to their mothers at the sound of danger. A few reflexes, such as blinking, breathing, and swallowing, persist throughout a person's life, but most reflexes disappear from the infant's repertoire of skills during the first few months. Their disappearance, in fact, helps doctors to judge whether a baby is developing normally. Newborn reflexes that persist over many months may suggest damage to the nervous system or generally retarded development (Menkes, 1994).

Rooting and Sucking   If you gently stroke the cheek of a newborn, he will turn his head to the side you are stroking. This searching behavior is called **rooting.** Under normal circumstances, rooting helps the baby to locate his mother's breast, because he will nose around for it if it brushes the side of his face just prior to nursing. If the baby then finds the nipple, he will begin **sucking** powerfully and rhythmically—and without having been taught. Actually, any object will elicit sucking if it intrudes far enough into his mouth; a finger, for example, makes a good pacifier. Later in the infant's first year, the sucking reflex comes under more voluntary control and broadens to become *mouthing*, a mixture of gnawing and chewing. The baby begins using his mouth as a primary way to learn about new objects; for a time, it seems, he puts just about everything in his mouth!

• • •

reflexes Simple, automatic movements displayed by infants, and which appear to be inborn.

skills Voluntary movements which are learned and performed deliberately.

motor abilities The set of reflexes and skills of which an infant or child is capable.

rooting A reflexive searching behavior that orients an infant to the mother's breast or to a bottle.

sucking One of the neonate's first and most powerful reflexes, triggered by any object intruding into the mouth.

Mouthing is one of the first reflexes infants exhibit. As they get older, they begin mouthing objects voluntarily to "get the feel" of them. Still later, mouthing is replaced with intentional handling of objects as a way of learning about the environment.

• • •

Moro reflex The reflexive startle response of newborns. Healthy infants fling their arms out suddenly and sometimes shake all over or cry in response to a sudden loud noise or sudden loss of support.

survival reflex An inborn behavioral response of newborn infants that serves a clear physical purpose, such as breathing.

primitive reflex An inborn behavioral response of newborn infants that serves no obvious physical purpose; contrasted to a survival reflex.

motor skills Physical skills using the body or limbs, such as walking and drawing.

gross motor skills Voluntary movements of the body that involve the large muscles of the arms, legs, and torso.

fine motor skills Voluntary movements of the body that involve the small muscles located throughout the body.

Moro Reflex   A newborn will startle dramatically in response to a sudden loss of support, even if the loss does not really threaten to hurt her. The startle response is called the **Moro reflex.** Normally the infant will thrust her arms outward, shake, make horrible faces, and possibly cry. Gradually she will bring her arms together again, as though to grab at something. The response looks much like the startle of children and adults, and may in fact be a precursor to it.

At some time earlier in human evolution, the Moro reflex may have helped infants who were being carried to grab more tightly when they experienced a sudden loss of support. At present, however, it is significant mostly because it helps doctors to diagnose normal development of the nervous system. Healthy infants show the response when they are born, but lose much of it as they approach their sixth month. Well before their second birthday, their startle responses come to resemble those of normal adults: they startle less often, and their responses become more abbreviated and less dramatic.

Grasping   If you place something firm, such as a finger, in a neonate's palm, he will grasp it. Like some other reflexes, the early grasping may facilitate later, more intentional versions of the same behavior, such as the grasping needed to explore toys and hang on to a railing for balance.

Table 5.3 summarizes these and other reflexes of newborn babies. Some, such as breathing, serve obvious physical needs; in Table 5.3, they are called **survival reflexes.** Others, such as the tonic neck reflex, serve no obvious physical purpose, although they may be vestiges of important reflex behaviors at earlier stages of human evolution; these are called **primitive reflexes.** Among both survival and primitive reflexes, some may set the stage for developing more refined versions of the behavior later in childhood. Even if they do facilitate later learning, though, infants must also have appropriate later experiences. For example, the grasping reflex may develop into mature grasping only if a child has chances to grasp actual objects as she grows toward toddlerhood.

The First Motor Skills

Motor skills are voluntary movements of the body or parts of the body. They can be grouped conveniently according to the size of the muscles and body parts involved. **Gross motor skills** involve the large muscles of the arms, legs, and torso. **Fine motor skills** involve the small muscles located throughout the body. Walking and jumping are examples of gross motor skills, and reaching and grasping are examples of fine motor skills.

Viewed broadly, the sequence in which skills develop follows two general trends. The *cephalocaudal principle* ("head to tail") refers to the fact that upper parts of the body become usable and skillful before lower parts do. Babies learn to turn their heads before learning to move their feet intentionally, and they learn to move their arms before they learn to move their legs. The *proximodistal principle* ("near to far") refers to the fact that central parts of the body become skillful before peripheral, or outlying, parts do. Babies learn to wave their entire arms before learning to wiggle their wrists and fingers. The former movement occurs at the shoulder joint, near the center of the body, and the latter occurs at the periphery. Stated differently, the shoulder movement is relatively proximal, whereas the finger movement is relatively distal.

Gross Motor Development in the First Year   Almost from birth, and before reflex behaviors disappear, babies begin doing some things on purpose. By age four weeks or so, most babies can lift their heads up when lying on their stomachs. At six or seven months, many babies have become quite adept at using their limbs; they can stick their feet up in the air and "bicycle" with them while a parent struggles valiantly to fit a diaper on the moving target. At ten months the average baby can stand erect, but only if an adult helps. By their first birthday, one-half of all babies can dispense with this assistance and stand by themselves without toppling over immediately (Savelsbergh, 1993). By age seven months, on the average, babies become able to locomote, or move around, on their own. At first, their methods are crude and slow; a baby might simply pivot on her stomach, for example, to get a better view of something interesting. Consistent movement in one direction develops soon after this time, although the movement does not always occur in the direction the baby intends!

Crawling and creeping offer new opportunities and make new demands on parents. On the one hand, locomotion lets babies entertain themselves better than before. They can relieve boredom on their own initiative simply by traveling to a new location or reaching and grasping a toy for themselves. On the other hand, parents discover that babies who move can get into everything, including poisons hidden in a low cupboard and electrical outlets. "Childproofing" becomes a major concern for many parents at this point as they continually scrutinize their living quarters for hazards to their mobile infants.

TABLE 5.3	**Major Reflexes in Newborn Infants**		
Reflex	**Description**	**Development**	**Significance**
Survival Reflexes			
Breathing reflex	Repetitive inhalation and expiration	Permanent, although becomes partly voluntary	Provides oxygen and expels carbon dioxide
Rooting reflex	Turning of cheek in direction of touch	Weakens and disappears by six months	Orients child to breast or bottle
Sucking reflex	Strong sucking motions with throat, mouth, and tongue	Gradually comes under voluntary control	Allows child to drink
Swallowing reflex	Swallowing motions in throat	Permanent, although becomes partly voluntary	Allows child to take in food and to avoid choking
Eyeblink reflex	Closing eyes for an instant ("blinking")	Permanent, although gradually becomes voluntary	Protects eyes from objects and bright light
Pupillary reflex	Changing size of pupils: smaller in bright light and bigger in dim light	Permanent	Protects against bright light and allows better vision in dim light
Primitive Reflexes			
Moro reflex	In response to a loud noise, child throws arms outward, arches back, then brings arms together as if to hold something	Arm movements and arching disappear by six months, but startle reaction persists for life	Indicates normal development of nervous system
Grasping reflex	Curling fingers around any small object put in the child's palm	Disappears by three months; voluntary grasping appears by about six months	Indicates normal development of nervous system
Tonic neck reflex	When laid on back, head turns to side, arm and leg extend to same side, limbs on opposite side flex	Disappears by two or three months	Indicates normal development of nervous system
Babinski reflex	When bottom of foot stroked, toes fan and then curl	Disappears eight to twelve months	Indicates normal development of nervous system
Stepping reflex	If held upright, infant lifts leg as if to step	Disappears by eight weeks, but later if practiced	Indicates normal development of nervous system
Swimming	If put in water, infant moves arms and legs and holds breath	Disappears by four to six months	Indicates normal development of nervous system

Before learning to walk, infants use all sorts of ways to move about; crawling on all fours is only one of them. New locomotion allows investigation of objects, like the baby on the right, and stimulates grasping reflexes, which develop into voluntary grasping skills suitable for a variety of objects and situations.

Reaching and Grasping   As pointed out earlier in this chapter, even newborn infants will reach for and grasp objects they can see immediately in front of them. They often fail to grasp objects successfully; they may make contact with an object but fail to enclose it in their fingers. This early, crude reaching disappears fairly soon after birth, only to reappear at about four or five months of age as two separate skills, reaching and grasping (Pownall & Kingerlee, 1993). These skills soon serve infants in many ways. For example, by their second birthday most babies can turn the pages in large picture books one at a time, at least if the paper is relatively indestructible. But they can also point at the pages without grasping for them.

Walking   A reasonably predictable series of events leads to true walking in most children; Figure 5.5 describes some of these milestones. By about twelve to thirteen months, most children take their first independent steps. Well before two years, they often can walk not only forward but backward or even sideways. Some two-year-olds can even walk upstairs on two feet instead of on all fours. Usually they use the wall or a railing to do so. Usually, too, coming downstairs proves more difficult than going up; one solution is to creep down backward, using all four limbs.

How do these changes develop? To some extent, the earlier skills may stimulate and give practice in the later ones. Sitting, for example, may give practice in balance, which helps in standing next to furniture; standing by furniture, in turn, improves balance and muscle development so that standing alone becomes possible; and so on. Each step in such a sequence rewards the child simply by giving her new opportunities to explore her body and see her world from new perspectives. The practice and sense of accomplishment may be their own rewards.

As reasonable as this explanation sounds, however, it has certain flaws. Not all children learn movement skills according to a predictable sequence; some, for example, creep only after they have mastered walking. And individual children who are normal in all respects learn motor skills at rather different ages: full-fledged walking, for example, may occur as early as nine months or as late as eighteen months. Yet all these children presumably have access to the crucial learning tool, namely their own legs and feet. Do some infants therefore practice harder or simply have an inborn ability to learn faster?

Variations in Motor Skill Development

The question about the origins of walking illustrates the issue of *nature* (genetic endowment) versus *nurture* (life experience) in children's growth, an important question throughout developmental psychology and one that we discussed in Chapter 1. A reasonable position on this issue is that most changes, including walking, depend on both genetics and experience. But the *way* in which each factor contributes often seems unclear. The problem is illustrated by a classic study that "taught" infants basic motor skills (Gesell & Thompson, 1929). One member of a pair of identical twins was taught to climb stairs beginning at age forty-six weeks. Her training began with assistance from an adult at moving from one step to the next, often at first simply by being lifted. Her twin received no training and in fact was prohibited from all encounters with stairs until she was fifty-three weeks old. At this point, the trained twin could climb stairs much better than her inexperienced sister. Yet even on her very first attempt, at fifty-three weeks, the untrained sister managed to climb the stairs! After just three weeks more, both girls performed equally well despite their prior differences in training.

Although the study suggested that maturation (or effects due to the aging process) matters more than learning (acquired knowledge and skill), it may really show only how children can learn a skill indirectly. The untrained twin encountered no stairs during her waiting period, but she was free to crawl every day and to practice any other motor techniques she chose. Such crawling may have given her preparation relevant for climbing stairs, even if the preparation was indirect; so experience and maturation may both account for the results.

Cultural Differences in Motor Development Similar ambiguities exist if we compare motor development across cultures or societies. Differences do sometimes occur, but sometimes also do not last, and sometimes no differences occur even where we might expect them. Certain African cultures, for example, give their infants unusually frequent chances to sit upright and to practice their "walking" reflex when held at a standing position by adults and older children (LeVine, 1994; Munroe et al., 1981). These opportunities seem to stimulate toddlers in these societies to learn to walk earlier and better than North American toddlers. Early walking, in turn, may prove especially valuable in these societies, which do not rely heavily on cars, bicycles, or other vehicles that make walking less important. Yet early walking may also be a genetic trait (at least partially) for these groups; without comparable training in reflex walking for North American infants, there is no way to be sure.

Yet differences in motor skills do not always appear where they might be expected. Take the Navaho Indians, whose infants spend nearly all of their first year bound and swaddled tightly to a flat board, with their arms and legs extending straight down along their bodies (Whiting, 1981). Apparently as a result, Navaho toddlers do tend to acquire walking a little later than Anglo American children. But they do not show delays in other skills inhibited by swaddling, notably reaching and grasping, and the deficit in walking disappears by the end of the preschool years in most cases (Connelly & Forssberg, 1997).

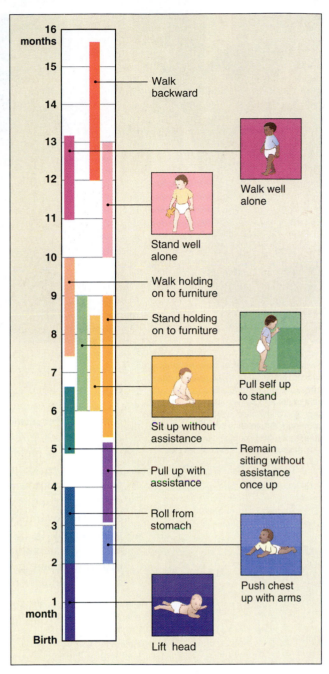

● ● ● ● ● ● ● ● ● ● ● ● ● ● ●

FIGURE 5.5

Milestones of Motor Development

Walking alone is one of the major physical achievements of the first year of life. Quite a few other physical skills usually develop prior to walking, as the figure shows. Note, though, that skills appear at different times for different individuals. As a result, some skills may even appear "out of sequence" in some children.

Swaddling infants, as is done with this Navajo infant, is practiced in many cultures. Swaddling tends to slow motor development at first, but not permanently. It may also allow caregivers to carry infants with them during daily activities—a circumstance that could make vocalizing a less urgent skill for infants to develop.

Gender Differences   Do boys and girls differ, on the average, in motor development? The answer depends on distinguishing what infants *can* do from what they typically *do* do. What they can do—their competence—has relatively little relationship to sex. Boy and girl babies sit upright at about the same age, for example, and stand and walk at about the same time. Similar equality exists for all of the motor milestones of infancy.

How infants use their time is another matter. Almost as soon as they can move, boys show more activity than girls. The trend begins even before birth, when male fetuses move about in their mothers' wombs more than female fetuses do (Moore & Persand, 1998). After birth, the trend continues: infant boys remain more active than infant girls, using what locomotor skills they have developed thus far, whereas girls spend more of their time using their emerging fine motor skills. Of course, the differences in use of time may stem partly from parents' encouragement (praise) for "gender-appropriate" behaviors. Given the young age of the children, though, and the fact that activity actually precedes birth, part of the difference must come from genetic endowment: an inborn tendency to be more (or less) active.

By their second birthday (and onward throughout childhood), boys and girls tend to differ in motor skills even in optimal, testlike situations; what they *can* do motorically begins to differ, on the average. Girls excel more often at fine motor skills, such as building a tower of blocks with fewer mistakes; boys excel more often at gross motor skills, such as running or throwing. But the origins of the gender differences—nature or nurture—remain obscure. Practice must surely contribute, with each gender accumulating more time with its "favorite" sorts of skills. But emerging awareness of gender roles may also contribute, with each gender beginning to know the skills in which society expects it to excel. With these influences operating on all children, it is noteworthy that boys and girls grow up more alike than different: many boys have good balance, and many girls pound their play dough (and occasionally another child) very hard indeed.

WHAT DO YOU THINK?   If motor skills develop partly through learning, why not just deliberately teach infants to walk? What do you think would be the result of doing so? Do similar considerations apply for certain other important developments in infancy?

Nutrition During the First Two Years

Of course, the growth described so far depends on good nutrition during the first two years. Like adults, babies need diets with appropriate amounts of protein, calories, and specific vitamins and minerals. For various reasons, however, infants do not always get all the nutrients they need. Often poverty accounts for malnutrition: parents with good intentions may be unable to afford the right foods. In other cases, conventional eating practices interfere: despite (or perhaps because of) relatively expensive eating habits, such as going to fast-food restaurants, some families may fail to provide their children with a balanced diet.

Compared to older children, infants eat less in overall or absolute amounts. A well-nourished young baby in North America might drink somewhat less than one liter (about .95 quarts) of liquid nourishment per day. This amount definitely would not keep an older child or a young adult well nourished, although it might prevent starving. In proportion to their body weight, however, infants need to consume much more than older children or adults do. For example, every day a three-month-old baby ideally should take in more than two ounces of liquid per pound of body weight, whereas an eighteen-year-old needs only about one-third of this amount (Queen & Lang, 1993).

Breast Milk Versus Formula

Someone (usually parents) must provide for an infant's comparatively large appetite. Whenever breast feeding is possible, health experts generally recommend human milk as the sole source of nutrition for at least the first six months or so of most infants' lives and as a major source for at least the next six months. In some cases, of course, this recommendation proves difficult or impractical to follow. Babies who need intensive medical care immediately after birth cannot be breast fed without special arrangements. Also, for one reason or another, some women may choose not to breast feed, and certain babies and mothers may not succeed in this activity even after trying it. For these infants, formulas can be prepared and fed in bottles.

Why do pediatricians recommend breast feeding? Studies of infants and mothers suggest four major reasons. First, human milk seems to give young infants more protection from diseases and other ailments. Breast-fed infants catch fewer colds and viruses of all types, experience fewer allergies, and suffer fewer serious illnesses. The ways in which human milk confers this benefit are not understood completely, but one reason is that human milk is always sterile, even at comfortable, lukewarm temperatures at which bottle milk may begin to grow bacteria. In addition, the protein in human milk contains substances that may bind or attach themselves to viruses and bacteria in the infant's intestine, thereby rendering them harmless. In any case, the disease resistance benefit of milk is so important that many hospitals now try to offer human milk in bottles to infants needing intensive care.

In recent decades, increasing numbers of mothers in our society have chosen to breast-feed their babies as recommended by most pediatricians. For a significant number of infants, however, partial or complete bottle feeding remains a better option—for example, if fathers wish to be involved in feedings.

The second reason concerns the nutritional composition of human milk. Overall, such milk matches the nutritional needs of human infants more closely than formula preparations do. Human milk contains more iron (an important nutrient for infants) but less casein (a protein prominent in cow's milk that many infants have trouble digesting). Human milk also contains helpful amounts of cholesterol, a form of fat that contributes to heart problems in later life but seems to protect against this possibility when digested in early infancy.

A third reason for preferring breast feeding is physical. Breast feeding better develops the infant's jaw and mouth muscles because it requires stronger sucking motions than bottle feeding does. For much the same reason, the breast also tends to satisfy infants' intrinsic needs for sucking better than a bottle does. This fact makes pacifiers less necessary, and it makes excessive sucking, and therefore overeating, less likely to occur.

A fourth reason for preferring breast feeding is more speculative: advocates of breast feeding argue that it benefits mother-infant relationships (La Leche League International, 1991; Mason & Ingersoll, 1997). Breast-fed infants spend more time snuggling close to their mothers, and vice versa. A breast-feeding mother and child undeniably spend a lot of time gazing into each other's eyes, like two people in love, and the mother appears to offer feeding sessions in closer response to the infant's true hunger demands. These behaviors may promote

A Multicultural View ·····················

Breast Feeding among the Gusii

The Gusii are an agricultural and sheep-herding people living in the hills of Kenya, a country in eastern Africa, and have been observed and interviewed extensively by Robert Levine and his associates (1994). Gusii mothers might find the discussion of breast feeding in this chapter strange: why, they might ask, are the authors trying so hard to show its merits? Among the Gusii, mothers universally breast-feed their infants for at least the first eighteen months of life, eventually interrupting the process only to care for their next baby.

This routine may sound grueling by North American standards, but consider the context. Throughout Africa (and including among the Gusii), parents widely regard infancy as the most life-threatening period of life—and with good reason, since the majority of deaths do in fact occur during that developmental period. Therefore, the best defense against the dangers of infancy is close, continuous contact between mother and infant. A mother will carry her young baby everywhere, often strapped in swaddling clothes to her back, soothe it at the least sign of discontent, and breast-

feed it frequently and on demand. These practices pay dividends in the form of healthier and more contented babies toward the end of infancy. Observations of Gusii infants in the waiting room of a community health clinic in Kenya, for example, found almost no crying among the babies, a situation unheard of for comparable groups of sick infants in the United States (Levine et al., 1994).

Anthropologists who have observed the Gusiis' approach call it the "pediatric model" of infant care and contrast it to the "pedagogical model" of care that prevails in North America. The pediatric model of care centers on protecting the child from life-threatening illness, whereas the pedagogical model of care emphasizes promoting active exchange between parent and child. A North American mother sees herself as her child's first teacher (among other things). So she talks with her child long before the child is able to understand language; she procures interesting toys for the child to play with even before the youngster's motor skills have developed very much; and she generally arranges for "quality" (meaning "highly interactive") time with her infant (Harkness & Super, 1992). These non-Gusii priorities are possible, of course, because she takes the

strong, secure attachments between mother and child, which enhance the infant's social and cognitive development later in childhood. (However, mothers in societies other than ours might find these comments odd; see the accompanying Multicultural View box.)

After about six months, infants can be introduced gradually to solid foods such as strained cereals and strained fruits. As babies become tolerant of these new foods, parents can introduce others that sometimes require a more mature digestive system, such as strained meats and cooked eggs. Overall, the shift to solid foods

TABLE 5.4	Changing Nutritional Needs During Infancy
Age in Months	**Parents May Begin**
Birth–4	Complete diet of breast milk or baby formula
4–6	Introduce puréed single-grain cereal, preferably iron-fortified. Begin with 1–2 teaspoons, work up to ½ cup, twice per day.
5	100% fruit juices, could be diluted, ½ cup serving per day.
6–8	Introduce puréed vegetables or fruit, one at a time. Begin with 1–2 teaspoons, work up to ¼–½ cup per serving, twice per day. Introduce "finger" foods (e.g., chopped banana, bits of dry cereal).
10–12	Introduce puréed meats or poultry, beginning with 1–2 teaspoons, working up to ¼–½ cup per serving, 3–4 times per day. Introduce soft but chopped foods (e.g., lumpy potatoes). Introduce whole milk, ½ cup per serving, 4–5 times per day.
24	Introduce low-fat milk, ½ cup per serving, 4–5 times per day.

Source: Adapted from International Food Information Council, 1993.

health of her baby for granted and feels little fear that the baby will die unexpectedly.

But there is more to this story than just mothers' fear of their infants' death. As an agricultural and sheep-herding people, the Gusii need able-bodied persons to work in the fields and pastures and to ensure that their large and widely scattered homesteads run smoothly. Families (and therefore mothers) who bear more children can accomplish these goals more successfully; children, in effect, are an economic asset. Gusii mothers therefore rarely practice birth control, even though government officials have made information and birth control materials widely available in the area. From the time a Gusii mother gets married (around age fifteen or sixteen) until menopause, she is usually either pregnant or nursing a young infant.

Again, this may sound grueling by North American standards, but consider again the context. A typical Gusii homestead is an extended family, or a grouping of one or two dozen relatives. Therefore, as the youngest infant moves into toddlerhood, many people are readily available to take partial responsibility for the newest member of the family. Typically the mother will assign primary responsibility to an older sibling (age six to eight), but these children will in turn be the responsibility of still older siblings or other relatives. It is this larger group, rather than the mother (or father) alone, that introduces the child to the ways of the (Gusii) world. Under these conditions, Gusii children become genuine contributors to their homesteads' wealth at very early ages. Anthropologists have observed children as young as eight years planting and successfully harvesting a large field of flaxseed.

Eventually, of course, these patterns will have to change. If all Gusii mothers continue to bear numerous children, the Gusii people will overpopulate themselves in time. If they respond by limiting the number of births, however, they will give up the economic benefits of bearing large numbers of children. Once those benefits decrease, further changes may occur that at this point are hard to foresee. What, for example, will happen to the extended family and to the child care that it makes possible?

often takes many months to complete (see Table 5.4 for guidelines about how to do this). As it occurs, parents must begin paying more attention to their baby's overall nutritional needs, since many solid foods lack the broad range of nutrients that breast milk and formula provide.

Malnutrition in North America

Often North American diets fail to provide enough of three specific nutrients: vitamin A, vitamin C, and iron. Prolonged deficiencies of vitamins A and C seem to create deficits in motor ability, and deficiency of iron appears to create deficits in cognitive performance (Pollitt, 1995). For about 4 to 5 percent of infants, these nutritional deficiencies are serious and require immediate remedy. For another group of about the same size, the nutritional deficiencies are less severe but are still a cause for concern.

Even when undernourished infants appear healthy and "bright," they may be at risk for later problems in development because poorly nourished families often experience other serious deprivations, such as poor sanitation, inadequate health care, and lack of educational opportunities. Under these conditions, it may not take much to turn mild undernourishment into severe malnutrition and thus reduce cognitive and motor performance to below satisfactory levels.

Overnutrition

In affluent, calorie-loving societies such as our own, the problem often is not lack of food but too much of calorie-rich, nutrient-poor foods. Social circumstances make it hard for parents to keep convenience foods and "junk" foods from their children

Parents should introduce solid foods slowly to ensure that their infants have developed enough to digest the food comfortably. The sensory experience of food remains a primary motive for eating throughout infancy—as indeed it does throughout life.

(or to avoid it themselves!). Food manufacturers and fast-food restaurants have discovered that foods sell better if they contain high amounts of fat, sugar, and salt, and low amounts of fiber—all of which violate well-established nutritional guidelines (Wootan & Liebman, 1998). The short-term result during infancy can be **overnutrition**: too many calories, too much of the wrong nutrients, and not enough of other nutrients. The longer-term result can be to establish food preferences that can create health risks when the infant becomes a child and later an adult. A toddler who eats too much ice cream and chips may be "cutely" chubby; an adult who does so experiences greater risk for heart problems, diabetes, and certain forms of cancer (Bronner, 1997).

Note that although overnutrition can increase an infant's weight, weight itself is not a cause of *medical* concern in infancy as long as the baby is only moderately above (or below) the average. Infants born bigger or heavier than usual tend to have diets higher than normal in calories. They also tend to drink more milk and other liquids than usual (either breast or bottle), and to shift earlier to solid foods. Contrary to what some parents fear, though, weight in infancy correlates little with weight in childhood and even less with weight in adulthood (Williams & Kimm, 1993). Babies born heavy stand only a slightly greater chance than lighter ones of becoming heavy children, and then only if they are very heavy indeed to begin with. This fact does not stop parents from sometimes feeling concerned about a heavy infant for essentially social and psychological reasons: the paradox of a society that makes overnutrition too easy is that it also overvalues thinness in physical appearance. As an infant grows into a child and adolescent, he will inevitably be affected by the social value placed on thinness. We discuss the results of the child's encounter with this problem in Chapter 11 in conjunction with discussing weight problems in middle childhood. In the meantime, it will be the child's parents who worry about weight on her behalf.

● ● ●

overnutrition Consumption of more calories than necessary for good health.

WHAT DO YOU THINK ?   If you (or your spouse) were expecting a child, would you prefer to breast feed or bottle feed? Is your answer affected by whether you are male or female?

Impairments to Infant Growth

Within broad limits, healthy infants grow at various rates and become various sizes, and most of the time the differences are no cause for concern. But a small percentage do not grow as large as they should, beginning either at birth or a bit later during infancy. When a baby's size or growth is well below normal, it is a major cause for concern for both the infant and the parents. At the extreme, it can contribute to infant mortality.

Low Birth Weight

For medical purposes, newborns are considered to be **low birth weight** if they are born weighing less than 2,500 grams, or about 5½ pounds. Such low weight can occur for either of two reasons. First, some babies do not develop as quickly as is normal, even though they are carried for about the usual term of forty weeks. These babies are called **small-for-date** infants. Second, some babies develop at about normal rates but are born significantly earlier than usual. If they are born sooner than about thirty-seven weeks from conception, they are called **preterm,** or *short-gestation,* infants. Until recently, medical research did not distinguish clearly between small-for-date and preterm infants; both were simply regarded as "premature" infants (Phelan, 1992).

Preterm infants face many more medical risks than do small-for-date infants. The extent of the risks depends on the infant's physical maturity. Physically immature infants look different from normal full-term infants: they tend to be redder and darker than normal, whatever their race, and their skin often is transparent enough to see blood vessels through it. Often they are covered with a downy hair called *lanugo* and a white, waxy substance called *vernix.* And, of course, immature newborns are smaller than usual; an infant will weigh only about two pounds if born two months early.

Causes of Low Birth Weight   Low birth weight, whether the infant is preterm or small for date, can result from several factors. As we saw in Chapter 4, one of the most common causes is malnourishment of the mother during pregnancy. But other harmful practices, such as smoking cigarettes, drinking alcohol, or taking drugs, also can depress birth weight. Mothers from certain segments of the population, such as teenagers and the very poor, are especially likely to give birth to preterm babies, most likely because of their own poor nourishment or their lack of access to good prenatal care. But even mothers who are well nourished and well cared for sometimes have infants who are smaller than is medically desirable. Multiple births (e.g., twins, triplets) usually result in small-for-date babies; so do some illnesses or mishaps, such as a serious traffic accident that causes damage to the placenta.

Consequences for the Infant   Despite recent advances in helping preterm infants survive and develop, their neurological abilities are initially impaired by early birth (Brooten, 1992). In general, the reflexes of preterm infants tend to be sluggish, weak, and poorly organized. Preterm infants do not startle as reliably or grasp as automatically and strongly at objects. Their muscles often seem flabby or overly relaxed, which is a sign not only of immature muscle development but also of nerve impulses insufficient to stimulate good muscle tone. Preterm infants tend to lie fully extended instead of with their arms and legs slightly flexed or bent. If someone pulls gently on their arms to extend them, their arms do not recoil as completely or smoothly as those of a full-term infant; jerky, random movements dominate instead, and sometimes there is no recoiling movement at all. At comparable points in their

* * *

low birth weight A birth weight of less than 2,500 grams (about 5½ pounds).

small-for-date infant An infant who develops more slowly than normal during pregnancy; can be born full term or preterm.

preterm baby Premature baby.

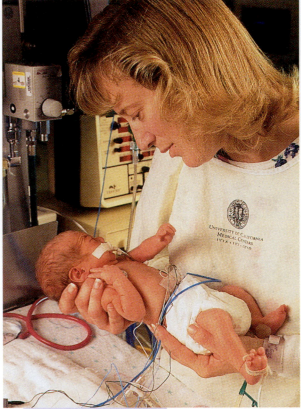

Low-birth-weight infants, like this one being held by its mother, are at risk for breathing problems for the first few weeks or months after birth. Modern medical techniques, however, have increased survival rates substantially, and also shown the value of handling and cuddling a low-birth-weight infant just as any other.

gestation, full-term infants presumably have these limitations too, but they are still inside their mothers' wombs at the time.

Outside that protected environment, preterm infants must cope with many tasks for which they are inadequately prepared. These tasks include the obvious vital processes, such as breathing and digesting food. But they also include some less obvious ones. Preterm infants suddenly must regulate the amount of sensory stimulation they receive. Just as full-term babies do, they need to see things and hear things to stimulate the development of their senses. But they also need to avoid overloading their senses with too many sights and sounds. One way to avoid overstimulation is to sleep periodically and deeply; yet even though preterm infants sleep more than full-term infants do, they have more trouble keeping their sleep peaceful and smooth. For example, they experience **sleep apnea,** periods when breathing stops for perhaps fifteen or twenty seconds, more frequently.

In some preterm infants, neurological limitations persist for the first two or three years of life, causing the babies to develop specific motor skills a bit later than full-term infants. Some of the delay is more apparent than real. A four-month-old born two months preterm, for example, in many ways resembles a two-month-old born at full term; both infants have lived eleven months from conception. Other delays may reflect stresses associated with preterm birth (such as parents' overprotectiveness) rather than the physical effects of early birth as such.

For the most part, however, preterm infants develop into normal children. Only infants with *very* low birth weight (less than 1,000 grams, or 2.2 pounds) show a significant risk of permanent impairment of motor or cognitive skills (Atkinson & Zucker, 1997), and even among these tiny babies only about 10 to 20 percent are affected by the time they reach school age. For newborns in the range of 1,000 to 2,500 grams, research suggests that toddlers and preschoolers who were preterm develop normal attachments to their parents despite their initial unresponsiveness as newborn infants. By school age, the "big" preterm children show slightly more risk of encountering learning disabilities, but their overall cognitive ability seems indistinguishable from that of full-term children.

Consequences for Parents and Health Care Providers   Because conventional hospital routines often fail to help preterm infants to regulate their sensory needs, health care providers have begun experimenting with ways to do so. For example, some hospitals can provide such babies with miniature waterbeds, which rock gently and slowly at about the same speed as a mother's normal breathing. In theory, the arrangement simulates a normal experience in the womb. Other programs have tried stimulating preterm infants with extra handling despite their initial unresponsiveness (Chestnut, 1998). Both approaches have shown very encouraging results. Infants raised in waterbeds were healthier and physically larger after several months than preterm infants raised in conventional, stationary hospital cribs. Infants who received extra handling were more responsive to sounds and displayed more normal motor behaviors. All in all, these techniques seem promising.

Even after low-birth-weight babies go home, their parents may continue to worry about their health and face challenges in forming close relationships with them. Low-birth-weight infants tend to respond to their parents less intensely than normal babies do, such as by smiling, at least at first. Under good conditions, however, these initial differences need not become lasting problems, and the parents and children eventually develop relationships that are healthy and gratifying. But if the parents face other stresses, such as insufficient economic resources, they may

• • •

sleep apnea Temporary stoppage of breathing during sleep.

lack the time or energy to overcome the initial difficulties in making contact with their baby (Gross et al., 1997). To avoid forming a permanently poor relationship, such parents may need help from a social worker or a nurse to understand their infant's development so that they can enjoy that development as it unfolds.

Failure to Thrive

An infant or a preschool child who fails to grow at normal rates for no apparent medical reason suffers from a condition called **failure to thrive.** About 6 percent of North American children show this condition at one time or another, although not necessarily continuously (Woolston, 1993). In some ways the condition resembles malnutrition, especially when it occurs in developing nations. Failure-to-thrive and malnourished children both develop motor and cognitive skills more slowly than usual; both experience higher rates of school failure and learning disabilities; and both are more likely to live in disadvantaged circumstances and to have parents who are enduring physical or emotional stress.

At one time, professionals tended to attribute failure to thrive to lack of nurturing and love between parent and child. A more complex picture may be closer to the truth: failure to thrive may have many sources, both physical and psychological, and depend on both the child and the environment. Consider this pattern. An infant has a genetically quiet, slow-to-respond temperament, making it more difficult for her mother to establish emotional contact. If the mother also is experiencing a number of other stresses (low income, illness, or disapproval of the new baby from others), the relationship between mother and infant is put at risk. A vicious cycle may develop of poorly timed feedings and ineffective efforts to nurture the infant, who persistently resists the mother's love—and even her food. However, the cycle may not develop at all, and even when it does, it does *not* develop because the mother does not care about her infant or because the infant does not want food or affection. Intentions are usually good. Partly for this reason, parents and children eventually can get out of such awkward, frustrating relationships if professionals help the parents to understand how the situation developed.

Infant Mortality

In the past several decades, health care systems in North America and around the world have substantially improved their ability to keep infants alive. The **infant mortality rate,** the proportion of babies who die during the first year of life, has declined steadily during this century. In 1950 in the United States, about twenty-nine out of every one thousand infants died; four decades later, this number was fewer than ten out of every one thousand infants (U.S. National Center for Health Statistics, 1998). The averages conceal wide differences within society, some of which are listed in Table 5.5. Families with very low incomes are about twice as likely to lose an infant as are families with middle-level incomes (about eighteen to twenty babies per one thousand versus nine per one thousand). Likewise, African American families are twice as likely as Caucasian families to lose an infant, perhaps because of the historical correlation of race with income level and access to health care in American society (Pritchett, 1993). As a result, mortality rates in some non-white, low-income areas of major cities rival the rates found in less developed countries around the world.

On average, the infant mortality rate in the United States and Canada is two or three times lower than that in many less developed countries. Even so, infant mortality in the United States actually is *higher* than in nineteen other developed nations, including Canada, Japan, Sweden, France, and Great Britain (United Nations International Children's Emergency Fund, 1998). The high mortality rate comes as

• • •

failure to thrive A condition in which an infant seems seriously delayed in physical growth and is noticeably apathetic in behavior.

infant mortality rate The frequency with which infants die compared to the frequency with which they live.

TABLE 5.5	Infant Mortality in Selected Nations

Nation	Infant Mortality (per 1,000 live births)
Finland	5.5
Japan	6.3
Sweden	6.7
Switzerland	6.9
Hong Kong	7.5
Canada	7.9
Denmark	7.9
Netherlands	7.9
France	8.0
United States, white	**8.5**
Norway	8.5
Germany	8.9
Ireland	8.9
Singapore	9.3
United Kingdom	9.3
Belgium	9.4
Australia	10.0
Spain	10.5
United States, average	**10.6**
New Zealand	10.8
Italy	10.9
Austria	11.0
Israel	12.3
Greece	14.0
Czechoslovakia	14.0
United States, nonwhite	**17.5**

Sources: UNICEF (1998); U.S. Bureau of the Census (1998).

a surprise, because the United States generally is more affluent than many of these other nations, and the American medical system originated many of the life-saving techniques that have lowered infant mortality rates around the world. Distribution of infant health care, it seems, is far from ideal in the United States.

A prime example of the problem concerns childhood immunizations against serious illnesses such as polio, diphtheria, or measles, among others. Survey research has found that only about half of all children in the United States receive immunizations against these (and other) diseases (Centers for Disease Control, 1997). This rate is higher than those in many less developed countries (but not all!), and significantly lower than those in Canada and most European countries, which typically have immunization rates of 80 to 95 percent. Several reasons probably operate jointly to account for the comparatively low rate in the United States. One is that free and low-cost immunization programs are not always well advertised. Another is that the United States is a society represented by many language, religious, and cultural groups, which makes communication about the benefits and availability of immunizations more difficult. A third is that many sources of immunization (e.g., a family doctor) cost money, which reduces their accessibility to families that lack sufficient financial resources or medical insurance.

Cross-cultural investigations of infant mortality rates in European countries have given further clues about the reasons for the relatively high U.S. rate and have suggested ways to improve it. The research overwhelmingly indicates that parents need social supports as much as they need access to basic medical services and knowledge. In Europe, this support takes several forms. Most European countries provide pregnant mothers with free prenatal care. Frequently this care is provided by medically trained (and usually female) midwives, who are better able to give the time needed to establish a supportive relationship with pregnant women.

Most European countries also protect working mothers by law. Pregnant women get special, generous sick leave, get at least four months of maternity leave with pay, and are protected from doing dangerous or exhausting work (such as night shifts). Every European country also begins a regular cash payment to parents when their child is born, the amount and duration depending on the condition of the child and the number of children already in the family. Altogether, these policies and practices communicate emotional support to pregnant mothers and their spouses in ways not currently available in the United States.

WHAT DO YOU THINK? It is common for parents to blame themselves if their child is born with low birth weight. What would you say to a parent who reacted this way? Would you say essentially the same things to a parent whose child showed failure to thrive?

Infancy: The Real End of Birth

During the first two years of life, several changes make infants seem much more like individuals, or "real" people, than they did on the day they were born. As children approach their second birthday, for example, many of their basic physical needs and skills have stabilized. Now they can swallow and even chew a variety of foods, even if they still lack a lot of teeth and make a mess out of eating. And now they can (sometimes!) sleep through the night.

Complementing this new stability are new behaviors. Two-year-olds can move around freely, even if they are sometimes still clumsy. Most important, a lot of their movement is voluntary; a toddler may wander away in a department store, for example, because he wants to. Such movements are facilitated by infants' physical growth during the first two years. By their second birthday, they can use their hands and feet to help them implement choices, however crudely at first. As the next two chapters show, the first two years also make infants seem more human in two other major ways: by preparing them to think in symbols and by helping them to form definite attachments to parents and peers.

Summary of Major Ideas

Appearance of the Young Infant

1. The average newborn born at full term weighs about 7½ pounds. Newborns' bodily proportions, such as their large heads, make them look appealing. These proportions may foster the formation of attachments with adult caregivers.

2. The health of newborns born in hospitals is assessed quickly after delivery with the Apgar scale.

Development of the Nervous System

3. A child's brain grows rapidly during infancy, and at the same time parts of it begin to develop special functions.

4. Infants sleep almost twice as much as adults do, but the amount gradually decreases as they get older. They also experience distinct states of arousal from deep sleep to full alertness.

Sensory Development

5. At birth infants already can see and hear, but with less accuracy or acuity than adults can.

6. All of the senses develop rapidly and reach adult levels of acuity and sensitivity by the end of infancy.

Motor Development

7. Infants are born with a number of physically useful reflexes, such as rooting and sucking.

8. Infants are also born with several reflexes, such as the Moro reflex, whose primary significance is to indicate normal development of the nervous system.

9. Motor skills appear during the first year of infancy and include reaching, crawling, walking, and grasping.

10. Motor skills develop differently depending on special learning experiences, cultural background, and sex, though the precise nature of these influences is ambiguous.

Nutrition During the First Two Years

11. Infants need more protein and calories per pound of body weight than older children do.

12. Compared to formula and bottle feeding, breast feeding has a number of practical and psychological advantages.

13. After weaning from breast or bottle, infants need a diet rich in protein and calories. Most North American families can provide these requirements, but many cannot.

14. A common problem in North American diets is overnutrition, which can create health risks in the long term.

Impairments to Infant Growth

15. One of the most important impairments to early growth is low birth weight, because the condition leads to difficulties with breathing, digestion, and sleep, and impairs normal reflexes.

16. The problems experienced by low-birth-weight infants sometimes puts stress on their relationships with parents, but not necessarily.

17. For a variety of reasons, infants sometimes fail to thrive normally.

18. Infant mortality has decreased in the recent past, but in the United States it is still higher than it should be.

Key Terms

Apgar scale (137)
attachment (139)
brainstem (139)
central nervous system (139)
cerebellum (139)
cerebral cortex (143)
failure to thrive (159)
fine motor skills (148)
gross motor skills (148)
infant mortality rate (159)
low birth weight (157)
midbrain (139)
Moro reflex (148)
motor abilities (147)
motor skills (148)
neonate (136)

neurons (139)
non-REM sleep (143)
overnutrition (156)
preterm (157)
primitive reflex (148)
reflexes (147)
REM sleep (143)
rooting (147)
skills (147)
sleep apnea (158)
small for date (157)
sucking (147)
sudden infant death syndrome (SIDS) (143)
survival reflex (148)

Cognitive Development in the First Two Years

Focusing Questions

- What clues do infants give about their cognitive processes? How can we learn about infants' thinking?

- Do infants see and hear in the same way adults do?

- What does "thinking," or cognition, consist of at different periods of infancy?

- What are the three types of learning, and how do infants demonstrate them?

- What steps do infants and toddlers go through in acquiring language, and how do adults affect this language acquisition?

From birth, infants begin acquiring knowledge about their environment. Consider William and Greta:

William, nine months old, laughs when his father puts on a Halloween mask. But two days later, when a family friend tries on the same mask, William cries in distress. Six months later he laughs when the friend tries on the mask again, but he shies away from trying it on himself. The same mask seems to have changed meaning for him more than once.

One day Greta, eighteen months old, cannot find a favorite toy, a stuffed cat. For a time she forgets everything else to look for her cat—under her bed, on the shelves, in the closet. She is so engrossed that her mother cannot get her to stop until the cat is found.

These examples illustrate two psychological processes: perception and cognition.

Perception refers to the processes involved in the brain's immediate or direct organization and interpretation of sensations. Perceptual processes occur when an infant notices that a toy car is the same car no matter which way he orients it. As the infant turns the car upside down in his hands, his visual image of it changes; yet he still perceives the changing patterns as one unchanging car. He is not fooled into thinking that the car has acquired a different identity when he turns it upside down. Perception has an automatic, involuntary quality as well, such as when William cannot help noticing that different people wearing the same mask look similar but also just a bit different.

Cognition refers to all the processes involved in thinking and other mental activities. It includes reasoning, attention, memory, problem solving, and the ability to represent objects and experiences. Greta uses cognitive skills when she searches for her favorite stuffed cat. William, on the other hand, is so young that his reaction to the mask may be based more on perception than on conceptual thinking; the mask has violated the constancy and stability that his brain automatically provides for the objects he encounters. Preschool children and adults almost surely would feel less distress than William does, because they would do more than perceive the mask. They might also consciously wonder who was behind the mask each time, why the person had put it on, and the like. They would *conceptualize* the experience and, in doing so, perhaps alter their perceptions of it as well.

Whatever your age or maturity, most of your activities include both perception and cognition. When you hear a university professor lecture, you may perceive the sounds she or he makes as language, but you probably also apply cognitive skills to make sense of them; otherwise, the lecture is only so much linguistic noise. Research on infancy suggests that infants may be more influenced by perception than older individuals are, but the difference is only a matter of degree. The fact that babies can imitate behaviors and search for a favorite toy suggests that they also experience deliberate conceptual thought.

perception The neural activity of combining sensations into meaningful patterns.

cognition All processes by which humans acquire knowledge; methods for thinking or gaining knowledge about the world.

163

In this chapter, we look at how infants develop conceptual and perceptual abilities. We begin by examining how such abilities can be discovered and studied, even at remarkably early ages and well before infants are able to express themselves with language. Then we describe the major cognitive achievements of infancy. Among these milestones are the beginnings of language, a topic so important that we discuss it further in Chapter 9, with reference to language developments in the preschool years.

Ways of Studying Perception and Cognition in Infants

How can we know whether a very young infant, who mostly just sleeps, is actually noticing an interesting sight or sound, much less thinking about it? Consider Jenny, who is only two months old:

> For two hours Jenny had slept. Now she lay in her mother's arms with eyes barely open, while her mother talked affectionately to her. The mother nodded her head while she talked, exaggerated her voice to a singsong, and even dangled a key chain in front of Jenny's eyes for a moment. Jenny stared more or less in the direction of all these events. She did not respond in an obvious way, but she did not avert her eyes from it all or go back to sleep.

Maybe Jenny noticed her mother's efforts, but then again maybe she did not. Either way, we could not find out by simple observation; a more complex investigation would be required. Infant psychologists have developed several interrelated techniques for inferring the perceptions and "thoughts" of babies. One measures changes in infants' states of arousal; another assesses how they respond to especially familiar sights and sounds; and still another measures their readiness to habitually perform those behaviors they find rewarding.

Arousal and Infants' Heart Rates

One way to understand an infant's cognition is to measure his heart rate (HR) with a small electronic stethoscope attached to his chest. The changes in HR are taken to signify variations in the baby's arousal, alertness, and general contentment.

Psychologists who study infants make this assumption because among adults, HR varies reliably with attention and arousal. Typically HR slows down, or decelerates, when adults notice or attend to something interesting but not overly exciting, such as reading the newspaper. If adults attend to something *very* stimulating, their HRs speed up, or accelerate. Watching a lab technician draw blood from your own arm, for example, often causes your HR to speed up. On the whole, novel or attractive stimuli produce curiosity and a slower HR, whereas potentially dangerous or aversive stimuli produce defensiveness, discomfort, and a faster HR, at least among adults.

Very young infants, from one day to a few months old, show similar changes, but we need to take several precautions when we study their HRs. For one thing, observations of infants' attention should be made when infants are awake and alert, and, as we already pointed out, newborn babies often spend a lot of time being drowsy or asleep. For another, newborn and very young infants are much more likely to respond to relatively gentle and persistent stimuli, such as a quiet, continuous sound or a soft light that moves slowly or blinks repeatedly (Slater & Morrison, 1991). Many stimuli that lead to deceleration in adults or older children lead to acceleration in infants. Many one-month-olds show a faster HR at familiar sights, such as their mothers, even though the infants may look like they are just staring calmly

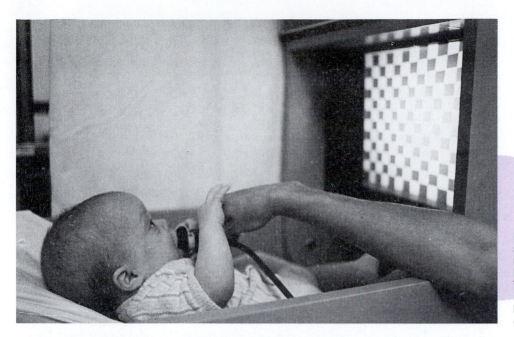

Babies often show preferences for novel stimuli. By sucking on a special nipple, the baby in the experiment pictured here brings a visual pattern into or out of focus. Typically a new pattern prompts intense and rapid sucking at first, but as the baby habituates or gets used to the pattern, she or he sucks less frequently.

into space. Despite these problems, however, studies of HR have provided a useful way to measure infants' attention, perception, and memory.

Recognition, Memory, and Infant Habituation

Although infants cannot describe what they remember, they often indicate recognition of particular objects, people, and activities. Familiar people, such as mothers, bring forth a special response in one-year-olds, who may coo suddenly at the sight of them, stretch out their arms to them, and even crawl or walk to them if they know how. Less familiar people, such as neighbors or the family doctor, tend not to produce responses like these and in fact may even produce active distress, depending on the age of the infant.

Babies' responses to the familiar and the unfamiliar offer infant psychologists a second way to understand infant perception and conceptual thought. Psychologists study infants' tendency to get used to and therefore ignore stimuli as they experience them repeatedly; this tendency is often called **habituation** by psychologists (Mazur, 1994). One habituation strategy repeatedly offers a baby a standard, or "study," stimulus—a simple picture to look at or a simple melody to hear. Like most adults, the baby attends to the study stimulus carefully at first, but on subsequent occasions gradually pays less attention to it. As this happens, the baby is said to be *habituating* to the stimulus. After she has become habituated, the investigators present the original study stimulus along with a few other stimuli. If the baby really recognizes the original, she probably will attend to the others *more* because they are comparatively novel. Her HR will slow down as well.

This method has shown that young babies recognize quite a lot of past experiences. One classic habituation study found that four-month-old girls recognized a familiar visual pattern among three others that differed from the original (McCall & Kagan, 1967). Still another found habituation even in newborns: they "noticed" when a light brush on their cheeks changed location, as revealed by changes in their HRs (Kisilevsky & Muir, 1984). Sometimes, too, recognition persists for very long periods. Three-month-olds, it seems, can still recognize a picture or toy two weeks after they first see it, as long as the objects are presented in a familiar context the second time—a performance that matches adults' recognition memory (Hayne et al., 1991).

● ● ●

habituation The tendency to attend to novel stimuli and ignore familiar ones.

Habituation is important not only because it provides a way to study infants' learning and development but also because it suggests that infants have memories well before they acquire language. And habituation has interesting, though speculative, implications for parent-child relationships: it suggests that young babies may begin recognizing their parents quite quickly—perhaps as quickly as they exhibit the habituation that psychologists have observed in laboratory experiments. Parents may not simply be imagining it, that is, when they become convinced that their baby responds differently or more fully to them than to other adults; the child may really be doing so even at the age of just a few weeks.

WHAT DO YOU THINK ?   Talk to a parent (preferably of an infant) about when he or she felt sure of being recognized. Do the parent's experiences suggest that the infant truly does remember the parent? Do the infant's signs of recognition apply only to his or her primary caregiver, or do they extend to other relatives?

Infant Perception and Cognition

As mentioned earlier, *perception* refers to how the brain organizes and interprets sensations. Perception operates relatively automatically: when your best friend walks up to you, your brain almost instantly converts an oval-shaped pattern of colors and lines from an unorganized batch of sensations into an organized whole called your friend's face. The automatic quality of perception has made many psychologists suspect that it is either genetically programmed or learned very early in infancy. Either way, it would be a primary feature of infant cognition.

Children indeed acquire a number of important perceptual skills during infancy. Each skill corresponds to one or another of the five human senses: vision, hearing, touch, taste, and smell. The first sense, vision, has been studied more than any of the others, and vision and hearing together account for the large majority of research about infants' perception. This emphasis reflects society's widespread (but probably unjustified) belief that touch, taste, and smell are "minor" senses, ones we can live without more easily than vision and hearing.

Visual Thinking in Infancy

Given that children can see at least to some extent during infancy, what do they perceive? Some of the earliest research on this question stirred up a lot of interest because it seemed to show that infants, even those just two days old, could discriminate between human faces and abstract patterns and that they looked at faces longer than at either patterned disks or plain, unpatterned disks (Fantz, 1963). The researchers presented infants with various combinations of these stimuli side by side and carefully observed which object the babies spent the most time looking at. At all ages studied (birth to six months), the infants showed a clear preference: they stared at a picture of a human face almost twice as long as at any other stimulus picture. Young infants, it seemed, were inherently interested in people.

More recent studies of visual preferences, however, have qualified this conclusion substantially (Yonas, 1988). It is not the humanness of faces that infants enjoy looking at but their interesting contours, complexity, and curvature. Newborns are particularly attracted to contours, or the edges of areas of light and dark. But such edges can be provided either by the hairline of a parent's head or by a properly constructed abstract drawing. When infants reach age two or three months, their perceptual interest shifts to complexity and curvature. At this age, infants prefer looking at a pattern of many small squares rather than one of just a few large squares. They also prefer looking at curved lines to looking at straight ones. These qualities too are conveniently provided to most babies by human faces, but not by faces alone.

Young infants concentrate longer on certain shapes and contours, even when these are not part of a human face. Newborns are especially attracted to contours and to patches of light and dark. A few months later, they prefer complex patterns over simpler ones, and curved lines over straight ones. Such changes are one reason (among many) that a baby's interest in crib toys waxes and wanes over time.

Also by age two or three months, infants can distinguish at least some of the colors that adults normally perceive (Teller & Lindsey, 1993). They even show a preference for red and blue over green and yellow, as judged by how long they choose to look at sample patches of each of these colors. The color preferences parallel those of adults, suggesting that they are at least partly inborn and not entirely the result of cultural learning. What infants conceptualize about colors at such a young age, however, remains ambiguous; it would seem they have much learning and experience to undergo before they can associate *red* with *fire,* for example.

Object Perception   A more complex form of perception—one that is a step closer to cognition—is *object constancy,* the perception (or is it a "belief"?) that an object remains the same despite constant changes in the sensation it sends to the eye. A baby's favorite toy duck never casts exactly the same image on her retina from one second to the next. The image continually varies depending on its distance and its orientation, or angle of viewing. Somehow the baby must learn that this kaleidoscope of images really refers to only one constant duck—that the duck always *is* the same but keeps *looking* different.

In general, research on infant perception suggests that infants begin perceiving objects as constant very early indeed (Granrud, 1993). Consider the development of *size constancy,* the perception that an object stays the same size even when viewed from different distances. In a typical study, newborn babies are conditioned to suck on pacifiers (see Chapter 2 for an explanation of this process) at the sight of a cube of some specified size and placed at some precise distance. During conditioning training, sucking at the sight of cubes of other sizes or distances is deliberately not reinforced so that the sucking provides an indicator of the baby's recognition of an object of a particular size and at a given distance.

Later the conditioned infants are shown several cubes of different sizes and placed at different distances. The test cubes include one that casts an image exactly the size of the original but is in fact larger and farther away. Typically, the babies are not fooled by this apparent identity of retinal images. They prefer to look at the original cube regardless of its distance; that is, they suck on their pacifiers more vigorously while looking at the original cube than while looking at any substitute. Apparently they know when an object really is the same size and when it only looks the same size.

Infants' behavior on a visual cliff reflects both their knowledge and their feelings about depth. Even babies too young to crawl or creep find the deep side of the cliff more interesting than the shallow side. But only babies who have begun crawling or creeping show fear or wariness of the deep side.

But size constancy is imperfect. Regardless of an object's size or shape, infants prefer objects at certain distances, especially nearby ones; objects with contrasting hues and brightnesses; and objects near their center line of vision (Banks & Sharman, 1993). Anything that meets these conditions attracts a newborn's attention especially well and therefore can create the impression of attentiveness just described. When all these factors are controlled, infants still show some size constancy, but not as much as in everyday life when hue, brightness, and distance tend to work together to confirm the size constancy of most objects.

Do babies perceive an object as being the same even when its shape changes because the angle from which it is viewed changes? This particular perception, sometimes called *shape constancy*, depends on the ability to recognize apparent but unreal changes in shape. A rubber doll held upright casts a different image on the eye than the same doll lying down. But this change in shape is only apparent; compare it with the real change caused by squeezing the rubber doll hard with both hands.

In general, research on this skill suggests that infants acquire shape constancy gradually, beginning at around three months of age. Typically they demonstrate this skill, as they do many others, by habituating—in this case, to shapes viewed at various angles or orientations, or undergoing various motions or rotations (Columbo, 1993). A variety of experiments have shown that during their first year, infants prefer to watch the same object under different orientations and movements rather than some other object undergoing comparable changes.

Infants begin their first year showing shape constancy only for simple shapes, such as spheres or cubes. As the year goes on, they develop constancy for increasingly complex forms, such as faces or abstract drawings presented at sidelong or tilted angles (Aslin, 1993). For the most complex figures, gentle movement or rotation seems to help infants identify shapes. In these cases, older infants react somewhat like adults who are viewing a piece of sculpture: they must see all sides of it to be able to perceive its full identity.

All of these qualifications make it hard to name a precise age at which babies acquire either shape or size constancy. A young infant's daily expression of various object constancies is likely to seem tentative and ambiguous to a parent or other adult. One day the child responds as though an object were the "same" at different distances or orientations, yet the next day the child conveys ignorance of constancy. The variability occurs because object constancy depends partly on the child's attentiveness and partly on the child's prior memories of the object, both of which are somewhat fragile in early infancy.

Whatever the timing of their appearance, shape and size constancies serve important functions in babies' long-term development. These skills help infants to distinguish familiar objects from novel ones and to begin seeing the world as predictable and secure. Gradually mother is mother and father is father, whether viewed from the side or from the front and whether viewed from ten feet or two feet. Shape and size constancies also help infants learn about new, inanimate objects more efficiently. Familiar objects are recognized more often and more quickly, allowing the baby to concentrate on newer, unexplored objects.

Depth Perception   Even if the infant perceives the sizes and shapes of objects fairly accurately, he or she still must navigate successfully from one place to another. Consider Joel, who recently learned to crawl around his house. Joel must realize that the rooms in his house stay put when he crawls or walks, even though they look like they move. And he must notice that stairs differ from floors. Such realizations require Joel to orient his actions to the world or space outside his own body and to understand its layout accurately. In other words, he must perceive depth and spatial orientation accurately. Each of these perceptions appears and then changes during the course of infancy.

Depth perception refers to a sense of how far away objects are or appear to be. Infants begin acquiring this kind of perceptual skill about as soon as they can focus on objects at different distances, at around two or three months of age. This conclusion is suggested by research that has developed out of the now classic experiment with the visual cliff (Gibson & Walk, 1960). In its basic form, the **visual cliff** consists of a table covered with strong glass under which is a textured surface with colored squares, such as that shown in the photograph on page 168. Part of the textured surface contacts the glass directly, and another part is separated from it by several feet. Visually, then, the setup resembles the edge of a table, but the glass provides ample support for an infant, even in the dropped-off area. A baby who is placed onto it will seem to float in midair.

On this apparatus, even babies just two months old discriminate between the two sides of the visual cliff. They find the deep side more interesting, as suggested by the extra time they take to study it. Young babies show little fear of the deep side, judging either by their overt behavior or by their heart rates, which tend to decrease during their investigations of the cliff. This finding implies they are primarily curious about the cliff rather than fearful of it.

Babies old enough to crawl, however, show significant fear of the visual cliff. Their heart rates increase markedly, and they will not crawl onto the deep side despite coaxing from a parent and the solid support they feel from the glass. Why the change? Perhaps infants' crawling skills allow them to perceive distances more accurately than before, since the motion of crawling causes faraway objects (including the deep side of the cliff) to move less than nearby objects (such as the shallow side). Perhaps, too, infants old enough to crawl are also old enough to focus their eyes more accurately for each side of the cliff, a physical skill that provides further perceptual information about the difference in distance of the two sides (Kermoian & Campos, 1988). And, of course, experiences with crawling may have led in the past to experiences with falling, so the older infants may wisely be cautious about heights.

Anticipation of Visual Events   Even closer to deliberate cognition than perception of contours, objects, and depth are infants' anticipations of visual events that have not yet occurred. Signs of "looking forward" to an interesting sight are visible by observing a child's eye movements carefully. Infant psychologists have developed

● ● ●

visual cliff The classic laboratory setup of a ledge covered by a sheet of glass; used to test the acquisition of depth perception. Young babies crawling on the glass discriminate between the two sides of the "cliff."

infrared video cameras to assist with this task, as well as a modified form of the habituation procedure, called a *visual expectation paradigm,* designed to elicit (or encourage) eye movements by the child. Typically, the infant sits in front of a large computer screen, which displays a series of interesting drawings at different locations on the screen, such as on the lefthand or righthand sides. Meanwhile a video camera films the baby's eye movements as she directs her gaze toward the drawings. By linking the camera with the computer, it is possible to know whether the child's eyes change direction *following* the appearance of a picture at a new location or actually *precede,* or anticipate, its appearance.

This procedure shows clearly that infants as young as two months do not merely follow but often anticipate the locations of pictures, and in this sense develop expectations about the environment that "foresee the future" (Canfield et al., 1997). Their anticipations, furthermore, show a variety of rule-governed qualities. By one year of age, for example, infants anticipate locations that portray numerical sequences. If a series of drawings contain various numbers of items at random, and the drawings are located alternately on the left and right sides of the screen, infants tend to look for the spot where a drawing with "one more" in it *should* be displayed if it were alternating in a regular pattern. They do not look for the spot that displays some other number of items (Canfield & Smith, 1995).

Infants' visual anticipations suggest that infants "think" in some way about what they see (engage in cognition) and do not merely register what they see automatically (engage simply in perception). For example, in their scanning of interesting visual patterns and contours mentioned earlier, they may be forming rudimentary generalizations, or rules, about what they see, such as where precisely to look to see another smiling face.

All of this verges on implying that infants process visual information in the same ways older children do. But do they really? Later in this chapter, we will describe opposition to the idea of strong continuity from Jean Piaget, whose views of developmental stages of thinking were discussed in Chapter 2 and will be discussed again in Chapter 9. Not, though, that the research on infants' visual expectations implies neither *full* continuity with children's visual processing nor uniformity among infants as individuals. Research on visual expectations also shows important individual differences among infants, with some babies anticipating events faster, more reliably, and at earlier ages than others (Haith et al., 1997). Whether the differences predict later variations in children's thinking, motor coordination, or other skills is a good question, but one that research has not yet answered. At this point, it is better not to assume that babies who anticipate visual events faster are in some sense destined to become "more intelligent" or skillful than others as they grow older.

Auditory Thinking in Infancy

Infants respond to sounds even as newborns. But what do they perceive from sounds? What sense do they make of the sounds they hear? These questions are important, because infants' ability to discriminate among sounds makes a crucial difference in their acquisition of language, as discussed later in this chapter.

Gaining skill at discriminating among sounds takes many months. Consider LaVonne and Daniel:

> At about five o'clock each day LaVonne, two months old, cries unaccountably. Her father finds that running the vacuum cleaner quiets her down immediately. He also finds it keeps her quiet more or less indefinitely, or at least until he cannot stand the sound of the vacuum any longer.
>
> Daniel, fourteen months old, sometimes gets fussy. His mother finds that playing music quiets him down rapidly. Familiar melodies and vocal singing seem to keep him quiet the longest, although every kind of music works for at least a little while.

Most adults would guess that Daniel perceives some sort of meaning from what he hears, such as the melodic structure of the songs or some of the words being sung. But LaVonne cannot get meaning from what she hears; more likely she quiets because she tunes out, or "averts her ears" from, the noise of the vacuum cleaner.

Localization of Sounds   Research confirms these informal impressions. Under certain conditions infants can indeed organize the sounds they hear, and in this sense they can hear as well as perceive what they hear. For example, infants just two months old can locate sounds, as suggested by the fact that they orient their heads toward certain noises, such as a rattle (Morrongiello, 1994). But they often take much longer to respond than do older children or adults. Instead of needing just a fraction of a second, as adults do, full-term infants require an average of two to three seconds before orienting toward ("looking at") a sound that occurs off to one side. Infants born one month preterm require even more time to respond. These delays may explain why pediatricians and others used to believe newborn infants cannot hear: the sounds they offered to the babies, such as a single hand clap, may not have lasted long enough for the infants to respond.

Although infants can locate sounds, their skill at doing so is somewhat limited. They are better able to locate relatively high-pitched sounds, such as those made by a flute or a small bird, than low-pitched sounds, such as that made by a foghorn (Spetner & Olsho, 1990). This fact has sometimes led some experts to suggest that infants have a "natural" preference for female—or at least high-pitched—human voices. Studies of voice preferences, however, have not confirmed this possibility consistently, probably because newborns' range of special sensitivity lies well above the pitch of even female voices and because male and female voices usually are more similar in overall quality than gender stereotypes suggest. Instead, it is more accurate to say that infants prefer sounds in the middle range of pitches, which is the range most similar to human voices, male or female.

Coordination of Vision and Hearing   The localization of sounds suggests that even very young babies coordinate what they see with what they hear; they seem to use sound to direct their visual gaze. But is this what really happens? As reasonable as this interpretation seems, the evidence suggests a more complicated story (Morrongiello, 1994). In their first efforts to turn their heads, very young babies (one or two months old) act more as though head turning is a reflex than a search for something to see. The behavior does not habituate, meaning a young baby is just as likely to turn toward a sound after many presentations as she was after the first presentation. Also, the behavior occurs even in the dark, when there is no chance to actually see the source of a sound. Only by age five or six months do these reflexive qualities change: by that age, babies habituate quickly to repeated presentations and search only in the light, when there is something to see. In these ways, then, hearing and vision have become coordinated, but it has taken several months of learning for the change to occur.

Categorical Thought: The Reversal Shift

The coordination of visual and auditory perception makes possible forms of deliberate learning that are definitely cognitive and not simply perceptual. One series of research studies used the sound of human speech to reward nine-month-old infants for learning complex visual discriminations (Coldren & Colombo, 1994). In the first part of the studies (which we will call Phase 1), infants viewed pairs of drawings on a computer screen. The images differed randomly in at least two dimensions at the same time, such as shape and color. The experimenters chose one of the dimensions (for example, color) and reinforced one of the "values" of that dimension (for exam-

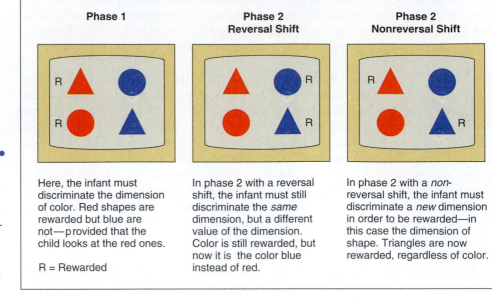

● ● ● ● ● ● ● ● ● ● ● ● ● ● ● ● ●

FIGURE 6.1

The Reversal Shift

There is little doubt that most infants can attend to specific features of their environment, such as the particular color or particular shape of an object. The reversal shift experiment helps to assess whether they can also attend to its underlying qualities, such as color or shape. The figure explains how this is done.

● ● ●

nonreversal shift An experimental procedure in which reinforcement shifts to discriminating a new dimension of difference between objects (e.g., shape versus size).

reversal shift An experimental procedure in which reinforcement continues for discriminating a new value of a dimension (e.g., large versus small) but the dimension itself (e.g., size) remains constant.

ple, they chose red to be reinforced rather than blue). If the baby looked at the correct value of the dimension (in this case, any one of the red shapes), she was reinforced with a brief recording of adult speech; otherwise she received no reinforcement. In essence, the baby had to figure out the "correct" figure to look at, but without being told. Figure 6.1 illustrates the procedure for Phase 1.

Under these conditions, all of the nine-month-olds learned to look at the correct figures. So far the experiment resembled a traditional example of operant conditioning such as those described in Chapter 2: a behavior (or operant) was reinforced and therefore began happening more often. But the experimenters then introduced a second phase of the experiment that altered this interpretation. In Phase 2, they changed the rule by which to earn a reinforcement. For some infants, the rule underwent what the experimenters called a *reversal shift*. In a **reversal shift,** reinforcement still occurred for the same underlying dimension, but took on a new "value"; for example, color was still rewarded regardless of the object's shape, but it was now blue color instead of red color. For other infants, reinforcement underwent a **nonreversal shift,** which meant that it became attached to an entirely new dimension; for example, all triangles were now rewarded, regardless of color. Figure 6.1 illustrates the two versions of Phase 2—one with a reversal shift and one with a nonreversal shift.

The subtle difference between a reversal and a nonreversal shift provided a way to test whether the infants responded to Phase 1 of the experiment in terms of the underlying dimensions of the problem or responded simply in terms of the specific sensations they perceived. If they responded in terms of the dimensions, a reversal shift should have proven easier for them during the second phase of the experiment. In that case it would be as though, for example, they had initially said to themselves, "This is a problem about color identification, and I just have to figure out which color to identify." When some infants encountered a reversal shift, it simply confirmed their hypothesis, and they were left with the relatively minor task of figuring out *which* color had now become the rewarded color. When other infants encountered a nonreversal shift, however, they faced the more difficult task of determining not only which new dimension was now being rewarded ("Is it shape? Size?") but also the specific *expression* of the dimension. The reversal shift ought to have been easier, but the advantage should have occurred only if the infants actually responded in terms of underlying dimensions. If they simply learned as operant conditioning theory predicts—by responding to the specific sensations presented to them—reversal and nonreversal shifts should have proven about equally challenging. In that case, it would be as though the infants were oblivious to the underlying dimensions and were simply hunting for specific correct answers.

What actually happened? The reversal shift proved significantly easier for nine-month-olds to learn (Coldren & Colombo, 1994), suggesting that the infants "thought" about this problem in terms of underlying, abstract categories of this particular problem. The result would not be remarkable if it had occurred with older children or adults; in fact, a long history of research about reversal and nonreversal shifts documents our tendency to solve problems by seeking underlying cognitive structures to them (Gholson, 1994; Kendler & Kendler, 1962). What makes the result important is the young age of the participants: just nine months old. Cognition, in the sense of deliberate reasoning, seems to be active even from infancy, and therefore something that parents and other caregivers can—and should—support even from birth. They can do so by providing interesting challenges for infants, such as playing peek-a-boo or offering them unfamiliar objects to manipulate.

WHAT DO YOU THINK ?   But wait: there have to be some qualifications or limits on the conclusion we reached in the sentence just above. What do you think they are? Maybe infants do "reason," as we suggest, but even if they do, how might their reasoning change as they get older? Would it be just by learning more facts, or would the fundamental nature of their reasoning also change somehow?

Cognitive Change During Infancy: Piaget's Stage Theory

The two preceding sections highlighted continuities between infants' and adults' cognitive abilities. Infants can perceive object constancies, anticipate what they are about to see, locate sounds, and categorize certain experiences—all abilities that they share with adults. Most of the research cited is framed by some version of information-processing theory, the approach described in Chapter 2 (and elsewhere in this book) that emphasizes the importance of organizing specific input so that it becomes more meaningful, much as a computer is sometimes thought to do.

Yet infants obviously do not think "just like adults." For one thing, they use little or no language to assist them in solving problems. Proud parents notwithstanding, they often also seem slow and highly error prone in figuring things out. Their skills are still limited and seem worlds away from the cognitive behaviors of older children or adults. How do they transform their budding infant skills into the comparatively smooth expertise of an adult? And during infancy, in particular, how does the transformation begin?

Stages of Sensorimotor Intelligence

Jean Piaget, whose approach was described in Chapter 2, offers one of the most complete descriptions and explanations of cognitive development available (Piaget, 1963). According to Piaget, infants begin life thinking in terms of *sensory* perceptions and *motor* actions, by doing things to and with the objects around them. Piaget called this activity **sensorimotor intelligence.** He identified stages during infancy that mark significant developments in sensorimotor intelligence, as summarized in Table 6.1.

In general, these stages show two trends as infants grow older. First, infants show a trend toward symbolic thinking. Instead of needing to handle a toy car to understand it, an infant becomes increasingly able to visualize, or think about, a car without actually touching or seeing one. This ability becomes very strong by the end

• • •
sensorimotor intelligence According to Piaget, thinking that occurs by way of sensory perceptions and motor actions; characteristic of infants.

During the first year, infants explore objects with their senses, often through mouthing or chewing. Gradually they shift their attention from these sensorimotor actions to the objects on which they perform the actions—an important sign that they are developing mental representations of objects.

of the first two years of life; for Piaget, it helps mark the end of infancy. Changes in infants' toys reflect this developmental trend, as indicated in Table 6.2.

Second, infants form cognitive structures that Piaget called *schemes*. In relation to infants, **schemes** are organized patterns of actions or concepts that help the baby to make sense out of and adapt to the environment. Schemes develop well before infants can represent objects or events through language or motor skills. A newborn baby's initial grasping motions constitute an early scheme, as do her earliest sucking motions. Eventually, as described shortly, internal, or mental, concepts and ideas develop out of such patterns of behavior. These too are sometimes called *schemes* (or sometimes *schemas* or *schemata*); but Piaget himself more often called cognitive structures and patterns that develop later by names such as *operations* or *systems*, depending on their exact nature (P. Miller, 1993).

As we discuss more fully in Chapter 2, Piaget argued that sensorimotor intelligence develops by means of two complementary processes, assimilation and accommodation. **Assimilation** consists of interpreting new experiences in terms of existing schemes. A baby who is used to sucking on a breast or bottle may use the same action on whatever new, unfamiliar objects he encounters, such as a rubber ball or his own fist. **Accommodation** consists of modifying existing schemes to fit new experiences. After sucking on a number of new objects, the infant may modify this action to fit the nature of each new object; he may chew on some new objects (his sweater) but not on others (a plastic cup).

The interplay of assimilation and accommodation leads to new schemes and eventually to the infant's ability to symbolize objects and activities. Let's see how Piaget believed this transition occurs.

Stage 1: Early Reflexes—Using What You're Born With (Birth to One Month)

According to Piaget, cognitive development begins with reflexes, those simple, inborn behaviors that all normal babies can produce at birth. As it happens, the majority of such reflexes remain just that—reflexes—for the individual's entire life; sneezing patterns and blinking responses, for example, look nearly the same in adults as they do in infants. But a few are notable for their flexibility, chiefly suck-

scheme According to Piaget, a behavior or thought that represents a group of ideas and events in a child's experience.

assimilation According to Piaget, a method by which a child responds to new experiences by using existing concepts to interpret new ideas and experiences.

accommodation According to Piaget, the process of modifying existing ideas or action-skills to fit new experiences.

TABLE 6.1	Piaget's Stages of Infant Cognition		
Stage	**Age in Months**	**Characteristics**	
1: Early reflexes	Birth–1	Reliance on inborn reflexes to "know" the environment; assimilation of all experiences to reflexes	
2: Primary circular reactions	1–4	Accommodation (or modification) of reflexes to fit new objects and experiences; repeated actions focusing on infant's own body	
3: Secondary circular reactions	4–8	Repeated actions focusing on objects; actions used as means toward ends, but haphazardly; early signs of object permanence	
4: Combined secondary circular reactions	8–12	Deliberate combinations of previously acquired actions (or schemes); AnotB error; early signs of sense of time	
5: Tertiary circular reactions	12–18	Systematic application of previously acquired actions (or schemes); well-organized investigation of novel objects, but always overt	
6: The first symbols	18–24	First symbolic representations of objects; true object permanence; deferred imitation	

Source: Piaget (1963).

ing, grasping, and looking. These behaviors resemble reflexes at birth, but they quickly begin to be modified in response to experiences such as sucking on the mother's breast, on toys, and on the child's own hand. They give infants a repertoire from which to develop more complex skills, and their susceptibility to influence makes them especially important to cognitive development during infancy.

Take sucking. Mothers who have breast fed know the first feeding or two can be awkward: the infant noses around inefficiently for the nipple and may fail to connect with it even when the nipple is right under her nose, so to speak. But within a week or two she finds it noticeably faster, usually to the relief of her mother. In the same period, she probably also has begun sucking on other objects: her fist, the corners of her blanket, her daddy's little finger. Sometimes she simply sucks on air. All these sucking motions differ slightly from one another in style or form, and each evolves into a *scheme* in the Piagetian sense.

Stage 2: Primary Circular Reactions—Modifying What You're Born With (One to Four Months)

Soon after the baby begins modifying his early reflexes, he begins to build and differentiate action schemes quite rapidly. In fact, within a month or so he sometimes repeats them endlessly for no apparent reason. Because of its repetitive quality, Piaget calls this behavior a **circular reaction.** The baby seems to be stimulated by the outcome of his own behavior, so he responds for the mere joy of feeling himself act. At this point the circular reactions are called **primary circular reactions,** because they still focus on the baby's own body and movements. Waving an arm repeatedly constitutes a primary circular reaction; so does kicking again and again.

During this period, the young infant practices her developing schemes widely, and the behaviors rapidly become less reflexive. The baby may shape her mouth differently for sucking her fist and for sucking her blanket. In this sense she begins to recognize the objects all around her, and implicitly she also begins to remember previous experiences with each type of object. But this memory has an automatic or object-focused quality, unlike the large variety of more conscious memories children have later in life.

Stage 3: Secondary Circular Reactions—Making Interesting Sights Last (Four to Eight Months)

As they practice their first schemes, young infants broaden their interests substantially. Before long, in fact, they move their attention beyond their own bodily actions to include objects and events immediately around them. Shaking his arm, for example, no longer captivates a baby's attention for its own sake; he has become too skilled at arm shaking for it to do so. Now a behavior like this becomes useful rather than interesting. A baby at this stage may accidentally discover that shaking his arm will make a mobile spin over his head in his crib, or create an interesting noise in a toy he happens to be holding, or make parents smile with joy. In all these cases, shaking an arm becomes a means to other ends. At

* * *

circular reaction Piaget's term for an action often repeated, apparently because it is self-reinforcing.

primary circular reaction According to Piaget, a behavior that is repeated and focuses on the baby's own body and movements; occurs during the second stage of infant cognition (usually at about one to four months of age).

TABLE 6.2 Toys That Support Cognitive Development in Infancy		
Birth–2 Months	**6–12 Months**	**12–24 Months**
Mobile in crib	Squeeze toys	Dolls, especially large ones
Rattle	Nested plastic cups	Toy telephone
	Boxes with lids	Puzzles (5–10 pieces)
	Soft ball	Vehicles (cars, boats, train)
	Stuffed animals	Sandbox, shovel, and pail
	Pots and pans	Water toys (cups, funnel, etc.)
	Picture books (especially cloth or cardboard)	Picture books with simple words

As infants get older, their toys tend to involve more complex motor skills, as well as language and make-believe. Can you see how these trends are reflected in these lists?

Playing peek-a-boo becomes popular with babies as they approach their first birthday. Even though the father disappears for a moment, the baby seems to believe that he still exists behind the door, as shown by the baby's delight when he reappears.

best it is a primitive means, however, because the usefulness of the behavior originally develops by chance.

Once primitive means are discovered, a baby at this stage will repeat a useful procedure endlessly to sustain and study the interesting results. The repetition is a circular reaction like those in the previous stage, but with an important difference: now the circular reactions orient toward external objects and events rather than to the baby's own body and actions. Now results matter. If arm shaking fails to keep the mobile spinning, the baby will soon stop her effort. If she finally figures out the nature of the mobile, she will also stop. Either way, the repetition is not governed by her earlier motivation simply to move. To differentiate this new orientation from the earlier one, Piaget called such repetitions **secondary circular reactions:** repetitions motivated by external objects and events.

Secondary circular reactions create two parallel changes in the child's motor schemes. On the one hand, the infant uses existing schemes even more widely than before. He tries to suck on more and more of the toys that come his way. On the other hand, he begins to discover that schemes can be combined to produce interesting results. He may happen to reach toward an object (one scheme) and discover that doing so makes it possible to grasp the object (another scheme). At first, the combination occurs accidentally; but once it does occur, the baby at this stage can produce the new combination of schemes deliberately on future occasions.

Secondary circular reactions also implicitly show that the infant is now acquiring at least a hazy notion of **object permanence,** a belief that objects exist separately from her own actions and continue to exist even when she cannot see them. In the first two stages of infant cognition, objects often seem to disappear from the baby's mind as soon as she loses sight of them or no longer touches them. She may stare at or grasp a toy duck, but a parent or an older sibling sometimes can take it from her without causing distress; at most, the baby will simply keep staring blankly where the duck used to be and then turn to other activities. As Piaget might have claimed, out of sight is out of mind in early infancy.

This is not so, however, as babies enter the second half of their first year. By stage 3, they will look for an object briefly if they have been watching it carefully or manipulating it just beforehand. Naturally, their first searching skills leave something to be desired, so it helps if the hidden object is actually partly visible and

secondary circular reaction According to Piaget, the third stage of infant cognition, which occurs at age four to eight months; repeated behaviors that are motivated by external objects and events.

object permanence According to Piaget, the belief that people and things continue to exist even when one cannot experience them directly; emerges around age two.

within easy reach: the toy duck's tail should stick out from under a blanket if that is where the toy is hidden. But the first signs of symbolic thought are there, because the infant must have some idea of the toy duck if she is going to bother searching for it.

Stage 4: Combined Secondary Circular Reactions—Deliberate Combinations of Means and Ends (Eight to Twelve Months)

At this stage, instead of just happening on connections among schemes by accident, the infant intentionally chooses to use a scheme as a means toward an end. In stages 1 and 2, he may have developed separate schemes for opening his mouth and for chewing food. In stage 3, he may have accidentally discovered that the first scheme is a means toward the other: mouth opening is a means toward eating. Now, in stage 4, the baby starts using this means-end connection purposefully. Like a young bird in a nest, he opens his mouth to "produce" food to chew on. Of course, he may eventually discover that the connection does not always work: sitting with his mouth wide open may sometimes produce no food at all or occasionally produce bad-tasting medicine instead of good-tasting food.

At this stage, the infant still lacks alternatives to the single-purpose, fragmented schemes he has developed so far. As he encounters the limitations of these schemes, he gradually modifies and expands (or accommodates, as Piaget would say) his initial schemes that connected means with ends. He may learn to open his mouth at the sight of some foods but not others. He may also add other behaviors to the mouth-opening scheme, such as pointing to favorite foods, thereby turning the original scheme into a more general food-requesting scheme. As these accommodations occur, the infant moves into the next stage of cognition.

The relatively fixed, stereotyped quality of schemes at this stage may derive from the infant's heavy reliance on motor action as a means for understanding objects. One of the most dramatic illustrations of this possibility is the **AnotB error** (read "A, not B, error"), illustrated by the following sequence. Hide a toy under a blanket while the infant carefully watches. Normally she can retrieve the toy easily at this stage. But then make the problem more complicated: hide the toy under blanket A, then transfer it to blanket B. Do this in full view of the infant. Where does the child look first for it? Not under the correct blanket, B, but under blanket A, where she previously retrieved the toy successfully. Figure 6.2 illustrates the procedure.

The infant makes this mistake, Piaget argues, because her knowledge of the toy really amounts to memories of the actions she has taken with it, especially memories of successful actions. Some studies of the AnotB error support this interpretation, but overall, the research suggests that several other factors—the number of locations to search, for example, or delays before the baby can begin searching—also can influence success at the task (Wellman et al., 1987). In one variation of the

• • •

AnotB error The tendency of infants to look for a hidden object in the first place it disappears (at "A") rather than where they have seen it most recently (at "B").

• • • • • • • • • • • • • • • •

FIGURE 6.2

The AnotB Error

The AnotB error occurs during sensorimotor stage 4 (about eight to twelve months), when the baby is still learning to combine means (searching behaviors) with ends (finding a hidden object). Even though the baby has watched a toy being moved to a new spot, he will search for it where it was first hidden.

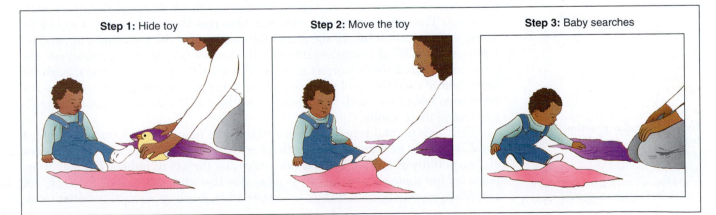

Step 1: Hide toy   **Step 2:** Move the toy   **Step 3:** Baby searches

task, babies watch while the toy is moved among three locations: from blanket A to blanket B to blanket C. Under these conditions the babies tend to reach for blankets A and B about equally, even though Piaget would have predicted that their fixed motor response would lead them to reach primarily for blanket A.

Stage 5: Tertiary Circular Reactions—Active Experimentation with Objects (Twelve to Eighteen Months)   At stage 5, the infant deliberately varies the schemes for producing interesting results, or ends. Previously, at stage 4, he could intentionally combine schemes, but only one pair at a time and only if an appropriate situation for using the combination happened to occur. Now, in dealing with a new object, the baby can run through a repertoire of schemes in a trial-and-error effort to learn about the object's properties. Piaget called the variations **tertiary circular reactions,** meaning third-level circular reactions, to distinguish them from the simpler forms of repetition that dominate the earlier stages.

These variations in behavior, however, are still organized largely by trial and error rather than by systematic plans. Given a rubber ball, for example, some babies may try dropping it from different heights and onto different objects. But no matter how delighted these infants are with the results of these variations, they will not think to vary the dropping conditions carefully or experimentally. Such actions require planning and consequently also require considerably more ability to represent objects and situations than the infant has yet developed.

Meanwhile, babies still cannot solve problems by running through solutions in their heads prior to overt action. Their belief in object permanence at stage 5 shows this limitation. They no longer make the AnotB error, but they still can be fooled if the search problem is made a little harder. A ball shifted from blanket A to blanket B still can baffle infants if they do not actually see it moved. They may not think to look under blanket B if they did not actually see the ball put there. Instead, they simply stare at the situation, perhaps looking surprised and confused. Babies respond this way even if a moment earlier they successfully solved a classic AnotB problem in which they did see the ball get moved. Taken together, these behaviors suggest two things. First, infants are tied less than before to previous successful actions for help in solving problems. Second, they may still fail to mentally form the solutions to problems in the absence of action.

Stage 6: The First Symbols—Representing Objects and Actions (Eighteen to Twenty-Four Months)   At this stage, the motor schemes the child previously explored and practiced overtly begin to occur symbolically. For the first time, the infant can begin to envision, or imagine, actions and their results without actually having to try them out beforehand.

Consider a stage 6 child who wants a favorite toy that is just barely out of reach on a high shelf. Near the shelf sits a small stool that she has played with numerous times. How to get the toy? Earlier in infancy, the baby might simply have stared and fussed and eventually either given up or cried. At this later stage, things are quite different. The baby surveys the situation, observes the stool, and pauses briefly. Then, with a purposeful air, she places the stool under the toy, climbs up, and retrieves the toy. What is important here is the lack of false starts or, conversely, the presence of only a single, correct attempt. The infant may succeed even though she never before used the stool to reach high-up objects. According to Piaget, trial and error is no longer the method of choice; now the infant tries out solutions mentally to envision their results.

Skill with mental representations makes true object permanence possible. A child at the end of infancy will search for a toy even after it has been fully hidden and even if it was hidden without his witnessing the act of hiding. If a ball disappears behind some shelves, he will go around to the other side to look for it. He will search appropriately, even though he cannot know in advance exactly where to look.

• • •

tertiary circular reaction According to Piaget, repeated variations of action schemes, organized by trial and error; the fifth stage in infant cognition, occurring between ages twelve and eighteen months.

That is in essence what Greta did (one of the infants described at the opening of this chapter). In the ball-and-blanket situation described earlier, the child can now play more complex games of hide-and-seek. She usually looks first under the blanket where the toy disappeared; if she fails to find it there, she will search under any and all other blankets, and sometimes even under the table and in the experimenter's pockets. Relatively extensive search is made possible in part by the child's new conviction that toys and other objects have a permanent existence independent of her own activities with them. In other words, they do not just disappear.

All these behaviors depend on the child's ability to form and maintain representations (thoughts or memories) of the relevant experiences, which later become available for expression again. As we will see, representational skill proves crucial in early childhood. It contributes to children's play, because much play involves re-enactment of previous experiences and roles. It makes possible much language development, because the child must learn to use words and expressions when they are appropriate and not just at the time he hears them uttered. And it makes possible the first real self-concept, because sooner or later the child realizes that he too has a (relatively) permanent existence akin to the permanence of all the things and people in his life, whether toys, pet dogs, or parents.

Baby Jill's Intelligence: An Example

The relationships among the six stages of sensorimotor intelligence become clearer if we look at how an infant might use the same object differently at different ages. Baby Jill acquired a ball when she was born and used it for the next several years. During that time, of course, her ways of using the ball changed dramatically, as shown in the following descriptions (comments are in italics). The ball was about four inches in diameter and was made out of rubber, but had a cloth covering. Mostly it was red, but it had a large black spot on each side, so it looked rather like an eyeball when viewed from the proper angle.

1. *Stage 1: Early reflexes*   When Jill first came home from the hospital, her mother suspended the ball over Jill's diaper-changing table so that the black spot looked down at Jill directly. Day after day, Jill stared hard at the ball and its black spot and followed it whenever her mother made it swing gently.

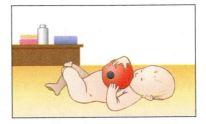

Here Jill used one of her earliest reflexes, in this case visual tracking of objects.

2. *Stage 2: Primary circular reactions*   At two months, Jill sucked on the ball a lot and grabbed at it whenever one of her parents put it directly into her hands. The ball was just soft enough for Jill to do these things. She still liked to look at the ball swinging above her changing table, but she was starting to find her parents' faces more interesting.

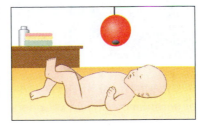

Jill was modifying, or accommodating, her reflexes—sucking, grasping, tracking—to fit new experiences she was undergoing. Her interest still lay primarily in her own actions rather than in the objects she was encountering.

3. *Stage 3: Secondary circular reactions*   At six months, Jill discovered that she could make the ball swing above her changing table simply by waving her hands and feet. Every once in awhile, one of her limbs would accidentally catch the ball and send it spinning and swinging wildly.

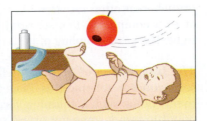

By now her attention had shifted away from her own body (primary circular reactions) to an object outside herself and to what it could do (secondary circular reactions).

Jill had become interested in combining schemes or actions. Her exploration of the effects of these schemes, however, was still guided primarily by chance discoveries.

4. *Stage 4: Combining secondary circular reactions*   When Jill was ten months old, her father took the ball down one day during a diaper change and put it behind a bottle of talcum powder. Jill looked hard at the partially hidden ball, then firmly knocked over the bottle of powder and got hold of the ball. Her father was dismayed at how hard she had hit the bottle but also was somewhat impressed. He did not remember her acting so purposefully before just to get something else.

Jill's investigations of the ball now had become rather deliberately varied, as though she were purposely trying out a conscious repertoire of actions to see what effect each would have on the ball.

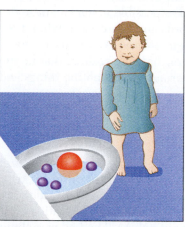

5. *Stage 5: Tertiary circular reactions*   At fifteen months, Jill preferred to have the ball down on the floor where she could get at it. One day she gathered together all the balls in the house—five, to be exact. She tried bouncing each one down the stairs in turn and noticed that some seemed to bounce higher than others. Another time she tried floating the balls in the toilet. They all floated well except for her original red-and-black ball, whose cloth covering got waterlogged. (For some reason, her parents did not enjoy her putting the balls in the toilet.)

In searching for the lost ball, Jill showed a perception of object permanence—a belief that the ball continued to exist even when out of sight. To hold this belief, she must have formed some sort of symbolic representation of the ball in her mind.

6. *Stage 6: Symbolic representation*   Just before her second birthday. Jill lost her red-and-black ball. She looked in her usual storage spots: her bottom dresser drawer and her (now little used) changing table. Where was it, anyway? When she could not find it, she asked her parents for help because she knew it had to be around somewhere.

By this point, both Jill and the ball had gone through a lot together. At the end of her infancy, Jill had considerable skill at motor manipulation of objects as well as some beginnings of mental representation of objects. She no longer needed to have an object such as the red-and-black ball literally in hand. The ball had assisted in this development, as had several other toys and numerous sensory and manipulative experiences with them.

Assessment of Piaget's Theory of Infant Cognition

Piaget's theory stimulated considerable study of infant cognition from the 1960s through the 1980s. A lot of the research has confirmed the main features of the theory, whereas other research has called attention to additional aspects of infancy that at least complicate Piaget's original presentation, if they do not contradict it outright. Here is a sampling of both the confirmations and the complications.

The Integration of Schemes   Do infants begin life with fundamentally separate sensorimotor schemes, as Piaget argued, and only gradually learn to combine them? Some such combining surely must occur, but there is also evidence for the opposite trend: some important schemes may begin as integrated wholes and only later become differentiated into parts (Lewkowicz & Lickliter, 1994). Newborn infants will reach for and grasp a small object placed in front of them at the proper distance, and will do so even if the object is only a projected image of one. Such behavior implies that young babies tend to regard sight and touch as connected rather than separate, or, in Piagetian terms, that they have a single early scheme for seeing and reaching rather than one scheme for seeing and another, separate scheme for reaching.

Vision and hearing also may have inborn integrated schemes. As pointed out earlier, infants just a few days old will turn, as though by reflex, to look at the source of a sound as long as the direction lies within their physical capacity to turn. In addition, they show signs of connecting their parents' faces and voices within two or three weeks: they will look longer at a photograph of their mothers, for example, if a recording of the mothers' voices is playing. And infants just a few months old prefer looking at sights that match a soundtrack to sights that do not match. Suppose a young infant looks at two films side by side, one with a kangaroo bouncing up and down and the other with a toy donkey doing the same thing but at a different speed. If a soundtrack of bouncing rhythms is made to coincide with one film but not the other, the infant will spend more time watching the soundtrack-coordinated picture.

Such evidence complicates Piaget's assertion that schemes begin primarily as separate, discrete reflexes and do not begin to be integrated until midway through infancy. At the same time, however, the evidence does not really contradict Piaget. Given the complexity of human beings, it is perfectly possible for both trends to occur at once. Some schemes may begin as integrated wholes and develop that way in at least certain situations, and others may begin as relatively specific reflexes and combine later.

Motor Versus Cognitive Limitations Some infant psychologists question Piaget's account because they believe it confuses the child's motor abilities with cognitive or thinking abilities (Meltzoff et al., 1991). Object permanence, for example, implicitly depends on a child's capacity to conduct a manual search: to walk around the room, lift and inspect objects, and the like. Perhaps younger infants "lack" classic object permanence, this argument goes, simply because they lack motor skills, or at best use them only clumsily.

To test this possibility, psychologists have designed new tests of object permanence that require only visual search rather than motor coordination (Baillargeon, 1993). In one experiment, infants were habituated to (repeatedly shown) the sight of a toy car sliding down an inclined track from the left and then rolling off to the right, as shown in Figure 6.3. In the middle of this track was a small screen concealing the middle portion of the track and obstructing a view of the car for part of its trip along the track. During habituation, the babies watched the car slide down the ramp, behind the screen, and out the other side. Between car trips, the screen was lifted temporarily to show that there was nothing behind it that might affect the car's movements.

After the infants had gotten used to seeing this setup and watching the car disappear and reappear predictably, they were shown one of two test events. In the first event, the screen was lifted and a toy mouse was placed directly behind the tracks. Then the screen was lowered, and the car made its usual run down the ramp and out the right side of the screen. This was called the "possible test event." The second test event was the same, except that the toy mouse was placed directly *on* the tracks. Then the screen was lowered, the car was released, it disappeared behind the screen, and—surprise!—it reappeared out the right side of the screen anyway, even though the mouse had been placed on the tracks. This was called the "impossible test event." In reality, the experimenters secretly removed the toy mouse before the car could hit it, using a hole concealed in the back of the test apparatus.

Under these conditions, infants as young as 3½ months looked significantly longer at the *im*possible test event than at the possible test event. The most plausible interpretation is that the impossible event violated assumptions the infants made about the permanence of objects: they seemed to assume the toy mouse should cause a collision, presumably because they believed it continued to exist behind the screen even when they could not see it. They also seemed to assume objects retain their usual physical properties even when invisible—that the car could not simply pass through the mouse, for example, just because it was hidden.

This evidence of early object permanence, though, does not mean young infants are ready yet to reason about hidden objects in the ways older children or adults might do. If a preschool child experienced the experiment just described, he or she would very likely suspect a trick of some sort and consciously puzzle over what the trick might be. The three- or four-month-old infant still has much developing to do before being able to do this kind of thinking. By requiring manual search skills, Piaget's tasks may have delayed children from displaying their preexisting object permanence until rudimentary reasoning skills had become established. Hence Piaget's assertion that full object permanence (the stage 6 described earlier) involves conscious problem solving: a deliberate search for the object.

● ● ● ● ● ● ● ● ● ● ● ● ● ● ● ● ● ●

FIGURE 6.3

Evidence of Object Permanence in Infants

First, the infant becomes habituated to watching a car roll down a track, behind a screen, and out the other side. In one test condition, a toy mouse is placed behind the tracks but is hidden while the car rolls past. In the other test condition, the mouse is placed on the tracks but is secretly removed after the screen is in place so that the car seems to roll "through" the mouse. Infants stare longer at the second impossible event, suggesting that they already "believe in" object permanence.

Source: Baillargeon (1991).

Memory Limitations   Piaget explains most infant thinking in terms of motor schemes: repeated, familiar actions that allow infants to understand their environment. The AnotB error in particular supposedly reflects the child's dependence on overt actions or motor schemes of this type. But does it really? Maybe the error really shows the infant's poor memory, which has not yet developed very far. After all, in the AnotB task, the baby at least has to remember, first, that the toy has been moved recently, and second, that it began by lying under the first blanket. As obvious as these ideas may seem to adults, a young infant may have trouble remembering them.

Considerable evidence suggests that memory does in fact affect infants' performance on many tasks, including, but not limited to, the AnotB task (Baillargeon, 1993). Imposing slight delays—just a few seconds—on the infant's search interferes

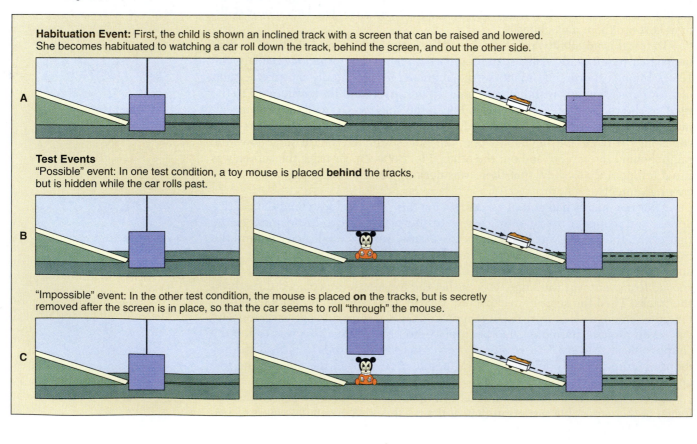

with appropriately searching for an object much more for younger infants than for older ones. Much of the change may reflect younger infants' difficulties in attending to and retaining relevant cues about the object to be searched for. Younger babies seem to remember less of what they are looking for.

These trends imply that infants may have a notion of object permanence, but find it demanding to remember the relevant facts needed to search: where they last saw the object and when and whether the object was in fact moved. The most complete explanation of the AnotB error, therefore, may involve both motor and memory development: infants probably use memory when they can, but supplement it with Piagetian motor schemes whenever necessary (Case, 1992). If an infant cannot recall where a toy is hidden, at least she can reenact the means she used to find it in the past. This multiple strategy actually resembles the way adults sometimes search for a lost object: if you cannot recall where you left it, you may retrace your steps up to the time you remember seeing it last—in essence, using an action scheme.

Notice that motor skill and memory limitations can affect the appearance of competence not only in infants but in adults as well. By showing that the limitations happen to infants, the research once again strengthens the idea of continuity in development (that infants resemble adults) and weakens the idea of change (that infants are somehow different from adults). It also suggests that the "belief in object permanence" that Piaget identified may mean something different to a young infant than to an older one. For a three- or four-month-old, an "object" is anything that remains visible when tracked with the eyes and whose movements meet reasonable expectations when tracked. For an eighteen-month-old, an "object" is whatever becomes visible when sought with your hands or feet and meets expectations to reappear after a reasonable physical search. We will see that still later in life, concept of an "object" changes meaning again, sometimes even referring to thoughts rather than things. But that is a story for later, when we discuss adolescent thought in Chapter 16.

WHAT DO YOU THINK ?   Between about eight and twelve months of age, many babies show distress at separations from their primary caregiver (usually the mother). Some psychologists suggest that the distress is a partial result of their budding belief in object permanence. Do you think this might be true? How might you explain your position to a new parent who is concerned about her baby's distress?

Behavioral Learning in Infancy

One framework for studying the specific performance of infants has come from **behaviorism,** or what psychologists sometimes also call *learning theory.* As described in Chapter 2, learning theory focuses on changes in particular behaviors (sometimes called *responses*) and on the specific, observable causes and consequences (reinforcements, or lack thereof, and punishments) of those behaviors. Typically, learning theorists identify three kinds of behavioral learning: classical conditioning, operant conditioning, and imitation.

Infants show signs of all three types of learning, at least by about age three months. Infant psychologists have not concentrated equally on each type of learning, however; rather, the majority of studies of infant learning concern operant conditioning (Lipsitt, 1990). This fact makes conclusions about operant conditioning in infants more definite than those about the other types.

Classical Conditioning

As described in Chapter 2, classical conditioning consists of transferring control of a reflex response by pairing two stimuli together. One of the stimuli (the uncondi-

• • •
behaviorism A learning theory that focuses on changes in specific observable behaviors and their causes.

tioned stimulus, or US) is chosen from among those that automatically produce a particular unconditioned response (UR). The other (the conditioned stimulus, or CS), is chosen from among those that do not.

Although it may matter little whether an infant blinks to music, certain other classically conditioned behaviors may significantly affect an infant's long-term development. One example is the conditioning associated with a parent's face, a stimulus that initially is relatively neutral. Looking at a parent usually occurs together with a variety of emotional and physiological responses. Hunger pangs and hunger satisfaction often *both* occur in the presence of the parent's face, because the parent usually approaches the baby when she is hungry and stays with her until she has finished feeding. The process is shown in Figure 6.4.

Eventually, therefore, the mere sight of the parent can trigger both positive and negative responses in the child. Classical conditioning occurs reliably and clearly from about age six months onward (Lipsitt, 1990). Before that age, however, efforts to demonstrate this kind of conditioning have produced conflicting results. Some infant reflexes prove conditionable to some neutral stimuli, but not all combinations of stimuli and responses can be conditioned. For example, a musical tone can be conditioned to an eyeblink response even in three-month-old infants, but it cannot be successfully conditioned to a reflexive change in infants' pupil size. A change in lighting can reliably make infants' pupils shrink, but pairing a tone with the change in lighting does not condition this reflex, no matter how many pairings occur.

These irregularities imply that young infants may be genetically prepared to learn certain kinds of connections from their environment and genetically constrained from or limited in learning others. Perhaps they are especially sensitive to some connections in their world, such as a tone and a puff of air, but not to others, such as a tone and a change in brightness. Because such constraints have long been recognized in studies of conditioning among animals, it seems reasonable to expect analogous limitations among human beings (Harper, 1988, Chapter 3). As infants become toddlers, they presumably overcome some of these limitations in classical conditioning, because their ability to think and reason begins to govern their responses to stimuli as well as classical conditioning.

Operant Conditioning

In operant conditioning as most infants experience it, a child gets a reward, or positive reinforcement, if she performs some simple action or set of actions. By turning her head, for example, she may get to see an interesting toy or picture. In this case the reinforcement is viewing the interesting toy, and head turning becomes the learned, or conditioned, behavior. Such actions tend to be performed more often than actions that are not reinforced.

As the examples of research in this chapter show, infants are quite capable of learning through operant conditioning. Newborns will learn to suck on their hands longer if doing so yields a tiny amount of sugar water delivered through a tube in the corners of their mouths. Or they will learn to blink their eyes more often if doing so causes a pleasant voice to speak or a melody to play. One reason infants seem to learn to breast feed so easily is the strong reinforcement the behavior brings in the form of mother's milk and being touched and held closely.

● ● ● ● ● ● ● ● ● ● ● ● ● ● ● ● ●

FIGURE 6.4

Classical Conditioning in Infancy

With infants (as with other human beings), more than one response can sometimes be conditioned to the same stimulus, creating ambivalent, or mixed, responses. In this case, the infant has learned to associate his caregiver with both hunger and hunger satisfaction.

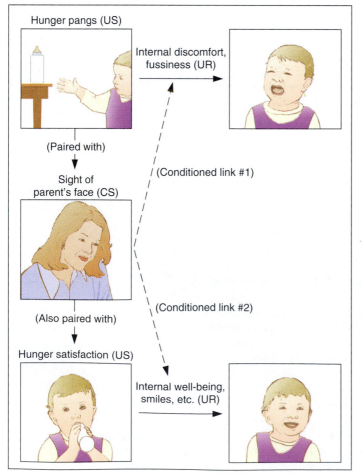

WORKING WITH

Gillian Luppiwiski, **Infant Care Provider**

Fostering Infants' Thinking

Gillian Luppiwiski has worked as a caregiver in an infant day care center for ten years. She made numerous comments about her work: the changes she sees in the babies as they grow, the responses of mothers and fathers, the interest that even infants and toddlers show in one another. When I asked her to comment on infants' thinking abilities, she began talking about their language and problem-solving behaviors and about how she and other caregivers support it.

Kelvin: *What do you notice most about these children when you're working here?*

Gillian: They change so much! Like day and night. Last fall Jocelyn could hardly move; she got so frustrated watching the older children walk around! But now she's all over the place, into *everything*—and happy as a lark.

Kelvin: *Can you figure out what she thinks about? Does it even make sense to ask about her "thoughts"?*

Gillian: Oh, yes. Like when we get out the play doh, and she starts using it—poking it with her fingers, talking about it. She just started naming it, you know; she says "doh" and looks at you with a smile. And "wed" when it's red. That's her favorite color.

Kelvin: *So her language is developing?*

Gillian: Yes, and the play doh helps with that. It gives her something to talk about. We support her comments, saying things like "That's right! We've got red play doh today."

Kelvin: *What about other times? Even when she's not talking, does it seem like Jocelyn's "thinking"?*

Gillian: Definitely! Take the climber: she loves to climb up there and sit with Joel. That teaches her about space and depth, but she learns more by *doing* it than by talking about it. Shelley (another caregiver) might talk about it, comment on it verbally when she sees Jocelyn climbing. But Jocelyn mainly learns it by doing it.

Kelvin: *Do you ever "teach" them anything directly?*

Gillian: We don't so much teach them as make it possible for them to learn. That's how I'd put it. Shelley or I might put out a few puzzles one day, and talk with a child when she chooses to work on one—encourage her to persist in putting it together, maybe give a hint or two, but not do it for her.

Or the other day Danny started getting out *all* the trucks! He lined them all up with the big ones at one end and the smaller ones at the other end. Sorted them! It was great to see. He needed help, though, in finding enough room to do this without tripping over Jocelyn and the others. He commented on the lineup: "All the trucks!" And so did I, by challenging him gently: "Are you sure you have them *all*?"

Kelvin: *So he was grouping? Classifying things?*

Gillian: Yes. In his own way, his own two-year-old way. "Developmentally appropriate practice"—that's what educators are always talking about. That's what makes us a real *infant* center, and different from a preschool center. We try to provide developmentally appropriate things and support the children for using them.

What Do You Think?

1. Considering what Gillian said, how important is an infant care center for fostering a child's thinking ability? How does it compare to experiences that an infant or toddler might have at home?

2. Gillian says, "We don't so much teach them as make it possible for them to learn." How comfortable are you with this idea? Can it apply to working with older children (preschoolers, school-age, adolescents) or only to infants and toddlers? Consult with a few classmates about this question; what do they think about it?

3. At times Gillian seems to equate language development with cognitive development. Is there some way to distinguish these two processes in an infant center? Brainstorm an example or two of how you might do this if you were a caregiver.

As with classical conditioning, infants are predisposed to learn these particular behaviors. All examples of operant conditioning in infants rely on those few behaviors that young babies already exhibit, which are mainly their inborn reflexes. By nature, reflexes occur easily—in fact, almost *too* easily. As parents often discover, any slight provocation, such as a touch on the baby's cheek, can stimulate sucking movements in young babies. Such readiness to respond creates confusion about when infant responses really constitute learning rather than general excitement. For example, when do sucking movements show true operant learning: a specific behavior performed more often because a particular reinforcement results from it? And when do sucking movements simply amount to a reflex that is itching to occur, so to speak, and would occur in response to almost any stimulus?

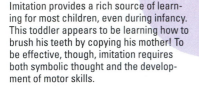

Imitation provides a rich source of learning for most children, even during infancy. This toddler appears to be learning how to brush his teeth by copying his mother! To be effective, though, imitation requires both symbolic thought and the development of motor skills.

The confusion between learning and excitement diminishes as babies grow older, because they acquire behaviors that are more truly voluntary. Even as babies get older, however, they acquire many behaviors, both desirable and regrettable, through what appears to be operant conditioning. A six- or nine-month-old will babble longer and more frequently if parents smile and express praise when he does so. A twelve-month-old will learn to wave good-bye sooner and more frequently if reinforced with praise or encouragement. And a two-year-old may learn to scream at her older sibling when she wants a toy the older child has because her screaming has been inadvertently reinforced: it causes the older child to simply abandon the toy, or it summons a parent who assumes (not always accurately) the older child somehow caused the screaming.

Of course, these effects refer primarily to immediate, short-term ones, which sometimes differ from long-term effects of reinforcement. An example often important to parents is crying: will picking up the baby to quiet his crying actually reinforce him for crying in the long term? Conditioning theory would predict that it would, but most research on the impact of crying has found that fast, sensitive response to crying actually leads to *less* crying (St. James-Roberts et al., 1993). However, the quieting is not reliable in the short term, but may take many months to become a definite, obvious response to being picked up. This is a long enough delay to cause parents a lot of worry about whether they are "spoiling" their child by responding to her crying.

Imitation

As make-believe play demonstrates, children obviously learn to imitate at some point in development. But exactly how early, and by what processes? Early research on these questions generally suggested that infants can engage in different kinds of imitation at different points during infancy (Piaget, 1962). Infants imitated actions they could literally see themselves perform (for example, in a mirror) sooner than those they could observe only in a model. Much research over the past two decades confirms this hypothesis. Imitating a hand gesture such as waving, for example, proves easier than imitating an unusual face made by an adult (Meltzoff & Kubl,

1994). Also, deferred imitation may not appear until close to a child's second birthday; by that time, the child can imitate a gesture an entire day after seeing a model perform it.

Despite their preference for visible actions, infants sometimes imitate actions that are relatively invisible to themselves. One-week-old babies tend to stick out their tongues in imitation of adults and to wiggle their fingers after seeing adults model this behavior. Distinguishing voluntary imitation from general, automatic excitement, however, remains a problem, as it does with other studies of very young babies. One research study highlighted this ambiguity especially well. It showed babies pictures of human faces depicting various emotions (Kaitz et al., 1988). Although the babies responded with emotional facial expressions of their own, their expressions did not match those in the pictures. In fact, the emotions on the babies' faces were hard to classify at all; they just looked "wrought up" at the sight of expressive human faces. At present, therefore, we still have more to learn about the origins of imitation during the newborn period.

WHAT DO YOU THINK ?   How do you suppose *mothers* might become conditioned to breast feeding, either positively or negatively? Think about "what's in it" for them, as well as what hassles breast feeding can create. If possible, talk to one or two breast-feeding mothers about their experiences (preferably one who has breast fed more than one baby). Then write an "advice sheet" to help expectant mothers to maximize the satisfactions of breast feeding (operant conditioning) as well as associate breast feeding with positive experiences and feelings (classical conditioning).

Language Acquisition

When Michael, the son of one of the authors, was an infant, he went through several phases in using language:

> At twelve weeks, Michael made open-mouthed, cooing noises when he was feeling content. Sometimes these sounds were vaguely similar to ordinary vowel sounds, but they seemed to vary unpredictably. Michael cooed a lot in the morning when he first woke up, which pleased his father and mother.
>
> By six months, Michael had added consonant sounds to his vocalizations to produce complicated babbling noises. His most productive time for this activity continued to be the morning, although he "said" quite a lot whenever he was feeling generally content. Certain sounds seemed to be favorites: *da* and *gn.* Sometimes Michael repeated these and other sounds—*da, da, da, da.* His father thought Michael repeated sounds when he was feeling especially happy.
>
> At fifteen months, Michael could produce about six words, but he did not pronounce them as adults would. The family cat was *dat;* his favorite food, yogurt, sounded like *yugun;* and airplanes were simply *der!* (as in "Look there!"). He seemed to understand dozens of words and sentences, although it was hard to be sure because he probably picked up clues about meaning from the behavior of his parents. When Michael was tired one day, he came immediately when his mother said, "Come sit here" in a sympathetic tone of voice. But when she said the same thing in a cross tone of voice the next day, he looked at her with an impish smile and went the other way.
>
> One day close to his second birthday, Michael sat "reading" a children's book to himself. Occasionally real phrases could be heard ("bug ate leaf"), but mostly Michael sounded as though he were mumbling or talking in the next room. When he finished, he walked to the kitchen and phrased a three-word question: "What's for lunch?"

As these examples show, language is a fundamental feature of infant and child development and an equally fundamental concern for parents, teachers, and other professionals who work with children (see the accompanying Perspectives box for a discussion of some of these concerns). A great deal of language develops during infancy; indeed, language is one of the most clearly human of all developments of this age period and perhaps of the entire lifespan.

PERSPECTIVES

Extremes in Language Acquisition: What Do They Mean?

As mentioned in this chapter and again in Chapter 9, children vary enormously in the rate at which they acquire language. Figure 6.5 shows dramatic differences for one aspect of language, vocabulary. The graph compares the top 10% of infants with the bottom 10% as judged by the number of words each group understands and produces in normal conversation (Fenson et al., 1994). At age 10 months, the low group can understand about 10 words and produce none, but the high group already understands about 150 words and can produce about 10. By 16 months, the low group understands about 90 words, compared to the high group's 350 words. At 16 months, the low group can also produce about 10 words (similar to the high group at 8 months), but the high group has begun using about 180 words. Equally dramatic diversity exists for other features of language acquisition, such as the acquisition of syntax and the use of the nonverbal gestures that accompany normal discourse.

Should parents and other caregivers be concerned about such extremes? Are the "slow" infants showing some sort of language disorder and the "fast" infants showing signs of genius? Although it is tempting to think so, the research evidence suggests a more complicated interpretation (Bates et al., 1995). For one thing, children often follow individual pathways toward full language acquisition that do not necessarily parallel the path taken by children as a group. Whereas children as a group experience a burst in vocabulary learning during the second year of life, for example, individual children actually experience this increase in a variety of ways: slowly and steadily, in sudden but small steps, and delayed for several months (Bates & Carnevale, 1993).

Second, different features of language are normally learned at different times and have different rates and patterns of acquisition. Receptive vocabulary (words understood) is generally learned sooner than expressive vocabulary (words produced), though not necessarily. Vocabulary that refers to objects is generally learned quickly before a baby's first birthday, after which vocabulary that refers to feelings undergoes a period of rapid growth (Bates et al., 1994), but again not for every child. In reality, an individual infant or toddler may acquire one feature of language more quickly than another, yet still end up with serviceable language skills in the end.

Extreme delay or acceleration is also ambiguous, because most observations of it are relative only to average trends in English. Do infants in other language communities acquire individual features of language at a pace and sequence similar to those of English-speaking infants? Language researchers have begun to study this question, but will have to do much more work on many languages before they have definitive answers. Part of the problem stems from the differences in structure of the world's languages. Compared to English, for example, some languages have more numerous verb forms (look at the multiple verb conjugations in French!), which may pose special challenges to a one-year-old infant even if her parents or older siblings are quite capable of learning and using them.

What Do You Think?

Suppose you are a caregiver at an infant day care center, and a parent expressed concern about whether his two-year-old was learning enough vocabulary compared to other children her age. What would you say? Would you say something different if you were a kindergarten teacher, and a parent expressed concern about the vocabulary learning of her five-year-old?

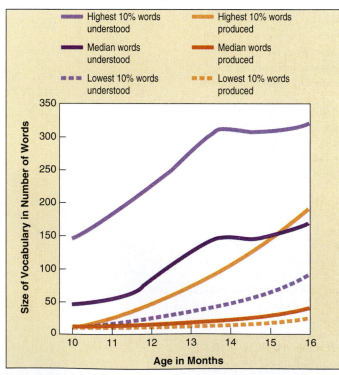

FIGURE 6.5   Extremes in Vocabulary Acquisition Vocabulary is one of the most variable features of language acquisition. Some infants produce more words at 10 months than other infants produce at 16 months, and the diversity is almost as dramatic for words understood (but not produced). However, the differences do not necessarily persist into later childhood.
Source: Fenson et al. (1994).

Language has several aspects, and infants must acquire them all to become verbally competent. When listed separately, the array is an impressive set of achievements for such young people!

- They must learn the sounds of the language (its **phonology**).

- They must learn its words (its **lexicon**).

- They must learn the meanings of words (**semantics**).

- They must learn the purposes and ways in which words and sentences normally get used in conversation (**pragmatics**).

- They must piece together the organization of words into sentences and connected discourse (**syntax**).

Infants must acquire all of these aspects of language to be able to express their feelings, get what they want, and describe their activities to others.

Phonology and semantics develop rapidly during infancy, and therefore are the focus of this chapter. Syntax begins rapid development only late in infancy, when children begin combining words into phrases and sentences. Pragmatics begins early but continues to undergo important developments throughout childhood. Because of these differences in timing, we discuss syntax along with other aspects of early childhood cognition in Chapter 9. We briefly discuss language use (pragmatics) in this chapter, but also say more about it in Chapter 9. In this section, we emphasize how children acquire phonology and describe their earliest achievements in semantics and the pragmatic uses of language.

Phonology

Every language uses a finite number of **phonemes,** or sounds that speakers of the language consider distinctive and that combine to make the words of the language. English has about forty-one phonemes; other languages have more or fewer than this number. Specific phonemes result from particular physical arrangements of the vocal apparatus: the tongue, mouth, nose, throat, and vocal cords. Often very small physical changes in the apparatus can create distinctly different phonemes. The sounds /th/ and /t/, for example, differ primarily in how tightly the tongue is held against the upper teeth. Other equally small changes may be routinely ignored by native speakers. The /k/ in *key,* for example, actually sounds different than the /k/ in *ski.* The first is made by releasing a puff of air (called *aspiration*) from the roof of the mouth; the second involves little or no puff of air and sounds closer to a clicking noise. What matters is not the objective, auditory features of the sound but whether speakers of the language normally perceive occurrences of the sound as equivalent. If they do, as in the examples of /k/, the sounds are defined as examples of one phoneme. If they do not, as in /t/ and /th/, the sounds are defined as different phonemes.

Perceiving Phonemes   In acquiring language, infants must be sensitive to phonemes and ignore any meaningless variations. Although the task may seem demanding, it actually proves surprisingly easy, even for a baby—so easy, in fact, that some language specialists suspect human beings are genetically and physiologically predisposed toward noticing phonemic differences (Archibald, 1995).

A variety of evidence supports this possibility. As mentioned earlier, infants just one month old can distinguish between vocalizations and nonhuman sounds. They tend to turn toward the source of the vocalizing and to show other physical signs of attending to human voices even in the midst of nonhuman noise. At the very least, such attention should make learning phonemic distinctions possible, although not inevitable.

phonology The individual vocal sounds of a language.

lexicon The words or units of meaning of a language.

semantics The purposes and meanings of a language.

pragmatics The ways in which words and sentences are normally used in ordinary conversation.

syntax The organizational rules of words and phrases in a language; its grammar.

phoneme A sound that combines with other sounds to form words.

Infants also seem predisposed to hear certain phonemes categorically, meaning they perceive sounds as belonging completely to one phoneme or another and never as somewhere in between (Jusczyk et al., 1990). Such categorical perception should make language acquisition inherently easier. However, it is not a uniquely human ability. Similar perceptual abilities exist in rhesus monkeys and even in chinchillas (Kuhl & Padden, 1983); yet monkeys and chinchillas do not learn to talk! Presumably they lack other crucial skills, anatomy, and experiences that human infants normally have. So perception of phonemes must be necessary to language acquisition but not sufficient for it.

Babbling   Although skill at producing phonemes takes longer to develop, it too seems biologically influenced. Sometime between four and eight months of age, infants begin **babbling** in increasingly complex ways, much the way Michael does in the earlier example. They apparently do so for the sole reward of hearing themselves vocalize, a form of play with sound and an example of a Piagetian primary circular reaction.

What suggests that babbling is motivated intrinsically? The most important evidence is the fact that all physically normal infants begin babbling at about the same age (about six months), regardless of the culture or language to which they are exposed. Furthermore, an observational study of deaf infants found the babies "babbling" with their hands. These infants could not babble orally, but they had been exposed to American Sign Language and were observed to make repetitive hand gestures analogous to the oral babbling of hearing infants (Pettito & Marentette, 1991).

Despite this finding, most research suggests a significant influence on babbling by parents and other members of an infant's language community. Although the study on deaf infants observed a type of babbling in these babies, the fact that the babbling was gestural rather than oral suggests that the infants' language environment influenced the form their babbling took. Other research on deaf infants has confirmed this conclusion. Contrary to a long-held belief, deaf infants do *not* babble orally in the same way hearing infants do; rather, they begin oral babbling some months later, and even then babble only if they hear sound that is amplified, such as through a hearing aid (Marschark, 1993).

Research on hearing infants also shows that the language environment shapes oral babbling significantly (Emmorey & Reilly, 1995). If you ask listeners to guess

• • •
babbling Infant vocalizations produced prior to acquiring language and without verbally meaningful intent.

TABLE 6.3	Milestones in Language Acquisition During Infancy
Approximate Age	**Vocal Accomplishment**
4 weeks	Cries of displeasure
12 weeks	Contented cooing, squealing, gurgling; occasional vowel sounds
20 weeks	First signs of babbling; most vowel sounds, but only occasional consonants
6 months	Babbling well established: full range of vowel sounds and many consonants
12 months	Babbling includes the melody or intonation of the language; utterances signal emotions; first words are produced; the child understands several words and simple commands
18 months	Expressive vocabulary of between 3 and 50 words; intricate babbling interspersed with real words; occasional two- and three-word sentences
24 months	Expressive vocabulary of between 50 and 300 words, although not all used accurately; babbling gone; many two-word sentences or even longer; nonadult grammar; the child understands most simple language intended for him or her

Source: DeVilliers & Devilliers (1978).

the language background of a babbling baby from hearing a tape recording of the child, their success rates are not perfect, but success is much better than chance. If the infant belongs to French-speaking parents, for example, she seems to produce sounds characteristic of French speakers rather than sounds of some other language group.

Despite this evidence of bias, babies make many babbling sounds unrelated to their native language. When infants finally limit their sounds to their own language, they apparently do so partly by their own choice and in an effort to produce their first real words. At that point, which occurs around the first birthday, parents' language also starts influencing infants' language more directly, as we explain later in this chapter. Overall, therefore, infants who babble do not use sounds as symbols. In playing with sounds, they show an important prerequisite for later communication with people.

Semantics and First Words

The semantics (or meanings) of a language, and of words in particular, are never mastered fully even by adults. To test this idea on yourself, scan any page of a large, unabridged dictionary and see how far you go before you encounter an unfamiliar word. Most people, it seems, never learn even a majority of the words or terms in their native language. This is because words get much of their meanings from the real world rather than from other words. Most of us simply do not live long enough to learn all of these relationships with the real world.

Learning semantics, therefore, is something children begin in infancy but do not nearly complete (see Table 6.3). Somewhere around their first birthday, most infants will use their first words or at least make sounds that parents take to be words. For a few months after that, new words are comparatively rare; but beginning around eighteen to twenty-one months, additions begin occurring at a dramatic rate. By their second birthday, infants may be using as many as fifty words appropriately, though some may still be acquiring their first words by this date and most still have only a limited command of many words. From ages two to three years vocabulary increases rapidly, thanks partly to the child's newly emerging skill in constructing longer sentences. An average three-year-old may know several hundred words; an average five- or six-year-old can use a few thousand words, or about one-half the vocabulary she or he will ever command, even as an adult (Anglin, 1993). Note, however, that these averages hide large differences among individual children, both in the overall size of their vocabularies and, as explained next, in the types of words they learn.

These figures refer only to children's **expressive language,** their ability to actually use words and sentences appropriately in conversation. Expressive language is complemented by **receptive language,** the ability to comprehend language used by others. Generally, receptive language develops sooner than expressive language does; put in plainer terms, babies can understand more than they can say (Bates et al., 1988). The difference in receptive and expressive capacities shows up in many exchanges between parents and their infants. For example, if a father asks his ten-month-old, "Can I have a bite of your cookie?", the baby may offer him one. But the infant may not use any of those words himself for several more months and may not combine them into a sentence for another year or more.

Individual Differences in First Words   What words do children use first? On the whole, they prefer nominals—labels for objects, people, and events—much more than other kinds of words, such as verbs or modifiers (Hart, 1991). Among nominals, they are most likely to name things that are used frequently or that stand out in some way. The child's own mother or father therefore may be named early,

• • •

expressive language Language that a child can actually use appropriately in conversation.

receptive language Language that is understood or comprehended when used by others.

Siblings serve as important models of behavior and language for younger infants as they grow and develop. What do you suppose this girl is saying to her infant sister, and what do you suppose the infant will learn from it?

but not always as early as the parents expect. *Dog* may appear as an early word more often than *sun* or *diaper* does, even though children probably experience the latter two objects more frequently than they do dogs.

Other research has found that children vary in how much they emphasize different language functions in their first utterances (Bloom, 1993). Most children have a *referential style,* meaning their first words refer to objects and objective events—*car, book,* and so on. Others have an *expressive style,* using words to express feelings and relationships—*hello* and *goody!* During the second year of life, infants with a referential style tend to make more rapid advances in vocabulary, though whether this advantage continues into the preschool years is unclear. Presumably these differences are encouraged partly by differing family environments. Some families may speak of objects more often than they do of feelings, or vice versa. But to some extent, word preferences may also represent a learning strategy adopted by the child; just as she may find a word easier if she already knows the phonemes in it, she may also find an utterance easier if she already has used similar ones on previous occasions.

Influencing Language Acquisition

Many of the preceding comments make language acquisition seem beyond human influence, and indeed many psychologists do consider language development beyond influence in important respects. Yet adults do in fact affect this process. The most important people exercising influence are parents, as you might expect. But other adult caregivers also make a difference when they have regular contact with infants and toddlers.

Parental Influences   Even when infants are very young, parents often talk to them as though they were full-fledged adult partners in a conversation (though not equally in all cultures; see the accompanying Multicultural View box). Consider this mother speaking to her three-month-old child:

MOTHER: How is Kristi today? *(pause)* How are you? *(pause)* Good, you say? *(pause)* Are you feeling good? *(pause)* I'm glad for that. *(pause)* Yes, I am.

(pause) What would you like now? *(pause)* Your soother? *(pause)* Um? *(pause)* Is that what you want? *(pause)* Okay, here it is.

By asking questions in this "conversation," the mother implies that Kristi is capable of responding, even though her infant is much too young to do so. Furthermore, the mother leaves pauses for her baby's hypothetical responses. Observations of these kinds of pauses show that they last just about as long as in conversations between adults (Haslett, 1997); it is as though the mother is giving her baby a turn to speak before taking another turn herself. When her child remains silent, the mother even replies on her behalf. In all these behaviors, the mother teaches something about turn taking in conversations, and she expresses her faith that the infant eventually will learn these conventions herself.

When infants finally begin speaking, parents continue this strategy. At the same time, however, parents also simplify their language significantly. Sentences become shorter, although not as short as the child's, and vocabulary becomes simpler, although less restricted than the child's (Gallaway & Richards, 1994). These extra strategies help teach a new lesson, namely that words and sentences do, in fact, communicate and that language is more than interesting noises and babbling. By keeping just ahead of the infant's own linguistic skills, parents can stimulate the further development of language.

This style is called **infant-directed speech,** or *caregiver speech,* or "motherese," meaning a dialect or a version of language characteristic of parents talking with young children. In addition to shorter sentences and simpler vocabulary, speech in motherese has several unique features. It tends to unfold more slowly than speech between adults and to use a higher and more variable, or singsong, pitch; it generally contains unusually strong emphasis on key words ("Give me your *cup*"). Parents speaking motherese also tend to repeat or paraphrase themselves more than usual ("Give me the cup. The cup. Find the cup, and give it."). These features seem to make the speech more understandable to the child. When adults listen to sentences with the words acoustically muffled, they can guess the emotional tone or "message" from the pitch patterns of the muffled words. More important, though, is that they can do so most accurately if the sentences have the exaggerated pitch patterns of infant-directed speech (Fernald, 1989).

Research shows clearly that parents' conversations with babies are extremely important to the infants' development. The Harvard Preschool Project, a longitudinal study conducted at Harvard University, observed the contacts between parents and their infants that occurred naturally in the families' own homes (White, 1993). At various intervals, the infants were assessed for both intelligence and social skills. When the assessments were correlated with the results of the home observations, one result stood out clearly: the most intellectually and socially competent infants had parents who directed large amounts of language at them. The most competent babies received about twice as much language as the least competent infants in this study did. But the most competent infants also stimulated interactions with their parents, primarily by procuring various simple kinds of help, such as in pouring a glass of juice or placing the final block on a tower. These "services" probably benefited the infants by offering many opportunities for parents to talk with them ("Shall I put the block on top?").

More recent research shows that certain types of conversation can encourage children's language development (Bloom, 1993). One helpful kind is *contingent dialogue,* or conversation that responds sensitively, specifically, and immediately to

Parents alter their style of speaking almost automatically when addressing an infant. As the text explains, the simplifications of grammar and exaggerations in tone may help a baby to acquire language. But it may also demonstrate parents' optimism about their baby's abilities to learn and parents' own commitment to assisting that learning.

• • •

infant-directed speech The style or register of speech used by adults and older children when talking with a one- or two-year-old infant.

A Multicultural View ....

Cognitive Effects of Talking to Infants: A Cross-Cultural Perspective

Although the text implies strong support for mothers' talking with their infants, a different impression of this practice occurs if you view it in a cross-cultural context. Then the frequent one-way "conversations" and direct gazing between mother and baby seem a bit less natural or inevitable, and even a bit strange.

In North America, the practice is widely regarded as a positive experience: talking with and gazing at a nonverbal infant increases in frequency until the child begins producing her own language, around the first birthday, and cuddling and holding close decrease at the same time. Parents are even given professional assistance when these changes in interaction do not occur (Yoder & Warren, 1993)! Mothers themselves believe that talking with and gazing at infants stimulates infants' intellectual competence.

Research evidence seems to support the mothers' belief. Children who have verbally interactive mothers during infancy do show better language comprehension as four-year-olds and do show higher competence at solving simple problems involving both verbal and nonverbal reasoning (Samter & Haslett, 1997). But there is contrary evidence as well. In China, for example, mothers talk to infants relatively little but cuddle and hold them relatively a lot (Ho, 1994). Yet Chinese culture values educational success and Chinese children perform well in school.

The fact is that the effects of maternal talk on infants are not really clear. But it is probably not a matter of stimulating thinking and language development, as many mothers themselves might believe. Maternal talk probably is much too complex for a two- or three-month-old infant to learn by hearing it directly. Instead of providing a language model directly, therefore, early verbal interaction may serve other purposes in infants' development: maybe it simply reflects the mother's general interest in and responsiveness to her child. Parents who enjoy talking to their babies as newborns are likely to still enjoy talking to them several years later, when the babies have become capable of learning and using language more effectively. If so, the relationship between early talk and later competence is a good example of a *correlation* (an association) that is not also a *cause.* In that case, too, North American mothers could (in theory) talk with their newborns a good deal less in the earliest months and

children's verbalizations. When an infant says "Teddy?" to his parent, for example, the parent does not ignore the comment but replies or extends it meaningfully, perhaps by saying, "I'm not sure where Teddy is; I haven't seen him this morning" or "Would you like Teddy now?"

Another valuable kind of conversation is "scripted" or *textual dialogue,* routine or ritualized language embedded in a highly familiar situation. The setting itself is so familiar that it assists in interpreting the language. Many everyday routines promote this kind of language: bathing and diapering, for example, encourage the same predictable remarks time after time ("Are you wet?"; "First let's take your shirt off"). So do children's songs and nursery rhymes. Despite their repetitiveness—in fact, precisely because of it—textual dialogues allow children to place language in a larger, more meaningful context.

Paradoxically, however, a bit of parental *insensitivity* or conversational *incompetence* also may help infants to develop their language skills. Expressing moderate ignorance about an infant's intended meanings can challenge the infant to speak more fully and explicitly. This sort of "beneficial ignorance" may account for how fathers and siblings assist in the development of infant language. Because fathers and siblings tend to know an infant less well than mothers do (despite today's changing family roles), they speak relatively explicitly and elaborately with one- and two-year-olds and prompt relatively explicit language from the infants in return ("Do you want another drink?" instead of "Another drink?").

Influences of Professional Caregivers   Language acquisition can also be supported by other adults who interact with infants extensively, notably professional caregivers in family child care or infant care centers. Their forms of influence parallel those of parents (Koralek et al., 1993). Contingent dialogue (extending the child's ver-

Constant close contact between caregiver and infant, as between this mother and her children, may encourage more nonverbal communication and result in infants who fuss relatively little. Crying and fussing, which we associate with infancy in our society, may actually be a precursor to verbal communication, which parents tend to encourage in North American society.

still expect the babies to end up with good language skills eventually! This would be true, though, only if a mother were responsive and caring throughout the child's infancy, and only if the mother did begin interacting verbally as soon as the infant showed signs of actually understanding and using language. This developmental pattern in fact describes mother-infant relationships in China to a certain extent (though not perfectly).

These ideas remain speculation, though, because mothers' language practices cannot, and probably should not, be manipulated simply to explore their effects on children. In any society, parents need to interact with their babies in ways they consider natural. But comparing cultural beliefs can nonetheless give clues about the deeper, less obvious effects of particular cultural practices (Greenfield, 1994). Mother-infant "conversations" are a good example of a culture-bound practice: virtually all parent advice books urge parents to talk with their babies. Yet in doing so, the books join parents in assuming a particular cultural value: that skillful oral expression is desirable and should be encouraged as much as possible.

bal initiatives), for example, can easily take place at an infant care center: a toddler may name objects in the room ("Book!") or pictures displayed on the wall ("Cat!"), and the caregiver can extend those early initiatives into longer dialogues ("Yes, it's a pretty cat. Do you like cats?"). Contextual dialogue (familiar language routines or rituals) can also occur: a caregiver and child may engage in predictable exchanges in preparing to go home each day ("Have you found your coat?"; "Now zipper it up"). To succeed, these dialogues must be simplified; that is, they should rely on infant-directed or "caregiver" speech that takes the infant's early stage of language into account. Table 6.4 lists some additional ways caregivers can assist in language development.

TABLE 6.4   Interactions That Support Language Development

Interaction	Purpose
Sitting on the floor with infant and reading books, telling stories, or singing songs	Builds trust, models interesting activities using language
Holding infant close, looking into infant's face, smiling, and talking to infant	Builds trust, models dialogue or conversation
Responding to infant's first words and gestures using caregiver's own words and gestures	Encourages dialogue and conversation, shows respect for infant's language initiatives
Offering simple choices to infant verbally ("Do you want to paint or to play outside?")	Stimulates infant to attend to language; calls attention to relationship between language and actions
Encouraging infant (especially if a toddler) to express desires and resolve differences using words ("What do you want to do?")	Encourages child to practice language; demonstrates power of verbal expression

But important differences also exist between caregiver influences and parental influences. One concerns intensity and frequency: caregivers usually do not see a particular infant or toddler for as many hours as a parent does, nor do they develop relationships as emotionally intense as parents'. Another difference concerns cultural expectations: it is common for caregivers (but rare for parents) to come from a cultural or language background that differs from the children's. The gap can create confusion and misunderstanding between caregiver and child or between caregiver and parent. If a caregiver and a child speak different primary languages, one may lack facility with some of the words and expressions needed to communicate with the other.

At a more subtle level, a language gap may contribute to differences in fundamental attitudes or values. In observing parent-teacher conferences for how language is used between white (Anglo) teachers and Hispanic parents, Patricia Greenfield found that teachers focused much more on a child's individual achievement, whereas parents focused on the child's social compatibility (Greenfield, 1995). Jean Van Keulen and her colleagues identified the potential for a similar language gap between white American adults in general and African American children of any age (Van Keulen et al., 1998). In both cases, the result can be misunderstanding and dissatisfaction with dialogue—with how language is used by both parties—even though both are capable, in principle, of understanding each other's concerns and feelings.

All things considered, parents, caregivers, and others constitute a far more positive than negative influence on language development. Given their importance to the process, it should not be surprising that nearly all children acquire high verbal competence in just a few years. Language acquisition is "overdetermined": society supports language learning in so many ways that if a child fails to experience that support in one way, she or he is likely to experience it in some other way. So most of us do learn to talk!

 WHAT DO YOU THINK? Work with five or six classmates to discover the first few words each of you spoke. Find out, too, something about the situation in which you spoke your first words. Pool your results. Are there any features common to either the words or the settings? Any ideas about why there was (or was not) common ground? If possible, pool your group's results with those from other groups until you have information from the entire class.

The End of Infancy

The word *infant* comes from a Latin term meaning "not speaking." By this standard, a child approaching his second birthday is no longer an infant. He is now talking and often using more than one word at a time.

Almost from birth, the child communicates nonverbally: she smiles and frowns, gestures and babbles. She uses these skills to both develop and demonstrate her cognitive abilities, but she also uses them to develop social relationships, as described in the next chapter. Both by thinking and by communicating, the two-year-old learns who she is as well as who her parents and siblings are. At the same time, when all goes well, she becomes attached to these people as individuals, and her early, vague emotions turn into feelings with more focus. Pleasure becomes love, rage becomes anger, and anxiety becomes fearfulness. As the next chapter shows, these are not mere changes in labels; they signify real emotional and social growth.

Summary of Major Ideas

1. Perception is the immediate organization and interpretation of sensation, whereas cognition is the set of processes by which humans acquire and organize knowledge.

Ways of Studying Perception and Cognition in Infants

2. Infants' arousal and attention can be studied by noting changes in their heart rates.

3. Infants' recognition and memory of familiar things can be studied by observing their habituation to stimuli, or tendency to attend to novel stimuli and ignore familiar ones.

Infant Perception and Cognition

4. Studies of visual perception suggest that infants under six months of age perceive a variety of patterns, including those usually found on a human face.

5. Young infants, including newborns, show object constancy in visual perception, as well as visual anticipation of events.

6. Infants also show sensitivity to depth, as indicated in the visual cliff experiments.

7. Infants can localize sounds to some extent at birth, but do not do so accurately until about six months of age.

8. Categorical thought can be demonstrated during infancy by using the reversal shift procedure.

Cognitive Change During Infancy: Piaget's Stage Theory

9. Piaget has proposed six stages of infant cognitive development during which infants' schemes become less egocentric and increasingly symbolic and organized.

10. Research on Piaget's six stages generally confirms his original observations, but it also raises questions about the effects of motor skills and memory on infants' cognitive performance.

Behavioral Learning in Infancy

11. Like older children and adults, infants can learn through behavioral conditioning and imitation.

12. Behavioral learning tends to be ambiguous in infants less than three months old because it is difficult to distinguish true learning from general, automatic excitement.

Language Acquisition

13. Babbling begins around six months of age and becomes increasingly complex until it disappears sometime before the infant's second birthday.

14. Infants show important individual differences in their selection of first words, but generally they use words for objects in their environment that are distinctive in some way.

15. Adults influence language acquisition mainly through modeling simplified utterances, recasting their infants' own utterances, and directing considerable language at the child as she or he grows.

16. Professional caregivers influence language acquisition in ways similar to parents, but they must also recognize the potential effects of cultural gaps between caregiver and child.

Key Terms

accommodation (174)
AnotB error (177)
assimilation (174)
babbling (190)
behaviorism (183)
circular reaction (175)
cognition (163)
expressive language (191)
habituation (165)
infant-directed speech (193)
lexicon (189)
nonreversal shift (172)
object permanence (176)
perception (163)
phoneme (189)
phonology (189)

pragmatics (189)
primary circular reaction (175)
receptive language (191)
reversal shift (172)
scheme (174)
secondary circular reaction (176)
semantics (189)
sensorimotor intelligence (173)
syntax (189)
tertiary circular reaction (178)
visual cliff (169)

Psychosocial Development During the First Two Years

Focusing Questions

- What emotional capabilities does an infant have? How do differences in infants' temperaments affect their social development?

- In what ways is a newborn infant capable of participating in the social world? How does caregiver-infant synchrony expand an infant's social capabilities?

- What experiences enable infants to develop secure emotional attachments with their caregivers? What are the consequences if secure attachments fail to develop?

- How do an infant's interactions with father, siblings, and peers differ from those with his or her mother? What are the effects of day care and maternal employment on infant and toddler development?

- Why is autonomy so central to development during toddlerhood? What qualities of parenting contribute to its successful development?

Even as a newborn, Alberto was an easy baby to feed and comfort. He was also very active and responsive to the sights and sounds in his environment. Even when tired or overstimulated by the people around him, he seemed able to calm himself with just a little help from his caregiver. When he was five weeks old, Alberto just loved attention. His smiles and excitement were irresistible, and he responded to anyone who paid attention to him—from his parents to his older brother and sisters to Luisa, the family dog. However, a special mutual responsiveness seemed to be present whenever Alberto interacted with his mother, Maria, or his father, José. With either of them, Alberto's smiles, sounds, and movements seemed so highly in tune with theirs that they appeared to be having a real conversation.

By the time Alberto was four months old, he began to show a preference for his mother and his oldest sister, Lydia, who helped Maria care for him. When he saw or heard either of them, he became especially happy, active, and vocal, which caused some jealousy among other family members.

Between ages nine and eleven months, Alberto's preferences for specific people became much stronger and more obvious. He clearly preferred his mother to any other adult and responded to his sister Lydia more than to any of the other children. Now able to crawl, he tried to follow his mother wherever she went, and he cried when she left the room. During this period, he also began to do something he had never done before: he sometimes became upset when unfamiliar people visited, even if they were friendly to him.

By the time he was almost two, Alberto was walking and talking well, had begun toilet training, and could do many things himself. He continued to be an active and happy child, but sometimes he became frustrated and upset if he did not succeed at a task. Fortunately, talking to him and giving him just the right amount of helpful guidance usually worked. Although he still demanded a good deal of attention from his mother and still preferred to play with Lydia, he rarely got upset when other family members cared for him. He also seemed quite happy to socialize with almost all friendly visitors, even those he had never met before.

These changes in Alberto are typical of some of the important psychosocial changes that occur during infancy. Infancy is the time when children learn to walk, think, talk, and, in a very broad sense, become more fully "human." From the moment of birth, infants differ in their temperaments—their characteristic activity levels and stylistic patterns of responding to the people and events in their new environment. As we will see in this chapter, temperamental differences in children and how well they fit with the temperaments and expectations of their parents, other family members, and society may influence development not only in infancy but through childhood, adolescence, and adulthood as well. And although infants highly depend on their caregivers to meet their needs, they are anything but passive. Infants become active, sophisticated observers and participants in their own psychosocial development.

Each member of a family has a unique style of interacting with a new infant.

As an infant grows older, she comes to form close and enduring emotional attachments with the important people in her life and sometimes shows her concerns about them very dramatically. She wails when a strange nurse approaches her in the doctor's office, and she greets her mother or father warmly when one of them "rescues" her from the nurse. At other times, the baby may participate in relationships in more subtle ways, such as attending closely to older brothers and sisters while they play—more closely than her siblings attend to her. At still other times, she may express her needs or feelings in ways that confound the people around her; for example, she may refuse particular foods when a parent offers them but take them happily from a baby sitter.

These behaviors convey two major tasks of psychosocial development in infancy: the development of trust and of autonomy. Infants learn what to expect from the important people in their lives. They develop strong feelings about whom they do (and do not) like to be with and what foods they prefer. The conflicts of trust versus mistrust and autonomy versus shame and doubt intertwine closely during their first two years, although many observers of children believe trust develops earlier than autonomy does.

In this chapter, we first discuss the essential role of early social relationships with family and others in the development of trust and in the achievement of autonomy. Next, we examine the importance of early infant emotions and temperament. Then we explore the ways in which attachments are formed and consider their short- and longer-term developmental consequences. Finally, we look at sources of autonomy and the development of self during later infancy and toddlerhood.

Early Social Relationships

Infants seem to have a natural tendency to be social participants. Not only do newborns show preferences for their mothers' voices shortly after birth; some evidence also suggests that their perception of speech can be influenced by prenatal exposure to their mothers' speech (DeCasper et al., 1994). Immediately after birth, infants are capable of many social responses. For example, a newborn will turn his head toward the sound of a human voice and actively search for its source, attend to and show preference for a voice with a female pitch, and pause regularly in his sucking pattern for human voices but not for similar, nonhuman tones. He will even prefer the smell and taste of human milk over those of formula, water, or sugar water (Brazelton, 1976).

Transition to Parenthood

Parent-child relationships begin even before a child is born. Almost as soon as pregnancy is confirmed, parents form *images* of the child, images of what she or he will be like and of how they as parents will respond and cope with this new human presence (Galinsky, 1987). They often experience both excitement and fear, the precise mix depending on how much support they have for becoming parents as well as the history of support, or lack thereof, that they had for being children themselves years ago. Even after the baby is born, these images can influence the parents' internal experiences and expectations regarding a child, although this "mental portrait" is now subject to ongoing revision based on the parents' ongoing interactions and experiences with their baby (Anderson, 1996; Ferholt, 1991; Stern, 1995).

Having a child, particularly if it is the first, represents a major life transition that is accompanied by personal, familial, social, and, for many people, professional changes. For most parents, having a child leads them to become less concerned about themselves and more concerned with the well-being of others and about the future as embodied in their child. This shift away from self-centeredness usually comes at some emotional cost, however. During the first two years of rearing an infant, many mothers find themselves removed from much of their normal contact with other adults to devote themselves to infant care, and fathers report working harder at their jobs (Bronstein, 1988; Cowan et al., 1991; Hyman, 1995).

To accommodate the additional family tasks involved in caring for a new infant, the division of roles between husband and wife tends to become more traditional, regardless of the wife's employment, educational level, pre-existing arrangements, or beliefs about gender roles. Social and emotional patterns between parents also appear to change, as reflected in significant decreases in shared leisure and sexual activities, in fewer positive interactions with each other, and in decreased marital satisfaction and greater marital conflict (Cowan et al., 1991; Monk et al., 1996; Vandell et al., 1997).

To better understand these changes, Rachel Levy-Shiff (1994) studied marital adjustment in 102 couples from diverse sociocultural backgrounds from pregnancy through the first eight months following the birth of their first child. She found that higher levels of *paternal involvement* with the baby, especially in caregiving, was the most important factor in sustaining marital satisfaction for *both* spouses. Levy-Shiff suggests that during the transition to parenthood, men and women must first solve the internal and interpersonal dilemmas of reorganizing their lives to adjust to the new demands and responsibilities of childrearing. In most families, the birth of a first child results in gender roles becoming more differentiated and traditional, with women assuming both the main responsibilities for child care and the majority of housework. The physical and emotional drain that new mothers experience may lead them to feel negative toward their husbands because of "overload" and because of unfulfilled prenatal expectations that caring for the new baby would be more fully shared.

Fathers who are more involved in *coparenting* (sharing child care) and sharing housework demonstrate that they are not just husbands but also good friends who are committed to meeting their partners' needs in ways that are caring and fair. It is

With the birth of a new baby, parents must suddenly think about their personal priorities in new ways—ways that take the child's needs into account. Getting to know the child's temperament and habits is a major challenge at first, but one at which most parents succeed.

WORKING WITH
Rachelle Turner, Infant Day Care Coordinator

Understanding Infant Social Development

Rachelle is the infant coordinator in a day care center, where she has taught for the past four years. She began working as a day care teacher during her college years and plans to eventually work as a therapist in a program serving young children and their families. Rachelle was interviewed in my office.

Rob: *What do you like most about working with infants?*

Rachelle: I find working with infants fascinating because so much is packed into the first year of life. It's amazing to see how rapid the changes are. Because you're with the children eight hours a day, five days a week, you can observe the very small changes in development that happen, even on a week-to-week basis.

Rob: *What differences in early infant temperament do you find?*

Rachelle: There are differences in napping patterns, for example. If, as an infant, a child needs you to rub his back or rock him gently to go to sleep, often he will want the same kind of thing as a three-year-old when he is going down for a nap on a cot. Or you might see him rocking himself to go to sleep. On the other hand, there's the child you can just put in his crib, and he'll just grab his blanket and go to sleep. When he's older, you can say, "OK, it's nap time," and he'll get on his cot and go to sleep. It often seems like children are their own person from day one.

Rob: *Do you have another example?*

Rachelle: Some infants aren't happy until they can crawl and go get what they want, while others seem perfectly content with just sitting up and having you plop toys in front of them. Infants can really differ in how active or passive they are in learning to crawl or walk and in their style of exploring their physical and social world. They also differ in their moods and in whether they are irritable or not.

Rob: *What about their social relationships?*

Rachelle: Their changing interactions with other children are interesting. A five-month-old infant will be attracted to another child, but will not, of course, play with the child. She'll pull the other infant's hair and touch its face and clothes. She'll want to explore it and see what it is, just like a doll. Toward the end of the first year, infants recognize their friends, and smile and laugh when they see them. They now want to go on the climber or play blocks together.

Rob: *So their social skills change from exploring each other as objects to interacting with each other as unique individuals?*

Rachelle: Yes.

Rob: *What changes do you see during the second year?*

Rachelle: Once they can actually say the child's name, they'll call him to come play. Games like hide-and-seek, chasing each other, or knocking blocks over together. They interact because the child makes it fun. It's not the imagination that three-year-old friends have, but it's definitely play and excitement when they see each other. They'll run up to each other, and they'll hug and kiss and be affectionate, and they know the other child isn't a doll. And if one gets hurt, they'll say, "Oh, Anne has a boo-boo," because she's a person in their life.

Rob: *What have you observed about infants' ability to form attachment relationships with nonparental adult caregivers?*

Rachelle: If you are affectionate and responsive to an infant's unique habits and needs around feeding, changing, and sleeping, and comforting and stimulation, she'll quickly come to know you and form an attachment to you. Particularly if a child is in day care full time, if an unfamiliar parent or delivery person comes into the center, or if a child is upset for some other reason, she will crawl or run to a caregiver or want to be held or to sit in your lap.

Rob: *How does it feel from the caregiver's perspective?*

Rachelle: Very strong feelings of attachment develop. Remember, unlike a typical household where laundry, cooking, and other tasks compete with child care, we spend almost all of our time observing and interacting with the children. I get very attached. When children leave, it's very hard to have children coming in and out of your life. You think about them constantly.

Rob: *Are parents sometimes jealous of your relationship with their baby?*

Rachelle: Yes. A parent might give the child excessive gifts, or become critical of the teacher, or make a point of telling the teacher something she didn't know about the child. I try to reassure parents by asking them for information about their child and by being interested in changes they have observed rather than just focusing on changes I have noticed.

What Do You Think?

1. What qualities do you think make a good day care teacher?

2. As a current or prospective parent, how comfortable would you feel putting your child in Rachelle's care? Why?

3. How closely do Rachelle's examples of temperamental differences and attachment fit your own understandings based on reading the chapter?

also likely that shared involvement in child care and the burdens of housework increase a husband's empathy and appreciation for his wife's experience. Such participation also likely reduces the guilt he would feel if he failed to share these new burdens. Interestingly, by freeing up their wives' time and conveying a spirit of cooperativeness, husbands create opportunities for more high-quality time with their wives, the lack of which is a major cause of upset for many new fathers (Belsky et al., 1995; Levy-Schiff, 1994; Vandell et al., 1997).

Caregiver-Infant Synchrony

Frequently the social interactions between parent (or other caregiver) and infant involve a pattern of close coordination and teamwork in which each waits for the other to finish before beginning to respond. This pattern of closely coordinated interaction is called **caregiver-infant synchrony.** Recall the description of Alberto at the beginning of this chapter. Even infants only a few weeks old are able to maintain and break eye contact with their mothers at regular intervals and to take turns with them in making sounds and body movements. Furthermore, videotape studies reveal that mother and baby have "conversations" that resemble adult dialogue in many ways, except for the child's lack of words (De Wolff & van IJzendorn, 1997; Fish et al., 1993; Stern, 1992).

How do such exchanges occur? A mother may gaze steadily at her baby, waiting patiently for her to vocalize, move, or at least look. When the action eventually occurs, the mother may respond by imitating the infant's gesture, smiling, or saying something to her. She times her responses to allow the baby a turn in this game, just as though the child were a fully competent person in a social exchange. As the interaction continues, the baby typically shows increasing tension: her movements and sounds become not only more frequent but more sudden and jerky as well. At some point, the infant becomes overstimulated and breaks the tension by looking away from her mother and spends the next few moments looking at or touching objects instead of the mother. This provides a break from sociability, although, of course, social exchanges may serve equally well as rest periods from nonsocial interactions. In any case, after a suitable interval, mother and infant recapture each other's attention, and the cycle of turn taking begins all over again (Stern, 1985b, 1992).

Until an infant is several months old, responsibility for coordinating this activity rests with the caregiver. But after a few months, the baby becomes capable of initiating social interchanges and influencing the content and style of his caregiver's behavior. Some of this continuity is created by the baby rather than the mother. The smiles, gazes, and vocalizing of a friendly infant prove hard for his mother to resist, and after several months of experience with such a baby, the mother becomes especially responsive to her infant's communications, further reinforcing the infant's social tendencies.

During the infant's second year, parent and baby use gestures such as pointing, vocalizing, and alternating their gaze between objects and their partner to coordinate and sustain periods of joint attention and maintain each other's interest. High levels of joint attention and reciprocal turn taking in parent-infant interaction, which are sometimes referred to as *coregulation,* are associated with sensitive parenting and help children to develop skills at self-regulation and the regulation of others that are central to becoming socially competent in relationships with family members and peers (Denham, 1998). Additional discussion of infant-caregiver communication is found in Chapter 6.

As we will see shortly, a good caregiver-infant temperament "fit" and a well-developed capacity for caregiver-infant synchrony are both important aspects of the development of the high-quality caregiver-infant relationships that serve as the basis for healthy development. Caregiver-infant relationships that lack the mutual

● ● ●

caregiver-infant synchrony Patterns of closely coordinated social and emotional interaction between caregiver and infant.

The closely coordinated interactions or caregiver-infant synchrony displayed by the mother and baby in this picture are an important aspect of the development of early social relationships.

awareness and responsiveness that makes synchrony possible may reflect childrearing difficulties and can place an infant at risk for developmental problems. Studies of interactions between depressed mothers and their infants, for example, have found that mothers' negative moods influence their babies' moods, and can affect their longer-term relationships and vulnerability to depression later in life (Nolen-Hoeksema et al., 1995).

Social Interactions with Other Family Members

Although infants may interact more with their mothers than with anyone else, they actually live in a network of daily social relationships in which a number of other people make at least minor—and sometimes major—contributions to their social lives. Fathers often belong to this network, and so do siblings. How do a baby's contacts with these people compare to those with his or her mother?

Father-Infant Interactions   Fathers have become increasingly involved in the care of infants and young children, spending around two or three hours per day compared with nine hours for mothers. In a small but significant number of instances, fathers assume the role of primary caregiver, reversing the traditional expectations that fathers should set personal and professional goals over investing time and care in their children and the paternal role (Garbarino, 1993; Hyman, 1995; Lamb, 1997). Infants' social episodes with their fathers follow the same cycle of buildup and withdrawal that characterizes infants' interactions with their mothers. Success at maintaining high levels of caregiver-infant synchrony is related to the degree of fit between their stress levels, personality characteristics, attitudes and expectations, and the characteristics and needs of the babies (Bridges et al., 1997; Noppe et al., 1991). In an interesting naturalistic study of fathers' interactions with their infants in their homes, Anju Jain, Jay Belsky, and Keith Crnic (1996) observed four groups of fathers. Caregiver fathers were involved in a broad range of infant care activities, including feeding, changing, playing, and disciplining, and were generally aware of their infants' needs. Playmate-teacher fathers focused on play and teaching activities when interacting with their infants. Disciplinarian fathers emphasized setting limits and imposing discipline. Finally, disengaged fathers had only minimal interaction with their infants and little awareness of their infants' needs. Caregiver and playmate-teacher fathers generally were more educated, had more prestigious occupations, were better adjusted emotionally, were better able to rely on others, and experienced fewer daily hassles than the disciplinarian or disengaged fathers.

Although mothers and fathers play many of the same games, their styles differ. Play episodes with fathers tend to have sharper peaks and valleys: higher states of excitement and more sudden and complete withdrawals by the baby. Fathers tend to jostle more and talk less than mothers do, and they roughhouse more and play ritual games such as peek-a-boo less. Fathers also devote more time with their babies to play than mothers do. These differences in style also appear in middle childhood, and such playful interactions may help to prepare infants for future play with peers (Parke, 1996).

How do we explain these differences? Past experience with infants, the amount of time routinely spent with young children, difficult work schedules, and fathers' expectations about the stresses and responsibilities of parenting may all play a role.

When researchers compared fathers who served as primary, full-time caregivers with fathers who took the more traditional secondary-caregiver role, they found differences in how the two groups played with their infants. Primary-caregiver fathers acted very much like mothers, smiling more and imitating their babies' facial expressions and vocalizations more than secondary-caregiver fathers did. However, all the fathers were quite physical when interacting with their infants (Field, 1987; Geiger, 1996; Noppe et al., 1991). These findings suggest that cohort effects may be at work here. (*Cohort effects* refer to developmental changes shared by individuals growing up in a particular time or place, or under a specific set of historical circumstances.) As successive generations of fathers assume greater involvement in the care of infants, it is likely that differences in how fathers and mothers interact with their babies will decrease.

Interactions with Siblings   Approximately 80 percent of children in the United States and Europe grow up with siblings. The time they spend together in their early years frequently is greater than the time spent with their mothers or fathers. In many cultures, children are cared for by siblings. From age one or two they are fed, comforted, disciplined, and played with by a sister or brother who may be only three or four years older (Dunn, 1985; Teti, 1992). First-born children are likely to monitor the interactions of their mother and the new baby very closely and try to become directly involved themselves. Children as young as eighteen months attempt to help in the bathing, feeding, and dressing of their sibling. At times they also try to tip over the baby's bath, spill things, and turn the kitchen upside down when they feel jealous of their mother's attention to the new baby. Conflict between siblings is most likely to occur when parents are seen as giving preferential treatment to one child (Dunn et al., 1994; Stewart et al., 1987).

In talking to their younger siblings, children make many of the same adjustments their parents do, using much shorter sentences, repeating comments, and using lots of action-getting techniques (baby talk, or "parentese"). In turn, infants tend to respond to their siblings in much the same way they do to their parents. But they also quickly learn the ways siblings differ from parents, particularly young siblings. Because younger children lack their parents' maturity and experience, they are less able to focus consistently on meeting the baby's needs rather than their own. For example, a four-year-old who is playing with his eight-month-old sister may not notice that she is becoming overstimulated and tired and needs to stop. On another occasion, he may become jealous of the attention she is getting and "accidentally" fall on her while giving her a hug. If parents (and other caregivers) keep in mind the needs and capabilities of each of their children and provide appropriate supervision, interactions with siblings are likely to benefit the development of both their new infant and his or her brothers and sisters. Secure infant-mother relationships and warmth toward both children is associated with positive relationships between siblings, whereas parental coldness is linked to sibling conflict (Volling & Belsky, 1992).

Grandparents   For the majority of well-functioning families, and in most cultural groups in North America, grandparents become welcome companions for the new child (Werner, 1991), as well as secondary sources of practical advice and child care. This is especially true when the grandparents live geographically close to the parents, they are relatively young and in good health, and the family itself belongs to a cultural group (such as Mexican Americans) that values the participation of the extended family in raising children (Ramirez, 1989; Slomin, 1991).

Interactions with Nonfamily Caregivers

In recent years, caregiving has become increasingly important in the lives of preschool children because many more mothers have started working outside the home, even before their children have begun public school. By 1995, about 55 to 60 percent of all mothers with children less than six years of age worked outside the home, and experts predict the proportion will rise even higher by the end of the century (Scarr, 1998). All of these parents require suitable, high-quality care for their children for either all or part of the day. The arrangements they actually make depend on the age of the child, on their own preferences (usually familylike settings), and on the kinds of services available in the community. Among all parents who work at least part time or more, about 45 percent arrange for a relative to come into the home or take the child to the relative's home (U.S. Bureau of the Census, 1996). Another 40 percent arrange for a nonrelative to care for the child in the child's home or, more commonly, in the caregiver's home.

That leaves only about 15 percent of infants, toddlers, and preschoolers to be cared for in formal child care centers. Figure 7.1 summarizes current child care arrangements for children under two years of age. In addition to good physical facilities and developmentally appropriate programs, high-quality care for infants is best ensured by employing caregivers who are well trained and supervised and responsive to the physical, cognitive, social, and emotional needs of infants and their families (Scarr, 1998).

Infant and Toddler Center Care   Almost one-half of all mothers with infants work and therefore need care for their babies. One relatively recent solution, though still not common, is child care centers that specialize in serving infants and toddlers (Scarr, 1998). These centers usually are regulated more strictly than centers for preschoolers are. Typically child care authorities require a closer ratio of adults to children, such as one adult for every three or four infants, as well as facilities for changing diapers, washing clothes, preparing food, and providing places for children to sleep. Often a licensed infant or toddler center must have a registered nurse on its staff, whereas a preschool center need have only a nurse or a doctor to call at a nearby clinic. Activities involve a mixture of supervised play, projects to stimulate language development, and physical routines such as sleeping, bathing, and eating. Since these requirements are relatively expensive to provide, and because controversy surrounds the very idea of out-of-home care for infants, infant and toddler centers remain much scarcer than centers for preschoolers.

Family Day Care Homes   Family day care homes care for only limited numbers of children—usually fewer than six—in the homes of the caregivers. The hours and activities tend to be similar to those for child care centers, but children's activities

FIGURE 7.1

Current Child Care Arrangements for Working Mothers with Children under One Year and with Children Between One and Two Years

The majority of infants and toddlers whose mothers work are cared for in their own or another home. Somewhat more toddlers than infants go to child care facilities. Infants are more likely than toddlers to be cared for in "other" situations, such as accompanying their parents to work.

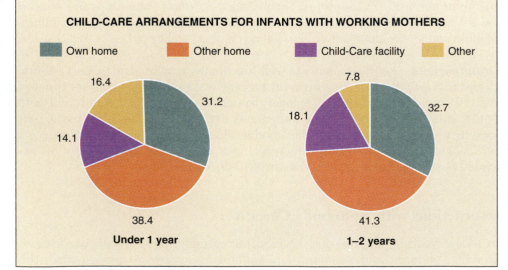

Good infant and toddler care requires a safe and developmentally appropriate play environment and caregivers who respond to each child with warmth and sensitivity, such as the one pictured here.

usually are organized in ways more similar to families. Children still engage in supervised play or crafts, for example, but they are more likely to do it together as a single group. Because the number of children and adults is smaller, the environment can feel more intimate than at a larger center and transitions between activities often occur more spontaneously and quickly.

Research on the effectiveness of family day care has found that compared to child care center programs, their success depends less on professional training and more on the family caregiver's own pride and motivation in serving children and on her or his "sense of mission" in providing particular kinds of experiences for children (Pence & Goelman, 1991). This may be partly because family caregivers work more autonomously than staff at centers do. By working at home, they are more likely to work alone rather than as part of a team and to have less opportunity to receive and therefore benefit from training. The autonomy of family day care homes is also reflected in the large number of family day care providers who operate with no official license or government regulation. Most are women who take in a few children of friends or neighbors, sometimes simultaneously caring for their own preschool children or infants. Government child care authorities usually deplore the lack of licensing in family day care homes (Kontos, 1992; Scarr, 1998), but because homes necessarily entail privacy, it is difficult to enforce licensing regulations.

What are the effects of family day care and infant center care? The fact that many family day care homes are unlicensed and unregulated has tended to focus research away from evaluating their long-term benefits and toward the more pressing tasks of assessing the qualities of family caregivers (Fischer & Eheart, 1991) and increasing the percentage of licensed family day care programs (Leavitt, 1991; Nelson, 1991). Judgments of the relative success of programs have been made (Pence & Goelman, 1991), but they have focused primarily on the daily processes of programs—the quality of conversation between caregiver and child, for example—rather than on long-term outcomes.

Characteristics of Good Child Care   What makes for good child care? Small group size, a high staff-to-child ratio, and a well-trained staff certainly are important. The number of children in the group should be small enough to allow caregivers to interact with each child in a stimulating and sensitive fashion. An adult-child ratio of one to four or less for children two years and younger and one to seven or less for children between two and three years are recommended. Caregiver stability and continuity also are important, because they help ensure that each child can form attachments with caregivers. Lack of continuity may make it difficult for an infant to continue to form multiple attachments and adversely affect his or her development. A turnover rate of no more than one or two primary caregivers over a year is recommended (Howes et al., 1993; Scarr, 1998).

Finally, caregivers should have formal training in child development. Well-trained caregivers are more likely to plan care based on expectations of developmentally appropriate behaviors and to distinguish such behaviors from maladaptive ones. They are also more likely to be aware of the factors that help to foster emotional relationships that are secure and developmentally supportive.

What preparation is needed to become an effective child care teacher? A study of three hundred teachers from randomly selected child care centers in five representative metropolitan areas of the United States found that for preschool teachers, a bachelor's degree in any subject or specialized training at the college level is sufficient, whereas infant and toddler teachers are more likely to need specialized college-level training (Kontos et al., 1996). For parents who are considering day care for their infant, knowing what to look for in a center is extremely important. Table 7.1 presents guidelines for choosing infant day care. Additional discussion of day care appears in Chapter 9.

Interactions with Peers

Young babies show considerable interest in other infants and in much the same ways they show interest in their parents: by gazing, smiling, and cooing. Sociability of this kind develops with peers at the same time and at the same rate that it does with parents. As you might expect, babies become more social with experience. In one study of infants and toddlers in a nursery school class, all the children became friendlier with one another during the four-month semester, vocalizing, smiling, and exchanging toys more frequently. Interestingly, the infants came close to equaling the toddlers (who were fifteen months older) in both types and amounts of social behavior (Hartup, 1989; Roopnarine & Field, 1982). When given the choice, infants often prefer playing with their peers to playing with their mothers. In play situations, infants more frequently look at and follow their peers, and toddlers are more likely to talk with, imitate, and exchange toys with their peers than with their mothers (Howes, 1996).

TABLE 7.1   Guidelines for Choosing a Good Infant Daycare Program

- Children are most likely to thrive intellectually and emotionally in programs that offer a balance between structured educational activities and an open, free environment.
- The caregiving environment should provide ample physical space (at least twenty-five square feet per child) and a variety of materials and activities to foster sensorimotor, social, and cognitive development.
- Class size should be small (fewer than ten children) and should include children within a two-year age range. Small centers (fewer than thirty children) usually have better staff-child ratios than centers with more children.
- The interaction style of the caregiver is a key aspect of quality care. The caregiver should be actively involved but not restrictive with the children. The caregiver should also be responsive and offer positive encouragement.
- Caregivers who have training in child development and continuing opportunities for education are most likely to provide high-quality care.
- The individual characteristics of the child should be taken into account. Some children will probably do well in a program that balances structure and openness; others may profit from either more structure or a more flexible and relaxed program.
- High staff-child ratio and low staff turnover is important. Research shows, for example, that when the staff-child ratio is at least one to three for infants, one to four for toddlers, and one to nine for preschoolers, the quality of caregiving and of children's activities within the center are both good.

Source: Adapted from Clarke-Stewart (1993).

Infants show considerable interest in interacting with other infants and, when given the opportunity, may prefer playing with their peers to playing with their parents.

During toddlerhood, parents, teachers, and other adults play a major role in the development of relationships with peers: through their relationships with their toddlers, through direct instruction about social interactions, and by providing their toddlers with appropriate opportunities to be with peers in extended family, play group, and day care situations (Fagot, 1997; Howes et al., 1994; Parke et al., 1994). Not surprisingly, the quality of infant-parent relationships appears to be related to young children's behavior with peers. For example, children who have secure relationships with their parents receive more positive responses from unfamiliar peers, are better liked by peers, and have more positive friendships with peers than children whose relationships are insecure (Belsky & Cassidy, 1994; Cassidy et al., 1996).

Toddlers in day care spend about 25 percent of their time interacting positively with other toddlers. They are more likely to express positive feelings and play competently with peers than with adults or when by themselves. Repeated contact with a peer in a familiar setting with a familiar caregiver and minimal adult interference appears to facilitate the development of peer friendship. Peers also support the autonomy of toddler from mother and offer the toddler an alternative source of stimulation and comfort (Hartup, 1989, 1996; Howes, 1996). Peer relationships during toddlerhood may in turn promote the development of positive friendships later in childhood. A recent longitudinal study of the quality of children's relationships between infancy and nine years of age found that children's formation of close friendships as toddlers predicted their positive ratings of their friendship quality as nine-year-olds (Howes et al., 1998). So far, there is no evidence that toddlers who have attended day care relate with peers differently than children who have had equal access to peer experiences in their homes.

In conclusion, although infants' social interactions with their parents and other adult caregivers generally are their most important early social experiences, interactions with other family members, nonfamily caregivers, and peers also contribute to their social development. The quality and developmental impact of experiences with siblings and peers will reflect to some extent the degree to which parental supervision of such contacts considers the needs of both the baby and the other children.

WHAT DO YOU THINK?   What advice would you give to prospective parents about maternal employment and child care arrangements for infants?

Emotions and Temperament in Infancy

The healthy cries of a newborn infant make it clear that infants are capable of feeling and expressing their emotions even at birth. During the first three months, infants spend about two hours crying during a typical day. Healthy babies produce four types of cries—the basic hunger cry, the angry cry, the pain cry, and the fussy irregular cry—all of which provide their caregivers with useful information about their physiological states of discomfort (St. James-Roberts & Halil, 1991). For most parents, however, the pattern of caregiving behaviors is not highly correlated with the specific causes of the infant's cries, meaning mothers and other caregivers tend to use the same basic routines to respond to the infant's different cries. These include rocking or moving the baby in a rhythmic manner; talking or making soothing sounds; holding the baby upright against their shoulder; touching him by patting, rubbing, kissing, and hugging; cradling him in their arms; checking his diaper or feeding him; giving him a pacifier; or showing him a toy or some other feature of the environment. Parents and other caregivers also use context (such as how recently the baby was fed or changed) to determine the meanings of the baby's cries (Gustafson & Harris, 1990). Over time, as infants gain better control over their crying, crying serves to convey a wider range of messages to their caregivers (Barr, 1995; Green et al., 1998). In the following sections, we discuss the role of early emotions and *temperament*—the infant's characteristic way of feeling and responding.

Emotions in Infancy

While researchers have long recognized changes in infants' crying, smiling, frustrations, and fear of strangers and novel stimuli, there is now a growing appreciation of the range and complexity of infant emotions. This appreciation has taken some time to develop because infants' limited awareness of their emotions and ability to communicate their feelings has made the scientific study of infant emotions difficult. For example, videotape studies reveal that an infant only a few weeks old is able to produce facial expressions corresponding to the range of adult emotional states, even though the infant's expressions of emotion, particularly negative emotions, do not always result from the same events that typically produce them in adults. Similarly, while physiological aspects of emotion, such as changes in heart rate, can be reliably measured, their relationships to specific emotions are not always clear (Camras et al., 1993; Oster et al., 1992). One reason for this lack of specificity is that babies' expectations and understandings appear to play an important role in their emotional reactions. For example, an incongruous stimulus, such as a mother's face covered with a mask, will produce a fear response in some situations but smiling and laughter in others.

While researchers still disagree about the earliest age at which particular emotions are present, they generally agree that most babies can reliably express basic joy and laughter by three or four months, fear by five to eight months, and more complex emotions such as shame, embarrassment, guilt, envy, and pride during toddlerhood (Izard, 1994; Kochanska et al., 1998; Lewis, 1992; Weinberg & Tronick, 1994). Table 7.2 shows the approximate ages at which certain infant emotions appear.

Expressions of emotion play an important role in development by providing vital information to infants and their caregivers about ongoing experiences and interactions. Caregivers "read" these messages and use them to

TABLE 7.2 Development of Infant Emotions	
Approximate Age (in months)	**Emotion**
0–1	Social smile
3	Pleasure smile
3–4	Wariness
4–7	Joy, anger, sadness
4	Surprise
5–9	Fear
18	Shame

Sources: Izard (1994); Lewis (1992).

guide their actions in helping the infant to fulfill his needs. Very young infants also appear to be sensitive to the positive and negative emotions of their caregivers; they are quite capable of responding to adult fears and anxieties. These responses are likely based on cues similar to those adults use, such as slight variations in voice quality, smell, and touch, as well as variations in facial expression and body language. As they get older, infants display these feelings with increasing frequency and predictability (Eisenberg et al., 1995; Tronick, 1989).

Another important change in the emotional life of an infant is the baby's growing ability to *self-regulate* her own emotional states. During the first year of life, an infant's emotional activities also serve as coping behaviors that allow the baby to regulate her own expressive behaviors and associated emotional states, especially negative ones. These *self-directed regulatory behaviors* include looking away, self-comforting, and self-stimulation. They allow the infant to control her negative feelings by shifting her attention away from a disturbing event or by substituting positive for negative stimuli. This helps the infant adjust her emotional state to a comfortable level at which she can successfully maintain interaction with her surroundings (Bass & Goldsmith, 1998; Grolinck et al., 1996). During the second year, increases in the capacity for emotional self-regulation also reflect her growing ability to respond to the feelings and needs of others through helping, sharing, and providing comfort (Zahn-Waxler et al., 1992). Claire Kopp (1982, 1989) has proposed that the modulation, or self-regulation, of behavior develops over a series of five successive phases (see Table 7.3). Emotional self-regulation in infancy from the viewpoint of development theorists was discussed in Chapter 2. As we will see in later chapters, emotional regulation continues to play an important developmental role in childhood and adolescence (Caspi et al., 1995; Eisenberg, 1997).

Temperament

Temperament refers to an individual's consistent pattern or style of reacting to a broad range of environmental events and situations. Most researchers agree that differences in primary reaction tendencies such as sensitivity to visual or verbal stimulation, emotional responsiveness, and sociability appear to be present at birth,

• • •

temperament Individual differences in quality and intensity of emotional responding and self-regulation that are present at birth, are relatively stable and enduring over time and across situations, and are influenced by the interaction of heredity, maturation, and experience.

During phase 1 (neurophysiological modulation), the infant becomes able to regulate its patterns and states of sleep, arousal, and waking activity. During phase 2 (sensorimotor modulation), the sensorimotor schemes described by Paiget are used to regulate behavior. During phase 3 (control), the infant intentionally controls and directs its behavior and is aware of the social demands of others. During phase 4 (self-control), language and representational thinking allow increased behavioral self-control. During phase 5 (self-regulation), self-control becomes more conscious, purposeful, and flexible in response to changing demands of the situation.

TABLE 7.3	**Development of Behavioral Self-Regulation (modulation) During Infancy: Phases of Self-Regulation**		
Approximate Ages	**Phases**	**Features**	**Cognitive Requisites**
Birth to 2–3 months	1. Neurophysiological modulation	Modulation of arousal, activation of organized patterns of behavior	
3 months–9 months+	2. Sensorimotor modulation	Change ongoing behavior in response to events and stimuli in environment	
12 months–18 months+	3. Control	Awareness of social demands of a situation and initiate, maintain, cease physical acts, communication, etc. accordingly; compliance, self-initiated monitoring	Intentionality, goal-directed behavior, conscious awareness of action, memory of existential self
24 months+	4. Self-control	As above; delay upon request; behave according to social expectations in the absence of external monitors	Representational thinking and recall memory, symbolic thinking, continuing sense of identity
36 months+	5. Self-regulation	As above; flexibility of control processes that meet changing situational demands	Strategy production, conscious introspection, etc.

Source: Kopp (1982), p. 202, Table 2.

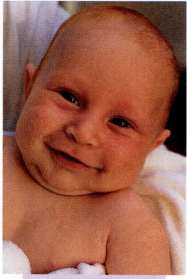

Infants vary in temperament, from easy-going to difficult; these variations may affect their long-run development significantly.

prior to any significant interaction with the external environment. However, researchers disagree on how much such differences are due solely to genetic inheritance and how much they reflect prenatal influences and more subtle environmental experiences during and shortly after birth (Kagan & Snidman, 1991; Kagan et al., 1995).

Parents certainly report differences in their newborn infants' temperaments. The parents of Alberto and his sister Lydia, for example, clearly remember that unlike Lydia, who was a fussy and somewhat difficult baby to care for and comfort during her first few months, Alberto was a very easy baby who was no trouble at all. In a now classic study of temperament, Alexander Thomas and Stella Chess used parents' reports of differences in their babies on the following nine dimensions: (1) activity level, (2) rhythmicity (regularity of eating, sleeping, and elimination), (3) approach-withdrawal to or from novel stimuli and situations, (4) adaptability to new people and situations, (5) emotional reactivity, (6) responsiveness to stimulation, (7) quality of mood (positive or negative), (8) distractibility, and (9) attention span (Chess & Thomas, 1986; Thomas & Chess, 1981). They found three general patterns of temperament. *Easy babies* (40 percent of the sample) showed mostly positive moods, regular bodily functions, and good adaptation to new situations. *Difficult babies* (10 percent) displayed negative moods, irregular bodily functions, and high stress in new situations. *Slow-to-warm-up babies* (15 percent) resembled the difficult ones, but were less extreme; they were moody and relatively unadaptable, but did not react vigorously to new stimuli. Finally, *mixed-pattern babies* (35 percent) did not fall neatly into any of the first three groups.

Because the original classification of temperaments was based solely on parents' reports, which tend to be unreliable, more recent studies have used two additional measures of temperament: multiple behavior ratings (by pediatricians, nurses, teachers, and other individuals familiar with the child) and direct observation of the child. These studies have confirmed earlier findings of temperamental differences at birth (Plomin, 1989; Seifer et al., 1994).

Classifying babies by temperamental pattern has been helpful in predicting problems for children who are difficult or slow to warm up, but not for the majority of children whose temperaments are less extreme. Newborn infants whose biological rhythms are irregular, who experience discomfort during feeding and elimination, and who do not communicate their needs clearly tend to be more difficult for their parents and are more likely to experience problems in developing close relationships with them. For example, mothers of temperamentally easy infants have been found to be more positive in their caregiving—including the amount and quality of visual and physical contact and stimulation, soothing, and responsiveness to their babies' positive signals—than mothers of difficult babies (Kerr et al., 1994; van den Boom & Hoeksma, 1994).

How stable are early differences in temperament? Temperamental differences observed toward the end of the first year, including reactivity to stress, irritability, sociability, shyness, inattentiveness, and activity level, are somewhat predictive of later temperament, although predictions based on temperamental differences among newborns are considerably less reliable (Carlson et al., 1995; Gunnar et al., 1995; Rothbart & Ahadi, 1994). Temperamental characteristics such as lack of control, approachability, and sluggishness in early childhood have been associated with similar characteristics and with behavior problems in adolescence (Caspi et al., 1995). Based on the current evidence, infant temperament alone does not appear to be very predictive of later behavior.

This may in part reflect the influence of experience and context on temperament. Temperamental qualities, much like other characteristics observable at birth (see Chapter 3), do not operate in a vacuum. In most cases, the degree to which an infant's early temperamental style contributes to personality development is likely to be influenced by the reactions the child evokes from parents and other caregivers and by how good a *fit* exists between her temperamental style and the attitudes, ex-

A TALK WITH

Jennifer, Age Eight Months, and Her Parents

Infant Temperament

The following is part of an interview conducted with the Granoff family in the living room of their apartment. Members of the family are Jennifer, age eight months; her brother, Thomas, age three; her sister, Loretta, age fifteen; and her parents, Joyce and Michael.

Interviewer: *You mentioned earlier that Jennifer has been an easy baby from the time she was born. Please tell me more about that.*

Michael: She has always had a very even disposition. The only time she is ever cranky is when she needs to sleep or when she's hungry, but we usually feed her often enough, so that doesn't happen too much.

Joyce: She is an extremely regular baby. She goes to bed every night at about the same time and sleeps all night long. When she wakes up, she is cheerful and waits patiently in her crib until we get there. Sometimes we don't even know that she's awake. Some babies are grumpy. They wake up screaming and crying. Her brother is sometimes that way. People I used to work with have a little girl who's a little younger than Jennifer, and a completely different baby—wiry, squirmy, and difficult to hold and to comfort.

Interviewer: *Is it harder or easier to have that kind of baby?*

Joyce: I don't know. I think that her parents find her more difficult. She seems to need to interact with her parents all of the time and constantly demands attention. Jennifer is remarkably independent. And although she'll fuss a little if she realizes that you have left her by herself in her room for more than a couple of minutes, once you come back, then she'll be all right. Her brother, Thomas, was very different. It was always a struggle to put him to sleep, and he was much more difficult to comfort.

Interviewer: *What calms Jennifer when she's unhappy?*

Michael: Singing, food, walking with her, rocking her, sitting with her on the couch.

Interviewer: *Do different things work for different children?*

Michael: I think that many of the same things work, but there are also differences. One of the things that worked for her brother was patting him on the back, which she doesn't like. It has never worked for her. She could care less. I keep trying to do it, and it's never worked.

Joyce: The astonishing thing about having more than one kid is how unique they are.

Interviewer: *How early can you tell that?*

Joyce: From the first day.

Michael: I probably can't say the first day, though I'm sure that Joyce can. I would say I definitely noticed it in the first week, though.

Interviewer: *Your husband mentioned earlier that Thomas was much more active and communicative from the start.*

Joyce: Oh, he was. It was clear very early that he was tuned into exactly what we were doing. His doctor called him a very visual kid. He was always looking, looking, looking at everything. You could always see that he was intensely interested in things around him. Jennifer is also interested and curious. Her brother was more focused. She'll get interested and curious, but without that intensity. She'll get interested in things that come her way or will play by herself. He reaches out. He'll look out at things, for example, when he's riding in a car.

Interviewer: *You seem to have a strong feeling that temperamental differences are important.*

Joyce: Yes, I do. Often I feel that kids turn out to be the way they are. You really can't do much about it. Their temperaments seem to come with them. You can mold and shape other things, but temperament seems to be pretty much set.

What Do You Think?

1. How can you explain Jennifer's qualities that her parents describe without referring to the concept of temperament?

2. How closely does Joyce and Michael's understanding of temperament fit with the discussion in this chapter? In what ways does it differ?

3. If you could talk with them, what additional questions would you ask the Granoff family?

pectations, and responses of her parents. For example, the fit between an infant who is very active and demanding and parents who expect this of their new baby is likely to be much better than the fit between a similar baby and parents who expect their infant to be more passive and less demanding (Chess & Thomas, 1986; Rickman & Davidson, 1995).

In the last decade, researchers have begun thinking of temperamental differences in infancy more broadly, as early-appearing behavioral styles that influence social and personality development and psychological adjustment in childhood, adolescence, and adulthood (Caspi & Silva, 1995; Hartup & van Lieshout, 1995; Lengua et al., 1998; Newman et al., 1997; Rothbart & Ahadi, 1994). For example, Denise Newman and her colleagues found that temperamental differences observed in children at age three were linked to interpersonal functioning in four important social contexts as young adults: at work, at home, with a special romantic partner, and in the wider social network. Based on behavioral observations of each child in an individual testing session, children were divided into five temperamental groups. Children who were judged to be temperamentally well adjusted, reserved, or confident at age three displayed a normal range of adjustment in all four social contexts as young adults. Children who were temperamentally inhibited as three-year-olds had lower levels of social support but normal adjustment in romantic relationships and at work as adults. Children who had been temperamentally undercontrolled (who had difficulty regulating their emotional states) at age three reported lower levels of adjustment and greater interpersonal conflict in all four social contexts as young adults (Newman et al., 1997).

WHAT DO YOU THINK ?   What advice would you give to parents about how to respond to differences in their children's temperaments? What temperamental differences have you noticed among members of your own family?

Attachment Formation

Attachment refers to the strong and enduring emotional bond that develops between infant and caregiver during the infant's first year of life. This relationship is characterized by reciprocal affection and a shared desire to maintain physical closeness (Ainsworth, 1991; Ainsworth & Bowlby, 1991; Main, 1995).

The concept of attachment has been most strongly influenced by the ethological perspective and, to a lesser extent, by the psychoanalytic approach. In the ethological view, the ties between infant and caregiver develop from the activation of a biologically based motivational system that is an inherited adaptation of human evolution. This system helped to ensure survival by protecting infants from environmental dangers. Because the nature of the child-caregiver relationship is widely viewed as being central to successful child development, studies of attachment have come to play an important role in developmental theory, research, and application. Another influence has been the work of theorists who emphasize the importance of "working models," internalized social relationships with significant caregivers (Biringen, 1994; Mahler et al., 1994).

Although attachment cannot be observed directly, it can be inferred from a number of commonly observed infant behaviors that help to establish and maintain physical closeness with caregivers. Three of these behaviors—crying, cooing, and babbling—are *signaling behaviors;* four others—smiling, clinging, nonnutritional sucking, and following—are *approach behaviors.* While researchers do not agree as to whether these *specific* attachment behaviors are biologically inherited, many believe that the tendency to seek proximity is biologically determined and essential to infant survival in much the same way food is (Main, 1995).

One important source of support for attachment theory comes from a well-known series of studies of infant rhesus monkeys by Harry Harlow (Harlow, 1959; Harlow & Zimmermann, 1996). Infant monkeys who were taken away from their mothers at birth and raised with artificial wire and terrycloth substitute mothers displayed many of the attachment behaviors just mentioned. When forced to choose, they preferred physical *contact comfort* with a warm, soft, terrycloth substitute mother that did not provide food to contact with a cold, hard, wire mother that provided milk from a bottle but was not soft and huggable. Harlow also found that infant monkeys that were deprived of physical closeness but were otherwise well

• • •
attachment the strong and enduring emotional bond that develops between an infant and his or her caregivers during the infant's first year of life.

Attachment—the tendency of young infants and their caregivers to seek physical and emotional closeness—provides an important basis for secure and trusting relationships during early childhood.

cared for exhibited extreme fear and withdrawal, an inability to establish social relations with peers, and much higher rates of illness and death.

Although we must be cautious about drawing conclusions about human infants from studies of monkeys, Harlow's findings suggest that contact comfort, a key attachment behavior, may be a primary need during infancy that is relatively independent of the need for food and the other sources of oral pleasure that psychodynamic theorists such as Freud thought to be the basis of emotional development. They also suggest that severe deprivation of physical closeness with a caregiver may have major negative consequences for subsequent development. The work of René Spitz (1945, 1946), who studied infants reared in institutional settings, suggests that consistency and reliability of caregiver responsiveness is also important. Spitz found that infants who experienced frequent changes in caregivers and who lacked at least one caregiver who was consistently responsive to their needs found it extremely difficult to establish social and emotional infant-caregiver connections.

Currently most developmental psychologists believe attachment relationships develop over time as a cumulative product of the infant's repeated experiences in interaction with her main caregiver during the first year. They also believe attachment involves a highly mutual and interactive partnership between caregiver and child, both of whom have strong, although unequal, needs to achieve physical and emotional closeness with each other. This view is influenced by recent discoveries about the interactive nature of social relations between infants and their caregivers (Belsky, 1996; Isabella, 1993). Recall that both Margaret Mahler and Daniel Stern (see Chapter 2) report that infants begin to develop mental images or representations of their relationships with their primary caregivers at age two to four months.

According to attachment theory, once attachment with the mother (or other primary caregiver) is established, the infant uses her as a *secure base* from which to explore the environment. As the infant gradually increases his distance from the mother, the *attachment behavioral system* and accompanying feelings of fear and anxiety are more likely to be activated, and the infant begins to seek proximity (closeness) to the mother once again. This pattern is also activated when the infant encounters dangers such as strangers, darkness, or approaching animals. The balance between activation of the attachment system and activation of exploratory behaviors varies with the particular context and developmental level of the child (Biringen, 1994).

TABLE 7.4   **Four Stages of Attachment Formation**

Phase 1: Indiscriminate Sociability (birth–2 months)

Responds actively with cries, smiles, coos, and gazes to promote contact and affection from other people; uses limited attachment behaviors less selectively than when older.

Phase 2: Attachments in the Making (2–7 months)

Increasing preference for individuals most familiar and responsive to needs; preferences reinforce parents' affection; accepts certain forms of attention and care from comparative strangers; tolerates temporary separations from parents.

Phase 3: Specific, Clear-cut Attachments (7–24 months)

Preferences for specific people become much stronger due to ability to represent persons mentally (Piaget's fourth stage of sensorimotor development; see Chapter 6); ability to crawl and walk enables toddler to seek proximity to and use caregiver as a safe base for exploration; increasing verbal skills allow greater involvement with parents and others; both *separation anxiety*—an infant's disturbance at being separated from the caregiver—and *stranger anxiety*—a wariness and avoidance of strangers— appear near the beginning of this phase.

Phase 4: Goal-coordinated Partnerships (24 months onward)

By age two, increasing representational and memory skills for objects and events; growing ability to understand parental feelings and points of view and to adjust his or her own accordingly; growing capacity to tolerate short parental absences and delays and interruptions in parents' undivided attention makes possible cooperation with others to meet needs; changing abilities are related to secure attachment relationships grounded in a sense of basic trust.

Source: Bowlby (1969).

Phases of Attachment Formation

John Bowlby believes that attachments develop in a series of phases determined partly by cognitive changes (described in the previous chapter) and partly by interactions that appear to develop quite naturally between infants and their caregivers (Ainsworth & Bowlby, 1991). Table 7.4 presents these four phases. Note that *separation anxiety,* an infant's disturbance at being separated from her caregiver, and *stranger anxiety,* a wariness and avoidance of strangers, appear near the beginning of phase 3. The achievement of object permanence (see Chapter 2) is thought to be an important basis for separation anxiety and attachment development.

Stranger anxiety is exhibited by many infants between age six and nine months and often continues through the first year. It is thought to be tied to infants' increasing ability to recognize and distinguish between familiar and unfamiliar people and to actively make sense of their interpersonal world. Whether or not a particular infant becomes wary of strangers and the strength of the reaction may vary with his temperament, the familiarity of the setting, the friendliness of the stranger, the caregiver's reaction, and how accustomed the child is to meeting strangers (Dickstein & Parke, 1988; Mangelsdorf et al., 1995).

Separation anxiety, which generally appears between nine and twelve months, involves displays of fear, clinging, crying, and related distress when an infant's parent or other caregiver leaves her (recall Elizabeth's protest when left at nursery school by her mother in Chapter 2). Separation anxiety appears to be related to how well the infant is prepared for the parent's departure and to her past experiences with separation. However, the responsiveness of the caregiver she is left with may be most important, especially if the infant tends to react strongly to separation (Gunnar et al., 1992).

Assessing Attachment: The "Strange Situation"

Strange Situation (SS) A widely used method for studying attachment; confronts the infant with a series of controlled separations and reunions with a parent and a stranger.

The most widely used method for evaluating the quality of attachment to a caregiver is called the **Strange Situation (SS).** Originally developed by Mary Ainsworth for infants who are old enough to crawl or walk, the procedure consists of eight brief social episodes with different combinations of the infant, the mother, and a strange adult (Ainsworth et al., 1978). It presents the infant with a cumulative series of stressful experiences: being in an unfamiliar place, meeting a stranger, and being separated from the caregiver. The steps in the Strange Situation are outlined in Table 7.5.

Based on the infants' patterns of behavior in the Strange Situation, Ainsworth and her colleagues identified three main groups. Most of the infants studied (approximately 65 to 70 percent) displayed a **secure attachment** pattern. When first alone with their mothers, they typically played happily. When the stranger entered, they were somewhat wary but continued to play without becoming upset. But when they were left alone with the stranger, they typically stopped playing and searched for or crawled after their mothers; in some cases, they cried. When the mothers returned, the babies were clearly pleased to see them and actively sought contact and interaction, staying closer to them and cuddling more than before. When left alone with the stranger again, the infants were easily comforted; although signs of distress were stronger, they quickly recovered from the upset by actively seeking contact with their mothers on their return.

The second group of infants (about 10 percent) were classified as displaying an **anxious-resistant attachment** or *ambivalent* pattern. They showed some signs of anxiety and, even in the periods preceding separation, stuck close to their mothers and explored only minimally. They were intensely upset by separation. When reunited with their mothers, they actively sought close contact with them, but at the same time angrily resisted the mothers' efforts to comfort them by hitting them and pushing them away. They refused to be comforted by the stranger as well.

The third group of infants (about 20 percent) displayed an **anxious-avoidant attachment** pattern. They initially showed little involvement with their mothers, treating them and the stranger in much the same way. They rarely cried when

It is hard to tell whether this baby's upset is due to the anxiety of being separated from his mother or to meeting a strange new daycare provider.

TABLE 7.5	Episodes in the Strange Situation (SS)		
Episode	Duration	Events	Observed Attachment Behaviors
1	30 seconds	Parent and infant enter the room with the experimenter.	
2	3 minutes	Parent is seated; baby plays with toys and explores the room.	Parent as a secure base
3	3 minutes	A stranger enters room, sits down, talks with parent.	Reaction to unfamiliar adult
4	3 minutes	Parent leaves infant alone with stranger, who responds to the baby and offers comfort if baby is upset.	Separation anxiety
5	3 minutes	Parent returns, greets (comforts) baby; stranger leaves room.	Reaction to reunion
6	3 minutes	Parent leaves baby alone in room.	Separation anxiety
7	3 minutes	Stranger again enters the room and offers comfort to the baby.	Reaction to being comforted by a stranger
8	3 minutes	Parent returns; stranger leaves; parent greets/comforts baby and tries to interest her in toys.	Reaction to reunion

Source: Ainsworth et al., (1978).

• • •

secure attachment A healthy bond between infant and caregiver. The child is happy when the caregiver is present, somewhat upset during the caregiver's absence, and easily comforted upon the caregiver's return.

anxious-resistant attachment An insecure bond between infant and caregiver in which the child shows signs of anxiety preceding separation, is intensely upset by separation, and seeks close contact when reunited while at the same time resisting the caregiver's efforts to comfort.

anxious-avoidant attachment An insecure bond between infant and caregiver in which the child rarely cries when separated from the caregiver and tends to avoid or ignore the caregiver when reunited.

A Multicultural View

Cross-cultural Variations in Attachment

Almost all infants become attached to their parents in some way. However, the patterns by which they do so vary around the world. Studies on the Strange Situation report that whereas 60 to 65 percent of children studied appear to be securely attached, rates of insecure attachment are much more variable (van IJzendoorn & Kroonenberg, 1988). Among infants from northern Germany, for example, anxious-avoidant attachment patterns occur twice as often as they do among North American infants. Among infants from Japan, on the other hand, anxious-resistant responses occur approximately three times as often as they do in the United States, while anxious-avoidant attachment is virtually nonexistent (Bretherton & Waters, 1985; Takahashi, 1990).

These variations result partly from differences in cultural values around the world and partly from the childrearing practices these values foster. In northern Germany, people value personal independence especially strongly (Grossmann et al., 1985) and believe children should obey parents more consistently than is usually expected in North America. As a result, infants need to learn not to make excessive demands on parents; they must minimize crying and fussing and do without extra bodily contact. During early infancy, mothers encourage these qualities by remaining relatively unresponsive to their infants' moment-by-moment behav-

ior. Thus, in northern Germany, unresponsiveness may not signify personal rejection of the child as much as a desire to raise a good citizen. The results show up in the Strange Situation as anxious-avoidant attachment: a larger than usual number of young children seem indifferent when reunited with their mothers.

Childrearing practices probably also influence the attachment responses of Japanese children. Separations between Japanese infants and their mothers are quite rare by North American standards. Most Japanese infants have very little experience with strangers. Typically they are left alone or with another adult only two or three times per month on average, usually someone already intimate with the child, such as the father or a grandparent (Mikaye et al., 1985). Their extreme protests to the Strange Situation resemble the anxious-resistant pattern of crying, anger, fear, and clinging when the mother returns. As with the German infants, however, it is more likely that these behaviors represent the fulfillment of typical cultural practices rather than failures in childrearing.

Some researchers have also noted that distribution of attachment types may vary within as well as across cultures. In a study of infants from southern Germany, the distribution of attachment types did not differ significantly from those reported for infants in the United States (Grossmann & Grossmann, 1990; van IJzendoorn & Kroonenberg, 1988). Studies of attachment among Israeli infants raised in kibbutz communities provide further evidence of cultural dif-

---

separated and, when reunited, showed a mixed response of low-level engagement with their mothers and a tendency to avoid them.

A fourth category, **disorganized-disoriented attachment,** has also been investigated. This pattern, which was not included in earlier studies because coding procedures were not available, indicates the greatest degree of insecurity. When reunited with their parents, these infants exhibit confused and contradictory behaviors. They may be unresponsive and turn away when held, display odd, "frozen" postures, and cry out unexpectedly after being comforted (Lyons-Ruth & Block, 1996; Lyons-Ruth et al., 1997; Main & Solomon, 1990).

All four attachment patterns have been studied in many other countries. In all cases, around 60 to 65 percent of the children are reported to be securely attached, whereas rates of insecure attachment are much more variable (van IJzendoorn & Kroonenberg, 1988). The accompanying Multicultural View box discusses cross-cultural variations in attachment.

disorganized-disoriented attachment An attachment pattern in which an infant exhibits confused and contradictory behaviors when reunited with the parent. The infant may be unresponsive and turn away when held, display odd, frozen postures, and cry out unexpectedly after being comforted.

Consequences of Different Attachment Patterns

Secure attachment early in infancy benefits babies in several ways during their second year. For one thing, securely attached toddlers tend to cooperate better with their parents than other babies do. They comply better with rules such as "Don't

ferences in attachment within a particular society. Kibbutz children were raised in communal peer groups by *metapelot* (nurse/educators), spending regular time with their families during evenings, weekends, and holidays. Kibbutz infants successfully formed attachments to both their parents and their communal caregivers, but a larger proportion displayed insecure attachment patterns compared to Israeli infants raised in the city or infants raised in the United States. This difference appears to be related to kibbutz sleeping arrangements, which differ among kibbutz communities. When Abraham Sagi and his colleagues compared infants from kibbutz infants' houses with home-based sleeping arrangements with infants who slept in their infants' houses (communal sleeping arrangements), they found that although the two groups of infants did not differ in temperament or life events, only 48 percent of the infants with communal sleeping arrangements were rated as securely attached to their mothers compared to 80 percent of the infants who slept at home. These researchers conclude that although group care and multiple caregiving of high quality do not necessary interfere with the formation of close relationships between parents and children or with the development of social skills, it appears that the sleeping arrangements in the kibbutz communities that were studied did (Aviezer et al., 1994; Ora et al., 1994; Sagi et al., 1995, 1997).

Cultural differences in childhood socialization and attachment also have been found within the United States. For example, studies have found that while both Anglo American and Puerto Rican mothers rated securely attached children as more typical and likable than insecurely attached children, the mothers differed in their reasons. Anglo American mothers focused on the self-confidence and independence of the child, whereas Puerto Rican mothers emphasized the child's obedience and the quality of his or her relatedness to others (Harwood, 1992; Zayas & Solari, 1994).

Cultural values and practices, however, cannot explain all the differences. Even in northern Germany, for example, many babies become securely attached even though their mothers follow culturally approved practices of aloofness. In Japan, some infants become anxious-resistant even though their mothers follow essentially Western childrearing styles, which include considerable experience with baby sitters and other nonparental caregivers. Observations of these babies in their homes suggest that they were born with somewhat irritable or fussy temperaments, which may predispose them to becoming anxious-resistant despite their mothers' practices.

On balance, attachment seems to result from the combination of several influences, including cultural values, inborn temperament, and the childrearing practices of the particular family. The developmental meaning of attachment may vary too. What looks like an attachment failure for one child may be a success for another, depending on the circumstances.

run in the living room!", and they are also more willing to learn new skills and try new activities their parents show them (such as when a parent says, "Sit with me for a minute and see how I do this"). When faced with problems that are too difficult for them to solve, toddlers who are securely attached are more likely than others to seek and accept help from their parents. At age five, these children tend to adapt better than other children to changes in preschool situations (Arend et al., 1979; Slade, 1987).

Less securely attached infants may not learn as well from their parents. Anxious-resistant infants often respond with anger and resistance to their parents' attempts to help or teach them. Such babies may at times invest so much time and energy in conflicts that they are unable to benefit from their parents' experience and to explore their environment. Given a roomful of toys and a mother who has recently returned from an absence, for example, a child may use up a lot of time alternating between being angry at and snuggling with his mother instead of getting on with his play. Anxious-avoidant infants do not have this particular problem, but because of their tendency to avoid interaction with their parents, they also miss out on parental efforts to teach or help them, and ultimately may discourage parents from even trying to help (Matas et al., 1978).

The disorganized-disoriented attachment pattern generally is found in seriously disturbed caregiving situations where interactions between mothers and infants are inconsistent, out of tune with, or inappropriately responsive to the infant's physical, social, and emotional needs. Parents who display disorganized-disoriented attachment behaviors may think of and experience their infants in inappropriate ways. For instance, they may display role reversal (in which the parent inappropriately expects to be cared for by the infant) or respond to their infants in overly intrusive, withdrawing, or rejecting ways. An infant's attempts to communicate or modify this behavior are often ignored and overridden, leading to the disorganized-disoriented infant attachment behaviors noted earlier. Disorganized-disoriented infant attachment behavior increases with the severity of family risk factors and places infants at risk for future problems with aggression, conduct disorder, and other developmental difficulties (Lyons-Ruth & Block, 1996; Lyons-Ruth et al., 1997; Main & Solomon, 1990).

Differences in attachment appear to persist into the preschool years. One study found that children rated as securely attached at age one seemed more likely to seek attention in positive ways in nursery school at age four (Sroufe et al., 1983). When they needed help because of sickness or injury, or just wanted to be friendly, they found it easy to secure attention by approaching their teachers fairly directly, and they seemed to enjoy the attention when they received it. Anxious-avoidant or anxious-resistant infants tended to grow into relatively dependent preschool children. They sought more help more frequently, but seemed less satisfied with what they got. However, methods of seeking attention differed between these two groups. Anxious-resistant children showed signs of chronic complaining or whining, whereas anxious-avoidant children tended to approach their teachers very indirectly, literally taking a zigzagging path to reach them. Having done so, they typically waited passively for the teachers to notice them. As noted above, disorganized-disoriented infants often are at risk for developmental difficulties.

These findings do not necessarily imply that secure attachments are set early in infancy once and for all. Instead, attachment is likely to be an extended process, one that in fact takes years to unfold fully, and prediction of future adjustment based on early attachment patterns will depend on the *continuity of caregiving* the child receives (Main et al., 1985).

Influences on Attachment Formation

So far we have emphasized the general aspects of attachment. In this section, we discuss some of the factors that appear to influence the quality of attachment between infants and their mothers, as well as other important caregivers.

The Role of the Mother   A major determinant of individual differences in attachment is the quality of the infant-mother relationship during the child's first year. A mother's capacity to respond sensitively and appropriately to her infant and to feel positively about him and his strengths and limitations appears to be more important than the amount of contact or caregiving. Mothers of securely attached infants are more responsive to their babies' crying, more careful and tender in holding them, and more responsive to their particular needs and feelings during both feeding and nonfeeding interactions than are mothers of less securely attached infants (Ainsworth, 1991; De Wolff & van IJzendoorn, 1997).

Differences in infant temperament are likely to affect the mother-infant relationship and the quality of attachment. Infants with irritable temperaments tend to receive less maternal involvement, which in turn may negatively influence the quality of attachment. With appropriate interventions, however, such negative cycles may be interrupted.

In one study of the influence of temperament and mothering on attachment, Dymphna van den Boom (1994) helped mothers to respond to their temperamentally difficult six-month-old infants in more sensitive and developmentally appropriate ways by adjusting their behaviors to the infants' unique cues. Mothers gained practice in imitating their infants' behaviors and repeating their own verbal expressions. They also learned to notice when their infants were gazing at them and when they were not, and to coordinate the pace and rhythm of their own behavior with their infants'. Mothers who received such help were found to be significantly more responsive, stimulating, visually attentive, and controlling of their infants' behavior than a similar group of mothers who did not get assistance. Intervention infants had higher scores on sociability, self-soothing, and exploration, cried less, and at twelve months of age were much more likely to be securely attached.

Being securely attached herself makes the mother more likely to have a child who is securely attached. The quality of the mother-child relationship is influenced by the mother's *working models*—her perceptions, expectations, and assumptions about her infant, herself, and their relationship. (Working models are discussed in Chapter 2.) Past mother-infant interactions, the mother's memories of her own childhood, and similar factors also may play a significant role in mother-child attachment relationships (Bretherton, 1995; Mahler et al., 1975; Stern, 1997; van IJzendoorn & Bakermans-Kroonenberg, 1997).

The Role of the Father   Studies of father-infant attachment in the United States and other countries suggest that the processes involved are similar and that fathers display the same range of attachment relationships mothers do. Most studies have found no differences in most babies' preferred attachment figures during the first two years. Infants appear to be equally attached to both mother and father, even though the mother typically is the primary caregiver (Lamb, 1997; van IJzendoorn & De Wolff, 1997).

As we pointed out earlier in the chapter, however, fathers and mothers interact with their infants somewhat differently. Fathers generally are more vigorous and physical in their interactions, and mothers are quieter and more verbal. Such differences in the quality of mother-infant versus father-infant attachment relationships are likely to reflect gender-related differences in caregiving opportunities, experience, and expectations, as well as in the division of child care and other household responsibilities within the family (Akande, 1994; Ferketich & Mercer, 1995; Owen & Cox, 1997; Volling & Belsky, 1992).

For example, Martha Cox and her colleagues (1992) found that the security of father-infant attachment at twelve months can be predicted from the qualities of their interactions at three months, the father's attitudes toward and reports about the infant and the paternal role, and the amount of time spent with the infant. In addition, a study by Nathan Fox and his colleagues (1991) found that security of attachment to one parent also appears to be closely related to the security of attachment to the other parent. Thus, an infant with a secure (or insecure) attachment to her mother was likely to have the same quality of attachment relationship to her father.

Overall, the better the psychological and social adjustment and life circumstances of the infant and her parents, the greater the chances of a secure attachment. For example, fathers of secure infants tend to be more extroverted and agreeable than fathers of insecure infants, to have more positive marriages, and to experience more positive emotional spillover between work and family. Chronic marital conflict before and after the birth of a child can interfere with sensitive, involved parenting and thereby predict insecurity in attachment relationships, particularly for fathers. An infant's ongoing exposure to parents who are upset and angry and the distress that such exposure causes may contribute to disorganized-disoriented infant-caregiver attachment behavior (Belsky, 1996; Owen & Cox, 1997).

The Effects of Maternal Employment   As we noted earlier, in 1995 approximately 50 percent of mothers with infants one year old or under and around 60 percent of mothers with three-to-five-year-olds were in the work force. The number of working mothers with young children is expected to continue to increase (U.S.

PERSPECTIVES

Family-Leave Policies in the United States and Europe

• • • • • In 1993, the United States enacted its first national Family and Medical Leave Act, guaranteeing up to twelve weeks of unpaid leave per year to any worker who is employed for at least twenty-five hours per week at a company with more than fifty employees. Family leaves are allowed after the birth of a child or an adoption, to care for a child, spouse, or parent with a serious health condition, as well as for a health condition that makes it impossible for the worker to perform a job. After the leave, the worker is assured of his or her old job or an equivalent position (Hyde et al., 1996).

How does U.S. family-leave policy compare with that in other countries? Most industrialized countries have much more generous policies than those in the United States, providing not only more extended leaves of absence so that working parents can take care of their young children but also financial support for part or all of the leave period (Frank & Zigler, 1996). In Sweden, West Germany, and France, one parent can take a paid infant care leave supported by the employer or a social insurance fund. If both parents choose to continue to work, they are guaranteed access to high-quality day care for their child. In Sweden, either the mother or the father is entitled to a twelve-month paid leave to stay home with a new infant. The parent on leave is reimbursed 90 percent of her or his salary for the first nine months following the child's birth, receives $150 per month for the next three months, and then is allowed to continue with an unpaid leave and a job guarantee for six additional months until the child is eighteen months old. An interesting sidelight is that only a very small percentage of fathers actually take advantage of this opportunity,

and when they do, the bulk of feeding and nurturance during nonwork hours still appears to be performed by the mother (Frank & Zigler, 1996: Hyde et al., 1996).

In France, a working parent is entitled to 90 percent reimbursement for four months through the social security system and then up to two more years of unpaid leave with a job guarantee, provided she or he works for a company with more than two hundred employees. In West Germany, a parent taking a leave of absence from work is entitled to 100 percent reimbursement for three months and then $287 per month for four more months.

It seems evident that while the twelve weeks of unpaid leave provided by the recent U.S. family-leave policy is a step in the right direction, policies in Europe go much farther in helping parents to directly meet the needs of their babies without undue economic hardship and risk to their jobs.

In a recent review of research on the impact of the Family and Medical Leave Act, Christopher Ruhm (1997) found that because the leaves are short and unpaid and only half of the work force is eligible under the current law, it has had little impact. Ruhm suggests that coverage of more workers, extension of the number of weeks of leave allowed, and payment during all or part of the leave would greatly increase the benefit to families and children.

What Do You Think?

What arguments would you make to support raising family-leave policies in the United States to the level of many European countries? What other examples of family support policies (e.g., health care) that fall short of what is needed for children's healthy development can you think of? Would you make the same arguments for these that you did for family leave?

Bureau of the Census, 1996). Length of maternity leave may influence the quality of mother-infant interactions. Roseanne Clark and her colleagues interviewed and videotaped employed mothers of four-month-old infants in their homes during feeding time. They found that shorter maternity leaves were associated with lower quality of mother-infant interactions. This was especially true for mothers who reported more depressive symptoms or who perceived their infants as having a more difficult temperament. These mothers expressed less positive affect, sensitivity, and responsiveness in interactions with their infants compared to mothers who had longer leaves (Clark et al., 1997). Family-leave policies in the United States and Europe are discussed in the accompanying Perspectives box.

Most infants of mothers who are employed either full or part time are securely attached, although full-time employed mothers are somewhat more likely than part-time employed and nonemployed mothers to have insecurely attached infants (Clarke-Stewart, 1989; Hoffman, 1989). However, these results must be viewed with caution, since the effects of maternal employment on the infant or young child are rarely direct. They are almost always based on a variety of family factors, including economic and cultural differences, the mother's "morale," the father's attitude toward his wife's employment, the type of work and number of hours it demands, the husband-wife relationship, the father's role in the family, the availability and quality of nonmaternal care, and the mother's and father's feelings about separation from the child (Scarr, 1998; Silverstein, 1991).

Cynthia Stifter and her colleagues compared mother-child interactions and attachment patterns in families in which mothers returned to full- or part-time employment outside the home before their infants were five months old with those in families in which mothers remained home full time, and found that employment did not directly affect attachment. However, employed mothers were experiencing high levels of separation anxiety as a result of the severe time constraints imposed by work schedules and were more likely to have infants who developed anxious-avoidant attachments. Although they were equally sensitive and responsive to their infants as working mothers who were not anxious, highly anxious mothers were much more likely to be "out of synch" and overcontrolling when interacting with their infants (Stifter et al., 1993).

Good-quality day care can play an important role in the lives of working mothers and their children.

The Effects of Day Care and Multiple Caregivers

The growing number of dual-wage and single-parent families and changing views about childrearing and family life have led to increased interest in nonmaternal child care to supplement the care given within families. Increased use of infant center care has also raised questions about its effects on infant and toddler development. The effects of day care and other forms of nonmaternal care on attachment in infants and toddlers are difficult to evaluate for many of the same reasons cited in the discussion of maternal employment. A child's gender, her or his temperament, the mother's (and father's) feelings about both day care and maternal employment, and the mother's reasons for working all play a role. Other factors include the type of child care arrangement (day care center, in-home day care, relative), the stability of the arrangement, the child's age of entry, the quality of day care, and the quality of the child-caregiver relationship (Belsky & Rovine, 1988; Scarr, 1998).

While some infant care researchers have found evidence that one-year-olds who attend centers more than twenty hours per week tend to form less secure attachments to their parents (Belsky & Nezworski, 1988; Belsky & Rovine, 1988), others have reported that negative attachment outcomes tend to be associated with little or part-time rather than full-time infant care. Babies in infant care centers show *more* social confidence than do infants reared at home (Anderson, 1989; Roggman et al., 1994).

A recent large-scale study of more than one thousand infants and their mothers at ten different sites supports the finding that an infant's child care experience alone is neither a risk nor a benefit for the infant-mother attachment relationship as measured by the Strange Situation. However, child care that is of poor quality or unstable may increase the developmental risks to an infant whose caregiving already lacks sensitivity and responsiveness. Thus, the effects of child care on attachment and the attachment relationship itself depend primarily on the nature of ongoing interactions between mother and child and on the family, neighborhood, and other contexts that either support or undermine the quality and reliability of the infant-mother relationship (Belsky, 1996; Cowan, 1997; NICHD, 1997; Owen & Cox, 1997).

Day care, even for infants and toddlers, has few negative effects on children, as long as the care is of high quality and parents feel satisfied with it.

What about attachments to multiple caregivers? While expectations based on infant-mother attachment relationships may help guide an infant in forming new attachments, infants and nonmaternal caregivers are capable of establishing unique and independent relationships based more on their reciprocal exchanges and individual qualities than on a "model" developed from mother-child interactions (Zimmerman & McDonald, 1995). The attachments infants form with their center caregivers, for example, appear to be no less secure than their attachments to their parents, and the two sets of attachments are relatively independent of each other. Thus, even an infant who exhibited an insecure pattern of attachment relationships with his family might still form secure attachments with other caregivers (Goosens & van IJzendoorn, 1990).

There is also evidence that in a variety of other contexts, including extended families and communal childrearing settings such as the Israeli kibbutz and the Efe people of Zaire, secure relationships with multiple professional and nonprofessional caregivers are not only possible but may also contribute to the child's well-being by either adding to a network of secure attachments or compensating for their absence (Sagi et al., 1997; Tronick et al., 1992). On the Israeli kibbutz, infants and toddlers are raised in same-age peer groups by community child care providers. Among the Efe, infants and toddlers experience a pattern of multiple relationships—with mother, father, other adults, and children. In such cases, the extended family or community childrearing network may be more predictive of attachment relationships than the mother-child relationship alone.

Long-Term Effects of Attachment

The long-term and intergenerational effects of attachment have been of growing interest to developmental researchers. Attachment patterns in infancy are predictive of attachment in childhood, adolescence, and even adulthood, and the attachment relationships parents experienced in their own childhoods are related to the attachment relationships they develop with their own children (Main, 1995; Mickelson et al., 1997; Trinke & Bartholomew, 1997; van IJzendoorn & Bakermans-Kroonenburg, 1997).

The Adult Attachment Interview (AAI) has been used to evaluate the childhood attachment relationships adults had with their own parents and other caregivers

(Main, 1995; van IJzendoorn, 1995). Based on their responses, adults are classified into four main attachment patterns: *autonomous* (secure), *dismissing* (insecure), *preoccupied* (insecure), and *unresolved-disorganized*. Adults classified as *autonomous* are generally thoughtful, value attachment experiences and relationships, and provide balanced, noncontradictory descriptions of both of their parents as loving during childhood, or, if they experienced rejection or abuse, have forgiven their parents for the maltreatment. Adults classified as *dismissing* tend to deny the influence of attachment experiences on their own development or their relationships with their own children. They may insist they cannot remember their childhood experiences or can recall them only in contradictory or overly idealized ways. Individuals classified as *preoccupied* often are still emotionally entangled in their early experiences and relationships with their families and have difficulty explaining them in a clear and understandable way. The *unresolved-disorganized* pattern is similar to the disorganized-disoriented type of attachment described for infants. Table 7.6 describes each of the adult AAI attachment patterns and the infant attachment patterns based on the Strange Situation (SS) that they parallel. Marinus van IJzendoorn (1995) analyzed eighteen studies of how well parents' AAI attachment classifications predicted their own infants' attachment classifications in the Strange Situation. He found that in approximately 75 percent of the cases, the security of the parent's own attachment classification predicted the security of the infant's attachment.

In one recent longitudinal study, AAI classifications of expectant mothers and fathers predicted the attachment classifications of the infants at twelve and eighteen months in the SS. Mothers and fathers with a dismissing attachment pattern were more likely to have an insecure-avoidant pattern of infant-parent attachment in the Strange Situation. An autonomous-secure pattern for both parents predicted secure infant-parent patterns of attachment. Mothers whose adult attachment patterns were classified as unresolved were likely to show a disorganized pattern of

TABLE 7.6   Patterns of Infant and Adult Attachment

Infant or Adult	Attachment Pattern	Description of Pattern
Infant	Secure	Displays positive affect when nondistressed
Adult	Autonomous (secure)	Gives coherent description of childhood relationship experiences in which both positive and negative aspects of relationships are acknowledged; relationships are valued and important
Infant	Avoidant (insecure)	Avoids caregiver despite high levels of internal distress; suppresses attachment behaviors and focuses on external environment
Adult	Dismissing (insecure)	Fails to recall details of childhood relationships or minimizes the effects of negative experiences; relationships are not valued or important
Infant	Resistant (insecure)	Seeks closeness when distressed but resists caregiver attempts to soothe while at the same time appealing for soothing; behaves ambivalently about contact, both signaling for it and rejecting it
Adult	Preoccupied (insecure)	Describes childhood relationship experiences incoherently and exhibits angry preoccupation or passive thought processes
Infant	Disorganized-disoriented	Exhibits one or more strange or bizarre conflict behaviors, directed toward caregiver, especially during stress; may have other classification as an underlying pattern
Adult	Unresolved-disorganized	Lacks resolution of mourning after a significant loss or severely traumatic experience; description of these experiences is incoherent, confused, or emotionally unintegrated

Source: Adapted from van IJzendoorn & Bakermans-Kroonenburg (1997).

attachment to their infants in the SS (Steele et al., 1996). Diane Benoit and Kevin Parker (1994) studied the transmission of attachment across three generations: infants, mothers, and grandmothers. They found that mothers' AAI classifications during pregnancy predicted infants' SS classifications in approximately 68 percent of the cases, and grandmothers' AAI classifications did so in 49 percent of the cases.

What accounts for the long-term, transgenerational transmission of attachment? One important factor is the caregiver's sensitivity in reliably and appropriately responding to the baby's signals. Another is living in families and communities that provide the economic, social, and emotional conditions that support and promote the working models and interactions that are the basis for secure attachment and adequate parent-child relationships.

WHAT DO YOU THINK ?   What advice would you give new parents about the roles of fathers, maternal employment, and infant day care in supporting secure and responsive attachment relationships and optimal social/emotional development for their infants? What recommendations would you give to your representatives in Congress regarding programs to make infant day care available to families with both working and nonworking mothers?

Toddlerhood and the Emergence of Autonomy

By the second year of life, infants who have experienced sufficient caregiver-infant synchrony and achieved relatively secure attachment relationships with their parents and other caregivers have developed a sense of *basic trust* (versus *mistrust*) about the world. According to Erik Erikson (1963, 1982), by resolving this crisis in the first stage of psychosocial development, an infant's trusting view of the world leads to the development of *hope,* the enduring belief that one's wishes are attainable. (See Chapter 2's review of Erikson's theory of psychosocial development.) Despite lingering anxieties about separations, the achievement of a basic sense of trust in their relationships with their caregivers enables toddlers to become increasingly interested in new people, places, and experiences. For example, an eighteen-month-old may no longer bother to smile at his mother while he plays near her, and he does not need to return to her for reassurance as often as he used to.

Parents may welcome these changes as a move toward greater independence and at the same time experience a loss of intimacy for which they may not be quite ready. This shift is both inevitable and developmentally important. For one thing, an older infant can move about rather easily and therefore find much to explore without help from others. The newfound abilities to crawl, climb, and walk make her more interesting as a playmate for other children and thus less dependent on her parents for her social life. For another, her rapidly developing thinking and communication skills contribute to her increasing autonomy.

These competencies create new challenges for both toddlers and their families as a new developmental crisis emerges: the psychosocial crisis of *autonomy versus shame and doubt.* According to Erikson (1963), **autonomy** refers to a child's capacity to be independent and self-directed in his activities and his ability to balance his own demands for self-control with demands for control from his parents and others. *Shame* involves both a loss of approval by people important to the child and a loss of self-respect due to a failure to meet one's own standards (Lewis, 1992). Toddlers must somehow practice making choices—an essential feature of autonomy—in ways that cause no serious harm to themselves or others.

Parents must learn to support their child's efforts to be autonomous, but must do so without overestimating or underestimating capabilities or the external dangers and internal fears he faces. If they are unable to provide such support and instead show their disapproval of failures by shaming their child, a pattern of self-

• • •
autonomy In Erikson's theory, a child's ability to govern and regulate her or his own thoughts, feelings, and actions freely and responsibly while at the same time overcoming feelings of shame and doubt.

After their first birthday, infants begin to show increasing autonomy in their play and others activities, which sometimes leads them to unsafe situations. This autonomy is fostered by their improving motor skills and cognitive development.

blame and doubt may develop. In such a case, the child is more likely to be either painfully shy and unsure of himself or overly demanding, self-critical, and relatively unable to undertake new activities and experiences freely.

Parents must help their infant to master this crisis of autonomy by continually devising situations in which their relatively mature baby can play independently and without undue fear of interference—by putting the pots and pans within reach but hiding the knives, for instance. Children also need social as well as physical safety. Chewing on a sister's drawing or dumping the dirt out of the flowerpots may not have dangerous physical consequences, but it can have negative social effects. Thus, parents must help their infants learn how to avoid social perils by being selective about their activities.

Sources of Autonomy

Why should infants and toddlers voluntarily begin to exert self-control over their own behavior? Developmental psychologists have suggested several possible answers to this question based on the various theories outlined in Chapter 2. Each has some plausibility, although none are complete in themselves.

Identification   According to psychoanalytic theory, **identification** is the process by which children wish to become like their parents and other important attachment figures in their lives. The intensity of a young child's emotional dependence on her parents creates an intense desire to be like them to please them and guarantee their love. This dependence also creates anger because of the helplessness and fear of abandonment the infant inevitably experiences during even brief periods of separation. Because it is so upsetting to be angry at the very person you depend on for love and care, identification can also be motivated by the unconscious desire to protect oneself from the distress by being like the person who is the object of that anger. Both mechanisms, of course, may operate at once, and either may function without the child's awareness.

Operant Conditioning   **Operant conditioning** stresses the importance of reinforcement for desirable behaviors. According to this view, adults will tend to reinforce a child for more grown-up behaviors, such as independent exploration ("What did you find?") and self-restraint ("I'm glad you didn't wet your pants"). Operant conditioning resembles identification in assuming parents can motivate

identification In psychoanalytic theory, the conscious and unconscious ways in which children experience themselves as being like their parents and other important role models and strive to be like them.

operant conditioning According to Skinner, a process of learning in which a person or an animal increases the frequency of a behavior in response to repeated reinforcement of that behavior.

This toddler's responses to her own reflection in the mirror are an important indicator of her developing self-knowledge and self-awareness.

children, but it also assumes their influence occurs in piecemeal ways; that is, the child acquires specific behaviors rather than whole personality patterns, and the behaviors eventually add up to autonomy and self-control.

Observational Learning   According to the theory of **observational learning,** the key to acquiring autonomy and self-control lies in the child's inherent tendency to observe and imitate parents and other caregivers. If parents act gently with the child's baby sister, for example, the child will come to do so too (although his interpretation of *gently* may occasionally be influenced by feelings of sibling rivalry). Similarly, if a young child observes her mother taking pots and pans from the kitchen cabinet, it is a fair bet that she will attempt to do the same. In fact, much home "childproofing" is necessitated by a young child's skill at observational learning. The process of observational learning implies that autonomy and self-control are acquired in units, or behavioral chunks, that are bigger than those described by operant conditioning but smaller than those acquired in identification.

Social Referencing: A Common Denominator   All three explanations of the development of autonomy have something in common: they involve **social referencing,** the child's sensitivity to the feelings of his parents and other adults and his ability to use these emotional cues to guide his own emotional responses and actions (Baldwin & Moses, 1996; Bretherton, 1992). For example, infants and toddlers exhibit social referencing when they visit a strange place. Should they be afraid of the new objects and people or not? How safe is it to be friendly and to explore? In the absence of past experiences of their own, they evaluate such situations based on their parents' responses: if their parents are relaxed and happy, they are likely to feel that way too; if their parents are made tense or anxious by the situation, the children probably will feel that way also. Even very young infants use their caregivers and even strangers to guide their responses—for example, approaching and playing with unfamiliar toys if a nearby stranger is smiling and avoiding them if the person looks fearful (Klinnert et al., 1986).

Development of Self

The sense of self that develops late in infancy shows up in everyday situations as well as in situations involving self-control. Its development appears to follow a sequence that begins with *physical self-recognition and self-awareness,* followed by *self-description and self-evaluation,* and then by *knowledge of standards and emotional response to wrongdoing* (Kochanska et al., 1995; Stipek et al., 1990).

Self-Recognition and Self-Awareness   One interesting series of studies explored this phenomenon in infants nine to twenty-four months old by testing their ability to recognize images of themselves in mirrors, on television, and in still photographs (Asendorf et al., 1996; Lewis et al., 1985). Because most of the infants could not verbally indicate whether or not they recognized themselves, the researchers secretly marked each infant's nose with red rouge. When placed in front of a mirror, infants from fifteen to twenty-four months of age touched their bodies or faces more frequently than they did before they were marked. Infants around fifteen to eighteen months also began to imitate their marked images by making faces, stick-

• • •

observational learning The tendency of a child to imitate or model behavior and attitudes of parents and other nurturant individuals.

social referencing The child's sensitive awareness of how parents and other adults are feeling and ability to use these emotional cues as a basis for guiding his or her own emotional responses and actions. Social referencing is important for the development of autonomy.

ing out their tongues, or watching themselves disappear and reappear at the side of a mirror. These self-recognition behaviors never occurred in infants younger than fifteen months and increased from 75 percent at eighteen months to 100 percent at twenty-four months. When presented with videotaped images of themselves in which a stranger sneaked up on them, infants as young as nine months displayed self-recognition based on *contingent cues,* that is, connections between their own movements and the movements of the image they were viewing. By approximately fifteen months, infants were increasingly able to distinguish themselves from other infants by using *noncontingent cues* such as facial and other physical features (Lewis & Brooks-Gunn, 1979a; Lewis et al., 1985).

Self-Description, Self-Evaluation, and Emotional Response to Wrongdoing
Between nineteen and thirty months of age, children develop the cognitive competence and vocabulary to describe and represent themselves in terms of physical characteristics such as size (*little, big*), type of hair (*curly, red*), and eye color. By the end of their second year, most children show an increasing appreciation of standards. For example, a broken toy can trouble a child even if he did not break it; he may show it to an adult and verbally express concern and a need for help ("Broken!" or "Daddy fix?"). A crack in the kitchen linoleum may now receive close scrutiny, even though several months earlier it went unnoticed and several months later it may go unnoticed again. Language that implies *knowledge of standards*—evaluative vocabulary such as *bad, good, dirty, nice*—appears as well (Bretherton, 1993). Such knowledge combines with other behaviors to suggest that the child is beginning to sense an identity for herself. There is also reason to believe that verbal and nonverbal reactions of toddlers to flawed objects are associated with the early development of a sense of morality. When faced with situations in which they believe they have been responsible for a "mishap" such as breaking a toy, toddlers' responses include acceptance of responsibility, apologies, focus on reparations (repairing the wrong), and distress (Kochanska et al., 1995).

By age two, children show satisfaction in purposely *initiating challenging activities* or behaviors for themselves, and they often smile at the results. A child builds a tower of blocks higher than usual and smiles broadly the moment she completes it. Another makes a strange noise—say, a cat meowing—and then smiles with pride. In each case, the child confronts a task that is somewhat difficult by her current standards, but attempts it anyway. Her behavior suggests an awareness of what competent performance amounts to and of her own ability to succeed. This knowledge reflects part of her sense of self and contributes to its further development.

Development of Competence and Self-esteem

From the beginning of infancy through the end of toddlerhood, children achieve a growing sense of basic trust, autonomy, competence, and ultimately self-esteem. In fact, these developments go hand in hand. Autonomy, as we discussed, is made possible by a child's secure and basically trustworthy relationships with his primary caregivers. **Competence** (skill and capability) develops as a result of the child's natural curiosity and desire to explore the world and the pleasure he experiences in successfully mastering and controlling that world (White, 1993). Much like the infant's need for proximity and attachment to caregivers, his motivation to explore and master the world is thought to be relatively autonomous and independent of basic physiological needs for food, water, sleep, and freedom from pain.

Based on many years of observational study, Burton White (1993) suggests that a socially competent toddler is likely to display capabilities in the following areas:

1. Getting and holding the attention of adults in socially acceptable ways
2. Using adults as resources after first determining that a task is too difficult

competence According to Robert White, children's increased skill and capability in successfully exploring, mastering, and controlling the world around them.

3. Expressing affection and mild annoyance to adults

4. Leading and following peers

5. Expressing affection and mild annoyance to peers

6. Competing with peers

7. Showing pride in personal accomplishments

8. Engaging in role play or make-believe activities

What everyday rules for behavior guide parents' efforts to socialize their toddlers and preschool-age children? To answer this question, Heidi Gralinski and Claire Kopp (1993) observed and interviewed mothers and their children in these age groups. They found that for fifteen-month-olds, mothers' rules and requests centered on ensuring the children's safety and, to a lesser extent, protecting the families' possessions from harm; respecting basic social niceties ("Don't bite"; "No kicking"); and learning to delay getting what they wanted (versus getting it immediately). As children's ages and cognitive sophistication increased, the numbers and kinds of prohibitions and requests expanded from the original focus on child protection and interpersonal issues to family routines, self-care, and other concerns regarding the child's independence. By the time children were three, a new quality of rule emerged: "Do not scream in a restaurant, run around naked in front of company, pretend to kill your sister, hang up the phone when someone is using it, fight with children in school, play with guns, or pick your nose."

Not surprisingly, a toddler's social competence is influenced by the nature of the parent-toddler relationship. Even though they do not spend more time interacting with their children than mothers of less competent children, mothers of highly competent children support and encourage their toddlers' curiosity and desire to explore the world around them by providing a rich variety of interesting toys and experiences that are both safe and appropriate to the children's level of competence. They also play with their toddlers in ways that are responsive to the children's interests and needs and use language their children can clearly understand.

Observations of mothers and their two-year-olds found that toddlers' capacity for both compliance with parental directions and self-assertion was associated with *authoritative parenting* relationships (see Chapter 10), consisting of a combination of control and guidance and an appropriate sharing of power with warmth, sensitivity, responsiveness, and child-centered family management techniques. High levels of defiance and parent-toddler conflict were most likely to be associated with more authoritarian, power-assertive control strategies. In situations where the toddler had said "no" to the mother, maternal negative control was most likely to elicit defiance (White, 1993; Crockenberg & Litman, 1990).

Mothers of competent toddlers are also more likely to encourage their children to accomplish the tasks they had initiated themselves by actively guiding them and praising them for achievements rather than actually performing the tasks for them (White, 1975, 1993). As you might expect, this approach requires considerable patience, the ability to tolerate the child's frustration when things do not work out the first few times, and a firm belief in the child's need and potential to be an autonomous and competent person. Perhaps the most important quality of these mothers is their ability to interact sensitively and appropriately with their children and to experience pleasure and delight (at least most of the time) in these interactions. The same quality appears to be most important in the development of secure attachment relationships and continues to be important throughout childhood.

Toddlers who grow up in supportive environments are likely to be better adjusted in their development than children whose environments are less supportive. A natural outcome of such parenting is the early emergence of a strong sense of **self-esteem:** a child's feeling that she is an important, competent, powerful, and worthwhile person whose efforts to be autonomous and take initiative are respected and valued by those around her (Erikson, 1963; Harter, 1983). The development of

• • •
self-esteem An individual's belief that he or she is an important, competent, powerful, and worthwhile person who is valued and appreciated.

self-esteem during infancy and toddlerhood is closely tied to the achievement of a positive ratio of autonomy versus shame and doubt and initiative versus guilt during the developmental crises that, according to Erikson, occur during this period (Erikson, 1963). As we will see, the childhood experiences that follow infancy continue to make major contributions to this important aspect of identity.

WHAT DO YOU THINK? If you were the primary person responsible for the care of a toddler for a week, which toddler needs and behaviors would provide the biggest challenges for you? Which would be the easiest for you? Why? If you have cared for a toddler, answer in terms of your own experience.

The Competent Toddler

In a matter of just months, a baby may have tripled in weight and doubled in height. He has learned to move about freely and independently, and has formed important relationships with particular people and places. The mature toddler is starting to know that he is a unique individual like everyone else. As we saw in Chapter 6, he has also made a good start in developing his capacities to think, listen, and talk. It generally becomes clear somewhere around his second birthday that he is definitely not a baby anymore!

But what, then, has the child become? For convenience, the next several chapters simply call him a "preschooler," a child who is too young to begin elementary school. Note, however, that a considerable number of children who are not yet school age attend day care centers, family day care, or nursery school on a regular basis. Although a preschool child may be too young for elementary school, he definitely is ready—and eager—to learn more about the physical and social worlds outside his immediate family. If all has gone reasonably well up to now, he can use his family as a secure base from which to explore these larger worlds, which include the children next door, the department store downtown, and the children and teachers at a nursery school or day care setting.

From the two-year-old's point of view, home is still a very important place, but it is no longer the entire world. From her parents' point of view, the daily burden of child care has declined markedly, although it certainly has not disappeared yet. A toddler may not need to have her diapers changed for much longer, but she will still need prepared meals for years to come. She may no longer seek attention several times per hour, but she will continue to seek it many times a day. The child still has a lot of growing and learning to do in the preschool years that follow.

Summary of Major Ideas

Early Social Relationships

1. A newborn infant has a natural tendency to actively participate in her social world.

2. *Infant-caregiver synchrony* refers to the closely orchestrated social and emotional interactions between an infant and his caregiver, and provides an important basis for the development of attachment relationships.

3. The similarities in the type and quality of an infant's interactions with both her mother and her father are much greater than the differences.

4. The effects of nonmaternal care and maternal employment on infant and toddler development depend on the specific circumstances, but in general do not appear to have negative effects.

5. When given the opportunity to do so, infants engage in active social interactions with their siblings and peers, and often prefer them to their parents as playmates.

Emotions and Temperament in Infancy

6. Infants appear to be capable of a complex range of emotional responses and are quite sensitive to the feelings of their caregivers. They probably use cues similar to those adults use, such as variations in voice quality, smell, touch, facial expression, and body language.

7. Even at birth, infants exhibit differences in temperament—their patterns of physical and emotional responsiveness and activity level. These differences both influence and are influenced by their caregivers' feelings and responses.

Attachment Formation

8. Attachment, the tendency of young infants and their caregivers to seek and maintain physical and emotional closeness with each other, is thought to provide an important basis for achieving secure and trusting relationships during early infancy.

9. Attachment develops in a series of phases from indiscriminate sociability at birth to goal-coordinated partnerships at two years.

10. The *Strange Situation,* in which the infant is confronted with the stress of being in an unfamiliar place, meeting a stranger, and being separated from his parent, has been used to study the development of attachment.

11. Secure attachment is most likely to develop when the caregiver responds sensitively and appropriately to the infant and the infant can use the caregiver as a safe base for exploration.

12. Infants are equally capable of forming secure attachments to their mothers and to their fathers, and to other caregivers as well, even though in the majority of families, the mother is the primary caregiver.

13. The effects of both maternal employment and day care on attachment depend largely on how the mother feels about herself and her role as a parent and how the situation helps or hinders her ability to care for and enjoy the baby. The quality of the infant's experience and the quality and consistency of the day care are also important.

14. Insecurely attached infants tend to be less able than securely attached infants to get help from parents and teachers when they need it or to accept it when offered.

15. Attachment patterns can be long term, often affecting three generations of parents and their children.

Toddlerhood and the Emergence of Autonomy

16. Sources of the growing autonomy that characterizes the second year of infancy include identification, operant conditioning, observational learning, and social referencing.

17. Toddlerhood also brings significant increases in self-knowledge and self-awareness. These changes are reflected in the toddler's increasing awareness of adult standards, levels of distress at behaviors modeled by unknown adults, and tendencies to smile following an accomplishment, and to speak self-descriptively.

18. Toddlers are strongly motivated to achieve greater competence through successfully mastering and controlling the physical and social worlds around them. Competence is fostered by parents who encourage their infant's curiosity by providing opportunities that are challenging, safe, and appropriate to the child's capabilities.

19. Increasing self-esteem in the infant is the natural outcome of supportive parenting.

Key Terms

anxious-avoidant attachment (217)

anxious-resistant attachment (217)

attachment (214)

autonomy (226)

caregiver-infant synchrony (203)

competence (229)

disorganized-disoriented attachment (218)

identification (227)

observational learning (228)

operant conditioning (227)

secure attachment (217)

self-esteem (230)

social referencing (228)

Strange Situation (SS) (216)

temperament (211)

PART 4

Early Childhood

Although most of us remember relatively little of our early childhood years, parents often believe those years are among the most gratifying for their children. Perhaps this is because children begin participating in their families more fully during this time. Now they talk and play with parents and siblings much more—and, of course, they sometimes infuriate everyone more, too. In all of these senses, they "belong" more fully than ever.

Preschoolers become more social during this period, partly because of the more complex motor skills they acquire; riding a trike or climbing a jungle gym can impress parents as well as friends. In addition, their new cognitive skills allow them to engage in extended conversations and try out new social roles in play. The preschooler's world is a rapidly expanding one, and for parents as well as children, the early childhood years are both exhausting and exhilarating.

Physical Development in Early Childhood

Focusing Questions

- What influences how rapidly preschool children grow, and why do they develop different bodily proportions?

- How does the brain become organized during early childhood?

- What motor skills do children acquire during the preschool years, and what refinements do they undergo?

- How do children's physical and motor development affect relationships between parents and young children?

During the preschool years, from ages two to five, children grow more slowly than they did during infancy, but growth continues to have a major impact on their lives as a whole. Physical growth not only makes new motor skills possible but also affects children's social, emotional, and cognitive development. To understand something of these relationships, consider two children, Maria and Kimberly, learning to swim. Each enrolls in the same swimming class, but before long Maria is swimming better than Kimberly. Why?

Most of the time such a difference stems from a mixture of physical, social, emotional, and cognitive factors. Maria is larger than Kimberly; even at the beginning of the swimming class, she was able to hold her breath longer and paddle more powerfully. She also gets more social support from home for learning to swim; her parents are devoted swimmers and take her to the pool between lessons. Because of differences such as these, Maria has developed a concept of herself as a good swimmer, one who is strong, holds her breath well, and can count on help at swimming when she needs it.

In this chapter we look closely at such factors, investigating how physical growth and motor skills influence each other and psychological processes during early childhood. First, we examine the overall nature and extent of physical growth. Then we look at some motor skills typically acquired during early childhood. Some of these skills, such as learning to walk, are relatively universal among all children. Other skills, such as ice skating, are rather unique to particular groups of children. Woven into our discussion are implicit notions of what constitutes typical, or "normal," physical development. As we point out repeatedly, however, such norms do not in and of themselves dictate how children *should* develop physically. Evaluating growth is also important, but it differs from describing growth. Throughout the chapter, we will keep this distinction in mind.

Influences on Normal Physical Development

Physical growth in the preschool years is relatively easy to measure and gives a clear idea of how children normally develop during this period. Table 8.1 shows the two most familiar measurements of growth, standing height and weight. At age two, an average child in North America measures about thirty-three or thirty-four inches tall, or about two feet and ten inches. Three years later, at age five, he measures approximately forty-four inches, or about one-third more than before. The typical child weighs about twenty-seven pounds on his second birthday but about forty-one

TABLE 8.1	Average Height and Weight During Early Childhood	
Age (Years)	Height (Inches)	Weight (Pounds)
2	34.5	27.0
3	37.8	31.5
4	40.9	36.0
5	43.6	40.5

Source: Engels (1993).

pounds by his fifth. (See also Figure 8.1.) Meanwhile, other measurements change in less obvious ways. The child's head grows about one inch in circumference during these years, and his body fat decreases as a proportion of his total bodily tissue.

For a preschool child who is reasonably healthy and happy, physical growth is remarkably smooth and predictable, especially compared to many cognitive and social developments. All in all, physical growth involves no discrete stages, plateaus, or qualitative changes such as those Piaget proposed for cognitive development. At the same time, however, differences develop among individual children and among groups of children. Often the differences simply create interesting physical variety among children, but sometimes they do more than affect appearance. Being larger (or smaller) than usual, for example, can make a child stronger (or less strong) than others of the same age, and therefore more (or less) able to master certain sports or other physical activities. Size can also affect how parents and other adults respond to the child: larger children may seem older, and be treated as such, whether or not they are psychologically ready. For both reasons, a child might gain (or lose) self-confidence and even gain (or lose) popularity among peers.

The overall smoothness of growth means that childhood height and weight can predict adult height and weight to a significant extent, although not perfectly. A four-year-old who is above average in height tends to end up above average as an adult. Nevertheless, correlation between childhood height and adult height is imperfect because of individual differences in nutrition and health and, most of all, in the timing of puberty. In particular, children who experience puberty later than average tend to grow taller than children who experience it early (Sanfilippo et al., 1994)—a source of diversity with implications for adolescence, which we will therefore discuss further in Chapter 14.

FIGURE 8.1

Growth in Height and Weight from Two to Eighteen Years

Girls and boys continue to grow during early childhood, but not as rapidly as during infancy. During early childhood, the genders overlap much more than they differ, in spite of social stereotypes that sometimes suggest a physical gap even among preschoolers.

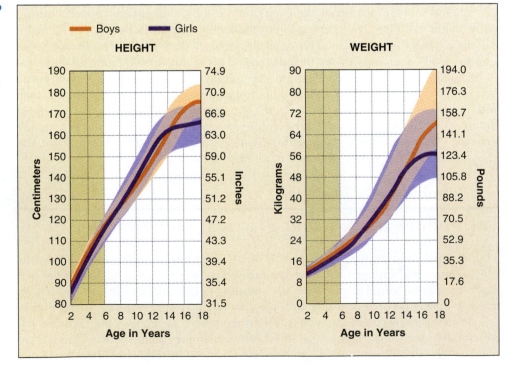

Genetic Background

Most dimensions of growth are influenced substantially by heredity. Tall parents tend to have tall children, and short parents typically have short children. Weight shows similar patterns, although it can be influenced strongly by habits of exercise and diet. Nevertheless, a tendency to be heavy or thin is inherited to a significant extent. Contrary to popular belief, both parents contribute equally to these tendencies. Sons do not necessarily resemble their fathers' growth patterns more than their mothers', nor do daughters resemble their mothers' more than their fathers'. A child with one tall parent and one short parent therefore stands equal chances of being either tall or short. On the average, in fact, such children are middling in height, although they vary widely as individuals.

Races and ethnic groups around the world also differ slightly in average growth patterns (Eveleth & Tanner, 1990). Children from Asiatic groups, such as Chinese and Japanese, tend to be shorter than European and North American children. The latter, in turn, tend to be shorter than children from African societies. Shape differs among these groups as well, although the differences do not always become obvious until adolescence. Asiatic children develop short legs and arms relative to their torsos, and relatively broad hips. African children do just the opposite: they develop relatively long limbs and narrow hips. Keep in mind, though, that these differences are only *average* tendencies. Racial and ethnic groups tend to overlap in size and shape more than they differ (that's what makes us all human!). From the point of view of parents, teachers, and other professionals, the most important physical differences among children are individual ones: there are large and small children in every racial and ethnic group, among both boys and girls, and in every community (Doherty, 1996). If you are responsible for children as individuals, recognizing their individual differences is likely to be your priority.

As a result of improvements in nutrition and health care, children in industrialized nations are often taller than in earlier times. But there are important variations among societies—even among industrialized ones—that apparently are genetically influenced.

Disease

Although serious illnesses interfere with growth, it often is hard to judge exactly how much. The trouble is that children with serious illnesses often have other conditions that retard growth; they may have been small for date or suffered from chronically poor nutrition during infancy. These conditions can lead not only to slow growth but also to various illnesses, which in turn may contribute to the problem.

To hold back growth, an illness must be fairly major. Preschool-age children in certain impoverished rural parts of Central America tend to be shorter and lighter in weight if they suffered continually from diarrhea during infancy (Pinstrup-Anderson et al., 1995), but similar children are not shorter and lighter if their illnesses consisted mainly of upper respiratory tract infections (colds). Children from affluent parts of the same societies usually do not get sick enough to suffer impaired growth, nor do children from societies that are generally well off. Middle-class American children are just as likely to grow large (or small) if they catch colds frequently as they are if they do not.

Certain specific diseases and conditions do retard growth, in many cases by reducing the normal absorption of nutrients over a long period of time. Childhood diabetes can hinder growth, at least partly, by interfering with the normal use of sugars in the body. So can any chronic infection of the intestine, such as amoebic

A Multicultural View ....

Cultural Influences on Children's Sleep

The development of children's sleep is a primary worry for American parents. One study found that it is the most commonly discussed single issue during periodic well-child visits to pediatricians and that concern about children's sleep remains high throughout both infancy and early childhood (Harkness et al., 1995a). Parents of three- and four-year-olds worry almost as much as parents of six-month-old infants about whether their children are falling asleep quickly enough, staying asleep long enough, and resting peacefully enough. Bedtime routines evolve to help meet these goals: they are supposed to calm children down and help them sleep better.

Doctors and parenting experts in our society tend to assert that sleep cycles depend on physical maturity and that interruptions and irregularities are something children will eventually "grow out of." Yet the fact that parents continue to worry about sleep even when their children become preschoolers suggests that more than physical maturity is at stake. In some sense, it seems, children must be "learning" to sleep.

Cross-cultural comparisons support this possibility. A comparison of families from the Netherlands with families from Boston, for example, found important differences between children's sleep in the two societies (Harkness et al.,

1995b). Dutch infants and preschoolers went to bed more than an hour earlier, on average, than their American counterparts, and they got significantly more sleep throughout infancy and the preschool years. They also experienced less variation in their bed times and waking times. In these ways, children from the Netherlands were sleeping "better" than children from the United States.

Why the difference? In this and another study, interviews with American and Dutch parents offered clues (Harkness et al., 1992). In describing their children's sleep patterns, American mothers referred frequently to the "innateness" pattern: they seemed to believe that regularity in a child's sleep is determined genetically. Children are born more or less regular, and parents can alter the innate regularity only in limited ways. Mostly they must learn to live with the pattern nature has prescribed.

The Dutch parents, on the other hand, often talked about the need for "the three Rs" of parenting: *Rust, Regelmaat,* and *Reinheid* (rest, regularity, and cleanliness). They commented relatively frequently on the child's need to learn how to organize his or her day and, therefore, to become independent eventually. Consistent with this view, the Dutch parents arranged for more regularity in children's daily lives than did the American parents; they more often arranged family errands, for example, so as not to interrupt or alter naps or mealtimes.

---

dysentery or worms, by preventing the normal digestion of foods. Nutritional deficits can also result from chronic intolerance to certain foods, such as the gluten in wheat products or the lactose in milk products. Children with these conditions suffer in various ways, but to a large extent they simply become malnourished and, like other malnourished children, do not grow as rapidly as usual.

Not all diseases that influence growth do so by affecting nutrition. About one preschool child in ten thousand develops a deficiency in the **endocrine glands,** the glands that produce growth hormones (Sanfilippo et al., 1994). As a result, growth simply slows down considerably; by age five, an afflicted child may measure only about 2½ feet tall (or 85 centimeters), which is about 9 inches (or 15 centimeters)

TABLE 8.2   Typical Ages Recommended for Immunizations

Birth–2 months	Hepatitis
2–6 months	Diphtheria, tetanus, and pertussis (DPT), polio, and haemophilus
6–18 months	Hepatitis booster, haemophilus booster
15–18 months	DPT booster, polio booster
4–6 years	DPT booster, polio booster
10–12 years	Measles, mumps, and rubella (MMR)
14–16 years	Tetanus and diphtheria booster

Source: American Academy of Pediatrics (1992).

endocrine glands Glands that produce growth hormones.

Research has found that Dutch children sleep more soundly at night than American children, apparently because their daytime routines are more regular and predictable. This father, for example, takes his son to school every morning without fail—and perhaps without knowing it, contributes to his regular sleep at night.

American parents certainly talked about establishing regular sleep patterns, but in doing so they focused mostly on the regularity of *nighttime* routines and ignored regularity during the day. Although parents themselves seemed unaware of it, daytime priorities contradicted the belief in regular sleep: parents emphasized responsiveness to the child and provision of stimulating activities filled with novelty. A stimulating day, in this view, fosters the child's cognitive and social development. In addition, American parents had more hectic, varied schedules themselves, making it hard to provide regularity for their children. As a result, compared to Dutch parents, American parents developed relatively elaborate bedtime rituals to calm their children down and compensate for the excitement (and relative unpredictability) of the day.

Of course, even some American parenting experts see a connection between regularity during the day and regularity at night. One best-selling book on children's sleep (Ferber, 1986) urges parents to develop regular daytime routines as soon as possible after childbirth if they wish their child to have a regular nighttime sleeping experience. But for now this advice will be hard for many parents to follow, given the competing cultural belief in providing stimulation for the child and the continuing cultural tolerance for hectic daytime schedules for parents.

shorter than average. Occasionally doctors can trace such growth deficiencies to an anatomical disorder (such as a tumor) of the glands that control growth. More often, however, they can find no obvious cause. In either case, the condition usually can be treated with injections of whatever hormones the child appears to be missing.

However, injections of hormones are a useful strategy only for children who have a diagnosed hormone deficiency and do not deviate far from normal height or weight. Because growth hormones are powerful medicines full of unknown side effects, doctors tend to prescribe them only in situations where their benefits are certain and their risks are small. Hormones do not make a desirable treatment for children who are merely shorter than average but want to become taller or whose parents want them to grow taller.

Once the causes of slow growth are diagnosed correctly and treated, children often can recover by growing much faster than usual until they have reached the normal range of size for their age. At that point, growth slows down again to comparatively normal rates and becomes relatively immune to short-term and minor changes in the child's health and nutrition. This process often is called **catch-up growth.** It suggests that genetics may influence the rate of physical growth significantly as long as children receive basically good nutrition and physical care. Immunizations during infancy and childhood probably also promote normal growth by preventing major diseases, whether or not a child happens to be slow growing. Table 8.2 lists the most common immunizations and the ages at which children typically receive them.

catch-up growth The process by which children recover from slow growth by growing faster than usual until they reach the normal size for their age.

Nutritional Needs During the Preschool Years

For a time, a young preschooler (such as a three-year-old) may eat less than he or she did as a toddler and become much more selective about foods as well. Michael, the son of one of the authors, ate every meal voraciously as a two-year-old; a year later he rarely finished a meal, even though he was significantly taller and heavier by then. Elizabeth, his sister, followed a similar pattern, except more pronounced. As a toddler she ate most foods except ice cream ("Too sweet," she said!), but as a young preschooler she sometimes hardly ate at all—though she did decide then that she liked ice cream. Later both children's appetites returned. As a nineteen-year-old, Michael routinely eats about twice as much as other members of the family do. Elizabeth, at sixteen, is no longer a picky eater, and has become especially enthusiastic about ice cream.

Parents may worry about such changes, but in fact they are normal and result from the slowing down of growth after infancy. Preschool children simply do not need as many calories per unit of their body weight as they did immediately after birth. They do need variety in their foods, however, just as adults do, to ensure adequate overall nutrition. Given preschoolers' newfound selectiveness about eating, providing the variety needed for good nutrition sometimes can be a challenge to parents and other caregivers.

How can one ensure healthy variety in a preschool child's diet? Experts generally discourage coercion ("Eat your vegetables because I say so!"), since it teaches children to associate undesired foods with unpleasant social experiences (Endres & Rockwell, 1993). They also discourage using sweet foods as a reward for eating undesired foods ("If you eat your vegetables, you can have your ice cream"), because it implicitly overvalues the sweets and undervalues the undesired food still further. The best strategy seems to be casual, repeated exposure to the food without insisting that the child eat it (Andrien, 1994). Observations of children's eating habits confirm what parents often suspect as well: children's food preferences are influenced by the adult models around them. In the long term, preschoolers tend to like the same foods as their parents and other important adults.

WHAT DO YOU THINK? How do you suppose parents evaluate their child's height and weight? Explore this issue by asking parents three questions: (1) "How tall is your child?"; (2) "How much does she or he weigh?"; and (3) "Are that height and weight about right, or too high or too low?" Try to involve as many classmates as possible in this survey, and pool your results. Then focus on this question: Do parents' evaluations of height and weight have any relationship to the actual size of their child?

The Connection Between Health and Poverty

In economically well-off settings, preschool children as a group are among the healthiest human beings alive, though not as healthy as they will become later in childhood and in adolescence. They experience comparatively few major illnesses as long as they get enough of the right things to eat and as long as their parents have reasonable access to modern medical care. As parents often note, preschoolers do experience frequent minor illnesses: various respiratory infections, ear infections, and stomach flu. These typically strike a young child several times per year, which is three or four times as often as for adults and about twice as often as for school-age children (Engels, 1993). For well-nourished children whose families have access to medical care, however, these illnesses rarely prove serious or life threatening. Colds and flu do cause worry, as well as create challenges in arranging child care for parents.

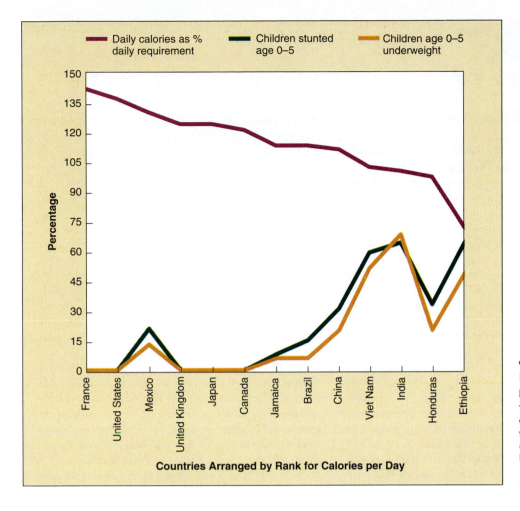

● ● ● ● ● ● ● ● ● ● ● ● ● ● ●
FIGURE 8.2
Physical Impact of Poverty on Growth
The percentage of children who are underweight and stunted (excessively short) tends to be smaller in countries where children receive more food calories, but the relationship is far from perfect.
Source: United Nations International Children's Emergency Fund (1998).

Poverty as a Health Problem

But this optimistic picture of preschool health poses a problem: about 30 percent of families in the United States, and even greater numbers in many other countries worldwide, have poor access to medical care, mainly because they live at or near the poverty level. Young children from these families are substantially less healthy than those from middle- and high-income families. Low-income preschoolers contract 25 to 50 percent more minor illnesses than do preschoolers as a group, and they are more often malnourished, meaning they chronically lack essential vitamins, iron, or protein (American Academy of Pediatrics, 1993; Wilkinson, 1996). Figure 8.2 illustrates the impact of child poverty on some aspects of health.

Whether in North America or around the world, minor illnesses combined with malnourishment put children's health at risk for additional illnesses, both minor and major. Malnourishment also contributes to delays in social, language, and cognitive development, possibly because it leads to lack of energy and lack of interest in new experiences. In one study based in Kenya (Africa), even a temporary food shortage (a few months of local drought) hurt children's health and school performance two years later (McDonald et al., 1994).

Responding to Child Poverty

How can we counteract these problems? In general, strategies can focus either on individuals and their particular communities or on systematic reorganization of the health care system as a whole. Among individually oriented strategies, an important

PERSPECTIVES

Reforming Children's Health Care

• • • • • In all modern societies, the health care system provides less help to poor families than to better-off ones. The gap begins before birth and continues after birth: low-income mothers receive less medical attention during pregnancy, their and their fetuses' health problems are overlooked, their infants receive fewer checkups from a doctor and are less likely to be seen by a doctor if they get sick (Wilkinson, 1996; Bury, 1997).

Why does access to health care depend so heavily on personal income? In the United States, medical services for the poor are paid through Medicaid, a federally sponsored insurance program created in the 1960s. Medicaid pays for basic health services up to a point; it will reimburse a doctor only a certain amount for seeing a child with an earache. Doctors may charge more but in the process price themselves out of the market for low-income families. In effect, low-income parents have significantly fewer doctors and clinics to choose from than higher-income parents do, even though (as pointed out in this chapter) their children experience more illnesses than do children from middle- and upper-income families (Fitzgerald et al., 1995). For this and other reasons, low-income parents are more likely than others to wait until a child's illness is serious, or even life threatening, before seeking medical help.

Efforts to limit the soaring costs of medical services have led many states to tighten the standards for eligibility for Medicaid (U.S. Congressional Budget Office, 1993). Recently, therefore, a person or a family has had to be "poorer" than before, in some states living at only one-half the income level of the official federal poverty line. Some states have set limits on services, such as the number of days a person can stay in a hospital or visits permitted to a doctor per year. Still others have required preauthorization from state health authorities for services that exceed a certain cost (say, $500).

What can society and concerned individuals do to reduce these inequalities in health care? Numerous reforms have been proposed, most centering on one of three ideas: community involvement, prevention, and reorganization of services. Reforms that focus on community involvement seek to reduce the psychological and geographical distance between medical staff and the people they serve. Some hospitals and cities have established small community health clinics in areas of greatest need (the inner city). They hire medical staff who try to establish rapport with the parents and children who seek help, recruit local community members to serve on their governing and advisory boards, and charge low fees based on families' ability to pay.

Reforms that focus on prevention seek to keep disease from striking in the first place. These actions often deal with relatively healthy children (who have not gotten sick yet) and with the conditions that make illness likely rather than with illness itself. Lead poisoning is a good example: community health experts often cite this substance as the most hazardous health threat to preschool children in modern society (Tesman & Hills, 1994). Lead accumulates in the body and eventually causes damage to the nervous system, sickness, and even death. Children (and adults) pick it up accidentally from many sources, but the most prominent culprit is the interior wall paint used in about 75 percent of all homes and apartments built before 1980. Since there is no real cure for lead poisoning, prevention strategies have dominated the response of the health care profession: educating parents to the dangers, pressing for legislation outlawing lead-based paints (and also lead-based gasoline), and even removal of leaded paint in some homes.

Reforms that focus on reorganization generally involve more self-conscious planning of medical services. Immunization and health screening programs based in schools, for example, reach a higher percentage of children than programs based in a community health clinic (R. Behrman, 1998; J. Behrman & Stacey, 1997). Also, making better use of "front-line" professionals can improve access dramatically without compromising quality of care: the majority of childhood illnesses, for example, can be treated effectively by a nurse rather than a medical doctor, as long as the nurse knows when a particular illness deserves referral to the doctor and appropriate specialized services are indeed available.

What Do You Think?

1. Look back on your medical-screening experiences (for example, an eye or a hearing test) as an elementary-age student—not from your point of view as a student but as the teachers and nurses might have experienced it. What might be the limitations and advantages to "mass screening"?

2. Is there a case to be made for *limiting* health care to the poor? If so, what would it be?

3. The most common reason individuals are admitted to a hospital is to give birth to a child. What might be the pros and cons of limiting access to hospitals for this purpose?

one is to educate children and families about health and nutrition. For example, pamphlets can be distributed in schools or medical clinics, and public health nurses can make presentations in classrooms, community clubs, or churches.

Educational activities can be effective if they build on the knowledge of health and nutrition low-income parents and their children already have and avoid assuming that the public is completely ignorant about these matters. Mexican American children as young as four years, for example, have good knowledge about the effects of cleanliness, but often need more information about nutrition (Olvera-Ezzell et al., 1994). A similar pattern exists among their parents (Sanjur, 1995). In this sort of situation, it is helpful to organize intervention programs aimed at providing parents and children with the knowledge they need. However, such programs must respect the culture and economic situations of the families, which usually influence food preferences in major ways. Put simply, certain foods acquire symbolic meanings (such as turkey at white American Thanksgiving) regardless of their precise nutritional value. Other foods may never be tried, no matter how worthwhile they are nutritionally, because they cost too much or seem too alien to a particular family or cultural group.

Another individually oriented intervention is direct aid to families to prevent illness. Food distribution centers ("food banks"), for example, give food away to needy families in specific communities. Typically they rely heavily on volunteers from churches or other community agencies and receive their supplies from local grocery stores, restaurants, or farmers with surpluses to give away. Typically, too, they fail to meet the demand for their services (U.S. Congress Select Committee on Hunger, 1992). Because of this problem, many experts favor reorganizing the health care system in broader, more systematic ways than is possible through individual action (see the accompanying Perspectives box).

WHAT DO YOU THINK ?   Given the correlation between health and poverty, how could you respond to a parent, teacher, or other member of the public who asserts a belief that "the United States is the healthiest nation on earth"? What would be the basis, in your opinion, for this belief?

Brain Development

By the preschool years, the brain has grown to nearly its final adult size and begins to function physically in adultlike ways (Brierley, 1994). Nerve fibers continue to interconnect among themselves. Therefore, even though no new nerve cells actually are created, a young child's brain looks increasingly dense and complex when viewed under a microscope.

Organization of the Brain

Given its complexity, how does the brain sort out and perform the diverse functions of being human? Contrary to a widespread belief, it does *not* work like a telephone switchboard; individual stimuli or thoughts do not confine themselves to selected nerve fibers, as though the fibers acted as wires. Instead, a stimulus generates neural activity over wide areas of the brain and sometimes even in the entire brain. Some of this response shows itself when electrodes are placed on a person's head. But the locations of brain activity can be mapped even more accurately by injecting tiny, harmless amounts of radioactive substances into the blood and measuring which parts of the brain then accumulate especially large amounts of the substances. Active brain cells and fibers, which require larger amounts of blood, therefore give off more radiation and can be "photographed" with this technique, a medical procedure called *tomography* (Seeram, 1994).

visual cortex The area of the brain located near the back of the head in the cerebral cortex, where visual images produce the strongest activity.

auditory cortex An area of the brain, located near the left side of the cerebral cortex, where the sounds of speech produce their primary response.

Wernicke's area The part of the auditory cortex in which the sounds of speech produce their primary response.

motor cortex The area of the brain, located just forward of the top of the head, where simple voluntary movements produce their largest neural activity.

Broca's area An area of the brain located on the left side of the cerebral cortex; vital to the production of language. See also *Wernicke's area.*

hemispheric lateralization A tendency for the left and right halves of the brain to perform separate functions.

lateralized behavior An action that individuals prefer to perform with one side of their bodies more than the other.

FIGURE 8.3

Areas of the Brain

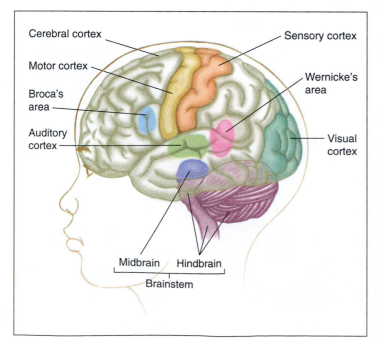

What does tomography show about brain activity in preschoolers? For one thing, it shows that most stimuli (sights and sounds) cause at least some neural activity throughout the brain; activity is never fully localized. At the same time, though, particular areas do respond more strongly to certain types of stimuli. A visual image, such as the sight of a cat, produces the strongest activity in an area called the **visual cortex,** located near the back of the head in the cerebral cortex. The sounds of speech produce their primary response in the **auditory cortex** and specifically in a place called **Wernicke's area,** located near the left side of the cerebral cortex. Simple voluntary movements, such as lifting an arm, produce their largest neural activity in the **motor cortex,** located just forward of the top of the head. The child's own speech usually produces its primary activity in a region called **Broca's area,** located on the left side of the cerebral cortex and somewhat to the front. Figure 8.3 illustrates these and other areas of specialized activity.

Hemispheric Lateralization

During the preschool years, children begin showing definite **hemispheric lateralization,** the tendency for the left and right halves of the brain to perform separate functions. In general, the left hemisphere deals increasingly with information on an item-by-item or linear basis, and the right hemisphere identifies relationships or patterns among the items (Bianci, 1993).

The difference in function is quite noticeable in a task called *dichotic listening.* In this task, a child wears headphones that feed sounds or information to each ear separately. Because of the layout of the nerve cells in the brain, the experimental sounds are conducted to particular hemispheres for processing. The sounds initially go to the hemisphere *opposite* the ear that receives each sound. Under these conditions, if the information given to each ear is provided sequentially, such as a string of random digits, the ear connected to the left hemisphere tends to hear its sounds relatively earlier and with fewer errors. But if the information emphasizes patterns, such as melodies, the right hemisphere functions better.

Observations such as these imply that the hemispheres specialize in certain functions even in young children. However, most everyday tasks probably obscure hemispheric specialization simply because they usually require the activity of both halves of the brain. A child in nursery school, for example, might discover that a shape is a cube, but most likely he will handle it with both hands, look at its overall shape, and count the corners—all at once.

Lateralized Behaviors

In contrast to hemispheric lateralization, lateralized behaviors are quite evident in everyday life, even among preschool-age children. **Lateralized behaviors** are actions individuals prefer to perform with one side of their bodies more than with the other. The best example is handedness: offer a toy to a five-year-old, and most likely she will take it with her right hand rather than her left. But people of all ages show lateral preferences (usually right-sided) for a variety of behaviors. Most of us have a favorite eye for looking through a telescope or keyhole, a preferred ear for listening on the telephone, and a preferred foot for squashing a bug on the floor (Gabbard, 1989).

Most children show a number of lateralized behaviors—apparently a genetic trait. One of these children, for example, prefers gluing with his right hand, and the other prefers gluing with her left hand. In addition to hand preference, most children have a preferred foot, a preferred eye, and a preferred ear.

Lateral preferences emerge during the preschool years and become stable about the time children begin school, and must have at least partly biological or genetic origins. It is hard to tell what experiences might cause a majority of three-year-olds to choose to use their right ears for listening to a seashell. Hand preference runs in families: siblings and twins are much more likely than other individuals to prefer the same hand, as are parents and their children. Boys are left-handed significantly more often than girls are, and children with genetically caused mental retardation are much more likely than usual to be left-handed (Coren, 1992). All of these facts imply genetic influences on lateralized behaviors.

But learning probably does affect lateral preferences somewhat. Among preschool children, right-hand bias is strongest for behaviors that are taught explicitly, such as eating with a spoon or using scissors, and weakest for behaviors children usually learn spontaneously, such as digging in a sandbox. Also, right-hand bias increases during the lifespan. About 85 percent of children favor their right hand during the preschool years, but more than 95 percent of adults do so during old age. This shift may not seem like much, but it is too large to occur by chance. Learning must account for it.

WHAT DO YOU THINK ? Is it a problem to be left-handed? Talk with a left-handed classmate about this, or offer your opinions about the problem if you yourself are left-handed. In view of left-handers' complaints, do you think teachers should support left-handedness in young children or encourage left-handers to switch?

Other Bodily Changes

Preschool Sensory Development

Changes in a preschooler's brain do not, of course, happen by themselves. They are accompanied by a host of other physical changes. Two of these that are especially important to parents are preschoolers' development of their senses and their development of bladder control. *Visual acuity*, or sharpness of vision, improves during

In the long run, successful bladder control depends on both physical growth and the child's own motivation. Forcing a child prematurely to control herself may produce results, but only in the immediate future.

the preschool years. For toddlers, acuity for distant, stationary objects or shapes, such as the letters on a traditional eye examination chart, is only about 20/60, meaning a two-year-old recognizes shapes at twenty feet that an adult can recognize at sixty feet. Paradoxically, children's near vision often is imperfect as well: many preschoolers have trouble focusing on shapes that are less than about two feet away. By about age five, distant vision improves substantially for most preschoolers, but near vision remains a problem for some during the early school years. About one child in ten needs glasses by age seven, even after vision has matured (Engels, 1993). The proportion continues to rise throughout childhood, especially around puberty.

For most children *auditory acuity*, or sharpness of hearing, is more fully developed by the preschool years than visual acuity. But hearing a specific tone in the midst of other tones can be confusing. Inability to isolate sounds may account for some children's apparent distractibility when they first enter school. In a classroom, even accidental rustling noises can compete strongly with the teacher's voice for the child's attention, especially if a child's native language is not English (Christenson & Delgado, 1993).

Bladder Control

Sometime during the preschool years, most children acquire control of their bladder. As parents will testify, the process includes many false starts and accidents. Most commonly, daytime control comes before nighttime control, sometime before a child's third birthday, although individuals vary widely and somewhat unpredictably. Typically, too, daytime control of the bladder occurs at very nearly the same time. Some pediatricians believe this fact implies that children decide when they wish to begin exercising control, perhaps to begin feeling more grown up. In the early stages of toilet training, therefore, reminders and parent-led visits to the toilet may make little difference to most toddlers. Nonetheless they may help in the long term as a form of behavioral conditioning: a child comes to associate seeing and using the toilet with the relief of emptying a full bladder, as well as with the praise parents confer on the child for successes.

Nighttime bladder control often takes much longer to achieve than daytime control. About one-half of all three-year-olds still wet their beds at least some of the time, and as many as one in five six-year-olds do the same (American Psychiatric Association, 1994). The timing of nighttime control depends on several factors, such as how deeply children sleep and how large their bladders are. It also depends on anxiety level; worried children tend to wet their beds more often than relaxed children do. Unfortunately, parents sometimes contribute to young children's anxieties by becoming overly frustrated about changing wet sheets night after night.

Achieving bladder control reflects the large advances children make during these years in controlling their bodies in general. As infants, they could not always be sure of reaching successfully even for a nearby object, and their first efforts to crawl and to walk often ended in falls or moves in the wrong direction. During the preschool years, those problems no longer occur. Instead of concentrating on whether they can simply get their bodies to move, children of this age can begin focusing on what they actually want to do with their bodies.

WHAT DO YOU THINK ?   Imagine how you would talk to a parent who was concerned about the child's bed wetting at night. What would you say? If you are not sure, you may first want to read one or two parent advice books (such as Dr. Spock) on this topic. If you or your instructor can arrange it, try acting out a meeting between a concerned parent and a child care center worker or director to discuss bed wetting.

Motor Skill Development

As young children grow, they become more skilled at performing basic physical actions. Often a two-year-old can walk only with considerable effort; hence the term *toddler*. But a five-year-old can walk comfortably in a variety of ways: forward and backward, quickly and slowly, skipping and galloping. A five-year-old also can do other vigorous things that were impossible a few years earlier. He can run, jump, and climb, all with increasing smoothness and variety. He can carry out certain actions that require accuracy, such as balancing on one foot, catching a ball reliably, or drawing a picture.

In this section, we examine in more detail how children reach milestones such as these. Because family conditions vary a great deal in real life, we will make certain assumptions. In particular, we will assume children have no significant fears of being active—that they have a reasonably (but not excessively) daring attitude toward trying out new motor skills, they are in good health, and their physical growth has evolved more or less optimally. For some children, unfortunately, these conditions are not met. For them, we may need to modify the following descriptions.

After examining motor development, we look at the effects of altering such conditions. Can very young children be taught motor skills? Can they become skillful sooner or more fully by receiving training from adults? Will such training affect physical skill development later on in childhood and adolescence? As you will see, the answers to these questions are not definite, but they do have interesting implications for people who care for young children.

Fundamental Motor Skills

Healthy preschool children obviously have moved well beyond the confines of reflex action, which constituted the first motor skills of infancy. From ages two to about five, they experiment with the simple voluntary actions that adults use extensively for their normal activities, such as walking, running, and jumping (Kalverboer et al., 1993). For older children, these actions usually are the means to other ends. For very young children, they lie very much in the foreground and frequently are goals in themselves. Table 8.3 summarizes some of these activities.

Walking and Running   From a young child's point of view, walking may seem absurd at first: it requires purposely losing balance, then regaining balance rapidly

---

TABLE 8.3   Milestones in Preschool Motor Development

Approximate Age	Gross Motor Skill	Fine Motor Skill
2.5–3.5 years	Walks well; runs in straight line; jumps in air with both feet	Copies a circle; scribbles; can use eating utensils; stacks a few small blocks
3.5–4.5 years	Walking stride 80 percent of adult; runs at one-third adult speed; throws and catches large ball, but stiff-armed	Buttons with large buttons; copies simple shapes; makes simple representational drawings
4.5–5.5 years	Balances on one foot; runs far without falling; can "swim" in water for short distance	Uses scissors; draws people; copies simple letters and numbers; builds complex structures with blocks

Note: The ages given above are approximate, and skills vary with the life experiences available to individual children and with the situations in which the skills are displayed.

Source: Kalverboer et al. (1993).

Providing Full-Time Child Care in the Home

Abigail Appleton is employed forty hours per week as a nanny in a home where both parents work. The children she works with are Elizabeth, ten months, and Gregory, three years. Abigail described her work to me (Kelvin), as well as its satisfactions and frustrations.

Kelvin: *Tell me about what you do, about how you spend your work days.*

Abigail: I like to follow some routine so that the children feel a sense of structure, but at the same time I stay flexible. I arrive about 8:00 in the morning and help get the children up and give them breakfast. Their mother is getting ready for work at that time, but often sits with us for breakfast. We both feel this helps the transition into the day.

After breakfast, the children and I usually play for a few minutes and then head upstairs for a bath and to get them dressed. What we do from there depends—on the weather, on Gregory's attitude that day, and so on. One of his favorites is to do crafts. We often stay in to do them, rain or shine. When the weather's good, we may head out

to the local park or do something else outdoors, like go to the zoo. On rainy days we've been to the museum—or even to McDonald's for lunch!

Kelvin: *Sounds like a mixture of the predictable and the variable.*

Abigail: The only constant each week is to go to the library on Thursday mornings. After lunch there is more play time, and then it's time for a nap for both of them. (Elizabeth naps in the morning, too, but we don't plan around it because she'll sleep anywhere.) After nap we usually watch a little TV—Gregory loves National Geographic shows—and then have unstructured play for the rest of the afternoon. Dad is the first to get home, usually around 6:00.

Kelvin: *Do the outings give you a chance to get to know them better?*

Abigail: Definitely—though really *all* the different times help me gradually to know them as individuals. Elizabeth—even though she's still an infant—has the calmer disposition. Gregory's the worrier, the more anxious one. He gets bothered if something doesn't work

right—like if he can't make a puzzle fit the way it's supposed to.

But he loves going to the library. He always looks for books about bugs and fish. We often look in the juvenile section, even though he can't read yet, to find books with more detailed pictures and more information on a topic. Bugs are one of his favorite topics, and he just seems to absorb any information you give him about bugs. Then he remembers later, when the time is appropriate.

Kelvin: *And what about Elizabeth? What do you notice about her?*

Abigail: She's changed so much in just a few months! When I started she couldn't even feed herself. I had to hold her bottle completely, and spoon-feed everything else. But lately she's handling finger food herself, like bits of cookies or banana. Her coordination is much better now.

Kelvin: *So she can feed herself now?*

Abigail: No, not quite yet. I still have to feed her most of her meal, but she often does feed herself dessert. One

enough to keep from falling (Rose & Gamble, 1993). As older infants, children still must pay attention to these facts, even after a full year or so of practice. Each step is an effort in itself. Children watch each foot in turn as it launches (or lurches) forward; they may pause after each step before attempting the next. Typically, too, infants are top-heavy; this requires them to plant their feet far apart, as though straddling a horse, to keep from falling down. Despite these precautions, spills are plentiful in infancy, and walking often is rather slow.

But after a year or so of experience, children usually can walk without looking at their feet. Around their second or third birthday, their steps become more regular and their feet get closer together. Stride, the distance between feet in a typical step, remains considerably shorter than that of a normal adult. This makes short distances easy to walk but long distances hard to navigate for a few more years.

Running appears early in the preschool years, shortly after walking begins to smooth out. At first it looks more like a hurried walk than a true run, and the child may have trouble stopping herself once she has begun. Also, at first the run may not really involve one of its defining features, namely a brief instant of complete separation from the ground. Not until the end of the preschool period, around age five,

problem is that she often gets distracted by what Gregory is doing. She just loves to watch him. Often she becomes very vocal, almost rowdy watching him play. She's definitely getting more independent.

Kelvin: *Is that ever a problem for Gregory? Maybe she crawls over and wrecks something he's making or doing?*

Abigail: Actually no, it's not. They mostly get along really well. He often will come over to her or hold her hand. I think he likes her better now that she's starting to move around and to respond to us more than she used to do.

Kelvin: *Seems like you function almost like a substitute parent for them.*

Abigail: In some ways I do. It's gratifying to see them changing and growing. I imagine their mom and dad feel that as well. And sometimes, at the end of the day, they act like they want *me* to stay and are annoyed by the father's arrival home from work!

Kelvin: *Are there also frustrations about being a full-time "nanny"?*

Abigail: On some days, I wish I saw more people. I can go for considerable stretches with only the company of Elizabeth and Gregory, and nice as they are, it's not enough. But I suspect that any parent would react the same way in similar circumstances. It helps to get out—to go to the library or the park, or other outings.

Kelvin: *How about your relationships with the parents? Is that helpful, or frustrating, or . . .*

Abigail: They are *very* supportive of me, constantly thanking me for what I'm doing for their children! I'm lucky that way. Occasionally something happens that I feel I would handle differently if they were *my* children. Like how long Elizabeth should continue using a bottle. Mom's very eager to wean her before her first birthday, and I don't see what the big rush is about. And Gregory recently reverted back to needing diapers after we thought he had "graduated" from them. It makes me wonder if he's feeling he's not getting enough attention, or whether he's just

stressed about something. But I really can't be sure.

Kelvin: *Will they be wanting to move their children to a day care center when they get a little older?*

Abigail: I doubt it. They keep saying that they prefer having a nanny—one person to look after their children. And I guess I'm it!

What Do You Think?

1. If you were Gregory and Elizabeth's caregiver, what kinds of motor skills could you reasonably expect from them? How would their skills affect daily activities, such as eating or going to the park?

2. How would you compare Abigail's role with the role of an actual parent? How would her relationship with the children be similar, and how would it be different?

3. If you were a parent, what do you think would be the practical advantages and problems of having a full-time baby sitter for your children? How would you feel about hiring one compared to the alternatives (e.g., a child care center or relying on relatives for baby sitting)?

---

are these problems corrected. By then the child probably is swinging her arms as she strides to counterbalance the large, twisting motions of her legs. These arm motions also help the child to stop. Without their counterbalancing effect, children go into a sort of uncontrolled spin at the end of the run.

Jumping   At first, a jump is more like a fast stretch: the child reaches for the sky rapidly, but his feet fail to leave the ground. Sometime around his second birthday, one foot, or even both feet, may finally leave the ground. Such early successes may be delayed, however, because the child may put his arms backward to help himself take off, as though trying to push himself off the floor. Later, perhaps around age three, he shifts to a more efficient arm movement—reaching forward and up as he jumps—which creates a useful upward momentum.

Success in these actions depends partly on the type of jump the child is attempting. Jumping down a step is easier than jumping across a flat distance, and a flat or broad jump is easier than a jump up a step. By age five or so, most children can broad-jump across a few feet, although variations among individuals are substantial.

Throwing and Catching   For infants and toddlers, first throws may happen by accident. The child may just be waving an object and happen to release it suddenly, and away it goes. Once intentional throwing begins, however, children actually adopt more stereotyped methods initially than they do later in childhood. At first, they launch all balls in much the same way—usually with a general forward lurch—regardless of the balls' size or weight. As skill develops, children vary their movements according to the balls' characteristics: they give more wrist movement to small balls and more arm movement to large ones. At the same time, children begin to vary among themselves even in how they throw the same type of ball. Some develop a persistent wrist twist over and above the twist needed for particular balls, whereas others develop a special torso turn all their own.

Catching proceeds through similar phases. Early in the preschool period, children may extend their arms passively to receive an oncoming ball. Naturally this method works only if the thrower aims the ball perfectly. By around age four, children introduce flexibility to their methods by moving their hands in last-minute responses to the oncoming ball, and so forth. By school age, some children have become very skillful at catching: their arms and hands remain flexible until the ball actually arrives and therefore can compensate for unexpected angles and speeds as the ball approaches. Not surprisingly, this technique demands far less accuracy by the thrower.

• • •

fine motor coordination The ability to carry out smoothly small movements that involve precise timing but not strength.

During the preschool period, most motor skills—like catching a ball—develop through children's own informal activities, a fact that makes free play and exploration especially important for this age group. But there is an important role for adults to encourage play and exploration.

Can Motor Skills Be Taught?

In general, caregivers and parents can influence the learning of motor skills by providing opportunities to practice them. But the specific skills adults encourage vary a lot, depending on the needs of the child and the priorities of the adults. A physically normal child is not likely to receive "instruction" in a fundamental skill such as walking, whereas a child with a physical disability is likely to receive help in this very skill. Some children, with or without disabilities, may acquire specialized motor skills, such as ballet or swimming, that cannot be practiced unless opportunities are provided deliberately.

Preschool children respond well to specialized training to the extent that the training respects their current stage of development and takes advantage of their growing abilities to plan and coordinate fundamental motor actions (Poest et al., 1990). The result is unusually early learning of specialized skills before many adults would expect it to be possible. Later, during the school years, specialized skills may acquire social value because they confer status and respect on a child and help to win friends. A good baseball player usually is in demand, and children who know how to swim are more likely to be invited to swimming parties.

Fine Motor Coordination: The Case of Drawing Skills

Not all motor activities of young children involve the strength, agility, and balance of their whole bodies. Many require the coordination of small movements but not strength. Tying shoelaces calls for such **fine motor coordination;** so do washing hands, buttoning and zipping clothing, eating with a spoon, and turning a doorknob.

One especially widespread fine motor skill among young children is drawing. In North American culture, at least, virtually every young child tries using pens or pencils at some time and often tries other artistic media as well. The scribbles or drawings that result probably serve a number of purposes. At times they may be used mainly for sensory exploration; a child may want to get the feel of paintbrushes or felt-tip pens. At other times, drawings may express thoughts or feelings; a child may suggest this possibility by commenting, "It's a horse, and it's angry." Children's drawings also probably reflect their knowledge of the world, even though they may not yet have the fine motor skills they need to convey their knowledge fully. In other words, children's drawings reveal not only fine motor coordination but also their self-concepts, emotional and social attitudes, and cognitive development.

Drawing shows two overlapping phases of development during the preschool period. From about 2½ to 4 years, children focus on developing nonrepresentational skills, such as scribbling and purposeful drawing of simple shapes and designs. Sometime around age four, they begin attempting to represent objects (Coles, 1992). Yet although representational drawings usually follow nonrepresentational ones, the two types stimulate each other simultaneously. Children often describe their early scribbles as though they referred to real things, and their practice at portraying real objects helps them to further develop their nonrepresentational skills.

Prerepresentational Drawing Around the end of infancy, children begin to scribble. A two-year-old experiments with whatever pen or pencil is available to him, almost regardless of its color or type. In doing so, he behaves like an infant and like a child. As with an infant, his efforts focus primarily on the activity itself: on the motions and sensations of handling a pen or pencil. But like an older child, a two-year-old often cares about the outcome of these activities: "That's a mommy," he says, whether it looks much like one or not. Contrary to a popular view of children's art, even very young children are concerned not only with the process of drawing but with the product as well (Broughton et al., 1996).

A child's interest in the results of her drawing show up in the patterns she imposes on even her earliest scribbles. Sometimes she fills up particular parts of the page quite intentionally—the whole left side, say, or the complete middle third. And she often emphasizes particular categories of strokes: lots of straight diagonals or many counterclockwise loops. Different children select different types of motions for emphasis, so the motions are less like universal stages than like elements of a personal style.

Representational Drawing While preschool children improve their scribbling skills, they also develop an interest in representing people, objects, and events in their drawings. This interest often far precedes their ability to do so. A three-year-old may assign meanings to scribbles or blobs in his drawing; one blob may be "Mama," and another may be "our house." Events may happen to these blobs, too: Mama may be "going to the store" or "looking for me." During the preschool years, and for a long time thereafter, the child's visual representations are limited by his comparatively rudimentary fine motor skills. Apparently he knows more, visually speaking, than his hands can portray with pens or brushes. Figure 8.4 shows this tendency for one particular child, Elizabeth, the daughter of one of the authors. Only as the child reaches school age do her drawings of people become relatively realistic. What happens to drawing skills beyond the preschool years depends on a child's experiences and on the encouragement (or lack thereof) from others. As Figure 8.4 suggests, Elizabeth's drawings in later years became even more realistic—more "photographic" or draftsmanlike in style. But she did not stay with art in the

Skills that require fine motor coordination, like painting, develop through identifiable steps or stages. At first children tend to make random marks or scribbles; later they coordinate these into patterns; still later they become increasingly recognizable as such.

long term. The final picture in the figure (the one from age fourteen) was one of the last she ever made due to the combined influence of competing academic interests, the priorities of friends, and a particular art teacher whom she disliked. We will discuss these sorts of influence again in Chapter 10 in connection with social and motivational changes during middle childhood.

Sex and Gender Differences in Physical Development

As is true during infancy, preschool boys and girls develop at almost exactly the same average rates. This applies to practically any motor skill of which young children are capable, and it applies to both gross and fine motor skills. Any nursery classroom therefore is likely to contain children of both sexes who can run very well and children of both sexes who can paint well or tie their shoelaces without help. This is especially true among younger preschool children (age three or four).

By the time children begin kindergarten (usually at age five), slight gender differences in physical development and motor skills appear, with boys tending to be (slightly) bigger, stronger, and faster (Kalverboer et al., 1993). Yet these differences are noticeable only as averages, and only by basing the averages on very large numbers of children. Despite the slight differences, therefore, more than 95 percent of children are more skillful and bigger than some members of *both* sexes and less skillful and smaller than certain others of both sexes. The small variation in the average makes no practical difference in the everyday lives of most children or in the lives of the teachers and parents who sometimes plan physical activities for them.

Nonetheless, the fact remains that by the time children start school, a few children in any community are bigger, stronger, and faster than *any* other children, and the majority of them are boys. Furthermore, these few individuals may get much more than their share of attention because of their superior physical skills. This contributes to the (mistaken) impression that boys are larger and more skillful than girls in general. In this way (among others), gender stereotypes are born.

As differences in motor skills emerge, they might be more accurately called *gender* differences than *sex* differences, because they probably derive partly from the social roles boys and girls begin learning early in the preschool years. Part of the role differences includes how preschool children spend their time. Preschool boys do spend more time than girls in active and rough-and-tumble play, and girls spend more time doing quiet activities such as drawing or playing with stuffed animals. Children of both sexes, furthermore, reinforce or support one another more for engaging in gender-typed activities (Davies, 1991). These differences create the twin impressions that boys are less capable of fine motor skills and girls are physically weaker, or at least are less inclined toward activities that require strength.

Perhaps such differences develop for some children by the end of the school years simply as a result of differences in practice that have accumulated over a period of years. Perhaps, too, boys choose active play partly for genetic or hormonal reasons. In any event, five-year-olds have only begun to accumulate these differences in motor experience and to make appropriate gender-typed choices in their play. Taken as groups, preschool girls and boys really differ very little.

Individual Variations in Motor Skill Development

Although the preceding sections may have implied that young children acquire motor skills at highly similar rates, in reality they show considerable variability in both fundamental and fine motor skill development. At age three, some children already can walk fast and catch a ball skillfully, but others are still having trouble with both tasks. At age five, some children can use scissors skillfully to cut out shapes for kindergarten art projects, but others still find scissors difficult or even mystifying. Whatever the motor skill, individual children will vary at it.

3 years, 2 months

3 years, 7 months

4 years

4 years, 2 months

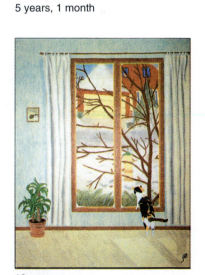

5 years, 1 month

11 years

13 years

FIGURE 8.4

Samples of a Elizabeth's Drawings (Ages Three to Five but also including two later works)

On the average, boys and girls develop motor skills at almost the same rate during the preschool years. But marked differences emerge among individuals within each sex even at this age.

Like other human differences, these probably result from variations in experience, motivation, and biological endowment. Because of family background or preschool educational experiences, some children may be encouraged more than others toward active play; not surprisingly, they develop the skills for active play—such as running, jumping, or throwing—sooner than children whose experience gives less encouragement for active play. Likewise for drawing or other fine motor activities: some children receive more encouragement and opportunity than others. Early successes breed satisfaction with the emerging skills and encourage the development of motivation to develop the initial skills further. Before long, as we saw in the case of gender differences in motor skill development, small initial differences in opportunity and skill become larger differences in skill and motivation.

Biological and genetic background probably also plays a role in motor skill development, although for most children it is hard to sort out how strong these influences are. The most obvious evidence for biological influence—as well as for the ambiguity of its importance—is the experiences of children with physical disabilities. A child born with cerebral palsy (a disorder of the nervous system that impairs motor coordination) may not learn to walk, jump, throw, or draw at the same times or to the same extent as a child who never experiences this condition. Yet contrary to common stereotypes of children with disabilities, the motor development of a child with cerebral palsy is *not* determined solely by the disability; it also depends on the child's opportunities and encouragement to learn new motor skills. The final motor achievements of children with disabilities will show diversity just as the achievements of nonhandicapped peers do, and some of the diversity will be the result of education, not biology (Smith, 1998).

WHAT DO YOU THINK? Suppose you are a child care center worker, and one of your four-year-olds seems especially clumsy at throwing and catching a ball. Should you do something about this, and if so, what should you do? Consult with a few classmates for their opinions. Would you feel the same way if the child seemed clumsy or "uninspired" at drawing?

Effects of Children's Physical Growth

The physical and motor developments that affect a child during the preschool years also affect the adults in the child's life, most notably parents or other caregivers. The changes in the child create, or at least encourage, major changes in how these people deal with him (Luster & Okagaki, 1993). This happens in two ways: through changes in the child's facial features and through changes in his overall size and motor ability.

Changes in Facial Features

From birth—and despite the biases from their own parents—children vary in how attractive their faces seem to adults and other children. As a rule, some individuals look younger than others of the same age. In general, having a young-looking face depends on having large features and a large forehead; that is, facial features should be wide-set and located relatively low on the front of the skull. Even slight changes in these proportions (just a fraction of an inch) can make an adult seem many years older or younger, an infant seem six months older or younger, or a preschooler seem one or two years older or younger.

In general, younger-looking children are also rated as more attractive than older-looking children by both adults and peers, and adults tend to expect more mature behaviors from older-looking children. This coincidence of stereotypes—of youthfulness and attractiveness—may contribute to differences in how parents and other adults respond to preschoolers as individuals. A three-year-old who looks like a four-year-old therefore may be expected to speak more fluently at nursery school or to behave more confidently in new or strange situations, even if the child is not yet ready to do so. Since the child is also more likely to be considered relatively unattractive, there is some risk that a vicious cycle of social interactions will develop: the less attractive child is disliked more to begin with, but disliked even more for failing to do what she supposedly is "able" to do. To overcome this risk, parents and other caregivers need to be made aware of the impact of facial attractiveness, even when the impact stems from innate human reactions to infantile (or babylike) appearance, such as described in Chapter 5 (Macrae et al., 1996).

The new motor skills that preschoolers develop bring new risks and create new safety concerns for parents and other caregivers. What hazards may be waiting for this girl? And how should adults deal with them?

Changes in Size and Motor Skill

Consider the changes in size that preschool children experience. A two-year-old often is still small enough to be handled. When necessary, parents can pick him up and move him from one place to another, physically remove him from danger, and carry him (at least partway) if a distance is too far for him to walk. By age five, the child often has outgrown these physical interactions, not only figuratively but literally. Parents or other adults may still lift and cuddle him sometimes in play or in an emergency, but they probably are beginning to avoid doing so on a regular basis. To a significant extent, the child may now simply be too bulky and tall. More and more rarely can parents save a child from danger by picking him up suddenly or speed him along a long hallway by carrying him piggyback. They must somehow get the child to do these things for himself.

Usually, of course, parents succeed at this task. By age five, a child can think and talk about her own actions much more than before, and these improvements help to guide her own actions. The handling that used to be literal now becomes mostly figurative: now *handling* means negotiating and discussing with the child rather than lifting her up or carting her around.

Improvements in motor skills also change the agenda for a child's daily activities. A two-year-old may spend a good part of his day experimenting with fundamental skills: walking from one room to another, tearing toilet paper to shreds, or taking pots and pans out of a cupboard. These activities often are embedded in an active social and cognitive life: the child may smile (or frown) at his parents while he works and may "talk" about what he is doing as well. But the motor aspects of his

---

TABLE 8.4   Common Accidents, Remedies, and Preventions among Preschoolers

Accidents	What to Do	How to Prevent
Drowning	Unless you are trained in water safety, extend a stick or other device. Use heart massage and mouth-to-mouth breathing when and as long as needed.	Teach children to swim as early in life as possible; supervise children's swim sessions closely; stay in shallow water.
Choking on small objects	If a child is still breathing, do not attempt to remove object; see a doctor instead. If breathing stops, firmly strike child twice on small of back. If this does not help, grab child from behind, put your fist just under his or her ribs, and pull upward sharply several times.	Do not allow children to put small objects in mouth; teach them to eat slowly, taking small bites; forbid vigorous play with objects or food in mouth.
Cuts with serious bleeding	Raise cut above level of heart; apply pressure with cloth or bandage; if necessary, apply pressure to main arteries of limbs.	Remove sharp objects from play areas; insist on shoes wherever ground or floor may contain sharp objects; supervise children's use of knives.
Fractures	Keep injured limb immobile; see a doctor.	Discourage climbing and exploring in dangerous places, such as trees and construction sites; allow bicycles only in safe areas.
Burns	Pour cold water over burned area; keep it clean; then cover with *sterile* bandage. See a doctor if burn is extensive.	Keep matches out of reach of children; keep children well away from fires and hot stoves.
Poisons	On skin or eye, flush with plenty of water; if in stomach, phone poison control center doctor for instructions; induce vomiting only for selected substances.	Keep dangerous substances out of reach of children; throw away poisons when no longer needed. Keep syrup of ipecac in home to induce vomiting, but use *only* if advised by doctor.
Animal bites	Clean and cover with bandage; see a doctor.	Train children when and how to approach family pets; teach them caution in approaching unfamiliar animals.
Insect bites	Remove stinger, if possible; cover with paste of bicarbonate of soda (for bees) or a few drops of vinegar (for wasps and hornets).	Encourage children to recognize and avoid insects that sting, as well as their nests; encourage children to keep calm in presence of stinging insects.
Poisonous plants (e.g., poison ivy)	Remove affected clothing; wash affected skin with strong alkali soap as soon as possible.	Teach children to recognize toxic plants; avoid areas where poisonous plants grow.

Source: Adapted from O'Keefe (1998).

activities absorb a significant part of his attention through-out the day. The child may return repeatedly to a staircase, for instance, as though compelled to get the hang of climb-ing it; no reward needs to lie at the top step except the satis-faction of a job well done.

A two-year-old's parents therefore must spend a lot of time ensuring that the child comes to no physical harm in her motor explorations. They must make sure she does not fall down the stairs, tumble into the toilet bowl, or discover a sharp knife among the pots. Their role as safety experts can dominate their contacts with the child, particularly if she is active.

By the end of the preschool period, minute-to-minute physical surveillance recedes in importance, even though, of course, a concern about safety remains (see Table 8.4 for common accidents and their remedies). Rules about dangers make their appearance ("Don't climb on that fence; it's rick-ety"), along with the hope that a five-year-old can remember and follow the rules at least some of the time. The shift to-ward rules also results from increasing confidence in the child's motor skills. Now parents are apt to believe their child can go up and down stairs without stumbling very of-ten—and they are usually right.

During the preschool period, many parents discover a special need for patience in their dealings with their chil-dren. Simple actions such as tying shoelaces or putting on socks may take longer than before simply because chil-dren now insist on doing many of these things themselves. For similar reasons, walking to the store may now take longer; a three- or four-year-old may prefer to push the stroller rather than ride in it, thus slowing everyone down. And preschoolers may have their own agenda on a walk, such as noticing little rocks on the sidewalk or airplanes in the sky, that differs from parents' goals. On good days these behaviors offer some of the joys of raising children, but on bad days they often irritate even well-meaning parents.

Perfecting new motor skills allows preschoolers to take care of many ac-tions and routines for themselves, when only months earlier they had to be super-vised and assisted. But the resulting inde-pendence can also challenge parents to make sure that children are doing what they now can do.

Physical development changes recreation and play too. At age two, a child prob-ably cannot play baseball; by age five, he may make something of a start at it. At age two, he may enjoy looking at pictures in a book and drawing a few lines of his own; by age five, he may spend long periods making elaborate pictures himself. At age two, he may listen and bounce to music in a general way; by age five, he may swing to it with more refined movements.

These new skills often have teachable elements, and that fact can create new relationships with parents and other caregivers. Now adults can begin showing and encouraging the practice of new skills in a more active, sustained, and focused way than before; in fact, depending on their personal interests and values, they may even feel obligated to do so. Both adult and child may find such teaching and learn-ing easier because the adult no longer has to monitor the child's every fundamental physical action. A few years before, one false step might have made a young child fall. But now this term has a metaphorical meaning. False steps for a five-year-old usually mean mistakes rather than actual physical stumblings. And while a fall may still mean just a physical tumble to a parent, it is also beginning to be experienced as a failure by the child.

WHAT DO YOU THINK ? All things considered, is it more relaxing to be the parent of a preschooler or the parent of an infant? Or are the stresses neither greater nor smaller, but just dif-ferent? This question makes a great topic for a class debate, particularly if you can get a panel of actual parents to judge the success of it afterward!

The Growing Child

As the preceding discussion implies, physical growth gives preschool children many opportunities for increased self-esteem. Now they can walk, skip, and run reliably, whereas before they could only "toddle." Now they can reach for specific objects without fear of breaking, dropping, or crushing them. Now they can write their own names, whereas before they could at most only say them. All these developments, as well as others, give a young child reason to feel proud.

By age five, as long as they have been well supported emotionally, children are firm believers in the value of physical growth. Parents admonish preschoolers to "act like a big boy/girl." Peers emulate older children by showing off their best motor skills to one another—their best ball throws, their best tricks on a swing set at the park, or their best chalk drawings on the sidewalk. "Growing up" becomes a goal, one that more children approach with optimism because the hassles, worries, and limitations of adulthood still seem invisible, incomprehensible, or at least far away. For a number of years longer, many young children concentrate on consolidating their cognitive and social talents because their physical development, for now at least, seems to be both reliable and vigorous.

Yet a child's growth turns out quite differently depending on the circumstances and priorities of the child's parents and community. What seems like a risky behavior to one parent (e.g., climbing up on a large boulder) may seem like constructive skill building to another, with consequent differences in encouragement or prohibitions for the child. What seems like a healthy amount of weight for a child to one parent may seem skinny (or plump) to another, with consequent differences in the parents' unconscious appraisals of the child's attractiveness.

Settings and circumstances matter as well. In families with many children and few adults, child minding may become the responsibility of older siblings as much as (or more than) adults. In extended families—those with nonparental relatives living at home or nearby—child minding may become partly the responsibility of other adult relatives. If parents work (or if a single parent works), relatives or other "caregivers for hire" take on much of the responsibility. All of these circumstances alter the settings in which preschoolers grow up and the relationships that become prominent during early childhood. Some settings may allow the child safer places for physical exploration than do other settings, with fewer worries about safety expressed by caregivers as a result. Some families may include so many children that differences in a particular child's physical appearance matter little simply because caregivers are distributing their attention among many children or activities. Differences like these are very real, and make important differences in the kind of person a child becomes (Canella, 1997). Yet many individual parents and children will scarcely be aware of them or, because of unfamiliarity, hold sketchy, stereotyped impressions of the alternatives. Professionals can help to remedy this problem by learning as much as possible about diversity among children and families, and by sharing that knowledge in appropriate and fair-minded ways.

Summary of Major Ideas

Influences on Normal Physical Development

1. Between ages two and five, growth slows down and children take on more adult bodily proportions.

2. Usually growth is rather smooth during the preschool period. Genetic and ethnic background affect its overall rate, as do the quality of nutrition and children's experiences with illness.

3. Children's appetites often are smaller in the preschool years than in infancy, and preschoolers become more selective about their food preferences.

4. If children fall behind in growth because of poor nutrition or hormonal deficiencies, they often can achieve catch-up growth if slow growth has not been too severe or prolonged.

The Connection Between Health and Poverty

5. A substantial proportion of children, even in well-off countries, live in families with poor access to medical care and therefore experience greater risk of illness and inadequate nutrition.

6. Some of the health risks of poverty can be counteracted by programs aimed at nutrition education and by direct distribution of food to families in need.

Brain Development

7. Although the brain continues to function as a whole, certain areas develop special importance for particular mental and motor functions.

Other Bodily Changes

8. Visual acuity and auditory acuity increase during the preschool period.

9. Children tend to achieve daytime bladder control early in the preschool period and nighttime bladder control late in this period.

Motor Skill Development

10. Preschoolers acquire and refine many fundamental motor skills, including walking, running, jumping, hopping, climbing, throwing, and catching.

11. Adults can teach some motor skills, but many skills seem to develop simply through young children's natural daily experiences.

12. Fine motor skills such as drawing also emerge during the preschool years.

13. Children's drawings begin with scribbles or prerepresentational drawings and later include representational drawings as well.

14. Boys and girls develop almost identical motor skill competence during the preschool years, but social influences lead each gender to practice and improve separate gender-related skills to some extent.

Effects of Children's Physical Growth

15. Between ages two and five, children's increasing physical competence causes parents to monitor their safety in new ways and to make up and revise rules for their children to follow.

16. Preschoolers' increasing physical independence can challenge parents' patience in a variety of situations.

17. In general, children's growth and motor development help them learn about their world and help parents teach their children as well.

18. Preschoolers' physical accomplishments are a source of pride and self-esteem.

19. Diversity in physical circumstances among families accounts for important differences in the long-term development of children.

Key Terms

auditory cortex (244)
Broca's area (244)
catch-up growth (239)
endocrine glands (238)
fine motor coordination (250)
hemispheric lateralization (244)

lateralized behavior (244)
motor cortex (244)
visual cortex (244)
Wernicke's area (244)

CHAPTER 9

Cognitive Development in Early Childhood

Focusing Questions

- What are the special strengths and limitations of preschoolers' thinking?

- How does the language of preschool children differ from that of older children and adults?

- What factors influence pre-school children's language development?

- What is early childhood education like, and how is it influenced by children's cognitive development and by cultural differences?

hile a child is growing physically, another miracle unfolds: when he is just about two years old, he begins representing the world to himself and others in ways that were unknown during infancy. For one thing, he can talk and understand much of other people's speech. "Kitty run!" the boy says, pointing to the neighborhood cat. "Yes," replies his father. "She's chasing a bird." The young boy nods and says, "Bird gone now. Bad kitty?", and looks to his father for confirmation. "It's okay this time," the father says. "The bird flew away soon enough." Unlike an infant, this child does not really need to handle or manipulate the objects he is thinking about. He can comment on the cat even after it has disappeared.

For another thing, this young preschool child can reenact experiences in new and creative ways through make-believe, a form of pretend play in which he simulates people, objects, animals, and activities in his efforts to understand them. The next day, this child may "become" the cat—crouching down, ready to pounce. If asked what he is doing, he will probably know that it is "just pretend." He is not likely to think he has actually become a cat, no matter how convincing his performance. Through make-believe, he is beginning to create and understand symbols.

Although this child's symbolic, or representational, skills still leave much to be desired, they mark a major achievement. In this chapter and the next, we look at several kinds of symbolic skills and at how young children use them. In this chapter we concentrate on thinking, or problem solving, and on early language acquisition. In Chapter 10 we focus on more social activities, such as play, family relationships, and early relationships outside the family. As we will see, these topics are far more inseparable in real life than they are in textbooks.

Thinking in Preschoolers

During the preschool years, young children extend their ability to represent objects and experiences into many new realms of activity and thinking. They begin to notice, for example, that their particular way of viewing the objects across a room differs from the perspective of a family member already sitting on the other side. They begin to distinguish between appearances and reality; that is, when you cover a doll with a costume, it still is "really" the same doll. They even develop implicit theories of how the human mind works: that other minds experience both beliefs and desires, and that people's actions are the joint product of both rather than of just one or the other.

Much of the research on these developments owes its intellectual roots to the observations and theorizing of Jean Piaget. During the 1960s and 1970s, considerable effort went toward testing his ideas about cognitive development. On the whole, the research led first to modifications of, and in some cases challenges to, Piaget's major proposals, such as the existence of comprehensive cognitive stages that unfold in a predictable order or the idea that thinking is really an individual rather than a social activity. To put these later findings in proper context, however, we must first keep in mind Piaget's key ideas about the changes young children experience during the preschool years.

Piaget's Preoperational Stage

At about age two, according to Piaget, children enter a new stage in their cognitive development (Piaget, 1963; Wadsworth, 1996). Infancy has left them with several important accomplishments, such as the belief that objects have a permanent existence and the capacity to set and follow simple goals, such as removing all the clothes from every drawer in the house. Infancy has also left them with the knowledge that of all their senses register the same world; now a child knows that hearing her mother in the next room means the child will probably see her soon and that seeing her probably also means she will hear from her.

The preoperational stage, roughly ages two through seven, extends and transforms these skills. During this stage, children become increasingly proficient at using **symbols,** words or actions that stand for other things. During this period, they also extend their belief in object permanence to include **identities,** or constancies, of many types: a candle remains the same even as it grows shorter from burning, and a flower growing out of the sidewalk remains the same flower even though its growth changes its appearance from day to day.

Preoperational children also sense many **functional relationships,** or variations in their environments that normally occur together. Preschool children usually know that the hungrier they are, the more they will want to eat; the bigger they are, the stronger they tend to be; and the faster they walk, the sooner they will arrive somewhere. Of course, they still do not know the precise functions or relationships in these examples—exactly how *much* faster they will arrive if they walk a particular distance more quickly—but they do know that a relationship exists.

These are all cognitive strengths of preschool children, and they mark cognitive advances over infancy. But as the *pre-* in the term *preoperational* implies, Piaget's original theorizing actually focused on the limitations of young children's thinking relative to that of older, school-age children. The term *operations* referred to mental actions that allow a child to reason about events he or she experiences. Piaget's

• • •

symbol A word, object, or behavior that stands for something else.

identities (1) Piagetian term for the constancy of an object. (2) A unique and relatively stable set of personal characteristics.

functional relationships Variations in an environment that normally occur together.

Preschoolers' play often relies on their growing abilities to represent objects and events symbolically. A sandbox becomes a boat, and a playground becomes the surrounding ocean.

observations suggested that from age two to seven, children often confuse their own points of view with those of other people, cannot classify objects and events logically, and often are misled by single features of their experiences. As later sections of this chapter point out, however, more recent research has substantially qualified this perspective; in essence, it has found that children often are more cognitively astute than Piaget realized. Their specific cognitive skills are all based on a key ability that Piaget *did* recognize: the ability to represent experiences symbolically.

Symbolic Thought

As we just noted, *symbols* are words, objects, or behaviors that stand for something else. They take this role not because of their intrinsic properties but because of the intentions of the people who use them. A drinking straw is just a hollow tube and does not become a symbol until a preschooler places it in the middle of a mound of sand and declares it to be a birthday candle. Likewise, the sound /bahks/ lacks symbolic meaning unless we all agree that it refers to a hollow object with corners: *box*.

Probably the most significant cognitive achievement of the preoperational period is the emergence and elaboration of **symbolic thought,** the ability to think by making one object or action stand for another. Throughout their day, two-year-olds use language symbolically, such as when they say "Milk!" to procure a white, drinkable substance from the refrigerator. They also use symbolic thought in make-believe play by pretending to be people or creatures other than themselves. By about age four, children's symbolic play often combines complex actions (getting down on all fours), objects (using a table napkin for a saddle), language (shouting "Neigh!"), and coordination with others (getting a friend to be a rider).

Symbolic thinking helps preschool children to organize and process what they know (Goldman, 1998; Nelson, 1996). Objects and experiences can be recalled more easily if they have names and compared more easily if the child has concepts that can describe their features. Symbols also help children to communicate what they know to others, even in situations quite different from the experience itself. Having gone to the store, they can convey this experience to others either in words ("I went shopping") or through pretend play ("Let's play store, and I'll be the clerk."). By its nature, communication fosters social relationships among children, but it also fosters cognitive development by allowing individual children to learn from the experiences of others. More precisely, communication allows individuals to learn from the symbolic representations of others' experiences. Not surprisingly, these benefits do not occur all at once. Preschool children need time and practice to hone symbolic skills to high levels of proficiency.

Egocentrism in Preschool Children

Egocentrism refers to the tendency of a person to confuse his or her own point of view and that of another person. The term does not necessarily imply selfishness at the expense of others, but a centering on the self in thinking. Young children often show egocentrism in this sense, but not always. Piaget illustrated their egocentrism by showing children a table on which models of three mountains had been constructed and asking them how a doll would see the three mountains if it sat at various positions around the table. Three-year-olds (the ones in Piaget's preoperational stage) commonly believed the doll saw the layout no differently than they did (Piaget & Inhelder, 1967).

On the other hand, when the task concerns more familiar materials and settings, even preschool children adopt others' spatial perspectives (Steiner, 1987). For example, instead of using Piaget's three-mountain model, suppose we use a "police officer" doll that is searching for a "child" doll and place them among miniature barriers that sometimes obscure the dolls' "view" of each other and sometimes do not. When

• • •

symbolic thought Cognition that makes one object or action stand for another.

egocentrism The inability of a person to distinguish between his or her own point of view and that of another person.

these procedures are followed, four-year-olds have relatively little difficulty knowing when the two dolls can "see" each other and when the barriers truly are "in the way".

In oral communication, preschoolers also show distinct but incomplete egocentrism. A variety of studies have documented that preschoolers often explain tasks rather poorly to others, even though their language and understanding are otherwise skillful enough to explain them better (Nelson, 1996). Copying a simple diagram according to instructions from a preschooler can prove next to impossible, no matter how sensitive the listener is. On the other hand, preschool children do show awareness of the needs of a listener. They explain a drawing more clearly, for example, to a listener who is blindfolded, apparently because the blindfold emphasizes the listener's need for more complete information. And preschoolers show ability to simplify their language when speaking to an infant—a cruder version of *infant-directed speech* used by parents and described later in this chapter (Messer, 1994).

In these studies, young children show both similarity to and difference from the adults they will become. All of us, young or old, show egocentrism at times; indeed, our own thinking often is the only framework on which we can base our actions and conversations with others, at least initially. As we mature, though, we learn more about others' thoughts, views, and feelings, as well as more about how to express ourselves more precisely. In these ways, we (hopefully!) differ from four-year-olds.

Children's Theories of Mind

As part of their growing symbolic abilities, preschool children develop ideas about how thinking itself occurs and how thinking leads to action in everyday activities. These ideas often are called a **theory of mind,** a stable, though informal framework with which to understand others' beliefs and desires and to predict their actions (Carruthers & Smith, 1996). Unlike truly scientific theories, a child's theory of mind is not based on systematic experimentation, nor are the terms in it defined as carefully. But a child's theory of mind shares important characteristics with any scientific theory. It contains a core of key ideas that are relatively resistant to change or disproof, as well as other ideas that are more peripheral and more subject to change as a result of experience. For example, a core idea of a child's theory of mind might be that people *have* ideas, beliefs, and desires, and these are fundamentally more intangible than everyday objects: the thought of a dog is intangible, even though the dog itself is very tangible. A peripheral idea—one subject to disproof by experience—might be that the thought of a dog necessarily leads a person to seek out a real, live dog to play with.

Considerable evidence exists that preschool children have a simple "theory" of mind in the sense just described. They clearly understand that other people have thoughts and feelings and that these mental entities are distinct from the reality of everyday objects. In one experiment, investigators asked three- and four-year-olds several versions of the following story (Bartsch & Wellman, 1995):

> Sam wants to find his puppy. It might be hiding in the garage or under the porch. Sam thinks his puppy is under the porch. Where will Sam look for his puppy—in the garage or under the porch?

In some versions, the story mentioned only where the puppy was *not* (i.e., not in the garage); in others, it mentioned that Sam changed his mind ("his mother tells Sam that she saw the puppy in the garage"); in still others, the investigators first asked the child where *she* thought the puppy was, and then she described Sam as thinking the puppy was in the opposite place. In all of these versions, children performed extremely well—with 85 to 90 percent accuracy—suggesting that they knew the only relevant consideration in solving the problem is what was in Sam's mind. It was not relevant, for example, whether the child being interviewed believed the puppy was in a particular place.

• • •

theory of mind Coherent, theory-like beliefs about how human thinking occurs that develop during the first few years of life.

On the basis of this study and others, Henry Wellman proposed a basic *belief-desire psychology* for young (three-year-old) preschoolers (Wellman, 1990). In this theory of mind, the child distinguishes between beliefs (what you know or think) and desires (what you want), and distinguishes both of these from actions (what you do). As children grow older, they elaborate on this basic, informal psychology by adding other sorts of mental entities—emotions that influence thinking, such as boredom or fear—to their theories of mind. The elaborations allow older preschoolers to solve problems that would be beyond the understanding of three-year-olds.

One such problem is the **false-belief task,** in which the child is expected to know how a person would respond despite having false or incorrect information (Olver & Ratner, 1994). A relatively basic false-belief task would pose the problem of misinformation explicitly: "Jane wants to find her kitten. Jane's kitten is really in the playroom, but Jane thinks her kitten is in the kitchen. Where will Jane look for her kitten? Where is the kitten really?" Another version might only imply that Jane is mistaken, for example, by having her mother move the kitten without Jane's knowledge. In either version, however, this problem proves very hard for three-year-olds: they consistently think Jane will look where the kitten *really* is rather than where she *thinks* it is. Not until age five do children solve the problem with a high degree of accuracy.

Why should children need this extra maturity? One possibility is that preschoolers' theories of mind are not fully elaborated; a preschooler may know that thoughts exist, but does not yet appreciate their consequences for behavior (Flavell et al., 1995). Another explanation is that false-belief tasks make heavy demands on cognition: the child must attend not only to where the kitten *really* is but also to where Jane *thinks* it is. This relatively complicated task is sometimes called **metacognition,** meaning an ability to "think about thinking," and it takes many years to develop fully.

The Appearance-Reality Distinction

One result of developing a theory of mind is that preschoolers gradually realize that things are not always what they seem to be. This realization is the **appearance-reality distinction:** a knowledge of when and why an object looks different than it "really and truly" is. This concept is surprisingly difficult for many three-year-olds but very easy for most six-year-olds.

In one of many experiments to investigate this ability, three-year-olds were shown a cutout of an animal, such as a pink-colored seal; then the investigators slid a green filter over the cutout. They asked the children, "What color does the seal look like now? Is it really and truly green?" More than half of the children answered the second question incorrectly; they knew the seal had changed color, but claimed it was "really" green. In another part of the experiment, the investigators showed objects that looked exactly like another object, such as an eraser that was shaped and painted to look like a banana. They asked, "Does it look like an eraser or a banana? Is it really an eraser or a banana?" On this task, three-year-olds over-identified with reality: they knew the object was really an eraser, but they now denied that it looked like a banana.

In general, three-year-olds seem unable to hold *both* the appearance and the reality of an object in mind at the same time. Interestingly, they find it much easier to make distinctions between pretense and reality (Harris & Kavanaugh, 1993). Suppose an investigator asks a child to pretend that a seal is "really" a different color or that a string is "really" a snake. When questioned about these pretenses, the child clearly distinguishes between the real color of the seal and its pretend color, and between the real string and the pretend snake. The reason for the greater success in identifying pretense is not clear, but it may be related to engaging in make-believe play, an almost universal activity during early childhood. Distinguishing appearance

false-belief task A type of research design that tests children's awareness of the difference between what they know and what other persons might believe.

metacognition Knowledge and thinking about cognition, how learning and memory operate in everyday situations, and how one can improve cognitive performance.

appearance-reality distinctions The ability to distinguish apparent perceptions from real qualities of objects; acquired during the preschool period.

from reality, on the other hand, requires developing the additional knowledge of the nature of false beliefs.

Other Aspects of Children's Conceptual Development

In addition to the concepts described in the previous sections, preschool children develop specific cognitive skills as a result of their growing symbolic ability. As Piaget originally pointed out, for example, they become able to classify objects, and by the end of the preschool period some can even attend to changes in objects involving more than one feature at a time. They move beyond rote counting to a meaningful understanding of the concept of *number*. They also acquire an intuitive sense of the differences among fundamentally different types of concepts, such as the difference between a living dog and a toy robot made to act like a dog.

Classification Skills   **Classification** refers to the placement of objects in groups or categories according to some specific standards or criteria. Young preschool children, even those just three years old, can reliably classify objects that differ in only one dimension, or feature, especially if that dimension presents fairly obvious contrasts. Given a collection of pennies and nickels, a preschooler usually can sort them by color, which is their most obvious dimension of difference. Given a boxful of silverware, a young child might sort the items by type: knives, forks, and spoons. Or she might group dishes by how they are used in real life, putting each cup with one saucer rather than separating all the cups from all the saucers. These simple groupings represent cognitive advances over infancy. Later, during middle childhood, she will become able to group objects by more than one dimension at the same time. But that will be later.

Reversibility and Conservation   Some classification problems require **reversibility** in thinking, or the ability to undo a problem mentally and go back to its beginning. If you accidentally drop a pile of papers on the floor, you may be annoyed, but you know that in principle the papers are all there: you believe (correctly) that the papers that have scattered can be "unscattered" if you pick them up and sort them into their correct order again. Reversibility, it turns out, contributes to a major cognitive achievement of middle childhood: **conservation,** or the ability to perceive that certain properties of an object remain the same, or constant, despite changes in the object's appearance. On average, children do not achieve conservation until about age six.

To understand reversibility and conservation, consider the following task. First, you show a preschool child two tall glasses with exactly the same amount of water in

classification Putting objects in groups or categories according to some set of standards or criteria.

reversibility Piaget's term for the ability to undo a problem mentally and go back to its beginning.

conservation A belief that certain properties (such as quantity) remain constant despite changes in perceived features such as dimensions, position, and shape.

FIGURE 9.1

Conservation of Liquid Quantity

Does a child believe liquid quantity remains constant (is "conserved") despite changes in its shape? The method illustrated here, or some variation of it, is often used to answer this question. Several additional conservation experiments are illustrated and discussed in Chapter 12 (see Figure 12.1).

First, you show a preschool child two tall glasses with exactly the same amount of water in each.

Then the child watches you pour the water from one of the glasses into a third, wide glass.

Finally, you ask the child, "Is there more water in the wide glass than in the (remaining) tall glass, or less, or just as much?"

A child who lacks reversibility (is non-conserving) in thinking about liquids says either, "The tall glass has more," or "The wide glass has more." She is fooled by its appearance.

each (see Figure 9.1). Then the child watches you pour the water from one of the glasses into a third, wide glass. Naturally, the water line in the wide glass will be lower than it was in the tall one. Finally, you ask the child, "Is there more water in the wide glass than in the [remaining] tall glass, or less, or just as much?"

Children less than five years old typically say that the tall glass has either less or more water than the wide glass, but not that the two glasses are the same. According to Piaget, this happens because the child forgets the identity of the water levels that he saw only a moment earlier; in this sense, he is a nonreversible thinker and cannot imagine pouring the water back again to prove the glasses' equality. Instead he is limited to current appearances. More often than not, a big difference in appearance leads him to say that the amount of water changes as a result of its being poured. In Piagetian terms, he fails to conserve, or believe in the constancy of the amount of liquid despite its visible changes (Inhelder & Piaget, 1958). Not until the early school years do conservation and reversibility become firmly established.

In the meantime, tasks that require conservation are affected significantly by how they are presented or described to the child. When given a series of conservation tasks, for example, a child tends to alternate conserving with nonconserving responses (Elbers et al., 1991). Why? Perhaps repeating the question makes some children believe the experimenter wants them to change their response; after all, why else would she repeat herself? Because most children begin the conservation task by agreeing that the glasses hold equal amounts of water, obliging children may feel compelled to give nonconserving responses against their own better judgment. It seems, therefore, that children may take Piagetian tasks as social events as well as cognitive ones.

The Concept of Number   Like many parents, Piaget correctly noted that children do not fully grasp how the conventional number system works during the first few years of life (Piaget, 1952). Preschoolers may, of course, count, such as when a three-year-old says, "One, two, three, blast off!" before tossing a ball high into the air. But such counting, Piaget argued, lacks understanding; it essentially is a rote activity. To fully understand number, a child must comprehend three ideas. The first is that a one-to-one correspondence exists among items in a set and number names; the second is *cardinality*, the idea that the total number of a set corresponds to the last number named when the items are counted; and the third is *ordinality*, the concept that numbers always occur in a particular order (the second item to be counted is always called the "second," for example).

Research stimulated by these ideas about number generally has concluded that Piaget underestimated preschoolers' knowledge of number. Many four-year-olds, and even some three-year-olds, can reliably say the numbers in sequence, at least up to some modest limit such as *five* or *six*. They also know that different sets of items should be counted with the same sequence of numbers, that each item should be counted only once, and that any set can be counted in more than one order. For this and other reasons, some psychologists have argued that children may have an innate conception of number, or at least that they can learn underlying notions of number from appropriate experiences during infancy (Case, 1998; Kirschner, 1997).

This evidence is persuasive, but it may not justify concluding that number knowledge is innate. Experiments by Karen Wynn (1990) suggest that children as young as three years understand something of the notion of numerosity—that numbers refer to specific amounts. In one study, a three-year-old was shown pairs of pictures, each portraying a different number of animals. In one pair, one picture showed a single animal and the second showed several (such as five); in the other pair, one picture showed exactly one *more* animal than in the other picture (such as five in one picture and six in the other). The procedure is illustrated in Figure 9.2. For both pairs of pictures, children were asked to point to the picture that showed a particular number ("Can you show me the five animals?").

This procedure produced several interesting results. First, even three-year-olds who could count had trouble choosing between the pictures that were closely matched in numerosity; choosing between five animals and six animals, for example, was difficult, even for children who could count to six or beyond. On the other hand, the same three-year-olds reliably identified which picture had "more" when several animals were paired with just a single animal; choosing between five animals and one animal, for example, was relatively easy. Only older preschoolers (four years and up) could reliably choose "more" when the numbers were very close, and when they did so, they tended to solve them for *all* possible numbers rather than for only selected numbers. A four-year-old who could point to six animals instead of five, for example, was likely to also point correctly to seven instead of eight or four instead of five.

These results imply that young children first acquire a general notion of numerosity whether or not they can count yet. They also suggest that it takes a relatively long time—about a year—to acquire knowledge of precise numerosities (exactly what *five* really means) and that children seem to acquire knowledge of all of these precise numbers at about the same time.

Distinguishing Natural Kinds and Artifacts

Piaget observed that preschool children often express **animism,** the belief that non-living objects are in fact alive or conscious or both. If asked, "Why do the clouds move?", a child might answer, "Because they want to" or "Because the wind tries to move them." Underlying the charm of these remarks is an implication that the clouds and the wind have desires and goals just as people do.

What leads to this sort of behavior? Research has approached this question by reframing Piaget's original observations as a problem concerning how children learn to distinguish between natural kinds and artifacts. **Natural kinds** are things with an intrinsic essence and with origins in other things of the same kind. A cat, for example, is a natural kind because it has an essential "catness," perhaps related to its genetic structure and genetic origins, that still exists even if the cat is painted to look like a skunk. **Artifacts,** on the other hand, are things created and defined by external causes. A hammer is an artifact because it is manufactured to be a hammer; it is not born from a mother and father hammer as a cat is born from a mother and father cat.

How early do children learn to distinguish between natural kinds and artifacts? Is there an early age at which the two concepts are confused or regarded as the same? If so, the confusion may account for some of the animism Piaget observed: if a child calls a small clock a "baby clock" and a large one a "mother clock," for exam-

animism A belief that nonliving objects are alive and human.

natural kind An object that is born from another of the same kind and cannot be constructed artificially from other materials.

artifact A manufactured or humanly crafted object; often distinguished from a "natural kind."

FIGURE 9.2

Judging Numerosity Without Counting

Even when they could count, three-year-olds often failed to identify the picture with only one more item in it. But they could identify the picture that contained many more items.

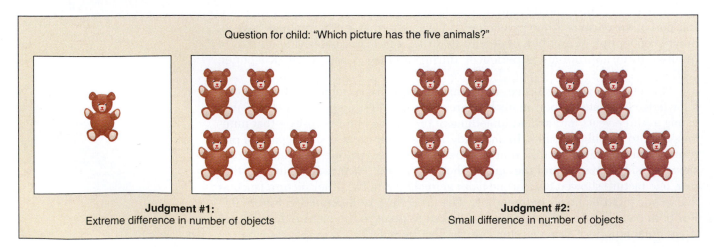

Question for child: "Which picture has the five animals?"

Judgment #1:
Extreme difference in number of objects

Judgment #2:
Small difference in number of objects

FIGURE 9.3

Children's Understanding of Artifacts and Natural Kinds

Children do not clearly distinguish artifacts and natural kinds until well into middle childhood. In the experiment illustrated here, five-year-olds tended to think the animal was still a raccoon, even though its *essential* features were really those of a skunk. Such confusion may contribute to the animism that Piaget observed in young children's thinking.
Source: Adapted from Keil (1989).

ple, she may be on her way to viewing these artifacts as living creatures. Another child who (unfortunately) pulls the wings off an insect out of sheer curiosity may be showing similar confusion: the insect is considered just a "thing"—an artifact.

Research provides some support for these possibilities, though with qualifications. In one series of studies, preschool children confused the truly defining features of natural kinds with more superficial features but seemed to understand the nature of artifacts clearly (Keil, 1989; Keil et al., 1998). Investigators showed children two sets of pictures. One set showed a raccoon and a skunk (see Figure 9.3), and the other showed a coffeepot and a bird feeder that had roughly the same shape as the coffeepot. The investigators showed the raccoon in the first set to children and said, "Some scientists studied this animal very carefully and found that they had the blood of a skunk and that their insides were like a skunk. They also found out that this animal's mommy and daddy were skunks, and when they have babies, the babies will be skunks. What do you think this animal is, a raccoon or a skunk?" Strictly speaking, therefore, the "raccoon" had the defining features of a skunk. Nevertheless, five-year-olds still tended to regard the animal as a raccoon; not until about age nine or ten did children discount its appearance and believe the information in the verbal description qualified the animal to be a skunk. Confusion about what constituted a truly "natural" kind seemed widespread well into middle childhood.

On the other hand, five-year-olds in the same study were clear about what qualified an object to be an artifact. After being told that scientists discovered that the bird feeder had really been made from a coffeepot, all the children asserted that it was nonetheless "really" a bird feeder, not a coffeepot. They did not need five more years of maturity to develop this certainty as they did for the concept of natural kinds.

It is tempting to conclude, as Piaget did, that five- and six-year-olds indeed show animism and that they do so because they find the nature of natural kinds—and especially living creatures—difficult to understand. Young children seem to develop an informal "theory" of natural kinds as early as their third or fourth year. The informal theory grows out of their knowledge of human bodily behaviors and functions, and generalizes to other living creatures: a natural kind is one that (like the child) breathes, eats, sleeps, and the like (Hickling & Gelman, 1995). As their knowledge of human functioning and anatomy increases, a theory develops ("animals are physically like people") that guides their thinking about differences among creatures and between natural kinds and artifacts.

Cognition as Social Activity

Variations in cognitive performance occur partly because young children depend on the social context or circumstances to develop new thinking skills. In spite of our stereotypes of thinking as a solitary, independent activity, children learn not only from interacting with objects and the physical environment but also from interacting with adults or others with more experience. Psychologists who study this sort of thinking often call it **situated cognition,** and call their perspective **social constructivism** (Kirschner & Whitson, 1997; Rogoff et al., 1993). A parent who is cooking dinner, for example, may invite a four-year-old to "help" with preparations, during which the child observes and works on a number of cognitive tasks: measuring amounts for ingredients, sequencing the steps in the preparations, attending to the time needed for each task. Interactions about the tasks being pursued in common form a context, or **activity setting,** for learning (Lave, 1997). In an activity setting, the older or more experienced individual provides problems and activities, as well as tasks, that allow a younger, less experienced person to become a legitimate—though perhaps marginal, or peripheral—participant in the situation. When cooking, for example, the parent determines the menu and in other ways sets the agenda for the activity: "We will make X instead of Y tonight." The parent also provides tasks for the apprentice-cook (in this case, the child) to do. The tasks ensure that the child "belongs" or participates successfully, although they also provide only a marginal role for the child

A lot of cognitive change occurs because of the mutual development of meaning that happens in the "zone of proximal development," where two people focus on a common activity. In this case, the father stimulates his son to learn about the son's growing knowledge and abilities.

at first, in keeping with his immaturity and lack of experience with the challenges of cooking.

Viewed this way, thinking seems far less solitary than Piaget pictured it, and far more social. Children figure things out not by manipulating objects and observing the results of the manipulations but by interacting (in activity settings) with a community of people, including parents, teachers, and peers. In doing so, the young, inexperienced preschooler is able to work on problems or tasks that might prove too difficult to attempt alone; yet the support and guidance of others allow considerable success! The interactions that allow the child to succeed are sometimes called the **zone of proximal development** (or **ZPD**). The concept of the ZPD originated with the Russian psychologist Lev Vygotsky (Newman & Holzman, 1993) and has created a lot of interest among developmental psychologists because it suggests ways in which knowledge and thinking skills may originate and evolve. Consider this conversation between a four-year-old girl and her grandfather while the two of them sort some scrap lumber piled behind the grandfather's hardware business:

GRANDFATHER: We have to put the spruce here and the pine over there.

GIRL: Spruce here? *(Tosses one piece, but to the wrong pile)*

GRANDFATHER: No, there. *(Moves her piece to the correct pile)*

GIRL: What's this? *(Notices letter S scribbled in pencil on a piece)*

GRANDFATHER: That's for *spruce.* Put it with the spruce.

GIRL: *(Pondering the letter S).* Spruce. I see. *(Tosses piece correctly)* So this must be pine. *(Looks at a piece with a P written on it)*

GRANDFATHER: Yep. Put it over there. *(The two continue sorting for awhile. Girl examines each piece for letters. Eventually she finds one with no letter written on it.)*

GIRL: Someone should write the name on this one. *(Notices a knothole in the piece)* I think it's pine.

GRANDFATHER: You're right about that. Here's a pencil. *(Tosses her a pencil)*

GIRL: *(Writes P on the piece of scrap pine)* Know what? I can write *pine!* *(Smiles)* I bet I can write *spruce,* too.

GRANDFATHER: *(Looks at the letter P she has written)* Yeah, says *pine* all right. You might say it says *pine.*

---

situated cognition Thinking that occurs jointly with others and is embedded in a particular context or activity setting.

social constructivism A theory that views learning as resulting from active dialogue and interaction between an individual and his or her community.

activity settings Group situations in which a shared focus of attention and common goals facilitate learning by an individual from others in the group.

zone of proximal development (ZPD) According to Vygotsky, the level of difficulty at which problems are too hard for children to solve alone but not too hard when given support from adults or more competent peers.

In this example, the grandfather (and his pile of scrap wood) provide an activity setting in which the girl learns about differences between two woods, spruce and pine, as well as a way to represent the differences with letters. Without his presence and comments, she might not have succeeded as well in this task. On the other hand, the grandfather does not simply "teach" the girl how to sort wood or read the letters *S* and *P,* as a teacher might conventionally do in a classroom. Instead he provides a task needed in his world (sorting the scrap wood is part of his business) and a way to involve the girl in the task. The interactions create a zone of proximal development for the girl. When she makes a mistake, the grandfather either simply corrects it matter-of-factly (such as when she tosses a piece in the wrong pile) or revises his own goals temporarily to fit hers (such as when she claims, mistakenly, that she has spelled the whole word *pine* using only its first letter).

As you might suppose, the nature of the ZPD depends on the child's experiences and circumstances. Parents with "bookish" interests, for example, and with the resources and time to provide book-related activity settings will more often provide ZPDs that encourage bookish and school-oriented skills in their children. Those with an outgoing, social disposition will provide ZPDs that encourage interpersonal interest and sensitivity in their children. Yet reproduction of parents' priorities is not inevitable. Much also depends on how a child interprets an activity setting. An opportunity to learn to play the piano, for example, can be experienced as either attractive or boring, or as either an invitation or burdensome drudgery. What is provided is not necessarily what the child takes up or appropriates (Cobb et al., 1997).

Neostructuralist Theories of Cognitive Development

As the studies described so far suggest, preschoolers show considerable new strengths in using symbolic thought. They can take others' perspectives to some extent, they develop a usable theory of how the human mind works, and they can distinguish between appearances and reality at least some of the time. Many of Piaget's classic observations of Swiss children have proven true: preschool children have trouble focusing on two dimensions of an object at once and therefore have difficulty with conservation tasks throughout most of the preschool period. Other Piagetian observations have underestimated children's ability and stimulated research that has led to new ways of thinking about children's capacities. For example, unlike Piaget's claims, preschool children do have a partial understanding of number and can make important distinctions between living and nonliving objects, as shown by the studies about natural kinds.

Strictly speaking, much of the research on children's conceptual development does not really contradict Piaget's general approach; it just complicates our picture of children's cognitive development. Many psychologists have sought to keep Piaget's commitment to stagelike progressions in development and at the same time revise the content or details of those progressions (Case, 1998). Instead of proposing comprehensive, "grand" stages of thinking, as Piaget did, they argue that stages may be much more focused in content. Research based on this premise has in fact identified stages of spatial representation, of mathematical ability, and of interpersonal awareness, among others (Case, 1992). Each of these skills seems to develop through predictable stages, but does so independently of the other domains. As individuals, children therefore show unique patterns and timing of development across many areas of thinking and skills (Wozniak & Fischer, 1993).

This newer view of cognitive stages is sometimes called **neostructuralist** or **neo-Piagetian theory** because of its roots in the ideas of Piaget. As a result of focusing on more specific cognitive achievements, it has also paid more attention to *how,* or by what processes, children acquire new cognitive skills. One neostructuralist line

• • •

neostructuralist (neo-Piagetian) theories Theories of cognitive development that are based on the general notion of stagelike development but focus on more precise areas of thinking and mechanisms of development than Piaget's original theory proposed.

of research explored the process of learning to draw by noting how it consists of the successive coordination of simpler skills (Dennis, 1992). An infant begins his second year of life able to visually track objects as well as reach for objects. With practice, by the time he reaches age three, the child has learned to coordinate these two schemes into a single cognitive skill that enables scribbling. As the child continues to practice with this newly consolidated scheme, he begins coordinating it with other, more advanced schemes, such as *comparing* scribbles with the orientation and edges of the paper. When tracking edges of a paper and tracking scribbles eventually become coordinated, the child can finally begin controlling lines and curves. Now the stage is set for his first representational drawings, such as stick-figure people.

From the neostructuralist perspective, then, cognitive development during the preschool years is not all of one piece when it unfolds but has many components—many forms of thinking, as well as perceptual and language developments. As a result, it is important to understand each piece separately from the others and to combine them to get a well-rounded picture of young children. Therefore, in the next section we look at another major piece of the puzzle of children's thinking: language acquisition.

WHAT DO YOU THINK ?   What do you think parents of young children *believe* about preschoolers' cognitive abilities? What if you asked them (1) how much their children know when parents are happy or upset and (2) whether children and adults outside the family know when other children are happy or upset? Would parents' beliefs about these questions coincide with the research described in this section? If possible, interview a few real-life parents to test your predictions.

Language Acquisition in Early Childhood

For most children, language expands rapidly after infancy. They learn words, form ever-longer sentences, and engage in increasingly complex dialogue. Fairly early in the preschool years, most children have mastered the basic sounds, or *phonology*, that make their first language meaningful and distinctive. They have also made a good beginning at acquiring a vocabulary of single words. We described both of these achievements in Chapter 4, in connection with infants' cognitive development. Now, during early childhood, children's most striking achievements involve *syntax*, or the way one organizes utterances, and *pragmatics*, knowledge about how to adjust utterances to the needs and expectations of different situations and speakers. As it turns out, these twin achievements show both diversity and uniformity among children, and therefore they raise important questions about language acquisition and about how parents and caregivers can influence it. In this section we look at these questions, beginning with preschoolers' achievements in the area of syntax.

The Nature of Syntax

The **syntax** of a language is a group of rules for ordering and relating its elements. Linguists call the elements of language *morphemes*. **Morphemes** are the smallest meaningful units of language; they include words as well as a number of prefixes and suffixes that carry meaning (the /s/ in *houses* or the /re/ in *redo*) and verb-tense modifiers (the /ing/ in *going*).

Syntactic rules operate on morphemes in several ways. Sometimes they mark important relationships between large classes or groups of words. Consider these two pairs of sentences:

syntax The organizational rules of words and phrases in a language; its grammar.

morphemes The smallest meaningful units of language; include words as well as a number of prefixes and suffixes that carry meaning.

1a. John kissed Barbara *and*   2a. Frank kisses Joan.

1b. Barbara kissed John.   2b. Frank kissed Joan.

These sentences differ in meaning because of syntactic rules. In the first pair, a rule about the order, or sequence, of words tells us who is giving the kiss and who is receiving it: the name preceding the verb is the agent (the kisser), and the name following the verb is the recipient (the "kissee"). In the second pair, the morphemes /es/ and /ed/ tell something about when the event occurred; adding /es/ to the end of the word signifies that it is happening now, but adding /ed/ means it happened in the past. These rules, and many similar ones, are understood and used by all competent speakers of the language. Unlike textbook authors, however, the speakers may never state them and may be only barely aware of them.

Syntactic rules vary in how regular or general they are. Most apply to large, open-ended groupings or classes of words. This quality makes them **generative;** that is, speakers can create or generate brand-new sentences almost infinitely by applying the rule to brand-new morphemes. The preceding examples are generative in this sense. Replacing *John* with *fish*, for example, and *Barbara* with *water* creates the strange sentence "Fish kissed water." This sentence may sound odd, but it nevertheless conveys some idea of who was doing the kissing and who was receiving it. Even nonsense words can fit into the same syntactic framework: "Gokems kissed splibs." We may have no idea of who (or what) *gokems* and *splibs* are, but the syntax of the sentence still tells us which was the kisser and which the kissee. To this extent, the syntax conveys meaning independently of the words slotted into the sentence form.

Unfortunately for a child learning to talk, some syntactic rules have only a small range of application, and still others have irregular exceptions. Most words, for example, signal pluralization (the existence of more than one) by having an /s/ or /es/ added at the end; *book* means one volume, and *books* means more than one. But a few words use other methods to signal the plural. *Foot* means one, and *feet*, not *foots*, means more than one; *child* means one and *children* more than one; and *deer* can mean either one animal or several.

Thus, in acquiring syntax, a young child confronts a mixed system of rules. Some apply widely and regularly, and others apply narrowly and exceptionally. Added to these complexities is the fact that the child often hears utterances that are grammatically incomplete or even incorrect. Somehow he or she must sort these out from the grammatically acceptable utterances while at the same time trying to sort out the various syntactic rules and the contexts for using them. On the face of it, the child's task seems daunting; yet somehow most children manage it within a few years' time. Their success makes a powerful argument that human beings are innately predisposed to acquire language. No other cognitive task is achieved with so little deliberate effort or direct teaching in such a short time, either during early childhood or in any other period of life.

Beyond First Words: Semantic and Syntactic Relations

Before age two, children begin linking words when they speak. Initially the words seem to be connected by their *semantic relations*, or the meanings intended for them, rather than by *syntactic relations*, the relations among grammatical classes of words such as nouns, verbs, and adjectives. This is particularly true when the child is still speaking primarily in two-word utterances (sometimes called **duos**). As

In addition to learning how language is structured, preschoolers acquire skill with communication, or how language is used. In discussing their picture books, for example, these children are practicing not only vocabulary and grammar but also how to have a conversation.

• • •

generative rules Syntactic rules that allow speakers to generate new sentences almost infinitely by applying them to new morphemes.

duo A two-word utterance.

TABLE 9.1   Semantic Relations in Two-Word Utterances

Relationship	Example
Agent + action	Baby cry
Action + object	Eat cookie
Agent + object	Bobby cookie
Action + locative (location)	Jump stair
Object + locative	Teddy bed
Possessor + possessed	Mommy sandwich
Attribute + object	Big dog
Demonstrative + object	There Daddy

A child's earliest utterances are organized not according to adultlike grammar but according to particular semantic or meaning-oriented relationships such as those listed in this table. Often the intended, underlying relationships are ambiguous and can be discerned only by an attentive, observant adult at the time of the utterance.

the mean length of a child's utterances increases to three words and more, syntactic relations become much more noticeable.

Duos and Telegraphic Speech   These ideas were documented in a classic set of three case studies of early language acquisition by Roger Brown (1973). When the children Brown observed were still speaking primarily in two-word utterances, their utterances were organized around eight possible semantic relationships; these are listed in Table 9.1, along with examples. The meanings of the utterances were determined by the intended relationships among the words, and the intentions of the preschool speakers often were discernible only by observing the context in which the utterances were made. "Mommy sandwich" could mean "the type of sandwich Mommy usually eats," or "Mommy is eating the sandwich," or "Mommy, give me a sandwich," all depending on the conversational context.

The reason for the ambiguity is that two-word utterances leave out indicators of syntactic relationships. One syntactic indicator is word order: due to word order, "the boy chased the girl" means something different than "the girl chased the boy." Children who still speak in duos do not use word order randomly, but they do tend to be less predictable about it than more linguistically mature children, whose utterances can be several words long. Another indicator of syntactic relationships is inflections, prepositions, and conjunctions. An older child will add *'s* to indicate possession (as in "Mommy's sandwich") and use words such as *in* and *on* to indicate location (as in "jump on the stair"). Leaving these indicators out makes the speech sound stilted and ambiguous; therefore, it is also called **holographic speech** or **telegraphic speech,** presumably because it sounds like a telegram. Telegraphic speech is characteristic of children's first efforts to combine words (around eighteen months to two years), but it can persist well after children begin using longer, more syntactic utterances some of the time.

Regularities and Overgeneralizations   After highly individualized beginnings, certain aspects of syntax develop in universal and predictable patterns. The present progressive form *-ing* occurs quite early in most children's language, the regular plural morphemes *-s* and *-es* somewhat later, and articles such as *the* and *a* still later (Marcus et al., 1992).

At a slightly older age, most children begin using auxiliary verbs to form questions, but they do so without inverting word order, as adults normally do. At first, a child will say, "Why you are cooking?" and only later "Why are you cooking?" This suggests that language acquisition involves more than just copying adult language; after all, adults rarely model incorrect forms. To a certain extent, children's language seems to compromise between the new forms children hear and old forms they already can produce easily.

Sometimes, in fact, early syntax becomes *too* regular, and children make **overgeneralizations.** Around age three, a preschool child may say, "I runned to the store" or "All the childs came." In each case, the child uses the wrong but more regular form as opposed to the correct but irregular forms of an earlier age. Usually, by early school age he shifts back again, although not necessarily because anyone teaches him or forces him to do so. Apparently his overgeneralizations represent efforts to try out new rules of syntax that he has finally noticed.

The Predisposition to Infer Grammar   Research confirms what these examples suggest: that young children seem to infer grammatical relationships rather than simply copy others' speech (Marcus et al., 1992). Few parents try purposely to teach talking, and those who do usually discover that direct efforts tend to fail.

holographic speech Early one- or two-word utterances that serve the function of entire sentences at later stages of language acquisition; also called *telegraphic speech.*

telegraphic speech See *holographic speech.*

overgeneralizations Utterances in which a child shifts from using correct but irregular forms to using wrong but more regular forms; represent efforts to try out newly noticed rules of syntax.

Consider this example:

CHILD: My teacher holded the rabbits, and we patted them.

MOTHER: Did you say your teacher held the baby rabbits?

CHILD: Yes.

MOTHER: What did you say she did?

CHILD: She holded the rabbits, and we patted them.

MOTHER: Did you say she held them tightly?

CHILD: No, she holded them loosely.

Despite her mother's apparently unsuccessful attempt to encourage adult grammar in this situation, the child almost certainly will switch from *holded* to *held* eventually. The child, not the adults around her, seems to control the timing of this change; she, not her mother, must solve the grammatical puzzles posed by language.

A classic study of early syntax showed the importance of the child's own inferences about grammatical rules. Instead of asking children about real words, the experimenter showed them pictures of imaginary creatures and actions that had nonsense words as names (Berko, 1958). With one picture, a child was told, "Here is a wug." Then he was shown two pictures and told, "Here are two of them. Here are two ——." Most children, even those as young as 2½, completed the sentences with the grammatically correct word, *wugs*. Because they could not possibly have heard the term before, they must have applied a general rule for forming plurals, one that did not depend on copying any language experiences specifically but came from inferring the underlying structure of many experiences taken together. The rule most likely operated unconsciously, because these children were very young indeed. The tendency to infer and apply grammatical rules is robust (or reliable) enough that it forms the basis for many current tests of children's language development (McDaniel et al., 1996).

The Limits of Learning Rules   Such skill at acquiring syntactic rules, however, obscures a seemingly contradictory fact about the acquisition of syntax: much syntax must be learned by rote. As we have pointed out, most children use irregular forms (such as *foot/feet*) correctly before they shift to incorrect but more regular forms. The most reasonable explanation for the change is that they pick up the very first sentence forms simply by copying, word for word, the sentences they hear spoken. Presumably they copy many regular forms by rote, too, but the very regularity of these forms hides the haphazard, unthinking way in which children acquire them.

"We don't say 'I losed my dime.' We say 'I LOSTED it.'"

As children acquire language, they sometimes overregularize their grammar, as the girl in the cartoon is doing by insisting that *-ed* be added to make the past tense. Since errors like this are never (or only rarely) spoken by adults, they suggest that children actively—though unconsciously —search for grammatical rules or syntax of language.

"I runned to the store."

"Unpour the water, please."

"All the childs came!"

Although children eventually rely on rule-governed syntax, they probably still learn a lot of language by rote. Many expressions in a language are *idiomatic,* meaning they bear no logical relation to normal meanings or syntax. The sentence "How do you do?", for example, usually is not a literal inquiry as to how a person performs a certain action; and the sentence "How goes it?", meaning "How is it going?", does not even follow the usual rules of grammar. Because words and phrases such as these violate the rules of syntax and meaning, children must learn them one at a time.

Mechanisms of Language Acquisition

Exactly how do children learn to speak? For most children, several factors may operate at once. In general, current evidence can best be summarized as follows: language seems to grow through the interaction of an active, thinking child with certain key people and linguistic experiences. The preceding sections describe in part this active, thinking child; the following sections describe some possible key interaction experiences.

Reinforcement   A commonsense view, one based essentially on behaviorist principles, is that children learn to speak through reinforcement. According to this idea, a child's caregiver reinforces vocal noises whenever they approximate a genuine word or utterance, and this reinforcement causes the child to vocalize in increasingly correct (or at least adultlike) ways (Skinner, 1957). In the course of babbling, an infant may happen to say "Ma-ma-ma-ma," to which his proud parent smiles and replies cheerfully, "How nice! You said 'Mama'!" The praise reinforces the behavior, so the infant says "Ma-ma-ma-ma" more often after that. After many such experiences, his parent begins to reinforce only closer approximations to *mama,* leading finally to a true version of this word.

Among preschool children, the same process could occur if parents reinforced correct grammatical forms and ignored or criticized errors or relatively immature utterances. Parents might respond more positively to the sentence "I have three feet" than to the sentence "I have two foots." According to the principles of reinforcement (see Chapter 2), the child would tend not only to use the correct version more often but also to generalize the correct elements of this sentence to other, similar utterances.

Analysis of conversations between parents and children confirms this possibility, at least in indirect form and for the early stages of language acquisition. One study compared parents' responses to simple but grammatical sentences made by their two- and three-year-old children to their responses to ungrammatical utterances (Penner, 1987). Parents did not correct their children's grammar directly, but they were more likely to elaborate on the child's topic if the utterance was a grammatical one. The tendency was most pronounced, however, when preschoolers were just beginning to use syntactic forms, speaking in sentences that vacillated between two and three words in length rather than in much longer sentences. Other research has documented that these elaborations seem to involve a two-way influence (Moerk, 1992): on the one hand, the child speaks more as a result of the parent's elaborations; on the other, the parent is more likely to fine-tune his or her own utterances to match the child's growing syntactic skills.

Imitation and Practice   In some sense, children obviously must imitate their native language to acquire it. This is an idea borrowed from the social learning variety of behaviorism. In daily life, though, the process of imitation is subtle and often indirect. Children do not imitate everything they hear, but most copy certain selected utterances, often immediately after hearing them. Sometimes the utterances chosen for imitation involve familiar sentence forms that contain new, untried terms, and sometimes they contain familiar terms cast into new, untried forms. The imi-

A lot of learning happens through imitation and practice. One of these boys sees and practices the reading and social skills demonstrated by his grandfather. The other sees and practices cooking skills demonstrated by his mother.

tated terms and forms return later in the child's spontaneous speech. At first these utterances resemble the rote learning mentioned earlier, and they seem to help the child by emphasizing or calling attention to new morphemes and syntax.

The following four-year-old child had never before heard the form -*ish*, meaning "something similar to":

FATHER: We need to paint the fence soon. Maybe a kind of brownish-red.

CHILD (*Pauses, listening*): Brownish-red. What's brownish-red?

FATHER: It's what you get when you mix brown and red. Brownish-red, or reddish-brown, or brownish-reddish.

CHILD (*Smiles and pauses again*): Brownish-red. Brownish-red.

Imitation may also help children acquire language by initiating playful practice with new expressions. The child in essence plays around with the new forms she learns and in doing so consolidates her recently acquired knowledge, just as she does in other forms of play, such as discussed in Chapter 10. Because quite a bit of language play remains unobserved by adults, its extent is hard to judge, but a lot obviously does go on even in children as young as two years (Messer, 1994). For example, the four-year-old just mentioned was talking to herself a few days later, just before falling asleep at night:

CHILD: You know what you get when you mix blue and red? Bluish-red. Bluish-reddish. Bluish-radish. Reddish, radish. You know what you get when you mix white and red? Whitish-red. Reddish-white. What do you get when you mix white and white? Whitish-white. Whitish-white?

The earlier discussion of colors evidently set the stage for this monologue. At the least, the earlier, imitative encounter helped to call the form -*ish* to the child's attention, and at the most it precipitated practice with this form.

Innate Predisposition to Acquire Language: LAD

The ease and speed children show in acquiring language have caused some linguists and psychologists to conclude that children have an innate predisposition, or built-in tendency, to learn language (Chomsky, 1994). For convenience, the innate tendency is sometimes called the **language acquisition device, or LAD**. According to this viewpoint, LAD functions as a kind of inborn road map to language. It guides the child to choose appropriate syntactic categories as he tries to figure out the comparatively confusing examples of real speech that he ordinarily hears. It helps him find his way through the mazelike structure of language with relatively few major errors instead of having to explore and construct his own language map, as the Piagetian viewpoint implies.

The most persuasive reason for postulating the LAD is the *poverty of content* in the speech to which most infants and preschoolers are exposed. According to this argument, the language children encounter is too incomplete and full of everyday grammatical errors (too "impoverished") to serve as a satisfactory guide in learning the grammatical structure of the language (Baker, 1995). Parents sometimes speak in incomplete sentences, sometimes make grammatical errors, and sometimes do not speak at all when speaking might prove helpful to a child learning the language.

Despite the poverty of content, children seem remarkably resilient about acquiring language. Children isolated from language through parental neglect, for example, have learned some language later in life, but their language usually is limited in amount and complexity. In a less tragic example, identical twins often create a private language that they speak only with each other. In many cases their private language seems to delay normal language development, though the delay rarely causes serious lasting damage to their development (Mogford, 1993).

A final piece of evidence that a LAD exists is that preschool children do not simply copy their parents' language directly, yet they seem to figure out and use many of its basic syntactic relationships remarkably well. The classic "wug" experiment discussed earlier illustrates this ability dramatically. In forming plurals they had never heard spoken before, children suggest that they have a grammatical skill that is more innate than learned.

The Limits of LAD   Although this evidence suggests that children have a built-in ability to acquire language, it does not show that experience plays no role at all. The evidence from twins and neglected children emphasizes just the opposite: that certain experiences with language may be crucial, especially early in life. Ordinarily practically every preschooler encounters these experiences. They may consist of hearing others talk and of being invited to respond to others verbally. But the fact that they happen to everyone does not mean children do not learn from them; it means only that what children learn is universal.

Furthermore, experiences affect the version of language children acquire, even when they supposedly grow up in the same language community. As pointed out earlier, children vary in the vocabulary they learn and in the grammar they use; even by age three or four, children often do not define grammatical categories as abstractly as adults do or necessarily in the same way other children do. Most preschoolers eventually revise their grammatical categories to coincide with conventional adult grammar, thus obscuring their individuality. But as we will see in Chapter 12, large differences persist in older children's styles of communicating, even after children have mastered the basic structure of language.

All things considered, the fairest conclusion we can draw is a moderate one: that children are both predisposed to acquire language and in need of particular experiences with it. Skill with language is neither given at birth nor divorced entirely from other cognitive development. A special talent for language may be given to all normal children, however, and many crucial experiences for developing that talent may happen to occur rather frequently among infants as they grow up.

language acquisition device (LAD) In Chomsky's theory of language development, a term that refers to the innate processes of language acquisition.

Parent-Child Interactions

Certain kinds of verbal interactions apparently help children to acquire language sooner and better. Parents can help by speaking in relatively short sentences to their

A TALK WITH

Audrey, Age Four

Cognitive Development in the Preschool Years

Audrey was interviewed shortly after she returned from her day care center. She asked me to come with her to the porch, where her toys were.

Interviewer: *Audrey, you were saying that you like to eat chicken. What is chicken?*

Audrey: Chicken is animal. And when it's dead it turns into food chicken.

Interviewer: *When it's dead it turns into food?*

Audrey: Yes.

Interviewer: *And then you eat it up?*

Audrey: Yes.

Interviewer: *Where does the food go after you put it in your mouth?*

Audrey: First we put it in the oven.

Interviewer: *And then what?*

Audrey: And then we eat it all up.

Interviewer: *Audrey, you seem to be very big. Are you growing?*

Audrey: Yes, I'm four. First I was one, then I was three, and then four. And now I'm almost five.

Interviewer: *And what happens when you get to be four? Do you get bigger?*

Audrey: Yes. And I get five. You get 1, 2, 3, 4, 5, 6, 7, 8, 9, 10, 11, 12, 13, 14, 15, 16, 17, 18, 19, 20, 21, 22, 23, 24, 25, 26, 27, 28. We die when we get to be thirty.

Interviewer: *We die when we get to be thirty? Why?*

Audrey: 'Cause we're old. We're too much. We're too much numbers.

Interviewer: *Audrey, do you know any stories you can tell me?*

Audrey: No, I can't read stories. I'm going to sing "Somewhere over the Rainbow."

Interviewer: *Okay.*

Audrey (singing): Somewhere, over the rainbow, clouds are blue, and the land that I love, the one thing I love about . . . it's happy little bluebird fly beyond the rainbow, fly away . . . goodbye!

Interviewer: *That was a lovely song.*

Audrey: When am I going to come on the tape recorder?

Interviewer: *You are on the tape recorder. You can see, when the little red light went on, it shows you are on the tape recorder.*

Audrey: When is my voice going to come on it?

Interviewer: *You want to hear your voice?*

Audrey: Yes.

Interviewer: *Okay, I'll turn it off and I'll let you hear yourself, and then we can talk some more. Okay?*

Audrey: Okay. When we turn it off, we can hear my voice gonna come on the tape recorder.

Interviewer: *Now, I'm going to play it back so you can hear your voice. . . . Now I have turned the recorder on again.*

Audrey: I curled my hair today.

Interviewer: *You did? Why did you do that?*

Audrey: Because I wanted a haircut. I got hair in my eye.

Interviewer: *Why are you holding your hair up now?*

Audrey: So it can't get inside my ear.

Interviewer: *Oh, when you put the earphones on to hear yourself on the tape recorder.*

Audrey: So I can hear myself sing "Somewhere over the Rainbow."

Interviewer: *Okay, I'm going to stop the tape recorder now. . . . Now the tape recorder is back on again.*

Audrey: Do you want to see me do letters in Spanish?

Interviewer: *You can do letters in Spanish?*

Audrey: Yes. Uno, dos, tres, quatros, cinquo . . .

Interviewer: *How did you learn to do that?*

Audrey: I didn't. Sammy told me because Sammy can do that.

Interviewer: *And Sammy is your friend.*

Audrey: Yes.

What Do You Think?

1. What specific comments of Audrey are good examples of the characteristics of preschool thinking discussed in this chapter?

2. In what ways are Audrey's comments examples of typical preschooler speech?

3. Why does Audrey seem so un-self-conscious about being tape recorded? How would you interpret her behavior differently if she were equally un-self-conscious as an adult?

preschoolers and using more concrete nouns than pronouns, though this also depends on whether the task or topic at hand calls for concrete or abstract ideas (Hoff-Ginsberg, 1997). In the following pair of comments, the first helps a child learn language more than the second does:

PARENT 1: Take your shoes off. Then put your shoes in the closet. Then come kiss Mama goodnight.

PARENT 2: After you take off your shoes and put them in the closet, come kiss me goodnight.

It can be hard to estimate children's cognitive abilities from their conversations. More often than not, though, parents are apt to overestimate rather than underestimate their children. This bias may indirectly assist the children's further development by leading parents to provide relatively stimulating conversations and tasks.

As we note in Chapter 6, the simplified style of the first set of comments is one aspect of a version of language called **infant-directed speech,** or sometimes "motherese." Another aspect of this version is the use of a high-pitched voice. Infant-directed speech is used intuitively by adults with young children and even by older children with younger children (Messer, 1994).

One of the most helpful kinds of verbal interactions is **recasting** a child's utterances: repeating or reflecting back what the child says, but in slightly altered form. For instance:

CHILD: More milk.

PARENT: You want more milk, do you?

Recasting helps because it highlights slight differences among ways of expressing an idea. In doing so, it may make the child more aware of how she expresses her idea—its form or organization—as well as call attention to the idea itself.

The techniques for stimulating language development have in common the fact that they provide young preschoolers with a framework of language that simultaneously invites them to try new, unfamiliar language forms and simplifies and clarifies other aspects of language. Some psychologists call this framework **scaffolding** (Bruner, 1996; Reeder, 1996); like real scaffolds used in building construction, parents' language scaffolds provide a temporary structure within which young children can build their own language structures. As such, scaffolding functions much like Vygotsky's zone of proximal development mentioned earlier: helpful scaffolding changes and grows in response to the child's continuing development, always building a bit beyond the child's current independent abilities but never very far beyond.

These and similar findings have been translated into curricula for education of young children and even of infants (Spodek & Saracho, 1993). Fortunately, the most useful methods of interaction often are those that parents and teachers use intuitively anyway; training for them therefore really consists of emphasizing and refining their use.

WHAT DO YOU THINK?   Suppose you were asked to speak to a parent group, and a parent complained of her four-year-old's use of poor grammar. What advice could you give to this parent? Rehearse your comments with a classmate to determine how appropriate they are.

infant-directed speech The style or register of speech used by adults and older children when talking with a one- or two-year-old infant.

recasting Rephrasing or restating an utterance expressed by a child; a process thought to encourage language acquisition and development.

scaffolding Providing a framework or cognitive support for a child's learning and thinking.

Language Variations

Not surprisingly, parents vary in how they talk to their children, and these differences may influence the version of language children acquire as they grow up. It is unclear, however, how language variations affect other aspects of children's development, such as thinking ability. Later, in Chapter 12, we discuss variations related to cultural differences—for example, the "Black English" that some African Americans speak in certain situations. First, though, consider three other sources of language variation: gender, socioeconomic status, and hearing impairments.

Gender Differences in Language

Within any one community, girls learn nearly the same syntax boys do, but they acquire very different pragmatics, or discourse patterns. On the whole, the differences reflect society's gender stereotypes. For example, girls phrase requests indirectly more often than boys do; girls more often say, "Could you give that to me?" instead of "Give me that." Also, they more frequently expand on comments made by others rather than initiating their own. These differences appear especially in mixed-gender groups and are noticeable not only in adults but in children as soon as they are old enough to engage in conversation (Coates, 1993). In some Asian societies, these differences are even more marked, resulting in separate female and male speech styles.

The sexes reinforce their language differences with certain nonverbal gestures and mannerisms. Girls and women tend to maintain more eye contact than boys and men do; they blink their eyelids at more irregular intervals and tend to nod their heads as they listen (Arliss, 1991). Boys and men use eye contact a good deal less in ordinary conversation, blink at regular intervals, and rarely nod their heads when listening. When these actions accompany the verbal differences, boys and girls (and men and women) run a distinct risk of misunderstanding each other. A boy talking to a girl may find the girl overly agreeable because she nods her head so much and never changes the subject, whereas a girl talking to a boy may find him self-centered because he seems not to acknowledge her comments and tends to change the topic.

Gender differences in discourse patterns may contribute to gender segregation: members of each sex may feel that members of the other sex do not really understand them, that they do not "speak the same language." Boys and girls therefore begin drifting apart during the preschool years almost as soon as they begin using language (Ramsey, 1995) and as a partial result of acquiring language. The emerging segregation, in turn, reinforces gender differences in language patterns (Fagot, 1994). Boys reinforce one another for their assertive discourse style, and girls and their (mostly female) teachers reinforce one another for their "considerate" style. In the end, then, cognitive development supports social development, and social development supports cognitive development.

Socioeconomic Differences in Language

Most research has found children of low socioeconomic status (SES) to be less skilled in using formal, school-like language than middle- or high-SES children (Heath et al., 1991). In practice, this means low-SES children perform less well in verbal test situations, but outside of those situations their language differences are less clear-cut. These facts have created controversy about the importance of socioeconomic differences in language development.

What is the significance of socioeconomic differences in tests of language development? Some psychologists point out that most tests of language skills favor middle-class versions of English in both vocabulary and style of *discourse*, or conversational patterns (Gopaul-McNicol & Thomas-Presswood, 1998; Miramontes et al., 1997). This bias is due to the content selected for individual test questions and to the ways tests are normally conducted. A question on one of these tests might ask

Introducing Sign Language to Young Children

Carolyn Eaton teaches in a nursery school that serves only children who are deaf or who have moderate or severe hearing impairment. Everyone in the school communicates in American Sign Language (ASL): teachers, the children themselves, and (as much as possible) the parents. When they start the program, the children and parents often know very little ASL.

Kelvin: *How do they acquire this new language? Carolyn talked about some of the ways.*

Carolyn: In a lot of ways the program really looks like any other nursery program, though maybe one with a lot of language emphasis. We always have a theme for the week. That's how we organize the vocabulary, the signs.

Kelvin: *Can you give an example of a theme?*

Carolyn: Last week's theme was "The Three Little Pigs." I told the story in ASL and read a picture book—one of the children had to hold it because I needed two hands to sign with. I emphasized key signs, like the ones for pig and three and the signs for brick, and straw, and house. I invited the children to make those signs with me when I came to them in the story.

Kelvin: *Do you do other things related to the week's theme?*

Carolyn: We'd have other conversations—in ASL, of course—about pigs and animals. And about trusting strangers, for that matter—that's in that story too! We might act out the story at some point, with signs instead of words. It depends partly on the vocabulary and fluency of the children.

Kelvin: *Is it harder to understand preschoolers' signing than adults'?*

Carolyn: It varies with the child, just like oral language. Most three- and four-year-olds tend to use less complex sign vocabulary and simpler expressions than adults. I found it hard at first to simplify my signing appropriately, the way you simplify oral language for young hearing children. There's a signing equivalent of "motherese" that you have to learn, or you won't be understood.

Kelvin: *I noticed a parent today in the class signing to the kids. Does that happen a lot?*

Carolyn: We have a parent volunteer just about every day. Since not all parents can volunteer, we have the kids take home a page each day that describes what's going on in the class and shows drawings of the signs we're currently emphasizing. We encourage the parents to learn them and use them at home. We also run two signing classes for the families of the preschoolers to help them communicate with their signing child.

Kelvin: *Is it hard for them to learn?*

Carolyn: Like everything else, people vary a lot. Some start learning immediately as soon as they learn that their child will always be deaf, and they're fluent by the time the child is a toddler. Others still haven't learned by the time the child is in grade school.

Personally, I think it has a lot to do with how accepting the parents are of the child's hearing impairment. If they're still grieving over the child's loss, they make less progress at ASL.

Kelvin: *Your program does seem language oriented—ASL oriented, that is.*

Carolyn: It really is, though we also deal with all the other stuff that happens to children—friendships among peers, for example. Did you see that argument between two kids that was going on just as you were arriving today?

Kelvin: *It looked fierce, judging by the children's faces. What was it about?*

Carolyn: Well, Billy wrecked a roadway that two other kids had made in the sand table. They were upset, signed Billy to get lost, and that got Billy upset. That's when I stepped in.

Kelvin: *I noticed how intently you were looking at Billy when you gave him a "talking to."*

Carolyn: I sure was—but in all ASL conversations, not just scoldings, you have to look to see the signs. You get good at reading people's moods that way too, especially if you learn signing as early as these children did.

What Do You Think?

1. Judging by Carolyn's comments, how does the acquisition of ASL resemble the acquisition of oral language? How does it differ?

2. Among speech-language pathologists and deaf people generally, there has been heated debate about whether to emphasize ASL experiences, even if they sometimes segregate children from the hearing community, or to emphasize oral language experiences, even if hearing-impaired children have trouble acquiring them. How might you decide between these alternatives? Compare your thoughts on this issue with one or two classmates' thoughts.

children to describe a dishwasher, but few low-SES families own this appliance. Other questions might draw on experiences that only middle-SES children usually enjoy, such as trips on airplanes or visits to museums.

Other psychologists point out that conventional methods of testing are inherently more threatening to low-SES children. For one thing, the people who give such tests (teachers, graduate students) usually have more power and status (John-Steiner et al., 1994). The greater inherent threat of test taking makes some low-SES children more cautious in their responses and hence less verbal. Moreover, some cultures consider it rude to ask questions if one does not understand what to do.

Perhaps most important, middle-SES families use styles of discourse that include many "test" questions, or questions to which parents already and obviously know the answers. At the dinner table, parents may ask their preschooler, "What letter does your name begin with?" even though they already know the answer and their child knows that they know. Exchanges such as these probably prepare young children for similar exchanges on genuine tests by making testing situations seem more natural and homelike.

In contrast, low-SES children more often lack prior experience with "test" question exchanges. They can give relatively elaborate answers to true questions such as "What did you do yesterday morning?" when the adult really does not know the answer. But they tend to fall silent when they suspect the adult already can answer the question (for example, "What are the names of the days of the week?"). Their silence is unfortunate, because rhetorical, or "test," questions become especially common when preschoolers enter school and because active participation in questioning and answering helps preschoolers' learning substantially.

Language of Deaf and Hearing-Impaired Children

Children with hearing impairments often do not develop oral language skills as fully as other children do, but they are quite capable of acquiring a language of gestures called **American Sign Language (ASL).** In fact, language development in ASL children provides much of the reason for considering ASL a true language, one as useful for communication as any verbal language, such as English. In the accompanying "Working With" box, Carolyn Eaton has come to the same conclusion from her work as a preschool teacher of children who are deaf.

What is the basis for considering ASL a language? How can this be so? Signing consists of subtle gestures of the fingers and hands made near the face. In general, each gesture functions like a morpheme. For example, holding the fingers together gently (which signers call a "tapered O") can mean either *home* or *flower,* depending on whether it is placed near the cheek or under the nose. Other sign-morphemes affect the syntax of expressions: gestural equivalents of *-ing* and *-ed.* Individual signs are linked according to syntactic rules, just as in English. After some practice, signers can "speak" (or gesture) as quickly and effortlessly as people who use English can.

What happens to infants and young children with hearing impairments who grow up learning ASL from their parents as their first language? Studies show they experience the same steps in signing development that speaking children do in language development. At about the age when infants begin to babble, signing children begin "babbling" with their hands, making gestures that strongly resemble genuine ASL signs but that signers recognize as gestural "nonsense" (Marschark, 1993). As with verbal babbling, signing infants apparently engage in gestural babbles playfully when waking up in the morning or going to sleep at night.

When signing infants reach ages two and three, they experience a phase of one-word signing similar to the holophrases described in Chapter 6 and often observed among speaking children. They also experience two-word, telegraphic signing. As with speech, their signs at this point often omit important syntactic gestures and do not follow the usual conventions of word order (or, in this case, signing order) (Bellugi et al., 1993). Signing vocabulary increases rapidly during the early preschool period, in amounts comparable to the increases speaking children experience. Even the kinds of words acquired parallel those speaking children acquire; signing preschoolers tend to learn signs for dynamic, moving objects first, as is true for speaking children.

• • •

American Sign Language (ASL) A system of gestures used in place of oral language by individuals with hearing impairments.

Sign language has the qualities of oral language, including grammar, subtlety, and expressiveness. This mother and child are communicating about the child's day at nursery school. Unfortunately, in hearing communities (such as classrooms), it can be hard to appreciate the capacities of sign language.

Still another reason to consider ASL a true language comes from observations of hearing preschoolers whose parents purposely used both English and ASL during the period when the children normally acquired language (Erting, 1998). During their preschool years, these children became thoroughly bilingual, using ASL and English interchangeably. Especially significant, however, were their patterns of language development, which essentially paralleled those shown by conventionally bilingual children. A clear example concerned vocabulary. Like verbal bilinguals, these children first acquired a single vocabulary that intermingled elements from both ASL and English but included few direct translations. If a child understood and used the sign for "tree," she or he would be unlikely to understand and use the spoken word *tree*. The children eventually acquired translations and thus finally possessed duplicate vocabularies. But acquiring duplicate terms took several years, just as it does for verbally bilingual children.

Language Deficits or Language Differences?

Although we have presented gender differences, socioeconomic differences, and American Sign Language as variations on language development that are equally worthy, society as a whole does not always agree with our assessment. In certain situations, each variation tends to be considered unsatisfactory, and the speaker (or, for ASL, the signer) may be considered deficient in linguistic or cognitive ability. The discourse patterns associated with females are often considered less satisfactory for learning and discussing mathematics, for example, compared to the discourse patterns associated with males (Walkerdine, 1997). In school, therefore, some girls are more likely to be judged less competent in math than they really are. Students with a language background other than English—whether it is Spanish, ASL, or something else—are at risk for being considered "unintelligent" simply because they cannot communicate fluently in the particular kind of language—middle-class oral and written English—that historically has dominated schooling at all levels. Language biases pose a challenge for anyone who works with children professionally (Gopaul-McNicol & Thomas-Presswood, 1998). However, as we will see in Chapter 12, where we look further at bilingualism and its effects, there are ways to overcome language biases and to honor the diversity and talents of all children.

WHAT DO YOU THINK ?   How do you think early childhood teachers should respond to language variety in preschoolers? Should they encourage it, discourage it, or simply accept it? This is an important issue in education and would make for a lively debate in class!

Relationships Between Language and Thought

The variations observed in language suggest a crucial issue: how are language and thought related? Is language just another type of thought or a skill in itself? The close connection between these two activities makes this question important but at the same time hard to answer. If you are talking, chances are you are also thinking (but see the accompanying Perspectives box for an exception); and if you are thinking, you are probably either talking to others or verbalizing inwardly, at least a little.

Despite the potential confusion between these activities, psychologists have often attempted to explain their relationship (Piatelli-Palmarini, 1994). One explanation, often associated with Piaget, emphasizes the importance and priority of action in creating both language and thought. Another, often associated with the psychologists Jerome Bruner and Lev Vygotsky, proposes more equal roles for language and thought in which they develop independently but eventually become interdependent. Let us look briefly at each of these viewpoints.

Piaget: Action as the Basis for Both Language and Thought

Piaget and his supporters argue that action or activity promotes initial language development. Children need to manipulate objects and to have a rich variety of concrete experiences (Piaget & Inhelder, 1971). This idea makes considerable sense to anyone who works with preschool children; such children, for example, often learn the concepts of *heavier* and *lighter* more easily if they have lots of actual experiences with lifting and observing objects of different weights. If young children are taught the definitions of these words without having such experiences, they often just learn the words by rote—presumably an inferior way to learn them.

According to the Piagetian viewpoint, children's language can achieve no greater sophistication or complexity than their general level of cognitive development permits. Cognitive ability consists of several interrelated symbolic skills, such as those described earlier in this chapter. All symbolic skills supposedly develop together, and their mutual dependence results in the general cognitive stages of development described by Piaget. But their mutual dependence also means that language cannot, in principle, become more complex than a child's other symbolic skills. Piagetians and many language specialists point out that language has no priority in the normal timetable of development; for twelve to eighteen months, in fact, an infant obviously thinks with little help from language (Bloom, 1993). When language does appear, it develops in conjunction with other symbolic activities, most notably make-believe and dramatic play. But it does not necessarily lead to or cause these activities.

In most situations, language seems to be both an accompaniment and a stimulus to cognitive development. This girl uses her existing knowledge to tell a story about these dolls, but telling the story also encourages her to think about them in new ways.

Vygotsky: The Gradual Integration of Language and Thought

As plausible as these facts and arguments sound, they ignore important evidence that language can also guide other cognitive developments, including both early sensorimotor development and later symbolic thinking. Three-year-old Paloma seems to talk to herself to improve her sensorimotor skill at making a sand castle:

PALOMA: Now pour this *here*. Now little more. Oops! Too much. No spill. First I clean this up, then start again. Like this. (*Pouring*)

Events such as this led Lev Vygotsky to propose that language and thought develop independently at first, but gradually become integrated with each other sometime during childhood (Vygotsky, 1987; Newman & Holzman, 1993). In his view, early speech is learned with little understanding; toddlers imitate words and grammatical constructions, but with only superficial comprehension of what they hear. At this point in development, toddlers' thinking occurs with little help from language, resembling a sort of mental shorthand.

As two- and three-year-old children acquire more verbal skill, they begin using speech overtly to guide their actions. But this self-guiding speech does not show egocentrism, as Piaget argued, as

PERSPECTIVES

Christopher, the Multilingual Savant: Speaking Without Understanding

• • • • •   Christopher is a striking example of a *savant,* a person with exceptional talent in one area of human functioning but serious limitations in other areas. Christopher's particular talent was languages. He could read English, his first language, by age three (even when printed upside down!) and became able to read and speak two or three foreign languages during elementary school with no explicit tutoring from anyone. As a young adult, Christopher could read, speak, and translate among the following languages with at least some fluency: Danish, Dutch, Finnish, French, German, Greek, Hindi, Italian, Norwegian, Polish, Portugese, Russian, Spanish, Swedish, Turkish, and Welsh.

Yet when observed carefully, Christopher showed many signs that he could not understand most of what he said or read in any language he used (Smith & Tsimpli, 1995). He failed most forms of the false-belief tasks described in this chapter. In one of these tasks, for example, experimenters hid a toy in full view of Christopher and a five-year-old girl. The girl was asked to leave the room and, unbeknownst to her, the toy was moved from one location to another, again in full view of Christopher. Where did Christopher think the *girl* would look for the toy afterward? Christopher responded in the same way a three-year-old might, even when he was an adult: he believed the girl would look in the *new* location, even though it was unknown to her. In essence, Christopher seemed not to understand the question being posed: he did not reflect on the girl's thoughts, as requested.

Christopher also seemed unable to reflect on his own thinking. He was incapable of lying, even in fun, and incapable of either making or understanding remarks that were ironic, sarcastic, or otherwise full of double meanings. In general, meaning one thing and thinking another was impossible. His translations among languages lacked attention to linguistic pragmatics, to the subtleties and social context of communication, even though his vocabulary and syntax were good.

Finally, Christopher failed completely to learn artificial languages that were structured in ways that were logically simple but linguistically unnatural. For example, he failed to learn an artificial language in which negation was indicated by adding a particular word after the *third* word of a sentence, whatever that word happened to be, rather than before or after the verb as in most naturally occurring languages. Even though this language rule is logically simple, and even though Christopher had learned many other languages, he could not learn to use it even haltingly.

Considered together, these observations have important implications for language and cognitive development. First, they provide a partial answer to the relationship between language and thought: it may not be true, as Piaget proposed, that thinking ability must develop prior to linguistic ability. Language may sometimes develop much further than thought. Second, these observations suggest that second languages may be learned differently than first languages. With a first language in particular, a child may be predisposed toward, or "hard-wired" for, acquisition; she or he may possess a language acquisition device (LAD) such as the one proposed by Chomsky (1994). With later languages, however, the child may draw on his or her thinking abilities more fully, comparing vocabulary, syntax, and pragmatics in the new language with these features in the original language (Ellis, 1994). The more underlying parallels that exist between the new language and the old one, the less the child will have to think or reason to acquire it. A child who cannot reason easily therefore will have trouble with an artificial language structured in ways that are uncharacteristic of traditional human languages.

Christopher's story suggests that human intelligence may exist in *modules,* discrete abilities that function somewhat autonomously. An ability to coordinate cognitive modules (language and reasoning) may itself prove to be a type of cognitive module (Gunnar & Maratsos, 1992). For professionals and parents, this may mean discovering those modules for individual children and adjusting expectations to fit the realities of their cognitive "architecture": not every child who is good with words should be expected to be good with reasoning, vice versa.

What Do You Think?

1. If you were a teacher rather than a parent, how much could you support the final conclusion of this box? Should there be a limit on how much teachers should adjust their expectations to the pre-existing strengths of their students? Or should teachers uphold certain standards of success regardless of students' talents and backgrounds?

2. If the story of Christopher suggests that it is possible to speak without understanding, do you think it is possible to understand something without being able to express your understanding verbally? Explain how this might happen and what it might feel like.

3. What other cognitive "modules," or discrete talents, may exist? Music? Drawing? Mathematical skill? Explain why these might (or might not) really constitute talents that can be isolated from other cognitive talents.

much as it shows preschool children's need for external support in solving problems—as Paloma perhaps needs. Paloma had this conversation with her mother at about the same time she built the sand castle:

PALOMA: What's an eggplant?

MOTHER: A purple thing that people eat.

PALOMA: Does it have eggs on it?

MOTHER: No, but it's long like an egg.

PALOMA: *(Pausing)*: When can I see one?

MOTHER: Tomorrow at the store. I'll show you.

In this conversation, Paloma's and her mother's language and thought work together closely, one guiding the other to benefit Paloma's thinking. As she gains maturity, however, Paloma will more often tend to hold such conversations with herself to guide her own thinking. At first these monologues will be spoken out loud, but gradually they will become internalized into a mental dialogue, a term Vygotsky calls **inner speech.**

Inner speech becomes common late in the preschool period and indicates that the child's language and thought have at last become fused, with each guiding the other (Diaz & Berk, 1992). But some situations still prompt their separation. Even adults sometimes use their verbal knowledge to guide further learning when they are not sure of what they are doing. Following the instructions on an income tax form, for example, may prompt considerable overt self-talk ("Add line 23 to line 24 and enter on line 25") to ensure that you truly understand what you are doing.

Whatever their precise relationship, language and thought remain only partly coordinated during the preschool years and especially during the early part of this period. This partial degree of coordination may actually account for some of preschoolers' most delightful qualities: often they can say exactly what they think, even though at other times their verbal comments carry *more* meaning than they realize. "Are you my friend?" asked one four-year-old of a playmate at nursery school. "Yes," replied the other child, "but only until 11:30" (when school ended and she went home). The reply served as a matter-of-fact statement of the extent of the children's friendship. Interpreted from an adult perspective, though, it carries extra meaning, since adult notions of friendship usually assume a continuing relationship, even during absences.

WHAT DO YOU THINK? Do you ever think without talking or talk without thinking? Collect a list of these incidents from yourself and a friend or classmate. What practical implications do such separations of talking and thinking have for professionals (such as teachers) who rely heavily on verbal communication with children?

Early Childhood Education

Developing cognitive skills influence an important experience for many preschool children: early childhood education. Programs for three- and four-year-olds take many forms. Look at these experiences:

- Juan goes to *family day care* for three full days each week. His care occurs in his caregiver's home, with only four other children.

- Denzel goes to a *child care center* full time, five days a week. The center consists of two rooms modified from a church basement. About twenty children attend the center and are cared for by four adults.

- Cary goes to a part-time *nursery school* four mornings per week. There are twelve children and two adults.

● ● ●
inner speech Toddlers' "mental shorthand"; thinking that occurs with little help from language.

Early Education and Cognitive Theories of Development

Despite the diversity these examples imply, high-quality early education programs are usually based on some sort of developmental perspective. Some programs draw heavily on Piaget's ideas about cognitive development, especially that children construct knowledge by interacting with the environment actively (Marlowe, 1998). They provide sensorimotor activities, such as sand and water play, as a basis for fostering preoperational activities such as make-believe play.

Other programs organize cognitive activities around structured materials, which teachers guide children to use in particular ways. Nurseries and centers inspired by Maria Montessori (Montessori, 1964; Cuffaro, 1991) give children sets of cylinders graded by size and designed to fit snugly into a set of size-graded holes in a board. A child experiments with the cylinders and holes to discover the best way to fit them.

Still other early education programs borrow from Vygotsky's views of cognition as originating in social and cultural activities. These programs emphasize cooperative problem-solving activities and *emergent literacy,* a way of introducing reading and writing by situating it in everyday, valued experiences (Morrow, 1993). For example, instead of teaching children to recognize letters or familiar words at a special time each day, the early childhood teacher might simply provide a classroom rich in print materials and encourage children to come to him with words or letters that they themselves want to learn.

Effectiveness of Early Childhood Education

Evaluations of early childhood programs suggest that a wide range of approaches, including those just mentioned, are about equally effective in promoting overall cognitive growth, although the choice of curriculum does seem to influence the *pattern* of skills that children acquire (Schweinhart et al., 1993).

Three factors seem to underlie successful early childhood programs, whatever their format and curriculum. First, the staff of successful programs regard themselves as competent observers of children's educational needs and as being capable of making important decisions in tailoring a curriculum to particular children. Second, the vast majority of successful programs and teachers view an early childhood curriculum as an integrated whole rather than consisting of independent subject areas or skills. Singing a song, for example, is not just "music"; it also fosters language development, motor skills (if the children dance along), arithmetic (through counting and rhythm), and social studies (if the words are about people and life in the community).

Third, successful early childhood programs involve parents, either directly as volunteers in the classroom or indirectly as advisers on governing boards, in certain school activities or in additional services that support families. The federally sponsored program of early education called *Head Start,* for example, owes much of its effectiveness to parent involvement (Ames, 1997). To get federal funding, local centers are required to create parent advisory boards to guide policy and practice at the centers. They are also encouraged to provide other family support services, such as parent support groups and dental screening for children.

Cultural Diversity and Best Practice in Early Education

A careful look at successful programs for young children raises an important question: are there "best" ways to support children's learning despite the cultural and

Providers of early childhood programs face the challenge of making activities developmentally appropriate. One way is to include classroom materials that invite exploration by the children. Another is to allow children to choose among activities.

individual diversity among children? A major professional association for early childhood education, the National Association for the Education of Young Children (NAEYC), argues that there are and has described its recommendations in detail in an influential book called *Developmentally Appropriate Practice: Birth to Age Eight* (Bredekamp & Copple, 1997; Gestwicki, 1995). **Developmentally appropriate practices** are ways of assisting children's learning that are consistent with children's developmental needs and abilities. Table 9.2 lists a few of the practices recommended by the NAEYC as they relate to the preschool years.

The NAEYC recommendations seem reasonable in many ways. Who can object, for example, to providing children with choices for their preschool play or to supporting their dialogues and initiatives with comments from the teacher or caregiver? Yet cross-cultural comparisons of early childhood programs complicate the picture somewhat by revealing that some practices in early education in North America are really culture bound rather than universally beneficial to children.

In Japan, for example, preschool programs are more likely to value large-group activities (such as singing or putting on a skit) in the belief that such activities develop commitment to the child's community—in this case, the community of the classroom (Kotloff, 1993). The time given to large-group activities, however, would probably seem excessive to some preschool educators in North America, where the development of individual initiative is more highly valued.

In Italy, preschool programs emphasize involvement of parents much more heavily than do most North American programs. They also place children in permanent groups from their entrance at age three until they leave the program for public school at age six. Unlike in North America, little effort is needed to maintain and justify these practices, because Italian culture already supports them: women (but not men) are expected to avoid paid employment and to form extended social networks of support with other relatives, with one another, and (in this case) with their children's teachers (Edwards et al., 1993).

These comparisons suggest that the best practices in early education may need to take account of cultural differences and values regarding children's development (Mallory & New, 1994). For programs in ethnically diverse societies such as the

• • •

developmentally appropriate practice Methods and goals of teaching considered optimal for young children given current knowledge of child development.

A Multicultural View ························

Parents' Beliefs About Intelligence: A Cross-cultural Perspective

In our society, parents mean particular things when they refer to children's *intelligence:* they are usually talking about a child's verbal skills and reasoning abilities, especially as they occur in school or school-like tasks. This view of intelligence is so deeply grounded in our culture that an entire psychological field has developed to measure it, complete with standardized "intelligence" tests and experts to help teachers and parents interpret the tests.

But not all societies think of intelligence in this way. The Kipsigis in East Africa frame the idea of intelligence rather differently, placing it more explicitly in its social context (Harkness & Super, 1992). They speak of a child being *ng'om,* meaning not only verbally skilled and sociable but also responsible to others. A child who is *ng'om* is quick to learn household tasks, for example, but also reliable about doing them without being reminded. The Kipsigis recognize, in principle, that a child can have verbal skill in the abstract. In practice, however, they regard such an isolated or abstract

skill as a unique ability that requires a special term to describe it: *ng'om en sukul,* or "smart in school." Furthermore, *ng'om* is a quality shown only by preschoolers; neither an infant nor an adult can be *ng'om,* since she or he is not expected to be responsible to others in the same way preschoolers are.

Such a socially embedded notion of intelligence differs radically from the usual North American idea. In our society, parents are likely to distinguish clearly between a child's sense of responsibility to others and his or her intelligence (Goodnow, 1995). They may consider the former desirable but not an intrinsic part of intelligence as such. When interviewed about the qualities shown by preschoolers, parents of preschoolers tend to name relatively "cognitive" features: an intelligent child is inquisitive, curious, imaginative, self-reliant, and able to play independently (Harkness & Super, 1992). These features of intelligence take individual autonomy for granted rather than social harmony: being intelligent is something you do by or on behalf of yourself, not with or on behalf of others.

These cultural differences begin to make sense if we consider the settings in which Kipsigis and North American

United States, this means more than including songs and brief mentions of the holidays of various cultural groups. The central values and attitudes of cultural groups served by a particular center or nursery school must find their way into the daily activities of the program. Particular centers therefore will experience cultural diversity in different ways:

- A program serving a rural community of Amish or Hutterite children will need to take seriously the value of learning outdoors from the natural environment, sometimes even in the winter (Wardle, 1995).

TABLE 9.2	**Developmentally Appropriate Practices with Preschoolers**
Principle	**Examples**
Caregivers provide ample space for active play	Program has access to outdoor space or gymnasium with climbing apparatus, tricycles, etc.
Caregivers allow children choices in activities	Classroom has several learning centers: dramatic play (dress-up), block building, books and reading area, art area, etc.
Caregivers provide long periods of uninterrupted time	Group transitions (e.g., from indoor to outdoor activities) are kept to a minimum; activities tend to begin and end individually
Activities and materials are relevant to children's experiences	Books are gender fair and culture fair; relevant cultural holidays are noted and celebrated through appropriate activities in class
Caregivers ensure that the environment is safe and free of hazards	Climbing apparatus has soft mats underneath (if indoors) or soft sand (if outdoors); furniture is sturdy; sharp objects (knives, scissors) are supervised carefully when used

Source: Adapted from Bredekamp & Copple (1997).

parents and preschoolers live. A Kipsigis preschooler typically is part of an extended family. There are likely to be children of all ages close at hand, related to one another in largely complex ways; older children typically care for younger children from an early age; and children's chores are likely to take on "real" economic importance as children get older. Such a setting seems sure to reward children for showing responsibility to others.

In our own society, a preschooler is likely to live with a small family; relatively few or even no immediate relatives may be close at hand; parents expect that school will figure prominently in the preschooler's future; and parents themselves (including mothers) are likely to be working for a living. This sort of setting favors children who can "teach themselves" to a certain extent, that is, play with and learn from materials on their own. It also favors children who orient themselves toward school-like activities—toward number and memory games, for example, and books and letters. An "intelligent" child is one who can do these things, which have much less to do with responsibility to others than is the case for a Kipsigis child (Harkness et al., 1992). Cultural differences such as these can pose problems for many preschoolers in our own society when they finally enter school. Historically, modern schooling has encouraged the culturally conventional definitions of intelligence as individual activity and those of cognitive activity as separate from the daily needs of the community. Students generally "do their own work" and focus on tasks (such as a set of math problems) that are created specially for school settings.

When these assumptions do not fit the cultural expectations of particular children or their families, however, teachers are challenged to modify them. Teachers must then find other ways for children to "be intelligent"—ways that involve greater responsibility to others, for example, and greater concern for the real needs of the child's community (Gopaul-McNicol & Thomas-Presswood, 1998). Though it takes effort, there are ways to accomplish these changes in teaching philosophy; some of these changes are discussed in Chapter 8 in connection with bilingualism and the influence of school in the middle years.

- A program serving urban Appalachian children in northern schools will have to recognize and honor the importance of religion in the lives of many Appalachian families, even if these families now live in a much more secular, urban environment (Klein, 1995).

- A program serving Native American children in the Northwest will need to recognize the importance of cooperation to many of these children and their families and their aversion to individual striving to "better" oneself (Soldier, 1993).

In these culturally diverse programs, cognition or thinking itself can take on diverse meanings (see the accompanying Multicultural View box). Educators who work with young children therefore need to do more than understand preschool cognition: they also need to explore how it might be understood and used by particular children and communities with specific social relationships and values. The next chapter turns to these important topics.

WHAT DO YOU THINK?   Is early childhood education a "social" or a "cognitive" activity? After you have formed an opinion about this question, try to discuss it with one or two experienced teachers of young children. Has your opinion changed at all as a result?

From Preschooler to Child

The cognitive changes we have talked about in this chapter create new relationships with parents and other caregivers, who in turn stimulate further changes. New cognitive abilities create increasing individuality in children: in spite of differences in temperament among infants, it is not they but preschoolers who have more

Early childhood programs often serve children from differing cultural backgrounds. The diversity can be enriching if caregivers encourage cooperative activities, like the game these two children are playing, and if caregivers include stories, activities, and information that recognize and respect children's cultural differences.

identifiable personalities. By age four or five, conversations become possible; moods can be expressed not only through gestures and body language but also through words; and a child's lasting interests become more obvious to those who know the child. All of these changes create new meanings for the idea of parenting. Attending to physical needs begins to recede in importance (though not completely), and attending to psychological needs comes more to the fore. As parents shift their relationship to accommodate these changes, they are more likely to remember their own childhoods once again, and with renewed vividness. The memories can be good, bad, traumatic, or mixed; but whatever they are like, they force reassessment of parents' *own* personal histories and identities, and of their relationships with their *own* parents, the preschooler's grandparents. We saw aspects of this in Chapter 7's discussion of attachment formation, and we will explore these themes further in Chapters 11 and 12, which explore where preschoolers' new physical growth and cognitive skills lead them during middle childhood. First, though, we must complete the portrait of the young child by discussing the development of his or her social relationships and emotional growth in the next chapter.

Summary of Major Ideas

Thinking in Preschoolers

1. The preoperational stage of thinking, defined by Piaget, is characterized by increased symbolic thinking.

2. Children's new reliance on symbolic thought helps them to recall experiences, solve problems more effectively, and communicate with others about their experiences.

3. Preschool children have developed a simple theory of the human mind by the time they are three years old.

4. Young preschool children have trouble distinguishing between appearances and reality, but by the end of the preschool period they have made substantial improvements in this skill.

5. Preschool children can classify objects accurately as long as the system or criteria used for classifying are relatively simple.

6. Preschoolers often cannot solve problems that require reversible thinking, such as the classic Piagetian tasks of conservation.

7. Preschoolers' distinctions between natural kinds and artifacts suggests that they may hold informal theories about biological functioning.

8. Social constructivism is a perspective that sees cognitive development as happening in social activity settings and sees concepts and knowledge as inevitably situated or tailored to those settings.

9. Neostructuralist theories of cognitive development use Piaget's belief in stages, but focus on relatively specific cognitive skills of the child.

Language Acquisition in Early Childhood

10. During the preschool years, children make major strides in acquiring the syntax, or grammar, of their native language.
11. Young children's first word combinations are related by semantics and omit syntactic relationships.
12. One important syntactic error preschool children make is overgeneralization.
13. Although preschoolers learn a great deal of language through the process of inference, they also learn some language by rote.
14. Infants and preschoolers are reinforced, but only indirectly, for using correct syntax in their earliest utterances.
15. Children probably acquire some syntax through imitation and practice of language models.
16. The ease with which children acquire language despite the poverty of the content of speech that they hear may mean children possess an innate language acquisition device, or LAD.
17. Parents probably assist children's language acquisition by recasting their children's own utterances, using a special style of talk called *infant-directed speech,* and providing scaffolding that supports their children's language efforts.

Language Variations

18. Language varies among children according to gender in ways that support gender stereotypes.
19. Language varies according to socioeconomic class in ways that prepare middle-class children better than low-SES children for school settings.
20. Children who are deaf or hearing impaired often learn American Sign Language, which has all of the properties of an oral language.
21. Language variations raise issues about when, and whether, a particular child's language is deficient or merely different from the norm.

Relationships Between Language and Thought

22. Two major theories have been proposed to explain the relationship between language and thought: Piagetian and Vygotskian.
23. According to Piaget, language develops only as rapidly and as far as other symbolic functions, such as dramatic play, do.

24. According to Vygotsky, language and thought begin as independent functions and gradually become integrated during the preschool years.
25. Piaget's viewpoint implies that language reflects primarily general cognitive development, whereas Vygotsky's suggests that language and thought eventually come to assist each other's development equally.

Early Childhood Education

26. Early childhood education programs come in a variety of forms, many of which have been influenced by theories of cognitive development.
27. Three factors characterize successful programs in early childhood education: a staff that is oriented toward observing the children, an integrated view of the curriculum, and significant involvement of parents in the program.
28. Cultural diversity challenges early childhood educators to identify teaching practices that are not only developmentally appropriate but also culturally appropriate.

Key Terms

activity settings (270)
American Sign Language (ASL) (283)
animism (268)
appearance-reality distinctions (265)
artifact (268)
classification (266)
conservation (266)
developmentally appropriate practice (289)
duo (273)
egocentrism (263)
false-belief task (265)
functional relationships (262)
generative rules (273)
holographic speech (274)
identity (262)
infant-directed speech (280)
inner speech (287)

language acquisition device (LAD) (278)
metacognition (265)
morphemes (272)
natural kind (268)
neostructuralist (neo-Piagetian) theories (271)
overgeneralizations (274)
recasting (280)
reversibility (266)
scaffolding (280)
situated cognition (270)
social constructivism (270)
symbol (262)
symbolic thought (263)
syntax (272)
telegraphic speech (274)
theory of mind (264)
zone of proximal development (ZPD) (270)

Psychosocial Development in Early Childhood

Focusing Questions

- How do different styles of parenting influence preschoolers' relationships with peers?

- How do preschoolers manage conflicts with peers?

- Why is play so important in preschoolers' development, and how does play change as children approach school age?

- How does a child's understanding of gender differences change during the preschool years? What factors influence a child's flexibility about gender-role stereotypes?

- What factors appear to contribute to child abuse and neglect? What are the consequences of maltreatment, and how might child maltreatment be prevented?

W hen Melissa was two, she used to crouch down on the floor with her rear end sticking out in imitation of the prominent haunches of Tigger, the family cat.

From time to time, she made a noise sort of like a cat's meow. Keeping her head low, she looked around carefully for acknowledgment from her parents. Occasionally she walked like a cat, although her walk looked more like a rabbit's hopping. Tigger herself was not impressed by all of this.

Melissa's skills as a performer and her active awareness of her audience illustrate an important milestone during the preschool years: the development of psychological and social skills. During the preschool years, many activities and events that occupy a child's waking hours involve social interaction with other people. These others include parents, grandparents, and siblings, as well as friends and acquaintances in the neighborhood and community. Many of these interactions also involve play. The nature of our play and its role in our lives change with age and experience, but the capacity to engage in playful activity and the social skills that make this possible continue to develop throughout our lives. The social skills and unique personality a preschool child develops are largely a result of social interactions within and outside his or her family.

In this chapter, we explore the process through which preschoolers develop the capacity to relate to others in empathic and prosocial ways and to successfully deal with conflict and aggression. As with play, psychosocial development is a lifelong process. We will examine the conditions that foster or undermine such development and their consequences for human development. We will also explore an aspect of early childhood development with profound and lifelong impact: the development of gender. Finally, we will discuss the serious problem of child maltreatment, including its causes, long-term consequences, treatment, and prevention.

Relationships with Family

Are your earliest memories of yourself alone, or do they include other people? Chances are it's the latter, for young children spend a good deal of their time relating to others. In this section, we discuss children's relationships with their parents and siblings—relationships that in many ways set the stage for social interactions beyond the family sphere.

Relationships with Parents

During the preschool years, the attachment relationships between children and their parents and other caregivers discussed in Chapter 7 continue to play a central

P E R S P E C T I V E S

Extended Family Supports for Childrearing

• • • • •   In American society in particular, parents are held, and hold themselves, responsible for the physical care of their children. Whether parents are rich or poor, Caucasian or African American, divorced or married, society expects them to provide food for their children as well as clothing and a place to sleep. In reality many families share these responsibilities with relatives, friends, and professionals of various kinds. In a typical week, a child may spend significant time not only with his biological parents but also with a grandparent, a neighbor, and (depending on the child's age) a teacher or day care center worker. The mixture of responsibility depends partly on the local circumstances of the particular family. It also reflects cultural and economic differences. Mexican American families, for example, value the participation of grandparents and other relatives in childrearing. Many nonwhite families report the participation in family life of *fictive kin,* neighbors or friends who develop a relationship with the family that closely resembles that of a blood relative (Ramirez, 1989, 1998). Though fictive kin are more common among ethnic and racial minorities, they are also an important part of the white, European American experience.

These additional adults supplement what parents provide, often literally by providing alternative persons to cook meals and arrange other daily routines and by bolstering the psychological goals and emotional supports provided by the biological parents. A study of African American families confirmed this conclusion by investigating the emotional climate in two- and three-generational families (Tolson & Wilson, 1990). Interviews with all members of the families, including the children, found that three-generational families (those with a resident grandparent) saw themselves as organized more informally and spontaneously than two-generational (two-parent)

families, which in turn saw themselves as organized more informally and spontaneously than one-parent families. In other words, the greater the number of parents (including a grandparent), the *fewer* the rules for children to follow and the *more* flexible the daily scheduling of activities, even though larger families had to coordinate the activities of more individuals. While this trend may seem contradictory, the family members themselves suggested the reason when interviewed: more adults in the house meant individual parents had more back-up support in carrying out their functions as parents and therefore needed to rely on preset procedures less heavily.

The benefits of back-up support are psychological as well as physical. The interviews just described also found that African American families with more than one parent placed significantly greater emphasis on moral and ethical issues and on determining how best to deal with both individual members and people outside the family (Tolson & Wilson, 1990; Wilson et al., 1995). To achieve this benefit, however, it did not matter whether the second "parent" was a father; it occurred just as frequently when a mother and a grandmother were the resident parents. Other research, in fact, suggests that it may not even matter whether the additional parents live at home, as long as they participate actively in the life of the family. In another interview study, successful minority single parents reported developing and depending on networks of family and personal relationships (Lindblad-Goldberg, 1989). What mattered was not the form or pattern of the networks but their existence and importance in helping the parent carry out the roles of childrearing.

What Do You Think?

What types of extended family supports did you experience during your childhood and adolescence? In what ways were they beneficial to you, and in what ways were they not?

role in their social and emotional development. Although the conflict of autonomy versus shame and doubt, which Erikson saw as central to infancy, can still be observed, the main psychosocial challenge of early childhood is to master the conflict of *initiative versus guilt.* Preschoolers explore their expanding verbal and physical powers by testing the limits of what they can and cannot do. Children's expanding abilities to initiate verbal and physical activity and their exploding powers of imagination can at times be a challenge to their parents. On the one hand, parents must support their children's efforts to take on the world. On the other hand, they must also appreciate young children's limitations, and avoid inducing guilt by establishing appropriate restraints that protect their children's physical and emotional safety and self-esteem. Preschoolers often test the limits their parents impose on their behavior, and they are often inconsistent in their ability to understand and conform to parental wishes. At times they express their strong desire to control their environment by refusing to eat certain foods or wear certain clothing, or by insisting on playing the same game or having the same story read to them over and over again. How effectively parents respond to this "limit testing" depends partly on their beliefs and characteristic styles of parenting and partly on the quality of the parent-child relationship.

Understanding the need for family rules poses a challenge to preschoolers, but making those rules also creates a challenge for parents, at least those living in the individualistic culture of mainstream North America. In this society, unlike most others, parents are expected to devise their own standards for rearing children, largely independently of other families' standards or expectations—a kind of "private enterprise" system of childrearing. For instance, it is up to parents as individuals to decide how much anger their child should be allowed to express, how early and well she should learn manners, or how much candy she can eat. Parents' independence in deciding these standards increases their power in shaping their child's behavior in the short run. But it also increases their dilemma over which standards to choose, since they observe that other parents often make choices different than their own (Piatrowski, 1997). These factors may help to explain why community members often are reluctant to say something to someone else's child who misbehaves or to offer advice or assistance to a parent who might find it useful. And, as we will see in Chapters 13 and 16, the lack of clear standards for good parenting leads to precisely the kind of ambiguous role that creates stress during middle childhood and adolescence.

Enforcing family rules may be less of a problem in cultures and societies that encourage less individualism and stronger, more prolonged interdependence among kin, community, or both. In Chinese American and Japanese American families, for example, grandparents and other relatives retain considerable prestige and influence in childrearing matters even after a couple has married and given birth to children (Chao, 1994; Huang & Ying, 1989; Nagata, 1989). Even as preschoolers, children are taught ways to show respect for their elders, such as caution in asking questions and readiness to obey orders. In such a situation, parents lose some decision-making authority to grandparents, in-laws, or "the community." But parents also gain family and community backing for their position: it is not just an adult or two, Mom and (sometimes) Dad, who decide whether talking in a loud voice is rude but an extended array of relatives and friends (Skolnick & Skolnick, 1989). (See the accompanying Perspectives box for a discussion of extended family members' participation in childrearing.)

In general, parent-child relationships during early childhood that are warm, respectful, empathic, and mutually responsive generally work best for children and their families. This is revealed both by how children and their parents interact and by the perceptions they have about each other. Grazyna Kochanska (1997) found that when mothers shared a mutually responsive orientation with their young children, children better internalized maternal rules and values and mothers less often relied on power to influence their children. Preschoolers who have more positive mental representations of the mothering they receive, as revealed in the stories they make up about a mother and her child, have fewer behavior problems and less psychological distress than children whose mental representations are more negative (Oppenheim et al., 1997; Stocker, 1994). In the following section, we discuss the main patterns of parental authority observed among North American families and their developmental impact.

Patterns of Parental Authority

One of the most important aspects of a parent-child relationship is the parent's style of authority. Observations of North American families of preschoolers suggest that childrearing styles can be classified into four groups: *authoritative, authoritarian, permissive-indulgent,* and *permissive-indifferent* (Darling & Steinberg, 1993; Grusec et al., 1997; Maccoby & Martin, 1983). In most families, however, none of these styles exist in a "pure" form, and parenting styles can change as children grow older and as other family changes occur. Table 10.1 summarizes the main patterns of parental authority.

Authoritative Parenting   Parents who exert a high degree of control over their children and demand a lot of them, but are also responsive, child centered, and respectful of their children's thoughts, feelings, and participation in decision making, are called **authoritative**. For example, although it may be easier for a parent to respond to her child's request for help in building something or getting dressed by doing it for him, an authoritative parent is likely to provide only the amount of help that will enable him to successfully accomplish the task himself. Such parents tend to be democratic and rational in their decision making and to respond to their children with warmth and empathy.

When it comes to discipline, authoritative parents assume their preschooler should be treated with respect, even when she has misbehaved severely. They believe discipline should be a positive learning experience, focused on helping their child to understand and take age-appropriate responsibility for her misbehavior and to internalize parental standards and develop competence so that she can make better decisions about how to behave in the future. For example, when faced with a preschooler whose water play at the sink has resulted in a flood, an authoritative parent is likely to ask the child how it happened, what he was thinking, and what he remembered about the rules about using the sink for water play. The parent's response would focus on helping the child understand why the parent was upset (the flood could damage the floor and downstairs ceiling, and be costly to repair), helping him to assume age-appropriate responsibility for his actions (perhaps by having him help mop up the floor), and having him explain how such "catastrophes" could be avoided in the future. The consequences would also be designed to increase the child's understanding of the misbehavior (for example, requiring him to help clean up the mess and removing water play privileges for the rest of the week).

Preschoolers of authoritative parents tend to be self-reliant, self-controlled, and able to get along well with their adult caregivers and peers (Hart et al., 1992; Kuczynski & Kochanska, 1995; Pettit et al., 1988). For example, Leon Kuczynski and Grazyna Kochanska (1995) found that children who experienced authoritative childrearing as toddlers were more responsive to parental guidance and had fewer behavior problems at age five. In particular, these authoritative mothers made demands that emphasized competence, prosocial behavior, and positive actions ("Ask

• • •

authoritative parenting A style of childrearing characterized by a high degree of control, clarity of communication, maturity demands, and nurturance.

Authoritative parents display high levels of control, clarity of communication, demands for mature behavior, and nurturance. Authoritarian parents also show high levels of control and maturity demands but are low on clarity of communication and nurturance. Permissive-indulgent parents are low on control and maturity demands, high on nurturance, and inconsistent in how clearly they communicate with their children. Permissive-indifferent parents display low levels of all four dimensions.

TABLE 10.1   Patterns of Parental Authority

Pattern	Control	Clarity of Communication	Maturity Demands	Nurturance
Authoritative	High	High	High	High
Authoritarian	High	Low	High	Low
Permissive-indulgent	Low	Mixed	Low	High
Permissive-indifferent	Low	Low	Low	Low

him to share"; "Pour the milk carefully"; "Put away your toys") rather than demands to inhibit behavior ("Don't hit"; "Don't spill the milk"; "Don't leave a mess").

Authoritative parenting is also associated with high self-esteem, internalized moral standards, psychosocial maturity, autonomy, and academic success. In addition, it appears to foster relationships with peers and family that display the same qualities of warmth and respect for others during middle childhood, adolescence, and beyond (Baumrind, 1991; Darling & Steinberg, 1992; Franz et al., 1991). The relationship between authoritative parenting and prosocial behavior is discussed later in this chapter.

Authoritarian Parenting   Like authoritative parents, **authoritarian** parents also are demanding of their children and exert high control over them. However, they tend to be less warm and responsive than authoritative parents, and more arbitrary and undemocratic in decision making. They frequently impose their rules or views on their children based on their own greater power and authority, with little sensitivity to their children's thoughts and feelings. Parent-child relationships that depend on arbitrary, "power-assertive" control and ignore children's thoughts, emotions, and need for independence often have a negative effect on children. Children of authoritarian parents tend to be relatively distrustful of others and unhappy with themselves and to have poorer peer relations, poorer school adjustment, and lower school achievement than do children with authoritative parents (Hart et al., 1990; Lamb et al., 1992). Longitudinal research by Kenneth Dodge and his colleagues found that children who experienced family violence, harsh, punitive (and potentially abusive) parenting styles, and parental rejection or hostility in their preschool years were much more likely to be both aggressive and victims of bullying in middle childhood than peers who received more supportive parenting (Deater-Deckhard et al., 1996; Schwartz et al., 1997). Further discussion of these issues appears in Chapter 16.

The disciplinary techniques authoritarian parents use differ from those of authoritative parents, in part because they do not see the development of responsibility in young children as a collaborative process and place less emphasis on mutual respect. When faced with misbehavior, they are more likely to focus on the arbitrary assertion of parental power and authority than on understanding the child's thoughts and feelings about the misbehavior or on helping the child to understand and take responsibility for it. In the extreme, the combination of rigid and arbitrary power assertion and insensitivity to a child's thoughts and feelings can increase the likelihood of child maltreatment, discussed later in this chapter. By modeling disrespectful and insensitive behavior, such parenting can elicit and reinforce similar behavior in children and lead to escalating cycles of negative reinforcement and coercion (Patterson, 1982).

Authoritarian parenting is more frequent in large families and in working-class families (Greenberger et al., 1994), and fathers are more likely to be authoritarian than mothers. Beliefs about how children should be raised and parenting styles differ across societies and cultures (Bornstein et al., 1998; Stevenson-Hinde, 1998). For example, authoritarian parenting is more common in cultures in which family relations are hierarchically structured based on age, family role, and gender. Ruth Chao (1994) has questioned the validity of Western European concepts of authoritative and authoritarian parenting for Chinese families. Chinese childrearing is based on Confucian principles that require children to show loyalty to and respect for their elders and require elders to responsibly train, discipline, and otherwise "govern" young children. High degrees of parental authority and control are viewed

All parents discipline their children sometimes. Their methods make a difference; calling attention to the consequences of misbehavior generally is more effective than spanking, at least in the long run.

• • •

authoritarian parenting A style of childrearing characterized by a high degree of control and demands on children's maturity and a low degree of clarity of communication and nurturance.

as positive and essential aspects of the *chiao shun*, or "training," needed to set a standard of acceptable family and community conduct. Chao suggests that cultural differences such as these may explain why authoritarian parenting, which is associated with poor school achievement among European American children, is linked to high school achievement among Chinese children. Central to such cultural differences are differences in values and assumptions about what kind of people parents want their children to be and what kinds of parenting and other developmental influences will best help them to get there.

Permissive Parenting   *Permissive parents* appear to show two patterns. **Permissive-indulgent** parents are warm, sensitive, caring, and generally responsive to their children's thoughts and feelings. However, they exert low levels of control and make relatively few demands, permitting their children to make almost all of their own decisions. Also, while they clearly communicate their warmth, love, and caring, their communication tends to be less clear in situations requiring that they set limits on their children's behavior. **Permissive-indifferent** parents are detached and emotionally uninvolved. They are inconsistent in setting and maintaining age-appropriate standards and expectations for their children and in fulfilling their parental responsibilities (Lamb et al., 1992; Maccoby & Martin, 1983). Permissive-indulgent parents rarely assert their disciplinary control directly. They tend to rely on their child to learn and conform to what is expected and to internalize parental values on her own, based on observing her parents and reacting to their expressions of disapproval or satisfaction regarding her behavior. Discipline by permissive-indifferent parents tends to be inconsistent, erratic, and out of step with the developmental needs of their child.

Children with permissive-indulgent parents tend to lack self-reliance and self-control and to have lower self-esteem as they enter adolescence. This is also true of children with permissive-indifferent parents, who seem to be emotionally detached and not to care what their children do (Loeb et al., 1980). These children tend to have various degrees of developmental difficulties, including a low ability to tolerate frustration and to control their impulsive and aggressive behavior. They also tend to have difficulty in making life choices and in setting long-term goals. At the extreme, permissive-indifferent parents neglect their children's physical and emotional needs, leaving them with more serious developmental and emotional problems associated with child maltreatment (discussed later in this chapter).

Mixed Parenting Styles   Most parents, of course, do not fit neatly into any one of these categories; rather, most show mixtures of all four parenting styles. At one time or another, even the best parents ignore their child's misbehavior and justify themselves on the basis of sheer power—perhaps when they (or their child) are too tired to explain for the tenth time why it is time to go to bed. In addition, the situations in which families live may influence the effectiveness of a particular parenting style. For example, the clear-cut expectations and standards of behavior associated with authoritarian parenting may offer certain advantages to families living in neighborhoods where drug use and violence leave little margin for error (Grusec & Lytton, 1988).

Changes over Time   Patterns of childrearing also tend to change over time. Authoritarian parents, for instance, often ease up and shift to a more permissive or authoritative style as their children grow older. Changes in the family situation, such as the birth of another child also can make a difference. The experience gained from rearing their first child frequently enables parents to become more comfortable and flexible in rearing the children who follow. Help from older children in caring for younger siblings can also reduce the stresses of parenting. On the other hand, additional children increase the family's overall child care and economic burdens, so more relaxed parenting is not always the outcome. Other changes within a

permissive-indulgent parenting A style of parenting in which parents make relatively few demands on their children but clearly communicate their warmth and interest and provide considerable care and nurturance.

permissive-indifferent parenting A style of parenting in which parents' permissiveness reflects an avoidance of childrearing responsibilities, sometimes with detrimental results.

family, such as in employment, standard of living, and health, also may influence childrearing. Families that are under stress tend to be more rigid, arbitrary, and authoritarian in rearing their children than families that are not. Finally, because they lack confidence and competence in clearly setting or negotiating limits, permissive parents may find it more difficult to move to being authoritative and democratic than authoritarian parents, who in turn must ease up on their unilateral limit setting and learn to be more democratic.

Although parenting styles influence early childhood development, they alone do not determine a child's developmental course. First, these styles reflect average patterns and do not describe the unique pattern of interactions and experiences that characterizes the relationship between any particular parent and child. The quality and developmental impact of a particular parent-child relationship will be influenced by the unique qualities of the parent, the child, and their interactions and experiences in the relationship. Second, although parents are certainly important, other individuals both within and outside of the family may contribute in vital ways to psychosocial development during early childhood.

Relationships with Siblings

Brothers and sisters are major participants in the social activities of many preschoolers. Though adjustment to the birth of a sibling often leads to increased behavior problems in older siblings, these increases tend to be temporary (Baydar et al., 1997). Studies of children's behavior toward their siblings have shown that most young children are very interested in babies and speak to their baby brothers and sisters in ways that are very similar to those of adult caregivers. Preschoolers also listen carefully to conversations between their parents and older brothers and sisters, as reflected in their efforts to join in family conversations. Both the friendly and the aggressive interactions of siblings contribute to the development of preschoolers' understandings of the feelings, intentions, and needs of people other than themselves (Brown & Dunn, 1992; Slomkowski & Dunn, 1992). Preschoolers' awareness of caregiving interactions between parents and younger siblings contributes to their own capacity to respond to their younger siblings' distress with appropriate caregiving behaviors (Garner et al., 1994).

Studies of several societies have found that older siblings serve two psychological functions for younger brothers and sisters. First, they help transmit customs and

Sibling relationships are important to social development. The warm and relaxed relationship between this preschooler and his school-age brother is likely to contribute positively to the quality of their other social relationships.

family expectations. Second, they provide challenges that (hopefully) lead the younger children to new learning (Ervin-Tripp, 1989; Weiser, 1989). Both functions may occur unconsciously. In North American society, for example, an older child may demonstrate to a sibling that athletic ability is important simply by choosing to use free time playing softball or hockey with neighborhood friends. But what happens when the younger child attempts to play these same games with the older sibling? The older child may try to assist, but may set tasks that the younger child finds challenging or even impossible at first, such as batting a ball or staying upright on a pair of skates while swinging a hockey stick. Older siblings do make allowances for lesser competence due to a sibling's younger age, but generally not as much as parents do. In explaining a task to a younger sibling, for example, older children simplify their language somewhat, but less so than their parents do (Hoff-Ginsberg & Krueger, 1991).

Influences on Sibling Relationships   Sibling relationships do not occur in a vacuum. For example, they are influenced by the quality of the relationships their parents have with their children and with each other. A recent observational study of interactions between pairs of 3½- to 8½-year-old siblings found that negative behaviors of both older and younger siblings were linked to negative aspects of the mother-child relationship and, for older siblings, to negative aspects of the parent's marital relationship (Erel et al., 1998). The quality of young children's social relationships with siblings also influences the quality of their relationships with friends, not only in early childhood but in middle childhood, adolescence, and adulthood as well (Bank et al., 1996; Volling et al., 1997). In a seven-year longitudinal study of the relationships between thirty-nine sibling pairs from mixed-SES families, Judy Dunn, Cheryl Slomkowski, and Lynn Beardsall (1994) followed the children from preschool through middle childhood and early adolescence. Sibling pairs included older male–younger female, older female–younger male, boy-boy and girl-girl dyads. The average ages of the sibling pairs were 3 years and 6½ years at the beginning of the study and 10 years and 13½ years when the study was completed. Sibling pairs were studied at four points in time: when the younger sibling was three years old, six years old, eight years old, and ten years old.

Dunn and her colleagues found considerable continuity in siblings' positive feelings and behaviors (affection, warmth, intimacy, cooperation) and negative feelings and behaviors (competition, jealousy, fighting) toward one another from early childhood and through early adolescence. Their detailed interviews with the children and their mothers revealed that the majority of children provided support for one another when faced with such problems as difficulties with other children at school, maternal illness, or accidents and illnesses that they themselves had suffered. Good relationships between siblings also helped to protect children who were experiencing the stress of parental conflict. Finally, both siblings and their mothers attributed negative changes in sibling relationships to new friendships that children formed outside the family during middle childhood.

Given the social opportunities siblings offer, one might expect children growing up with brothers and sisters to develop social skills earlier and more rapidly, and perhaps end up with better skills, than children who lack siblings. But having siblings can have its down side as well. For instance, an older sister can be an excellent teacher and role model for her younger brother, but her relative competence and need to outshine him may make it more difficult for him to develop certain social skills than if he were not in his older sister's shadow. Similarly, caring for a younger sibling is likely to enhance the younger child's social competence, but being burdened with her care may also limit the older child's opportunities to spend time with his peers. How siblings will affect a particular child's social development is likely to depend on the degree to which parents recognize and respond appropriately to the social needs of all of their children.

Only Children   Of course, not every child has a sibling. What impact does growing up as an "only child" have on development? Two widely held but conflicting views exist regarding this question. One view suggests that being an only child is a negative experience since it deprives only children of the advantages of having siblings and "spoils" them because they are the sole focus of their parents' attention. The second view sees only childhood as an advantage, allowing parents to be more responsive and attentive than they would be if they had to share their time and resources with other children (Rosenberg & Hyde, 1993). Research suggests that only children perform as well as or somewhat better than those from two-child families on various measures, including self-esteem, achievement motivation, and academic success, than children who must share their parents with siblings, and that the greatest problem only children and their families face may be the prejudicial views about them (Falbo, 1992; Laybourn, 1990).

WHAT DO YOU THINK ?   What style of parental authority best describes what you experienced as a child? How did it change as you grew older? Which pattern of parenting do you currently provide or plan to provide for your children? Why?

Relationships in an Expanding Social World

As we have just seen, parents and siblings have a profound and long-lasting impact on the child's developing social skills. In early childhood, the child's social world expands and changes, providing new opportunities for testing out these skills, and new challenges as well. Children learn from many sources that they can influence their social relationships through their own helpful or aggressive behavior, as we now explore.

Empathy and Prosocial Behavior

Empathy, the ability to vicariously experience the emotions of another person, is thought to play an important role in the successful development of friendships and other close emotional relationships (Eisenberg et al., 1989). *Prosocial behavior* refers to positive social actions that benefit others, such as sharing, helping, and cooperating. Some prosocial behaviors are *altruistic*, meaning they are voluntarily aimed at helping others with no expectation of rewards for oneself. The development of both empathy and prosocial behavior is related to sound parent-child relationships and secure attachment during infancy and toddlerhood (see Chapter 7).

The Extent of Empathy and Helpfulness   Preschool children usually will respond helpfully to another person's distress in a variety of situations. For example, observational reports by mothers of the prosocial behavior of their four- and seven-year-olds at home indicate that spontaneous helping occurred in both age groups more frequently than did sharing and giving, affection and praise, or reassuring and protecting (Grusec, 1991). Young children show a strong tendency to empathize in other situations as well. One study of children at a day care center playground found that more than 90 percent of the time, a crying child generated concerned and mostly helpful responses from the other children (Sawin, 1979). About half of the children who were near the distressed child looked as though they would cry themselves. Almost 20 percent of the nearby children tried to console the child directly (and their actions did, in fact, help to reduce the crying); other children sought out an adult on the playground; still others threatened revenge on the child who caused the upset. In contrast, naturalistic studies by Carolee Howes and her colleagues of

empathy A sensitive awareness of the thoughts and feelings of another person.

These three toddlers are concerned about the unhappy baby. Important gains in children's capacity for empathy and emotional support occur during the preschool years.

young children's responses to crying in day care settings found that somewhat fewer than 20 percent of crying incidents received a response, 70 percent were ignored, and fewer than 40 percent of the children intervened prosocially by mediating, consoling, or offering information to a teacher (Howes & Farver, 1987; Phinney et al., 1986).

Development of Prosocial Behavior   **Prosocial behavior**, or helpfulness, is well established by the time a child reaches the preschool years. An early, classic study found that all of the following helping behaviors occurred with significant frequency among four-year-olds (Murphy, 1937): assisting another child; comforting another child; protecting another child; warning another child of danger; giving things to another child; and inquiring of a child in trouble. Fifty years later, these and similar helping behaviors are still quite evident, not only among preschool children but even among children younger than two (Eisenberg & Mussen, 1989; Radke-Yarrow & Zahn-Waxler, 1987).

Between ages two and six, children give increasingly complex reasons for helping and are more strongly influenced by nonaltruistic as well as altruistic motives and concerns (Eisenberg et al., 1989; Yarrow & Waxler, 1978). An older child may justify her helpfulness in terms of gaining approval from peers in general rather than in terms of her concern for the well-being of the child in distress. Or she may justify withholding help because of fear of disapproval from adults, for example, if she has been instructed to let the day care or nursery school teachers handle children in trouble. In fairness to older preschoolers, however, younger children also may have reasons such as these but are not yet able to verbalize them clearly (Fabes et al., 1988).

Sources of Prosocial Behavior   Potential sources of individual differences in prosocial responses include age, gender, temperament, child care experience, social competence with peers, and friendship status (Farver & Branstetter, 1994). Prosocial behaviors increase with age due to gains in cognitive functioning, social skills, and moral reasoning and to more socialization experiences that enhance prosocial responsiveness (Eisenberg & Mussen, 1989). No consistent gender differences in prosocial responses have been found, although some studies have found girls to be more prosocial than boys.

There is some evidence that differences in temperament affect children's prosocial behavior. Young children who display high levels of prosocial behavior tend to be active, outgoing, and emotionally expressive. This pattern is similar to the temperamentally *easy child,* whose high levels of adaptiveness, positive mood, and approachfulness may help him to initiate and sustain more peer interaction than *difficult* or *slow-to-warm-up children,* who are more likely to avoid peer contact (Buss & Plomin, 1984; Farver & Branstetter, 1994).

Early exposure to prosocial experiences with peers, parents, and other important individuals may be the best predictor of subsequent prosocial behavior. Jo Ann Farver and Wendy Branstetter (1994) studied prosocial behavior among preschoolers ages 3 to 4½ in three child care programs. They found that it was the type and quality of peer contact children experienced, rather than the length of time children spent in their prior or current preschool programs, that most influenced their prosocial tendencies. Early peer relationships are most likely to foster prosocial responsiveness when teachers, parents, and other adults create an environment that supports it and provides models for children to observe and imitate.

Prosocial competence among preschoolers may also depend on how often parents initiate informal play activities. Gary Ladd and Craig Hart (1992) found that

prosocial behavior Positive social contacts; actions that benefit others.

children whose parents frequently arranged for them to play with peers and actively involved them in arranging play activities displayed higher levels of prosocial behavior. Children who more frequently initiated informal peer contacts were better liked by their classmates.

Overall differences in parenting styles also appear to influence preschoolers' prosocial behavior. Children whose parents are authoritative in their disciplinary styles engage in more prosocial, empathic, and compassionate behavior and less antisocial behavior in day care, playground, and other play settings than children whose parents have authoritarian discipline styles (Hart et al., 1992; Main & George, 1985; Zahn-Waxler et al., 1979).

Cross-cultural studies have provided some additional insights about the significance of parental support and encouragement. In mainly rural societies where mothers worked in the fields and children assumed major child care and household responsibilities, children had greater opportunity to experience prosocial roles and to behave prosocially. Firstborn children, who had the most helping experience, tended to be more prosocial than lastborn or only children. Children raised in close-knit, communal Israeli kibbutz communities, which place high value on cooperation and prosocial behavior, exhibited higher levels of cooperation and prosocial behavior than children from rural or big-city areas (Eisenberg et al., 1990; Whiting & Edwards, 1988).

What practical steps can parents and teachers take to increase altruism and prosocial behavior in the children they care for? Two techniques that have proven successful in increasing such behavior among preschoolers are (1) verbal approval and encouragement and (2) arranging play opportunities that allow children to discover firsthand the benefits of cooperation and helping.

Conflict and Aggression

So far our discussion of social relationships has focused on the ability of preschoolers to get along reasonably well with one another. However, preschoolers also get very angry and express their feelings in aggressive ways: grabbing one another's toys, pushing, hitting, scratching, and calling names. What types of interpersonal conflicts make preschoolers angry, and how do they cope with their angry feelings? Richard Fabes and Nancy Eisenberg (1992) observed the causes of anger and reactions to provocations among preschool children between ages 3 and 6½ while the children were at play. Conflict over possessions was the most common cause of anger, and physical assault was the second most frequent cause. In most types of anger conflicts, most children responded by expressing angry feelings (particularly boys) or by actively attempting to defend themselves in nonaggressive ways (particularly girls). Active resistance was most likely in conflicts over material things such as toys and least likely in conflicts involving compliance with teachers and other adults. In contrast, venting of angry feelings was least likely for material conflicts and most likely for compliance conflicts with adults, suggesting that the particular coping strategy chosen depends in part on how controllable the child sees the situation to be. Children's use of aggressive revenge (hitting or threatening) and tattling was most frequent when their anger was caused by physical assault.

Aggression refers to actions that are intended to harm another person or an object. Aggressive actions frequently are divided into two types. **Overt aggression** harms others through physical damage or the threat of physical damage, such as pushing, hitting, kicking, or threatening to "beat up" a peer. In contrast, **relational aggression** harms others through damage or threat of damage to their peer relationships—for example, by threatening to withdraw friendship to get one's way or by using social exclusion or rumor spreading as a form of retaliation. Children tend to express their aggression in ways that are most likely to interfere with or damage the social goals of their target. Since there is a lot of same-gender play at this age,

aggression A bold, assertive action that is intended to hurt another person or to procure an object.

overt aggression Actions that harm others through physical damage or threat of such damage, such as pushing, hitting, kicking, or threatening to beat up after.

relational aggression Actions that harm others through damage or threats of damage to their peer relationships.

Overt aggression among preschoolers frequently is associated with frustrations at being unable to solve a conflict over toys and with angry and jealous feelings that may result when excluded from a desired activity with peers.

the targets of aggression usually are peers. Consequently, boys are more likely to use overt, physical forms of aggression that hinder the dominance goals of boys, whereas girls are more likely to use more verbal, relational forms of aggression that effectively hinder the social intimacy goals that are more typical of girls' peer relationships (Crick et al., 1997). Although the harmful effects of overt aggression have long been obvious, recent studies indicate that relationally aggressive behaviors are also highly aversive and damaging to both victims and aggressors. The majority of children view these behaviors as mean, hostile acts that cause harm and are often carried out in anger, and children who are frequently the target of relationally aggressive acts experience more psychological distress, such as depression and anxiety, than do their nontargeted peers. Relationally aggressive boys and girls have poorer social and emotional adjustment and report higher levels of loneliness, depression, and negative self-perceptions than do their non–relationally aggressive peers. Children who frequently engage in relational aggression are also far more likely to experience peer rejection as preschoolers and at later ages (Crick, 1996; Crick & Grotpeter, 1996; Grotpeter & Crick, 1996). Finally, there is some evidence that school-age girls who are overtly aggressive and boys who are relationally aggressive are significantly more maladjusted than children who conform to gender norms or children who are nonaggressive, although norms may vary with peer group and culture (Crick, 1997; Hart et al., 1998; Tomada & Schneider, 1997).

When expressed in acceptable ways, aggression may be not only tolerable but even desirable. Aggressive actions allow a child to communicate and fulfill legitimate needs, such as when he takes back a toy that is rightfully his or stands up for his integrity against unfair insults. Often, however, hostile motivations complicate matters and create additional distress. The anger and rage children sometimes experience can be quite upsetting to them as well as to their parents and others. For example, a mother who observes her four-year-old attack a playmate, perhaps biting her or pulling her hair, is likely to be upset for multiple reasons, including her own child's unhappiness, the pain and distress of the other child, her belief that biting is "dirty fighting," and concerns about how all of this reflects on her as a parent.

Temperamental Differences in Aggression   Temperamental differences that are present at birth may make aggressive behavior more likely during early childhood. For example, babies who are low in their ability to regulate their physical and emotional states and high in emotional intensity may be especially prone to overt expressions of anger, frustration, and aggressive behavior, whereas babies with a high ability to regulate these states are more likely to cope more constructively with their anger and frustration.

Consistent with this view, Nancy Eisenberg and her colleagues found that babies with especially "difficult" temperaments at six months of age experienced significantly more conflict with their mothers at age three than babies with less difficult temperaments. At six months, temperamentally difficult infants displayed irregular levels of activity, including sudden bursts of arm waving and general restlessness (Eisenberg & Fabes, 1992; Eisenberg et al., 1994). At age three years, these children responded less cooperatively than did children who had easier temperaments as infants. They were also more likely to get into trouble a second time, ignore their parents' disciplinary efforts, and respond in unpleasant ways. Their parents used a wide variety of methods to attempt to control them, including forbidding certain activities, threatening punishment, and using physical restraint. Thus, the ongoing interactions between these difficult children and their parents seemed likely to be escalating a cycle of aggression (Eisenberg et al., 1994). Of course, many active or difficult babies do not become aggressive three-year-olds, perhaps because the expression of temperament is largely a product of child-caregiver interactions.

A fifteen-year longitudinal study conducted by Avshalom Caspi and his colleagues found a relationship between early childhood temperament, including emotional instability, restlessness, impulsiveness, and negativism, and teacher and parent reports of problems with aggression in middle childhood and adolescence (Caspi et al., 1995). Temperamental and family characteristics at age three have also been found to predict convictions for violent criminal activities at age eighteen (Henry et al., 1996).

Childrearing Style and Aggression   As in the case of prosocial behavior discussed earlier, styles of childrearing and the overall quality of the parent-child relationship are likely to significantly influence children's use of aggression in coping with interpersonal anger. There is some evidence that both permissive-indifferent and extremely authoritarian parenting styles are associated with higher levels of aggression and lower levels of prosocial behavior (DeKlyen et al., 1998; Herrenkohl et al., 1997). In one study, children who were abrasive and aggressive in interacting with their mothers and whose mothers used control tactics that were negative and ambiguous were more likely to be aggressive, low in prosocial behavior, and unsuccessful with their peers compared to children of mothers whose guidance was more respectful (Kochanska, 1992).

All of the following childrearing characteristics have been found to contribute to aggressiveness in preschoolers, especially when they are part of an ongoing pattern (Baumrind, 1971; Martin, 1975):

1. Lack of acceptance of the child, dislike of the child, and criticism of the child for being the sort of person she or he currently is or is becoming

2. Excessive permissiveness, particularly if it includes indifference to the child's true needs for reasonable but consistent limits and emotional support

3. Discipline that does not respect the child's ability and need to understand the reasons for the punishment and its meaning to the parent

4. Inconsistent discipline, which fails to provide the child with a reasonable and predictable basis for learning to regulate his or her behavior

5. A "spare the rod and spoil the child" belief that *too little* physical discipline would be harmful, which often results in impulsive and overly harsh use of discipline

6. Unclear rules and expectations for the child, particularly those regarding interactions with other family members

Peer Influences on Aggression   Peers can also contribute to aggression by acting in ways that provoke aggressive retaliation. Presumably a child surrounded by provocative peers eventually will acquire a similar style herself and, in doing so, will stimulate further aggressive behavior in her peers.

Some preschool children are continually involved in conflicts. They constantly either lose battles and arguments or lose potential friends by depending too much on hostile, aggressive actions to get what they need. Kenneth Dodge and his colleagues have proposed that a combination of low peer status and lack of social competence in the preschool period may contribute to a child's tendency to behave aggressively. When entering a new group, aggressive children have difficulty in accurately processing and evaluating information about what is expected and generating appropriate responses when faced with threat or provocation. Such children may have a biased pattern of thinking that leads them to overestimate the harmful intentions of their peers and to respond aggressively in situations that do not warrant it (Dodge & Coie, 1987; Schwartz et al., 1997). The aggressive, hostile behavior of an unpopular preschooler may also be his way of externalizing any anger and distress he is experiencing due to similar problems at home.

Media Influences on Aggression   As many concerned parents realize, television, films, and other media exert a strong influence on children, and much of that influence centers on physical violence. Researchers estimate that three-to-four-year-olds watch two or more hours of television each day and that viewing TV violence increases children's aggressive behavior, at least in the short run (Clarke & Kutz-Costes, 1997; Huston et al., 1989). Numerous well-documented studies indicate that watching violence *disinhibits*, or releases, violent behavior in children who are already prone to anger and aggression. Longitudinal studies have found that the amount of TV violence viewed at age eight may predict the seriousness of boys' aggressiveness at age nineteen and the average severity of criminal behavior at age thirty for both males and females (Eron, 1987; Huesmann et al., 1984). Media are so pervasive in many preschoolers' lives that we consider their impact separately in the next section.

Responding to Aggressive Behavior

Children who have difficulty controlling their aggression experience considerable problems. Often they become aggressive at inappropriate times and in self-defeating ways, getting into fights with children and adults who are stronger than they are. Peers and parents alike find it difficult not to attribute malicious motives to children who seem out of control and appear unresponsive to generally agreed-on standards of behavior (Kutner, 1989). Children who are overly aggressive can stimulate strong feelings of inadequacy, guilt, anger, and loss of control in their parents, leading to an increased risk that parents will respond in angry, punitive ways.

Spanking and Other Forms of Punishment   In general, preschoolers conform to parental expectations, especially if those expectations are communicated in a clear, understandable way that conveys warmth and respect for the child. Even when a child resists, patient explanation and responsiveness to the child's feelings and perceptions generally resolve the problem. In instances when a preschooler "loses it" and throws a tantrum or refuses to comply with a parent's reasonable and necessary demands, firm but respectful physical restraint and guidance may also be needed until the child has regained self-control. In dangerous situations requiring immediate action, such as when a child runs into the street or is about to touch something hot, parents may use strong reprimands or spanking to stop the risky behavior and prevent it from happening again.

Some parents, however, rely on spanking and punishment as a regular part of their childrearing discipline. James Comer and Alvin Poussaint, two prominent child psychiatrists, point out that children who were spanked by thoughtful, loving parents rarely have problems as a result of the spanking. Nevertheless, Comer and Poussaint caution that punishment is not the best way to provide discipline, especially in cases where parents are having difficulty with their preschoolers (Comer & Poussaint, 1992). A better alternative is to physically remove the child from the dangerous situation and talk with her about why the parent is upset, why the child's behavior is unacceptable, and how she is expected to behave in the future.

What problems are associated with spanking and punishment in general? Although verbal or physical punishment can suppress misbehavior in the short run, it is not an effective or desirable long-run strategy, particularly if it is harsh or frequent. One obvious problem is that preschoolers are very likely to imitate the behavior of the adult models who punish them (Bandura, 1991; Emery, 1989). Using aggressive behavior such as verbal threats or spanking to reduce a child's unacceptable behavior is likely to increase the very behavior it seeks to control. A child who is hit by an angry parent learns to act on his own anger in similar ways, which is surely not the lesson his parents intend. Even moderate use of spanking appears to contribute to child aggression. One large-scale study conducted by Robert Larzelere (1986), using a nationally representative sample of parents with at least one child age three to seventeen living at home, found that the use of physical punishment was positively associated with child aggression. In situations where spanking was frequent and reasons were rarely provided, the association between spanking and child aggression dramatically increased. Excessive reliance on spanking and other forms of punishment is strongly associated with child maltreatment, discussed later in this chapter.

A second problem with spanking and other forms of punishment is that a child quickly learns to fear and avoid the punishing adult, thus reducing opportunities for adult supervision and constructive adult-child interactions. Third, because punishment quickly suppresses the child's undesirable behavior in the short run, it serves to reinforce adult reliance on punishment and reduce the likelihood of exploring other ways to respond to the child's unacceptable behavior. Fourth, to the extent that punishment reduces the guilt a child feels for misbehaving, it reinforces the child's reliance on external (parental) control rather than internal, self-control of his behavior (Comer & Poussaint, 1992).

Helping Aggressive Children and Their Parents Several principles have emerged from work with aggressive children and their families that aim to help them learn more constructive ways of interacting. The most successful approaches frequently involve working with the entire family. The first step is to carefully observe the child's interactions with peers and adults to discover consistent patterns in what triggers the aggression and how each family member may unintentionally reinforce the patterns of problem behavior (Kutner, 1989; Patterson et al., 1989).

Structure, predictability, and consistency of routine are important for all preschoolers, especially for children who have difficulty controlling their aggressive behavior. For such children, aggressive outbursts are most likely to occur in unstructured and ambiguous situations. Such circumstances aggravate their tendency to distort information about potential harm and to perceive themselves as being at risk. Thus, neutral behavior, such as the approach of another child, is misinterpreted as an aggressive act (Dodge et al., 1994).

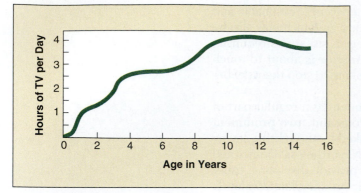

● ● ● ● ● ● ● ● ● ● ● ● ● ● ● ● ● ●

FIGURE 10.1

Changes in the Amount of TV Viewing with Age

Daily TV viewing time increases during the preschool and school years, with children viewing 1.5 hours daily at age two, 2.5 hours at age four, 3.5 hours at age eight, and a peak of 4.0 hours at age eleven.
Source: Adapted from Bukatko & Daehler (1995, p. 626).

Once the patterns of aggression are discovered, parents can learn to recognize the early signs and intervene by either changing the situation or removing their preschooler before things escalate. The most successful methods involve reinforcement of positive behaviors through warmth, affection, and parental approval, assertiveness training to help the child meet her needs for attention in less self-destructive ways, and increasing predictability and consistency in the child's everyday life (Kutner, 1989; Patterson et al., 1989).

Another successful approach to modifying destructive family processes and problems with childhood aggression uses social learning theory methods such as coaching, modeling, and reinforcing alternative patterns of parent-child interaction. After carefully observing the parent-child interaction, the therapist describes and then demonstrates alternative ways to deal with the child's hostile, aggressive, or disobedient behaviors. As parents gain more confidence in their competence, they become more effective parents; as children learn to resolve conflicts in more appropriate ways, their problematic behavior decreases (Patterson, 1982, 1985).

The Effects of Television on Preschoolers' Development

As influential as parents and family are in the lives of preschoolers, television has become a potent force in teaching them about the wider world. An exploration of preschoolers' TV viewing patterns will show the extent to which TV has become a part of daily life. We will also explore the impact of television watching on several areas of development.

Viewing Patterns   Ninety-eight percent of American homes have at least one television set, and a TV set is on for a total of 7.1 hours per day in a typical household (Huston et al., 1992). Most children are exposed to television from the time they are born, and American children spend more time, on average, watching TV than in any other waking activity, including play.

As Figure 10.1 shows, a typical six-month-old is in front of a TV set almost 1.5 hours per day, and by three years most children avidly watch their favorite shows. Viewing time increases during the preschool years and peaks at about 2.5 hours per day just before a child enters elementary school. Viewing then decreases slightly with the beginning of school, but at about age eight it increases steadily, reaching an average of about four hours per day during adolescence. Boys and girls appear to watch equal amounts of television. The same basic developmental pattern has been found in a number of European countries, Canada, and Australia, although the amount of viewing time varies with program availability and the number of broadcast hours (Liebert & Sprafkin, 1988).

Not surprisingly, the types of programs children prefer to watch change with age. Until they are three or four, children prefer programs such as "Sesame Street" and "Mister Rogers' Neighborhood," which are designed for children and feature language, characters, and events at a level children can readily understand. Children ages three to five tend to watch more cartoons, and children ages five to seven increasingly watch comedies, action shows, and special-interest programs that are more cognitively demanding and aimed at general audiences (Huston et al., 1990).

Differences in family circumstances significantly affect young children's TV viewing. Children from lower socioeconomic levels watch more television than those from families that are better off (Greenberg, 1986). Having a mother who works outside the home and attending day care or preschool, however, may decrease the amount of TV viewing. And while having an older brother or sister to play with may decrease TV watching, having younger siblings may increase it (Pinon et al., 1989).

Both the types of programs TV networks provide and the choices parents make about what their children may or may not view appear to be the most important factors affecting young children's viewing patterns (Huston et al., 1992). Families vary considerably in their attitudes toward television and in the amount and type of guidance they provide for their children. While nearly 40 percent of parents of preschoolers sometimes use TV to keep their children occupied, almost 40 percent regularly limit the number of hours their children can watch, and close to 50 percent have consistent rules regarding which types or which specific programs their children are allowed to view (Comstock, 1991).

Michelle St. Peters and her associates conducted a two-year longitudinal study of television-viewing patterns of families with five-year olds (St. Peters et al., 1991). Whereas the majority of children's programs were viewed without parents, most adult programs were watched with parents, although watching programs together declined with age. Based on the degree to which parents regulated their children's TV viewing (high versus low regulation) and to which they encouraged TV watching (high versus low), St. Peters and her colleagues classified families into four types. *Laissez-faire* parents provided low levels of regulation or encouragement; *restrictive* parents provided high regulation and low encouragement; *promotive* parents had few regulations and high levels of encouragement; and *selective* parents highly regulated their children's TV watching and encouraged specific types of viewing (see Table 10.2).

As Table 10.2 indicates, the number of hours of TV children viewed per week was highest for the promotive style (21.2) and lowest for the restrictive style (11.9), with selective (19.2) and laissez-faire (17.6) supervisory styles falling in between. The same pattern was evident for the types of programs children watched. For example, children whose parents encouraged TV watched more educational programs, such as "Sesame Street" and "Mister Rogers' Neighborhood," and more adult programs, including comedy, game shows, and action-adventure shows, than children who were not encouraged. Children whose TV viewing was regulated watched similar amounts of educational programs but significantly fewer adult programs. These findings suggest that parents can substantially influence their children's TV viewing by providing appropriate supervision and guidance.

Many older preschoolers, especially those with school-age brothers and sisters, also spend a lot of time watching prerecorded videos and playing video and computer games. In a recent survey of households with at least one child in the two-to-twelve-year range, 33 percent reported that the child watched videos, 33 percent indicated that the child had used a personal computer, and 14 percent reported that

TABLE 10.2	Styles of Parental Regulation and Number of Hours of Television Children Watch Each Week		
Style of Supervision	Degree of Regulation	Degree of Encouragement	Hours of TV Viewed per Week
Laissez-faire	Low	Low	17.6
Restrictive	High	Low	11.9
Promotive	Low	High	21.2
Selective	High	High	19.2

Source: Adapted from St. Peters et al. (1991), p. 1419.

Children whose parents do not encourage TV viewing (laissez-faire and restrictive) watch the fewest hours of TV; children whose parents encourage viewing (promotive and selective) watch the most hours.

the child had played video games "some or a lot" during the previous day. Since 1984, industry studies have found a 1 percent decrease in the average number of hours of TV viewing among children ages two to eleven, due largely to their increased viewing of videos and use of computer games (Roland & Gross, 1995).

Influences on Development   Television viewing has been found to influence children's social development in a number of areas, including aggression, gender stereotypes and prosocial behavior (Huston & Wright, 1996). The relationships between viewing aggression on TV and children's aggressive behavior are notable.

Preschoolers have a special problem in coping with violence in the media: their lack of skill in figuring out the motives of characters portrayed and the subtleties of plots. A heinous murder on television may look the same to a preschooler as one committed in self-defense or to protect innocent people. Also, some of the most violent TV programs are those produced for children; Saturday morning cartoons average more than twenty violent acts per hour (Gerbner et al., 1986). Programs such as "Spider Man," "Xena, Warrior Princess," "Mighty Morphin Power Rangers," "Masked Rider," and "X-Men," and many videotapes that young children view, also contain substantial amounts of violence. Violent video and computer games pose similar problems for young children and their parents (Emes, 1997; Roland & Gross, 1995). Adult supervision and help in understanding television programs therefore are especially important for very young children. Unfortunately, one of television's main attractions for some parents is that it makes adult supervision less necessary by keeping children passively occupied.

Recent widespread concern about children's exposure to television violence has led to a U.S. communications law stipulating that all new TV sets be equipped with a "violence chip," or V-chip. The V-chip "reads" TV programming and allows parents to tune out shows that they consider too violent for their children based on a rating system (Andrews, 1996). Several unanswered questions remain, however: Will the V-chip really give parents control over their children's exposure to TV violence? What criteria should be used to decide which programs are too violent for preschoolers? Are the same criteria appropriate for older children or adolescents?

In addition, television programs designed for children (and adults) often convey a highly stereotyped and distorted social world that values being male, youthful, handsome, and white over being female, old, handicapped, dark-skinned, or foreign born (Huston & Wright, 1996). Despite recent efforts to broaden the portrayals of gender roles, women continue to be cast in strongly sex-typed roles: teachers, secretaries, nurses, or (most commonly) homemakers. On television, women solve problems less frequently, need help more often, listen better and talk less than men do, and behave in other gender-stereotypical ways. These patterns also prevail for children's television despite widespread concern about the ways gender stereotypes limit girls' expectations. One reason for this may be that boys, who are reinforced largely by their peers, show much greater interest in shows with action heroes than in programs that present less stereotypic male activities. The significance of these patterns is not lost on advertisers, who are interested in buying time on programs that most effectively sell their products (Huston & Alvarez, 1990; Wright et al., 1995).

However, television is also a very useful educational tool for supporting children's intellectual and social development. Studies have found, for example, that programs modeling cooperative, prosocial behavior are likely to increase children's prosocial behavior and that children who are exposed to non-gender- and non–racially stereotyped programs are more likely than other children to behave in less stereotypic ways (Liebert & Sprafkin, 1988).

WHAT DO YOU THINK?   When you were a child, how did your family deal with the issues of prosocial behavior, aggression, and television? If you become a parent (or are now a parent), what might you change and what might you keep the same? Why?

Play in Early Childhood

In our society and many others, play dominates the preschool years. Every child plays, it seems, and virtually all observers of young children see lots of examples of play. What are the play activities of a preschooler like, and what important contributions does play make to a child's development? Before we tackle these questions, we must first agree on what we mean by *play*.

The Nature of Play

One useful approach to defining *play* focuses on the attitudes and dispositions of children themselves (Rubin et al., 1983; Sarachs & Spodak, 1998). First, play is *intrinsically* (rather than *extrinsically*) motivated. Children engage in play mainly because it is enjoyable and reinforcing for its own sake rather than because it is useful in achieving external goals.

Second, play is *process oriented* rather than *product oriented*. At the local playground, for instance, children may care very little about the goal of using the slide, to get from top to bottom, but they likely care a lot about their style of sliding—whether they go head first or feet first, or how fast they go.

Third, play is *creative* and *nonliteral*. Although it resembles real-life activities, it differs from them in that it is not bound by reality. For example, a child who is "play fighting" looks different than one who really is fighting, and a child playing Mommy typically acts differently than one who is actually caring for a baby brother or sister. The features that reveal an activity as play rather than the real thing vary with the particular type of play and the situation; a play fight may include smiles and laughter, and a make-believe mother may be overly bossy. Whatever the signs, they communicate the message that "this behavior is *not* what it first may appear to be." Even so, it is common for a preschooler to become so caught up in a round of dramatic play that he forgets for a moment that it is not real and becomes truly frightened when his make-believe mother tells him he has been bad and must sit in the corner.

Fourth, play tends to be governed by *implicit rules,* that is, rules that can be discovered by observing the activity rather than rules that are formally stated and exist independently of the activity. For example, although no rule book exists for playing house, children implicitly understand that there can be only one mother and one

In early childhood, the process of doing things often matters more than the outcome. Even taking a bath can seem like play.

Constructive play, such as block building, probably is the most common form of play in early childhood.

father and that these actors must live up to certain expectations. If one player deviates too widely from the expected role, the other children are likely to correct her for it ("Hey, mommies don't suck on baby bottles; only babies do!").

Fifth, play is *spontaneous* and *self-initiated,* meaning it is engaged in only under a child's own free will and is not evoked or controlled by others. Sixth, play is *free from major emotional distress.* Play does not normally occur when a child is in a state of fear, uncertainty, or other kinds of significant stress. It might be interesting to think about play in your own childhood, adolescence, and adulthood and see to what degree it has involved these six qualities.

Theories of Play

There are four main theoretical approaches to play: psychoanalytic, learning, ethological, and cognitive. Although each theory emphasizes a somewhat different aspect of play, all hold that play activities make a major contribution to the development of important social and emotional skills and understandings during the preschool years. Moreover, play during early childhood has important implications for the development and refinement of social information processing, empathy, emotional regulation, conflict management, perspective taking, and skilled social interaction (Creasey et al., 1998).

Psychoanalytic Theory   Psychoanalytic theories emphasize the social and emotional importance of play in early childhood. For one thing, play gives a child an opportunity to *gain mastery* over problems by rearranging objects and social situations in ways that allow him to imagine he is in control. Following an especially painful and upsetting experience such as being suddenly separated from a parent who is hospitalized for a serious illness, a child may display *repetition compulsion,* repeating the experience over and over in her symbolic play with dolls or other toys to gain greater control or resolution of her distress.

Play also allows a child to use fantasy to *gain satisfaction for wishes and desires* that are not possible to fulfill in reality due to limitations in the child's abilities and life situation. Another function of play is to provide an opportunity for *catharsis,* the release of upsetting feelings that cannot be expressed otherwise. Finally, play allows a child to *gain increased power* over the environment by rearranging it to suit his own needs and abilities (Lewis, 1993).

A major strength of the psychoanalytic approach is that it helps us appreciate the importance of fantasy and inner life in children's play. A limitation is its vagueness about precisely how developmental changes result from play.

Learning Theory   Learning theorists view play as an opportunity for children to safely try out new behaviors and social roles. In their view, play is a major means by which children progressively learn adult social skills, either through successive reinforcement of behaviors that come closer and closer to correct adult behaviors or through the processes of observational learning and imitation described in Chapter 2. A good example is pretend play, be it playing "house," "school," "doctor," or some other interpersonal situation familiar to young children. Whether a child is playing the role of mother, father, or baby brother, teacher or student, doctor, nurse, or patient, he or she will draw heavily on observational learning and imitation to create the role. And as the pretend-play episode unfolds, the child will learn through her own experience of receiving praise or encouragement for her actions (direct reinforcement); through observations of others being reinforced for their activities (vicarious reinforcement); and through the experience of setting a goal and achieving it (cognitive or self-reinforcement). Finally, early childhood play will also expose the child to adult expectations and practices regarding the play activity itself, such as when and where the play can occur, what props can be used, and when items must be picked up and shared.

Ethological Theory   Theorists such as A. D. Pellegrini and Peter Smith (1998) believe that children's **physical activity play**—vigorous physical activity that occurs in a playful context—has a basis in human evolution and serves several adaptive developmental functions. Examples include running, climbing, chasing, and play fighting. Physical activity play begins in early infancy, peaks during childhood, declines during adolescence, and all but disappears by adulthood. It appears to take three forms. The first is *rhythmic stereotypies*. These repetitive movements, such as the body rocking and foot kicking displayed by infants and the repetitive play interactions between parents and older infants, such as bouncing the baby on one's knee or tossing and catching him, are thought to help infants improve their sensorimotor skills. A second form of physical activity play, *exercise play*, emerges at the end of the first year. Exercise play includes chasing, jumping, pushing and pulling, lifting, and climbing. It appears to peak in the preschool and early primary grades, and is thought to contribute to the development of physical strength, endurance, and coordination. The third form, *rough-and-tumble play*, includes vigorous behaviors such as wrestling, grappling, kicking, tumbling, and chasing in a playfully aggressive way. Rough-and-tumble play increases through the preschool years and peaks at around eight to ten years, just prior to early adolescence. It is thought to provide a way for children to assess their own physical strength compared to the strength of others, establish dominance status in peer groups, and gain skill at recognizing and responding appropriately to the emotional states of others.

Cognitive Theory   Cognitive theorists have identified four major kinds of play that they believe develop sequentially in parallel with the major stages of cognitive development (Piaget, 1962; Johnson & Christie, 1998). Table 10.3 describes the different types of cognitive play.

Cognitive Levels of Play: Developmental Trends

Functional Play   **Functional play,** which involves simple, repeated movements such as splashing water or digging in a sandbox, is most common during the sensorimotor period. Because it requires no symbolic activity, functional play makes up an especially large part of the play activity of older infants and toddlers—more than one-half, in fact. By the time a child reaches kindergarten or first grade, however,

TABLE 10.3	Types of Cognitive Play
Type	**Description and Examples**
Functional play	Simple, repetitive movements, sometimes with objects or own body. Example: shoveling sand; pushing a toy
Constructive play	Manipulation of physical objects to build or construct something. Example: building with blocks
Pretend play	Substitutes make-believe, imaginary, and dramatic situations for real ones. Example: playing house or Superman
Games with rules	Play is more formal and governed by fixed rules. Example: jumping rope; hide-and-seek

physical activity play Vigorous physical activity that occurs in a playful context and is thought to have a basis in human evolution, serving several adaptive developmental functions.

functional play A cognitive level of play that involves simple, repeated movements and a focus on one's own body.

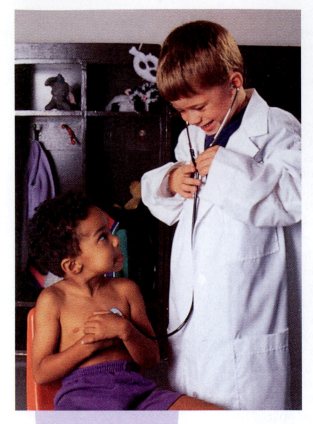

In dramatic play, children take on pretend roles, like the doctor and patient here. Realistic props, such as the uniform and stethoscope, in this photograph, encourage dramatic play, but they are not always necessary.

functional play has decreased to less than one-quarter of his total play (Hetherington et al., 1979; Sponseller & Jaworski, 1979). The shift occurs partly because many symbolic activities incorporate some of the physical activities characteristic of functional play. Functional play does not disappear in later childhood as much as it becomes combined with other playful ends.

Constructive Play   **Constructive play** involves manipulation of physical objects, such as using blocks to build or construct something. This form of play is evident in older infants and preschoolers, although it is not always clear where functional play ends and constructive play begins. For example, a child who at first appears to be building a mountain out of sand may forget about her goal and end up just shoveling the sand for the fun of it. As the child grows older, however, the constructive elements of play become quite clear. Not only does she build a mountain; she builds it in a certain shape and adds a road leading to it, and perhaps a car or two to make the trip.

Pretend Play   **Pretend play** (also called *fantasy* or *dramatic play*) substitutes imaginary situations for real ones, as in playing house or Superman, and dominates the preoperational period. Pretend play occurs even among toddlers and probably begins as soon as a child can symbolize, or mentally represent, objects. Family roles (including mother, father, brother, sister, baby, and even family pet) and *character roles* based on fictionalized heros such as Batman, Xena, Warrior Princess, and Power Rangers are most likely to be dramatized by preschool children. Pretend play grows in frequency and complexity during the preschool years and eventually decreases again later in childhood, when social pressures to act more "grown-up" reduce it in public settings (Dunn, 1985; Howes & Matheson, 1992; Kavanaugh & Engel, 1998). The complexity, flexibility, and elaborateness of preschoolers' fantasy play also appear to be positively related to the quality of their family relationships, to the support and the nurturance preschoolers receive from their parents, and to the specific reinforcement parents give them for such play (Howe et al., 1998; Ladd & Hart, 1992). Jerome Singer (1995) suggests that early pretend play, when suitably nurtured by family members and other individuals or settings in which a child participates, plays an important role in the development of fantasy and make-believe in middle childhood.

Pretend play is a good example of how new forms of experience are assimilated into existing schemes of cognitive understanding. In addition to allowing the child to practice and expand schemes already acquired, such play contributes to the consolidation and expansion of cognitive skills during the preschool years (Piaget, 1962; Vygotsky, 1967). The alternation between pretense and reality involved in pretend play also gives children an opportunity to practice and more fully understand these distinctions. Through their play with nonrealistic toys and objects, children become better able to internally represent and manipulate objects in the form of symbols and fantasy rather than solely in terms of realistic representations (Flavell et al., 1986; Rubin et al., 1983).

Games with Rules   **Games with rules,** such as Simon Says and hide-and-seek, first appear during the concrete operational period, when children are five or six years old, and peak in frequency toward the end of elementary school (Rubin & Krasnor, 1980). The rules for many such games apparently develop out of the more flexible, "made-up" rules of pretend play. Instead of continuing to negotiate roles and behaviors as they go along, young children gradually learn to agree on them beforehand and to stand by their agreements throughout a play episode. Due to their

• • •

constructive play A type of play that involves manipulation of physical objects to build or construct something.

pretend play Play that substitutes imaginary situations for real ones. Also called *fantasy* or *dramatic play*.

games with rules A cognitive level of play involving relatively formal activities with fixed rules.

greater formality, games with rules can become traditions handed down from one sibling to another, from older to younger playmates, and from generation to generation (Opie, 1993). Hopscotch, for example, has been around in some form for decades.

Social Levels of Play

Play also varies according to how social it is, that is, how much and in what ways children involve others in their play activities. Several decades ago, Mildred Parten studied social participation among children ages two to five and proposed that children's play develops in six stages, or levels, of sociability (Parten, 1932). Although subsequent researchers have questioned whether Parten's categories actually form a developmental sequence, her distinctions continue to be useful to people who study young children. Table 10.4 describes the six types of play that Parten identified.

How Play Changes with Age   Social participation in different types of play also varies with age. Even very young infants actively interact with the objects and people in their environment, and by twelve months their play interactions with peers become more frequent, particularly those that involve toys. Access to peers through play groups or day care and parental support tend to increase the likelihood of peer play.

Mildred Parten found that parallel play accounted for almost half of the observed play activity of preschoolers, whereas solitary play accounted for about one-fourth, associative play one-fifth, and cooperative and unoccupied play less than one-tenth of the total. Parallel and solitary play appeared to decline throughout the preschool years, whereas associative play and cooperative play, which involve greater social participation, increased with age.

Often a preschooler's play combines several of the types Parten described. For example, among three-year-olds, parallel play is frequently followed by associative or cooperative group play and serves as a transitional, or warm-up, strategy that enables a child to move into play involving others (Bakeman & Brownlee, 1980). The ability to cooperate appears to develop sequentially, and this sequence of play styles probably helps children to successfully cooperate with others in new situations. The ability to cooperate with others is an important aspect of successful social relationships throughout one's life.

By early elementary school, most children can play games with rules. Not only do these games cultivate motor skills, but they also teach social skills, such as learning to take turns and knowing how to be a good winner or loser.

TABLE 10.4   Parten's Social Levels of Play

Type	Description and Examples
Unoccupied play	The child wanders about, watching whatever is of momentary interest, but does not become involved in any activity
Solitary play	The child plays alone with different toys or other objects and with no direct or indirect awareness of or involvement with other children, even if nearby
Onlooker play	The child watches others play without actually entering into the activities; is clearly involved with what is happening and usually is within speaking distance of the participants
Parallel play	Involves two or more children playing with the same toys in a similar way, in close proximity and with an awareness of each other's presence; do not share toys, talk, or interact except in very minimal ways
Associative play	Children engage in a common activity and talk about it with each other, but do not assign tasks or roles to particular individuals and are not very clear about their goals
Cooperative play	Children consciously form into groups to make something, attain a goal, or dramatize a situation; one or two members organize and direct the activity, with children assuming different roles and responsibilities

Source: Parten (1932).

As preschoolers get older, play involving coordinated interactions increases. These interactions include imitation; complementary exchanges in which playmates take different roles, such as driver or passenger in pretend play; and more complex combinations of imitation and complementary exchanges (Eckerman, 1996; Eckerman et al., 1989). Preschoolers' highest level of peer social play also increases with age, progressing through a sequence of parallel play, simple social play, complementary and reciprocal play, cooperative social pretend play, and finally complex social pretend play. Children who spend more of their play time in complex forms of play appear to have greater overall social competence with their peers (Howes & Matheson, 1992). The nature and number of available playmates are also important (Benenson et al., 1997). See the accompanying interview with Javier Hernandez for a discussion of play and friendship during early childhood.

Although play involving high degrees of social participation increases during childhood and adolescence and tends to dominate throughout the rest of one's life, all forms of play continue to be important to various degrees. For example, the random, nondirected activity of a shy teenager at a party has much in common with the unoccupied play of a preschooler; devotees of jigsaw or crossword puzzles clearly engage in forms of solitary play; television viewing and involvement in spectator sports are basically onlooker play activities; and aerobics, weightlifting, and in-line skating sometimes have strong parallel-play aspects.

Play and Friendship in Early Childhood

Preschoolers are simultaneously pulled in two directions. On the one hand, they seek the security and intimacy that come from playing continually with a familiar friend; on the other, they want to participate in the variety of activities that many different children make possible. Although preschool friendships often involve shared activities and recognition of similarities, solidarity between two children sometimes results in exclusion of a third. In the following example, which takes place at a sink in a preschool classroom, Yolanda's alliance with Deanne involves exclusion of Shawn:

YOLANDA: I have some gum and candy—not for Shawn.

SHAWN: Why not?

YOLANDA: 'Cause you won't help.

SHAWN: I'm rinsing.

DEANNE: These are hardly even clean. I have a whole bunch of lollipops.

YOLANDA: Me too. I'm not giving Shawn any gum.

SHAWN: Yes, you are.

YOLANDA: No, I ain't. I'm going to give Deanne gum 'cause . . .

DEANNE: 'Cause I don't fight with you?

YOLANDA: Yes.

DEANNE: I'll give Shawn a little teeny piece.

YOLANDA: Yes, give him a little teeny piece. . . . See, you're not helping.

SHAWN: I'm rinsing.

DEANNE: I already rinsed it twice.

The Evolution of Friendship   Even infants and toddlers show preferences for particular children of their own age. Given a choice among several peers in a play-room, a one- or two-year-old is likely to smile at and approach his particular friend more often than a nonfriend. He will also be more skillful at taking turns with a friend than with a nonfriend. If two friends are playfully making noises or move-ments, for example, they will wait longer for each other to finish and generally co-ordinate their activity better than two children who are not friends might (Furman, 1982; Howes & Mueller, 1984; Vandell, 1980).

John Gottman and Jennifer Parkhurst (1980) made extensive home observations of preschoolers between ages three and six as the children played with friends and new acquaintances. Play between younger children and their friends included fre-quent and extensive fantasy role playing, whereas older children's friendships focused more on the actual activities they were doing than on make-believe roles. Younger children communicated more clearly with their friends than did older children and were more responsive to their friends' requests for information or explanation. They also worked harder to create a "climate of agreement" by avoiding disagreements. They did this by immediately discussing the reasons for a disagreement or explaining

These children are involved in parallel play. They probably are aware of each other's presence, but they are using sepa-rate toys and are preoccupied primarily with their own activities.

WORKING WITH

Javier Hernandez, **Preschool Program Coordinator**

Play and Friendships Among Preschoolers

Javier Hernandez coordinates a privately run preschool program that serves a middle- and working-class community. A parent himself, he has a degree in early childhood education and has worked in preschool and day care programs for almost six years. Javier was interviewed during nap time in the day care center office and talked about ways in which children's playing styles evolve over time.

Rob: *Your program serves a pretty wide age range. Do you see the kids' play change as they grow older?*

Javier: Yes, I do. Most of the two-year-olds' play involves sharing toys and turn taking—"it's my turn, it's your turn." They might share building blocks or share crayons when they draw. They can follow simple directions, like for circle time at the beginning and end of the day and for various other activities.

Rob: *How do three-year-olds play differently?*

Javier: Between 3 and 3½, you see an amazing increase in dramatic and fantasy play. The games become more complex and are rarely what they appear to be. The two-year-olds see the climber as just a climber, but the three-year-olds see it as a car, a spaceship, a house, or anything else they decide. The kids all make up different names and are deeply into imaginative role playing. They're always trying to involve you in their fantasy play.

Rob: *What about rules?*

Javier: They're very interested in rules—setting them and following them. They'll tell each other, "Oh, we can't do that now" or "We can't go that way" or "That's not the way we do it," or "You have to sit down." They're really into structure and delight in pointing out the right and wrong way to do things. There's a lot of tattling; I'll frequently overhear "You're going to get in trouble if you do that" or "You can't walk up the slide."

Rob: *This is quite different behavior than the two-year-olds.*

Javier: Yes. The two-year-olds are more apt to hit or push another kid, who will cry until the teacher comes over. With three-year-olds, the one who gets hit or pushed cries, but goes and then tells the teacher, "He hit me" and watches to see what you're going to do about it.

Rob: *So this also reflects the superior verbal and cognitive abilities of three-year-olds?*

Javier: Yes. The two-year-olds do a lot of copycatting. What one wants, the other one wants, and they want everything to be the same. Their attention spans are much shorter, and they change their minds quickly. They often forget what they want, and you can never be sure just what they're after.

Rob: *And the three-year-olds?*

Javier: They have much longer attention spans. They'll get so involved in a story that they won't move a muscle. And you have to point out and explain every detail of every picture in the book.

Rob: *You have to satisfy their desire to fully understand exactly what is going on?*

Javier: Exactly. Two-year-olds will keep on saying *why* just for the sake of it. Three- and four-year-olds really want a solid answer and are generally satisfied once they hear one they like. They're really listening to what you're saying, whereas the two-year-olds are mainly practicing their verbal skills.

Rob: *What about friendships and prosocial behavior among preschoolers?*

Javier: If one two-year-old is aggressive toward another and you say, "That wasn't very nice, you hurt his feelings and I think you need to say you are sorry," she may go over to the child and say, "sorry," but five minutes later might do the same thing again. Three- and four-year-olds tend to be more aware of other children's feelings and of their own. They base their friendships on who is nice to them and are better able to appreciate how it feels to be hurt. If you say, "Well, would you like it if she did that to you?" they are likely to say, "No, I wouldn't like it."

Rob: *Are they better able to take care of each other?*

Javier: Yes. We have two children who started in the infant room and went all the way up to kindergarten together. By the last few months they were here, if Larry said anything to Jenelle that she was sensitive about, she would just fall apart because "He's my best friend." She would get very sad and look to us to help them make up and mend their friendship. Then Larry would apologize, and they would hug. Older preschoolers seem to know a lot about each other's personalities. They know what to expect of each other and are very aware of what other children are doing.

What Do You Think?

1. In what ways do Javier's examples of preschool play and peer interactions demonstrate the interplay of cognitive and social development?

2. In what ways do Javier's descriptions of preschool friendships parallel the discussion of preschool friendship and its management in the chapter?

3. How do Javier's observations of preschoolers' play compare with those of Pamela Mitchell, the primary school teacher whose interview appeared in Chapter 1?

them away and by using positive social comparisons with their friends to create a sense of common ground and solidarity. Older children were better able to tolerate differences and disagreements and had less need to use positive social comparisons to manage conflict in their friendships.

Due to the "management" problems just noted and the emphasis on overt, concrete, shared activities—such as whether to build a sand castle, how to draw a dog, how to cook a pretend dinner—early friendships tend to be somewhat unstable and may change on a weekly or even daily basis. A preschooler will drop a friend relatively easily and later make up to her just as easily. Sometimes she will even exchange goods for friendship: "If you give me a piece of candy, I'll be your best friend!"

Preschoolers are also capable of sustaining relationships with playmates that last for a year or more (Howes, 1988; Howes et al., 1998). These preferences are an important step toward forming more lasting friendships later in childhood, as well as a basis for learning to get along with others. By age three to four, friendships become more involved and durable. Certain pairs of children develop a liking for each other and purposely try to spend time together.

During early childhood, friendships depend heavily on shared activities that children enjoy. Only later do more abstract qualities, such as intimacy and mutual loyalty, become important.

In fact, approximately 80 percent of three-to-four-year-olds spend a substantial amount of time with at least one special "associate" or playmate. Children in nursery school spend at least 30 percent of their time with one other peer. Typically, the pairings develop in situations that encourage physical proximity, such as the children's neighborhood play group, day care center, or preschool classroom (Hinde et al., 1985). Pairs of preschool friends exhibit greater reciprocity and interdependence with each other in their parallel play, requesting and following or imitating activities, than they do with mere acquaintances (Goldstein et al., 1989).

About 75 percent of nursery school children are involved in reciprocated friendships, as reflected in time spent in each other's company, nursery school teachers' reports, and interviews with their mothers. This number increases through adolescence, with 80 to 90 percent of teenagers reporting having mutual friends and several "close" or "good" friends. Friendship networks are small among preschool children, consisting of one or two best friends. School-age children, in contrast, average three to five best friends, a figure that remains fairly constant during adolescence (Hartup & Stevens, 1997).

The development of social competence and the ability to understand others' emotions and mental states during early childhood depend in part on the frequency with which playmates, parents, and other children initiate informal play activities. During the preschool years, children begin to imitate their own peer contacts and receive play invitations from peers, a trend that increases through early childhood (Bhavnagri & Parke, 1991; Maguire & Dunn, 1997).

Conceptions of Friendship   During the preschool years, a friend is someone who does certain things with you; she is someone (anyone, in fact) whom you like to play with, share toys with, or talk with a lot. "A friend," as one preschooler put it, "lets you hold his doll or truck or something." Young children form internal representations of peer and friendship relations in much the same way that they form internal rerpresentations of adult caregivers and attachments (Howes, 1996).

As children near school age, more permanent, personal qualities enter into their conceptions (Howes, 1996). Now the crucial features of a friend are more often dispositional, that is, related to how the friend is likely to behave in the future. A friend is still very much "someone you like," but she is also someone whom you trust, whom you can depend on, and who likes and admires you. To be friends in this sense, two children must know each other's likes and preferences better than before, and they must also be increasingly aware of thoughts and feelings that the friend may keep hidden. Nevertheless, each child is still likely to focus primarily on his own needs to the exclusion of his friend's. As one child said, "A friend is someone who does what you want"; and as another said, "A friend doesn't get you in trouble." Neither of these children understands that sometimes he or she should return these favors; later, during the school years, they will likely think of this.

Other Influences on Play and Friendship

The composition of a particular child's is likely to be influenced by the range of play opportunities that caregivers provide and the types of play they encourage. For example, a parent or caregiver who insists that the child always be learning something or trying something new may make play a stressful rather than a rewarding experience for the child. Outside the home, children who attend child care centers with qualified staffs, developmentally appropriate programs, and safe, well-designed, and well-equipped play areas have been found to develop more complex forms of pretend play at earlier ages, engage in much less unoccupied and solitary play, and interact more positively with adults than do children in less adequate centers (Howes & Matheson, 1992; Susa & Benedict, 1994).

Having adequate time for play is also important. Large amounts of television viewing can reduce the amount of time available for play, and watching programs with high levels of violence has been associated with decreased levels of fantasy play (van-der-Voort & Valkenburg, 1994).

Although play is a universal activity and occurs in all cultures, its frequency, forms, and functions also vary with cultural and socioeconomic contexts (Farver & Shin, 1997; Roopnarine et al., 1994). For example, in countries such as Kenya, India, Ecuador, and Brazil, where many children spend a large part of the day doing household chores and assisting their families in gathering food or earning money, time and opportunity for play are far more limited than for children in Mexico, the Philippines, or the United States (Campos et al., 1994; Hoffnung, 1992; Whiting & Edwards, 1988).

Even when free time, space, and toys are limited, however, most children find a way to play. They use common household objects such as pots, pans, and furni-

TABLE 10.5	General Characteristics and Appropriate Play Materials for the Preschool Child	
Age	General Characteristics	Appropriate Play Materials
2	Uses language effectively. Large-muscle skills developing, but limited in the use of small muscle skills. Energetic, vigorous, and enthusiastic, with a strong need to demonstrate independence and self-control.	Large-muscle play materials: Swing sets, outdoor blocks, toys to ride on, pull toys, push toys. Sensory play materials: Clay, fingerpaints, materials for water play, blocks, books, dolls and stuffed animals.
3	Expanded fantasy life, with unrealistic fears. Fascination with adult roles. Still stubborn, negative, but better able to adapt to peers than at age two. Early signs of product orientation in play.	Props for imaginative play (e.g., old clothes). Miniature life toys. Puzzles, simple board games, art materials that allow for a sense of accomplishment (e.g., paintbrushes, easels, marker pens, crayons).
4	Secure, self-confident. Need for adult attention and approval—showing off, clowning around, taking risks. More planful than threes, but products often accidental. Sophisticated small-muscle control allows for cutting, pasting, sewing, imaginative block building with smaller blocks.	Vehicles (e.g., tricycles, Big Wheels). Materials for painting, coloring, drawing, woodworking, sewing, stringing beads. Books with themes that extend well beyond the child's real world.
5	Early signs of logical thinking. Stable, predictable, reliable. Less self-centered than at four. Relaxed, friendly, willing to share and cooperate with peers. Realistic, practical, responsible.	Cut-and-paste and artistic activities with models to work from. Simple card games (e.g., Old Maid), table games (e.g., Bingo), and board games (e.g., Lotto), in which there are few rules and the outcomes are based more on chance than on strategy. Elaborate props for dramatic play.

Source: Hughes (1991), p. 70.

A TALK WITH

Larry, Age Four

• •

Play and Friendship in Early Childhood

Larry, age four, was interviewed in his bedroom after he returned from his day-care center.

Interviewer: *Tell me about your friends, Larry. Do you have a best friend?*

Larry: No.

Interviewer: *Who are some of the friends you play with?*

Larry: Kimmy, Judy. Nobody else.

Interviewer: *And what do you do with your friends? What do you play?*

Larry: Play dough. . . . You make it into things.

Interviewer: *Why is someone your friend?*

Larry: We play together. With baseball cards.

Interviewer: *How?*

Larry: We put doubles together.

Interviewer: *What do you do with your doubles?*

Larry: You pile them together.

Interviewer: *What do you do during the day?*

Larry: I like to play games and Mouse-trap and Safely Home and Wheel of Fortune and go to that store across the street.

Interviewer: *What do you do when you get up in the morning?*

Larry: Get dressed. Sometimes I watch TV.

Interviewer: *And then what do you do?*

Larry: I eat breakfast. I have all kinds of food. What you want. Bubble gum!

Interviewer: *I mean for regular breakfast, not silly breakfast. What would you have?*

Larry: Cereal.

Interviewer: *And then what happens, after you have your breakfast?*

Larry: I go to day care.

Interviewer: *Tell me about day care. What is day care?*

Larry: You play and there's a lot of toys and there's bikes and balls. A lot of bikes. And Big Wheels. Tricycles. A train. And drinks.

Interviewer: *And drinks?*

Larry: Right. And food. And there's a couch there. And there's a closet.

Interviewer: *What about people? Who else is there?*

Larry: Kimmy and Judy.

Interviewer: *How many other kids are there at day care?*

Larry: Ten people. And two new kids. Eric and Jason. And Aaron.

Interviewer: *And are there grown-ups at day care too?*

Larry: Yes. Lots and lots and lots.

Interviewer: *What do the grown-ups do at day care?*

Larry: They tell us what to do.

Interviewer: *What do they tell you?*

Larry: Don't do bad things. Like hit or bite.

Interviewer: *No hitting, no biting.*

Larry: No throwing pillows, but you can make a hideout.

Interviewer: *Do you make a hideout?*

Larry: No. But you can if you want to. If you ask them if it's okay, you can make a hideout. And if they say no, we can't. And if they say yes, we can. And we play and go outside.

What Do You Think?

1. In Larry's view, what is the basis of friendship? How does this fit with the discussion of preschool friendships in this chapter?

2. Which social and cognitive levels of play described in this chapter characterize Larry's play?

3. How typical are the types of aggression that Larry reports of children his age?

ture, as well as outdoor items such as trees, sticks, rocks, sand, empty cans, and discarded equipment, as props for their make-believe and sociodramatic play. However, the range and developmental appropriateness of play activities under such circumstances are likely to be more restricted than in the case of children who play in more supportive settings.

Table 10.5 summarizes age-appropriate recommendations for preschool play materials for children growing up in the United States.

Now that we have concluded our discussion of play in early childhood, we turn to discussing gender development, which profoundly affects almost all other developmental changes in early childhood and the years that follow.

WHAT DO YOU THINK? Many political leaders (and a significant number of parents who have voted for them) have criticized spending money on preschool programs where children spend their time playing rather than learning important preschool skills. How would you respond to such critics regarding the importance of play for preschool children?

Gender Development

Gender influences important aspects of social development in early childhood. As used here, the term **gender** refers to the behaviors and attitudes associated with being male or female. Most children go through at least three steps in gender development (Shepherd-Look, 1982). First, they develop beliefs about **gender identity,** that is, which sex they *are.* Second, they develop **gender preferences,** attitudes about which sex they *wish to be;* gender preference does not always coincide with gender identity. Third, they acquire **gender constancy,** a belief that the sex of a person is biologically determined, permanent, and unchanging, no matter what else about the person changes. All three aspects of gender contribute to a child's general knowledge of society's expectations about **gender-role stereotypes** (also called *sex roles*), or the culturally "appropriate" patterns of gender-related behaviors.

Learning Gender Schemata

From age two onward, preschoolers use gender-role stereotypes to guide their behaviors. Children's gender preferences and knowledge of stereotypes increase significantly with age: whereas twenty-four-month-olds typically do not show consistent gender preferences in toys and activities, thirty-month-olds consistently prefer "same-gender" over "opposite-gender" objects. In contrast to gender-based preferences for toys and activities, preschool children develop gender stereotypes about personal qualities relatively slowly. Only by age five or so do children begin to know which gender is "supposed" to be aggressive, loud, and strong and which is "supposed" to be gentle, quiet, and weak. Knowledge of gender stereotypes about personal qualities continues to develop throughout childhood and adolescence (Bailey & Zucker, 1995; Huston & Alvarez, 1999).

Most children acquire gender identity, the ability to label themselves correctly as boys or girls, between ages two and three, and are able to correctly label other children and adults as well (Huston, 1983). Some children develop gender identity early, before age twenty-eight months, and others not until later. Early identifiers exhibit significantly more gender-stereotyped play, such as building and car play for boys and doll play for girls, than later identifiers do (Fagot & Leinbach, 1989; Fagot et al., 1992).

Gender constancy, the understanding that one's sex is permanent and will never change, first appears by age four or five. A young preschool child may say she can switch gender just by wanting to or say that even though she is a girl now, she was a boy as an infant or may grow up to become a man as an adult. And a two-year-old may have only a hazy notion of what defines gender, believing, perhaps, that certain hairstyles, clothing, and toys make the crucial difference. Most children, however,

gender The thoughts, feelings, and behaviors associated with being male or female.

gender identity One's beliefs about what sex one is.

gender preference Attitudes about the sex one prefers to be.

gender constancy A belief that a person's sex is biologically determined, permanent, and unchanging, no matter what else about that person changes.

gender-role stereotypes The culturally "appropriate" patterns of gender-related behaviors expected by society. Also called sex roles.

Gender-role stereotyping starts early.

achieve a reliable sense of gender constancy between ages seven and nine (Bem, 1989; Emmerich & Sheppard, 1982).

A *gender schema* (plural schemata) is a pattern of beliefs and stereotypes about gender that children use to organize information about gender-related characteristics, experiences, and expectations. A child's gender schema is thought to develop through a series of stages. First, a child learns through social experiences what kinds of things are directly associated with each sex, such as "boys play with cars" and "girls play with dolls." Around age four to six, the child moves to the second stage and begins to develop more indirect and complex associations for information relevant to her own sex but not for the opposite sex. By age eight or so, the child moves to the third stage, where she has also learned the associations relevant to the opposite sex and has mastered the gender concepts of masculinity and femininity that link information within and among various content areas (Bem, 1983; Martin et al., 1990; Ruble, 1988).

Influences on Gender Development

If gender development is largely a process of learning socially constructed definitions of "boy" and "girl," we would expect the child's social circle of parents and peers to influence that process. In the following sections, we explore how this occurs.

Parents   Many theorists hold parents responsible for the development of gender differences, either blaming or congratulating them depending on the theorist's point of view. A close look suggests that parents do deserve some credit, but perhaps not as much as is commonly thought. When asked about their childrearing philosophies, parents tend to express belief in gender equality, but their actions often differ from their statements. Observations of parents playing with their preschool children reveal that parents support their children for gender-stereotyped activities more than for cross-gender activities; a boy gets praised more for playing with blocks than for playing with dolls. Parents generally support physical activity in boys more than in girls, by both praising it and participating in it. Possibly as a by-product of these differences, boys get punished more often and more physically than girls do. Also, as children approach school age, parents begin assigning household chores according to gender: girls more often fold the laundry, and boys more often take out the trash. Parents are also more likely to reward sons for being assertive, independent, active, and emotionally unexpressive and to reward daughters for being accommodating, dependent, more passive, and emotionally expressive (Fagot & Hagan, 1991; Lytton & Romney, 1991).

Socialization of females appears to emphasize interpersonal relatedness and emotional expressivity, whereas socialization of males emphasizes autonomy and rationality. These orientations have been associated with gender-typed differences in the ways parents talk to and interact with their children. In emphasizing causes and consequences of emotions with boys, mothers might orient them toward seeing emotions as problems to be solved and controlled rather than experienced and understood. Mothers' conversations with girls focus on the emotional states themselves, perhaps encouraging girls to directly focus on their own feelings and reactions and orienting them toward an interpersonal approach involving emotional sensitivity (Cervantes & Callanan, 1998; Leaper et al., 1998).

Nancy Chodorow (1995) has proposed that the gender differences between girls and boys are related to differences in their experiences of identity formation during their early years, when women are usually their exclusive caregivers. In this view, girls' identities and personality development are based on similarity and attachment to their mothers, who provide models for nurturing, caregiving, and closeness. Boys' identities and personality development are based on difference, separateness, and independence from these qualities, for to be male in our society means possessing qualities that are incompatible with those traditionally associated with being female. Thus, Chodorow believes, women's capacity to nurture, raise children, and develop close relationships and men's capacity to separate themselves from their feelings and participate in the often isolating and alienating world of work are rooted in these early experiences.

According to this view, the task of identity formation for a boy may be more difficult in that it requires a certain degree of rejection of essential qualities of his primary female caregiver. At the same time, the higher degree of similarity and continuity of experience between daughter and mother may make it more difficult for a girl to separate from her mother and establish an independent and separate identity.

Peers   In some ways, peers may shape gender differences more strongly than parents do. Early in the preschool years, even before age three, children respond differently to partners of the opposite sex than to those of the same sex (Maccoby, 1990). In play situations, girls tend to withdraw from a boy partner more often than from a girl partner, and boys heed prohibitions made by another boy more often than they do those that come from a girl. Even when preschoolers are not playing actively, they watch peers of the same sex more often than they do peers of the opposite sex.

Children of this age also respond to a reinforcement more reliably if it comes from a child of their own sex. If a boy compliments another boy's block building, the second boy is much more likely to continue building than he is if a girl compliments it. Conversely, if a boy criticizes the building, the other boy is more likely to stop than if a girl criticizes it. Parallel patterns occur for girls, who tend to persist in whatever other girls compliment or praise and to stop whatever they criticize or ignore. For both sexes, teachers' reinforcements have less influence than peers' in determining children's persistence at activities (Maccoby, 1990). What makes these patterns important is that children tend to reinforce play activities that are considered appropriate for their own sex. Children who deviate from expected gender-stereotyped activities, such as boys playing with dolls, often find themselves largely ignored, even after they return to expected activities. Thus, peer pressures to practice conventional gender roles are both strong and continuous, and they occur even if teachers and other adults try to minimize gender-typed play. As we noted earlier, the content of many children's TV shows—and the toys they promote—also send powerful messages about gender stereotypes.

The ease with which these three-year-olds adopt both stereotyped and non-stereotyped roles in playing "house" at preschool illustrates the flexible qualities associated with androgyny.

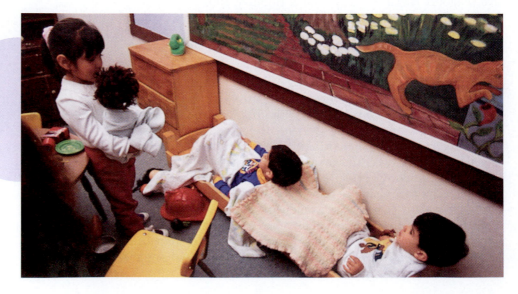

Androgyny

How we choose to define *gender* also can affect our understanding of what it means to be male or female. On the one hand, definitions that tend to exaggerate positive gender differences run the risk of perpetuating gender-role stereotyping and inequality; on the other hand, definitions that minimize real differences may be used to deny boys and girls the physical, cognitive, and social developmental opportunities appropriate to their different gender-related needs. One positive consequence of focusing on differences associated with gender is that it increases our awareness and appreciation of feminine (and masculine) qualities. A positive consequence of efforts to minimize gender differences is to help equalize treatment under the law and access to equal opportunity for males and females (Hare-Mustin & Marecek, 1988).

Androgyny refers to a situation in which gender roles are flexible, allowing all individuals, male and female, to behave in ways that freely integrate behaviors traditionally thought to belong exclusively to one or the other sex. In this view, both girls and boys can be assertive *and* yielding, independent *and* dependent, instrumental (task oriented) *and* expressive (feelings oriented). Sandra Bem (1981, 1987) and others (e.g., Lamke, 1982a, 1982b) have found that adolescent and young adult males and females use both masculine and feminine characteristics to describe their own personalities. Bem believes androgynous individuals are less concerned about which activities are appropriate or inappropriate and therefore are more flexible in their responses to various situations.

What are the implications of androgyny? Because the notion of androgyny challenges certain fundamental beliefs that individuals hold about gender, it has the potential to reduce gender-role stereotyping and its detrimental developmental effects in early childhood and beyond (Stake, 1997). The idea of androgyny also contributes to our understanding of sexual orientations that are not traditionally heterosexual, a topic discussed in Chapter 16.

WHAT DO YOU THINK? In what ways have you been personally influenced by gender-role stereotyping? What advice might you give to parents and teachers for reducing such stereotyping? Should they encourage children to be more androgynous?

Child Maltreatment

Child abuse and neglect by parents and other caregivers are a serious social problem, with more than 1 million new cases reported each year. A significant number of these cases involve infants, toddlers, and preschoolers, who are particularly vulnerable because of their immaturity and dependence. *Child abuse* may be physical, sexual, or emotional; *neglect* may be physical or emotional (Finkelhor, 1995; Wolock, 1998).

Causes

The causes of physical child abuse and neglect are best understood within the developmental-ecological contexts within which they occur. These include parent and child characteristics, parenting and parent-child interactions, and the broader context of family, community, and culture (Belsky, 1993; Helfer et al., 1997; Wolock, 1998).

Parent and Child Characteristics   One explanation for the transmission of maltreatment from one generation to the next is that the aggressive and antisocial

• • •
androgyny A tendency to integrate both masculine and feminine behaviors into the personality.

behavior involved in abuse was previously learned through modeling and direct reinforcement by the parent during her or his own childhood. The risk of maltreatment is much higher when parenting is extremely authoritarian (overly harsh and lacking in empathy) or when it is permissive-indifferent and neglectful of a child's needs. This explanation, however, fails to explain why two-thirds of parents who were abused themselves do not abuse their own children.

A second, more promising explanation of the causes of abuse is based on the idea of *internal working models*, the mental representations that organize and guide a parent's experiences, relationship, and interactions with the child (Bowlby, 1988; Farrangy et al., 1991; Stern, 1985b). The internal working models of an abusive parent are based on past experiences with the child, the parent's own childhood experiences, and the beliefs and expectations held by his or her own abusive parents. The working models of an abusing parent are often characterized by a distorted, unbalanced view of the child (overly negative or overly positive) and are associated with pervasive failures in parental empathy, parent-infant synchrony, and attachment (Belsky, 1993; Ferholt, 1991; Main & Goldwyn, 1989).

Mothers who are at risk for being abusive because they themselves were abused as children are much less likely to abuse their own children if they experienced one nonabusive, supportive, and close relationship while growing up. These mothers are also likely to display greater self-awareness regarding their own abuse, to be involved in a satisfying social relationship, and to have more extensive social supports than mothers who do abuse (Belsky, 1993; Caliso & Milner, 1992).

Personality characteristics that significantly undermine the ability to provide good parenting may also increase the risk of abuse, particularly if they interfere with getting social and emotional support from others. Difficulty with impulse control, emotional instability, high levels of depression, anxiety, or hostility, and alcohol and drug abuse can all impair a parent's capacity to respond to a child in empathic and responsible ways.

Finally, although a young child is never to blame for his or her own abuse, in some circumstances certain characteristics, such as a difficult temperament, prematurity, a physical disability, hyperactivity, or other developmental problems, may contribute to an increased risk of abuse (Belsky, 1980).

Parenting and Parent-Child Interactions   Parenting and parent-child interactions also play a role. Abusive parents are more likely than nonabusive parents to rely on physical punishment and negative control strategies such as hitting, grabbing, and pushing, or threats and disapproval, rather than on reasoning to guide or discipline their children. They are also less likely to appropriately adjust their disciplinary techniques to different kinds of misbehavior (Belsky, 1993; Herenkohl et al., 1997). During an abusive episode, the *overtly* aggressive behavior (physical punishment) on which an abusive parent relies is transformed into an act of interpersonal violence. A parent with a strong predisposition toward anxiety, depression, and hostility may become so irritated with the child that she or he loses control and physical or verbal punishment escalates into abuse.

Family, Community, and Cultural Factors   Poverty, unemployment, marital conflict, social isolation, and family dysfunction can increase the risk of abuse; so can shorter-term stressors such as emotional distress, economic or legal problems, or the birth of a new baby (Belsky, 1988; Cicchetti & Olson, 1990; Garbarino, 1992). Economic conditions, child and family social welfare policies, and cultural values and expectations regarding the care and protection of children can indirectly contribute to the risk of abuse and neglect (Black & Krishnakumar, 1998). For example, societies that condone the use of violence against women (who are the primary caregivers of children) are likely to have higher rates of child abuse than societies that treat women with respect. The role of differing cultural values and expectations regarding child maltreatment is discussed in the Multicultural View box on page 330.

Consequences

Neglected infants, toddlers, and preschoolers often are deprived of sufficient food, clothing, shelter, sanitation, and medical care, which may interfere with their physical, intellectual, social, and emotional development and place them at risk of serious illness and even death (Egeland, 1988). Abused or neglected preschoolers often develop emotional problems that include insecure attachment relationships, lack of empathy, and emotional detachment. They are also more likely to exhibit behavioral problems, such as aggressiveness and withdrawal, toward peers than other children are (Cicchetti & Olson, 1990; Dodge et al., 1990; Klimes-Dougan & Kistner, 1990; Pianta et al., 1989). Physical abuse in early childhood is linked to aggressive and violent behaviors in adolescents and adults, including violence toward nonfamily members, children, dating partners, and spouses (Kendall-Tackett et al., 1993; Malinosky-Rummell & Hansen, 1993).

The most common symptoms reported for preschoolers who have been sexually abused include nightmares, general posttraumatic stress disorder, depression and emotional withdrawal, regressive and immature behavior, anxiety disorders, and problems with aggression and inappropriate sexual behavior (Kendall-Tackett et al., 1993). The developmental stage at which sexual abuse occurs is particularly significant in determining longer-term outcomes. For example, incest (sexual abuse by a parent or other family member) disrupts the development of social functioning and self-esteem and increases risk for borderline and multiple personality disorders, eating disorders, and substance abuse in adolescence and adulthood (Finkelhor, 1995; Spaccarelli, 1994). (See Chapter 16 for a discussion of special problems of adolescence.)

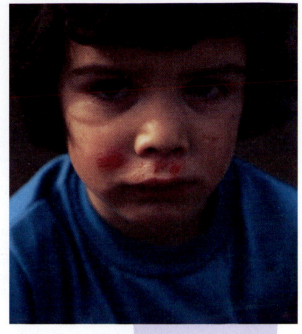

Preschoolers are particularly vulnerable to child abuse because of their immaturity and dependence. The destructive impact of abuse is often serious and long term.

Treatment and Prevention

Treatment of child abuse and neglect involves working directly with the abused infant, toddler, or preschooler, the parents, and the family after abuse (or the threat of abuse) has been discovered. One goal is to protect the child from further mistreatment and help her recover from the physical and psychological consequences. Another is to assist the abusing parent(s) in establishing a parent-child relationship and family environment that adequately ensures the preschooler's safety and supports his developmental needs.

Intensive professional help, including family counseling and psychotherapy, often can help parent and child understand the causes, consequences, and personal meanings of their destructive feelings and behaviors so they will be able to live together in less destructive ways. A key aspect of treatment is to help parents improve their parenting skills. Self-help groups such as Parents Anonymous, parent aides who assist abusive and neglectful families in their homes, crisis nurseries, foster care for the abused child, and short-term residential treatment for family members or the entire family unit are among the treatment alternatives that have met with some success (Willis et al., 1992; Wolfe et al., 1997).

Early intervention programs that target "high-risk" families, including those headed by low-SES teenage mothers, have focused on helping parents improve their parenting skills, the family climate, and their ability to better cope with the stressful life events and conditions. Such programs include early and extended contact between parents and their newborn infants to improve the early parent-child relationship, parent education about child development and everyday child care problems, and home visitors and parent aides who assist parents with young

A Multicultural View ....

The Cultural Context of Child Abuse and Neglect

Can the ideas one culture holds about child abuse and neglect be validly applied to others? According to Jill Korbin, who has extensively studied child abuse and neglect in many different cultural and societal contexts, culturally appropriate definitions of child abuse and neglect require an awareness of both the viewpoint of an "insider" to a particular culture, termed the *emic* perspective, and the viewpoint of an "outsider" to that culture, or the *etic* perspective (Korbin, 1991, 1987, 1981). Such definitions must include three dimensions: (1) cultural differences in childrearing practices, (2) treatment of children that deviates from cultural norms, and (3) societal abuse and neglect.

Cultural differences in childrearing include practices considered acceptable in the culture in which they occur but abusive or neglectful by outsiders. For example, most middle-class American parents believe it is developmentally important for young children to sleep separately from their parents, but traditional Japanese and Hawaiian-Polynesian cultures, which highly value interdependence among family members, view isolating children at night as potentially dangerous to healthy child development. Another example concerns a woman in London who cut the faces of her two young sons with a razor blade and rubbed charcoal into the cuts. She was arrested for child abuse, but officials soon learned that she and her children belonged to an East African tribal group that traditionally practiced facial scarification. When viewed from within her culture, her actions were an attempt to protect her children's cultural identity, for without such markings they would be unable to participate as adults in the culture of their birth (Korbin, 1987).

Many cultures have practiced such initiation rights as a normal part of childrearing before and during adolescence. Where, for example, is the line drawn between male circumcision during adolescence and circumcision at birth? How would a European or an American convince traditional people in highland New Guinea that circumcision is more painful for an adolescent than for an infant? How would traditional highland New Guinea people convince Europeans or Ameri-

children. They also offer training and support in home safety, money management, job finding, health maintenance and nutrition, leisure time counseling, and help in developing stronger social support networks (Rosenberg & Reppucci, 1985; Wolfe et al., 1997).

Other prevention efforts attempt to reduce or eliminate the causes of abuse by changing more general conditions that affect *all* children and families. These *social policy* efforts include education for parenthood programs, elimination of corporal punishment, the development of a bill of rights for children, and various social policy supports for parents and their children, including more and better jobs, funding for preschools and day care centers, affordable health care, and so forth.

WHAT DO YOU THINK ?   If you were a preschool teacher, what behaviors in a child might lead you to suspect child maltreatment? What advice might you give to parents who may be at risk for abusing or neglecting their children?

The End of Early Childhood

Although the early childhood period, considered as a whole, may not bring about physical changes as dramatic as those of infancy, the cognitive, social, and emotional changes that occur may be even more striking. By age five or six, a child has both worked and played with symbolic skills quite a lot, and sometimes is beginning to do so according to prearranged rules. He can form friendships that last at least a bit beyond the here and now and that both foster and draw on genuine understanding of others. His increasing social sophistication may also allow him to use less aggressive means of asserting his needs and dealing with conflict. All of these new skills, both positive and negative, are strongly guided by the child's gender role, a concept

cans that (1) circumcision has no meaning for an infant, who cannot understand its deep cultural significance, and (2) infancy is a time when the child should be spared all discomfort? How is the line drawn between facial scarification and orthodontia (braces), both of which cause pain and discomfort but are intended to enhance the child's attractiveness?

Idiosyncratic child abuse and neglect involves treatment of children that deviates from established standards of acceptable treatment within a particular culture. Although they may differ, all societies have such standards. For example, in one Polynesian culture known for its indulgence of children, a child can be pinched lightly on the mouth for misbehavior, but more severe punishments are prohibited. When one man left a scratch on the lip of his grandchild, he was severely criticized by his cultural group. By their *emic* standards his behavior was abusive, although from the *etic* perspective of American parents it is unlikely that such behavior would be of great concern.

Societal abuse and neglect refers to harm caused to children by societal conditions such as poverty and inadequate housing, health care, and nutrition, all of which either con-

tribute significantly to abuse or neglect or are considered abusive or neglectful in themselves. For example, the widespread famine in Ethiopia and Somalia and the inadequate nutrition in India and Chile have had devastating effects on the physical, cognitive, and socioemotional development of millions of children. In many countries physical, sexual, and emotional exploitation and abuse of children are very common. Even in affluent countries such as our own, social policy regarding aid to parents with dependent children, early childhood health care and nutrition, child care, and employment can significantly harm (or help) the development of young children. Where does responsibility lie, and what should be done about this?

It seems likely that neither a single, universal standard nor a completely relativistic, "anything goes" standard for determining abuse and neglect is acceptable. The challenge, then, is to develop an approach that incorporates developmental values and standards for "good enough" care and treatment of children that should be universal and values standards that afford more room for cultural and societal diversity

to which the child himself makes important contributions during the preschool years.

But human development is far from over at this point. The child's social world broadens widely in the years ahead, most obviously through her entry into school and the development of important social relationships outside her family. Major changes also occur in the child's cognitive abilities and in her physical growth and ability to use her body. The following three chapters explore these and other important features of the child's development as she progresses through middle childhood.

Summary of Major Ideas

Relationships with Family

1. In early childhood, a child's relationships with parents and other family members are a central source of psychosocial development.
2. Parenting styles differ in their maturity demands, need for control, and responsiveness to children's feelings and needs. Such differences are associated with differences in parent-child relationships and developmental outcomes.
3. Authoritative parents display high levels of control, maturity demands, and responsiveness to their children's feelings and needs. Their children tend to show greater self-reliance, self-control, and achievement.
4. Authoritarian parents display high levels of control and maturity demands but low levels of responsiveness to their children's feelings and needs. Their children tend to be

more distrustful and unhappy with themselves and to show lower school achievement than children of authoritative parents.
5. Permissive-indulgent parents display high levels of responsiveness but very low levels of control and maturity demands. Their children tend to lack self-reliance and self-control.
6. Permissive-indifferent parents are detached, uninvolved, and inconsistent. They display low levels of control, maturity demands, and responsiveness. Their children tend to lack self-reliance and self-control, and may be at risk for more severe social and emotional problems.
7. Parents often use mixtures of parenting styles, and the preferred parenting style may change as children grow older.

8. Both siblings and friends also make an important contribution to social development during the preschool years. The quality of children's social relationships with siblings is predictive of the quality of their relationships with friends. Ultimately, however, it is the parents' responsibility to help their children establish and maintain positive social relationships.

Relationships in an Expanding Social World

9. As children grow older, the support and judgments of parents and other adults contribute increasingly to children's feelings of empathy and prosocial activities.

10. Preschoolers commonly exhibit both overt and relational aggression to assert their needs and resolve conflicts. As they grow older, verbal methods replace physical ones and overall aggression declines.

11. Children who cannot control their aggression can be helped to do so with methods such as assertiveness training and social learning theory strategies. Parents can learn to spot the triggers of their children's aggression and respond effectively.

12. Television viewing and video and computer game playing significantly influence preschoolers' social development in such areas as aggression, prosocial behavior, and gender stereotyping.

Play in Early Childhood

13. Play for its own sake is the major waking activity of preschoolers.

14. Psychoanalytic theory emphasizes the mastery and wish fulfillment functions of play, whereas learning theory stresses the acquisition of social skills through imitation and observation.

15. The ethological approach emphasizes the evolutionary roots and adaptive developmental functions of physical play.

16. Cognitive theory emphasizes that play develops in a sequence that generally parallels the major stages of cognitive development. It includes functional play, constructive play, pretend play, and play involving games with rules.

17. Mildred Parten has identified six social levels of play: unoccupied, solitary, onlooker, parallel, associative, and cooperative play. The type of setting is important to the development of social play.

18. Whereas early friendships are unstable and depend on specific shared play activities, friendships among older preschoolers involve expectations about future behavior.

19. Preschoolers' friendships become more durable and involve a greater degree of shared activity with age. As they near school age, the more permanent and personal qualities of friendship become increasingly important.

Gender Development

20. During early childhood, children acquire an understanding of gender-typed behaviors and gender identity. A sense of gender constancy, the belief that being male or female is biologically determined and permanent, typically is not achieved until ages seven to nine.

21. Because the development of stereotypes about personal qualities appears to depend on the ability to think abstractly, children do not gain a clear and stable concept of gender until the school years.

22. Influences on gender development include differential expectations and treatment of boys and girls by parents, peers, and the media.

23. A more flexible approach to gender roles enables children to adopt more androgynous behaviors and attitudes.

Child Maltreatment

24. More than 1.5 million cases of child abuse are reported annually. Types of abuse include physical, psychological, and sexual abuse. Neglect can be physical or emotional.

25. Causes of maltreatment occur at the levels of the individual parent, the family, the community, and the culture.

26. Consequences of abuse and neglect include a range of developmental, adjustment, and emotional problems.

27. Responses to abuse and neglect frequently focus on treating the victims and their families. Prevention efforts include early intervention programs targeting "high-risk" families and attempts to change more general conditions that affect all children and families.

Key Terms

aggression (305)
androgyny (327)
authoritarian parenting (299)
authoritative parenting (298)
constructive play (316)
empathy (303)
functional play (315)
games with rules (316)
gender (324)
gender constancy (324)
gender identity (324)
gender preference (324)

gender-role stereotypes (324)
overt aggression (305)
permissive-indifferent parenting (300)
permissive-indulgent parenting (300)
physical activity play (315)
pretend play (316)
prosocial behavior (304)
relational aggression (305)

Middle Childhood

Because growth slows after the preschool years, children in middle childhood have more time and energy to develop skills of all sorts, from riding a skateboard to making friends. All their years of language practice and symbolic play finally pay off: School-age children often can think rather logically, even if only about concrete matters. Partly because of these new competencies and partly due to school life, peers take on more importance than ever before.

Perhaps because children are now old enough to be aware of these changes, as adults they often remember middle childhood as the best years of their childhood. For most children of this age, the world seems secure, their health is excellent, and their abilities improve visibly and steadily year by year.

11

Physical Development in Middle Childhood

Focusing Questions

- What trends in height and weight occur among school-age children?

- How do differences in growth affect children's feelings about one another and about themselves?

- What improvements in motor skills do children usually experience during the school years, and how do they affect children's involvement in athletic activity?

- What kinds of illnesses, accidents, and physical conditions tend to occur among schoolchildren? How do children's family and community circumstances affect them?

- What is the relationship between physical growth and psychological development during middle childhood?

C armen and Mercedes were sisters. When Carmen was four and Mercedes eight, they found an old pair of roller skates in a trash can behind their apartment building. The skates were too small for Mercedes, so Carmen got to keep them. Carmen could not believe her good fortune; their mother had always said they could not afford "extras" like skates.

But Carmen's pride was short-lived. To Carmen's dismay, their mother bought Mercedes a brand-new pair of skates. "It's more practical," their mother tried to explain to Carmen, "because Mercedes won't grow out of them as fast as you will. And anyway, she'll work at them, use them a lot." Carmen thought *she* would use skates a lot too. But time proved her mother was right: Carmen used her skates only occasionally, but Mercedes was outside on hers almost every day. One time she even took lessons for a week when the city offered them as part of its summer recreation program. In these ways, Mercedes eventually acquired quite a talent for roller-skating.

In general, as Carmen and Mercedes' mother observed, children's physical growth slows down during middle childhood (ages six to twelve) even more than it does during early childhood. But as with Mercedes' skating talents, the results of growth begin to show more than ever before. Specific physical skills are easier to teach than they used to be because children now find them easier to learn. For a school-age child, instruction and practice in baseball make a more obvious difference in skill development than they did when he was still a preschooler. This means the child can now acquire physical and athletic skills that may give him a lifetime of satisfaction. But children *can* get hurt during physical activity, and athletic games can emphasize competition that is unrealistic or unpleasant.

Children are relatively healthy during the school years, but they do sometimes have accidents or get sick. A few children also develop problems that have ambiguous physical causes, and such children may show excessive motor activity even in quiet situations or difficulties in learning specific academic skills. Such problems may originate from subtle differences in how the nervous system operates in these children, although this is far from certain.

In this chapter, we review these ideas in more detail. We begin by looking at normal trends and variations in overall growth during middle childhood. Then we examine specific motor skill and athletic development and their psychological effects on children. Finally, we discuss health in the school years, with special reference to children who are overly active.

Trends and Variations in Height and Weight

As Figure 11.1 shows, children grow steadily during middle childhood, from about forty-six inches and forty-five pounds at age six to almost sixty inches and eighty pounds at age twelve (Engels, 1993). At the same time, variations among children often are significant. Figure 11.2 shows, for example, that the average height of eight-year-old girls varies from forty-five inches in South Korea to almost fifty-one

FIGURE 11.1

Growth in Height and Weight from Two to Eighteen Years

During the early middle childhood, children continue to grow at a smooth rate, though more slowly than in early childhood and infancy. By the middle and later parts of this period, however, weight and height begin to accelerate as children move into puberty. The growth spurts usually begin sooner for weight than for height and sooner for girls than for boys.

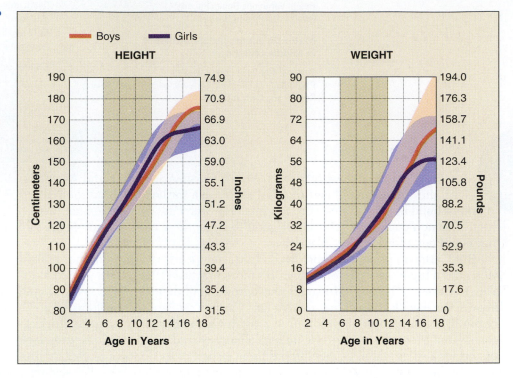

Late in childhood, girls often grow taller and faster than boys of the same age. The disparity can create awkward moments for members of both sexes, though many children do not seem to be concerned about it at all.

inches in Russia. And any age within any one society, individual variations are even more dramatic. The shortest and tallest six-year-olds in North America differ by only two or three inches, but the shortest and tallest twelve-year-olds differ by more than one foot. The changes are a source of both pride and dismay to individual children.

Growth gives children the potential to participate in activities with new skillfulness: whether playing softball or hiking in the woods, they can do it better than ever before. But growth can also create problems for them, and the difficulties typically have both physical and psychological aspects. Stereotypes about size and shape exist among school-age children as well as among adults. Wearing glasses may typecast some children as "geeks," and big ears may typecast others as "clowns." The most prominent physical stereotypes, however, concern overall size and weight. Very small children may seem younger than they really are, and as a result their teachers and friends may treat them with less respect than they deserve. An overweight child may be regarded as unattractive, so friends and teachers may not respond to her as warmly as they otherwise would. Such reactions may occur unconsciously. And even though physical appearance may really stem largely from biological influences, children with the "wrong" looks may blame themselves.

Height Variations Due to Puberty

As we have noted, toward the end of the elementary school years, girls tend to become significantly taller than boys of the same age. The difference results partly from girls' earlier puberty and partly from the timing of the growth spurt associated with puberty for each gender. For boys, a spurt in height tends to follow the other physical changes of adolescence, such as the growth of pubic hair and the deepening of the voice. For girls, a spurt in height usually occurs before the growth of breasts and pubic hair.

Inevitably these changes create temporary embarrassment for at least some girls and boys. Late in childhood, most children become aware of social expectations or stereotypes about attractiveness, such as the idea that men "should" be taller than women. But this awareness dawns precisely when many children exhibit the opposite pattern. This discrepancy undoubtedly is felt more acutely by some children than by others; it may feel worse for children who seek the attentions of the opposite sex most strongly, yet find they are the "wrong" height. The exact amount by which a child deviates from height standards may matter little, except at the extremes. Very tall girls and very short boys are most likely to feel out of place, though numerous exceptions exist.

Excess Weight and Obesity

At least one American child in ten suffers from **obesity,** meaning the child weighs more than 130 percent of the normal weight for his or her height and bone size (Cassell, 1994). This means that a child who is fifty-four inches tall weighs more than eighty-five pounds instead of a normal weight of about sixty-five pounds. How does such a child feel about her size? Accepting social stereotypes about weight means regarding herself as unattractive. But rejecting those standards means disagreeing with peers about what makes a person good looking. The dilemma is particularly acute for girls, since cultural norms emphasize physical appearance, especially thinness, more heavily in females than in males. Note, though, that in some other cultures, physical size is not important to individuals' social success. (See the accompanying Multicultural View box.)

In the long run, obesity causes physical problems as well. Children who continue to be obese into adulthood run more risk of a variety of minor illnesses, as well as of a few major ones such as heart disease and diabetes (Dalton, 1997). Partly as a result, they also tend to live shorter lives. Overweight people tend to be significantly less active than people of normal weight, even by the standards of our relatively sedentary society, and their lack of exercise can further aggravate their weight problem and the risks connected with it. For all these reasons, obese children deserve help, even if their problem cannot be resolved easily.

Most people (including most medical professionals) assume that these problems are *caused by* (rather than merely associated with) excess weight as such, and therefore assume that a primary goal for such people is to lose weight. A careful look at medical research about obesity and weight control, however, suggests that the link between weight and health is not so simple (Gaesser, 1996). Sometimes excess weight is the result rather than the cause of an ailment (as in the case of diabetes). Other times it is the result not of eating too much but of insufficient activity. Inactivity, in turn, may be caused not by simply personal "laziness" but by social prejudices. An overweight person may feel quite self-conscious about exercising in public, since he correctly senses the social biases against the "wrong" type of body; yet he is also unmotivated to exercise privately, where no social support is available. These attitudes are essentially social problems, not personal ones; and as the accompanying Multicultural View box indicates, the attitudes are *not* shared by all societies.

For a child, losing weight can be difficult for other reasons as well. Any dieting or exercise scheme must have the full support of the child's parents and siblings, because they usually have a substantial influence on meal preparation and on the child's daily lifestyle (Pittman & Kaufman, 1994). Yet family members may find support difficult to sustain over the long periods of time most weight control programs require. The collective willpower may just not be there, especially because overweight children tend to have siblings and parents who are overweight themselves. But help for these challenges is widely available (Shaw et al., 1996). Table 11.1 lists some additional guidelines for assisting a child with a weight problem.

Whether a child has a weight problem or not, establishing good nutrition in childhood can pave the way for a lifetime of healthy eating. A child in the middle years needs about 2,200 calories per day (similar to what an average active woman or a sedentary man requires, although fewer calories than a growing adolescent

EIGHT-YEAR-OLD GIRLS

Height (in Inches)

- 51
- Moscow, Russia 50.8
- 50 — United States, African ancestry 50.0
- United States, European ancestry 49.6
- 49 — Brussels, Belgium 49.0
- United States, Asian ancestry 48.7
- 48
- Monrovia, Liberia (Africa) 47.6
- 47 — Hong Kong 47.2
- 46
- 45 — South Korea 45.1

FIGURE 11.2

Ethnic and Cultural Differences in Growth

Differences in height are associated strongly with cultural and ethnic background. This chart summarizes the heights of eight-year-old girls from a number of nations and regions of the world. Girls from eastern and northern Europe are nearly six inches taller than girls of the same age from India and South Korea. Similar trends occur for boys.
Source: Adapted from Meredith (1981).

obesity The state of being extremely overweight, specifically more than 130 percent of normal weight for height and bone size; affects one American child in ten.

A Multicultural View

Dieting in Cross-Cultural Perspective

In our society, self-administered dieting and exercise has become a major industry. Countless books have been published to help individuals lose weight and gain muscle, and many of them are intended for children (see, for example, Schwarzenegger & Gaines, 1994). Attaining a culturally valued bodily "look" can become a major personal project, one that for many children begins in late childhood and continues well into adulthood.

At the heart of North Americans' preoccupation with body image is not only a concern with nutrition and health but also a commitment to crucial cultural values. One of these values is *individualism*, a belief that people are fundamentally autonomous and responsible for themselves. From this notion comes the belief that your body indeed belongs to you and that you personally are responsible for how it looks. How it compares to social ideals of physical beauty therefore indicates your success as a member of society as well as your ongoing commitment to participation in society. A lean, thin body (supposedly) shows self-discipline and re-straint, two socially admired qualities, because it implies that you have been eating and exercising responsibly. To achieve these things, numerous individuals embark on exercise and diet programs for varying periods of time. Girls and women are especially likely to do so, since they are almost certain to be judged by their physical appearance repeatedly, even during childhood (Bordo, 1993).

Yet a preoccupation with diet and exercise is not universal. The Fiji islanders in the South Pacific, for example, seem generally indifferent to the size or weight (Becker, 1994). At the same time, they have definite ideals about physical appearance: a person should have sturdy calf muscles, for example, and generally look "well fed" (a bit plump by our standards). Furthermore, despite their indifference to size and weight, the Fijians comment on one another's physical looks constantly and directly. Everyday greetings often include teasing about whether a person looks fatter (or thinner) than in the past. Daily conversations about persons not present ("gossip") also refer frequently to a person's size, particularly if his or her size seems to have changed.

The paradox of personal indifference combined with public frankness is accounted for by the Fijians' fundamen-

---

TABLE 11.1   Guidelines for Responding to a Child's Weight Problem

1. *Make sure the child really needs to lose weight.* Weighing only a little (10%) more than average poses no medical risk and may cause a child few social problems in the long term. If a child is teased for his or her weight, learning ways to cope with the teasing may be more effective than trying to lose weight.

2. *Consult with a doctor or a trained nutritionist before starting the child on a diet program.* A diet should aim at stabilizing weight or causing a loss of only about one pound per week at most. It should be balanced nutritionally and include snacks. Crash diets or food fads should be avoided at all costs; they are not effective and can seriously jeopardize a child's health.

3. *Develop a program of exercise appropriate for the child.* Start slowly and build up gradually. Try to incorporate activities that the child enjoys and that can fit into his or her daily routines conveniently.

4. *Seek support from the child's whole family, as well as from teachers or others whom the child sees regularly.* These people must show respect for the child's efforts, offer encouragement, and avoid tempting the child to break a diet or give up on exercise. Most of all, participate *with* the child in programs of activity or programs to control eating.

---

needs). The child's diet should emphasize breads, cereals, rice, and pasta, including about six servings a day of these foods (a slice of bread is a full serving). Also include moderate amounts of fresh fruits and vegetables each day, aiming for two to three servings (a piece of fruit or a half cup of vegetables each constitute a serving). Go easy on fatty and sugary foods such as butter, margarine, candy, and soft drinks, saving them for occasional treats rather than eliminating them altogether.

WHAT DO YOU THINK? Do you think concern about height and weight is really a gender issue? Why or why not? Check your perceptions by polling ten male and ten female acquaintances (it's easier if you collaborate in doing this task) about whether they weigh more than the ideal, less than the ideal, or close to it. Then ask them how they think members of the opposite sex would rate themselves, on average.

tal orientation to their *community* rather than to themselves as individuals. What is important to an individual Fijian is not personal achievement or standing out from the average but showing a nurturing and caring attitude toward friends, family, and children. A primary vehicle for attaining these goals is food: serving food is a major way to show interest and attention to others' needs, both physical and emotional. According to custom, Fijians open their windows and doors during mealtimes so that the event becomes more truly public, and anyone passing by is cordially (and sincerely) invited in to share the food. Extra food is routinely prepared for each meal to allow for this possibility, because it is considered a social disgrace to be unable to share food generously with whoever happens to come by.

The Fiji islanders, therefore, consider dieting to be self-centered and irresponsible because it prevents a person from either giving or receiving nurturance from the community. In a sense, a person's body "belongs" to the community rather than to the individual. Secret eating is a serious social mistake, as is secret noneating (dieting). Parents observe their children carefully for changes in appetite, as well as for changes in weight (either up or down) that may imply fluctuations in appetite. They do so not because they want their children to achieve a certain size but because they want them to participate fully in both the giving and receiving of community care, and an important way of participating is through food.

In Fiji, it is not the cultivation of a certain body image that confers prestige, as in North American society. Instead, it is the cultivation of social relationships, particularly those that make nurturance possible. Is this orientation preferable to our own? The focus on caregiving spares most Fijian children from worries about their physical appearance, as well as from discouragement caused by unsuccessful dieting or exercise programs to improve physical looks (Sault, 1994). But a negative effect also is possible: the focus on community can create problems for children who *must* limit their eating for health reasons, such as diabetes or intestinal flu. In a strongly communal society, these situations can prove especially worrisome to both child and family, since they require deliberately limiting participation in a central social practice: the daily abundant sharing of food.

Motor Development and Athletics in Middle Childhood

Motor skills continue to improve during the school years and gradually become specialized in response to each child's particular interests, physical aptitudes, and life experiences, and the expectations of others. The improvement and specialization occur both in fundamental or gross motor skills, such as running, jumping, and throwing, and in fine motor skills, such as writing and putting on clothing every day. In Chapter 6 we saw a detailed example of fine motor skills: Elizabeth's growing ability to draw, which improved not only throughout the preschool years but on into the school years and adolescence. In this chapter, we look at the changes in fundamental motor skills during middle childhood and the psychological impact of those changes.

Unlike a preschooler, an older child no longer is content simply to run, jump, and throw things; now she puts these skills to use in complex, active play. Sometimes this consists of informal, child-organized games, such as hide-and-seek, in which the child uses her motor skills. At other times, as described next, active play involves formal sports such as gymnastics, swimming, or hockey. During the school years, children develop the ability to play games with rules. Some of these games are informal, such as after-school hopscotch, and some are formal and adult sponsored, such as Little League softball. In any case, traditional team sports now begin to have meaning for children because they can understand and abide by a game's rules. At the same time, children's improvements in co-ordination and timing enhance their performance in all kinds of sports, whether individual or group. Swimming, for instance, reveals the benefits of increasing coordination: some preschoolers can swim quite well, but usually only school-age children achieve

In middle childhood, children continue to refine fundamental motor skills, such as running, walking, or throwing. But they show the biggest improvements in activities like gymnastics or hockey that require not only fundamental skills, but coordination and timing as well.

adultlike coordination, speed, and grace in their strokes and breathing. The same holds for other informal, individual activities, such as riding a bicycle, roller blading, and jumping rope.

What lasting physical and psychological effects do early athletics have on children? This question has not been studied as thoroughly for children as it has for adolescents and adults, but a few tentative answers are possible. On balance, athletic activity probably helps children much more than it hurts them. However, it does carry a few significant risks.

Physical Effects of Early Athletics

The most obvious physical risks in athletics are sports-related injuries: bruises of various kinds and severity, damage to muscles (sprains), and broken or dislocated bones (Backx, 1996). Do such injuries actually pose a problem for child development? Some researchers express concern about the frequency of athletic injuries, even in childhood. The injuries usually receive only short-term medical attention: once bones or muscles appear to be healed, they are promptly ignored, and the athlete is encouraged to return to play. Given the special stresses of athletic activity, this short-run approach may allow minor but long-term disabilities to develop (Smith, 1996).

Other researchers point out that most children who are injured during sports have relatively minor injuries, and the benefits of participation therefore considerably outweigh the risks. They cite the physical benefits of athletics. For example, children involved in regular athletics may develop better physical endurance than nonathletic children; this means their hearts and large muscles may function more efficiently (Rowland, 1993). As a result, they may be better able to undertake ordinary daily activities with less effort.

Psychological Effects of Early Athletics

The immense popularity of early athletics probably stems at least in part from the psychological benefits attributed to participation. Sports, it is hoped, develop achievement motivation, teamwork, and a tolerance for or even enjoyment of competition. How well do early athletics in fact realize these goals?

WORKING WITH

Katherine Paterson, Pediatric Occupational Therapist

Diagnosing Children's Coordination Difficulties

Katherine Paterson is a pediatric occupational therapist. She works with children who have difficulties carrying out age-appropriate activities. Typically the problems have a physical basis, but they also affect everyday responsibilities (like schoolwork) or social relationships (like making friends) significantly. The challenge, as Katherine points out, is to pinpoint the nature of these links as clearly as possible and then devise a program that will help the child overcome his or her difficulties. Here is how she described this process.

Katherine: When the kids first come to you, they might present just one or two "simple" problems. Take Paul, who's nine. A few months ago, his teacher referred him to me because he had trouble following directions and couldn't print words. But he had great people skills! He tried to get along and didn't act up in class. I suspect that's why he was nine years old by the time I saw him. He probably faded into the woodwork.

Kelvin: *What did you do once you started seeing him?*

Katherine: It's like detective work. You've got to figure out what's behind the "official" problem that you first hear about. I started out by talking at length with Paul's classroom teacher and the school's special ed consultant. And I talked with his parents; you've got to involve them a lot from the first, because they know so much about their kids and potentially can help them so much in the future.

Kelvin: *Were Paul's parents at all defensive about Paul's being sent to an occupational therapist?*

Katherine: Well, they were sure worried. But they also wanted the best for Paul. We'd work out a plan together that helps Paul use his strengths to address his needs.

Kelvin: *Could you give some specifics?*

Katherine: Well, for instance, when I did my standardized assessments I discovered that Paul did really well at perceiving shapes. He could pick them out easily even when they were imbedded in a complicated drawing, rotated, or oriented in unusual ways. That skill will eventually help him with his reading at school.

Kelvin: *Is standardized testing always part of your initial assessment?*

Katherine: Usually. I use tests that look at underlying physical and cognitive processes—visual perception, for example, and motor coordination. I also test for auditory perception, but only enough to figure out whether a child needs to see a speech-language pathologist as well as see me.

Kelvin: *Don't kids get pretty impatient and restless with being tested?*

Katherine: Well, it does take time. Sometimes I break the testing into several sessions, especially if the child is very young or impulsive—has trouble sitting still. But it's worth it! The test results give clues about what might be wrong. Paul's tests revealed that he had some trouble remembering sequences of information; recalling several shapes in series, for example, often mixed him up. I suspect that may relate to his reading and writing problems at school. Maybe he can't keep letter or word sequences in mind reliably.

Kelvin: *What else do you do when a child first comes to you?*

Katherine: Observe him—you know, I keep saying "him," not "her," but they do tend to be boys!—when he's drawing or playing with the toys we have here. I interact during these times, too, to see how he responds to my directions and suggestions. Sometimes a child behaves differently during these informal times compared to the more formal testing times.

Kelvin: *Once the initial assessments are done, what happens?*

Katherine: It depends on the child, of course. I recommended that Paul visit an occupational therapist regularly—me, in this case—and some further consultations with the school staff. The visits with me will actually serve two purposes: helping Paul with his visual sequencing and motor coordination and providing a good time to talk with Paul's parents about his needs and progress. I invite parents to the sessions so I can show them what we're doing. I try to give parents one or two activities to do with the child between visits, some sense of a goal that's realistic. That's so important, both for the child's self-esteem and for the parents.

With the school staff, I discuss what my assessment turned up and we brainstorm ideas that might help Paul in class. For instance, we considered if it might help Paul to get some practice writing on a computer. That way, he doesn't have to perfect his penmanship before he can begin writing longer pieces.

What Do You Think?

1. Think about the major domains of development (physical, cognitive, and social). Chapter 1 pointed out that these are not necessarily separate. How does Paul's case seem to support this idea?

2. Katherine noted that the children she sees tend to be boys, and research indeed confirms this gender imbalance among children with school-related learning difficulties. Consult with several classmates about this fact, and generate some possibilities about why it may be true.

3. How might a family's income level influence a child's chances of success with an occupational therapist?

Athletic activity can support the development of achievement motivation. But it can also foster competitiveness. What do the children think who do not win a judo award in the top picture? And what do team members feel in the bottom picture if their team loses a game?

Training in Achievement Motivation   Most sports provide standards against which children can assess their performances. Goals can be scored, distances measured, and times clocked. Children's performances can then be compared with the youngsters' own previous scores, with those of their peers, or with those of top-scoring individuals or teams.

Whether this information really encourages higher athletic achievement depends on how a child uses it. A kindergarten child tends to remember her sports history poorly. She therefore approaches each performance as a unique event. For example, she may find each swim meet enjoyable in its own right, but think little about bettering a past performance or correcting previous mistakes. During the school years, however, comparing herself to standards becomes a prominent concern (Weiss, 1993). This concern does motivate some children to better their performances, but it also undermines motivation for children who believe athletic standards are arbitrary, externally imposed, or unreasonably difficult to meet.

Teamwork and Competition   Many sports promote teamwork, that is, cooperation with a selected group of individuals. This goal certainly is a positive one, but it comes only if a child's team wins. What happens to losers? Among schoolchildren,

A TALK WITH

John, Age Eleven

Growing Older

John was interviewed after school in his bedroom, which contained three fish tanks, plants, a cat, and a number of models and other construction projects he had worked on.

Interviewer: *John, how old are you now?*

John: I was eleven in August.

Interviewer: *What is it like to be eleven? Have you noticed yourself getting bigger?*

John: I don't know. You do grow more.

Interviewer: *How do you know?*

John: I just have. My parents tell me, too. They say I've grown a lot.

Interviewer: *Can you notice some things about your body compared with the way you were at nine or ten?*

John: I don't know. I can reach things better. And I can run better, faster, and for a longer time if I go for a jog with my mom and dad.

Interviewer: *What other things can you do better?*

John: It's easier to play my guitar with bigger hands. It used to be harder to reach my fingers around the neck to make chords, and now it's getting easier. It's still not that easy, though.

Interviewer: *What about sports?*

John: I like to play baseball, soccer, and basketball. Getting bigger and stronger helps there. You can hit the ball farther and throw better. In soccer, being able to run and kick hard are important, and I can play much better than I did a couple of years ago. Of course, I also have more experience at playing.

Interviewer: *What other things can you do that you couldn't do a couple of years ago?*

John: I'm a better bike rider than I used to be. It's easier for me to ride. My legs are longer, and my seat is as high as it can go. Some of my clothing is also too small for me.

Interviewer: *How is your size compared with other kids your age?*

John: I think about the same size. Some kids are smaller and some are bigger . . . taller and heavier.

Interviewer: *What does an eleven-year-old do to stay healthy and strong?*

John: They don't want to get too fat.

Interviewer: *Do you think about that?*

John: Yes.

Interviewer: *What would make you too fat?*

John: Not getting any exercise and maybe eating too much candy and things like that. I don't think that will happen to me, but some kids are overweight, and that's not healthy.

Interviewer: *What other changes have you noticed in yourself?*

John: My parents used to have to tell me to clean up my room, but I just keep it clean now. And I do my work and my parents don't have to tell me to do it.

Interviewer: *Do you think differently about your work now? Does it feel different?*

John: I still don't like it—I never have, and I probably never will. I just do it before my parents tell me, and then I'm done. And that way I don't get nagged.

Interviewer: *Do people treat you differently now that you're older?*

John: Yes. They treat me more like an adult than a little kid. Instead of just telling me to do something, now they sometimes talk about it. They discuss it with me. I also have more responsibilities. I have to take care of my sister when I get home from school and sometimes till five o'clock, when my parents get home.

Interviewer: *Any other changes?*

John: I can go to my friend's house by myself. And I can stay home alone. And I can have my own room, too.

What Do You Think?

1. What physical changes seem most important to John?

2. What effects have athletics had on John's development?

3. In what ways has John's physical development affected his psychosocial development?

---

even the most gracious loser shows significant stress. Research has found that losers become less sociable, refuse to talk about the game, and miss game practices more often than winners do (Petlichkoff, 1996). Losing teams also show a marked tendency to pinpoint blame by scapegoating individual members or events during a sporting season. If one "big play" seemingly lost a crucial basketball game, the players may dwell on that event more than it deserves, and they may stew about one or two players who seemed most responsible for that play.

For some children, the path away from being a loser consists of training harder to win. For substantial numbers of others, however, it consists of learning not to take a sport too seriously—to treat it as "just a game" played for social and health reasons rather than for competitive success. Unfortunately the historical association of athletics with competition, glory, and "manliness" (for boys) can make this

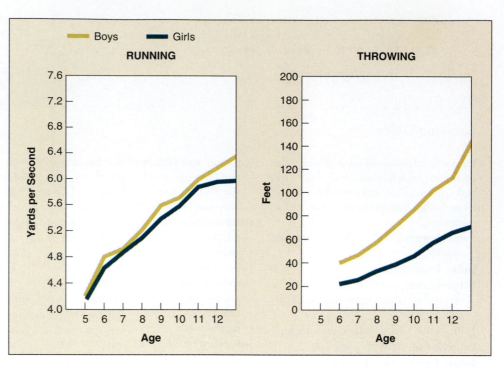

FIGURE 11.3

Running Speed and Throwing Distance for Boys and Girls at Different Ages

As the data indicate, despite changing gender roles in society, boys still tend to run faster and throw farther than girls during middle childhood. The data summarize a number of studies carried out since 1960. The gender gap increases as children enter adolescence.

Source: Gallahue (1993).

transition difficult for certain sports in some communities (Messner & Sabo, 1994). When a truly recreational approach to sports proves impossible, some children may adopt new interests and activities (such as watching television) that have fewer health benefits than sports do.

Gender and Early Athletics

In North America, girls are especially likely to drop out of athletic activity late in their school years. On the whole, they do so for cultural rather than physiological reasons (Scraton, 1992). Throughout childhood, they compare favorably with boys in strength, endurance, and motor skill, and late in childhood girls also tend to be physically more mature than boys. But beginning at about age twelve, they begin to perform less well than boys on tests of physical skills: they run slower, jump less far, and lift less weight (see Figure 11.3). Because physical training can eliminate these differences, their relatively poor performance most likely results from social expectations about gender. At the time of puberty, some girls begin to emphasize nonathletic pursuits such as listening to rock music, reading, or talking with friends. (Some boys, of course, do the same.) Fortunately, gender-role standards may be shifting, and athletic activity may be getting more attractive for both girls, as well as for boys than in the past (Ontario Ministry of Culture, Tourism, and Recreation, 1994).

WHAT DO YOU THINK?   Do childhood athletics by nature foster a competitive spirit among players? Or does competitiveness simply depend on stimulation by coaches and parents? This issue can spark a good in-class debate, particularly if individuals have to advocate the position *opposing* their usual point of view!

Health and Illness in Middle Childhood

In middle childhood, children usually are relatively healthy in the sense that they rarely experience serious illnesses or accidents with medical consequences (but see also the accompanying Perspectives box). They also have colds and minor viral illnesses less often than preschool children and infants do. But illnesses and accidents still occur in this age group, which partly accounts for why medical professionals and parents sometimes disagree about whether or not schoolchildren are really healthy. From a doctor's perspective, schoolchildren do not need advanced medical services as much as most other age groups do. From a parent's perspective, though, the illnesses schoolchildren do get can still be very disruptive.

Death Rates and Accidents Among Schoolchildren

One sign of good health in schoolchildren is their very low **mortality,** or the proportion who die at a given age. In recent years, only about three or four children in every ten thousand between ages six and thirteen die, compared to twice this number among preschoolers and four times this figure among adolescents (U.S. Department of Commerce, 1998). The low rate for school-age children is part of a long decline extending back over the past century.

The decline in mortality has changed the relative importance of various causes of death. Infectious diseases, such as pneumonia and chronic diarrhea, have become very infrequent among children from middle-income families in North America. As a result, accidents have become relatively more important as a cause of death among children. The largest number of childhood deaths in recent years have resulted from motor vehicle accidents (National Safety Council, 1995). A majority of those deaths were children who were not wearing seat belts while riding with their parents or other relatives.

mortality As used in population studies and developmental studies, the relative frequency of death in a community, society, or population.

FIGURE 11.4

Selected Causes of Death in Childhood and Adolescence

For both children and adolescents, deaths by accidents outnumber deaths by life-threatening illness, as these figures on mortality rates show. Both causes of death occur more frequently during adolescence, reflecting typical changes in lifestyle that lead to risks (e.g., driving an automobile). *Sources:* Adapted from U.S. Department of Commerce (1998) and World Health Organization (1998).

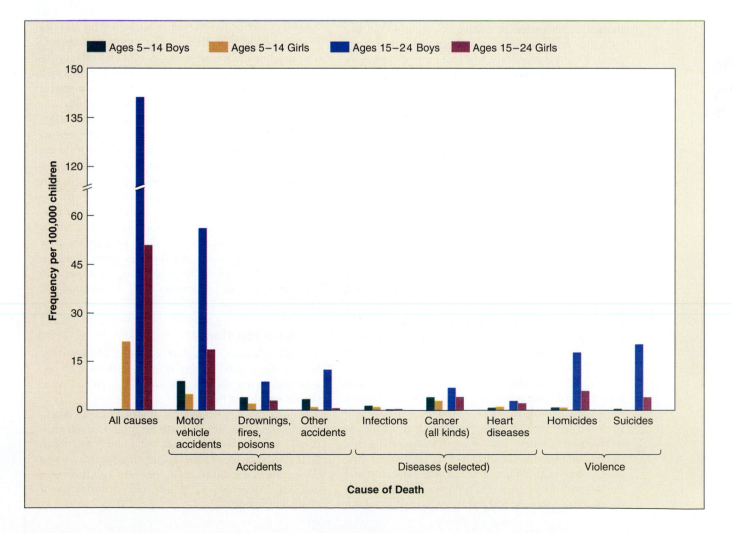

PERSPECTIVES

How Children Understand Death

• • • • • In modern society, death has become rare in childhood and common in old age. This seemingly natural state of affairs actually is quite unusual: throughout history and around the world, most deaths have occurred in infants and children. Today's reversal of this trend has had benefits, of course, but it may also leave children unprepared to understand and cope with death when they do experience it at close hand. Instead of seeming natural, inevitable, and universal, death may seem a rare and arbitrary event, a catastrophe that befalls only a few people. Such a view may create confusion about the nature and meaning of death.

Studies confirm that children have a hazy understanding of death, even well into middle childhood. Early in this period, around age six, they describe death with analogies that are often reversible: "Death is when you go to sleep," said one six-year-old, as though death ended in waking up again. Often the analogies refer not to universal events but to special ones: "Death is going on a trip," for example, implying that not everyone will die since not everyone goes on trips (Webb, 1993). Perhaps for these reasons, young children do not seem to fear death as much as older children and adults do. They reveal concern and distress about the general idea of death, but unless they experience the death of a close relative (such as a parent) directly, their concerns tend to be limited. Not until around age ten do most children realize that death is irreversible, permanent, and universal. But even then concern is rather abstract and emphasizes physical inevitability rather than psychological repercussions: "Dying is when your heart stops beating forever."

These developments occur more rapidly and vividly if a child has had a life-threatening illness (such as leukemia) or lost a close relative, especially a parent (Bertoia, 1993). These children face challenges that develop their understanding of death quickly. First, they must *understand* the death as realistically as possible: it indeed has occurred, cannot be ignored, and will never be undone. Younger children may have trouble grasping this reality because their general cognitive understanding is limited. Second, children must have chances to *grieve,* or mourn their loss, and work through feelings they still have about the person who died. The extent and nature of their grieving will depend on how emotionally attached they were to the deceased person, their overall cognitive maturity, and the support they receive for expressing their sadness. As one nine-year-old girl put it, "What bothered me most about my mother's death was that no one gave me a chance to talk about it; they were too busy with their own problems." Another child said, "My little brother didn't seem to react when my sister died [of meningitis]—but I can't tell if it's because he wasn't very close to her emotionally, or because he was only four at the time, or because Mom and Dad kept telling him how 'strong' he was not to cry."

Either despite or because of their cognitive limitations, children react strongly to the death of the most important people in their lives—usually their parents. Research shows that the effects can be long-lived (Silverman & Worden, 1993). Even 10 years after losing a parent, bereaved children tend to be more submissive and introverted and less aggressive than other children, even children who have lost a parent through divorce. The extent and nature of a child's reactions depend on the circumstances: losing a mother can be harder for a child than losing a father, on average, because the remaining parent (the father) more often has had less practice in expressing his own grief and has fewer social relationships to offer emotional support. The reactions of the surviving parent and other relatives also affect the child's ability to come to terms with the death. A parent absorbed in his or her own grief is less able than usual to comfort a school-age child.

What can professionals do to help children come to terms with death in general and a specific person's death in particular? The answer depends partly on the extent of their own involvement. Social workers and nurses who assist families following particular deaths can encourage children to talk about the death, say what they think and feel, and ask about what perplexes them. Teachers and school counselors can do this too when a classmate has died. In addition, they can explore the issues and feelings about death in more general ways by incorporating the topic into the overall school curriculum (U.S. Department of Health and Human Services, 1993).

What Do You Think?

1. Suppose you are a teacher or a nurse and have just learned that a child you are working with recently lost a parent. What should you say to the child? What should you do for the child?

2. Given the importance of understanding death, should education about death be offered to all children, even those who have *not* lost a family member?

3. If you favor some form of "death education," who do you think should teach it, and how can it respect cultural differences in beliefs and attitudes about death and dying?

As children get older, their everyday activities make them more likely to experience accidents. The risks are greatest, as with these boys swimming, when activities take them to unfamiliar places and when peers challenge one another to attempt risky behaviors.

But school-age children do sometimes die from other kinds of accidents (see Figure 11.4). Some children face much greater risk for certain accidents than others do, either because their environments pose more risks or because their parents and other adults responsible for them do not recognize the risks and therefore fail to teach the children proper safety precautions.

What are the reasons for the greater number of accidents? During the school years, children begin playing in and exploring larger territories. In particular, they investigate the neighborhood around their homes and schools, despite its unknown dangers. Because the improvised games (usually sports) children play at this age require more space than the play of preschoolers does, children in urban and some suburban areas often play in the street. They may do their best to avoid traffic, but games such as baseball may require sudden sprints and allow no time to check for cars.

When not playing at formal and informal games, school-age children are deeply curious about the wider world that has become available since their preschool years. Poking around neighbors' backyards, they may find old equipment or machinery that looks too interesting not to investigate. Or they may find flammable or toxic substances, such as gasoline or paint thinner, that supposedly have been stored away safely. Construction sites are especially inviting: they contain pieces of debris and partially completed nooks and crannies that make good hiding places. Unfortunately, these interesting spaces often lack structural strength; children can slip and fall in them, and pieces of steel or wood can land on their heads.

Most of the time, accidents from such sources are relatively minor. But a significant number cause fractures, poisoning, or open wounds that require medical attention. Somewhere between 5 and 10 percent of all visits to doctors by schoolchildren, in fact, are for treatment of accidents such as these (Wright & Leahey, 1994).

Illnesses

On the average, schoolchildren get sick only about one-half as often as preschoolers do. From their parents' point of view, however, illnesses probably still seem rather frequent; nearly one-quarter of the parents in one survey reported that during the preceding two weeks their children were "too sick to carry on as normal" (Coiro, 1994), meaning the children stayed home from school for at least one day. As parents often point out, a sick child has a substantial impact on the work and leisure schedules of the rest of the family, especially parents.

Acute Illness   Most common childhood diseases are **acute illnesses,** meaning they have a definite beginning, middle, and end. Most childhood acute illnesses, such as colds, gastrointestinal flu, chicken pox, and measles, develop from *viruses,* complex protein molecules that come alive only when they infect a host tissue (such as a child's nose). Despite popular belief, no drugs can combat viral infections. (This is not the case with bacteria that invade the body; they can be effectively fought off with antibiotic drugs.) Instead, viral illnesses must run their course, and the child's natural immunities must work the real cure.

For such diseases, doctors usually prescribe simple bed rest. Sometimes they also prescribe medications, more to prevent complications than to cure the illness. Many ear infections, for example, arise from viral infections, but doctors sometimes prescribe antibiotic drugs to prevent a more serious bacterial ear infection from developing. This practice is somewhat controversial, though, since it reduces the effectiveness of antibiotics when they are needed more urgently for true bacterial illnesses.

Chronic Illness   By the school years, about 5 to 10 percent of children develop **chronic illnesses,** or conditions that persist for many months without significant improvement. In the United States and other developed countries, the most common chronic conditions occur in the lungs and affect breathing (United Nations International Children's Emergency Fund, 1998). Some children develop *asthma,* or persistent congestion in the lungs; others develop chronic coughs or allergies. Still other chronic complaints concern specific sensory organs. About one child in one hundred, for example, experiences problems in hearing or seeing.

Social Influences on Illness   The seriousness and frequency of illnesses vary a lot according to children's social and economic circumstances. Consider income differences among families. In general, parents in higher-income families report that their school-age children get sick just about as often as parents from lower-income families do for their children. But the higher-income parents also report keeping their children at home for shorter periods of time. In the highest 25 percent of families, children stay at home for an average of only 1½ days per illness, whereas in the lowest 25 percent, they stay at home for nearly 5 days per illness (Fitzgerald et al., 1994).

What accounts for this difference? Low-income families probably lack money for doctors' visits, access to special child care when a child is sick, and permission to take time off from work to tend to a sick child. Therefore, to merit staying home from school or visiting a doctor, a child must have a relatively major illness, such as a seriously high fever or severe diarrhea. The result of these circumstances shows in the longer average stay at home when illness finally receives special attention.

Race and gender appear to matter too. African American families report fewer illnesses per child than do white families of similar income, and all families of both races report more illnesses for girls than for boys of the same age (Johnson, 1995). In fact, school-age girls appear to get sick almost as often as preschool children of both sexes do; boys, however, get sick less frequently as they get older.

Note, however, that these trends result partly from families' beliefs about illness as well as from real differences. Girls may not necessarily get sick more often than boys do; rather, training in gender roles may lead them to talk about their ailments and request medical treatment more often. For similar reasons, parents may be more apt to consider girls to be physically delicate and therefore to keep them home for minor illnesses they would not consider serious in boys. These facts may mean that girls exaggerate the extent of their illnesses, that boys hide the extent of theirs, or both.

• • •

acute illness A disease with a definite time of onset and lasting for a fixed and relatively short period of time.

chronic illness A disease lasting a long period of time (such as several months or more) and changing only very slowly.

AIDS and the School-age Child

Acquired immunodeficiency syndrome (AIDS) is a viral illness that gradually destroys the body's ability to combat other diseases. In all officially recorded cases so far the disease has proven fatal, although often not for several years. Its frequency has increased dramatically since the 1980s. In 1981–1982 only 838 cases of AIDS were reported in the entire United States, but by the 1990s the number had grown to about 30,000 new cases per year (U.S. Department of Commerce, 1998). Approximately ten times these numbers of people become infected every year with **human immunodeficiency virus (HIV),** the virus that eventually triggers the actual symptoms of AIDS.

So far only about 1 to 2 percent of AIDS victims have been schoolchildren, but concerns about the disease have spread throughout society and filtered down into the elementary schools and homes of this age group. Without doubt, some fears come from prejudice against the populations in which AIDS first appeared in North America, namely male homosexuals and heavy users of addictive drugs that are injected intravenously. (In some other parts of the world, such as Africa, AIDS first appeared among heterosexuals.) Fear of catching the disease from casual contact at school has become common, even though current medical evidence shows that AIDS is not spread in this way (Cohen & Durham, 1993). Some parents therefore have demanded the immediate, complete removal from school of any child known to have contracted the disease.

Such demands raise difficult issues about civil rights and fairness in education. Should school leaders respect parents' wishes, even if the wishes are based on clearly mistaken notions about AIDS? Or should they keep a child with AIDS in school out of respect for the child's right to an education, even at the risk of alienating significant numbers of parents? In the short term, these questions have no easy answers.

But longer-term solutions may be possible. One is to offer education at school and other community agencies about sexuality in general and AIDS in particular. Curricula concerning AIDS already have been written and published (Rowe & Hanvey, 1997), and some school districts have begun using them. It is hoped that an AIDS curriculum can help to correct students' misinformation about the disease and therefore help them avoid contracting AIDS and encourage them to respond sensibly when and if they learn of classmates who have the disease.

Another long-term solution lies with school staff, whose own attitudes and actions can make a major difference in a community's reactions to news of a child with

• • •

acquired immunodeficiency syndrome (AIDS) A viral illness that gradually destroys the body's ability to combat other diseases.

human immunodeficiency virus (HIV) The virus known to cause the disease AIDS. See *acquired immunodeficiency syndrome.*

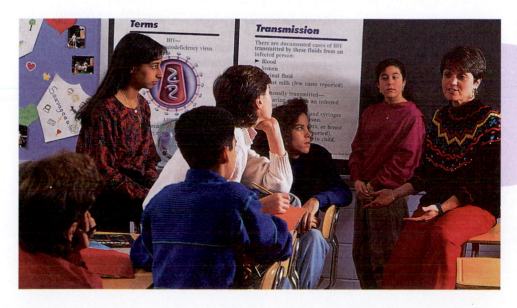

As the problem of AIDS has reached public awareness, some schools have begun AIDS education programs even in elementary schools. Questions remain, however, about this practice: How much should be taught at this age? How explicit about sexuality should it be?

AIDS. For teachers and principals, the key responses seem to be a calm attitude about the child, accurate knowledge about AIDS, and active efforts to communicate its lack of contagiousness through casual contact (see Table 11.2).

Attention Deficit Hyperactivity Disorder

A small number of school-age children seem extremely active and have considerable trouble concentrating on any one activity for long (American Psychiatric Association, 1994). Their problem is called **hyperactivity,** or **attention deficit hyperactivity disorder (ADHD).** A second-grade teacher described one student with ADHD like this:

> Joey was friendly when you greeted him; "Hi!" he would say brightly, and smile. But he would never settle down. First he dumped the class's main supply of pencils out on a table; he sort of lunged at one of the pencils, but before he began writing, he left the table, looking for something new. During a reading lesson, I asked Joey to read silently until I finished helping another child; but Joey found this hard to do. He glanced in my direction; tapped a neighboring child on the shoulder; giggled; and kept scanning the room for "more." A child happened to drop a book; Joey laughed at this harder than the others, and jumped up quickly to pick the book up. He was probably trying to help, but in doing so he knocked his own papers all over the floor. Instead of picking up the papers, he only picked up his pencil, and headed off to sharpen it. And the morning was still only half over!

In the long run, behavior such as this both results from and contributes to emotional problems, conflicts with teachers and other adults, and poor relationships with peers. Such social problems eventually aggravate the child's troubles with concentrating. Joey, for example, may become wrought up over conflicts with teachers and self-conscious about what peers think of his behavior. He may become so upset, in fact, that he gets even more fidgety than before.

Reactions to Children with ADHD   Overly active children cause parents and teachers a lot of worry, and excessive activity is one of the most common reasons for referring children to psychiatrists and other health professionals (Weiss & Hechtman, 1993). How many children really have ADHD, however, depends somewhat on who is doing the estimating. Professional school psychologists usually estimate that around 5 to 10 percent of school-age children are seriously overactive. Teachers give a somewhat higher figure, and parents may give the highest figure of all. All estimates agree that the majority of highly active children are boys.

Excessive activity presents more problems in some situations than in others. During outdoor play, very active children hardly stand out at all and seem to make friends about as well as any other children do. The structured atmosphere of most school classrooms poses more problems. During class, children with ADHD often get out of their seats, respond aggressively to teachers and peers, and run the risk of losing not only opportunities to learn but also the affection and respect of friends.

Note that *most* children show excessive activity *some* of the time. This fact may not make dealing with ADHD any easier, but it does make the disorder seem more understandable and manageable. Only a few children really exhibit extremely high activity levels consistently enough to warrant professional attention. Experts suggest five criteria for deciding when activity poses a truly serious problem (Ingersoll, 1998):

hyperactivity Excessive levels of activity and an inability to concentrate for normal periods of time. See *attention deficit hyperactivity disorder.*

attention deficit hyperactivity disorder (ADHD) A disorder of childhood characterized by impulsivity, excessive motor activity, and an inability to focus attention for appropriate amounts of time.

TABLE 11.2   Important Facts about AIDS

1. AIDS can be, and has been, contracted by heterosexuals as well as homosexuals.
2. Quarantining (isolating) people with AIDS is both impractical and unethical.
3. AIDS does not spread by casual contact, such as a handshake or exposure to a sneeze by an infected person.
4. Uninfected people can protect themselves from AIDS by avoiding contact with other people's blood for any purpose (sharing drugs, piercing ears, becoming "blood brothers"), avoiding specific sexual practices, and using latex condoms during all forms of sexual intercourse.
5. There is no known cure for AIDS, and it takes many years for a person infected with the AIDS virus (HIV) to begin experiencing symptoms.

1. The overactivity occurs even when it is clearly inappropriate, such as when the child is riding in a car or sitting at a meal.

2. Seriously overactive children consistently fail to respond to pressures to inhibit their activity.

3. Seriously overactive children seem to always respond at the same rapid pace, even when they are trying to respond more slowly, such as when drawing a picture.

4. Seriously overactive children show other, related problems, such as high distractibility and difficulties in making friends.

5. Seriously overactive children exhibit poor academic achievement without evidence of sensory, physical, or cognitive disability.

Only children who meet all or most of these criteria warrant the often misused label *hyperactive;* all others probably should be considered simply *very active* or *overactive.*

Causes of ADHD   Most psychologists and medical researchers agree that ADHD has biological roots, but they do not know for sure what those roots are (Rutter, 1995). It seems likely that ADHD in individual children has different causes: one child may have suffered oxygen deprivation during birth, for example, whereas another child may have been exposed to toxic substances such as lead (found in the paint in many older houses). Certain foods, especially those with artificial additives, may contribute to hyperactivity in some children, but probably only to a minority of ADHD children and possibly only to those who already are predisposed to ADHD for other reasons. Head injuries are more common among children with ADHD than among other children, but it is not clear whether the injuries caused high activity or whether hyperactivity made children prone to the injuries (by bumping into things at high speed, for example).

In addition to biological explanations, it is tempting to believe that a child's parents or social environment may accidentally precipitate hyperactivity in some way, such as by setting rules for behavior that are too rigid. For example, forbidding children to wiggle in their seats in class actually makes many children more rather than less restless. Riding in a car for a long time may make a child restless. A child with a naturally active temperament may comply with these restrictions only with great difficulty, especially if they are imposed repeatedly over a long period.

However, research evidence is ambiguous about whether certain parents or teachers are so strict in their treatment of children that they singlehandedly cause or lead to hyperactivity in individual children. It is true that parents of ADHD children tend to impose strict behavioral requirements on their children, but this style may be as much a response to the child's behavior as a cause of ADHD in the first place. It is also true that many parents are strict without their children becoming hyperactive. The most reasonable conclusion, then, is that parents or teachers probably do not cause hyperactivity directly, but they may accidentally aggravate it in some cases by responding to very active children inappropriately (Cohen, 1998). What adults need are not new personalities but specific techniques and advice for dealing with such children.

Helping Children with ADHD and Their Families   Because no one is sure what makes some children overactive, and because ADHD usually persists throughout an individual's childhood and beyond, no single strategy for treating or dealing with the condition exists (Rutter, 1995). However, a group of strategies have proven helpful for the majority of children with this problem.

To reduce immediate symptoms, the most effective treatment is a stimulant medication. One common and effective stimulant has been *Ritalin* (also called

The new physical skills of middle childhood allow new social activities, whether they are formal athletics or spontaneously running a line, as these girls are. When all goes well, new physical skills also promote a child's belief in himself or herself as an increasingly competent person who can make independent decisions.

methylphenidate), which, paradoxically, quiets the child's behavior by "waking up" the central nervous system, that is, making it more alert. When used properly, Ritalin has no short-term, negative side effects; contrary to popular belief, it does not make the child lethargic, depressed, drowsy, or lacking in spontaneity (Cherkes-Julkowski et al., 1997). Instead, it makes the child less bossy, argumentative, and noisy, and better able to focus on tasks. As you might suppose, these changes allow more positive relationships to develop with both adults and peers, especially when combined with a diet that reduces the child's mood changes.

In addition to medication, behavior modification often helps to alter some of the most undesirable or counterproductive behaviors of an ADHD child. As the term implies, **behavior modification** is a psychotherapeutic technique that identifies specific behaviors that need changing, as well as straightforward techniques for eliminating or reducing them (Kazdin, 1994). In classrooms, one behavior modification technique consists of using high-status peers to model or demonstrate appropriate behaviors. The active child simply watches a classmate complete an assignment slowly instead of at lightning speed; then the child tries to copy the same slow style in doing the assignment himself. The teacher, of course, reinforces (usually with praise) the modulated behavior when it occurs.

One key quality of behavior modification is its consistency and predictability, and parents and teachers can help significantly by striving to provide these qualities in the child's everyday environment. At home this means meals, play times, and bedtimes should come at about the same times every day and follow roughly the same pattern. At school, lessons should have a regular, predictable format. In either setting, rules of acceptable and unacceptable behavior should be clear, simple, and relatively consistent. All of these strategies help the ADHD child by temporarily reducing the demands on her attention-directing capacities and allowing these abilities to develop at the child's own pace.

When these strategies are followed, about half of all ADHD children eventually outgrow the problem, although they often report continuing to feel restless and distractible as adults (Weiss & Hechtman, 1993). The remaining ADHD children show some greater risk as adults for minor antisocial behaviors, such as driving too fast or carrying (but not using) a weapon. Psychiatric experts generally believe, however, that such behavior may result not so much from ADHD itself as from the extensive interpersonal conflicts these individuals experience in growing up: many

• • •

behavior modification Techniques based on the principles of learning theory that can be used by parents, teachers, therapists, and other professionals to help children, adolescents, and adults to reduce or eliminate undesirable behaviors and learn desirable ones.

ADHD children live in chronic conflict with teachers and parents for years and, as one expert put it, are "driven to distraction" (Hallowell & Ratey, 1994).

 WHAT DO YOU THINK ? Some experts argue that children with ADHD are not so much "disturbed" as "disturbing." What do you suppose they mean by this comment? Speculate about ways in which home and school could be made less "disturbing" for a hyperactive child. Try out your ideas on a teacher or some other person who has experience with children's behavior problems.

Effects of Growth on Thinking and Feeling

This chapter has shown us some ways in which physical growth can influence the other aspects of a child's development during the elementary school years. Growth may seem slower or less eventful than either before or after this period, but this is true only in a strictly physical sense. Psychologically, a child's growth makes new social opportunities possible, such as participation in sports. When growth problems such as childhood obesity do develop, they often cause serious psychological side effects during the school years. Also, some abnormal physical developments, such as brain damage, have effects that closely resemble purely psychological developments—so closely, in fact, that distinguishing between the physical and mental aspects may confuse our understanding of the child as much as help it. Real children consist of minds, bodies, and feelings combined; only textbooks separate these three elements. Keeping this idea in mind may help to clarify the next two chapters, which concern school-age children's thinking and social relationships.

Summary of Major Ideas

Trends and Variations in Height and Weight

1. Although growth slows during middle childhood, children still exhibit significant differences in height and weight by the end of this period.

2. Toward the end of the elementary school years, girls tend to grow taller than boys, and the difference can create embarrassment for some children.

3. Weight can become a significant problem for some school-age children, because of both fears of social rejection and (in extreme cases) risks of medical problems.

Motor Development and Athletics in Middle Childhood

4. Motor skill development during middle childhood emphasizes coordination and timing rather than strength and fundamental skill.

5. Athletics during middle childhood involve physical risks as well as experience in achievement motivation, teamwork, and competition—with both good and bad effects.

Health and Illness in Middle Childhood

6. Overall, schoolchildren are among the healthiest people in society, as shown by their low mortality.

7. Compared to preschoolers, school-age children catch fewer minor acute illnesses, but a small percentage suffer from significant chronic medical problems.

8. Family SES and parents' beliefs about illness affect how long children stay at home as a result of getting sick.

9. AIDS is a concern among some educators and health officials because of its perceived potential to spread among school-age children, as well as because of concerns for protecting human rights of both ill and healthy individuals.

10. Attention deficit hyperactivity disorder (ADHD) affects a small percentage of school-age children and may result from a combination of genetic, physical, and social causes.

11. Treatment of ADHD sometimes includes medications and behavior modification techniques.

Key Terms

acquired immunodeficiency syndrome (AIDS) (349)
acute illness (348)
attention deficit hyperactivity disorder (ADHD) (350)
behavior modification (352)
chronic illness (348)
human immunodeficiency virus (HIV) (349)
hyperactivity (350)
mortality (345)
obesity (337)

Cognitive Development in Middle Childhood

Focusing Questions

- What new cognitive skills do children acquire during the school years? What are the psychological and practical effects of these new skills?

- How does memory change during the middle years? How do these changes affect thinking and learning?

- What new changes in language emerge during the middle years?

- What is general intelligence, and how can it be measured?

- How does acquiring two languages affect a child's cognitive development?

- How does school affect children's cognitive development?

One day two brothers, ages seven and nine, constructed a "science museum" in their living room. They systematically selected all the best chairs and blankets as building materials. Then they found all their stuffed animals and put them on display in the museum, grouping them both by color and by size. They finished the museum by hanging a sign reading "ANIMAL MUSEUM. TIKETS $1." Not many people bought tickets, but this did not stop the boys from having a lively conversation about their project.

This activity drew on the kinds of cognitive skills school-age children have in greater abundance than preschool children do. It required the boys to make the building and to remember where to find particular stuffed animals. Making the sign took a rudimentary knowledge of reading and writing. The project also required the knowledge that museums store interesting objects in systematic ways and often cost money to visit.

In this chapter, we examine the development of cognitive skills such as these. We pay special attention to how parents and teachers influence their development, both unconsciously and deliberately. First, we look at Piaget's now classic research on thinking during middle childhood and at how and why this research has influenced education even though newer research has not fully supported Piaget's ideas. Then we discuss an alternative to Piagetian theory called *information-processing theory,* a viewpoint that focuses on how children use memory and learning strategies during the school years—and sometimes fail to use them. Next, we look at how children differ in their thinking and learning styles and how these styles influence their success in school. We will examine three topics that have implications for children's social relationships and therefore provide a bridge to Chapter 13. The first topic is language: how children differ in their styles of speaking and how these variations can affect children's educational and social success. The second is intelligence: what developmental psychologists mean by the concept, how they measure it, and how measurement practices have influenced school-age children and their families, both for better and for worse. The third is school itself: how its organization and goals affect both children's ways of thinking and their ways of forming and developing social relationships.

Piaget's Theory: Concrete Operational Skills

As we discussed in Chapter 2, Jean Piaget developed a comprehensive theory of cognitive development from birth through adolescence. During middle childhood,

Decentration

Sensitivity to Transformation

Reversability of Thought

according to this theory, children become skilled at **concrete operations,** mental activities focused on real, tangible objects and events. Concrete operations have three interrelated qualities, none of which is reliably present among preschool children: decentration, sensitivity to transformations, and reversibility (Piaget, 1965; Wadsworth, 1996). *Decentration* means attending to more than one feature of a problem at a time. For example, in estimating the number of pennies spread out on a table, a school-age child probably will take into account not only how large the array is but also how far apart individual pennies seem to be. *Sensitivity to transformations* means having different perceptions of the same object and combining them in logical ways. For example, when judging whether the amount of liquid in a glass stays the same after being poured into a new container, a school-age child concentrates on the actual process of change in appearance—the transformation—rather than on how the liquid looks either before or after pouring. *Reversibility of thought* means understanding that certain logical operations (for example, addition) can be reversed by others (subtraction). All in all, the concrete operational child constructs a view of the world that emphasizes quantitative relationships for the first time. Now many facts seem logically necessary that earlier appeared arbitrary or even incomprehensible. In judging whether the amount of liquid stays the same when transferred to a new container, the child now reasons that the amount *must* be the same if nothing was added or taken away when the liquid was poured.

To understand these features of concrete operations, let's compare how preschool and concrete operational children solve the same problem. Consider how Ken and Maria each got started making a batch of muffins:

> Ken, age four, needed guidance from his day care teacher to cook, but even with her help he kept coming dangerously close to ruining the recipe. The teacher set out the ingredients Ken needed—flour, sugar, salt, baking powder—and some containers. Ken liked the bag of flour (it was bright red), so he picked it up and happily began pouring flour into a large bowl. His teacher stopped him from overdoing it: "We need only one cup," she said. "But there isn't as much in the bowl," said Ken, meaning the flour had spread out in the bowl and therefore looked like less. "Okay," said the teacher, "but we still need to measure one cup. How can we do that?" Ken took a *two*-cup measuring cup, filled it to overflowing, and dumped the contents into the bowl. Now there was far too much flour! Apparently the teacher's comment about the amount and her implied advice to measure the flour had meant nothing to Ken.
>
> Maria, age ten, worked much more independently than Ken had and had a better sense of what she was doing. After setting out all the ingredients and containers she needed, Maria poured exactly one cup of flour into the bowl. Just then her teacher came by. "Hmm," she said, "that doesn't look like very much flour." (It was a big bowl, so the flour had spread out pretty far.) "It's what the recipe said," replied Maria. "Are you sure?" the teacher asked. "Yep," insisted Maria. To prove it, she poured the flour back into the one-cup measuring cup she had first used. "See? Nothing added, nothing taken away. So it's *got* to be right."

There are many reasons that these two children differed in their cooking performances, including different prior experiences with cooking, measuring, and even reading. But for Maria, part of the difference was likely the development of concrete operations. She was less distracted by immediate sensory cues, such as the color of the flour bag and the exhilaration of pouring out large amounts of flour. Most important, though, Maria felt a certainty about the quantity of flour that was based on an explicit logical principle. "Nothing added, nothing taken away" implied that the amount had not changed even though it looked smaller at the bottom of a big bowl.

Concrete operations cause important transformations in the cognitive skills children develop in the preoperational period. In classifying objects, children can group things in more than one way at a time by about age seven. They know that a person can be *both* a parent and a teacher at the same time, for example, rather

concrete operations Logical thinking about concrete or tangible objects and processes; especially characteristic of children in the school years.

than just one or the other. They also understand that some classifications are inclusive of others—for example, that a particular animal can be both a dog and a pet. As a result, they usually can answer correctly a question such as "Are there more boys in your class or more children?" Preschool children, in contrast, often fail to answer such a question correctly unless it is further simplified or clarified.

Conservation in Middle Childhood

Some cognitive skills make their first real appearance during middle childhood. Probably the best known of these skills is **conservation,** a realization that certain properties of an object necessarily remain constant despite changes in the object's appearance. An example of conservation of quantity is the one described in Chapter 9 involving two tall, narrow glasses containing exactly the same amount of water. If you empty one glass into a wide, low tray, you create a substantial perceptual change in the water; it looks quite different than before and quite different than the water in the remaining tall glass (see Figure 12.1). Will a child know that the wide tray has the same amount of water the tall glass does? If he does, he conserves, meaning he shows a belief in the water's underlying constancy despite a perceptual change.

conservation A belief that certain properties (such as quantity) remain constant despite changes in perceived features such as dimensions, position, and shape.

FIGURE 12.1

Conservation Experiments

As Piaget demonstrated, conservation (or the perception of invariance) emerges on a wide scale in middle childhood. In some cases, the child realizes that amounts of liquid or of solid mass remain constant; in other cases, he or she realizes that length or number remain constant. Early in middle childhood, however, the child often holds one of these beliefs without necessarily holding another, or holds one belief only on some occasions and not on others.

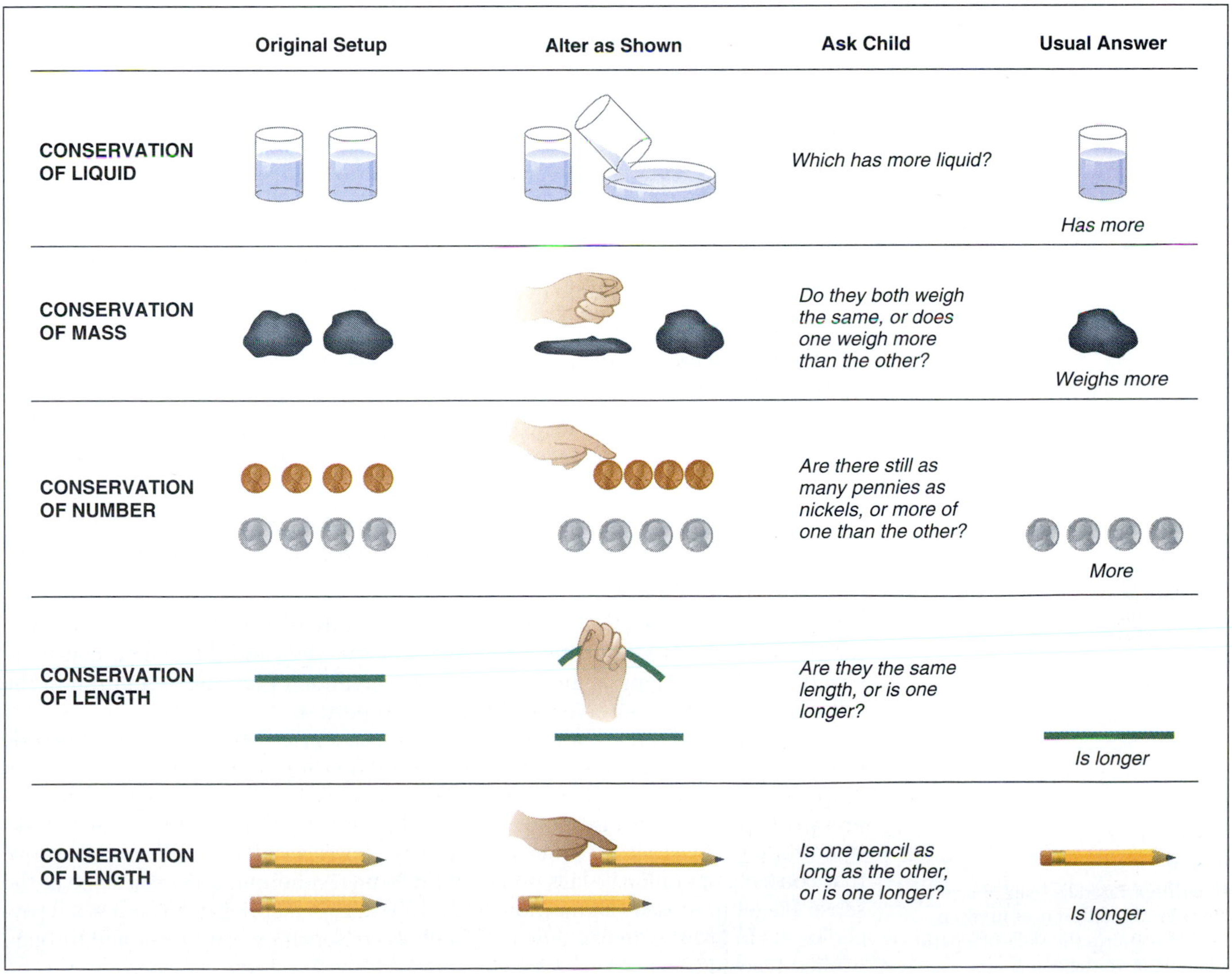

	Original Setup	Alter as Shown	Ask Child	Usual Answer
CONSERVATION OF LIQUID			Which has more liquid?	Has more
CONSERVATION OF MASS			Do they both weigh the same, or does one weigh more than the other?	Weighs more
CONSERVATION OF NUMBER			Are there still as many pennies as nickels, or more of one than the other?	More
CONSERVATION OF LENGTH			Are they the same length, or is one longer?	Is longer
CONSERVATION OF LENGTH			Is one pencil as long as the other, or is one longer?	Is longer

School-age children can often use their spatial relations skills to make accurate maps of familiar places, such as their own neighborhoods. But like some adults, they often have trouble using a map as a guide to an *un*familiar place.

Piaget (1965) found that after about age seven, most children did indeed conserve quantity in the water glass experiment. In fact, he found that by a year or two later, children conserved on a lot of other tasks as well, including the following (also illustrated in Figure 12.1):

1. *Pennies and nickels* Lay out two matching rows of coins, one row of pennies and the other of nickels. The rows should have the same number of coins, and each penny should be set next to one of the nickels. Then bunch up the coins in one row, but not those in the other. Ask, "Are there still as many pennies as nickels, or are there more of one than the other?"

2. *Bent wires* Start with two identical wires or pipe cleaners. Then bend one of them in an arc or circle. Ask, "Is one wire just as long as the other, or is one of them longer?"

3. *Overlapping pencils* Set two identical pencils parallel to each other. Then shift one pencil up or down by an inch or so. Ask, "Is one pencil just as long as the other, or is one of them longer?"

4. *Clay balls* Start with two identical clay balls. Flatten one so that it looks like a pancake. Ask, "Do these two pieces of clay weigh the same, or does one weigh more than the other?"

Each of these tasks requires some form of conservation. The clay balls, like the water glasses, require conservation of mass, the bent wires and the pencils conservation of distance or length, and the coins conservation of number. Children in the school years tend to conserve on all of these properties.

Typically a child does not acquire all of these conservation concepts at exactly the same time, a phenomenon Piaget called **décallage,** a French term meaning "gap." Piaget believed such gaps occur because children do not yet grasp the general principles underlying conservation and therefore do not apply them to tasks that are logically similar. Critics have argued, however, that *décallage* may prove that concrete operational skills do not really form a coherent, universal stage in the sense Piaget proposed (Demetriou et al., 1992). This skepticism has led some psychologists to investigate whether skills such as conservation can be learned through explicit teaching.

● ● ●

décallage Literally "gap"; Piaget's term for the differences in when a child acquires the skills of a particular cognitive stage.

Conservation Training

Specialists agree that children do not begin life conserving but instead acquire this skill somehow. How do they do it? Piaget argued that biological maturation and countless experiences with physical objects that show conservation properties enable children to mentally construct conservation. These experiences are numerous and diverse, and although they can be taught explicitly, Piaget believed they have a fuller, more general influence on development if allowed to emerge naturally.

But many psychologists have tried to teach conservation anyway. In recent studies, investigators tried to prevent children from being distracted by coaching them to talk about what was happening ("Nothing is being added or taken away") or to compare the important dimensions closely ("Watch the height *and* the width"). Such efforts do produce greater conserving in a large number of children, though not in all (Wadsworth, 1996). Conservation has even been taught successfully to children with mental retardation (Hendler & Weisberg, 1992).

Piaget's idea that thinking begins with manipulation and active exploration has been interpreted to support many elementary education programs that emphasize active learning. Here, these first-graders discover the properties of soap bubbles, thanks to the opportunity to explore on their own.

However, trained children often do not maintain conservation concepts the same way "natural" conservers tend to do; they are more likely to give up their belief at even a slight provocation. When experimenters surreptitiously remove a bit of clay in the clay balls experiment, for example, most children easily accept the change. "Natural" conservers are more steadfast in their commitment to conservation, although even they frequently give up their belief. All in all, it seems conservation may not unfold during childhood as inevitably as Piaget first believed.

Other Concrete Operational Skills

Piaget described many other forms of knowledge that emerge during middle childhood (Piaget, 1983). For one thing, children become able to *seriate*, or arrange objects in sequence according to some dimension such as length or size. For another, they understand *temporal relations*, or the nature of time, better than they did as preschoolers; an eight-year-old knows that time unfolds in a single, constant flow marked by calendars, clocks, and landmark events. Children at this age can also represent the *spatial relations* of their surroundings. They can make maps and models of familiar places, such as their homes, their classrooms, or the local shopping mall.

Piaget's Influence on Education

Although Piaget commented on educational issues (Piaget, 1970), he never intended his research to serve as a theory of education. At no time, in particular, did he offer advice about problems that normally concern teachers, such as how to teach reading or other conventional school subjects, how to motivate students, or how to evaluate students' learning. Nonetheless, his ideas and approach have significantly influenced educators, particularly those in early childhood education (Elkind, 1994a). At the heart of this influence is Piaget's *constructivist philosophy:* the assumption that children develop their own concepts through active engagement with the environment. Also at the heart is Piaget's emphasis on stages of cognition. These two ideas have jointly influenced teaching methods, curriculum content, and methods for assessing student progress.

Teaching Methods   Educators have borrowed Piaget's idea that true knowledge originates from active manipulation of materials (Seifert, 1993). Children learn about weights, for instance, by actually weighing various objects on a scale rather than by reading about weights in a book or hearing their teacher talk about them. A commitment to active learning, in turn, encourages teachers and curriculum planners to put more tangible activities into educational programs wherever possible, as well as to sequence activities from the tangible to the abstract. Reading about insects still has a place in learning about those creatures, but collecting (and handling) some real bugs probably should come first.

Curriculum Content   Piagetian theory has influenced particular curriculum content by providing many specific ideas about what cognitive competencies to expect from children of particular ages or levels of development (Kamii, 1994; Wait-Stupiansky, 1997). The conservation skills described earlier imply that elementary school children should develop a greater ability to solve problems no matter *how* the problems are presented. Compared to preschoolers, older children should be less distracted by seemingly small changes in drawings in their books or seemingly insignificant changes in how a teacher phrases assignments. In Piagetian terms, the children have become more "decentered."

Likewise, acquisition of concrete operations should help school-age children in a number of other ways. For instance, many academic tasks require multiple classification, which preschoolers often do not understand reliably. A written assignment may ask children to "list all the machines you can think of that begin with *c*." This task requires classifying objects in two ways at once: first, by whether or not something is in fact a machine, and second, by whether or not it begins with the letter *c*.

Piaget's cognitive theory has guided many curriculum planners and teachers to select and evaluate academic tasks such as these. The theory itself does not, of course, lead to accurate selections for all children, because not all children move through Piagetian stages at the same rate. In addition, most children are capable of abstract thinking to a certain extent, even if they are not as skilled as adolescents or adults are (Metz, 1995). Despite these limitations, though, Piagetian theory gives us valuable guidance about how children gradually adapt and reorganize their thinking as they grow older.

Assessment of Students' Progress   Throughout his work, Piaget emphasized the importance of children's actual thought processes and what those processes actually allow children to accomplish. This approach is evident in Piaget's heavy use of partially structured interviews and problem-solving tasks. Many educators believe such dialogues and tasks offer a much better way to assess students' progress than do traditional classroom tests and assignments, which tend to emphasize knowledge that is rote and taken out of context (Hill & Ruptic, 1994). Recent revisions to Piaget's approach, sometimes called "neo-Piagetian" theory, have made the approach even more attractive to educators by focusing more closely on *how* children learn and

Traditional methods of assessment create complex responses in students. As with Calvin in this cartoon, responses are not always constructive. Piaget has inspired some educators to shift to assessment that emphasizes the process of thinking rather than the outcomes—for example, by interviewing students or by examining portfolios of their work rather than single polished products.

proposing cognitive stages that are more specific, and therefore more accurate, than Piaget's original proposals (Case & Edelstein, 1994).

 WHAT DO YOU THINK?   Given Piaget's ideas about how thinking develops in middle childhood, what would be a good way to evaluate students' academic work in elementary school? Work with a classmate or two to devise an evaluation plan for a favorite grade level and subject. Then see how your plan compares to plans devised by classmates and (if possible) to those composed by an experienced teacher.

Information-Processing Skills

A major alternative to Piaget's way of understanding the cognitive changes of middle childhood is in terms of **information-process theory** (described in Chapter 2), which focuses on how children organize and remember information. By school age, children's short-term memories already are well developed—though not perfectly, as we will see shortly. Their long-term memories, however, have significant limitations at the beginning of this period. For most children, the limitations diminish with age, but for a few, information processing remains a problem serious enough to interfere with school performance throughout elementary school and beyond. As with the development of concrete operational thinking, then, children simultaneously show both common trends and individual diversity in developing this form of thinking.

Memory Capacity

According to popular wisdom, children remember better as they get older. But how true or universal is this idea really? In everyday life, children obviously do not perform as well as adults do on some tasks, such as remembering to put away their clothes at the end of the day. But in other ways they seem to perform equally well; they will remember their grandparents when they see them again after months or even years of absence.

Short-Term Memory   Some of these differences in memory may depend on which parts of the information-processing model the children happen to be using. Some tasks rely primarily on *short-term memory (STM)*, a feature of thinking that holds information only for a short period, perhaps up to twenty seconds (see Chapter 2). On tasks that emphasize short-term recognition memory, school-age children perform less well than adults do. This tendency can be demonstrated by showing a group of children and adults a set of digits briefly and then immediately asking them whether the set included a particular digit (Cowan, 1997). Under these conditions, recognition of a test digit improved steadily, with eight-year-olds remembering only about three digits and adults remembering about seven. Not surprisingly, too, the time it took an individual to recognize a test digit *did* depend on how many digits were shown in the original set, regardless of the person's age. Showing six digits made the task take longer than showing just three, no doubt because the subject evaluated the test digit against a larger number of alternatives.

This study assessed a variation of **recognition memory,** in which a person merely compares an external stimulus or cue with pre-existing experiences or knowledge. Recognition memory is involved when children look at snapshots of a holiday celebration months in the past: their faces light up, and they may describe aspects of the celebration they had apparently forgotten. **Recall memory,** in contrast, involves remembering information in the absence of external cues, such as when trying to remember a friend's telephone number without looking it up. Recall

• • •
information-processing theory Explanations of cognition that focus on the precise, detailed features or steps of mental activities. These theories often use computers as a model for human thinking.

recognition memory Retrieval of information by comparing an external stimulus or cue with preexisting experiences or knowledge.

recall memory Retrieval of information by using relatively few external cues.

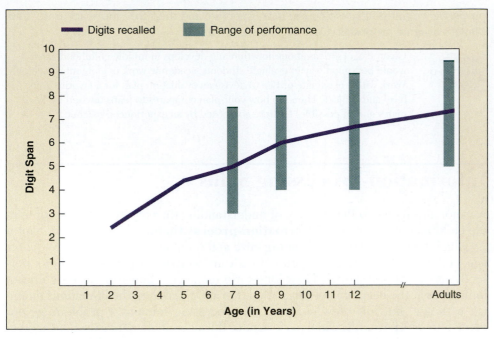

FIGURE 12.2

Developmental Changes in Recall Memory

In the study represented here, children were asked to recall a series of digits shortly after hearing them. The points on the graph represent the average number of digits subjects were able to recall, and the bars represent the ranges of typical performance at each age. Recall of digits improves during middle childhood and almost reaches adult levels by age twelve, though not quite.

generally is more difficult than recognition, but it shows the same developmental trend recognition does: school-age children can recall better than preschoolers, but not as well as adults (see Figure 12.2).

Long-Term Memory   *Long-term memory (LTM)* is the feature of thinking that holds information for very long periods, perhaps even indefinitely. It is not clear how much long-term memory changes during childhood, or even whether it changes at all, because LTM relies increasingly on complex strategies of information storage and retrieval. Younger children may remember less because they have experienced fewer memorable events or because they use fewer methods of deliberately remembering information and experiences.

To understand how LTM changes during childhood, consider how children and adults recall short stories they have heard (Wolf, 1993). By age six, children already understand the basic narrative structure of stories—that such stories contain characters, situations, and plots with a beginning, a middle, and an end. Not surprisingly, therefore, children show many similarities to adults in recalling stories. Like adults, they recall important features of a story ("Goldilocks was not supposed to enter the bears' house") and ignore or forget trivial details ("Goldilocks was wearing brown shoes"). They also recall the essences of sentences rather than their exact wording.

But compared to adults, the recollections of school-age children include fewer inferences based on the sentences they actually hear (McNamara et al., 1991). If adults hear the two sentences "Red Riding Hood's grandmother was baking" and "Grandmother set the cookies out on the table," they automatically infer that (1) grandmother had an oven and (2) she was the one who took the cookies out of the oven. Because of these inferences, adults are relatively likely to think they actually heard this information and to remember a sentence that actually was not used, such as "Grandmother finished her baking in the oven before she put the cookies out." Schoolchildren are far less likely to include such inferred sentences, although they are more likely to do so than preschool children are. As children get older, they seem to read between the lines more frequently, at least when recalling stories. This tendency lends color and detail to their retellings as they get older, although they sometimes risk misstating the "facts" of a story.

Implications for Elementary Education   The "architecture" of memory may affect how children can learn during the school years. A younger student who can remember only three bits of information needs to have information organized in smaller chunks than an older student who can remember six bits at a time. The younger child may have trouble remembering a phone number long enough to dial it, for example, unless the teacher can offer some learning strategies for doing this task (see the next section for some suggested strategies). More significant for learning, research shows that elementary students' ability to solve arithmetic problems is correlated with the extent of their short-term memories: in one study, "larger" short-term memory meant greater accuracy in solving problems (Swanson et al., 1993). Children's limitations on long-term memory, on the other hand, pose a different challenge: school-age children *can* remember ideas and facts for long periods, but their teachers may need to help them to see connections among the stories, ideas, and other material they learn in school.

Influences on Memory Development

As many of the preceding examples imply, LTM develops partly because other, related cognitive changes occur during childhood. One of these changes is an improvement in logical reasoning, such as that described by Piaget. Another is an increase in specific knowledge or facts. Still another is an improvement in the learning strategies used in solving problems, including problems that depend on long-term memory.

The Effects of Logical Reasoning on Memory   Reasoning skills affect children's memory, and because reasoning often improves with age, memories of specific experiences sometimes actually improve gradually rather than deteriorate. In a classic Piagetian study that illustrates this fact, experimenters showed children a series of sticks of various lengths (see Figure 12.3); then they asked the children to reproduce the series from memory by drawing pictures of it (Piaget & Inhelder, 1973). Several months later, they asked the children to draw the series from memory again.

As you might expect, on both occasions preschool children reproduced the series with considerably less accuracy than older, school-age children did; the younger ones simply drew a random group of sticks, or correctly sequenced only part of the series. The later drawings, however, showed a surprising result: nearly three-quarters of the children's drawings actually improved in accuracy over the first ones. Although some of the change probably reflected improvements in motor skills, the drawings were too simple to have depended on motor development entirely. Some of the improvement probably also reflected the children's increasing understanding of the underlying concept of seriation. Development of this concept apparently aided their later drawings, at least in part.

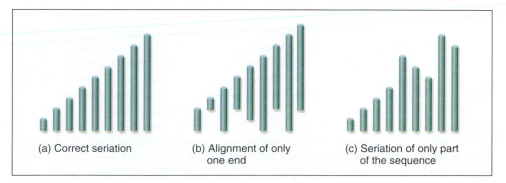

(a) Correct seriation   (b) Alignment of only one end   (c) Seriation of only part of the sequence

• • • • • • • • • • • • • • • •
FIGURE 12.3
Seriation of Sticks
Concrete operational children can arrange a series of sticks by length much more accurately than younger, preoperational children can. Piaget found, however, that performance by preoperational children improved spontaneously over a period of several months: later seriations were more accurate than earlier ones, even when no practice occurred between trials.

Expertise includes a rich knowledge base in a specific area, as with this young expert in raising chickens. Her elaborate knowledge of this activity fosters better organized, longer-lasting memory and probably allows her to remember many details about these chicks and their behavior.

Other research suggests that children's ability to make inferences affects what they remember. Consider this task, which calls for recognition of sentences. Ask children to listen to a set of sentences that express simple relationships, such as "Carlos is older than Bill," "Bill is older than Nicole," and so on. Later, ask them to recognize whether certain sentences were in fact part of the original list. Some of the test sentences should indeed be identical to the originals ("Bill is older than Nicole"); some should be logically true but worded differently ("Bill is younger than Carlos"); and some should be logically false but worded similarly ("Nicole is older than Carlos"). On a task such as this, people of all ages will falsely "recognize" some sentences that were not in the first list. As it turns out, their mistakes suggest how memory and reasoning may affect each other.

What determines which sentences they falsely recognize? The sophistication of their reasoning skills is partly responsible (Howe et al., 1992). Among young children (around age five), the similarity of wording seems to matter the most; in the preceding examples, a kindergartner is comparatively likely to think she heard "Bill is older than Carlos." By the middle elementary school years, logical consistency matters more; a third- or fourth-grader will think he heard "Carlos is older than Nicole." Apparently his more developed reasoning skills color his memory. In reality, he may have heard only "Carlos is older than Bill" and "Bill is older than Nicole." From these he reasons immediately that Carlos must be older than Nicole, but he apparently forgets that a sentence about Carlos and Nicole was not given.

Studies of both false recognition and spontaneous improvements in recall suggest that memory is not passive but active; it is not inert and unchanging (a memory "bank") but growing, developing, and changing. This fact can help children as they grow older: in school, for example, material learned five years earlier can seem more meaningful than it did when recalled immediately after it was learned. But it can also pose serious problems in situations where accuracy is at a premium. Children who have been sexually abused, for example, sometimes must testify in court about abusive events they experienced or witnessed in the distant past. How much can their testimony be trusted as accurate? There is no simple answer to this question, but research suggests that the overall theme, or "message," of children's memories remains accurate over the long term even though their recollection of details may change significantly (Zaragoza, 1995). In other words, a child may be accurate in recalling being abused during a period of childhood but not be accurate about all of the specific times and places the abuse occurred.

Familiarity and Richness of Knowledge   Common sense suggests that prior knowledge influences what a child can learn and remember. A child who knows a lot about animals will have an easier time learning the concepts of *mammal* and *reptile* than will a child who knows little about animals, even if neither child has dealt with these concepts before. In this sense, knowledge leads to more knowledge—an obvious advantage in school learning, in particular.

Familiarity matters not only during learning but during recall. One widely cited study showed this to be true by observing a young child who had expert knowledge about dinosaurs (Chi & Ceci, 1987). The child could name and describe forty-six different dinosaurs, telling about their size, appearance, eating habits, and behavior. He could do so, however, only if given ample time (literally hours) and encouragement from adults. In a short, straightforward test of his recall, he named familiar dinosaurs far more often than he named less familiar ones. Being "familiar" in this case meant the child had had more prior experience with reading about a particular species in books, playing with toy models of it, and viewing its skeleton in a museum (although *not*, presumably, more experience with seeing it on the hoof).

More often than not, older children show greater familiarity than younger ones with, or richness of knowledge about, a variety of topics simply because they have lived longer and therefore have accumulated more facts. But this is not always true. Like the dinosaur expert, many young children have special areas of knowledge or experience that outstrip those of older children and therefore promote unusually good memory. There are child experts in baseball and chess and among music lovers and performers (see the accompanying Multicultural View box).

Metacognition and Learning Strategies

As children grow older, they pick up more knowledge about thinking itself, about how learning and memory operate in everyday situations and how a person can improve his or her cognitive performance. Psychologists sometimes call this type of knowledge **metacognition,** meaning "knowledge about cognition" (Volk, 1995).

Compared to older children, young children are notably oblivious of factors that can affect their problem-solving performance. For example, ask two children of different ages which set of numbers will be harder to remember:

$$815 \quad \text{or} \quad 39268147$$

Both preschool and school-age children will tell you that the first set is easier to remember than the second set. They will differ, though, in how accurately they predict their chances of actually remembering each set. In general, the younger the child, the less accurate the prediction: a six-year-old might tell you she can remember the eight-digit set, but in fact be unable to do so.

By age ten or so, a child's predictions are much more accurate. He might tell you he can remember the eight digits, but also qualify the prediction: he might remember it only for awhile or only if he can use some supplementary strategy such

• • •

metacognition Knowledge and thinking about cognition, how learning and memory operate in everyday situations, and how one can improve cognitive performance.

STONE SOUP

While expert skill and knowledge often do correlate with age, it is more accurate to say that they correlate with amount of experience with the skill or knowledge. A child with more experience with computers like the girl in this cartoon may be more of an expert in this area than many adults.

A Multicultural View

Cultural Differences in Learning Mathematics

Research consistently shows that children from China and Japan learn mathematics sooner and more thoroughly than children from North America do. The advantage occurs not only in basic written computation (problems such as "How much is 34 × 26?") but in a range of other mathematical skills, such as knowledge of concepts, graphing, estimating amounts, and mental calculations. The differences favoring Chinese and Japanese children emerge as early as first grade, widen considerably by the end of the elementary school years, and persist throughout high school (Stevenson et al., 1993). Furthermore, international differences in mathematics achievement are wide and substantial: the highest-achieving percentage of American students perform mathematics only about as well as the lowest-achieving percentage of Chinese or Japanese students.

The clearest explanations for these differences center on cultural influences, especially on educational practices and attitudes toward achievement. One obvious cultural difference is the priority given to mathematics. Observations of

Chinese and Japanese classrooms reveal that Asian teachers devote double or triple the amount of time to mathematics instruction each week than their U.S. counterparts do. Most of this extra time involves the class as a whole group: the teacher gives verbal explanations of mathematical procedures and ideas and illustrates them using simple, concrete materials such as blocks and sticks of fixed, known sizes.

In American classrooms, in contrast, teachers spend more time with children individually or in small groups and simultaneously assign tasks or seatwork to occupy the remainder of the class. These practices reflect American teachers' strong belief in individualizing instruction. But they also encourage students to concentrate on getting paperwork done to the exclusion of interacting with the best-educated person in the classroom, the teacher.

Differences in mathematics achievement may also stem from broader cultural beliefs about the sources of educational success. Comparisons of parents in Japan and the United States, for example, show that Japanese parents tend to attribute success to students' effort and motivation and failure to lack of motivation or family problems (White, 1993). In the United States, parents tend to attribute suc-

---

as writing the numbers down. These ideas are metacognitive in that they imply increasingly accurate knowledge of how thinking and memory operate.

Types of Learning Strategies   Improvements in metacognitive knowledge are correlated with, but do not necessarily bring about, improvements in broad **learning strategies,** or general methods or techniques that help in solving a variety of problems. Typically such strategies draw not only on pre-existing skills, such as the language skills developed during early childhood, but on brand-new ones, such as the emerging conservation abilities described by Piaget and neo-Piagetian theorists. Learning strategies give school-age children major advantages over younger children in solving certain types of problems (Rafoth, 1993).

Attention to Detail   During the school years, children notice details much more frequently. For example, try showing children several similar pictures, only two of which are exactly the same. On the whole, younger children will make relatively more errors in finding the identical pictures. Observing their eye movements carefully shows they get sidetracked more often by the most noticeable aspects of the drawings. As a result, they sometimes forget to check all the details systematically, even when the details are crucial to solving the problem.

Rehearsal   The term *rehearsal*, which literally means "hearing again," refers to a purposeful repetition of information, either silently or aloud. Older children engage in rehearsal more often and with less prompting than younger children do (Bjorkland, 1990). To see this difference, ask children of different ages to remember a set of numbers (1, 2, 3, 5, 8, 13, . . .), and take note of how they do so. Older children are more likely to review the digits to themselves somehow, perhaps by whispering them, looking at them, or pointing to each one repeatedly. If younger children use any of these strategies at all, they are likely to apply them haphazardly.

learning strategies General methods or techniques that help to solve a variety of problems.

cess to ability and failure to lack of ability. They are also more likely to believe a failing child has a physical impairment, such as minimal brain damage or some other condition that is strictly "within" the child. The differences in attitudes can be seen in parental responses to homework: apparently because Asian parents believe more strongly that effort pays off, they tend to involve themselves in helping their children with homework more heavily than American parents do (Stevenson & Stigler, 1992).

All in all, international differences in mathematics learning challenge a widely held belief in North American society that mathematical knowledge is inherently more formal, difficult, and inaccessible than other kinds of knowledge and that success in math therefore depends on an innate, unchanging ability held by only a select number of individuals (Restivo et al., 1993). This belief may reduce the effectiveness of many American teachers in teaching math compared to many other subjects and cause many American parents to give up relatively easily on supporting their children's efforts to learn mathematics.

Japanese students have some of the highest scores on mathematics tests of any students in the world. Japanese teachers spend much more time at mathematics than do American teachers, and Japanese parents are more likely than their American counterparts to treat nightly tutoring and assistance as a high priority.

Organizing Tactics   Older children more often notice the structure, or organization, of new information and exploit that structure more effectively. For example, older children are more likely to notice that each number in the preceding list is the sum of the two numbers preceding it, and may simply use this relationship to remember the entire series. The ability to organize information helps older children to concentrate attention on cognitive tasks for longer periods.

Elaboration   Older children more often relate new information to their prior knowledge, as well as embellish it and add complexities to it. This strategy is really the outcome of the other three: elaboration inevitably results from attention to detail, rehearsal, and organization of new information.

Strategies such as these explain much of the advantage older children have over younger ones in learning new material. Not only do older children know more strategies; they also use them more widely, spontaneously, and appropriately. The developmental difference is especially obvious when they are learning arbitrary information, the kind that takes deliberate effort to remember.

However, young children do not completely lack learning strategies; often they merely use overly simple or unreliable ones (Uljens, 1997). For example, a three- or four-year-old often will point at and label the objects and words in a book, but will not do so consistently. Also, preschool children can be trained to use strategies such as rehearsal, even if they never do so as effectively as older children do. Simply reminding them to say each name on a list makes a big difference in later recall. So does recasting a problem in more familiar terms; school-age children, especially younger ones, can learn a list of "things to buy at the store" much more effectively than they would if the same list were presented as an arbitrary memory task.

Much of the difference between younger and older children concerns how reliably and automatically they invoke learning strategies. Older children are less likely to need special coaching or specially designed problems to remember successfully. They can extract organization from material that is not already well organized, and they can do so more often even when not explicitly asked for such behavior. In this sense, they are more able learners than younger children are.

Mechanisms for Acquiring Learning Strategies   Children acquire these strategies in at least three ways: trial and error, logical construction, and observational learning (Siegler, 1995). Each strategy can be seen in children's own naturally occurring activities, sometimes in combinations, and each can be assisted by parents and teachers.

Trial and Error   Sometimes children encounter effective strategies more or less by accident, or through trial and error. Often this process occurs in the midst of pre-existing, more logical learning strategies. Some schoolchildren write many essays and follow all the advice of their teachers before they discover, by accident, the methods that work best for them. Even though their teachers advise them to make an outline first, and even though the children do so repeatedly, they eventually may discover that simply writing a first draft produces better results.

Logical Construction   A lot of so-called random learning of strategies may really reflect logical construction of knowledge instead. *Logically constructed* knowledge refers to one form of children's active efforts to understand the world—the type of learning Piaget emphasized and sometimes also called *schemas.* Such thinking may especially help children extend learning strategies to brand-new situations. For example, children sometimes demonstrate knowledge of certain social relationships even though they rarely see people acting out such relationships. They can dramatize the behavior of firefighters even though they have not seen actual fires or observed firefighting behaviors. Even what they see of fires in the media tends to lack the detail they put into their reenactments. Instead, they seem to follow mental scripts, or inferences constructed from knowledge of what fighting a fire *must* be like.

Observational Learning   These examples may also involve observational learning, as described in Chapter 2. In many situations, children watch others talking and acting, and witness the consequences of those activities as well. Such observations provide models for children's learning strategies at other times and places, even those far from the original demonstrations.

Siblings often learn by observation. A younger sister may watch her older sibling plead with their parents for an extra cookie. If the pleading proves successful, the younger child is likely to use the same method herself later; but if the pleading does not work, she is relatively unlikely to imitate this particular behavior.

Helping Children to Acquire Learning Strategies   All of the processes just described can, and often are, assisted by adults. Parents may purposely demonstrate effective ways to remember the time of an appointment by writing it down as soon as they hear it and pointing out the fact that they have done so to their child. Teachers may help children solve a problem in long division by encouraging them to whisper each step in the process to themselves as they do it.

When interventions such as these are carried out systematically, they constitute various forms of *strategy training,* or coaching in when and how to apply learning strategies to new and difficult problems. Evaluations of strategy training have concluded that it improves learning substantially (Rosenshine & Meister, 1994), although the amount of improvement depends on exactly how much a child understands the purposes and potential benefits of the training. The simplest forms—what might be called **blind training**—lead children to use particular learning strategies, but do not give them any reasons for doing so or even explain that they

• • •

blind training The teaching of learned strategies without informing the learner of the benefits of the strategies.

As children gain educational experience, they acquire new strategies for learning, such as attending to important details and knowing how much attention to give to specific subtasks. Teachers and parents can help by modeling these strategies and encouraging children to use them, particularly if they explain the advantages of strategic thinking.

are actually using strategies. More complex forms not only lead children to use strategies but also emphasize the advantages of using them. Sometimes they also teach children ways to monitor the progress of their own learning. These more complex forms might be called **informed training.**

In any case, learning strategies do seem to help children to organize and process information, at least for problems similar to those for which they first learn the strategies. In and of themselves, however, learning strategies do not ensure metacognition. In fact, children do not show metacognition or learning strategies in a wide variety of situations until adolescence or even adulthood, and such strategies do not enhance problem-solving performance reliably until then either. Given the rather abstract quality of knowledge *about* thinking, we should not be surprised at this. After all, a child cannot judge a math problem's difficulty or select strategies for solving it—that is, use metacognitive skills—before he has accumulated some basic experience with math problems, and accumulating that experience may simply take more time than most children have had by age ten or twelve.

Difficulties with Information Processing: Learning Disabilities

Improvements to information processing do not occur uniformly for all children. During middle childhood, about 5 percent of children develop **learning disabilities,** disorders in basic information processing that interfere with understanding or using language, either written or spoken (Lerner, 1993). Usually a learning disability causes poor academic achievement, although low achievement is not in and of itself evidence of a learning disability. Learning disabilities have no obvious physical cause, as blindness or hearing impairment do, and do not result from a general slowness of thinking, as mental retardation does.

Learning disabilities take many forms. One of the more common forms is called *dyslexia*, literally an inability to read. The diversity of symptoms among children with dyslexia reflects the diversity among learning disabilities in general. For some children, dyslexia consists of "word blindness": they can read letters singly (such as *c, a,*

• • •

informed training The teaching of learning strategies that includes telling and showing the learner the reasons for using the strategies.

learning disability Difficulty in learning a specific academic skill such as reading or arithmetic.

Giving Children a Second Chance to Learn

Terry Wharton has a wide range of experience in classroom teaching and special education. He currently teaches a class of second to fourth graders who have shown significant behavioral and emotional problems in regular classrooms. There are only eight students in his class, all of them boys, and two teacher assistants—definitely not the typical teacher-to-student ratio. Terry spoke about the philosophy guiding his program and about how he and his assistants reconcile it with conventional academic expectations for the primary grades.

Terry: We emphasize making the class nonpunitive and nonaversive. For these kids, school has been a disaster socially—lots of fights with classmates, conflicts with teachers and other adults. We have to provide successes and confidence to counteract the downward spiral of their self-esteem.

Kelvin: *How do you do that without leading to further fights and conflicts? Eight of these kids in one room could be explosive!*

Terry: Well, we do have to plan activities carefully and guide their choices more than usual. At the start of the year, the children only come for half a day, and I plan a series of activities they are sure to enjoy and to be able to do, like setting up a personal datebook or calendar to use later in the year. By the end of that first day, they really feel successful.

Kelvin: *Given your students, how much is it like ordinary school?*

Terry: Oh lots, actually! Academics is a priority. We have a "news" time where everyone relates some interesting personal experience. Then I read to them

for a few minutes. Then they write in journals, either about the story or about something else that concerns them.

Kelvin: *Do the kids like the journals?*

Terry: I must admit, at first they resisted. They seemed very self-conscious about their writing skills and about revealing their thoughts and feelings. But lately it's been amazing; you should read them! Their growth with the journals is impressive. They talk about the story, or about their fears and hopes for their family.

Kelvin: *What about math?*

Terry: They don't seem as uncomfortable about math as they do about writing and reading; I'm not sure why. We work on basic arithmetic skills using some of the latest manipulatives.

Kelvin: *Manipulatives?*

Terry: Like sets of unit blocks that you can combine to illustrate addition problems. They seem to like that. But you know what surprised me the most? Workbooks! When I taught a regular primary-grade class, I tried to avoid those because I felt they were too structured, but these students love them; they even ask to do them! I think it gives them a feeling of clear progress and a sense of control over their own efforts. They can see clearly that they are getting work done.

Kelvin: *So your program is indeed academic? You do work on cognitive skills?*

Terry: Absolutely. The cognitive skills develop only because we're also supporting these students socially, though. The two go hand in hand. I think that's true for all children, but working with

these kids with behavior problems has really brought that idea home to me.

Kelvin: *Where else do you see academic and social connections?*

Terry: With the parents, certainly. We make a big effort to involve the parents in our program. Several times a year we have "family celebrations," lunches where the child's whole family is invited. The parents have responded enthusiastically. Some parents work as volunteers in the school. They've been a real help, and even if they are not in the same classroom, it's reassuring to be in the same building as their child.

Kelvin: *These sound like good ideas for all classrooms and parents. Do you agree?*

Terry: Yes, I do. But they're especially valuable for these particular parents because they've had so many bad experiences with schools, either because of their child's problems or when they were students themselves. It builds their confidence as parents.

What Do You Think?

1. Do you think Terry would define the word *cognitive* the same way this chapter does?

2. Terry did not comment on the fact that his class is all boys. Do you think gender is important to consider in teaching a class like this? Why or why not?

3. Terry mentions that his students enjoy workbooks for mathematics, even though he personally does not consider them a good idea initially. How do you feel about this issue? What do you suppose Piaget or an information-processing theorist would say about using workbooks?

or *t*) but not in combinations that make words, such as *cat*. In other forms of dyslexia, children can read words but fail to comprehend them. They can copy words accurately or transcribe them from oral dictation, but they cannot explain what they have written afterward, no matter how simple the vocabulary. Some children with dyslexia can read combinations of digits that make large numbers; for example, they can read

123 as "one hundred and twenty-three" but not as "one, two, three," even when they try. Most children with dyslexia have these problems in combination. Yet they seem normal in every other respect; their everyday conversations seem perfectly intelligent and their motor skills just as developed as other children's.

Causes of Learning Disabilities   What causes some children to have a learning disability such as dyslexia? The symptoms sometimes resemble what happens to individuals who suffer injuries to their brains (Rourke & Del Dotto, 1994). For this reason, some professionals have suggested that many learning disabilities, including dyslexia, may reflect undetected minimal brain damage that occurred during the birth process or even before birth. This hypothesis is extremely hard to prove, however. It also discourages some parents and professionals from helping children with learning disabilities on the grounds (probably mistaken) that organically based problems are beyond control.

A more helpful explanation for learning disabilities focuses on cognitive functions rather than on brain anatomy. In this view, disabilities may result from subtle differences in how the mind of a child normally organizes and processes information. To see what this idea means, consider what children must do to read an ordinary page of print. First, they must perceive the letters and words as visual patterns. Then they must combine those patterns into larger strings that constitute phrases and sentences. Finally, they must connect those strings with meanings to form ideas. While all of these steps are going on, they must also scan ahead to recognize the upcoming visual patterns on the page. If any of these steps fails to occur or occurs in the wrong sequence or at the wrong speed, a child may appear dyslexic.

Such problems in processing information may lie at the heart of many learning disabilities. Some children with dyslexia may, for example, find visual recognition especially difficult or time consuming. Several researchers have reached this conclusion after studying a phenomenon called *perceptual masking,* in which some letters are hard to read because of the presence of other letters nearby. To understand this problem, consider the following arrangement of letters:

w e k
q w e k l
a q w e k l m
s a q w e k l m n
d s a q w e k l m n p
g f d s a q w e k l m n p y b
c v g f d s a q w e k l m n p y b h t

If you look at the *e* in the top line, you probably will still be able to see the letters *w* and *k* clearly using your peripheral vision (the corner of your eye). If you look at the *e* in a line farther down, you can still see the end letters relatively clearly, but the middle letters become almost impossible to pick out clearly. Trying to notice the middle letters does help you to perceive them, but when you make this effort, the end letters become hard to discern. Perceiving one set of features in this display masks others; hence the term *perceptual masking.* Without a lot of practice, few people, adults or children, can see very many letters at once.

Some (though not all) children with dyslexia show especially strong perceptual masking (Snowling & Stackhouse, 1996). Compared to normal readers, they must stare at words for rather long periods, consciously shifting attention from one subset of letters to another in a way similar to the staring required to "see" the letters displayed on this page. Once they figure out the letters in a word, however, they can connect meanings with them fairly quickly and accurately. For these children, verbal association may occur much sooner than visual perception.

The gap in speed between perceiving and associating may account for many errors made by children with dyslexia. A ten-year-old may look at the word *conceal* and say something like "concol," or look at *alternate* and say "alfoonite." In making

There are numerous ways to help children with learning disabilities, but no single way is guaranteed to be effective. This teacher, for example, is helping a girl with a specially designed tutorial that combines graphics and other information in ways meant to facilitate learning.

these mistakes, children may literally be reading what they see and guessing about the rest. Unfortunately, they may see fewer letters than normal readers usually discern. To put it differently, trying to see all letters clearly may simply take too much time and effort, and overall reading comprehension breaks down as a result.

Helping Children with Learning Disabilities   Because learning disabilities become a problem primarily in school settings, school professionals have taken increasing responsibility in recent years for helping children who develop these problems. Most commonly, help consists of careful diagnosis of which steps of thinking cause difficulty for a child, followed by individual educational plans to strengthen those particular steps (Lyon, 1993). For instance, children with problems in perceptual masking can be given exercises in which they purposely work to improve this skill. Often such special work can be done in a regular class during a normal school day, but at least some of it requires individual tutoring so that the professional can monitor and give precise assistance to the child's thinking as it actually occurs. Depending on the child's needs and the school's circumstances, regular classroom teachers, parents, or trained special educators can act as tutors, as well as additional sources of encouragement and support for the child.

Note that children with learning disabilities usually are old enough to have feelings and opinions about their problems. Eventually, in fact, the major problem in some learning disabilities may become *self-consciousness* about failing to learn, in addition to any cognitive or perceptual problems as such. A child who cannot read well usually becomes painfully aware of this fact sooner or later and worries about what teachers, parents, and peers may think of her as a result. Parents can help with this problem by being optimistic about the child's eventual capacity to learn academic skills, in spite of current difficulties, and by being supportive rather than critical of the child's efforts to do so. Teachers can help in these same ways. In addition, they can encourage a positive, supportive climate in the child's classroom and school. The social impact of school is so important, in fact, that we discuss it again later in this chapter. First, though, let us look at another major cognitive change of middle childhood: the development of language. As we will see, this development also has both cognitive and social effects.

WHAT DO YOU THINK?   Think about the methods you yourself have used to remember new information. What are they, and how are they consistent with the discussion in this chapter about how memory develops during middle childhood? Compare your own memory strategies with those of classmates. Are they similar or different?

Language Development in Middle Childhood

As we saw in Chapters 6 and 9, language development is a gradual process, one that continues to unfold during middle childhood. Vocabulary keeps growing, of course, and the ways children use words and sentences become more subtle and complex and more like adults' (Anglin, 1993). Contrary to the impressions young school-age children sometimes give, though, they have not necessarily mastered syntax. They often are confused by a number of common sentence forms until well into the elementary school years. To six-year-olds, for example, the sentence *The baby is not easy to see* means "The baby cannot see very well"; the sentence *I don't think it will rain tomorrow* is likely to mean "I know for a fact that it won't rain."

Mistakes like these may hardly be noticeable to parents and teachers if a child otherwise has normal language ability and has been acquiring only one language since birth. A school-age child can make himself or herself understood for most everyday purposes, and can express basic feelings. What is primarily still missing at this age is an extended vocabulary and skill in the more subtle or specialized uses of language—needs that therefore become the focus of many elementary school programs. The fact that language is actually changing or "developing" during middle childhood, in fact, may seem obvious only if a child is acquiring *two* languages during this period. In that case, all of the basic issues of language acquisition come to the fore: problems in phonology (the sounds of a new language), in lexicon (vocabulary), in syntax (grammar), and in pragmatics (language use). Although we do not have enough space to review all of these issues in this chapter, two aspects merit attention: the development of metaphorical thinking and the cognitive and social effects of bilingualism.

Understanding Metaphor

One of the most interesting language developments in middle childhood concerns understanding metaphor. A **metaphor** is a figure of speech in which a word or an expression ordinarily used for one thing is used for another ("the perfume is bright sunshine"). Children can understand a variety of metaphors even in the preschool years, comparing color and personality ("He is blue") and objects and personality ("It was a friendly house"), among other things (Broderick, 1991). At first, however, they often assume a metaphor refers to a physical similarity rather than to an underlying conceptual relationship. The sentence *My brother is a rock*, for example, is taken to mean "My brother sits very still, like a rock" or "My brother is very hard when you touch or punch him, like a rock."

Children do not reliably interpret a metaphor in conceptual or relational terms until about age ten (Winner, 1988). By that age, the sentence *My brother is a rock* is taken psychologically rather than physically: now the term *rock* is assumed to refer to a personality trait, so the sentence might mean "My brother is unfeeling or reserved." The sentence *Your words are music to my ears* no longer means literally that you are singing, as some preschoolers assume, but that "Your ideas produce a pleasurable feeling in me, like the feeling I get listening to music."

At least two factors explain the developmental changes in children's understanding of metaphor. One is the child's growing sensitivity to the context of communications: calling a person a *butterfly* means one thing when the person is beautifully dressed but another when the person is behaving restlessly. Older children take enough time to note such variations in the context of a metaphor to be able to interpret it correctly (Anderson, 1992). The other factor is the significant information-processing demands of metaphor: to understand it, the child must grasp not only the literal meaning of the sentence and its terms but also the speaker's intended meaning. This is basically an example of metacognition, discussed earlier, since the child must treat the metaphor itself as an object of thought in trying to discern its nonliteral, intended meaning. It is not surprising, therefore, that children do not become proficient in understanding metaphors until well into middle childhood. It is also not surprising that research has found that school-age children who fail to comprehend metaphorical language tend also to experience language and learning disabilities (Smith & Tsimpli, 1995). Their failure probably is not a cause of their disabilities, but it may be a symptom of a more general difficulty with metacognitive thinking and with applying the learning strategies that metacognition makes possible.

● ● ●

metaphor A word, phrase, or sentence containing an implied comparison.

Bilingualism and Its Effects

Although most monolinguals may not realize it, a majority of children around the world are able to speak two languages and therefore are bilingual (Romaine, 1995). Bilingualism is common in the United States even though the nation is officially monolingual; somewhere between 30 million and 35 million individuals (about 10 to 15 percent) regularly use another language in addition to English (U.S. Department of Commerce, 1998) (see Figure 12.4). Does this skill benefit their cognitive development? Research suggests that it does, but primarily when they acquire both languages equally well and when both languages are treated with respect by teachers and other representatives of the community (Bialystok & Hakuta, 1994). Language specialists call such individuals **balanced bilinguals.**

Cognitive Effects of Bilingualism   For one thing, balanced bilingual children show greater cognitive flexibility—skill at detecting multiple meanings of words and alternative orientations of objects—than monolingual children do. Bilingual children can substitute arbitrary words for normally occurring words relatively easily without changing any other features of the sentence. If asked to substitute *spaghetti* for *I* in the sentence "I am cold," bilingual children more often produce the exact substitution ("Spaghetti am cold") and resist the temptation to correct the grammar ("Spaghetti is cold"), thereby violating the instructions for the task. Presumably such a skill stems from bilinguals' special experience with the arbitrary, conventional nature of words and language.

In part, such flexibility shows **metalinguistic awareness,** the knowledge that language—and in this case individual words—can be an object of thought. Metalinguistic awareness develops because bilingual experiences often challenge children to think consciously about what to say and how to say it (Jimenez et al., 1995). A question such as "What if a dog were called a cat?" therefore poses fewer conceptual problems for bilinguals. So do follow-up questions such as "Would this 'cat' meow?" or "Would it purr?"

However, all of these cognitive advantages apply primarily to balanced bilingual children, those with equal skill in both languages. What about the unbalanced bilinguals, those with more skill in one language than in the other? Does knowledge of a second language help, even if it is limited? Evidence is scarce, but what there is suggests that unbalanced bilingualism has mixed effects on children's thinking skills, largely because of the interplay of social attitudes surrounding language differences in society (Pease-Alvarez, 1993).

---

balanced bilingual A person who is equally fluent in two languages rather than more fluent in one language than in the other.

metalinguistic awareness The ability to attend to language as an object of thought rather than attending only to the content or ideas of a language.

● ● ● ● ● ● ● ● ● ● ● ● ● ● ● ● ● ●

FIGURE 12.4

Children Five Years and Older from Homes Where a Language Other Than English Is Spoken, 1980 and 1990

The percentage of homes in which a non-English language is spoken has been growing. The single most common non-English language is Spanish. In some cities and regions, the proportion of non-English speakers is far higher than shown in this graph. *Source:* U.S. Department of Commerce, 1998.

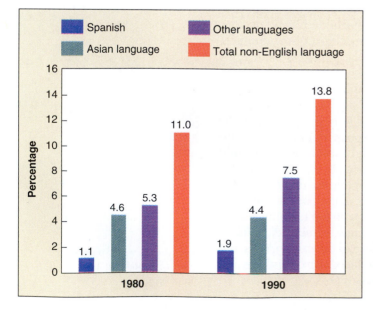

Social Effects of Bilingualism   When children acquire two languages, one language usually has more prestige than the other. In the United States, the "best," or most important, language almost always is English. Its prestige results not only from its widespread use but also from its association with success and power: all the important people in American society, it seems, speak English fluently. These circumstances create negative attitudes or stereotypes about people who speak other languages and challenge educators to overcome social prejudices at the same time they facilitate learning new grammar, vocabulary, and usage (Soto, 1997).

The influence of language on attitudes can be documented through experiments using the *matched guise technique.* In this procedure, perfectly balanced and fluent bilinguals tape record standard messages in each of their two languages, and the messages are interspersed among other tape-recorded messages to dis-

Fully bilingual children have cognitive advantages over monolinguals, but only as long as both languages and their related cultures are treated with respect by teachers and society. These Vietnamese children are well on their way to becoming bilingual; what attitudes will they encounter about their language and heritage?

guise the identities of the bilingual speakers. Then listeners evaluate the competence and social attractiveness of each speaker. Time after time, two consistent trends occur in studies of this type. First, speakers of English are rated more highly than speakers of other languages. Second, listeners from non-English-speaking cultural groups rate the English speakers more highly than they do speakers of their own language. The prestige of English, in other words, comes from sources in addition to English speakers themselves.

Negative attitudes toward non-English languages reduce children's school performance by making them less willing to use their primary, or first, language in public and reducing their self-confidence about linguistic skills in general. Fortunately, however, educational programs exist that can counteract these effects by treating children's first language as an educational resource rather than a liability. Overall, research favors *additive bilingual education,* programs that develop language skills in *both* of a child's languages rather than attempting to replace a first language with English (Hernandez, 1997). As a practical matter, such programs usually are conducted partly in each language, depending on children's current language skills, but they do not confine either language to isolated "lessons" lasting only short periods each day. The challenge is a double one: to foster new language skills while also promoting respect for a child's original language and culture. In countries where language is less strongly associated with economic or social status (for example, Canada, where about 25 percent of the population speaks French as a first language), bilingual education often does not include this double agenda (Johnson & Swain, 1997). Therefore, successful bilingual programs more often emphasize simple immersion in a second language and tend to ignore a child's first language without negative educational effects.

Black English

In the United States, some African Americans use a dialect, or version of English, called **Black English,** that differs from the middle-class dialect that linguists call *Standard English.* The two versions differ in three ways (Guy, 1996). First, certain sounds occur differently: for example, the sound /th/ becomes /d/, making the word *this* sound like *dis.* Second, certain grammatical forms differ. The verb *to be* is used

• • •

Black English A dialect or version of English spoken by many African Americans.

to indicate a continuing situation or condition. The sentence "The coffee be cold" means approximately "Every day the coffee is always cold"; but the sentence "The coffee cold" is closer to meaning "The coffee is cold this time." Third, Black English contains many words and expressions that have meanings very different than those in Standard English. The word *bad* can mean something undesirable ("I have a bad cold") but also something highly desirable ("She look bad" usually means "She looks very good").

Studies of Black English have found it to be as complex as any other language, including Standard English, and equally capable of expressing the full range of human thought and emotion (Smitherman-Donaldson, 1994). Unfortunately, society's attitudes toward it remain rather negative, which has created dilemmas for teachers of students who use Black English. Should students be allowed to speak this dialect in class, or even be encouraged to do so, because they know it best? Or should they always be expected to use Standard English to prepare them to function better in mainstream (white) society? Educators typically recommend a compromise: teachers should respect Black English, appreciate its richness, and allow students to use it in class some of the time. But they should also show students how Black English has influenced and enriched Standard English (van Keulen et al., 1998)—where, for example, did the term *cool*, meaning "terrific," come from? Teachers should also encourage students to practice Standard English because it probably will help them in situations where they must communicate more formally.

WHAT DO YOU THINK ?   Think about a language you wish you could speak fluently. Why would you like to be able to use this language? In forming your opinion, what assumptions are you making about the culture or people who use this language?

Defining and Measuring Intelligence

Intelligence refers to adaptability, or, put differently, to a general ability to learn from experience. Usually intelligence also refers to the ability to reason abstractly, sometimes using language to do so, and it includes the ability to integrate old and new knowledge. In recent years, some psychologists have also used the term *intelligence* to refer to social skills, talents of various kinds (such as a talent for music), or bodily skills. The traditional orientation toward reasoning and problem solving, however, still dominates discussions of intelligence, and partly as a result, many standardized tests have been developed to measure these forms of intelligence.

Issues Regarding Intelligence

Because so many definitions of *intelligence* exist, it is not surprising that psychologists continually debate a number of issues related to it. Here is a sampling.

How Many Abilities?   Both common sense and research suggest that abilities come in many forms. But do these forms add up to one truly general intelligence or to an assortment of "intelligences"? Some theories of intelligence emphasize relatively specific skills; others stress one rather general ability, sometimes called *g* (Spearman, 1927). In practice most psychologists acknowledge the presence of both general and specific factors, although they differer in emphasis and in the number of specific factors proposed.

How Are Abilities Related?   Assuming specific skills contribute to intelligence in some way, how do they do it? Are they a loose conglomeration, even a hodgepodge, of diverse skills? The contents of some psychometric tests of intelligence,

intelligence A general ability to learn from experience; also refers to ability to reason abstractly.

which often contain a wide range of discrete problems, seem to imply a diverse conglomeration. Are they a discrete number of moderately general but unrelated abilities? That idea is implied by some information-processing views of intelligence, as well as other views. Or do the elements of intelligence bear logical, structured relationships to one another in which each requires the others for its full expression? The most widely known version of this view is Piaget's theory of cognitive stages, explained in Chapter 2.

What Role Does Experience Play in Developing Intelligence?   Most psychologists argue that certain experiences can modify intelligence, that is, give a person more of one ability or less of another. But since they disagree about the nature of abilities, they also differ over the influence of experience on intelligence. Attending a cognitively enriching preschool program, one designed to stimulate problem-solving and verbal skills, has been shown to raise children's scores on traditional, standardized tests of intelligence (or IQ) in the short term and sometimes even in the long term (Schweinhart et al., 1993). At the same time, though, children's IQ scores correlate with, or tend to parallel, the IQ scores of close relatives, such as parents and siblings, even when children do not live in the same household as the relatives. Thus, heredity also influences intelligence, at least in the specific form expressed on IQ tests.

In answering the major questions about intelligence, psychologists have worked from a number of perspectives. The oldest and therefore best developed is the **psychometric approach,** which is based on standardized, quantitative measurement of abilities and achievement. More recently, researchers oriented toward *information processing* and toward *sociocultural* issues also have developed theories of intelligence, although these approaches have not been tied to standardized testing to any significant extent.

Psychometric Approaches to Intelligence

Psychometric definitions of intelligence have developed out of *standardized tests,* all of which share three important features. First, they always contain clearly stated questions that have relatively specific answers. The questions usually draw on logical reasoning and verbal skills, which schools typically require. Second, standardized tests always include clear, standard procedures for administration and scoring. Often they provide a script for the person giving the test, as well as specific printed advice about when and how to credit particular answers. Third, such tests present information about how large groups of comparable individuals perform to allow evaluation of the performances of particular groups or individual children (Aiken, 1996).

Kinds of Standardized Test   Standardized tests serve many purposes, but for convenience we can classify them into two major groups: achievement tests and aptitude, or ability, tests. **Achievement tests** measure individuals' existing skills or knowledge; they try to assess current attainment in a particular realm of human behavior. Children often encounter such tests in the form of scholastic achievement tests, such as tests of reading achievement or of arithmetic achievement. By nature, such tests usually draw heavily on the typical curriculum content of the subject area being tested.

Aptitude tests measure ability or try to estimate future performance in some realm of behavior. A test of scholastic aptitude, for instance, tries to estimate a child's potential for success in school. Because of their goal, aptitude tests contain a broader range of questions than achievement tests do. A scholastic aptitude test probably would include questions from several major school subjects and draw on basic academic skills such as reading and mathematical reasoning.

• • •

psychometric approach to intelligence A view of intelligence based on identifying individual differences in ability through standardized test scores.

achievement test A test designed to evaluate a person's current state of knowledge.

aptitude test A measurement of ability that estimates future performance in some realm of behavior.

In practice, aptitude and achievement tests are less distinct than these definitions make them sound. Often achievement tests are very effective predictors of future performance; children's current skills in arithmetic, for instance, predict their future mathematical performance about as well as any aptitude test can do. Also, aptitude tests can successfully predict future progress only by sampling skills and knowledge children have already attained. Nonetheless, the distinction remains useful for those who develop and use tests. In general, measuring aptitude means looking to the future, whereas measuring achievement means assessing the past.

Once norms have been calculated, standardized tests, and especially achievement tests, can serve two purposes. On the one hand, they can help educators know how well particular schools or classrooms are functioning in general. For example, all classrooms using a particular curriculum can be compared with classrooms using another curriculum, or all classrooms in one school can be compared with all classrooms in the city or even with a national cross-section.

On the other hand, standardized tests sometimes can aid individual children. The most common approach involves screening students who need special educational help. If teachers find that a certain student is learning the curriculum very slowly, they may ask a school psychologist to test her general scholastic ability in the hope of diagnosing or clarifying her learning problems. Although the results of such a test cannot stand alone, they often contribute to the complex process of assessing the learning needs of a particular child.

As you may suspect, standardized tests serve neither of these purposes perfectly. Factors other than ability, such as a child's health or motivation to succeed, affect performance. So do physical disabilities, such as visual impairment. More indirectly, cultural and language differences among children affect performance on standardized tests. These additional influences deserve special discussion because they affect all children throughout society.

Biases of Intelligence and General Ability Tests   Although they attempt to measure general qualities, tests of ability and intelligence contain various biases. For example, many intelligence tests rely heavily on language in all of its forms— listening, speaking, and reading. Many also emphasize problems that have specific answers and that play down divergent or creative thinking. Also, although they do not focus on speed, intelligence tests tend to favor children who answer fairly rapidly and take little time to mull over their solutions.

Because schools also emphasize all of these features, intelligence tests measure academic ability better than they do any other skill. Some psychologists, in fact, have suggested calling them measures of *academic intelligence* or of school ability to make this limitation clear (Anastasi & Urbina, 1997).

The biggest problem with intelligence tests, however, comes from their cultural assumptions, which have originated entirely from white, middle-class experiences in Western Europe and North America. The tests show their assumptions or biases in at least two ways. First, individual questions often demand knowledge that children can gain only by thorough immersion in white, middle-class society. One question might ask children to describe the purpose of a garden hose, thereby assuming previous contact with a garden in their backyards. Another question might ask children to define the word *drama* or *concerto*, thereby assuming the sort of education that provides this information.

Even when tests avoid this type of bias, they suffer from other, more subtle cultural assumptions. For example, some ethnic groups and cultures do not value conversations that emphasize abstract or general propositions, as is common in classrooms or intellectual discussions; using this style may seem rude or at least boring (Heath, 1993). Children from these groups therefore cannot be expected to take tests that rely heavily on this form of dialogue. Also, in some cultural groups contact with strange adults is extremely rare, so children from such groups may find sitting alone in a room with an unfamiliar test administrator perplexing or even frightening. For such children, any questions the administrator asks may seem much less important than figuring out this adult's real motives.

Common Misinterpretations of Intelligence Tests   Because of these problems, intelligence tests sometimes have been strongly criticized. Some school districts and states have even banned the less reliable group tests altogether. Individual intelligence tests generally have remained in use, however, because they are especially helpful in diagnosing children with special learning needs and are always administered by relatively well-trained psychologists.

A lot of criticism has stemmed from misinterpretations of the results of intelligence tests. In one way or another, all of the following mistakes have turned out to be all too easy to make:

1. *Equating test scores with all forms of ability*   As we already pointed out, intelligence tests primarily measure academic talent. Yet life abounds with many other kinds of talent, from cooking or playing the piano to always saying the tactful thing. The further removed these talents are from academics, the less accurately intelligence tests can measure or predict them.

2. *Confusing intellectual differences with levels of intelligence*   Most intelligence test scores reflect how much a child differs from other, comparable children. They usually do *not* report how much a child actually knows at any given point in time. Yet in many situations, actual knowledge may matter more than differences in knowledge, such as when a child tries to fix a bicycle or find his way home along an unfamiliar street.

3. *Assuming too much validity*   Because intelligence tests give numerical scores, adults are tempted to think they are more precise than they really are. In reality, small differences in scores among children often reflect random variations rather than true differences in intelligence. Test manuals usually point out this fact, but unfortunately the information does not always reach parents, and even teachers or school psychologists may forget it.

4. *Assuming too much reliability and stability*   Likewise, because intelligence tests give numerical scores, it is tempting to assume that the numbers are fixed and stable and that one administration of a test will yield the same score that a subsequent administration does. In reality, intelligence test scores are not perfectly reliable or stable, and in fact may vary significantly across test occasions. Administrations separated by long periods (several years) are particularly likely to produce different scores for the same individual.

Information-Processing Approaches to Intelligence

Psychologists have responded to these criticisms by developing other definitions and theories of intelligence. One way or another, all of the newer approaches broaden the nature and sources of intelligence. From these perspectives, more children seem to qualify as "intelligent" than is the case when children are assessed psychometrically.

The Triarchic Theory of Intelligence   An approach that draws explicitly on principles of information-processing theory is the **triarchic theory of intelligence** proposed by Robert Sternberg (Sternberg, 1994, 1997). This theory broadens the psychometric approach by incorporating recent ideas from research on *how* thinking occurs. To do this, Sternberg proposed three realms of cognition or, in his words, "subtheories" (hence the name *triarchic*), each of which contributes to general intelligence.

triarchic theory of intelligence A view of intelligence as consisting of three components: (1) adaptability, (2) information-processing skills, and (3) the ability to deal with novelty.

The first realm of intelligence concerns the *components* of thinking. These resemble the basic elements of the information-processing model described in Chapter 2. Components include skills at coding, representing, and combining information, as well as higher-order skills such as planning and evaluating one's own success in solving a problem or performing a cognitive task.

The second realm of intelligence concerns how individuals cope with their *experiences.* How effectively do they respond to novelty in solving new problems? For example, a person may follow a dinner recipe accurately when it is written in imperial measurements (ounces, teaspoons) but fail miserably when the same recipe is presented in metric units (milliliters, grams). How quickly can that person adjust to the new form of the task and solve it as automatically as was possible with the old form?

The third realm of intelligence concerns the *context* of thinking. A person shows this form of intelligence to the extent to which she can adapt to, alter, or select environments relevant to and supportive of her abilities (Sternberg & Wagner, 1994). In taking a university course, for example, a student may try diligently to complete the course assignments as given, in essence adapting herself to the environment of the course. If this strategy does not work satisfactorily, the student may complain about the assignments to the professor in an effort to alter them. If the altered assignments do not work for her, the student may drop the course and select another. All of these behaviors show contextual intelligence (though not necessarily of a kind that may please professors!).

Table 12.1 summarizes the three realms of thinking or cognition. These realms describe the processes of intelligence in more detail than classic psychometric approaches to intelligence have done. They also suggest an explanation for why individuals sometimes seem intelligent in different ways: perhaps one person has an advantage at internal processing of information, another adjusts to new experiences especially well, and a third has a knack for adapting, altering, or selecting appropriate environments in which to work. Given these possibilities, it would not be surprising if psychometric tests favored certain children and cultural groups more than others, since the environments of some families and cultures foster the learning of testlike behaviors more than others do.

Gardner's Theory of Multiple Intelligences   Like Sternberg, Howard Gardner (1993a) has proposed that general ability consists of several elements or factors. However, Gardner has defined these factors in ways that reflect the influence of culture and society even more explicitly than the triarchic theory does. He argues that not one but **multiple intelligences** exist and take the following forms:

1. *Language skill* A child with this talent speaks comfortably and fluently and learns new words and expressions easily. She also memorizes verbal materials, such as poems, much more easily than other children do.

2. *Musical skill* This child not only plays one or more musical instruments but also sings and discerns subtle musical effects. Usually musical talent also includes a good sense of timing, or rhythm.

• • •

multiple intelligences According to Howard Gardner's theory of intelligence, alternative forms of intelligence or adaptability to the environment.

The triarchic theory of intelligence, developed by Robert Sternberg, identifies three different realms of thinking: componential, experiential, and contextual. Philosophically, the theory is rooted in information-processing theory.

TABLE 12.1 The Triarchic Theory of Intelligence	
Realm of Intelligence	**Examples**
Componential	Coding and representing information; planning and executing solutions to problems
Experiential	Skill with novel problems and familiar problems in novel settings; skill at solving problems automatically as they become familiar
Contextual	Deliberate adaptation, alteration, and selection of learning environments to facilitate problem solving

Musical intelligence is not well assessed on most classical tests of general ability, even though some psychologists (for example, Howard Gardner) believe it constitutes a unique form of talent or intelligence. Children who play an instrument may—or may not—be particularly studious at school.

3. *Logical skill* A child with this skill organizes objects and concepts well. Using a microcomputer, for example, comes easily, as does mathematics.

4. *Spatial skill* This child literally can find his way around. He knows the streets of the neighborhood better than most children his age do; if he lives in the country, he can find his way across large stretches of terrain without getting lost.

5. *Kinesthetic, or body balance, skill* This child is sensitive to the internal sensations created by body movement. As a result, she finds dancing, gymnastics, and other activities requiring balance easy to learn.

6. *Interpersonal and intrapersonal skills* A child with interpersonal skill shows excellent understanding of others' feelings, thoughts, and motives. A child with intrapersonal skill has a good understanding of his own. For children with either or both of these skills, handling social encounters comes relatively easily. (Interpersonal and intrapersonal skills may really amount to two distinct forms of intelligence, but the research evidence has made Gardner unsure about this.)

Gardner argues that the various intelligences are distinct, for several reasons. First, some of them can be physically located within the brain. Certain language functions occur within particular, identifiable parts of the brain, as do kinesthetic or balance functions. Second, the intelligences sometimes occur in pure form; some individuals with mental retardation play a musical instrument extremely well, even though their language ability may be limited and they cannot reason abstractly. Third, each intelligence involves particular, core skills that clearly set it off from the others. Being musical requires a good sense of pitch, but this skill contributes little to the other intelligences.

Like Sternberg's ideas, the theory of multiple intelligences implies criticisms of psychometric definitions of intelligence and of the standardized intelligence testing associated with psychometric definitions. Strictly speaking, however, the notion of multiple intelligences may really criticize the *use* of conventional tests beyond their intended purposes. As we pointed out earlier, such tests are designed to predict academic skills and therefore heavily emphasize verbal and logical activities. But school is not everything in life, despite its prominence in children's lives. Perhaps, as Gardner himself argues, the fact that school attendance is compulsory has actually interfered with understanding intelligence because it may have made us all value verbal and mathematical skills more highly than we should (Gardner, 1993b). The accompanying Perspectives box discusses this possibility as it relates to the experiences of gifted students.

Sociocultural Approaches to Intelligence

Sociocultural definitions of intelligence give even more importance than information-processing theories do to the social setting. In the **sociocultural perspective,** intelligence is not actually "in" individual persons but instead is to be found in the interactions and activities that occur *among* individuals (Wertsch et al., 1995). In this view, it is not the individual who adapts to, learns, and modifies knowledge but the person and his or her environment in combination. For example, a child may make many mistakes on a test of arithmetic computation but be able to locate the most economical items at the local candy store almost infallibly, even if the items come in odd sizes (1⅞ versus 2¼ ounces) or odd prices (34 cents versus 49 cents) (Chaiklin & Lave, 1993). That is because the knowledge needed for comparison shopping is contained not only in the shopper's mind but also in the overall structure of shopping in the candy store's environment. With practice, a child learns how to sort out pricing clues that depend very little on the computational procedures learned in grade school. Some of the clues involve rough estimations, such as when the prices of two items differ widely but their sizes differ only a little. Others involve nonarithmetic knowledge, such as recommendations from other shoppers or memories of where the store kept the bargains on previous visits. The intelligence needed for comparison shopping thus is only partly "in" the child; the rest is more accurately said to be distributed among the store shelves, the conversations with other shoppers, and the history of events at the store.

A key concept in understanding the sociocultural view of knowledge is the *zone of proximal development (ZPD)*, originated by the Russian psychologist Lev Vygotsky and discussed in Chapter 9 (Vygotsky, 1978, 1997). The ZPD refers to the level of problem solving at which a child cannot solve a problem alone but can do so when assisted by an adult or a more competent peer. For example, a six-year-old may find the telephone directory too difficult to use alone but may be quite able to look up a phone number when given a bit of help from a parent. Implicit in the ZPD is the idea of shared knowledge, or shared cognition. Knowledge of how to use

sociocultural perspective on intelligence A view of intelligence that emphasizes the social and cultural influences on ability rather than the influence of inherent or learned individual differences.

Even though repairing a fishnet may be too difficult for this boy to do alone, he is able to make repairs successfully when assisted by a more experienced adult. Changes in performance because of such assistance is part of what Vygotsky means by the zone of proximal development.

PERSPECTIVES

Gifted Students: Victims or Elite?

• • • • For years some educators have worried that *gifted students* (those capable of high performance in some or all academic areas, social leadership, or the performing arts) (see Table 12.2) become bored with the normal curriculum, isolated from their peers socially, and sometimes unproductive in school and career (Ross, 1993). Their "problem" was too much talent, but gifted students were believed to be potential victims of conventional schooling in the way students with learning or physical disabilities are.

In response to these concerns, some schools have created programs of gifted education. Typically these include a "pull-out" program: for an hour or two each week, students designated as gifted work in a separate classroom on activities designed to meet their needs. Often students work independently on projects of their own choosing, such as learning about local butterflies, designing a computer program, or creating a portfolio of paintings. Sometimes they are also linked with community experts (called *mentors*) who help them develop these interests. Regular classroom teachers are encouraged to recognize their interests and abilities by allowing time to pursue the projects and periodically grouping gifted children together for tasks related to the regular curriculum (Gallagher & Gallagher, 1994).

This portrait of gifted education is attractive but highly controversial. A number of educators, parents, and political leaders argue that gifted education creates an overprivileged group of students (Margolin, 1994). In the pull-out programs, students receive much more time and attention from teachers than in a typical classroom and enjoy more freedom in using their time. Ironically, it is argued, the curriculum for gifted students is much *less* rigorous than that for regular students; gifted children do not necessarily read more books, write more essays, or learn more mathematics than others do.

Furthermore, the gifted programs tend to treat students as if they were broadly talented in all areas, even though research and professional teachers' experiences suggest that almost all students have selected talents—math but not English, for example, or music but not athletics (Gardner, 1997). This makes gifted programs more compatible with the preexisting strengths of high-SES families and white, English-speaking families, which may constitute a subtle form of racism.

Gifted education responded to these criticisms by making entrance into gifted programs more flexible: relying less on standardized test scores and more on students' own interest in volunteering for the program. Another is to arrange more activities for gifted students in the regular classroom and fewer in pull-out situations (Maker, 1993). A third is to redefine gifted education as *enrichment:* activities that tie conventional curriculum goals (reading, arithmetic) to students' own prior interests and talents. All students may be invited to pull-out activities, and activities focus on particular areas of the normal curriculum.

Integrating gifted and regular education in these ways is more equitable but does not eliminate the basic educational controversy underlying gifted education: fostering excellence and fostering equality of education. Some researchers argue, for example, that having highly talented students work with less talented ones may accentuate rather than reduce elitism. Differences between higher and lower performers become obvious to all students, day in and day out, and may create tensions within the classroom (Gallagher, 1993). Students may still prefer classmates with similar levels of academic motivation, both to work with and to be friends with; so informal social segregation may develop even in a room that is officially integrated. Enrichment activities also are harder to schedule if they invite volunteers and focus on specific school subjects; they cannot overlap with regular class times since some students are ahead and motivated in the enrichment subject but may need extra help in the "regular" subject that they miss. That leaves lunch periods and before and after school for enrichment periods, times that teachers may need for class preparations and "refueling." Despite problems, many excellent enrichment programs exist in schools and have succeeded reasonably well in creating flexible yet challenging learning opportunities.

What Do You Think?

Some educators argue that the idea of a "bored gifted student" is a contradiction in terms. Why do you think they believe this? What do *you* think of this possibility?

TABLE 12.2	Some Characteristics of Gifted Students Renzulli (1994)

Characteristic	Examples
Well-above-average ability	Can think abstractly; skilled at verbal and numerical reasoning; adapts well to novel situations; rapid and accurate memory
Task commitment	Shows high level of interest, enthusiasm, perseverance, and self-confidence; sets high standards for success
Creativity	Shows original thoughts; open to new experiences and information; curious, speculative, sensitive to detail and to aesthetic characteristics of ideas and things

the directory exists at first in the interaction or relationship between two people—parent and child—and only gradually becomes located fully within the developing child. Likewise, knowledge of academic skills such as reading and mathematics also begins in the interactions between adults and children and only later becomes internalized by individual children. In fact, as the internalization progresses, children tend to perform better on tests of reasoning and language, and therefore seem more "intelligent" in the psychometric sense.

Note that in emphasizing the social context of intellectual development, the sociocultural approach turns the issue of cultural bias on psychometric tests into an outcome to be expected and explored rather than a problem to be overcome or minimized. This changes the key question about intelligence from one about individuals to one about groups and communities. Instead of wondering why some individuals seem more intelligent than others, the sociocultural view points out that some social *settings* may nurture and encourage individuals who show extra measures of talent, skill, and knowledge more than individuals from other settings. In this sense, some families, classrooms, and workplaces may be more "intelligent" than others. The differences are well known by all psychologists interested in intelligence, including those who do not approach the topic from a sociocultural perspective. What is unique about the sociocultural perspective is the priority it gives to the impact of the community on individuals' cognitive development (Salomon & Perkins, 1998).

WHAT DO YOU THINK ?   Should standardized tests of ability be used in schools? If so, when and with whom, and for what purpose? Consult with several classmates about this issue. Then, if possible, compare the opinions of several professionals, such as a special education teacher and an occupational therapist. How do you think their work affects their opinions?

School Influences

Next to the family, school probably is the single most important influence during middle childhood. Each year children spend about eleven hundred hours at school and often many additional hours in school-related activities. Experiences at school give children opportunities to develop cognitive skills, language, and various talents and abilities. School also provides an arena for social development—for developing a self-image and self-esteem, cultivating peer relationships, and learning to deal with the inevitable diversity and conflicts that are part of most lives. In the next chapter we look at such social developments more fully, not only as they unfold in school but also in terms of their broader impact on the lives of children. First, though, we will look at how school affects children's learning, and therefore their cognitive development. Schools—and classrooms in particular—affect learning in three main ways: through fostering particular patterns of discourse, through the social biases of students and teachers, and through assessment (or evaluation) of students' learning. These factors also influence students' social development, but for now we will focus on how they affect learning and cognition.

discourse Extended verbal interaction.

participation structures Regular patterns of discourse or interaction in classrooms with unstated rules about how, when, and to whom to speak.

Participation Structures and Classroom Discourse

Classrooms provide particular patterns and styles of **discourse,** or language interaction, that influence how, when, and with whom children can speak (Gee & Green, 1998). Recurring patterns of classroom interaction are sometimes called **participation structures,** and probably seem familiar if you have attended school for many years. They correspond roughly to common teaching strategies, except that participation structures include the behavior not only of the teacher but of students as well. Table 12.3 lists several common participation structures.

As you may have noted from your own experience as a student, however, participation structures do not always work as intended, nor do they always have the same effect on all students. One reason is that different students bring to a classroom different expectations about discourse language and about work relationships: what seems like an invitation to work on a group project to one student may seem like an invitation to relax to another, in spite of a teacher's explicit efforts to focus students on work per se. This can be a problem if the discourse that a student experiences at home has differed significantly in style from the discourse typically used at school.

Another reason is that teachers' discourse is always heavily laced with **control talk**—patterns of speech that collectively remind students that the teacher has power over students' behavior and their verbal comments. Even during "indirect" participation structures such as discussion or group work, teachers regularly do all of the following, among other things, to remind students of the teacher's influence:

- Designate speakers (calling on one student rather than another)

- Declare when a comment is valuable or irrelevant ("That's a good idea" or "How can you relate [your comment] to what we were just talking about?")

- Changing the topic or activity (Now let's do X [instead of Y]")

Hopefully teachers' control talk empowers rather than silences students by providing fair opportunities for individual children to express ideas and ask questions (O'Connor & Michaels, 1996). There is a constant danger, however, that control talk will empower only certain students at the expense of others. The inequity can occur when certain students get called on more than others, or the ideas of certain students tend to be declared irrelevant or inappropriate more often than the ideas of others. As we note in the next section, such inequities sometimes do occur in practice as a result of social biases on the part of both teachers and classmates. But they are not inevitable.

Social Biases That Affect Learning

Observations of classroom teaching show that both teachers and classmates sometimes respond differently to a student on the basis of gender, race, or ethnic background in ways that parallel gender, racial, and ethnic biases in society at large. On average, for example, teachers are more likely to speak to boys from a physical distance, such as from across the room, and to speak to girls at close range, such as at

control talk A style or register of speech used by teachers to indicate their power over activities, discussion, and the behavior of students.

Structure	Teacher's Behavior	Students' Behavior	Assumptions
Lecture	Talk; tell ideas; answer questions	Listen; take notes; ask questions	Students think about what teacher says; do not daydream
Discussion	Set topic or broad question	Say something relevant; take others' comments into account	Know something about the topic before beginning class
Group work	Set general task; select group members	Work out details of solution to task	Do a fair share of the work; cooperate; compromise as needed

TABLE 12.3   Common Participation Structures in Classrooms

Educational research has found important benefits when students have cooperative rather than competitive goals. Individuals learn from each other, both slower and faster students feel more motivated, and students become more tolerant of each other's differences.

arm's length (Delamont, 1996; Wilkinson & Marrett, 1985). During discussions and question-and-answer sessions, furthermore, teachers tend to call on boys 10 to 30 percent more often than on girls, depending on the subject and grade level (Measor & Sykes, 1992). Both behaviors create an impression in the minds of students that boys are somehow more important—more worthy of public notice—than girls are.

Fellow students too show biases like these. During group work, for example, teammates sometimes reproduce society's gender and racial biases: speaking and listening to boys more than girls, for example, and to white children more than to children of color (Cohen, 1994). A related pattern sometimes occurs during "free" times: as we saw in Chapter 7's discussion of gender development, children tend to reinforce one another for gender-appropriate behavior, including being assertive if (and only if) you are a boy and cooperative (or nonassertive) if and only if you are a girl (Maccoby, 1995). But the biases are not inevitable. Some teachers and classmates do not express them at all, and educational interventions have been successful in training teachers, and even classmates, to include all students equitably, regardless of gender, race, or ethnic background (Cohen & Latan, 1997; Leaper, 1994).

The Impact of Assessment

For most children, school becomes a primary setting for **assessment,** which refers to teachers' diagnosis and evaluation of students' strengths, weaknesses, and progress at learning. Assessment has a profound impact on students' perceptions of themselves and of one another (Wigfield et al., 1998)—either positive, negative, or both at once. The nature of the influence depends on the structure of goals experienced by the child. Most schools and teachers use some combination of individualized, competitive, and cooperative goals, and educational research has found that each has distinct effects both on students' learning and on their social relationships.

Individualized Goals   These occur when each student is judged on his or her own performance, regardless of the performance of others. In principle, therefore,

• • •
assessment The diagnosis of an individual's strengths, needs, and qualities.

every student could achieve top evaluations, failing evaluations, or any mixture in between. Sometimes this kind of assessment is called "grading on an absolute standard," since the performance of each individual is compared to a standard rather than to other students. It is common in the teaching of relatively structured subjects, such as elementary arithmetic, where standards can be defined clearly. Research on individualized goal structures generally has found that this arrangement heightens students' attention to mastering content and skills, and makes them relatively indifferent to judging their overall abilities or those of other students (Johnson & Johnson, 1994). Unfortunately, individualized goals also make students less interested in what they can teach one another and less appreciative of (because less focused on) one another's diverse knowledge and skills. Individualized goals also do not lend themselves equally well to all content or topics; performing in a school play or on a sports team, for example, depends as much on good coordination among individuals as it does on skills possessed by individuals themselves.

Competitive Goals   These occur when students are assessed in comparison to one another, and some individuals therefore are judged better than others; there are "winners" and "losers." Competitive goals are common in school sports competitions (only one person or team can take first place), but also in many nonathletic tournaments and contests of all kinds (e.g., a schoolwide spelling bee). They are also implied, though not stated, when teachers post marks or scores in rank order for students' inspection. Competitive goals make students concerned with how they expect to perform relative to others, regardless of how well they perform in any absolute sense. Competitive goals also tend to make students think of their own abilities as fixed entities ("You either have it or you don't") rather than as the result of effort and hard work on their own part. For both of these reasons, competitive goals can interfere with sustained motivation to learn, and therefore eventually reduce engagement with activities that develop thinking skills like the ones described earlier in this chapter. They can also reduce the self-esteem of "losers" as well as diminish the status of losers among peers. For example, every year about 35 percent of children drop out of competitive athletics, and the most common reason is a feeling of discouragement about losing (Gould & Eklund, 1996; Petlichkoff, 1996).

Cooperative Goals   These occur when individuals share in rewards or punishments, and when a group's overall performance is the key to success. Cooperative goals are commonly used, for example, for major group projects or presentations in elementary school (e.g., a term project about "castles and dragons"). They focus attention on helping other group members and on attending to and accepting diversity among fellow students, and away from judging differences along some single scale of performance. They also promote a belief that learning or knowledge is intrinsically a shared or group phenomenon rather than something that exists only inside the heads of individuals (Salomon & Perkins, 1998).

Cooperative goals became increasingly common in elementary schools during the 1980s and 1990s, partly because research strongly suggests that they benefit students' learning, motivation, and social relationships more than either individualistic or competitive goals do, particularly in classrooms that are multicultural or otherwise diverse (Slavin, 1996). But cooperative learning does have problems. If cooperative groups of students are not supervised closely enough, they can reproduce the gender and racial biases of the larger society, as described earlier in this section. This problem can be alleviated if the teacher chooses tasks that truly do call for a diversity of talents for completion (e.g., a project that needs an artist, a good writer, and a good oral presenter) and highlights this fact to students. Some individuals in a cooperative work group may also "overspecialize," meaning they focus only on their own task and ignore helping and learning from others. Other individuals may "freeload," or take advantage of others' hard work without contributing their own fair share of effort. Both of these problems can be alleviated by combining individualized and cooperative assessments; some part of students' final grade depends on their own efforts and another part on the group's combined performance.

WHAT DO YOU THINK ?   What participation structures worked best for you in elementary school? Is there a single answer to this question, or did your answer depend on the topic, the teacher, and/or your classmates? If you were a teacher, which participation structure(s) would you try to emphasize, and why?

Cognition and Social Development

Among all the ideas discussed in this chapter, one especially stands out: cognition rarely develops in isolation from social and emotional experiences. To use memory strategies successfully, for example, children must want to use them, must believe that others value their use, and must enjoy the effort involved in solving memory-related problems. These requirements encompass social and emotional issues, and they influence cognition significantly. Partly for this reason, the next chapter looks more closely at social and emotional influences on development during middle childhood. To do so effectively, the chapter temporarily places cognitive development in the background. We return to issues in cognition when we discuss adolescence later in the book.

Summary of Major Ideas

Piaget's Theory: Concrete Operational Skills

1. School-age children develop concrete operational thinking, or reasoning focused on real, tangible objects.

2. A very important new skill is conservation—the belief that certain properties, such as size or length, remain constant in spite of perceptual changes.

3. Efforts to train children in conservation have had moderate success, although when applied in a variety of circumstances, training does not persist as strongly as naturally developed conservation.

4. Concrete operational children also acquire new skills in seriation, temporal relations, and spatial relations.

5. Piaget's ideas about cognitive development have influenced educators' styles of teaching and the content of early childhood curricula.

Information-Processing Skills

6. Both short-term and long-term memory improve with age, partly as a result of other cognitive developments such as growing skills in using learning strategies.

7. Improvements in logical reasoning sometimes assist the development of long-term memory, as does increasing richness or familiarity of knowledge as schoolchildren grow older.

8. Learning disabilities can be understood in part as the result of problems in information processing. Providing learning assistance that focuses on specific aspects of information processing sometimes can benefit students.

Language Development in Middle Childhood

9. Although school-age children already are quite skillful with language, they continue to have difficulties with certain subtle features of syntax.

10. During middle childhood, children become better able to understand metaphorical uses of language.

11. Bilingual children develop certain cognitive advantages over monolingual children, at least if their bilingualism is relatively balanced; the advantages include cognitive flexibility and metalinguistic awareness.

12. Often, however, bilinguals must cope with prejudices against one of their two languages and against the culture of that language.

13. Black English is an important dialect of English spoken by some African Americans in some situations, but not by all or in all circumstances.

Defining and Measuring Intelligence

14. Intelligence is a general ability to learn from or adapt to experience.

15. Traditionally, intelligence has been studied from the perspective of psychometric testing, but newer perspectives based on information-processing theory and on sociocultural principles have challenged this perspective.

16. A view of intelligence based on information-processing theory is the triarchic theory of Robert Sternberg, which divides intelligence into components, experiences, and the context of thinking.

17. Howard Gardner's theory of multiple intelligences identifies six distinct cognitive capacities: language skill, musical skill, logical skill, spatial skill, kinesthetic skill, and interpersonal and intrapersonal skills.

18. The sociocultural view of intelligence regards thinking as being distributed among individuals who interact and communicate, and it locates cognitive development in the zone of proximal development.

School Influences

19. School provides experiences with particular patterns of language interaction called *participation structures*.

20. Teachers' language is marked by large amounts of control talk, which are comments or other linguistic markers that remind students of the power difference between students and teachers.

21. Classroom interaction is also marked by a gender bias in which both teachers and students favor comments made by boys more than those made by girls.

22. School is also a primary arena of assessment for children, as well as a place that provides experience with individualized, competitive, and cooperative goals.

Key Terms

achievement test (377)
aptitude test (377)
assessment (386)
balanced bilingual (374)
Black English (375)
blind training (368)
concrete operations (356)
control talk (385)
conservation (357)
décallage (358)
discourse (384)
information-processing theory (361)
informed training (369)
intelligence (376)
learning disability (369)
learning strategies (366)
metacognition (365)
metalinguistic awareness (374)
metaphor (373)
multiple intelligences (380)
participation structures (384)
psychometric approach to intelligence (377)
recall memory (361)
recognition memory (361)
sociocultural perspective on intelligence (382)
triarchic theory of intelligence (379)

Psychosocial Development in Middle Childhood

Focusing Questions

- What major psychological challenges do children face during middle childhood?

- What important changes occur in a child's sense of self during middle childhood?

- What is *achievement motivation*, and what forms does it take?

- How have changes in the nature of the family, such as increases in the proportion of single-parent and dual-wage-earner families, affected children's psychosocial development?

- How do peers contribute to development during middle childhood?

- How do children deal with death, loss, and grieving during the school years?

N ickie is nine years old and in second grade. Between practicing soccer, baseball, and basketball, playing with his friends, playing video games, or watching TV with his older brother Alex, doing his homework, walking the dog, and carving a model race car for his Cub Scout den with his father, he is always on the go. Until recently, if asked about his popularity or how he was doing at school or sports, Nickie would answer with a noncommittal "OK" or "I don't know." Lately, however, he has begun to talk more about himself: who he is and how well he is (or is not) doing as a ballplayer, a friend, a student, a brother, and a son.

Middle childhood, approximately ages six through twelve, is a time when the developmental changes of early childhood are rapidly consolidated and children ready themselves for adolescence and the movement to full adulthood. By the time they start school, most children have learned something about human nature and are beginning to learn the psychological and social skills needed to successfully deal with an increasingly complex world. Children's increasing involvements outside the family and their growing capacity for independence and self-direction contribute to changes in their relationships with parents and other family members.

Middle childhood also brings about an increased focus on peer relationships, and school offers the primary arena for contacts with **peers**, children of about the same age and development level who share common attitudes and interests. Peers offer certain benefits, such as freedom from the watchful eyes of parents and teachers. But they also demand loyalty and conformity. "Be nice to everyone except Rachel" may be a rule in one circle of friends; "Homework is for geeks" may be a rule in another. School-age children must learn to coordinate these expectations with those of parents, who sometimes disagree with peers.

To meet all of these demands simultaneously, children must learn to regulate their behavior from within. Somehow they must find ways to control their expressions of aggression, impatience, grief, and other strong impulses and emotions. Doing so becomes easier as they develop concepts of themselves as individuals, knowledge of their own needs and values, and a sense of how these needs and values compare with those of other people. In this chapter, we will explore how the changes that occur during middle childhood build on the achievements of early childhood and provide the groundwork for the major changes that accompany adolescence, which will soon follow.

peers Individuals who are of approximately the same age and developmental level and who share common attitudes and interests.

Psychosocial Challenges of Middle Childhood

During the school years, children's psychosocial development includes five major challenges: the challenge of knowing who you are, the challenge to achieve, the challenge of family relationships, the challenge of peers, and the challenge of school. We will first summarize the nature of those challenges and then discuss the first four in greater detail in the sections that follow. We explored school influences in Chapter 12.

The Challenge of Knowing Who You Are   Throughout middle childhood, children develop a deeper understanding of the kinds of people they are and what makes them unique. They also acquire a more fully developed sense of self as a framework for organizing and understanding their experiences. These notions do not yet constitute a final, stable identity, such as that developed during adolescence and adulthood, but they do lay the groundwork for later development. During the school years, a child at least can ask, "Am I a popular sort of person?" or "Am I a good athlete?" The answers may still be rather simplistic, but they are beginning to take on meaning nonetheless.

The Challenge to Achieve   Some psychologists consider the major crisis of this age period to be the development of competence, self-confidence, and willingness to achieve to the best of one's ability. Of course, children care about their competence even in infancy. But during middle childhood, this motive is complicated by children's growing awareness of others' opinions about their efforts.

The older of two siblings showed this awareness one afternoon when talking with his sister about their paintings. Michael, age seven, said, "That's a nice painting, Elizabeth, but not as nice as usual." Elizabeth, age three, seemed unaware of his insult; she simply smiled and continued to discuss her picture. Then she tried to be friendly by reciprocating: "That's a nice picture too, Michael, but not as nice as yesterday's." Michael looked pained and insisted, "It is *so* a good one!"

Both Elizabeth and Michael revealed some understanding of achievement in this interchange. They seemed to know that paintings vary in quality and that painters need encouragement for their work. But Michael seemed more concerned about meeting certain standards of achievement. He worried about Elizabeth's implication that he might have fallen below these standards, and he also worried about whether Elizabeth had noticed this fact.

The Challenge of Family Relationships   We discuss several important aspects of family life in this chapter, including recent changes in family roles and family membership due to changing employment patterns and divorce rates. These changes in the traditional family structure have raised the questions of who is responsible for doing what within a family and what constitutes a family in the first place. Furthermore, all too often school-age children must share the challenge of holding the family together. While family relationships have far from disappeared from the lives of schoolchildren, peers become increasingly important.

The Challenge of Peers   The fourth major challenge of middle childhood is relationships with other children, or peers. As we point out later in this chapter, peers serve even more important purposes for schoolchildren than they do for preschoolers, and most school-age children choose to spend a great deal of their time in peer-related activities.

The Challenge of School   During middle childhood, school plays a major role in children's social and emotional development. Observing and interacting with a large number of diverse children and adults other than their parents give children an opportunity to develop a fuller sense of identity through their experiences with teachers and peers. As we saw in Chapter 12, participation structures, gender and social biases, and assessment goals can influence cognitive development as well as the child's sense of self.

The Sense of Self

Throughout infancy, childhood, and adolescence, children actively construct a **sense of self,** a structured way of thinking about themselves that helps them to organize and understand who they are based on the views of others, on their own experiences, and on cultural categories such as gender and race. This structure rapidly evolves during middle childhood and becomes increasingly organized and complex. In fact, although a sense of self often is called a *self-concept,* it functions more as a theory that organizes a pattern of related ideas than as a single concept. A child actively constructs and continually revises his or her sense of self based on increasing age and experience (Damon & Hart, 1992).

For example, at age six, Mina loved playing with dolls and also loved holding and caring for babies. She noticed that her parents and others commented on this preference, so nurturance became part of Mina's idea of herself: "I'm someone who likes babies," she sometimes thought. But later experiences modified this idea. Toward the end of elementary school, Mina discovered that she often preferred playing softball to playing house. Somehow, at age ten or eleven, she had to incorporate this reality into her sense of self: "I'm a good ballplayer," she realized. By the start of adolescence, she still was not sure how to reconcile these two concepts of herself: her interest in child care and her interest in sports. Someday she may succeed in doing so, but not at age twelve.

To a large extent, a child's notion of self grows out of social experiences with other selves or, put more plainly, out of contacts with other children and adults. Learning what it means to be female, for example, occurs as girls meet other individuals who also are female. Learning what it means to be happy occurs as children see other people express happiness. As personal and individual as a sense of self is, then, it reflects generalizations about others, and it cannot develop without considerable social contact.

The Development of Self in Childhood

How do children acquire a sense of self? The first step involves basic social labels or categories. By the end of their second year, most children can correctly label their gender ("I'm a boy" or "I'm a girl"), their age ("I'm two"), and their species ("I'm a person"). Labels such as these pave the way for later, more complete knowledge of self.

At first, however, most such labels lack permanence. At age two or three, a boy may claim he can become a girl under certain circumstances—"when I grow up" or "if I grow my hair long." Or a very young child may say she can become a different individual "if I change my name." **Self-constancy,** the belief that identity remains permanently fixed, does not become firm until the early school years, sometime after age six. At this time, the child becomes convinced that she will stay the same person indefinitely into the future, will remain human in all circumstances, and will keep her gender forever. Beliefs such as these are what a sense of self means.

• • •
sense of self A structured way children have of thinking about themselves that helps to organize and understand who they are based on the views of others, their own experiences, and cultural categories such as gender and race.

self-constancy The belief that one's identity remains permanently fixed; established sometime after age six.

During middle childhood, children develope preliminary notions of their personal qualities and phychological identity. What do you suppose this girl's sense of herself might be?

The First Beliefs in Psychological Traits   Younger children, up to age five or six, tend to define themselves in terms of observable features and behaviors such as hairstyles or how fast they can run (Rosenberg, 1979). Around age eight, some children form a more stable sense of self by including psychological traits in their self-descriptions. At first, the traits are feelings and qualities that have no apparent reference to other human beings; "I am brave," says the child, or "I am cheerful." By implication, these traits describe him as an entire personality and in all possible situations, with little recognition of people's usual variations in moods. At first, too, the child describes the traits in bold, global terms that ignore the possibility that opposing feelings or qualities sometimes exist within the same person. The child may vacillate in describing his own qualities without realizing it. Sometimes he will say, "I am dumb," meaning *completely* dumb, and other times he will say, "I am smart," meaning *completely* smart (Harter, 1977). Neither statement suggests the child recognizes that both descriptions contain an element of truth.

By the end of middle childhood, fuller integration of contradictory traits occurs. Around age ten or twelve, children begin to recognize that they can feel more than one way about any particular situation or person; they can both like and hate their teachers or enjoy and dislike school more or less at the same time (Selman, 1980). With this recognition comes the ability to use trait labels in less global ways and to express qualities in particular situations. When an older child says, "I am smart," she no longer means "I am always smart in every possible way and in every activity." Now she more likely means "I am smart in a number of significant situations, but not in all." During the school years, children become increasingly able to interrelate the different categories of traits and develop more patterned and integrated self-descriptions (Damon & Hart, 1988; Fischer et al., 1990).

These changes contribute to the development of a more flexible sense of self, in which the same individual can be characterized in a variety of ways depending on the circumstances. The situation-bound qualities that school-age children express usually describe them more accurately than the global traits and observable features that younger children rely on. But a school-age child's consciousness of inner traits still lacks the subtlety and flexibility found in adolescents and adults, who recognize that the stability of self involves multiple dimensions and ongoing change.

However, significant cultural differences exist in how the concept of self is constructed, and the idea of self probably is not a discrete psychological entity in all cultures (Hoare, 1994). In Asian countries such as India, Japan, and Nepal, for example, three distinct senses of self appear to exist simultaneously even in adulthood: a familial self, in which one's sense of self is defined almost exclusively in relationship to one's family; a spiritual self, which is defined and organized in terms of religious beliefs; and an individualized self, which is closer to the European-American sense of self just described (Roland, 1988).

Processes in Constructing a Self

To a large degree, the process of developing an identity and a sense of self during middle childhood reflects a growing awareness of relationships with other people (Damon & Hart, 1988). Children construct their identities by distinguishing their thoughts and feelings from those expressed by others. When children of various ages are asked how they would feel if their parents expressed certain emotions, such as sadness, anger, or happiness, preschoolers are likely to say they would feel the same emotions: they would be angry if their parents were angry, sad if they were sad, and so on. Older children, however, are more likely to name complementary rather than identical emotions; if their parents felt angry, for example, they would feel fearful (Harter & Barnes, 1983).

Additional evidence comes from studies of how children gradually acquire a fuller understanding of shame and pride. By age six or seven, children begin explicitly mentioning an external audience in defining these two terms (Seidner et al., 1988). For example, one seven-year-old's definition was "My teacher was proud when I earned 100 percent on the test"; another's was "My mother was ashamed when I lost my temper at the neighbor." Such attention to others implies awareness that others sometimes observe the child's self. More important, it suggests that school-age children distinguish between their own emotions and those of others—something they must do to develop a mature sense of self.

A child's emerging sense of self during middle childhood is part of a broader process of personality development. In the following section, we briefly discuss how two major developmental theorists, Sigmund Freud and Erik Erikson, view this process.

WHAT DO YOU THINK ?   What do you remember about changes in your sense of self during your school years? What conflicting traits do you recall, and how did you integrate them?

The Age of Industry and Achievement

When viewed as part of the overall life span, the years from six to twelve seem especially important to the achievement of competence. Children spend countless hours in school acquiring skills in reading, writing, and mathematics. Many of these hours also contribute to learning of the unofficial curriculum of school: how to get along with teachers and with other children. Outside of school, children often devote themselves to the long, slow mastery of particular skills. One child may spend years learning to play baseball; another may devote the same amount of time to learning how to care for a zoo of pet hamsters, dogs, and birds.

Latency and the Crisis of Industry Versus Inferiority

Psychodynamic theories such as those proposed by Freud and Erikson explain such behavior in terms of the emotional relationships that precede it in early childhood. Preschool children feel envy, awe, and competitiveness with respect to their parents. At first, these feelings have a magical quality: children simply want to be like their parents. Inevitably they are disappointed to learn that merely wanting such things does not make them come true.

In this regard, Freud emphasized the emotional hardship of preschoolers' disappointment and their consequent repression of their magical wishes toward their parents (Freud, 1983). A five-year-old, he argued, cannot continue indefinitely to wish for intimacy with his opposite-sex parent and for success in competition with his same-sex parent. These feelings (which Freud termed the *Oedipus* and *Electra conflicts*) disrupt life if they persist too long. Thus, the child eventually represses the feelings, meaning he pushes them completely out of awareness. As it happens, this repression occurs at about the time most children begin school—around age six or seven—and continues until adolescence. Freud called this the **latency** period, meaning a child's earlier unresolved feelings have gone underground and are waiting to resurface in the future (at the beginning of adolescence). During this period, the schoolchild focuses on building competencies and skills as a defense—an unconscious, self-protective behavior—against his earlier romantic feelings toward his parent. Developing talents, whether in sports, art, academics, or whatever, also helps to keep the child's mind off his earlier disappointment, which lingers on unconsciously.

Erikson agreed with Freud's account up to this point, but he went beyond it to stress not only the defensive, negative functions of skill building but its positive functions as well. (Erikson, 1963, 1968). According to Erikson, children respond to

• • •
latency In Freud's theory, the period between about six and twelve years of age when sexual activity is suspended and energies shift to physical, intellectual, and social activities.

School-age children often devote themselves to the long, slow mastery of complicated skills, such as learning to play the
violin.

their romantic feelings toward their parents not only by repress-
ing them but also by trying consciously to become more like their
parents and more like adults in general. Becoming competent
helps children reach this goal in two ways. First, it helps them
through *identification,* a process by which they experience themselves as being like their parents and thus capable of becoming
genuine adults; second, it helps them to gain similar recognition
from others.

Erikson called this process the crisis of **industry versus inferiority,** meaning children of this age concern themselves with
their capacity for *industry,* or the ability to do good work. Children who convince themselves and others of this capacity develop
relatively confident, positive concepts of themselves. Those who
do not tend to suffer from feelings of poor self-esteem and *inferiority,* a sense of inadequacy or general lack of competence. According to Erikson, most children end up with a mixture of
self-confidence and feelings of inferiority, but self-confidence
predominates in most cases (we hope) (see Chapter 2).

In addition, the crisis of industry versus inferiority gives healthy
school-age children a more or less permanent motivation to achieve
particular, definable standards of excellence. A child's continuing
sense that she can achieve and that her industry will pay off is
shaped by her earlier successes and failures in school. No longer is
she happy just to draw pictures, for example; now she must draw
well. With persistence and support, children often do reach higher
standards of excellence in many activities than they did as preschoolers, and most of
the time they are happy about doing so.

Partly because of the connection between industry and increasing competence,
psychologists have devoted a lot of attention to the development of achievement
motivation in middle childhood. The next section describes some of this work.

Achievement Motivation

Achievement motivation is the tendency to show initiative and persistence in attaining certain goals and increasing competence by successfully meeting standards
of excellence. What matters most is the approach to a task rather than the importance of the task itself. An individual can reveal achievement motivation as either a
student or a college professor, for example, and as either an amateur chess player or
a world-class chess grand master. As long as the individual strives toward a standard
of excellence that is reasonable for him, he possesses achievement motivation. Usually, too, his motivation leads to increased competence compared to his previous
level.

Differences in Achievement Motivation   There appear to be two distinct kinds
of achievement motivation: one that focuses on competence as such and one that
emphasizes the judgments people make about competence (Dweck & Leggett,
1988; Ginsburg & Bronstein, 1993). The first type of motivation, called **learning
orientation,** relies on *intrinsic motivation,* that is, motivation that comes from
within the learner and relates directly to the task and its accomplishment. A learning orientation leads children to concentrate on learning as an end in itself; they will
practice jumping rope just to see whether they can do it. The second type of motivation, called **performance orientation,** involves *extrinsic motivation,* meaning
motivation comes not from the learner but from other individuals who see and evaluate her. In this instance, the person the child is trying to please or satisfy is not her-

industry versus inferiority Erikson's fourth crisis, during which
children concern themselves with
their capacity to do good work and
thereby develop confident, positive
self-concepts or else face feelings of
inferiority.

achievement motivation Behavior
that enhances competence or enhances judgments of competence.

performance orientation Achievement motivation stimulated by other
individuals who may see and evaluate the learner rather than by the intrinsic nature of the task itself.

self but others (Dweck & Leggett, 1988; Erdley et al., 1997; Ginsburg & Bronstein, 1993).

The differences between the two orientations can be seen in children who are learning to swim. To the extent that they adopt a learning orientation, they enjoy the actual activity: practicing new strokes, working up to higher speeds, and so on. They also feel relatively free to invite criticisms from coaches or other swimmers because these comments often can help them improve.

But for children who adopt a performance orientation, swimming is less enjoyable in itself and more a means of winning approval from others. Such children are more concerned about receiving compliments from coaches and swimming friends or performing well in competitive swim meets. If others criticize aspects of their swimming, the comments are not welcome. Ironically, too much concern with pleasing others may indirectly limit these children's ability to learn.

Motivational orientations play an important role in children's development. For example, higher levels of intrinsic motivation have been found to be related to an internal sense of control, feelings of enjoyment, and various mastery-related characteristics such as curiosity, creativity, exploration, and persistence in completing tasks and a preference for taking on challenges. They are also associated with higher academic performance and learning, feelings of academic competence, and perceptions of what contributes to academic success or failure (Cain & Dweck, 1995; Ginsburg & Bronstein, 1993; Masten & Coatsworth, 1995).

Achievement Motivation in Middle Childhood   During the school years, children become more performance oriented than they were at earlier ages. At the beginning of this period, children express considerable optimism about their abilities. Kindergartners tend to rank themselves at the top of their class in scholastic ability, even though they rank other children relatively accurately (Stipek & Hoffman, 1980). This implies a learning orientation; for young children, achievement is something they do without either the involvement or the evaluations of others (Frieze et al., 1981).

During the next several years, however, children begin to believe that having an ability depends partly on whether other people give them credit for having it. This belief lies at the core of the performance orientation. It does not replace a learning orientation; rather, it takes a place alongside it. Now being "smart" means partly that a child's teachers, parents, and friends *say* she is smart and partly that she possesses certain skills in reading, mathematics, and the like regardless of what others say.

Successful achievement becomes more complicated in middle childhood. Consider swimming. Late in infancy and during the preschool years, a child may be motivated to learn to swim simply by being given chances to experiment in the water. In middle childhood, however, he may ask himself what other people, especially parents and friends, will think about his learning to swim. Will they consider this skill a true achievement? Most people will value swimming to some extent, of course. But even very respectable progress in swimming may not look like much of an achievement if the child's family and friends hold very high athletic standards or place little value on athletics in the first place.

Environmental factors can also influence motivational orientation. Environments that provide optimal challenge, provide feedback that promotes competence, and support children's autonomous and independent behaviors are likely to facilitate the development of intrinsic motivation, whereas environments that strongly emphasize extrinsic rewards, deadlines, and adult control tend to undermine intrinsic motivation and foster an extrinsic motivational orientation (Deci & Ryan, 1987; Masten & Coatsworth, 1998; Reynolds & Temple, 1998).

Differences in cultural backgrounds also can influence children's achievement orientations. For example, Chinese and Japanese mothers believe more strongly

A Multicultural View

Parental Expectations and Academic Achievement

Differences in academic achievement among African American, white, and Hispanic children appear early during the elementary school years and continue throughout elementary, junior, and senior high school. One study found that at second grade, about 5% of white children and more than 15% of African American and Hispanic children were performing below grade level in mathematics, and by sixth grade 20% of white children, more than 40% of Hispanic children, and 50% of African American children were performing below grade level (Norman, 1988).

One popular explanation is that lower achievement of minority children is due to low levels of achievement motivation resulting from poverty, family disruption, inadequate academic support, and low parental expectations for children's academic success. This view has been challenged by a large-scale study of African American, Hispanic, and white urban elementary school children and their mothers (Stevenson et al., 1990). In that study, Harold Stevenson and his colleagues examined the role parents played in their children's education and parents' and children's beliefs about children's current school performance and their educational future. Mothers and teachers were also asked how the children's performances might be improved.

What did the researchers find? First, when only families from similar economic and educational backgrounds were compared, the achievement levels of the African American and Hispanic children were *not* substantially lower than those of the white children. Second, beliefs about the children's educational achievement held by both the Hispanic and African American children and their mothers were very similar to those typically associated with higher rather than lower levels of achievement.

When the entire sample was looked at, the following findings emerged. All mothers agreed that parents should work closely with their children on schoolwork. African American mothers expressed the greatest interest in helping their children, followed by Hispanic and then white mothers. Hispanic mothers were less confident about their knowledge of English and of the American school system, but were still eager to help their children with schoolwork, stressed the importance of school, and had high regard for their children's intellectual abilities and academic achievement. They also shared with the African American mothers (and their children's teachers) a strong belief in the importance of homework and competency examinations, and the potential value of a longer school day. They held high expectations for their children's futures, though not as high as those of the African American and white mothers.

Most of the African American mothers were familiar with what teachers expected of their children. They reported spending more time teaching their children academic skills than the other parents and evaluated their children's skills, abilities, and academic achievement in

than American mothers do that academic success depends on one's own efforts rather than on factors beyond one's control, such as inborn ability or external conditions. This intrinsically motivated, achievement-oriented view is likely shared by their children and may help account for the higher academic achievement of Asian students over American students (Stevenson & Lee, 1990). The accompanying Multicultural View box discusses ethnic differences in parental expectations for academic achievement.

Family factors are also important. Golda Ginsburg and Phyllis Bronstein examined how parental monitoring of homework, parental reactions to grades, and general family style influenced achievement motivation orientation among fifth-grade children (Ginsburg & Bronstein, 1993). When parents heavily supervised their children's homework (by helping, checking, reminding, or insisting), reacted to grades with punishment, criticism, uninvolvement, or extrinsic rewards, and displayed overcontrolling (authoritarian) or undercontrolling (permissive) styles of parenting, children were more likely to have extrinsic (performance) motivational orientations and lower academic performance. On the other hand, children whose parents responded to grades with encouragement and were supportive of their children's autonomy (authoritative parenting style) were more likely to have intrinsic motivational orientation and higher academic performance. The contributions of socioeconomic level and social class to these differences will be discussed shortly.

Active encouragement and support from parents plays an important role in fostering academic achievement during middle childhood.

students' evaluations of their school performances were unrelated to their actual levels of achievement in reading and math, which suggests they had not received or internalized realistic feedback about their academic performances from either their parents, their teachers, or both (Alexander & Entwisle, 1988; Bock & Moore, 1986).

These findings challenge the view that the low performances of African American and Hispanic elementary school children are due to low levels of achievement motivation, parental expectations, or parental support. What, then, accounts for the decreasing academic achievement of minority elementary school children and increasing rates of academic failure and dropping out in junior and senior high school? One possibility is that teachers and staff may have lower academic expectations for minorities, who are overrepresented in the low academic tracks compared with other student groups, leaving these students with both inadequate preparation and unrealistic expectations about the academic demands of junior and senior high school (Reed, 1988). As these children approach adolescence, the schools they attend and the families in which they live fail to adequately meet their emerging needs for intellectual challenge and academic support, for adult supervision and independence, and for relationships with teachers and parents that enable them to believe a relationship exists between their academic efforts and the rewards available to them in American society (Eccles, 1993; Stevenson et al., 1990).

reading and math very highly. Their children rated their own performances very highly as well and believed they were working hard. Surprisingly, though, African American

As children grow older, they shift toward a performance orientation and become more similar to adults in their achievement motivation. This in part reflects the increasing importance of peers and children's changing perceptions of social comparisons (Pomerantz et al., 1995). At this stage, children take others' opinions more and more seriously, and often seek out those opinions on a variety of matters. As we will see in the section that follows, the opinions of family members are quite important in this regard.

WHAT DO YOU THINK ?   Survey several classmates about their current learning orientations and the extent to which those orientations grew out of middle childhood experiences. What advantages and disadvantages do you see in each of these orientations?

Family Relationships

Despite the growing importance of peers, families continue to influence children's development strongly during middle childhood. However, parental influence differs from that of peers due both to their greater experience and psychological maturity and to the greater material resources and power they possess. In this section,

This father's willingness to help his son pursue his interests—in this case, build a robot—illustrates an important aspect of effective parent-child relationships during middle childhood.

we discuss how the particular circumstances and characteristics of families affect family relationships and psychosocial development during middle childhood.

The Quality of Parent-Child Relationships in Middle Childhood

During middle childhood, as children gradually learn more about their parents' attitudes and motivations and the reasons for family rules, they become better able to control their behavior. This change has a major impact on the quality of relations between school-age children and their parents (Galinsky, 1987). Parents find themselves monitoring the moment-to-moment behavior of their children less closely than in earlier years. They need not always watch carefully as their child pours a glass of milk, and they do not always have to remind him to use the toilet before getting in the car.

Nevertheless, parents do continue to monitor children's efforts to take care of themselves, but in more indirect ways. Instead of simply arranging for a child's friend to visit, parents increasingly use comments such as "If you want to have Lin sleep over next week, you'd better call by tomorrow." Instead of helping their child put on each item of clothing in the morning, they will more likely confine themselves to some simple reminder ("It's time to get dressed") on the assumption that the child can take care of the details of dressing.

These changes contribute to one stereotype of parenting during middle childhood: the notion that parenting consists only of fixing meals, providing taxi service, and enforcing a few rules. In reality, this stereotype does not take into account the activities parents and children often still do together, from shopping to watching television to holiday celebrations. It also fails to consider the emotional ties underlying these activities. If children have become securely attached during the preschool years, they and their parents often enjoy each other's company more than ever during middle childhood.

By this period, parents and children have accumulated a history of experiences together that makes family relations increasingly unique and meaningful. One study documented this idea by analyzing letters school-age children wrote to a local newspaper about "What Makes Mom Great" (Weisz, 1980). Many of the children said they valued their mothers' enduring presence in their lives: "She is always there to listen," said one child. They also valued the empathy or sensitivity their mothers provided: "She always seems to know how I feel." These comments imply that the bonds between parents and children typically are very strong during middle childhood.

The Changing Nature of Modern Families

The stereotypical family—a father who works, a mother who cares for the family full time—shows little similarity to families of today. In 1955, 60 percent of families in North America fit this popular stereotype. By the early 1990s, only 7 percent of North American families conformed to this model (Children's Defense Fund, 1995).

Today an increasing number of mothers work outside the home. Currently two out of three married women with children under eighteen are employed, more than double the rate in 1960 (Statistical Abstracts of the United States, 1995a). When both single and married women with children under eighteen are considered, more than half are employed outside the home, a trend that is expected to increase through the early 21st century (U.S. Bureau of the Census, 1995c; U.S. Bureau of Labor Statistics, 1995). Figure 13.1 summarizes this trend.

Divorce also has become much more common as Figure 13.2 shows. Between 1960 and 1993, the U.S. divorce rate tripled, with half of all marriages in the United States ending in divorce. Approximately 25 percent of children younger than eighteen live in single-parent households, 88 percent with their mothers and 12 percent with their fathers. It is estimated that children of divorce spend an average of six of their first eighteen years in a single-parent home (Children's Defense Fund, 1993; U.S. Bureau of the Census, 1995). Because approximately two-thirds of divorced parents remarry, most children of divorce will live in a *reconstituted family* consisting of parent, stepparent, siblings, and stepsiblings. And in almost half of these cases, the second marriage will end in divorce as well (Hetherington et al., 1998).

"During the next stage of my development, Dad, I'll be drawing closer to my mother—I'll get back to you in my teens."

During middle childhood, the quality of parent-child relationships may vary with changing developmental needs and family circumstances.

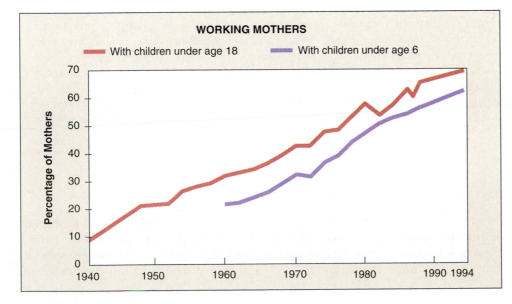

WORKING MOTHERS

— With children under age 18   — With children under age 6

(y-axis: Percentage of Mothers, 0 to 70)
(x-axis: 1940, 1950, 1960, 1970, 1980, 1990 1994)

● ● ● ● ● ● ● ● ● ● ● ● ●

FIGURE 13.1

Percentage of Working Mothers, 1940–1994

The long-term trend for working mothers with children is expected to increase through the year 2000.
Source: U.S. Bureau of the Census (1995)

PERSPECTIVES

The Quality of Parenting and Family Life During Middle Childhood

• • • • • As in the early childhood years that precede and the adolescent years that follow, the quality of the parent-child relationship and overall family life play an important developmental role in middle childhood. A seven-year longitudinal study conducted by Gregory Pettit, John Bates, and Kenneth Dodge (1997) found that supportive, authoritative-style parenting involving high levels of mother-to-child warmth, active teaching of social skills, positive interest and involvement in their children's peer relationships, and use of discipline based on reasoning rather than power assertion observed when children were five years old predicted higher levels of adjustment at age 12.

High levels of supportive parenting also helped reduce the negative developmental effects of low SES, family stress, and single parenthood. In a study of school-age African American children living in both two-parent and single-parent families, Gene Brody and her colleagues found that children's academic and psychosocial competence was positively related to harmonious family interactions, emotional caregiving and support, low levels of overt conflict between parents (in two-parent households), family involvement with children's school activities, parental optimism and religious involvement, and adequacy of family financial resources predicted (Brody & Flor, 1997, 1998; Brody et al., 1994). For single-parent, mother-headed households, *no-nonsense* parenting, which included high levels of physical and emotional control and displays of warmth and affection, helped to protect children from dangerous neighborhood surroundings and involvement in antisocial activity and promoted the development of self-regulation. This type of parenting falls between the authoritative and authoritarian parent styles, employing a higher level of control than authoritative parenting style and greater warmth and nurturance than authoritarian parenting style (Brody & Flor, 1998).

The goals that parents hope to achieve also play an important role in determining how they interact with their children, especially when faced with parent-child disagreements. Paul Hastings and Joan Grusec (1998) studied a sample of 78 fathers and 110 mothers to explore how their parenting goals influenced interactions during disagreements with their young children. Parenting goals reflected three main areas of parental concern: *relationship-centered* goals, focused on maintaining and improving the parent-child relationship; *child-centered* goals, focused on concern with understanding the child's viewpoint and promoting the child's happiness and well being; and *parent-centered* goals focused on controlling or changing the child to meet the parent's wishes or agenda. The interventions parents reported using also depended on whether their focus was on the short-term or long-term consequences. Table 13.1 shows descriptions and examples of these three parenting goals, both short-term and long-term.

Hastings and Grusec found that women were more likely than men to focus on relationship-centered goals. Short-term, parent-centered goals were more likely when parent-child disagreements occurred in public situations (e.g., while grocery shopping, visiting friends, playing in the park). Long-term, child- and relationship-centered goals were associated with higher levels of parental empathy. Parent-centered goals were associated with power assertion, child-centered goals with reasoning, and relationship-centered goals with warm, negotiating, and cooperative parenting behavior. Parents who focused on solving parent-child disagreements that fulfilled their own needs (parent-centered goals) were most likely to be punitive and controlling and least likely to resolve conflicts by talking with their children, working out a compromise, or being warm and accepting. When parents' concerns were centered on children's needs, however, open communication and providing explanations were the strategies most preferred, and coercion, punishment, and negative criticism were avoided. Strong power assertion was even less likely when parents were highly

Divorce and Its Effects on Children

Most parents who divorce must make major adjustments in their lives, and these adjustments often affect their children deeply. First, many divorcing parents face sudden economic pressures. Some find themselves financially responsible for two households, that of their former spouse and children and that of the new spouse and children.

invested in promoting the quality of family relationship. Instead, negotiation, compromise, shared control, and affection were the strategies of choice.

Parenting goals were related not only to what the child had done but to the parents' judgments about their child's motivations and to parents' feelings about the situation. Parents who were focused on parent-centered, long-term goals were more likely to believe that their children's misbehaviors were deliberate, to experience annoyance, upset, and concern, and to have decreased sympathy for their child's wishes compared to parents who focused on child-centered, short-term goals. Although changes occur in parental goals and in the context of parent-child disagreements as children move through adolescence and adulthood, parenting goals continue to play an important role in how parents and their children interact with and experience each other.

What Do You Think?

1. What is your view of the "no-nonsense" parenting described above? How successfully do you think it joins the advantages of authoritative and authoritarian parenting styles?

2. Thinking back to conflicts with your parents in your own middle childhood, what long-term and short-term goals best describe the parenting you experienced?

TABLE 13.1   Immediacy and Focus of Parental Concerns and Parenting Goals

Focus of Parental Concern	Immediacy of Parental Concern	
	Short Term	**Long Term**
Focus on relationship	Wanting to reach fair and equitable resolutions to an interaction; wanting to promote everyone's happiness	Wanting to build or maintain love, trust, and close family connections.
	Example: I want us to be able to enjoy doing this together.	*Example:* I hope she realizes that I'll always be here to help her through hard times.
Focus on child	Wanting to understand the child's point of view in a given situation; wanting to promote the child's happiness.	Wanting to teach the child values, social rules or important lessons for the child's future benefit
	Example: I want to find out what's making him so upset.	*Example:* She needs to understand that she can't give up on things so easily.
Focus on parent	Wanting to control, change, or end a child's current behavior; wanting to meet the parent's wishes or agenda	Wanting to have an obedient or respectful child; wanting to ensure a given behavior isn't repeated in the future.
	Example: I need to have peace and quiet.	*Example:* I'll make sure he listens next time.

Source: Adapted from Hastings & Grusec (1998), p. 470.

Two dimensions on which parenting goals may vary are the immediacy of a parent's concern (short term versus long term) and the focus of concern (parent, child, or relationship). This table presents the six types of parenting goals that result when two dimensions are combined and examples of the goals a parent might have when dealing with a child's tantrum during the shared activity.

Many divorced mothers must take on new or additional employment to meet their household responsibilities, but even so their standard of living frequently declines. For many of these women, a reduction of economic resources often is accompanied by dependence on welfare; poorer-quality housing, neighborhoods, schools, and child care; and the need to move to a neighborhood they can afford, which often leads to loss of social support for the child from familiar friends, neighbors, and teachers. In contrast,

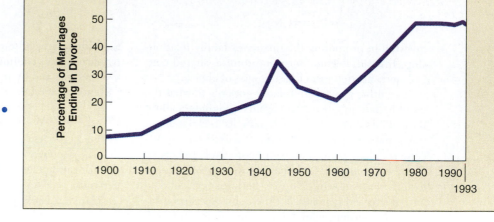

FIGURE 13.2

Percentage of U.S. Marriages Ending in Divorce, 1900–1993

Since the mid-1980s, approximately half of all marriages in the United States have ended in divorce.
Source: U.S. Bureau of the Census (1995)

both noncustodial and custodial fathers are more likely to maintain or improve their standard of living following divorce (Hetherington et al., 1998).

Divorce involves many psychological pressures as well. The parent who takes primary custody of the children must learn to manage a household alone, which is a major physical and psychological burden. Some parents may feel deeply isolated from relatives or friends to whom they used to feel close. If relatives do live nearby, divorcing parents often must rely on them for the first time, simply to procure help with child care and household work. Even before actual separation and divorce, many such families go through long periods of distress, tension, and discord. For most, these pressures continue to create stress for two or three years following separation (Coley, 1998; Hetherington et al., 1998).

Divorce is especially hard for school-age children. Having outgrown the self-centeredness of the preschool years, school-age children increasingly identify with and rely on their parents as role models to help them establish their own sense of who they are and how they should behave. At a time when children are just learning to be independent from home life, divorce threatens the safe base they have come to rely on to help make increasing independence possible. The loyalty conflicts frequently created by parents who are competing for their children's allegiance can make children fearful that they will lose one of their parents in the process.

Judith Wallerstein and Sandra Blakeslee (1996) conducted a long-term follow-up study of middle-SES children who were between six and eight years old at the time of their parents' divorce. She found that even ten years later, these children were burdened by fear of disappointment in love relationships, lowered expectations, and a sense of powerlessness. When compared to children who were older or younger at the time of the breakup, school-age children fared far worse in their emotional adjustment and overall competence, including school and social relationships. The profound unhappiness with current relationships and concerns regarding future ones that these children experienced often were masked by their overall conformity to social expectations (see Table 13.2).

Some critics have questioned the degree to which Wallerstein & Blakeslee's findings, which were based on naturalistic, case study techniques with a middle-class sample, represent the entire population of parents and children of divorce. Future research using more quantitative approaches and families from a broader range of backgrounds will help determine the validity of their findings (Hetherington et al., 1998).

TABLE 13.2	The Psychological Tasks of Children of Divorce
Task 1: Understanding the divorce	Children must first learn to accurately perceive the immediate changes that divorce brings. Later they learn to distinguish between fantasized fears of being abandoned or losing their parents and reality so that they can evaluate their parents' actions and draw useful lessons for their own lives.
Task 2: Strategic withdrawal	Children and adolescents need to get on with their own lives as quickly as possible and get back, physically and emotionally, to the normal tasks of growing up. This poses a dual challenge to children, who must actively remove themselves emotionally from parental distress and conflict to safeguard their individual identities and separate life course.
Task 3: Dealing with loss	Children must overcome two profound losses: the loss of the intact family, together with the symbolic and real protection it provided, and the loss of the presence of one parent, usually the father, from their lives. They must overcome the powerful sense of rejection, humiliation, unlovableness, and powerlessness they feel and feelings of self-blame for causing the divorce.
Task 4: Dealing with anger	The major task for children is to resolve their anger at being hurt by the very people they depend on for protection and love. They must recognize their parents as human beings capable of making mistakes and respect them for their efforts and courage.
Task 5: Working out guilt	Young children often feel responsible for divorce, thinking their misbehavior may have caused one parent to leave. They need to separate from guilty "ties that bind" them too closely to a troubled parent and go on with their own lives.
Task 6: Accepting the permanence of the divorce	At first, children's strong need to deny the divorce can help them cope with the powerful realities they face. Over time, they must accept the divorce as a permanent state of affairs.
Task 7: Taking a chance on love	Achieving realistic hope regarding relationships may be the most important task for both the child and society. Children must create and sustain a realistic vision of their own capacity to love and be loved, knowing that separation and divorce are always possible. Mastering this last task—which depends on successfully negotiating all of the others—leads to psychological freedom from the past and to a second chance.

Source: Adapted from Wallerstein & Blakeslee (1989, 1996).

Different Effects on Boys and Girls On the whole, girls and boys tend to respond differently to divorce. Boys often express their distress in *externalizing* ways, becoming more aggressive, willful, and disobedient during the period surrounding separation and divorce. They often lose access to the parent with whom they identify more strongly—their father—because the majority of divorced children live with their mothers and are more frequently victims of parental power struggles and inconsistencies in matters of discipline. In a study of children six years after divorce, Mavris Hetherington (1988, 1991) found that whereas mothers and daughters had reestablished close and positive relationships, problems between mothers and sons persisted. Whereas the most common parenting style for divorced mothers with daughters was authoritative, the most common style with sons was authoritarian and the next most common permissive, suggesting that mothers either tried to control their sons' behavior with power assertiveness or gave up trying.

Girls appear to become less aggressive as a result of divorce, tend to worry more about schoolwork, and often take on more household responsibilities. This suggests they are *internalizing,* or holding inside, their distress by trying to act more helpful and responsible than usual (Block et al., 1981). Daughters of divorced parents may also become overly preoccupied with their relationships with males. They are more likely to become involved in dating and sexual activities at an early age, sometimes before the end of elementary school, and more likely to get pregnant and have conflict-ridden relationships with males during their teen years. Girls may also encounter increased risk of sexual abuse from stepparents and parents' dating partners in the period following divorce (Wallerstein & Blakeslee, 1996).

Perhaps the most important effort parents can make to minimize the negative effects of divorce is to try to reduce their own conflicts and to cooperate in providing the best parenting possible for their children. Also important is the appropriate use of professional help to successfully work out postdivorce arrangements, resolve emotional conflicts more effectively, and develop the skills needed to sustain strong and supportive parent-child relationships. Finally, close relationships with mothers who are warm and supportive but still provide firm, consistent control and supervision

Dear Daddy,
This was supposed
to be a Mothers day
card but since
Mommy doesn't live
with us I made it
a card for you.

For children of divorce, Mother's Day and other family holidays serve as painful reminders of the changes and losses that have occurred. Children often respond to such challenges in creative ways.

(similar to the no-nonsense parenting described in the Perspectives box), particularly in the period immediately following divorce, are associated with positive adjustment for both girls and boys (Armatz et al., 1995; Simons & Johnson, 1996; Stolberg & Walsh, 1988).

Custody Arrangements   Relationships between parents and children frequently deteriorate during and immediately after a divorce. The parent with physical custody of the children (usually the mother) finds herself dealing not only with her children but also with major new responsibilities for earning a living and making peace—at least in her mind—with the reality of divorce. Parents without physical custody of the children (usually fathers) do not face these daily hassles, but they do report feeling rootless, dissatisfied, and unjustly cut off from their children. Seeing his children every other week or on school vacations may prevent a father from knowing them intimately and being part of their everyday lives, and lead him to become increasingly reliant on special events (such as going to Disney World), when contacts do occur. Noncustodial parents may also believe their financial and emotional support for their children goes unappreciated. Perhaps for these reasons, although fathers often increase the amount of time they spend with their children immediately after divorce, they soon decrease such time well below what it was before the divorce (Hetherington et al., 1998).

For noncustodial fathers and mothers alike, both the quantity and quality of parent-child relationships differ from those of parents who have custody. Noncustodial mothers are, on the average, less competent than custodial mothers in controlling and monitoring their children's behavior, although they are more effective than noncustodial fathers. Noncustodial mothers are also more interested in and better informed about their children's activities; more supportive, sensitive, and responsive to their children's needs; and better able to communicate with their children than noncustodial fathers are (Hetherington et al., 1998). The postdivorce parenting of fathers is less predictable than that of noncustodial mothers. Some fathers who were previously attached to and involved with their children find their new role too limited and painful, and drift away from their children. Others, however, rise to the occasion and become more involved with their children. The quality of the noncustodial father's relationship with his children and the circumstances in which contacts with them occur are much more important than frequency of visits. When noncustodial fathers remain actively involved in their children's activities and emotional lives, positive developmental outcomes are likely. Even limited contact with noncustodial fathers can enhance children's adjustment when it occurs under supportive, low-conflict conditions (Clarke-Stewart & Hayward, 1996; Simons & Beaman, 1996).

Sometimes parents are able to establish *joint custody,* a legal arrangement in which parental rights and responsibilities continue to be shared in a relatively equal manner. The mechanics of the arrangement vary with the child's age and the family's circumstances. The children may live with each parent during alternate weeks, parts of weeks, or even parts of the year. Or, when the children are older, one or more may live with one parent and the rest with the other parent. Joint custody tends to promote greater contact with both parents after divorce, facilitate fathers' involvement, and make mothers' parenting responsibilities less burdensome. Its success, however, depends on parents' willingness and ability to rearrange their lives and maintain the levels of mutual respect and cooperation required to make this arrangement work (Arditti, 1992).

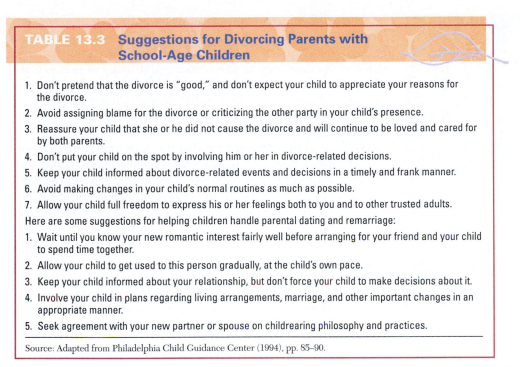

TABLE 13.3   Suggestions for Divorcing Parents with School-Age Children

1. Don't pretend that the divorce is "good," and don't expect your child to appreciate your reasons for the divorce.
2. Avoid assigning blame for the divorce or criticizing the other party in your child's presence.
3. Reassure your child that she or he did not cause the divorce and will continue to be loved and cared for by both parents.
4. Don't put your child on the spot by involving him or her in divorce-related decisions.
5. Keep your child informed about divorce-related events and decisions in a timely and frank manner.
6. Avoid making changes in your child's normal routines as much as possible.
7. Allow your child full freedom to express his or her feelings both to you and to other trusted adults.

Here are some suggestions for helping children handle parental dating and remarriage:

1. Wait until you know your new romantic interest fairly well before arranging for your friend and your child to spend time together.
2. Allow your child to get used to this person gradually, at the child's own pace.
3. Keep your child informed about your relationship, but don't force your child to make decisions about it.
4. Involve your child in plans regarding living arrangements, marriage, and other important changes in an appropriate manner.
5. Seek agreement with your new partner or spouse on childrearing philosophy and practices.

Source: Adapted from Philadelphia Child Guidance Center (1994), pp. 85–90.

Remarriage and Blended Families   Most divorced parents remarry within a few years, creating **blended families** consisting of the remarried parents and their children. The most common type of blended family results when a mother marries a man who does not have custody of his children by a previous marriage, but families with stepmothers occur as well. In both situations, the stepparent and stepchildren must somehow acknowledge the previous attachments they bring to the new family. Children must recognize and accept the fact that their new stepparent has other children, about whom he or she cares a great deal, living somewhere else. Also, the new stepparent must accept the fact that the stepchildren have another, "real" father or mother somewhere and strong attachments to that parent.

Younger children appear to eventually form an attachment with a competent stepparent and to accept the stepparent in a parenting role. Older children and young adolescents are more vulnerable and less able to adapt to the transition of remarriage due to the developmental tasks they face. In the early stages of remarriage, stepfathers often act like polite strangers, trying to win over their stepchildren by showing less negativity but also less control, monitoring, and affection than do fathers in nondivorced families. In longer-established stepfamilies, a distant, disengaged, parenting style is common for stepfathers, but conflict and negativity can remain high or increase, particularly for stepparents and stepdaughters and particularly with adolescents. Conflict between stepfathers and stepchildren is not necessarily precipitated by the children. Rates of physical abuse of stepchildren by stepfathers is seven times higher than those for fathers with their biological children (Daly & Wilson, 1996; Hetherington et al., 1998). Stepfathers who establish parent-child relationships based on warmth, friendly involvement, and mutual respect rather than on assertion of parental authority are more likely to be accepted by both boys and girls, although daughters, especially those approaching adolescence, appear to have a more intense and sustained negative psychological reaction to their mothers' remarriage and more difficulty accepting and interacting with their new stepfathers (Hetherington et al., 1998; Vuchinich et al., 1991). Stepmothers generally are more emotionally involved and take a more active role in discipline than stepfathers do, but gaining acceptance from the stepchildren is not easy for them either (Ganong & Coleman, 1987; Hetherington et al., 1989).

● ● ●
blended family A family created from a combination of stepchildren, stepparents, and stepsiblings.

In families in which mothers work, other family members often share household responsibilities. Sometimes this results in less stereotypic role models of male and female behavior.

More difficult challenges arise when both parents bring children from previous marriages to live in the same household. The children must learn to get along not only with the parents but also with one another, despite the prolonged distress of previous divorces. Parents in this type of blended family report especially high rates of stress and daily conflict, at least during the first year or two of the new marriage (Hetherington et al., 1989; Hobart, 1987; Santrock & Sitterle, 1987).

Table 13.3 presents suggestions for parenting during or following divorce. Because divorce affects development throughout life, we will return to this issue when we discuss psychosocial development in adolescence. In the next section, we look at the developmental effects of work on families during middle childhood.

The Effects of Work on Families

Work affects family life profoundly, although not always in simple or straightforward ways. Jobs determine daily schedules, of course, which in turn affect how much time parents have for their children. Job schedules also influence which parent or child does particular household chores. At a more subtle level, work affects parents' self-esteem and thus their happiness as human beings and as parents. Jobs also determine income and therefore affect many aspects of family life (Greenberger et al., 1994; Kohn et al., 1986). All of these effects are magnified by the fact that an increasing number of families are headed by two working parents or by a single parent who works.

Effects of Maternal Employment   Despite the once popular view that mothers should stay at home to care for their children, research suggests that maternal employment as such usually does children no developmental harm (Gottfried et al., 1994; Hoffman, 1989). What does matter is whether a woman chooses to work or not to work. Mothers who can make this choice and who live in relatively supportive families apparently suffer no setbacks in their relations with their children. Mothers who feel forced either to work or not to work are less fortunate; they report more stressful relations with their children.

However, maternal employment often does influence children's development in some ways. Most of these influences are positive, or at least not negative. For example, families with working mothers divide housework and child care more evenly than do families without employed mothers (Hoffman, 1983). In dual-earner families, fathers do some household chores relatively more often and spend more time alone with their children (although mothers still do the majority of housework and child care). In families with working mothers, children often are expected to help with household chores and caring for younger brothers and sisters. It is quite common for a parent to instruct her ten-year-old to pick up several things from the grocery store, set the table, and put the casserole in the oven.

The blend of housework and breadwinning seems to create less stereotyped attitudes in the children of working mothers regarding the "proper" roles of mothers and fathers. Both sons and daughters witness nurturant behavior in their fathers and occupational competence in their mothers. Especially as they approach adolescence, children are likely to support women's employment in general, and daughters usually expect to work outside the home when they get older. Studies of school-age children of employed women indicate that they are as well or better adjusted and hold less rigid views of gender roles than do children of women who do not work outside the home (Hoffman, 1984a, 1984b, 1989; Moorehouse, 1991).

Many working mothers compensate for potential negative effects of their employment through more frequent shared activities or "quality time" with their children. A high level of shared mother-child activities serves as a buffer against the long hours and other disruptive demands of full-time jobs. Also, children are likely to match or exceed their peers in school achievement and adjustment when shared mother-child activities are more frequent (Gottfried et al., 1994; Moorehouse, 1991).

Effects of Paternal Unemployment   When a father loses his job, significant economic, social, and psychological disruption for children and their families can result. Loss of income can require parents and their children to make major sacrifices in their lifestyles. In many cases, the search for a new job or for affordable housing may cause a family to uproot itself, forcing children and parents to leave behind their friends and social support network. Leaving their existing school and neighborhood peers and gaining acceptance in a new neighborhood and school is particularly difficult during middle childhood (Cooksey et al., 1997; Liem & Liem, 1988; Price, 1992).

Children who experience family economic hardship are vulnerable to a broad range of difficulties, including negative peer relations, academic performance, and psychological adjustment. However, the impact of such hardships is significantly influenced by how severe they are, how long they last, and how well parents can mobilize their material and psychological resources to deal with adversity while continuing to provide good parenting for their children (Bolger et al., 1995).

After-School Care   Dividing energies between home and work can be challenging. One common challenge working parents face is finding after-school supervision for their children. In cases where after-school programs do not exist and siblings, friends, and other relatives are not available, older (and sometimes younger) elementary-school-age children are left at home by themselves. Many parents in this situation carefully work out after-school procedures, including strict limits on what a child may do and a checkup phone call from work to ensure that everything is okay; others leave their children to their own resources.

Jill Posner and Deborah Vandell (1994) compared the effects of formal after-school programs with three other arrangements (mother care, informal adult supervision, and self-care) for a sample of low-SES third-graders from nine urban

Well-run after school-programs such as this one provide a safe, supervised environment and interesting activities for children whose parents work schedules prevent them from being at home after the school day.

schools. They found that attending after-school programs was associated with better grades and conduct in school as well as better peer relations and emotional adjustment. Children who attended such programs were exposed to more learning opportunities, spent more time in enrichment lessons (such as music and dance), and spent less time watching TV and in unstructured neighborhood activities than children in other forms of care.

Formal after-school programs may be less important for children who live in communities that provide safe and constructive after-school opportunities. Nevertheless, even for these children, close parental monitoring of their after-school plans and activities and authoritative parenting (respectful acceptance and firm control) tend to promote good academic performance and social adjustment as well as keep them out of trouble. Lower levels of such parental involvement and stressful, unsupportive family circumstances are associated with poorer academic and social adjustment and more problem behaviors (Galambos & Maggs, 1991; Steinberg, 1986; Vandell & Ramanan, 1991).

Other Sources of Social Support

Most school-age children establish sources of social support other than parents, including siblings and other adults. A study documented this fact by interviewing schoolchildren about people, places, and activities that they found satisfying and helpful in conducting their lives (Bryant, 1985). To stimulate the children's thinking, the interviewers took them on long walks around their neighborhoods. From time to time, the interviewers asked questions about what they saw ("Do you know who lives there?"; "Is this where you go to relax?"). This approach revealed a large number of social supports for school-age children, as shown in Table 13.4.

Sibling Support   Perhaps most noteworthy is the high frequency with which siblings (as well as peers) were named as sources of support. As in early childhood, during middle childhood brothers and sisters provide one another with companionship, friendship, social support, and mentoring. Older children frequently serve as role models and mentors to younger siblings, helping to transmit customs and family expectations and providing challenges that (hopefully) lead the younger children to new learning (Azmitia & Hesser, 1993; Ervin-Tripp, 1989; Weiser, 1989). As well will see in later chapters, siblings continue to serve as an important source of social support through adolescence and adulthood as well.

TABLE 13.4 Sources of Support Reported by School-Age Children	
Support	**Average Number Mentioned in Interviews**
Homes and informal meeting places where child feels free to visit	5.5
Peers and siblings named among ten most important individuals	4.5
Formally sponsored activities (public library, community pool, church or temple)	4.5
Adults (including parents) named among ten most important individuals	3.0
Hobbies that child attributes to self	2.3
Special places to go to be alone	2.1
Pets (including neighbors') considered as a special friend	1.7
Make-believe friends and make-believe identities	1.6
Grandparents and others of grandparents' generation named among ten most important individuals	1.3

Source: Bryant (1985).

During the school years, grandparents and other adults and older children within and outside the immediate and extended family provide invaluable sources of social support for children.

In a study comparing the impact of siblings and peers on learning to construct toy models, Margarita Azmitia and Joanne Hesser (1993) found that young school-age children conferred a unique role on their older siblings by selecting them as models and guides and prompting them to use effective teaching strategies such as explaining and transferring responsibility. Compared to interactions with their older peers, children were better able to "coregulate" their interactions with their older siblings. In unstructured learning situations, they were more likely to observe, imitate, and consult their older siblings, who in turn were more likely to spontaneously offer guidance and support. In more structured "teaching" situations, older siblings provided more explanations and positive feedback and gave learners more control over the task than did older peers; young children more often prompted the siblings' explanations, pressured them into giving them more control over the task, and performed at higher levels than when taught by their older peers.

It is not surprising that older brothers and sisters tend to develop relationships with younger siblings that combine dominance and nurturance, the two major elements of mentoring relationships. However, a survey by Duane Buhrmeister and Wyndol Furman (1990) with third-, sixth-, ninth-, and twelfth-graders found that as children moved toward the end of middle childhood, relationships between siblings became less domineering any more egalitarian, and reported levels of intensity and conflict decreased.

Siblings also tend to be less domineering and more nurturant in families in which children feel secure and parents get along well together (Brody et al., 1992; Dunn et al., 1994). For example, Gene Brody and his colleagues (1992) found that school-age siblings whose fathers treat them with equality and impartiality during problem-solving discussions, whose families are generally harmonious even when discussing problems, and whose parents perceive family relationships to be close are less likely to experience sibling conflict than children in families functioning less effectively.

Beyond Siblings   In her research on social support, Brenda Bryant, found that many of the children reported seeking our adults other than their parents, especially grandparents, to talk with and confide in. Family pets, and sometimes even neighbors' pets, also served as confidants. Children also reported using hobbies to unwind and feel better about themselves (although some of the hobbies, such as collecting stamps or playing a musical instrument, were relatively nonsocial). Other children reported having special hideaways where they went to be alone for awhile. Many children sought out peers for activities when they needed an emotional lift or felt confused; but this was not the case on every occasion, and not all of the children did so (Bryant, 1985, 1994).

In general, Bryant found that as children moved through the school years, their sources of support increasingly broadened. This made them better able to manage particular stresses, whether inside or outside their families. At all ages during the elementary school years, children seemed happiest when they reported the widest range of social supports and when that range emphasized informal rather than formal supports.

As the preceding discussions imply, family members offer significant support in middle childhood. So do peers, as we explore in the next section.

WHAT DO YOU THINK?   What are your views about the impact of maternal employment on child development? In what ways do your views reflect your own experiences as a child?

Peer Relationships

The peer group is second only to the family as a context within which developmental changes occur. Throughout childhood, some of children's most important relationships involve peers. As early as age two, children enjoy playing with or next to one another, and by age three or four they often prefer the company of peers, even when adults are available. Time spent with peers increases steadily during middle childhood. By the late elementary school years, about one-half of children's social interactions are with peers (Hartup & Stevens, 1997).

What Theorists Say About Peer Relationships

Piaget   According to Jean Piaget, one important function of peers is to help school-age children overcome their *egocentrism,* or their tendency to assume everyone views the world in the same way they do (Piaget, 1963). In the course of playing together, children inevitably run into conflicts over toys and priorities, arguing over who should use a new set of felt pens or over what and where they should draw. In settling such disagreements, children gradually come to understand and value different points of view, a capacity that is central to living successfully in a pluralistic, democratic society.

Sullivan   The most comprehensive theory about peers was proposed by Harry Stack Sullivan (Sullivan, 1953; Youniss, 1980). Like Piaget, Sullivan argued that relationships with peers have fundamentally different qualities than those with adults. In particular, peers foster skills in compromise, cooperation, and competition. But unlike Piaget, Sullivan emphasized the value of peers in promoting emotional health. Peers create a life for children outside their families, and in doing so they help to correct the emotional biases families inevitably instill in their children, biases that Sullivan called emotional **warps.** For instance, an eight-year-old with shy, reserved parents may learn from peers that not all people are shy and reserved. Or a ten-year-old whose parents care little about competitive athletics may discover from peers that athletic competition matters quite a lot to some people.

• • •

warps The emotional biases that families instill in their children regarding how they think about and experience themselves.

According to Sullivan, this form of learning occurs during the **juvenile period,** which begins around age five and continues until nine or ten. In this period, children show increasing interest in playmates of similar age and status. As they near the end of the elementary school years, they supposedly focus this interest on just a few select friends of the same sex, whom Sullivan called *chums*. These relationships provide children with models for later intimate relationships.

Support for Theories About Peer Relationships   Research on peer relationships supports Piaget's and Sullivan's ideas in broad outline, but not in certain specifics. Conflict with peers does stimulate children's progress in solving cognitive problems, as Piaget proposed. Two seven-year-olds do learn from a discussion with each other about whether "the oldest people are always the tallest," but they learn only if they are already thinking at about the same level of maturity (Bell et al., 1985). Otherwise, such discussions easily turn into confrontation and browbeating as the more advanced child forces the other to comply with her point of view.

Research also supports Sullivan's claim that playmates and peers matter a lot to school-age children. Some relationships become closer and more important than others, of course, but few actually become intimate in the sense that Sullivan proposed. Children's comments about intimacy in friendship do increase greatly between childhood and adolescence, although friendships in which children share their most private or personal thoughts and feelings probably are relatively rare (Berndt, 1988; Youniss, 1980).

Peer relationships acquire a special intensity during late childhood and the transition to adolescence that typically occurs between fifth and seventh grades. During this period, children have increased unsupervised contact with peers and begin to place greater importance on peers' approval, views, and advice. At the same time, they spend less time with their parents and display greater emotional distance and psychological independence from them (Brown, 1990; Larson & Richards, 1991).

The Functions of Friends

Children's relationships with peers consist of multiple levels of interpersonal experiences. At one level, a child interacts with a group of peers in the classroom or neighborhood and occupies a social position among those peers. This level, which is referred to as *social status, group acceptance,* or *popularity,* is group oriented and reflects the social acceptance, or popularity, of the individual from the peer group's perspective. Another level of peer relationship involves *friendship*, a subjectively defined, voluntary, and reciprocal relationship between two individuals. Peer popularity and friendship are distinct but interrelated, and success or failure in one does not necessarily dictate success or failure in the other (Bukowski & Hoza, 1989; George & Hartman, 1996). During the early school years, friendships provide an arena for "activity and opportunity": children base friendships on shared interests and activities, exchanges of possessions, and concrete, supportive behaviors. By second or third grade, children become better able to live with differing perspectives within their friendships and feel less pressure to chose between one or the other (Hartup, 1997; Hartup & Stevens, 1997).

As children move into later childhood and preadolescence, *equality* and *reciprocity* become key elements of friendship interactions. Exchanging favors and sharing activities continue to matter as children get older, but by the time they enter fifth and sixth grades, they place greater emphasis on psychological qualities such as intimacy, trust, mutual support, and loyalty. Friendship begins to involve a concept of a relationship based on a reciprocity between equals, each with distinct but compatible personalities. Sharing between friends shifts from an unreflective,

• • •

juvenile period The period between approximately age five and ten during which children show increasing interest in playmates the same age, status, and gender.

symmetrical reciprocity based on "tit-for-tat" to a *cooperative reciprocity* based on mutual and deliberate sharing of assistance and resources that are intended to serve as tokens of friendship. Actually doing the same things or sharing the same objects becomes correspondingly less important (Keller & Wood, 1989; Rawlins, 1992).

By fifth or sixth grade, children can even adopt an independent, or third-party, perspective, comparing their own points of view with those of their friends. As one eleven-year-old put it about a good friend, "He thinks that I don't study enough, and that he studies just about the right amount for schoolwork. But you know what *I* think? I think that I'm just trying to keep schoolwork from bothering me too much, and that *he* works too hard. I wonder what the teachers think." Judging by statements such as this, friendship at this stage appears to be an intimate collaboration between two people who are mutually committed to building the relationship, which has acquired an importance beyond the particular needs of either friend.

In a recent review of the current literature on friendships and their developmental significance, Willard Hartup (1997) argues that the developmental implications of friendships cannot be specified without distinguishing among *having friends*, the *identity of one's friends,* and *friendship quality*. He concludes that friends provide one another with cognitive and social *scaffolding* that differs from what nonfriends provide, and that having friends supports good developmental outcomes across *normative transitions*, predictable changes that almost all children experience, such as entering school, starting middle school, and puberty. However, predicting developmental outcomes also requires knowledge of the attitudes and behavioral characteristics of children's friends as well as the qualitative features of these relationships. Cognitive and social scaffolding is similar to Vygotsky's zone of proximal development, which is discussed in Chapter 2.

The Functions of Other Peers

Like friendships, peer relationships, which generally are group oriented and less intimate than friendships, appear to serve several main functions. First, they provide a context for sociability, enhancement of relationships, and a sense of belonging. Second, they promote concern for achievements and a reliable and integrated sense of who one is. Finally, they provide opportunities for instruction and learning (Zarbatany et al., 1990).

Children's reliance on peers versus parents for help appears to increase with age. According to fourth-graders, friends provide support less frequently than do mothers and fathers, the most frequent providers. Seventh-graders, however, believe same-sex friends and parents are equally supportive, whereas tenth-graders view same-sex friends as the most frequent source of support (Furman & Buhrmester, 1992).

Although the functions of children's relationships with peers show considerable similarity to those with adults, several features are unique to peer relationships. Attachments with parents and other adults or older children are "vertical and complementary," meaning they involve individuals who have greater knowledge, competence, and social power. Peer relationships, in contrast, are "horizontal and symmetrical" in that they involve individuals of approximately equal knowledge, competence, and social power (Hartup, 1989). They are by nature voluntary and involve reciprocal relationships among comparative equals. These facts mean that a child must act in a way that explicitly supports the relationship—be friendly, that is—if he expects the relationship to survive. And he must do so with another individual whose social skills may be little better or even a bit worse than his own. Children apparently understand these differences intuitively, because they typically attribute an obedience orientation to relationships between adults and children but attribute play and recreation orientations to relationships among children (Berndt, 1988; Youniss, 1980).

During the school years, children tend to associate with peers of the same gender. Girls' friendships tend to be more intimate, whereas boys' friendships often reflect male stereotypes.

Influences on Peer Group Membership

Most of children's peer interactions occur in groups. In defining a peer group, elementary school children emphasize the importance of shared activities such as talking, hanging out, walking to school, talking on the telephone, listening to music, playing games, and just acting silly; however, sharing attitudes becomes most important as children approach adolescence (O'Brien & Bierman, 1988; Zarbatany et al., 1990). Living in the same neighborhood, attending the same school, and participating in the same community organizations all contribute to the likelihood that peer groups will form.

Children's peer groups are not simply random assortments of individuals but are influenced by many factors. Three of the most important factors are age, gender, and racial or ethnic background. Let us look briefly at each of these in turn.

Age   Children play mostly with others of approximately the same age and, when asked, say they prefer to be friends with their agemates. But contrary to a common impression, schoolchildren may spend anywhere from one-quarter to one-half of their time with companions who are more than two years older or younger and say they prefer to seek help and comfort from older children (Ellis et al., 1981; French, 1984). School imposes an upper limit on these cross-age contacts, however, because classrooms usually group children according to age.

Groups with mixed ages have certain special qualities. Older children show more nurturant behavior, such as tying the shoelaces of a younger child or buttoning the child's sweater. Younger children show greater dependence by asking for help with schoolwork or agreeing to older peers' preferences for play activities. However, mixed-age groups also tend to be less "sociable" than same-age groups; they chat or have friendly conversations less often, for example. Same-age groups encourage the opposites of all of these qualities: children give and receive less practical help, show more friendliness to one another, and get into conflicts more often (Brody et al., 1983; Furman & Buhrmester, 1992).

Gender   Although mixed-gender play occurs during the elementary school years, first-graders generally name children of their own gender as best friends. Observations of younger schoolchildren during free play show that during cooperative play periods, they interact about four times as often with children of their own gender as they do with those of the opposite gender (Golombok & Fivush, 1994; Maccoby & Jacklin, 1987). This ratio actually increases as children get older; by third grade most peer groups contain only one gender, and by fifth grade virtually all do. As children move into middle school and adolescence, however, the trend reverses (Shrum et al., 1988).

How do we interpret this tendency toward gender-based separation during middle childhood? Eleanor Maccoby argues that gender differences emerge primarily in social situations and vary with the gender composition of the dyads (two-person relationships) and groups involved. She suggests that children spontaneously choose same-gender playmates even in situations where they are not under pressure from adults to do so because they find same-gender play partners more compatible (Maccoby, 1990).

During the preschool years, two factors seem to be important. First, the rough-and-tumble style and emphasis on competition and dominance that is characteristic of boys appear to be unappealing to most girls, who in general prefer play that is more cooperative and less aggressive. Second, girls discover that boys are becoming increasingly unresponsive to their influence and therefore avoid playing with them. At a time when children are actively involved in learning how to influence their play partners and integrate and coordinate activities with those of others, girls discover that their growing reliance on polite suggestion to influence others is increasingly ineffective with boys, and therefore avoid choosing boys as playmates (Maccoby, 1990).

Further support for the idea that playmate selection may be more heavily influenced by sharing gender-based play activities than by merely being of the same gender comes from a laboratory study of choice of playmates among six-to-eight-year-olds reported by Gerianne Alexander and Melissa Hines. When given the choice of selecting a playmate based on gender versus preferred style of play, style of play appeared to be more important for both boys and girls. Boys chose female playmates who had masculine play styles (including toys, rough-and-tumble play, and activity level), whereas girls chose male playmates with more feminine play styles (Alexander & Hines, 1994).

Over time, children find same-gender play partners more compatible and segregate themselves into same-gender groups. As children enter adolescence, childhood patterns carry over into cross-gender interactions in which girls' styles may put them at a disadvantage. Though patterns of mutual influence may be more symmetrical in intimate male-female couples, the distinctive styles of the two genders are still present and subsequently manifest themselves in the roles and relationships of parenthood (Maccoby, 1990).

Despite the pervasiveness of gender segregation in peer relationships, a small but stable subgroup of children maintain cross-gender relations beyond the age when such relationships are the norm. Donna Kovacs, Jeffrey Parker, and Lois Hoffman (1996) studied cross-sex friendships among more than seven hundred third- and forth-grade boys and girls from diverse SES backgrounds. They found that 14 percent of the children had one or more reciprocal opposite-gender friendships. Children with primarily opposite-gender friendships had poorer social skills than other children with friends, but held fewer stereotypes about gender roles than other children did and were better adjusted than children with no friends. Children involved in opposite-gender friendships that were secondary to their same-gender friendships were as well adjusted as children with only same-gender friendships. African American children, who comprised about one-third of the children studied, were more likely than European American children to have opposite-gender friends. African American children from single-parent homes had more opposite-gender friends than those from two-parent homes, perhaps because they were likely to live in extended, multigenerational family settings in which they interacted with many female family members and few adult males.

Differences between school-age girls and boys sometimes reflect culturally supported gender stereotypes.

Gender Boundaries   Alan Sroufe and his colleagues have used the concept of gender boundaries to help explain the influence of gender on peer relationships during middle childhood and preadolescence. *Gender boundaries* refer to the elaborate system of rules and rituals that surround cross-gender interactions between boys and girls. The cycle of teasing and retaliation that a ten-year-old boy endures from his peers at summer camp when he is seen leaving a girls' tent (where he went only to get his radio) reflects the seriousness of the boundaries and of the consequences if they are crossed. The boy is obligated to retaliate by chasing and hitting his tormenters to reestablish his place in the group (Sroufe et al., 1993).

Based on extensive videotaped observations of ten-to-eleven-year-olds participating in summer day camps, Sroufe and his colleagues found that preadolescents face a complex developmental task of maintaining a clear gender boundary while simultaneously finding opportunities to express interest in and learn about members of the other gender. Same-gender friendships promote the learning of skills for group functioning and prevent premature heterosexual intimacy, while the taunting, name calling, and chase games that occur between groups of boys and girls allow them a safe, protected way to explore cross-gender relationships. Table 13.5 lists some of the "rules" that appear to regulate middle childhood gender boundaries in a day camp setting.

TABLE 13.5	Gender Boundary Rules of Middle Childhood: Under What Circumstances Is Contact with the Other Gender Permissible?
Rule:	The contact is accidental.
Example:	You're not looking where you are going and you bump into someone.
Rule:	The contact is incidental.
Example:	You go to get some lemonade and wait while two children of the other gender get some. (There should be no conversation.)
Rule:	The contact is in the guise of some clear and necessary purpose.
Example:	You may say, "Pass the lemonade," to persons of the other gender at the next table. No interest in them is expressed.
Rule:	An adult compels you to have contact.
Example:	"Go get that map from X and Y and bring it to me."
Rule:	You are accompanied by someone of your own gender.
Example:	Two girls may talk to two boys, though physical closeness with your own partner must be maintained and intimacy with the others is disallowed.
Rule:	The interaction or contact is accompanied by disavowal.
Example:	You say someone is ugly or hurl some other insult or (more commonly for boys) push or throw something at them as they pass by.

Source: Sroufe et al. (1993), Table 1, p. 456.

WORKING WITH

Lisa Truong, **Fourth-Grade Teacher**

Reducing Gender-Role Stereotyping in Play

Lisa Truong is a fourth-grade teacher at a "follow-through" elementary school that serves students from citywide head-start preschool and kindergarten programs as well as children from the local neighborhood. Her classroom is a well-organized, friendly, cheerful place filled with children's drawings and other projects. Lisa provides richly detailed observations of gender differences in peer group and play activities among fourth-graders.

Rob: *How would you describe peer relations among fourth-graders?*

Lisa: Often children's academic ability sets the tone and pace for their friendships. Children who do well academically tend to be friends with other kids who are bright.

Rob: *Why do you think this is so?*

Lisa: In part because of parent pressure. Parents are interested in their children having good friends. Another reason may be that much of the teaching here occurs in small skill groups. These group children with the same academic needs together. They also focus on group dynamics, teaching the children to work with other people. When we go outside for recess, the children do tend to stay in those same groups.

Rob: *What other factors seem to influence peer groups?*

Lisa: Boy-girl differences are very important. As much as I've tried to encourage girls to play football or soccer and boys to do things like four-square and jump-rope, it really does break down by gender as to how they play outside. Girls tend to play jump-rope, and boys tend to play soccer on the field—it's almost automatic. Girls also tend to go to the swings and slide much more than the boys.

Rob: *Why do you think this happens?*

Lisa: At this age, girls are getting more social and interactive. Often I see girls walking slowly and talking. Even their jump-rope is more consistently interactive and coordinated—with turn taking and things like that—than the boys' play. You should see the girls play four-square! It involves a lot of verbal interaction and social coordination.

Rob: *How so?*

Lisa: Four people stand in a 10-foot-by-10-foot square drawn in chalk and divided into four smaller squares. The person in the fourth square is in control of whatever the category will be. So, for example, that person will say "Colors" and then bounce the ball into any of the other players' squares. They will have to name a color and catch the ball, or they're out.

Rob: *There's a rhythm to it?*

Lisa: You have to keep the rhythm, and you can't name the same color twice—or animal, country, movie star, or whatever the category is. The categories get more complex as the year goes on. The kids almost always start the year with colors, and by the end of the year it will be something much more specific, like Spice Girls songs or names of rock stars. This group of girls also made up a great hand-clapping game about music groups; the way they thought it through and the rules they made up were fascinating.

Rob: *What are the boys doing?*

Lisa: They're playing soccer and kick-ball, building forts, or skateboards, if they can. Or they'll collect things and investigate the environment. At the beginning of the year, we studied insects and their natural habitats in science. Once the boys got outside, they tried to find every single little bug they could, and they would come in and show it.

Rob: *It seems fourth-grade boys are less interested in make-up games than girls.*

Lisa: Yes, that's true. Boys tend to play games that emphasize physical rather than social interaction and where they follow rules that are already made up for them.

Rob: *How permanent are these peer group patterns?*

Lisa: They seem long-lasting. The group I described was made up of five girls who are very, very close. They're all good students, and all happen to be white. I've been trying to encourage them to be less of a clique and interact with other people more.

Rob: *How else might teachers encourage greater interaction?*

Lisa: Our school is committed to helping children interact in a way that doesn't break down along sex role or racial lines. I talk to them about it very up-front, and I say I think there should be more interaction between boys and girls and blacks and whites. When we have social studies activities, the rule is that groups will be mixed. The children understand this and help make it work.

What Do You Think?

1. Lisa's observations of her students illustrate how closely play and social development are interrelated. What examples in the interview demonstrate this?

2. How has Lisa attempted to reduce gender-role stereotyping in her fourth-graders' peer group and play activities? Based on this chapter, what additional things might she consider trying?

3. Discuss how Lisa's observations demonstrate the interaction of physical, cognitive, and social domains in her fourth-graders' development. How are the three domains reflected in gender differences in peer groups and play activities?

Adult norms and expectations regarding gender stereotyping can also make a significant difference. For example, children growing up in families that downplay gender typing in their childrearing values and practices are less stereotyped in their activities, interests, and gender-typed beliefs. Such children seem able to understand and use *both* gender-typed and non-gender-typed beliefs and behaviors related to gender. However, gender flexibility in children's play behavior or friendship preferences is more likely to be evident in situations where it is supported, or at least not actively discouraged, by parents, teachers, and other adults (Hoffman, 1989; Maccoby, 1990; Moorehouse, 1991; Weisner & Wilson-Mitchell, 1990).

For interesting firsthand observations and discussion of the role of gender in peer group play, see the Working With interview on page 418.

Racial and Ethnic Background   Patterns of segregation and preferences based on racial and ethnic differences are a fact of life in much of our society (Asher et al., 1982; Shrum et al., 1988). Racial and ethnic awareness are especially important during middle childhood, because children of this age are in the process of committing themselves to society and to the values and standards of the majority culture. They are also developing their own self-concepts.

Racial segregation and racial preference often reflect certain types of prejudice. *Prejudice* is a positive or negative attitude toward an individual based solely on the person's membership in a particular group. Prejudices are frequently based on *stereotypes,* patterns of rigid, overly simplified, and generally inaccurate ideas about the characteristics of another group of people. Stereotypes often involve negative ideas associated with racial, ethnic or cultural background, religion, social class, age, gender, and sexual orientation. Although prejudices based on stereotypes do not necessarily determine a person's overt behavior, they often do. Frequently prejudice is associated with *discrimination*—actions toward members of the targeted group, such as exclusion or mistreatment, that reflect prejudicial attitudes toward that group.

Studies that asked children to name their friends have found that children are more likely to name peers of their own race, particularly if that race is the majority one. This trend begins in the preschool years and increases over middle childhood until children reach junior high school (Asher et al., 1982; Shrum et al., 1988). The degree to which family, neighborhood, and school settings are supportive (or unsupportive) of cross-race friendships is also likely to influence a child's peer preferences. Among children and adolescents, social contact both inside and outside of school may influence intergroup attitudes. Maureen Hallinan, Roy Texeira, and Richard Williams studied black-white interracial friendships among fourth-through-seventh-graders in integrated classrooms. They found that the more African American students a classroom contained, the more likely European American students were to choose a black peer as a best friend. However, having a higher proportion of white students in a classroom did not increase the likelihood of a black student choosing a white friend. Yet cross-race friendships are more likely to develop in integrated schools, for example, but are difficult to maintain outside of school unless the children live in interracial neighborhoods or participate in team sports or other integrated activities (DuBois & Hirsch, 1990; Hallinan & Texeira, 1987; Hallinan & Williams, 1989; Howes & Wu, 1990).

Elementary school programs that emphasize multicultural competence and awareness by integrating multicultural activities in both academic and extracurricular activities and actively involve children's families and other community members in school activities can successfully foster friendship and peer acceptance among students from different racial, ethnic, and cultural backgrounds (Bojko, 1995). *Magnet schools* that use specialized programs in science, language, or the arts to attract students from school districts representing a variety of ethnic and cultural backgrounds have also succeeded in increasing diversity on a long-term basis (Rossell, 1988).

A school or neighborhood setting that is ethnically diverse may foster peer interactions and friendships among children from different ethnic groups. The steps of their school provide an excellent place for these boys from one fifth-grade class to "hang out".

Cooperative learning experiences that allow mixed groups of children to work as a team to achieve common academic goals also have had some success in fostering cross-race acceptance and enhancing children's self-esteem. In one program based on this "jigsaw" technique, children from different racial and ethnic backgrounds were assigned to different parts of a single project. They quickly learned to work together to complete the task and developed more positive feelings about both themselves and one another (Johnson et al., 1984; Slavin, 1996).

Popularity and Rejection

When peers are asked to evaluate one another's popularity, or likability, by "nominating" whom they like most or would choose to play with, children generally are classified as "popular" or as occupying one of three unpopular statuses: "rejected," "controversial," or "neglected." Popular children receive many positive and very few negative votes from their peers; rejected children receive many negative and few positive peer nominations; controversial children receive many positive and negative peer nominations; and neglected children receive few positive or negative nominations (Coie et al., 1982).

The Popular Child   Easily noticed characteristics, such as having the "right" hairstyle or an attractive-sounding name, are quite important to acceptance in the early grades. As children get older, they increasingly choose their friends on the basis of personal qualities such as honesty, kindness, humor, and creativity (Bukowski et al.,1996; Furman & Bierman, 1983). However, they still evaluate one another and confer more popularity on some children than on others.

Popular children are viewed by their peers as being confident, good-natured, kind, outgoing, and energetic. Highly visible abilities and achievements help, especially in athletics, but also in academics or social activities. Stylish clothing and special material possessions, such as an expensive pair of athletic shoes, also influence status with peers. Popular children are well liked; they easily initiate and maintain social interactions and understand social situations. They possess a high degree of interpersonal skills and tend to behave in ways that are prosocial, cooperative, and in tune with group norms (Marsten & Coatsworth, 1998).

Some of these assets, such as peer competence and athletic ability, remain valuable to children as they move into adolescence, and others (such as athletic shoes) may not. But during childhood, such advantages create prestige for individual children within particular peer groups and also make membership in the "best," or highest-status, groups possible. Because of the importance of peer relationships during the school years, the interpersonal competencies associated with peer acceptance and popularity are likely to have a positive impact not only on a child's current adjustment but also on her or his longer-term psychological well-being (Bukowski et al., 1996; Marsten & Coatsworth, 1998).

The Unpopular Child   Peers describe unpopular children, particularly those classified as "rejected," as unpleasant, disruptive, selfish, and having few positive characteristics. Such children are likely to exhibit socially inappropriate aggression, hyperactivity, inattention or immaturity, and, not surprisingly, behavioral and academic problems in school (Bierman et al., 1993). Because they lack the social skills needed to successfully join and participate in peer groups, they are blamed by peers for their own deviance and are often actively disliked and excluded from activities (Coie et al., 1991; Marsten & Coatsworth, 1998).

Thomas George and Donald Hartmann (1996) studied the friendship networks of popular, average, and unpopular fifth- and sixth-graders. They found that all children reported having at least one *unilateral* friend, a person whom they considered to be a friend but who did not feel the same way about them. Unpopular children were less likely than popular children to have at least one *reciprocal* friend, someone who shared their view that a mutual friendship existed. The unilateral friendship networks of unpopular children contained more younger school-age friends and fewer same-age friends than the friendship networks of popular children. The reciprocal friendship networks of unpopular children were smaller, more evenly distributed within and outside of the classroom, and contained fewer average and popular friends or friends of the opposite gender than those of popular children.

In a twelve-year longitudinal study that followed fifth-graders to young adulthood, Catherine Gabwell, Andrew Newcomb, and William Bukowski (1998) found that peer-rejected children were at risk for later difficulties. Children who were rejected by their peers and had no good friend at age ten had lower aspiration levels, participated in fewer organizations and activities with others, had a less active social life, and experienced more psychological problems, including depression and anxiety, in adolescence and young adulthood compared to children who were not rejected and who had at least one friend.

Aggression   Among both boys and girls, the highest levels of aggression are displayed by children who are classified as unpopular-rejected. However, girls and boys appear to differ in the form their aggressive behavior most typically takes. As described in Chapter 10, boys are more likely to attack peers through *overt aggression* (such as hitting, pushing, or verbally threatening to hurt others), whereas girls are more likely to display *relational aggression* (harming others through purposeful manipulation and damage of their peer relationships) (Crick, 1997; Crick & Grotpeter, 1995).

Gender differences in aggression, as expressed by frustration and rage, are not found in infancy, but do emerge in the preschool period, when boys are more likely than girls to dispaly both overt

Unpopular children may behave aggressively or selfishly without realizing it. Ironically, since they tend to be excluded from groups, they find few chances to learn new ways of relating.

(physical) aggression and relational (emotional) aggression. During the school years, girls display significantly more relational aggression, whereas boys exhibit substantially more overt aggression, including, in the extreme, group and gang fighting, aggravated assault, sexual violence, and homicide (Loeber & Stouthamer-Loeber, 1998).

Jennifer Grotpeter and Nicki Crick (1996) conducted a study to discover whether the social problems that relationally aggressive and overtly aggressive children typically experience in peer group situations also occur in their one-to-one friendships. Children who were relationally aggressive in their peer group did exhibit high levels of relational aggression, intimacy, exclusivity, and jealousy within their friendships. In contrast, children who were overtly aggressive with their peers exhibited low levels of intimacy but greatly valued companionship and spending time with their friends, and placed great importance on having friends who joined them in using aggression to harm children outside the friendship. Thus, children who are not themselves aggressive but develop friendships with overtly aggressive peers may nevertheless be pulled into aggressive encounters against other children. Children who possess high levels of emotional expressiveness, emotional insight, and empathy are better able to manage their own anger in social interactions and to display higher levels of empathy and prosocial behavior with friends than children who lack such qualities (Roberts & Strayer, 1996).

The likelihood of aggressive behavior is also influenced by social context. For example, one study of seven-to-nine-year-old African American boys found that aggressive behavior between two children was more likely in group situations characterized by a tense, negative atmosphere; high levels of aversive verbal and nonverbal behavior, such as criticizing, teasing, grabbing, and pushing; high levels of competitiveness; and low levels of cooperation and group cohesion (DeRosier et al., 1994).

Family, culture, and neighborhood contexts also are important. Research by Carol MacKinnon-Lewin and her colleagues found that in families in which mothers and their elementary-school-age sons judged each other to be hostile and treated each other in a coercive, disrespectful manner, boys tended to be more aggressive and less socially competent with their peers. Siblings with rejecting mothers treated one another more aggressively than siblings with less rejecting mothers, and boys who experienced aggressive interactions with their siblings were more likely to be viewed as aggressive and to be rejected by their peers (MacKinnon-Lewis et al., 1994; MacKinnon-Lewis et al., 1997). In a large-scale study of second-through-fifth-graders, Janis Kupersmidt and her colleagues found that problems with aggression and peer rejection are most likely for low-income African American children from single-parent homes and least likely for middle-class white children (Kupersmidt et al., 1995). Living in middle-class neighborhoods had a strong protective effect on aggressive behavior and peer rejection, particularly among those African American children from low-SES, single-parent homes who also lived in such neighborhoods.

For children living in war zones or in other dangerous environments such as communities where gang and drug activity and the wounding and killing of friends and relatives are everyday occurrences, the developmental toll on children and their parents is immense (Wandersman & Nation, 1998). Youngsters who are exposed to ongoing violence suffer from chronic emotional distress, learning problems, sleep disturbances, and preoccupation with their own safety and the safety of those they depend on and care about. They are also more likely to have problems with aggression, impulse control, and conflict resolution with peers and others in both school and nonschool settings. Children may cope with chronic danger by adopting a world view that is dysfunctional in any "normal" situations in which they are expected to participate. For example, although being hyperaggressive may help to ensure survival in a dangerous neighborhood, it is likely to be nonfunctional and to stimulate peer and teacher rejection if used to cope with disappointments and disputes in most school situations (Garbarino & Kostelny, 1996; Kozol, 1995; Marsella, 1998; Masten & Coatsworth, 1998; McCloyd, 1998). In addition, some adaptations to chronic danger, such as emotional withdrawal, may cause problems for the next generation, when the individual himself becomes a parent.

Conformity to Peers

Because peer groups involve social equals, they give children unique opportunities to develop their own beliefs without having parents or older siblings dominate or dismiss them. But in doing so, peer groups also present challenges. Acceptance and support by groups matter intensely to children, who are still learning what kind of people they are and acquiring the skills they need to interact with others. As a result, peer groups often influence their members very strongly indeed: they demand conformity to group expectations in return for continued acceptance and prestige.

Pressures to conform sometimes lead children to violate personal values or needs or those of parents and other adult authorities. One child might feel pressured into paying dues she cannot afford, joining fights she does not want to participate in, or shunning children who do not belong to her own group. Another might feel pressured to wear clothes that his parents consider outrageous or to perform poorly at school. In return for these behaviors and attitudes, the children remain in good standing with their peers. Despite these differences, however, there tends to be high agreement between peer group and parents on important issues such as moral and ethical standards, standards of appropriate behavior, schooling, and future goals (Damon, 1988; Fine, 1982).

Peer groups can exert positive pressures as well. For example, they can encourage athletic achievement above and beyond what physical education teachers can generate in their students, and they can create commitments to fairness and reciprocity, at least within an immediate circle of peers: "When someone buys a candy bar at the drugstore, she shares it with the rest of us. Then we do the same thing the next time if *we* get something nice." Whether the pressures are positive or negative, however, peer groups offer a key setting for acquiring social skills, evaluating and managing personal relationships, and handling competition and cooperation.

A study of the natural, self-selected peer groups of fourth- and fifth-graders conducted by Thomas Kinderman (1993) found that children tend to associate with peers who share similar norms regarding involvement in school. Children who were academically oriented and highly engaged in school tended to affiliate with classmates who had similar motivational orientations; the same was true for children who were disengaged from school and lacked academic motivation. Although their memberships changed somewhat during the year, peer groups remained quite stable with regard to their norms concerning academic orientation.

School Influences on Peer Relationships

According to Erik Erikson, school is one of the main arenas in which children resolve the crisis of industry versus inferiority. Interactions with teachers and other children provide important opportunities to develop cognitive and social skills, gain knowledge about the world, and cultivate peer relationships that are central to the development of self-concept during middle childhood.

School Culture   Each school has its own culture, which includes the values, beliefs, traditions, and customary ways of thinking and behaving that make it unique and distinguish it from other schools and institutions. One school may especially value its innovative academic programs and the high achievement levels of is students, another the degree of student involvement in school-sponsored activities, and a third the active involvement of parents in providing special resources. The closer the fit between the school culture and the values and expectations of the children (and families) it serves, the more likely the school's developmental impact will be positive. Students function better both academically and socially in classrooms in which the instructional approach, pattern and rhythm of verbal interaction and student participation, and strategies for motivating students are in tune with their family and cultural expectations (Vygotsky, 1997; Wigfield et al., 1998).

Clearly, teachers strongly influence a school's culture—and its children. In fact, with the exception of their parents, most elementary school children spend more time with their teachers than with any other adults. Teachers therefore play a very significant role in the lives of school-age children. Observational studies of daily classroom life reveal that the elementary school teacher engages in as many as one thousand interpersonal exchanges with pupils each day (Cazden, 1988). As we saw in Chapter 12, teachers' styles of classroom management vary considerably. However, all effective teachers establish learning environments that are calm, predictable, and engaging, and provide smooth transitions from one activity to the next. They also stay on top of the classroom situation by keeping in tune with their students, in both their communication of academic content and their responses to the constantly changing social and emotional needs of thirty or more children (Linney & Seidman, 1989). In other words, they create an environment with clear rules and expectations, effective controls, open communicaton, high nurturance, and respectful relationships that encourage students to participate as fully as possible in school and classroom life and to maintain positive relationships with their peers. Not surprisingly, effective teacher-student relationships tend to be authoritative in that their qualities parallel those of the authoritative parenting style discussed in Chapter 10.

The Student's Experience   What do students experience in the classroom? According to Philip Jackson, particularly in traditional, teacher-centered classrooms, students spend a great deal of time waiting for the teacher or other students, delaying fulfillment of their needs until given permission to do so by the teacher, and contending with distractions and social disruption. Students must wait to ask a question, wait to get permission to leave their seats, wait to have a question answered, wait for the next assignment, or wait for their turn to use the stapler (Jackson, 1986).

Although these observations are cause for concern, many classrooms are conscientiously organized to minimize such difficulties and provide a learning environment that is academically stimulating and supportive of children's developmental needs. Though the teaching styles may vary, the experiences of the great majority of students in well-run classrooms are largely positive. Students in such classrooms feel like respected members of their classroom and school communities. They are eager to learn and are active participants in classroom activities, both academic and nonacademic. Effective school environments also provide children with opportunities to freely interact with and form developmentally beneficial relationships both with peers and with children of different ages, developmental levels, and backgrounds. The Working With interview with fourth-grade teacher Lisa Truong (page 418) is a good example of how a teacher uses her authoritative relationships with her students and her awareness of school and classroom culture to reduce gender-role stereotyping in peer group activities.

WHAT DO YOU THINK ?   Children's growing exposure to peer group influences during middle childhood is a source of concern for both parents and teachers. What advice might you give to parents and teachers regarding the best ways to deal with this challenge?

Death, Loss, and Grieving During the School Years

Approximately 1.5 million children in the United States live in single-parent families because the other parent has died (U.S. Bureau of the Census, 1995). One study of death, loss, and grieving among middle school children found that 41 percent had been personally involved with death within the previous year, with the death of a grandparent or great-grandparent most frequently mentioned (Glass, 1991). However, parents, other relatives (including siblings and family friends), other children, and pets, are also noted. Though the loss of a parent may be the most difficult for children, the death of a sibling due to an illness such as sudden infant death syndrome (SIDS), AIDS, cystic fibrosis, or cancer, or to accidents or suicide, can also have a profound effect on children at various ages (Birenbaum et al., 1991; Davies, 1995; Fangos & Nickerson, 1991; Powell, 1991).

The Process of Grieving for a Childhood Loss

Loss refers to being separated from someone to whom one was emotionally attached; *grieving* refers to the complex emotional, cognitive, and perceptual reactions and experiences that accompany the loss (Mullan et al., 1995). John Baker and his colleagues propose that the grief process for bereaved children consists of three phases, each involving certain psychological tasks (Baker et al., 1992).

Early-phase tasks for children who are grieving include developing an understanding of the fact that someone has died and of the implications of the death, and protecting themselves and their families both from physical harm and from the full emotional impact of the loss. Children need information at an age-appropriate level about death in general and about the nature of the particular death. Euphemistic explanations (e.g., "Mother has gone to sleep") should be avoided because they tend to interfere with children's need to understand what really happened. Bereaved children listen intently and watch others' reactions, ask questions, and reenact elements of the events in their play; if there are gaps in their understanding, they tend

Approximatery 1.5 million children in the United States live in single-parent families because the other parent has died, and experiences with death have developmental impact throughout the lifespan.

to fill in the missing pieces with fantasy. Children also need to feel that they are safe and in a secure environment. Because of fears that they too will die or that their families will disintegrate, children and their families may engage in a variety of self-protective mechanisms such as denial, distortion, emotional numbing, and even physical isolation from people.

Middle-phase tasks of grieving include accepting and emotionally acknowledging the reality of the loss, exploring and reevaluating the relationship to the person who died, and bearing the intense psychological pain involved. *Late-phase tasks* require that the child achieve the following: consolidate a new sense of personal identity that includes both the experience of the loss and identifications with the deceased person; safely develop new emotional relationships without excessive fear of loss or guilt; construct his or her own inner representation of the deceased, based on past and current experiences, thoughts, and feelings that enable the child to maintain an ongoing emotional connection (attachment) with the deceased; wholeheartedly resume the age-appropriate developmental tasks and activities that were interrupted by the loss; and successfully cope with the periodic resurgence of painful memories associated with the loss that are likely to occur at points of developmental transition or on specific anniversaries, such as the date of the person's death.

Just as the adopted child faces the question "How could my parent(s) give me up?" and the child of divorce faces the question "Why did my father (or mother) leave me?", the child who has lost a parent to death must deal with how and why the parent died and what the parent's presence may have been like had it continued over time. Children's efforts to remain connected to the deceased parent include locating the deceased (e.g., in "heaven"), experiencing the deceased (e.g., believing the parent is watching them), reaching out to the deceased (e.g., visiting the cemetery, "speaking" to the parent), having waking memories of the deceased, and cherishing physical objects linked to the deceased (Silverman et al., 1992).

Children's Understanding of Death

As we noted in Chapter 11, it isn't until around age ten that most children realize that death is irreversible, permanent, and universal. Even then there are a wide range of individual differences based on children's particular experiences. For example, children who have faced a life-threatening illness such as leukemia or have lost a close relative, may develop an understanding of death as much as two or three years earlier than those who have little first-hand experience with death (Bertoia, 1993; Webb, 1993).

Developmental Impact   The developmental impact of death experienced during childhood depends on a number of factors, including the significance of the person to the child, the nature of the death and the conditions surrounding it, the child's strengths and vulnerabilities at the time of the loss, the amount of support available to the child to successfully grieve the loss, the amount of material and psychological disruption in the child's family as a result of the loss, and the quality of the child's relationships with the surviving parent and family members. Studies of college students and older adults who experienced the death of a parent during childhood have found that being able to talk freely with the surviving parent about the circumstances surrounding the death, to express sorrow about the death, or to ask questions about the deceased parent helped to protect against the development of depression in adulthood. Greater involvement in activities such as attending funeral-related events, keeping mementos of the dead parent, openly expressing anger about the death to someone else, hearing stories about the deceased parent, seeing pictures in the home of the dead parent, and visiting the grave also decreased the risk of subsequent depression (Saler & Skolnick, 1992).

Helping Children with Bereavement   The work of Kelly Lohnes and Neil Kalter (1994) is an excellent example of preventative intervention with groups of parentally bereaved elementary school-age children. Groups of five to seven children met for twelve weeks of one-hour sessions designed to achieve the following: (1) normalize the children's reactions to and experiences of the death of a parent; (2) clarify confusing and frightening death-related issues; (3) provide a safe place for children to experience and rework emotionally painful aspects of the death and the stresses of living in a single-parent household; (4) help the children to develop coping strategies for particularly troubling feelings and family and peer dynamics; (5) help the children to maintain an emotional connection (attachment) to the deceased parent; and (6) share the children's concerns about parental death and its aftermath with surviving parents (and stepparents) through newsletters.

Group activities included bereavement stories, drawings, role playing, and discussion to help the children express and understand their feelings and experiences related to loss and bereavement. Some of the thoughts, feelings, and experiences of these children, which in other contexts might have raised concerns about psychopathology, were in fact common for parentally bereaved children who were otherwise developmentally normal. For example, children typically reported hallucinations of the dead parent, believed the parent would return, and wished to be "dead" in order to be reunited with the parent. If ignored or misunderstood by adults, such fantasies, distortions, and symptoms may contribute to psychopathology. Knowledge that such behaviors are normal for this age group, however, can enable mental health professionals, surviving parents, school personnel, pediatricians, and other concerned individuals to more effectively help these children mourn their loss and minimize negative developmental effects such as health problems, decline in school performance, and emotional difficulties (Lohnes & Kalter, 1994).

WHAT DO YOU THINK?   Based on your own experience with death during your middle childhood, how well does the chapter's description of the grieving process fit with what you remember? In what ways are the challenges of dealing with loss due to death similar to the challenges of dealing with the losses due to divorce discussed earlier in this chapter?

Beyond Childhood

In a variety of ways, middle childhood is the time when a child becomes a person in a more adult sense than ever before. This happens partly because the child has begun accumulating considerable experience with other people of roughly the same age and maturity and partly because of cognitive developments. Children begin setting goals and working toward them in more adult ways by taking into account others' opinions about their achievements as well as their own interest in learning.

As we point out several times in this chapter, the developments of middle childhood do not always result in happy feelings and experiences. With their newly developed maturity, children are able to hurt and snub some of their peers as well as make new friends, and they are now able to worry about peer evaluations as well as be commendably open-minded. Life has not gotten happier just because the child has gotten older, but it is not necessarily unhappier either.

Taken together, these experiences create a new, more mature sense of self within children of this age, one that has more inward or psychological properties than that of early childhood. In the years ahead, during adolescence, this psychological self becomes still more elaborate. Contrary to widespread belief, the adolescent years do not necessarily prove any more or less difficult than the middle childhood or early childhood years do, although some individuals, for special reasons, encounter unique challenges.

Summary of Major Ideas

Psychosocial Challenges of Middle Childhood

1. During the school years, children face challenges concerning the development of an identity or a sense of self, achievement, family relationships, peer relationships, and school.

The Sense of Self

2. During the school years, children develop a sense of self, acquire a belief in self-constancy and in relatively permanent psychological traits, and learn to distinguish their thoughts and feelings from those of others.

The Age of Industry and Achievement

3. According to some psychodynamic theorists, schoolchildren repress their earlier romantic attachments to their parents and focus instead on developing a sense of industry and achievement.

4. During the school years, children shift their achievement orientation from an exclusive focus on learning, or task orientation, to a performance orientation that includes others' responses to their achievements.

Family Relationships

5. Divorce is common in North American families and usually creates stress for all members of the family, although girls and boys react differently.

6. Blended families that result from remarriage pose considerable challenges. Younger children form attachments with stepparents more easily than adolescents do.

7. Many mothers now work at least part time, and their employment generally does not seem to have any negative effects on their children. Nevertheless, maternal employment influences the division of household labor and children's attitudes about gender roles.

8. When fathers are unemployed, both they and their families experience significant stress.

9. Providing good after-school supervision is a challenge for working parents. For children in unsupportive environments, formal after-school progams offer considerable benefits.

10. Schoolchildren often find emotional support from adults other than parents, as well as from siblings, friends, pets, and hobbies.

Peer Relationships

11. Piaget believed that peers help children to overcome their egocentrism by challeging them to deal with perspectives other than their own.

12. According to Sullivan, peers help children to develop democratic ways of interacting and also offer the first opportunities to form close relationships with others.

13. In general, peers seem to serve unique functions by creating voluntary relationships of equality among children.

14. Groups of peers vary in membership and behavior in terms of age, gender, and racial or ethnic group. Peer groups tend to segregate themselves by both gender and race.

15. Popular children possess a number of socially desirable qualities, including well-developed social skills and confidence in themselves. Unpopular children exhibit less desirable qualities, such as aggressiveness, selfishness, and bossiness.

16. Early in the school years, a friend is someone with whom a child shares activities and toys, but later in this period, a friend becomes someone whom the child can count on and with whom she or he can share intimacies.

17. Peers exert pressure to conform on individual children, and this pressure can have either positive or negative effects.

18. School culture influences children's peer relationships. This influence is more likely to be positive if the school's culture and the child's familial culture are compatible.

Death, Loss, and Grieving During the School Years

19. At about age ten, most children realize that death is irreversible, permanent, and universal, although individual differences in experience mean that some children may develop this understanding earlier.

20. Intervention groups help parentally bereaved children to normalize their reactions to and experiences with death, clarify confusing and frightening death-related issues, and safely deal with emotionally painful aspects of the death and stresses of living in a single-parent household. They also enable children to better cope with family and peer dynamics and to maintain an emotional connection (attachment) to the deceased parent, and help surviving parents (and grandparents) to better understand their children's concerns.

Key Terms

achievement motivation (396)
blended family (407)
industry versus inferiority (396)
juvenile period (413)
latency (395)

learning orientation (396)
peers (391)
performance orientation (396)
self-constancy (393)
sense of self (393)
warp (412)

PART 6

Adolescence

The adolescent years present new and unique challenges for children. They must come to terms with their bodies as they suddenly grow taller and become sexually mature. They must establish more equal relationships with their parents. And they must come to grips with the need to leave home eventually and become independent individuals.

How stressful these challenges prove to be depends on a variety of circumstances. For some teens, the timing of puberty can make these years especially hard (or easy). For others, their newly forming ability to reason abstractly can make life seem suddenly confusing at the same time it reveals exciting new possibilities for the future. For most young people, dating, or even just talking to, the opposite sex proves both intriguing and frustrating as they slowly overcome childhood tendencies to relate only to members of their own sex. All in all, the changes of adolescence can be difficult, but on average they are neither more nor less challenging than those children face during other periods of life.

Physical Development in Adolescence

Focusing Questions

- What is meant by *adolescence,* and how did it come to be recognized as a developmental stage?

- What changes in height, weight, and appearance can be expected during adolescence, and how do they differ for girls and boys?

- What is puberty, and what important physical changes occur for boys and girls during this process?

- What are the effects of early, "on-time," and late pubertal development, and how do the effects differ for girls and boys?

- What major health problems do adolescents face, and in what ways are adolescents more at risk than other age groups?

D illon is fourteen. Ever since last summer, he has started looking and acting different than before. He has grown nearly two inches in the last six months, a fact that his mother comments on with pride, but also with a note of dismay when his clothing no longer fits. Sometimes Dillon would prefer that no one notice the changes. He was well coordinated and athletic in school sports just a year or two ago, but now he feels clumsy, trips over himself, and bumps into things. He can't even count on his voice. Sometimes it sounds normal, and other times it sounds as deep as his father's; worst of all, it sometimes bounces out of control, cracking and breaking at embarrassing moments.

Yet physically, Dillon feels very optimistic. So far he has experienced no major illnesses, accidents, or violence; in fact, he secretly feels invulnerable to these mishaps, as if they could happen only to others, not to him. Feeling physically invulnerable allows him to be careless about his body in small but significant ways. He sometimes eats more "junk food" than he should, fails to brush his teeth, or goes a few days without enough sleep. Sometimes, especially when his parents aren't aware of it, he drives a car without wearing a seat belt, not realizing that driving is statistically the most dangerous current activity in his life. Eventually he may pay a price for these behaviors. But for now he has other things on his mind.

The Concept of Adolescence

Dillon is experiencing one version of **adolescence,** the period of development from about ages twelve to twenty that leads from childhood to adulthood. As you might imagine, Dillon's is not the only possible experience of adolescence; in this and the next two chapters, we will catch glimpses of other, very different experiences, as well as look at key programs of research meant to describe adolescence in general terms. As we will see, adolescents sometimes resemble children and at other times resemble young adults. For any one teenager, the particular mix of qualities and behaviors depends on the teenager's age and on the unique roles and responsibilities that he or she encounters.

Compared to adolescent roles and responsibilities in many other societies of the world, those in modern industrial societies are relatively unpredictable, and young people often feel ill prepared to meet them as a result. Most male teenage Australian aborigines, for example, go on a year-long walkabout through the desert, carrying only a few simple weapons for protection; their chances of survival are high, though, because they have spent much of childhood learning skills that help them to meet this challenge. Most adolescent girls in the hunting-and-gathering society of the Inuit of Alaska and Northern Canada have a good idea of what it takes to be an adult woman: they have already witnessed bearing of and caring for children, gathering and preparing food, and the like. But because of technology, urbanization, and other social changes, teenagers in modern North America often have little

adolescence The stage of development between childhood and adulthood, around ages twelve to twenty-two.

431

idea of what kind of work they will do as adults, what kind of family they will live in, or even where they will live.

In fact, some psychologists have proposed that adolescence be defined primarily as a time of transitions (Graber et al., 1996). Friendships for teenagers, for example, share qualities with friendships in childhood (friends *are* not yet a primary source of advice and support on the most important questions of life), but also some qualities with friendships in adulthood (friends are a source of support about many matters, such as clothing styles and assessments of mutual acquaintances). Thinking skills are in some ways childlike (the limits of thinking and reasoning are not yet noticed) and in other ways adultlike (much thinking can now be abstract). Physically, adolescents can sometimes look like children and sometimes like adults, and sometimes like a cross between the two; for confirmation, simply attend a social event at any junior high school.

Because viewing adolescence as a transition highlights the place of this period in human development as a whole, we will often use it to frame the discussion in this chapter. But sometimes we will also use two other widely held views of adolescence.

Adolescence: From Idea to Social Fact

Most of us take the idea of adolescence for granted, but in fact it is a relatively modern concept. Its discovery, or recognition, in technological societies was largely a response to the social changes that accompanied industrial development in the nineteenth century in Europe and the United States (see Chapter 1 for a discussion of this development).

In fact, some researchers have proposed that adolescence was defined as a separate stage of development primarily to prolong the years of childhood so that the aims of the new urban-industrial society that rapidly developed after the Civil War could be fulfilled (Bakan, 1975). According to this view, the spread of railroads and the telegraph, accompanied by a general shift in population from the country to the industrial cities and the addition of a huge number of immigrants, threatened the American way of life. Because so much was changing so fast, people felt a growing fear that society would get out of control—that the country would be overrun by foreigners and the crowded, dirty cities would breed crime and immorality. There were three major legal responses to this national "identity crisis": compulsory education, requiring children to attend school; child labor laws, regulating the age and hours children and adolescents could work; and special legal status and procedures for juveniles, including those who were "delinquent." Together these developments played a major role in making adolescence a social reality.

Theoretical Views of Adolescence

Since the "discovery" of adolescence in the United States, two somewhat conflicting views about its basic nature have emerged. One view sees adolescence is a time of "storm and stress," a period when major physical, intellectual, and emotional

Although some teenagers experience periods of turmoil during adolescence, for most, adolescence is neither more nor less difficult than earlier periods of life.

changes create tremendous upset and crisis within the individual and conflict between the person and society. As you may recall, Sigmund Freud believed development is full of conflict, especially in adolescence. Erik Erikson and others have suggested that a lack of stable and predictable role expectations due to rapid changes in society may make the transition from childhood to adulthood more difficult (Erikson, 1963, 1968; Elkind, 1994).

Freud/Erikson

The "storm and stress" view of adolescence is still a popular stereotype, reinforced by media reports of teenage drug use, school dropout, pregnancy, and crime, but most teens do not fit this image. Most do not abuse drugs, drop out of school, become pregnant, or engage in criminal activity. Most adolescents in the United States adapt to the changes in themselves quite well and adjust to the changing demands and expectations of parents and society in a relatively smooth and peaceful way. The same appears to be generally true in a number of other cultures, both Western and non-Western, where the majority of teenagers have been found to have positive self-images and good emotional adjustment (Arnett, 1999; Hurrelmann, 1994).

While adolescence is not an unusually problematic period for the great majority of youngsters, in the United States and Great Britain the onset of adolescence is associated with more frequent negative feelings among many teenagers and increased rates of behavioral and psychological problems for some (Brooks-Gunn & Warren, 1989; Hamburg, 1994; Larson & Ham, 1993). In certain ethnic groups, for example, between 15 and 20 percent of adolescents in the United States drop out of school before completing high school; adolescents have the highest arrest rate of any age group; and a large number of adolescents use alcohol and drugs on a regular basis (Eccles et al., 1993). How negative or positive the changes associated with adolescence are likely to be will depend on the degree of fit between adolescents' developing needs and the opportunities offered them by their social environments, school and home being two of the most important. And the increased stress some adolescents experience may not be due simply to the external environment but may also result from developmental changes in adolescents' subjective construction of their environments (Larson & Ham, 1993).

We discuss these and other social aspects of adolescence in greater detail in the next two chapters. First, let's look more closely at the physical changes of adolescence and their effects on development.

WHAT DO YOU THINK ?   In what ways has the "discovery" of adolescence as a developmental stage been helpful for teenagers and their families? In what ways has it been a problem? What has your personal experience with adolescence been?

Growth in Height and Weight

Although nearly everyone—including Dillon at the start of this chapter—experiences a rapid growth spurt during adolescence, the period includes less growth in height and weight *overall* but significantly *more* irregularity in the pattern and pace of growth. As Figure 14.1 shows, the average height for both boys and girls at twelve years is about fifty-nine or sixty inches. By age eighteen, the average height for boys is sixty-nine inches, whereas the average for girls is only sixty-four inches. These are big changes, but not as big as the ones during the six previous years.

Most of the impression of rapid change is due to a dramatic **growth spurt,** which is preceded and followed by years of comparatively little increase. The change in height is particularly striking, as Figure 14.2 shows. The maximum rate of growth occurs around age eleven or twelve for girls and about two years later for boys. In those years, many girls grow three inches in a single year and many boys grow more than four inches (Merenstein et al., 1997).

The reason for males' greater average height is that boys start their growth spurt two years later than girls do and thus undergo two additional years of childhood growing. The average girl is around fifty-four or fifty-five inches tall when she begins her growth spurt, whereas the average boy is fifty-nine or sixty inches tall when he begins his. Because both boys and girls add around nine or ten inches during adolescence and grow relatively little afterward, women end up being shorter than men on average.

Weight also increases during adolescence, as a result of both overall growth and the adolescent growth spurt in particular (see Figure 14.1). But weight is more strongly influenced than height by diet, exercise, and general lifestyle, and therefore changes in weight are less predictable from past size and growth patterns. What *is* relatively predictable, however, is the impact of diet, exercise, and lifestyle on a young person's future: more calories and less exercise contribute to heavier weight as an adult. Unfortunately, teenagers' social habits often contribute to the problem, because "junk food" and sedentary activities (like watching television) are both inexpensive and easily available, not to mention socially preferred, or "in."

• • •

growth spurt A rapid change in height and weight that occurs in puberty and is preceded and followed by years of comparatively little increase.

FIGURE 14.1

Growth in Height and Weight from Two to Eighteen Years

During adolescence, young people reach their final adult size. On average, young men end up significantly taller and heavier than young women, though of course many exceptions to this trend exist.

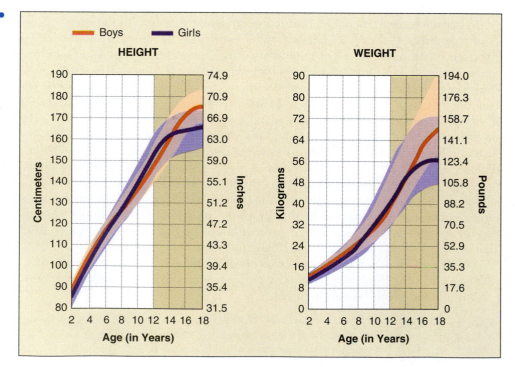

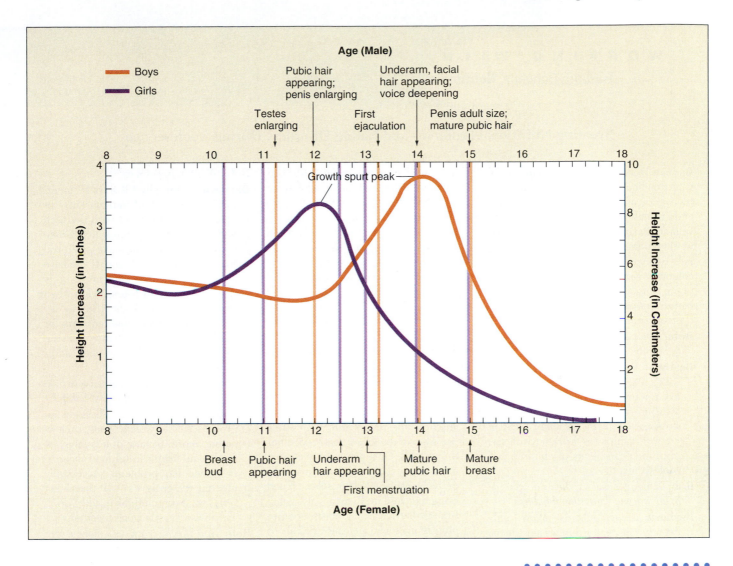

Age (Male)

Boys

Girls

Testes
enlarging

Pubic hair
appearing;
penis enlarging

First
ejaculation

Underarm, facial
hair appearing;
voice deepening

Penis adult size;
mature pubic hair

Growth spurt peak

Height Increase (in Inches)

Height Increase (in Centimeters)

Breast
bud

Pubic hair
appearing

Underarm
hair appearing

First menstruation

Mature
pubic hair

Mature
breast

Age (Female)

● ● ● ● ● ● ● ● ● ● ● ● ● ● ● ●

FIGURE 14.2

**Physical Development
During Adolescence**

Puberty involves a number of specific changes in both boys and girls, as this graph shows. One of the most obvious changes, the "growth spurt" or rate of increase in height, occurs significantly sooner in girls than in boys. But as with trends in final adult size, many individual exceptions exist.

These changes in weight tend to affect girls more than boys because of society's gender-role expectations. In general, girls are expected to look slender, while at the same time a bit curvaceous. Yet girls, not boys, are the ones who experience the greatest gains in body fat as a part of the adolescent growth spurt. During this period, total body fat for boys declines from an average of 18 or 19 percent to 11 percent of body weight, whereas for girls it increases from about 21 percent to around 26 or 27 percent (Sinclair, 1990). The average weight gain during the growth spurt is about thirty-eight pounds for girls and forty-two pounds for boys. These pounds are distributed differently among individuals, of course, but in general girls end up with more fat tissue than boys at the end of adolescence, a sex difference that continues into adulthood.

Whether male or female, most teenagers do not end up with the height, weight, or other physical characteristics that match either society's ideals or their own. Teenage boys may worry about not looking muscular or tall enough. But because of social pressures to "look good," girls will worry even more: at some time or other, most may feel they are too heavy, and many may worry about being too tall as well. The Perspectives box on page 456 describes how such concerns contribute to eating disorders in some young athletes; later in this chapter, we will discuss how chronic worries about physical appearance affect many adolescent girls. In the "Working With" interview, Barbara Donohue, nutritionist, discusses her work with adolescents who have eating problems.

WORKING WITH
Barbara Donohue, **Nutritionist**

Treating Nutritional Problems and Eating Disorders During Adolescence

Barbara Donohue is a nutritionist in private practice. She works with children, teenagers, and adults, both individually and in small groups, and is a school consultant. Barbara was interviewed in the waiting room of her office. Her interest in kids is revealed by the books, toys, and computer games and the informal atmosphere. Our discussion focused on Barbara's approach to helping adolescents overcome eating disorders.

Rob: *What kind of training is required to become a nutritionist?*

Barbara: You need four years of college, with a major in nutrition and food service. You then do an eighteen-month internship, after which you must pass certification exams. A major focus of my internship was working with the nutritional problems of children and adolescents.

Rob: *What general problems do you see in adolescents' nutritional habits?*

Barbara: Since schools allow only twenty minutes for lunch, most teens skip lunch or eat very little so they have more time to socialize with their friends. More and more adolescent girls are cutting back on protein intake and eating just vegetables and fruits to lose weight and be thin enough to feel they will be accepted. This pressure to diet causes many overweight teens to eat a lot of high-fat foods secretively. Sometimes it's only when parents find candy and other food wrappers that they discover why their child is overweight.

Rob: *How are teenagers referred to your practice for help?*

Barbara: Sometimes they're referred at their own request. An overweight youngster who's experiencing problems at school may finally bring it up with a parent, and then they decide together to get help. Or a parent may contact me and say, "My child has a weight problem; can you help us solve it?" and bring the child in. Referrals also come from pediatricians, therapists, or other professionals who are concerned about a child's nutrition and weight.

Rob: *What happens next?*

Barbara: Generally I'll start by meeting with the child and parents together. Then I'll meet with the teen and the parents separately to evaluate whether I'll need to make a referral for psychological help too. If you have a teen who's emaciated or severely obese, and nobody listens to her when she's talking—or if she tries to say something and someone answers for her—there's a good chance that the teen or the family may need additional help.

Rob: *What techniques do you use to help teens change their nutritional habits?*

Barbara: Usually I use a behavioral approach. We set weekly goals, such as eating more fruit and less high-fat foods, and keep careful food records. If a teen has problems successfully meeting the goals, I say, "If that didn't work, what do you think *would* work?" Then we revise the goals together.

Rob: *How do you work with more severe problems such as anorexia?*

The Secular Trend

The **secular trend** refers to the tendency of succeeding generations to achieve physical maturation at an earlier age and to end up heavier and taller than their parents. These generational differences include body weight, height, body build, body fat, strength, age of growth spurt onset, and age of menarche (first menstrual period). For example, today's boys generally reach their full height between ages eighteen and twenty and girls between thirteen and fourteen, whereas in 1880 the average male did not reach full height until between ages twenty-three and twenty-five and the average female between nineteen and twenty (Tanner, 1998).

Perhaps even more significant, the average age at which girls have their first menstrual period has dropped from between fifteen and seventeen a hundred years ago to between twelve and fourteen today in both the United States and Western Europe. This is of considerable concern, since no evidence exists that earlier onset of puberty is accompanied by earlier gains in social and emotional development that would equip children to successfully manage their sexuality. Also, the first ovulation can occur before the first menstrual period, and some girls as young as eight years (third grade) are becoming fertile. The secular trend also helps to explain why adolescence in industrial societies occurs over a longer period of time than in less developed countries, where puberty may begin much closer to the beginning of adulthood.

secular trend (1) In general, any long-term historical trend. (2) In human development, the tendency of each new generation in industrialized countries to grow larger and heavier and to experience puberty earlier than their parents did.

Barbara: For starters, I'll take a thorough medical and social history. For example, I might find out that my client's compulsion to avoid eating fat started after her aunt died of heart disease; the disorder was an attempt to protect herself from dying. My job is to help teenagers learn about good nutrition and how to be more flexible about their eating. I'll often use issues the teen raises as support. For example, I might tell this girl that vitamin E may help prevent heart disease, that fats contain vitamins A, D, E, and K, and that some fats are necessary for a healthy diet.

Rob: *Are the issues always so straightforward?*

Barbara: Well, no. I saw one fourteen-year-old girl who refused to get psychological help. My work focused on helping her increase her food intake enough so that she could think more clearly and come to see that food was not the main issue. I helped her realize that her confused thinking and mood swings were related to her starvation diet and that her constant obsession with food made it difficult to think about anything else. I asked her, "How often during the day do you think about food?" "All the time," she said. "Well, that's because you're starving. If you can eat just a little more, that will help."

Rob: *This must be difficult, given how afraid anorectics are of gaining weight.*

Barbara: My approach is to help them to eat just a little more each time and understand what is actually happening if the scale moves. For a starving person, a small increase in food intake may cause a temporary weight gain of three or four pounds due to fluid shifting. They take one look and can't eat again. So I have to help them understand that this doesn't reflect a real weight gain. The anorectic teen may have a hard time accepting that, so to help I'll say something like "Let's figure out what you ate and how much of the weight gain could be due to your additional food intake and how much to fluid retention." Careful food records and clear, logical explanations are both important here.

Rob: *This must be a very slow process.*

Barbara: Usually the best you can count on is an average gain of about four ounces per week, with many ups and downs. Anorectics aren't really safe until fats are part of their regular diet and they're comfortable with it. Generally it's a two-to-three-year process to get back to a healthy weight and develop a healthy approach to food that they can rely on.

What Do You Think?

1. In what ways do Barbara Donohue's observations of adolescents' eating behaviors coincide with your own behaviors or observations?

2. What other concepts from behavioral theory discussed in Chapter 2 may be useful in understanding Barbara's approach?

How can the secular trend be explained? Improvements in health care, diet, and overall living conditions are thought to be the major reasons for earlier maturation. Because the onset of puberty usually depends on reaching a certain body weight, improvements in diet have led to achievement of that weight at earlier ages than in previous generations. In addition, early childhood diseases that limit growth have been largely eliminated, and nutrition and medical care have greatly improved for children in developed countries. We can expect that a similar trend will occur

The considerable growth in height and weight during adolescence is generally accompanied by significant increases in the amount of food that is consumed.

A TALK WITH

Jason, Age Fourteen

Physical Development at Age Fourteen

Jason agreed to be interviewed if I would give him a ride to soccer practice afterward. The interview was conducted in the kitchen of his home over an after-school snack.

Interviewer: *What physical changes have you noticed in kids your age?*

Jason: When we were in fifth grade, all the guys were taller than the girls, or at least the same height. And then, in sixth grade, the girls shot up and all got much taller than us.

Interviewer: *How did that feel?*

Jason: We didn't grow in seventh grade. We had sex education, so we started to understand it. So in sixth grade, seventh, and part of eighth grade, all the guys were much less developed than the girls and much less tall and less heavy and everything. And then the later part of eighth grade we all shot up.

Interviewer: *I noticed. How tall are you now?*

Jason: Five-eleven.

Interviewer: *Almost as tall as me.*

Jason: We all shot up. I'm as tall as my older brother.

Interviewer: *Are there other differences besides height that you've noticed in kids your age?*

Jason: Weight, for example, because some people were heavy before. The weight was not really part of them. It was excess. Now people have become heavier but more solid. I'm gaining weight, not a lot of weight. I've gained weight and it's in my bones, in my muscle, and in my skin and just a little bit of fat. I'm gaining it all over as opposed to gaining it in just fat. I'm gaining it in muscle.

I think that as you get older, guys become less ashamed of their bodies and more likely to expose them. Not necessarily all the way, but just to take off your shirt. It's easier for them to do that because now they're bigger . . . now they feel that they can expose their chest and they don't have to be embarrassed about it.

Interviewer: *Have you noticed differences in how rapidly people develop?*

Jason: Different parts of people develop at different times. Some people stay shorter but get a full beard sooner. But they're not gonna shoot up as far. And some people shoot up and grow a beard at about the same time, but people in all four years of high school are getting interested in shaving and stuff like that. And usually it would seem ridiculous to an outsider to shave the little hair that you grow on your mustache, but it's a big thing to someone to have to shave, or at this age it's important to look the best you can even if it's just a few hairs to get off.

Interviewer: *How do kids your age deal with staying healthy?*

Jason: They know what is healthy, but they don't necessarily follow what is always healthy.

Interviewer: *Why do you think that is?*

Jason: 'Cause, you know, there's the simple fact that junk food tastes good. And the other thing is that it is overemphasized that kids shouldn't eat that much junk food. I don't eat that much junk food. I eat a little bit, but I also eat really good food, too. I eat plenty of it to survive. So anything above that really doesn't matter.

Interviewer: *Do you think that most kids basically eat a good diet and that junk food is on top of it?*

Jason: A lot of girls don't need to eat as much, because they have stopped growing. But they still need to eat more than they do eat. They starve themselves to a certain extent when they are hungry because they think, "Oh, God, I have to lose weight!" I think it's just a fad just to be able to say it. It makes people feel better about themselves to say, "I'm fat, look at me, I'm fat," because they really want other people to say, "No, you're not." I think a lot of girls in the teenage years eat a crummy breakfast and then don't eat lunch and then go all day without eating. They eat at night. And then they go to sleep. Which is the wrong method. If you're only going to eat one meal a day, you should eat breakfast.

Interviewer: *Why is that?*

Jason: Because you need the nutrition more during the day when you are active. At night you don't really need that much.

What Do You Think?

1. How does Jason feel about the effects of physical maturation? How consistent are his views with those presented in the chapter?

2. What nutritional problems might be related to the eating habits of Jason's peers?

3. How typical of adolescents his age are Jason's views about health?

---

wherever adequate nutrition and living conditions are available to all children and their families (Malina, 1990).

WHAT DO YOU THINK ? What pattern (timing, rate) did changes in your own height and weight follow during adolescence? What do you remember thinking and feeling about those changes?

Puberty

Puberty is a set of physical changes that marks the completion of sexual development, or reproductive maturity. The changes that contribute directly to making sexual reproduction possible are called **primary sex characteristics.** Other changes, which are simply correlated or associated with the primary changes, are called **secondary sex characteristics.**

Primary sex characteristics make sexual reproduction possible. For girls, these include complex changes in the vagina, uterus, fallopian tubes, and ovaries; the most obvious sign of these changes is the beginning of menstrual periods. For boys, changes in primary sex characteristics include development of the penis, scrotum, testes, prostate gland, and seminal vesicles, which lead to the production of enough sperm to enable successful reproduction. Secondary sex characteristics include enlargement of the breasts, growth of body hair, and deepening of the voice. Associated with these developments are important changes in the levels of hormones present in the bloodstream. These powerful chemicals play a major part in initiating and regulating all of the changes associated with puberty.

The Development of Primary Sex Characteristics

For boys, the most significant sign of sexual maturation is rapid growth of the penis and scrotum (the sack of skin underneath the penis that contains the testicles), which begins at around age twelve and continues for about five years for the penis and seven years for the scrotum (Kagan, 1998). The penis typically doubles or triples in length, so locker room comparisons are almost inevitable as boys become increasingly aware of obvious changes in themselves and their friends. Although penis size has almost nothing to do with eventual success at overall sexual functioning, for adolescent boys it sometimes seems to be an all-important sign of their new status as men (Malina, 1990; Merenstein et al., 1997).

During adolescence, enough live sperm are produced in the testes to make reproduction a real possibility for the first time. Sometime around age twelve, boys are likely to experience their first ejaculation of **semen,** a sticky fluid produced by the prostate gland, which is located near the penis just inside the body cavity. Semen carries the sperm to the penis and provides it with a medium in which to live after ejaculation. Most boys have their first ejaculation during masturbation; as **nocturnal emissions,** or "wet dreams," during sleep; or, less frequently, as emissions that occur spontaneously upon waking. Most males report experiencing nocturnal emissions about one or two years before puberty; the accompanying dreams are frequently but not always erotic in nature. The sexual changes just discussed and the unexpected erections and uncomfortable sexual fantasies and sensations that boys sometimes experience are common sources of embarrassment. Less frequently, they are a source of more serious discomfort and conflict.

For girls, the appearance of the first menstrual period, called **menarche,** signals sexual maturity. In most societies, menarche also symbolizes the shift from girlhood to womanhood. Nevertheless, menarche occurs rather late in a girl's sexual maturation and is preceded by a number of other changes, including enlargement of the breasts, the appearance of pubic hair, and broadening of the hips and shoulders. Next, as the growth spurt peaks, the uterus, vagina, labia, and clitoris develop, as do the ovaries.

Adequate information about menstruation, including practical details about the purchase and use of sanitary napkins and tampons, personal hygiene, and birth control, is important. The same holds for knowledge about *dysmenorrhea* (menstrual cramps) and *premenstrual syndrome (PMS)*, a pattern of behavioral, emotional, and physical symptoms that may occur approximately a week before menstruation

• • •

primary sex characteristics Characteristics that make sexual reproduction possible. For girls, consist of the vagina, uterus, fallopian tubes, and ovaries; for boys, consist of the penis, scrotum, testes, prostate gland, and seminal vesicles.

secondary sex characteristics Sex characteristics other than the sex organs, such as extra layers of fat and pubic hair.

semen A sticky fluid produced by the prostate gland; carries sperm to the penis and provides it with a medium in which to live after ejaculation.

nocturnal emission Ejaculation of semen during sleep.

menarche The first menstrual period.

For girls, breast development is one of the major occurrences of puberty, and getting a first bra can be an important event. Likewise, the growth of facial hair—and thus the need to shave—is a significant milestone for adolescent boys.

(Wilson & Keye, 1989). In addition, contact with women who have positive feelings about their monthly cycles will help make menarche a positive experience and allay fears and negative attitudes about it (Brooks-Gunn & Warren, 1989). As we will see, the same informative and supportive climate can also help girls deal with the other physical changes of puberty. Later in this chapter, we will look at the various psychological effects of physical growth in adolescence.

The Development of Secondary Sex Characteristics

Both boys and girls experience a number of physical changes that create secondary sex characteristics, notably in their breasts, body hair, and voices. These changes do not directly contribute to their physical ability to reproduce, but they do make the two sexes look more adultlike and more stereotypically masculine or feminine.

Breasts   Girls first develop breast "buds," or slightly raised nipples, at the beginning of puberty. During the following several years, the nipples grow darker, the areolas (the pigmented areas surrounding the nipples) increase in size, and the breasts continue to grow until they reach their full size. Given the attention our culture devotes to breasts, it is not surprising that breast development is a potential source of concern for many adolescent girls. Breasts that are "too big," "too small," or the "wrong" shape may cause embarrassment, and in some cases girls experience outright harassment due to these physical developments.

Boys too undergo a small amount of breast development, and their areolas become larger and darker much as they do in girls. A few boys experience enough tissue growth to cause them some embarrassment, but these "breasts" usually return to typical male size in a year or two.

Body Hair   When their genital development is relatively advanced, both boys and girls acquire more body hair, although boys generally grow more of it than girls do. The first growth is simply a fine fuzz around the genitals called *pubic hair*, which then darkens and becomes coarser. At the same time, underarm or *axillary hair* begins to appear; this eventually becomes dark and coarse as well.

Although considerable differences exist among individuals, in girls pubic hair and axillary hair begin to appear around age eleven and are fully grown by about age fourteen; in boys they begin around age twelve and continue until about age eighteen. At age fifteen or so, many boys begin growing facial hair, which usually appears first as a mere suggestion of a mustache that begins on the outer corners of the lips and gradually grows inward toward the nose. For both girls and boys, however, there are inherited ethnic and individual differences in the amount of facial and body hair that develops. For example, some boys have little or no facial hair, or hair growth is limited to their upper lips or chins. Eventually boys may grow real whiskers on the chin and cheeks, as well as hair on the chest and back, although these later developments usually do not become obvious until around age seventeen or older (Tanner, 1990). Cultural attitudes and expectations influence women's feelings about axillary hair during puberty. For example, whereas many women in our culture spend considerable time and money to rid themselves of "unsightly" underarm, leg, and facial hair, women in a number of European countries believe this hair is attractive and do not attempt to remove it.

Voice   In both sexes, the voice deepens near the end of puberty and becomes richer in overtones so that it sounds less like a flute or whistle and more like a violin or clarinet. These changes make the adolescent's voice sound more truly adult, but the fluctuations in voice qualities that some adolescents experience can be a cause of considerable (although usually temporary) embarrassment.

Hormonal Changes: Physical and Social Consequences

For both boys and girls, the onset of puberty brings increases in the levels of all sex hormones in the blood, but the pattern by which it does so differs for each sex. **Testosterone** (also called *male sex hormone*), a particular type of androgen, and **estrogen** (or *female sex hormone*) are two of the most important sex hormones. Although both hormones are present in males and females, the high concentration of testosterone in boys stimulates the growth of the penis and related male reproductive organs, and the high concentration of estrogen in girls stimulates the growth of the ovaries and vagina. Androgens are thought to influence the strength of the sex drive in both sexes.

Hormones affect more than just sexual characteristics. For example, they are responsible for the typical differences between girls' and boys' overall body builds. In general, the sex that has shorter bones and more rounded curves (female) also has higher estrogen levels, and the sex that has longer bones and larger muscles (male) also has higher levels of testosterone (Tanner, 1990).

Testosterone stimulates muscle and bone growth in both sexes. Throughout childhood, boys and girls are about equally muscular. They have roughly the same number and sizes of muscle fibers, and they can exert about the same amount of strength with their muscles. Although individual children vary around the averages, as groups the two sexes differ very little (Malina, 1990).

Puberty changes this equality to some extent, at least when the sexes are compared on average. The average boy becomes more muscular compared to the average girl, even though girls also tend to become more muscular compared to their childhood selves. From early childhood to adolescence, boys experience close to a fourteenfold increase in the size of the largest muscles in their bodies (for example, in their thighs), but girls experience only a tenfold increase (Froberg & Lammert, 1996; Malina, 1990). Since these changes are only averages, many adolescent girls are actually stronger than some boys.

Individual differences in muscularity probably result in part from differences in life experiences that either promote or interfere with muscular growth. Some of the differences in experiences are linked to society's gender-role expectations. In particular, teenage boys more often receive encouragement (or even pressure) to participate in sports and to take on jobs and responsibilities that involve physical work (Coakley, 1996). The higher level of activity leads to greater bone and muscle mass

testosterone A sex hormone; sometimes called the *male sex hormone* because its high concentration in boys stimulates the growth of the penis and related male reproductive organs.

estrogen A sex hormone, sometimes called the *female sex hormone* because its high concentration in girls stimulates the growth of the ovaries and vagina during puberty.

as boys mature and become adults. In recent years, some girls have received encouragement and support for being active, though for girls in general it has been less intense and less widespread.

In spite of these social effects, a lot of the physical differences between the sexes result from genetically programmed development. Genetically triggered changes in estrogen levels during adolescence, for example, lead to increases in the fat deposited under the skin, as well as final maturation of bones. The higher concentration of estrogen in girls, combined with the higher concentration of testosterone in boys mentioned earlier, means that girls end up with more fat tissue than boys as a proportion of their body weight and boys end up with more muscle tissue than girls. Hence the tendency toward conventional sex differences in physical appearance: boys look more muscular and girls have more curves (Kagan, 1998)—though these are only average trends.

WHAT DO YOU THINK ?   Talk with one or two classmates about how the timing of their own maturation affected their adolescence. Did it fit any of the patterns described here, or did it show variability? On balance, what implications do you see for teachers and parents given that puberty creates patterns and variability at the same time?

Psychological Effects of Physical Growth in Adolescence

Given how rapid the physical changes of puberty are, it is not surprising that adolescents often are preoccupied—and dissatisfied—with how they look. When dissatisfaction occurs, it is most noticeable early in adolescence, but it is also common during the later teen years (Connolly et al., 1996; Fox, 1997). It would seem, then, that a milestone as important as puberty should affect individuals deeply, perhaps leading to long-term effects that last even into adulthood. Psychologists therefore have searched for predictable psychological effects of physical growth, both short term and long term; however, the results of this research have not been fully conclusive.

Timing of Puberty

During the 1980s, a series of longitudinal studies explored the impact of the timing of puberty on individuals' well-being (Livson & Peskin, 1981a, 1981b; Tobin-Richards et al., 1983). Was it better to experience puberty earlier than usual, or later, or "on time"? And did these timings have a different effect depending on whether you were a boy or a girl? Because these studies were longitudinal—teenagers were followed for several years, and eventually even for several decades—they were especially helpful in determining the effects of timing. This research suggested intriguing trends in the effects of timing and gender, as summarized in Table 14.1. The trends

For adolescents who begin puberty early, initial reactions among males tend to be positive and later reactions are negative, while the reverse is true for females. Late-maturing males first react negatively and later react positively. Late-maturing females first react positively, and later reactions are mixed. These trends, however, conceal variability among individuals.

TABLE 14.1   Trends in Adolescents' Reactions to the Onset of Puberty

Time of Onset	Time of Reaction	Reaction of Male	Reaction of Female
Early	Initial	Positive	Negative
	Later	Mixed	Positive
Late	Initial	Negative	Positive
	Later	Positive	Mixed

themselves, however, also masked important individual differences in responses to puberty, which more recent research has highlighted.

What did the original longitudinal research find? First, it suggested that *early-maturing boys* seemed to experience initial advantages as teenagers. They enjoyed a head start on muscle growth compared to their peers, a change that apparently stimulated peers, teachers, and others to treat them like adults sooner. The boys responded positively to this treatment and, through a sort of self-fullfilling prophecy, actually became more confident and mature in their behavior. By the same token, though, they were more conforming to adult standards than usual for adolescents and less open to the minor risk taking characteristic of adolescents as a group (Lighfoot, 1997). These differences continued into young adulthood: a decade after puberty, early-maturing men were still more responsible and self controlled, but also more rigid in relating to peers. Most important, though, was a lowering of their self-esteem; as later-maturing boys caught up with them physically, the early-maturing boys received less attention and respect from others, and experienced a loss of self-esteem.

Late-maturing boys, on the other hand, still resembled children as late as age sixteen, and tended to be judged as children as a result. Teachers and parents rated these individuals as impulsive, immature, and lacking self-confidence. Their ratings may have been partly stereotypes based on how the boys looked, but partly also based on accurate observations. The late-maturing boys generally had less access to key social activities, such as sports and sports-focused social activities, and therefore had fewer opportunities to learn social skills. The good news, however, was that these boys tended to feel less pressure to become socially or sexually active. Perhaps as a result, they feel better about themselves as young adults than did the early maturers.

What about girls? *Early-maturing girls* did not experience early timing as an advantage as boys did. Their early physical change put them out of step with gender-role expectations for girls. Because they now looked like sexual beings, parents and teachers worried about their behavior; and because they were relatively short when they acquired normal female fat tissue and "curves," they tended to look plumper than average. Both changes tended to create stress for early-maturing girls. Yet the effect did not last into adulthood: at age thirty, the early maturers reported feeling *more* poised and self-directed than usual, perhaps *because* of experiencing and surviving social disapproval as teenagers.

Late-maturing girls experienced a complementary trend. As teenagers, they were rated by parents and teachers as more attractive and as better social leaders. In fact, the girls actually did become school leaders more often than usual. By age thirty, though, they reported feeling *less* poised than early maturers, and less sure of where their lives were heading.

Nonnormative Effects of Puberty   Although the trends regarding the timing of puberty are intriguing, they also mask variability in teenagers' experiences. Newer research about the psychological impact of puberty has highlighted this fact, and has been more cautious in generalizing about both the short- and the long-term effects of timing. In reviewing studies about this question, the psychologist Sucheta Connolly and her colleagues concluded that puberty has little lasting psychological impact on adolescents (Connolly et al., 1996). In the short term, while these physical changes are actually occurring, family relationships tend to be more stressful: both children and their parents worry about the significance of the changes and feel unsure about whether to welcome them. In the long-term—meaning later in adolescence and during young adulthood—family relationships return to whatever quality they had before puberty, whether happy, conflict ridden, or mixed. Other social and emotional effects, such as changes in self-esteem or in peer relationships, are much more variable than similar, both in the short term and in the long term.

A Multicultural View ······················

How Do Ethnic Differences in Physical Appearance Affect Social Development During Adolescence?

Physical appearance plays a very important role in adolescent development, especially during the junior and senior high school years, when attitudes about physical differences can significantly affect social acceptance and popularity. How ethnic differences in physical appearance affect social development was one of the questions addressed by Jeannie Kang in her recent study of identity development in eighteen Korean-American female college students, ages eighteen to twenty-one, from a variety of regional backgrounds (Kang, 1990).

For the majority of these young women, junior high was the hardest and most confusing time. They reported being very concerned with how they looked and whether they could fit in, but having little awareness or understanding of conflicts regarding their ethnic identity during that period. Very few remembered feeling socially successful or accepted as part of the "popular crowd" during their high school years. For many, it was not until they were sophomores or juniors in college that they experienced mainstream social acceptance and more fully explored the meaning of bicultural identity.

Regional differences played an important role in how differences in physical appearance affected their social and emotional experiences. For girls who grew up as part of a small and isolated ethnic minority in all-white communities in the Midwest, the "blue-eyed, blond hair, cheerleader" type was the sole standard of beauty and popularity—a standard they could never hope to achieve. Girls from these communities were more likely to feel ostracized and less likely to succeed in their social adjustment during their high school years than girls who grew up in more heterogeneous communities that provided alternative models of beauty and popularity and greater social acceptance of ethnic differences.

The majority of these young women reported withdrawing from the coed social scene during high school. During this period, they rechanneled their energies into other activities. Academic achievement, extracurricular activities, work, and friendships rather than group social life became their major sources of self-esteem. Even so, many found that ethnic differences were still important because their choices of activities reinforced the stereotypic notion that Korean Americans (and other Asian Americans) are "naturally" adept in math, science, and music.

These women also experienced considerable conflict between the cultural values, traditions, and expectations of their immigrant parents (who spoke little English) and those of mainstream American culture as represented by schools, peer groups, and the media. This conflict of cultures was particularly difficult for many of the girls, whose limited knowledge of Korean language and traditions made it difficult to communicate with their parents and other relatives.

As older adolescents move into adulthood, furthermore, the effects of puberty become even more obscure and harder to generalize about. For example, in a longitudinal study based on interviews of women from college age through midlife, the psychologist Ruthellen Josselson found that self-esteem and attitudes about self commonly changed markedly—either for good or for ill—regardless of what they were initially (Josselson, 1996).

Body Image and Self-esteem

For many adolescents, and especially for females, judgments about their physical appearance may be the most important factor in their self-esteem (Harter, 1990b). Even the most attractive teenager worries about her hair, her nose, or a pimple on her chin. What determines how much discomfort a particular adolescent feels about her own body?

For one thing, conventional standards of attractiveness have considerable influence. In our culture, people of all ages find certain body builds more attractive than others. Although individuals obviously differ, most children and adolescents clearly consider the muscular, athletic body type most attractive for males and a more slen-

Even something as simple as getting a suntan, a major leisure time activity for many American adolescents, proved a source of cultural conflict. A beautiful, golden tan has long been highly valued in mainstream American culture, but most Korean American parents forbid tanning because in Korea being tan is associated with being uneducated and lower class. In fact, one of the most rebellious things a Korean girl can do is get a really deep tan.

Most of the women said that they did not really begin to come to terms with the meanings of these ethnic differences until their college years. Often it was not until their second or third year of college that they were able to more actively explore personal issues of bicultural identity and acceptance (or lack of it) by both minority and mainstream cultures. College was the first time many of these women found themselves with a sizable peer group of Korean Americans among whom they could explore issues of identity and cultural difference.

The task of forging a coherent bicultural identity out of these two conflicting cultural experiences was a challenging one that potentially influenced every aspect of a Korean American adolescent's experience. Even during the college years, physical difference remained a metaphor for the women's efforts to achieve a comfortable resolution of the dilemma of bicultural identity. Several girls recalled how they were reminded of this by being called a "banana" and a "twinkie," derogatory terms occasionally used by Korean Americans to criticize a person who they believe has embraced a mainstream, white American identity to the exclusion of her or his identity as a Korean.

Not surprisingly, a review of research on body image and eating disorders among Asian and Asian American women by Christine Iijima Hall (1995) found that many of these women judged their own attractiveness by the media image that portrayed the "perfect" woman as tall, blonde, buxom, thin, and with Northern European skin color, hair, eyes, nose, mouth, and other facial features. The influence of such standards has led to increased dissatisfaction with body image and lowered self-esteem, and increased use of cosmetic surgery, chemical processing of hair, and intensive use of cosmetics to more closely approximate the Northern European ideal. These standards have also increased the pursuit of thinness and unrealistic estimates of personal body weight, both of which are associated with eating disorders, a topic discussed later in this chapter.

By the end of this decade, the majority of children and adolescents in the United States will be from non-European backgrounds (Carnegie Council on Adolescent Development, 1992). Hopefully this increasing cultural pluralism will bring greater acceptance of multiple standards of beauty and of bicultural identity among Koreans as well as other Asian and non-Asian cultural groups.

der body type most attractive for females, and view a rounder, more padded body type as less than ideal for either. However, the majority of males and females do not have body types that fit these ideals, and many are concerned that they are too fat, especially girls. An adolescent girl's body is becoming rounder and fuller due to the normal increases in fat associated with puberty; yet our society holds a standard of slenderness for female beauty and still values physical attractiveness as a woman's most important asset (Koff & Benavage, 1998; Rierdon & Koff, 1997).

Adolescents evaluate themselves and their peers according to such stereotypes. Conventionally attractive youngsters may develop greater self-esteem than others because of the appreciation they receive. Under the wrong conditions, however, a youngster who receives approval for something that is a result of genetic chance may come to believe he is not appreciated for other important qualities and cannot influence the opinions of his friends by his conduct. On the other hand, teenagers who are physically "unattractive" may compensate by developing other desirable qualities, such as being energetic and outgoing, having a good sense of humor, and being a good listener.

Social contexts such as family, school, and community also can play a role. For example, a study of pubertal girls and boys from two different communities found that girls from one community were less satisfied with their bodies and weight than

For these girls, participating in after-school activities such as soccer can make an important contribution to a comfortable body image and sense of self-esteem.

girls from the other community. Greater involvement and satisfaction in after-school activities, including sports, and more positive perceptions of their school environments were related to higher satisfaction with body weight and appearance.

As we have noted, perceptions about attractiveness are strongly influenced by the existing cultural stereotypes for feminine and masculine beauty. (See the Multicultural View box on p. 444 for a discussion of the effects of ethnic differences in physical appearance on adolescents' social development.) Role models from fashion magazines, movies, and television help to create and cultivate these stereotypes. Although there may be more than one "ideal" type for men and women—which may reflect trends such as our society's growing appreciation for physical fitness—only a very small percentage of teenagers have bodies that come even reasonably close. In recent years, for example, the benchmark of feminine beauty has been the "prepubertal look": lean, long-legged, and lithe. But puberty and the associated increases in fat deposits and redistribution of fat make this ideal impossible to maintain for the majority of girls (Abell & Richards, 1996).

One consequence is that successive generations of teenagers have attempted to modify their bodies to fit the prevailing ideals, sometimes with tragic results. Obsessive concern with being slender has led many teenage girls to adopt diets that are seriously deficient in nutrition (Fowler, 1989). Anorexia nervosa and bulimia are eating disorders that involve distorted relationships between eating and body image; they appear to be connected, at least in part, to cultural stereotypes. We discuss these conditions more fully later in this chapter and in the Perspectives box on page 456.

Compulsive efforts to increase muscle mass may combine body building, unsafe dieting, and use of steroids and other drugs. Such a regimen poses serious health hazards to an increasing number of male and, more recently, female athletes. Steroids have been banned in most athletic programs because they have been shown to cause liver damage, testicular shrinkage, increased cholesterol levels, and elevated blood pressure. Use of steroids has also been linked to emotional problems, including depressive and psychotic symptoms (Pope & Katz, 1994).

Adolescents who have atypical physical characteristics because of inherited or acquired abnormalities sometimes face more serious psychological problems regarding their bodies. For example, children who are badly scarred or whose movements are spasmodic must learn to cope with these added burdens. As suggested by the film *Mask*, which portrays an adolescent whose face and head are grossly disfigured, strong, loving, support from parents and friends can help a child with a disability to feel good about himself and his body. Although physical appearance certainly is important, beauty and positive self-concept really *are* more than skin deep.

WHAT DO YOU THINK?   In what ways does the discussion of body image and self-esteem fit your own understanding and experience? In what ways does it differ?

Health in Adolescence

In some ways, adolescents are among the healthiest of all people. They tend to have fewer colds and ear infections than young children or adults do. And compared with adults, they suffer fewer of the illnesses and physical damage associated with prolonged exposure to physical and emotional stress and with aging.

Nevertheless, adolescents actually experience certain health risks more than either younger children or adults do. Compared to either age group, they are much more likely to be injured in motor vehicle accidents, misuse alcohol and other substances, experience unwanted pregnancy, have unhealthy diets and have inadequate health and mental health care (Balk & Corn, 1996).

These statistical realities may contribute to teenagers' common dismissal of risky behavior in themselves and to a belief in their personal invulnerability. Since death and serious disability usually originate from unusual or "untimely" events, some adolescents are tempted to think death and disability happen only to others and cannot happen to themselves. Ironically, therefore, accidents, drug abuse, and pregnancy can seem less risky—at least to some teenagers—than they really are.

Continuity with Health in Childhood

The health and health care patterns of most children show considerable consistency and continuity from early childhood through adolescence. This is true of common, recurring illnesses, patterns of use of medical services, and children's overall levels of health as judged by doctors and other health care professionals. Children who visit the doctor frequently when young continue to do so as adolescents, whereas those who visit less frequently early in life tend to maintain this pattern (Takanishi & Hamburg, 1997).

Factors such as socioeconomic status and the quality and accessibility of services play a major role in adolescent patterns of use (and underuse) of health and mental health services and health-related behaviors (Hamburg, 1994). Because health care and health insurance are extremely expensive, many families cannot afford to pay for care that adequately meets their needs. If such families receive inferior medical care and are treated in belittling ways (as is often the case), their children are more likely to develop negative attitudes toward doctors and hospitals. In contrast, children and adolescents from families whose financial resources allow them more regular and positive contacts with the health care system are likely to have more favorable attitudes and better health habits, and these continue into adulthood.

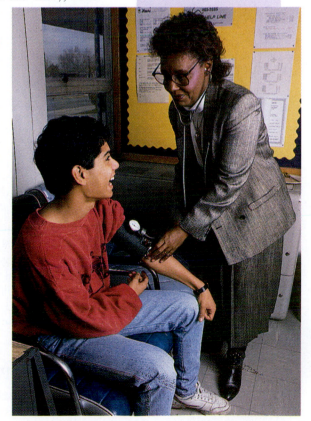

School-based health care programs that are responsive to the special needs and vulnerabilities of adolescents can make an important contribution to helping teenagers to take responsibility for their own health care.

Inadequate understanding of the relationship between their behavior and their health may also affect how much responsibility adolescents assume for their own health. As noted in Chapter 11, not until adolescence are children able to understand health in terms of multiple causes and cures and to realize that interrelationships among thoughts, feelings, and changes in physical health are important (Hergenrather & Rabinowitz, 1991; Millstein, 1989; Sigelman et al., 1993). But although adolescents may be similar to their parents in their estimates of risks to their health and in their cognitive decision-making processes regarding health care, they (and their parents) still frequently display significant gaps in their knowledge about what does and does not cause illness and how to safeguard their health (Quadrel et al., 1993).

For many teenagers, health care that is affordable, accessible, and responsive to their particular developmental needs and level of understanding appears to be the most important factor in determining whether they receive adequate care. Consider Genelle, a teenager from a poor family who recently discovered she was pregnant. It is very likely that her family's lack of health insurance and a regular doctor, along with the difficult psychological issues

Danger and opportunity. Automobiles give teenagers a great deal of independence. But they also have drawbacks: auto collisions are the leading cause of death in adolescence.

involved, will substantially reduce her chances of seeking or receiving adequate prenatal care. There is growing evidence, however, that under the right circumstances, adolescents (and even younger children) from a broad range of backgrounds can become very competent managers of their own health. Programs to encourage self-care have had significant success, especially when they are based in junior and senior high schools and offer comprehensive health care and family planning to teenagers. The success of such programs is due not only to the quality and appropriateness of the health services provided but also to their accessibility, assurances of confidentiality, and the reduction or elimination of financial barriers (Hamburg, 1994; Takanishi & Hamburg, 1997).

Causes of Death Among Adolescents

Although adolescents are less affected by the health problems that lead to death in younger children and adults, the death rate during adolescence is one of the highest for all age groups. Both the risky environments in which teenagers live and the risk-taking behavior associated with adolescence undoubtedly contribute to this statistic (Lightfoot, 1996; Noppe & Noppe, 1996).

Because of their lifestyles, males are significantly more at risk than females are. Middle- and working-class males are likely to believe that risk-taking behaviors, such as aggressive driving and experimentation with alcohol and drugs, are signs of masculinity. Poor and minority males are at still greater risk for accidental death and homicide, because the dangerous inner-city environments in which many of them live and the lifestyles they often lead are likely to involve the use and sale of drugs, participation in gangs, and exposure to various forms of physical violence, including the use of lethal weapons (Takanishi, 1993). Leading causes of adolescent deaths are motor vehicle accidents (more than fifteen thousand per year), homicide and other forms of intentional violence (more than six thousand per year), and self-inflicted harm or suicide (more than five thousand yearly) (Balk & Corn, 1996).

Health-Compromising Behaviors

Although adolescents are not prone to the infectious diseases of childhood, they often adopt habits that are damaging to their health. Poor diet, lack of sleep, use of

TABLE 14.2   Common Infectious Diseases During Adolescence

Disease	Cause	Symptoms	Incidence	Treatment
Non–Sexually Transmitted Diseases				
Infectious mononucleosis	Virus	Sore throat, fever, swollen glands, extreme fatigue, enlarged spleen		Rest and good nutrition
Hepatitis	Virus transmitted through blood transfusions, injections, or sexual activity; also, inadequate sanitation	Acute infection of liver		Antiviral drugs
Sexually Transmitted Diseases				
Syphilis	Bacteria; transmitted by direct sexual contact with infected individual	Sores and lesions on genitals and mucous membranes; if untreated, CNS damage	134,000 new cases per year	Antibiotics
Gonorrhea	Bacteria; transmitted by direct sexual contact with infected individual	Infection of mucous membrane of urethra and genital areas; pain in urinating, vaginal discharge; if untreated, may cause pelvic inflammatory disease and sterility in women	1.9 million new cases per year	Antibiotics
Genital warts	Virus; transmitted by direct sexual contact	Small, painless growths on penis, urethra, rectal areas in males, genitals and anus in females; if untreated, increased risk of cervical cancer	1 million new cases per year	Removal
Genital herpes	Virus; transmitted by direct sexual contact with infected individual	Chronic, painful inflammation and lesions on genitals and other areas of sexual contact	200,000 to 500,000 new cases per year	Antiviral drugs; no cure as yet
Chlamydia	Bacteria; transmitted by direct sexual contact	Pain in urination, discharge from penis; vaginal discharge, abdominal discomfort; if untreated, may cause pelvic inflammatory disease, sterility	4 million new cases per year; most common STD	Antiviral drugs
Acquired immunodeficiency syndrome (AIDS)	Virus transmitted by body fluids from infected person		As of 1992, 671 males and 275 females age thirteen to nineteen, and 7,820 males and 1,762 females ages twenty to twenty-four. In the late 1990s, about 5,000 deaths per year and 15,000 new cases per year.	Antiviral drugs such as AZT may slow replication of the virus. No fully effective treatment has been developed so far.

Sources: Barchardt & Noble (1997); Centers for Disease Control (1998); DeVita et al. (1997).

alcohol or drugs, and unsafe sexual practices can all lead to a number of serious diseases. Infectious mononucleosis, hepatitis, and a variety of *sexually transmitted diseases (STDs)* constitute major health risks during adolescence (see Table 14.2).

Sexually Transmitted Diseases   Teenagers and young adults under age twenty-five account for more than 50 percent of the 20 million STD cases reported annually.

The growing danger of AIDS and other sexually transmitted diseases during adolescence has led to many new educational programs designed to reduce these risks. These ninth-grade students are working on an AIDS project in health class.

It is estimated that 25 percent of adolescents will become infected with an STD before graduating from high school (Moore et al., 1996). With the exception of prostitutes and homosexual men, adolescent females have the highest rates of gonorrhea, cytomegalovirus, chlamydia, and pelvic inflammatory disease of any age group. STDs can cause pelvic inflammatory disease, which places young women at risk for subsequent ectopic pregnancy and infertility (Shafer & Moscicki, 1991).

Risk factors for STDs include the increased acceptability of early sexual activity throughout our culture and inadequate use of contraceptives. Use of the birth control pill has replaced condoms as the favored method for birth control among teenagers. But condoms provide significant protection against venereal diseases and HIV, whereas the pill provides none. Inadequate health and sex education at home and in the schools must also be held accountable. As we discuss next, sexual experimentation and unprotected sex, particularly in the case of poor and minority adolescents who participate in the sex-for-drugs exchanges common in the drug subculture, place adolescents at great risk for all STDs, including AIDS.

First diagnosed in the United States in the early 1980s, *AIDS (acquired immunodeficiency syndrome)* is perhaps the best-known and most feared sexually transmitted disease today. AIDS destroys the body's ability to maintain its normal immunity to diseases; death often results from pneumonia or related complications. The disease is transmitted through introduction of the *human immunodeficiency virus (HIV)* through body fluids from an infected person. The most common methods of transmission are sexual intercourse with an infected person, contact with the blood of an infected person (through sharing of needles or through a blood transfusion), and contact of a child with an infected mother during pregnancy, birth, and breast feeding (Shafer & Moscicki, 1991). Because the virus cannot survive in air, water, or things people touch, it does not spread through casual, day-to-day contact. AIDS has *never* been transmitted by sharing food; shaking hands; hugging; using the same dishes and utensils; being spit, drooled, or cried on; or having any form of casual contact. The risk of contracting AIDS is extremely high for the large number of poor and minority adolescents and young adults who engage in intravenous drug use. One group of particular concern is the 1.5 million homeless adolescents in the United States whose sexual and substance abuse behaviors place them at an especially high risk for AIDS.

AIDS Education and Prevention   A growing number of teenagers now receive formal instruction about AIDS in school. Most know that sexual intercourse and sharing needles are the main routes to getting AIDS and that condoms reduce the risk of transmission. However, for a variety of social and psychological reasons, the use of condoms has not increased as rapidly as youngsters' knowledge of why they are important. Sexually active adolescents need to know ways to protect themselves against AIDS. Perhaps most important is practicing safe sex, including massage, petting, masturbation, and kissing (provided there is no chance of direct contact between the body fluids of the partners). Kissing on the lips also is safe. No cases of AIDS have been traced to deep-tongue, "French" kissing, but because small amounts of HIV have been found in saliva, people who have open sores in their mouths or wear braces on their teeth are better off avoiding this practice. There is no such thing as "100 percent safe" sexual intercourse, but some sexual practices and behaviors are *safer* than others in that they significantly reduce (but do not eliminate) the risk of contracting AIDS. One such practice is to correctly use latex condoms along with a spermicide and water-based lubricant. A second is to be monogamous—to have sexual intercourse with only one person—and that person should have no history of intravenous drug use or sexual contact with high-risk individuals. A third alternative is to screen and limit the number of one's sexual partners. A fourth is abstinence, that is, refraining from sexual intercourse altogether (DeVita et al., 1997).

Drug and Alcohol Abuse   As of 1991, 88 percent of high school seniors had used alcohol, 36.7 percent had tried marijuana, and 7.8 percent had used cocaine at least once. Figure 14.3 shows more general trends in drug use; it indicates a decline in the use of marijuana, stimulants, and sedatives by high school students in recent

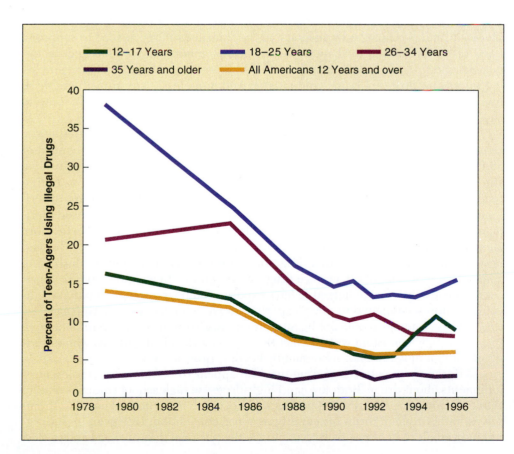

● ● ● ● ● ● ● ● ● ● ● ● ● ● ● ●
FIGURE 14.3
Drug Use by Teen-Agers Falls
Percentage of each age group that used any illegal drug* in the month before the survey was taken.
Includes marijuana or hashish, cocaine (including crack), inhalants, hallucinogens, heroin, or the nonmedical use of any prescription psychotherapeutic drug.
Source: Department of Health and Human Services (1997).

years after a brief increase in the mid-1990s. The overall trend, however, is downward (L. Johnston et al., 1992). High rates of experimentation with drugs and of drug abuse are typical of adolescence. In our society, as in many others, drinking alcoholic beverages represents a rite of passage associated with the adolescent's transition to adulthood. Although drugs differ in many ways, experimentation with psychedelics and other "mind-altering" drugs, such as LSD, psilocybin, and mescaline in the 1960s and traditional use of peyote among Native American cultures in the southwestern United States, can also be thought of as serving a rite of passage function. Choices of drugs and patterns of use may, of course, change over time. More important, drug use has great potential for harm, particularly for adolescents.

Developmental Effects of Drug Abuse   For several reasons, the effects of drug abuse on development are extremely destructive, particularly if the use is prolonged or chronic. First, even short-term use of illegal drugs such as heroin, cocaine, crack, and Quaaludes exposes the user to considerable physical risk of injury or death due to overdose, contamination of the drug, or both. Second, even moderate use of certain drugs may have destructive physical and psychological effects; they may disrupt normal patterns of eating, sleeping, and physical activity and mask psychological problems that require attention. Third, a number of these drugs cause physical addiction and psychological dependence. Physical addiction involves a biological dependence on the drug; withdrawal can be painful and sometimes life threatening. In most cases, tolerance to the drug increases with prolonged use, requiring higher doses to maintain the same level of effect and thus increasing the user's exposure to the drug's negative effects (Weinberg et al., 1998).

Finally, even if a proper medicinal dose of the drug itself is not physically dangerous, as is true with heroin, the physical, social, and psychological risks involved in supporting a habit are enormous. Teenagers addicted to heroin are, with few exceptions, forced to sell drugs and steal to support their habit. They are at great risk for using unreliable and contaminated drugs and for contracting hepatitis or even AIDS from dirty and infected needles. They are exposed to situations that are both physically and psychologically violent, and the time and energy needed to support a habit often force them to abandon normal social, emotional, and intellectual endeavors and threaten to halt their identity development prematurely. Teenagers living in poverty-stricken, crime-ridden areas and homeless teens are vulnerable to involvement in the drug trade, which to them may appear to be the only route to success or even survival (World Bank, 1997).

Causes of Drug Abuse   Problem drug use often is both a symptom and a cause of personal and social maladjustment and is best understood in the context of an individual's personality and developmental history. For example, a longitudinal study of marijuana and related drug use among eighteen-year-olds who were first recruited at age three found three different drug use groups: frequent users, experimenters, and abstainers (Shedler & Block, 1990). *Frequent users,* who used marijuana once a week or more and had tried at least one other drug, were more alienated, impulsive, and anxious than *experimenters* were. *Abstainers,* who had never tried marijuana or any other drug, were more anxious, emotionally constricted, and lacking in social skills than were drug experimenters. In addition, both frequent users and abstainers were judged to have experienced poorer maternal parenting as young children compared to drug "experimenters," who had used marijuana a few times. These findings should not be interpreted as advocating drug experimentation; they are simply consistent with the fact that the majority of adolescents who experiment with marijuana do not subsequently become drug abusers.

Differences in patterns of drug use also appear to be related to adolescents' judgments about drugs. Both low- and high-drug-use high school students tend to think of drug use primarily as a personal issue, involving potential harm to themselves, rather than in terms of morality or social convention. However, high-drug-use individuals seem more likely to minimize the personal risks involved and to view

Cigarette smoking makes some teenagers feel more grown-up and more sociable and accepted by their friends. As a result, cigarettes are used by many more teenagers in spite of the health risks.

themselves as the only authority on drug use, undermining the views of parents, the law, and other sources of authority (Shedler & Block, 1990).

Alcohol and Tobacco   What is the impact of the two drugs most commonly used by teenagers, alcohol and tobacco? In many ways their effects are more serious than the effects of more exotic drugs, simply because they are used so widely and therefore affect a wider range of both users and nonusers. For example, the use of alcohol is associated with nearly half of all deaths from motor vehicle crashes involving adolescents (Tillman, 1992) and with numerous other vehicle accidents, violent crimes, and suicides (Hunt & Zakhari, 1995). Chronic alcohol use can lead to severe health problems, including destruction of the liver and damage to the central nervous system. It also seriously disrupts the drinker's ability to function effectively in school, at work, at home, and in other settings. Because alcohol is heavily advertised and socially valued as a sign of adulthood and independence, is readily available at low cost, and is a potent short-term reducer of anxiety, it continues to be very popular among adolescents.

The use of tobacco products also has been widely advertised as a sign of adulthood. Early adolescents are particularly susceptible to this "ready-made" symbol of maturity. Although most adolescents are aware that smoking causes cancer and heart disease, about half of all students in grades nine through twelve report using tobacco (U.S. Department of Health and Human Services, 1994). While overall smoking rates for teenagers have decreased over the last two decades, smoking among females and minorities has risen, at least in part because advertisers have targeted them as a highly lucrative market (Becker, 1996).

Patterns of both drinking and smoking are strongly influenced by the lifestyles of family members and peers and by the environments in which they live. Among family members, minimal, moderate, and heavy levels of drinking, smoking, and drug use, including legally prescribed medications, are strongly associated with very similar patterns of use among adolescents. Peer pressure is also thought to significantly influence which drugs a teenager uses, in what circumstances, and how much and how often, although there is some indication that its contribution may be over-estimated (Bauman & Ennett, 1994).

Because most initial experiences with cigarettes, alcohol, and illicit drugs occur during the early teenage years, prevention efforts are now being directed at this age group. These efforts have focused on reducing exposure to drugs, altering the social environment, and changing the attitudes and behaviors of the drug user (or potential user). In general, however, drug prevention programs have not proven very effective. Those that show promise are peer programs and school-based prevention efforts involving life skills training designed to increase knowledge and build confidence and overall social competence in areas such as risk assessment, decision making, self-directed behavior change, capacity to cope with anxiety, and conflict resolution (Hamburg, 1997; Lynch & Bonnie, 1994).

Nutritional Problems   Consider these two students:

- Michael, age sixteen, leaves school at 4:00. On his way home, he stops by a convenience store with his friends and buys himself a large soft drink (three hundred calories) and a bag of French fries (four hundred calories). As a result, he is not hungry when dinner is served at 6:00; in fact, he doesn't finish his dinner. By the next morning, he is hungry again because he has not eaten for more than fourteen hours. He is too rushed to have breakfast, but on his way to school he buys a candy bar at the same convenience store he visited yesterday.

- Susan, also age sixteen, leaves school at 4:00. On her way home, she stops by a convenience store with her friends, where they buy various snacks. Susan buys nothing, though, because she believes she is slightly overweight. Later, for the same reason, she eats almost none of her dinner, causing mild worry for her parents. Still later, she sneaks out of the house without telling anyone, goes to the convenience store, and buys herself several candy bars, which she consumes on the spot. She feels sick, but doesn't throw up—this time.

Michael and Susan are not unusual in their eating habits. Of all age groups in society, adolescents have some of the most unsatisfactory nutrition (Barness, 1993). Many of their eating habits—a tendency to skip meals, to snack (especially on "junk" foods), to consume fast foods, and (especially for girls) to diet—place them at dietary risk. Inadequate nutrition can interfere with a teenager's ability to concentrate at school or work, and it can interfere with activities with peers. The negative effects may not seem serious to many teenagers, since their youth gives them comparative resilience to bounce back after a period of poor nutrition, preventing them from feeling ill as a consequence. In the short term, furthermore, many (but not all) teenagers neither gain weight from eating too many calories nor lose it from too much dieting. Yet poor nutritional habits definitely contribute to serious health problems in adulthood if they persist on a long-term basis.

Like dependence on drugs, dependence on "empty calories" and the obesity that sometimes results are problems that affect a significant portion of the teenage population. Currently an estimated 15 percent of today's teenagers are significantly overweight. Major causes of obesity include a biologically inherited tendency to be overweight, childhood diet and family attitudes and habits regarding food, and lack of exercise (Mella & Rogers, 1998). Adolescents and young adults who are overweight suffer increased health risks, including hypertension, respiratory disease, orthopedic disorders, and diabetes.

Obesity is particularly difficult for adolescents who already are struggling to develop a comfortable and realistic view of their changing bodies. It can significantly impair teenagers' sense of themselves as physically attractive people and their overall identity development. In some cases, obesity can severely limit social opportunities due to both exclusion by peers and self-isolation. Because overweight adolescents do not conform to the social ideal of thinness, they also suffer from dis-

Although most teenagers suffer no shortage of calories, their diets often lack balance and rely heavily on "fast foods," which are high in fat.

crimination that limits their access to education, employment, marriage, housing, and health care (DeJong, 1993; Gortmaker et al., 1993).

Kelly Brownell and his colleagues (Battle & Brownell, 1996; Liebman, 1998) believe that, along with eating disorders, obesity now constitutes a serious national health problem, not just an individual one. They base this conclusion in part on the disturbing 25 percent increase in obesity since 1980, a health problem that now affects one-third of all Americans. Brownell believes the major cause of this "epidemic" is the unprecedented success of leading fast-food corporations in promoting ready access to a good-tasting but poor-quality diet of high-calorie, high-fat, low-cost foods through restaurants and school cafeterias located in almost every community. He suggests that this "toxic food environment" helps to ensure that children, adolescents, and adults are exposed to the unhealthy diet that is largely responsible for the national epidemic of eating disorders, obesity, and other diet-related problems.

According to Brownell, halting this epidemic will require that our nation adopt the same aggressive approach to the toxic food environment that it has for tobacco. To accomplish this, he suggests that the government subsidize the cost of healthy foods so they cost less, tax the sale of unhealthy foods so they cost more, regulate food advertising aimed at young children and adolescents, and develop more opportunities for people to be more physically active (Battle & Brownell, 1996; Liebman, 1998).

Eating Disorders Excessive thinness is also a problem, especially for girls. Despite a growing appreciation of physical strength and fitness in women, a lean body is still the dominant cultural standard for feminine beauty. Many adolescent girls try to lose weight to achieve a degree of slenderness that may not be possible for them. Inadequate knowledge about dietary requirements and poor judgment lead to inadequate nutrition for many teenage girls.

In its exteme form, the quest for thinness can become an eating disorder. **Anorexia nervosa** and **bulimia** are two emotional disorders characterized by severely abnormal eating patterns, an obsession with food and weight, and a relentless pursuit of excessive thinness (Robertson, 1992). Anorexia nervosa affects

• • •

anorexia nervosa A physical and psychological disturbance that causes a person to refuse to eat sufficient food and to develop an increasingly unrealistic view of his or her body; most individuals with anorexia are teenage girls.

bulimia A disorder in which a person, usually a teenage girl, eats huge amounts of food and then vomits it to avoid gaining weight.

PERSPECTIVES

Female Athletes and Eating Disorders

• • • • • Statistics show that athletic activities requiring a lean physical body predispose serious, competitive female participants to eating disorders. In figure skating, gymnastics, and ballet, more than half of competitive females report some form of pathological dieting, and as many as 25% are dangerously underweight or undernourished (Graber et al., 1996; Zerbe, 1993). This figure is more than double that for other women athletes (e.g., softball or basketball) and many times higher than for women in general. Eating disorders among skaters, gymnasts, and ballet dancers usually take the form of either *anorexia nervosa* or *bulimia*.

Several factors contribute to the prevalence of eating disorders among women in the "lean" sports. Competitive skating and ballet require much practice and pencil-like proportions to make turns and lifts, setting the stage for excessive exercise and a compulsion to prove one's worth through competitions. Most winners of Olympic competitions in these sports are teenagers, and the females are 5 to 10 years younger than their male counterparts (Ryan, 1995). Youth makes them likely to be slender, both because some have not yet fully experienced puberty and exercising so intensely delays the onset of puberty. Their immaturity makes them less likely to question the intense exercise needed to succeed at skating or gymnastics.

These young females may seem not obviously troubled because their activities support society's gender-role expectations. Both their talent and appearance are what the public often wants to see: a childlike body combined with a cooperative spirit, one that performs on demand and does not mind being looked at intently or even erotically (Guttmann, 1996; Hesse-Biber, 1996). Under these conditions, it becomes easy to hide an eating disorder. The public at large is

Some young women—like Christy Henrich, at one time a successful gymnast—are at risk for anorexia and bulimia. Their compulsive dieting and exercise may be attempts to attain culturally imposed standards of female beauty and gain control over their lives. No matter how thin they become, they are likely to view themselves as "too fat."

eager *not* to hear about the down-side to its image of perfection. And coaches, parents, and the girl herself find it easier to interpret symptoms as normal signs of stress or as normal self-discipline associated with training. At the beginning of the girl's sports career, in fact, they may be right: self-disciplined practice only later deteriorates into an addiction to public acclaim.

The experience of these athletes suggests ways to prevent and treat girls with eating disorders. For example, both girls and their families need to understand the pervasiveness of gender-role expectations and social conventions that value thinness, docility, and youth for females (Hesse-Biber, 1996). This goal usually takes two strategies. One is to control and simplify a girl's environment to eliminate behaviors and stimuli that contribute to weight loss—by counseling family members about appropriate behavior or arranging for the girl or woman to live away from her family for a time. Unsolicited compliments on thinness should be reduced. So should criticisms for *not* eating, which can be interpreted as personal attacks and contribute to feeling helpless. The second strategy is to encourage a sense of autonomy and self-direction so that the girl feels less at the mercy of others' expectations and admiring (and sometimes envious) gazes. Accomplishing this goal usually requires counseling or therapy for the girl herself (Zerbe, 1993). To the extent that a girl can understand the link between an action as personal as eating and broad social issues about gender equity and about respect for the young, she can begin to see that eating problems are widespread and that her growing insights about her experiences, if shared appropriately, can sometimes help others with similar experiences.

What Do You Think?

1. Not everyone with an eating disorder is a young female. How would the experiences of others with this problem differ from those presented here?

2. If you knew someone who you suspected had an eating disorder, how might you deal with it? Compare your answer with that of a classmate.

3. When boys participate in sports that fit traditional male gender stereotypes (e.g., football), what price do they risk paying for participation analogous to the experience of some girls with eating disorders?

approximately 0.2 percent, or one in five hundred, adolescent girls and young women, and bulimia affects between 1.0 and 2.8 percent. Also, it is estimated that about 20 percent of adolescent girls (2.5 million) exhibit less extreme bulimic behaviors and an additional 20 percent engage in less extreme but still unhealthy dieting behaviors (Grabor et al., 1996).

The major symptom of anorexia is extreme weight loss (about 20 to 25 percent of body weight) through self-starvation that is tied to an obsessive fear of becoming fat. Anorexic youngsters experience severe disturbances in three areas of psychological functioning. The first is in *body image*. A girl (call her Jill) is five feet, six inches tall and weighs eighty-seven pounds. Jill looks like a walking skeleton, but when she views herself in a mirror, she sees someone who is too fat and needs to continue dieting. The second disturbance is *misinterpretation of internal and external stimuli*: although she is literally starving to death, Jill enjoys the feeling of hunger and her flat, empty stomach, both of which make her feel thinner. The third disturbance is a *pervasive sense of ineffectiveness and helplessness* about her ability to direct her life. Other symptoms of anorexia include excessive, compulsive exercise; amenorrhea (the cessation of menstruation); hyperactivity; social isolation; and feelings of insecurity, loneliness, inadequacy, shame, and guilt (American Psychological Association, 1996).

Bulimia is a related eating disorder that frequently involves a recurrent "binge-purge" syndrome in which as many as 4,800 calories are eaten at a time, mostly in the form of sweets and other "forbidden" and fattening food, and then immediately purged by forced vomiting, laxatives, and other cathartics. About half of all anorexics also have bulimic eating patterns (Fairburn & Wilson, 1993). Women at greatest risk for bulimia are those who have most deeply accepted and internalized the social and cultural norms that equate fat with the bad and ugly, and thinness with the good and beautiful (Hesse-Biber, 1996).

Most anorexics are girls from financially and socially successful upper-middle-class and upper-class families. Many feel burdened by their parents' success and an overwhelming obligation to be at least as special and as successful as their parents were. Their eating behaviors serve as a means of forestalling and/or avoiding the physical, sexual, and psychosocial changes and challenges of puberty and adolescence, which they do not feel ready to face. The behaviors also give them means of asserting control over their own bodies and daily activities and of resisting the intense pressure to conform to the parental expectations they experienced throughout their childhood.

Anorexia and bulimia are frequently associated with a serious family disturbance, and in particular with a mother-daughter relationship that is overprotective, rigid, and rejecting or hostile, and with mothers who themselves are preoccupied with thinness and have disturbed eating patterns. There is also evidence that sexual abuse may be involved in some cases (Vanderlinden, 1997).

Successful treatment of anorexia generally requires a multiple focus. First, it must deal with the starvation problem in a way that addresses both the anorexic's need for control and the distortions in her thinking. This typically requires a highly restricted hospital environment that allows careful observation and the use of behavior modification to reduce or eliminate rewards for behaviors leading to weight loss and reinforce more appropriate eating behaviors. Antidepressant medications have also proven helpful in reducing the depression and risk of suicide that are present in many cases. Second, the treatment must address the underlying family problems and abnormal interactions among family members that are invariably related to anorexia. Finally, individual therapy with the anorexic adolescent must focus on helping her to uncover her own abilities and resources for independent thinking, judging, and feeling. It must help her to achieve autonomy and self-directed identity by helping her to become aware of, express, and act on her own impulses, feelings, and needs. The accompanying Perspectives box looks at how these issues and solutions express themselves in the lives of competitive athletes. In the "Working With" interview on pg. 436, Barbara Donahue, a nutritionist, discussed her work with adolescents with eating problems.

WHAT DO YOU THINK ?   Why do you think adolescents are at such high risk for injury, death, and health problems? What recommendations regarding these issues might you make to a group of high school students and their parents?

Finally Young Adults?

After all the bodily changes adolescents experience, they certainly look like adults. But as we have pointed out, they do not consistently *feel* like adults yet. Especially early in adolescence, teenagers are often uncomfortable with their new physical features, which take up the foreground of their thinking, feeling, and acting. Young people often are self-conscious, meaning (among other things) they are highly conscious of their bodies. The nature and strength of that self-consciousness depend in part on the nature, strength, and timing of puberty in all of its facets.

Given the newness of their physical changes, it is not surprising that adolescents lack awareness of or concern for their health. So far in life, they have had little reason to be aware or concerned. Soon, however, this perspective changes. Just as their bodies develop during the teen years, so do their thoughts, feelings, and social relationships. These developments eventually help them to become truly adult in the physical sense as well as in other realms.

Summary of Major Ideas

The Concept of Adolescence

1. Adolescence, which begins around age twelve and lasts until about age twenty-two, is a developmental period of transition between childhood and adulthood.

2. Adolescence was "discovered" in the early part of this century as a way of prolonging childhood in a period of rapid social and economic change. Compulsory education, child labor laws, and special laws to combat "juvenile delinquency" helped to solidify the idea of adolescence.

3. Some theories of adolescence emphasize the "storm and stress" of this period, whereas others portray it as a continuation of developmental trends begun in childhood.

Growth in Height and Weight

4. Adolescents experience significant increases in height and weight, but variations in the timing of the "growth spurt" among teenagers are even more striking.

5. On average, boys start their growth spurt later than girls. Individual variations create worries about personal appearance for some adolescents.

6. During the last century, children have tended to begin physical maturation and puberty earlier and to grow taller and heavier than their parents. This *secular trend* is thought to reflect improvements in diet, health, and overall living conditions.

Puberty

7. In addition to increases in height and weight, a larger pattern of changes occurs that leads to full physical and sexual maturity, or puberty.

8. Primary sexual maturation among boys includes rapid growth of the penis and scrotum and the production of fertile semen.

9. Among girls, primary sexual maturation is marked by menarche, or the beginning of menstrual cycles. In many cultures, including our own, the onset of menarche can be stressful, in part due to the strong personal and cultural expectations associated with it.

10. Maturation of secondary sex characteristics includes enlargement and development of the breasts, growth of body hair, deepening of the voice, and increased production of sex-related hormones.

11. Male and female hormones affect both sexes, although in differing degrees and with different effects.

12. Although girls and boys are equally muscular prior to adolescence, during puberty boys experience significantly greater increases in muscle tissue than girls do, and girls experience a somewhat greater increase in body fat.

Psychological Effects of Physical Growth in Adolescence

13. The physical sex differences of puberty are accentuated by differences in life experiences related to gender-role expectations.

14. For boys, the effects of early maturation tend to be positive in the short run but negative in the long run. Late maturation appears to have the reverse effects.

15. For girls, early maturation is more stressful in the short term but positive in the long term. Late maturers tend to experience immediate benefits during adolescence, but report being less poised and more uncertain about their lives than early-maturing girls.

16. The timing of puberty affects only average response to puberty; individuals with identical timing vary widely in their responses, depending on their circumstances.

17. Most adolescents are preoccupied with their physical appearance; a teenager's body image is influenced by conventional standards of attractiveness. An adolescent's feelings of attractiveness depend on the evaluations of peers, parents, and self, and affect self-esteem.

Health in Adolescence

18 There is considerable continuity between childhood and adolescent patterns of illness and health care. Both are influenced by individual and family attitudes and resources.

19. Adolescents are a high-risk group for injury and death due to risky lifestyles and their myth of invulnerability. Major health-compromising behaviors of adolescence include exposure to sexually transmitted diseases; alcohol, tobacco, and drug abuse; inadequate diet; and behaviors associated with eating disorders.

Key Terms

adolescence (431)
anorexia nervosa (455)
bulimia (455)
estrogen (441)
growth spurt (434)
menarche (439)
nocturnal emission (439)
primary sex characteristics (439)

puberty (439)
secondary sex characteristics (439)
secular trend (436)
semen (439)
testosterone (441)

Cognitive Development in Adolescence

Focusing Questions

- To what extent and in what situations are adolescents capable of abstract reasoning?

- How does cognitive development affect adolescents' knowledge and beliefs about political processes, religion, and morality?

- How can one support or foster skillful and critical thinking in adolescents?

- How do adolescents show improved information-processing skills in everyday activities?

- How does school affect adolescents, both cognitively and socially?

J acob and Maria, both twelfth-graders, were discussing abortion.

"What's the big deal about abortion, anyway?" asked Jacob. "Why not just let anybody get one who wants one? It's a personal choice, like deciding which college to go to."

"You sound like you don't care about the people involved," said Maria. "How would you feel if *you* needed an abortion?"

"But I won't ever need one," Jacob replied smugly. "Only girls get pregnant, you know."

"That's why you don't understand," said Maria. "What if it's *your* body that can grow babies, and everybody expects *you* to grow one at the right time, like when you get married? And everybody expects you *not* to grow one at the wrong time, like during high school. How do you deal with all those people—your parents and friends, and the baby's father too?"

Jacob looked thoughtful at this comment. Then he said, "You're getting bogged down in what other people think. Try to imagine what you yourself would want to do with your life if you found out you were pregnant."

"I do that," said Maria, "and I also try to think about what the baby would want to do with *his* or *her* life if I allowed it to live."

This example reveals a number of new cognitive competencies that adolescents acquire. Jacob and Maria reason about possibilities rather than about actual events; neither of them has ever experienced an abortion. They also make generalizations as a basis for specific conclusions; for Jacob, abortion is generally "a personal choice" and should always be treated as such. School-age children also show these cognitive abilities in some situations, but not as often or as reliably. Thinking in middle childhood is more closely tied to the concrete than it is in adolescence.

In this chapter, we look at thinking in the adolescent years. We do so from two general viewpoints. The first is the *cognitive developmental viewpoint*, often associated with the work of Piaget. The second is the more recent approach of *information-processing theory*, which analyzes human thinking as a complex storage, retrieval, and organizing system for information, much like a computer. Because each of these theories is discussed elsewhere in this book, we focus here on their relevance to adolescence.

In real life, of course, thinking is always "about" something in particular. In recognition of that fact, we also discuss adolescents' ideas about themselves and about morality, politics, and religion. The two general theories about adolescent cognition help us to understand how adolescents (and others) make decisions about right and wrong, about the consequences of political actions, and about the nature of God.

Compared to children, teenagers think more often about possibilities and about the future; they also daydream and fantasize more. What do you suppose this adolescent is thinking about?

General Features of Adolescent Thought

Teenagers' new cognitive competencies broaden the horizons of their world substantially. For example, the question "What if a nuclear war broke out?" is more meaningful to an adolescent than to a child, even though both are equally inexperienced with actual nuclear war. So is the question "What if I had been born really poor or fabulously rich?" Adolescents can imagine what these situations might be like even though they have not experienced them in a concrete way. In general, thinking about the possible creates a new skill for speculating about important events and guessing about daily experiences (Keating & Sasse, 1996). It also stimulates adolescents to daydream or fantasize about their actions and feelings. It helps them to make more astute inferences about human motivations ("Perhaps she did that because . . . "), and to critique their own and others' actions.

Tied to this ability is a greater capacity to plan ahead. Contrary to what frustrated parents sometimes claim, adolescents can set and plan goals for themselves, and they can do so much more competently than children can. Sometimes such goals are socially approved ones, such as making sure to take the best courses to get into a desirable college. Just as often, however, goals seem to lack redeeming value by conventional adult standards, such as when an adolescent carefully plans and finances an expensive trip to a rock concert in a faraway city.

Another way to state these competencies is to say that during adolescence, young people develop an ability to think about thoughts and to do so in a logical way. Most of the time such thinking serves some purpose, such as developing a better understanding of human nature or figuring out the best way to have fun. But sometimes thinking about thoughts has no concrete content at all. Many adolescents are quite capable of thinking simply about the forms of statements or propositions, even when the statements lack content entirely:

Some wugs are glibs.

All glibs are bots.

From these two statements, some adolescents can decide, and even enjoy deciding, whether or not any "wugs" are in fact "bots." (The answer, incidentally, is that some "wugs" are indeed "bots," though not necessarily all of them.)

WHAT DO YOU THINK?   How did your thinking change when you became a teenager compared to when you were in elementary school? Consider both *what* you thought about and *how* you thought, and compare your experiences with those of a few friends or classmates.

Beyond Concrete Operational Thinking

formal operational thought
Thinking based on previously acquired concrete mental operations and involving hypothetical reasoning and attention to the structure or form of ideas.

During adolescence, many teenagers go beyond the *concrete operational thought* described in Chapters 6 and 8, and begin to develop a more abstract way of thinking called **formal operational thought.** This new form of thinking frees individuals from reasoning only about the here-and-now, and allows them to be more fully logical and systematic in analyzing ideas. When using formal operational thought, individuals show some combination of three skills: they emphasize the possible rather than the real, they use scientific reasoning, and they combine ideas skillfully. But although these represent cognitive advances over the concrete thinking of childhood, they are neither the "final" form of cognition nor the only stepping stone toward fully adult thinking. Some teenagers (and adults) never develop formal operational thought at all, although later in life they may develop other kinds of thinking that might best be called "wisdom." Formal thought involves a style of thinking that closely resembles scientific reasoning, a form of thought that most people probably do not use in everyday activities. Keep this proviso in mind as you read this section, where we look in more detail at the main features of formal operational thought.

Possibilities Versus Realities

Formal thought involves attention to possibilities rather than merely to actual realities. A parent discovered this feature when he tried to get his two children to make suggestions about how to improve the humdrum weekly chicken dinner. "Fried is fine," said his nine-year-old. "I like it the way we always have it." But the fourteen-year-old insisted on a more complicated response: "Let me think about that," she said. Later she remarked, "Can we make some brand-new sauce for it? Maybe one of the cookbooks has some ideas." Even though the older child had never eaten chicken cooked this way, she thought about trying it.

Scientific Reasoning

Formal thought also involves scientific reasoning, the same kind psychologists use in designing many of their studies of human development. This quality reveals itself when adolescent students must solve some problem systematically. For example, how do youngsters in an art class figure out methods for mixing basic colors of paint to produce various intermediate shades and other colors? Those capable of formal operations in effect design an experiment to test all the available combinations of colors. They form hypotheses, or hunches, about how certain colors affect one

Many teenagers become able to solve problems scientifically. But like these students in a biology laboratory class, and like most adults, they still need ample concrete experiences to support their abstract thinking. Commonly, too, they may have trouble using scientific thought outside a structured school situation.

another when mixed. Then they try out their hypotheses by mixing each basic color with every other basic color, being careful to try every possibility. By carefully observing the results of this procedure, they can draw logical conclusions about how to mix colors. This procedure in effect uses the scientific method.

In contrast, concrete operational children rarely act so systematically. Like the formal operational thinkers, they probably would mix colors, but they would do so haphazardly and might not take careful note of the results of their experiments. As a result, they may not learn to mix colors as rapidly as older, formal operational thinkers do. When confronted with this problem, of course, some younger children might draw on previous experience with art materials to solve it; but then their performance would reflect memory about how to mix colors rather than true scientific reasoning.

Logical Combination of Ideas

The third feature of formal operational thought involves combining ideas logically. Unlike less cognitively mature children, formal thinkers can hold several ideas in mind at once and combine or integrate them in logical ways. When asked to explain why some students perform better in school than others do, concrete operational thinkers are likely to latch on to one reason or another: "Some kids are smarter" or "Some kids work harder." In contrast, formal operational thinkers often give combinations of reasons, as this college freshman did:

> Well, I think it depends. Sometimes it pays just to be smart. But it also helps to work hard—except when the teacher doesn't notice. Some kids do better too because they have taken courses before in the same area. Your first class in literature is likely to be harder than your fifth class in that subject.

As this example shows, the ability to combine ideas sometimes makes formal operational thinkers qualify their opinions more than pre–formal operational thinkers do.

Concrete Versus Formal Thought: Reasoning About Bending Rods

To understand the features of formal thought, consider how children at different stages of cognitive maturity approach a problem that Piaget designed (Inhelder & Piaget, 1958). A set of flexible rods is attached to the side of a basin of water. The rods differ in length, thickness, and material (metal or wood). In addition, a number of small weights are attached to the ends of the rods (see Figure 15.1). A friendly experimenter, perhaps a teacher, asks the child to determine what factor or factors control how far the rods bend toward the water. Does the amount of bending depend on the rods' length, on their thickness, on what they are made of, or on the weight attached to them?

Imagine you are a school-age child asked to solve this problem. Your attention would be captured primarily by the apparatus itself. You would enjoy varying anything that seemed to vary—in this case, the length of the rods and the attached weights. You would also enjoy comparing one rod with another—wooden rods with metal ones and thick rods with thin ones. But your observations and comparisons would lack a system. You might vary more than one factor at a time (length *and* thickness) or forget to vary one of the factors at all. This haphazardness would likely prevent you from solving the problem fully, although you nevertheless might make a number of useful observations about the apparatus. The haphazard quality would also mark your efforts as concrete operational. At this age and stage, you would still be closely tied to the real, or concrete.

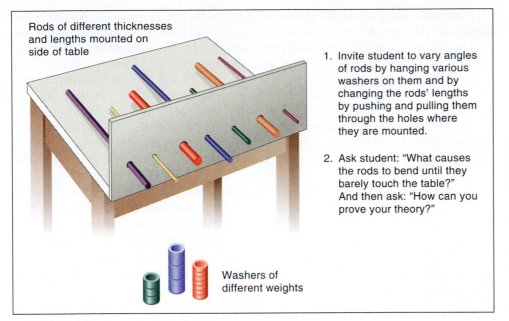

Rods of different thicknesses and lengths mounted on side of table

1. Invite student to vary angles of rods by hanging various washers on them and by changing the rods' lengths by pushing and pulling them through the holes where they are mounted.

2. Ask student: "What causes the rods to bend until they barely touch the table?" And then ask: "How can you prove your theory?"

Washers of different weights

FIGURE 15.1

Experiment Requiring Formal Operational Thought

In this experiment, originally conducted by Piaget, the participant is asked to discover the factors that influence how far various rods bend toward the surface of a table, as shown here. Individuals who have developed formal operational thinking are able to test several factors (e.g., thickness of rods, length of rods, weights on rods) systematically and describe the bases for their explanation in a logical manner.

As a formal operational thinker, however, you would approach the problem much more systematically. First, you would make some good guesses (or hypotheses) about the solution to the problem. You would take mental note of several factors that looked as though they might affect how far the rods bend: length, thickness, and weight, as well as whether the rods were made of wood or metal. Having noticed these possibilities, you would go on to the next step: devising and carrying out an informal experiment for testing each hypothesis in turn while holding all of the other factors constant. If you began by varying the weights on the rods, you would make sure to use only rods of the same thickness, length, and material. Otherwise you could not be sure whether any variations in bending came from differences in weight or from differences in one of the other factors. Having checked for the effects of weight in this way, you would go on to test the effects of each remaining factor, keeping the other three factors constant in every case.

The formal operational approach contrasts sharply with the less systematic efforts of younger children. It guarantees that, given enough time, you will find a solution to the problem if a solution actually exists. It also makes more cognitive demands on you: you must devise hypotheses, plan a way to test them, and draw reasonable conclusions from your observations. Using concrete operations, in contrast, simply requires careful observation of events as they unfold; in thinking concretely, the child in essence asks from moment to moment, "Is what I am looking at a solution?"

Cognitive Development Beyond Formal Thought

Piaget and other psychologists have identified formal, or abstract, thought as a major achievement of adolescence. But for most human beings, it may not be the final or highest cognitive achievement. One clue to this possibility comes from adolescents themselves: some teenagers overuse logical thinking when they first achieve facility with it. They may believe all problems, including ambiguous ones such as achieving world peace, can be solved by the proper application of rational principles and careful reasoning. Teenagers may fail to notice that some problems by nature resist the application of general logic and may inherently have multiple, partial solutions. Later, as adults, they will take a more *ad hoc*, pragmatic approach to most problem solving (Sinnott, 1998).

Consider Ana, a twelfth-grader who recently has begun sleeping with her boyfriend. Ana gets along well with her parents, and she knows they will worry and feel hurt if they learn of her sexual involvement. She also believes that in general, friends and family should have no secrets. By continuing her sexual activities, she seems to be violating this principle. On the other hand, she and her boyfriend regard their intimacy as a private matter, and she worries that telling her parents would violate this privacy, which she also considers her right. Telling her parents might also create a lot of bad feelings among Ana, her boyfriend, and her parents. In this case, her principles do not seem to point her toward a good solution: Ana believes that no matter what she does, somebody will get hurt, some ethical principle will be violated, or both.

Ana's situation suggests the importance of nonrational choices or judgments in solving real-life problems. Like Ana, many people may wish to be reasonable; that is, they may wish to rely on formal logic and may even believe they use it a lot. But in practice, most people use formal logic consistently only when solving academic problems posed by teachers, especially when the problems are deliberately scientific in nature (Bartsch, 1993). Less systematic reasoning serves as well or better for solving daily problems.

For older adolescents, the cognitive challenge consists of converting formal reasoning from a goal in itself to a *tool* used for broader purposes and tailored to the problems at hand (Myers, 1993). Ana cannot reach a sound decision about informing her parents of her sexual activities if she focuses on formal principles about truthfulness and privacy to the exclusion of more personal facts, which in this case include her knowledge of her boyfriend's and her own parents' probable responses and feelings. Taking these circumstances into account leads to the "best," or most mature, solution, but it may not lead to a solution that is fully logical in Piaget's sense.

Implications of the Cognitive Developmental Viewpoint

According to Piaget, formal operations begin developing early in adolescence and are fully formed by the end of the high school years. All teenagers supposedly develop wide-ranging thinking abilities that have a formal, abstract nature and apply to many specific experiences and daily problems. In reality, however, the actual cognitive performances of adolescents fail to conform to this picture in several ways. First, a majority of adolescents (and even adults) use formal thinking inconsistently or even fail to use it at all (Lakoff, 1994). In explaining why a car is not working properly, for example, many adolescents and adults merely describe the car's symptoms: "The brakes are making a weird noise" or "It won't shift into third gear." By focusing only on visible symptoms, such comments are in effect concrete operational; even a school-age child could make them. They cast doubt on whether formal thinking really develops as universally as concrete operational thinking does.

Most experimental studies of formal operational thinking have confirmed that cognitive performance depends a lot on how it is observed or measured (Overton, 1994). In a typical study, adolescents solve a Piagetian task, such as describing why a pendulum swings faster or slower. Is it affected by the length of the cord holding it, by the amount of weight on the end, or by the angle from which it starts? (The actual solution is length: shorter pendulums swing faster and longer ones swing slower, with the other variables having no effect.) In a task such as this, adolescents do best at demonstrating and drawing a solution and worst at describing a solution verbally, although many exceptions occur. For example, more individuals can show the importance of length by actually displaying swinging pendulums of different lengths, but fewer people can explain the ideas underlying the demonstration verbally and coherently.

The result is that formal operational thought does describe adolescents' thinking, but only partially or intermittently. Formal thought helps teenagers to argue with their parents more skillfully than they could as children, thereby contributing to the stereotype of teenagers as being relatively "rebellious." Formal thought also makes teenagers more skillful at cultivating friendships, potential dates, and social contacts; now they can imagine and anticipate the consequences of various friendly (and unfriendly) strategies. And formal thought means teenagers are more ready than children are to grapple with philosophical and abstract topics at school: literary analysis can now begin to make sense, for example, and so can at least some theoretical concepts in science.

At other times, however, especially when not using formal thought, adolescents can seem much younger than their years. They may argue with parents skillfully, but sometimes their goal may be petty, such as permission to stay out just a few minutes longer than usual. Social encounters may be planned to facilitate meeting a potential date, but the new date himself or herself may be a dubious choice of acquaintance. And broad concepts and principles learned in school can be treated as irrelevant to teenagers' everyday concerns (Forlizzi, 1993). The accompanying Working With box describes how these changes look from the point of view of one high school mathematics teacher, Jerry Acton.

WHAT DO YOU THINK ? Outside of school- or job-related tasks, most people actually use formal operational thinking rather little in their everyday lives. How much do *you* actually use it? Think of a situation other than school (shopping, visiting a friend, cooking) in which you need to use abstract thinking to function effectively. What does your answer imply about the place of formal thought in adolescents' overall development?

Moral Development: Beliefs About Justice and Care

As adolescents gradually develop formal thought, they also develop a personal **morality,** or sensitivity to and knowledge of what is right and wrong. Moral thinking develops in two ways: in the form of increasingly logical and abstract principles related to fairness and justice and in the form of increasingly sophisticated ways of caring about the welfare of friends, family, and self (Noam & Wren, 1993). (See the accompanying Perspectives box.) Each of these trends is somewhat related to gender, with boys emphasizing ethical thinking about justice rather abstractly and girls emphasizing ethics of care. But the gender difference is not large; most individuals develop both kinds of ethical thinking to a significant extent. A major theory of the development of justice was originated by Lawrence Kohlberg, and a major theory of the development of care was conceived by Carol Gilligan. Both are stage theories in the cognitive developmental tradition, reminiscent of Piaget's approach to cognitive development.

Kohlberg's Six Stages of Moral Judgment

Lawrence Kohlberg proposed six stages of moral judgment that develop slowly, well into middle age (Schrader, 1990). The stages were derived from interviews conducted in much the same style as Piaget's classic interviews about cognitive development: children and adults of various ages responded individually to hypothetical stories that contained moral dilemmas. The original interviewees were all males, but in later studies Kohlberg and his associates extended the research to include females.

• • •
morality In developmental psychology, the sense of ethics or of right and wrong.

Table 15.1 summarizes the six proposed stages. The stages form a progression in two ways. First, earlier stages represent more egocentric thinking than later stages do. Second, earlier stages by their nature require more specific or concrete thinking than later stages do. For instance, in stage 1 (called *heteronomous morality*), a child makes no distinction between what he believes is right and what the world tells him is right; he simply accepts the perspectives of the authorities as his own. By stage 4 (social system orientation), when the child is an adolescent, he realizes that individuals vary in their points of view, but he still takes for granted the existing overall conventions of society as a whole. He cannot yet imagine a society in which those conventions might be purposely modified, for example, by passing laws or agreeing on new rules. Only by stages 5 and 6 (ethics) can he do so fully.

In the school years, children most commonly show ethical reasoning at stage 2, but some may begin showing stage 3 or 4 reasoning toward the end of this period (Colby & Kohlberg, 1987). For the majority of youth and adults, stage 3 (interpersonal orientation) and stage 4 (social system orientation) characterize their most advanced moral thinking. In stage 3, a person's chief concern is with the opinions of her peers: an action is morally right if her immediate circle of friends says it is right. Often this way of thinking leads to helpful actions, such as taking turns and sharing toys or materials. But often it does not, such as when a group of friends decide to let the air out of the tires of someone's car. In stage 4, the person shifts from concern with peers to concern with the opinions of community or society in the abstract: now something is right if the institutions approve. This broader source of moral judgment spares stage 4 children from the occasional tyranny of friends' opinions; now they will no longer steal hubcaps just because their friends urge them to do so. This change makes teenagers less *opportunistic* than children are, less inclined to judge based on immediate rewards or punishments they experience personally. Instead they evaluate actions on the basis of principles of some sort. For the time being, the principles are rather conventional; they are borrowed either from ideas expressed by immediate peers and relatives or from socially accepted rules and principles, whatever they may be. If friends agree that premarital sex is permissible, many teenagers are likely to adopt this idea as their own, at least as a general principle. But if friends or family believe premarital sex is morally wrong, teenagers may adopt this alternative belief as a principle. (Note, however, that whether a teenager really *acts* according to these principles is another matter. Moral action does not always follow from moral belief.)

TABLE 15.1   Kohlberg's Stages of Moral Judgment

Stage	Nature of Stage
Preconventional Level (*emphasis on avoiding punishments and getting awards*)	
Stage 1 Heteronomous morality; ethics of punishment and obedience	Good is what follows externally imposed rules and rewards and is whatever avoids punishment
Stage 2 Instrumental purpose; ethics of market exchange	Good is whatever is agreeable to the individual and to anyone who who gives or receives favors; no long-term loyalty
Conventional Level (*emphasis on social rules*)	
Stage 3 Interpersonal conformity; ethics of peer opinion	Good is whatever brings approval from friends as a peer group
Stage 4 Social system orientation: conformity to social system; ethics of law and order	Good is whatever conforms to existing laws, customs, and authorities
Postconventional Level (*emphasis on moral principles*)	
Stage 5 Social contract orientation; ethics of social contract and individual rights	Good is whatever conforms to existing procedures for settling disagreements in society; the actual outcome is neither good nor bad
Stage 6 Ethics of self-chosen universal principles	Good is whatever is consistent with personal, general moral principles

WORKING WITH

Jerry Acton, Math and Science Teacher

Blending the Social and Emotional with the Cognitive

Jerry Acton teaches math, chemistry, and physics in high school. I wanted to interview him to learn more about how students think about these traditionally "cognitive" subjects. What I learned, though, was that success in these subjects depended heavily on social and emotional factors—on students' attitudes and motivations, and not just on their thinking abilities as such. The blending of the domains of development was especially evident in Jerry's tenth-grade math class, the one we spent most time discussing.

Kelvin: *I've heard a lot of generalizations about math—stereotypes about learning it, so to speak. I've heard that math is inherently abstract, for example, and that it's very sequentially organized, and that you have to be willing to work independently if you want to do well in math. What do you think about these ideas? Do they explain why some students do better in math than others? Tell me about your own classes.*

Jerry: For my classes, I would say that *maturity* makes the biggest difference. Maybe it's because these are tenth-graders—people who have just arrived at senior high school and are still getting used to it. The more successful students in math classes are the ones who are the most mature.

Kelvin: *What do you mean by "mature"?*

Jerry: I mean the ones who are prepared to come to class to work, to listen, to ask questions, and to do work in class, as opposed to coming to class because it is a convenient place to socialize with friends. The mature ones already seem to see value and usefulness to math, without my having to persuade them of that idea.

Kelvin: *That makes it sound like there's not much need for you as the teacher— students either choose to work or they don't, and you don't have much to do about it. Surely that's not what you mean?*

Jerry: Oh no, there's still lots to do! One thing I do to motivate the less self-motivated students is give them a structured environment: where tasks are predictable, where there's routine. With a good routine, they know what to expect and tasks are organized into steps they understand and can do. We always do mental math first, then review the day's homework, then start a new lesson, and so on. I find that variations from the format inevitably throw some students "off their stride," and less gets done.

Kelvin: *That reminds me of the sequencing idea. People sometimes say that you have to learn math concepts in a certain sequence or else you risk getting hopelessly lost in the long term. Is that true?*

Jerry: Yes, in a sense it *is* true. But teachers can do things to keep students from getting lost as a result. In our new curriculum, for example, we use "spiral sequencing," where we revisit topics periodically and give daily review in between visits. If you're sick for a whole week, you don't miss out altogether on a particular math topic. And all the teachers in my school now use cumulative testing, which gives students incentives for consolidating what they know so that there are no "holes" in their math knowledge at the end of the course.

Kelvin: *Still, by its nature, math must be pretty abstract, even in tenth grade.*

Jerry: You're right about that. Especially in the course called "pre-calculus," which actually says in its advertising that it *is* abstract and is intended for students who already enjoy math. How do you offer concrete, hands-on activities related to factoring? What are the everyday uses for factoring? [*Smiles.*] Most students *do* learn better if you can make the material more down to earth and relate it to familiar activities.

But I have found ways to move in that direction. This year we used graphing calculators, for example, which the students really enjoy. The calculators make it a lot easier to create graphs—much faster and less laborious. With the calculators, you can actu-ally play around with graphing different functions instead of taking fifteen minutes just to draw one by hand. When we get the computer lab set up properly, we'll be able to do even more.

Kelvin: *Sounds like with the calculators, students could even work together. They could do problems and projects cooperatively.*

Jerry: That's indeed the case. Students can do problems independently, for example, and compare their results. We'll be able to do more joint work, in fact, when we get the computer lab set up.

Kelvin: *I often think of math as being an especially "solitary" activity, not one that lends itself to working with others. Would you agree?*

Jerry: I've found that there are ways for students in math to work together, like with the graphing calculators. Sometimes, in fact, I've actually had trouble with students cooperating *too* much; it seems like they're always wanting to consult with each other how to do certain problems, or about what the answers are. Then I wish they would function more independently of each other. A mix is best: cooperation combined and independence combined.

What Do You Think?

1. Given Jerry Acton's comments, would you describe mathematical success as a "cognitive" skill, a "social" skill, or as some combination? Explain your reasoning.

2. Do you believe there is indeed truth in the stereotypes or expectations about mathematics that Kelvin expressed at the beginning of the interview? How would you qualify these ideas, taking into account both Jerry's comments and your own knowledge and beliefs?

3. Sometimes mathematics is traditionally thought of as a "boy's" subject more than a "girl's." Judging by Jerry's comments, do you think this is true for his class? Do you still think it could be true for mathematics students in general?

PERSPECTIVES

What Creates a Life of Moral Commitment?

• • • • • Both Kohlberg's and Gilligan's theories concern moral beliefs rather than moral actions: they describe what people know and believe about right and wrong, without predicting whether in fact they will actually do what they believe. In everyday life, of course, we often do *not* choose what we believe is the most moral course of action. The gap between actions and beliefs exists even though we gradually come to be very consistent in our beliefs and even in knowing what actions we should take, whether or not we take them (Keller & Edelstein, 1993).

Yet some individuals do seem to act according to their beliefs relatively consistently—so consistently, in fact, that they make a way of life out of their moral commitments. Take Suzie Valadez, a resident of the border city of El Paso, Texas. Every morning for the past thirty years, Suzie has packed sandwiches and other supplies and driven to Cuidad Juarez, the neighboring town on the Mexican side of the border. Along with friends and members of her family, she distributes the food to the poor and homeless at the town dump; later she often visits a school and a medical clinic that she helped to organize for the area. Naturally, she has become a valued part of the community, and residents have affectionately nicknamed her "Queen of the Dump" to honor her efforts.

What motivates someone like Suzie Valadez to work so untiringly on behalf of the poor? Anne Colby and William Damon have studied this question at length and suggested several explanations in a book called *Some Do Care: Contemporary Lives of Moral Commitment* (1992). After interviewing Suzie and other highly committed individuals at length, they concluded that developing sophisticated moral *beliefs* has little to do with leading a committed life. When asked to solve hypothetical moral problems (such as "Should a husband steal a drug to save his dying wife?"), Suzie and others like her reasoned about the problems in a range of ways, but ways that were typical of the population as a whole. When analyzed according to Kohlberg's six-stage framework of moral judgment, for example, the morally committed individuals stated beliefs that clustered around the "conventional" levels of development.

Rather than finding predictable stages of development, a number of authors (including Colby and Damon) have found that moral commitment is a lifelong evolution, one that merely begins during childhood and adolescence (Wilson, 1993). Suzie Valadez's childhood, for example, was consistent with her later commitment to the poor and to children, but her childhood would also have been consistent with some other form of adult life. As a child and youth, for example, Suzie showed great liking for others and an outgoing personality. She also received tremendous support for this quality from her parents, friends, and other relatives. But many other young people have these experiences in childhood without becoming particularly committed to serving the poor as adults.

What factors propelled Suzie's movement toward moral commitment? One factor was her interest in listening to others' concerns, even when their lives and perspectives differed from her own. By listening to the needs of the poor in particular, she could respond more appropriately, and eventually—and paradoxically—she became a better leader and independent advocate in the long term. Other factors were more accidental: one of her sisters died as a young adult, for example, and this event deepened Suzie's religious commitments and led her to affiliate with a new church community that supported its members more actively.

Although the details of her life were unique, Suzie Valadez shared important underlying qualities with other people leading morally committed lives. Colby and Damon (1992) identified several of these qualities. For example, in addition to a desire to listen closely to others, these people seem to enjoy collaborating with others even when their goals or values differ, and they actively seek new knowledge and skills from others who differ from them. These involvements stimulate the person to rethink his or her own values at increasingly profound and permanent levels and eventually to transform them into lasting moral commitments and lifestyles. But the process of transformation takes more than the seventeen-odd years or so of childhood and adolescence; it requires a lifetime.

What Do You Think?

Given that moral beliefs and moral actions are not necessarily consistent with each other, is there any reason to be concerned with children's moral *beliefs*? Should parents and teachers in particular try to encourage moral belief in youngsters or simply concern themselves with their moral actions?

A few older teenagers and young adults develop **postconventional moral judgment,** meaning that for the first time ethical reasoning goes beyond the judgments society conventionally makes about right and wrong. Adolescents' growing ability to use abstract formal thought stimulates this development, though it does not guarantee it. Unlike schoolchildren, teenagers can evaluate ethical ideas that *might* be right or wrong, given certain circumstances that can only be imagined.

Issues in the Development of Moral Beliefs About Justice

Kohlberg's six stages of moral judgment have held up well when tested on a wide variety of children, adolescents, and adults (see Figure 15.2). The stages of moral thinking shown in Table 15.1 do seem to describe how moral judgment develops, at least when individuals focus on hypothetical dilemmas posed in stories. When presented with stories about risky but fictional sexual behaviors, adolescents of both sexes evaluated the actions of the stories' characters in line with Kohlberg's stages (Jadack et al., 1995).

Even so, Kohlberg's theory of moral judgment leaves a number of important questions unanswered. One is whether the theory really recognizes the impact of prior knowledge on beliefs; another is whether the theory distinguishes clearly enough between conventions and morality. The most important lingering question has to do with gender differences: does Kohlberg's theory really describe the moral development of girls as well as that of boys?

Form Versus Content of Moral Beliefs   Despite the theory's plausibility, a number of developmental psychologists have questioned important aspects of it. Can the form of ethical thinking really be separated from content to the degree Kohlberg proposes? Perhaps not. Some studies have found that when people reason about familiar situations, they tend to have more mature (that is, higher-stage) ethical responses (Lickona, 1991). For instance, children have a better sense of fairness about playing four-square on the playground than about whether to steal a drug for a spouse who is dying (one of Kohlberg's fictional dilemmas). In addition, young women think in more mature (more "developed") ways about ethical problems of special concern and familiarity to women, such as whether to engage in premarital sex or whether to have an abortion (Bollerud et al., 1990). To some extent, therefore, what someone thinks about affects the ethics she applies.

Conventions Versus Morality   According to some psychologists, some inconsistencies in moral beliefs may arise because the theory does not fully distinguish between social conventions and morality (Nucci & Turiel, 1993). **Social conventions** refer to the arbitrary customs and agreements about behavior that members of society use, such as table manners and forms of greeting and of dressing. *Morality*, as we already pointed out, refers to the weightier matters of justice and right and wrong. By nature, social conventions inevitably generate widespread agreement throughout society, whereas morality does not necessarily do so. Yet Kohlberg's six-stage theory glosses over these differences by defining some of its stages in terms of social conventions and others in terms of morality. Stage 4 (social system orientation),

• • •

postconventional moral judgment In Kohlberg's theory, an orientation to moral justice that develops beyond conventional rules and beliefs.

social conventions Arbitrary customs and agreements about behavior that members of a society use.

A youth's level of moral judgment depends on the reasoning used, not on the judgments as such. In this cartoon, Ben may express ideas that seem principled, but if they have been adopted simply to conform, as his mother implies, then Ben's level of moral thinking is closer to Kohlberg's middle, conventional level.

"Ben is in his first year of high school, and he's questioning all the right things."

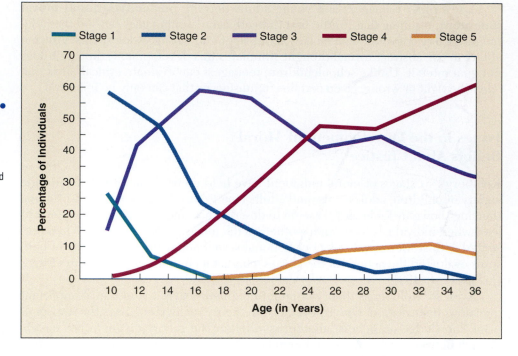

● ● ● ● ● ● ● ● ● ● ● ● ● ● ●

FIGURE 15.2

The Development of Moral Reasoning

In a longitudinal follow-up study of Kohlberg's original sample, Colby and her colleagues confirmed that subjects showed consistent upward advances in moral reasoning with age. The graph shows the extent to which subjects gave responses characteristic of each of Kohlberg's six stages from age ten through adulthood. With development, responses associated with the preconventional level (stages 1 and 2) declined, whereas responses associated with the conventional level (stages 3 and 4) increased. Few young adults moved to the postconventional level of moral reasoning.
Source: Adapted from Colby et al. (1983).

for example, seems to refer to social conventions as well as to moral matters, but stage 5 (social contract orientation) refers only to moral judgment.

Studies that have in fact distinguished between convention and morality have produced a less stagelike picture of moral development. Suppose children are asked questions such as these:

Is it wrong to steal? *(morality related)*

Is it wrong to hit another person? *(morality related)*

Is it wrong for a group to change the rules of a game? *(convention related)*

Is it okay for a country to make the traffic lights blue and purple instead of red and green? *(convention related)*

Throughout the middle childhood and beyond, most children believe hitting and stealing are wrong but changing the rules of a game or changing the color of traffic lights is acceptable (Smetana et al., 1991a). If true morality develops at all, then, it seems to begin doing so even before the school years. By kindergarten, children already clearly distinguish between moral and conventional behavior.

Gender Differences in Morality?   One especially important criticism of Kohlberg's theory of moral justice has to do with possible gender bias: Do Kohlberg's stages describe both genders equally well? And does his theory undervalue ethical attitudes that may develop more fully in girls and women than in boys and men? The best-known investigations of these questions have been pursued by Carol Gilligan and her associates, described next.

Gilligan's Ethics of Care

According to Gilligan and others, boys and girls tend to view moral problems differently (Gordon et al., 1996; Taylor et al., 1995). As they grow up, boys learn to think more often in terms of general ethical principles that they can apply to specific moral situations. They might learn that deceiving is always bad in principle and evaluate a specific instance of deception of a friend against this generalization. The principles boys learn also tend to emphasize independence, autonomy, and the rights of others. This orientation biases boys to ignore or minimize others' possible needs: if a friend is at home sick with a cold, it may seem better to leave him alone until he gets better rather than check on how well he is recovering.

Girls tend to develop a different sort of morality as they grow up. Instead of seeing moral judgment as a set of abstract principles to apply to specific situations, girls tend to develop an *ethics of care,* a view that integrates principles with the contexts in which judgments must be made (see Table 15.2). A girl therefore may think deception is usually bad but also believe deception is ethical in certain circumstances, such as when a friend needs reassurance about the quality of a term paper that is actually mediocre but took a lot of time and effort. Viewing ethics in context grows out of a general concern for the needs of others more than for one's independence. A friend who is depressed therefore deserves a visit or a phone call; leaving her alone seems more like neglect than like respect for her privacy.

These differences are only tendencies, not dramatic or sharply drawn gender differences. But they are enough, argues Gilligan, to make Kohlberg's theory seem to underrate the moral development of girls and women. Concern with context and with others' needs causes girls to score closer to the middling, conventional levels of moral judgment, where peers' opinions matter most. Asked if a child should inform authorities about a friend who often shoplifts small items from a local department store, a girl is likely to give priority to one part of the problem in particular: that of balancing each person's views and needs in the particular situation. Doing so means wondering, among other things, whether informing will alienate peers not only from the shoplifter but also from the informer. On the other hand, it also means wondering whether keeping silent will make her risk losing the trust and respect of important adults, such as parents and teachers. It also means considering the amount of emotional pain that will befall the shoplifting friend at the hands of either angry parents or the police. Taking all of these considerations into account can make the final decision seem hesitant, tentative, and apparently lacking in principle, whichever way it goes.

Reviews of moral judgment have qualified Gilligan's ideas somewhat but have also lent them support. When faced with hypothetical dilemmas, females show as much capacity as males to reason in terms of abstract ethical principles (Gilligan & Wiggins, 1987). When faced with real-life dilemmas, however, girls make different choices (Taylor et al., 1995). For example, adolescent girls who personally confront the decision of whether to engage in premarital intercourse often show more concern than do boys for the context in which they make their decisions and for the impact of their decisions on relationships with others. As with Kohlberg's justice-oriented stages, however, a needs-oriented ethics of care takes time—years, in fact—to develop.

TABLE 15.2   Gilligan's Stages of Moral Development

Stage	Features
Stage 1 *Survival orientation*	Egocentric concern for self, lack of awareness of others' needs; "right" action is what promotes emotional or physical survival
Stage 2 *Conventional care*	Lack of distinction between what others want and what is right; "right" action is whatever pleases others best
Stage 3 *Integrated care*	Coordination or integration of needs of self and of others; "right" action takes account of self as well as others

Source: Gilligan (1982).

Moral development involves more than learning to reason about moral principles. It also involves learning to care about others and to reconcile their needs with your own. This girl seems to be on her way to learning to care, by providing companionship for elderly residents.

The Ethics of Care During Adolescence

As with the morality of justice, young people develop an ethics of care during adolescence, but like ethical justice, it remains somewhat conventional during the teenage years. As school-age children, they develop significant concern about others' needs and welfare, and begin viewing actions as good if the actions take others' needs and welfare into account (Larrabee, 1993). However, egocentrism persists in that teenagers often fail to distinguish between actions that merely *please* others and actions that are "right" in a deeper, ethical sense. For example, if parents will be pleased if their adolescent enrolls in complex science and mathematics courses in high school, doing so may seem "right" to the youngster, even if he has little interest or aptitude in those areas.

As with the ethics of justice, a few individuals move beyond conventional pleasing of others toward *integrated care,* in which the young person realizes that pleasing everyone is not always possible but it is important to balance everyone's needs, including her own (Larrabee, 1993). Deciding whether or not to take a part-time job, for example, now becomes a matter of reconciling the impact of the job on family, friends, and self. Some individuals may gain (the teenager herself may earn more money and make new friends), but others may lose (parents and friends may see less of her). The gains and losses must be balanced rather than viewed completely as gains.

Overall, then, the moralities of justice and care begin taking into account a broader array of both interpersonal circumstances and general principles than was true during the school years. Teenagers more often refer to principles in evaluating actions, although they still do not always act on those principles. Often they also regard pleasing others as ethically good or right, even though they are learning to deal with the impossibility of pleasing everyone perfectly. Like many other cognitive developments, these changes result from adolescents' growing capacities to reason abstractly.

WHAT DO YOU THINK ?   Suppose you are starting your first job in a helping profession, such as nursing or teaching. How much would you want your work to be guided by an ethics of justice and how much by an ethics of care? Exchange your views on this question with a classmate or a friend.

The Development of Social Cognition

No matter which approach they take, most developmental psychologists agree that the new cognitive skills of adolescents have important effects on their **social cognition**, their knowledge and beliefs about interpersonal and social matters. In this section, we look at the most important forms of social cognition. We begin with a description of the special form of self-centeredness, or **adolescent egocentrism**, that affects teenagers' reactions to others and their beliefs about themselves. We consider what causes this form of egocentrism and how those causes affect three other important kinds of social cognition: moral beliefs, political attitudes, and religious orientation.

Egocentrism During Adolescence

When adolescents first begin reasoning abstractly, they often become overly impressed with this skill; it seems to them that anything can be solved "if only people would be reasonable" (that is, logical). This attitude can make teenagers idealistic and keep them from appreciating the practical limits of logic (Bowers, 1995). They may wonder why no one has ever "realized" that world war might be abolished simply by explaining to all the world powers the obvious dangers of war. Or they may wonder why their parents have not noticed the many "errors" they have made in raising children.

The development of formal thought also leads to a new kind of confusion between an adolescent's own thoughts and those of others. This confusion of viewpoints amounts to a form of egocentrism. Unlike the egocentrism of preschoolers, which is based on concrete problems, adolescent egocentrism concerns more abstract thoughts and problems. Consider what happened to Neira. When she was fourteen, she had to perform at a figure-skating recital. For weeks beforehand, she practiced daily to prepare. As the performance date drew near, she naturally began to worry about how well she would do. In fact, she became convinced that

• • •

social cognition Knowledge and beliefs about interpersonal and social matters.

adolescent egocentrism The tendency of adolescents to perceive the world (and themselves) from their own perspective.

These teenagers illustrate two aspects of adolescent egocentrism: a preoccupation with the reactions of others and a belief that serious catastrophes may happen to others but never to them.

"everyone" was talking about her particular performance and wondering how good it would be. Her parents encouraged her not to worry and assured her that "people always like what you do on your skates." To Neira, however, these comments suggested that her parents did not appreciate the unique importance of *her* performance. Even after the recital, Neira fretted about others' reactions to it: Had they liked it? What were they saying about it?

The Imaginary Audience   Adolescent egocentrism such as Neira's sometimes shows itself in teenagers' preoccupation with the reactions of others. Thirteen-year-olds often fail to differentiate between how they feel about themselves and how others feel about them. Instead, they act as though they are performing for an **imaginary audience,** one that is as concerned with their appearance and behavior as they themselves are (Elkind, 1985).

Teenagers also reveal concern with an imaginary audience through *strategic interactions* with their peers, encounters that aim to either reveal or conceal personal information indirectly. Telephoning often serves as a strategic interaction, especially for younger teenagers. Frequent phone calls help to sustain a belief in personal popularity with an imaginary audience, so a teenager may subtly encourage others to phone by casually promising to share special gossip or secrets "if you call me tonight." An adolescent can also create the appearance of popularity by talking on the phone for very long periods of time so that potential callers get a "busy" signal, implying that the youngster is too popular to reach easily by telephone. This message can also be conveyed to the person on the line with an offhand comment such as "Gotta go; I'm expecting some other calls."

The Personal Fable   As a result of their egocentrism, teenagers often believe in a **personal fable,** or the notion that their own lives embody a special story that is heroic and completely unique. For example, one high school student may be convinced that no love affair has ever reached the heights of romance of his involvement with a classmate. Another may believe she is destined for great fame and fortune by virtue of (what she considers to be) her unparalleled combination of charm and academic talent. Still another may "know" that even though serious catastrophes happen to others, they will never happen to him; he will never get seriously ill, or have trouble finding a job, or die.

In experiencing these feelings and ideas, adolescents fail to realize how other individuals feel about themselves as well. Early in adolescence, they still have only limited empathy, or the ability to understand reliably the abstract thoughts and feelings of others and compare those thoughts and feelings with their own. In fact, much of adolescence consists of developing these social skills. So does most of adulthood, for that matter; we never really finish learning how to understand others or comparing our own experiences with those of others. But adolescence serves as the time when most people begin learning to consider other viewpoints in relation to their own and developing complex ideas about moral, political, and religious questions, among others, in response.

However, not all teenagers seem to be equally egocentric, and even those who do show this quality only when compared to adults, not to younger children. Investigations of adolescents' belief in an imaginary audience show that teenagers are just as likely to develop greater empathy, or interpersonal sensitivity, during this developmental period as they are to develop greater self-centeredness (Lapsley, 1991). Accurate awareness of others' opinions about oneself apparently develops alongside, and sometimes even instead of, self-conscious preoccupation with others' opinions. The relative balance between these two developments depends, among other things, on the quality of relationships between parents and the adolescent: closer and more supportive relationships lead to greater realism and less self-consciousness.

- - - •

imaginary audience A characteristic of young adolescents in which they act as though they are performing for an audience and believe that others are as concerned with their appearance and behavior as they themselves are.

personal fable Adolescents' belief that their own lives embody a special story that is heroic and completely unique.

The Development of Political Ideas

Perhaps not surprisingly, political thinking develops in ways that parallel other forms of cognition and continually reveals both progress and limitations. Teenagers often hold more sophisticated political ideas than children do; they handle political ideas and opinions more abstractly and see more relationships among them. They view the formation of laws and legal regulations more democratically, seeing them as something that applies equally to everybody in society rather than to isolated individuals or selected groups (Haste & Torney-Purta, 1992). In these ways, adolescent political thinking draws on elements of formal operational thought and the relatively advanced forms of moral thinking. At the same time, however, adolescents reveal substantial gaps and inconsistencies in their political thinking. These suggest that political thinking is not acquired in an all-or-nothing, stagelike way but involves acquiring large amounts of specific political knowledge—an idea consistent with the information-processing viewpoint, discussed later in this chapter.

To understand these developments, consider a common political issue: poverty. What must be done to eliminate it? Can it really ever be eliminated? The answers given by two (imaginary) children, one in sixth grade and one in twelfth grade, differ in significant ways that reflect the children's cognitive development. The answers also have some common limitations despite the six years of living and learning that separate the two youngsters. First, the sixth-grader:

INTERVIEWER: Do you know what I mean by *poverty*?

SIXTH-GRADER: No.

INTERVIEWER: It means being poor—not having any money. Could you make it so no one was poor?

SIXTH-GRADER: Um . . . if they got people to really work hard, then maybe. But if you were retired or just lazy, I don't know. You've already put in lots of years working.

INTERVIEWER: Do you think we could make it so that there wouldn't be poor people any more?

SIXTH-GRADER: Maybe, in the future, if they could enforce the law that all lazy people should work.

The twelfth-grader answered in this way:

INTERVIEWER: Do you think we could ever eliminate poverty?

TWELFTH-GRADER: Yes, because this country is highly advanced and rich. I mean, we give away money for all kinds of things—roads, starving nations, and such. Why not spend some money at home here? Buy fewer bombs, make more jobs—even for young kids like me!

Aside from obvious differences in content, how do these two responses differ in cognitive form? First, because the adolescent can hold several ideas in mind at once, he seems to better understand that a political problem may concern many aspects of society at once (Torney-Purta, 1990b). Unlike the younger child, he points out how poverty may be related to or aggravated by activities beyond the borders of his own particular country, the United States, by implying that poverty abroad may worsen poverty at home by stimulating foreign aid and thereby draining away dollars. In contrast, the younger child implies that poverty is simply the fault of the individuals who experience it. If only they would work harder, they might escape their problem with little or no help from the rest of society and with little impact on society.

The two children also have different views of how governments can help ordinary people. The sixth-grader implies that the most helpful thing government can do about poverty is to act like the police: the government should make poor people work harder ("enforce the law that all lazy people should work"). The twelfth-grader, on the other hand, suggests a less concrete solution: that government and citizens can genuinely cooperate with each other. In his view, the government should identify the people or groups who need money the most and give it to them; after all, these are the domestic poor, not the foreign poor.

Although the twelfth-grader's ideas are more abstract and less personal than the sixth-grader's, neither youngster expresses a true *ideology,* or coherent philosophy, about poverty. Admittedly, neither has a chance to do so in the short interviews quoted earlier; longer talks might allow them to show their political knowledge and sensitivities more completely. But probably not; studies show that most adolescents lack a consistent, conscious system of beliefs about politics (Haste & Torney-Purta, 1992). Instead, they tend to approximate consistency, frequently contradict themselves, and often base political ideas on values that are unconscious to some extent. The twelfth-grader in this example may freely contradict himself when the topic shifts to the problems of strategic planning for national defense by deciding that foreign economic aid does serve a useful, if indirect, purpose by gaining allies abroad.

Of course, in a highly individualistic society such as the United States, lack of a coherent ideology may also represent a final or true maturity rather than a failure to attain one. Like most adolescents, very few adults really have explicit, complex political philosophies, and many tend to hold rather personalized beliefs on specific issues. The attitudes of the sixth-grader have been stated publicly in the U.S. Congress, as well as in many other adult forums. Yet sophisticated ideas about aspects of the political process often are expressed by young people as well, as long as they are speaking from experiences they have actually had (Coles, 1993).

Religious Beliefs and Orientation

During adolescence, cognitive development also affects both specific religious beliefs and overall religious orientation. In general, specific beliefs become more sophisticated or complex than they were during childhood. The concept of religion, for example, evolves from relatively superficial notions to subtler and more abstract ones. A child of ten is more likely to identify a religion by observable behaviors (a Catholic is "someone who goes to mass every Sunday"), whereas a teenager is more likely to identify it according to beliefs (a Jew is "someone who believes in one God and doesn't believe in the New Testament"). These changes occur partly due to young people's developing cognitive skills and partly because they are accumulating greater general knowledge of the world of ethical issues, of religion in particular (Molnan, 1997).

For those involved in religious education and development, children's acquisition of specific beliefs such as these often matters less than their development of an overall view of the world, or of a *faith*—a coherent orientation to religious experiences that guides their responses to life. Faith is much more general than "mere" beliefs are: it usually involves feelings as well as thoughts. Due to its breadth, faith often touches on topics and problems that are not explicitly religious in content, such as the meaning of birth and death or the best ways to handle personal relationships (Noddings, 1993).

In childhood, religious orientation amounts largely to loose groupings of concrete religious beliefs and images, often with relatively little coordination and seemingly little relevance to daily experiences (Fowler, 1996). A ten-year-old might describe God like this, for example:

INTERVIEWER: Can you tell me what God is?

MILLIE: God is a like a saint. He's good and he like—he like rules the world, but in a good way. And . . .

INTERVIEWER: How does he rule the world?

MILLIE: Well, he—not really rule the world, but um—let's see, he like—he lives on top of the world, and he's always watching over everybody. At least he tries to. And he does what he thinks is right. He does what he thinks is right and tries to do the best and—he lives up in heaven and . . .

INTERVIEWER: What does God look like?

MILLIE: I imagine that he's an old man with a white beard and white hair wearing a long robe and that the clouds are his floor and he has a throne. And he has all these people, and there's angels around him. (Fowler, 1981, pp. 138–140)

Millie describes God in concrete terms that have little relevance to daily life. In contrast, a fifteen-year-old offers fewer visual images; for her, God is more of a universal presence that she believes permeates her life and helps her:

INTERVIEWER: What do you think God is?

LINDA: God is different to a lot of people . . . I just feel . . . he's there. There might not be any material proof, but I *know*. I can bet my life on it. Really. I know because he *has* talked to me. . . . [Once when I had trouble with my friends,] I remembered that, you know, there was *God*, and I just asked him to tell me something, tell me what I could do, because why can't I be good friends with everybody? Go places with her one time, and then with her and him, and you know, with everybody? (Fowler, 1981, pp. 155–156)

For this adolescent, God is not so much a person living in a specific place as an abstraction. God is a relationship that transcends specific situations and experiences and that helps to give those specifics fuller meaning.

Religious orientation need not come out of an organized religion, of course, and for many adolescents and adults it does not. Many teenagers prefer to develop a personal faith without reference to other groups' or individuals' beliefs. Take this sixteen-year-old, who grew up attending an unusually liberal Protestant church and whose ideas resemble those of many people who never attend church at all:

INTERVIEWER: What means the most to you?

BRIAN: Just life. It fascinates me. I don't know what goes on before or after birth or death. And some things scare me. The unknown is really a factor in my life because I like to think about it a lot and the reason why everything got here. It really bothers me a lot because I don't know the answers and no one knows the answers, and I can't turn to anyone to get the answers—except to God, if there is a God. Maybe someday I'll get a vision from the Almighty! *(spoken sarcastically)* (Fowler, 1981, p. 159)

These ideas have much of the scope of Linda's comments. Despite appearances, however, they may partly reflect social conformity rather than true, spontaneous conviction. Paradoxically, Brian may be conforming to an ideal of nonconformity or independent thinking. He implies this possibility elsewhere in the interview by stating that the worst thing that could happen to him would be to agree with conventional, majority opinions. But although Brian and Linda differ dramatically in the source of their religious orientation—Brian comes from a relatively secular, humanist social environment and Linda from a more traditional Christian denomination—they are not entirely opposite in their thinking. Compared to Millie, they share a quality of comprehensiveness; their specific beliefs range relatively widely over life's issues and fit together at least some of the time.

These developments may result from changes both in general cognitive structures and in knowledge and information-processing strategies (discussed next). As Piaget predicted for other realms of knowledge, Brian and Linda have developed the capacity to think abstractly, and as a result they may have reconstructed their childhood beliefs and faith to use their new abilities. At the same time, they have had several years in which to acquire new knowledge about religion, God, and the

Participation in social causes like these youths signing the wall for the Walk for Hunger both reflects and builds adolescents, involvement in community and society. It also builds more sophisticated thinking about societal needs. But it probably also serves personal needs, like making new friends.

meaning and dilemmas of life (Heller, 1994). Along with this knowledge may have come new, broad strategies for dealing with and organizing this knowledge, strategies similar in scope to Piaget's formal operations but with greater application to religious problems. Therefore, in their own ways, Brian and Linda may have become modest experts about faith, although not about the same kind of faith.

As these comments suggest, cognition significantly influences many areas of adolescent life that are essentially social in nature. And vice versa: a motivation to have many friends, for example, can foster the strong development of empathy, which is in part a cognitive skill. Similarly, deep involvement with a religion can promote relatively sophisticated knowledge and thinking about religious beliefs, at least as they exist in that particular religion. In real life, cognitive and social development do not divide up neatly as they are made to do in textbooks such as this one. (See, for example, the Perspectives box on lives of moral commitment on page 470.) Their blending shows up again in the next chapter, in which we discuss adolescents' psychosocial development. As we will see there, most psychosocial developments assume the types of cognitive accomplishments discussed in this chapter. Some, such as identity development, do so rather explicitly, but all at least imply an awareness of teenagers' growing ability to think.

WHAT DO YOU THINK?   A young person once said, "My parents get smarter every year." In what sense is this probably true? In what sense is it probably the young person who is getting smarter? If possible, after articulating your ideas about these questions, consult with a parent to get her or his own views about them.

Information-Processing Features of Adolescent Thought

As we saw in Chapter 2, information-processing theory sees human cognition as a complex storage and retrieval system, governed largely by an "executive" control system that transfers information between short- and long-term memory and organizes information for more efficient and meaningful handling and retrieval. When cognition is viewed this way, development consists largely of overcoming the bottlenecks in processing information, especially those caused by the limited capacities of the executive and short-term memory. As children mature into adolescents, they develop strategies for taking in, organizing, and remembering larger amounts of information more quickly and with less effort. The most important of these strategies are included in Figure 15.3 and explained more fully next.

Improved Capacity to Process Information

Typically an adolescent can deal with, or process, more information than a child can. A first-grader may remember three or four random digits (3 9 5 1), but a teenager usually can remember six or seven. And when a first-grader asks an adult how to spell a word, he can hold only two or three letters in his mind at a time; the adult has to dole them out singly or in very small groups (*LO . . . CO . . . MO . . . TI . . . VE*). A teenager can more often encounter much longer groupings of letters and still reconstruct the word accurately.

These differences may result from either of two sources. The first source is what information-processing psychologists sometimes call *structural capacity,* meaning a person's basic "mental power," or cognitive ability (Case & Okamoto, 1996). Differences in structural capacity are like the differences in physical strength between adolescents and children: because teenagers have bigger and more powerful muscles, they naturally can accomplish more physically. The same is true for performance on cognitive tasks: adolescents may be able to handle longer-term projects than children can, partly because their brains can handle more information at any one time.

The second source of differences between children and adolescents is sometimes called *functional capacity,* the ability to make efficient use of existing mental abilities. Differences in functional capacity are more like the improvements in physical performance that come to a gymnast who already is perfectly conditioned: at a certain point in her training, her performance improves mainly because she learns to coordinate her movements more precisely, rest her muscles when she does not really need them, and take into account the unique features of the gymnasium in which she is performing. Similarly, functional capacity on cognitive tasks requires coordinating existing skills to best advantage—recalling facts about World War II by grouping them according to theme or topic, for instance.

In terms of cognitive development, it usually is hard to discriminate between the relative influences of structural and functional capacity, that is, between how much of an adolescent's improved thinking comes from a greater ability to hold information in mind and how much comes from greater efficiency in processing information (King & Kitchener, 1994). Almost any cognitive task allows an individual to perform it more efficiently with practice; yet the person himself may not be aware that he is trying to do so. For example, many adolescents can write term papers much more easily than they could when they attended elementary school, but try as they may, they may be unable to explain *why* they can do so. Did their extra years of practice make them smarter than before or simply more efficient at using skills they have always had? Research on information processing suggests that cognitive development consists of a bit of both.

Compared to younger children doing a science experiment, these teenagers are more planful about carrying out a complicated science project. The changes happen both because they can now hold more ideas in mind at once because they can coordinate and delegate activities between partners more effectively and because their motor skills for handling the equipment may be better than ever.

Expertise in Specific Domains of Knowledge

By adolescence, many individuals have become comparative experts in specific domains of knowledge or skill. These domains may or may not have much to do with school learning. One teenager excels in knowledge of mathematics, whereas another excels in knowledge of baseball and still another excels in getting along with people.

Much of such expertise may depend not on generalized development of cognitive structures, as Piagetian theorists would claim, but on the long, slow acquisition of large amounts of specific knowledge, along with better organization of that knowledge. Studies of experts and novices among adults suggest this possibility. Experts in physics know many more concepts about physics than beginners do, but they do not necessarily know more about geography, English grammar, or other areas of knowledge (Gregg & Leinhardt, 1995). Experts also know more about problem solving in their particular field of expertise. A mathematician remembers countless formulas, equations, and solution methods, thanks to years of experience in memorizing them. Her memories naturally help her to solve new problems as they come up; she may realize that a new equation is similar to one she has worked with before and simply recall how she responded to the earlier formula.

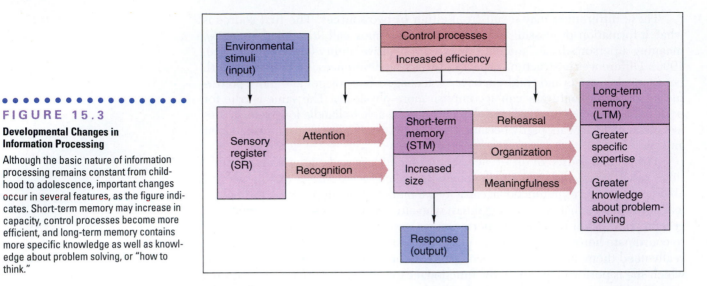

FIGURE 15.3

Developmental Changes in Information Processing

Although the basic nature of information processing remains constant from childhood to adolescence, important changes occur in several features, as the figure indicates. Short-term memory may increase in capacity, control processes become more efficient, and long-term memory contains more specific knowledge as well as knowledge about problem solving, or "how to think."

Ironically, then, expertise often makes creative problem solving unnecessary. Instead of using valuable energy in thinking through a solution, the expert can simply recall *heuristics*, or general strategies for solving classes or types of problems. (Table 15.3 illustrates the use of heuristics for solving problems in two different academic areas.) This advantage, however, is confined to specific domains or types of problems. An expert's performance therefore contradicts a widespread (but not entirely justified) impression of Piaget's theory: that it proposes powerful, abstract strategies that develop across many domains at once. Outside of his field, an expert must struggle for solutions just like the rest of us. Within his field, on the other hand, he often may only look as though he is reasoning at a high level, when in reality much of his performance amounts to a simple recall—the kind we all engage in when we remember the letters of the alphabet or a phone number.

This conclusion does not mean, however, that experts work only by simple recall. On the contrary, their larger number of memories may free them to focus on more difficult aspects of a problem or on aspects they have never encountered before. If you have to make an oral presentation on a topic that you already know well, for example, you may spend *more* time planning its overall design and purpose and relatively *less* time on the details of final preparation. To a large extent, the final preparations take care of themselves because you can draw on a rich array of ideas and concepts about your topic.

TABLE 15.3   Examples of Problem-Solving Strategies (Heuristics) in Two Academic Subjects

Problem in Social Studies

What have the media been saying about the impact of computers on society?
Novice-level strategy: Search all of the headlines in the newspaper for the past year.
Expert-level strategy: Search the headlines for the past week or two; look for references to and dates of references further back in the past; check only those dates.

Problem in Algebra

How to factor the equation $12x^2 - xy - 6y^2$?
Novice-level strategy: Try multiplying every possible set of linear combinations—$(x + y)$, $(x - y)$, $(2x + y)$, $2x - y)$, $(x + 2y)$, $(x - 2y)$, etc.—until you find one that gives the correct answer.
Expert-level strategy: Search for clues that eliminate the need to try every possible linear combination; e.g., try only combinations in which the final terms multiply to −6.

Implications of the Information-Processing Viewpoint

By focusing on the detailed features of problem solving, the information-processing viewpoint provides a valuable complement to the broader approach of cognitive developmental theory. By focusing on the fine details of thinking, information-processing theory offers more insights into why individuals vary in their thinking performances from one occasion to the next. Some psychologists have also tried to identify developmental trends in information processing (Case & Edelstein, 1993). Their research has emphasized specific sequences within particular domains of thinking rather than the more global stages of the cognitive develop-

A TALK WITH
Joan, Age Fifteen

. . . .

Thinking in Adolescence

Joan is a slender, poised young woman of fifteen with a friendly but serious manner. She was interviewed on the back porch of her home after school.

Interviewer: *How have your thinking and intellectual activity changed over the past several years?*

Joan: For some kids it looks like they haven't changed very much, but for me they have. You read and think about different things—like George Orwell's *1984*—more than you did before, and the discussions you have are a lot different . . . about bigger things.

Interviewer: *Why does a book like 1984 appeal to you now?*

Joan: Well, you can understand it now. I mean, you can start thinking about all the different . . . the big questions . . .

Interviewer: *What would be an example?*

Joan: Like . . . the type of government. Serious things. Now if I read a fairy tale it's fun, but I'm not so into it. It's not quite as interesting, while before it was exciting.

Interviewer: *Have there been changes in the way you use your mind to figure out problems at school?*

Joan: I don't think so. I mean, it's like I do more advanced math and stuff, but it doesn't seem to me that I couldn't have understood it before if someone had taught it to me. Of course, now you don't just deal with facts. You sort of write essays and things and read. You have to think about the connections. Which I'm not sure I couldn't have done before.

Interviewer: *How has your thinking about problems changed?*

Joan: It's hard to remember. I mean, I talked about problems before, but I suppose that I didn't think about so many realistic things. I remember thinking about "what if" after I read something or saw something, but it was generally about fantasy rather than something like world war or the nuclear threat. I think I could have learned what I am learning now in sixth grade. When we get into more interesting things like in history and English, I end up talking about it out of school more. Like with my parents and with some friends. When it's not just facts. I mean, you never talk about math and French out of school, but you may talk about a book you read in history or something connected with other things.

Interviewer: *Do you feel more like an intellectual equal with adults?*

Joan: I don't ever remember feeling like I was not an equal. I always thought that if I didn't know it now, I'd learn it in a few months, and then I would definitely be as smart or smarter.

Interviewer: *Are all kids able to think the same way you do?*

Joan: Well, it sort of divides up more. I mean, before there were lots of different levels, and it was basically who could learn faster. And it's not like some kids just never get that far and some kids, even if they don't get that far fast, are able to think about things. . . . So I think it does divide up more into two separate groups instead of many levels.

Interviewer: *Have you thought about the reasons for this?*

Joan: Well, sometimes I think it might be just like who spends time thinking about things. And sometimes I think the upper group are just extremely smart. I mean, I think a lot of it's how much energy you're putting into it and how much interest you have in thinking about it.

Interviewer: *So the lower group may spend less time thinking . . .*

Joan: Or at that time in their lives, they're not bothering to think so much about these things; they're worrying about other things. And some people look like they're thinking about things, and when you talk to them, . . . they're not, really.

Interviewer: *Do you get fooled the other way too?*

Joan: Yes. And then you talk to them and they say something really smart that they thought of, and you say, "Hmmm!"

What Do You Think?

1. What signs of adolescent egocentrism do you see in Joan?

2. Which of Piaget's stages of cognitive development best describes Joan's thinking? How typical do you think she is of children her age?

3. Joan mentions her increasing interest in what she calls the "big questions." What might this interest signify about her cognitive approach to moral and political issues?

---

mental approach. In this way, the information-processing viewpoint resembles research on adolescents' cognition about interpersonal and social knowledge.

WHAT DO YOU THINK? Think of an activity or area of knowledge in which you consider yourself a relative expert. How much of your expertise has resulted from knowing a lot of specific facts about the area? How much has resulted from organizing your knowledge better than other people do? Compare your opinions with those of a classmate or friend who is an expert in an area other than yours.

A Multicultural View ·····················

Cross-cultural Misunderstandings in the Classroom

- Student 1 is quiet when his teacher speaks to him, but he generally looks down at the floor or away from her when she speaks. Even when the teacher encourages him to express his own ideas, the Student pauses and looks away for what feels like an eternity to the teacher.

- Student 2 writes an essay for a social studies class entitled "Jobs in the Coming Global Economy." To the teacher, the essay seems to meander all over the place and does not state its theme until the final paragraph. "It's as if you were telling me what you were thinking," the teacher wrote on the essay afterward, "instead of stating and then justifying a position."

- Student 3 rarely answers questions completely when the teacher calls on her in class; she just mumbles an answer or remains silent. But when collaborating with a small group on a project or an activity, she is lively, talkative, and focused on the task.

There are many possible reasons for these situations. One common explanation is *cross-cultural miscommunication*, culturally based differences in how individuals interpret comments and behaviors. Observations of conversations show that cultures vary in communication styles and that children acquire the styles in the course of learning their native language (Scollon & Scollon, 1994).

Cultural communication styles can vary in the following ways, among others:

1. *Timing:* speakers expect different lengths of pauses between conversational turns, from many seconds to only a fraction of a second or even to a "negative" pause (overlapping comments).

2. *Deductiveness/inductiveness:* in some cultures, speakers are expected to state their point immediately (use a "topic sentence") and then justify their position; in others, speakers more often lead up to the main point indirectly, describing their thought processes along the way.

3. *Politeness indicators:* in some cultures, it is especially important to indicate respect for those in authority, chiefly

The Influence of School

In modern, industrialized countries, school plays a formal role in developing many forms of thinking and expertise while at the same time introducing young people to new social relationships. From the point of view of adolescents, school is *both* cognitive and social, and activities often serve both purposes at once. Participating in the annual Spanish-language play may improve your foreign language skills, but it will also facilitate making new friends. Listening attentively to a math teacher may help to clarify some part of the math curriculum, but it will also create new respect for the teacher herself as a model of inquisitive, open-minded learning. Unfortunately, the converse can also happen: an activity may fail either to teach, to provide desirable social contact, or both. To clarify the connections between the cognitive and social effects of schooling, we look at each area separately in this section. As you will see, each area influences the other significantly, though not always in ways teachers and parents desire. Part of the variation in school influence is based on cultural differences, as the accompanying Multicultural View box indicates, but part of it also has to do with the intrinsic universal qualities of schooling.

Cognitive Effects of Schooling

School influences adolescents' thinking primarily through both a formal curriculum and an informal curriculum. The *formal curriculum* refers to a school's official program: the courses offered, the books required for reading, and the assignments expected for completion. The *informal curriculum* consists of the unplanned activities and relationships that influence students' academic knowledge and motivation to

by listening quietly and allowing an authority to determine the topic and length of a conversation.

These cultural differences can pose problems whenever members of more than one culture come together to interact. For children and adolescents, therefore, cultural mismatch is especially likely in classrooms, particularly in contacts between teachers and students. If the teacher "speaks the culture" of white, mainstream English, she or he will tend to use and expect relatively short pauses between conversational turns in classroom discussions. The teacher will also tend to use and expect a deductive style of turn taking, with the topic stated immediately by whoever initiates a conversational exchange. And although the teacher may expect moderate indications of respect for his or her right to initiate topics of conversation, she or he may also expect students to initiate ideas and concerns of their own.

When a student's culture supports other communication styles, the teacher may get the impression that the student is either unintelligent, lacking in confidence, or deliberately resistant to learning (Lustig & Koester, 1993). Yet these sorts of mismatches are precisely what occur, and always to the disadvantage of the student. What the teacher sees and hears are pauses that are too long, eye contact that is poor, comments that stray from the topic, and silence in response to invitations to speak. What the student experiences, though, may be quite different: he or she may see and hear a teacher who is too talkative, stares at individuals too much, and seems insincere in issuing invitations to ask questions.

But such misunderstandings can be overcome. Training in intercultural communication exists and is effective when focused on the key cultural misunderstandings of particular conversational partners. In the teaching profession, some of the most elaborate training occurs for teachers of English as a Second Language (Paulston, 1992), but programs are also developing in many business communities (Brislin & Yoshida, 1994; O'Hara-Devereaux & Johansen, 1994), where economic activity increasingly spans more than one country, language, and cultural community. The programs vary in detail, of course, but share a common assumption: that awkwardness between culturally different speakers is likely the result of legitimate differences in communication styles rather than of inferiority of one style or the other.

learn—their relationships with teachers, for example, or the "gossip" and other tips related to schoolwork picked up from classmates. Both the formal and the informal curriculum are extremely diverse. What one student learns can be quite unlike what another student learns because of differences in students' experiences in school as well as in their personal backgrounds. As a result, Joe may learn to excel at sports while Jill learns to hate them; Sara may begin to thrive on science courses and study these subjects aggressively while Stan becomes bored by science and chooses to learn the material strictly by rote.

In spite of the normal diversity among teachers, students, and classroom experiences, most schools *seek* to develop students' broad ability at **critical thinking,** or the ability to solve problems and to think reflectively and creatively about ideas and issues, usually for purposes of making decisions or taking actions (Keating & Sasse, 1996). Whether they actually succeed is another question, which we will return to soon. First, we'll look at what critical thinking involves and what therefore may be required to encourage it in students.

The Nature of Critical Thinking

Despite its name, critical thinking refers not to thinking that is negative or full of complaints but to reflections and insights that provide a basis for intelligent choice. Critical thinking is a broad, practical skill: it can help a person figure out why an unfamiliar appliance broke down, compose a term paper, resolve a conflict with a friend, or decide what kind of career to pursue. As the examples suggest, not all critical thinking occurs in school settings, and this fact poses a challenge to teachers and curriculum experts, whose access to students generally is limited to classrooms and related environments.

critical thinking Reflection or thinking about complex issues, usually to make decisions or take actions.

Critical thinking must be caught by a youngster through his or her own active efforts, not absorbed passively as implied in this cartoon. But teachers and parents can stimulate and encourage critical thinking in a number of ways.

What does critical thinking involve? Educators and psychologists have analyzed it in various ways, but usually point out these elements (King & Kitchener, 1994):

1. *Basic operations of reasoning* To think critically, a person must be able to classify, generalize, deduce conclusions, and perform other logical steps mentally.

2. *Domain-specific knowledge* To deal with a problem, a person must know something about its topic or content. To evaluate a proposal for a new, fairer tax system, a person must know something about the existing tax system. To resolve a personal conflict, a person has to know something about the individual with whom he is having the conflict.

3. *Metacognitive knowledge* (knowledge about how human thinking works, including one's own). Effective critical thinking requires a person to monitor when she really understands an idea, know when she needs new information, and predict how easily she can gather and learn that information.

4. *Values, beliefs, and dispositions* Thinking critically means valuing fairness and objectivity. It means having confidence that thinking does in fact lead to solutions. It also means having a persistent and reflective disposition when thinking.

Interestingly, research has found that students themselves understand these elements of critical thinking (Nichols et al., 1995). Furthermore, compared to grade-school children, adolescents regard critical thinking as a fairer and more appropriate purpose of schooling (see Figure 15.4).

Programs to Foster Critical Thinking Educators have devised a number of programs intended to foster the qualities needed for critical thinking (Adams & Hamm, 1996), many of which serve adolescents. The programs differ in their particulars: they last for various lengths of time, emphasize different thinking skills, and draw on content from different areas of the standard school curriculum. Some programs are integrated into the curriculum, meaning they replace a traditional course in some subject area; others are taught separately and draw content from several areas at once.

But experts do agree on several general principles that enhance the quality of programs that teach critical thinking. First, teaching thinking is best done directly and explicitly. Critical thinking does not develop on its own by unconscious osmosis, so to speak (Keefe & Walberg, 1992). Watching the teacher or a classmate think critically does not guarantee that a student will become a better thinker. Neither does giving a student a lot of practice in simple mental operations, such as basic addition or simple logical puzzles.

Second, good programs for teaching thinking offer lots of practice at solving actual problems. Merely describing the elements of critical thinking (as this text is doing) does not turn students into skillful thinkers. To accommodate the need for practice, the most successful educational programs last at least a full academic year and sometimes also weave the thinking skills into other, related courses to extend the effects of the program still further.

Third, successful programs try to create an environment conducive to critical thinking. Typically they expect teachers to model important critical thinking skills themselves, such as thinking out loud while they explain a solution to a problem. The programs also expect teachers to convey confidence in students' ability to think while providing constructive, explicit criticism of ideas, whether their own or the students'. For example, one technique is to invite individual students to temporarily act as teacher or constructive critic (Slavin, 1995). To make time for these activities, most critical thinking programs tend to minimize individual seatwork, a time-consuming activity that is found in much traditional classroom instruction but gives students little on-the-spot feedback about the quality of their thinking processes.

Programs that teach critical thinking draw on the spirit, if not the literal research findings, of several strands of cognitive theory concerning the adolescent years. One strand is Piagetian, with its concern for how logic and reasoning gradually develop. Another is information-processing theory, with its focus on specific ways of organizing ideas and coordinating new ideas with preexisting ones. A third strand is the concern with the human context of cognitive development in adolescence: how people and settings affect a young person's thinking.

Social Effects of Schooling

For early adolescents, the graduation from elementary school can be a period of increased social and emotional stress: their new school is usually larger, teachers are more numerous, new friendships must be formed, and students must adjust to being the youngest, least knowledgeable members of the school community. In the United States, these problems are particularly frequent and acute in junior high schools, which tend to be organized in ways similar to senior high schools, but serve the sixth through ninth grades. Over the course of their first year of junior high, students report less positive attitudes about school, poorer achievement, and lower levels of participation in extracurricular activities (Eccles et al., 1996; Finders, 1997). New students (especially girls) report feeling less positive about themselves. Instances of both bullying and being bullied—often with sexual overtones—are widespread (Lee et al., 1996).

A major response to these stresses has been to create **middle schools,** which are organized deliberately to take students' developmental needs into account. Middle schools typically span fifth through eighth grades, though there is variation among school districts in the exact span used. They share features of both elementary schools (e.g., smaller size and fewer class changes per day) and high schools (e.g., specialization in class subjects). A particularly characteristic feature of middle schools is the assignment of students to a "home-base" or homeroom class that students visit every day and where the teacher acts as an adviser to help them navigate the new challenges of postelementary education (Galassi et al., 1997). Studies of the impact of middle schools suggest that these changes can indeed help young adolescents to adjust—but only if the teachers actually understand students' developmental needs and adjust their ways of relating to students accordingly. In general, adjustment is more likely to succeed if teachers work together collegially, supporting one another's efforts to innovate in classroom practices (Louis et al., 1996; Peterson et al., 1996).

middle school A school intended to meet the needs of early adolescents (students from about fifth through eighth grade, or about age ten through thirteen).

FIGURE 15.4

Students' Ratings of Fairness of Critical Thinking as a Goal of School

As students get older, they perceive critical thinking to be a fairer or more appropriate goal of schooling. In other parts of this particular study, students also increasingly rated critical thinking as more likely to get students excited about learning and to get them to help one another more.

Source: Adapted from Nichols et al. (1995).

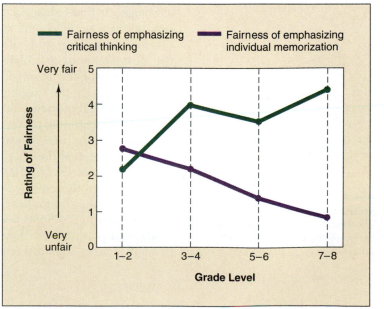

Dropping Out of High School

A bit more than 11 percent of all high school students drop out of school, although for several reasons the significance of this percentage is somewhat hard to interpret (Ianni & Orr, 1996). First, school jurisdictions vary in how they define "dropping out" (some leave students who are over age eighteen out of their records). Second, some dropouts—possibly as many as a third—return to complete school in any one year; they might better be called temporary school leavers rather than permanent dropouts. Third, students drop out for a variety of reasons, ranging from general alienation from school, to family crises, to difficulties fitting in with friends and teachers. Some of the reasons are more serious and long-lasting than others, and contribute to variations in students' tendency to return to school to obtain a diploma.

Although dropout rates vary considerably among schools and communities, the significance of concentrations of dropouts, like that of the overall percentage of dropouts, is surprisingly ambiguous. A few large, inner-city high schools have high dropout rates, for example; as much as 50 percent of each entering ninth-grade class may not graduate. But this concentration masks the fact that nationwide, dropping out is only slightly more likely among urban students (about 13 percent) than among suburban or rural students (10 and 11 percent, respectively). Dropping out is also more frequent among nonwhite students (14 to 29 percent) than among white students (8 percent); yet this trend, too, obscures the fact that half of all dropouts are white. And dropping out is more frequent among low-income families (25 percent) than among middle- and high-income families (10 and 2 percent, respectively); yet this trend can distract from the fact that nationwide, half of all dropouts are from middle-income families. These somewhat paradoxical statistics suggest an especially important point for teachers and other people who work with youth professionally: that although social categories (race, SES, urban residence) *correlate with* dropping out, they do not *cause* it. (See Chapter 1 for a discussion of the difference between correlation and causation.) Most adolescents *do* graduate from high school, even in the inner city, as do most youth who are nonwhite or poor.

Educational research therefore has looked for factors contributing to **resilience** in youth, that is, to the factors that allow individual adolescents to cope with and overcome difficult circumstances. In general, the studies point to the importance of adults seeing and responding to the potential of individual teenagers, whether the adults be parents, school personnel, members of the community, or some combination of the three (Altenbaugh, 1995; Catterall, 1998). The research also suggests that teenagers do not necessarily get discouraged, or necessarily drop out, because they become aware of belonging to social categories that have high dropout rates. One study of urban African American youth found that those with the most conscious, articulate knowledge of racial oppression were precisely the individuals most likely to *stay* in school and to perform well (O'Connor, 1997)!

Even though the existence of dropouts implies that high schools may be limiting the potential of some students, in reality many high schools are successfully providing both academic and social opportunities to which many students might not have access otherwise. A variety of educational observers and researchers have identified the qualities that lead to school effectiveness and success (Gallagher, 1996; Sizer, 1996; Slavin, 1998). For one thing, both teachers and students must be able to work in their own ways, even when these may be unconventional. Only by doing so can they honor the developmental diversity in most high school communities. For another, schools need to focus the attention of everyone—teachers, students, and parents—on their primary purpose of promoting learning. Given the diversity among students, teachers, and communities, it can be challenging to rec-

resilience A quality or ability that allows some children and youth to cope with unusually difficult circumstances.

oncile this second purpose with the first. Yet most high schools manage to do so, even if not perfectly.

WHAT DO YOU THINK ? Some educators argue that you cannot teach thinking skills in *general*, since a person always thinks about something in *particular*. Why do you think they take this position? This issue makes for a useful debate in class. Try adopting a position contrary to the one you truly embrace!

Summary of Major Ideas

General Features of Adolescent Thought

1. During adolescence, teenagers become better able to consider hypothetical possibilities and to plan ahead.

Beyond Concrete Operational Thought

2. During adolescence, some teenagers (though not all) develop formal operational thought, or the ability to reason about ideas regardless of their content.
3. Formal thought is characterized by an ability to think about possibilities, by scientific reasoning, and by an ability to combine ideas logically.
4. In general, formal thought fosters systematic solutions to many cognitive problems.
5. In daily life, however, adolescents (and adults) often do not use formal thinking to solve everyday problems.
6. Research on adult thinking suggests that formal operations are not the final point of cognitive development or an inevitable step toward mature thinking.

Moral Development: Beliefs About Justice and Care

7. Adolescents develop two forms of morality, one oriented toward justice and one oriented toward caring for self and others.
8. Lawrence Kohlberg proposed six stages in the development of moral judgments oriented toward justice.
9. A number of issues about Kohlberg's theory have not been resolved, including the significance of the content (versus the form) of moral beliefs, differences between conventions and morality, and the possibility of gender differences in moral development.
10. Carol Gilligan proposed forms of moral development oriented toward interpersonal caring; on average, these forms may be slightly more characteristic of females than males, though many exceptions exist.

The Development of Social Cognition

11. Despite their improved cognitive skills, adolescents still sometimes show egocentrism by believing in an "imaginary audience" and in a "personal fable," or biography of their lives.
12. Teenagers also begin seeing more relationships among political problems and developing a greater sense of society as a community.

13. During adolescence, youngsters develop relatively abstract understandings of God and begin forming a personal faith, or a coherent guiding orientation to religious experiences.

Information-Processing Features of Adolescent Thought

14. During adolescence, information-processing skills continue to improve.
15. Teenagers acquire greater expertise in particular areas of knowledge or skill, a trend that continues into adulthood.
16. Both structural and functional capacities improve as a result of development, and both probably contribute to improved cognitive performance.

The Influence of School

17. School has significant effects on adolescents' lives, both cognitively and socially.
18. Cognitively, school encourages the development of critical thinking, or the ability to reflect about complex issues to make decisions or take actions.
19. Educational programs to foster critical thinking usually do so explicitly, offering practice in solving problems and creating an environment conducive to critical thinking.
20. Socially, school can be stressful for youngsters, especially early in adolescence.
21. A significant percentage of teenagers drop out of high school each year, though their reasons vary. However, the majority complete school with reasonable success.

Key Terms

adolescent egocentrism (475)
critical thinking (485)
formal operational thought (462)
imaginary audience (476)
middle schools (487)
morality (467)

personal fable (476)
postconventional moral judgment (471)
resilience (488)
social cognition (475)
social conventions (471)

Psychosocial Development in Adolescence

Focusing Questions

- What conflicts do adolescents typically experience in their search for identity? What factors support or hinder successful identity development?

- What special challenges does adolescence pose for parents? How do differences in parenting style affect parent-teenager relationships?

- In what ways do adolescent friendships and peer groups play a constructive role, and how are concerns about their negative influence justified?

- What changes in sexual activities and attitudes occur among teenagers, and how are they related to other aspects of adolescent development?

- Why are adolescents at risk for problems such as pregnancy, depression, and delinquency?

As we have discovered, a number of dramatic physical and cognitive changes occur during puberty and adolescence. Although the rate at which these changes occur varies greatly, by the end of this period most adolescents look like adults and are physically and intellectually capable of most adult activities. But as important as these physical changes are, the changes that occur in the psychosocial domain may be even more significant. Perhaps the most important change is the progress adolescents make in achieving a full-fledged and integrated psychological identity that is mature, adult, unique, and separate from those of parents, friends, and other important childhood figures. An identity gives teenagers a more integrated and more permanent sense of who they really are, what they really need, what they believe in, and what they are and are not capable of doing. Barbara, who has just begun her senior year of high school, put it this way:

> It's not just that I'm all grown up now—physically, I mean. It's that I have grown up inside, too. I feel different, more like a grownup than a child. Although there are still many things I'm unsure of, I finally have a much clearer sense of who I am and what is important to me and what I believe in. And this may sound strange, but the sense of independence and separateness that I now feel means I can often be close to my parents and friends without losing a sense of who I am and my confidence in my ability to succeed at achieving the things I really want. In a way, it feels like I'm at the end of a long journey and ready to start off on a new one.

As Barbara's thoughts suggest, an enhanced capacity for psychological autonomy, intimacy, and relatedness to parents, family, and friends and significant strides in achievement and self-esteem are also important accomplishments of adolescence (Allen et al., 1994).

In this chapter, we explore the process of adolescent identity development as well as the related processes by which adolescents develop a healthy sense of autonomy, industry and achievement, intimacy, and sexuality. We explore several important aspects of the teenager's social world, including relationships with parents and peers, the development of friendships, and the impact of school and work. We also look at adolescent sexuality and how it is influenced by current social trends and personal beliefs. Finally, we explore the special problems adolescents face today and some strategies for preventing them.

Theories of Identity Development

Parents often are surprised at how much careful thought an eighteen- or nineteen-year-old has given to who he is and how strong his sense of personal direction can be. For example, in a two-hour discussion with his mother that occurred quite by chance, Jorge, a high school senior, revealed that first and foremost he thought of

At times, conflicting needs for both closeness and separateness can make life confusing for both adolescents and their families.

himself as an artist and worked very hard to develop a special way of seeing and translating what he saw into creative works. He also considered himself a person who was good at helping others. He said that he planned on first attending art school and becoming an artist, but thought he would eventually earn his living as a social worker or some other type of mental health professional. How did Jorge develop this strong sense of identity? Several theorists have explored this process.

Ruthellen Josselson: Individuation and Identity Development

Individuation is the process by which an adolescent develops a unique personal identity or sense of self, one distinct and separate from all others. Individuation is thought to consist of four separate but overlapping subphases: differentiation, practice and experimentation, rapprochement, and consolidation of self. During the *differentiation* subphase, which occurs early in adolescence, the teenager recognizes that she is psychologically different from her parents. This discovery often leads her to question and reject her parents' values and advice, even if they are reasonable. For example, although as a twelve-year-old Barbara enjoyed and did well in her music lessons, she refused to continue them because they were her parents' idea rather than her own. During this period, the realization that parents are not as wise, powerful, and all-knowing as she earlier thought sometimes leads a youngster to overreact and reject *all* of their advice (Josselson, 1994).

In the *practice and experimentation* subphase, the fourteen- or fifteen-year-old believes he knows it all and can do no wrong. He may deny any need for caution or advice and actively challenge his parents at every opportunity. He also increases his commitment to friends, who provide the support and approval he previously sought from adults. In a discussion of plans to go to a heavy-metal rock concert, for example, Alonzo will completely dismiss his parents' concerns about the dangers in attending, insisting that his friends, who went to last year's concert, have assured him that it was perfectly safe.

During the *rapprochement* subphase, which occurs toward the middle of adolescence, a teenager has achieved a fair degree of separateness from her parents and is able to *conditionally* reaccept their authority. Often she alternates between experimentation and rapprochement, at times challenging her parents and at other times being conciliatory and cooperative. Although Maria, who has just turned fifteen, goes to great lengths to accept responsibility around the house, she often becomes highly indignant when her parents still insist on a curfew and on knowing where she is going when she leaves the house in the evening.

During the final, *consolidation-of-self* subphase, which lasts until the end of adolescence, youngsters develop a sense of personal identity, which provides the basis for understanding self and others and for maintaining a sense of autonomy, independence, and individuality. Shannon, a high school junior who will soon be applying to colleges, is a good example. Viewed by her family (and to some extent

● ● ●
individuation The process by which an adolescent develops a unique and separate personal identity. Consists of four subphases: differentiation, practice and experimentation, rapprochement, and consolidation.

herself) as somewhat disorganized and lacking maturity and life direction, Shannon in fact surprised them with the sense of independence and self-awareness she displayed in the college application process. After meeting with a school guidance counselor on her own initiative, Shannon used her computer skills to access college websites and to select schools from a CD-ROM database. Based on what she referred to as her "self-evaluation plan," she listed the academic and social qualities she was looking for in a school; her own strengths and weaknesses as a student and overall; and college location, cost, admission standards, and other factors. Then she ordered information from colleges that seemed to be a good fit. She did all of this largely without her parents' awareness. When school catalogues began to arrive, she proudly sat down with her parents' and explained her plan and how it fit with her views about herself and her future.

The process of individuation continues throughout the teenage years and often into young adulthood. As we will see shortly, it dovetails with Erikson's theory, which holds that the major task of adolescence is to resolve the crisis of identity successfully.

Erik Erikson: The Crisis of Identity Versus Role Confusion

According to Erik Erikson (see Chapter 2), the key developmental challenge of adolescence is to resolve the crisis of **identity versus role confusion** (Erikson, 1963, 1993). In forming an identity, an adolescent selectively accepts or rejects the many different aspects of herself that she acquired as a child and forms a more coherent and integrated sense of unique identity (Damon & Hart, 1988; Harter, 1989; Harter & Monsour, 1992). During middle childhood, she may have simply formed disconnected, relatively separate impressions about herself: on one occasion she noticed that she excelled at hockey and on another that she excelled at swimming. In adolescence, however, she mulls over the significance of all of these impressions

• • •

identity versus role confusion
The fifth of Erikson's psychosocial crises, in which one must integrate one's many childhood skills and beliefs and gain recognition for them from society.

For each of these adolescents, it is likely that their willingness to engage in activities that diverge from cultural expectations reflects a strong sense of individual identity and self-direction.

taken together: Do they mean that I am generally athletic? That I am popular? Intelligent? Or that I am merely a conformist, just devoting myself to whatever others value?

An adolescent's increasing capacity for abstract thought and self-understanding (see Chapter 15) plays a central role in this process. As adolescents experiment with different roles in their search to create a coherent sense of identity, many experience a sense of *false self*, that is, a sense that one is acting in ways that do not reflect one's true self as a person, or the "real me." Each of the many different role-related selves that adolescents experience, such as self with parents, self with friends, self as a classmate, and self with a girlfriend or boyfriend, contains qualities that seem to contradict one another. For example, an adolescent may be outgoing with friends but shy with a romantic partner, or cheerful with friends and depressed with parents (Harter et al., 1996).

Susan Harter and her colleagues (Harter et al., 1996) asked middle school and high school students to describe their true and their false selves. Descriptions of their true selves included "the real me inside," "my true feelings," "what I really think and feel," and "behaving the way I want to behave and not how someone else wants me to be." False selves were described as "being phony," "putting on an act," "expressing things you don't really believe and feel," or "changing yourself to be something that someone else wants you to be." Adolescents who reported high levels of positive support from parents and peers engaged in less false-self behaviors than those who experienced lower levels and poorer-quality support. Teens who engaged in false-self behavior as a healthy way to experiment with new roles reported more positive feelings about themselves, higher self-worth, greater hopefulness about the future, and more knowledge of their true selves than teens who engaged in false-self behavior to please, impress, or win the approval of parents and peers or because they were experiencing depression or other problems.

Psychosocial Moratorium   According to Erikson, adolescence provides a **psychosocial moratorium,** a period during which the young adult is free to suspend or delay taking on adult commitments and to explore new social roles. The goal of role experimentation is to find a place, or niche, that is clearly defined and yet seems uniquely made for him. He may devote this time to academics, to trying out different jobs, to travel, to social causes, or even to delinquency, depending on prevailing social, cultural, and economic conditions as well as on his individual capacities and needs.

The type of psychosocial moratorium an adolescent encounters (or whether she encounters one at all) will largely depend on the opportunities for exploring a variety of roles that are provided by her family, culture, society, and the particular historical period in which she lives. For example, children growing up under conditions of poverty and deprivation or during periods of war and social upheaval are likely to experience more limited and less supportive moratorium opportunities than children living under more optimal circumstances. As mentioned in Chapter 2, a successful resolution of the crisis of identity is the development of the virtue of *fidelity*, the ability to sustain loyalties to certain values despite the inconsistencies and conflicts that inevitably arise. Individuals who have successfully resolved their identity crises possess a sufficiently reliable and well-integrated identity to allow them to undertake the challenges of young adulthood, including physical, intellectual, religious, career, and family, without undue conflict or anxiety. According to Erikson, adolescents whose life circumstances severely limit their opportunity to explore new social roles and values may develop identities that lack sufficient flexibility and reliability to allow them to fully undertake the challenges of the adulthood.

Identity Diffusion   **Identity diffusion,** or the failure to achieve a relatively coherent, integrated, and stable identity, may take a number of forms. The first is *avoidance of closeness* with others. A second form, *diffusion of time perspective*, in-

psychosocial moratorium According to Erikson, the period during adolescence when youngsters are free to suspend or delay taking on adult commitments and to explore new social roles.

identity diffusion A failure to achieve a relatively coherent, integrated, and stable identity.

volves the belief that one is out of step with others, that important opportunities may be lost forever. It is sometimes accompanied by feelings of depression and despair over whether the pain and confusion surrounding identity will ever end and a comfortable sense of identity will finally be achieved. The third form, *diffusion of industry,* may involve an inability to concentrate on school- or work-related tasks or an excessive preoccupation with a single activity, such as reading or dating, that interferes with accomplishing other things. A final form of identity diffusion is the choice of a negative identity. A **negative identity** involves the disparagement and rejection of the roles and opportunities that are valued and made available by one's family and community and an acceptance of socially undesirable roles, such as that of juvenile delinquent. Problems of identity confusion are more likely to occur and are more difficult to resolve in families experiencing serious problems such as alcoholism or drug abuse, physical or sexual abuse, marital conflict, and parental separation or divorce.

Various historical, cultural, and personal events and experiences may affect how one resolves one's identity. For example, many people who grew up during the Great Depression developed identities that were preoccupied with work, economic survival, and self-sacrifice. Some people who grew up in the 1960s, when many challenged or rejected traditional social roles, developed identities based on alternative roles. Similarly, individuals who are deprived of adequate opportunities and resources because they are poor or belong to a disadvantaged minority group may face special challenges in their identity development (McLoyd, 1998; Spencer & Markstrom-Adams, 1990).

The Relationship Between Identity and Intimacy   Successful resolution of the crisis of identity versus role confusion prepares the adolescent for the crisis of intimacy versus isolation, which occurs in early adulthood. A clear and coherent sense of identity provides a basis for achieving intimacy in friendships and love relationships and for tolerating the fear of losing one's sense of self when intimacy becomes very intense and of experiencing loneliness and isolation if a relationship ends. During the later teen years and in early adulthood, the establishment of an intimate relationship with a partner frequently occurs prior to or simultaneously with the resolution of identity issues. The tendency for teenage couples to break up suddenly and then unexpectedly reconcile may in part reflect a level of identity resolution that is not yet up to the task of sustaining intimacy. It is much more difficult to work out conflicting needs and expectations with someone who lacks a clear picture of who she is and what she needs. It is also harder to meet someone else's needs if one is unclear about one's own needs and identity. Thus, the development of identity provides an important basis for intimacy.

Identity Status   Guided by Erikson's ideas, researchers such as James Marcia have been able to empirically study identity development during adolescence. Marcia interviewed students ages eighteen to twenty-two about their occupational choices and religious and political beliefs and values, all central aspects of identity (Marcia, 1993; Marcia et al., 1993). He classified students into four categories of **identity status** based on judgments about (1) whether or not they had gone through an "identity crisis" as described by Erikson and (2) the degree to which they were now committed to an occupational choice and to a set of religious and political values and beliefs (see Table 16.1):

1. *Identity-achieved* individuals had experienced and successfully resolved a period of crisis concerning their values and life choices and were now able to feel commitment to an occupation and to a religious and political ideology. Their occupational choices and their religious and political beliefs were based on serious consideration of alternatives and were relatively independent of those of their parents.

negative identity A form of identity diffusion involving rejection of the roles preferred by one's family or community in favor of socially undesirable roles.

identity status Marcia's four categories of identity development: identity achievement, identity diffusion, moratorium, and foreclosure.

2. *Identity-diffused* individuals may or may not have experienced a crisis, but showed little concern or sustained commitment regarding occupational choice and religious and political beliefs.

3. *Moratorium* individuals were presently *in* crisis, actively struggling to make commitments and preoccupied with achieving successful compromises among their parents' wishes, the demands of society, and their own capabilities.

4. *Foreclosed* individuals had "prematurely" committed themselves to important aspects of identity without having experienced any significant conflict or crisis. Consequently, it was difficult for them to tell where their parents' goals for them ended and where their own goals began. Their college experiences served mainly to confirm the childhood beliefs to which they rigidly held rather than provide challenging alternatives.

Most adolescents seem to progress toward a status of identity achieved. Researchers using Marcia's categories have found that for both males and females, identity achievement is rarest among early adolescents and most frequent among older high school students, college students, and young adults. During junior and senior high school, identity diffusion and identity foreclosure are the most common identity statuses. Although diffused and foreclosed statuses significantly decrease during the later high school and college years, only about one-third of college juniors and seniors and one-quarter of adults studied are found to be identity achieved (Archer & Waterman, 1988; Kroger, 1995; Marcia, 1993; Marcia et al., 1993).

Differences in social class, culture, and ethnicity may also affect identity development, depending on the context. Adolescents growing up during the Depression were much less likely to have the opportunity to experience a moratorium than the typical adolescent today. The same is likely to be the case for minority youth living in poverty today, for whom opportunities for the exploration associated with moratorium are likely to be much more limited than for middle-class adolescents attending college. Youngsters who live in poor neighborhoods where gangs, drugs, and violence are common and rates of school dropout and unemployment are high, and who lack positive adult and peer role models, are more likely to encounter difficulties in forming positive identities than adolescents growing up in more supportive life circumstances (Bat-Chava et al., 1997; McCloyd, 1998).

The proportion of individuals at each identity status appears to vary with the specific identity area involved. Identity achievement was the most frequent status in the area of *religious beliefs;* identity achievement and moratorium were the most frequent statuses where *vocational choice* was concerned; identity foreclosure was the most common status in the area of *gender-role preferences;* and identity diffusion was the most frequent status in the area of *political philosophies* (Archer, 1982; Marcia, 1993). For example, when Jean Phinney and her colleagues conducted in-depth interviews with Asian American, Hispanic, and white American-born male and female high school students to assess stage of ethnic identity development, they

According to James Marcia, adolescents can be classified into four categories of identity status based on the presence or absence of an identity crisis and whether or not they are committed to an occupational choice and a set of religious values and beliefs.

TABLE 16.1   Crisis and Commitment in Marcia's Theory of Identity Status

Identity Status	Crisis	Commitment
Achieved	Present	Present
Diffused	Present/absent	Absent
Moratorium	In process	In process
Foreclosed	Absent	Present

Source: Marcia (1980).

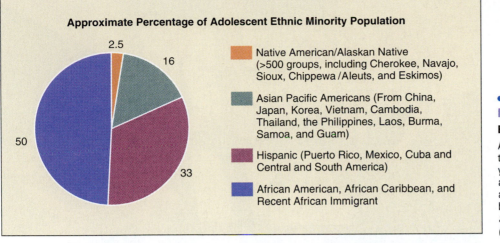

Approximate Percentage of Adolescent Ethnic Minority Population

2.5 — Native American/Alaskan Native (>500 groups, including Cherokee, Navajo, Sioux, Chippewa/Aleuts, and Eskimos)

16 — Asian Pacific Americans (From China, Japan, Korea, Vietnam, Cambodia, Thailand, the Philippines, Laos, Burma, Samoa, and Guam)

33 — Hispanic (Puerto Rico, Mexico, Cuba and Central and South America)

50 — African American, African Caribbean, and Recent African Immigrant

● ● ● ● ● ● ● ● ● ● ● ● ● ● ●
FIGURE 16.1
Ethnic Minority Youth in the United States
Adolescents with African origins make up the largest percentage of ethnic minority youth in the United States, followed by adolescents from Hispanic, Asian Pacific, and Native American/Alaskan Native backgrounds.
Source: Adapted from Harrison et al. (1990), p. 350.

found no significant differences based on either ethnic group or gender in the percentages of youngsters who were in the diffusion/foreclosure stage, moratorium stage, or achievement stage of ethnic identity development (Phinney, 1989; Phinney et al., 1997). Groups did differ, however, in which issues were of most concern in resolving their identity crisis. Nearly one-third of all adolescents in the United States are from non-European American backgrounds (see Figure 16.1).

Few differences between males and females have been found on measures of identity. Both genders are equally represented among the four identity statuses and seem to develop in similar ways. Although early studies suggested that the identity statuses may have different psychological meanings and consequences for males and females, more recent research indicates that the meanings and implications appear to be quite similar for both sexes (Archer & Waterman, 1988; Gilligan, 1987; Marcia, 1993).

Whereas high school students often begin as foreclosed due to their lack of autonomy and dependence on others for direction, or diffused because they still are not thinking in a long-term manner about careers and future plans, many students engage in active role experimentation (moratorium) throughout high school and college, as reflected in the increased frequency of casual dating, changes in majors and shifts in career plans, and the like. Movement toward identity achievement increases during early adulthood.

During late adolescence and early adulthood, both identity achievement and moratorium statuses are generally viewed as healthy outcomes, whereas foreclosed and diffused identities are seen as more problematic. Being identity achieved in today's society is probably rarer among teens than in previous eras. First, today's adolescents have far more options than ever before. Second, technological and social changes are becoming so rapid and complex that identity resolution takes a longer time to achieve.

WHAT DO YOU THINK? To what degree have you experienced the developmental crisis of identity versus role confusion proposed by Erikson? Which of Marcia's four identity statuses best describes your own at the present time?

Family Relationships During Adolescence

The search for identity and the achievement of a mature psychological sense of autonomy and relatedness affect all of an adolescent's relationships. Ties with parents must make room for an increasing interest in peers and a new commitment to the

Although leaving home is often accompanied by mixed feelings, the overall quality of adolescent-parent relationships often improves after teenagers have left.

life among comparative equals that peers provide. A young teenager's efforts to become more physically and emotionally separate from his parents and closer to his friends may be stressful, but more often than not the problems and conflicts of this period are relatively minor. Full-blown upheavals and more serious problems of adolescence are most likely to occur in families and communities in which a poor fit exists between the developmental needs of adolescents and the opportunities and supports that are available (Eccles et al., 1993; Offer & Schonert-Reichl, 1992). In this section, we first explore relationships within the family, then look at social relationships in the wider world.

Relationships with Parents

Even though the majority of teens get along well with their parents on a daily basis, parent-teenager relationships are likely to feel slightly "unstable" or "out of joint" some of the time. This is in part a result of the increasingly stressful pace of modern family life and the different ways adolescents and their parents choose to spend their time. Both adolescents and their parents tend to agree that differences in the activities, expectations, and interests of each family member make it difficult for them to find times to do things together and find activities that are of mutual interest (Larson & Richards, 1994).

The disconnectedness that parents and teenagers sometimes feel may also reflect teenagers' sensitivity to the discrepancies between their own and their parents' views of how their families function—whether individuals really get along with one another, for example, and who really makes decisions around the house (Carlson et al., 1991). Parents may think they listen to their teenager's opinions about what household chores she should do, but she herself may regard the "listening" as shallow or meaningless, since parents evidently decide who does what chores anyway. When and if discrepancies such as these come into the open, conflicts usually arise ("You always say X, but you really mean Y!"). That is the bad news. The good news is that the conflicts frequently serve as catalysts for further growth in teenagers' social maturity and to reconcile gaps between parents and their nearly grown children (Holmbeck & O'Donnell, 1991). An important task of adolescence is to achieve adequate psychological separation, or independence, from one's parents.

Achieving psychological separation from one's parents entails four important accomplishments: *functional independence,* the ability to manage one's own personal and practical affairs with minimal help from one's parents; *attitudinal independence,* a view of oneself as unique and separate from one's parents and having a personal set of values and beliefs; *emotional independence,* freedom from being overly dependent on parents for approval, intimacy, and emotional support; and *conflictual independence,* freedom from excessive anxiety, guilt, resentment, anger, or responsibility to one's parents (Moore, 1984, 1987; Sullivan & Sullivan, 1980). From the perspectives of adolescents themselves, the most significant indicators of successful separation from parents are gaining economic independence, living on their own, graduating from school, and being free to make their own life choices without being overly concerned about what their parents may think (Moore, 1987).

Although the majority of college students expect to live with their parents after graduation, in our culture leaving home is still a powerful metaphor for achieving psychological separation, and differences in how parents and adolescents understand and react to this experience are fairly common. Many of the everyday conflicts between adolescents and their parents over chores, curfews, school, and social activities reflect different perspectives about the approaching separation. Adolescents' tendency to view themselves as increasingly emancipated from their parents' conventional perspectives and control may create conflict between a parent's need to maintain the usual family norms while allowing the child increasing independence (Smetana, 1995).

In recent studies by Reed Larson and his colleagues, fifth-through-twelfth-graders from white working- and middle-class backgrounds carried electronic beepers and provided reports on their experiences when contacted at random times over the course of a week (Larson, 1997; Larson et al., 1996). As Figure 16.2 shows, the amount of time adolescents spent with family decreased from 35 percent of waking hours in fifth grade to just 14 percent in twelfth grade. By the end of senior high school, these teenagers were spending significantly less time in leisure and daily manitenance activities with family, and this decline was greatest for time spent with

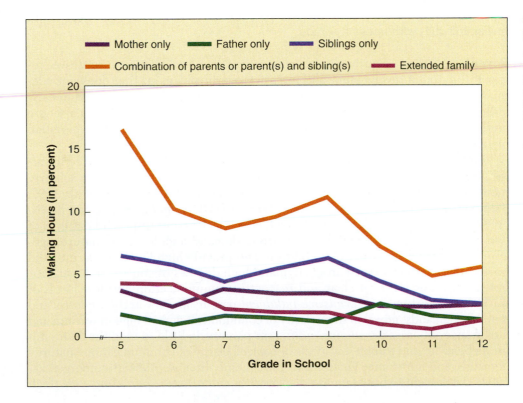

● ● ● ● ● ● ● ● ● ● ● ● ● ● ● ● ●

FIGURE 16.2

Age Differences in Time Spent by Adolescents with Family Members

Between fifth and twelfth grades, the amount of time spent with various family members decreases. The greater decrease is in time spent with the entire family. *Source: Adapted from Larson et al. (1996, p. 748).*

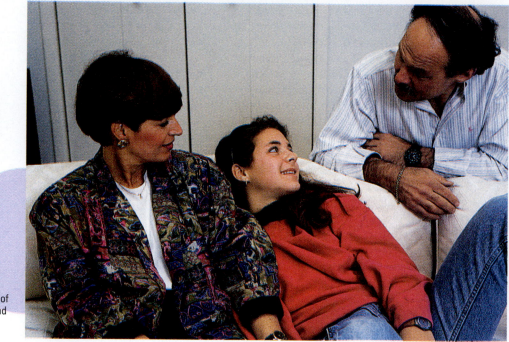

Most parents and teenagers have plenty of disagreements and conflicts, but they tend to share long-run interests, goals, attitudes, and values.

the entire family group and time spent with siblings. Despite these changes, however, the connection between these adolescents and their parents remained stable over time, as reflected in the amount of time they spent talking with and being alone with their parents. The teens' increasing disengagement was unrelated to levels of family conflict; rather, the decline in adolescents' family time appeared to be related to pulls from outside the family. Early adolescents replaced family time with time spent alone at home, whereas for older adolescents access to friends, having a car, having a job, and receiving permission from parents to stay out later all affected time spent away from home. Table 16.2 presents the changes in percentage of different activities with family by grade.

Parenting Styles   During adolescence, a fine line exists between sensitive, respectful parental involvement and intrusive overinvolvement that does not adequately respect adolescents' need for separateness and independence. As in early and middle childhood, a parent-adolescent relationship that establishes a secure emotional base provides a context within which a mutually satisfactory exploration of autonomy and relatedness is most likely to occur (Allen et al., 1994).

Not surprisingly, the parenting styles discussed in Chapter 10 are related to various aspects of adolescent development, including personality, academic achievement, and social and emotional adjustment. (Ge et al., 1997; Glasgow et al., 1997; Steinberg et al., 1994; Weiss & Schwarz, 1996). Recall that *authoritative* parents exercise high degrees of appropriate control, develop clear and respectful patterns of two-way communication with their children, demand high levels of mature, age-appropriate behavior from their children, and provide high levels of warmth and nurturance. *Authoritarian* parents demand high degrees of control and maturity, but provide low levels of clear and respectful communication and low levels of warmth and nurturance. *Permissive-indulgent* parents are low in their control and maturity demands, mixed in their clarity of communication, and high in warmth and nurturance, whereas *permissive-indifferent* parents do little to monitor their children's behavior and exhibit low levels of control, clarity of communication, maturity demands, and nurturance (Baumrind, 1991; Lamborn et al., 1996; Steinberg et al., 1994). Adolescents whose families displayed an *authoritative parenting style* (high levels of acceptance, supervision, and respect for children's autonomy) and a high degree of parental involvement in schooling experienced better relationships at home and better performance and social adjustment at school (Smetana, 1995; Steinberg et al., 1992). Adolescents with permissive-indifferent (neglectful) parents experience the lowest level of adjustment. For example, in a one-year longitudinal study of 2,300 fourteen- to eighteen-year-olds from different ethnic and SES backgrounds, Laurence Steinberg and his colleagues discovered that differences in parenting styles were related to differences in psychosocial development, school achievement, internalized distress, and behavior problems (Steinberg et al., 1994).

These developmental differences continued or increased over time. Teenagers raised in authoritative homes maintained or improved in all areas. Youngsters from authoritarian homes maintained good adjustment in all areas except internalized distress, which increased during the year studied. Adolescents from permissive-indulgent homes were psychologically well adjusted in interactions with peers and family, but showed declines in school adjustment and increases in school misconduct over the year. Finally, teens raised in permissive-indifferent homes showed the poorest adjustment in all areas at the beginning of the year, with sharp drops in work and school adjustment and increases in delinquency and drug and alcohol abuse one year later.

Of course, not all families provide an authoritative relationship. While warm, caring, and supportive parenting appears to be associated with constructive and effective solutions to family problems, parent-child relationships that are hostile and uncooperative frequently result in conflict and failure (Rueter & Conger, 1995).

Parenting style and the quality of the parent-child relationship can exert influence far beyond the boundaries of the family. This is important, since during adolescence youngsters spend increasing amounts of time outside the home. Contact among parents in a community and between adolescents and nonfamilial adults can benefit (or harm) children by creating and supporting shared community expectations regarding adolescent behavior (Coleman, 1988). For example, adolescents whose friends described their parents as authoritative earned higher grades in school, spent more time on homework, felt more academically competent, and reported lower levels of delinquency and substance abuse (Fletcher et al., 1995).

The changes and conflicts teenagers experience often stimulate similar unresolved feelings in their parents. As one parent put it, "Sometimes I'm not sure

TABLE 16.2	Percentage of ESM Reports in Different Activities with Family, by Grade							
	Percent of ESM Reports by Grade Level							
Activity	**5**	**6**	**7**	**8**	**9**	**10**	**11**	**12**
Homework	3.1	1.4	1.5	2.2	1.7	0.9	0.3	0.4
Chores	1.5	1.8	1.7	1.4	2.0	1.2	0.9	1.1
Eating	3.9	2.6	1.8	2.6	2.2	1.6	1.4	1.8
Transportation	1.5	1.5	0.9	1.1	1.6	1.4	0.9	0.8
Personal maintenance	3.5	2.1	1.7	2.0	2.1	1.6	1.1	1.7
Watching TV	9.9	7.6	6.0	6.7	6.9	4.5	2.9	3.4
Active leisure	5.4	3.4	3.5	2.0	2.4	1.2	0.5	1.2
Talking	2.3	3.1	2.8	2.7	3.0	2.2	2.1	2.3
Idling	2.1	1.3	1.3	0.8	1.6	1.1	0.5	0.4
	33.2	24.8	21.2	21.5	23.5	15.7	10.6	13.1

Note: ESM = experience sampling method.
Source: Larson et al. (1996).

All activities with family decrease with increasing grade level, except talking and transportation.

which is more upsetting to me, my teenage daughter's pain and confusion about who she is or similar feelings that are stirred up from my own difficult adolescence." Higher levels of parent-adolescent conflict are more likely to occur in families experiencing divorce, economic hardship, or other serious stressors (Flanagan, 1990; Heatherington et al., 1996; Smetana et al., 1991b). Despite the many changes taking place, however, the majority of adolescents and parents continue to get along rather well together. They also tend to share similar attitudes and values about important issues and decisions such as ideas of right and wrong, what makes a marriage good, or the long-run value of education (Collins, 1991; Larson, 1997; Larson & Richards, 1994).

Where adolescents and parents do differ is in the emphasis, or strength, of those attitudes and values. Most disagreements between teens and parents are about matters affecting the teenager's current social life and behavior, such as styles of dress, hair length, choices of friends, dating, curfews, telephone use, participation in household chores and family activities, and choice of music. For preferences such as these, teenagers agree more with their peers than with their parents. Yet when it comes to the basic attitudes and values that guide long-term life choices, adolescents have consistently rated their parents' advice more highly than their friends' (Carlson et al., 1991; Grusec et al., 1996).

How children perceive their relationships with their parents may also influence their relationships with peers, particularly during early adolescence. As children enter early adolescence, they desire relationships with parents that are more mutual, are less restrictive, and provide increased opportunities to participate in making decisions that affect their own lives. Children who do not perceive these qualities in their relationships with their parents may come to believe that their parents will never acknowledge that they are maturing and deserve to be treated more like adults. These teenagers may sacrifice other developmentally important experiences with adults for the sake of peer relationships that appear to offer greater opportunity for mutually respectful and supportive interactions. They are less likely to seek advice from their parents and more likely to consult with friends about important issues. In some cases, they may orient toward peers so strongly that they are willing to forgo their parents' rules, their schoolwork, and even their own talents to ensure peer acceptance (Fuligni & Eccles, 1993).

Craig Mason and his colleagues found that the style of parental control that the African American mothers they studied employed depended on who their children's peers were (Mason et al., 1996). For teenagers whose peers engaged in a relatively low level of problem behaviors—such as gang activity, drug use, stealing, truancy, and fighting, with or without a weapon—the optimal level of parental control required to influence their problem behaviors was relatively low, and remained relatively low, even if parents increased or decreased their control. But for adolescents who associated with peers involved in higher levels of problem behavior, the optimal level of parental control was higher, and deviations from this level led to significant increases in their own problem behavior.

Although parent-adolescent alienation and excessive orientation toward peers can have serious negative long-term implications, this is the exception rather than the rule. More commonly, the parent-child relationship undergoes positive changes during middle and later adolescence, frequently aided by constructive relationships that teenagers develop with other adults, including relatives, teachers, coaches, camp counselors, and other community members.

In summary, parents and adolescents get along best when decision making is consistent and collaborative, decisions are perceived as being fair and reasonable rather than arbitrary, and the developmental needs and sensitivities of all family members, both parents and children, are respected. Self-reliance and self-control and the successful academic and social achievement associated with authoritative parenting during childhood are also fostered by these qualities during adolescence (Baumrind, 1989, 1991; Hart et al., 1990).

SES and Ethnic Differences in Families   As noted earlier, adolescents are significantly influenced by the type of family in which they grow up. One useful way to describe families is by **SES** (*socioeconomic status or social class*), which is determined by parents' level of education, income, and type of work, as well as by their lifestyle and cultural values. Studies of SES and conformity among families in the United States, Great Britain, and Italy have found that differences between the values, childrearing practices, and expectations of middle-class parents and those of working- and lower-class parents closely parallel differences in the amount of autonomy, independence, and satisfaction experienced in their day-to-day work experiences (Greenberger et al., 1994; Kohn et al., 1986). These studies found that adolescents in middle-SES families were encouraged to be independent and to regulate or control their own behavior rather than rely on the rewards or punishments of others to determine how they would act. The parents' childrearing styles tended to be democratic or authoritative rather than authoritarian. Working-class parents were much more authoritarian than middle-class parents in their childrearing patterns and were less likely to support their children's attempts to be independent and participate in family decision making until their children were ready to leave home.

Recent research supports these findings (Glasgow et al., 1997; Greenberger et al, 1994; Steinberg et al., 1991; Steinberg et al., 1994). For example, Laurence Steinberg and his colleagues found similar relationships among parenting styles, social class, ethnicity, and family structure in a sample of ten thousand ninth-through-twelfth-grade students from white, African American, Hispanic, and Asian backgrounds. Authoritative parenting (based on student reports of high levels of parental acceptance, control, and autonomy) was generally more common in middle-class than in working-class families, although ethnic differences and differences in family structure were also important. Table 16.3 gives the percentages of authoritative families for each social class and ethnic group. In addition, for all ethnic groups and family types, adolescents from authoritative families had better school grades, were more self-reliant, and exhibited less delinquent behavior than those from nonauthoritative families (Steinberg et al., 1991).

There is, however, some reason for caution in drawing conclusions. For one thing, it is unlikely that the categories the researchers used to classify family structure, SES, culture, and parenting style adequately capture the range of relationships and contexts that are at work. For another, these categories don't adequately take into account changes in family structure and parenting style and differences in parenting styles when more than one parent is involved. (In thinking about your own adolescence, how accurately is the parenting style in your family, including the family structure, cultural, SES, and community contexts in which you were raised, captured by the categories just mentioned?)

• • •

SES Socioeconomic status.

SES differences: Middle-class parents were more likely to be authoritative than working-class parents in all ethnic groups, with the exception of white biological parents.

Ethnic differences: The highest percentage of authoritative parenting occurred for whites, followed by African Americans, Hispanics, and Asians.

Differences in family structure: In both working-class and middle-class Hispanic and Asian families and for working-class white and African American families, authoritative parenting occurred more frequently with biological parents than with other parenting arrangements. For both middle-class white and African American families, however, authoritative parenting was less frequent with biological parents than with other parenting arrangements.

TABLE 16.3	**Percentages of Families with Authoritative Parenting Styles in Different SES Levels, Ethnic Groups, and Parenting Situations**			
	Working-Class Family Structure		**Middle-Class Family Structure**	
Ethnic Group	**Biological Parents**	**Other***	**Biological Parents**	**Other**
White	17.2	11.5	15.0	17.6
African American	13.4	12.2	14.0	16.0
Hispanic	10.7	9.8	15.8	12.9
Asian	7.5	6.1	15.6	10.8

Adapted from Steinberg et al. (1991), Table 1, p. 25.
*Includes single-parent households, stepfamilies, and other family arrangements.

The Role of Ethnicity and Community in Family Decision Making   Susie Lamborn, Sanford Dornbusch, and Laurence Steinberg (1996) conducted a two-year longitudinal study of the relationship among ethnicity, community context, and styles of family decision making and adolescent adjustment among European American, Hispanic American, African American, and Asian American high school students. Three types of family decision making were studied: *unilateral teen* (decisions made by the teenager alone), *unilateral parent* (decisions made by the parent alone), and *joint parent-teen* (decisions made jointly by parent and teenager). For all four ethnic groups, unilateral teen decisions were associated with poorer adolescent adjustment one year later, whereas joint parent-teen decision making was associated with improved adjustment. Teens whose parents allowed them a great deal of decision-making autonomy over a wide range of issues reported higher rates of deviant behavior, lower academic competence, and poorer psychosocial functioning, whereas those whose parents engaged in joint decision making with them reported higher academic competence and more positive psychosocial functioning.

Community context interacted with ethnic background in three distinct patterns of influence. For Hispanic Americans living in ethnically mixed neighborhoods, the impact of joint decision making on adjustment was more positive and the impact of unilateral teen decision making more negative. Among African American youth, however, the negative impact of unilateral teen decision making was greater for those living in predominantly white communities compared to those in ethnically mixed communities. Finally, for European and Asian Americans, living in an ethnically mixed versus an all-white or Asian American neighborhood did not appear to affect the impact of type of decision making on adolescent adjustment (Lamborn et al., 1996)

Divorce, Remarriage, and Single Parenthood

Almost half of all marriages in the United States end in divorce, with about 1 million children experiencing their parents' divorce each year. Divorce changes the family context in which the adolescent develops. Since 75 percent of divorced men and 66 percent of divorced women remarry, approximately half of all children whose parents divorce will have a stepfather within four years of parental seperation and 10 percent will experience at least two divorces before turning sixteen years of age (Hetherington et al., 1998).

Based on their extensive review of the literature on the impact of divorce and remarriage on children and adolescents, Mavis Hetherington and her colleagues proposed a transactional model similar to the ecological model used by Uri Bronfenbrenner (see Chapter 1) to understand how the many complex factors work together to influence children's adjustment (Hetherington et al., 1998). Figure 16.3 diagrams how these factors interact. The main factors to consider include (1) the individual characteristics of the parents, including their personality, education, and psychological problems; (2) the nature of the marital transition (marriage and remarriage); (3) stressful life experiences and economic changes associated with divorce (and remarriage); (4) the family following divorce or remarriage; (5) the types and amount of social support available to family members; (6) the amount of parental distress; (7) the family process, including the nature and the quality of the relationships among family members; (8) the individual characteristics of the children, including age, gender, temperament, and intelligence, as well as strengths and vulnerabilities; and (9) the adjustment of the child or adolescent. This "transactional model" helps us to understand the risks associated with divorce and remarriage to the adjustment of children, adolescents, and adults. Chapter 13 includes additional discussion of the impact of divorce on school-age children.

Marital Conflict   Marital conflict is a well-known source of distress for both parents and children, and particularly for adolescents, whose struggles to separate from their families to establish an independent and autonomous identity often involve an increased need for a safe "home base" from which to separate and a heightened awareness of hostility and conflict between their parents (Harold & Conger, 1997; Hetherington et al., 1998). Some conflict is normal in marriages; in fact, children learn the strategies and skills needed to deal with conflict in their own lives by observing their parents' successful strategies for coping with marital discord. However, in families where levels of conflict and disagreement are excessive because parents are unable to resolve them, children and adolescents are negatively affected (Cummings & Cummings, 1988). A majority of divorces involve a failure of parents to successfully resolve their conflicts, a problem that often intensifies during the process of separation and divorce, and may persist even after the marriage has ended, when the need to share parenting responsibilities may continue.

The Impact of Divorce and Remarriage   Between one-quarter and one-third of adolescents in divorced and remarried families become disengaged from their families, minimizing the time they spend at home and avoiding interactions, activities, and communication with family members. When this disengagement is associated with lack of adult support and supervision and with involvement with a delinquent peer group, antisocial behavior and school problems are more likely. However, if the adolescent has a relationship with a caring adult outside the home, such as the parent of a friend, a teacher, a neighbor, or a coach, disengagement may be a positive solution to a disrupted, conflictual family situation (Hetherington et al., 1998).

Children in divorced families tend to "grow up" faster due in part to early assignment of responsibilities, more autonomy in making decisions, and the lack of adult supervision. Whether this is a positive or negative developmental

● ● ● ● ● ● ● ● ● ● ● ● ● ● ● ● ●
FIGURE 16.3

A Transactional Model of the Predictors of Children's Adjustment Following Divorce and Remarriage

The arrows connecting the boxes indicate their influence on one another in together contributing to children's and teens' adjustment to marital transitions.
Source: Hetherington et al. (1998).

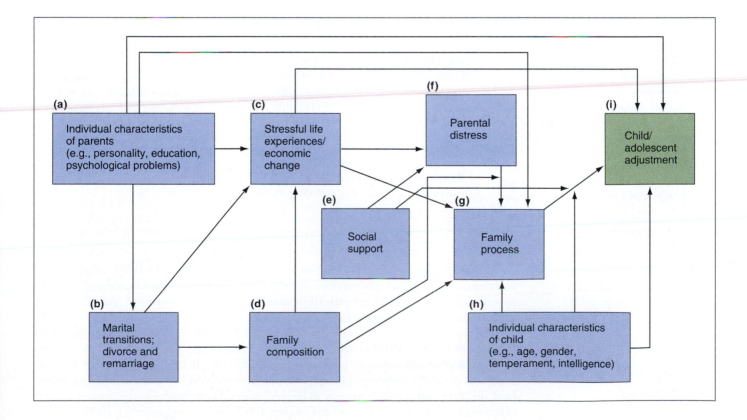

A TALK WITH
Don, Age Eighteen

Social Relationships among Adolescents

Don took time out between homework and football practice to be interviewed. He is athletically built and of average height.

Interviewer: *In general, what do kids your age look for in friends?*

Don: Right now, a friend to me can be anybody. I don't care if they have a drinking problem. That's up to them, although I wouldn't like a person to drink too much. I have a lot of friends who are college freshmen already, I have friends who are my own age, and I have friends who are sophomores and juniors in high school.

Interviewer: *What are relationships with parents like for kids your age?*

Don: I think they give you a lot more freedom when you're a freshman or sophomore and come down on you when you're a junior or senior. They tell you that once you get your license, you can drive me around and you can do this or that once you start dating; they won't be as strict. But it tends to be somewhat the opposite. Like I didn't get my license until I was almost eighteen years old.

Interviewer: *How come?*

Don: My father, who I am living with right now, my only parent, kind of uses a two-way street. He tends to say, "Don't bring up the past when you're trying to prove your point," but when he's trying to prove his point, he always brings up the past. He'll say something

like "You're almost grown, but while you're living under my roof, you'll play by my rules." So you're in a no-win situation. It's plain and simple.

Interviewer: *How did this affect your getting a license?*

Don: My father would not let me go for my license test until he thought that I drove at a level that he was proud of. He said, "I don't want you to be like all those other kids who can barely drive." I wouldn't say I'm a pro or specialist, but I was at a higher level and my skills were more refined when I got my license. That's how my father wanted it to be, and I'm happy now because of it. And I say, "Hey, well, he was right." I can drive better. I can drive on the highway and in the city and take control of certain situations where another person might freeze.

Interviewer: *What other hassles do older teenagers have with their parents?*

Don: Being a senior now, I find that I never really know what my father is going to say. I mean, I'll come in and he'll say, "Ah, it's one-thirty," and you start to say, "The movie didn't get out until this time, we had a flat tire, we ran out of gas . . ." and he goes, "It's okay, just be in a little bit earlier next time." And you go upstairs and you sit there and go, "Huh?" And then another time, you come in and he says, "It's two-thirty—where have you been?", and you're saying, "We were just all over

Freddie's house, we rented a couple of movies and we watched them on the VCR, and after that we sat and talked about our teachers. Nothing really big; it was a boring night." And he says. "It's two-thirty, you should have been in here a long time ago," and this time he really gets on me. So you say, "I really don't understand this." And it gets a lot trickier, too. They start saying things like "You're going to be in college next year. You should work on this because when you go to college, your roommate won't want you to have a messy room."

Interviewer: *Is your father worried about your leaving?*

Don: Maybe not worried too much, but worried to a point of thinking, "Have I taught him the right way, or have I taught him enough to make his own way?"

What Do You Think?

1. Which parenting style best characterizes the relationship between Don and his father?

2. What indications of a generation gap between Don and his father do you see?

3. Which of Josselon's four subphases of individuation does Don's description of his social relationships reflect?

consequence depends on whether or not the demands are within the adolescent's capabilities. If adolescents perceive themselves as being unfairly burdened with responsibilities that interfere with their other activities, resentment, rebellion, and noncompliance may result (Hetherington et al., 1998).

Adolescents who grow up in troubled families that remain together but have high levels of unresolved marital conflict and hostility are likely to experience negative developmental consequences as well. For families in which destructive and unresolved conflicts between parents cannot be resolved, divorce may provide the best solution and result in improved developmental outcomes for the teenagers and other children involved (Harold & Conger, 1997; Hetherington et al., 1998).

The effects of divorce and remarriage are experienced throughout the lifespan. Compared to children from two-parent, nondivorced families, children, adolescents, and adults from divorced and remarried families are at increased risk for developing difficulties in adjustment, including academic problems, psychological disorders, lower self-esteem, and problems in their relationships with parents, siblings, and peers. The normative developmental tasks of adolescence and young adulthood—developing intimate relationships and autonomy—are especially hard. In addition to experiencing some of the same behavior problems found in childhood, adolescents are more likely to drop out of school, be unemployed, become sexually active at an earlier age, have children out of wedlock, associate with antisocial peers, and be involved in delinquent activities and substance abuse. Both male and female adolescents whose parents have divorced are more likely to become teenage parents, and single parenthood most adversely affects the lives of adolescents who experience declining SES and who drop out of school (Conger & Chao, 1996; Demo & Acock, 1996; Hetherington et al., 1998; Simons & Chao, 1996; Whitbeck et al., 1996).

WHAT DO YOU THINK ?   Think about your own separation and individuation with regard to your parents. How similar were your concerns to those described in the text?

Social Relationships During Adolescence

We already touched on the interplay among peer group, ethnic, and community context, parenting styles, and family decision making, and their impact on development. Now we will consider the direct influence of friends, peers, and work on adolescent development in more detail.

Friendship

Friends matter a lot during adolescence. Unlike most adults, who often try to "improve" many of a teenager's behaviors and skills, friends offer easier and more immediate acceptance and thus ease the uncertainty and insecurity of the adolescent years. They also offer reassurance, understanding, advice, and emotional and social support in stressful situations. The opportunity to share inner feelings of disappointment as well as happiness with close friends enables the adolescent to better deal with her emotional ups and downs. Furthermore, a capacity to form close, intimate friendships during adolescence is related to overall social and emotional adjustment and competence (Buhrmester, 1990; Reid et al., 1989).

Sam, age thirteen, describes a best friend this way:

> A best friend to me is someone you can have fun with and you can also be serious with about personal things, about girls or what you're going to do with your life or whatever. My best friend, Jeff, and I can talk about things. His parents are divorced too, and he understands when I feel bummed out about the fights between my mom and dad. A best friend is someone who's not going to make fun of you just because you do something stupid or put you down if you make a mistake. If you're afraid of something or someone, they'll give you confidence. (Bell, 1980, p. 62)

Especially during early and middle adolescence, youngsters' unquestioning appreciation of friends helps them to become more independent of parents and other representatives of authority and to resist the seemingly arbitrary demands of family living. Friends provide one another with cognitive and social scaffolding that differs from what nonfriends provide. Having good friends supports positive developmental outcomes during periods of developmental change (Hartup, 1996). Friends also

Sharing interests with friends is important to teenagers, as it is to children. At the same time, though, less tangible qualities such as loyalty, mutual respect, and intimacy become increasingly important in friends, especially among older adolescents.

promote independence simply by providing knowledge of a world beyond the family. Teenagers learn through their friends that not every young person is required to be home by the same hour every night, that some parents expect their children to do more household chores than other parents do, and that other families hold different religious or political views. The processes of sharing feelings and beliefs and exploring new ideas and opinions with friends play an important role in helping adolescents to define their sense of self (Rawlins, 1992).

Qualities of Adolescent Friendships   Friends strongly influence an adolescent's development by virtue of their positive and negative characteristics, attitudes, values, and behaviors and through the quality of the friendship. A friendship based on mutual respect and trust, intimacy, and prosocial behavior is likely to help the adolescent cope with stressful situations in the family and in school. Friendships that lack these qualities are likely to be less helpful or even destructive (Dusek, 1991; Hartup, 1996).

During the teenage years, the basis of what makes a close friendship changes. When asked to define close friendships and how they are initiated, maintained, and ended, adolescents report that *mutual understanding* and *intimacy* are most important, whereas school-age children emphasize shared activities. Unlike cooperation between younger children, adolescent mutuality depends on the understanding that other people share some of one's own abilities, interests, and inner experiences and on an appreciation of each person's uniqueness. In fact, early adolescents share a fascination with the particular interests, life histories, and personalities of their friends; young teenagers want to understand friends as unique individuals and be understood by them in the same way. The ability of adolescents to recognize the advantages of complementary relationships—relationships in which two people with different strengths and abilities cooperate for mutual benefit—makes possible friendships that involve greater commitment, permanence, and loyalty (Damon & Hart, 1992, 1988; Youniss, 1994).

Intimacy in adolescent friendships includes self-revelation, confidence (in keeping secrets), and a sense of exclusivity. Here is how Taisha, age fifteen, and Cherell, age sixteen, describe a friend:

> A friend is a person you can talk to, you know, show your feelings and she'll talk to you. You can talk more freely to a friend. Someone you can tell your problems to and she'll tell you her problems. They are open. . . . A friend is a person you can really tell your feelings to. . . . You can be yourself with them.
>
> Friends can keep secrets together. They can trust that you won't tell anybody. You won't expect them to tell anybody else. You know she won't tell anybody anything. If you tell somebody something, they won't use it to get revenge on you when you get into a fight. You talk about things you wouldn't tell other people. (Youniss, 1980, p. 181)

The quality of friendships during early adolescence appears to have long-term effects on development. Catherine Bagwell, Andrew Newcomb, and William Bukowski (1998) conducted a twelve-year longitudinal study of thirty young adults who had a stable, reciprocal best friend or "chum" in fifth grade and thirty young adults who had been without a chum. Adults who had close friends in early adolescence experienced better adjustment in school and family relationships and had less difficulty with authority figures than those who did not. Adults who had been rejected by peers in early adolescence did more poorly in school, had greater difficulty with authorities, had lower levels of aspiration, and participated in fewer organizations and social activities in later adolescence and early adulthood. Finally, lower levels of peer rejection during early adolescence predicted more successful overall life adjustment and feelings of self-worth in adulthood.

Gender and Friendship   How do friendships differ for girls and boys? Friendships formed by boys generally involve lower levels of intimacy than those of girls, who are better able to express feelings and more comfortable with giving emotional support to one another. During the junior high and early high school years, girls appear to develop greater intimacy with the opposite sex than boys do. They also tend to have one or two close friends, whereas adolescent boys often have many friends with whom they are less intimate. These differences are likely influenced by traditional gender-role stereotyping, which defines and values intimacy much more strongly as a feminine than a masculine quality. Adolescent boys may be more likely to equate intense intimacy exclusively with heterosexual friendships, whereas girls at this age can be comfortably close with both male and female friends. To better understand developmental changes in the patterns and gender differences in the activities, thoughts, and feelings associated with friends during adolescence, Maryse Richards and her colleagues had 218 adolescents in fifth through eighth grade carry electronic pagers for one week and complete self-report forms in response to signals received at random times during their waking hours (Richards et al., 1998). When paged, the teens responded to questions about whom they were talking with, whom they were thinking about, and what their subjective experiences were, including body image, mood, motivation, self-esteem, and excitement, at the moment they were paged. These same adolescents underwent the same procedure four years later, when they were in grades nine through twelve.

The researchers found that both the amount of time adolescents spent with and thought about same-sex friends and the positive feelings they experienced did not decline across adolescence and into high school. Compared to fifth- and sixth-graders, adolescents in high school spent more time with opposite-sex friends and more time thinking about them. Fifth- and sixth-grade girls spent approximately an hour a week in the presence of a boy and less than two hours thinking about an individual of the opposite sex, while fifth- and sixth-grade boys spent less than an hour in the presence of a girl and less than an hour thinking about girls. By eleventh and twelfth grades, however, girls were spending almost ten hours a week with a male companion, whereas boys were spending approximately five hours a week with a female companion.

Compared to boys, girls' opposite-sex companionship and frequency of thoughts about boys had increased dramatically from eighth to twelfth grade. The oldest girls spent roughly eight hours each week thinking about a boy, while the oldest boys spent approximately five to six hours a week thinking about a girl. During early adolescence, seventh- and eighth-graders spent more time thinking about the opposite sex (four to six hours) than actually being with the opposite sex (thirty to eighty minutes). By eleventh and twelfth grades, this trend had shifted, and more time was spent in the actual presence of the other sex. In general, girls spent more time interacting with and thinking about both boys and girls, whereas boys, when not with their peers, spent very little time thinking about either.

According to Richards and her colleagues, it is developmentally normative for pre- and young adolescents to be more romanticaaly involved in fantasy than in reality. The adolescents in their study reported that time spent with opposite-sex peers was more exciting and that they felt more attractive and important, enjoyed more positive feelings, and felt much more "in love" than when they were same-sex peers. However, when alone and thinking about the opposite sex, subjective experiences were less positive. Older adolescents felt especially negative and unmotivated, perhaps because they missed the company of their girlfriend or boyfriend. We take a closer look at these and related issues later in this chapter.

Interethnic Friendships   Friendships between adolescents from different ethnic groups tend to be the exception. One national study of students enrolled in more than one thousand public and private high schools in the United States found that fewer than 3.5 percent of the eighteen thousand friendships identified by students involved friendships between African American and white teens (Hallinan & Williams, 1989). However, the social contexts in which potential friendship interactions occur seem to make an important difference. In one study of school and neighborhood friendship patterns of African American and white students who attended an integrated junior high school, most students reported having a close other-race school friend, but only about one-quarter saw such a friend frequently outside of school (DuBois & Hirsch, 1990).

Living in a neighborhood with children from other ethnic groups appears to increase the likelihood of having close other-race friends outside of school. Having a higher proportion of neighborhood friends attending one's school also affected other-race friendship. Living in a racially mixed neighborhood may help to create more positive attitudes toward members of other ethnic groups and provide a meeting ground on which cross-race friendships can develop outside of school. The informal peer activities that occur in neighborhood settings are more likely to promote close friendships across groups than the more formal, teacher-directed activities in school. Interethnic friendships are stongly influenced by the attitudes adolescents hold about their own and other ethnic groups (DuBois & Hirsch, 1993; Giordano et al., 1993; Phinney et al., 1997)

Peer Groups

Peer groups play an even greater role in the everyday lives of adolescents than they do for younger children. They also tend to be more structured and organized, frequently include individuals from a relatively wide age range, and are much less likely to be all male or all female (Dusek, 1991; Furman, 1989). Peer groups are an important component of an adolescent's *social convoy*, the network of social relationships that follow a person over his or her lifetime, changing in structure but providing continuity in the exchange of support. Who is included in this social convoy is determined by the adolescent's emotional attachment to the person and by the person's role in the adolescent's life (Levitt et al., 1993). Peers provide a teenager with critical information about who he is, how he should act, what he is like, and so

It is probably no coincidence that all these teenagers wear similar clothing. Adolescent peer groups do encourage conformity, although they also allow for a certain amount of diversity and role distinctions among their members.

forth. They offer him an environment for making social comparisons between his own actions, attitudes, and feelings and those of others. These are important ingredients in an adolescent's development of self-concept and identity. Most important, peer groups provide a support base outside of the family from which the teenager can more freely try on the different identity roles that ultimately will contribute to his adult personality: popular, jock, brain, normal, druggie, outcast, partyer, punk, grind, clown, banger, nerd, lover, and so forth (B. Brown et al., 1993; Durbin et al., 1993; Stone & Brown, 1998). Peer groups can also exert powerful pressures to conform. Especially when the family fails to serve as a constructive corrective force, such pressures may contribute to a prolonged period of identity diffusion or to premature identity foreclosure, for example, as a teenage parent, drug addict, or gang member (Dishion et al., 1988; Patterson & Dishion, 1985). Conformity to peer pressure can be particularly disruptive during early adolescence. Frank Vitaro and his colleagues examined how the characteristics of their friends affected delinquency among eleven- and twelve-year-old boys who were judged by their teachers to be either highly disruptive, moderately disruptive, moderately conforming, or highly conforming. They found that only moderately disruptive boys appeared to be negatively influenced by hostile-aggressive friends and exhibited more delinquent behavior at age thirteen. Highly disruptive boys were most delinquent at age thirteen, regardless of their friends' characteristics, and boys who were judged to be moderately or highly conforming appeared to be unaffected by their friends' characteristics. We will explore the contribution of peers to negative developmental outcomes more fully when we discuss juvenile delinquency later in this chapter (Vitaro et al., 1997).

Peer Group Structure   Adolescent peer groups generally are of two types: the clique and the crowd. The **clique** is a small, closely knit group of two or more members (with an average of six members) who are intimately involved in a number of shared purposes and activities and exclude those who are not. The **crowd** is a larger, less cohesive group of between fifteen and thirty members (with an average of twenty members) and generally consists of from two to four cliques.

Clique membership allows a teenager to have a few select friends whom she knows well and who share important interests and activities, whereas membership in a crowd provides contact with a much broader group of peers on a more casual

• • •

clique A small, closely knit peer group of two or more members (average of six members) who are intimately involved in a number of shared purposes and activities and exclude those who are not.

crowd A large, loosely knit peer group of between fifteen and thirty members (average of twenty members) that generally consists of from two to four cliques.

basis. The small size and intimacy of a clique make it like a family in which the adolescent can feel comfortable and secure. The major clique activity seems to be talking, and cliques generally meet during the school week. Advantages of clique membership include security, a feeling of importance, and acquisition of socially acceptable behaviors (such as academic, social, or athletic competence) that are part of conforming to the clique's norms. However, conformity can also suppress individuality and may promote "in-group" snobbishness, intolerance, and other negative values and behaviors. Involvement with a clique of antisocial peers is associated with various adolescent adjustment problems, including substance abuse, school dropout, delinquency, and gang membership, although which is cause and which is effect is uncertain (Dishion et al., 1988; Patterson & Dishion, 1985). Clique membership peaks in early adolescence and then declines; the percentage of adolescents who are connected with several cliques but are not themselves clique members increases (Schrum & Cheek, 1987).

Crowds usually gather at parties and other organized social functions, which typically take place on weekends. They tend to include both males and females, thereby providing opportunities for mixed-gender interactions and promoting transition from same-gender to mixed-gender cliques. Crowd membership also provides opportunities to interact with individuals from a broad range of backgrounds and experiences, but can also promote snobbishness and can pose real or imagined threats to parental and teacher authority.

How are cliques, crowds, and friendship related? Kathryn Urberg and her associates (1995) studied the school-based peer networks of more than three thousand sixth-to-twelfth-graders from varying SES and ethnic backgrounds. Peer networks became more exclusive with increasing age. Female students were more connected to the peer network than were male students, and ethnic groups that were in a numeric minority were less integrated into school peer networks than the majority group. Best friends were in the same clique about 90 percent of the time but in the same crowd only about 50 percent of the time, and the average clique or loose group had members with two to four different crowd affiliations.

Popularity and Social Acceptance   Popularity is very important to teenagers. Often it is linked with membership in a particular clique or crowd and, in ethnically diverse schools, to peer groups that are identified by ethnic categories such as Asian, Puerto Rican, Mexican American, and African American (Brown, 1990; Clark & Ayers, 1988). Personal qualities also influence popularity. In general, both boys and girls who are popular are perceived as being tolerant, flexible, lively, cheerful, energetic, self-confident, and physically attractive. They are also described as sympathetic, helpful to others, and committed to their friends. Adolescents who are ill at ease and lacking in self-confidence and who respond to uncomfortable situations by acting timid, nervous, or withdrawn are more likely to be neglected and socially ignored by peers, whereas teens who appear to be conceited and demanding are apt to be more actively disliked and rejected (Clark & Ayers, 1988; Youniss et al., 1994).

Residential instability also can reduce chances of being popular. Adolescents who began the academic year in a new school due to a change in family residence were found to have fewer friends and less intimacy with their best friends than those who were residentially stable. Boys who had moved encountered more instances of peer rejection than did those who had not (Vernberg, 1990). Unpopular children are most likely to face peer rejection when their overaggressiveness or oversubmissiveness is accompanied by unresponsiveness to the needs of others. Unpopular students generally report higher levels of loneliness and concern about their relationships with others (Parkhurst & Asher, 1992).

Parental Influence   Parents of adolescents frequently are concerned that their children will be excessively influenced by peer pressure and that peer influence will replace their own guidance (Youniss et al., 1992). Laurence Steinberg and Anne Levine (1990) suggest that parents can help their adolescents with their friendships and relationships with peers in a number of ways (see Table 16.4). The accompanying Perspectives box discusses recent research findings on parental influence.

Adolescents in the World of Work

Adolescents balance many roles: son or daughter, friend, peer, student. Many also add "employee" to the mix. As we saw in Chapter 15, work has an impact on cognitive development and on identity formation as well. Participation in work within and outside the family provides a major base for the development of competence and sense of identity and self, especially during adolescence. Working with others can produce a broad range of benefits, from sound work habits to the development of helpfulness toward others, responsibility for the welfare of others, a sense of agency or personal efficacy, and an appreciation of the needs and feelings of others (Call et al., 1995; Goodnow et al., 1995; Grusec et al., 1996).

For both male and female adolescents, participation in household work and the consequences of such involvement depend on the helper's motivations, the meaning of the work activity, and the social context in which it occurs. In a two-year longitudinal study of one thousand ninth-graders and their parents, Kathleen Call, Jeylan Mortimer, and Michael Shanahan (1995) found that adolescents from large families with fewer financial resources and mothers who were employed responded to the needs of their families by taking on more household responsibilities than adolescents from smaller families with with more resources. Girls who were more competent to begin with chose work that allowed them to be helpful to others, and the opportunity to be helpful to others at work strengthened their sense of competency. Doing household chores increased a sense of competency for African American and Hispanic American boys, but decreased such feelings for European American boys, perhaps because the former group saw helping out as being important to their families' functioning, whereas the latter saw chores as burdensome and lacking in value.

TABLE 16.4   Guidelines for Parents Concerning Their Adolescents' Friends

Helping Adolescents to Deal with Peer Pressure

- Build self-esteem by helping your adolescent discover her or his strengths and special talents.
- Encourage independence and decision making within the family.
- Talk about situations in which people have to choose among competing pressures and demands.
- Encourage your adolescent to anticipate difficult situations and plan ahead.
- Encourage your adolescent to form alliances with peers who share his or her values and your family's values.
- Know your adolescent's friends.
- Don't jump to hasty conclusions based on peers' appearance, dress, language, or interests.
- Allow time for peer activities.
- Remain close to your adolescent.

When to Be Concerned

- If your adolescent has no friends at all.
- If your adolescent is secretive about her or his social life.
- If your adolescent suddenly loses all interest in friends.
- If all of your adolescent's friends are much older than him or her.

Source: Adapted from Steinberg & Levine (1990), pp. 183–187.

PERSPECTIVES

Can Parents Influence Their Adolescent's Choice of Group?

• • • • •   It has long been accepted that parental influence declines sharply during adolescence due to the increasing counterinfluence of peer groups over which parents have little control. However, recent large-scale studies of high school students challenge this view.

Bradford Brown and his colleagues studied parenting practices and peer affiliation in a sample of more than 3700 high school students drawn from a variety of socioeconomic, ethnic, and family backgrounds (e.g., first-time two-parent, divorced, remarried) and types of communities (urban, suburban, rural) (B. Brown et al., 1994; Brown & Huang, 1996). To determine peer group affiliation, school administrators identified a set of boys and girls in each grade and within each ethnic group who represented a cross-section of the student body. Researchers interviewed students in small groups composed of individuals of the same sex, grade level, and ethnic background. Each group listed the school's major crowds and identified two boys and two

This small, closely knit clique of high school students hangs out at this table during lunch period on a fairly regular basis to relax, talk, and play cards.

girls in the same grade who were the leaders or most prominent members of each crowd.

Identified leaders then individually placed each student in the same grade level in one of the crowds that had been named. In addition, all students in the sample were surveyed about family characteristics, parenting practices, and adolescent behaviors related to academics, drug use, and self-reliance.

Brown and his colleagues found that levels of authoritative parenting (as reflected by parental monitoring, encouragement of achievement, and support

for joint decision making) were significantly associated with teenagers' levels of academic achievement, drug use, and self-reliance. These factors, in turn, were closely related to the type of crowd an adolescent belonged to (popular, jock, brain, normal, druggie, and outcast).

The authors concluded that parents can indirectly influence the behaviors by which teenagers become associated with a particular crowd and that peer group norms serve to reinforce behaviors and predispositions that parenting strategies and/or family background characteristics influence. Although parenting practices and family background cannot *determine* a teenager's crowd affiliation, their influence should be taken seriously.

How might this parental influence work? Anne Fletcher and her colleagues (Fletcher et al., 1995) asked students about parenting practices in their families and about their academic achievement, psychosocial competence, behavior problems, and personal distress. Each student's friends independently evaluated the degree to which authoritative parenting was present in the peer network, as indicated by parental acceptance and involvement, behavioral supervision and strictness, and granting of psychological autonomy.

What did they find? Adolescents whose friends described their parents as authoritative earned higher grades in school, spent more time on homework, had more positive perceptions of their academic competence, and reported lower levels of delinquency and substance abuse. Fletcher and her colleagues suggest that authoritative parenting is associated with adolescent competence; competent, well-adjusted adolescents with authoritative parents select (and are selected by) peers similar in competence and background; and within-peer-group experiences maintain and strengthen a higher level of adjustment. Less competent adolescents with nonauthoritative parents are more likely to select peers who are similar to themselves, thus maintaining and amplifying their limitations. Adolescent delinquent activities may be unlikely due to the higher level of shared social control provided by a network of authoritative parents.

What Do You Think?

What role did your parents play in your peer relationships? What role did the parents of your friends play? If you were the parent of a teenager, how would you help your child make wise choices about peers?

For many high school students, working a moderate number of hours provides an opportunity outside of the home for gaining experience and the material rewards needed to have an independent life with peers.

Family dynamics also affected the relationship between helping with household work and feelings of competency and concern for others. For girls living in families where the father-daughter relationship was not supportive and the mother's manner of assigning household tasks diminished the girl's sense of autonomy and independence, participating in household chores undermined rather than enhanced feelings of competency (Call et al., 1995). Teenagers who were expected to do household work that benefited members of the family and expected to do it on a routine or self-regulated basis were more likely to show spontaneous concern for the welfare of others. Work that focused on what is one's "own," such as cleaning one's own room, or was based on frequent requests for assistance (i.e. nagging) was not associated with increased concern for others (Grusec et al., 1996).

How work outside the family influences adolescent development depends on how well it fits the developmental needs of the individual and his or her family, including the type and level of workplace stress, the relevance of job-related skills to future careers, and the compatibility between the demands and experiences of work and those of school. Further discussion of the relationship between work and school activities appears in Chapter 15.

WHAT DO YOU THINK ?   In what ways are your own experiences similar to the text's description of friendship, peer groups, and work during adolescence? In what ways do they differ?

Sexuality During Adolescence

The popular idea that adolescence is a highly sexual period of life is correct. However, people tend to focus on sexual intercourse and the risks of pregnancy rather than consider the broader pattern of interrelated changes involved. During adolescence, the expression of sexual urges interacts closely with the need to establish a secure sexual identity that is reasonably free from anxiety and with the need for intimate relationships with others.

Reasons for dating vary widely, from a desire to "be seen" and thus gain status or to have a good time, to intrinsic interest in friendship with a particular member of the opposite sex.

Sexual Fantasies and Masturbation

Sexual fantasies about real or imaginary situations often accompany masturbation, although adolescents of all ages report having sexual fantasies throughout their waking hours. Both sexes have reported that they most commonly fantasize about "petting or having intercourse with someone [they] are fond of or in love with" (P. Miller & Simon, 1980). Regarding the second most common fantasy, however, males reported imagining anonymous sex ("petting or having intercourse with someone you don't know"), whereas females reported imagining intimate but not explicitly sexual activity ("doing nonsexual things with someone you are fond of or in love with").

Approximately 70 percent of boys and 45 percent of girls surveyed have reported having masturbated by age fifteen, and about 65 percent of boys and 50 percent of girls ages sixteen to nineteen have reported masturbating once a week or more. Sexually experienced adolescents tended to masturbate more than those who were less experienced, but boys tended to give up masturbation when they were involved in an ongoing sexual relationship, whereas girls tended to masturbate more often (Coles & Stokes, 1985; Dreyer, 1982). Feelings of discomfort and guilt resulting from cultural and religious beliefs about masturbation have decreased in recent years. However, many teenagers still find the subject embarrassing; fewer than a third of teenagers questioned in one study reported that they felt no guilt at all (Coles & Stokes, 1985). It is likely that current efforts to encourage safe sexual practices to reduce the risk of AIDS will lead to increased acceptance of and decreased guilt about masturbation.

Sexual Experience

Recent trends in adolescent sexual activity in the United Satates include earlier initiation of intercourse, a greater number of partners, and ineffective and inconsistent use of contraceptives. But despite these changes, the rate of teenage sexual activity is about the same in the United States as in Western European nations (Coley & Chase-Lansdale, 1998; Seidman & Rieder, 1994). In a sequential longitudinal study of the timing of first intercourse and psychosocial adjustment, Raymond Bingham and Lisa Crockett (1996) surveyed seventh-, eighth-, and ninth-grade adolescents annually through their graduation from twelfth grade. They found that for both boys and girls, earlier timing of first sexual intercourse was associated with longitudinal patterns of greater difficulty with the transition to adolescence and with poorer psychosocial adjustment. Previous psychosocial adjustment and life circumstances rather than timing of first intercourse accounted for negative consequences of early sexual involvement, and the effescts of early intercourse were no more severe for girls than for boys. Timing of first sexual intercourse was related neither to self-esteem nor to adolescents' emotional reactions to first intercourse, which were probably related to socialization, life circumstances, and family beliefs regarding sex.

The median age of first intercourse was 15.5 years for girls and 14.75 years for boys. Longitudinal patterns of development differed for early (before the median age), middle (after the median age), and late (still virgins) initiators of intercourse. Adolescents who had first sexual intercourse early demonstrated the poorest psychosocial adjustment in ninth grade, and the same negative pattern persisted through twelfth grade. Adolescents who postponed first sexual intercourse the longest (were still virgins) had the most positive ninth-grade adjustment and the most positive developmental trajectory through the twelfth grade. They reported more postive psychosocial development, more positive family relationships, more frequent church attendance, greater commitment to education, and lower involvement with problem behaviors than those who initiated intercourse earlier. These longitudinal outcomes were not associated with the timing of first intercourse; rather, they appeared to be a continuation of enduring developmental paths based on childhood differences in temperament, personality, and family and life circumstances that were already well established before ninth grade (Bingham & Crockett, 1996; Dorius et al., 1993).

Table 16.5 presents sexual activity rates by gender, ethnic group, and grade based on data collected by the U.S. Centers for Disease Control (1992). As the table indicates, rates of intercourse increase from ninth through twelfth grade for both males and females, with a higher percentage of males reporting intercourse at each grade level and overall. African American high school students report the highest overall rate of sexual intercourse (72.3 percent), followed by Hispanic teens (53.4 percent) and white teens (51.55 percent). For each ethnic group, a higher percentage of males than females report having had sexual intercourse.

Sexual Attitudes   The "sexual revolution" of the 1960s and 1970s resulted in greater acceptance of premarital intercourse, masturbation, and homosexuality and a decline in the double standard holding that sexual activity outside of marriage is less acceptable for females than for males. In the 1980s and 1990s, however, teenagers appear to have had more cautious attitudes concerning sexual activity.

By and large, girls still tend to be more conservative than boys in their sexual attitudes, values, and actions. Boys tend to be more sexually active and to have more sexual encounters. Girls are more likely to emphasize intimacy and love as a necessary part of sexual activity and less likely to engage in sex merely as a physically pleasurable activity (Leigh, 1989; White & DeBlassie, 1992).

When asked to recall their reasons for first intercourse and how they felt about the experience, female and male college students differ. Though both frequently report that "we both wanted to," were curious, and loved or cared deeply about their partners, many more women cite partner pressure and many more men report sexual arousal and a desire to "score" as reasons (Koch, 1988).

Women and men also differ in their emotional reactions to their first experience with intercourse. College women are significantly more likely to report that their first sexual experience left them feeling less pleasure, satisfaction, and excitement than men and more sadness, guilt, nervousness, tension, embarrassment, and fear. Women also are more likely than men to have been in a committed relationship and to have had intercourse again with their first partner (Darling et al., 1992; Guggino & Ponzetti, 1997).

TABLE 16.5   Rates of Adolescent Sexual Activity by Gender, Ethnic Group, and Grade

| Gender | Ethnic Group | | | Grade | | | | Total |
	White	African American	Hispanic	9	10	11	12	
Male	56.4%	87.8%	63.0%	48.7%	52.5%	62.6%	76.3%	60.8%
Female	47.0	60.0	45.0	31.9	42.9	52.7	66.6	48.0
Total	51.6	72.3	53.4	39.6	47.6	57.3	71.9	54.2

Note: Percentages are of high school students who report ever having sexual intercourse.
Source: Centers for Disease Control (1992).

For these teenage couples, the junior/senior prom is an opportunity to experiment with intimacy, sexuality, and commitment, as well as other complex activities and roles associated with adulthood.

Motivations for teenage sex are not only sexual. Adolescents report that in addition to offering pleasure, sex helps them to confirm masculinity or femininity, get affection, rebel against parents, feel better about themselves, get revenge or degrade someone, express anger, alleviate boredom, and ensure the loyalty of a partner (Coley & Chase-Landsdale, 1998; Hajcak & Garwood, 1989). Nevertheless, while pregnancy and sexually transmitted diseases have always been a concern to parents and adolescents, the risk of AIDS has greatly increased the importance of initiating sexual activity in a safe and age-appropriate manner.

Dating   Since the beginning of this century, dating has tended to begin earlier, thus increasing the time span over which teenage dating takes place. Currently many adolescent girls begin dating at age twelve and boys at age thirteen, with almost one-half of boys and more than one-half of girls reporting dating at least once a week and approximately one-third dating two or three times per week. Only 10 percent of male and female seniors report never having dated (Savin-Williams & Berndt, 1990).

Dating is a major avenue for exploring sexual activity. In recent years, there has been a growing awareness that dating situations may lead to sexual activity that is coerced. *Date rape* refers to a situation in which a person, usually a female, is forced to have sex with a person she is dating. It is estimated that as many as 25 percent of sixteen-to-nineteen-year-old females are victims of date rape (Sorenson & Bowie, 1994). In one large-scale study of college men and women, more than three-quarters of the women reported having been treated in a sexually aggressive way (being forced to engage in sexual acts ranging from kissing to petting to sexual intercourse) and more than one-half of the men reported acting in a sexually aggressive manner on a date, either in high school or in college (Muehlenhard & Linton, 1987).

Date rape and other forms of sexual aggression were most likely to occur between two partners who knew each other fairly well, often for almost a year prior to the incident. Sexual aggression was most likely when a man initiated the date, provided transportation, and paid for the date, and was also more likely if both people got drunk and ended up in the man's dorm room or apartment (Sipe & Hall, 1996). It is likely that the cultural expectation that the boy initiate and the girl limit sex and the persistent tendency in our culture to blame the victim continue to contribute to this problem.

Nagayama Hall and Christy Barongan (1997) suggest that mainstream cultural experiences in the United States place men at risk for sexually aggressive behavior. Among the risk factors are the conditioning of sexual arousal to deviant stimuli, the development of cognitive distortions that reduce the perceived impact of sexual aggression, the condoning of anger toward women, and developmentally related personality problems that may lead to sexual aggression as well as to other problems. Hall and Barongan propose that a feminist and multicultural socialization, which accepts feminine attributes as a component of masculine gender identity and promotes cultural values and attitudes that deter sexual aggression, can help to reduce this problem.

The rate of date rape and other forms of violence among older adolescents does not differ substantially from the rate of such violence among college students, and there appears to be considerable overlap in the causes of both types of violence. In one recent study of 463 high school students, 43 percent reported being the victim of either sexual violence or severe physical violence by peers in the past year. Perpetrators were more likely to be known than unknown to the victim, or to be dating or ex-dating partners, and 70 percent of those who experienced violence by peers were girls. Findings support the view that both physical and sexual violence among high school peers is influenced by relationship, gender, effects on the victim, and beliefs about both male role power and personal power (Bennett & Fineran, 1998).

Sexual Orientations

Our discussion so far has centered on issues related to heterosexual orientation. But in the population at large, not all adolescents are heterosexual. Reliable statistics on sexual orientation are difficult to obtain. A study of thirty-eight thousand adolescents in grades seven through twelve found that 88.2 percent described themselves as predominantly heterosexual (exclusively interested in the other sex), 1.1 percent as predominantly homosexual or bisexual (interested in members of both sexes), and 10.7 percent as uncertain about their sexual orientation (Remafedi et al., 1992). Other studies have found that between 3 and 6 percent of teenagers report they are lesbian or gay (Patterson, 1995).

Due largely to the political and educational efforts of the "equal rights" and "gay rights" movements, public acceptance of nonheterosexual orientations has increased significantly during the past several decades. This acceptance acknowledges the right of individuals to freely practice their own sexual orientations and lifestyles and to receive protection from discrimination. However, other researchers have found that **homophobia** (dislike and fear of homosexuals) remains strong among adolescents. One study found that 75 percent of females and 84 percent of males expressed disgust for homosexual acts; however, females seemed to be more tolerant of homosexuality and less fearful about being identified as homosexual than males were (Stokes, 1985). Another study found that most heterosexual college students, both male and female, would not want to marry someone who had had even a single homosexual experience (Williams & Jacoby, 1989).

Because the widespread homophobia in their environments makes communication seem dangerous, gay, lesbian, and bisexual adolescents are likely to experience feelings of attraction for members of the same gender for several years before *coming out*, or publicly acknowledging their sexual orientation (Patterson, 1995). A study by Ritch Savin Williams found that for gay males, initiation of sexual behavior with same-sex partners appeared to be closely associated with biological changes of puberty (early maturers initiated same-sex encounters earlier than did late maturers), whereas sexual behavior with opposite-sex partners began according to a youngster's age and level of social and emotional development (Savin-Williams,

homophobia Fear and dislike of homosexuals.

1995). Disclosure of sexual orientation to family members is a complex challenge. In a study of 194 lesbian, gay, and bisexual adolescents ages fourteen to twenty-one and living at home, Anthony D'Augelli and his colleagues found that three-quarters had told at least one parent, more often the mother than the father. Only half of the mothers and siblings and one-quarter of fathers were fully accepting, and 25 percent of fathers and 10 percent of mothers were actively rejecting. In many cases, coming out within the family was associated with threats and verbal abuse from family members (D'Augelli et al., 1998).

The challenging task of achieving a secure sexual identity is considerably more difficult for nonheterosexual adolescents, who have the added burdens of grappling with their difference and the anxieties and dangers involved. Homosexual and bisexual teenagers often experience rejection by their families, peer groups, schools, places of worship, and other community institutions—the very groups that adolescents depend on for support. The verbal abuse, the AIDS-related stigmatization, the threat of physical attack, and other forms of victimization they experience also put them at greater risk for mental health problems. Strong family support and self-acceptance, however, can serve as buffers against these negative outcomes (Hershberger & D'Augelli, 1995).

As yet no agreement exists on the specific pattern of factors that leads to the development of nonheterosexual orientations. Experiences within the family have long been considered an important contributor. Cross-gender behavior in childhood appears to be strongly associated with nonheterosexual orientations in adolescence and adulthood for both males and females, but a substantial proportion of gay and lesbian adults report no or few cross-gender behaviors in childhood (Bailey & Zucker, 1995; Golombok & Tasker, 1996; Green, 1987). In a unique longitudinal study, Susan Golombok and Fiona Tasker (1996) compared the sexual orientations of twenty-five adults who had been raised as children by lesbian mothers with a group of twenty-one adults who had been raised by heterosexual single mothers. Although children from lesbian families were more likely to explore same-sex relationships, all but two children raised by lesbian mothers (and all children raised by heterosexual mothers) identified themselves as heterosexual in adulthood, a difference that was not statistically significant.

A number of researchers are also exploring the contributions of biological and genetic predispositions to the development of nonheterosexual orientations. (Byne, 1994; LeVay & Hamer, 1994; Patterson, 1995). One approach has sought to discover physical differences between the brains of male and female animals and humans; the second has explored the role of genes by using family and twin adoption studies to analyze the frequencies with which homosexuality occurs in families and by directly examining DNA. To date, there is little reliable evidence of differences in brain structure that correlate with differences in sexual orientation and no reason to think that the discovery of such differences would explain the cause of sexual orientation. The search for genetic causes of homosexuality suffers from the same methodological and conceptual problems discussed in Chapter 3.

Sex and Everyday Life

Although sexuality plays an important role in adolescents' feelings, fantasies, and social relationships, it does not necessarily dominate their lives. Sexual experience involving intercourse is the exception for most junior high school students. And although sexual activity increases during high school, most adolescents have intercourse on a rather sporadic, unpredictable basis, if at all. Masturbation and various forms of petting appear to be the mainstay of many adolescents' sexual activity.

As we noted earlier, changes in sexuality during adolescence involve not only physical maturation and the development of new social skills; they also play a major role in the development of intimacy and personal identity. Sometimes identity development is complicated by sexual issues. It can also be affected by social problems specific to teenagers, as we will see in the next section.

 WHAT DO YOU THINK?   When you were an adolescent, what were your attitudes toward premarital sex, dating, and nonheterosexual orientations? In what ways, if any, have your attitudes changed since then?

Special Problems of Adolescence

In Chapter 14, we looked at the special physical and health risks adolescents face as a group. Their lack of experience, their need to experiment with new and sometimes risky social roles, and the lack of educational and economic opportunities and social support they frequently encounter can place adolescents at high risk for developing certain psychosocial problems. In the following section, we discuss three special problems of adolescence: teenage pregnancy and parenthood, adolescent depression and suicide, and juvenile delinquency.

Adolescent Pregnancy and Parenthood

In 1990, 1,040,000 adolescents under age twenty became pregnant, and approximately 530,000 (51 percent) of them gave birth (Alan Guttmacher Institute, 1994). Birth rates for nineteen-year-olds were double those for fifteen- to seventeen-year-olds, and rates for those under fifteen years were extremely low. In 1995, birth rates for white fifteen- to nineteen-year-olds were 39.3 per 1,000 compared to 106.7 per 1,000 for Hispanics and 99.3 per 1,000 for African Americans (Ventura et al., 1997).

Causes of Teen Pregnancy   Causes of teen pregnancy include individual, family, neighborhood, and societal characteristics, suggesting that a contextual or ecological approach similar to that used in our discussion of the impact of divorce earlier in this chapter will be useful here. Female adolescents who live in communities with high rates of poverty and who themselves are raised in poverty by single parents with low levels of education are at higher risk of becoming pregnant. In fact, in 1988, 60 percent of adolescent mothers lived in poverty at the time of their babies' birth (Alan Guttmaacher Institute, 1994; Coley & Chase-Landsdale, 1998). The majority of teen pregnancies are thought to involve experiences of poverty and perceptions of limited life opportunities and choices. Life experiences associated with poverty, such as alienation at school, being surrounded by role models of unmarried parenthood and unemployment, and lack of educational opportunities and stable career prospects, tend to lower the perceived costs of early motherhood (Coley & Chase-Landsdale, 1998). In addition, the loss of most low-skill, high-paying manufacturing jobs due to changes in the U.S. economy has increased unemployment and poverty in our inner cities and strikingly changed the context and course of development during the teenage years and the early twenties. Although median ages of completing school, marriage, and childbearing have significantly increased for middle-class adolescents, lower-SES populations have not adapted to these changes by delaying starting their families. Adolescent childbearing, which in the past occurred mostly in the context of marriage with an employed husband, is now occurring among unmarried teenagers with few prospects for economic security (Coley & Chase-Landsdale, 1998; Rosenheim & Testa, 1992; Wilson, 1996).

Decisions About Contraception   Although American teenagers do not exhibit different patterns of sexual activity than adolescents in many industrial countries, they use contraception less consistently and effectively. In 1990 the rate of teenage

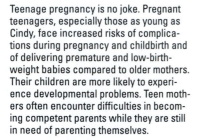

Teenage pregnancy is no joke. Pregnant teenagers, especially those as young as Cindy, face increased risks of complications during pregnancy and childbirth and of delivering premature and low-birth-weight babies compared to older mothers. Their children are more likely to experience developmental problems. Teen mothers often encounter difficulties in becoming competent parents while they are still in need of parenting themselves.

births in the United States was almost twice that of Great Britain, the country with the next highest rate; more than four times greater than those of Sweden and Spain; seven times greater than those of Denmark and the Netherlands; and fifteen times greater than that of Japan (Coley & Chase-Landsdale, 1998).

The great majority of teenage pregnancies are the result of inadequate or no contraception. Many teenagers are startlingly uninformed about the basics of reproduction, believing they are "immune" to pregnancy, or at least at very low risk. Approximately one-third of all teenagers do not use contraceptives the first time they have sex, and many, particularly younger adolescents, delay contraception for a year or more after the first intercourse (Coley & Chase-Landsdale, 1998).

Although birth control pills are popular, they are not reliable during the first month of use. Only foam and condoms or a diaphragm and contraceptive jelly are really effective for first intercourse. But adolescents do not like to use these contraceptives because they imply a preparedness for sex, are expensive or unavailable when needed, can be messy, reduce pleasure, and increase anxiety due to inexperience in their use. As one female high school senior put it "When you carry condoms, all the boys think you want it." Irregular use of contraception is associated with low economic status, poor communication with parents, lack of knowledge about contraceptives, having teenage friends who became parents, low educational achievement and aspirations, high levels of anxiety, low self-esteem, and feelings of fatalism, powerlessness, and alienation (Coley & Chase-Landsdale, 1998; Hiller et al., 1998).

Parent-Teen Communication About Sexual Behavior   The helplessness that many parents feel about influencing their teens' sexual behavior may in part reflect a failure to communicate effectively about such matters. This is illustrated in a recent study by James Jaccard and his colleagues of African American adolescents ages fourteen to seventeen, which found little agreement between the mothers' perceptions and reports of their teenagers' sexual behavior and the teenagers' self-reports (Jaccard et al., 1998). Adolescent perceptions and reports were more predictive of actual sexual behavior than maternal reports. Mothers significantly underestimated the sexual activity of their teens, and teens tended to underestimate their mothers' level of disapproval of their sexual activity. While 58 percent of the teens in the study had engaged in sexual intercourse, only 34 percent of the mothers thought that was the case. This was particularly true for older mothers who were satisfied with their parent-teen relationship but did not talk with their teens about sex and strongly disapproved of premarital sex. Teens were more likely to underestimate their mothers' opposition to premarital sex if the mothers were not religious, if the teens' friends viewed it favorably, if they reported little communication about sex with their mothers, and if they were male.

Parent-teen communication is a complex process, especially when adolescent sexual behavior is the topic. It takes good communication, which allows both parties to share their needs and expectations to negotiate differences, for parents to successfully influence their teens. Efforts to improve parent-teen communication must address five important aspects: (1) the *extent* of the communication, as indicated by the frequency and depth; (2) the *style* or manner in which the information is communicated; (3) the *content* of the communication; (4) the *timing* of the communication; and (5) the *general family environment* in which the communication takes place, as reflected in the overall quality of the parent-teen relationship (Jaccard et al., 1998).

Choosing Between Abortion and Parenthood   Although most teenage mothers report that they did not plan to become pregnant and would not choose to do so if they had a choice, the more than 50 percent who decide to have their babies become increasingly committed to motherhood during the course of the pregnancy. A teenager's reactions to unplanned pregnancy are influenced by a variety of factors, including her feelings about school, her relationship with the baby's father, her relationship with her parents, perceived family support for keeping the child, how many of her peers have become parents, and her sense of self-esteem (Faber, 1991; Furstenberg et al., 1989).

Approximately 44 percent of all teenage pregnancies end in abortion, which is roughly 25 percent of all abortions performed in the United States (Hayes, 1987; U.S. Bureau of the Census, 1992). The experience of an abortion may be psychologically stressful for teenagers. How an abortion will affect a particular teenager depends on her feelings and attitudes about pregnancy and abortion; the attitudes of and support available from parents, other adults, peers, and her sexual partner; and her overall personal adjustment and life circumstances (Franz & Reardon, 1992; Hardy, 1991).

Consequences of Teenage Parenthood   Many teenage mothers may see having a baby as a way to prematurely crystallize their identity, because motherhood and marriage promise to establish them in a secure adult role and help them to escape role confusion. For some, teenage parenthood and marriage also promise an intense, intimate, and lasting relationship with another person, a relationship that they themselves may have been deprived of and may figure heavily in their search for identity. Such fantasies generally are not realized, however. Teenage mothers are less likely to finish high school, find a stable-paying job, enter secure marriages, or achieve equal job status or income in their lifetimes. Teenage fathers are less negatively affected, largely because they generally do not assume responsibility for raising their children (Coley & Chase-Landsdale, 1998; Furstenberg et al., 1989).

Teenage mothers are more likely than older women to experience complications such as anemia and toxemia during pregnancy, as well as prolonged labor. Their babies are more likely to be premature, have low birth weight, and have neurological defects, and are also more likely to die during their first year. For some children of teenage mothers, delays in cognitive development begin to emerge during the preschool years and continue into the school years. Many children show behavioral problems, including aggression and impulse control. In adolescence, they have higher rates of grade failure, delinquency, incarceration (for males), and early sexual activity and pregnancy than their peers born to older mothers. Both teenage

For teen couples who are expectant or who have an infant such as this one, a good high school pregnancy and parenting program and support from family, friends, and each other can have a major impact on how well they cope with the challenges of early parenthood.

mothers and their children, however, display a wide range of diversity in their development and functioning. Although children of teenage mothers are at risk for becoming teenage parents, it is estimated that only between one-quarter and one-third of the daughters and one-tenth of the sons of teen parents become teen parents themselves. The lower SES experienced by the majority of teen parents appears to be a more important predictor of children's and adolescents' functioning than is maternal age at birth (Coley & Chase-Lansdale, 1998).

Involvement of Grandmothers   The transition to parenthood is a challenging one, even for married young adults who are well educated and enjoy economically and socially supportive circumstances. For single teenage mothers, the transition often is much more difficult. Many teenage mothers end up living with their own mothers. The quality of childrearing practices for teenage parents living in three-generation families appears to be positively related to the quality of their relationships with their own mothers (their babies' grandmothers). Adolescent mothers whose own mothers provided authoritative parenting, helped them care for their new babies, and modeled appropriate behaviors in a way that respected their daughters' autonomy became better parents themselves than teen mothers without such support. However, although living in the same household as their mothers resulted in positive mother-grandmother relationships for younger teen mothers, mother-grandmother relationships were better for older teenage mothers when the adolescent daughter and her mother lived in separate households (Apfel & Seitz, 1991; Chase-Landsdale et al., 1994; Wakschlag et al., 1996).

Prevention and Support Programs   Programs to prevent teen pregnancy must be responsive to adolescents' developmental needs and life contexts. Teaching abstinence appears to be most effective in dealing with preteens and young adolescents, while providing information and access to contraceptives works better with older adolescents (Frost & Forrest, 1995). For teens who are at high risk because of their life circumstances, programs that include comprehensive, developmentally oriented services—medical care and contraceptive services, social services, family and educational support, and school-linked parenting education—appear to be most effective. One such program conducted at John Hopkins University was successful in delaying the age at which sexual activity was initiated, increased contraceptive use, reduced the frequency of sexual relations, and reduced the pregnancy rate by 30 percent, while comparison school rates increased by 58 percent (Hardy & Zapin, 1991).

Effective support programs for pregnant teenagers and teenage parents generally focus on providing pre- and postnatal health care, economic support, child care and parenting support, education, and job training. The Prenatal/Early Infancy Projects (Olds, 1988) still stands as a model for assisting teenage parents and their children and for reducing the likelihood of unplanned pregnancies in the future. It clearly demonstrates close connections between issues in adolescent development and themes associated with prenatal development, infancy, and early childhood development. It also highlights the interconnectedness of the three main developmental domains of physical, cognitive, and psychosocial development discussed in Chapter 1.

This five-year longitudinal study focused on single, first-time-pregnant adolescents from low-SES circumstances. The program (1) provided prenatal parent education; (2) helped to involve family members and friends in the pregnancy, birth, early care of the child, and support of the mother; and (3) helped to link family members with formal health and human services. Prenatal and pediatric care was available through a local team of private obstetricians and pediatricians. A central feature of the program was an ongoing caregiving relationship with an experienced nurse who made regular home visits during and for two years following the pregnancy. During the pregnancy, the nurse provided parenting education focused on helping the pregnant teen to improve her diet and monitor her weight gain, identify signs of pregnancy complication, adopt a healthy lifestyle (e.g., eliminate use of cigarettes), prepare for labor and delivery, prepare for the early care of the newborn, make appropriate use of the health care system, and make plans regarding subsequent pregnancies, returning to school, and finding employment. After the baby was born, the nurse provided home-based infancy education designed to improve the young mother's understanding of her infant's temperament and to promote the infant's physical, cognitive, and psychosocial development.

To evaluate the long-term impact of the program, the teen mothers and their children were followed from early pregnancy until their children were four years old. Adolescent mothers who received postnatal home nursing care made better use of formal health and social services, experienced greater informal social support, improved their diets more, and reduced the number of cigarettes smoked compared to a similar group of women who had not received such nursing care. High-risk teen mothers benefited the most. For very young teenagers, there was 335-gram improvement in their babies' birth weight and, for women who smoked, a 75 percent reduction in preterm delivery. Among poor, unmarried, high-risk teens who received postnatal home nursing care, there was a 75 percent reduction in reported cases of child abuse and neglect (from 19 to 4 percent). These at-risk mothers found their children easier to care for, used less punishment and restriction and a greater number of growth-promoting playthings, needed to use the emergency room fewer times for their babies' health care, and, during the children's second year, used the emergency room 56 percent fewer times for children's accidents than did similar mothers who did not receive home nursing care (Olds, 1988). The Working With interview with Janet Whallen, a nurse practitioner, provides a first-hand view of what it is like to work with pregnant teenagers.

Teenage Depression and Suicide

Depressive disorders involve disturbances of emotion that affect an individual's entire mental life. Two key subtypes of depressive disorder exist: major depressive disorder (MDD), which involves a single episode or recurrent episodes of depression, and dysthymic disorder (DD), which involves chronic depressive symptoms. Individuals with either type of depressive disorder experience a pervasive mood disturbance that involves feelings of sadness and loss of interest or pleasure in most activities; feelings of fear, anger, self-criticism, and hopelessness; and disturbances in sleep, appetite, ability to concentrate, sexual interest, and energy level. Depression is frequently accompanied by other problems such as anxiety, social withdrawal, disruptive disorder, and substance abuse (American Psychiatric Association, 1994; Cicchetti & Toth, 1998; Peterson et al., 1993).

It is estimated that at any point in time, between 0.4 and 2.5 percent of children and from 0.4 and 8.3 percent of adolescents suffer from MDD, and between 15 and 20 percent of adolescents suffer from MDD over their lifetimes. Approximately 0.6 to 1.7 percent of children and 1.6 to 8.0 percent of adolescents suffer from DD at any point in time. Depression during childhood and adolescence are nonnormative experiences that interfere with children's development. The average length of an episode of MDD in children and adolescents is from seven to nine months. Approximately 90 percent of MDD episodes end within two years following their onset, and the remaining 10 percent last longer. MDD frequently recurs in children and adolescents. DD episodes last much longer than MDD episodes, with the average length being four years. Because the development of DD often leads to a recurrent depressive disorder, early diagnosis and treatment are important. There is some evidence that a significant increase in the prevalence of depression during early to middle adolescence occurs among both males and females and that rates are higher for girls, who may be more likely to deal with their stresses by internalizing them rather than externalizing them in a more aggressive manner (Cicchetti & Toth, 1998).

Causes of Depression in Adolescence   Dante Cicchetti and Sheree Toth (1998) suggest that the causes of depression are best understood from an ecological systems perspective similar to that of Uri Bronfenbrenner (see Chapter 1). In this view, the development of depression is related to the multiple, dynamic interactions among environmental forces, caregiving characteristics, and the characteristics of the developing child and adolescent. At each ecological level of influence, certain risk and preventative factors may influence the development of depressive problems. At the individual level, some infants may be born with a biological vulnerability to depression due to genetic or nongenetic factors. Family influences include the unique family circumstances, both biological and psychosocial, in which the child and adolescent develops. Although genetic factors account for some within-family depression, genetics alone cannot fully explain the development of depression. For one thing, many depressed children display rapid recovery when hospitalized, even without additional interventions. For another, a number of family characteristics have been associated with the development and maintenance of depression, including parental depression, anxiety, substance abuse, and maltreatment. Family transitions, low SES, and acute and chronic negative life events involving significant losses through parental death, divorce, or separation or involving child maltreatment have been associated with the occurrence of depression during childhood and adolescence (Cicchetti & Toth, 1998; Downey & Coyne, 1990).

Children and adolescents who live in a family in which one or more parents are depressed, have other serious emotional problems, or experience a serious and pervasive disturbance in the parent-child relationship, including physical or emotional abuse, are at much greater risk for depression as well as other forms of psychopathology. In addition, the environments provided by the schools and neighborhoods in which a child grows up can play an important role in the development of depression. Neighborhoods that are unsafe and unsupportive may create levels of stress that are developmentally disruptive, particularly during early and middle adolescence. Especially during the early adolescent transition to middle school, school

WORKING WITH

Janet Whallen, **Nurse Practitioner**

Helping Pregnant Teenagers

Janet Whallen was interviewed in her office, which is located in a neighborhood health care center serving disadvantaged Hispanic and African American individuals and families. Janet's warm, low-key style made it easy to see why teenagers would find her easy to talk with. Our interview focused on the experiences of pregnant teens.

Rob: *What special problems do pregnant teenagers face?*

Janet: Most of the sexual relationships these teenagers are involved in are fairly short-lived. A young woman or man might have three or four partners in a year. When a young woman becomes pregnant, the chances that she'll still be with the same boyfriend when she delivers nine months later are fairly slim.

Rob: *Nine months would be a long relationship?*

Janet: For someone who is only fourteen or fifteen, it is. Very few of these girls have the baby's father with them in any way, shape, or form at the time of delivery.

Rob: *Why is this so?*

Janet: Sometimes the guy gets scared or loses interest because the girl is starting to get fat. Or the girl or guy was already losing interest even before the pregnancy occurred. Whatever the reason, I think shorter relationships are fairly typical of early adolescent behavior.

Rob: *In what other ways are the experiences of pregnant teenagers typical of adolescents in general?*

Janet: They have very little sense of the implications of the decisions they make. They make most choices based on short-term consequences, and those choices are tightly connected to peer approval. There are also lots of rebellion issues against important adults, whether parents or teachers.

Rob: *How does this rebelliousness affect pregnancy?*

Janet: Teenagers are very sensitive about many things, from small issues to big ones: being told to eat certain things or to wear certain clothes—you know, "you're going to look fat if you wear that"—about smoking or not smoking, getting home on time after school or staying out late on Friday night, about how their parent will feel about their being sexually active or getting pregnant. I have to be very careful to give advice in a way that they don't find threatening.

Rob: *Sounds like typical adolescent behavior.*

Janet: I have kids who will come in for an appointment with four or five giggling teenage friends, who'll sit outside the office and heckle and laugh. They'll all be talking about who is going out with whom, who passed notes to whom in class, who cut class for what reasons, where they bought their clothes. You would never know you were in the middle of an inner-city clinic for pregnant teenagers.

Rob: *Are these pregnant teenagers in danger of losing connection with their peer culture?*

Janet: Not as much as you might think. Unlike in middle-class communities, where teenagers are expected to complete high school and go to college, there is relatively little stigma attached to becoming pregnant during high school—although there may be a little bit more if pregnancy occurs in junior high.

Rob: *Why do teenagers become pregnant in the first place?*

Janet: I wish I knew the answer to that one! Failure to use effective birth control is, of course, the immediate factor. And some teenagers want to have a little baby to care for and be close to and to feel important and needed, or they see pregnancy as a way to gain adult status. Another reason is that sex is a big deal and getting pregnant isn't.

Rob: *What do you mean?*

Janet: Many of these kids become sexually active at age twelve or thirteen, and some even before they start having their periods. Most of them have little extra money, so they don't go shopping, or buy CDs, or collect this or that. A lot of them are involved in Pentecostal or Baptist churches, so they don't do drugs and they don't drink. But they do sex.

Rob: *It's an enjoyable activity, and it's inexpensive.*

Janet: Well . . . intimacy is involved too, but for many young teens, sex is mainly a way to have immediate fun. Getting pregnant simply happens, with little thought about its deeper social, emotional, or philosophical significance.

Rob: *What social supports are available to these youngsters?*

Janet: Family or extended family members often will babysit and share other child care responsibilities. Sometimes the boyfriend's family will also become involved, even when he's out of the picture. Many teen moms are back to being teenagers fairly soon after having their babies. Some graduate from high school and get a job, and a few go on to college. A significant number do not finish school. Unfortunately, we are finding that an increasing number get pregnant again soon after the first baby.

What Do You Think?

1. If Janet Whallen were working with pregnant teens in the community in which you spent your adolescence, in what ways might her observations be different? In what ways might they be the same? Why?

2. What are your views about the causes of teenage pregnancy?

3. What strategies might you recommend for preventing teen pregnancy among low-SES, inner-city youth?

environments that respond inappropriately to adolescents' academic and psychosocial needs can alienate them from academic activities and from prosocial activities with peers, and contribute to school failure, antisocial behavior, drug abuse, and depression (Cicchetti & Toth, 1998; Downey & Coyne, 1990; Eccles, 1993; Garbarino, 1992b; Jacobvitz & Bush, 1996). Depression is often a factor in adolescent suicide.

Suicide in Adolescence   Suicide is the third leading cause of death among children ages fifteen to nineteen. Between 6 and 13 percent of adolescents have reported attempting suicide at least once in their lives, and the ratio of attempted to successful suicides is estimated to be as high as fifty to one. Suicide attempts are estimated to be three to nine times more common among girls, but boys succeed three times as often, in part because they use more effective methods such as knives and guns (Garland & Zigler, 1993; Meehan et al., 1992).

The majority of teenagers who attempt suicide have experienced serious family difficulties, including parent-child conflict, divorce, neglect, and abuse. Suicide attempts almost always represent cries for help with the personal turmoil and feelings of intense loneliness, isolation, and hopelessness that such youngsters experience. Although most teenagers who are not depressed still experience moments of unhappiness, and most who are depressed do not attempt suicide, signs of unhappiness and depression should not be dismissed, particularly if they persist. Also, because a large percentage of those who attempt suicide have threatened or attempted it before, such threats should be taken very seriously (Blumenthal & Kupfer, 1988; Rubenstein et al., 1998).

Attempts to prevent suicide include early detection and intervention in family and personal crises, school-based education about depression and suicide risk factors, training in problem-solving and coping skills, crisis counseling, and emergency hot lines. Treatment for teens who attempt suicide generally involves therapy with both the adolescent and his or her family (Garland & Zigler, 1993; Rubenstein et al., 1998). The film *Ordinary People* provides an excellent portrayal of a teenager's suicide attempt, the events and family circumstances involved, and the treatment received.

In the following section we discuss another serious problem of adolescence: juvenile delinquency.

Juvenile Delinquency

Juvenile delinquency refers to a pattern of destructive or antisocial activities and lawbreaking offenses committed by adolescents. In 1990, more than 1.75 million juveniles were arrested for less serious *status offenses* such as vandalism, joy-riding, drug abuse, or running away, and almost 650,000 for more serious crimes such as larceny or theft, robbery, or forcible rape (Federal Bureau of Investigation, 1991; Patterson et al., 1989). Between 1988 and 1994, arrests for violent offenses by juveniles increased by 61 percent (Snyder & Sickmund, 1995). Cultural expectations also affect rates of delinquent behavior among adolescents, as discussed in the accompanying Multicultural View box.

There is some evidence that the route to chronic delinquency may follow a predictable developmental sequence of experiences. The first step involves ineffective parenting and problematic family interaction processes, both of which frequently contribute to childhood conduct disorders. In the second step, the conduct-disordered behaviors lead to academic failure and peer rejection. During later childhood and early adolescence, continuing failure at school and peer rejection lead to a third step: increased risk for depressed mood and involvement in a deviant peer group. Children who follow this developmental sequence are assumed to be at high risk for engaging in chronic delinquent behavior (Flannery et al., 1998).

• • •
juvenile delinquency A pattern of destructive or antisocial activities and lawbreaking offenses committed by adolescents.

Factors associated with delinquency include a caregiver-child relationship characterized by hostility, lack of affection, underinvolvement, and lack of supervision; overly harsh and authoritarian methods of discipline; a high degree of family conflict and disorganization; a parent with a personality disturbance and a delinquent history of her or his own; impoverished living conditions; lack of attachment to any prosocial institution such as school, job, or religious organization; lack of positive adult role models; and exposure to neighborhood environments in which violence, crime, and delinquent behavior are prevalent (Dishion et al., 1995; Huff, 1996).

Longitudinal studies of delinquency and antisocial behavior have found that aggression during the preschool period is predictive only of serious forms of antisocial behavior in adolescence and adulthood. For these children, who are mostly boys, the onset of minor aggression (annoying others and bullying) tends to presede the onset of physical fighting (including gang fighting), which in turn precedes the onset of more extreme violence (aggravated assault, robbery, and rape) (Loeber, & Stouthamer-Loeber, 1998). The majority of violent male adults exhibited a life course pattern initially characterized by both aggressive behavior and symptoms of attention deficit hyperactivity disorder (ADHD) during their preschool years, followed by more serious forms of conduct disorder and antisocial behavior during adolescence and adulthood. A second, limited-duration pattern is shown by individuals who outgrow aggression either during the preschool–elementary school age period or in late adolescence–early adulthood. A third, late-onset pattern accounts for individuals who become violent during adulthood but do not have a history of aggression earlier in their lives (Loeber, & Stouthamer-Loeber, 1998).

Gangs   Many delinquent youngsters belong to gangs. A *gang* is a relatively permanent group of individuals with a clearly identified leadership and organizational structure and clear role expectations for its members. Gangs identify with or claim control over "territory" in the community and engage in violence and other forms of illegal activities such as fighting, vandalism, theft, and drug dealing on an individual or group basis (Miller, 1990). A gang is likely to have a group name, an initiation rite, nicknames for members, and gang symbols such as colors, tattoos, hand signs, or jewelry (Winfree et al., 1994).

Typically gangs are formed by individuals from poor and racial or ethnic minority and immigrant backgrounds. Traditionally gang members have mainly been adolescent males, but the growth of gangs in prisons and increased gang involvement in the drug trade have expanded the age range to include children as young as nine as well as adults, and also increased female involvement to some degree (Flannery et al., 1998; Goldstein & Soriano, 1994).

Gangs are thought to provide alternative economic opportunities and social supports for disadvantaged and alienated youths who face high levels of uncertainty, instability, and danger in their families and neighborhoods. For such adolescents, gang membership offers a surrogate "family," a sense of identity and belonging, and status, power, and protection, as well as the material benefits of criminal activity (Flannery et al., 1998).

A gang typically reinforces its members for associating exclusively with other members, conforming to pro-gang attitudes and behaviors, and rejecting the values of parents, teachers, and mainstream peers (Winfree et al., 1994). Many of the individual, family, and social factors associated with gang membership, gang activity, and their prevention are similar to those associated with juvenile delinquency.

Reducing and Preventing Delinquency   Most adolescents, of course, do not become delinquents or join gangs. Adolescents who are at risk for delinquency sometimes can be helped by programs that make available the support and opportunities that will allow successful experimentation with other roles and identities. These include community houses, YMCAs, police athletic leagues, summer camps,

A Multicultural View ....

Differing Cultural Views of Delinquency

Cultures differ widely in how they judge the appropriateness of adolescents' delinquent behavior and how they respond when it occurs. Jeffrey Arnett (1992) suggests that this is largely due to important forces outside of the microsystem of family and peer group that strongly influence adolescent socialization. As we saw in Chapter 1's discussion of ecological systems of development, mesosystem, exosystem and macrosystem influences include the school community, legal system, cultural beliefs, and the media. In Arnett's view, some cultures value independence and free self-expression more highly than they value conformity. These *broad socialization* cultures have no commonly accepted belief systems by which to judge right and wrong behavior. Such cultures tolerate a wide range of deviations from cultural expectations without severe upset or punishment. In contrast, *narrow socialization* cultures subscribe to ideologies that strictly set forth what constitutes right and wrong behavior. Such cultures value conformity and adherence to standards of the community over individual autonomy, and are more likely to severely punish deviations from community standards or norms. This helps explain why behaviors considered delinquent in one society are tolerated in others.

A study by Jeffrey Arnett and Lene Jensen (1997) which compared socialization and risk behavior among middle class adolescents in Denmark and the United States lends support to this view. Overall, socialization was narrower among the Danish youth, who had more household obligations, greater community stability, and more adults beyond their immediate families involved in their socialization. Rates of risk-taking and delinquent behavior were higher for American teens, who were raised in a more broadly socialized culture. American teens had higher rates of high-speed and drunk driving and of minor criminal behavior such as shoplifting and vandalism, whereas Danish youth had higher rates of riding a bicycle or moped while intoxicated. Danish adolescents also had higher rates of sexual intercourse than American adolescents, but because Americans were less likely to use contraception, overall rates of unprotected sex (without contraception) were almost identical.

Another good example of cultural difference with regard to delinquent behavior is the use of alcohol. While adolescent drinking of alcoholic beverages is a cause of great concern in the United States, in Jamaica, adolescent drinking is not a sign of delinquent behavior and there are few legal restrictions against it (Smith & Blinn Pike, 1994). In European countries, attitudes about teenage drinking and the amount of weekly drinking that occurs vary widely. Adolescents in Greece and Italy, for example, drink almost twice as much alcohol per week than teenagers in Ireland, and adolescents in Spain are able to consume considerably more alcohol per week than are adolescents in the United States before they are categorized as "drinkers" (Recio Adrados, 1995; van Reek et al., 1994). Studies of juvenile delinquency in England, France, Germany, Japan, South Africa, and the United States also find that differences in cultural tradition and national character play an important role in how delinquency is defined, how prevalent it is, and how it is treated (Corley & Smitherman, 1994; McCall, 1995).

Whether or not adolescent social behavior is viewed as deviant is also affected by the status of the particular adolescent subculture within the majority culture and by how ado-

---

crisis drop-in centers, and telephone hot lines, as well as outpatient and residential treatment programs to assist more disturbed teenagers and their families. Unfortunately, such interventions have been found to produce mostly short-term effects and to lose their impact unless continued on a long-term basis (Hamburg, 1994).

Intensive early childhood intervention programs for at-risk preschool children and their families have achieved significant success at reducing delinquency and related problems later in life (Ramsey & Ramsey, 1998; Zigler et al., 1992). The High/Scope Perry Preschool Program, for example, provided a high-quality preschool, weekly home visits by teachers, and extensive parent involvement for three- and four-year-olds from low-SES families. Long-term longitudinal follow-up studies of these children at age nineteen found significantly lower rates of school dropout, illiteracy, unemployment, welfare dependence, and arrests for delinquent or criminal behavior than for a comparable group of children who did not participate in the program (Hamburg, 1994; Schweinhart & Weikart, 1988). Parent training programs designed to improve family management practices with at-risk preadolescents have also yielded promising results (Kazdin, 1987).

lescents view that culture. For example, Mexican American teenagers may decide to join a gang as a way of retaining their own culture of origin and rejecting the majority values found in American public schools (Calabrese & Noboa, 1995). A large-scale international survey of youth-related offenses among 14- to 21-year-old boys and girls from 13 countries found that youth from low educational and low-SES circumstances reported more violent and property-related-offenses than did those from more mainstream social and economic circumstances, but that drug offenses and more minor youth-related offenses were equally distributed across all SES backgrounds (McQuoid, 1996).

Most of the research discussed above focuses on Western industrialized countries. To what extent is adolescent antisocial behavior an expected occurrence in nonindustrial societies? To answer this question, cultural anthropologists Alice Schlegel and Herbert Barry (1991) analyzed cross-cultural differences regarding such expectations in a sample of 186 nonindustrial societies from around the world. The antisocial behaviors studied included hostile speech, fighting, crimes against persons, theft, sexual misbehavior, destruction of property, and drunkenness or misuse of other drugs. Direct information about antisocial behavior among adolescent boys was available for 54 societies, 24 of which expected antisocial behavior to occur and 30 of which did not. Similar information was available for adolescent girls in 34 societies, six of which expected it to be present and 28 of which did not. In general, antisocial behavior was less likely in societies in which adolescent boys spent a significant amount of time with adults, and was more likely in societies in which adolescents spent much of their time in organized peer groups, particularly when peer activities were highly competitive.

Schlegel and Barry also found that some societal organizations appear to promote adolescent misbehavior, either because the conditions that contribute to it are not recognized or because preventing such conditions would be too costly or disrupt other arrangements. For example, when it is economically advantageous to have groups of adolescent boys working apart from adults and adult supervision, risk of aggressive and other antisocial activities is likely to increase. They cite the case of the African Masai, who live in the highlands of Kenya and Tanzania. Masai adolescent boys are responsible for herding cattle and are sometimes suspected of stealing cattle to add to their own herds. Among Abkhaz adolescent boys, who live in the Georgian Republic (formerly part of the Soviet Union) and spend much of their time with peers, theft is a central feature of economic and political life and boys are trained to steal. However, if this thievery is turned against community members and even other peers, it is then punished. Antisocial behavior, while publicly deplored, may also be tolerated or even condoned if it serves individual family interests, such as fighting with an enemy's child or stealing from a disliked or envied neighbor.

Antisocial behavior, particularly among adolescent boys, is more likely in cultures that define adolescence as a new stage that involves a sharp break from childhood and includes a rapid transition to adult character, the development of new roles in the family and in the community, and increased opportunities to own property and to choose a spouse. Adolescent antisocial behaviors are also more likely when such behavior is prevalent among adult men.

WHAT DO YOU THINK ?   What advice might you give to concerned parents regarding how they can protect their children from teenage pregnancy and delinquency? What advice might you give to the governor of your state regarding programs to prevent these problems?

The Emerging Adult

We have reached the end of our discussion of adolescence. We saw how relationships with parents, friendships, and activities with groups of peers contribute to the development of identity during this stage. We also discussed the important contribution of sexuality and sexual experiences to identity formation and explored several special problems that can interfere with identity achievement. Just as the growth spurt and physical changes of puberty and the development of formal cognitive thinking at the beginning of adolescence culminate the long series of maturational and cognitive changes that begin with conception and birth, the achievement

By the end of adolescence, most young people have achieved a much more coherent sense of who they are and are ready to face the challenges of early adulthood.

of identity culminates the psychosocial developments that precede it.

Although adolescence marks both the end of childhood and the last developmental stage covered in this book, it by no means marks the end of development. As we note at the beginning of this section of the text, adolescence is a period of transition to adulthood, and many other important developmental changes are yet to come.

The social changes of adolescence show vividly one of the major themes of this book: individuals change dramatically as they grow. As we have seen, in a matter of months an infant who smiles at everyone becomes devoted to particular adults and siblings, and in just a few years more people well outside the family compete seriously with these attachments. The other domains of development show equally dramatic changes. In just a few years, a child grows physically from wearing diapers to climbing trees and riding a bicycle; in just a few years more, she or he starts looking (almost) like an adult. Cognitive changes are equally sweeping: individuals change from infants who think by looking and touching to children who can reason out concrete problems to teenagers who can imagine possibilities they have never personally experienced.

Yet no matter how dramatic they are, developmental changes remain whole, continuous, and human. For convenience, this book has divided human change into topics and discussed the topics one at a time. But real children and youths do not come so divided. As this book has tried to show, children and adolescents not only grow, think, and feel; they also do all of these things at once and in a pattern that makes each person truly unique.

Summary of Major Ideas

Theories of Identity Development

1. According to Ruthellen Josselson, the process of individuation, or becoming a separate and independent person, appears to follow a fairly predictable pattern: differentiation, practice and experimentation, rapprochement, and consolidation of self.

2. A key task of adolescence is successful resolution of Erikson's psychosocial crisis of identity versus role confusion.

3. According to Erik Erikson, adolescent identity formation involves selectively keeping and integrating certain aspects of one's earlier childhood identity while discarding others.

4. Successful resolution of the identity conflicts typical of adolescence depends in part on having adequate opportunities to experiment with different identities and roles.

5. Erikson named the period of experimentation and uncertainty that precedes the achievement of a firm adult identity the psychosocial moratorium.

6. James Marcia and his colleagues studied four identity statuses among older adolescents: identity-achieved, identity-diffused, moratorium, and foreclosed. The proportion of adolescents at each identity status varies with the area of identity involved, such as religious beliefs, vocational choice, gender-role preferences, and political philosophies.

Family Relationships During Adolescence

7. Achieving psychological separation from one's parents during adolescence entails four important accomplishments: functional independence, attitudinal independence, emotional independence, and conflictual independence.

8. Teens and their parents tend to share similar attitudes and values about important issues and decisions, and most disagreements are about matters affecting current social life and behavior.

9. Adolescents from authoritative homes appear to display positive developmental outcomes in all areas, while youngsters from authoritarian homes are well adjusted in all areas except internalized distress. Teens from permissive-indulgent homes are well adjusted in peers and family interactions but show declines in school adjustment, while those raised in permissive-indifferent homes display the poorest developmental outcomes in all areas.

10. Differences in SES, ethnicity, and community context influence choice of parenting style and the educational and career expectations that parents have for their adolescent children as well as the expectations adolescents have for themselves.

11. A growing number of adolescents experience family transitions and conflict associated with divorce, remarriage, or single parenthood. Factors that determine the impact of these transitions include parent, family, and child characteristics; the nature of the transition; economic circumstances; and the social support available.

Social Relationships During Adolescence

12. During adolescence, friendships become increasingly stable, intimate, and mutual. Friends provide one another with cognitive and social scaffolding that differs from what nonfriends provide.

13. The quality of friendships during early adolescence appears to have long-term effects on development.

14. Both small, cohesive cliques and larger, less intimate crowds appear to be important in peer group participation. Peers provide teenagers with critical information about who they are and how they differ from others, as well as a support base for exploring different identity roles outside the family.

15. Teenagers participate in peer groups to please parents and teachers and to gain peer acceptance and popularity. Conformity to peer pressure can be particularly disruptive during early adolescence.

16. Parents can indirectly influence the behaviors by which teenagers become associated with a particular crowd, and peer group norms reinforce behaviors and predispositions to which parents have already contributed.

17. Work both inside and outside the family can also make an important contribution to development during adolescence.

Sexuality During Adolescence

18. Adolescents' sexual needs are closely tied to their need to establish a secure identity and to achieve both intimacy and independence.

19. Masturbation and sexual fantasies play a significant role in adolescents' sexual development.

20. Recent trends in adolescent sexual activity include earlier initiation of intercourse, increased premarital intercourse, a greater number of partners, and ineffective and inconsistent use of contraceptives.

21. Girls and boys differ in their reasons for and feelings about first sexual intercourse and in their attitudes toward sexual experiences in general.

22. In the United States, adolescent dating is the major avenue for exploring sexual activity. High rates of dating violence occur during both high school and college. Risk factors include cultural and personal values and attitudes regarding gender, sexuality, and power.

23. Although acceptance of homosexuality has increased, homophobia still exists, placing bisexual, lesbian, and gay sexual orientations at risk for rejection, discrimination, and violence from peers, family members, and other adults.

Special Problems of Adolescence

24. Pregnancy and parenthood continue to be major problems faced by adolescents. Individual, family, neighborhood, and societal characteristics affect the causes as well as the wide range of developmental outcomes displayed by teenage parents and their children.

25. Two other major problems that are common during adolescence are depression and juvenile delinquency.

26. It is estimated that between fifteen and twenty percent of adolescents suffer from major depressive disorder over their lifetime and eight percent suffer from dysthymic disorder at any point in time. Depression is a significant risk factor for suicide.

27. Juvenile delinquency continues to be a serious problem of adolescence. Its multiple causes include dysfunctional family, school and peer relationships, poverty, gang involvement, and violent neighborhood environments. Successful preventative efforts require intervention at all of these levels.

Key Terms

clique (511)
crowd (511)
homophobia (519)
identity diffusion (494)
identity status (495)
identity versus role confusion (493)

individuation (492)
juvenile delinquency (530)
negative identity (495)
psychosocial moratorium (494)
SES (503)

Glossary

accommodation According to Piaget, the process of modifying existing ideas or action-skills to fit new experiences. *(48, 174)*

achievement motivation Behavior that enhances competence or enhances judgments of competence. *(396)*

achievement test A test designed to evaluate a person's current state of knowledge. *(377)*

acquired immunodeficiency syndrome (AIDS) A viral illness that gradually destroys the body's ability to combat other diseases. *(349)*

activity settings Group situations in which a shared focus of attention and common goals facilitate learning by an individual from others in the group. *(270)*

acute illness A disease with a definite time of onset and lasting for a fixed and relatively short period of time. *(348)*

adaptation Piaget's term for the process by which development occurs; concepts are deepened or broadened by assimilation and stretched or modified by accommodation. *(48)*

adolescence The stage of development between childhood and adulthood, around ages ten to twenty-two. *(431)*

adolescent egocentrism The tendency of adolescents to perceive the world (and themselves) from their own perspective. *(475)*

adoption study A research method for studying the relative contributions of heredity and environment in which genetically related children reared apart are compared with genetically unrelated children reared together. *(85)*

ageism Prejudice or bias against an individual on account of the individual's age. *(12)*

aggression A bold, assertive action that is intended to hurt another person or to procure an object. *(305)*

allele One of several alternative forms of a gene. *(67)*

American Sign Language (ASL) A system of gestures used in place of oral language by individuals with hearing impairments. *(283)*

amniocentesis A prenatal diagnostic method in which a sample of amniotic fluid is withdrawn and tested to detect chromosomal abnormalities. *(79)*

amniotic sac A tough, spongy bag filled with salty fluid that surrounds the embryo, protects it from sudden jolts, and helps to maintain a fairly stable temperature. *(96)*

androgyny A tendency to integrate both masculine and feminine behaviors into the personality. *(327)*

animism A belief that nonliving objects are alive and human. *(268)*

anorexia nervosa A physical and psychological disturbance that causes a person to refuse to eat sufficient food and to develop an increasingly unrealistic view of his or her body; most individuals with anorexia are teenage girls. *(455)*

AnotB error The tendency of infants to look for a hidden object in the first place it disappears (at "A") rather than where they have seen it most recently (at "B"). *(177)*

anxious-avoidant attachment An insecure bond between infant and caregiver in which the child rarely cries when separated from the caregiver and tends to avoid or ignore the caregiver when reunited. *(217)*

anxious-resistant attachment An insecure bond between infant and caregiver in which the child shows signs of anxiety preceding separation, is intensely upset by separation, and seeks close contact when reunited while at the same time resisting the caregiver's efforts to comfort. *(217)*

Apgar scale A system of rating newborns' health immediately following birth based on heart rate, strength of breathing, muscle tone, color, and reflex irritability. *(137)*

appearance-reality distinctions The ability to distinguish apparent perceptions from real qualities of objects; acquired during the preschool period. *(265)*

aptitude test A measurement of ability that estimates future performance in some realm of behavior. *(377)*

artifact A manufactured or humanly crafted object; often distinguished from a "natural kind." *(268)*

assessment The diagnosis of an individual's strengths, needs, and qualities. *(386)*

assimilation According to Piaget, a method by which a child responds to new experiences by using existing concepts to interpret new ideas and experiences. *(48, 174)*

attachment The strong and enduring emotional bond that develops between an infant and his or her caregivers during the infant's first year of life. *(41, 139, 214)*

attention deficit hyperactivity disorder (ADHD) A disorder of childhood characterized by impulsivity, excessive motor activity, and an inability to focus attention for appropriate amounts of time. *(47, 350)*

auditory cortex An area of the brain, located near the left side of the cerebral cortex, where the sounds of speech produce their primary response. *(244)*

authoritarian parenting A style of childrearing characterized by a high degree of control and demands on children's maturity and a low degree of clarity of communication and nurturance. *(299)*

authoritative parenting A style of childrearing characterized by a high degree of control, clarity of communication, maturity demands, and nurturance. *(298)*

autonomy In Erikson's theory, a child's ability to govern and regulate her or his own thoughts, feelings, and actions freely and responsibly while at the same time overcoming feelings of shame and doubt. *(226)*

autonomy versus shame and doubt According to Erikson, the psychosocial crisis of children ages one to three involving the struggle to control their own thoughts, feelings, and actions; the second of Erikson's developmental stages. *(36)*

babbling Infant vocalizations produced prior to acquiring language and without verbally meaningful intent. *(190)*

baby biography A detailed narrative or history of an infant's development. *(12)*

balanced bilingual A person who is equally fluent in two languages rather than more fluent in one language than in the other. *(374)*

behavior genetics The scientific study of the relationship between genotype and phenotype, especially with regard to intelligence, personality, and mental health. *(82)*

behaviorism A learning theory that focuses on changes in specific observable behaviors and their causes. *(183)*

behavior modification Techniques based on the principles of learning theory that can be used by parents, teachers, therapists, and other professionals to help children, adolescents, and adults to reduce or eliminate undesirable behaviors and learn desirable ones. *(47, 352)*

Black English   A dialect or version of English spoken by many African Americans. *(375)*

blended family   A family created from a combination of stepchildren, stepparents, and stepsiblings. *(407)*

blind training   The teaching of learned strategies without informing the learner of the benefits of the strategies. *(368)*

brainstem   A relatively primitive, or "lower," area of the brain; along with the midbrain, this area regulates relatively automatic functions such as breathing, digestion, and consciousness. *(139)*

Broca's area   An area of the brain located on the left side of the cerebral cortex; vital to the production of language. See also *Wernicke's area*. *(244)*

bulimia   A disorder in which a person, usually a teenage girl, eats huge amounts of food and then vomits it to avoid gaining weight. *(455)*

caesarean section   A childbirth procedure in which the baby is removed surgically from the mother's abdomen. *(127)*

canalization   The tendency of many developmental processes to unfold in highly predictable ways under a wide range of conditions. *(83, 105)*

caregiver-infant synchrony   Patterns of closely coordinated social and emotional interaction between caregiver and infant. *(203)*

case study   A research study of a single individual or small group of individuals considered as a unit. *(26)*

catch-up growth   The process by which children recover from slow growth by growing faster than usual until they reach the normal size for their age. *(239)*

central nervous system   The brain and nerve cells of the spinal cord. *(139)*

cerebellum   The part of the brain that coordinates muscles and maintains physical balance. *(139)*

cerebral cortex   The "higher" part of the brain; along with the cerebrum, it controls vision, hearing, and touch, as well as motor actions such as lifting an arm. *(143)*

chorionic villus sampling (CVS)   A medical procedure for detecting genetic abnormalities before birth in which a small bit of tissue surrounding the embryo is removed and examined microscopically. *(79)*

chromosome   A threadlike, rod-shaped structure containing genetic information that is transmitted from parents to children; each human sperm or egg cell contains twenty-three chromosomes, and these determine a person's inherited characteristics. *(63)*

chronic illness   A disease lasting a long period of time (such as several months or more) and changing only very slowly. *(348)*

circular reaction   Piaget's term for an action often repeated, apparently because it is self-reinforcing. *(175)*

classical conditioning   According to Pavlov, learning in which a neutral stimulus gains the power to bring about a certain response by repeated association with another stimulus that already elicits the same response. *(44)*

classification   Putting objects in groups or categories according to some set of standards or criteria. *(266)*

clique   A small, closely knit peer group of two or more members (average of six members) who are intimately involved in a number of shared purposes and activities and exclude those who are not. *(511)*

cognition   All processes by which humans acquire knowledge; methods for thinking or gaining knowledge about the world. *(163)*

cognitive development   Long-term continuities and changes related to thinking and learning. *(4)*

competence   According to Robert White, children's increased skill and capability in successfully exploring, mastering, and controlling the world around them. *(229)*

conception   The moment at which the male's sperm cell penetrates the female's egg cell (ovum), forming a zygote. *(94)*

concordance rate   The percentage of instances in which both members of a genetically similar pair of individuals (e.g., identical twins) display a particular all-or-none trait such as cystic fibrosis, Huntington's disease, or schizophrenia. *(85)*

concrete operations   Logical thinking about concrete or tangible objects and processes; especially characteristic of children in the school years. *(356)*

conservation   A belief that certain properties (such as quantity) remain constant despite changes in perceived features such as dimensions, position, and shape. *(266, 357)*

constructive play   A type of play that involves manipulation of physical objects to build or construct something. *(316)*

context-specific development   Continuities or changes that happen only to certain individuals because of unique circumstances that they experience. *(15)*

continuity   Long-term stability in a human quality, behavior, or ability. *(14)*

control group   In an experimental study, the participants who experience conditions similar or identical to the experimental group, but without experiencing the experimental treatment. *(23)*

control talk   A style or register of speech used by teachers to indicate their power over activities, discussion, and the behavior of students. *(385)*

correlation   An association between two variables in which changes in one tend to accompany changes in the other without implying that one variable causes changes in the other. *(24)*

critical period   Any period during which development is particularly susceptible to an event or influence, either negative or positive. *(105)*

critical thinking   Reflection or thinking about complex issues, usually to make decisions or take actions. *(485)*

cross-sectional study   A developmental study that compares individuals of different ages at the same point in time. *(20)*

crowd   A large, loosely knit peer group of between fifteen and thirty members (average of twenty members) that generally consists of from two to four cliques. *(511)*

décallage   Literally "gap"; Piaget's term for the differences in when a child acquires the skills of a particular cognitive stage. *(358)*

deficit   In human development, a continuity or change regarded as limiting the competence and potential of an individual. *(17)*

deoxyribonucleic acid (DNA)   A molecule containing hereditary information; has a chemical structure of two chains of polynucleotides arranged in a double helix or spiral. *(63)*

dependent variable   A factor measured in an experimental study that depends on or is controlled by one or more independent variables. *(23)*

developmentally appropriate practice   Methods and goals of teaching considered optimal for young children given current knowledge of child development. *(289)*

dichotic listening   A task in which an individual is fed information or sounds to each ear separately; demonstrates hemispheric lateralization. *(244)*

difference   In human development, a continuity or change regarded as making an individual distinctive but not better or worse than other individuals. *(17)*

discontinuity   Long-term gaps or changes in a human quality, behavior, or ability. *(14)*

discourse   Extended verbal interaction. *(384)*

disorganized-disoriented attachment   An attachment pattern in which an infant exhibits confused and contradictory behaviors when reunited with the parent. The infant may be unresponsive and turn away when held, display odd, frozen postures, and cry out unexpectedly after being comforted. *(218)*

domains of development   The major realms or types of human development—physical, cognitive, and psychosocial. *(4)*

dominant gene   In any paired set of genes, the gene with greater influence in determining physical characteristics that are physically visible or manifest. *(67)*

duo   A two-word utterance. *(273)*

ego   According to Freud, the rational, realistic part of the personality; coordinates impulses from the id with demands imposed by the superego and by society. *(34)*

egocentrism   The inability of a person to distinguish between his or her own point of view and that of another person. *(263)*

ego integrity versus despair   According to Erikson, the final psychosocial crisis, reached during late adulthood and old age, in which one looks back on one's life with dignity, optimism, and wisdom while facing the despair resulting from the negative aspects of old age. *(39)*

embryo   The fully implanted blastocyst; refers specifically to the developing human from the second to eighth week after conception. *(95)*

embryonic stage   Stage in prenatal development that lasts from week 2 through week 8. *(93)*

empathy   A sensitive awareness of the thoughts and feelings of another person. *(303)*

endocrine glands   Glands that produce growth hormones. *(238)*

estrogen   A sex hormone, sometimes called the *female sex hormone* because its high concentration in girls stimulates the growth of the ovaries and vagina during puberty. *(441)*

experimental group   In an experimental study, the participants who experience an experimental treatment while in other ways experiencing conditions similar or identical to those of the control group. *(23)*

experimental study   A research study in which circumstances are arranged so that only one or two known factors influence the participants at a time. *(22)*

expressive language   Language that a child can actually use appropriately in conversation. *(191)*

failure to thrive   A condition in which an infant seems seriously delayed in physical growth and is noticeably apathetic in behavior. *(159)*

false-belief task   A type of research design that tests children's awareness of the difference between what they know and what other persons might believe. *(265)*

fetal alcohol syndrome (FAS)   A congenital condition exhibited by babies born to mothers who consumed too much alcohol during pregnancy. They do not arouse easily and tend to behave sluggishly in general; they also have distinctive facial characteristics. *(108)*

fetal presentation   Refers to the body part of the fetus that is closest to the mother's cervix; may be head first (cephalic), feet and rump first (breech), or shoulders first (transverse). *(118)*

fetal stage   The stage in prenatal development that lasts from the eighth week of pregnancy until birth. *(93)*

fetus   An embryo that has developed its first bone cells, after about eight weeks of gestation. *(96)*

fine motor coordination   The ability to carry out smoothly small movements that involve precise timing but not strength. *(250)*

fine motor skills   Voluntary movements of the body that involve the small muscles located throughout the body. *(148)*

first stage of labor   In childbirth, the stage that begins with relatively mild and irregular contractions of the uterus. As contractions grow stronger, the cervix dilates enough for the baby's head to begin fitting through. May take from eight to twenty-four hours for a first-time mother. *(119)*

formal operational thought   Thinking based on previously acquired concrete mental operations and involving hypothetical reasoning and attention to the structure or form of ideas. *(462)*

freestanding birth center (FBC)   Nonhospital facilities organized to provide family-centered maternity care for women who are at low risk for obstetrical complications. *(121)*

functional play   A cognitive level of play that involves simple, repeated movements and a focus on one's own body. *(315)*

functional relationships   Variations in an environment that normally occur together. *(262)*

games with rules   A cognitive level of play involving relatively formal activities with fixed rules. *(316)*

gamete   A reproductive cell (sperm or ovum). *(63)*

gender   The thoughts, feelings, and behaviors associated with being male or female. *(324)*

gender constancy   A belief that a person's sex is biologically determined, permanent, and unchanging, no matter what else about that person changes. *(324)*

gender identity   One's beliefs about what sex one is. *(324)*

gender preference   Attitudes about the sex one prefers to be. *(324)*

gender-role stereotypes   The culturally "appropriate" patterns of gender-related behaviors expected by society. Also called sex roles. *(324)*

gene   A molecular structure, carried on chromosomes, containing genetic information; the basic unit of heredity. *(63)*

gene-environment relationship   May be passive, active, or evocative, depending on whether an infant or a child passively accepts, stimulates (evokes), or actively seeks and creates situations and experiences that support or increase genetically influenced behavioral traits such as shyness or intelligence. *(84)*

generative rules   Syntactic rules that allow speakers to generate new sentences almost infinitely by applying them to new morphemes. *(273)*

generativity versus stagnation   The seventh of Erikson's psychosocial crises, reached in middle adulthood, in which one must balance the feeling that one's life is personally satisfying and socially meaningful with feelings of purposelessness. *(39)*

genetic imprinting   A method of genetic transmission in which genes are chemically marked to result in a different phenotype if inherited from the mother than if inherited from the father. *(70)*

genotype   The set of genetic traits inherited by an individual. See also *phenotype*. *(66)*

germinal stage   The stage in prenatal development that occurs during the first two weeks of pregnancy; characterized by rapid cell division. Also called the *period of the ovum*. *(93)*

glia   Brain cells that emit a sheathing that encases neurons and their fibers; helps to transmit impulses more quickly and reliably.

gross motor skills   Voluntary movements of the body that involve the large muscles of the arms, legs, and torso. *(148)*

growth spurt   A rapid change in height and weight that occurs in puberty and is preceded and followed by years of comparatively little increase. *(434)*

habituation   The tendency to attend to novel stimuli and ignore familiar ones. *(165)*

hemispheric lateralization   A tendency for the left and right halves of the brain to perform separate functions. *(244)*

hemophilia   A disease in which the blood fails to clot properly and therefore is characterized by excessive bleeding; example of a sex-linked recessive trait. *(70)*

heritability estimate   The degree to which variation among an individual's phenotypic behaviors can be attributed to genetic influences. *(85)*

heterozygous   Describes a genotype consisting of distinct forms of chromosomes for the same gene. *(67)*

holographic speech   Early one- or two-word utterances that serve the function of entire sentences at later stages of language acquisition; also called *telegraphic speech*. *(274)*

homophobia   Fear and dislike of homosexuals. *(519)*

homozygous   A genetic condition in which an individual inherits two identical genes at a particular location on a particular chromosome. *(67)*

human development   Long-term continuities and changes in growth, thinking, and social relationships. *(4)*

human immunodeficiency virus (HIV)   The virus known to cause the disease AIDS. See *acquired immunodeficiency syndrome*. *(349)*

hyperactivity   Excessive levels of activity and an inability to concentrate for normal periods of time. See *attention deficit hyperactivity disorder*. *(350)*

hypothesis   A statement that expresses a research question precisely and is capable of being tested scientifically. *(19)*

id   In Freud's theory, the part of an individual's personality that is present at birth, unconscious, impulsive, and unrealistic, and that attempts to satisfy a person's biological and emotional needs and desires by maximizing pleasure and avoiding pain. *(34)*

identification   In psychoanalytic theory, the conscious and unconscious ways in which children experience themselves as being like their parents and other important role models and strive to be like them. *(227)*

identity   (1) Piagetian term for the constancy of an object. (2) A unique and relatively stable set of personal characteristics. *(262)*

identity diffusion   A failure to achieve a relatively coherent, integrated, and stable identity. *(494)*

identity status   Marcia's four categories of identity development: identity achievement, identity diffusion, moratorium, and foreclosure. *(495)*

identity versus role confusion   The fifth of Erikson's psychosocial crises, in which one must integrate one's many childhood skills and beliefs and gain recognition for them from society. *(38, 493)*

imaginary audience   A characteristic of young adolescents in which they act as though they are performing for an audience and believe that others are as concerned with their appearance and behavior as they themselves are. *(476)*

implantation   The attachment of the blastocyst to the wall of the uterus. *(95)*

independent variable   A factor in an experimental study that a researcher manipulates (or varies) to determine its influence on the participants. *(23)*

individuation   The process by which an adolescent develops a unique and separate personal identity. Consists of four subphases: differentiation, practice and experimentation, rapprochement, and consolidation. *(492)*

industry versus inferiority   Erikson's fourth crisis, during which children concern themselves with their capacity to do good work and thereby develop confident, positive self-concepts or else face feelings of inferiority. *(38, 396)*

infant-directed speech   The style or register of speech used by adults and older children when talking with a one- or two-year-old infant. *(193, 280)*

infant mortality rate   The frequency with which infants die compared to the frequency with which they live. *(159)*

information-processing theory   Explanations of cognition that focus on the precise, detailed features or steps of mental activities. These theories often use computers as a model for human thinking. *(50, 361)*

informed consent   An agreement to participate in a research study based on understanding the nature of the research, protection of privacy, and the right to withdraw from the study at any time. *(27)*

informed training   The teaching of learning strategies that includes telling and showing the learner the reasons for using the strategies. *(369)*

initiative versus guilt   Erikson's third crisis, during which a child's increasing ability to initiate verbal and physical activity and expanding imaginative powers lead to fantasies of large and sometimes frightening proportions. *(38)*

in loco parentis   In developmental research, the principle that investigators should act in the best interests of the child at all times. *(28)*

inner speech   Toddlers' "mental shorthand"; thinking that occurs with little help from language. *(287)*

intelligence   A general ability to learn from experience; also refers to ability to reason abstractly. *(376)*

interview   A face-to-face, directed conversation used in a research study to gather in-depth information. *(25)*

intimacy versus isolation   The sixth of Erikson's psychosocial crises, in which young adults must be able to develop intimate relationships with others while dealing with the fear of loss of identity that such intimacy entails. *(39)*

juvenile delinquency   A pattern of destructive or antisocial activities and lawbreaking offenses committed by adolescents. *(530)*

juvenile period   The period between approximately age five and ten during which children show increasing interest in playmates of the same age, status, and gender. *(413)*

language acquisition device (LAD)   In Chomsky's theory of language development, a term that refers to the innate processes of language acquisition. *(278)*

latency   In Freud's theory, the period between about six and twelve years of age when sexual activity is suspended and energies shift to physical, intellectual, and social activities. *(395)*

lateralized behavior   An action that individuals prefer to perform with one side of their bodies more than the other. *(244)*

learning disability   Difficulty in learning a specific academic skill such as reading or arithmetic. *(369)*

learning strategies   General methods or techniques that help to solve a variety of problems. *(366)*

lexicon   The words or units of meaning of a language. *(189)*

longitudinal study   A developmental study that compares the same individual(s) with themselves at earlier or later ages. *(20)*

low birth weight   A birth weight of less than 2,500 grams (about 5½ pounds). *(129, 157)*

meiosis   A complex process by which gametes form; involves duplication and division of reproductive cells and their chromosomes. *(66)*

menarche   The first menstrual period. *(439)*

metacognition   Knowledge and thinking about cognition, how learning and memory operate in everyday situations, and how one can improve cognitive performance. *(51, 265, 365)*

metalinguistic awareness   The ability to attend to language as an object of thought rather than attending only to the content or ideas of a language. *(376)*

metaphor   A word, phrase, or sentence containing an implied comparison. *(373)*

midbrain   The area of the brain that, together with the brainstem, regulates relatively automatic functions such as breathing, digestion, and consciousness. *(139)*

middle school   A school intended to meet the needs of early adolescents (students from about fifth through eighth grade, or about age ten through thirteen). *(487)*

midwife   A woman experienced in pregnancy and childbirth who traditionally served as the primary caregiver during pregnancy, childbirth, and the month or two following delivery. *(121)*

mitosis   The creation of new cells through duplication of chromosomes and division of cells. *(66)*

morality   In developmental psychology, the sense of ethics or of right and wrong. *(476)*

Moro reflex   The reflexive startle response of newborns. Healthy infants fling their arms out suddenly and sometimes shake all over or cry in response to a sudden loud noise or sudden loss of support. *(148)*

morphemes   The smallest meaningful units of language; include words as well as a number of prefixes and suffixes that carry meaning. *(272)*

mortality   As used in population studies and developmental studies, the relative frequency of death in a community, society, or population. *(345)*

motor abilities   The set of reflexes and skills of which an infant or child is capable. *(147)*

motor cortex   The area of the brain, located just forward of the top of the head, where simple voluntary movements produce their largest neural activity. *(244)*

motor skills   Physical skills using the body or limbs, such as walking and drawing. *(148)*

multifactorial disorders   Disorders that result from a combination of genetic and environmental factors. *(75)*

multiple intelligences   According to Howard Gardner's theory of intelligence, alternative forms of intelligence or adaptability to the environment. *(380)*

natural kind   An object that is born from another of the same kind and cannot be constructed artificially from other materials. *(268)*

naturalistic study   A research study in which behavior is observed in normal or natural circumstances and without significant intervention by the researcher. *(22)*

nature   In the study of human development, the essential and/or inborn qualities of a person. *(14)*

negative identity   A form of identity diffusion involving rejection of the roles preferred by one's family or community in favor of socially undesirable roles. *(495)*

neonate   A newborn infant. *(136)*

neostructuralist (neo-Piagetian) theories   Theories of cognitive development that are based on the general notion of stagelike development but focus on more precise areas of thinking and mechanisms of development than Piaget's original theory proposed. *(271)*

neurons   Nerve cell bodies and their extensions or fibers. *(139)*

nocturnal emission   Ejaculation of semen during sleep. *(439)*

non-REM sleep   A relatively quiet, deep period of sleep. See also *REM sleep.* *(143)*

nonreversal shift   An experimental procedure in which reinforcement shifts to discriminating a new dimension of difference between objects (e.g., shape versus size). *(172)*

norms   Behaviors typical at certain ages and of certain groups; standards of normal development. *(12)*

nurture   In the study of human development, the environmental influences and experiences that affect a person's development. *(14)*

obesity   The state of being extremely overweight, specifically more than 130 percent of normal weight for height and bone size; affects one American child in ten. *(337)*

object permanence   According to Piaget, the belief that people and things continue to exist even when one cannot experience them directly; emerges around age two. *(176)*

object relations   The child's relationships with the important people (called *objects*) in his or her environment and the process by which their qualities become part of the child's personality and mental life. *(31)*

observational learning   The tendency of a child to imitate or model behavior and attitudes of parents and other nurturant individuals. *(45, 228)*

operant conditioning   According to Skinner, a process of learning in which a person or an animal increases the frequency of a behavior in response to repeated reinforcement of that behavior. *(44, 227)*

overgeneralizations   Utterances in which a child shifts from using correct but irregular forms to using wrong but more regular forms; represent efforts to try out newly noticed rules of syntax. *(274)*

overnutrition   Consumption of more calories than necessary for good health. *(156)*

overt aggression   Actions that harm others through physical damage or threat of such damage, such as pushing, hitting, kicking, or threatening to beat up a peer. *(305)*

ovum   The reproductive cell, or gamete, of the female; the egg cell. *(63)*

participation structures   Regular patterns of discourse or interaction in classrooms with unstated rules about how, when, and to whom to speak. *(384)*

peers   Individuals who are of approximately the same age and developmental level and who share common attitudes and interests. *(391)*

perception   The neural activity of combining sensations into meaningful patterns. *(163)*

performance orientation   Achievement motivation stimulated by other individuals who may see and evaluate the learner rather than by the intrinsic nature of the task itself. *(396)*

period of transition   A very brief period between the first and second stages of labor during which the cervix approaches full dilation, contractions become more rapid and intense, and the baby's head moves into the birth canal. *(119)*

permissive-indifferent parenting   A style of parenting in which parents' permissiveness reflects an avoidance of childrearing responsibilities, sometimes with detrimental results. *(300)*

permissive-indulgent parenting   A style of parenting in which parents make relatively few demands on their children but clearly communicate their warmth and interest and provide considerable care and nurturance. *(300)*

personal fable   Adolescents' belief that their own lives embody a special story that is heroic and completely unique. *(476)*

phenotype   The set of traits an individual actually displays during development; reflects the evolving product of genotype and experience. See also *genotype*. *(66)*

phoneme   A sound that combines with other sounds to form words. *(189)*

phonology   The individual vocal sounds of a language. *(189)*

physical activity play   Vigorous physical activity that occurs in a playful context and is thought to have a basis in human evolution, serving several adaptive developmental functions. *(315)*

physical development   Long-term continuities and changes related to growth, motor skills, and sensory perception. *(4)*

placenta   An organ that delivers oxygen and nutrients from the mother to the fetus and carries away the fetus's waste products, which the mother will excrete. *(96)*

postconventional moral judgment   In Kohlberg's theory, an orientation to moral justice that develops beyond conventional rules and beliefs. *(471)*

pragmatics   The ways in which words and sentences are normally used in ordinary conversation. *(189)*

preoperational stage   In Piaget's theory, the stage of cognition characterized by increasing use of symbolic thinking, but not yet by logical groupings of concepts. *(262)*

prepared childbirth   A method of childbirth in which parents have rehearsed or simulated the actual sensations of labor and delivery well before the actual delivery date. *(122)*

pretend play   Play that substitutes imaginary situations for real ones. Also called *fantasy* or *dramatic play*. *(316)*

primary circular reaction   According to Piaget, a behavior that is repeated and focuses on the baby's own body and movements; occurs during the second stage of infant cognition (usually at about one to four months of age). *(175)*

primary sex characteristics   Characteristics that make sexual reproduction possible. For girls, consist of the vagina, uterus, fallopian tubes, and ovaries; for boys, consist of the penis, scrotum, testes, prostate gland, and seminal vesicles. *(439)*

primitive reflex   An inborn behavioral response of newborn infants that serves no obvious physical purpose; contrasted to a survival reflex. *(148)*

prosocial behavior   Positive social contacts; actions that benefit others. *(304)*

psychometric approach to intelligence   A view of intelligence based on identifying individual differences in ability through standardized test scores. *(377)*

psychosocial development   Long-term continuities and changes related to personality, social knowledge, and emotions. *(4)*

psychosocial moratorium   According to Erikson, the period during adolescence when youngsters are free to suspend or delay taking on adult commitments and to explore new social roles. *(494)*

puberty   The period of early adolescence characterized by the development of full physical and sexual maturity. *(439)*

random sample   In a research study, a group of participants chosen from a larger population such that each has an equal chance of being chosen. *(23)*

range of reaction   The range of possible phenotypes that an individual with a particular genotype might exhibit in response to the particular sequence of environmental influences he or she experiences. *(83)*

recall memory   Retrieval of information by using relatively few external cues. *(361)*

recasting   Rephrasing or restating an utterance expressed by a child; a process thought to encourage language acquisition and development. *(280)*

receptive language   Language that is understood or comprehended when used by others. *(191)*

recessive gene   In any paired set of genes, the gene that influences or determines physical characteristics only when no dominant gene is present. *(67)*

recognition memory   Retrieval of information by comparing an external stimulus or cue with preexisting experiences or knowledge. *(361)*

reflex   An involuntary, automatic response to a stimulus. The very first movements or motions of an infant are reflexes. *(147)*

reflexes   Simple, automatic movements displayed by infants, and which appear to be inborn. *(147)*

relational aggression   Actions that harm others through damage or threats of damage to their peer relationships. *(305)*

REM sleep   A relatively active period of sleep, named after the rapid eye movements that usually accompany it. See also *non-REM sleep*. *(143)*

resilience   A quality or ability that allows some children and youth to cope with unusually difficult circumstances. *(488)*

reversal shift   An experimental procedure in which reinforcement continues for discriminating a new value of a dimension (e.g., large versus small) but the dimension itself (e.g., size) remains constant. *(172)*

reversibility   Piaget's term for the ability to undo a problem mentally and go back to its beginning. *(266)*

rooting   A reflexive searching behavior that orients an infant to the mother's breast or to a bottle. *(147)*

scaffolding   Providing a framework or cognitive support for a child's learning and thinking. *(280)*

scheme   According to Piaget, a behavior or thought that represents a group of ideas and events in a child's experience. *(47, 174)*

scientific methods   Systematic procedures for ensuring objective observations and meaningful interpretations of observations. *(19)*

second stage of labor   The period of labor that starts with "crowning," the first moment the baby's head can be seen, and ends with the baby's birth; usually lasts between sixty and ninety minutes. *(120)*

secondary circular reaction   According to Piaget, the third stage of infant cognition, which occurs at age four to eight months; repeated behaviors that are motivated by external objects and events. *(176)*

secondary sex characteristics   Sex characteristics other than the sex organs, such as extra layers of fat and pubic hair. *(439)*

secular trend (1) In general, any long-term historical trend. (2) In human development, the tendency of each new generation in industrialized countries to grow larger and heavier and to experience puberty earlier than their parents did. *(436)*

secure attachment A healthy bond between infant and caregiver. The child is happy when the caregiver is present, somewhat upset during the caregiver's absence, and easily comforted upon the caregiver's return. *(217)*

self-constancy The belief that one's identity remains permanently fixed; established sometime after age six. *(393)*

self-esteem An individual's belief that he or she is an important, competent, powerful, and worthwhile person who is valued and appreciated. *(230)*

semantics The purposes and meanings of a language. *(189)*

semen A sticky fluid produced by the prostate gland; carries sperm to the penis and provides it with a medium in which to live after ejaculation. *(439)*

sense of self A structured way children have of thinking about themselves that helps to organize and understand who they are based on the views of others, their own experiences, and cultural categories such as gender and race. *(393)*

sensorimotor intelligence According to Piaget, thinking that occurs by way of sensory perceptions and motor actions; characteristic of infants. *(173)*

sex-linked recessive traits Recessive traits resulting from genes on the X chromosome. *(70)*

sickle-cell disease A genetically transmitted condition in which a person's red blood cells intermittently acquire a curved, sickle shape. The condition sometimes can clog circulation in the small blood vessels. *(73)*

situated cognition Thinking that occurs jointly with others and is embedded in a particular context or activity setting. *(270)*

skills Voluntary movements which are learned and performed deliberately. *(147)*

sleep apnea Temporary stoppage of breathing during sleep. *(158)*

small-for-date infant An infant who develops more slowly than normal during pregnancy; can be born full term or preterm. *(157)*

social cognition Knowledge and beliefs about interpersonal and social matters. *(475)*

social constructivism A theory that views learning as resulting from active dialogue and interaction between an individual and his or her community. *(270)*

social conventions Arbitrary customs and agreements about behavior that members of a society use. *(471)*

social referencing The child's sensitive awareness of how parents and other adults are feeling and ability to use these emotional cues as a basis for guiding his or her own emotional responses and actions. Social referencing is important for the development of autonomy. *(228)*

social trajectory The pathway, or direction, that development takes over an individual's life course, which is influenced by the school, work, family, and other important social settings in which he or she participates. *(54)*

sociocultural perspective on intelligence A view of intelligence that emphasizes the social and cultural influences on ability rather than the influence of inherent or learned individual differences. *(382)*

sperm Male gametes, or reproductive cells; produced in the testicles. *(63)*

Strange Situation (SS) A widely used method for studying attachment; confronts the infant with a series of controlled separations and reunions with a parent and a stranger. *(216)*

sucking One of the neonate's first and most powerful reflexes, triggered by any object intruding into the mouth. *(147)*

sudden infant death syndrome (SIDS) "Crib death" syndrome in which apparently healthy infants stop breathing unaccountably and die in their sleep; most frequently strikes infants between ages two and four months. *(143)*

superego In Freud's theory, the part of personality that acts as an all-knowing, internalized parent. It has two parts: the conscience, which enforces moral and social conventions by punishing violations with guilt, and the ego-ideal, which provides an idealized, internal set of standards for regulating and evaluating one's thoughts, feelings, and actions. *(34)*

survey A research study that samples specific knowledge or opinions from a large number of individuals. *(25)*

survival reflex An inborn behavioral response of newborn infants that serves a clear physical purpose, such as breathing. *(148)*

symbol A word, object, or behavior that stands for something else. *(262)*

symbolic thought Cognition that makes one object or action stand for another. *(263)*

syntax The organizational rules of words and phrases in a language; its grammar. *(189, 272)*

telegraphic speech See *holographic speech.*

temperament Individual differences in quality and intensity of emotional responding and self-regulation that are present at birth, are relatively stable and enduring over time and across situations, and are influenced by the interaction of heredity, maturation, and experience. *(211)*

teratogen Any substance a pregnant woman is exposed to that can harm the developing embryo or fetus. *(105)*

tertiary circular reaction According to Piaget, repeated variations of action schemes, organized by trial and error; the fifth stage in infant cognition, occurring between ages twelve and eighteen months. *(178)*

testosterone A sex hormone; sometimes called the *male sex hormone* because its high concentration in boys stimulates the growth of the penis and related male reproductive organs. *(441)*

theory of mind Coherent, theorylike beliefs about how human thinking occurs that develop during the first few years of life. *(264)*

third stage of labor The final stage of labor, in which the afterbirth (placenta and umbilical cord) is expelled; normally lasts only a few minutes. *(120)*

triarchic theory of intelligence A view of intelligence as consisting of three components: (1) adaptability, (2) information-processing skills, and (3) the ability to deal with novelty. *(379)*

trust versus mistrust In Erikson's theory, the psychosocial crisis of children from birth to one year involving whether they can rely on their parents to reliably meet their physical and emotional needs. *(36)*

twin study A research method for studying the relative contributions of heredity and environment in which the degree of similarity between genetically identical twins (developed from a single egg) is compared with the similarity between fraternal twins (developed from two eggs). *(86)*

ultrasound A prenatal diagnostic method that allows medical personnel and others to view the fetus by projecting high-frequency sound waves through the mother's womb. *(78)*

umbilical cord Three large blood vessels that connect the embryo to the placenta, one to provide nutrients and two to remove waste products. *(96)*

universal development Changes or continuities that occur to all, or at least most, human beings. *(15)*

validity   The extent to which research findings measure or observe what is intended. *(23)*

visual cliff   The classic laboratory setup of a ledge covered by a sheet of glass; used to test the acquisition of depth perception. Young babies crawling on the glass discriminate between the two sides of the "cliff." *(169)*

visual cortex   The area of the brain located near the back of the head in the cerebral cortex, where visual images produce the strongest activity. *(244)*

warps   The emotional biases that families instill in their children regarding how they think about and experience themselves. *(412)*

Wernicke's area   The part of the auditory cortex in which the sounds of speech produce their primary response. *(244)*

working models   Internalized perceptions, feelings, and expectations regarding social and emotional relationships with significant caregivers based on experiences with those caregivers. *(45)*

zone of proximal development (ZPD)   According to Vygotsky, the level of difficulty at which problems are too hard for children to solve alone but not too hard when given support from adults or more competent peers. *(53, 270)*

zygote   The single new cell formed when a sperm cell attaches itself to the surface of an ovum (egg). *(66)*

References

Abell, S. C., & Richards, M. H. (1996). The relationship between body shape satisfaction and self-esteem: An investigation of gender and class differences. *Journal of Youth & Adolescence, 25,* 691–703,

Adams, D., & Hamm, M. (1996). *Cooperative learning: Critical thinking and collaboration across the curriculum.* 2nd ed. Springfield, Ill.: C. C. Thomas.

Aiken, L. (1996). *Assessment of intellectual functioning.* 2nd ed. New York: Plenum Press.

Ainsworth, M., Blehar, M., Waters, E., & Wall, S. (1978). *Strange-situation behavior of one-year-olds. Its relation to mother-infant interaction in the first year and to qualitative differences in the infant-mother attachment relationship.* Hillsdale, N.J.: Erlbaum.

Ainsworth, M. D. (1991). Attachments and other affectional bonds across the life cycle. In C. M. Parkes, J. Stevenson-Hinde, et al. (Eds.), *Attachment across the life cycle* (pp. 33–51). London: Tavistock/Routledge.

Ainsworth, M. S., & Bowlby, J. (1991). An ethological approach to personality development. *American Psychologist, 46,* 333–341.

Akande, A. (1994). What meaning and effects does fatherhood have in child development? *Early Child Development and Care, 101,* 51–58.

Alan Guttmacher Institute. (1994). *Sex and America's teenagers.* New York: Author. American Psychiatric Association (1994). *Diagnostic and statistical manual of mental disorders* (4th ed.). Washington, D.C.: Author

Aldis, O. (1975). *Play fighting.* New York: Academic Press.

Alexander, G. M., & Hines, M. (1994). Gender labels and play styles: Their relative contribution to children's selection of playmates. *Child Development, 65,* 869–879.

Alexander, K. L., & Entwisle, D. R. (1988). Achievement in the first 2 years of school: Patterns and processes. *Monographs of the Society for Research in Child Development, 53*(2, Serial No. 218).

Allen, J. P., Hauser, S. T., Bell, K. L., & O'Conner, T. G. (1994). Longitudinal assessment of autonomy and relatedness in adolescent-family interactions as predictors of adolescent ego development and self esteem. *Child Development, 65,* 179–194.

Altenbaugh, R. (1995). *Caring for kids: Critical studies of urban school leavers.* Washington, D.C.: Falmer Press.

Altman, L. K. (1998, June 30). U.N. plans to treat 30,000 HIV-infected pregnant women. *New York Times,* p. A–15.

Amato, P. R., Loomis, L. S., & Booth, A. (1995). Parental divorce, marital conflict, and offspring well-being during early adulthood. *Social Forces, 73,* 895–915.

American Academy of Pediatrics. (1991). *Facts about children with AIDS.* Elk Grove Village, Ill.: Author.

American Academy of Pediatrics. (1992). *Immunization protects children.* Brochure.

American Academy of Pediatrics. (1993). *Pediatric nutrition handbook* (3rd ed.). Elk Grove Village, Ill.: Author.

American College of Obstetricians and Gynecologists (ACOG). (1990). *Planning for Pregnancy, Birth, and Beyond.* New York: Dutton.

American Psychiatric Association. (1994). *Diagnostic and statistical manual of mental disorders* (4th ed.). Washington, D.C.: Author.

American Psychological Association. (1992). Ethical principles of psychologists and code of conduct. *American Psychologist, 47*(12), 1992.

American Psychological Association. (1996). *Body image, eating disorders, and obesity: Integrative guide for assessment and treatment.* Washington, D.C.: Author.

Ames, L. (1997). *Women reformed, women empowered: Poor mothers and the endangered promise of Head Start.* Philadelphia: Temple University Press.

Anastasi, A., & Urbina, S. (1997). *Psychological testing.* 7th ed. Upper Saddle River, N.J.: Prentice-Hall.

Anderson, A. M. (1996). The father-infant relationship: Becoming connected. *Journal of the Society of Pediatric Nurses, 1,* 83–92.

Anderson, B. (1989). Effects of public day care: A longitudinal study. *Child Development, 60,* 857–866.

Anderson, E. (1992). *Speaking with style: Sociolinguistic skills of children.* New York: Routledge.

Andrews, E. (1996, February 29). TV executives reach broad accord on rating violent shows. *The New York Times,* p. A15.

Andrien, M. (1994). *Social communication in nutrition: A methodology for intervention.* Rome: Food and Agricultural Organization of the United Nations.

Angier, N. (1994, May 17). Genetic mutations tied to father in most cases. *New York Times,* pp. B9, C12.

Anglin, J. (1993). Vocabulary development: A morphological analysis. *Monographs of the Society for Research on Child Development, 58*(10, Serial No. 238). Chicago: University of Chicago Press.

Apfel, N. H., & Seitz, V. (1991). Four models of adolescent mother-grandmother relationships in Black inner-city families. *Family Relations, 40,* 421–429.

Apgar, V. (1953). A proposal for a new method of evaluation in the newborn infant. *Current Research in Anesthesia and Analgesia, 32,* 260.

Archer, J. (1992). *Ethology and human development.* Lanham, MD: Harvester-Wheatsheaf.

Archer, S. L. (1982). The lower age boundaries of identity development. *Child Development, 53,* 1551–1556.

Archer, S. L., & Waterman, A. S. (1988). Psychological individualism: Gender differences or gender identity? *Human Development, 31,* 65–81.

Archibald, J. (Ed.). (1995). *Phonological acquisition and phonological theory.* Hillsdale, N.J.: Erlbaum.

Arditti, J. A. (1992). Differences between fathers with joint custody and noncustodial fathers. *American Journal of Orthopsychiatry, 62,* 186–195.

Arend, R., Gove, F., & Sroufe, L. (1979). Continuity of individual adaptation from infancy to kindergarten: A predictive study of ego-resiliency and curiosity in preschoolers. *Child Development, 50,* 950–959.

Arliss, L. (1991). *Gender communication.* Englewood Cliffs, N.J.: Prentice-Hall.

Arnett, J. (1992). Reckless behavior in adolescence: A developmental perspective. *Developmental Review, 12,* 339–373.

Arnett, J. J., & Jensen, L. A. (1997). Socialization and risk behavior in two countries: Denmark and the United States. *Youth & Society, 26,* 1994, 3–22.

Asendorpf, J. B., Warkentin, V., & Baudonniere, P. M. (1996). Self-awareness and other-awareness II: Mirror self-recognition, social contingency awareness, and synchronic imitation. *Developmental Psychology, 32,* 313–321.

Asher, S., Renshaw, P., & Hymel, S. (1982). Peer relations and the development of social skills. In S. Moore & C. Cooper (Eds.), *The young child: Reviews of research: Vol. 3.* Washington, D.C.: National Association for the Education of Young Children.

Aslin, R. (1987). Visual and auditory development in infancy. In J. Osofsky (Ed.), *Handbook of infant development* (2nd ed.) (pp. 5–97). New York: Wiley.

Aslin, R. (1993). Perception of visual direction in human infants. In C. Granrud (Ed.), *Visual perception and cognition in infants,* pp. 91–120. Hillsdale, N.J.: Erlbaum.

Atkinson, L., & Zucker, K. (1997). *Attachment and psychopatholgy.* Guilford, Conn.: Guilford Press.

Aviezer, O., van IJzendoorn, M. H., Sagi, A., & Schuengel, C. (1994). "Children of the Dream" revisited: 70 years of collective early child care in Israeli kibbutzim. *Psychological Bullletin, 116,* 99–116.

Azmitia, M. & Hesser, J. (1993). Why siblings are important agents of cognitive development: A comparison of siblings and peers. *Child Development 64,* 430–444.

Backx, F. (1996). Epidemiology of pediatric sports-related injuries. In O. Bar-Or (Ed.), *The child and adolescent athlete* (pp. 163–172). Oxford, U.K.: Blackwells.

Bagwell, C. L., Newcomb, A. F., & Bukowski, W. M. (1998). Preadolescent friendship and peer rejection as predictors of adult adjustment. *Child Development, 69,* 140–153.

Bailey, J. M., & Zucker, K. J. (1995). Childhood sex-typed behavior and sexual orientation: A conceptual analysis and quantitative review. *Developmental Psychology, 31,* 43–55.

Baillargeon, R. (1991). Object permanence in infants: Further evidence. *Child Development, 62,* 1227–1246.

Baillargeon, R. (1993). The object concept revisited: New directions in the investigation of infants' physical knowledge. In C. Granrud (Ed.), *Visual perception and cognition in infants,* pp. 265–316. Hillsdale, N.J.: Erlbaum.

Bain, L. (1993). *Parents' guide to childhood emergencies.* New York: Delta.

Bakan, D. (1975). Adolescence in America: From idea to social fact. In R. E. Grinder (Ed.), *Studies in adolescence* (3rd ed.). New York: Macmillan.

Bakeman, R., & Brownlee, J. (1980). The strategic use of parallel play: A sequential analysis. *Child Development, 51,* 873–878.

Baker, C. (1995). *English syntax* (2nd ed.). Cambridge, Mass.: MIT Press.

Baker, J. E., Sedney, M. A., & Gross, E. (1992). Psychological tasks for bereaved children. *American Journal of Orthopsychiatry, 62,* 105–116.

Baldwin, D. A., & Moses, L. J. (1996). The ontogeny of social information gathering. *Child Development, 67,* 1915–1939.

Bamford, F., Bannister, R., Benjamin, C., Hillier, V., Ward, B., & Moore, W. (1990). Sleep in the first year of life. *Developmental Medicine and Child Neurology, 32,* 718–724.

Bandura, A. (1989). Social cognitive theory. In R. Vasta (Ed.), *Annals of Child Development. Theories of child development: Revised formulations and current issues.* Greenwich, Conn.: JAI Press.

Bandura, A. (1991). Social cognitive theory of moral thought and action. In W. Kurtines & J. Gewirtz (Eds.), *Handbook of moral behavior and development: Vol. 1* (pp. 45–104). Hillsdale, N.J.: Erlbaum.

Bank, L., Patterson, G. R., & Reid, J. B. (1996). Negative sibling interaction patterns as predictors of later adjustment problems in adolescent and young adult males. In G. H. Brody et al. (Eds.), *Sibling relationships: Their causes and consequences. Advances in applied developmental psychology, 10* (pp. 197–229). Norwood, N.J.: Ablex.

Banks, M., & Sharman, E. (1993). Spatial and chromatic visual efficiency in human neonates. In C. Granrud (Ed.), *Visual perception and cognition in infants,* pp. 1–46. Hillsdale, N.J.: Erlbaum.

Barlow, D. H., & Durand, V. M. (1995). *Abnormal psychology: An integrative approach.* Pacific Grove, Cal.: Brooks/Cole.

Barnes, D. (1993). Central closure defects. In B. K. Rothman (Ed.), *The encyclopedia of childbearing.* New York: Henry Holt.

Barness, L. (Ed.). (1993). *Pediatric nutrition handbook* (3rd ed.). Elk Grove Village, Ill.: American Academy of Pediatrics.

Barr, H. M., Streissguth, A. P., Darby, B. L., & Sampson, P. D. (1990). Prenatal exposure to alcohol, caffeine, tobacco, and aspirin: Effects on fine and gross motor performance in 4-year-old children. *Developmental Psychology, 26,* 339–348.

Barr, R. G. (1995). The enigma of infant crying: The emergence of defining dimensions. *Early Development and Parenting, 4,* 225–232.

Bartol, B. (1986, July 28). Cocaine babies: Hooked at birth. *Newsweek,* pp. 56–57.

Bartsch, K. (1993). Adolescents' theoretical thinking. In R. Lerner (Ed.), *Early adolescence: Perspectives on research, policy, and intervention,* pp. 143–159. Hillsdale, N.J.: Erlbaum.

Bartsch, K., & Wellman, H. (1995). *Children talk about the mind.* New York: Oxford.

Bat-Chava, Y., Allen, L., Aber, J. L., & Seidman, E. (1997, April). *Racial and ethnic identity and the contexts of development.* Paper presented at the annual meeting of the Society for Research in Child Development, Washington, D.C.

Bates, E., Bretherton, I., & Snyder, L. (1988). *From first words to grammar.* Cambridge, U.K.: Cambridge University Press.

Bates, E., & Carnevale, G. (1993). New directions in research on language development. *Developmental Review, 13,* 436–470.

Bates, E., Dale, P., & Thal, D. (1995). Individual differences and their implications for theories of language development. In P. Fletcher & B. MacWhinney (Eds.), *Handbook of child language.* Oxford, U.K.: Blackwell.

Bates, E., Marchman, V., Thal, D., Fenson, L., Dale, P., Reznick, J., Reilly, J., & Hartung, J. (1994). Developmental and stylistic variation in the composition of early vocabulary. *Journal of Child Language, 21*(1), 85–124.

Battle, E. K., & Brownell, K.D. (1996). Confronting a rising tide of eating disorders and obesity: Treatment vs. prevention and policy. *Addictive Behaviors, 21,* 755–765.

Bauman, K. E., & Ennett, S. T. (1994). Peer influence on adolescent drug use. *American Psychologist, 49,* 820–822.

Baumrind, D. (1971). Current patterns of parental authority. *Developmental Psychology, 4,* 1–103.

Baumrind, D. (1989). Raising competent children. In W. Damon (Ed.), *Child development today and tomorrow* (pp. 349–378). San Francisco: Jossey-Bass.

Baumrind, D. (1991). Effective parenting during the early adolescent transition. In P. Cowan & M. Hetherington (Eds.), *Family transitions.* Hillsdale, N.J.: Erlbaum.

Baumrind, D. (1991). The influence of parenting style on adolescent competence and substance abuse. *Early Adolescence, 11,* 56–95.

Baydar, N., Hyle, P., & Brooks-Gunn, J. (1997). A longitudinal study of the effects of the birth of a sibling during preschool and early grade school years. *Journal of Marriage and the Family, 59,* 957–965.

Beauchamp, G., & Bartoshuk, L. (Ed.). (1997). *Tasting and smelling.* Orlando: Academic Press.

Becker, A. (1994). Nurturing and negligence: Working on others' bodies in Fiji. In T. Csordas (Ed.), *Embodiment and experience: The existential ground of culture and self* (pp. 100–115). New York: Cambridge University Press.

Becker, G. (1996). *Accounting for tastes.* Cambridge, Mass.: Harvard University Press.

Behrman, J. & Stacey, N. (Eds.). (1997). *The social benefits of education.* Ann Arbor, Mich. University of Michigan Press.

Behrman, R. (1998). *Nelson textbook of pediatrics.* 3rd. ed. Philadelphia: Saunders.

Bell, K., Allen, J., Hauser, S., & O'Connor, T. (1996). Family factors and young adult transitions: Educational attainment and occupational prestige. In J. Graber, J. Brooks-Gunn, & A. Petersen (Eds.), *Transitions through adolescence* (pp. 345–366). Mahwah, N.J.: Erlbaum.

Bell, N., Grossen, M., & Perret-Clermont, A.-N. (1985). Sociocognitive conflict and intellectual growth. In M. Berkowitz (Ed.), *Peer conflict and psychological growth.* New Directions for Child Development, No. 29. San Francisco: Jossey-Bass.

Bell, R. (1980). *Changing bodies, changing lives: A book for teens on sex and relationships.* New York: Random House.

Bellugi, U., Van Hoek, K., Lillo-Martin, D., & O'Grady, L. (1993). The acquisition of syntax and space in young deaf signers. In D. Bishop & K. Mogford (Eds.), *Language development in exceptional circumstances* (pp. 132–149). Hillsdale, N.J.: Erlbaum.

Belsky, J. (1980). Child maltreatment: An ecological integration. *American Psychologist, 35,* 320–335.

Belsky, J. (1988). Child maltreatment and the emergent family system. In K. Browne, C. Davies, & P. Strattan (Eds.), *Early prediction and prevention of child abuse* (pp. 291–302). New York: Wiley.

Belsky, J. (1993). Etiology of child maltreatment: A developmental-ecological analysis. *Psychological Bulletin, 114,* 413–434.

Belsky, J. (1996). Parent, infant and social-contextual antecedents of father-son attachment security. *Developmental Psychology, 32,* 905–913.

Belsky, J., Crnic, K., & Gable, S. (1995). The determinants of coparenting in families with toddler boys: Spousal differences and daily hassles. *Child Development, 66,* 629–642.

Belsky, J., & Nezworski, T. (Eds.). (1988). *Clinical implications of attachment.* Hillsdale, N.J.: Erlbaum.

Belsky, J., & Rovine, M. (1988). Nonmaternal care in the first year of life and the security of infant-parent attachment. *Child Development, 59,* 157–176.

Bem, S. L. (1981). Gender schema theory: A cognitive account of sex typing. *Psychological Review, 88,* 354–364.

Bem, S. L. (1987) Gender schema theory and its implications for child development: Raising gender-aschematic children in a gender-schematic society. In M. R. Walsh, et al. (Eds.), *The psychology of women: Ongoing debates* (pp. 226–245). New Haven, Conn.: Yale University Press.

Bem, S. L. (1989) Genital knowledge and gender constancy in preschool children. *Child Development, 60,* 649–662.

Benenson, J. F., Apostololeris, N. H., & Parnass, J. (1997). Age and sex differences in dyadic and group interaction. *Developmental Psychology, 33,* 538–543.

Bennett, L., & Fineran, S. (1998). Sexual and severe physical violence among high school students: Power beliefs, gender, and relationship. *American Journal of Orthopsychiatry, 68,* 645–652.

Benoit, D., & Parker, K. C. (1994). Stability and transmission of attachment across three generations. Child Development, 65, 1444–1456.

Beresford, T. (1993). Abortion counseling. In B. K. Rothman (Ed.), *The encyclopedia of childbearing.* New York: Henry Holt.

Berk, L. E. (1994, November). Why children talk to themselves. *Scientific American,* 78–83.

Berko, J. (1958). The child's learning of English morphology. *Word, 14,* 150–177.

Berndt, T. J. (1988). The nature and significance of children's friendships. In R. Vasta (Ed.), *Annals of child development: Vol. 5* (pp. 155–186). Greenwich, Conn.: JAI Press.

Bernhardt, J. S. (1990). Potential workplace hazards to reproductive health. *Journal of Obstetrical and Gynecological Nursing, 19,* 53–62.

Bertoia, J. (1993). *Drawings from a dying child: Insights into death from a Jungian perspective.* London: Routledge.

Beveridge, D. (1993) Violence against pregnant women. In B. K. Rothman (Ed.), *The encyclopedia of childbearing.* New York: Henry Holt.

Bhavnagri, N., & Parke, R. D. (1991). Parents as direct facilitators of children's peer relationships: Effects of age of child and sex of parent. *Journal of Social and Personal Relationships, 8,* 423–440.

Bialystok, E., & Hakuta, K. (1994). *The science and psychology of second language acquisition.* New York: Basic Books.

Bianci, V. (1993). *Mechanisms of brain lateralization.* Philadelphia: Gordon and Beach.

Bierman, K. L., Smoot, D. L., & Aumiller, K. (1993). Characteristics of aggressive-rejected, aggressive (nonrejected), and rejected (nonaggressive) boys. *Child Development, 64,* 139–151.

Bingham, C. R., & Crockett, L. J. (1996). Longitudinal adjustment patterns of boys and girls experiencing early, middle and late sexual intercourse. *Developmental Psychology, 32,* 647–658.

Birenbaum, L. K., Robinson, M. A., Phillips, D. Stewart, B., et al. (1991). The response of children to the dying and death of a sibling. *Omega: Journal of Death & Dying, 20,* 213–228.

Biringen, Z. (1994). Attachment theory and research: Application to clinical practice. *American Journal of Orthopsychiatry, 64,* 404–420.

Bjorklund, D. (Ed.). (1990). *Children's strategies.* Hillsdale, N.J.: Erlbaum.

Black, M., & Krishnakumar, A. (1998). Children in low-income, urban settings. *American Psychologist, 53,* 635–646.

Blackman, J. A. (1990). *Medical aspects of developmental disabilities in children birth to three* (2nd ed) Rockville, Md.: Aspen Publishers, Inc.

Blanck, G. (1990). The man and his cause. In L. C. Moll (Ed.), *Vygotsky and education: Instructional implications and applications of sociohistorical psychology.* Cambridge, U.K.: Cambridge University Press.

Blatt, R. J. R. (1988). *Prenatal tests.* New York: Vintage.

Block, J. H., Block, J., & Morrison, A. (1981). Parental agreement-disagreement on child-rearing orientations and gender-related personality correlates in children. *Child Development, 52,* 965–974.

Bloom, L. (1993). *The transition from infancy to language: Acquiring the power of expression.* New York: Cambridge University Press.

Blumenthal, S. J., & Kupfer, D. G. (1988). Overview of early detection and treatment strategies for suicidal behavior in young people. *Journal of Youth and Adolescence, 17,* 1–23.

Bock, R. D., & Moore, E. G. J. (1986). *Advantage and disadvantage: A profile of American youth.* Hillsdale, N.J.: Erlbaum.

Bogdon, J. C. (1993). Childbirth practices in American history. In B. K. Rothman (Ed.), *The encyclopedia of childbearing.* New York: Henry Holt, 1993.

Bojko, M. (1995). The multi-cultural program at O'Brien Elementary School. Personal communication.

Bolger, K. E., Patterson, C. J., Thompson, W. W., & Kupersmidt, J. B. (1995). Psychosocial adjustment among children experiencing persistent and intermittent family economic hardship. *Child Development, 66,* 1107–1129.

Bollerud, K., Christopherson, S., & Frank, E. (1990). Girls' sexual choices: Looking for what is right: The intersection of sexual and moral development. In C. Gilligan, N. Lyons, & T. Hanmer (Eds.), *Making connections: The relational worlds of adolescent girls at Emma Willard School* (pp. 274–285). Cambridge, Mass.: Harvard University Press.

Borchardt, K., & Noble, M. (Eds.). (1997). *Sexually transmitted diseases: Epidemiology, pathology, diagnosis, and treatment.* Boca Raton: CRC Press.

Bordo, S. (1993). *Unbearable weight: Feminism, Western culture, and the body.* Berkeley, Cal.: University of California Press.

Bornstein, M. H., Haynes, O. M., Azuma, H., Galperin, C., et al. (1998). A cross-national study of self-evaluations and attributions in parenting: Argentina, Belgium, France, Israel, Italy, Japan, and the United States. *Developmental Psychology, 34,* 662–676.

Boughton, D., Eisner, E., & Ligtvoet, J. (Eds.). (1996). *Evaluating and assessing the visual arts in education.* New York: Teachers College Press.

Bowers, R. (1995). Early adolescent social and emotional development: A constructivist perspective. In M. Wavering (Ed.), *Educating young adolescents,* pp. 79–110. New York: Garland.

Bowlby, J. (1969). *Attachment and loss: Vol. 1. Attachment.* New York: Basic Books.

Bowlby, J. (1988). *A secure base: Clinical applications of attachment theory.* London: Routledge.

Bowlby, J. (1988). Developmental psychology comes of age. *American Journal of Psychiatry, 145,* 1–10.

Brazelton, T. B. (1976). Early mother-infant reciprocity. In V. C. Vaughn III & T. B. Brazelton (Eds.), *The family: Can it be saved?* Chicago: Yearbook Medical Publishers.

Brazelton, T. B., & Nugent, J. (1997). *Neonatal behavioral assessment scale.* (4th ed.). New York: Cambridge University Press.

Bredekamp, S., & Copple, C. (Eds.). (1997). *Developmentally appropriate practice in early childhood programs.* Rev. ed. Washington, D.C.: National Association for the Education of Young Children.

Bretherton, I. (1992). Social referencing, intentional communication, and the interfacing of minds in infancy. In S. Feinman, et al., *Social referencing and the social construction of reality in infancy* (pp. 57–77). New York: Plenum Press.

Bretherton, I. (1993). From dialogue to internal working models: The co-construction of self in relationships. In C. A. Nelson et al. (Eds.), Memory and affect in development. *The Minnesota Symposia on Child Psychology, 26,* 237–263. Hillsdale, N.J.: Erlbaum.

Bretherton, I. (1995). A communication perspective on attachment relationships and internal working models. *Monographs of the Society for Research in Child Development, 60,* 310–329.

Bretherton, I., & Waters, E. (1985). Growing points in attachment theory. *Monographs of the Society for Research in Child Development, 50*(12, Serial No. 209).

Bridges, L. J., Grolnick, W. S., & Connell, J. P. (1997). Infant emotion regulation with mothers and fathers. *Infant Behavior and Development, 20,* 47–57.

Brierly, J. (1994). *Give me a child until he is seven: Brain studies and early childhood education.* Washington, D.C.: Falmer Press.

Brislin, R., & Yoshida, T. (1994). *Intercultural communication training: An introduction.* Thousand Oaks, Cal.: Sage.

Broderick, V. (1991). Young children's comprehension of similarities underlying metaphor. *Journal of Psycholinguistic Research, 20,* 65–81.

Brody, G. H., Graziano, W. G., & Musser, L. M. (1983). Familiarity and children's behavior in same-age and mixed-age peer groups. *Developmental Psychology, 19,* 569–576.

Brody, G. H., & Flor, D. L. (1997). Maternal psychological functioning, family processes, and child adjustment in rural, single-parent, African American families. *Developmental Psychology, 33,* 1000–1011.

Brody, G. H., & Flor, D. L. (1998). Maternal resources, parenting practices, and child competence in rural, single-parent African American families. *Child Development, 69,* 803–816.

Brody, G. H., Stoneman, Z., Flor, D. L., McCrary, C., Hastings, L., & Conyers, O. (1994). Financial resources, parent psychological functioning, parent co-caregiving, and early adolescent competence in rural two-parent African American families. *Child Development*, 65, 590–605.

Brody, G. H., Stoneman, Z., McCoy, J. K., & Forehand, R. (1992). Contemporary and longitudinal associations of sibling conflict with family relationship assessments and family discussions about sibling problems. *Child Development*, 63, 391–400.

Brody, J. E. (1993, February 10). Adult years bring new afflictions for DES "babies." *The New York Times*, p. C–12.

Brody, J. E. (1995). The use of alcohol linked to rise in fetal illness. *New York Times*, April 7, A-27, col. 1.

Bronfenbrenner, U. (1989). Ecological systems theory. In R. Vasta (Ed.), *Annals of child development: Vol. 6. Six theories of child development: Revised formulations and current issues*. Greenwich, Conn.: JAI Press.

Bronner, F. (Ed.). (1997). *Nutrition policy in public health*. New York: Springer.

Bronstein, P. (1988). Marital and parenting roles in transition. In P. Bronstein & C. Cowan (Eds.), *Fatherhood today: Men's changing role in the family* (pp. 3–12). New York: Wiley.

Brooks-Gunn, J., & Warren, M. (1989). Biological and social contributions to negative affect in young adolescent girls. *Child Development*, 60, 40–55.

Brooten, D. (Ed.). (1992). *Low-birth-weight neonates*. Philadelphia: Lippincott.

Brown, B. B. (1990). Peer groups and peer cultures. In S. S. Feldman & G. R. Elliot (Eds.), *At the threshold: The developing adolescent* (pp. 171–196). Cambridge, Mass.: Harvard University Press.

Brown, B. B., & Huang, B. (1995). Examining parenting practices in different peer contexts: Implications for adolescent trajectories. In L. J. Crockett, A. C. Crouter, et al. (Eds.), *Pathways through adolescence: Individual development in relation to social contexts: The Penn State series on child & adolescent development* (pp. 151–174). Mahwah, N.J.: Erlbaum.

Brown, B. B., Mocents, N., Lamborn, S. D., & Steinberg, L. (1993). Parenting practices and peer group affiliation in adolescence. *Child Development*, 64, 467–482.

Brown, J. L., & Pollitt, E. (1996, February). Malnutrition, poverty and intellectual development. *Scientific American*, 38–43.

Brown, J. R. (Ed.). (1990). *Plant population genetics, breeding, and genetic resources*. Sunderland, Mass.: Sinaeur Associates.

Brown, J. R., & Dunn, J. (1992). Talk with your mother or your sibling? Developmental changes in early family conversations about feelings. *Child Development*, 63, 336–349.

Brown, L., & Gilligan, C. (1992). *Meeting at the crossroads: Women's psychology and girls' development*. Cambridge, Mass.: Harvard University Press.

Brown, R. (1973). *A first language: The early stages*. Cambridge, Mass.: Harvard University Press.

Bruner, J. (1996). *The culture of education*. Cambridge, Mass.: Harvard University Press.

Bryant, B. (1985). The neighborhood walk: Sources of support in middle childhood. *Monographs of the Society for Research on Child Development*, 50 (3, No. 210).

Bryant, B. K. (1994). How does social support function in childhood? In F. Nestmann, & K. Hurrelmann et al. (Eds.), *Social networks and social support in childhood and adolescence: Prevention and intervention in childhood and adolescence*, 16 (pp. 23–35). Berlin, Germany: Walter De Gruyter.

Buckley, K., & Kulb, N. (Eds.). (1983). *Handbook of maternal-newborn nursing*. New York: Wiley.

Buhrmester, D. (1990). Intimacy of friendship, interpersonal competence, and adjustment during preadolescence and adolescence. *Child Development*, 61, 1101–1111.

Buhrmester, D. & Furman, W. (1990). Perceptions of sibling relationships during middle childhood and adolescence. *Child Development*, 61, 1387–1398.

Bukatko, D., & Daehler, M. W. (1995). *Child development: A thematic approach*. Boston: Houghton Mifflin.

Bukowski, W. M., & Hoza, B. (1989). Popularity and friendship: Issues in theory, measurement, and outcome. In T. J. Berndt & G. W. Ladd (Eds.), *Peer relationships in child development* (pp. 15–45). New York: Wiley.

Bukowksi, W. M., Newcomb, A. F., & Hartup, W. W. (1996). *The company they keep: Friendship in childhood and adolescence*. New York: Cambridge University Press.

Bury, M. (1997). *Health and illness in a changing society*. New York: Routledge.

Buss, A. H., & Plomin, R. (1984). *Temperament: Early developing personality traits*. Hillsdale, N.J.: Erlbaum.

Buss, K. A., & Goldsmith, H. H. (1998). Fear and anger regulation in infancy: Effects on the temporal dynamics of affective expression. *Child Development*, 69, 359–384.

Byard, R., & Cohle, S. (1994). *Sudden death in infants, children, and adolescents*. New York: Cambridge University Press.

Byne, W. (1994, May). The biological evidence challenged. *Scientific American*, 50–55.

Cain, K. M., & Dweck, C. S. (1995). The relation between motivational patterns and achievement cognitions through the elementary school years. *Merrill-Palmer Quarterly, 41*, 35–52.

Calabrese, R. L. & Noboa, J. (1995). The choice for gang membership by Mexican-American adolescents. *High School Journal*, 226–235.

Caliso, J., & Milner, J. (1992). Childhood history of abuse and child abuse screening. *Child Abuse and Neglect, 16*, 647–659.

Call, K. T., Mortimer, J. T., & Shanahan, M. J. (1995). Helpfulness and the development of competence in adolescence. *Child Development*, 66, 129–138.

Campion, M. J. (1993). Childbearing with a disability. In B. K. Rothman (Ed.), *The encyclopedia of childbearing*. New York: Henry Holt.

Campos, R., Raffaelli, M., Greco, W., Ruff, A., Rolf, J., Antunes, C., Halsey, N., & Greco, D. (1994). Social networks and daily activities of street youth in Belo Horizonte, Brazil. *Child Development*, 65, 319–330.

Camras, L. A., Sullivan, J., & Michel, G. (1993). Do infants express discrete emotions? Adult judgments of facial, vocal, and body actions. *Journal of Nonverbal Behavior, 17*, 171–186.

Cannella, G. (1997). *Deconstructing early childhood education: Social jusice and revolution*. New York: Peter Lang.

Canfield, R., & Smith, E. (1996). Number-based expectations and sequential enumeration by 5-month-old-infants. *Development Psychology, 32*, 269–279.

Canfield R., Smith, E., Brezsnyak, M., & Snow, K. (1997). Information processing through the first year of life: A longitudinal study using the visual expectation paradigm. *Monographs of the Society for Research in Child Development*, 62 (2, Serial No. 250).

Carlson, C. I., Cooper, C. R., & Spradling, V. Y. (1991). Developmental implications of shared versus distinct perceptions of the family in early adolescence. *New Directions for Child Development, 51*, 13–32.

Carlson, E. A., Jacobvitz, D., & Sroufe, A. L. (1995). A developmental investigation of inattentiveness and hyperactivity. *Child Development*, 66, 37–54.

Carnegie Council on Adolescent Development. (1992). A matter of time: Risk and opportunity in the nonschool hours. Report of the task force on youth development and community programs. New York: Carnegie Corporation of New York.

Carroll, J., & Siska, E. (1998). SIDS: Counseling parents to reduce the risk. *American Family Physician, 57*(9). [On-line]. Available: www.sids. org.

Carruthers, P., & Smith, P. (Eds.). (1996). *Theories of theories of the mind*. New York: Cambridge University Press.

Case, R. (1991a). *The mind's staircase: Exploring the conceptual underpinnings of children's thought and knowledge*. Hillsdale, N.J.: Erlbaum.

Case, R. (1991b). General and specific views of the mind, its structure, and its development. In R. Case (Ed.), *The mind's staircase* (pp. 3–16). Hillsdale, N.J.: Erlbaum.

Case, R. (1991c). A neo-Piagetian approach to the issue of cognitive generality and specificity. In R. Case (Ed.), *The mind's staircase* (pp. 17–36). Hillsdale, N.J.: Erlbaum.

Case, R. (1991d). Advantages and limitations of the neo-Piagetian position. In R. Case (Ed.), *The mind's staircase* (pp. 37–51). Hillsdale, N.J.: Erlbaum.

Case, R. (1992). Neo-Piagetian theories of intellectual development. In H. Beilin & P. Pufall (Eds.), *Piaget's theory: Prospects and possibilities*. Hillsdale, N.J.: Erlbaum.

Case, R. (1998, April). *Fostering the development of number sense in the elementary and middle grades*. Paper presented at the annual meeting of the American Educational Research Association, San Diego.

Case, R., & Edelstein, W. (1994). *The new structuralism in cognitive development: Theory and research on individual pathways*. New York: Kargar.

Case, R., & Okamoto, Y. (1996). The role of central conceptual structures in the development of children's thought. *Monographs of the Society for Research in Child Development*, Serial No. 246, Vol. 61, No. 1–2. Chicago: Society for Research in Child Development.

Caspi, A., Henri, B., McGee, R. O., Moffitt, T. E., & Silva, P. A. (1995). Temperamental origins of child and adolescent behavior problems: From age three to age fifteen. *Child Development*, 66, 55–68.

Caspi, A., & Silva, P. A. (1995). Temperamental qualities at age 3 predict personality traits in young adulthood: Longitudinal evidence from a birth cohort. *Child Development*, 66, 486–498.

Cassell, D. (1994). *Encyclopedia of obesity and eating disorders*. New York: Facts on File Press.

Cassidy, S. B. (1995). Uniparental disomy and genomic imprinting as causes of human genetic disease. *Environmental and Molecular Mutagenesis, 25*, 13–20.

Catterall, J. (1998). Risk and resilience in student transitions to high school. *American Journal of Education, 106*(2), 302–333.

Cazden, C. (1988). *Classroom discourse*. Portsmouth, N.H.: Heinemann.

Centers for Disease Control. (1992, January 3). Sexual behavior among high school students—United States, 1990. *Morbidity and Mortality Weekly Report, 40*, 885–888.

Centers for Disease Control. (1997). *Centers for Disease Control's national immunization program*. Washington, D.C.: U.S. Government Printing Office.

Centers for Disease Control and Prevention. (1998). *National vital statistics report, 47*(4). Bethesda, Md.: National Center for Health Statistics.

Cepecchi, M. R. (1994, March). Targeted gene replacement. *Scientific American*, 52–59.

Cernoch, J., & Porter, R. (1985). Recognition of maternal axillary odors by infants. *Child Development*, 56, 1593–1598.

Cervantes, C. A., & Callanan, M. A. (1998). Labels and explanations in mother-child emotion talk: Age and gender differentiation. *Developmental Psychology, 34*, 88–98.

Chafel, J. (1993). *Child poverty and public policy*. Washington, D.C.: The Urban Institute.

Chaiklin, S., & Lave, J. (Eds.). (1993). *Understanding practice: Perspectives on activity and context*. New York: Cambridge University Press.

Chan, S. (1991) *Asian Americans: An interpretive history*. Boston: Twayne Publishers.

Chao, R. K. (1994). Beyond parental control and authoritarian parenting style: Understanding Chinese parenting through the cultural notion of training. *Child Development*, 65, 1111–1119.

Chase-Landsdale, P. L., Brooks-Gunn, J., & Zamsky, E. S. (1994). Young African-American multi-generational families in poverty: Quality of mothering and grandmothering. *Child Development*, 65, 373–393.

Chasnoff, I. J., Griffith, D. R., MacGregor, S., Dirkes, K., & Burns, K. A. (1989). Temporal patterns of cocaine use in pregnancy: Perinatal outcome. *Journal of the American Medical Association, 262*, 1741–1744.

Cherkes-Julkowski, M., Sharp, S., & Stolzenberg, J. (1997). *Rethinking ADHD*. Cambridge, Mass.: Brookline Books.

Cherry, F. (1995). *"Stubborn particulars" of social psychology: Essays on the research process*. New York: Routledge.

Chess, S., & Thomas, A. (1986). *Temperament in clinical practice*. New York: Guilford.

Chestnut, M. (1998) *High-risk perinatal home care manual* (5th ed.). Philadelphia: Lippincott-Raven.

Chi, M. (1985). Interactive roles of knowledge and strategies in the development of organized sorting and recall. In S. Chipman, J. Segal, & R. Glaser (Eds.), *Thinking and learning skills: Vol. 2. Research and open questions* (pp. 457–483). Hillsdale, N.J.: Erlbaum.

Chi, M., & Ceci, S. (1987). Content knowledge: Its role, representation, and restructuring in memory. In H. Reese (Ed.), *Advances in child development and behavior: Vol. 20*. New York: Academic Press.

Chi, M., Glaser, R., & Farr, M. (1989). *The nature of expertise*. Hillsdale, N.J.: Erlbaum.

Children's Defense Fund. (1993). *Progress and peril: Black children in America: A fact book and action primer.* Washington, D.C.: Author.

Children's Defense Fund. (1995). *The state of America's children.* Washington, D.C.: Author.

Chodorow, N. J. (1995). Gender as a personal and cultural construction. *Signs, 20,* 516–544.

Chomsky, N. (1994). *Language and thought.* Wakefield, R.I.: Moyer Bell Publishers.

Chosak, R. (1998). Personal communication.

Christensen, K., & Delgado, G. (Eds.). (1993). *Multicultural issues in deafness.* White Plains, N.Y.: Longman.

Cicchetti, D., & Olson, K. (1990). The developmental psychopathology of child maltreatment. In M. Lewis & S. Miller (Eds.), *Handbook of development psychopathology.* New York: Plenum Press.

Cicchetti, D., & Toth, S. L. (1998). The development of depression in children and adolescents. *American Psychologist, 53,* 221–241.

Clark, M. L., & Ayers, M. (1988). The role of reciprocity and proximity in junior high school friendships. *Journal of Youth and Adolescence, 17,* 403–411.

Clark, R., Hyde, J. S., Essex, M. J., & Klein, M. H. (1997). Length of maternity leave and quality of mother-infant interaction. *Child Development, 68,* 363–383.

Clarke, A. T., & Kutz-Costes, B. (1997). Television viewing, educational quality of the home environment, and school readiness. *Journal of Educational Research, 90,* 279–285.

Clarke-Stewart, K. A. (1989). Day care: Maligned or malignant? *American Psychologist, 44,* 266–273.

Clarke-Stewart, K. A., & Hayward, C. (1996). Advantages of father custody and contact for the psychological well-being of school-age children. *Journal of Applied Developmental Psychology, 17,* 239–270.

Coakley, J. (1996). Socialization through sports. In O. Bar-Or, (Ed.), *The child and adolescent athlete* (pp. 353–363). London: Blackwell Science.

Coates, J. (1993). *Women, men, and communication* (2nd ed.). New York: Longman.

Cobb, P., Gravemeijer, K., Yackel, E., McClain, K., & Whitenack, J. (1997). Mathematizing and symbolizing: The emergence of chains of signification in one first-grade classroom. In D. Kirschner & J. Witson (Eds.), *Situated cognition: Social, semiotic, and psychological perspectives* (pp. 151–234). Mahwah, N.J.: Erlbaum.

Cohen E. (1994). *Designing group work: Strategies for the heterogeneous classroom* (2nd ed.). New York: Teachers College Press.

Cohen, E., & Latan, R. (Eds.). (1997). *Working for equity in heterogeneous classrooms.* New York: Teachers College Press.

Cohen, F., & Durham, J. (Eds.). (1993). *Women, children, and HIV/AIDS.* New York: Springer.

Cohen, M. (1998). *The attention zone: Parents' guide to ADHD.* Washington, D.C.: Brunner/Mazel.

Cohen, N. (1997). *The development of memory in childhood.* Hove, U.K.: Psychology Press.

Coie, J. D., Dodge, K. A., & Coppotelli, H. (1982). Dimensions and types of social status: A cross-age perspective. *Developmental Psychology, 18,* 557–570.

Coie, J. D., Dodge, K. A., Terry, R., & Wright, V. (1991). The role of aggression in peer relations: An analysis of aggression episodes in boys' play groups. *Child Development, 62,* 812–826.

Coiro, M. (1994). *Health of our nation's children.* Hyattsville, M.B.: United States Department of Health and Human Services.

Colby, A., & Damon, W. (1992). *Some do care: Contemporary lives of moral commitment.* New York: The Free Press.

Colby, A., & Kohlberg, L. (1987). *The measurement of moral judgment.* New York: Cambridge University Press.

Colby, A., Kohlberg, L., Gibbs, J., & Lieberman, M. (1983). A longitudinal study of moral development. *Monographs of the Society for Research on Child Development, 48*(1–2, Serial No. 200).

Coldren, J., & Colombo, J. (1994). The nature and processes of preverbal learning. *Monographs of the Society for Research in Child Development, 59*(2, Serial No. 241), 1–75.

Cole, M. (1990). Cultural psychology. In J. Berman (Ed.), *Nebraska symposium on motivation, 1989: Cross-cultural psychology* (pp. 279–336). Lincoln, Neb.: University of Nebraska Press.

Coleman, J. (1988). Social capital in the creation of human capital. *American Journal of Sociology, 94,* 95–120.

Coles, R. (1992). *Their eyes meeting the world: Drawings and paintings of children.* Boston: Houghton Mifflin.

Coles, R. (1993). *The call of service: A witness to idealism.* Boston: Houghton Mifflin.

Coles, R., & Stokes, G. (1985). *Sex and the American teenager.* New York: Harper & Row.

Coley, R. L. (1998). Children's socialization experiences and functioning in single-mother households: The importance of fathers and other men. *Child Development, 69,* 219–230.

Coley, R. L., & Chase-Lansdale, P. L. (1998). Adolescent pregnancy and parenthood: Recent evidence and future directions. *American Psychologist, 53,* 152–166.

Coll, C. G., Lamberty, G., Jenkins, R., McAdoo, H. P., Crnic, K., Wasik, B. H., & Garcia, H. V. (1996). An integrative model for the study of developmental competencies in minority children. *Child Development, 67,* 1891–1914.

Collins, W. A. (1991). Shared views and parent-adolescent relationships. *New Directions for Child Development, 51,* 103–110.

Columbo, J. (1993). Infant cognition: Predicting intellectual functioning (pp. 30–81). Newbury Park, Cal.: Sage Publications.

Comer, J. P., & Poussaint, A. F. (1992). *Raising black children.* New York: Plume.

Comstock, F. (1991). *Television and the American child.* San Diego: Academic Press.

Condry, J. (1993, Winter). Thief of time, unfaithful servant: Television and the American child. *Daedalus, 122,* 259–278.

Conger, R. D., & Chao, W. (1996). Adolescent depressed mood. In R. L. Simons et al. (Eds.), *Understanding differences between divorced and intact families: Stress, interaction, and child outcome* (pp. 81–93). Thousand Oaks, Cal.: Sage.

Connelly, K., & Forssberg, H. (Eds.). (1997). *Neurophysiology and neuropsychology of motor development.* London: MacKeith Press.

Connolly, J., White, D., Stevens, R., & Burstein, S. (1987). Adolescent self-reports of social activity: Assessment of stability and relations to social adjustment. *Journal of Adolescence, 10,* 83–95.

Connolly, S., Paikoff, R., & Buchanan, C. (1996). Puberty: The interplay of biological and psychosocial processes in adolescence. In G. Adams, R. Montemayor, & T. Gullotta (Eds.), *Psychosocial development during adolescence* (pp. 259–299). Thousand Oaks, Cal.: Sage.

Cooksey, E. C., Menaghan, E. G., & Jekielek, S. M. (1997). Life course effects of work and family circumstances on children. *Social Forces, 761,* 637–667

Coren, S. (1992). *The left-hander syndrome.* New York: Free Press.

Coren, S. (1996). *Sleep thieves.* New York: Free Press.

Corley, C. J. & Smitherman, G. (1994). Juvenile justice: Multicultural issues. In J. E. Hendricks, B. Byers, et al. (Eds.), *Multicultural perspectives in criminal justice and criminology* (pp. 259–290). Springfield, Ill.: Charles C. Thomas.

Cowan, C., Cowan, P., Heming, G., & Miller, N. (1991). Becoming a family: Marriage, parenting, and child development. In P. Cowan & M. Hetherington (Eds.), *Family transitions* (pp. 79–110). Hillsdale, N.J.: Erlbaum.

Cowan, N. (Ed.). (1997). *Development of memory in childhood.* Hove, U.K.: Psychology Press.

Cowan, P. A. (1997). Beyond meta-analysis: A plea for a family systems view of attachment. *Child Development, 68,* 571–591.

Cox, M. J., Owen, M. T., Henderson, V. K., & Margand, N. A. (1992). Prediction of infant-father and infant-mother attachment. *Developmental Psychology, 28,* 474–483.

Creasey, G. L., Jarvis, P. A., & Berk, L. E. (1998). Play and social competence. In O. N. Saracho & B. Spodek, et al. (Eds.), *Multiple perspectives on play in early childhood education. SUNY series, early childhood education: Inquiries and insights* (pp. 116–143). Albany, N.Y.: State University of New York Press.

Crick, N. R. (1996). The role of overt aggression, relational aggression, and prosocial behavior in the prediction of children's future social adjustment. *Child Development, 67,* 2317–2327.

Crick, N. R. (1997). Engagement in gender normative versus nonnormative forms of aggression: Links to social-psychological adjustment. *Developmental Psychology, 33,* 610–617.

Crick, N. R., Casas, J. F., & Mosher, M. (1997). Relational and overt aggression in preschool. *Developmental Psychology, 33,* 579–588.

Crick, N. R., & Grotpeter, J. K. (1995). Relational aggression, gender, and social-psychological adjustment. *Child Development, 66,* 710–722.

Crick, N. R., & Grotpeter, J. K. (1996). Children's treatment by peers: Victims of relational and overt aggression. *Development and Psychopathology, 8,* 367–380.

Crockenberg, S. B., & Litman, C. (1990). Autonomy and competence in 1-year-olds: Maternal correlates of child defiance, compliance, and self-assertion. *Developmental Psychology, 26,* 961–971.

Crosette, B. (1998, June 7). A global divide on abortion splits poor from rich. *New York Times,* p. C-3.

Cuffaro, H. (1991). A view of materials as the texts of the early childhood curriculum. In B. Spodek & O. Saracho (Eds.), *Issues in early childhood curriculum* (pp. 64–85). New York: Teachers College Press.

Cummings, E. M., & Cummings, J. L. (1988). A process-oriented approach to children's coping with adults' angry behavior. *Developmental Review, 8,* 296–321.

Cushman, P. (1991). Ideology obscured: Political uses of the self in Daniel Stern's infant. *American Psychologist, 46,* 206–219.

D'Alton, M. E., & DeCherney, A. H. (1993). Prenatal diagnosis. *New England Journal of Medicine, 32,* 114–120.

D'Augelli, A. R., Hershberger, S. L., & Pilkington, N. W. (1998). Lesbian, gay, and bisexual youth and their families: Disclosure of sexual orientation and its consequences. *American Journal of Orthopsychiatry, 68,* 361–371.

Dalglish, P. (1998). *The courage of children: My life with the world's poorest kids.* New York: HarperCollins.

Dalton, S. (Ed.). (1997). *Overweight and weight management.* Gaithersburg, Md.: Aspen Publishers.

Daly, M., & Wilson, M. I. (1996). Violence against stepchildren. *Current Directions in Psychological Science, 5,* 77–81.

Damon, W. (1988). *The moral child.* New York: Cambridge University Press.

Damon, W., & Hart, D. (1988). *Self-understanding in childhood and adolescence.* New York: Cambridge University Press.

Damon, W., & Hart, D. (1992). Self-understanding and its role in social and moral development. In M. C. Bornstein & M. E. Lamb (Eds.), *Developmental psychology: An advanced textbook* (3rd ed., pp. 421–464). Hillsdale, N.J.: Erlbaum.

Darling, C. A., Davidson, J. K., & Passarello, L. C. (1992). The mystique of first intercourse among college youth: The role of partners, contraceptive practices, and psychological reactions. *Journal of Youth and Adolescence, 21,* 97–117.

Darling, C. A., Kallen, D. J., & Van Dusen, J. E. (1984). Sex in transition, 1900–1984. *Journal of Youth and Adolescence, 13,* 385–399.

Darling, N., & Steinberg, L. (1993). Parenting style as context: An integrative model. *Psychological Bulletin, 113,* 487–496.

Davies, B. (1991). Accomplishment of genderedness in preschool children. In L. Weis, P. Altbach, G. Kelly, & H. Petrie (Eds.), *Critical perspectives in early childhood education.* Albany, N.Y.: State University of New York Press.

Davies, B. (1995). Sibling Bereavement Research: State of the Art. In I. B. Corless, B. B. Germino, & M. A. Pittman (Eds.), *A challenge for living: Dying, death, and bereavement.* Boston: Jones and Bartlett.

Davis, E. (1987). *Heart and hands: A midwife's guide to pregnancy and birth.* Berkeley, Cal.: Celestial Arts.

Davis, E. (1993). Common complaints of pregnancy. In B. K. Rothman (Ed.), *The encyclopedia of childbearing.* New York: Henry Holt.

Davis-Floyd, R. E. (1986). Birth as an American rite of passage. In K. L. Michaelson (Ed.), *Childbirth in America: Anthropological perspectives.* South Hadley, Mass.: Bergin & Garvey.

de Cubas, M. M., & Field, T. (1995). Children of methadone-dependent women: Developmental outcomes. *American Journal of Orthopsychiatry, 63,* 266–276.

Deater-Deckard, K., Dodge, K. A., Bates, J. E., & Pettit, G. (1996). Physical discipline among African American and European American mothers: Links to children's externalizing behaviors. *Developmental Psychology, 32,* 1065–1072.

DeCasper, A. J., Lecanuet, J. P., Busnel, M. C., & Granier-Deferre, C. (1994). Fetal reactions to recurrent maternal speech. *Infant Behavior and Development, 17,* 159–164.

Deci, E. L., & Ryan, R. M. (1987). The support of autonomy and the control of behavior. *Journal of Personality and Social Psychology, 56,* 1024–1037.

DeJong, W. (1993). Obesity as a characterological stigma: The issue of responsibility and judgments of task performance. *Psychological Reports, 73,* 963–970.

DeKlyen, M., Biernbaum, M. A., Speltz, M. L., & Greenberg, M. T. (1998). Fathers and preschool behavior problems. *Developmental Psychology, 34,* 264–275.

Delamont, S. (1996). *Women's place in education.* Brookfield, Mass.: Avebury Publishers.

Demetriou, A., Shayer, M., & Efklides, A. (Eds.). (1992). *Neo-Piagetian theories of cognitive development.* London: Routledge.

Demo, D. H., & Acock, A. C. (1996). Family structure, family process, and adolescent well-being. *Journal of Research on Adolescence, 6,* 457–488.

Denham, S. A. (1998). *Emotional development in young children.* New York: Guilford.

Dennis, S. (1992). Stage and structure in the development of children's spatial reasoning. In R. Case (Ed.), *The mind's staircase* (pp. 229–245). Hillsdale, N.J.: Erlbaum.

DeRosier, M. E., Cillessen, A. H. N., Coie, J. D., & Dodge, K. A. (1994). Group social context and children's aggressive behavior. *Child Development, 65,* 1068–1079.

DeVilliers, P., & DeVilliers, J. (1978). *Language development.* Cambridge, Mass.: Harvard University Press.

DeVita, V., Hellman, S., & Rosenberg, S. (Eds.). (1997). *AIDS: Etiology, diagnosis, treatment, and prevention* (4th ed.). Philadelphia: Lippincott-Raven.

DeWolff, M S. & van IJzendoorn, M. H. (1997). Sensitivity and attachment: A meta-analysis on parental antecedents of infant attachment. *Child Development, 68,* 571–591.

Diamond, A. (1993, July). Science meets practice on PKU studies' findings. *APA Monitor,* 16–17.

Diamond, J. (1989, February). Blood, genes, and malaria. *Natural History,* 8–18.

Diaz, R., & Berk, L. (1992). *Private speech: From social interaction to self-regulation.* Hillsdale, N.J.: Erlbaum.

Dickstein, S., & Parke, R. D. (1988). Social referencing in infancy: A glance at fathers and marriage. *Child Development, 59,* 506–511.

Dishion, T. J., Andrews, D. W., & Crosby, L. (1995). Antisocial boys and their friends in early adolescence: Relationship characteristics, quality, and interactional process. *Child Development, 66,* 139–151.

Dishion, T. J., Reid, J. B., & Patterson, G. R. (1988). Empirical guidelines for a family intervention for adolescent drug use. *Journal of Chemical Dependency Treatment, 1,* 181–216.

Dodge, K. A. (1986). A social information processing model of social competence in children. In M. Perlmutter (Ed.), *Minnesota symposia on child psychology: Vol. 18.* Hillsdale, N.J.: Erlbaum.

Dodge, K. A., Coie, J. D., Pettit, G. S., & Price, J. M. (1990). Peer status and aggression in boys' groups: Developmental and contextual analysis. *Child Development, 61,* 1289–1309.

Dodge, K. A., Pettit, G. S., & Bates, J. E. (1994). Socialization mediators of the relationship between socioeconomic status and child conduct problems. *Child Development, 65,* 649–665.

Doherty, D. (Ed.). (1996). *Measurement in pediatric exercise science.* Champaign, Ill.: Human Kinetics Press.

Dorius, G. L., Heaton, T. B., & Steffen, P. (1993). Adolescent life events and their association with the onset of sexual intercourse. *Youth and Society, 25,* 3–23.

Downey, G., & Coyne, J. C. (1990). Children of depressed parents: An integrative review. *Psychological Bulletin, 108,* 50–76.

Dreyer, P. H. (1982). Sexuality during adolescence. In B. B. Wolman (Ed.), *Handbook of developmental psychology.* Englewood Cliffs, N.J.: Prentice-Hall.

Dubois, D. L., & Hirsch, B. J. (1990). School and neighborhood friendship patterns of blacks and whites in early adolescence. *Child Development, 61,* 524–536.

Dubois, D. L., & Hirsch, B. J. (1993). School/nonschool friendship patterns in early adolescence. *Journal of Early Adolescence, 13,* 102–122.

Dunn, J. (1985). *Sisters and brothers.* Cambridge, Mass.: Harvard University Press.

Dunn, J. (1987). The beginnings of moral understanding. In J. Kagan & S. Lamb (Eds.), *The emergence of morality in young children* (pp. 91–111). Chicago: University of Chicago Press.

Dunn, J., Slomkowsky, C., & Beardsall, L. (1994). Sibling relationships from the preschool period through middle childhood and early adolescence. *Developmental Psychology, 30,* 315–324.

Durbin, D. L., Darling, N., Steinberg, L., & Brown, B. B. (1993). Parenting style and peer group membership among European-American adolescents. *Journal of Research on Adolescence, 3,* 87–100.

Dusek, J. B. (1991). *Adolescent development and behavior* (2nd ed.). Englewood Cliffs, N.J.: Prentice-Hall.

Dweck, C. S., & Leggett, E. L. (1988). A social-cognitive approach to motivation and personality. *Psychological Review, 95,* 256–273.

Eagle, M. (1984). *Recent developments in psychoanalysis: A critical evaluation.* New York: McGraw-Hill.

Eakins, P. S. (1992) Birthcenters. In B. K. Rothman (Ed.), *The encyclopedia of childbearing.* New York: Henry Holt.

Eakins, P. S. (1989, September). Obstetric outcomes at the birth place in Menlo Park: The first seven years. *Birth, 16,* 123–129.

East, M. C., & Steele, P. R. M. (1987). Inhaling heroin during pregnancy: Effects on the baby. *British Medical Journal, 296,* 754.

Eccles, J., Lord, S., & Buchanan, C. (1996). School transitions in early adolescence: What are we doing to our young people? In J. Graber, J. Brooks-Gunn, & A. Petersen (Eds.), *Transitions through adolescence* (pp. 251–284). Mahwah, N.J.: Erlbaum.

Eccles, J. S., Midgley, C., Wigfeld, A., Buchanan, C. M., Reuman, D., Flanagan, C., & MacIver, D. (1993). Development during adolescence: The impact of stage-environment fit on young adolescents' experiences in schools and families. *American Psychologist, 48,* 90–101.

Eckerman, C. O. (1996). Early social-communicative development: Illustrative developmental analyses. In R. B. Cairns, G. H. Elder, Jr., et al. (Eds.), *Developmental science.* Cambridge studies in social and emotional development (pp. 135–167). New York: Cambridge University Press.

Eckerman, C. O., Davis, C. C., & Didow, S. M. (1989). Toddlers' emerging ways of achieving social coordinations with a peer. *Child Development, 60,* 440–453.

Edwards, C., Gandini, L., & Furman, G. (Eds.). (1993). *The hundred languages of children.* Norwood, N.J.: Ablex.

Egeland, B. (1988). The consequences of physical and emotional neglect on the development of young children. In A. Cowan (Ed.), *Child neglect.* Washington, D.C.: National Center on Child Abuse and Neglect.

Eisenberg, N., & Fabes, R. A. (1992). Emotion, self-regulation, and social competence. In M. Clark (Ed.), *Review of personality and social psychology. Vol. 14: Emotion and social behavior* (pp. 119–150). Newbury Park, Cal.: Sage.

Eisenberg, N., Fabes, R. A., Murphy, B., Maszk, P., Smith, M., & Karbon, M. (1995). The role of emotionality and regulation in children's social functioning: A longitudinal study. *Child Development, 66,* 1360–1384.

Eisenberg, N., Fabes, R. A., Nyman, M., Bernzweig, J., & Pinuelas, A. (1994). The relations of emotionality and regulation to children's anger-related reactions. *Child Development, 65,* 109–128.

Eisenberg, N., Fabes, R. A., Schaller, M., & Miller, P. (1989). Sympathy and personal distress: Development, gender differences, and interrelations of indices. In N. Eisenberg (Ed.), *Empathy and related emotional responses: New directions for child development* (pp. 107–126). San Francisco: Jossey-Bass.

Eisenberg, N., Fabes, R. A., Shepard, S. A., Murphy, B. C., Guthrie, I. K., Jones, S., Friedman, J., Poulin, R., & Maszk, P. (1997). Contemporaneous and longitudinal prediction of children's social functioning from regulation and emotionality. *Child Development, 68,* 642–664.

Eisenberg, N., Hertz-Lazarowitz, R., & Fuchs, I. (1990). Prosocial moral judgment in Israeli kibbutz and city children: A longitudinal study. *Merrill Palmer Quarterly, 36,* 273–285.

Eisenberg, N., & Mussen, P. H. (1989). *The roots of prosocial behavior in children.* Cambridge: Cambridge University Press.

Elbers, E., Wiegersma, S., Brand, N., & Vroon, P. (1991). Response alternation as an artifact in conservation research. *Journal of Genetic Psychology, 152,* 47–56.

Elder, G. H., Jr. (1998). The life course as developmental theory. *Child Development, 69,* 1–12.

Elkind, D. (1985). Egocentrism redux. *Developmental Review, 5,* 218–226.

Elkind, D. (1994a). *A sympathetic understanding of the child* (3rd ed.). Boston: Allyn & Bacon.

Elkind, D. (1994b). *Ties that stress: The new family imbalance.* Cambridge, Mass.: Harvard University Press.

Ellis, R. (1994). *The study of second language acquisition.* New York: Oxford University Press.

Ellis, S., Rogoff, B., & Cromer, C. (1981). Age segregation in children's social interactions. *Developmental Psychology, 17,* 399–407.

Emery, R. E. (1989). Family violence. *American Psychologist, 44,* 321–328.

Emes, C. E. (1997). Is Mr. Pac Man eating our children? A review of the effect of video games on children. *Canadian Journal of Psychiatry, 42,* 409–414.

Emmerich, W., & Sheppard, K. (1982). Development of sex-differentiated preferences during late childhood and adolescence. *Developmental Psychology, 18,* 407–417.

Emmorey, K., & Reilly, J. (Eds.). (1995). *Language, gesture, and space.* Hillsdale, N.J.: Erlbaum.

Endres, J., & Rockwell, R. (1993). *Food, nutrition, and the young child* (4th ed.). Columbus, Ohio: Merrill.

Engels, J. (1993). *Pocket guide to pediatric assessment* (2nd ed.). St. Louis: Mosby.

Erdley, C. A., Cain, K. M., Loomis, C. C., Dumas-Hines, F., & Dweck, C. S. (1997). Relations among children's social goals, implicit personality theories, and responses to social failure. *Developmental Psychology, 33,* 263–272.

Erel, O., Margolin, G., & John, R. S. (1998). Observed sibling interaction: Links with marital and mother-infant relationship. *Developmental Psychology. 34,* 268-298.

Erikson, E. (1963). *Childhood and society* (2nd ed.). New York: Norton.

Erikson, E. (1968). *Identity, youth and crisis.* New York: Norton.

Erikson, E. (1975). "Identity Crisis" in autobiographical perspective. In E. Erikson, *Life history and the historical moment.* New York: Norton.

Erikson, E. (1982). *The life cycle completed: A review.* New York: Norton.

Erikson, E. H. (1993). The problem of ego identity. In G H. Pollock et al. (Eds.), *Pivotal papers on identification* (pp. 265–303). Madison, Conn.: International Universities Press.

Eron, L. D. (1987). The development of aggressive behavior from the perspective of a developing behaviorism. *American Psychologist, 42,* 435–442.

Erting, C. (1998, March). *Language acquisition in deaf preschool children.* Paper presented at the Seventeenth Annual Forum in Ethnography in Education, Philadelphia.

Ervin-Tripp, S. (1989). Sisters and brothers. In P. Zukow (Ed.), *Sibling interaction across cultures: Theoretical and methodological issues* (pp. 184–196). New York: Springer-Verlag.

Eveleth, P., & Tanner, J. (1990). *Worldwide variation in human growth* (2nd ed.). New York: Cambridge University Press.

Faber, N. B. (1991). The process of pregnancy resolution among adolescent mothers. *Adolescence, 26,* 697–716.

Fabes, R. A., & Eisenberg, N. (1992). Young children's coping with interpersonal anger. *Child Development, 63,* 116–128.

Fabes, R. A., Eisenberg, N., McCormick, S. E., & Wilson, M. S. (1988). Preschoolers' attributions of the situational determinants of others' naturally occurring emotions. *Developmental Psychology, 24,* 376–385.

Fagot, B. I. (1982). Adults as socializing agents. In T. Field, A. Huston, H. Quay, L. Troll, & G. Finley (Eds.), *Review of human development.* New York: Wiley.

Fagot, B. I. (1994). Peer relations and the development of competence in boys and girls. In C. Leaper (Ed.), *Childhood gender segregation: Causes and consequences: New directions for child development* (pp. 53–66). San Francisco: Jossey-Bass.

Fagot, B. I., & Hagan, R. (1991). Observations of parent reactions to sex-stereotyped behaviors: Age and sex effects. *Child Development, 62,* 617–628.

Fagot, B. I., & Leinbach, M. D. (1989). The young child's gender schema: Environmental input, internal organization. *Child Development, 60,* 663–672.

Fagot, B. I., Leinbach, M. D., & O'Boyle, C. (1992). Gender labeling, gender stereotyping, and parenting behaviors. *Developmental Psychology, 28,* 225–230.

Fagot, B. (1997). Attachment, parenting, and peer interactions of toddler children. *Developmental Psychology, 33,* 489–499.

Fairburn, C., & Wilson, T. (Eds.). (1993). *Binge eating.* Guilford, Conn.: Guilford Press.

Falbo, T. (1992). Social norms and the one-child family: Clinical and policy implications. In F. Boer, J. Dunn, et al. (Eds.), *Children's sibling relationships* (pp. 71–82). Hillsdale, N.J.: Erlbaum.

Fangos, J. H. & Nickerson, B. G. (1991). Long-term effects of sibling death during adolescence. *Journal of Adolescent Research, 6,* 70–82.

Fantz, R. (1963). Pattern vision in newborn infants. *Science, 140,* 296–297.

Farmer, J. A. M., & Shin, Y. L. (1997). Social pretend play in Korean- and Anglo-American preschoolers. *Child Development, 68,* 544–556.

Farrangy, P., Steele, H., & Steele, M. (1991). Maternal representations of attachment during pregnancy predict the organization of infant-mother attachment at one year of age. *Child Development, 62,* 891–905.

Farver, J. M., & Branstetter, W. H. (1994). Preschoolers' prosocial responses to their peers' distress. *Developmental Psychology, 30,* 334–341.

Federal Bureau of Investigation. (1991, August). *Uniform crime reports for the United States.* Washington, D.C.: U.S. Department of Justice.

Feinbloom, R. I., & Forman, B. Y. (1987). *Pregnancy, birth and the early months: A complete guide.* Reading, Mass.: Addison-Wesley.

Feld, S., Ruhland, D., & Gold, M. (1979). Developmental changes in achievement motivation. *Merrill-Palmer Quarterly, 25,* 43–60.

Feldman, S. S., & Quatman, T. (1988). Factors influencing age expectations for adolescent autonomy: A study of early adolescents and parents. *Journal of Early Adolescence, 8,* 325–343.

Fenson, L., Dale, P., Reznick, J., Bates, E., Thal, D., & Pethick, S. (1994). Variability in early communicative development. *Monographs of the Society for Research on Child Development, 59*(5, Serial No. 242).

Ferber, R. (1986). *Solve your child's sleep problem.* New York: Simon & Schuster.

Ferber, R., & Kryger, M. (Eds.). (1995). *Principles and practice of sleep medicine in the child.* Philadelphia: Saunders.

Ferholt, J. B. (1991). Psychodynamic parent psychotherapy: Treating the parent-child relationship. In M. Lewis (Ed.), *Comprehensive textbook of child psychiatry.* New York: Saunders.

Ferketich, S. L., & Mercer, R. T. (1995). Paternal-infant attachment of experienced and inexperienced fathers during infancy. *Nursing Research, 44,* 31–37.

Fernald, A. (1989). Intonation and communicative intent in mothers' speech to infants. *Child Development, 60,* 1497–1510.

Field, J. (1987). Development of auditory-visual localization in infants. In B. McKenzie & R. Day (Eds.), *Perceptual development in early infancy* (pp. 175–198). Hillsdale, N.J.: Erlbaum.

Field, T., Miller, J., & Field, T. (1994). How well preschool children know their friends. *Early Child Development and Care, 100,* 101–109.

Finders, M. (1997). *Just girls: Hidden literacies and life in junior high.* New York: Teachers College Press.

Fine, G. A. (1982). Friends, impression management, and preadolescent behavior. In S. Asher & J. Gottman (Eds.), *The development of children's friendships.* New York: Cambridge University Press.

Finkelhor, D. (1995). The victimization of children: A developmental perspective. *American Journal of Orthopsychiatry, 65,* 177–193.

Fischer, C. B., & Lerner, R. M. (Eds.) (1994). *Applied developmental psychology.* New York: McGraw-Hill.

Fischer, J., & Eheart, B. (1991). Family day care: A theoretical basis for improving quality. *Early Childhood Research Quarterly, 6,* 549–563.

Fischer, K. (1980). A theory of cognitive development: The control and construction of hierarchies of skills. *Psychological Review, 87,* 477–531.

Fischer, K., & Pipp, S. L. (1984a). The process of stage transition: A neo-Piagetian view. In R. Sternberg (Ed.), *Mechanisms of cognitive development.* San Francisco: Freeman.

Fischer, K., & Pipp, S. L. (1984b). Processes of cognitive development: Optimal level and skill acquisition. In R. J. Sternberg

(Ed.), *Mechanisms of cognitive development* (pp. 45–90). New York: Freeman.

Fischer, K., Shaver, P., & Carnochan, P. (1990). How emotions develop and how they organize development. *Cognition and Emotion, 4,* 81–127.

Fish, M., Stifter, C. A., & Belsky, J. (1993). Early patterns of mother-infant dyadic integrations: Infant, mother, and family demographic antecedents. *Infant Behavior and Development, 16,* 1–18.

Fitzgerald, H., Lester, B., & Zuckerman, B. (1994). *Children of poverty: Research, health, and policy issues.* New York: Garland.

Fivush, R. (1989). Exploring sex differences in emotional content of mother-child conversations about the past. *Sex Roles, 20,* 675–691.

Flanagan, C. A. (1990). Change in family work status: Effects on parent-adolescent decision making. *Child Development, 61,* 163–177.

Flannery, D. J., Huff, C. R., & Manos, M. (1998). Youth gangs: A developmental perspective. In T. P. Gullotta, G. R. Adams, et al. (Eds.), *Delinquent violent youth: Theory and interventions. Advances in adolescent development: An annual book series* (Vol. 9, pp. 175–204). Thousand Oaks, Cal.: Sage.

Flavell, J., Green, F., & Flavell, E. (1986). Development of knowledge about the appearance-reality distinction. With commentaries by M. Watson & J. Campione. *Monographs of the Society for Research on Child Development, 51*(1, Serial No. 212).

Flavell, J., Green, F., and Falvell, E. (1995). *Young children's knowledge about thinking.* Chicago: Society for Research in Child Development.

Fletcher, A. C., Darling, N. E., Steinberg, L., & Dornbusch, S. M. (1995). The company they keep: Relation of adolescents' adjustment and behavior to their friends' perceptions of authoritative parenting in the social network. *Developmental Psychology, 31,* 300–310.

Forlizzi, L. (1993). Transferring literacy between the classroom and life: Metacognition, personal goals, and interests. In R. Lerner (Ed.), *Early adolescence: Perspectives on research, policy, and intervention* (pp. 201–220). Hillsdale, N.J.: Erlbaum.

Forrest-Pressley, D., Mackinnon, G., and Waller, T. (1985). *Metacognition, cognition and human performance.* Orlando, Fla.: Academic Press.

Foster, S. (1990). *The communicative competence of young children.* New York: Longman.

Fowler, B. (1989). Relationship of body-image perception and weight status to recent change in weight status of the adolescent female. *Adolescence, 24,* 557–568.

Fowler, J. (1996). *Faithful change: The personal and public challenges of postmodern life.* Nashville: Abingdon Press.

Fox, N. A., Kimmerly, N. L., & Schafer, W. D. (1991). Attachment to mother/attachment to father: A meta-analysis. *Child Development, 62,* 210–225.

Frank, M., & Zigler, E. F. (1996). Family leave: A developmental perspective. In E. F. Zigler, S. L. Kagan, et al. (Eds.), *Children, families and government: Preparing for the twenty-first century* (pp. 117–131). New York: Cambridge University Press.

Franz, C. E., McClelland, D. C., & Weinberger, J. (1991). Childhood antecedents of conventional social accomplishment in midlife adults: A 36-year prospective study. *Journal of Personality and Social Psychology, 60,* 586–595.

Franz, W., & Reardon, D. (1992). Differential impact of abortion on adolescents and adults. *Adolescence, 27,* 161–172.

Frazer, A. M., Brockert, J. E., & Ward, R. H. (1995). Association of young maternal age with adverse reproductive outcomes. *New England Journal of Medicine, 332,* 113.

French, D. C. (1984). Children's knowledge of the social functions of younger, older, and same-aged peers. *Child Development, 55,* 1429–1433.

Freud, S. (1983). *A general introduction to psychoanalysis* (rev. ed.). New York: Washington Square Press.

Freund, H., Sabel, B., & Witte, O. (Eds.). (1997). *Brain plasticity.* Philadelphia: Lippincott-Raven.

Frieze, I., Francis, W., & Hanusa, B. (1981). Defining success in classroom settings. In J. Levine & M. Wang (Eds.), *Teacher and student perceptions.* Hillsdale, N.J.: Erlbaum.

Froberg, K., & Lammert, O. (1996). Development of muscle strength during childhood. In O. Bar-Or, (Ed.), *The child and adolescent athlete* (pp. 25–41). London: Blackwell Science.

Frost, J. J., & Forrest, J. D. (1995). Understanding the impact of effective teenage pregnancy prevention programs. *Family Planning Perspectives, 27,* 195–199.

Fuligni, A. J. & Eccles, J. S. (1993). Perceived parent-child relationships and early adolescent's orientation toward peers. *Developmental Psychology, 29,* 622–632.

Furman, W. (1982). Children's friendships. In T. Field (Ed.), *Review of human development.* New York: Wiley.

Furman, W. (1989). The development of children's social networks. In D. Belle (Ed.), *Children's social networks and social supports.* New York: Wiley.

Furman, W., & Bierman, K. L. (1983). Developmental changes in young children's conceptions of friendship. *Child Development, 54,* 549–556.

Furman, W., & Buhrmester, D. (1992). Age and sex differences in perceptions of networks of personal friendships. *Child Development, 63,* 103–115.

Furstenberg, F. F., Brooks-Gunn, J., & Chase-Lansdale, L. (1989). Teenaged pregnancy and childbearing. *American Psychologist, 44,* 313–320.

Gabbard, C. (1989). Foot lateralization and psychomotor control in four-year-olds. *Perceptual and Motor Skills, 68,* 712–715.

Gaesser, G. (1996). *Big fat lies.* New York: Fawcett-Columbine Books.

Galambos, N. L., & Maggs, J. L. (1991). Out-of-school care of young adolescents and self-reported behavior. *Developmental Psychology, 27,* 644–655.

Galassi, J., Gulledge, S., & Cox, N. (1997). Middle school advisories: Retrospect and prospect. *Review of Educational Research, 67*(3), 301–338.

Galinsky, E. (1987). *The six stages of parenthood.* Reading, Mass.: Addison-Wesley.

Gallagher, J. (1993). Comments on McDaniel's "Education of the Gifted and the Excellence-Equity Debate." In J. Maker (Ed.), *Programs for the gifted in regular classrooms* (pp. 19–22). Austin, Tex.: Pro-Ed Publishers.

Gallagher, J., & Gallagher, S. (1994). *Teaching the giftedchild* (4th ed.) Boston: Allyn & Bacon.

Gallagher, M. (1996). *Turning points in middle schools.* Thousand Oaks, Cal.: Corwin Press.

Gallahue, D. (1993). *Developmental physical education for today's children, 2nd edition.* Madison, Wis: Brown & Benchmark.

Gallaway, C., & Richards, B. (1994). *Input and interaction in language acquisition.* New York: Cambridge University Press.

Ganong, L. H., & Coleman, M. (1987). Effects of parental remarriage on children: An updated comparison of theories, methods, and findings from clinical and empirical research. In K. Pasley & M. Ihinger-Tallman (Eds.), *Remarriage and stepparenting: Current research and theory* (pp. 94–140). New York: Guilford Press.

Garbarino, J. (1982). Sociocultural risk: Dangers to competence. In C. Kopp & J. Krakow (Eds.), *Child development in a social context.* Reading, Mass.: Addison-Wesley.

Garbarino, J. (1992a). *Children and families in the social environment* (2nd ed.). New York: Aldine de Gruyter.

Garbarino, J. (1992b). *Children in danger.* New York: Jossey-Bass.

Garbarino, J. (1993). Reinventing fatherhood. *Families in Society, 74,* 52–54.

Garbarino, J. & Kostelny, K. (1996). The effects of political violence on Palestinian children's behavior problems: A risk accumulation model. *Child Development, 67,* 33–45.

Gardiner, H. W., Mutter, J. D., & Kosmitzki, C. (1998). *Lives across cultures: Cross-cultural human development.* Boston: Allyn & Bacon.

Gardner, H. (1993a). *Frames of mind: The theory of multiple intelligences* (2nd rev. ed.). New York: Basic Books.

Gardner, H. (1993b). *Multiple intelligences: Theory in practice.* New York: Basic Books.

Gardner, H. (1997). *Extraordinary minds: Portraits of exceptional individuals and an examination of our extraordinariness.* New York: Basic Books.

Garland, A. F., & Zigler, E. (1993). Adolescent suicide prevention: Current research and social policy. *American Psychologist, 48,* 169–182.

Garner, P. W., Jones, D. C., & Palmer, D. J. (1994). Social cognitive correlates of preschool children's sibling caregiving behavior. *Developmental Psychology, 30,* 906–911.

Garver, K. L., & Garver, B. (1994). The human genome project and eugenic concerns. *American Journal of Human Genetics, 54,* 148–158.

Ge, X., Best, K. M., Conger, R. D., & Simons, R. L. (1996). Parenting behaviors and the occurrence and co-occurrence of adolescent depressive symptoms and conduct problems. *Developmental Psychology, 32,* 717–731.

Gee, J., & Green, J. (1998). Discourse analysis, learning, and social practice: A methodological study. In D. Pearson & A. Iran-Nejad (Eds.), *Review of research in education* (Vol. 23, pp. 119–170). Washington, D.C.: American Educational Research Association.

Geiger, B. (1996). *Fathers as primary caregivers.* Westport, Conn.: Greenwood Press/Greenwood Publishing Group.

Gelles, R. (1998, August). Violence and pregnancy: Are pregnant women at greater risk of abuse? *Journal of Marriage and the Family, 50,* 841–847.

George, C., Kaplan, N., & Main, M. (1985). *The Adult Attachment Interview.* Unpublished manuscript, University of California at Berkeley, Department of Psychology.

George, T. P., & Hartman, D. P. (1996). Friendship networks of unpopular, average, and popular children. *Child Development, 67,* 2310–2316.

Gerbner, G., Gross, L., Signorielli, N., & Morgan, M. (1986). *Television's world: Violence profile No. 14–15.* University of Pennsylvania, Annenberg School of Communications, Philadelphia.

Gesell, A. (1926). *The mental growth of the preschool child* (2nd ed.). New York: Macmillan.

Gesell, A., & Thompson, H. (1929). Learning and growth in identical infant twins. *Genetic Psychology Monographs, 6,* 1–125.

Gestwicki, C. (1995). *Deveiopmentally appropriate practice: Curriculum and development in the early years.* Albany, N.Y.: Delmar.

Gholson, B. (1994). Cognitive processes explain learning across the life span: Infants and toddlers are people too. *Monographs of the Society for Research in Child Development, 59*(4, Serial No. 241), 76–89.

Gibson, E., & Walk, R. (1960). The visual cliff. *Scientific American, 202,* 64–71.

Gilbert, S. (1998, May 19). Benefits of assistant for childbirth go far beyond the birthing room. *New York Times,* p. F–7.

Gilligan, C. (1982). *In a different voice: Psychological theory and women's development.* Cambridge, Mass.: Harvard University Press.

Gilligan, C. (1987). Adolescent development reconsidered. In C. Irwin (Ed.), *Adolescent social behavior and health.* San Francisco: Jossey-Bass.

Gilligan, C., & Wiggins, G. (1987). The origins of morality in early childhood relationships. In J. Kagan & S. Lamb (Eds.), *The emergence of morality in young children* (pp. 277–305). Chicago: University of Chicago Press.

Ginsburg, G. S., & Bronstein, P. (1993). Family factors related to children's intrinsic/extrinsic motivational orientation in academic performance. *Child Development, 64,* 1461–1474.

Giordano, P. C., Cernkovich, S. A., & Demaris, A. (1993). The family and peer relations of black adolescents. *Journal of Marriage and the Family, 55,* 277–288.

Glasgow, K. L., Dornbusch, S. M., Troyer, L., Steinberg, L., & Ritter, P. L. (1997). Parenting styles, adolescents' attributions, and educational outcomes in nine heterogeneous high schools. *Child Development, 68,* 507–529.

Glass, J. C. (1991). Death, loss, and grief among middle school children: Implications for the school counselor. *Elementary School Guidance and Counseling, 26,* 139–148.

Glauser, B. (1997). Street children: Deconstructing a construct. In A. James & A. Prout (Eds.), *Constructing and reconstructing childhood* (2nd ed., pp. 145–164). London: Falmer Press.

Glick, P. C., & Lin, S. (1987). Remarriage after divorce: Recent changes and demographic variations. *Sociological Perspectives, 30,* 162–179.

Goldman, L. (1998). *Children's play: Mime, mimesis, and make-believe.* New York: Oxford.

Goldstein, A. P., & Soriano, F. I. (1994). Delinquent gangs. In L. Eron & J. Gentry (Eds.), *Violence and youth: Psychology's response: Vol. II. Papers of the American Psychological Association on Violence and Youth.* Washington, DC: American Psychological Association.

Goldstein, S., Field, T., & Healy, B. T. (1989). Concordance of play behavior and physiology in preschool friends. *Journal of Applied Developmental Psychology, 10,* 3337–3351.

Golombok, S., Cook, R., Bish, A., & Clare, M. (1995). Families created by the new reproductive technologies: Quality of parenting and social and emotional development of the children. *Child Development, 66,* 285–298.

Golombok, S., & Fivush, R. (1994). *Gender development.* New York: Cambridge University Press.

Golombok, S., & Tasker, F. (1996). Do parents influence the sexual orientation of their children? Findings from a longitudinal study of lesbian females. *Developmental Psychology. 32,* 3–11.

Goodnow, J. J. (1976). The nature of intelligent behavior: Questions raised by cross-cultural studies. In L. B. Resnick (Ed.), *The nature of intelligence.* Hillsdale, N.J. Erlbaum.

Goodnow, J. J. (1995). From household practices to parents' ideas about work and interpersonal relationships. In S. Harkness & C. Super (Eds.), *Parents' cultural belief systems: Their origins, expressions, and consequences.* New York: Guildford Press.

Goodnow, J. J., Miller, P. M., & Kessel, F. (Eds.). (1995). Cultural practices as contexts for development. *New directions for child development:* No. 67. San Francisco: Jossey-Bass.

Goosens, F. A., & van IJzendoorn, M. H. (1990). Quality of infants' attachments to professional caregivers: Relation to infant-parent attachment and day-care characteristics. *Child Development, 61,* 832–837.

Gopaul-McNicol, S., & Thomas-Presswood, T. (1998). *Working with linguistically and culturally different children.* Boston: Allyn and Bacon.

Gordon, E. W. (1995). Putting them in their place. *Readings: A Journal of Reviews and Commentary in Mental Health, 10,* 8–14.

Gordon, S., Benner, P., & Noddings, N. (1996). *Caregiving: Readings in knowledge, practice, ethics, and politics.* Philadelphia: University of Pennsylvania Press.

Gordon, T. H., & Conger, R. D. (1997). Marital conflict and adolescent distress: The role of adolescent awareness. *Child Development, 68,* 333–350.

Gorman, C. (1993, June 13). Thalidomide's return. *Time,* June 13, p. 67.

Gortmaker, S. L., Must, A., Perrin, J. M., Sobol, A. M., & Dietz, W. H. (1993). Social and economic consequences of overweight in adolescence and young adulthood. *New England Journal of Medicine, 329,* 1008–1012.

Gottesman, I. I. (1963). Heritability of personality: A demonstration. *Psychological Monographs, 77* (Whole No. 572).

Gottfried, A. E., Bathurst, K., & Gottfried, A. W. (1994). Role of maternal and dual-earner employment status in children's development: A longitudinal study from infancy through early adolescence. In A. E. Gottfried, A. W. Gottfried, et al. (Eds.), *Redefining families: Implications for children's development* (pp. 55–97). New York: Plenum Press.

Gottman, J., & Parkhurst, J. (1980). A developmental theory of friendship and acquaintanceship. In A. Collins (Ed.), *Minnesota symposia on child psychology: Vol. 13.* Hillsdale, N.J.: Erlbaum.

Gould, D., & Eklund, R. (1996). Emotional stress and anxiety in the child and adolescent athlete. In O. Bar-Or (Ed.), *The child and adolescent athlete* (pp. 383–398). Oxford, U.K.: Blackwells.

Graber, J., Brooks-Gunn, J., & Petersen, A. (1996). *Transitions through adolescence: Interpersonal domains and context.* Mahwah, N.J.: Erlbaum.

Gralinski, J. H., & Kopp, C. (1993). Everyday rules for behavior: Mothers' requests to young children. *Developmental Psychology, 29,* 573–584.

Granrud, C. (Ed.). (1993). *Visual perception and cognition in infancy.* Englewood Cliffs, N.J.: Erlbaum.

Grant, J. (1986). *The state of the world's children.* Oxford, U.K.: Oxford University Press.

Green, J. A., Gustafson, G. E., & McGhie, A. C. (1998). Changes in infants' cries as a function of time in a cry bout. *Child Development, 69,* 271–279.

Green, M. (1994). *Sigh of relief: A first-aid handbook for childhood emergencies.* New York: Bantam Books.

Green, R. (1987). *The "sissy boy" syndrome and the development of homosexuality.* New Haven, Conn.: Yale University Press.

Greenberg, B. S. (1986). Minorities and the mass media. In J. Bryant & D. Zillman (Eds.), *Perspectives on mass media effects.* Hillsdale, N.J.: Erlbaum.

Greenberger, E., O'Neill, R., & Nagel, S. K. (1994). Linking workplace and homeplace: Relations between the nature of adults' work and their parenting behaviors. *Developmental Psychology, 30,* 990–1002.

Greenfield, P. (1994). Independence and interdependence as developmental scripts: Implications for theory, research, and practice. In P. Greenfield & R. Cocking (Eds.), *Cross-cultural roots of minority child development* (pp. 1–40). Hillsdale, N.J.: Erlbaum.

Greenfield, P. (1995, March 30). *Independence and interdependence in school conferences between Anglo teachers and Hispanic parents.* Paper presented at the biennial meeting of the Society for Research on Child Development, Indianapolis.

Gregg, M. and Leinhardt, C. (1995). Mapping out geography: An example of epistemology and education. *Review of Educational Research, 64* (2), 311–361.

Gregg, R. (1993). "Choice" as a double-edged sword: Information guilt and mother-blaming in a high-tech age. *Women and Health, 20,* 53–73.

Greil, A. L. (1993a). Infertility: Overview. In B. K. Rothman (Ed.), *The encyclopedia of childbearing.* New York: Henry Holt .

Greil, A. L. (1993b). Infertility: Cross-cultural and historical aspects. In B. K. Rothman (Ed.), *The encyclopedia of childbearing.* New York: Henry Holt.

Grolinck, W. S., Bridges, L. J., & Connell, J. P. (1996). Emotional regulation in two-year-olds: Strategies and emotional expression in four contexts. *Child Development, 67,* 928–941.

Gross, R., Spiker, D., & Haynes, C. (1997). *Helping low-birth-weight, premature babies.* Stanford, Cal.: Stanford University Press.

Grossmann, K., Grossmann, K., Spangler, G., Suess, G., & Unzner, L. (1985). Maternal sensitivity and newborns' orientation responses as related to quality of attachment in northern Germany. In I. Bretherton & E. Waters (Eds.), Growing points of attachment theory and research. *Monographs of the Society for Research on Child Development, 50,* 233–256.

Grossmann, K. E., & Grossmann, K. (1990). The wider concept of attachment in cross-cultural research. *Human Development, 33,* 31–47.

Grotpeter, J. K., & Crick, N. R. (1996). Relational aggression, overt aggression, and friendship. *Child Development, 67,* 2328–2338.

Grusec, J. E. (1991). Socializing concern for others in the home. *Developmental Psychology, 27,* 338–342.

Grusec, J. E., Goodnow, J. J., & Cohen, L. (1996). Household work and the development of concern for others. *Developmental Psychology, 32,* 999–1007.

Grusec, J. E., & Lytton, H. (1988). *Social development.* New York: Springer-Verlag.

Grusec, J. E., Rudy, D., & Martini, T. (1997). Parenting cognition and child outcomes: An overview of implications for children's internalization of values. In J. E. Grusec, L. Kuczynski, et al. (Eds.), *Parenting and the internalization of values: A handbook of contemporary theory* (pp. 259–282). New York: Wiley.

Guggino, J. M., & Ponzetti, J. J. (1997). Gender differences in affective reactions to first coitus. *Journal of Adolescence, 20,* 189–200.

Guntheroth, W. (1995). *Crib death: The sudden infant death syndrome.* Armonk, NY: Futura Publishers.

Gunner, M. R., Larson, M. C., Hertsgaard, L., Harris, M. L., & Bodersen, L. (1992). The stressfulness of separation among nine-month-old infants: Effects of social variables and infant temperament. *Child Development, 63,* 290–303.

Gunnar, M. R., & Maratsos, M. (Eds.). (1992). *Modularity and constraints in language and cognition: The Minnesota symposia on child psychology: Vol. 25.* Hillsdale, N.J.: Erlbaum.

Gunnar, M. R., Proter, F. L., Wolf, C. M., Rigatuso, J., & Larson, M. C. (1995). Neonatal stress reactivity: Predictions of later emotional temperament. *Child Development, 66,* 1–13.

Gustafson, G. E., & Harris, K. L. (1990). Women's responses to young infants' cries. *Developmental Psychology, 26,* 144–152.

Guttmacher, A., & Kaiser, I. (1984). *Pregnancy, birth, and family planning.* New York: Signet.

Guy, G. (Ed.). (1996). *Variation and change in language and society.* Philadelphia: J. Benjamins.

Hagerman, R. J. (1996). Biomedical advances in developmental psychology: The case of fragile–x syndrome. *Developmental Psychology, 32,* 416–424.

Haith, M., Wass, T., & Adler, S. (1997). Infant visual expectations: Advances and issues. *Monographs of the Society for Research in Child Development, 62*(2, Serial No. 250).

Hajcak, F., & Garwood, P. (1989). Quick-fix sex: Pseudosexuality in adolescents. *Adolescence, 23,* 75–76.

Hall, C. C. I. (1995). Asian eyes: Body image and eating disorders of Asian and Asian American women. *Eating Disorders, 3,* 8–19.

Hall, C. S., & Lindzey, G. (1978). *Theories of personality* (3rd ed.) New York: Wiley.

Hall, G. C. N., & Barongan, C. (1997). Prevention of sexual aggression. Sociocultural risk and protective factors. *American Psychologist, 52,* 5–14.

Halliday, J. L., Watson, L. F., Lumley, J., Danks, D. M., & Sheffield, L. S. (1995). New estimates of Down syndrome risks of chorionic villus sampling, amniocentesis, and live birth in women of advanced maternal age from a uniquely defined population. *Prenatal Diagnosis, 15,* 455–465.

Hallinan, M., & Teixeira, R. (1987). The stability of students' interracial friendships. *American Sociological Review, 52,* 653–664.

Hallinan, M. T., & Williams, R. A. (1989). Interracial friendship choices in secondary schools. *American Sociological Review, 54,* 67–78.

Hallowell, E., & Ratey, J. (1994). *Driven to distraction.* New York: Pantheon Books.

Hamburg, D. (1997). Towards a strategy for healthy adolescent development. *American Journal of Psychiatry, 154* (6), 7–12.

Hamburg, D. A. (1994). *Today's children: Creating a future for a generation of crisis.* New York: Times Books.

Hamill, P., Drizd, T., Johnson, C., Reed, R., Roche, A., & Moore, W. (1979). Physical growth: National Center for Health Statistics percentiles. *Clinical Nutrition, 32,* 607–629.

Hamilton, N. G. (1989). *Self and others: Object relations in theory and practice.* Northvale, N.J.: Jason Aronson.

Hamilton, P. M. (1984). *Basic maternity nursing* (5th ed.). St. Louis: Mosby.

Hanshaw, J. B., Dudgeon, J. A., & Marshall, W. C. (1985). *Viral diseases of the fetus and newborn* (2nd ed.). Philadelphia: Saunders.

Hardy, J. B. (1991). Pregnancy and its outcome. In W. R. Hendee (Ed.), *The health of adolescents: Understanding and facilitating biological, behavioral, and social development* (pp. 250–281). San Francisco: Jossey-Bass.

Hardy, J. B., & Zabin, L. S. (1991). *Adolescent pregnancy in an urban environment: Issues, programs, and evaluaton.* Baltimore: Urban & Schwarzenberg.

Hare-Mustin, R. T., & Marecek, J. (1988). The meaning of difference: Gender theory, postmodernism, and psychology. *American Psychologist, 43,* 455–464.

Hareven, T. (1986). Historical changes in the family and the life course: Implications for child development. In A. Smuts & H. Hagen (Eds.), *History and research in child development. Monographs of the Society for Research on Child Development, 50* (4–5, Serial No. 211).

Harkness, S., & Keefer, C. (1995, February). *Cultural influences on sleep patterns in infancy and early childhood.* Paper presented at the annual meeting of the American Association for the Advancement of Science, Atlanta.

Harkness, S., & Super, C. (1992). Parental ethnotheories in action. In I. Sigel, A. McGillicuddy-DeLisi, & J. Goodnow (Eds.), *Parent belief systems: The psychological consequences for children* (2nd ed., pp. 373–392). Hillsdale, N.J.: Erlbaum.

Harkness, S., Super, C., & Keefer, C. (1992). Learning to be an American parent: How cultural models gain directive force. In R. D'Andrade & C. Strauss (Eds.), *Human motives and cultural models* (pp. 163–178). New York: Cambridge University Press.

Harkness, S., Super, C., Keefer, C., Raghavan, C., & Kipp, E. (1995a). Ask the doctor: The negotiation of cultural models in American parent-patient discourse. In S. Harkness & C. Super (Eds.), *Parents' cultural belief systems: Their origins, expressions, and consequences.* New York: Guilford Press.

Harkness, S., Super, C., Keefer, C., van Tijen, N., & van der Vlugt, E. (1995b, February). *Cultural influences on sleep patterns in infancy and early childhood.* Paper presented at the annual meeting of the American Association for the Advancement of Science, Atlanta.

Harlow, H. F., & Zimmermann, R. R. (1996). Affectional responses in the infant monkey. In L. D. Houck, L. C. Drickamer,

et al. (Eds.), *Foundations of animal behavior: Classic papers with commentaries* (p. 376–387), Chicago: University of Chicago Press.

Harold, G. T., & Conger, R. D. (1997). Marital conflict and adolescent distress: The role of adolescent awareness. *Child Development, 68,* 333–350.

Harper, L. (1988). *The nurture of human behavior.* Norwood, N.J.: Ablex.

Harris, P. (1983). Infant cognition. In Paul Mussen (Ed.), *Handbook of child psychology: Vol. 4.* New York: Wiley.

Harris, P., & Kavanaugh, R. (1993). *Young children's understanding of pretense.* Chicago: University of Chicago Press.

Harrison, A. O., Wilson, M. N., Pine, C. J., Chan, S. Q., & Buriel, R. (1990). Family ecologies of ethnic minority children. *Child Development, 61,* 347–362.

Harrison, A. O., Wilson, M. N., Pine, C. J., Chan, S. Q., & Buriel, R. (1995). Family ecologies of ethnic minority children. In N. R. Goldberger, J. B. Veroff, et al. (Eds.), *The culture and psychology reader* (pp. 292–320). New York: New York University Press.

Hart, B. (1991). Input frequency and children's first words. *First Language, 11,* 289–300.

Hart, C. H., DeWolf, D. M., Wozniak, P., & Burts, D. C. (1992). Maternal and paternal disciplinary styles: Relations with preschoolers' playground behavioral orientations and peer status. *Child Development, 63,* 879–892.

Hart, C. H., Ladd, G. W., & Burleson, B. R. (1990). Children's expectations of the outcomes of social strategies: Relations with socioeconomic status and maternal disciplinary styles. *Child Development, 61,* 127–137.

Hart, C. H., Nelson, D. A., Robinson, C. C., Olsen, S. F., & McNeilly-Chocque, M. K. (1998). Overt and relational aggression in Russian nursery-school-age children: Parenting style and marital linkages. *Developmental Psychology, 34,* 687–697.

Harter, S. (1977). A cognitive-developmental approach to children's expression of conflicting feelings and a technique to facilitate such expression in play therapy. *Journal of Consulting and Clinical Psychology, 45,* 417–432.

Harter, S. (1983). Developmental perspectives on self-system. In E. M. Hetherington (Ed.), *Handbook of child psychology: Vol. 4. Socialization, personality, and social development* (4th ed., pp. 275–285). New York: Wiley.

Harter, S. (1990a). Self and identity development. In S. Feldman & G. Elliot (Eds.), *At the threshold: The developing adolescent.* Cambridge, Mass.: Harvard University Press.

Harter, S. (1990b). Processes underlying adolescent self-concept formation. In R. Montemayor, G. R. Adams, & T. P. Gullotta (Eds.), *From childhood to adolescence: A transitional period?* Newbury Park, Cal.: Sage.

Harter, S., & Barnes, R. (1983). *Children's understanding of parental emotions: A developmental study.* Unpublished paper, 1981. Cited in S. Harter, *Developmental perspectives on the self-system.* In P. Mussen (Ed.), *Handbook of child psychology: Vol. 4.* New York: Wiley.

Harter, S., Marold, D. B., Whitesell, N. R., & Cobbs, G. (1996). A model of the effects of perceived parent and peer support on adolescent false self-behavior. *Child Development, 67,* 360–374.

Harter, S., & Monsour, A. (1992). Developmental analysis of conflict caused by opposing attributes in the adolescent self-portrait. *Developmental Psychology, 28,* 251–260.

Hartup, W. (1983). Peer relations. In P. Mussen (Ed.), *Handbook of child psychology: Vol. 4.* New York: Wiley.

Hartup, W. (1989). Social relationships and their developmental significance. *American Psychologist, 44,* 120–126.

Hartup, W. W. (1996). The company they keep: Friendships and their developmental significance. *Child Development, 67,* 1–13.

Hartup, W. W., & Stevens, N. (1997). Friendships and adaptation in the life course. *Psychological Bulletin, 121,* 335–370.

Hartup, W. W. , & Van Lieghart, C. F. M. (1995). Personality development in social context. *Annual Review of Psychology, 46,* 655–687.

Harwood, R. L. (1992). The influence of culturally derived values on Anglo and Puerto Rican mothers' perceptions of attachment behavior. *Child Development, 63,* 822–839.

Haste, H., & Torney-Purta, J. (Eds.). (1992). *The development of political understanding: A new perspective.* San Francisco: Jossey-Bass.

Hastings, P. D., & Grusec, J. E. (1998). Parenting goals as organizers of responses to parent-child disagreement. *Developmental Psychology, 34,* 465–479.

Hayes, C. (1987). Risking the future: *Adolescent sexuality, pregnancy and childbearing.* Washington, D.C.: National Academy Press.

Hayne, H., Rovee-Collier, C., & Borza, M. (1991). Infant memory for place information. *Memory and Cognition, 19,* 378–386.

Heath, S. (1993). *Identity and inner-city youth: Beyond ethnicity and gender.* New York: Teachers' College Press.

Heath, S., Mangolia, L., Schlecter, S., & Hull, G. (Eds.). (1991). *Children of promise: Literate activity in linguistically and culturally diverse classrooms.* Washington, D.C.: National Education Association.

Helfer, M. E., Kempe, R. S., & Krugman, R. D. (Eds.). (1997). *The battered child.* Chicago: University of Chicago Press.

Heller, D. (1994). *Talking to your child about God.* New York: Berkley Publishers.

Hellige, J. (1993). *Hemispheric asymmetry: What's right and what's left.* Cambridge, Mass.: Harvard University Press.

Helton, A., McFarlane, J., & Anderson, E. T. (1987). Battered and pregnant: A prevalence study. *American Journal of Public Health, 77,* 1337–1339.

Hendler, M., & Weisberg, P. (1992). Conservation acquisition, maintenance, and generalization by mentally retarded children using equality-rule training. *Journal of Experimental Child Psychology, 53,* 258–276.

Hendrick, H. (1997). Constructions and reconstructions of British childhood: An interpretative survey, 1800 to the present. In A. James & A. Prout (Eds.), *Constructing and reconstructing childhood* (2nd ed., pp. 34–62). London: Falmer.

Henry, B., Caspi, A., Moffitt, T. E., & Silva, P. A. (1996). Temperamental and familial predictors of violent and nonviolent criminal convictions: Age 3 to age 18. *Developmental Psychology, 32,* 614–623.

Hergenrather, J. R., & Rabinowitz, M. (1991). Age-related differences in the organization of children's knowledge of illness. *Developmental Psychology, 27,* 952–959.

Hernandez, D. J. (1997). Child development and the social demography of childhood. *Child Development, 68,* 149–169.

Hernandez, H. (1997). *Teaching in multilingual classrooms.* Upper Saddle River, N.J.: Merrill.

Hernstein, R. J., & Murray, C. (1994). *The Bell Curve: Intelligence and Class Structure in the American Life.* New York: The Free Press.

Herrenkohl, R. C., Egolf, B. P., & Herrenkohl, E. C. (1997). Preschool antecedents of adolescent assaultive behavior. A longitudinal study. *American Journal of Orthopsychiatry, 67,* 422–432.

Hershberger, S. L., & D'Augelli, A. R. (1995). The impact of victimization on the mental health and suicidality of lesbian, gay, and bisexual youths. *Developmental Psychology, 31,* 65–74.

Herzberger, S. (1996). *Violence within the family: Social psychological perspectives.* Boston: Westview Press.

Hesse-Biber, S. (1996). *Am I thin enough yet? The cult of thinness and commercialization of identity.* New York: Oxford University Press.

Hetherington, E. M. (1988). Family relations six years after divorce. In K. Pasley & M. Ihinger-Tallman (Eds.), *Remarriage and stepparenting: Current research and theory* (pp. 185–205). New York: Guilford Press.

Hetherington, E. M. (1991). The role of individual differences and family relationships in children's coping with divorce and remarriage. In P. A. Cowan & M. Hetherington (Eds.), *Family transitions* (pp. 165–194). Hillsdale, N.J.: Erlbaum.

Hetherington, E. M. (1995, March 30). *The changing American family and the well-being of children.* Paper presented at the biennial meeting of the Society for Research on Child Development, Indianapolis.

Hetherington, E. M., Bridges, M., & Insabella, G. M. (1998). What matters? What does not? Five perspectives on the association between marital transitions and children's adjustment. *American Psychologist, 53,* 167–184.

Hetherington, E. M., Cox, M., & Cox, R. (1979). Play and social interaction in children following divorce. *Journal of Social Issues, 35,* 26–49.

Hetherington, E. M., Stanley-Hagen, M., & Anderson, E. (1989). Marital transitions: A child's perspective. *American Psychologist, 44,* 303–312.

Hickling, A., & Gelman, S. (1995). How does your garden grow? Early conceptualization of seeds and their place in the plant growth cycle. *Child Development, 66,* 856–876.

Hill, B., & Ruptic, C. (1994). *Practical aspects of authentic assessment.* Norwood, Mass.: Christopher-Gordon.

Hiller, L., Harrison, L., & Warr, D. (1998). "When you carry condoms all boys think you want it": Negotiating competing discourses about sex. *Journal of Adolescence, 21,* 15–29.

Hinde, R. A. (1989). Ethological relationships and approaches. In R. Vasta (Ed.), *Annals of Child Development: Six theories of child development—Revised formulations and current issues.* Greenwich, Conn.: JAI Press.

Hinde, R. A., Titmus, G., Easton, D., & Tamplin, A. (1985). Incidence of "friendship" and behavior to strong associates versus non-associates in preschoolers. *Child Development, 56,* 234–245.

Ho, D. (1994). Cognitive socialization in confucian heritage cultures. In P. Greenfield & R. Cocking (Eds.), *Cross-cultural roots of minority child development* (pp. 285–314). Hillsdale, N.J.: Erlbaum.

Hoare, C. H. (1994). Psychosocial identity development in United States society: Its role in fostering exclusion of cultural others. In E. P. Salett & D. R. Koslow (Eds.), *Race, ethnicity and self: Identity in multicultural perspective.* Washington, D.C.: National Multicultural Institute, 1994.

Hobart, C. (1987). Parent-child relations in remarried families. *Journal of Family Issues, 8,* 259–277.

Hoff-Ginsberg, E. (1997). *Language development.* Pacific Grove, Cal.: Brooks/Cole.

Hoff-Ginsberg, E., & Krueger, W. (1991). Older siblings as conversational partners. *Merrill-Palmer Quarterly, 37,* 465–482.

Hoffman, L. W. (1983). Increased fathering: Effects on the mother. In M. Lamb & A. Sagi (Eds.), *Fatherhood and family policy.* Hillsdale, N.J.: Erlbaum.

Hoffman, L. W. (1984a). Maternal employment and the young child. In M. Perlmutter (Ed.), *The Minnesota symposium on child psychology: Vol. 17.* Hillsdale, N.J.: Erlbaum.

Hoffman, L. W. (1984b). Work, family, and the socialization of the child. In R. Parke (Ed.), *Review of child development research: Vol. 7.* Chicago: University of Chicago Press.

Hoffman, L. W. (1988). Cross-cultural differences in childrearing goals. In R. A. LeVine, P. M. Miller, & M. M. West (Eds.), *Parental behavior in diverse societies: New directions for child development.* San Francisco: Jossey-Bass.

Hoffman, L. W. (1989). Effects of maternal employment in the two-parent family. *American Psychologist, 44,* 283–292.

Hoffman, L. W., & Hoffman, M. (1973). The value of children to parents. In J. T. Fawcett (Ed.), *Psychological perspectives on population.* New York: Basic Books.

Hoffnung, A. (1992). *Shoeshine boys of Cuenca, Ecuador.* Unpublished paper, Reed College, Portland.

Hoffnung, M. (1992). *What is a mother to do? Conversations on work and family.* Pasadina, Cal.: Trilogy Books.

Holmbeck, G., & O'Donnell, K. (1991). Discrepancies between perceptions of decision making and behavioral autonomy. In R. Paikoff (Ed.), *Shared views of the family during adolescence* (pp. 51–70). San Francisco: Jossey-Bass.

Holmes, L. J. (1993). Midwives, southern black. In B. K. Rothman (Ed.), *The encyclopedia of childbearing.* New York: Henry Holt.

Horgan, J. (1993, June). Eugenics revisited. *Scientific American,* 120–128.

Houck, L. C. Drickamer, et al. (Eds.), *Foundations of animal behavior: Classic papers with commentaries* (pp. 376–387). Chicago: University of Chicago Press.

Hover-Kramer, D. (1996). *Healing touch: Resource for health professionals.* New York: Delmar.

Howe, M., Brainerd, C., & Reyna, V. (Eds.). (1992). *The development of long-term memory.* New York: Springer-Verlag.

Howe, N., Petrakos, H., & Rinaldi, C. M. (1998). "All the sheeps are dead. He murdered them": Sibling pretense, negotiation, internal state language, and relationship quality. *Child Development, 69,* 182–191.

Howes, C. (1988). Peer interaction of young children. *Monographs of the Society for Research in Child Development, 53*(Serial No. 2170), 1–78.

Howes, C. (1996). The earliest friendships. In W. M. Bukowski, A. F. Newcomb, et al. (Eds.), *The company they keep: Friendship in childhood and adolescence. Cambridge Studies in Social and Emotional Development* (pp. 66–86). New York: Cambridge University Press.

Howes, C., & Farver, J. M. (1987). Toddlers' responses to the distress of their peers. *Journal of Applied Developmental Psychology, 8,* 441–452.

Howes, C., Hamilton, C. E., & Matheson, C. C. (1994). Children's relationships with peers: Differential associations with aspects of the teacher-child relationship. *Child Development, 65,* 253–263.

Howes, C., Hamilton, C. E., & Philipsen, L. C. (1998). Stability and continuity of child-caregiver and child-peer relationships. *Child Development, 69,* 418–426.

Howes, C., & Matheson, C. C. (1992). Sequences in the development of competent play with peers: Social and social pretend play. *Developmental Psychology, 28,* 961–972.

Howes, C., & Mueller, E. (1984). Early peer friendships: Their significance for development. In W. Spiel (Ed.), *The psychology of the twentieth century.* Zurich: Kindler.

Howes, C., Phillips, D. A., & Whitebrook, M. (1993). Thresholds of quality: Implications for the social development of children in center-based child care. *Annual Progress in Child Psychiatry & Child Development,* 563–580.

Howes, C., & Wu, F. (1990). Peer interactions and friendships in an ethnically diverse school setting. *Child Development, 61,* 537–541.

Huang, L., & Ying, Y. (1989). Chinese-American children and adolescents. In J. Gibbs & L. Huang (Eds.), *Children of color* (pp. 30–66). San Francisco: Jossey-Bass.

Hubbard, R. (1993). Genetics. In B. K. Rothman (Ed.), *The encyclopedia of childbearing.* New York: Henry Holt.

Hudley, C., & Graham, S. (1993). An attributional intervention to reduce peer-directed aggression among African-American boys. *Child Development, 64,* 124–138.

Hurrelmann, K. (1994). *International handbook of adolescence.* Westport, Conn.: Greenwood Press.

Huesmann, L. R., Eron, L. D., Lefkowitz, M. M., & Walder, L. O. (1984). Stability of aggression over time and generations. *Developmental Psychology, 20,* 1120–1134.

Huff, C. R. (1996). The criminal behavior of gang members and nongang at-risk youth. In C. R. Huff et al., *Gangs in America* (2nd ed., pp.75–102). Thousand Oaks, Cal.: Sage.

Hunt, C. (Ed.). (1992). *Apnea and SIDS.* Philadelphia: Saunders.

Hunt, W., & Zakhari, S. (1995). *Stress, gender, and alcohol-seeking behavior.* Bethesda, Md.: National Institutes of Health/National Institute of Alcohol Abuse and Alcoholism.

Hurrelmann, K. (1994). *International handbook of adolescence.* Westport, Conn.: Greenwood Press.

Huston, A. C., & Wright, J. C. (1996). Television and socialization of young children. In T. M. MacBeth et al. (Eds.), *Tuning in to young viewers: Social science perspectives on television* (pp. 37–60). Thousand Oaks, Cal.: Sage.

Huston, A. C. (1983). Sex-typing. In P. Mussen (Ed.), *Handbook of child psychology: Vol. 4.* New York: Wiley.

Huston, A. C. (1994). *Children in poverty: Designing research to affect policy.* Social policy report, vol. 8(2). Ann Arbor, Mich.: Society for Research on Child Development.

Huston, A. C., & Alvarez, M. M. (1990). The socialization context of gender role development in early adolescence. In R. Montemayor, G. R. Adams, & T. P. Gullota (Eds.), *From childhood to adolescence: A transitional period?* Newbury Park, Calif.: Sage.

Huston, A. C., Donnerstein, E., Fairchild, H., et al. (1992). *Big world, small screen: The role of television in American society.* Lincoln: University of Nebraska Press.

Huston, A. C., Watkins, B., & Kunkel, D. (1989). Public policy and children's television. *American Psychologist, 44,* 424–433.

Huston, A. C., Wright, J. C., Rice, M. L., Kerkman, D., & St. Peters, M. (1990). Development of television viewing patterns in early childhood: A longitudinal investigation. *Developmental Psychology, 26,* 409–420.

Hyde, J. S., Essex, M. J., Clark, R., Klein, M. H., & Byrd, J. E., (1996). Parental leave: Policy and research. *Journal of Social Issues, 56,* 91–109.

Hyman, J. P. (1995). Shifting patterns of fathering in the first year of life: On intimacy between fathers and their babies. In J. L. Shapiro, M. J. Diamond, & M. Greenberg, (Eds.), *Becoming a father: Contemporary, social, developmental, and clinical perspectives.* Springer series, *Focus on Men,* Vol. 8. (pp. 256–267). New York: Springer.

Ianni, F., & Orr, M. (1996). Dropping out. In J. Graber, J. Brooks-Gunn, & A. Petersen (Eds.), *Transitions through adolescence* (pp. 285–322). Mahwah, N.J.: Erlbaum.

Ingersoll, B. (1998). *Daredevils and daydreamers: New perspectives on ADHD.* New York: Doubleday.

Inhelder, B., & Piaget, J. (1958). *The growth of logical thinking from birth to adolescence.* New York: Basic Books.

International Food Information Council. (1993). *Starting solids.* (On-line) Located at http://ificinfo.health.org.

Isabella, R. A. (1993). Origins of attachment: Maternal interactive behavior across the first year. *Child Development, 64,* 605–621.

Izard, C. E. (1994). Innate and universal facial expressions: Evidence from developmental and cross-cultural research. *Psychological Bulletin, 115,* 288–299.

Jaccard, J., Dittus, P. J., & Gordon, V. V. (1998). Parent-adolescent congruency in reports of adolescent sexual behavior and in communications about sexual behavior. *Child Development, 69,* 247–261.

Jackson, P. (1986). *The practice of teaching.* Chicago: University of Chicago Press.

Jacobvitz, D. B., & Bush, N. F. (1996). Reconstructions of family relationships: Parent-child alliances, personal distress, and self-esteem. *Developmental Psychology, 32,* 732–743.

Jadack, R., Hyde, J., Moore, C., & Keller, M. (1995). Moral reasoning about sexually transmitted diseases. *Child Development, 66,* 167–177.

Jain, A., Belsky, J., & Crnic, K. (1996). Beyond fathering behaviors: Types of dads. *Journal of Family Psychology, 10,* 431–442.

Jensen, A. R. (1969a, Winter). How much can we boost I.Q. and scholastic achievement? *Harvard Educational Review,* 1–123.

Jensen, A. R. (1969b). Reducing the heredity-environment uncertainty: A reply. *Harvard Educational Review, 39,* 449–483.

Jimenez, R., Garcia, G., & Pearson, D. (1995). Three children, two languages, and strategic reading: Case studies in bilingual/monolingual reading. *American Educational Research Journal, 32*(1), 67–97.

John-Steiner, V., Panofsky, C., & Smith, L. (Eds.). (1994). *Sociocultural approaches to language and literacy.* New York: Cambridge University Press.

Johnson, D., & Johnson, P. (1994). *Learning together and alone.* 4th ed. Boston: Allyn and Bacon.

Johnson, D. W., Johnson, R. T., & Maruyama, G. (1984). Goal interdependence and interpersonal attraction in heterogeneous classrooms: A meta-analysis. In N. Miller & M. B. Brewer (Eds.), *Groups in contact: The psychology of desegregation.* New York: Academic Press.

Johnson, J. E., & Christie, J. F. (1998). *Play and early childhood development.* New York: Addison-Wesley.

Johnson, R. (Ed.). (1995). *African-American voices: African-American health educators speak out.* New York: National League for Nursing.

Johnson, R., & Swain, M. (Eds.). (1997). *Immersion education: International perspectives.* New York: Cambridge University Press.

Joshi, M., & MacLean, M. (1994). Indian and English children's understanding of the distinction between real and apparent emotion. *Child Development, 65,* 1372–1384.

Josselson, R. (1980). Ego development in adolescence. In J. Adelson (Ed.), *Handbook of adolescent psychology.* New York: Wiley.

Josselson, R. (1994). The theory of identity development and the question of intervention: An introduction. In S. L. Archer et al. (Eds.), *Interventions for adolescent identity development. Sage focus editions* (Vol. 169, pp. 12–25). Thousand Oaks, Cal.: Sage.

Josselson, R. (1996). *Revising herself: The story of women's identity from college to midlife.* New York: Oxford University Press.

Jusczyk, P., Bertancini, J., Bijeljac-Babac, R., Kennedy, L., & Mehler, J. (1990). The role of attention in speech perception by young infants. *Cognitive Development, 5,* 265–286.

Kagan, J. (1984). *The nature of the child.* New York: Basic Books.

Kagan, J. (1998). *The Gale encyclopedia of childhood and adolescence: Puberty* (pp. 521–523). Detroit: Gale Research.

Kagan, J., Arcus, D., Snidman, N., Feng, W. Y., Handler, J., & Greene, S. (1995). Reactivity in infants: A cross-national comparison. *Developmental Psychology, 30,* 342–345.

Kagan, J., & Snidman, N. (1991). Temperamental factors in human development. *American Psychologist, 46,* 856–862.

Kaitz, M., Meschulach-Sarfaty, O., Auerbach, J., & Eidelman, A. (1988). A re-examination of newborns' ability to imitate facial expressions. *Developmental Psychology, 24,* 3–7.

Kalverboer, A., Hopkins, B., & Gauze, R. (Eds.). (1993). *Motor development in early and late childhood.* New York: Cambridge University Press.

Kamerman, S. B. (1991). Child care policies and programs: An international overview. *Journal of Social Issues, 47,* 179–196.

Kamii, C. (1994). *Young children continue to reinvent arithmetic.* 3rd ed. New York: Teachers College Press.

Kamin, L. M. (1995, February). Behind the curve. *Scientific American,* 99–103.

Kang, J. (1990). *Identity development in Korean-American college women.* Unpublished manuscript, Yale University.

Kao, G. (1995). Asian-Americans as model minorities? A look at their academic performance. *American Journal of Education, 103,* 121–159.

Kaplan, L. (1995). *No voice is ever wholly lost.* New York: Simon & Schuster.

Karpov, Y. V. & Haywood, H. C. (1998). Two ways to elaborate Vygotsky's concept of mediation: Implications for instruction. *American Psychologist, 53,* 27–36.

Kavanaugh, R. D., & Engel, S. (1998). The development of pretense and narrative in early childhood. In O. Saracho, B. Spodek, et al. (Eds.), *Multiple perspectives on play in early childhood education. SUNY series, early childhood education: Inquiries and insights* (pp. 80–99). Albany, N.Y.: State University of New York Press.

Kazdin, A. E. (1987). Treatment of antisocial behavior in children: Current status and future directions. *Psychological Bulletin, 102,* 187–203.

Kazdin, A. E. (1994). *Behavior modification in applied settings* (5th ed.). Pacific Grove, Cal. Brooks/Cole.

Keating, D., & Sasse, D. (1996). Cognitive socialization in adolescence: Critical period for a critical habit of mind. In G. Adams, R. Montemayor, & T. Gullotta (Eds.), *Psychosocial development during adolescence* (pp. 232–258). Thousand Oaks, Cal.: Sage.

Keefe, J., & Walberg, H. (Eds.). (1992). *Teaching for thinking.* Reston, Va.: National Association of Secondary School Principals.

Keil, F. (1989). *Concepts, kinds, and cognitive development.* Cambridge, Mass.: MIT Press.

Keil, F., Smith, C., Simons, D., & Levin, D. (1998). Two dogmas of conceptual empiricism. *Cognition, 65,* 103–135.

Keller, M., & Edelstein, W. (1993). The development of the moral self from childhood to adolescence. In G. Noam & T. Wren (Eds.), *The moral self* (pp. 310–336). Cambridge, Mass.: MIT Press.

Keller, M., & Wood, P. (1989). Development of friendship reasoning: A study of interindividual differences and intraindividual change. *Developmental Psychology, 25,* 820–826.

Kendall-Tackett, K. A., Williams, L. M., & Finkelhor, D. (1993). Impact of sexual abuse on children: A review and synthesis of recent empirical studies. *Psychological Bulletin, 113,* 164–180.

Kendler, H., & Kendler, T. (1962). Vertical and horizontal processes in problem solving. *Psychological Review, 69,* 1–16.

Kermoian, R., & Campos, J. (1988). Locomotor experience: A facilitator of spatial cognitive development. *Child Development, 59,* 908–917.

Kerr, M., Lambert, W. W., Stattin, H., & Klackenberg-Larsson, I. (1994). Stability of inhibition in a Swedish longitudinal sample. *Child Development, 65,* 138–146.

Kinderman, T. A. (1993). Natural peer groups as contexts for individual development: The case of children's motivation in school. *Child Development, 29,* 970–977.

King, P., & Kitchener, K. (1994). *Developing reflective judgment.* San Francisco: Jossey-Bass.

Kirschner, D. (1997). The situated development of logic in infancy: A case study. In D. Kirschner & J. Whitson (Eds.), *Situated cognition: Social, semiotic, and psychological perspectives* (pp. 83–96). Mahwah, N.J.: Erlbaum.

Kirschner D., & Whitson, J. (Eds.). *Situated cognition: Social, semiotic, and psychological perspectives.* Mahwah, N.J.: Erlbaum.

Kisilevsky, B. S., & Muir, D. W. (1984). Neonatal habituation and dishabituation to tactile stimulation during sleep. *Developmental Psychology, 20,* 367–373.

Kisilevsky, B. S., Muir, D. W., & Low, J. A. (1992). Maturation of human fetal responses to vibroacoustic stimulation. *Child Development, 63,* 1497–1508.

Kitzinger, J. (1997). Who are you kidding? Children, power and the struggle against sexual abuse. In A. James & A. Prout (Eds.), *Constructing and reconstructing childhood* (2nd ed., pp. 165–189). London: Falmer.

Klahr, D. (1992). Information-processing approaches in cognitive development. In M. H. Borenstein & M. E. Lamb (Eds.), *Developmental psychology: An advanced textbook* (3rd ed., pp. 273–335) Hillsdale, N.J.: Erlbaum.

Klein, H. (1995). Urban Appalachian children in northern schools: A study in diversity. *Young Children, 50*(3), 10–16.

Klimes-Dougan, B., & Kistner, J. (1990). Physically abused preschoolers' responses to peers' distress. *Developmental Psychology, 26,* 599–602.

Klinnert, M. D., Emde, R. N., Butterfield, P., & Campos, J. J. (1986). Social referencing: The infant's use of emotional signals from a friendly adult with mother present. *Developmental Psychology, 22,* 427–432.

Koch, P. B. (1988). The relationship of first intercourse to later sexual functioning concerns of adolescents. *Journal of Adolescent Research, 3,* 345–362.

Kochanska, C., Casey, R. J. & Fukumoto, A. (1995). Toddlers' sensitivity to standard violations. *Child Development, 66,* 643–656.

Kochanska, G. (1992). Children's interpersonal influence with mothers and peers. *Developmental Psychology, 28,* 491–499.

Kochanska G. (1997). Mutually responsive orientation between mothers and their young children: Implications for early socialization. *Child Development, 68,* 94–112.

Kochanska, G., Coy, K. C., Tjebkes, T. L., & Husarek, S. J. (1998). Individual differences in emotionality in infancy. *Child Development, 64,* 375–390.

Koff, E., & Benavage, A. (1998). Breast size perception and satisfaction, body image, and psychological functioning in Caucasian and Asian American college women. *Sex Roles, 38,* 655–673.

Kohn, M. L., Slomczynski, K. M., & Schoenbach, C. (1986). Social stratification and the transmission of values in the family: A cross-national assessment. *Sociological Forum, 1,* 73–102.

Kontos, S. (1992). *Family day care: Out of the shadows and into the limelight.* Washington, D.C.: National Association for the Education of Young Children.

Kontos, S., Howes, C., & Galinsky, E. (1996). Does training make a difference to quality in family child care? *Early Childhood Research Quarterly, 11,* 427–445.

Kopp, C. (1982). Antecedents of self-regulation: A developmental perspective. *Developmental Psychology, 18,* 199–214.

Kopp, C. (1989). Regulation of distress and negative emotions: A developmental view. *Developmental Psychology, 25,* 343–354.

Koralek, D., Colker, L., & Dodge, D. (1993). *The what, why, and how of high-quality early childhood education: A guide for on-site supervision.* Washington, D.C.: National Association for the Education of Young Children.

Korbin, J. (Ed.) (1981). *Child abuse and neglect: Cross cultural Perspectives.* Berkeley: University of California Press.

Korbin, J. E. (1987). Child abuse and neglect: The cultural context. In R. E. Helfer & R. S. Kemp (Eds.), *The battered child* (4th ed.). Chicago: University of Chicago Press.

Korbin, J. E. (1991). Cross-cultural perspectives and research directions for the 21st century. *Child Abuse and Neglect, 15,* 67–77

Kotloff, L. (1993). Fostering cooperative group spirit and individuality: Examples from a Japanese preschool. *Young Children, 48*(3), 17–24.

Kovacs, D. M., Parker, J. G., & Hoffman, L. W. (1996). Behavioral, affective and social correlates of involvement in cross-sex friendships in elementary school. *Child Development, 67,* 2269–2286.

Kozol, J. (1991). *Savage inequalities: Children in America's schools.* New York: Crown Publishers.

Kozol, J. (1995). *Amazing grace: The lives of children and the conscience of the nation.* New York: Crown Publishers.

Kroger, J. (1995). The differentiation of "firm" and "developmental" foreclosure identity statuses: A longitudinal study. *Journal of Adolescent Research, 10,* 317–337.

Kuczynski, L., & Kochanska, G. (1995). Function and content of maternal demands: Developmental significance of early demands for competent action. *Child Development, 66,* 616–628.

Kuhl, P., & Padden, D. (1983). Enhanced discriminability at the phonetic boundary for the place feature in macaques. *Journal of the Acoustical Society of America, 73,* 1003–1010.

Kupersmidt, J. B., Griesler, P. C., DeRosier, M. E., Patterson, C. J., & Davis, P. W. (1995). Childhood aggression and peer relations in the context of family and neighborhood factors. *Child Development, 66,* 360–375.

Kutner, L. (1989, March 16). Parent and child: Responding to aggressive behavior. *New York Times,* p. C–1.

La Leche League International. (1991). *The womanly art of breastfeeding* (5th ed.). New York: Plume Books.

Ladd, G. W., & Hart, C. H. (1992). Creating informal play opportunities: Are parents' and preschoolers' initiations related to children's competence with peers? *Developmental Psychology, 28,* 1179–1187.

Lakoff, G. (1994). What is a conceptual system? In W. Overton & D. Palermo (Eds.), *The nature and ontogenesis of meaning* (pp. 41–90). Hillsdale, N.J.: Erlbaum.

Lamaze, F. (1970). *Painless childbirth: Psychoprophylactic method.* Chicago: Henry Regnery.

Lamb, M. E. (1997). The development of father-infant relationships. In Michael E. Lamb (Ed.), *The role of the father in child development* (3rd ed., pp. 104–120). New York: Wiley.

Lamb, M. E., Keterlinus, R. D., & Fracasso, M. P. (1992). Parent-child relationships. In M. H. Bornstein & M. E. Lamb (Eds.), *Developmental psychology: An advanced textbook* (pp. 465–518). Hillsdale, N.J.: Erlbaum.

Lamborn, S. D., Dornbusch, S. M., & Steinberg, L. (1996). Ethnicity and community context as moderators of the relations between family decision making and adolescent adjustment. *Child Development, 67,* 383–301.

Lamke, L. K. (1982a) Adjustment and sex-role orientation. *Journal of Youth and Adolescence, 11,* 247–259.

Lamke, L. K. (1982b). The impact of sex-role orientation on self-esteem in early adolescence. *Child Development, 53,* 1530–1535.

Lane, C. (1994, December). The tainted sources of "The Bell Curve." *The New York Review of Books,* 14–19.

Lapsley, D. (1991). Egocentrism theory and the "new look" at the imaginary audience and personal fable. In R. Lerner, A. Petersen, & J. Brooks-Gunn (Eds.), *Encyclopedia of adolescence: Vol. 1* (pp. 281–286). New York: Garland.

Larrabee, M. (1993). *An ethic of care: Feminist and interdisciplinary perspectives.* New York: Routledge.

Larson, R., & Ham, M. (1993). Stress and "storm and stress" in early adolescence: The relationship of negative events with dysphoric affect. *Developmental Psychology, 29,* 130–140.

Larson, R., & Richards, M. H. (1991). Daily companionship in late childhood and early adolescence: Changing developmental contexts. *Child Development, 62,* 284–300.

Larson, R., & Richards, M. H. (1994). *Divergent realities: The emotional lives of mothers, fathers and adolescents.* New York: Basic Books.

Larson, R. W. (1997). The emergence of solitude as a constructive domain of experience in early adolescence. *Child Development, 68,* 80–93.

Larson, R. W., & Richards, M. H. (1994). *Emergent Realities.* New York: Basic Books.

Larson, R. W., Richards, M. H., Moneta, G., Holmbeck, G., & Duckett, E. (1996). Changes in adolescents' daily interaction with their families from ages 10–18: Disengagement and transformation. *Developmental Psychology, 32,* 744–754.

Larzelere, R. E. (1986). Moderate spanking: Model or deterrent of children's aggression in the family? *Journal of Family Violence, 1,* 27–37.

Lave, J. (1997). The culture of acquisition and the practice of understanding. In D. Kirschner & J. Whitson (Eds.), *Situated cognition: Social, semiotic, and psychological perspectives* (pp. 17–36). Mahwah, N.J.: Erlbaum.

Laybourn, A. (1990). Only children in Britain: Popular stereotype and research evidence. *Children and Society, 4,* 386–400.

Leaper, C. (Ed.). (1994). *Childhood gender segregation: Causes and consequences* (pp. 7-18). San Francisco: Jossey-Bass.

Leaper, C., Anderson, K. J., & Sanders, P. (1998). Moderators of gender effects on parents' talk to their children: A meta-analysis. *Developmental Psychology, 34,* 3–27.

Leary, W. E. (1995, January 31). Sickle cell trial called success, halted early. *The New York Times,* p. C–1.

Leavitt, R. (1991). Family day care licensing: Issues and recommendations. *Child Care and Youth Forum, 20,* 243–254.

Leckman, J., & Mayes, L. C. (1998). Understanding developmental psychopathology: How useful are evolutionary concepts?

Journal of the American Academy of Child and Adolescent Psychiatry, 37, 1011–1021.

Lee, F. R. (1995, May 9). For women with AIDS, anguish of having babies. *The New York Times,* pp. A1, B6.

Lee, V., Croninger, R., Linn, E., & Chen, X. (1996). The culture of sexual harassment in secondary schools. *American Educational Research Journal, 33*(2), 383–418.

Leifer, M. (1977). Psychological changes accompanying pregnancy and motherhood. *Genetic Psychology Monographs, 95,* 68.

Leigh, B. C. (1989). Reasons for having sex: Gender, sexual orientation, and relationship to sexual behavior. *Journal of Sex Research, 26,* 199–209.

Lengua, L. J., West, S. G., & Sandler, I. N. (1998). Temperament as a predictor of symptomotology in children: Addressing contamination of measures. *Child Development, 69,* 164–181.

Lerner, J. (1993). *Learning disabilities* (6th ed.). Boston: Houghton Mifflin.

Lerner, R. M. (1996). Relative plasticity, integration, temporality, and diversity in human development: A developmental contextual perspective about theory, process, and method. *Developmental Psychology, 32,* 781–786.

LeVay, S., & Hamer, D. H. (1994, May). Evidence for a biological influence in male homosexuality. *Scientific American,* 44–49.

Levine, G., & Parkinson, S. (1994). *Experimental methods in psychology.* Hillsdale, N.J.: Erlbaum.

LeVine, R. (1994). *Child care and culture: Lessons from Africa.* New York: Cambridge University Press.

Levine, R., Dixon, S., Levine, S., Richman, A., Leiderman, P., Levy, M., & *Schwartz* (Eds.). (1994). *Vagal control of the heart: Experimental basis and clinical implications.* Armonk, N.Y.: Futura Publishing Company.

Levitt, M. J., Guacci-Franco, N., & Levitt, J. L. (1993). Convoys of social support in childhood and early adolescence: Structure and function. *Developmental Psychology, 29,* 811–818.

Levy-Shiff, R. (1994). Individual and contextual correlates of marital change across the transition to parenthood. *Developmental Psychology, 30,* 591–601.

Lewis, J. M. (1993). Childhood play in normality, pathology and therapy. *American Journal of Orthopsychiatry, 63,* 6–15.

Lewis, M. (1992). *Shame: The Exposed Self.* New York: The Free Press.

Lewis, M., & Brooks-Gunn, J. (1979a). *Social cognition and the acquisition of self.* New York: Plenum Press.

Lewis, M., & Brooks-Gunn, J. (1979b). Toward a theory of social cognition: The development of the self. In I. Uzgiris (Ed.), *Social interaction and communication during infancy.* San Francisco: Jossey-Bass.

Lewis, M., Brooks-Gunn, J., & Jaskir, J. (1985). Individual differences in visual self-recognition as a function of mother-infant attachment relationship. *Developmental Psychology, 21,* 1181–1187.

Lewkowicz, D., & Lickliter, R. (1994). *The development of intersensory perception.* Hillsdale, N.J.: Erlbaum.

Lickona, T. (1991). Moral development in the elementary school classroom. In W. Kurtines & J. Gewirtz (Eds.), *Handbook of moral behavior and development: Vol. 3* (pp. 143–162). Hillsdale, N.J.: Erlbaum.

Liebert, R. M., & Sprafkin, J. (1988). *The early window: Effects of television on children and youth* (3rd ed.).New York: Pergamon Press.

Liebman, B. (July/August 1998). The pressure to eat: Why we're getting fatter. *Nutriion Action Health Letter,* 3–5.

Liebman-Smith, J. (1993). Infertility: Overview. In B. K. Rothman (Ed.), *The encyclopedia of childbearing.* New York: Henry Holt.

Liem, R., & Liem, J. H. (1988). Psychological effects of unemployment on workers and their families. *Journal of Social Issues, 44,* 87–105.

Lightbook, C. (1997). *The Culture of Adolescent Risk-Taking.* Guilford, Conn.: Guilford Press.

Lindblad-Goldberg, M. (1989). Successful minority single-parent families. In L. Combrinck-Graham (Ed.), *Children in family contexts* (pp. 116–134). New York: Guilford.

Lindell, S. G. (1988). Education for childbirth: A time for change. *Journal of Obstetrics, Gynecology, and Neonatal Nursing, 17,* 108–112.

Linn, S., Lieverman, E., Schoenbaum, S. C., Monson, R. R., Stubblefield, P. G., & Ryan, K. (1988). Adverse outcomes of pregnancy in women exposed to diethylstilbestrol in utero. *Journal of Reproductive Medicine, 33,* 3–7.

Linney, J. A., & Seidman, E. (1989). The future of schooling. *American Psychologist, 44,* 336–340.

Lipsitt, L. (1990). Learning and memory in infants. *Merrill-Palmer Quarterly, 35,* 53–66.

Lipsitt, L., & Kaye, H. (1964). Conditioned sucking in the newborn. *Psychonomic Science, 1,* 29–30.

Little, J., & Thompson, R. (1988). Descriptive epidemiology. In I. MacGillvray, D. M. Campbell & B. Thompson (Eds.), *Twinning and twins* (pp. 37–66). New York: Wiley.

Livingston, M. (1993a). Read method: Natural childbirth. In B. K. Rothman (Ed.), *The encyclopedia of childbearing.* New York: Henry Holt.

Livingston, M. (1993b). Psychoprophylactic method (Lamaze). In B. K. Rothman (Ed.), *The encyclopedia of childbearing.* New York: Henry Holt.

Livingston, M. (1993c). Bradley method: Husband-coached childbirth. In B. K. Rothman (Ed.), *The encyclopedia of childbearing.* New York: Henry Holt.

Livson, N., & Peskin, H. (1981a). Perspectives on adolescence from longitudinal research. In J. Adelson (Ed.), *Handbook of adolescent psychology.* New York: Wiley.

Livson, N., & Peskin, H. (1981b). Psychological health at 40: Predictions from adolescent personality. In D. Eichorn, J. Clausen, N. Haan, M. Honzik, & P. Mussen (Eds.), *Present and past in middle life.* New York: Academic Press.

Loeb, R. C., Horst, L., & Horton, P. J. (1980). Family interaction patterns associated with self-esteem in preadolescent girls and boys. *Merrill-Palmer Quarterly, 26,* 203–217.

Loeber, R., & Stouthamer-Loeber, M. (1998). Development of juvenile aggression and violence: Some common misconceptions and controversies. *American Psychologist, 53,* 242–259.

Lohnes, K. L. & Kalter, N. (1994). Preventative intervention groups for parentally bereaved children. *American Journal of Orthopsychiatry, 64,* 594–603.

Louis, K., Marks, H., & Kruse, S. (1996). Teachers' professional community in restructuring schools. *American Educational Research Journal, 33*(4), 757–800.

Lozoff, B. (1989). Nutrition and behavior. *American Psychologist, 44,* 231–236.

Luria, A. R. (1976). *Cognitive development: Its cultural and social foundations.* Cambridge, Mass.: Harvard University Press.

Luster, T., & McAdoo, H. (1996). Family and child influences on educational attachment: A secondary analysis of the High Scope Perry Preschool data. *Developmental Psychology, 32,* 26–35.

Luster, T., & Okagaki, L. (1993). *Parenting: An ecological perspective.* Hillsdale, N.J.: Erlbaum.

Lustig, M., & Koester, J. (1993). *Intercultural competence: Interpersonal communication across cultures.* New York: HarperCollins.

Lynch, B., & Bonnie, R. (Eds.). (1994). *Growing up tobacco free.* Washington, D.C.: National Academy Press.

Lyon, G. (1993). *Better understanding learning disabilities: New views for research and their implications for education and public policy.* Baltimore: Paul Brookes.

Lyons-Ruth, K., & Block, D. (1996). The disturbed caregiving system: Conceptualizing the impact of childhood trauma on maternal caregiving behavior during infancy. *Infant Mental Health Journal, 17,* 257–275.

Lyons-Ruth, K., Easterbrooks, M. A., & Cibelli, C. D. (1997). Infant attachment strategies, infant mental lag, and maternal depressive symptoms: Predictors of internalizing and externalizing problems at age 7. *Developmental Psychology, 33,* 681–692.

Lytton, H., & Romney, D. M. (1991). Parents' sex-related differential socialization of boys and girls: A meta-analysis. *Psychological Bulletin, 109,* 267–296.

Maccoby, E. E. (1995). The two sexes and their social systems. In P. Moen, G. Elder, & K. Luscher (Eds.), *Examining lives in context: Perspectives on the ecology of human development* (pp. 347–364). Washington, D.C.: American Psychological Association.

Maccoby, E. E. (1990). Gender and relationships: A developmental account. *American Psychologist, 45,* 513–520.

Maccoby, E. E., & Jacklin, C. (1987). Gender segregation in childhood. In H. Reese (Ed.), *Advances in child development and behavior: Vol. 20.* New York: Academic Press.

Maccoby, E. E., & Martin, J. A. (1983). Socialization in the context of the family: Parent-child interaction. In E. M. Hetherington (Ed.), *Handbook of child psychology: Vol. 4. Socialization, personality, and social development* (4th ed., pp. 1–101). New York: Wiley.

MacGregor, S. N., Keith, L. G., Chasnoff, I. J., Rosner, M. A., Chisum, G. M., Shaw, P., & Minogue, J. P. (1987). Cocaine use during pregnancy: Adverse perinatal outcome. *American Journal of Obstetrics and Gynecology, 1,* 66–90.

MacKinnon-Lewis, C., Starnes, R., Volling, B., & Johnson, S. (1997). Perceptions of parenting as predictors of boys' sibling and peer relations. *Developmental Psychology, 33,* 1024–1031.

MacKinnon-Lewis, C., Volling, B. L., Lamb, M. E., Dechman, K., Rabiner, D., & Curtner, M. E. (1994). A cross-contextual analysis of boys' social competence: From family to school. *Developmental Psychology, 30,* 325–333.

Macrae, C., Stangar, C., & Hawthorne, M. (1996). *Stereotypes and stereotyping.* Guilford, Conn.: Guilford Press.

Maguire, M. D., & Dunn, J. (1997). Friendships in early childhood and social understanding. *International Journal of Behavioral Development, 21,* 669–686.

Mahler, M., Pine, F., & Bergman, A. (1975). *The psychological birth of the human infant: Symbiosis and individuation.* New York: Basic Books.

Mahler, M. S., Pine, F., & Bergman, A. (1994). Stages in the infant's separation from the mother. In G. Handel, G. G. Whitchurch, et al. (Eds.), *The psychosocial interior of the family* (4th ed., pp. 419–448). New York: Aldine De Gruyter.

Main, M. (1995). Recent studies in attachment: Overview, with selected implications for clinical work. In S. Goldberg, R. Muir, & J. Kerr (Eds.), *Attachment theory: Social, developmental, and clinical perspectives* (pp. 407–470). Hillsdale, N.J.: Analytic Press.

Main, M., & George, C. (1985). Responses of abused and disadvantaged toddlers to distress in agemates: A study in the day care setting. *Developmental Psychology, 21,* 407–412.

Main, M., & Goldwyn, R. (1989). Predicting rejection of her infant from mother's representation of her own experience: Implications for the abused-abusing intergenerational cycle. *Child Abuse and Neglect, 8,* 203–217.

Main, M., Kaplan, N., & Cassidy, J. (1985). Security in infancy, childhood, and adulthood: A move to the level of representation. In I. Bretherton & E. Waters (Eds.), Growing points of attachment theory and research. *Monographs of the Society for Research on Child Development, 50*(1–2), 66–104.

Main, M., & Solomon, J. (1990). Procedures for identifying infants as disorganized/disoriented during the Ainsworth Strange Situation. In M. Greenberg, D. Cicchetti, & E. M. Cummings (Eds.), *Attachment in the preschool years: Theory, research and intervention* (pp. 121–160). Chicago: University of Chicago Press.

Maker, J. (Ed.). (1993). *Programs for the gifted in regular classrooms.* Austin, Tex.: Pro-Ed Publishers.

Makin, J., & Porter, R. (1989). Attractiveness of lactating females' breast odors to neonates. *Child Development, 60,* 803–810.

Malina, R. M. (1990). Physical growth and performance during the transition years (9–16). In R. Montemayor, G. R. Adams, & T. P. Gullotta (Eds.), *From childhood to adolescence: A transitional period?* (pp. 41–62). Newbury Park, Cal.: Sage.

Malinosky-Rummell, R., & Hansen, D. J. (1993). Long-term consequences of childhood physical abuse. *Psychological Bulletin, 114,* 68–79.

Mallory, G., & New, R. (Eds.). (1994). *Diversity and developmentally appropriate practice: Challenges for early childhood education.* New York: Teachers' College Press.

Mangelsdorf, S. C., Shapiro, J. R., & Marxolf, D. (1995). Developmental and temperamental differences in emotion regulation in infancy. *Child Development, 66,* 1817–1828.

Mann, J. M., & Tarantola, D. J. M. (1998, July). HIV 1998: The global picture. *Scientific American,* 82–83.

Marcia, J. (1980). Identity in adolescence. In J. Adelson (Ed.), *Handbook of adolescent psychology.* New York: Wiley.

Marcia, J. E. (1993). The relational roots of identity. In J. Kroger (Ed.), *Discussions on ego identity* (pp. 101–120), Hillsdale, N.J.: Erlbaum.

Marcia, J. E., Waterman, A. S., Matteson, D. R., Archer, S. L., & Osofsky, J. L. (1993). *Ego Identity: A handbook for psychosocial research.* New York: Springer-Verlag.

Marcus, G., Pinker, S., Ullman, M., Hollander, M., Rosen, T., & Xu, F. (1992). Overregularization in language acquisition.

Monographs of the Society for Research on Child Development, 57(4, Serial No. 228).

Margolin, L. (1994). *Goodness personified: The emergence of gifted children.* New York: Aldine de Gruyter.

Markman, H. J., & Kadushin, F. S. (1986). Preventive effects of Lamaze training for first-time parents: A short-term longitudinal study. *Journal of Consulting and Clinical Psychology, 54,* 872–874.

Marlowe, B. (1998). *Creating and sustaining the constructivist classroom.* Thousand Oaks, Cal.: Corwin Press.

Marschark, M. (1993). *Psychological development of deaf children.* New York: Oxford.

Marsella, A. J. (1998). Urbanization, mental health, and social deviancy: A review of issues and research. *American Psychologist, 53,* 624–634.

Martin, B. (1975). Parent-child relations. In F. Horowitz (Ed.), *Review of child development research: Vol. 4.* Chicago: University of Chicago Press.

Martin, C. L., Wood, C. H., & Little, J. K. (1990). The development of gender stereotype components. *Child Development, 61,* 1891–1904.

Mason, C. A., Cauce, A. M., Gonzales, N., & Hiraga, Y. (1996). Neither too sweet nor too sour: Problem peers, maternal control, and problem behavior in African American adolescents. *Child Development, 67,* 2115–2130.

Mason, D., & Ingersoll, D. (1997). *Breastfeeding and the working mother.* New York: St. Martin's Griffin Press.

Masten, A. S., & Coatsworth, J. D. (1998). The development of competence in favorable and unfavorable environments. *American Psychologist, 53,* 205–220.

Matas, L., Arend, R. A., & Sroufe, L. A. (1978). Continuity of adaptation in the second year: The relationship between quality of attachment and later competence. *Child Development, 49,* 547–555.

Mazur, J. (1994). *Learning and behavior* (3rd ed.). Englewood Cliffs, N.J.: Erlbaum.

Mazzocco, M. M., Nord, A. M., Van-Doorninck, W., Greene, C. L., et al. (1994). Cognitive development among children with early-treated phenylketonuria. *Developmental Neuropsychology, 10,* 133–151.

McCall, G. J. (1995). Juvenile delinquency in Germany, South Africa, and America: Explorations in national character. In J. Braun et al. (Eds.), *Social pathology in comparative perspective: The nature and psychology of civil society.* (pp. 117–132). Westport, Conn.: Praeger Publishers/Greenwood Publishing Group.

McCall, R. (1981). Nature-nurture and the two realms of development: A proposed integration with respect to mental development. *Child Development, 52,* 1–12.

McCall, R., & Kagan, J. (1967). Stimulus schema discrepancy and attention in the infant. *Journal of Experimental Child Psychology, 5,* 381–390.

McCloyd, V. C. (1998). Socioeconomic disadvantage and child development. *American Psychologist, 53,* 185–204.

McDaniel, D., McKee, C., & Smith, H. (1996). *Methods of assessing children's syntax.* Cambridge, Mass.: MIT Press.

McDonald, A. D., Armstrong, B. G., & Sloan, M. (1992). Cigarette, alcohol, and coffee consumption and congenital defects. *American Journal of Public Health, 82,* 91.

McDonald, M., Sigman, M., Espinosa, M., & Neumann, C. (1994). Impact of a temporary food shortage on children and their mothers. *Child Development, 65,* 404–415.

McKay, S. (1993). Labor: Overview. In B. K. Rothman, (Ed.), *The encyclopedia of childbearing.* New York: Henry Holt.

McKenzie, C. (1983). Risk factors in perinatology. In C. McKenzie & K. Vestal (Eds.), *High-risk perinatal nursing.* Philadelphia: Saunders.

McKussick, V. A. (1995). *Mendelian inheritance in man: Catalogs of autosomal dominant, autosomal recessive, and X-linked phenotypes* (10th ed.). Baltimore: Johns Hopkins University Press.

McLoyd, V. C. (1990). The impact of economic hardship on Black families and children: Psychological distress, parenting and socioemotional development. *Child Development, 61,* 311–346.

McLoyd, V. C. (1998). Socioeconomic disadvantage and child development. *American Psychologist, 53,* 185–204.

McNamara, T., Miller, D., & Bransford, J. (1991). Mental models and the construction of meaning. In P. Pearson (Ed.),

Handbook of reading research: Vol. 2 (pp. 490–511). New York: Longman.

McQuoid, J. (1996). The ISRD Study: Self-report findings from N. Ireland. *Journal of Adolescence, 19,* 95–98.

McTigue, J. (1993). Endometriosis. In B. K. Rothman (Ed.), *The encyclopedia of childbearing.* New York: Henry Holt.

Measor, L., & Sykes, P. (1992). *Gender and schools.* New York: Cassell.

Meehan, P. J., Lamb, J. A., Saltzman, L. E., & O'Carroll, P. W. (1992). Attempted suicide among young adults: Progress toward a meaningful estimate of prevalence. *American Journal of Psychiatry, 149,* 41–44.

Meins, E. (1997). *Security of attachment and the social development of cognition.* Hove, U.K.: Psychology Press.

Mela, D., & Roberts, P. (1998). *Food, eating, and obesity: Psychobiological basis of appetite and weight control.* New York: Chapman and Hall.

Meltzoff, A., & Kuhl, P. (1994). Faces and speech: Intermodel processing of biologically relevant signals in infants and adults. In D. Lewkowicz & R. Lickliter (Eds.), *The development of intersensory perception* (pp. 335–370). Hillsdale, N.J.: Erlbaum.

Meltzoff, A., Kuhl, P., & Moore, M. K. (1991). Perception, representation, and control of action in newborns and young infants. In M. Weiss & P. Zelazo (Eds.), *Newborn attention: Biological constraints and the influence of experience* (pp. 377–411). Norwood, N.J.: Ablex.

Menkes, J. (1994). *Textbook of child neurology* (5th ed.). Philadelphia: Williams and Wilkins.

Meredith, H. (1981). Body size and form among ethnic groups of infants, children, youth, and adults. In R. Munroe, R. Munroe, and B. Whiting (Eds.), *Handbook of cross-cultural human development.* New York: Garland Press.

Merenstein, G., Kaplan, D., & Rosenberg, A. (1997). *Handbook of pediatrics* (18th ed.). Norwalk, Conn.: Appleton and Lange.

Messer, D. (1994). *The development of communication: From social interaction to language.* New York: Wiley.

Messner, M., & Sabo, D. (1994). *Sex, violence, and power in sports.* Freedom, Cal.: Crossing Press.

Metz, K. (1995). Reassessment of developmental constraints on children's science instruction. *Review of Educational Research, 65(2),* 93–128.

Michelsson, K., Rinne, A., & Paajanen, S. (1990). Crying, feeding and sleeping patterns in 1 to 12-month-old infants. *Child: Care, health and development, 116,* 99–111.

Mickelson, K. D., Kessler, R. C., & Shaver, P. R. (1997). Adult attachment in a nationally representative sample. *Journal of Personality and Social Psychology, 73,* 1092–1106.

Mikaye, K., Chen, S., & Campos, J. (1985). Infant temperament, mother's mode of interaction, and attachment in Japan. In I. Bretherton & E. Waters (Eds.), Growing points of attachment theory and research. *Monographs of the Society for Research on Child Development, 50* (209).

Miller, M. A. (1993). Smoking in pregnancy. In B. K. Rothman (Ed.), *The encyclopedia of childbearing.* New York: Henry Holt.

Miller, P. H. (1993). *Theories of developmental psychology* (3rd ed.). New York: W. H. Freeman.

Miller, P., & Simon, W. (1980). The development of sexuality in adolescence. In J. Adelson (Ed.), *Handbook of adolescent psychology.* New York: Wiley.

Miller, W. B. (1990). Why the United States has failed to solve its youth gang problem. In C. R. Huff (Ed.), *Gangs in America* (pp. 263–287). Newbury Park, Cal.: Sage.

Millstein, S. G. (1989). Adolescent health: Challenges for behavioral scientists. *American Psychologist, 44,* 837–842.

Milunsky, A. (1992). *Heredity and your family's health.* Baltimore: Johns Hopkins University Press.

Miramontes, O., Nadeau, A., & Commins, N. (1997). *Restructuring schools for linguistic diversity.* New York: Teachers College Press.

Moerk, E. (1992). *A first language taught and learned.* Baltimore: Paul Brookes.

Mogford, K. (1993). Language development in twins. In D. Bishop & K. Mogford (Eds.), *Language development in exceptional circumstances* (pp. 80–95). Hillsdale, N.J.: Erlbaum.

Molnar, A. (Ed.). (1997). *The construction of children's character: 96th yearbook of the National Society for the Study of Education, Part 2.* Chicago: University of Chicago Press.

Monk, T. H., Essex, M. J., Smider, N. A., Klein, M. H., et al. (1996). The impact of the birth of a baby on the time structure and social mixture of a couple's daily life and its consequences for well-being. *Journal of Applied Social Psychology, 26,* 1237–1258.

Montagu, A. (Ed.) (1975). *Race and IQ.* New York: Oxford University Press.

Montessori, M. (1964). *The Montessori method.* New York: Schocken Books.

Moore, C., & Dunham, P. (1995). *Joint attention: Its origins and role in development.* Hillsdale, N.J.: Erlbaum.

Moore, D. (1984). Parent-adolescent separation: Intrafamilial perceptions and difficulty separating from parents. *Personality and Social Psychology Bulletin, 10,* 611–619.

Moore, D. (1987). Parent-adolescent separation: The construction of adulthood by late adolescents. *Developmental Psychology, 23,* 298–307.

Moore, K., & Persaud, T. (1998). *The developing human: Clinically oriented embryology* (6th ed.). Philadelphia: Saunders.

Moore, K. L. (1983). *Before We Are Born: Basic Embryology and Birth Defects* (2nd ed.). New York: Saunders.

Moore, S., Rosenthal, D., & Mitchell, A. (1996). *Youth, AIDS, and sexually transmitted diseases.* London: Routledge.

Moorehouse, M. J. (1991). Linking maternal employment patterns to mother-child activities and children's school competence. *Developmental Psychology, 27,* 295–303.

Morrongiello, B. (1994). Effects of colocation on auditory-visual interactions and cross-modality perception in infants. In D. Lewkowicz & R. Lickliter (Eds.), *The development of intersensory perception* (pp. 235–264). Hillsdale, N.J.: Erlbaum.

Morrow, L. (1993). *Literacy development in the early years* (2nd ed.). Boston: Allyn & Bacon.

Morrow, L. (1996). *Motivating reading and writing in diverse classrooms: Social and physical contexts in a literature-based program.* Urbana, Ill.: National Council of Teachers of English.

Morse, J. M., & Park, C. (1988). Differences in cultural expectations of the perceived painfulness of childbirth. In K. L. Michaelson (Ed.), *Childbirth in America: Anthropological perspectives.* South Hadley, Mass.: Bergin & Garvey.

Muehlenhard, C., & Linton, M. (1987). Date rape. *Journal of Counseling Psychology, 34,* 186–196.

Muir, B. (1983). *Essentials of genetics for nurses.* New York: Wiley.

Mullan, J. T., Pearlin, L. I., & Skaff, M. M. (1995). The bereavement process: Loss, grief, recovery. In I. B. Corless, B. B. Germino, & M. A. Pittman, (Eds.), *A challenge for living: Dying, death, and bereavement.* Boston: Jones and Bartlett.

Munroe, R., Munroe, R., & Whiting, J. (1981). Male sex-role resolutions. In *Handbook of cross-cultural human development.* New York: Garland.

Myers, J. (1993). Curricular designs that resonate with adolescents' ways of knowing. In R. Lerner (Ed.), *Early adolescence: Perspectives on research, policy, and intervention* (pp. 191–206). Hillsdale, N.J.: Erlbaum.

Nagata, D. (1989). Japanese-American children and adolescents. In J. Gibbs & L. Huang (Eds.), *Children of color* (pp. 67–113). San Francisco: Jossey-Bass.

National Safety Council. (1995). *Accident facts: 1994.* Chicago: Author.

Nelson, K. (1996). *Language in cognitive development: Emergence of the mediated mind.* New York: Cambridge University Press.

Nelson, M. (1991). A study of family day care providers: Attitudes toward regulation. *Child Care and Youth Quarterly, 20,* 225–242.

New York Times (1995a, April 7). Use of alcohol linked to rise in fetal illness, p. A27.

New York Times (1995b, April 13). 5,600 infant deaths tied to mothers' smoking, p. A–23.

Newman, D. L., Caspi, A., Moffitt, T. E., & Silva, P. A. (1997). Antecedents of adult interpersonal functioning: Effects of individual differences in age 3 temperament. *Developmental Psychology, 33,* 203–217.

Newman, F., & Holzman, L. (1993). *Lev Vygotsky: Revolutionary scientist.* New York: Routledge.

NICHD Early Child Care Research Network. (1997). The effects of infant child care on infant-mother attachment security: Results of the NICHD study of early child care. *Child Development, 68,* 860–879.

Nichols, J., Nelson, J., & Gleaves, K. (1995). Learning "facts" versus learning that most questions have many answers: Student evaluations of contrasting curricula. *Journal of Educational Psychology, 87*(2), 253–260.

Noam, G., & Wren, T. (1993). *The moral self.* Cambridge, Mass.: MIT Press.

Noddings, N. (1993). *Educating for intelligent belief or unbelief.* New York: Teachers' College Press.

Nolen-Hoeksema, S., Wolfson, A., Mumme, D., & Guskin, K. (1995). Helplessness in children of depressed and nondepressed mothers. *Developmental Psychology, 31,* 377–387.

Noppe, I. C., Noppe, L. D., & Hughes, F. P. (1991). Stress as a predictor of the quality of parent-infant interactions. *Journal of Genetic Psychology, 152,* 17–28.

Noppe, L., & Noppe, I. (1996). Ambiguity in adolescent understandings of death. In C. Corr & D. Balk (Eds.), *Handbook of adolescent death and bereavement* (pp. 25–41). New York: Springer Publishing.

Norman, C. (1988). Math education: A mixed picture. *Science, 241,* 408–409.

Northern, J. (1996). *Hearing disorders* (3rd ed.). Boston: Allyn and Bacon.

Nucci, L., & Turiel, E. (1993). God's word, religious rules, and their relation to Christian and Jewish children's concepts of morality. *Child Development, 64,* 1475–1491.

O'Brien, S. F., & Bierman, K. L. (1988). Conceptions and perceived influence of peer groups: Interviews with preadolescents and adolescents. *Child Development, 59,* 1360–1365.

O'Connor, C. (1997). Dispositions toward (collective) struggle and educational resilience in the inner city: A case analysis of six African-American high school students. *American Educational Research Journal, 34*(4), 593–629.

O'Connor, M., & Michaels, S. (1996). Shifting participant frameworks: Orchestrating thinking practices in group discussions. In D. Hicks (Ed.), *Discourse, learning, and schooling* (pp. 63–103). New York: Cambridge University Press.

O'Donnell, J., Hawkins, J. D., Catalano, R. F., Abbott, R. D., & Day, L. E. (1995). Preventing school failure, drug use and delinquency among low-income children: Long-term intervention in elementary schools. *American Journal of Orthopsychiatry, 65,* 87–100.

O'Hara-Devereaux, M., & Johansen, R. (1994). *Globalwork: Bridging distance, culture, and time.* San Francisco: Jossey-Bass.

O'Keefe, M. (Ed.) (1998). *Brady emergency care.* 8th ed. Upper Saddle River, N.J.: Prentice-Hall.

Offer, D., & Schonert-Reichl, K. A. (1992). Debunking the myths of adolescence: Findings from recent research. *Journal of the American Academy of Child and Adolescent Psychiatry, 31,* 1003–1014.

Olds, D. (1997). The Prenatal/Early Infancy Project: Fifteen years later. In G. W. Albee, T. P. Gullotta, et al. (Eds.), *Primary prevention works: Issues in children's and families' lives* (Vol. 6, pp. 41–67). Thousand Oaks, CA: Sage.

Olds, D. L. (1988). The prenatal/early infancy project. In R. H. Price, E. L. Cowen, R. P. Lorion, & J. R. McKay (Eds.), *14 ounces of prevention: A casebook for practitioners.* Washington, D.C.: American Psychological Association.

Olver, R., & Ratner, N. (1994). Children's understanding of false beliefs in two contexts. *Psychological Reports, 75,* 1136–1138.

Olvera-Ezzell, N., Power, T., Cousins, J., Guerra, A., & Trujillo, M. (1994). The development of health knowledge in low-income Mexican-American children. *Child Development, 65,* 416–427.

Ontario Ministry of Culture, Tourism, and Recreation. (1994). *Policy on full and fair access for women and girls in sport and physical activity.* Toronto: Author.

Opie, I. (1993). *The people in the playground.* Oxford, U.K.: Oxford University Press.

Oppenheim, D., Nir, A., Warren, S., & Ernde, R. (1997). Emotion regulation in mother-child narrative construction: Associations with children's narratives and adaptation. *Developmental Psychology, 33,* 284–294.

Oster, H., Hegley, D., & Nagel, L. (1992). Adult judgments and fine-grained analysis of infant facial expressions: Testing the validity of a priori coding formulas. *Developmental Psychology, 28,* 1115–1131.

Overton, W. (1994). Contexts of meaning: The computational and the embodied mind. In W. Overton & D. Palermo (Eds.),

The nature and ontogenesis of meaning (pp. 1–18). Hillsdale, N.J.: Erlbaum.

Owen, H., & Everly, G. S. (1988). Psychological factors in preterm labor: Critical review and theoretical synthesis. *American Journal of Psychiatry, 145,* 1507–1513.

Owen, M. T., & Cox, M. J. (1997). Marital conflict and the development of infant-parent attachment relationships. *Journal of Family Psychology, 11,* 152–164.

Page, D. C., Mosher, R., Simpson, E. M., Fisher, E. M., Mardon, G., Pillack, J., McGillivray, B., de la Chapelle, A., & Brown, L. G. (1987). The sex-determining region of the human Y chromosome encodes a finer protein. *Cell, 51,* 1091–1104.

Pakiz, B., Reinherz, H. Z., & Giaconia, R. M. (1997). Early risk factors for serious antisocial behavior at age 21: A longitudinal community study. *American Journal of Orthopsychiatry, 67,* 92–101.

Pappert, A. (1993). Preimplantation diagnosis. In B. K. Rothman, (Ed.), *The encyclopedia of childbearing.* New York: Henry Holt.

Parke, R. D. (1996). *Fatherhood.* Cambridge, Mass.: Harvard University Press.

Parke, R. D., Burks, V. M., Carson, J. L., Neville, B., & Boyum, L. A. (1994). Family-peer relationships. A tripartite model. In R. D. Parke & S. G. Kellam (Eds.), *Exploring family relationships with other social constructs* (pp. 115–146). Hillsdale, N.J.: Erlbaum.

Parkhurst, J. T., & Asher, S. R. (1992). Peer rejection in middle school: Subgroup differences in behavior, loneliness, and interpersonal concerns. *Developmental Psychology, 28,* 231–242.

Parten, M. (1932). Social play among preschool children. *Journal of Abnormal and Social Psychology, 27,* 243–269.

Patterson, C. J. (1995). Sexual orientation and human development: An overview. *Developmental Psychology, 31,* 3–11.

Patterson, G. R. (1982). *Coercive family processes.* Eugene, Ore.: Castilia Press.

Patterson, G. R. (1985). *A social learning approach to family intervention: Vol. 1. Families with aggressive children.* Eugene, Ore.: Castilia Press.

Patterson, G. R., DeBaryshe, B. D., & Ramsey, E. (1989). A developmental perspective on antisocial behavior. *American Psychologist, 44,* 329–340.

Patterson, G. R., & Dishion, T. J. (1985). Contributions of families and peers to delinquency. *Criminology, 23,* 63–79.

Paulston, C. (1992). *Linguistic and communicative competence: Topics in ESL.* Philadelphia: Multilingual Matters Ltd.

Pease-Alvarez, L. (1993). *Moving in and out of bilingualism: Investigating native language maintenance and shift in Mexican-descent children.* Santa Cruz, Cal.: National Center for Research on Cultural Diversity, University of California.

Pelligrini, A. D., & Smith, P. K. (1998). Physical activity play: The nature and function of a neglected aspect of play. *Child Development, 69,* 577–598.

Pence, A., & Goelman, H. (1991). The relationship of regulation, training, and motivation to quality of care in family day care. *Child Care and Youth Forum, 20*(2), 83–101.

Penner, S. (1987). Parental responses to grammatical and ungrammatical child utterances. *Child Development, 58,* 376–384.

Peterson, P., McCarthey, S., & Elmore, R. (1996). Learning from school restructuring. *American Educational Research Journal, 33*(1), 119–153.

Petlichkoff, L. (1996). The drop-out dilemma in youth sports. In O. Bar-Or (Ed.), *The child and adolescent athlete* (pp. 418–432). Oxford, U.K.: Blackwells.

Pettit, G. S., Bates, J. E., & Dodge, K. A. (1997). Supportive parenting, ecological context, and children's adjustment: A seven-year longitudinal study. *Child Development, 68,* 908–923.

Pettit, G., Dodge, K., & Brown, N. (1988). Early family experience, social problem solving patterns, and children's social competence. *Child Development, 59,* 107–120.

Pettito, L., & Marentette, P. (1991). Babbling in the manual code: Evidence for the ontogeny of language. *Science, 251,* 1493–1496.

Phelan, J. (Ed.). (1992). *Prevention of prematurity.* Philadelphia: Saunders.

Philadelphia Child Guidance Center. (1994). *Your child's emotional health: The middle years.* New York: Macmillan.

Phinney, J. S. (1989). Stages of ethnic identity development in minority adolescents. *Journal of Early Adolescence, 9,* 34–49.

Phinney, J. S., Ferguson, D. L., & Tate, J. D. (1997). Intergroup attitudes among ethnic minority adolescents: A causal model. *Child Development, 68,* 955–969.

Phinney, J. S., Feshbach, N. D., & Farer, J. (1986). Preschool children's response to peer crying. *Early Childhood Research Quarterly, 1,* 207–219.

Piaget, J. (1952). *The child's conception of number.* New York: Norton.

Piaget, J. (1959). *The language and thought of the child.* London: Routledge & Kegan Paul.

Piaget, J. (1962). *Play, dreams, and imitation in childhood.* New York: Norton.

Piaget, J. (1963). *The origins of intelligence in children.* New York: Norton.

Piaget, J. (1964). *The moral judgment of the child.* New York: The Free Press.

Piaget, J. (1965). *The child's conception of the world.* Totowa, N.J.: Littlefield, Adams.

Piaget, J. (1970). Piaget's theory. In P. Mussen (Ed.), *Carmichael's manual of child psychology* (3rd ed., vol. 1). New York: Wiley.

Piaget, J. (1970). *The science of education and the psychology of the child.* New York: Viking.

Piaget, J. (1983). Piaget's theory. In P. Mussen (Ed.), *Handbook of child psychology: Vol. 1.* New York: Wiley.

Piaget, J., & Inhelder, B. (1967). *The child's conception of space.* New York: Norton.

Piaget, J., & Inhelder, B. (1971). *Science of education and the psychology of the child.* New York: Viking.

Piaget, J., & Inhelder, B. (1973). *Memory and intelligence.* New York: Basic Books.

Pianta, R., Egeland, B., & Erikson, M. (1989). The effects of maltreatment on the development of young children. In D. Cicchetti & V. Carlson (Eds.), *Child Maltreatment.* New York: Cambridge University Press.

Piatelli-Palmarini, L. (1994). Ever since language and learning: Afterthoughts on the Piaget-Chomsky debate. *Cognition, 50,* 315–346.

Piatrowski, C. (1997). Rules of everyday family life: The development of social rules in mother-child and sibling relationships. *International Journal of Behavioral Development, 21,* 571–598.

Pinon, M. F., Huston, A. C., & Wright, J. C. (1989). Family ecology and child characteristics that predict young children's educational television viewing. *Child Development, 60,* 846–856.

Pinstrup-Anderson, P., Pelletier, D., & Alderman, H. (Eds.). (1995). *Children's growth and nutrition in developing countries.* Ithaca, N.Y.: Cornell University Press.

Pittman, T., & Kaufman, M. (1994). *All shapes and sizes: Promoting fitness and self-esteem in your overweight child.* Toronto: Harper Perennial Books.

Plomin, R. (1989). Environment and genes: Determinants of behavior. *American Psychologist, 44,* 105–111.

Plomin, R. (1990). *Nature and nurture: An introduction to human behavioral genetics.* Pacific Grove, Cal.: Brooks/Cole.

Plomin, R., & DeFries, J. C. (1998, August). The genetics of cognitive abilities and disabilities. *Scientific American,* 62–69.

Plomin, R., Emde, R., Braungart, J., Campos, J., Corley, R., Fulker, D., Kagan, J., Resnick, J., Robinson, J., Zahn-Waxler, C., & DeFries, J. (1993). Genetic change and continuity from 14 to 20 months. *Child Development, 64,* 1354–1376.

Plomin, R., Owen, M. J., & McGuffin, P. (1994). The genetic basis of behavior. *Science, 264,* 1733–1739.

Poest, C., Williams, J., Witt, D., & Atwood, M. (1990). Challenge me to move: Large muscle development in young children. *Young Children, 45*(5), 4–10.

Pollitt, E. (Ed.). (1995). *The relationships between undernutrition and behavioral development in children.* Washington, D.C.: American Institute of Nutrition.

Pomerantz, E. M., Ruble, D. N., Frey, K. S., & Greulich, F. (1995). Meeting goals and confronting conflict: Children's changing perceptions of social comparison. *Child Development, 66,* 723–738.

Pope, H. G., & Katz, D. L. (1994) Psychiatric and medical effects of anabolic-androgenic steriod use: A controlled study of 160 athletes. *Archives of General Psychiatry, 51,* 375–382.

Posner, J. K., & Vandell, D. L. (1994). Low-income children's after-school care: Are there beneficial effects of after-school programs? *Child Development, 65,* 440–456.

Powell, M. (1991). The psychosocial impact of Sudden Infant Death Syndrome on siblings. *Irish Journal of Psychology, 12,* 235–247.

Pownall, T., & Kingerlee, S. (1993). *Seeing, reaching, and touching: Relationships between vision and touching in infants.* New York: Harvester and Wheatsheaf.

Price, R. H. (1992). Psychosocial impact of joblessness on individuals and families. *Current Directions in Psychological Science, 1,* 9–11.

Priel, B., & Zeidman, O. (1990). Infant social behavior in front of a mirror in and in front of a familiar and unfamiliar peer. *Journal of Genetic Psychology, 151,* 483–493.

Primeau, M. R. (1993). Fetal movement. In B. K. Rothman (Ed.), *The encyclopedia of childbearing.* New York: Henry Holt.

Pritchett, L. (1993). *Wealthier is healthier.* Washington, D.C.: The World Bank.

Quadrel, M. J., Fischoff, B., & Davis, W. (1993). Adolescent (in)vulnerability. *American Psychologist, 48,* 102–116.

Queen, P., & Lang, C. (1993). *Handbook of pediatric nutrition.* Gaithersburg, Md.: Aspen Publishers.

Radke-Yarrow, M., & Zahn-Waxler, C. (1987). Roots, motives, and patterns in children's prosocial behavior. In J. Reykowski, J. Karylowski, D. Bar-Tal, & E. Staub (Eds.), *Origins and maintenance of prosocial behaviors.* New York: Plenum Press.

Rafoth, M. (1993). *Strategies for learning and remembering: Study skills across the curriculum.* Washington, D.C.: National Education Association.

Ramey, C. T., & Ramey, S. L. (1998). Early intervention and early experience. *American Psychologist, 53,* 109–120.

Ramirez, O. (1998). Mexican American children and adolescents. In J. T. Gibbs, L. N. Huang, et al. (Eds.), *Children of color: Psychological interventions with culturally diverse youth* (Rev. ed., pp. 215–239). San Francisco: Jossey-Bass.

Ramsey, P. (1995). Changing social dynamics in early childhood classrooms. *Child Development, 66,* 764–773.

Raphael, D. (1993). Doula. In B. K. Rothman, (Ed.), *The encyclopedia of childbearing.* New York: Henry Holt.

Raver, C. C. (1996). Relations between social contingency in mother-child interaction and 2-year-old's social competence. *Developmental Psychology, 32,* 850–859.

Rawlins, W. K. (1992). *Friendship matters: Communication, dialectics, and the life course.* New York: Aldine DeGruyter.

Reaves, J., & Roberts, A. (1983). The effect of type of information on children's attraction to peers. *Child Development, 54,* 1024–1031.

Reccio Adrados, J. L. (1995). The influence of family, school, and peers on adolescent drug misuse. *International Journal of the Addictions, 30,* 1407–1423.

Reed, R. J. (1988). Education and achievement of young black males. In J. T. Gibbs (Ed.), *Young, black and male in America: An endangered species* (pp. 37–93). Dover, Mass.: Auburn House.

Reeder, K. (Ed.). (1996). *Literate apprenticeships: The emergence of language and literacy in the preschool years.* Norwood, N. J.: Ablex.

Reid, M., Landesman, S., Treider, R., & Jaccard, J. (1989). "My family and friends": Six- to twelve-year-old perceptions of social support. *Child Development, 60,* 896–910.

Remafedi, G., Resnick, M., Blum, R., & Harris, L. (1992). Demography of sexual orientation in adolescents. *Pediatrics, 89,* 714–721.

Rennie, J. (1994, June). Grading the gene tests. *Scientific American,* 89–97.

Renzulli, J. (1994). *Schools for talent improvement.* Mansfield Center, Conn.: Creative Learning Press.

Restivo, S., VanBendegem, J., & Fischer, R. (1993). *Math worlds: Philosophical and social studies of mathematics and math education.* New York: State University of New York Press.

Reynolds, A. J., & Temple, J. A. (1998). Extended early childhood intervention and school achievement: Age thirteen findings from the Chicago Longitudinal Study. *Child Development, 69,* 231–246.

Richards, M. H., Boxer, A. M., Petersen, A. C., & Albrecht, R. (1990). Relation of weight to body image in pubertal girls and boys from two communities. *Developmental Psychology, 26,* 313–321.

Richards, M. H., Crowe, P. A., Larson, R., & Swarr, A. (1998). Developmental patterns and gender differences in the experience of peer companionship during adolescence. *Child Development, 69,* 154–163.

Richter, P. (1993). HIV and pregnancy. In B. K. Rothman (Ed.), *The encyclopedia of childbearing.* New York: Henry Holt.

Rickman, M. D., & Davidson, R. J. (1995). Personality and behavior in parents of temperamentally inhibited and uninhibited children. *Developmental Psychology, 30,* 346–354.

Rierdan, J., & Koff, E. (1997). Weight, weight-related aspects of body image, and depression in early adolescent girls. *Adolescence, 32,* 615–624.

Roberts, W., & Strayer, J. (1996). Empathy, emotional expressiveness, and prosocial behavior. *Child Development, 67,* 449–470.

Roggman, L. A., Langlois, J. H., Hubbs-Tait, L., & Rieser-Danner, L. A. (1994). Infant day-care, attachment, and the "file drawer problem." *Child Development, 65,* 1429–1443.

Rogoff, B. (1990). *Apprenticeship in thinking.* New York: Oxford University Press.

Rogoff, B., & Chavajay, P. (1995). What's become of research on the cultural basis of cognitive development? *American Psychologist, 50,* 859–877.

Rogoff, B., Mistry, J., Goncu, A., & Mosler, C. (1993). Guided participation in cultural activity by toddlers and caregivers. *Monographs of the Society for Research in Child Development, 58*(8, Serial No. 236).

Roland, A. (1988). *In search of self in India and Japan: Toward a cross-cultural psychology.* Princeton, N.J.: Princeton University Press.

Roland, I., & Gross, A. M. (1995). Cognitive tempo, violent video games, and aggressive behavior in young boys. *Journal of Family Violence, 10,* 337–350.

Romaine, S. (1995). *Bilingualism.* 2nd ed. Oxford, U.K.: Blackwells.

Rooks, J. P., et al. (1989, December). Outcomes of care in birth centers. *New England Journal of Medicine, 321,* 1801–1822.

Roopnarine, J. L., & Field, T. (1982). Peer-directed behaviors of infants and toddlers during nursery school play. In T. Field (Ed.), *Review of human development.* New York: Wiley.

Roopnarine, J. L., Johnson, J. E., & Hooper, F. H. (Eds.). (1994) *Children's play in diverse cultures.* Albany, N.Y.: State University of New York Press.

Rose, J., & Gamble, J. (1993). *Human walking* (2nd ed.). Baltimore: Williams and Williams.

Rosenberg, B. G., & Hyde, J. S. (1993). The only child: Is there only one kind of only? *Journal of Genetic Psychology, 154,* 269–282.

Rosenberg, M. S. (1979). *Conceiving the self.* New York: Basic Books.

Rosenberg, M. S., & Repucci, N. D. (1985). Primary prevention of child abuse. *Journal of Consulting and Clinical Psychology, 53,* 576–585.

Rosenheim, M. K., & Testa, M. F. (Eds.), (1992). *Early parenthood and coming of age in the 1990's.* New Brunswick, N.J.: Rutgers University Press.

Rosenshine, B., & Meister, C. (1994). Reciprocal teaching: A review of the research. *Review of Educational Research, 64*(4), 479–530.

Rosett, H., Weiner, L., Zuckerman, B., McKinlay, S., & Edelin, K. (1980). Reduction of alcohol consumption during pregnancy with benefits to the newborn. *Alcoholism: Clinical and Experimental Research, 4,* 178–184.

Ross, P. (1993). *National excellence: The case for developing America's talent.* Washington, D.C.: United States Department of Education.

Rossell, C. H. (1988). How effective are voluntary plans with magnet schools? *Educational Evaluation and Policy Analysis, 10,* 325–342.

Rothbart, M. K., & Ahadi, S. (1994). Temperament and the development of personality. *Journal of Abnormal Psychology, 103,* 55–66.

Rourke, B., & Del Dotto, J. (1994). *Learning disabilities: Neuropsychological perspectives.* Thousand Oaks, Cal.: Sage.

Rowe, W. and Hanvey, L. (Eds.). (1997). *Building a bridge: Challenges and opportunities in interdisciplinary HIV/AIDS education.* Ottawa, Ontario: Association of Canadian Medical Colleges.

Rowland, T. (1993). The physiological impact of intensive training on the prepubertal athlete. In B. Cahill & A. Pearl (Eds.), *Intensive participation in children's sports* (pp. 167–194). Champaign, Ill. Human Kinetics Press.

Rubenstein, J. L., Halton, A., Kasten, M. A., Rubin, C., & Stechler, G. (1998). Suicidal behavior in adolescents: Stress and protection in different family contexts. *American Journal of Orthopsychiatry, 68,* 274–284.

Rubin, K., & Krasnor, L. (1980). Changes in the play behaviors of preschoolers: A short-term longitudinal investigation. *Canadian Journal of Behavioral Science, 12,* 278–282.

Rubin, K. H., Fein, G. G., & Vandenberg, B. (1983). Play. In E. M. Hetherington (Ed.), *Handbook of child psychology: Vol. 4. Socialization, personality and social development* (4th ed.). New York: Wiley.

Ruble, D. N. (1988). Sex-role development. In M. H. Bornstein & M. E. Lamb (Eds.), *Developmental psychology: An advanced textbook* (2nd ed., pp. 411–460). Hillsdale, N.J.: Erlbaum.

Rueter, M. A., & Conger, R. D. (1995). Interaction style, problem-solving behavior, and family problem-solving effectiveness. *Child Development, 66,* 98–115.

Ruhm, C. J. (1997). Policy watch: The family and medical leave act. *Journal of Economic Perspectives, 11,* 175-186.

Rutter, M. (1995). *Psychosocial disturbances in young people.* New York: Cambridge University Press.

Ryan, J. (1995). *Little girls in pretty boxes: The making and breaking of elite gymnasts and figure skaters.* New York: Doubleday.

Sagi, A., van IJzendoorn, M. H., Aviezer, O., Donnell, F., et al. (1995). Attachments in a multiple-caregiver environment: The case of the Israeli kibbutzim. *Monographs of the Society for Research in Child Development, 60,* 71–91.

Sagi, A., van IJzendoorn, M.H., Scharf, M., Joels, T., et al. (1997). Ecological constraints for intergenerational transmission of attachment. *International Journal of Behavioral Development, 20,* 287–299.

Saler, L., & Skolnick, N. (1992). Childhood parental death and depression in adulthood: Roles of surviving parent and family environment. *American Journal of Orthopsychiatry, 62,* 504–516.

Salomon, G., & Perkins, D. (1998). Individual and social aspects of learning. In P. D. Pearson & A. Iran-Nejad (Eds.), *Review of research in education* (Vol. 23, pp. 1–24). Washington, D.C.: American Educational Research Association.

Samter, W., & Haslett, B. (1997). Family influences on communicative and social development. In B. Haslett & W. Samter (Eds.), *Children communicating: The first five years* (pp. 160–191). Mahwah, N.J.: Erlbaum.

Sanfilippo, J., Finkelstein, J., & Styne, D. (Eds.). (1994). *Medical and gynecological endocrinology.* Philadelphia: Hanley and Belfus.

Sanjur, D. (1995). *Hispanic foodways, nutrition, and health.* Boston: Allyn & Bacon.

Santrock, J., & Sitterle, K. (1987). Parent-child relationships in stepmother families. In K. Pasley & M. Ihinger-Tallman (Eds.), *Remarriage and stepparenting: Current research and theory.* New York: Guilford Press.

Saracho, O. N., & Spodek, B. O. (1998). A historical overview of theories of play. In O. N. Saracho & B. Spodek, et al. (Eds.), *Multiple perspectives on play in early childhood education. SUNY series, early childhood education: Inquiries and insights* (pp. 1–10). Albany, N.Y.: State University of New York Press.

Sato, D. (1983). DES: Diethylstilbestrol. In B. K. Rothman (Ed.), *The encyclopedia of childbearing.* New York: Henry Holt.

Sault, N. (Ed.). (1994). *Many mirrors: Body image and social relations.* New Brunswick, N.J.: Rutgers University Press.

Savelsbergh, G. (1993). *Development of coordination in infancy.* New York: North-Holland.

Savin-Williams, R., & Berndt, T. (1990). Peer relations during adolescence. In S. Feldman & G. Elliot (Eds.), *At the threshold: The developing adolescent.* Cambridge, Mass.: Harvard University Press.

Savin-Williams, R. C. (1995). An exploratory study of pubertal maturation timing and self-esteem among gay and bisexual male youths. *Developmental Psychology, 31,* 56–64.

Sawin, D. (1979). *Assessing empathy in children: A search for an elusive construct.* Paper presented at the meeting of the Society for Research on Child Development, San Francisco.

Scarr, S. (1998). American child care today. *American Psychologist, 53,* 95–108.

Scarr, S., & McCartney, K. (1983). How people make their own environments: A theory of genotype-environment effects. *Child Development, 54,* 424–435.

Schlegel, A., & Barry, H. (1991). *Adolescence: An anthropological inquiry* (pp. 133–156). New York: Free Press.

Schrader, D. (Ed.). (1990). *The legacy of Lawrence Kohlberg (New Directions in Child Development,* No. 47). San Francisco: Jossey-Bass.

Schrum, W., & Cheek, N. (1987). Social structure during the school years: Onset of the degrouping process. *American Psychological Review, 52,* 218–223.

Schwartz, D., Dodge, K. A., Pettit, G. S., & Bates, J. (1997). The early socialization of aggression and bullying. *Child Development, 68,* 665–675.

Schwarzenegger, A., & Gaines, C. (1994). *Arnold's fitness for kids, age 6–10: A guide to health, exercise, and nutrition.* New York: Doubleday.

Schweinhart, L., Barnes, H., & Weikart, D. (1993). Significant benefits: The High/Scope Perry Preschool Study through age 27. (*Monographs of the High/Scope Educational Research Foundation,* No. 10). Ypsilanti, Mich.: High/Scope Press.

Schweinhart, L., & Weikart, D. (1992). The High/Scope Perry Preschool Study, similar studies, and their implications for public policy in the United States. In D. Stagelin (Ed.), *Early childhood education: Policy issues for the 1990's* (pp. 67–88). Norwood, N.J.: Ablex.

Scollon, R., & Scollon, S. (1994). *Intercultural communication: A discourse approach.* Oxford, U.K.: Blackwell.

Scraton, S. (1992). *Shaping up to womanhood: Gender and girls' physical education.* Philadelphia: Open University Press.

Seeram, E. (1994). *Computed tomography: Physical principles, clinical applications, and quality control.* Philadelphia: Saunders.

Segall, M. H., Lonner, W. J., & Berry, J. W. (1998). Cross-cultural psychology as a scholarly discipline: On the flowering of culture in behavioral research. *American Psychologist, 53,* 1101–1110.

Seidel, H., Rosenstein, B., & Pathak, A. (Eds.). (1997). *Primary care of the newborn* (2nd ed.). St. Louis: Mosby.

Seidman, S. N., & Rieder, R. O. (1994). A review of sexual behavior in the United States. *American Journal of Psychiatry, 151,* 330–341.

Seidner, L. B., Stipek, D. J., & Feshbach, N. D. (1988). A developmental analysis of elementary school-aged children's concepts of pride and embarrassment. *Child Development, 59,* 367–377.

Seifer, R., Sameroff, A. J., Barrett, L. C., & Krafechuk, E. (1994). Infant temperament measured by multiple observations and mother reports. *Child Development, 65,* 1478–1490.

Seifert, K. (1993). Cognitive development in early childhood. In B. Spodek (Ed.), *Handbook of research on the education of young children* (3rd ed., pp. 7–40). New York: Macmillan.

Seifert, K. (1999). Uniformity and diversity in everyday views of "the" child. In S. Harkness (Ed.), *New directions in child development: Parental belief systems in cultural context.* San Francisco: Jossey-Bass.

Seitz, V., & Apfel, N. (1994). Parent-focused intervention: Diffusion effects on siblings. *Child Development, 65*(2), 677–683.

Selekman, J. (1993). Update: New guidelines for the treatment of infants with sickle cell disease. *Pediatric Nursing, 19,* 800–809.

Selman, R. (1980). *The growth of interpersonal understanding.* New York: Academic Press.

Selman, R. (1981). The child as friendship philosopher. In S. Asher & J. Gottman (Eds.), *The development of children's friendships.* New York: Cambridge University Press.

Sen, A. (1993, May). The economics of life and death. *Scientific American,* 40–47.

Shafer, M. B., & Moscicki, A. (1991). Sexually transmitted diseases. In W. R. Hendee (Ed.), *The health of adolescents: Understanding and facilitating biological, behavioral, and social development* (pp. 211–249). San Francisco: Jossey-Bass.

Shapiro, J. P. (1993). *No pity: People with disabilities forging a new civil rights movement.* New York: Random House.

Shaw, A., Fulton, L., Davis, C., & Hogbin, M. (1996). *Using the food guide pyramid: A resource for nutrition educators.* Rev. ed. Washington, D.C.: Center for Nutrition Policy and Promotion, United States Department of Agriculture.

Shedler, J., & Block, J. (1990). Adolescent drug use and psychological health. *American Psychologist, 45,* 612–630.

Sheldon, S., Spire, J., & Levy, H. (1992). *Pediatric sleep medicine.* Philadelphia: Saunders.

Shepherd-Look, D. (1982). Sex differentiation and the development of sex roles. In B. Wolman (Ed.), *Handbook of developmental psychology.* Englewood Cliffs, N.J.: Prentice-Hall.

Shrum, W., Cheek, N. H., & Hunter, S. M. (1988). Friendship in school: Gender and racial homophily. *Sociology of Education, 61,* 227–239.

Shure, M. B., & Spivak, G. (1988). Interpersonal cognitive problem solving. In R. H. Price, W. L. Cowen, R. P. Lorion, & J. Ramos-McKay (Eds.), *14 ounces of prevention: A casebook for practitioners* (pp. 69–82). Washington, D.C.: American Psychological Association.

Siegler, R. (1995, March). *Nothing is; everything becomes; recent advances in understanding cognitive-developmental change.* Paper presented at the biennial meeting of the Society for Research on Child Development, Indianapolis. USA.

Sigelman, C., Maddox, A., Epstein, J., & Carpenter, W. (1993). Age differences in understandings of disease causality: AIDS, colds and cancer. *Child Development, 64,* 272–284.

Silber, S. J. (1991). *How to get pregnant with the new technology.* New York: Warner Books.

Silverman, P., & Worden, J. (1993). Children's reactions to the death of a parent. In M. Stroebe, W. Stroebe, & R. Hansson (Eds.), *Handbook of bereavement: Theory, research, and intervention* (pp. 300–315). New York: Cambridge University Press.

Silverman, P. R., Nickman, S., & Worden, J. W. (1992). Detachment revisited: The child's reconstruction of a dead parent. *American Journal of Orthopsychiatry, 62,* 495–505.

Silverstein, L. B. (1991). Transforming the debate about child care and maternal employment. *American Psychologist, 46,* 1025–1032.

Simonds, W. (1993). Politics of abortion. In B. K. Rothman (Ed.), *The encyclopedia of childbearing.* New York: Henry Holt.

Simons, R. L., & Beaman, J. (1996). Fathers' parenting. In R. L. Simons et al. (Eds.), *Understanding differences between divorced and intact families: Stress, interaction and child outcome* (pp. 94–103). Thousand Oaks, Cal.: Sage.

Simons, R. L., & Chao, W. (1996). Conduct problems. In R. L. Simons et al. (Eds.), *Understanding differences between divorced and intact families: Stress, interaction, and child outcome* (pp. 81–93). Thousand Oaks, Cal.: Sage.

Simons, R. L., & Johnson, C. (1996). Mothers' parenting. In R. L. Simons et al. (Eds.), *Understanding differences between divorced and intact families: Stress, interaction and child outcome* (pp. 81–93). Thousand Oaks, Cal.: Sage.

Sinclair, D. (1990). *Human growth after birth* (5th ed.). New York: Oxford University Press.

Singer, J. L. (1995). Imaginative play in childhood: Precursor of subjunctive thought, daydreaming, and adult pretending games. In A. D. Pelligrini (Ed.), *The future of play theory: A multidisciplinary inquiry into the contributions of Brian Sutton-Smith. SUNY series, children's play in society* (pp. 187–219). Albany, N.Y.: State University of New York Press.

Sinnott, J. (1998). *The development of logic in adulthood: Postformal thought and its applications.* New York: Plenum.

Sipe, B., & Hall, E. J. (1996). *I am not your victim.* Newbury Park, Cal.: Sage.

Sizer, Theodore. (1996). *Horace's hope.* Boston: Houghton Mifflin.

Skinner, B. F. (1957). *Verbal behavior.* New York: Appleton-Century-Crofts.

Skolnick, A., & Skolnick, J. (1989). *Families in transition: Rethinking marriage, sexuality, child-rearing and family organization* (6th ed.). New York: Scott Foresman.

Slade, A. (1987). Quality of attachment and early symbolic play. *Developmental Psychology, 23,* 78–85.

Slater, A., & Morrison, V. (1991). Visual attention and memory at birth. In M. Weiss & P. Zelazo (Eds.), *Newborn attention: Biological constraints and the influence of experience* (pp. 256–277). Norwood, N.J.: Ablex.

Slavin, R. (1996). Research on cooperative learning and achievement: What we know, and what we need to know. *Contemporary Educational Psychology, 21,* 43–69.

Slavin, R. (Ed.). (1998). *Show me the evidence: Promising programs for American schools.* Thousand Oaks, Cal.: Corwin Press.

Slavin, R. E. (1990). Achievement effects of ability grouping in secondary schools: A best evidence synthesis. *Review of Educational Research, 60,* 471–499.

Slavin, R.E. (1995). *Cooperative learning* (2nd ed.) Boston: Allyn & Bacon.

Slomin, M. (1991). *Children, culture, and ethnicity: Evaluating and understanding the impact.* New York: Garland.

Slomkowski, C. L., & Dunn, J. (1992). Argument and relationships within the family: Differences in young children's disputes with mother and sibling. *Developmental Psychology, 28,* 919–924.

Sloper, P., Turner, S., Knussen, C., & Cunningham, C. C. (1990). Social life of school children with Down's syndrome. *Child Care, Health, and Development, 16,* 235–251.

Smetana, J. G. (1995). Parenting styles and conceptions of parental authority during adolescence. *Child Development, 66,* 299–316.

Smetana, J. G., Killen, M., & Turiel, E. (1991a). Children's reasoning about interpersonal and moral conflicts. *Child Development, 62,* 629–644.

Smetana, J. G., Yau, J., Restrepo, A., & Braeges, J. L. (1991b). Adolescent-parent conflict in married and divorced families. *Developmental Psychology, 27,* 1000–1010.

Smith, A. (1996). Rehabilitation of children following sport- and activity-related injuries. In O. Bar-Or (Ed.), *The child and adolescent athlete* (pp. 224–244). Oxford, U.K.: Blackwells.

Smith, D. (1998). *Inclusion: Schools for all students.* Belmont, Cal.: Wadsworth.

Smith, D. E., & Blinn Pike, L. (1994). Relationship between Jamaican adolescents' drinking patterns and self-image: A cross-cultural perspective. *Adolescence, 29,* 429–437.

Smith, N., & Tsimpli, I. (1995). *The mind of a savant: Language learning and modularity.* Oxford, U.K.: Blackwell.

Smitherman-Donaldson, G. (1994). *Black talk: Words and phrases from the hood to the amen corner.* Boston: Houghton Mifflin.

Snowling, M., & Stackhouse, J. (1996). *Dyslexia, speech, and language: A practitioner's handbook.* San Diego: Singular Publishers Group.

Snyder, H. N., & Sickmund, M. (1995). *Juvenile offenders and victims: A national report* (Document No. NJC-153569). Washington, D.C.: U.S. Department of Justice, Office of Juvenile Justice and Delinquency Prevention.

Soldier, L. (1993). Working with Native-American children. *Young Children, 47*(6), 15–21.

Sommerville, J. (1990). *The rise and fall of childhood* (2nd ed.). New York: Vintage Books.

Sorenson, S., & Bowie, P. (1994). Vulnerable populations: Girls and young women. In L. Eron & J. Gentry (Eds.), *Violence and youth: Psychology's response: Vol. II. Papers of the American Psychological Association on Violence and Youth.* Washington, D.C.: American Psychological Association.

Soto, L. (1997). *Language, culture, and power: Bilingual families and the struggle for quality education.* Albany, N.Y.: State University of New York Press.

Spaccarelli, S. (1994). Stress, appraisal, and coping in child sexual abuse: A theoretical and empirical review. *Psychological Bulletin, 116,* 340–362.

Sparshott, M. (1997). *Pain, distress and the newborn baby*. Oxford, U.K.: Blackwell Science.

Spassov, L., Curzi-Dscalovi, L., Clairambualt, J., Kauffman, F., Eiselt, M., Medigue, C., & Peirano, P. (1994). Heart rate and heart-rate variability during sleep in small-for-gestational-age newborns. *Pediatric Research, 35,* 500–505.

Spearman, C. (1927). *The abilities of man.* New York: Macmillan.

Speece, M. W., & Brent, S. B. (1984). Children's understanding of death: A review of three components of the death concept. *Child Development, 55,* 1671–1686.

Spencer, M. B., & Markstrom-Adams, C. (1990). Identity processes among racial and ethnic minority children in American. *Child Development, 61,* 290–310.

Spetner, N., & Olsho, L. (1990). Auditory frequency resolution in human infants. *Child Development, 61,* 632–652.

Spitz, R. A. (1945). Hospitalism: An inquiry in the genesis of psychiatric conditioning in early childhood. In D. Feneschel et al. (Eds.), *Psychoanalytic Studies of the Child: Vol. 1* (pp. 53–74). New York: International Universities Press.

Spitz, R. A. (1946). Hospitalism: A follow-up report. In D. Feneschel et al. (Eds.), *Psychoanalytic Studies of the Child: Vol. 1* (pp. 113–117). New York: International Universities Press.

Spodek, B., & Saracho, O. (Eds.). (1993). *Language and literacy in early childhood education.* New York: Teachers' College Press.

Sponseller, D., & Jaworski, A. (1979). *Social and cognitive complexity in young children's play.* Paper presented at the annual meeting of the American Educational Research Association, San Francisco.

Sroufe, L. A., Bennett, C., Englund, M., Urban, J., & Shulman, S. (1993). The significance of gender boundaries in preadolescence: Contemporary correlates and antecedents of boundary violation and maintenance. *Child Development, 63,* 455–466.

Sroufe, L. A., Fox, N., & Pancake, V. (1983). Attachment and dependency in developmental perspective. *Child Development, 54,* 1615–1627.

St. James-Roberts, I., & Halil, T. (1991). Infant crying patterns in the first year: Normal community and clinical findings. *Journal of Child Psychology and Psychiatry, 32,* 951–968.

St. James-Roberts, I., Harris, G., & Messer, D. (Eds.). (1993). *Infant crying, feeding, and sleeping: Development, problems, and treatments.* New York: Harvester Wheatsheaf.

St. Peters, M., Fitch, M., Huston, A. C., Wright, J .C., & Eakins, D. J. (1991). Television and families: What do young children watch with their parents? *Child Development, 62,* 1409–1423.

Stake, J. E. (1997). Integrating expressiveness and instrumentality in real-life settings: A new perspective on the benefits of androgyny. *Sex Roles, 37,* 541–564.

Steele, H., Steele, M., & Fonagy, P. (1996). Associations among attachment classifications of mothers, fathers, and their infants. *Child Development, 67,* 541–555.

Steiger, C. (1993). Midwifery: Overview. In B. K. Rothman (Ed.), *The encyclopedia of childbearing.* New York: Henry Holt.

Steiger, C. (1993). Midwifry: Overview. In B. K. Rothman (Ed.), *The encyclopedia of childbearing.* New York: Henry Holt.

Steinberg, L. D. (1986). Latchkey children and susceptibility to peer pressure: An ecological analysis. *Developmental Psychology, 22,* 433–439.

Steinberg, L. D., & Dornbusch, S. M. (1991). Negative correlates of part-time employment during adolescence: Replication and elaboration. *Developmental Psychology, 27,* 304–313.

Steinberg, L. D., Lamborn, S. D., Dornbusch, S. M., & Darling, N. (1992). Impact of parenting practices on adolescent achievement: Authoritative parenting, school involvement, and encouragement to succeed. *Child Development, 63,* 1266–1281.

Steinberg, L., Lamborn, S. D., Darling, N., Mounts, N. S., & Dornbusch, S. M. (1994). Over-time changes in adjustment and competence among adolescents from authoritative, authoritarian, indulgent, and neglectful families. *Child Development, 65,* 754–770.

Steinberg, L. D., & Levine, A. D. (1990). *You and your adolescent: A parent's guide to development from 10 to 20.* New York: Harper & Row.

Steiner, G. (1987). Spatial reasoning in small-scale and large-scale environments. In B. Inhelder, D. DeCaprona and A. Cornu-Wells, (Eds.), *Piaget today.* Hillsdale, NJ: Erlbaum.

Steininger, M., Newell, J. D., & Garcia, L. (1984). *Ethical issues in psychology.* Homewood, Ill.: Dorsey Press.

Stern, D. N. (1985a). *The first relationship: Infant and mother.* (4th ed.). Cambridge, Mass.: Harvard University Press.

Stern, D. N. (1985b). *The interpersonal world of the infant: A view from psychoanalysis and developmental psychology.* New York: Basic Books.

Stern, D. N. (1992). *Diary of a baby.* New York: Basic Books.

Stern, D. N. (1995). *The motherhood constellation: A unified view of parent-infant psychotherapy.* New York: Basic Books.

Stern, D. N., Bruschweiler-Stern, & Freeland, A. (1997). *The birth of a mother: Charting the the inner landscape of the motherhood experience.* New York: Basic Books.

Sternberg, R. (1994). *Thinking and problem solving.* San Diego: Academic Press.

Sternberg, R. (1997). *Thinking styles.* New York: Cambridge University Press.

Sternberg, R. (1998). Abilities are forms of developing expertise. *Educational Researcher, 27*(3), 11–21.

Sternberg, R. J. (1988). *The triarchic mind: A new theory of human intelligence.* New York: Penguin Books.

Sternberg, R., & Wagner, R. (Eds.). (1994). *Mind in context: Interactionist perspectives on human intelligence.* New York: Cambridge University Press.

Stevenson, H. W., Chen, C., & Lee, S. (1993). Mathematics achievement of Chinese, Japanese, and American children: Ten years later. *Science, 259,* 53–58.

Stevenson, H. W., Chen, C., & Uttal, D. H. (1990). Beliefs and achievement: A study of black, white and Hispanic children. *Child Development, 61,* 508–523.

Stevenson, H. W., & Lee, S. Y. (1990). Contexts of achievement: A study of American, Chinese, and Japanese children. *Monographs of the Society for Research in Child Development, 55.*

Stevenson, H. W., & Stigler, J. (1992). *The learning gap: Why our schools are failing and what we can learn from Japanese and Chinese education.* New York: Summit Books.

Stevenson-Hinde, J. (1998). Parenting in different cultures: Time to focus. *Developmental Psychology, 34,* 698–700.

Stewart, R. B., Mobley, L. A., Van Tuyl, S. S., & Salvador, M. A. (1987). The firstborn's adjustment to the birth of a sibling: A longitudinal assessment. *Child Development, 58,* 341–355.

Stifter, C. A., Coulehan, C. M., & Fish, M. (1993). Linking employment to attachment: The mediating effects of maternal separation anxiety and interactive behavior. *Child Development, 64,* 1451–1460.

Stipek, D., & Hoffman, J. (1980). Children's achievement related expectancies as a function of academic performance histories and sex. *Journal of Educational Psychology, 72,* 861–865.

Stipek, D. J., Gralinski, H., & Kopp, C. B. (1990). Self-concept development in the toddler years. *Developmental Psychology, 26,* 972–977.

Stocker, C. (1994). Children's perceptions of relationship with siblings, friends and mothers: Compensatory processes and links with adjustment. *Journal of Child Psychology and Psychiatry, 35,* 1447–1459.

Stokes, G. (1985). The social profile. In R. Coles & G. Stokes (Eds.), *Sex and the American teenager* (pp. 31–144). New York: Harper & Row.

Stolberg, A. L., & Walsh, P. (1988). A review of treatment methods for children of divorce. In S. A. Wolchik & P. Karoly (Eds.), *Children of divorce* (pp. 299–321). New York: Gardner Press.

Stone, M. R., Brown, B. B. (1998). In the eye of the beholder: Adolescents' perceptions of peer crowd stereotypes. In R. E. Muuss, H. D. Porton, et al. (Eds.), *Adolescent behavior and society; A book of readings* (5th ed., pp. 158–169). New York: McGraw-Hill.

Stout, B. C., (1993). Thalidomide. In B. K. Rothman (Ed.), *The encyclopedia of childbearing.* New York: Henry Holt.

Stratford, B. (1994). Down syndrome is for life. *International Journal of Disability, Development and Education, 41,* 3–13.

Streissguth, A. P., Barr, H. M., Sampson, P. D., Darby, B. L., & Martin, D. C. (1989). IQ at age 4 in relation to maternal alcohol use and smoking during pregnancy. *Developmental Psychology, 25,* 3–11.

Streissguth, A. P., Bookstein, F. L., Sampson, P., & Barr, H. (1995). Attention: Prenatal alcohol and continuities of vigilance and attentional problems from 4 through 14 years. *Development and Psychopathology, 7,* 419–446.

Striegel-Moore, R., Silberstein, L. R., & Rodin, J. (1986). Toward an understanding of bulimia. *American Psychologist, 41,* 246–263.

Strom, R., Collingsworth, P., Strom, S., & Griswald, D. (1995). Strengths and needs of black grandparents. In J. Hendricks (Ed.), *The ties of later life* (pp. 195–207). Amityville, N.Y.: Baywood.

Subramanian, S. (1995, January 16). The story in our genes. *Time,* 54–55.

Sue, S. (1998) In search of cultural competence in psychotherapy and counseling. *American Psychologist, 53,* 440–448.

Sue, S., & Zane, N. (1987). The role of culture and cultural techniques in psychotherapy: A critique and reformulation. *American Psychologist, 42,* 37–45.

Sue, S., Zane, N., & Young, K., (1994). Research on psychotherapy with culturally diverse populations. In A. E. Bergin & S. L. Garfield (Eds.), *Handbook of psychotherapy and behavior change* (4th ed., pp. 783–820). New York: Wiley.

Sullivan, H. S. (1953). *The interpersonal theory of psychiatry.* New York: Norton.

Sullivan, K., & Sullivan, A. (1980). Adolescent-parent separation. *Developmental Psychology, 16,* 93–99.

Susa, A. M., & Benedict, J. O. (1994). The effects of playground design on pretend play and divergent thinking. *Environment and Behavior, 26,* 560–579.

Swanson, H., Cooney, J., & Brock, S. (1993). The influence of working memory and classification ability on children's word

problem solution. *Journal of Experimental Child Psychology, 55,* 374–395.

Taffel, S. M. (1989). Cesarean sections in America: Dramatic trends, 1970 to 1987. *Statistical Bulletin, 70,* 2–11.

Taffel, S. M. (1993). Cesarean birth: Social and political aspects. In B. K. Rothman (Ed.), *The encyclopedia of childbearing.* New York: Henry Holt.

Takahashi, K. (1990). Are the key assumptions of the "Strange Situation" procedure universal? A view from Japanese research. *Human Development, 33,* 23–30.

Takanishi, R. (1993). The opportunities of adolescence—Research, interventions, and policy: Introduction to the special issue. *American Psychologist, 48,* 85–88.

Takanishi, R., & Hamburg, D. (Eds.). (1997). *Preparing adolescents for the 21st century.* New York: Cambridge University Press.

Tanner, J. M. (1990). *Fetus into man. Physical growth from conception to maturity* (rev. ed.). Cambridge, Mass.: Harvard University Press.

Tanner, J. M. (1998). Sequence, tempo, and individual variation in growth and development of boys and girls aged twelve to sixteen. In R. E. Muuss & H. D. Porton, et al. (Eds.), *Adolescent behavior and society: A book of readings* (5th ed., pp. 34–46). New York: McGraw-Hill.

Task Force on Pediatric AIDS. (1989). Pediatric AIDS and human immunodeficiency virus infection: Psychological issues. *American Psychologist, 44,* 258–264.

Taylor, J., Gilligan, C., & Sullivan, A. (1995). *Between voice and silence: Women and girls, race and relationship.* Cambridge, Mass.: Harvard University Press.

Teberg, A. J., Walther, F. J., & Pena, I. C. (1988). Mortality, morbidity, and outcome of the small-for-gestational-age infant. *Seminars in Perinatology, 12,* 84–94.

Teller, D., & Lindsey, D. (1993). Motion nulling techniques in infant color vision. In C. Granrud (Ed.), *Visual perception and cognition in infants* (pp. 47–75). Hillsdale, N.J.: Erlbaum.

Tesman, J., & Hills, A. (1994). Developmental effects of lead exposure in children. *Social Policy Report: Society for Research on Child Development, 8*(3).

Teti, D. M., (1992). *Sibling interaction.* New York: Plenum Press.

Thelen, E. (1995). Motor development: A new synthesis. *American Psychologist, 50,* 79–95.

Thomas, A., & Chess, S. (1981). The role of temperament in the contributions of individuals to their development. In R. Lerner & N. Busch-Rossnagle (Eds.), *Individuals as producers of their development: A life-span perspective.* New York: Academic Press.

Thompson, R. A. (1990a). On emotion and self-regulation. In R. A. Thompson (Ed.), *Nebraska symposium on motivation: Vol. 36* (pp. 383–483). Lincoln, Neb.: University of Nebraska Press.

Thompson, R. A. (1990b). Vulnerability in research: A developmental perspective on research risk. *Child Development, 61* (1), 144–148.

Tillman, P. (1992). *Adolescent alcoholism.* Bethesda, Md.: U.S. Department of Health and Human Services.

Tobin-Richards, M. H., Boxer, A. M., & Petersen, A. C. (1983). The psychological significance of pubertal change: Sex differences in perceptions of self during early adolescence. In J. Brooks-Gunn & A. C. Petersen (Eds.), *Girls at puberty: Biological and psychological perspectives* (pp. 127–154). New York: Plenum.

Tolson, T., & Wilson, M. (1990). The impact of two- and three-generational black family structure on perceived family climate. *Child Development, 61,* 416–428.

Tomada, G., & Schneider, B. H. (1997). Relational aggression, gender, and peer acceptance: Invariance across culture, stability over time, and concordance among informants. *Developmental Psychology, 33,* 601–609.

Torney-Purta, J. (1990a). Youth in relation to social institutions. In S. Feldman & G. Elliott (Eds.), *At the threshold: The developing adolescent* (pp. 457–477). Cambridge, Mass.: Harvard University Press.

Torney-Purta, J. (1990b). From attitudes and knowledge to schemata: Expanding the outcomes of political socialization research. In O. Ichilov (Ed.), *Political socialization, citizenship education, and democracy* (pp. 98–115). New York: Teachers' College Press.

Trinke, S., & Bartholomew, K. (1997). Hierarchies of attachment relationships in young adulthood. *Journal of Social and Personal Relationships, 14,* 603–625.

Tronick, E. Z. (1989). Emotions and emotional communication in infants. *American Psychologist, 44,* 112–119.

Tronick, E. Z., Morelli, G. A., & Ivey, P. K. (1992). The Efe forager infant and toddler's pattern of social relationships: Multiple and simultaneous. *Developmental Psychology, 28,* 568–577.

Turkheimer, E., & Gottsman, I. I. (1991). Individual differences and the canalization of human behavior. *Developmental Psychology, 27,* 18–22.

United Nations International Children's Emergency Fund. (1995). *The state of the world's children: 1995.* New York: Oxford University Press.

United Nations International Children's Emergency Fund. (1998). *State of the world's children—1998.* New York: Oxford University Press.

U. S. Department of Health and Human Services. (1994). *Preventing tobacco use among young people.* Washington, D.C.: Author.

U.S. Bureau of the Census. (1992). *Poverty in the United States, 1991.* Washington, D.C.: U.S. Government Printing Office.

U.S. Bureau of the Census. (1995). *Marital status and living arrangements: March, 1995* (Series P–20, No. 445). Washington, D.C.: U.S. Government Printing Office.

U.S. Bureau of the Census. (1996). *Statistical abstract of the United States:* (116th ed.). Washington, D.C.: U.S. Government Printing Office.

U.S. Congress Select Committee on Hunger. (1992). *Hunger in America: Who cares?* Washington, D.C.: United States Government Printing Office.

U.S. Congressional Budget Office. (1993). *Trends in health spending.* Washington, D.C: Author:

U.S. Department of Commerce. (1998). *Statistical abstract of the United States, 1997.* (118th ed.). Washington, D.C: U.S. Government Printing Office.

U.S. Department of Health and Human Services. (1990). *The health benefits of smoking cessation: A report of the Surgeon General.* Public Health Service, Centers for Disease Control, Center for Chronic Disease Prevention and Health Promotion, Office on Smoking and Health. DHHS Publication No. (CDC) 90-8416.

U.S. Department of Health and Human Services. (1993). *Talking to children about death.* Washington, D.C.: U.S. Government Printing Office.

U.S. Department of Health and Human Services. (1994a). *Creating a 21st century Head Start: Final report of the advisory committee on Head Start quality and expansion.* Washington, D.C.: U.S. Government Printing Office.

U.S. Department of Health and Human Services. (1994b). *Back to sleep: Reducing the risk of SIDS: What you can do.* Bethesda, Md.: Author.

U.S. General Accounting Office. (1993). *Preventive home care for children: Experience from select foreign countries.* Washington, D.C.: Author.

U.S. National Center for Health Statistics. (1998). *Vital statistics of the United States.* Washington, D.C.: U.S. Government Printing Office.

Uljens, M. (1997). *School didactics and learning.* East Sussex, U.K.: Psychology Press.

Urberg, K. A., Degirmencioglu, S. M., Tolson, J. M., & Halliday-Scher, K. (1995). The structure of adolescent peer networks. *Developmental Psychology, 31,* 540–547.

van den Boom, D. C. (1994). The influence of temperament and mothering on attachment and exploration: An experimental manipulation of sensitive responsiveness among lower-class mothers with irritable infants. *Child Development, 65,* 1457–1477.

van den Boom, D. C., & Hoeksma, J. B. (1994). The effect of infant irritability on mother-infant interaction: A growth-curve analysis. *Developmental Psychology, 30,* 581–590.

van IJzendoorn, M. H. (1992) Review. Intergenerational transmission of parenting: A review of studies in nonclinical populations. *Developmental Review, 12,* 76–99.

van IJzendoorn, M. H. (1995). Adult attachment representations, parental responsiveness, and infant attachment: A meta-analysis on the predictive validity of the adult attachment interview. *Psychological Bulletin, 117,* 387–403.

van IJzendoorn, M. H., & Bakermans-Kranenburg, M. J. (1997). *Intergenerational transmission of attachment: A move to the contextual level.* New York: Guilford Press.

van IJzendoorn, M. H., & De Wolff, M. S. (1997). In search of the absent father—Meta-analysis of infant-father attachment: A rejoinder to our discussants. *Child Development, 68,* 604–609.

van IJzendoorn, M. H., & Kroonenberg, P. M. (1988). Cross-cultural patterns of attachment: A meta-analysis of the Strange Situation. *Child Development, 59,* 147–156.

Van Keulen, J., Weddington, G., & DeBose, C. (1998). *Speech, language, learning, and the African-American child.* Boston: Allyn and Bacon.

van Reek, J., Adriaanze, H., & Knibbe, R. (1994). Alcohol consumption and correlates among children in the European Community. *International Journal of Addictions, 29,* 15–21.

van-der-voort, T. H. A., & Valkenburg, P. M. (1994). Television's impact on fantasy play: A review of research. *Developmental Review, 14,* 227–251.

Vandell, D. L. (1980). Sociability with peers and mothers in the first year. *Developmental Psychology, 16,* 355–361.

Vandell, D. L., & Ramanan, J. (1991). Children of the national longitudinal survey of youth: Choices in after-school care and child development. *Developmental Psychology, 27,* 637–643.

Vandell, D. L., Hyde, J. S., Plant, E. A., & Essex, M. J. (1997). Fathers and "others" as infant-care providers: Predictors of parents' emotional well-being and marital satisfaction. *Merrill-Palmer Quarterly, 43,* 361–385.

Ventura, S. J., Martin, J. A., Curtin, S. C., & Mathews, T. J. (1997). Report of final natality statistics, 1995. *Monthly Vital Statistics Report, 45*(11, Suppl. 2). Hyattsville, Md.: National Center for Health Statistics.

Vernberg, E. M. (1990). Experiences with peers following relocation during early adolescence. *American Journal of Orthopsychiatry, 60,* 466–472.

Vissing, Y. (1996). *Out of sight, out of mind: Homeless children and families in small-town America.* Lexington, Ky.: University Press of Kentucky.

Vitaro, F., Tremblay, R. E., Kerr, M., Pagani, L., & Bukowski, W. M. (1997). Disruptiveness, friends' characteristics, and delinquency in early adolescence: A test of two competing models of development. *Child Development, 68,* 676–689.

Volk, T. (1995). *Metapatterns across time, space, and mind.* New York: Columbia University Press.

Volling, B. L., & Belsky, J. (1992). Contribution of mother-child and father-child relationships to the quality of sibling interaction: A longitudinal study. *Child Development, 63,* 1209–1222.

Volling, B. L., Youngblade, L. M., & Belsky, J. (1997). Young children's social relationships with siblings and friends. *American Journal of Orthopsychiatry, 67,* 102–111.

Vorhees, C. W., & Mollnow, E. (1987). Behavioral teratogenesis: Long-term influences on behavior from early exposure to environmental agents. In J. D. Osofsky (Ed.), *Handbook of infant development* (2nd ed., pp. 913–971). New York: Wiley.

Vuchinich, S., Hetherington, E. M., Vuchinich, R. A., & Clingempeel, W. G. (1991). Parent-child interaction and gender differences in early adolescents' adaptation to stepfamilies. *Developmental Psychology, 27,* 618–626.

Vygotsky, L. (1962). *Thought and language.* Cambridge, Mass.: MIT Press.

Vygotsky, L. (1967). Play and its role in the mental development of the child. *Soviet Psychology, 12,* 62–76.

Vygotsky, L. (1978). *Mind in society: The development of higher psychological processes.* Cambridge, Mass.: Harvard University Press.

Vygotsky, L. (1987). *Thinking and speech.* New York: Plenum Press.

Vygotsky, L. (1997). *Educational psychology.* Boca Raton, Fla.: St. Lucie Press.

Waddington, C. H. (1966). *Principles of development and differentiation.* New York: Macmillan.

Wadsworth, B. (1996). *Piaget's theory of cognitive and affective development: Foundations of constructivism.* 5th ed. White Plains, N.Y.: Longman.

Waite-Stupiansky, S. (1997). *Building understanding together: A constructivist approach to early childhood education.* Albany, N. Y.: Delmar.

Wakschlag, L. S., Chase-Landsdale, P. L., & Brooks-Gunn, J. (1996). Not just "ghosts in the nursery": Contemporaneous intergenerational relationships and parenting in young African-American families. *Child Development, 67,* 2131–2147.

Waldman, S. (1993). Contraception: Defining terms. In B. K. Rothman (Ed.), *The encyclopedia of childbearing.* New York: Henry Holt.

Walkerdine, V. (1997). Redefining the subject in situated cognition theory. In D. Kirschner & J. Whitson (Eds.), *Situated cognition: Social, semiotic, and psychological perspectives* (pp. 57–70). Mahwah, N.J.: Erlbaum.

Wallerstein, J., & Blakeslee, S. (1996). *Second chances, Men, women and children a decade after divorce.* Boston: Houghton Mifflin.

Wandersman, A., & Nation, M. (1998). Urban neighborhoods and mental health: Psychological contributions to understanding toxicity, resilience, and interventions. *American Psychologist, 53,* 647–656.

Wang, V., & Marsh, F. H. (1992). Ethical principles and cultural integrity in health care delivery: Asian ethnocultural perspectives. *Journal of Genetic Counseling, 1,* 81–92.

Wardle, F. (1995). Alternatives . . . Bruderhof education: Outdoor school. *Young Children, 50*(3), 68–74.

Webb, N. (Ed.). (1993). *Helping bereaved children: A handbook for practitioners.* New York: Guilford Press.

Weinberg, M. K., & Tronick, E. Z. (1994). Beyond the face: The empirical study of infant affective configurations of facial, vocal, gestural, and regulatory behaviors. *Child Development, 65,* 1503–1515.

Weinberg, N. Z., Rahdert, E., Colliver J. D., & Glantz, M. D. (1998). Adolescent substance abuse: A review of the past 10 years. *Journal of the American Academy of Child and Adolescent Psychiatry, 37,* 252–261.

Weiser, T. (1989). Comparing sibling relationships across cultures. In P. Zukow (Ed.), *Sibling interaction across cultures: Theoretical and methodological issues* (pp. 11–25). New York: Springer-Verlag.

Weisner, T. S., & Wilson-Mitchell, J. E. (1990). Nonconventional family life-styles and sex typing in six-year-olds. *Child Development, 61,* 1915–1933.

Weiss, G., & Hechtman, L. (1993). *Hyperactive children grown up: ADHD in children, adolescents, and adults* (2nd ed.). New York: Guilford Press.

Weiss, L. H., & Schwarz, C. (1996). The relationship between parenting types and older adolescents' personality, academic achievement, adjustment, and substance abuse. *Child Development, 67,* 2101–2114.

Weiss, M. (1993). Psychological effects of intensive sport participation on children and youth: Self-esteem and motivation. In B. Cahill & A. Pearl (Eds.), *Intensive participation in children's sports* (pp. 39–70). Champaign, Ill.: Human Kinetics Press.

Weisz, J. (1980). Autonomy, control, and other reasons why "Mom is the greatest": A content analysis of children's Mother's Day letters. *Child Development, 51,* 801–807.

Wellman, H. (1990). *Children's theory of mind.* Cambridge, Mass.: MIT Press.

Wellman, H., Cross, D., & Bartsch, K. (1987). A meta-analysis of the AnotB error. *Monographs of the Society for Research on Child Development, 51*(3). Chicago: University of Chicago Press.

Wellman, H., & Hickling, A. (1994). The mind's "I": Children's conception of the mind as an active agent. *Child Development, 65*(6), 1564–1581.

Werner, E. (1991). Grandparent-grandchild relationships amongst US ethnic groups. In P. Smith (Ed.), *The psychology of grandparenthood* (pp. 68–84). London: Routledge.

Wertsch, J. V. (1985). *Vygotsky and the social formation of mind.* Cambridge, Mass.: Harvard University Press.

Wertsch, J. V. (1989). A socio-cultural approach to mind. In W. Damon (Ed.), *Child development today and tomorrow* (pp. 14–33). San Francisco: Jossey-Bass.

Wertsch, J. V., del Rio, P., & Alvarey, A. (1995). *Sociocultural studies of mind.* New York: Cambridge University Press.

Whitbeck, L. B., Simons, R. L., & Goldberg, E. (1996). Adolescent sexual intercourse. In R. L. Simons et al. (Eds.), *Understanding differences between divorced and intact families: Stress, interaction and child outcome* (pp. 81–93). Thousand Oaks, Cal.: Sage.

White, B. (1975). Critical influences in the origins of competence. *Merrill-Palmer Quarterly, 21,* 243–266.

White, B. (1993). *The first three years of life.* (Rev. ed.). New York: Simon & Schuster.

White, S. D., & DeBlassie, R. R. (1992). Adolescent sexual behavior. *Adolescence, 27,* 183–191.

Whitehurst, G., Epstein, J., Angell, A., Payne, A., Crone, D., & Fischel, J. (1994). Outcomes of an emergent literacy intervention in Head Start. *Journal of Educational Psychology, 86*(4), 542–555.

Whiting, B. B., & Edwards, C. P. (1988). *Children of different worlds.* Cambridge, Mass.: Harvard University Press.

Whiting, J. W. M. (1981). Environmental constraints on infant care practices. In R. Munroe, R. H. Monroe, & B. B. Whiting (Eds.), *Handbook of cross-cultural development.* New York: Garland Press.

Wigfield, A., Eccles, J., & Rodriguez, D. (1998). The development of children's motivation in school contexts. In P. Pearson & A. Iran-Nejad (Eds.), *Review of research in education* (Vol. 23, pp. 73–118). Washington, D.C.: American Educational Research Association.

Wilcox, A. J., Weinberg, C. R., & Baird, D. (1995). Timing of sexual intercourse in relation to ovulation: Effects on the probability of conception, survival of the pregnancy, and sex of the baby. *New England Journal of Medicine, 333,* 1517–1519.

Wilfert, C. M., & McKinney, R. E., Jr. (1988, August). When children harbor HIV. *Scientific American,* 94–95.

Wilkinson, L., & Marrett, C. (Eds.). (1985). *Gender influences in classroom interaction.* Orlando, Fla.: Academic Press.

Wilkinson, R. (1996). *Unhealthy societies: The afflictions of inequality.* New York: Routledge.

Williams, C., & Kimm, S. (1993) *Prevention and treatment of childhood obesity.* New York: New York Academy of Sciences.

Williams, J. D., & Jacoby, A. P. (1989). The effects of premarital heterosexual and homosexual experience on dating and marriage desirability. *Journal of Marriage and the Family, 51,* 489–497.

Willis, D. J., Holden, E. W., & Rosenberg, M. S. (Eds.). (1992). *Prevention of child maltreatment: Developmental and ecological perspectives.* New York: Wiley.

Wilson, C., & Keye, W. (1989). A survey of adolescent dysmenorrhea and premenstrual symptom frequency. *Journal of Adolescent Health Care, 10,* 317–322.

Wilson, J. (1993). *The moral sense.* New York: The Free Press.

Wilson, M. N., et al. (Eds.) (1995). *African American family life: Its structural and ecological aspects. New directions for child development, No. 68: The Jossey-Bass education series* (pp. 59–72). San Francisco: Jossey-Bass

Wilson, W. J. (1996). *When work disappears: The world of the new urban poor.* New York: Knopf.

Winfree, L. T., Backstrom, T. V., & Mays, G. L. (1994). Social learning theory, self-reported delinquency, and youth gangs. *Youth and Society, 26,* 147–177.

Winner, E. (1988). *The point of words.* Cambridge, Mass.: Harvard University Press.

Wolf, D. (1993). There and then, intangible and internal: Narratives in early childhood. In B. Spodek (Ed.), *Handbook of research on the education of young children* (pp. 42–56). New York: Macmillan.

Wolf, N. (1997). *The beauty myth.* New York: Vintage Books.

Wolfe, D. A., McMahon, R. D., & Peters, R. D. (Eds.). (1997). *Child abuse: New directions in prevention and treatment across the lifespan.* Thousand Oaks, Cal.: Sage.

Wolock, I. (1998). Beyond the battered child. *Readings: A Journal of Reviews and Commentary in Mental Health,* 4–9.

Woolston, J. (1993). *Eating and growth disorders.* Philadelphia: Saunders.

Wootan, M., & Liebman, B. (1998). Ten steps to a healthy 1998. *Nutrition Action Health Letter, 25*(1), 1, 6–10.

Worden, J. W. (1996). *Children and grief.* New York: Guilford.

World Bank. (1997). *Confronting AIDS: Public priorities in a global epidemic.* New York: Oxford University Press.

World Health Organization. (1998). *World health annual statistics: 1997.* Geneva: Author.

Wozniak, R., & Fischer, K. (1993). *Development in context: Acting and thinking in specific environments.* Hillsdale, N.J.: Erlbaum.

Wright, J. C., Huston, A. C., Truglio, R., Fitch, M., Smith, E., & Piemyat, S. (1995). Occupational portrayals on television: Children's role schemata, career aspirations, and perceptions of reality. *Child Development, 66,* 1706–1718.

Wright, L., & Leahey, M. (1994). *Nurses and families: A guide to family assessment and intervention.* Philadelphia: F. A. Davis Publishers.

Wyly, M. (1997). *Infant assessment.* Boulder, Colo.: Westview Press.

Wynn, K. (1990). Children's understanding of counting. *Cognition, 36,* 155–193.

Yarrow, M., & Waxler, C. (1978). The emergence and functions of prosocial behavior in young children. In M. Smart & R. Smart (Eds.), *Infants, development and relationships.* New York: Macmillan.

Yoder, P., & Warren, S. (1993). Can developmentally delayed children's language development be enhanced through prelinguistic intervention? In A. Kaiser & D. Gray (Eds.), *Enhancing children's communication: Vol. 2* (pp. 35–62). Baltimore: Paul Brookes.

Yonas, A. (1988). *Perceptual development in infants. Minnesota Symposium on Child Psychology: Vol. 20.* Minneapolis: University of Minnesota Press.

Youniss, J. (1980). *Parents and peers in social development: A Sullivan-Piaget perspective.* Chicago: University of Chicago Press.

Youniss, J. (1994). Children's friendship and peer culture: Implications for theories of networks and support. In F. Nestmann, K. Hurrelmann, et al. (Eds.), *Social networks and social support in childhood and adolescence. Prevention and intervention in childhood and adolescence, 16* (pp. 75–88). Berlin: Walter De Gruyter.

Youniss, J., DeSantis, J. P., & Henderson, S. H. (1992). Parents' aproaches to adolescents in alcohol, friendship, and school situations. In I. E. Sigel, A. V. McGillicuddy-DeLisi, et al. (Eds.), *Parental belief systems: The psychological consequences for children* (2nd ed., pp. 199–216). Hillsdale, N.J.: Erlbaum.

Youniss, J., McLellan, J. A., & Strouse, D. (1994). "We're popular, but we're not snobs": Adolescents describe their crowds. In R. Montemayor, G. R. Adams, et al. (Eds.), *Personal relationships during adolescence. Advances in adolescent development: An annual book series* (Vol. 6, pp. 101–122). Thousand Oaks, Cal.: Sage

Zahn-Waxler, C., Radke-Yarrow, M., & King, R. A. (1979). Child rearing and children's prosocial initiations toward victims of distress. *Child Development, 50,* 319–330.

Zahn-Waxler, C., Radke-Yarrow, M., Wagner, E., & Chapman, M. (1992). Development of concern for others. *Developmental Psychology, 28,* 126–136.

Zaragoza, M. (1995). *Memory and testimony in the child witness.* Thousand Oaks, Cal.: Sage.

Zarbatany, L., Hartmann, D. P., & Rankin, D. B. (1990). The psychological functions of preadolescent peer activities. *Child Development, 61,* 1067–1080.

Zayas, L. H., & Solari, F. (1994). Early childhood socialization in Hispanic families: Context, culture, and practice implications. *Professional Psychology, Research and Practice, 25,* 200–206

Zerbe, K. (1993). *The body betrayed: Women, eating disorders, and treatment.* Washington, D.C.: American Psychiatric Press.

Zigler, E. F., Taussig, C., & Black, K. (1992). Early childhood intervention: A promising preventative for juvenile delinquency. *American Psychologist, 47,* 997–1006.

Zimmerman, L., & McDonald, L. (1995). Emotional availability in infants' relationships with multiple caregivers. *American Journal of Orthopsychiatry, 65,* 147–152.

Acknowledgments

Part And Chapter Opener Photo Credits

Part 1: © Myrleen Ferguson/PhotoEdit; **Chapter 1:** © Dion Ogust/The Image Works; **Chapter 2:** © Shackman/Monkmeyer; **Part 2:** © Bob Daemmrich/The Image Works; **Chapter 3:** © Chip Henderson/Tony Stone Images; **Chapter 4:** © Lennart Nilsson/*A Child Is Born*, Dell Publishing Company; **Part 3:** © G.P.A./Petit Format/Photo Researchers; **Chapter 5:** © Sally Moskol/The Picture Cube; **Chapter 6:** © Elizabeth Crews/The Image Works; **Chapter 7:** © Andrew Cox/Tony Stone Images; **Part 4:** © Steve Hamblin/Tony Stone Images; **Chapter 8:** © Julie Bidwell/Stock Boston; **Chapter 9:** © Kindra Clineff; **Chapter 10:** © Elizabeth Crews; **Part 5:** © Bob Daemmrich/Stock Boston; **Chapter 11:** © David Madison/Tony Stone Images; **Chapter 12:** © Michael Newman/PhotoEdit; **Chapter 13:** © Bob Daemmrich; **Part 6:** © David R. Frazier Photolibrary; **Chapter 14:** © Lori Adamski Peek/Tony Stone Images; **Chapter 15:** © Bob Daemmrich/The Image Works; **Chapter 16:** © Don Smetzer/Tony Stone Images.

Chapter Photo Credits

Chapter 1: p. 5: *top,* © David Young Wolff/Tony Stone Images; *bottom,* © Dean Berry/The Picture Cube; p. 12: *left, Family Portrait (1830–1840),* Jacob Maentel, courtesy, Winterthur Museum; *right, Children Playing on Beach* (1884), Mary Cassatt, National Gallery of Art, Ailsa Mellon Bruce Collection; p. 15: *top,* © Sylvain Grandadam/Tony Stone Images; *bottom,* © Lawrence Migdale/Tony Stone Images; p. 17: ©Richard Pasley/Stock Boston; p. 21: *top and bottom,* © Bradley D. Lanphere/Stock Boston; p. 22: © M. K. Denny/PhotoEdit.

Chapter 2: p. 33: © Kevin Syms/David R. Frazier Photolibrary; p. 34: Mary Evans Picture Library; p. 35: © Myrleen Ferguson/PhotoEdit; p. 37: Stock Montage; p. 38: © Robert W. Ginn/The Picture Cube; 45: © Steven Stone/The Picture Cube; p. 46: © Lawrence Migdale/Stock Boston; p. 49: *left,* © Nita Winter; *right,* © J. Carini/The Image Works; p. 51: © Will Hart/PhotoEdit; p. 56: © Bill Aron/PhotoEdit.

Chapter 3: p. 64: Custom Medical Stock Photo; p. 66: © Dr. Yorgos Nikas/Science Photo Library/Photo Researchers; p. 69: © Lawrence Migdale; p. 71: © Paul Conklin; p. 79: © Lawrence Migdale/Photo Researchers; p. 80: © Med.Illus.SBHS/Tony Stone Images; p. 83: © Tony Freeman/PhotoEdit; p. 86: © Robert Ginn/PhotoEdit.

Chapter 4: p. 95: © Lennart Nilsson, Dell Publishing Company; p. 97: *top,* © Petit Format/Nestle/Science Source/Photo Researchers; *bottom,* © Lennart Nilsson, Dell Publishing Company; p. 100: © George Haling/Tony Stone Images; p. 109: © David Young-Wolff/PhotoEdit; p. 119: © SIU/Peter Arnold; p. 120: © SIU/Peter Arnold; p. 121: © Catherine Smith/Impact Visuals; p. 123: ©PhotoEdit; p. 129: CORBIS/Annie Griffiths Belt; p. 130: © Laura Dwight.

Chapter 5: p. 137: © Frank Siteman/The Picture Cube; p. 138: © David Young-Wolff/PhotoEdit; p. 140: © David Young-Wolff/Tony Stone Images; p. 148: © David C. Bitters/The Picture Cube; p. 150: *left,* © David J. Sams/Tony Stone Images; *right,* © Elizabeth Crews/Stock Boston; p. 152: © Rick Browne/Stock Boston; p. 153: © Myrleen Ferguson/PhotoEdit; p. 158: © Elizabeth Crews/The Image Works; p. 158: © Jonathan Nourok/PhotoEdit.

Chapter 6: p. 165: © Jason Laure/Woodfin Camp; p. 167: © Peter Southwick/Stock Boston; p. 168: © Birnbach/Monkmeyer; p. 174: © Sally Cassidy/The Picture Cube; p. 176: © James Prince/Photo Researchers; p. 186: © Bob Daemmrich; p. 192: © Merrim/Monkmeyer; p. 193: © David Young-Wolff/PhotoEdit; p. 195: AnthroPhoto File no. 6273.

Chapter 7: p. 200: © Lawrence Migdale/Photo Researchers; p. 201: © Paul Conklin; p. 204: © Richard Hutchings/PhotoEdit; p. 207: © Elizabeth Crews; p. 209: © Elizabeth Crews; p. 212: *top,* © Bob Daemmrich/Stock Boston; *bottom,* © Jeff Dunn/The Picture Cube; p. 215: © David Young-Wolff/PhotoEdit; p. 217: © Lawrence Migdale/Stock Boston; p. 223: © Nancy J. Pierce/Photo Researchers; p. 224: © B. Mahoney/The Image Works;

p. 227: © Robert E. Daemmrich/Tony Stone Images; p. 228: © Laura Dwight.

Chapter 8: p. 237: © Lawrence Migdale/Stock Boston; p. 239: © Andy Levin/Photo Researchers; p. 245: © Laura Dwight; p. 246: © Laura Dwight/PhotoEdit; p. 250: © N. Richmond/The Image Works; p. 251: © Esbin-Anderson/The Image Works; p. 254: © Bob Daemmrich/The Image Works; p. 255: © Jernigan/Monkmeyer; p. 257: © Richard Hutchings/Photo Researchers.

Chapter 9: p. 262: © Elizabeth Crews; p. 270: © Bob Daemmrich/Stock Boston; p. 273: © Rick Browne/Stock Boston; p. 277: *left,* © Blair Seitz/Photo Researchers; *right,* © Donna Day/Tony Stone Images; p. 284: © Bob Daemmrich/Tony Stone Images; p. 285: © Laura Dwight/PhotoEdit; p. 289: © Peter Southwick/Stock Boston; p. 292: © Paul Conklin.

Chapter 10: p. 299: © Ellen Senisi/The Image Works; p. 301: © Brian Haimer/PhotoEdit; p. 304: © Elizabeth Crews; p. 306: © Elizabeth Crews; p. 313: © Palmer/Brilliant/The Picture Cube; p. 314: © Elizabeth Crews; p. 316: © Michael Newman/PhotoEdit; p. 317: © Charles Thatcher/Tony Stone Images; p. 319: © Elizabeth Crews; p. 321: © Ellen Senisi/The Image Works; p. 326: © Elizabeth Crews; p. 329: © Robert Eckert/Stock Boston.

Chapter 11: p. 336: © Bob Daemmrich/Stock Boston; p. 340: *left,* © Esbin/Anderson/The Image Works; *right,* © David Hiser/Tony Stone Images; p. 342: *top,* © Elizabeth Crews; *bottom,* © Bob Daemmrich; p. 347: © Eastcott/M./The Image Works; p. 349: © Mugshots/Tony Stone Images; p. 352: © David Maung/Impact Visuals.

Chapter 12: p. 358: © Ulrike Welsch/PhotoEdit; p. 359: © Elizabeth Crews; p. 364: © Kevin Horan/Stock Boston; p. 367: © John Nordell/Picture Cube; p. 369: © David Young-Wolff/Tony Stone Images; p. 372: © Paul Conklin/PhotoEdit; p. 375: © Bob Daemmrich; p. 381: © Will McIntyre/Photo Researchers; p. 382: © Lawrence Migdale/Stock Boston; © Marc Pokempner/Impact Visuals.

Chapter 13: p. 393: © George Goodwin/The Picture Cube; p. 396: © Frank Siteman/The Picture Cube; p. 399: © Robert Brenner/PhotoEdit; p. 400: © Elizabeth Crews; p. 405: © Bob Daemmrich/The ImageWorks; p. 408: © Myrleen Ferguson/PhotoEdit; p. 409: © Elena Rooraid/PhotoEdit; p. 411: © David Young-Wolff/Tony Stone Images; p. 415: *left,* © Bill Aron/PhotoEdit; *right,* © David Young-Wolff/PhotoEdit; p. 420: © Ellen Senisi/The Image Works; p. 421: © Bob Daemmrich/Stock Boston; p. 425: © David Young-Wolff/PhotoEdit.

Chapter 14: p. 433: © Elizabeth Crews; p. 440: *left,* © Michael Newman/PhotoEdit; *right,* © Robert W. Ginn/The Image Works; p. 446: © David Young-Wolff/PhotoEdit; p. 447: © Bob Daemmrich; p. 448: © David R. Frazier Photolibrary; p. 450: © Will Hart/PhotoEdit; p. 453: ©Martin Rogers/Tony Stone Images; p. 455: © David R. Frazier Photolibrary; p. 456: © Reuters/Kansas/Archive Photos.

Chapter 15: p. 462: © Mary Kate Denny/PhotoEdit; p. 463: © Bob Daemmrich; p. 474: © David M. Grossman/Photo Researchers; p. 475: *left,* © Laima Druskis/Stock Boston; *right,* © Smiley/TexaStock; p. 480: © Kindra Clineff/The Picture Cube; p. 481: © Bob Daemmrich/Stock Boston.

Chapter 16: p. 493: *left,* © Syracuse Newspapers/Kevin Jacobus/The Image Works; *right,* © Elizabeth Crews; p. 499: © Andy Levin/Photo Researchers; p. 500: © Shackman/Monkmeyer; p. 508: © Laura Dwight; p. 511: © John Eastcott/YVA Momatiuk/The Image Works; p. 514: © PhotoEdit; p. 515: © Phil McCarten/PhotoEdit; p. 516: © Jim Whitmer Photography; p. 518: © Dan Habib/Impact Visuals; p. 524: © Bob Daemmrich/Tony Stone Images; p. 532: © Frank Siteman/The Picture Cube.

Text, Table and Line Credits

p. 4: Cartoon: For Better or Worse copyright 1994 Lynn Johnston Productions Inc. Reprinted with permission of Universal Press Syndicate. All rights reserved.

p. 87: Cartoon: © The New Yorker Collection 1981 Chas Addams from cartoonbank.com. All Rights Reserved.

p. 102: Figure 4.2 adapted from *Before We Are Born: Basic Embryology and Birth Defects,* 2nd ed., by K.L. Moore, p. 111, with permission of W.B. Saunders Company, © 1983.

p. 110: Table 4.3 from *Planning for Pregnancy, Birth, and Beyond* by American College of Obstetricians & Gynecologists. Copyright © 1990 by The American College of Obstetricians & Gynecologists. Used by permission of Dutton, a division of Penguin Putnam, Inc.

p. 141: Figure 5.4 reprinted with permission from Roffway, Muzin, & Dement, 1966 (revised, 1969), "Ontogenetic Development of the Human Sleep-Dream Cycle," *Science, 152,* pp. 604–619. Copyright 1966 American Association for the Advancement of Science.

p. 182: Figure 6.3 adapted from Renee Baillargeon and Julie De-Vos, "Object Permanence in Young Children: Further Evidence," *Child Development, 62* (1991), 1227–1246. Copyright © 1991 by the Society for Research in Child Development, Inc. Reprinted by permission.

p. 275: Cartoon: Reprinted with special permission of King Features Syndicate.

p. 280: Cartoon: Reprinted with special permission of King Features Syndicate.

p. 324: Cartoon: Cathy, copyright 1986 by Cathy Guisewite. Reprinted with permission of Universal Press Syndicate. All rights reserved.

p. 344: Figure 11.3 adapted from D. Bukatko, and M. Daehler, *Child Development: A Topical Approach,* 2nd ed., 1995, p. 188. Adapted from Haubenstriker and Siefeldt, 1986. Copyright © 1995 by Houghton Mifflin Company. Used with permission.

p. 360: Cartoon: Calvin and Hobbes, copyright 1989 Watterson. Distributed by Universal Press Syndicate. Reprinted with permission. All rights reserved.

p. 365: Cartoon: Stone Soup, copyright 1997 Jan Eliot. Distributed by Universal Press Syndicate. Reprinted by permission. All rights reserved.

p. 401: Cartoon: © The New Yorker Collection 1991 Lorenz from cartoonbank.com. All Rights Reserved.

p. 417: Cartoon: Calvin and Hobbes, copyright 1987 Watterson. Distributed by Universal Press Syndicate. Reprinted with permission. All rights reserved.

p. 432: Reprinted with special permission of North America Syndicate.

p. 435: Figure 14.2 reprinted from *Drug and Alcohol Dependence, 27,* Friedman et al., "Percentage of Subjects Reporting Current Cigarette Smoking by Race, Sex, and Alcohol Consumption, 1991, with permission from Elsevier Science.

p. 437: Cartoon: Foxtrot, copyright 1996 Bill Amend. Reprinted with permission of Universal Press Syndicate. All rights reserved.

p. 451: Figure 14.3 from NYT Graphics/NYT Pictures, *The New York Times,* August 7, 1997. Used by permission.

p. 471: Cartoon: © The New Yorker Collection 1992 Koren from cartoonbank.com. All Rights Reserved.

p. 486: Cartoon: DILBERT reprinted by permission of United Feature Syndicate, Inc.

p. 492: Cartoon: © Lynn Johnston Productions Inc./Distributed. by United Feature Syndicate, Inc.

p. 522: Cartoon: Reprinted with special permission of North America Syndicate.

Author/Name Index

Subject Index

Abortion
  adolescent pregnancy and, 523
  controversy over, 104
  counseling prior to, 104–105
  death rates from, 104
  legislation regarding, 102, 104
  statistics on, 102
Abuse. *See also* Child maltreatment
  idiosyncratic child, 331
  physical, 114
  sexual, 329, 518–519
  societal, 331
Academic achievement. *See also* Achievement motivation; Assessment; Education; School
  Asian cultural beliefs and, 366–367
  cultural differences and, 54
  factors related to, 25
Accidents
  in adolescence, 448
  in school-age children, 345, 347
  in young children, 256
Accommodation, 7, 48, 174
Achievement motivation. *See also* Academic achievement
  cultural differences in, 54, 397–399
  differences in, 396–397
  explanation of, 396
  in middle childhood, 397–399
Achievement tests, 377, 378. *See also* Standardized tests
Achondroplasis, 74
Acquired immunodeficiency syndrome (AIDS)
  educating children with, 349–350
  explanation of, 349, 450
  facts about, 350
  hemophilia and, 70
  pediatric, 112–113
  prenatal exposure to, 110
  prevention of, 451
Active gene-environment relationship, 85
Activity settings, 270
Acute illness, 348
Adaptation, 48
Additive bilingual education, 375
Adolescence. *See also* Cognitive development in adolescence; Physical development in adolescence; Psychosocial development in adolescence
  alcohol abuse and, 451, 453–454
  beyond formal thought and, 465–466
  body image and self-esteem and, 444–446
  causes of death among, 448
  cognitive competencies and, 461, 462
  concept of, 431–433
  delinquency and, 528–531
  depression and, 525–526, 528
  development of social cognition and, 475–480
  drug abuse and, 451–453
  eating disorders and, 436–437
  effects of puberty and, 439–442
  egocentrism and, 475–476
  employment and, 513, 515
  explanation of, 431
  family relationships and, 497–507
  formal operational thought and, 462–467
  friendship and, 506–510
  growth in height and weight and, 434–435
  health and, 446–447

health-compromising behaviors and, 448–449
  identity development theories and, 491–497
  information processing and, 480–484
  moral development and, 467–468, 470–474
  nutritional problems and, 454–458
  parenthood in, 523–524
  peer groups and, 510–514
  school and, 484–489
  secular trends and, 436–438
  sexuality and, 515–521
  sexually transmitted diseases and, 449–451
  suicide and, 528–529
  timing of puberty and, 442–444
  tobacco use and, 453–455
Adolescent pregnancy
  abortion and, 523
  adolescent parenthood and, 523–524
  causes of, 521
  contraception and, 521–522
  medical risks of, 114
  parent-adolescent communication and, 522–523
  prevention and support programs for, 524–525, 527
  statistics regarding, 521
Adoption studies
  explanation of, 85–86
  intelligence and, 87
  twin, 86
Adult Attachment Interview (AAI), 224–225
Adults, long-term attachment effects and, 224–226
African Americans
  academic achievement and, 398–399
  extended family supports for childrearing and, 296
  family decision making and, 504
  midwives and, 124
  parenting style and, 402, 502
  sickle-cell disease and, 73
After-school care, 409–410
Age
  maternal, 114
  peer group membership and, 415
  play and, 317–318
  of viability, 97
Ageism, 12
Aggression
  childrearing styles and, 307–308
  in dealing with divorce, 405
  explanation of, 305
  juvenile delinquency and, 530
  media influences on, 308
  peer influences on, 308
  in preschoolers, 305–306
  responses to, 308–310
  temperamental differences in, 307
  in unpopular-rejected children, 421–422
AIDS. *See* Acquired immunodeficiency syndrome (AIDS)
Alcohol abuse
  in adolescence, 451–452
  cultural differences in, 528
  effects of, 453
  prenatal exposure to, 108–109
Alleles, 67–68
American Sign Language (ASL), 283–284
Amniocentesis, 79, 80
Amniotic sac, 96

Androgyny, 327
Anemia, 523
Animal studies
  heredity and environment and, 87, 89
  of infant attachment, 214–215
Animism, 268
Anorexia nervosa, 455, 457
AnotB error, 177, 182
Anticipation, of visual events, 169–170
Anxious-avoidant attachment, 217–219
Anxious-resistant attachment, 217, 219
Apgar scale, 137
Appearance-reality distinctions, 265–266
Aptitude tests, 378, 379. *See also* Standardized tests
Arousal
  infant heart rates and, 164–165
  states of infant, 143–144
Artifacts, 268–269
Artificial insemination, 103
Asian Americans. *See also* Chinese children; Japanese children
  academic achievement among, 25
  genetic counseling and, 78, 79
Assessment. *See also* Academic achievement
  explanation of, 386
  impact of, 386–387
  Piagetian theory and, 360–361
Assimilation, 48, 174
Athletics
  eating disorders and, 456
  gender and early, 344
  physical effects of early, 340
  psychological effects of early, 340, 342–344
Attachment
  animal studies of infant, 214–215
  assessment of, 216–218
  consequences of patterns of, 218–220
  cultural differences in, 218–219
  development of, 215
  explanation of, 41, 138, 214
  infant-caregiver, 55
  long-term effects of, 224–226
Attachment formation
  effects of day care and multiple caregivers on, 223–224
  effects of maternal employment on, 221–223
  phases of, 216
  role of father in, 221
  role of mother in, 220–221
Attention deficit/hyperactivity disorder (ADHD)
  causes of, 351
  explanation of, 47, 350
  helping children with, 351–353
  reactions to children with, 350–351
Attention to details, 366
Attractiveness, 255
Auditory acuity, 145, 246
Auditory cortex, 244
Auditory thinking, 170–171
Authoritarian parenting
  adolescents and, 501
  aggression and, 307
  explanation of, 299–300, 500
  maltreatment and, 328
Authoritative parenting
  adolescents and, 500–501
  effects of, 402
  explanation of, 298–299
Authority. *See* Parenting styles
Autistic phase, 39

Autonomy
  emergence of, 226–227
  explanation of, 226
  sources of, 227–228
Autonomy versus shame and doubt stage, 36, 38, 296
AZT, 112

Babbling, 190–191
Baby biographies, 12
Balanced bilinguals, 374. *See also* Bilingualism; Non-native English speakers
Behavioral learning theories
  applications of, 47
  classical conditioning and, 44, 183–184
  comparisons of, 58
  explanation of, 43
  imitation and, 186–187
  operant conditioning and, 44–45, 184–186
Behavior genetics
  canalization and, 83–84
  explanation of, 82–83
  gene-environment relationship and, 84–85
  measures of hereditary influence and, 85
  range of reaction and, 83
Behaviorism, 183
Behavior modification, 47, 352
Biases
  affecting learning, 385–386
  of standardized tests, 378–379
  toward non-native English speakers, 284
Bilingual education, 375
Bilingualism. *See also* Non-native English speakers
  cognitive effects of, 374
  social effects of, 374–375
  statistics regarding, 374
Black English, 375–376
Bladder control, 246
Blended families, 407
Blind training, 368–369
Blood type, 68, 69
Body balance skill, 381
Body hair, 440–441
Body image, 444–446
Brain development
  in infants, 139–140
  in preschoolers, 243–245
Brainstem, 139
Braxton-Hicks contractions, 119
Breast development, 440
Breast feeding
  among Gusii, 154–155
  mother-infant relationships and, 153–154
  nutritional value of, 153
Breech presentation, 118, 127
Broca's area, 244
Bulimia, 455, 457

Caesarean section, 127–128
Canalization, 83–84, 105
Caregiver-infant synchrony, 203–204
Caregivers. *See also* Professional caregivers
  fathers as, 204–205
  language acquisition in infants and, 194–196
  multiple, 224
Caregiver speech, 193
Case studies, 26